Adrian Mitchell was born in London in 1932. An ex-reporter, he is widely acclaimed as a poet, lyricist, novelist and writer for television and the stage. He has adapted plays for, among other people, the Royal Shakespeare and National Theatre Companies as well as instigating and script-editing many shows written by groups of adults and children. He was one of the originators of the public poetry movement and now performs his poems extensively in Britain, Europe and the United States. He has won an Eric Gregory Award and was during 1980-81 Judith E. Wilson Fellow at Cambridge.

Adrian Mitchell's books include the poetry collections OUT LOUD, RIDE THE NIGHTMARE, THE APEMAN COMETH and FOR BEAUTY DOUGLAS (Collected Poems 1953-79) and the novels IF YOU SEE ME COMIN', THE BODYGUARD and WARTIME. His first collection of poems for children, NOTHINGMAS DAY, is published in 1984.

Also by Adrian Mitchell
and published by Allison and Busby

For Beauty Douglas: Collected Poems 1953-79

ON THE BEACH AT CAMBRIDGE
New Poems

by
ADRIAN MITCHELL

Allison & Busby

London   .   New York

First published in Great Britain in 1984 by
Allison & Busby Ltd
6a Noel Street
London W1V 3RB
and distributed in the USA by
Schocken Books Inc
200 Madison Avenue
New York, NY 10016

Copyright © 1984 Adrian Mitchell

British Library Cataloguing in Publication Data
Mitchell, Adrian
    On the beach at Cambridge.
    I. Title
    821'.914   PR6063.177

    ISBN 0–85031–563–8
    ISBN 0–85031–564–6 Pbk

Set in 11/12 Univers by
Falcon Graphic Art Ltd, Wallington, Surrey
Printed and bound in Great Britain by
Richard Clay (The Chaucer Press) Ltd, Bungay, Suffolk

Acknowledgements

Most of these poems have not been published before, but all of them have been used in my performances of poetry. My special thanks to those who organized those performances and those who came to them.

Dedication

This book is dedicated to the true socialists and anarchists of the world.

Educational Health Warning

None of the work in this or any of my other books is to be used in connection with any examination whatsoever. (But I'm happy if they're read aloud in schools by people who like them enough to read them aloud.)

Contents

ON THE BEACH AT CAMBRIDGE

What Is Poetry?

(for Sasha, Daniella, Vladko and Martin Shurbanov)

Look at those naked words dancing together!
Everyone's very embarrassed.
Only one thing to do about it —
Off with your clothes
And join in the dance.
Naked words and people dancing together.
There's going to be trouble.
Here come the Poetry Police!

Keep dancing.

Back In The Playground Blues

I dreamed I was back in the playground, I was about four
 feet high
Yes dreamed I was back in the playground, standing about
 four feet high
Well the playground was three miles long and the
 playground was five miles wide

It was broken black tarmac with a high wire fence all
 around
Broken black dusty tarmac with a high fence running all
 around
And it had a special name to it, they called it The Killing
 Ground

Got a mother and a father, they're one thousand years
 away
The rulers of The Killing Ground are coming out to play
Everybody thinking: "Who they going to play with today?"

Well you get it for being Jewish
And you get it for being black
Get it for being chicken
And you get it for fighting back
You get it for being big and fat
Get it for being small
Oh those who get it get it and get it
For any damn thing at all

Sometimes they take a beetle, tear off its six legs one by
    one
Beetle on its black back, rocking in the lunchtime sun
But a beetle can't beg for mercy, a beetle's not half the
    fun

I heard a deep voice talking, it had that iceberg sound
"It prepares them for Life" — but I have never found
Any place in my life worse than The Killing Ground.

To A Critic

You don't go to Shakespeare for statistics
You don't go to bed for a religious service
But you want poems like metal mental mazes —
Excuse me while I nervous.

A song can carry so many facts
A song can lift plenty of story
A song can score jokes and curses too
And any amount of glory

But if you overload your dingadong song
With theoretical baggage
Its wings tear along the dotted line
And it droppeth to earth like a cabbage

Yes it droppeth to earth like a bloody great cabbage
And the cabbage begins to rot.
My songs may be childish as paper planes
But they glide – so thanks a lot.

Lament For The Welsh Makers

WILLIAM DUNBAR sang piteously
When he mourned for the Makers of poetry.
He engraved their names with this commentary —
Timor mortis conturbat me.

DUNBAR, I'm Scot-begotten too,
But I would celebrate a few
Welsh masters of the wizardry —
The fear of death moves inside me.

''After the feasting, silence fell.''
ANEIRIN knew how the dead smell.
Now he has joined their company.
The fear of death moves inside me.

TALIESIN, born of earth and clay,
Primroses, the ninth wave's spray
And nettle flowers, where is he?
The fear of death moves inside me.

LLYWARCH's sons numbered twenty-four.
Each one was eaten by the war.
He lived to curse senility.
The fear of death moves inside me.

TALHAEARN and AROFAN,
AFAN FERDDIG and MORFRAN
Are lost, with all their poetry.
The fear of death moves inside me.

MYRDDIN sang, a silver bell,
But from the battlefield he fell
Into a deep insanity.
The fear of death moves inside me.

GWALCHMAI, who sang of Anglesey
And a girl like snowfall on a tree
And lions too, lies silently —
The fear of death moves inside me.

CYNDDELW's balladry was sold
For women's kisses and men's gold.
His shop is shut permanently.
The fear of death moves inside me.

HYWEL chanted Meirionnydd's charm.
His pillow was a girl's white arm.
Now he is whiter far than she.
The fear of death moves inside me.

PRYDYDD y MOCH would smile to see
An Englishman — if he was maggoty.
Now he is grinning bonily.
The fear of death moves inside me.

DAFYDD ap GWILYM did women much good
At the cuckoo's church in the green wood.
Death ended his sweet ministry.
The fear of death moves inside me.

GWERFYL MECHAIN wrote in cheerful tones
Of the human body's tropical zones.
She shared DAFYDD's hot philosophy.
The fear of death moves inside me.

IOLO GOCH wrote of any old thing —
Girls, feasts and even an English King.
They say he died most professionally.
The fear of death moves inside me.

GRUFFUDD GRYG wept desperately
For the North of Wales in her poverty.
He was a bird from heaven's country.
The fear of death moves inside me.

LLYWELYN GOGH's fist dared to knock
On the heavy door with the black steel lock.
A skull told him its history.
The fear of death moves inside me.

SION CENT, who sang thank you to his purse,
RHYS GOGH, who killed a fox with verse,
Sleep in the gravel dormitory.
The fear of death moves inside me.

IEUAN ap RHYDDERCH so scholarly,
GWERFUL MADOG of famed hospitality,
LEWYS GLYN COTHI who loved luxury –
The fear of death moves inside me.

DAFYDD ap EDMWND's singing skill
Thrilled through all Wales. Then it fell still.
LEWYS MON wrote his elegy.
The fear of death moves inside me.

BEDO BRWNLLYS, IEUAN DEULWYN,
GUTYN OWAIN, TUDUR PENLLYN,
All exiles in Death's monarchy.
The fear of death moves inside me.

Life was dark-coloured to TUDUR ALED.
WILLIAM LLYN brooded on the dead.
SION TUDUR mocked all vanity.
The fear of death moves inside me.

17

DIC HUWS dedicated a roundelay
To a girl by the name of Break of Day.
Night broke on both of them, remorselessly –
The fear of death moves inside me.

And hundreds have since joined the towering choir –
Poets of Wales, like trees on fire,
Light the black twentieth century.
The fear of death moves inside me.

Oh DYLAN THOMAS, as bright as nails,
Could make no kind of a living in Wales
So he died of American charity.
The fear of death moves inside me.

Terror of death, terror of death,
Terror of death, terror of death,
That drumbeat sounds relentlessly.
The fear of death moves inside me.

Since we must all of us ride down
The black hill into the black town,
Let us sing out courageously.
The fear of death moves inside me.

The black lungs swell, the black harp sighs,
Whenever a Welsh maker dies.
Forgive my nervous balladry.
Timor mortis conturbat me.

The Owl Song

(After watching a terrible battle, Merlin decides to live as
an owl in a wood.)

I have walked through the valley of slate
And the rain was blue
I have seen the sky like a hunter's net
Deepest darkest blue
I have seen the bit tight in the horse's teeth
And the bit was blue
I have heard swords sing on the battlefield
And the swords were blue
I have seen the eyes of my dead foe
They were round as the world and blue
I have seen the face of my friend in the dawn
On the sheep-shorn grass — his face was blue

      Blue grave
    Blue gravel on a grave
Blue flowers on the gravel on a grave

And I shall wake in the blue night
And sleep in the blue day
And I will live my own blue life
In the blue tree   In the blue tree

And my food shall be blue
And my wine shall be blue
And my mind shall be filled
With nothing but blue

blue   blue   blue   blue   blue   blue

19

Farm Animals

Clotted cream sheep
We troop in a dream
Through the steep deep wool
Of a yellow meadow
We are oblong and boring
We are all alike
Liking to be all alike

And the grass-like grass
Is alike, all alike, and all we think
Is grass grass grass
Yes grass is all we think
And all we do
Is wool

But that's the deal, the ancient deal,
The wonderful deal between sheep and men

Men give grass
We come across with wool

That agreement was signed
On the green baize table in Eden

What would happen if we broke the contract?
Oh that would be mutiny, we would be punished
By being eaten, we would deserve to be eaten.
But of course we never rebel, so we are never eaten.

On The Verses Entitled "Farm Animals"

The stereotypical tra-a-avesty opposite
Purports to speak for sheep
Nothing could be more cra-a-assly human

Despite our similar coiffures
Each sheep's a separate planet
With its own opinions and visions

All that we share is the furnace heart
Of all long-distance serfs
We're hot and getting hotter
So shepherds, you better watch your flocks

A. Ram.

December Cat

Among the scribbled tangle
of the branches of that garden tree
only about two hundred
lime-coloured leaves still shudder

but the hunting cat
perched in the middle of the scribble
believes he's invisible
to the few sparrows visiting
the tips of the tree

like a giant soldier
standing in a grey street at noon
wearing a bright ginger uniform
hung with guns
hung with grenades
who holds a sprig of heather up
as he shouts to the houses:
Come out! It's all right,
I'm only a hillside!

The Airline Steward's Spiel

Oxygen masks
Four at each side
Whenever you see one
You need one
So grab one

I've never
Seen them come down
And my wife and I
Would like to keep it that way

Have a pleasant flight

Commuting The Wrong Way Round Early Morning

Caught the Gospel Oak train
At the dog-end of Tuesday night.
Camden Town darkness
Laying like gravy on a plate . . .
But at Liverpool Street Station
They've got a smudgey brand of blue daylight.

Here comes half the Essex population
Tensed up for their desky work.
I'm struggling up a waterfall —
Bubbling secretaries, rocky clerks.
For I'm off to Billericay
Like a sausage on a fork.

The Call

(or Does The Apple Tree Hate Plums?)

i was standing in my room
the whirling tape was singing:
i'm never going back
i'm never going back.

i read four lines by Elaine Feinstein
the tears jumped in my eyes.
i read eight lines by Allen Ginsberg
and electricity sprang
from the soles of my feet
and the electric flames
danced on the roof of my skull.

someone calling
my self calling to myself
the call i'd been hoping for

let yourself sing it said
let yourself dance
let yourself be
an apple tree

i wrote this daftness down
then smiled and smiled
and said aloud
thank you thank you

you may want money
you may want pears
you may want bayonets
or tears

shake me as hard as you like
only apples will fall

apples   apples   and apples

For My Son

"The next best thing to the human tear" . . . advertising slogan for an eyewash.

The next best thing to the human tear
Is the human smile
Which beams at us reflected white
For a lunar while.
But smiles congeal. Two eyes alight
With water cannot glow for long,
And a better thing than the human tear
Is the human song.

If cigarette or city burn
The smoke breaks into air.
So your breath, cries and laughter turn
And are abandoned there.
Once I had everything to learn
And thought each book had pretty pages.
Now I don't even trust the sun
Which melts like butter through the ages.

Nevertheless, crack-voiced I'll sing
For you, who drink the generous light
Till, fat as happiness, you sing
Your gay, immortal appetite.
I bring you air, food, grass and rain,
Show you the breast where you belong.
You take them all and sing again
Your human song.

The Swan

The anger of the swan
Burns black
Over ambitious eyes.

The power of the swan
Flexes steel wings
To batter feeble air.

The beauty of the swan
Is the sermon
Preached between battles.

One More Customer Satisfied

He staggered through the cities moaning for melons:
"Green melons streaked with yellow!
Yellow melons tinged with green!
Don't try to fool me. They fooled me before
With tie-dyed green-and-yellow footballs
And the breasts of yellow women, green-tinted
nipples. . . ."

In his yellow rage and his green longing
He rolled himself into a melon-shaped heap of
hopelessness
Crying out: "Melons! Bring out your melons!"

So they took a million melons to Cape Kennedy,
Scooped them out, filled them with green and yellow
paint
And splattered them all over the bright side of the
moon.

They adjusted his face so it faced the face of the moon
And they told him: "There is your one true melon,
Your forever melon, your melon of melons."

Now, fully grateful, he watches the melon rise,
The setting of the melon, the new melon and the full
melon,
With a smile like a slice of melon in the green-and-
yellow melon-light.

Io, Io, It's Off To Work We Go

To be seduced by a cloud
It's like wrestling with a weightless bear
He was all around me in and out of me
Whispering his small rain everywhere

Now I am an old walking woman
My skin is like yellow leather
But I keep half an eye cocked at the sky
And I smile when they talk about the weather

So when the sky gets randy to rain
I never run for cover
For a man is only a fool on a stick
But a cloud is a total lover

Brazil Nut In Edinburgh

Strapping upon her head the brand-new sporran
Dolores hoped she did not look too foreign

For Julietta, Who Asked For An Epitaph

The half-dead shone with double life
When magicked by her liveliness.
Over the woods she used to go
Flying in her flying dress.

But Death was depressed.
He took Julietta.
She smiled and danced with him.
Now Death feels better.

A Wise Woman

Woman called Sarah born with nothing but looks and
    lust
I saw her on her deathbed she was smiling fit to bust
She said: I've lived my life on the Golden Triangle
    plan —
Don't play with razors, don't pay your bills, don't
    boogie with a married man.

Happy Fiftieth Deathbed

D H Lawrence on the dodgem cars
Sniffing the smell of the electric stars
Cool black angel jumps up beside
Sorry David Herbert it's the end of your ride

Thank you very much Mr D H Lawrence
Thank you very much
Thank you very much Mr D H Lawrence
For The Rainbow and such

D H Lawrence with naughty Mrs Brown
Trying to play her hurdy-gurdy upside-down
In comes Mr Brown and he says Veronica
May I accompany on my harmonica

Thank you very much Mr D H Lawrence
Thank you very much
Thank you very much Mr D H Lawrence
Back to your hutch

D H Lawrence met Freud in a dream
Selling stop me and buy one Eldorado ice cream
Siggie says you ought to call your stories
Knickerbocker Splits and Banana Glories

Thank you very much Mr D H Lawrence
Thank you very much
Thank you very much Mr D H Lawrence
Keep in touch

September Love Poem

I flop into our bed with Thee,
Ovaltine and warm milk-o
And there we lie in ecstasy
Watching Sergeant Bilko.

Astrid-Anna

(This piece was written especially for an Anglo-German audience at the Goethe Institute in London)

Here is a news item from a right-wing British paper — the *Daily Mail*.

"TERROR GIRL IS ILL"
"Baader Meinhof girl Astrid Proll, who faces extradition to Germany, is physically and mentally ill, her friends said yesterday. They gathered outside Bow Street magistrates court . . . and handed out leaflets saying she was having difficulty in breathing and had 'sensations of panic'. Carnations were thrown to her as she was led away."

If Astrid Proll, who is now a British citizen by marriage — Anna Puttick — is sent back to Germany, she will be dead within two years. There are special sections in special prisons in Germany where prisoners like Astrid-Anna find it easy to obtain revolvers. Even odder, they do not shoot their jailers. They shoot out their own brains. If the British hand over Astrid-Anna to the West German police, we will be collaborating in yet another murder. Well, we done a few before.

> Sensations of panic
> Carnations were thrown
> Free Astrid   Free Anna

Astrid-Anna was accused of the attempted murder of two policemen.
But she has never been found guilty of anything.
But she was the first prisoner in Germany to be kept in conditions of SENSORY DEPRIVATION. In the Silent Wing of the

Women's Psychiatric Unit at Ossendorf Prison in Cologne.

There are white walls, constant lighting, no external sounds — techniques designed to disorientate and subdue. She spent a total of FOUR AND A HALF MONTHS in the Silent Wing. About TWENTY-FOUR WEEKS in the Silent Wing. About ONE THOUSAND SEVEN HUNDRED HOURS in the Silent Wing.

Her trial was stopped by a doctor. He found the following complaints: weakness and exhaustion, the feeling of "being wrapped in cotton wool", dizziness, blackouts, headaches and no appetite, feelings of breaking down, an inability to concentrate, increasing signs of phobia and agoraphobia. Her blood circulation began to collapse, depriving her brain of oxygen. Continued imprisonment, said the doctor, would lead to PERMANENT AND IRREPARABLE DAMAGE.

> Four and a half months
> In the silent wing
> Four and a half months
> in the silent wing
>
> Shut in a white box
> Under the constant neon
> Being whitened in a box
> Under the silent neon
> Boxed in the white neon
> Of the silent box
> Under the constant wing.
>
> Silenced in the white
> Under the white wing
> Of the constant box of neon

In the white of the silent box
In the silence of the white box
In the constant silence
In the constant white
In the white of the white box

Your head starts exploding
Your skull is about to split
Your spine is drilling into your brain
You are pissing your brains away

In the white of the silent box
In the silence of the white box
In the constant silence
In the constant white
In the white of the white box

Under the Nazis an experiment was made in which they locked a man in a white cell with white furniture. He wore white clothes. And all his food and drink were white. He very soon lost his appetite. He could not eat. He could not drink. The sight of the white food and the white drink made him vomit.

Astrid came to England and began life again as Anna. She worked with young people in the East End as an instructor in car mechanics. One Englishwoman says: "Anna gave me and my children enormous support. . . . When I was drinking too much, it was Anna who cared enough to see why and then helped me to make decisions that I was drinking to forget."

This is the Terror Girl of the *Daily Mail*.

Now Anna is being kept under maximum-security conditions in a man's prison — Brixton. There are only two women in the prison. They are supervised by seven warders. They have no privacy. When Anna has a visitor, her conversation is listened to. When her lawyer visits her in her cell below the court, there is always a policeman in the cell. For three hours a day she is allowed to meet the other woman in Brixton jail. The rest of the time she spends on her own.

So will Anna be sent back by our rulers
to the white of the white box
to the silence of the white silence
to the constant silence and the constant white
to the whiteness of the silence
to the silence of the whiteness
to the whiteness of the whiteness
to the silence of the silence
to the whiteness of the whiteness
to the silence of the silence
to the whiteness to the silence to the whiteness to
the silence
whiteness whiteness silence silence

Stop. You can stop them. If Anna is extradited or not depends on the Home Secretary. Write to the Home Secretary. Demand she be allowed to stay. Demand that she be treated humanely. And if you are German, force your government to be satisfied with its revenge, to drop its demands for extradition, to drop the case against her, to close the Silent Wing forever.

We will walk out from here
into the blue-eyed, brown-faced, green-haired
world
our spinning, singing planet

but Anna who was Astrid lies chained in the box
   of the state
silent men in suits walk towards her with blank
   faces
they carry syringes and hooks and guns in their
   white briefcases

LET ANNA STAY HERE

LET HER WORK

LET HER REST

LET HER FIND LOVE

Screws and Saints

What's worse than the uniformed devils
When they trap you in a concrete hell?
The claws and boots of the angels
When you're savaged in a golden cell.

Nearly Nothing Blues

Well it's six o'clock and I done nearly nothing all day
Yes 6 p.m. — done nearly nothing all day
I'll do half as much tomorrow if I get my way

Four Sorry Lines

Sixteen years old, and you would sneer
At a baby or a phoenix.
Mock on, mock on, in your blue-lidded splendour —
Most well-paid jobs are reserved for cynics.

Action And Reaction Blues

Further back you pull a bow-string
            the further the arrow goes whooshin
Further back Maggie drags us
            the further the revolution

"Appendix IV

Requirements In The Shelter

    Clothing
    Cooking Equipment
    Food
    Furniture
    Hygiene
    Lighting
    Medical
    Shrouds"

What?

    "Shrouds.
    Several large, strong black plastic bags
    and a reel of 2-inch, or wider, adhesive tape
    can make adequate air-tight containers
    for deceased persons
    until the situation permits burial."

No I will not put my lovely wife into a large strong
    black plastic bag
No I will not put my lovely children into large strong
    black plastic bags
No I will not put my lovely dog or my lovely cats into
    large strong black plastic bags

I will embrace them all until I am filled with their
    radiation

Then I will carry them, one by one,
Through the black landscape
And lay them gently at the concrete door
Of the concrete block
Where the colonels
And the chief detectives
And the MPs
And the Regional Commissioners
Are biding their time

And then I will lie down with my wife and children
And my dog and my cats

And we will wait for the door to open

My Shy Di In Newspaperland

(All the lines are quoted from the British Press on Royal Engagement day, the only slight distortions appear in the repeats of the four-line chorus. Written in collaboration with Alistair Mitchell.)

Who will sit where in the forest of tiaras?
She is an English rose without a thorn.
Love is in their stars, says Susie.
She has been plunged headfirst into a vast goldfish
    bowl.

Did she ponder as she strolled for an hour through
    Belgravia?
Will they, won't they? Why, yes they will.
They said so yesterday.
He said: "Will you?"
She said: "Yes."
So did his mother — and so say all of us.

Who will sit where in the head of the goldfish?
She is an English forest without a tiara.
Love is in their roses, says Thorny.
She has been plunged starsfirst into a vast susie bowl.

Most of the stories in this issue were written
By James Whitaker, the *Daily Star* man
Who has always known that Diana and Prince Charles
    would marry.
He watched them fishing on the River Dee —
And Lady Diana was watching him too.
She was standing behind a tree using a mirror
To watch James Whitaker at his post,
James Whitaker, the man who always knew.

Who will sit where in the stars of Susie?
She is an English head without a goldfish.
Love is in their forests, says Tiara.
She has been plunged rosefirst into a vast thorn bowl.

All about Di.
Shy Di smiled and blushed.
Lady Di has her eyelashes dyed.
My shy Di.

She descends five times from Charles II —
Four times on the wrong side of the blanket
And once on the right side.

Who will sit where in the rose of thorns?
She is an English star without a susie.
Love is in their heads, says Goldfish.
She has been plunged forestfirst into a vast tiara bowl.

Flatmate Carolyn Pride was in the loo
When she heard of the engagement.
"Lady Diana told me through the door," she said last
    night.
"I just burst into tears. There were floods and floods of
    tears."

Who will sit where in the forest of tiaras?
She is an English rose without a thorn.
Love is in their stars, says Susie.
She has been plunged headfirst into a vast goldfish
    bowl.

Autumnobile

The forest's throat is sore.
Frost-work. Echoing shouts of friends.
October, in her gold-embroidered nightie,
Floating downstream, little mad flowers shimmering.

The silky fur of her
And her hot fingers curling,
Uncurling round and a sudden shove —
There goes my heart tobogganing,

Down snow, slush, ending stuck in the mud,
That's love! O dig me out of here
And glide me off down Pleasure Street
To the sparkle rink where bears go skating.

I ate pancakes at the funeral.
I ate pancakes and ice-cream too.
The mourners drank like musty flies,
All round Summer's coffin, sucking and buzzing.

The days of dust and nights of gnats
Are over and, covered with raindrop warts,
My friend, the most unpopular Season in school,
Smoking and spitting — Autumn's coming.

How do I love that fool, the Fall?
Like Paraquatted nettles. Like
A two-headed 50p. Like a sick shark.
Like a punchy boxer who can't stop grinning.

Sunshine's rationed. Get in the queue
For a yard of colour, a pound of warm.
Deathbed scenes on the video-sky,
Sunsets like Olivier acting dying.

I feel weightless as a child who's built
Out of nursery bricks with ducks and clocks on.
I eat more sleep. I slap more feet.
Autumn — my marzipan flesh is seething.

I open a book and splash straight into it.
The fire reads all my old newspapers.
I freak across the galaxy on Pegasus
And see the cracked old world, rocking and bleeding.

The saloon doors in my skull swing open,
Out stride a posse of cowboy children
Bearing a cauldron of the magic beans
Which always set my poems quivering.

Now my electric typer purrs,
And now it clackers under my fingers'
Flickering. And now the oily engine
Throbs into hubbub. The Autumnobile is leaving.

Nobody on earth knows where on earth they're going
. . . .

(a hell of a long way after Pushkin and Derzhavin)

To My Friends, On My Fiftieth Birthday

My darlings, my friends, makers of all kinds, what can
   I say to them?
Go on with your labours of love, for you build
   Jerusalem.
My friends, my darlings, what can I say about you?
I will love you forever, I would have died without you.

Sally Go Round the Ombelibus On A Thursday Afternoon

(for Sally Stephens)

First time I saw Sally
She was moving through the meadow
Lazing on her mother's lovely arm.

Together in the big marquee
She was just the right size for beauty
Held against my heart,
And I saw her daddy smile
A wider smile.

Milk was warm
Blue air was chilly
Trees and hedges
Danced circles round Sally

Green afternoon
Green afternoon
And my heart filled up again

For Gordon Snell — My Best, First And Finest Friend — On His Fiftieth Birthday

"By and by they all are dead" — stage direction at the end of an early play by Gordon Snell, writer for grown-ups and children.
"By and by is easily said" — Hamlet in *Hamlet*, a part once played by Gordon Snell.

By and by they all are dead —
The people, animals, earth and sky.
By and by is easily said.

Any child who has ever read
Knows that Book People cannot die.
By and by they all are dead?

Peter Rabbit's still raiding the potting shed
Under Long John Silver's laser eye.
By and by is easily said,

But Alice and the Golux tread
Emerald Oz where the Jumblies fly.
By and by they all are dead?

Lorna Doone and Just William wed
Where The Wild Things Are with Harriet the Spy.
By and by is easily said. . . .

Gordon — the creatures your fancy has bred
Shall live with them — that's the sweet By-and-
     By!
By and by they all are dead?
By and by is easily said!

51

Shoot-out At The Hebden Bridge Saloon

(for Joy Smedley)

Pony Express rider
leaned down and muttered:
Watch out for the Gold-Dust Kid,
gonna be the fastest. . . .
then he hit the horizon with his horse.

Waited awhile. . .
I'm takin a taste at the bar
when this gold-colour kid
kinda jumpy
but Apache eyes
moseys in, tosses a bag of dust on the bar —
Bourbon.

You the Gold-Dust Kid?

Yup.

Heard you're fast.

Yup.

Show me.

We locked eyes.
Made my move.

In through my ribs
out through my backbone.

Pour a last whiskey down me, Doc
And — watch out for the Gold-Dust Kid,
She. . . .

52

For Nigel And Delyth

Mumbles, June 1982

Nightfall: the harp is playing like a fountain.
The harp is dancing like a happy woman.
The heartbeat of the house is the harp
As it sings like the spinning world.

Young Merlin splashes in the generous fountain.
He eats and drinks happiness with his woman
And the sea lies below them like a mighty harp
And his making table is a brown field in a new world.

To Elizabeth Quinn on the First Night Of "Children Of A Lesser God" In London

25 August 1981

Tonight I saw a thousand birds
   Nobody knew their names
A thousand birds in flight
   a thousand birds
Tonight I saw a thousand birds

For the Eightieth Birthday of Hoagy Carmichael

22 November 1979

Hoagland — white waterfall piano keys!
Old rockin' chairs to help us all think mellow!
Always-Fall forests of star-tall trees
Growing chords of gold, brown, red and yellow!
Yes, Hoagland, friendliest of all countries.

Casual is, I guess, as casual does,
And you casually sing and casually knock us sideways.
Rolling songs riding the river's tideways,
Mist-songs gliding, city-songs that buzz.
I wander Hoagland pathways when dusk falls.
Celia strolls with me as wild and tame
Hoagland bird-folk enchant us with their calls.
Anyone who has ears grins at your name.
Eighty years of great songs! I wish you would
Live on as long as your good Hoagland life feels good.

Notes:
a. Hoagland is Mr Carmichael's official Christian name
b. Celia is my wife's name.

Sardinia, 1979

(for Boty)

Yellow lampshine through the leaves of the
  tambourine.
Black waves of jelly slapping the white jetty.
Forty grandfathers sit round a Victorian tree.
Five of us are discussing our spaghetti.

To Michael Bell

(my teacher at Greenways School whose motto was: "A Green Thought In A Green Shade.")

In the second year of the Slaughter
I attended a school in Hell
Feeling like King Lear's fourth daughter
Strapped down in a torture cell
Then my blue and white mother appeared to me
And she saw I was all afraid
So I was transported mysteriously
To a green school in a green shade

And there I met a great mechanic
And he mended my twisted wings
And he gentled away my panic
And he showed me how a vision sings
And I thank Michael Bell most lovingly
For the mountains and lakes he made
And the way he shone the light of peace on me
Like a green thought in a green shade

Loony Prunes

(an apology poem for my daughter)

We played the savage ludo which is known as Coppit,
Chatted, drank wine, ate lamb, played Beatle tunes
And then we started it, found we couldn't stop it —
A contest to eat maximum loony prunes.

They weren't just the ordinary, wrinkled, black,
Laxative fruit imported from — who knows?
But, floating in a stinging pool of Armagnac,
They were sozzled Français lunatic pruneaux.

Then, indoor fireworks, and the sharp flashes
Of three-second sparklers, dull horse-races,
A wonderful serpent, a frilly fern of ashes —
While the loony prune-juice flushed our faces.

As I was trying to put the fireworks out
We started arguing like sun and moon.
I grabbed you as the whole world seemed to shout.
You ran upstairs. I'm sorry. I'm a loony prune.

Falling Feathers

(for Andy and Gill on their wedding day
Saturday, 7 May 1983)

watch out for falling feathers
golden sailboats in the air
watch out for falling feathers
or they'll settle in your hair

and you'll look pretty silly with golden feathers
thrilling all over your nut
you'll never get a mentionable pensionable job
you'll live in a hut with a wooden water-butt

you'll have to sidle round the countryside side-
     ways
dancing to the music of bats
attempting to make a magical living
cutting rabbits in half producing girls out of hats

o watch out for falling feathers
golden rockinghorses in the air
watch out for falling feathers
or they'll settle in your hair

and you'll be no better than your singing
and no better than your audience too
and you'll be no better than feathers falling
golden golden down the blue

and you'll be no better than hedgehogs
who can only live like hedgehogs live
and you'll be no better than the holy Jumblies
who went to sea like you in a sieve

yes watch out for falling feathers
golden lions prowling down the air
watch out for falling feathers
or they'll settle in your hair

> ten miles overhead there's a couple of angels
> loving in a cloud on springs
> and they got a little archangelic
> and a couple of feathers jumped off of their wings

> so live like a couple of featherheads
> who got married on Uppendown Hill
> for the feathers fell off a pair of angels
> whose names coincidentally are Andy and Jill

watch out for falling feathers
golden cradles in the air
watch out for falling feathers
and catch them and save them
and take them and place them
golden in your children's hair

watch out for falling feathers
golden in the golden air
watch out for falling feathers
and they'll settle in your hair
in your happyeverafter hair

Bring Out Your Nonsense

A detective-sergeant walks into the police station
A woman with a floor at home inspects the carpet
    store
A train stops at the platform after deceleration
Librarians enter the library through the library door
Telephonists at the switchboard are answering
    telephones
A Telegraph reader buys the Telegraph from the paper
    shop
Cars drive, pedestrians walk and my heart groans
As out of the Billericay copshop steps a cop

But I'm wrong — the cop debags himself to give birth
    to a phoenix
Which zips down the High Street with Dizzy Gillespian
    squeals
And the silver and gold melts in all the jewellers'
    windows
And the town is crotch-deep in whirlpools of syrup
And you sail over the horizon in a pea-blue schooner
Bearing the wild good news you sail bearing the good
    wild food
Over the horizon with a ton of friends playing magical
    banjoes
And the people of Billericay dance in delirious dozens

First Poem Composed In A Dream

A snub-nosed woman holding a jug;
Maybe it will be empty
By 1969 or nineteen-sempty. . . .

Second Poem Composed In A Dream

"Let's get married!"
"But I can't remember my name."
"Let's get suffocated then!"

Daydream Number 157,423

In a quiet afternoon drinking club
In a leather-upholstered booth
I wish I was listening to Billie Holiday
Telling the poisonous truth

24 Orders With (Optional) Adjectives

fetch my (happy) screwdriver
smell those (sugary) goldfish
shut that (amazing) door
touch my (scrawny) statues
close your (intricate) eyes
fill up the (Russian) hole again
tell your (gaping) sister
put that (shining) bomb together
spare my (murky) child
show your (grey) feelings
put up your (smiling) hand
hide your (iron) face
hand over those (solemn) emeralds
don't try to get (red-handled) funny with me
wash their (impertinent) car
cut its (sweet) throat
eat your (exclusive) cabbage
take down your (little) trousers
make up your (agile) mind
get down on your (frightening) knees
stick to your own (pathetic) kind
take the (stupid) tea
polish those (harmonious) boots

Reassuring Song If Your Name Is Mitchell

A million Mitchells sing this song
A million Mitchells can't be wrong
We are a million Mitchells strong
Why don't you just sing along?
Why don't you just sing along?
    Happy-go-zombie,
    Hello Abercrombie!
With a million marching Mitchells

Chile In Chains

"Student demonstrators yesterday forced the Chilean Ambassador to clamber over roof-tops and hide in a kitchen after they broke up a meeting he was trying to address at St John's College, Cambridge.

"The Ambassador, Professor Miguel Schweitzer, was invited to talk to the Monday Club on diplomatic relations between Britain and Chile ..." *The Guardian*, 13 November 1980.

"Any victory for the people, however small, is worth celebrating" — a demonstrator.

"I've never seen an Ambassador running before, so I'm not quite sure how to rate him as a runner" — a Cambridge spectator.

There's eight men in Cambridge called the Monday
    Club,
It's like the British Movement with brains,
And they thought it cute to pay a sort of tribute
To the government of Chile in Chains.

So the Mondays invited the Ambassador
To St John's as their honoured guest —
But he must come unto them secretly
(At the Special Branch's special request).

The Ambassador was glad to get an invite —
He flicked off his electric shock machine,
Scrubbed the blood from under his fingernails
And summoned his bodyguard and limousine.

"What shall I tell them?" the Ambassador mused
As he flushed his better self down the loo,
"Allende was a mass murderer
But Pinochet is Jesus Mark Two?

"What shall I tell them?" the Ambassador thought
As his car snaked down Cambridgeshire lanes,
"That Victor Jara tortured himself to death
And Paradise is Chile in Chains?"

But as they were proffering South African sherry
The faces of the Monday Club froze —
For a mob of Lefties had assembled outside:
Socialist and Anarchist desperadoes!

So they switched their venue from the Wordsworth
  Room
To the Wilberforce Room, locked the doors
And the Monday Club gave its limp applause
To a pimp for fascist whores.

But the revolution never stops
(We even go marching when it rains),
And a Yale lock is no protection at all
For a salesman for Chile in Chains.

When the Left tumbled into the Wilberforce Room
The Ambassador was terrified.
His bodyguard shovelled him out the back door
And the Monday Club was occupied.

Oh they hurried him over the rooftops
And the pigeons gave him all they had.
Oh they hid him away in the kitchen
And all of the food went bad.

But the Left sat down in the Wilberforce Room.
The atmosphere smelled of shame.
Then a Don said: "This is private property.
Tell me your college and name."

"We didn't come to talk about property.
We came to talk about the pains

Of the poor and the murdered and the tortured and the
   raped
Who are helpless in Chile in Chains."

They grouped a scrum of cops round their honoured
   guest
And we jeered at him and his hosts
As he ran with the cops across the grass of the Court
Like a torturer pursued by ghosts.

He galloped with his minders to his limousine
But the stink of his terror remains
And everyone who watched his cowardly run
Knows — Chile will tear off her chains.

A Prayer For The Rulers Of This World

God bless their suits
God bless their ties
God bless their grubby
Little alibis

God bless their firm,
Commanding jaws
God bless their thumbs
God bless their claws

God bless their livers
God bless their lungs
God bless their
Shit-encrusted tongues

God bless their prisons
God bless their guns
God bless their deaf and dumb
Daughters and sons

God bless their corpuscles
God bless their sperms
God bless their souls
Like little white worms

Oh God will bless
The whole bloody crew
For God, we know,
Is a ruler too

And the blessed shall live
And the damned shall die
And God will rule
In his suit and his tie

Ode To George Melly

If Bonzo the Dog got resurrected he could leap like you
If Satan the Snake ate Adam's birthday cake he would
  creep like you
If Liz Bat Queen wasn't pound-note green she'd hand
  the Crown to you —
For nothing on earth falls down like George Melly do.

About Suffering They Were Never Wrong
The Old Mistresses

Bessie Smith
And Big Joe Turner
Make Othello
Sound like a learner

All Darks Are Alike In The Death

As you crouch on my chest
I'll stroke your fur
Funny old death
Purr   purr   purr   purr

Smilers

When Woody Allen smiles
From the attics of the town
The secretary tears
Come rolling down

When John Wayne smiles
Boy you better grin
Or he'll be obliged
To kick your feelings in

Buy A Sprig Of Haggis For Bad Luck, Sir?

Have you ever been pregnant on Euston Station?
And they said you'd be met at your destination
By a fixer who'd be wearing an Asian carnation
And you stare around the concourse in consternation
For it's the annual outing of the Royal Association
For the Propagation of the Asian Carnation.
Have you ever been pregnant on Euston Station?

A Sunset Cloud Procession Passing Ralph Steadman's House

1. A cigar-smoking porker drags a small hay-cart from which a jewelled crocodile smiles and waves.

2. A black fried egg struts by, one woolly eyebrow raised like Noel Coward.

3. An emaciated caribou clanks along.

4. An ant-eater inflates a smoker's-lung balloon.

5. Eskimo Jim pulls Auntie Hippo tail-first, but she hangs on to her perambulator full of hippolets.

6. They are pursued by a neolithic Hoover.

7. And followed by Leonardo's Tin Lizzie and Michelangelo as a tumescent frogman, pride of the Sexual Boat Service.

8. A simple mushroom shape, rising one inch every four seconds.

9. Father Time with a crumpled scythe.

10. A whale spouting black shampoo all over its own humpy head.

11. A cocker spaniel taking a free ride on the backbone of a boa-constrictor.

12. And up from out of the dark hill's shoulders rise the shoulders of another, larger, darker hill.

Dinner With The Dons of Saint Abysmas's College, Oxbridge

I am the spy from Ignorance,
In my thundercloud gown I dine.
I am the Elephant Man who sits
Between Will Hay and Wittgenstein.

Bury My Bones With An Eddy Merckx

live people don't often
have eyes for the overhead stars
but gloom down roads
in micro-wave cars

they dunno how the rippling
of the wild air feels
frowning round town
in tombs on wheels

but ghosts ride bikes
free-wheeling mostly
singing songs like
Give It To Me Ghostly

ghosts got no rooty-tooty
duty to be done
cars are for bloody business
bikes for fun

Give It To Me Ghostly

give it to me ghostly
close-up and long-distance
i've an open policy
of misty non-resistance

so give it to me ghostly
shudder up and lisp a
bogey-woman promise
to your will o' the whisper

give it to me ghostly
spook it to me somehow
haunt me haunt me haunt me
oooo thanks i've come now

Who Goes Where?

Oh who is that man who wishes he'd stuck to the path
His suede shoes uncomfortably soaked in the dews of
   the lawn?
Oh that is the man with the face of a sad sardine,
    And they call him Overdrawn.

Activities Of An East And West Dissident Blues

(Verses to be read by the Secret Police, the chorus to be read by anyone else.)

When I woke up this morning it was nothing
    o'clock
I erased all the dreams from my head
I washed my face in shadow-juice
And for breakfast I ate my bed

I said goodbye to my jailer and spy
Burnt letters from all of my friends
Then I caught the armoured bus for a mystery
    tour
To the street with two dead ends

and oh
I wish I had a great big shiny brass diver's helmet
and I wish I had great big leaden diver's boots on me
and I wish I had infallible mates upstairs at the
    air-pumps
as I wandered forever on the bottom of the great free
    sea

I arrived at my factory or office or field
I did what I was meant to do
I left undone what should be left undone
And all of the others did the same thing too
        And you too? Right.

In the evening I read whatever should be read
Listened to whatever should be heard
And I taught the top twenty government slogans
To my golden-caged security bird

And I changed into the pair of pyjamas
With a number stamped on brown and black bars
And I pulled down the blind to keep out of my
   mind
The excitement of the stars

but oh
I wish I had a great big shining brass diver's helmet
and I wish I had great big leaden diver's boots on me
and infallible mates upstairs with their hands on the
   air-pumps
as I wandered forever on the bottom of the great green
   flowing free and easy sea

New Skipping Rhymes

Good little Georgie
Worked like a madman
Three years at Oxford
Five years an Adman
Went on Mastermind
Did so well on that show
Now he's the Host
Of a TV Chat Show

My savings are my baby
Money is my boss
My mummy and my daddy
Were profit and loss
One thousand, two thousand, three
thousand, four. . . .

Meat on the hook
Powder in the jar
Mickey Jagger is a Star
S-T-A-R spells Star
He can whistle
He can hum
He can wriggle his umpumbum

Pretty little Pam
Passed her exam
What shall we give her?
Doughnuts with jam

Stupid little Sam
Failed his exam
What shall we give him?
Who gives a damn?

The High School Bikeshed

Yellow stairs
Do the zig-zag stagger.
In the red shed
The bikes are snogging.
Silver, they whisper to each other,
Silver, silver.

Staying Awake

Monday came so I fucked off to school
School is a big huge building
Where you're not supposed to get any fucking sleep
We hung around till they counted us in a room
With pictures of fucking owls and bats
Then we hung around some more

Miss Harburton ponced in and yelled about
How her fucking bike's gone missing who cares
Then we all fucked off to another room

It was Mister Collins from Outer Space
Talked about not leaving gum stuck around
And Queen Victoria up the Suez Canal
And how he wouldn't let us act out
The Death of General Gordon again
Not ever and no he never saw Chainsaw Massacre
And no didn't want to even free
On Goodgeman's sexy mother's video
And Beano Black said his mother was poorly
And started to give us the fucking grisly details
Saved by the bell and we hung around
Smoking in the bog and not getting any sleep

Then we all fucked off to another room
And it was Mrs Grimes Environmental Studies
So I finally got my fucking sleep.

I stay out of trouble but in my head
I'm bad I'm fucking bad as they come
When I die they'll punish me
For the things I done in my fucking head.

They'll send me off to a big huge building
And they won't let me get any fucking sleep.
Well that's what I reckon
Death is like fucking off
To another fucking school.

The Reindeer Rider In An Old Russian Photograph

The reindeer rider could only speak
A Russian brand of Turkish
While the best that I can manage
Is a sort of British English.
Besides the reindeer rider died
In the last century
While I'm in the top front left-hand seat
Of a double-decker called Mortuary.
But seeing him on that reindeer's back
I want to warn him to pin his ears back,
For, while he seems to think: so far so good,
That reindeer is obviously a no-good
And its eye is full of mischief
As an oak is full of oak-wood.

Carol During The Falklands Experience

In the blind midslaughter
The drowned sank alone
Junta set like concrete
Thatcher like a stone

Blood had fallen, blood on blood,
Blood on blood
In the blind midslaughter
In the madness flood

What shall I give them
Powerless as I am?
If I were a rich man
I wouldn't give a damn

If I were an arms dealer
I would play my part —
All I can do is point towards
The holy human heart.

Third Opinion

"Is he better off with it or without it?"
Said the doctor with the moustache.
Said the doctor with the beard:
"Well, frankly, Simon, I'm in two minds about it."
They turned to the bed.
The patient had disappeared.

Money And Booze

(a love song)

He was as filthy as fivepence
And vacant as ginger-beer shandy
But she was as naughty as ninepence
And she went through his system like brandy

Social Being

"Come to the party! Isn't it time
You faced the world again?"
So I clenched my face and entered the place —
A roomful of boozing Mister Men.

Remember Red Lion Square?

I haven't heard any Moderates lately
Mention the name of Kevin Gateley,
The student who, so the Coroner said,
Died from "a moderate blow to the head".

The Christians Are Coming Goodbye Goodbye

They fought the good fight on six continents,
Cutting down the godless foe.
The Christians were Super-Campbells,
The whole world – their Glencoe.

Ode To Her

You so draggy Ms Maggie
The way you drag us down
The way you shake your finger
Way you frown your frown
But a day's soon dawning
When all the world will shout
We're gonna catch yer Ms Thatcher
You'll be dragged out

You so draggy Ms Maggie
You tore this land apart
With your smile like a laser
And your iceberg heart
You teach the old and jobless
What poverty means
You send the young men killing
The Irish and the Argentines

You so draggy Ms Maggie
With your million cuts
You slashed this country
Till it spilled its guts
You crucified parents
And their children too
Nailed em up by the million
Here's what we'll do

You so draggy Ms Maggie
Madonna of the Rich
We're gonna introduce you
On the Anfield pitch
Oh you can talk your meanest
But you as good as dead
When Yosser Hughes butts you
With his poor old head. . . .

How To Be Extremely Saintly, Rarefied And Moonly

(For Becky, who, when I spoke about resisting my urge to lie around watching videotapes all day told me: "Let your temptation never fail you.")

Let your coconut be your guide
Let the sun stew in its own juice
Let your coat and rent your hat
And let your temptation never fail you

Let the good times roller-skate
Let me inside-out please, I forgot my keys
Let the flim-flam floogie with the floy-floy rock 'n' roll
But let your temptation never fail you

Let the lecturer be harangued by the blackboard
Let your letters stamp their footling feet to better letter
    music
Let us play soccer together with a bonny lettuce
And in the Beantime —
Let your temptation, Becky, never fail you.

Land Of Dopes And Loonies

William Shakespeare was loony
Burns was a maniac too
Milton was thoroughly crackers
Yeats was a looney all through
Edward Lear, Shelley and Coleridge,
Whitman and Lawrence and Blake
What a procession of nutters
Looning for poetry's sake
All of the poets were dafties
Dafter when the going got rough
All except William Wordsworth
Who wasn't nearly crazy enough

Leonardo was loopy
So was Toulouse Lautrec
Bosch had all of his screws loose
Van Gogh's head was a wreck
Pablo Picasso was batty
Just take a look at his work
Rembrandt was out of his windmill
Brueghel was bloody berserk
All of the painters were bonkers
In the barmy army of art
All except Sir Joshua Reynolds
And he was a wealthy old Humpty Dumpty. . . .

On The Beach At Cambridge

I am assistant to the Regional Commissioner
At Block E, Brooklands Avenue,
Communications Centre for Region 4,
Which used to be East Anglia.

I published several poems as a young man
But later found I could not meet my own high
    standards
So tore up all my poems and stopped writing.
(I stopped painting at eight and singing at five.)
I was seconded to Block E
From the Ministry for the Environment.

Since there are no established poets available
I have come out here in my MPC
(Maximum Protective Clothing),
To dictate some sort of poem or word-picture
Into a miniature cassette recorder.

When I first stepped out of Block E on to this beach
I could not record any words at all,
So I chewed two of the orange-flavoured pills
They give us for morale, switched on my Sony
And recorded this:

I am standing on the beach at Cambridge.
I can see a group in their MPC
Pushing Hoover-like and Ewbank-like machines
Through masses of black ashes.
The taller men are soldiers or police,
The others, scientific supervisors.
This group moves slowly across what seems
Like an endless car park with no cars at all.

I think that, in one moment,
All the books in Cambridge
Leapt off their shelves,
Spread their wings
And became white flames
And then black ash.
And I am standing on the beach at Cambridge.

You're a poet, said the Regional Commissioner,
Go out and describe that lot.

The University Library — a little hill of brick-dust.
King's College Chapel — a dune of stone-dust.
The sea is coming closer and closer.

The clouds are edged with green,
Sagging low under some terrible weight.
They move more rapidly than usual.

Some younger women with important jobs
Were admitted to Block E
But my wife was a teacher in her forties.
We talked it over
When the nature of the crisis became apparent.
We agreed somebody had to carry on.
That day I kissed her goodbye as I did every day
At the door of our house in Chesterton Road.
I kissed my son and my daughter goodbye.
I drove to Block E beside Hobson's Brook.
I felt like a piece of paper
Being torn in half.

And I am standing on the beach at Cambridge.
Some of the men in their MPC
Are sitting on the ground in the black ashes.
One is holding his head in both his hands.

I was forty-two three weeks ago.
My children painted me
Bright-coloured cards with poems for my birthday.
I stuck them with Blue-tack on the kitchen door.
I can remember the colours.

But in one moment all the children in Cambridge
Spread their wings
And became white flames
And then black ash.

And the children of America, I suppose.
And the children of Russia, I suppose.

And I am standing on the beach at Cambridge
And I am watching the broad black ocean tide
Bearing on its shoulders its burden of black ashes.

And I am listening to the last words of the sea
As it beats its head against the dying land.

Cambridge, March 1981

OXFORD CLINICAL NEPHROLOGY SERIES

Inherited Disorders of the Kidney

Oxford Clinical Nephrology Series

Editorial board
Professor J. Stewart Cameron, Dr Tilman Drüeke, Dr John Feehally,
Professor David N. S. Kerr, Professor Leon G. Fine, Professor David Salant,
and Dr Christopher G. Winearls

Prevention of Progressive Chronic Renal Failure
Edited by A. Meguid El Nahas, Netar P. Mallick, and Sharon Anderson

Analgesic and NSAID-induced Kidney Disease
Edited by J. H. Stewart

Dialysis amyloid
Edited by Charles van Ypersele and Tilman B. Drüeke

Infections of the Kidney and Urinary Tract
Edited by W. R. Cattell

Polycystic Kidney Disease
Edited by Michael L. Watson and Vicente E. Torres

Treatment of Primary Glomerulonephritis
Edited by Claudio Ponticelli and Richard J. Glassock

Inherited Disorders of the Kidney
Edited by Steven Morgan and Jean-Pierre Grünfeld

Complications of Long-term Dialysis
Edited by Edwina Brown and Patrick S. Parfrey

Inherited Disorders
of the Kidney

Investigation and Management

STEPHEN H. MORGAN

South Essex Renal Services, Basildon and Thurrock General Hospitals, Basildon, Essex, UK

and

JEAN-PIERRE GRÜNFELD

Department of Nephrology, Universite René Descartes, Hôpital Necker, Paris, France

Oxford   New York   Tokyo
OXFORD UNIVERSITY PRESS
1998

Oxford University Press, Great Clarendon Street, Oxford OX2 6DP

Oxford New York

Athens Auckland Bangkok Bogota Buenos Aires Calcutta
Cape Town Chennai Dar es Salaam Delhi Florence Hong Kong Istanbul
Karachi Kuala Lumpur Madrid Melbourne Mexico City Mumbai
Nairobi Paris São Paolo Singapore Taipei Tokyo Toronto Warsaw
and associated companies in
Berlin Ibadan

Oxford is a trade mark of Oxford University Press

Published in the United States
by Oxford University Press Inc., New York

A catalogue record for this book is available from the British Library

Library of Congress Cataloging in Publication Data
(Data available)

ISBN 0 19 262473 3

Typeset by Best-set Typesetter Ltd., Hong Kong
Printed in Great Britain by
Bookcraft (Bath) Ltd,
Midsomer Norton, Avon

PREFACE

The hereditary nephropathies have become increasingly important to the practising nephrologist. Economically, they represent another significant burden to the cost of provision of renal replacement therapy for paediatric and adult patients developing end stage renal failure (ESRF). Almost 50% of children and over 15% of adult patients requiring dialysis and/or transplantation have diseases with an underlying hereditary basis (Table 1).

Many of these hereditary diseases have the potential to affect all parts of the nephron either as primary disorders in their own right or, more often than not, as part of a more multisystem disease such as diabetes mellitus or some of the metabolic storage disorders. Whilst some of these diseases present and may be fatal early in infancy, many present in adolescence or early adult life. This monograph is therefore particularly directed at the adult nephrologist who may see or be referred such patients at first presentation or who pick up the care of growing patients previously managed by paediatric colleagues.

The first half of this monograph provides an insight into the development of the complex homeostatic organ whose failure provides us with many clinical challenges. It also deals with many of the general scientific and clinical aspects of investigation applicable to this particular subspecialist field. Chapter 6, on growth, development, and management, provides a link to the second half of the monograph which gives systematically a detailed description of specific diseases, addressing predominantly clinical issues.

This decade has seen many major clinical and scientific advances in this subject. The isolation of one of the mutant genes responsible for one of the commonest genetic diseases—autosomal dominant polycystic kidney disease (ADPKD)—and identification of the putative protein—polycystin—has captivated scientific audiences worldwide and shown how collaborative efforts between academic groups can work.

Table 1   Distribution of major causes of ESRF in patients starting renal replacement therapy between 1985–1987 according to age (1429 patients) (Wing 1992)

	All ages (%)	<15 years (%)	>65 years (%)
Uncertain	14.8	6.2	20.1
Glomerulonephritis	24.1	13.5	13.4
Tubulointerstitial nephritis (includes reflux)	17.3	24.7	19.6
Toxic causes	2.9	0.5	4.1
Cystic disease	8.3	3.0	5.3
Congenital	2.3	18.8	0.7
Renovascular/hypertension	10.3	1.1	16.2
Diabetes	12.0	0.4	12.7
Multisystem disease	4.6	8.3	4.8
Other	3.4	3.7	3.0

Although it would appear classical genetics has been overtaken by the molecular analysis of the genome, the classical approach still has a place in the practice of clinical nephrology. A detailed and knowledge-based clinical history and physical examination may prove invaluable in the diagnosis of unexplained renal disease. Identification of a heritable basis is vital for the identification of at-risk family members so that they can be offered the potential of presymptomatic screening and antenatal diagnosis. We trust that this monograph will provide a valuable reference source to clinicians and scientists alike.

Basildon, UK   S.H.M.
Paris, France   J-P.G.
May 1998

CONTENTS

CONTRIBUTORS

Ross R. Bailey[†], Department of Nephrology, Christchurch Hospital, Christchurch, New Zealand

Daniel G. Bichet, Research Center and Nephrology Division, Université de Montréal Hôpital du Sacre-Coeur de Montreal, Canada

R. W. Bilous, Diabetes Care Centre, Middlesbrough General Hospital, South Tees Acute Hospitals Trust, Middlesbrough, UK

Michel Broyer, Hôpital des Enfants-Malades, Universite René Alscartes, Paris, France

J. Stewart Cameron, Guy's Hospital, UMDS, London, UK

Martin d'A. Crawfurd, Lately Kennedy Galton Centre, Northwick Park Hospital, Harrow and MRC Clinical Research Centre, Northwick Park, Harrow, UK

Robert J. Desnick, Departments of Human Genetics and Pediatrics, Mount Sinai School of Medicine, New York, USA

Frances V. Elmslie, Mothercare Department of Clinical Genetics and Fetal Medicine, Institute of Child Health, UCL Medical School, London, UK

Christine M. Eng, Departments of Human Genetics and Pediatrics, Mount Sinai School of Medicine, New York, USA

T. G. Feest, The Richard Bright Unit, Southmead Hospital; Reader in Renal Medicine, University of Bristol, UK

Frances A. Flinter, Paediatric Research Unit, Division of Medical and Molecular Genetics, Guy's Hospital, London, UK

Patricia A. Gabow, University of Colorado Health Sciences Center, Denver, Colorado, USA

William A. Gahl, Heritable Disorders Branch, National Institute of Child Health and Human Development, National Institutes of Health, Bethesda, Maryland, USA

Linda K. Gallo, Heritable Disorders Branch, National Institute of Child Health and Human Development, National Institutes of Health, Bethesda, Maryland, USA

Jane Green, Department of Community Medicine, Memorial University, St. John's, Newfoundland, Canada

Jean-Pierre Grünfeld, Department of Nephrology, Université René Descartes, Hôpital Necker, Paris, France

Marie-Claire Gubler, INSERM U 423, Hôpital Necker-Enfants Malades, Paris, France

John D. Harnett, Division of Nephrology, Memorial University, St. John's, Newfoundland, Canada

[†] Died in 1997

D. S. Harry, Department of Medicine, and School of Medicine, The Royal Free Hospital, London, UK

George B. Haycock, UMDS Department of Paediatrics, Guy's Hospital, London, UK

Philippe Jaeger, Policlinic of Medicine, University Hospital, Berne, Switzerland

Stephen Jeffer, Medical Genetics Unit, St. George's Hospital Medical School, London, UK

Claire Kleinknecht, Hopital des Enfants-Malades, Paris, France

Jöry Laubenberger, Department of Radiology, University of Freiburg i.B., Germany

Philippe Lesavre, Département de Néphrologie and Unité 90 INSERM (Prévention et traitement de l'insuffisance rénale), Hôpital Necker, Paris, France

Micheline Lévy, Unite 155 INSERM (Epidémiologie génétique), Château de Longchamp, Paris, France

S. M. Mauer, Department of Pediatric Nephrology, University of Minnesota, Minneapolis, USA

Heather Maxwell, Renal Unit, Royal Hospital for Sick Children, Yorkhill NHS Trust, Glasgow, UK

D. S. Milliner, Division of Nephrology, Department of Internal Medicine, Mayo Clinic, Rochester, Minnesota, USA

Christopher Mitchell, Paediatric Oncology, Oxford Radcliffe Hospital, Oxford, UK

Stephen H. Morgan, South Essex Renal Services, Basildon and Thurrock General Hospitals, Basildon, Essex, UK

S. R. Nelson, St. George's Healthcare NHS Trust, St. George's Hospital, London, UK

Harmut P. H. Neumann, Department of Nephrology, University of Freiburg i.B., Germany

Patrick S. Parfrey, Dirision of Nephrology, Memorial University, St. John's, Newfoundland, Canada

Michael A. Patton, Department of Medical Genetics, St George's Hospital Medical School London, UK

Mordechai Pras, Department of Internal Medicine, Heller Medical Research; Director, Heller Institute, Tel Aviv University, Sheba Medical Centre, Israel

Anand K. Saggar-Malik, St. George's Hospital Medical School, London, UK

V. E. Torres, Division of Nephrology, Department of Internal Medicine, Mayo Clinic, Rochester, Minnesota, USA

G. C. Viberti, Unit for Metabolic Medicine, UMDS, Guy's Hospital, London, UK

R. W. E. Watts, Renal Section, Division of Medicine, Imperial College of Science, Technology and Medicine, Hammersmith Hospital, London, UK

Ulrich Wetterauer, Department of Urology, University of Freiburg i.B., Germany

A. F. Winder, Department of Chemical Pathology and Human Metabolism, The Royal Free Hospital, and School of Medicine, London, UK

Robin M. Winter, Mothercare Department of Clinical Genetics and Fetal Medicine, Institute of Child Health, UCL Medical School, London, UK

Adrian S. Woolf, Nephrology Unit, Institute of Child Health, London, UK

Berton Zbar, Laboratory of Immunobiology, National Cancer Institute, Frederick, Maryland, USA

PART I

Application of clinical genetics to renal disease

1

Developmental anatomy and physiology

Adrian S. Woolf

Introduction

> The more complicated an organ in its development the more subject it is to maldevelopment, and in this aspect the kidney outranks most other organs (Potter 1972).

Thus wrote Edith Potter in 1972 when she provided the most complete summary of the normal and abnormal development of the kidney, or nephrogenesis. Her work describes in detail the complex normal morphogenesis of the kidney and classifies the histopathology of diseases such as the renal dysplasias, cystic diseases, and Wilm's tumours that, she argued, appeared to arise from abnormal development. Two decades on, the science of molecular and cellular biology has begun to dissect both the pathways of normal nephrogenesis and the genetic mutations which lead to a wide range of inherited and congenital aberrations of renal anatomy and physiology (Woolf 1997).

The clinical importance of developmental disorders of kidney structure is enormous, and renal dysplasias and cystic diseases account for a large proportion of patients with end–stage renal failure, both in childhood and adulthood (Kaplan *et al.* 1991; Ehrich *et al.* 1992; McEnery *et al.* 1992; Holliday *et al.* 1993; Al-Khaldi *et al.* 1994). Similarly, a wide range of inherited metabolic disorders cause significant renal diseases. In some, such as oxalosis, the primary defect does not lie within the kidney, but in others, such as cystinuria and the renal tubular acidoses, molecular defects directly cause tubular disorders (Holliday *et al.* 1993). Recently, it has been suggested that essential hypertension, which manifests later in life, can be initiated before birth (Law *et al.* 1993), and this observation suggests an unexplained link between renal development and postnatal disease. Many of these diseases will be described in detail later in this book but I will allude to some of them in this chapter in the context of 'development gone wrong'.

This first part of this chapter summarizes some of the recent studies which attempt to explain the mechanism of nephrogenesis. It is a long-term aim of these studies that an understanding of molecular and cellular mechanisms will, in future, allow manipulation of disease processes either by conventional pharmacological means (Slotkin *et al.* 1992; Woo *et al.* 1994) or by the use of novel strategies such as cell transplantation (Woolf *et al.* 1990; Herzlinger *et al.* 1992) and genetic engineering (Bosch *et al.* 1993; Woolf *et al.* 1993; Moullier *et al.* 1994). Genetic screening for inherited disorders such as polycystic kidney diseases (Harris *et al.* 1994; Zerres *et al.* 1994) is an example of how basic biology is already contributing to the clinical practice of nephrologists.

Developmental anatomy of the kidney

The origin of the kidney

The mammalian embryo develops three sets of organs, all of which might be termed the 'embryonic kidneys' (Potter 1972; Saxen 1987). The pronephros and mesonephros are formed earlier in development than the metanephros, which is the direct precursor of the adult kidney. Although the mesonephros contains glomeruli which deliver ultrafiltrate into short tubules (Gersh 1937), both this structure, and the pronephros, degenerate by mid-gestation. This review considers metanephric development, and this is shown schematically in Figs 1.1 and 1.2. The bulk of the adult kidney is derived from the mesoderm, or the middle of the three embryological layers, whereas its innervation is derived from the embryonic ectoderm. In the mouse the metanephros is first noted at day 10.5 of pregnancy, midway through gestation, whereas in the human the metanephros has appeared by 5–6 weeks after fertilization. Most of the experimental data regarding the control of kidney morphogenesis is accrued from experiments in mice and rats.

The metanephros is formed by the interaction of two populations of cells: the ureteric bud and the renal mesenchyme. The former is a branch of the mesonephric or Wolffian duct, which is an

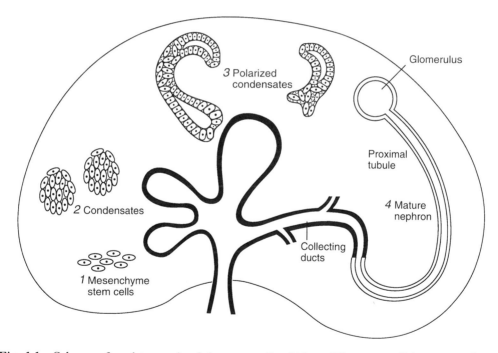

Fig. 1.1 Scheme of nephrogenesis of the mammalian kidney. The centre of the metanephros is occupied by the ureteric bud (*thick line*) which branches serially to form the ureter and collecting ducts. The development of the renal mesenchyme is shown serially from left to right. *1* and *2*: Nephrogenic mesenchyme stem cells condense to from a compact ball at the branch points of the ureteric bud. *3*: Next, the cells within the condensed mesenchyme polarize to form an epithelial nephron with a lumen surrounded by cells which have discrete apical and basal membrane domains. *4*: Finally, the primitive nephron forms specialized glomerular and tubular epithelia and fuses with the ureteric bud which itself has differentiated into the collecting ducts (*thick line*).

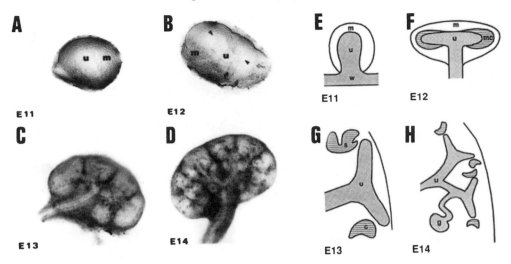

Fig. 1.2   Early development of the metanephros. Stereomicroscopic images of the mouse metaneph-ros (*A–D*) and cross-sectional diagrams of the metanrephros (*E–H*) at embryonic day 11 (E11; *A* and *E*), E12 (*B* and *F*), E13 (*C* and *G*), and E14 (*D* and *H*). Note the serial branching of the central ureteric bud and also the conversion to nephron epithelia by the surrounding undifferentiated renal mesen-chyme. The most primitive structures are located in the periphery of the E14 organ. Panels *A–D* would span approximately 5 to 9 weeks after fertilization in the human embryo. Key: ureteric bud (*u*), mesenchyme (*m*), mesenchymal condensate (*mc*), comma and S-shaped bodies (*c* and *s*), glomerulus (*g*), and wolffian duct (*w*). *E–H* are not drawn to scale. Arrowheads in *B* indicate the first branch tips of the ureteric bud. (Reproduced from Woolf *et al.* 1995 with permission from the Rockefeller University Press.)

epithelial tube located just lateral to the midline of the embryo. The ureteric bud will develop to form all the adult structures from the branching collecting ducts to the ureter. The ureteric bud grows and makes contact with a group of mesenchymal cells located near the embryonic perito-neal cavity, which coalesce or condense around the tip of the bud to form a cap. These nephro-genic mesenchymal progenitor cells resemble fibroblasts but some of them are destined to undergo an extraordinary transition of their phenotype to form the epithelial cells of the nephron tubules. Other cells within the renal mesenchyme will differentiate into the interstitial fibroblast cells which are found between the tubules of the adult kidney (Herzlinger *et al.* 1992). The remaining cell types of the adult organ, which comprise the vasculature and nerves, are currently considered to grow into the metanephros from the major vessels and spinal ganglia which lie adjacent to the organs (Saxen 1987).

The renal mesenchyme is induced to develop into nephrons

In simple terms, the whole of the development of the mesenchyme can be divided into two phases, called 'induction' and 'nephrogenesis'. 'Induction' refers to the process by which one tissue, in this case the ureteric bud, interacts with another, the nephrogenic mesenchyme, causing the latter to differentiate. Induction has been investigated using an organ culture model in which the metanephros is dissected from the embryo and is grown on the surface of a filter where it can be maintained for up to one week (Grobstein 1953; Saxen and Lehtonen 1987). If the whole metanephros is cultured intact, the mesenchyme undergoes a burst of cell proliferation followed by the formation of tubules and (non-vascularized) glomeruli. If, however, the mesenchyme is cultured in isolation, it fails to differentiate and then dies despite being provided with serum and nutrients. It is therefore apparent that the ureteric bud must be present for the mesenchyme to survive and grow. In general, when one tissue affects the behaviour of another, the 'cross-talk' must involve either a direct cell–cell or cell–matrix interaction, or it must be mediated by release of soluble molecules called 'cytokines' or 'growth factors'.

An early observation, using the organ culture model, shed light on the nature of inductive process. Grobstein (1953) found that the mesenchyme could be induced when embryonic spinal cord was placed on the opposite side of a filter to that of the kidney rudiment. At first it was thought that a soluble factor released by the neural tissue might mediate the process, but further investigations showed that neurones had penetrated the mesenchyme through the microscopic pores of the filter. If the neural tissue of the spinal cord was destroyed, leaving its supporting tissue intact, the induction did not occur (Sariola *et al.* 1989). Interestingly, neuronal cell bodies are observed around the ureteric bud *in vivo* and this supports the argument that the earliest stages of kidney development may be partly dependent on the early innervation of the organ (Sariola *et al.* 1988*a*).

The 'cross-talk' which occurs between the mesenchyme and the ureteric bud in tissue culture is also likely to be essential for normal nephrogenesis *in vivo*. Primary perturbations of these molecular mechanisms could contribute to the pathogenesis of human renal disorders such as agenesis and dysplasias in which kidneys respectively are absent or fail to mature, although it is often assumed (and stated in text books) that human renal malformations are usually caused by prenatal obstruction by lesions in the ureter or urethra. However, there has been some difficulty in reproducing these diseases experimentally using surgical obstruction in the fetal period (Berman and Maizels 1982; Gonzalez *et al.* 1990). The human disorders can occur sporadically or be inherited, suggesting as yet unknown genetic causes (Roodhooft *et al.* 1984; McPherson *et al.* 1987). It will become evident from reading the rest of this chapter that renal malformations may arise from the primary aberrant expression of master genes during early kidney development; in these cases there are no anatomical lesions which obstruct the developing organ.

Recently, Kreidberg *et al.* (1993) used transgenic technology to generate mice with homozygous null (non-functional) mutations of WT1, a gene expressed in induced renal mesenchyme. The WT1 gene is normally expressed in the induced mesenchyme and also in the podocytes of mature glomeruli; it codes for a series transcription factor proteins which regulate the transcription of a range of metanephric growth factors (Rauscher *et al.* 1990; Drummond *et al.* 1991). In the mutant mice the renal mesenchyme fails to survive, thus producing kidney aplasia. In humans, WT1 mutations occur in about 10% of sporadic Wilms' tumours, childhood renal malignancies which resemble undifferentiated kidney tissue, and in the majority of patients with the Denys–Drash syndrome (Coppes *et al.* 1993). The latter condition is characterized by early-onset nephrotic syndrome, perhaps suggesting that WT1 has a role in maintaining the normal filtration barrier within the glomerulus.

Death in the developing kidney

As mentioned above, the uninduced mesenchyme will rapidly die *in vitro*. This process is at least partly mediated by apoptosis (Koseki *et al.* 1992), which is widespread in the embryo and appears

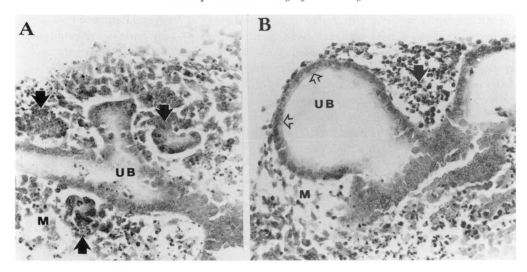

Fig. 1.3 Blockade of HGF/SF in metanephric organ culture. Embryonic day 11 mouse kidney rudiments after three days of growth in organ culture in either (*A*) serum-free basal media alone or (*B*) basal media with antisera to hepatocyte growth factor (HGF). Note that ureteric bud branching and nephron formation are limited in organs treated with anti-HGF antibody (*B*). Condensations of mesenchyme have formed around the tips of the ureteric bud in (*A*), but, in the presence of anti-sera to HGF (*B*), the ureteric bud is surrounded by undifferentiated mesenchyme with pyknotic nuclei. These data suggest that HGF is produced by the metanephros and that, under these *in vitro* conditions, the factor is necessary for the survival and differentiation of the organ. Arrowheads indicate the tips of the ureteric bud and arrows in (*A*) indicate primitive nephrons which have forming from undifferentiated mesenchyme. Ureteric bud and its derivatives are designated by *u* and renal mesenchyme by *m*. Bars are 100 μm. (Reproduced from Woolf *et al.* 1995, with permission from the Rockefeller University Press.)

to be an essential mechanism by which tissues are remodelled (Walker *et al.* 1988; Barres *et al.* 1992). When a cell dies by apoptosis its metabolism is highly active with messenger ribonucleic acid (mRNA) being transcribed in the nucleus and proteins synthesized in the cytoplasm. An early feature of apoptosis is the degradation of deoxyribonucleic acid (DNA) by a calcium-dependent endonuclease which restricts the molecule to segments approximately 200 base-pairs in lenght. For these reasons the process is also known as 'programmed cell death' or 'cell suicide' to contrast with toxic necrosis in which metabolic failure is an early event.

Koseki and colleagues (1992) found that the application of epidermal growth factor (EGF) to the uninduced renal mesenchyme could reduce the degree of apoptosis which occurred *in vitro*. This molecule is the adult homologue of transforming growth factor-α (TGF-α) which is known to be synthesized by the metanephros in the period after induction (Rogers *et al.* 1992). Although EGF can save the mesenchyme from cell suicide, it is not sufficient for the induction of nephrogenesis (Koseki *et al.* 1992). It is of interest that apoptosis continues after induction and is marked in two areas: in the zone of active nephrogenesis, where mitosis is marked, and in the medullary papilla where no correlation with mitosis is seen (Coles *et al.* 1993). Hepatocyte growth factor (HGF; Fig. 1.3) is expressed by the early mesenchyme and, among multiple roles, has also been shown to reduce cell death in metanephric organ culture (Woolf *et al.* 1995).

Early kidney growth and differentiation thus involves a fine balance of cell proliferation and cell death; an excess of these processes respectively causes renal neoplasms (e.g. Wilm's tumour) or failure of kidney growth and differentiation. There is preliminary evidence that in human dysplastic kidneys, which are malformations in which the mesenchyme fails to differentiate, there is an excess of cell death (Winyard *et al.* 1996a), suggesting that the pathogenesis might involve a lack of growth factors which prevent apoptosis. Interestingly, human dysplastic kidneys are often observed to completely involute (Mesrobia *et al.* 1993), and this might be explained be an excess of cell death versus proliferation. Mice which lack functional BCL2, a protein which blocks apoptosis by preventing lipid peroxidation, have excessive renal cell death *in vivo* and, intriguingly, also develop polycystic kidneys (Veis *et al.* 1993). In that animal model excessive cell death coexists with increased epithelial cell proliferation and similar observations have been made in human polycystic kidney diseases (Winyard *et al.* 1996a).

How does the ureteric bud branch?

Potter (1972) has described in detail the anatomy of the ureteric bud as it branches serially to form the collecting ducts. Grobstein (1953) noted that the ureteric bud did not develop in organ culture if it was separated from the adjoining mesenchyme, suggesting that the mesenchyme must communicate with the bud to cause proliferation and branching. Some progress has been made toward defining the molecular controls of morphogenesis of the ureteric bud. Importantly, the epithelia in the ureteric bud express various plasma membranebound tyrosine kinases which are considered to transduce differentiation signals after binding to growth factors produced by the adjacent renal mesenchyme (Sonnenberg *et al.* 1991; Pachnis *et al.* 1993; Woolf *et al.* 1995).

The most important of these signalling systems involves the c-ret protooncogene which is a receptor tyrosine kinase expressed in the branching tips of the bud (Pachnis *et al.* 1993). Its ligand is glial cell line-derived neurotrophic factor (Jing *et al.* 1996). Transgenic mice which do not express functional c-ret either fail to develop ureters and collecting ducts or have small dsyplastic kidneys (Schuchardt *et al.* 1994). As yet, mutations of this gene have not been been reported in patients with renal malformations although c-ret mutations do occur in some patients who have (1) isolated papillary thyroid carcinomas, (2) inherited medullary thyroid and adrenal tumours (multiple endocrine neoplasia IIA), and (3) Hirschprung's disease (reviewed by van Heyningen 1994).

In 1991, Montesano and co-workers reported that epithelial cysts, derived renal epithelial cell lines, branched serially when HGF was added to the medium. Within the metanephros HGF is secreted by mesenchymal cells and the c-met proto-oncogene, its receptor tyrosine kinase, is expressed by the adjacent ureteric bud. Moreover, antisera which block the bioactivity of HGF (Fig. 1.3) also prevent the branching of the ureteric bud when grown in organ culture (Woolf *et al.* 1995). Other mechanisms may contribute to the branching of the bud. For example, a macromolecule, the G_{D3} ganglioside, is expressed on the surface of mesenchyme adjoining the ureteric bud. Antisera to G_{D3} added to the metanephros in organ culture block subsequent development of the bud and mesenchyme (Sariola *et al.* 1988b). Currently the mode of action of this molecule is not known.

Formation of the nephron

Each nephron develops from a solid ball of cells which has condensed from the induced nephrogenic mesenchyme. These condensates appear at the tips of the ureteric bud (Figs 1.1 and 1.2) so that serial branching of the bud is associated with the fromation of sequential layers of nephrons. For this reaon, during nephrogenesis, the most mature nephrons are located towards the centre of the organ. In the mouse and rat nephron formation continues for one month after birth, but in humans the process is complete by 36 weeks after fertilization (Potter 1972; Saxen 1987). Listed below are three major areas in which control of nephron formation has been described.

The extracellular matrix

During the transition from metanephric mesenchyme to epithelium, progenitor cells lose the expression of neural cell adhesion molecule, a surface glycoprotein, and begin to express another cell membrane protein, uvomorulin, which contributes to the adhesion between cells in mature epithelia (Gumbiner *et al.* 1988; Klein *et al.* 1988*a,b*). If the gene coding for uvomorulin is transfected into fibroblasts they change their phenotype to resemble polarized epithelium (Mc-Neil *et al.* 1990). This involves the reorganization of the cytoskeleton and localization of proteins within the cell membrane (Rodriguez-Boulan and Nelson 1989). For example, the localization of the Na^+-K^+-ATPase pump to the basolateral membrane facilitates the net movement of solute out of the tubule lumen, and is characteristic of epithelial cells in the nephron. This development of cell asymmetry is essential for the differentiation of mesenchymal cells into a polarized epithelium.

Laminin is an extracellular matrix glycoprotein which anchors cells by binding to cell-surface receptors called 'intergrins'. In the mature epithelium, laminin is located in the basement membrane of epithelia and the laminin A chain protein can be first detected during nephrogenesis when the mesenchyme is induced and epithelia are forming (Klein *et al.* 1988*a*). Evidence for the role of laminin A chain in nephrogenesis come from the observation that tubule formation in metanephric organ culture is inhibited by antibodies against the laminin A chain but not against antibodies to uvomorulin (Klein *et al.* 1988*a*; Sariola *et al.* 1988*b*). The human KAL gene is located on the short arm of the X chromosome and encodes for a putative protein with homology to molecules which are known to be involved in cell–cell and cell–matrix adhesion (Franco *et al.* 1991). The gene is mutated in patients with Kallmann's syndrome, a disorder which comprises a complex of aberrations in neural development, resulting in anosmia and infertility. About 30% of these patients have unilateral renal agenesis (Hardelin *et al.* 1993) and it is interesting that KAL mRNA is expressed early in early human nephrogenesis (Legouis *et al.* 1993; Duke *et al.* 1995).

Growth factors

Experimental evidence from metanephric organ culture implicates a variety of growth factors and their receptors in the control of nephron formations. These include HGF (Woolf *et al.* 1995*a*), insulin-like growth factors (IGF) I and II and the IGFI receptor (Rogers *et al.* 1991), the low affinity nerve growth factor receptor (NGFR; Sariola *et al.* 1991), and TGF-α (Rogers *et al.* 1992) and TGF-β (Rogers *et al.* 1993) in nephron formation. All are secreted by the metanephros in organ culture and antibodies which bind to and sequester them will perturb of affect nephrogenesis *in vitro*. In this context, all the factors enhance nephrogenesis apart from TGF-β which inhibits nephron formation and branching morphogenesis; the latter molecule has similar inhibitory actions on the development of other embryonic organs (Hardman *et al.* 1994).

Despite the above data from a wide array of *in vitro* experiments, mice with transgenic homozygous null mutations of either HGF (Schmidt *et al.* 1995) or IGF II (De Chiara *et al.* 1992) or low-affinity NGFR (Lee *et al.* 1992) or TGF-α (Luetteke *et al.* 1993; Mann *et al.* 1993) or TGF-β (Letterio *et al.* 1994) appear to have grossly normal kidney development, suggesting that, in the context of the whole animal, nephrogenesis may proceed without any one of these factors. It is possible that an *in vivo* deficiency of more than one of these genes would be necessary to produce aberrant nephrogenesis (Stein *et al.* 1994). Finally, circulating factors such as the thyroid hormones, together with the metals selenium and iron, enhance nephrogenesis in organ culture and are presumed to be of importance to nephrogenesis *in vivo* (Avner *et al.* 1985).

Transcription factors

While extracellular matrix molecules and growth factors undoubtedly affect the survival, proliferation, and differentiation of the metanephros, the question arises 'What regulates the expression of those proteins?' The answer is likely to be the sequential expression of 'master' genes which code for proteins called transcription factors that bind to and regulate the expression of other genes. Such molecules are known to orchestrate the development of the *Drosophila* fruit fly where they determine the body axes and the genesis of specialized segments such as the head, thorax, and abdomen (Kessel and Gruss 1990). These transcription factors act as control elements in a cascade of gene activation and repression and their targets include genes which code for growth factors and their receptors, extracellular matrix molecules, and other transcription factors. Remarkably, many transcription factors expressed during *Drosophila* development have homologues in mouse and man (Kessel and Gruss 1990) and some, such as the PAX and HOX genes, are expressed in specific cell populations during nephrogenesis (Winyard *et al.* 1996*b*). One such transcription factor that is encoded by the WT1 gene has been discussed earlier in this chapter. PAX2 is a another transcription factor gene expressed in the metanephros. When gene function is abolished in organ culture using the technique of anti-sense olionucleotides which sequester PAX2 mRNA, nephron formation is abolished (Rothenpeiler and Dressler 1993). Moreover, overexpression of the PAX2 gene in transgenic mice results in aberrations of kidney development comprising epithelial overgrowth and a congenital nephrotic syndrome (Dressler *et al.* 1993). PAX2 is also overexpressed in human cystic dysplastic kidneys (Winyard *et al.* 1996*b*). These recent studies give an indication of how the sequential expression of genes which code for transcription factors may orchestrate both normal and pathological nephron formation and function.

Formation of glomerular blood supply and basement membrane

After the establishment of epithelial polarity in the primitive nephron, the characteristic glomerular, proximal, and distal epithelia are seen to develop but little is known about the mechanisms which generate this diversity. Tissue remodelling also occurs during this period and apoptosis may contribute to this process. Cell death is marked both at the reflection of the glomerular visceral and parietal epithelia and also in the medulla of the kidney where the loops of Henle will develop (Coles *et al.* 1993).

Factors which stimulate the proliferation and migration of capillary endothelial cells are produced by the developing kidney (Risau and Ekblom,. 1986); these include vascular endothelial growth factor (VEGF) which is also known as vascular permeability factor (Breier *et al.* 1992). When the metanephros is grown in organ culture the glomeruli which develop remain avascular, but when the early metanephric rudiment is grafted onto the avian chorioallantoic membrane the transplanted organ becomes vascularized by ingrowth from the host blood vessels (Sariola *et al.* 1983), a process known as angiogenesis. More recent evidence, however, suggests that at least some renal blood vessels may differentiate from precursors within the metanephros by the process of vasculogenesis. For example, the renal mesenchyme expresses receptors for VEGF when it contains no mature capillaries (Loughna *et al.* 1997) and when the metanephros is transplanted into the anterior chamber of the eye or into the neonated mouse nephrogenic cortex the vasculature originates from the donor rather than the host (Pinson *et al.* 1993; Loughna *et al.* 1997).

The matrix which separates the capillary endothelium from the glomerular visceral epithelium is at first generate by both of these tissues (Sariola *et al.* 1984), and as the nephron matures these matrices fuse to form the glomerular basement membrane. After fusion there are sequential changes in the isoforms of collagen IV chains which are expressed and which can be correlated with the progressive restriction of filtration of macromolecules (Abrahamson and Leard Kamolkarn 1991). In Alport's syndrome, which is an inherited form of glomerular disease, the structure of the glomerular basement membrane is abnormal and a large variety of mutations of the gene coding for the 5α chain of collagen IV have been detected (Zhou *et al.* 1991).

In addition to the epithelial and endothelial cells, the glomerulus contains another population called the mesangial cells which resemble fibroblasts and smooth muscle cells. They support the delicate capillary loops within the glomerular tuft and during development their growth and differentiation may be controlled in part by platelet-derived growth factor secreted by epithelial cells (Alpers *et al.* 1992). Mice which are deficient in the cell surface receptor for this growth factor fail to develop mesangial cells and consequently have glomeruli which lack complex capillary loops (Soriano 1994).

Developmental physiology of the kidney

Introduction

Kidney function can be broadly classified into three categories:

(1) glomerular filtration;
(2) tubular reabsorption and secretion;
(3) the endocrine function of the kidney.

Although it is known that glomerular filtration occurs as early as the mesonephric phase (Gersch 1937) and that tubular ion pumps are expressed in the fetal kidney (Minuth *et al.* 1987), it has proved difficult to perform physiological tests of renal function when animals are *in utero*. On account of this problem most reports have focused on physiological changes which occur in the neonateal period or compared neonatal renal function with adult kidney function. On reviewing these studies it is clear that the maturity of kidney anatomy, and therefore renal function, differs markedly between species at the time of birth. In humans, for example, no new nephrons are formed after 34–36 weeks of gestation, whereas in the mouse and the rat, nephro-genesis continues for about two weeks after birth. (Saxen 1987; Potter 1972). Comparisons of developmental renal function between species must therefore be interpreted with this caveat in mind. It should be noted that, in experimental animals, tubular cell differentiation and diversi-fication continue in the postnatal period and, using *in vitro* experiments, there is evidence of plasticity of tubular epithelial cell phenotype even in the adult (Evan *et al.* 1991; Fejes-Toth and Naray-Fejes-Toth 1992).

The maturation of renal haemodynamics

As discussed above, the glomerular capillary network is currently thought to be formed by *in situ* growth of enothelial cells in the primitive glomerular epithelium of the mesenchyme condensate (Loughna *et al.* 1997). Studies of renal plasma flow have been performed in human neonates and are based on the clearance of para-amino hippurate (PAH) (Gruskin *et al.* 1970; Aschinberg *et al.* 1975; Ichikawa *et al.* 1979). In full-term neonates, the tubular extraction of PAH is only two-thirds of the adult value and this reflects an inability of the pre-term kidney tubules to excrete organic acids. When factored for body surface area, renal plasma flow is only approximately 50% of the adult value. The total renal vascular resistance of the kidney exceeds adult values, and both the afferent and efferent glomerular arterioles appear to be constricted in the immature kidney.

The cause of the fall of renal vascular resistance which occurs after birth is not known but may be partly explained by a failling ratio of α adrenergic (constrictor) to β adrenergic (vasodilator) receptors which are located in the renal vasculature (Felder *et al.* 1983). in addition, the fall of high levels of circulating plasma renin activity and angiotensin II may contribute to the increase of plasma flow (Arant and Stephenson 1982; Grone *et al.* 1992). A striking feature of the fetal renal vasculature is the distribution of renin secreting cells which extend from the adult conformation, in the juxtaglomerular region, to a more proximal location within the afferent arterioles and larger renal afferent vessels (Jones *et al.* 1990). Funthermore, two angiotensin II receptor subtypes, AT_1 and AT_2, show a complex non-overlapping distribution during postnatal kidney development (Aguilera *et al.* 1994), perhaps suggesting multiple roles for this signalling system. Although the kidneys possess all the biochemical components necessary to generate angiotensin, the exact physiological function of this system within the fetal kidneys is not known. It is, however, of note that the use of angiotensin-converting enzyme inhibitors appears to reduce the rate of postnatal maturation of glomerular capillaries in rats (Fogo *et al.* 1990).

In human neonates, it is striking that glomerular filtration rate, usually assesseed by creatinine clearance, increases little before about 34 weeks of gestation, even though renal weight rises during that period: after this time glomerular filtration rate rises rapidly (Leake *et al.* 1976; Arant 1978; Stonestreet and Oh 1978; Arant and Stephenson 1982). It would appear that this increase of filtration may be partly explained by both the termination of nephrogeneis and also the fall of renal vascular resistance as described above. In human term neonates, plasma creatinine falls over the first month, and the failure of plasma creatinine to fall is an important early clinical indication of the presence of congenital renal disease.

Tubular function

Sodium and water homeostasis

Apart from the clearance of the waste proudcts of nitrogen metabolism, the most important function of the kidney is to maintain the balance of sodium in the body, which in turn determines the extracellular fluid volume, because it is the main cation within that compartment. Postnatally, term infants lose 10% of their extracellular volume because of a renal sodium 'leak' (Arant 1978; Al-Dahhan *et al.* 1983; Rodriguez-Soriano *et al.* 1983). The fractional excretion of sodium, which is urinary sodium clearance factored for glomerular filtration rate, is 0.2% in term neonates but is >5% of glomerular filtration rate in preterm infants born before 30 weeks of gestation. The mechanism of this natriuresis has been debated and two alternate hypotheses have been proposed.

If the preterm infant is considered to have an expanded extracellular fluid space then the high fractional excretion of soduium may be regarded as an appropriate physiological response. Certainly, plasma levels of atrial natriuretic factor are elevated birth and fall rapidly in the first two postnatal weeks (Tulassay *et al.* 1987). This homone is secreted by the heart in response to atrial stretch caused by an increase of blood volumen.

Alternatively, the high fractional sodium excretion had been considered to be an inappropriate renal response to a normal extracellular volume. This hypothesis postulates an imbalance between an excessive load of filtrate produced by relatively mature glomeruli and an impaired capacity for reabsorption by the less mature tubular epithelia. It has been demonstrated that distal tubule sodium reabsorption becomes enhanced during the neonatal period (Aperia and Elinder 1981) and that the loss of the ion by the immature kidney is partly accounted for by a failure of sodium reabsorption of more proximal nephron segments (Sulyok *et al.* 1979). There is also evidence that the natriuresis which is sometimes recorded in preterm infants might be due to an inability of the adrenal gland to secrete aldosterone in response to a fall of plasma volume (Spitzer 1982) combined with a diminished tubular sodium-retaining response to this hormone (Aperia *et al.* 1979).

The fetal kidney of the sheep is able to respond to plasma hypertonicity by an increase of urine osmolality, and fetal urine is concentrated in response to an infusion of arginine vasopressin (AVP) (Woods 1986; Woods *et al.* 1986). It is interesting that while full-term neonates can increase urine volumes in response to a high fluid intake, in one study this response was independent of a change of plasma AVP (Aperia *et al.* 1984).

Potassium homeostasis

The plasma potassium concentration of neonates tends to be higher than adult values, and it appears that the connecting tubule and cortical collecting ducts of the immature kidney are less able to excrete a potassium load compared to the mature organ even when the lower glomerular filtration rate is taken into account (Jones and Chesney 1992). It is interesting that although renal aldosterone receptors are present in the mammalian fetal kidney (Pasqualini *et al.* 1972), the kaliuretic response to aldosterone is blunted in the neonatal period (Kleinman and Banks 1983). Jones and Chesney (1992) have summarized a variety of factors which may contribute to the impaired potassium secretion of the immature kidney and these include reduced Na^+-K^+-ATPase activity in the basolateral membrane of principal cells and a limited permaeability to potassium in their luminal surface. The aforementioned ion pump is required to move potassium ions into the epithelial cells from where they can enter the tubular lumen.

Acid–base balance

With regard to hydrogen ion homeostasis by the kidney, the plasma bicarbonate level is lower in the neonate than in the adult and this is explained by the lower capacity of the proximal tubule to reabsorb HCO_3 (Edelmann *et al.* 1967). The capacity to reabsorb HCO_3 increases in parallel with total fluid reabsorption by this segment, which in turn correlates with a postnatal increase of the tubular basolateral surface area (Schwartz and Evan 1983). There is no impairment of carbonic anhydrase activity in the second trimester human kidney (Beck *et al.* 1991) and neonates are able to excrete an acid urine (Edelmann *et al.* 1967). Moreover, the capacity to excrete ammonium and titrable acid increases to adult values, when factored for glomerular filtration rate, by the first month post-term (Edelmann *et al.* 1967).

In brief, the ability of the neonatal kidney to concentrate urine, and reabsorb amino acids, glucose, and ß2 micraglobulin is impaired whereas phosphate reabsorption is enhanced compared to the adult (Arant 1978; Aperia *et al.* 1981; Jones and Chesney 1992). These aspects are considered in more detail in later chapters of this book in which inherited defects of these systems are reviewed.

Tubular cell polarity in normal and abnormal kidney development

The plasma membrane of a renal mesenchymal cell is uniform but, as these cells differentiate into nephron epithelia, they 'polarize' so that certain proteins become progressively restricted to specific membrane domains (Rodriguez-Boulan and Nelson 1989). For example, the apical brush border of the proximal tubule contains enzymes such as alkaline phosphatase, and the apical membrane of the α-intercalated cell of the cortical collecting duct contains H$^+$ pumps. Epidermal growth factor (EGF) is also targeted to the apical membrane of tubular cells and enters the urine from that point. In contrast, in mature epithelia the Na$^+$-K$^+$-ATPase ion pump is localized to the basolateral membrane, and provides the major electromotive force for the vectorial transport of solutes out of the tubule lumen. In mature epithelia, growth factor receptors are often located in the basolateral membrane and it is from the basal aspect of the epithelium that the components of the basal lamina matrix, including collagen IV, are secreted.

Recently, specific membrane proteins have been found to be mislocalized in a variety of renal disorders. Of relevance to genetic renal diseases are reports of the mislocation of both Na-K$^+$-ATPase and EGF receptors in patients and animals who suffer from inherited polycystic kidney diseases (Fig. 1.4). In the renal tubules and early cysts of patients with autosomal dominant polycystic renal disease (Wilson *et al.* 1991), and in animals with autosomal recessive polycystic kidney disease (Avner *et al.* 1992), the Na$^+$-K$^+$-ATPase pump is located in an atypical, apical location. The mislocation of the sodium pump may contribute to the vectorial transport of solutes and water into the cyst lumen. Cpk/cpk mice develop polcystic disease and have an apical location of the EGF receptor in renal tubules. This could activate an intrarenal paracrine loop because EGF secreted into the tubular lumen would access its receptor and stimulate the proliferation of cystic epithelia (Avner 1993). Finally, kidney cyst fluids in patients with polycystic diseases often contain high concentrations of low molecular weight molecules which are, in health, transported out of the tubule lumen (Foxall *et al.* 1992).

It can be argued that the cystic epithelia resemble a dedifferentiated or embryonic state with a less polarized and hyperproliferative phenotype (McKay *et al.* 1987; Trudel *et al.* 1991).

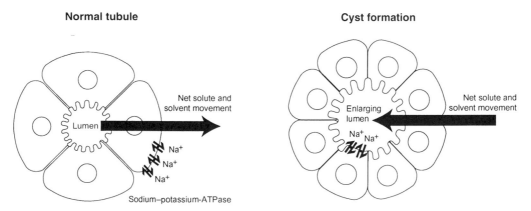

Fig. 1.4 Polarity in renal epithelia. A. Cross section of a normal adult nephron shows net movement of water and solute from the lumen into the renal interstitium. The energy for this process is provided by the Na$^+$-K$^+$-ATPase pumps in the basolateral cell membranes. B. In inherited cystic diseases there is evidence that this ion pump, and also the EGF receptor, are mislocalized to the apical membrane. Note also the hypercellularity of the tubule versus the normal epithelium in (A).

Interestingly, the administration of Taxol, a drug which can prevent the targeting of protein to the apical plasma membrane (Ojakian and Schwimmer 1992), and is also antimitotic, can retard the *in vivo* growth of renal cysts in cpk/cpk mice (Woo *et al.* 1994).

Acknowledgements

This work was supported by grants from the National Kidney Research Fund, the Wellcome Trust, Action Research, and the British Heart Foundation.

References

Abrahamson, D. R. and Leardkamolkarn, V. (1991). Development of kidney tubular basement membranes. *Kidney International*, **39**, 382–93.

Aguilera, G., Kapur, S., Feuillan, P., Sunar-Akbasak, B., and Bathia, A. J. (1994). Developmental changes in angiotensin II receptor subtypes and AT_1 receptor mRNA in rat kidney. *Kidney International*, **46**, 973–80.

Al-Dahhan, I., Haycock, G., Chantler, C., and Stimmler, L. (1983). Sodium homeostasis in term and preterm neonates. *Archives of Disease in Childhood*, **58**, 335–42.

Al-Khaldi, N., Watson, A. R., Zucollo, J., Twining, P., and Rose, D. H. (1994). Outcome of antenatally detected cystic dysplastic kidney disease. *Archives of Diseases in Childhood*, **70**, 520–2.

Alpers, C. E., Seifert, R. A., Hudkins, K. L., Johnson, R. J., and Bowen-Pope, D. R. (1992). Developmental patterns of platelet-derived growth factor B chain, PDGF receptor and α-actin expression in human glomerulogenesis. *Kidney International*, **42**, 390–9.

Aperia, A., Broberger, O., Herin, P., *et al.* (1979). Sodium excretion in relation to sodium intake and aldosterone excretion in newborn preterm and full-term infants. *Acta. Physiol. Scand.*, **68**, 813–19.

Aperia, A., Broberger, O., Elinder, G., Herin, P., and Zetterstrom, R. (1981). Postnatal development of renal function in preterm and full-term infants. *Acta. Paediatr. Scand.*, **70**, 183–7.

Aperia, A. and Elinder, G. (1981). Distal sodium reabsorption in the developing rat kidney. *American Journal of Physiology*, **240**, F487–F491.

Aperia, A., Herin, P., Lundin, S., Melin, P., and Zetterstrom, R. (1984). Regulation of renal water excretion in newborn full-term infants. *Acta. Paediatr. Scand.*, **73**, 717–21.

Arant, B. S. Jr. (1978). Developmental patterns of renal functional maturation compared in the human neonate. *Journal of Pediatrics*, **92**, 705–12.

Arant, B. S. Jr. and Stephenson, W. H. (1982). Developmental changes in systemic vascular resistance compared with prostaglandins and angiotensin II concentration in arterial plasma of conscious dogs. *Pediatric Research*, **16**, 120A.

Aschinberg, L. C., Goldsmith, D. I., Obling, H., *et al.* (1975). Neonatal changes in blood flow distribution in puppies. *American Journal of Physiology*, **228**, 1453–61.

Avner, E. D., Sweeney, W. E., Piesco, N. P., and Ellis, D. (1985). Growth factor requirements of organogenesis in serum-free metanephric organ culture. *In Vitro Cellular and Developmental Biology*, **21**, 297–304.

Avner, E. D., Sweeney, W. E., and Nelson, W. J. (1992). Abnormal sodium pump distribution during renal tubulogenesis in congenital murine polycystic disease. *Proc. Natl. Acad. Sci. USA*, **89**, 7447–51.

Avner, E. D. (1993). Renal developmental diseases, *Seminars in Nephrology*, **13**, 427–35.

Barres, B. A., Hart, I. K., Coles, H. S. R., Burne, J. F., Voyvodic, J. T., Richardson, W. D., *et al.* (1992). Cell death and control of survival in the oligodendrocyte lineage. *Cell*, **70**, 31–46.

Beck, J. C., Lipkowitz, M. S., and Albamson, R. G. (1991). Ontogony of Na/H antiporter activity in rabbit renal brush border vesicles. *Journal of Clinical Investigation*, **87**, 2067–76.

Berman, D. and Maizels, M. (1982). The role of urinary obstruction in the genesis of renal dysplasia. *Journal of Urology*, **128**, 1091–100.

Bosch, R. J., Woolf, A. S., and Fine, L. G. (1993). Gene transfer into the mammalial kidney: direct transduction of regenerating tubular epithelial cells. *Experimental Nephrology*, **1**, 49–54.

Breier, G., Albrecht, U., Sterrer, S., and Risau, W. (1992). Expression of vascular endothelial growth factor during embryonic angiogenesis and endothelial cell differentiation. *Development*, **114**, 521–32.

Coles, H. S. R., Burne, J. F., and Raff, M. C. (1993). Large-scale normal cell death in the developing rat kidney and its reduction by epidermal growth factor. *Development*, **118**, 777–84.

Coppes, M. J., Huff, V., and Pelletier, J. (1993). Denys–Drash syndrome: relating a clinical disorder to alterations in the tumor suppressor gene WT1. *Journal of Paediatrics*, **123**, 673–8.

De Chiara, T. M., Efstratiadis, A., and Robertson, E. J. (1990). A growth-deficiency phenotype in heterozygous mice carrying an insulin-like growth factor II gene disrupted by targeting. *Nature*, **345**, 78–80.

Dressler, G. R., Wilkinson, E. E., Rothenpieler, U. W., Patterson, L. T., Williams-Simons, L., and Westphal, H. (1993). Deregulation of *Pax-2* expression in transgenic mice generates severe kidney abnormalities. *Nature*, **362**, 65–7.

Drummond, I. A., Madden, S. L., Rohwer-Nutter, P., Bell, G. I., Sukhatme, V. P., and Rauscher III, F. J. (1991). Repression of the insulin-like growth factor II gene by Wilm's tumor suppressor WT1. *Science*, **257**, 674–7.

Duke, V., Winyard, P. J. D., Thorogood, P. V., Southill, P., Bouloux, P. M. G., Woolf, A. S., (1995). KAL, a gene mutated in Kallman's syndrome is expressed in the first trimester of human development. *Molec. Cell Endocrinol.*, **110**, 73–9.

Edelmann, C. M. Jr., Rodriguez-Soriano, J., Boichis, H., Gruskin, A. B., and Acosta, M. I. (1967). Renal bicarbonate reabsorption and hydrogenion excretion in normal infants. *Journal of Clinical Investigation*, **46**, 1309–17.

Ehrich, J. H. H., Rizzoni, G., Brunner, F. P., Fassbinder, W., Geerlings, W., Mallick, N. P., *et al.* (1992). Renal replacement therapy for end-stage renal failure before 2 years of age. *Nephrology Dialysis and Transplantation*, **7**, 1171–7.

Evan, A. P., Satlin, L. M., Gattone II, V. H., Connors, B., and Schwartz, G. J. (1991). Postnatal maturation of rabbit renal collecting duct. II. Morphological observations. *American Journal of Physiology*, **261**, F91–F107.

Fejes-Toth, G. and Naray-Fejes-Toth, A. (1992). Differentiation of renal β-intercalated cells to α-intercalated and principal cells in culture. *Proc. Natl. Acad. Sci. USA*, **89**, 5487–91.

Felder, R. A., Pelayo, J. C., Calcagno, P. L., *et al.* (1983). Alpha adrenoceptors in the developing kidney. *Pediatric Research*, **17**, 177–80.

Fogo, A., Yoshida, Y., Yared, A., and Ichikawa, I. (1990). Importance of angiogenic action of angiotensin II in the glomerular growth of maturing kidneys. *Kidney International*, **38**, 1068–74.

Foxall, P. J. D., Price, R. G., Jones, J. K., Neild, G. H., Thompson, F. D., and Nicholson, J. K. (1992). High-resolution proton magnetic resonance spectroscopy of cyst fluids from patients with polycystic kidney disease. *Biochemica. et. Biophysica. Acta.*, **1138**, 305–14.

Franco, B., Guioli, S., Pragliola, A., Incerti, B., Bardoni, B., Tonlorenzi, R., *et al.* (1991). A gene deleted in Kallmann's syndrome shares homology with neural cell adhesion and axonal path-finding molecules. *Nature*, **353**, 529–36.

Gersh, I. (1937). The correlation of structure and function in the developing mesonephros and metanephros. *Contributions to Nephrology*, **153**, 35–57.

Gonzalez, R., Reinberg, Y., Burke, B., Wels, T., and Vernier, R. L. (1990). Early bladder outlet obstruction in fetal lambs induces renal dysplasia and the prune-belly syndrome. *Journal of Pediatric Surgery*, **25**, 342–5.

Grobstein, C. (1953). Morphogenetic interaction between embryonic mouse tissues separated by a membrane filter. *Nature (London)*, **172**, 869–71.

Grone, H-J., Simon, M., and Fuchs, E. (1992). Autoradiographic characterization of angiotensin receptor subtypes in fetal and adult human kidney. *American Journal of Physiology*, **262**, F326–F331.

Gruskin, A. B., Edelmann, C. M. Jr., and Yuan, S. (1970). Maturational changes in renal blood flow in piglets. *Pediatric Research*, **4**, 7–13.

Gumbiner, B., Stevenson, B., and Grimalfi, A. (1988). The role of the cell adhesion molecule, uvomorulin, in the formation and maintenance of the epithelial junctional complex. *Journal of Cell Biology*, **107**, 1575–87.

Hardelin, J-P., Levilliers, J., Young, J., Pholsena, M., Legouis, R., Kirk, J., *et al.* (1993). Xp22.3 deletions in isolated familial Kallmann's syndrome. *J. Clin. Endocrinol. Metab.*, **76**, 827–31.

Hardman, P., Landels, E., Woolf, A. S., and Spooner, B. S. (1994*b*). Transforming growth factor β1 inhibits growth and branching morphogenesis in embryonic mouse submandibular and sublingual glands. *Dev. Growth Diff.*, **36**, 567–77.

Harris, P. and the European polycystic kidney disease consortium (1994). The polycystic kidney disease 1 gene encodes a 14 kb transcript and lies within a duplicated region on chromosome 16. *Cell*, **77**, 881–94.

Herzlinger, D., Koseki, C., Mikawa, T., and Al-Awqati, Q. (1992). Metanephric mesenchyme contains multipotent stem cells whose fate is restricted after induction. *Development*, **114**, 565–72.

Holliday, M. A., Barratt, T. M., and Avner, E. (1994). *Pediatric nephrology*. Williams and Williams, Baltimore.

Ichikawa, I., Maddox, D. A., and Brenner, B. M. (1979). Maturation development of glomerular ultrafiltration in the rat. *American Journal of Physiology*, **236**, F465–F471.

Jing, S., Wen, D., Yu, Y., Holst, P. L., Luo, Y., Fang, M., Tamir, R., Antonio, L., Hu, Z., Cupples, R., Louis, J. C., Hu, S., Atrock, B. W., Fox, G. M. (1996). GDNF-induced activation of the ret protein tyrosine kinase is mediated by GDNFR-alpha, a novel receptor for GDNF. *Cell*, **85**, 1113–24.

Jones, C. A., Sigmund, C. D., McGowan, R. A., Kane-Haas, C. M., and Gross, K. W. (1990). Expression of murine renin genes during fetal development. *Molecular Endocrinology*, **4**, 375–83.

Jones, D. P. and Chesney, R. W. (1992). Development of tubular function. *Clinics in Perinatology*, **19**, 33–57.

Kaplan, B. S., Kaplan, P., and Ruchelli, E. (1991). Inherited and congenital malformations of the kidneys in the neonatal period. *Clinics in Perinatology*, **19**, 197–211.

Kessel, M. and Gruss, P. (1990). Murine developmental control genes. *Science*, **249**, 374–8.

Klein, G., Langegger, M., Timpl, R., and Ekblom, P. (1988*a*). Role of laminin A chain in the development of epithelial cell polarity. *Cell*, **55**, 331–41.

Klein, G., Langegger, M., Garidis, C., and Ekblom, P. (1988*b*). Neural cell adhesion molecules during embryonic induction and development of the kidney. *Development*, **102**, 749–61.

Kleinman, L. I. and Banks, R. O. (1983). Segmental sodium and potassium reabsorption in newborn and adult dogs during saline expansion. *Proc. Soc. Exp. Biol. Med.*, **173**, 231–7.

Koseki, C., Herzlinger, D., and Al-Awqati, Q. (1992). Apoptosis in metanephric development. *Journal of Cell Biology*, **119**, 1322–33.

Kreidberg, J. A., Sariola, H., Loring, J. M., Maeda, M., Pelletier, J., Housman D., *et al.* (1993). WT-1 is required for early kidney development. *Cell*, **74**, 679–91.

Law, C. M., de Swiet, M., Osmond, C., Fayers, P. M., Barker, D. J. P., Cruddas, A. M., *et al.* (1993). Initiation of hypertension *in utero* and its amplification throughout life. *British Medical Journal*, **306**, 24–7.

Leake, R. D., Trygstad, C. W., Oh, W. (1976). Inulin clearance in the newborn infant: relationship to gestational and postnatal age. *Pediatric Research*, **10**, 762–6.

Lee, K-F., Li, E., Huber, J., Londis, S. C., Sharpe, A. H., Chao, M. V., *et al.* (1992). Targeted mutation of the gene encoding the low-affinity NGF receptor p75 leads to deficits in the peripheral sensory nervous system. *Cell*, **69**, 733–49.

Legouis, R., Ayer-Le Lievre, C., Leibovici, M., Lapointe, F., and Petit, C. (1993). Expression of the *KAL* gene in multiple neuronal sites during chicken development. *Proc. Soc. Natl. Acad. Sci. USA*, **90**, 2461–5.

Letterio, J. J., Geiser, A. G., Kulkarni, A. B., *et al.* (1994). Maternal rescue of TGF-β mice. *Science*, **264**, 1936–7.

Loughna, S., Hardman, P., Landels, E., Jussila, L., Altalo, K., Woolf, A. S. (1997). A genetic and molecular analysis of renal glomerular capillary development. *Angiogenesis*, **1**, 84–101.

Luetteke, N. C., Qui, T. H., Peiffer, R. L., Oliver, P., Smithies, O., and Lee, D. C. (1993). TGFα deficiency results in hair follicle and eye abnormalities in targeted and waved-1 mice. *Cell*, **73**, 263–78.

McEnery, P. T., Stablein, D. M., Arbus, G., and Tejani, A. (1992). Renal transplantation in children. *New England Journal of Medicine*, **326**, 1727–32.

McKay, K., Striker, L. J., Pinkert, C. A., Brinster, R. L., and Striker, G. E. (1987). Glomerulosclerosis and renal cysts in mice transgenic for the early region of SV40. *Kidney International*, **32**, 827–37.

McNeil, H., Ozawa, M., Kemler, R., and Nelson, W. J. (1990). Novel function of the cell adhesion molecule uvomorulin as an inducer of cell surface polarity. *Cell*, **62**, 309–16.

McPherson, E., Carey, J., Kramer, A., *et al.* (1987). Dominantly inherited renal adysplasia. *Am. J. Med. Genet.*, **26**, 836–50.

Maizel, M. and Simpson, S. B. (1983). Primitive ducts of renal dysplasia induced by culturing ureteral buds denuded of condensed renal mesenchyme. *Science*, **219**, 509–10.

Mann, G. B., Fowler, K. J., Gabriel, A., Nice, E. C., Williams, R. L., and Dunn, A. R. (1993). Mice with null mutation of the TGFα gene have abnormal skin architecture, wavy hair and curly whiskers and often develop corneal inflammation. *Cell*, **73**, 249–61.

Mesrobian, H-G. J., Rushton, H. G., and Bulas, D. (1993). Unilateral renal agenesis may result from *in utero* regression of multicystic dysplasia. *Journal of Urology*, **150**, 793–4.

Minuth, W. W., Gross, P., Gilbert, P., *et al.* (1987). Expression of alpha subunit of Na-K-ATPase in renal collecting duct epithelium during development. *Kidney International*, **31**, 1104–12.

Montesano, R., Matsumoto, K., Nakamura, T., and Orci, L. (1991). Identification of fibroblast-derived epithelial morphogen as hepatocyte growth factor. *Cell*, **67**, 901–8.

Moullier, P., Friedlander, G., Calise, D., Ronco, P., Perricaudet, M., and Ferry, N. (1994). Adenoviral-mediated gene transfer into renal tubular cells *in vivo*. *Kidney International*, **45**, 1220–5.

Ojakian, G. K. and Schwimmer, R. (1992). Antimicrotubule drugs inhibit the polarized insertion of an intracellular glycoptotein pool into the apical membrane of Madin-Darby canine kidney (MDCK) cells. *Journal of Cell Science*, **103**, 677–87.

Pachnis, V., Mankoo, B., and Constantini, F. (1993). Expression of the c-ret proto-oncogene during mouse development. *Development*, **119**, 1005–20.

Pasqualini, J. R., Sumida, C., and Gelly, C. (1972). Mineralocorticoid receprors in the fetal compartment. *Journal of Steroid Biochemistry*, **3**, 543–56.

Pinson, D. Y., St. John, P. L., Tucker, D. C., and Abrahamson, D. R. (1993). Origin of glomerular microvasculature in kidneys developing in oculo. *Journal of the American Society of Nephrology*, **4**, 474. (Abstract).

Potter, E. L. (1972). *Normal and abnormal development of the kidney*. Year Book Medical Publishers, Inc., Chicago.

Rauscher, J. R., Morris, J. F., Tournay, O. E., Cook, O. M., and Curran, T. (1990). Wilm's tumour locus zinc finger binds to the *EGR-1* concensus sequence. *Science*, **250**, 1259–62.

Risau, W. and Ekblom, P. (1986). Production of a heparin-binding angiogenesis factor by the embryonic kidney. *Journal of Cell Biology*, **103**, 1101–7.

Rodriguez-Boulan, E. and Nelson, W. J. (1989). Morphogenesis of the polarized epithelial cell phenotype. *Science*, **245**, 718–25.

Rodriguez-Soriano, J., Vallo, A., Oliveros, R., and Castillo, G. (1983). Renal handling of soldium in premature and full-term neonates: a study using clearance methods during water immersion. *Pediatric Research*, **17**, 1013–17.

Rogers, S. A., Ryan, G., and Hammerman, M. R. (1991). Insulin-like growth factors I and II are produced in the metanephros and are required for growth and development *in vitro*. *Journal of Cell Biology*, **113**, 1447–53.

Rogers, S. A., Ryan, G., and Hammerman, M. R. (1992). Metanephric transforming growth factor-α is required for renal organogenesis *in vitro*. *American Journal of Physiology*, **262**, F533–F539.

Rogers, S. A., Ryan, G., Purchio, A. F., and Hammerman, M. R. (1993). Metanephric-transforming growth factor-β1 regulates nephrogenesis *in vitro*. *American Journal of Physiology*, **264**, F996–F1002.

Roodhooft, A. M., Birnholz, J. C., and Holmes, L. B. (1984). Familial nature of congenital absence and severe dysgenesis of both kidneys. *New England Journal of Medicine*, **310**, 1341–5.

Rothenpieler, U. W. and Dressler, G. R. (1993). *Pax-2* is required for mesenchyme to epithelium conversion during kidney development. *Development*, **119**, 711–20.

Sariola, H., Ekblom, P., Lehtonen, E., and Saxen, L. (1983). Differentiation and vascularization of the metanephric kidney grafted onto the chorioallantoic membrane. *Developmental Biology*, **96**, 427–35.

Sariola, H., Timpl, R., Von de Mark, K., *et al.* (1984). Dual origin of the glomerular basement membrane. *Developmental Biology*, **101**, 86–96.

Sariola, H., Holm, K., Henke-Fahle, H. (1988a). Early innervation of the metanephric kidney. *Development*, **104**, 589–99.

Sariola, H., Aufderheide, E., Bernhard, H., Henke-Fahle, B., Dippold, W., and Ekblom, P. (1988b). Antibodies to cell surface ganglioside GD3 perturb inductive epithelial mesenchymal interactions. *Cell*, **54**, 235–45.

Sariola, H., Ekblom, P., and Henke-Fahle, H. (1989). Embryonic neurons as *in vitro* inducers of differentiation of nephrogenic mesenchyme. *Developmental Biology*, **132**, 271–81.

Sariola, H., Saarma, M., Sainio, K., *et al.* (1991). Dependence of kidney morphogenesis on expression of nerve growth factor receptor. *Science*, **254**, 571–3.

Saxen, L. (1987). *Organogenesis of the kidney*. Cambridge University Press, Cambridge, UK.

Saxen, L. and Lehtonen, E. (1987). Embryonic kidney in organ culture. *Differentiation*, **36**, 2–11.

Schmidt, C., Bladt, F., Goedecke, S., Brinkman, V., Zschiesche, W., Sharpe, M., Gherardi, E., Birchmeir, C. (1995). Scatter factor/hepatocyte grow factor is essential for liver development. *Nature*, **373**, 702–5

Schuchardt, A., D'Agati, V., Larsson-Blomberg, L., *et al.* (1994). Defects in the kidney and enteric nervous system of mice lacking the tyrosine kinase receptor Ret. *Nature*, **367**, 380.

Schwartz, G. J. and Evan, A. P. (1983). Development of solute transport in the rat proximal tubule. I: HCO_3^- and glucose reabsorption. *American Journal of Physiology*, **245**, F382–F390.

Slotkin, T. A., Seidler, F. J., Kavlock, R. J., and Gray, J. A. (1992). Fetal dexamethasone exposure accelerates development of renal function: relationship to dose, cell differentiation and growth inhibition. *Journal of Developmental Physiology*, **17**, 55–61.

Sonnenberg, E., Godecke, A., Walter, B., Bladt, F., and Birchmeier, C. (1991). Transient and locally restricted expression of the *ros 1* protooncogene during mouse development. *EMBO J.*, **10**, 3693–702.

Soriano, P. (1994). Abnormal kidney development and hematological disorders in platelet-derived growth factor β-receptor mutant mice. *Genes and Development*, **8**, 1888–96.

Spitzer, A. (1982). The role of the kidney in sodium homeostasis during maturation. *Kidney International*, **21**, 539–45.

Stein, P. L., Vogel, H., and Soriano, P. (1994). Combined deficiencies of Src, Fyn and Yes tyrosine kinases in mutant mice. *Genes and Development*, **8**, 1999–2007.

Stonestreet, B. S. and Oh, W. (1978). Plasma creatinine levels in low-birth-weight infants during the first three months of life. *Pediatrics*, 61, 788–9.

Sulyok, E., Varga, F., Gyory, E., Jobst, K., and Csaba, I. F. (1979). Postnatal development of renal sodium handling in premature infants. *Journal of Pediatrics*, 95, 787–92.

Trudel, M., D'Agati, V., and Costantini, F. (1991). *c-myc* as an inducer of polycystic disease in transgenic mice. *Kidney International*, 39, 665–71.

Tulassay, T., Seri, I., and Rascher, W. (1987). Atrial natriuretic peptide and extracellular volume contraction after birth. *Acta. Physiol. Scand*, 76, 444–8.

van Heyningen, V. (1994). One gene–four syndromes. *Nature*, 367, 319–20.

Veis, D. J., Sorenson, C. M., Shutter, J. R., and Korsmeyer, S. J. (1994). Bcl-2-deficient mice demonstrate fulminant lymphoid apoptosis, polycystic kidneys and hypopigmented hair. *Cell*, 75, 229 40.

Walker, N. I., Harmon, B. V., Gobe, G. C., and Kerr, J. F. R. (1988). Patterns of cell death. *Meth. Achiev. Exp. Pathol.*, 13, 18–54.

Wilson, P. D., Sherwood, A. C., Palla, K., Du, J., Watson, R., and Norman, J. T. (1991). Reversed polarity of the Na$^+$-K$^+$-ATPase: mislocalization to apical plasma membranes in polycystic kidney disease epithelia. *American Journal of Physiology*, 260, F420–F430.

Winyard, P. J. D., Nauta, J., Lirenman, D. S., Hardman, P., Sams, V. R., Risdon, A. R., Woolf, A. S. (1996*a*). Deregulation of cell survival in cystic and dysplastic renal development. *Kidney International*, 49, 135–46.

Winyard, P. J. D., Risdon, A. R., Sams, V. R., Dressler, G. R., Woolf, A. S. (1996*b*). The PAX2 transcription fator is expressed in cystic and hyperproliferative dysplastic epithelia in human kidney malformations. *Journal of Clinical Investigation*, 98, 451–9.

Woo, D. D. L., Miao, S., Pelayo, J., and Woolf, A. S. (1994). Taxol inhibits congenital polycystic kidney disease progression. *Nature*, 368, 750–3.

Woods, L. L. (1986). Fetal renal contribution to amniotic fluid osmolality during maternal hypertonicity. *American Journal of Physiology*, 250, R235–R239.

Woods, L. L., Cheung, C. Y., Power, G. G., and Brace, R. A. (1986). Role of arginine vasopressin in fetal renal response to hypertonicity. *American Journal of Physiology*, 251, F156–163.

Woolf, A. S., Palmer, S. J., Snow, M. L., and Fine, L. G. (1990). Creation of a functioning chimeric mammalian kidney. *Kidney International*, 38, 991–7.

Woolf, A. S., Bosch, R. J., and Fine, L. G. (1993). Gene transfer into the mammalian kidney: transplantation of retrovirus-transduced metanephric tissue. *Experimental Nephrology*, 1, 41–8.

Woolf, A. S. (1997). The biology of renal malformations. In: *Birth defects: perspectives from developmental biology* (ed. P. Thorogood), pp. 303–27. John Wiley and Sons Ltd. Chichester..

Woolf, A. S., Kolatsi, M., Hardman, P., Andermarcher, E., Moorby, C., Fine, L. G., *et al.* (1995). Roles of hepatocyte growth factor/scatter factor (HGF/SF) and met in early development of the metanephros. *Journal of Cell Biology*, 128, 171–84.

Zerres, K., Mucher, G., Bachner, L., Deschennes, G., Eggerman, T., Kaariainen, H., *et al.* (1994). Mapping of the gene for autosomal recessive polycystic kidney disease (ARPKD) to chromosome 6p21-cen. *Nature Genetics*, 7, 429–32.

Zhou, J., Barker, D. F., Hostikka, S. L., Gregory, M. C., Atkin, C. L., and Truggvason, K. (1991). Single-base mutation in a5 (IV) collagen chain gene converting a conserved cysteine to serine in Alport syndrome. *Gene*, 9, 10–18.

2

Gene structure and regulation and the application of laboratory techniques

Stephen Jeffery and Anand K. Saggar-Malik

Introduction

Cell activity is essential for cell survival and organ function and is determined by the integrated activity of almost 100 000 genes through control of protein synthesis at the nuclear and cytoplasmic level. It was first believed that proteins were more likely candidates than DNA as components of the genetic code, but by the beginning of the 20th century it was apparent that chromosomes determined inheritance. In the late 1940s, Linus Pauling demonstrated that gene function could be studied not only by gross phenotypic change but also through encoded protein products, e.g. by gel electrophoresis. In 1953, James Watson and Francis Crick, from x-ray crystallographic data, described the double helical structure for DNA of two intertwined chains running in opposite directions. These strands had varying pattern repeats of four nitrogenous bases—adenine, guanine, cytosine, and thymine—running in apparent random sequence along a deoxyribose phosphate backbone. Since there is an absolute requirement for specific base pairing between helical strands, each strand is complementary to the other in terms of base pair sequence. In 1956, the human diploid chromosome complement of 22 pairs of autosomal including 2 sex chromosomes was correctly identified. Females have two X and males one X and one Y sex chromosome.

The potential information content of the human genome is enormous and far greater than is necessary to determine the upper limit of functional genes. Furthermore, since all cells, with few exceptions, contain the full DNA complement present in all other cells of the body, there must be some mechanism of gene regulation that turns genes on and off in specific cells, allowing specialized functional control in different cell types. Additionally, different genes must be switched on or off as organ development proceeds so that different protein compositions can occur.

There appears to be nothing particularly unusual about the position of a given gene on a chromosome, with some exceptions, so genetic variation depends ultimately on physical and chemical alterations in the basic hereditary material. Certainly, the genome is not static. Point mutations, gross rearrangements such as insertions, deletions, or duplications of DNA are common. These constant changes form the basis of genetic disease. Thus, in order to understand the role of genes in such diseases, it is important to understand the structure and regulation of genes themselves and the ways in which information contained in DNA is passed on to the cell. This process involves the transcription of DNA into RNA and the translation of RNA in to proteins containing specific amino acid sequence residues.

Much of the early work on gene structure, regulation, and abnormality focused on the haemoglobinopathies, cystic fibrosis, the muscular dystrophies, and haemophilias. Thus, many examples relate to this. However, in this synopsis we hope to put more emphasis on the inherited renal diseases to better understand the role of gene expression and regulation in the inherited basis of renal disease.

Chromosomes, genes, and deoxyribonucleic acid (DNA)

Basic structure

Of the three thousand million bases that make up the DNA of the human genome, only about 10% code as genes. Most of the remainder are considered to be functionless, though it is probably more accurate to say that we do not yet know their function. DNA is complexed with protein in the cell nucleus in the form of chromosomes. Human somatic (diploid) cells contain 23 pairs of chromosomes, one of each pair being drawn from each parent. They are numbered from 1 to 22 in order of size. The sex chromosomes are not numbered, they are referred to as X and Y. All the chromosomes can be individually identified by their specific pattern of band staining which varies by number and size. This phenomenon of alternate dark and light banding is caused by 'hetero-chromatic' regions of DNA being more tightly supercoiled (condensed) and therefore staining darker than the 'euchromatic' areas, which are less tightly coiled.

During most of the cell cycle this DNA in the form of chromosomes is distributed randomly throughout the nucleus, but at cell division it condenses such that the chromosomes are visible under the light microscope, particularly so during the metaphase satge. Each chromosome can then be seen to be composed of two halves called chromatids. These chromatid halves are joined only at one point called the 'centromere'. Each chromatid is itself also divided into two parts called short and long arms or 'p' and 'q' respectively. From here the nomenclature gets compli-cated since each arm is then also divided and subdivided according to the number of light and dark bands seen (Paris Conference 1971). These bands are counted from the centromere. For example, the gene for tuberous sclerosis is placed on chromosome 16p13.3. Thus, it is on the 3rd

Table 2.1   The more common terms used for describing chromosome karyotype

cen	centromere
del	deletion
der	derivative of a chromosome rearrangement
dup	duplication
ins	insertion
inv	inversion
mat	maternal origin
pat	paternal origin
p	short arm
pter	tip of short arm
q	long arm
qter	tip of long arm
t	translocation
/	mosaicism
+/−	before a chromosome number, indicates gain or loss of that whole chromosome
+/−	after a chromosome number, indicates gain or loss of part of that chromosome

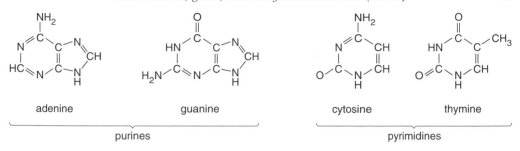

Fig. 2.1 The ring stucture of the four bases found in DNA.

part of the 3rd part of the 1st band of the short arm of chromosome 16. Table 2.1 summarizes some of the other symbols used for describing chromosomes. Identical positions on each pair of homologous chromosomes are refered to as alleles.

A chromosome is essentially an extremely long strand of supercoiled DNA. As most DNA has no known purpose, it is customary to restrict the term 'gene' to those parts of the chromosome that have a coding function, i.e. unique base sequences on the chromosomes which code for specific proteins. However, except for certain specific areas such as telomeres, required for ensuring complete replication of the DNA at the chromosome termini, and centromeres, essential for the correct movement of chromosomes into daughter cells following cell division, the remaining DNA, much of which is repetitive (see below), has no known purpose.

The DNA molecule exists in the form of a double helix. Each DNA strand has a backbone of 5-carbon sugar (deoxyribose) residues which are linked by covalent phosphodiester bonds. On each residue is a nitrogeneous base, either a pyrimidine (cytosine or thymine) or a purine (adenine or guanine) (Figure 2.1). A base linked to a sugar is called a nucleoside which combines with the phosphate group. Thus, the basic repeat unit of a DNA strand is a sugar with an attached base and phosphate group, termed a nucleotide. The phosphodiester bonds link carbon atoms 3' and 5' of successive sugar residues, thus one end of each DNA strand will have a terminal sugar residue on which carbon atom number 5' is not linked to a neighbouring sugar residue, the *five prime* (5') end. The other end is defined as a *three prime* (3') end because of a similar absence of phosphodiester bonding. The two strands of the DNA duplex always associate in such a way that the 5' to 3' direction of one DNA strand is opposite to that of its partner.

The two strands of the DNA duplex are complementary as adenine (A) specifically binds to thymine (T) and cytosine (C) specifically binds to guanine (G). It is conventional to describe a DNA sequence by writing the base pairs of one strand only and in the direction 5' to 3'.

Repetitive DNA

Approximately 30–40% of the nuclear genome is composed of sets of closely related non-allelic repetitive DNA sequences. Such repetitive sequences are known as sequence families whose individual members include functional gene families and also non-genic families. Within a DNA sequence family there is a high level of DNA sequence similarity (sequence homology) between individual members of the family. Repeated DNA sequences which do not include functional genes are composed of arrays of tandem repeats or individual repeat units interspersed with other

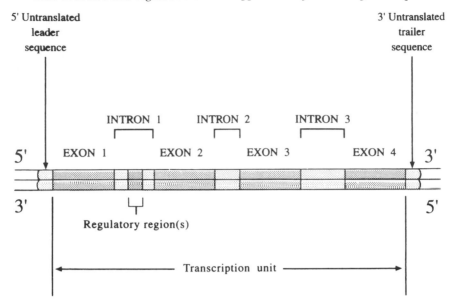

Fig. 2.2 The idealized structure of a gene.

DNA sequences. These may be subdivided according to the average size of the array of tandem repeat into satellite DNA, mini-satellite DNA, and micro-satellite DNA.

Non-repetitive DNA

The coding sequence, i.e. gene size, is only partly determined by the final size of the protein produced. This is in part because most genes are composed of 'exons and introns'. Figure 2.2 illustrates the structure of an idealized gene. The unique intragenic sequences which are expressed, i.e. the exons, are interspersed with smaller regions of non-coding and again often repetitive DNA. These intervening sequences are called introns. The precise significance in human genes is uncertain but it is possible that they have some form of regulatory role in controlling gene transcription. Often there is great variation between genes and the size of the introns. For example, the recently discovered gene for adult polycystic kidney disease on 16p13.3 produces an approximately 14 kb transcript from a gene about 55 kb in length, whereas the dystrophin gene on the X chromosome gives a similar sized messenger ribonucleic acid (mRNA) molecule from a gene of over 2000 kb. Occasionally, large introns can contain whole small genes which are transcribed from the opposite DNA strand to that used to express the larger gene, e.g. the factor VIII gene contains a small, single, intronless gene within one of its introns and one large intron of the NF1 (neurofibromatosis type 1) gene contains three small genes, each with two exons.

Gene expression

The production of proteins in a cell, known as translation, is the end product of a process that begins at the gene. Each stage in this process has numerous control mechanisms, many of which are still poorly understood, while many others are certainly not known. Gene expression begins in the nucleus where one DNA strand acts as a template to produce an RNA copy; a process called transcription. The exact position at which transcription starts varies, but is determined by regulatory elements, including promotors, enhances, silencers, and oncogenes. Furthermore, there are various DNA sequences or motifs, upstream and even downstream of the start of transcription, some of which control tissue-specific expression while others are concerned with quantitative mRNA production. The mode of action of these elements, and the molecules that interact with them, is the subject of current research.

Once an RNA copy of a gene has been produced it has to be modified to give the correct structure for its translation into protein. This process of modification is called 'post-transcriptional processing'. It involves capping, the addition of a polyadenosine 'tail', removal of introns, and the bringing together of exons in a contiguous sequence. Mature mRNA is then transported into the cytoplasm where the cellular machinery translates the DNA code to produce the required protein.

Transcription

The general principle of gene expression is not complicated and begins with the DNA in the nucleus. When a specific gene is to be transcribed the hydrogen bonds holding the complementary pairs of bases together separate and the two DNA strands unwind. One DNA strand, the 'anti-sense' strand, acts as a template, allowing the enzyme RNA polymerase II to transcribe a single-stranded mRNA molecule. This RNA molecule is complementary to the strand of DNA which has been copied, except that uridine interchanges with thymine. Transcription starts at the 5′ end (cap site) where there is a short untranslated leader sequence and a start sequence of codon (ATG). Untranslated sequences at the 3′ end (tail site) include a signal for the addition of a string of adenosine residues (poly-A tail). These primary RNA transcripts represent a true RNA copy of an individual gene with the entire sequence of contiguous exons and introns. Subsequent post-transcriptional processing must generate mRNA without the intervening introns. Only then can mRNA enter the cytoplasmic ribosomal system where it is translated into an amino acid sequence and so protein. In this way information from the nucleus is passed into the cytoplasm of the cell.

Transcriptional regulation

Gene expression is mostly regulated at the level of transcription. Of those genes specifying polypeptides, some are expressed at low levels in all somatic cells to give products which are required for general cell function (housekeeping genes). The expression of other genes, however, is tissue specific (for example, the beta globulin gene/dystrophin gene). Methylation of DNA is an important such control mechanism, determining transcription and regulating access to transcription factors which are present in all cells, although some are active only in specific cells or after exposure to particular stimuli.

DNA that is to be transcribed is marked by promoter sequences or 'regulatory boxes', usually located within a few hundred base pairs upstream of the gene. The first of these, 20–30 base pairs upstream, is the TATA box, and another sequence, 70–90 base pairs upstream, is called the CCAAT box. These boxes are responsible for the rate of DNA transcription into RNA, and, for some genes, the tissue-specific nature of the process.

Transcription factors

Many proteins that act as specific transcription factors have been discovered. These factors bind to regulatory sequences adjacent to specific genes and enable those genes to be transcribed. In haemophilia B, for example, the particular factor necessary for transcription of factor IX gene is present, but it fails to bind to the gene promoter owing to a mutation in the DNA sequence to which it would normally bind.

Promoters

These are combinations of very short sequence elements in the DNA region immediately upstream of genes. They govern the start position and the general level of transcription.

Cis-acting transcription factors are elements of defined DNA sequence or structure which are located on the same DNA strand as the genes they regulate and in the vicinity of the genes. They do not encode any product but often act as binding sites for trans-acting transcription factors. These latter factors are protein products encoded by other genes.

Enhancers/silencers

Combinations of sequence elements stimulate the transcription of genes (enhancers) or suppress transcription (silencers). Although they may be located near, or even within the gene whose expression they influence, they are usually located some distance away.

Proto-oncogenes/cellular oncogenes

Oncogenes are genes which can transform a normal cell to a tumourous cell. Their normal function as proto-oncogenes is to control cell growth. Many of the estimated 60–70 human proto-oncogenes have been characterized at the molecular level. Several oncogene products, oncoproteins, act as transcriptional factors, although the mode of action is largely unknown.

Tumour suppressor genes

Most inherited cancers involve gene defects in a class of genes which are being called tumour suppressor genes (anti-oncogenes). Inactivation of both gene copies of an autosomal tumour suppressive gene is thought to lead to tumourigenesis. Such disorders may occur in both hereditary and non-hereditary forms of cancer. The mode of action of tumour suppressive genes is presently unknown, but study of disorders such as retinoblastoma has shown that the mechanism underlying inactivation of a tumour suppresser gene is consistent with the two-hit mutation model (Knudson 1971). The first mutational hit is often a subtle mutation occurring either in the germ line or in a somatic cell precursor of the type of cell in which the tumour develops. The second mutational hit occurs subsequently in the somatic cell from which the tumour arises and is often a large-scale mutation. Such mutations are often detectable cytogenetically or by comparison of tumour and blood samples from the same individual to establish the loss in a tumour of constitutional heterozygosity.

Post-transcriptional processing

Intron sequences in primary mRNA transcript precursors have to be removed to generate mature mRNA. This post-transcriptional processing is undertaken by three major mechanisms: capping, polyadenylation, and splicing. The untranslated sequences at the 5′ end (cap site) and 3′ end (tail site) now signal for the addition of a methylated cap and a string of adenosine residues (poly-A tail). This capping and tailing is necessary to provide stability and to subsequently permit export of mRNA from the nucleus. Splicing now occurs. This is tightly controlled with the base sequences, GT and AG, dictating the splice donor and splice acceptor sites respectively. The mechanism for splicing out introns and the subsequent ligation of exons is not fully understood. Mutations in any of these four bases cause incorrect splicing so they are essential for the correct functioning of intron removal.

Translational regulation

In addition to transcriptional control, some human genes are controlled at the level of translation. For example, in a haploid (sex) cell, there is production of many new proteins in the egg immediately after fertilization. This translation into protein from mature mRNA that existed in the cytoplasm of the unfertilized egg was blocked before fertilization.

Once in the cytoplasm, mRNA functions as a template for the synthesis of proteins, in the 5′ to 3′ direction, from their constituent amino acid residues. The 5′ cap and 3′ poly-A tail are required in binding and stabilizing the mRNA on ribosomes. The remaining mRNA sequence is then translated into a polypeptide in a complex manner in which individual amino acids are specified by successive groups of three nucleotides (codons) which determine a particular amino acid. A family of cytoplasmic transfer RNA (tRNA) each carries a specific amino acid and has a specific three base pair recognition site (the anti-codon) for mRNA. Thus, the original information encoded in the exon sequence of the gene is transferred by mRNA to the correct amino acid sequence in a growing polypeptide chain. The polypeptide chain is synthesized from the amino terminal end. The first residue is always methionine but may be rapidly removed after incorporation into protein. Since there are a total of 64 possible codons and only 20 unmodified amino acids found in animal protein, there are, with the exception of methionine and tryptophan, more than one codon for each amino acid. Remarkably, many of the different codons for single amino acids differ only in the third nucleotide of the repeat. Other RNA codons (UAA, UAG, UGA) lead to a termination of translation and are called stop or termination codons.

Post-translational processing

Once translated, most proteins undergo a series of post-translational modifications, i.e. removal of leader sequences, glycosylation, phosphorylation, or attachment of co-enzymes. The maturation of human polypeptides, including plasma proteins, polypeptide hormones, neuropeptides, and growth factors, requires post-translational proteolytic cleavage of a precursor polypeptide with minor peptide cleavage products being discarded. In some cases this will yield more than one functional polypeptide chain, e.g. insulin. Such precursor formation is particularly important for all polypeptides whose ultimate destination requires passage through the cell membrane.

Mutations can also occur in non-coding sequences of the genome. These differences between allelic sequences or related non-allelic sequences are referred to as polymorphisms, if they occur with a frequency greater than 0.01 in a human population. Polymorphisms due to point mutation, i.e. single nucleotide substitutions, are the most common type of mutation in coding DNA sequences. The significance and use of such polymorphisms for locating the chromosomal position of a gene is discussed in the section on laboratory techniques, described later in this chaper. Differences in human gene products therefore reflect sequence alterations both at the level of the nuclear genome and gene expression, i.e. RNA processing. Variation must therefore represent the effect of chromosomal and genetic mechanisms, be it spontaneous mutations or errors in DNA replication, repair, or programmed modification. Furthermore, spontaneous alterations or abnormalities in meiosis, mitosis, or fertilization can generate cells with a different number of chromosomes or chromosome types than normal.

Classification of genetic diseases

Most genomic sequences show Mendelian inheritance whereby in somatic (diploid) cells, one of the two DNA sequences (alleles) which are located on identical positions (loci) on homologous chromosomes is inherited from each parent. An individual is homozygous or heterozygous at a specific locus if the two alleles at that locus are identical or different respectively. As Y chromosomes are transmitted exclusively by males, Y chromosome sequences exist as single copies in male diploid cells, as do X chromosome sequences. In general, the severity of the clinical phenotype reflects the degree to which a pathological mutation affects normal gene expression. This pathological contribution depends not only on the effect of the mutation on that gene's expression but also the dominance or recessivity of the mutant gene with respect to normal gene copies. Dominant allele disorders are characterized by the expression of clinical symptoms in the heterozygote because the disease allele is dominant over the normal allele. Such mutations often result in deficient or abnormal gene expression. Generally speaking, dominant pathological alleles occur in a gene which normally produces a non-enzymatic protein such as a receptor, carrier, structural or regulatory protein, e.g. many of the inherited disorders of collagen protein are dominant alleles. Autosomal dominant polycystic kidney disease, discussed later, is an example of a such a dominant allele disorder. Recessive disease alleles are normally non-functional or produce a limited amount of normal gene product so that the clinical phenotype is determined by the compound effect of gene product from the two alleles. In heterozygotes, one autosomal recessive disease allele and one normal allele can produce at least 50% or more of normal product. For many gene products, e.g. enzymes, this amount may be sufficient to avoid clinical symptoms, e.g. familial juvenile nephronophthisis. Table 2.2 shows some of human Mendelian disorders.

For clinical purposes, genetic disease can be divided into five major categories.

1. Single gene defects

Single gene defects (Mendelian) are caused by a mutant allele at a single locus. They may be inherited or be the result of new mutations. The inheritance patterns are classified as autosomal dominant, autosomal recessive, X-linked dominant, or X-linked recessive. Figure 2.3 shows examples of idealized patterns of monogenic inheritance for these traits and should be examined in concert with the following descriptions. Descriptions of standard pedigree symbols are shown in Table 2.3.

Autosomal dominant inheritance

Disorders inherited in this way manifest in the heterozygous state. The affected individual carries a mutant allele on one chromosome and a normal allele on the homologous chromosome. Since the relevant locus in on one of the 22 autosomes, both males and famales can be affected. Because alleles at any one locus segregate at meiosis, there is a 50% chance that any one child of an affected parent will also be affected. However, the clinical expression of the disorder may be quite variable.

Table 2.2 Common mendelian disorders in the UK population

Autosomal dominant inheritance
Adult polycystic kidney disease
Neurofibromatosis type 1
Tuberous sclerosis complex
Beckwith–Wiedeman syndrome
Von Hippel–Lindau disease
Charcot–Marie–Tooth disease*
Muckle–Wells syndrome
Nail–Patella syndrome
Renal tubular acidosis type I

Autosomal recessive inheritance
Wilms' tumour
Alpha-1 anti-trypsin deficiency (SZ)
Juvenile nephronophthisis
Juvenille polycystic kidney disease
Sickle cell disease
Retinitis pigmentosa
Alkaptonuria
Cystinuria

X-linked inheritance
Anderson–Fabry's disease
Renal tubular acidosis type II
Oro–facial–digital syndrome
Alport's syndrome*

---

*Inheritance not fully determined. Cases of autosomal recessive, dominant and/or X-linked have been reported.

Autosomal recessive inheritance

These disorders are clinically apparent only in the homozygote. Here, a mutant allele exists on each of the homologous chromosomes. Both sexes can be affected. Most cases arise because of union between two heterozygotes. In such cases there is a 25% chance of normal outcome, 50% chance of heterozygous outcome, and 25% chance of affected outcome. Most recessive conditions are quite rare and may make an isolated event in apparently normal families.

X-linked inheritance

Females have two X chromosomes and males only have one, so X-linked inheritance is usually recessive, with a frequent pattern of females as asymtomatic carriers who give birth to affected male children. Union between a normal father and a carrier mother has four possible outcomes, each with a 25% chance of occurring, i.e. an affected son, a normal son, a carrier daughter, or a normal daughter. This is because the father contributes only normal X chromosomes to his daughters and Y chromosomes to his sons, while the 'carrier' mother may or may not pass on the abnormal X. However, if the father were affected, all his daughters would be carriers and all his sons would be normal. There can be no male to male transmission of disease in X-linked inheritance.

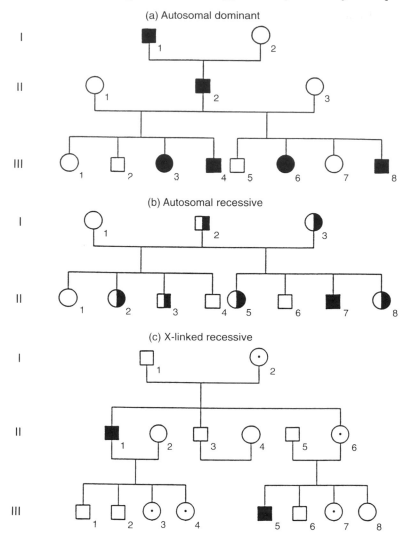

Fig. 2.3 (a) Typical examples of idealized patterns of inheritance for autosomal dominant disease; (b) autosomal recessive disease; and (c) X-linked disease.

Mosaicism

The expression of a pathological allele in some cells but not in others results in a variation in clinical severity proportional to the amount of relevant cells expressing the diseased allele. All women exhibit mosaicism because in some of their cells the paternal X sex chromosome is inactivated while in others the maternal X chromosome is inactivated. This phenomenon, called Lyonization (named after Mary Lyon's hypothesis in 1961), occurs in early embryonic life, in order that females do not express twice as much X-linked gene product as males. The choice of X chromosome is random so that either the paternal or maternal X chromosome can be inactivated. Therefore, under rare circumstances, female carriers of X-linked recessive disorders may show some clinical signs when Lyonization largely affects the normal X chromosome, allowing

Table 2.3 Some of the many standard pedigree symbols

☐	Male (unaffected)
●	Female (affected)
⬛ (diagonal)	Deceased (male)
☐—○	Mating
☐═○	Consanguinous mating
☐2 ○4	Two males, four females
◇4	Four sibs—sex not specified
☐⌃☐	Dizygotic (non-identical) twins
☐⌃☐	Monozygotic (identical) twins
	Spontaneous abortion or stillbirth
⊙	Unaffected heterozygous (female) (X-linked)
◧	Heterozygous (male) autosomal recessive trait

the abnormal X chromosome to be expressed. In this circumstance the carrier mother is known as a manifesting heterozygote. This can therefore blur the distinction between X-linked dominant and X-linked recessive inheritance since, in a small percentage of obligate female carriers of X-linked disease, expression of disease symptoms can occur if the unaffected X chromosome has been suppressed.

Co-dominant inheritance

Although most Mendelian disorders are classified as autosomal dominant, autosomal recessive, or X-linked, if one examines phenotypes at a biochemical or molecular level, the terms 'dominant' and 'recessive' are best replaced by the term 'co-dominant'. This means that the product of each allele at a locus can be individually distinguished, although the patient may clinically express a recessive disorder (compound heterozygote). Therefore, it is only gross phenotypes that shown dominance or recessiveness.

2. Chromosomal disorders

Chromosomal disorders are caused by a loss, gain, or breakage (translocation) of nuclear chromosomal material either in part or in whole. The majority of such disorders are *de novo* events because of major mutations in the parents' germ cells. A common example of such a disorder is Down's (trisomy 21) syndrome.

There are two broad categories of chromosome abnormality: numerical or structural. Gain (polyploidy) or loss (aneuploidy) of one or more chromosomes can occur although the latter of is most common. This is often the result of non-disjunction, i.e. the failure of paired chromosomes to separate during cell division. Such failure early in meiosis can result in an extra copy of a chromosome (trisomy) or a missing copy (monosomy).

Structural chromosome abnormalities all result from chromosomal breakage. This may lead to deletion (loss of material), duplication (gain of material), or inversion (rearrangement of material) when a single chromosome is involved. When a chromosome break involves more than one chromosome, the common result is a translocation. In reciprocal translocations, material distal to the breakage point is exchanged either between homologous or non-homologous chromosomes. In insertional translocations, material from one chromosome may be inserted into another chromosome. Very often, translocations are *balanced* in that there is no net loss of nuclear genetic material and the person may be perfectly normal. Offspring, however, have an increased risk of inheriting unbalanced chromosome constitutions.

3. Multifactorial disorders

Multifactorial disorders account for the majority of congenital malformations. In most common adult diseases, as well as in congenital malformations there is no suggestion of a Mendelian mode of inheritance and the abnormalities presumably result from genetic interaction with complex environmental factors, although the exact mechanism(s) are poorly understood. Evidence for this is provided by the fact that such disorders usually occur at higher frequencies in certain racial or ethnic groups, or they occur at a higher frequency in the immediate relatives of an affected person when compared to the general population. There is also often a high degree of concordance between monozygotic twins. Essential hypertension and diabetes mellitus are typical examples of such multifactorial disorders.

4. Mitochondrial disorders

Mitochondrial disorders arise from mutations in the mitochondrial genome which is distinct from the bulk of nuclear DNA carried by chromosomes. The mitochondrial genome accounts for approximately 1% of cellular DNA. It is wholly maternally inherited, unlike nuclear genes which are transmitted as allelic Mendelian traits. This is because at fertilization, only nuclear DNA from the father's sperm is transferred to the female zygote cell which contains the mitochondrial DNA within the cytoplasm. In principle, mitochondrial disease results from mutations in genes which specify mitochondrial products or mitochondrial DNA expression. Mitochondrial DNA code is essentially the same as that found in the nucleus but the genes contain no introns. The severity of the clinical phenotype is normally proportional to the number of mutant mitochondrial genome copies. This is well-demonstrated by the peroxisomal diseases, e.g. adrenoleucodystrophy and the mitochondrial myopathies such as Kearns–Sayre syndrome. Leber's hereditary optic atrophy is another example of mitochondrial disease inheritance.

5. Somatic genetic disorders

Somatic genetic disorders arise from mutations in specific somatic cells giving rise to tumours.

These events are not inherited even though they involve gene mutation.

We have discussed above the structure of genes, their regulation, and how genetic diseases are classified. The next section outlines methods used in the laboratory to localize genes and determine specific mutations.

Application of laboratory techniques

Investigations into the nature of genetic disorders are effectively a continuum, from finding the location of the responsible gene on a chromosome, to an eventual understanding of the physiological role of the protein produced by that gene, and then consideration of possible genetic or pharmacological therapies. In this section, methods used for finding genes which cause inherited disease will be considered, as well as methods for looking for mutations in those genes.

Localizing a gene

Chromosomal rearrangements

The easiest way to locate the position of a gene is to discover a chromosomal rearrangement in an individual who has the genetic disorder. Inversions, deletions, or translocations might all distrupt or remove a particular gene and produce the phenotype associated with an absence of one copy of the gene. Clearly, this kind of event is much more likely to expose the position of a gene responsible for a dominant disorder than it is a recessive one, where the chromosomal rearrangement would have to coincide with a mutation in the gene on the other chromosome to produce the condition. Of all the possible types of chromosomal rearrangement which could disrupt gene function in some way, the most useful for the molecular geneticist is a balanced translocation. This is because this situation removes only a small amount of DNA, if any, and if it produces the phenotype of a particular disorder then it probably disrupts the actual gene responsible for that condition. A chromosomal deletion, on the other hand, could remove numerous genes as well as the one responsible for the disease. A translocation might also give rise to 'junction fragments' when techniques for isolating the gene are used (discussed further below), thus making this search much easier.

Specific examples

A good example of a genetic disorder where the position of the gene was suggested by a translocation is neurofibromatosis type 1 (NF1). This is a dominant disorder characterized by neurofibromata, café au lait patches, and lisch nodules, plus an increased likelihood of malignancies in some cases. In 1987, an individual was discovered with NF1, without any family history, who had a chromosome 17/1 translocation (Schmidt *et al.* 1987). In 1989, another individual with a similar history showed a 17/22 translocation (Ledbetter *et al.* 1989). In both cases the breakpoint on chromosome 17 was at q11.2. This made it highly probable that mutations in a

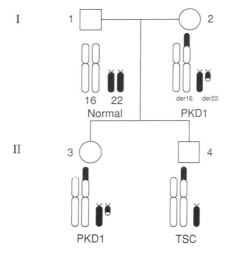

Fig. 2.4 A family with polycystic kidney disease and tuberous sclerosis where there was a chromosome 16/22 translocation. The phenotypes are described in the text. (with permission.)

gene in this position were responsible for NF1 in familial cases, and this was confirmed by linkage analysis, using probes for this region of the genome in families with NF1.

Very recently, the value of a patient with a chromosomal rearrangement has been shown in the search for the gene responsible for adult polycystic kidney disease type 1 (PKD1) on chromosome 16p13.3. The location of the gene at this position has been known since 1985 (Reeders *et al.* 1985), but in spite of extensive investigations into this region of the chromosome (Germino *et al.* 1992), the gene remained elusive. In 1994, a paper from The European Polycystic Kidney Disease Consortium finally identified the gene, mainly by means of a family with a 16/22 translocation (Fig. 2.4). This example is more complicated than that described above for NF1. A family was ascertained where the mother and one child had APKD, and the other child had tuberous sclerosis (TS) with cystic kidneys (one of the genes causing TS was known to be very close to the PKD1 locus). The chromosomes of each family member were examined. Both the mother and the child with APKD had a balanced 16:22 translocation, with the chromosome 16 breakpoint at 16p13.3, while the child with TS had an unbalanced translocation and was monosomic for 16p13.3 → 16pter, as well as for 22q11.2 → 22pter. Considerable investigation revealed that the breakpoint in the balanced translocation at 16p13.3 disrupted the PKD1 gene and this discovery led to the identification of that gene.

Although the chances of discovering a chromosomal rearrangement which disrupts the gene responsible for a given disease are small, the effort saved by such a discovery makes it worthwhile to examine the chromosomes from any sporadic cases of the disease and to conduct a similiar investigation into one affected member of each family ascertained with the disorder.

Candidate gene approach

If there are no chromosomal rearrangements to suggest the possible location of a gene for the disease under investigation, it may be necessary to conduct a random search of the genome using markers which are polymorphic in the population, coupled with linkage analysis using a computer (see Chapter 3). This is a very common and important method for gene location in inherited disorders and is discussed below, but it can be time-consuming. Any method which avoids this process is therefore often used first. One such method is the 'candidate gene' approach, whereby a gene thought highly likely to cause the disease is tested in families either for mutations (see below), or by linkage analysis to see if it is indeed the gene responsible for the condition.

A successful example of such an approach was the implication of the gene for a type IV collagen 'alpha' chain in classical X-linked Alport's syndrome. When the X-linked type IV collagen was identified, all that was known about the gene responsible for Alport's syndrome was its location in a 5 million base pair region of Xq22. The type IV collagen gene mapped to Xq22 and examination of the gene in patients with X-linked Alport's syndrome demonstrated mutations (Barker *et al* 1990). This was therefore identification by a combination of linkage analysis and the 'candidate gene' approach.

Linkage analysis using polymorphic markers

If candidate genes yield no results, it is necessary to conduct a linkage analysis using polymorphic markers throughout the genome, to discover a marker that co-segregates with the disease within families (see Chapter 3). There are a variety of markers but by far the most commonly used are 'CA repeat' or 'microsatellite' markers. The discovery of these markers in the genome, together with the development of the polymerase chain reaction (PCR), has revolutionized genetic linkage analysis. Prior to the discovery of microsatellites and PCR, linkage analysis primarily used restriction fragment length polymorphism (RFLP) markers, detected by Southern blotting.

Restriction fragment length polymorphisms (RFLPs)

These are fragments of DNA which vary in size in different individuals in the population. RFLPs are produced by the action of bacterial enzymes called restriction endonucleases. These enzymes recognize a specific sequence of bases in DNA and only cut where that exact sequence occurs. About 90% of human DNA is non-coding, i.e. does not contain genes, and variations in base sequence between individuals in this non-coding DNA can occur without any harmful effect. Thus, different individuals will show variations in the structure of their non-coding DNA, usually in the form of single base changes. Sometimes these changes occur in an existing recognition sequence for a restriction endonuclease and the site is then lost. Or, the change can create a new recognition site for a restriction endonuclease. When the DNA from an individual showing such a change is digested with the restriction endonuclease that cuts at that site, there will be a change in the size of the fragments produced compared with an individual not showing the change in base sequence. The DNA from the two individuals will therefore exhibit different fragment lengths when digested with the relevant restriction enzyme. These different-sized fragments are restriction fragment length polymorphisms (RFLPs). To be considered an RFLP, the most commonly found fragment size must occur in less than 99% of the population.

RFLPs are commonly detected after 'Southern blotting' by using a radioactive labelled DNA probe. These probes are small pieces of DNA that bind to the human DNA that has been cut into pieces by restriction endonucleases. The probes bind in the region where the RFLP occurs and are chosen for that reason.

In Southern blotting, DNA that has been cut by an endonuclease restriction enzyme is sorted into sized fragments in an agarose gel by electrophoresis. The DNA is made sngle-stranded and

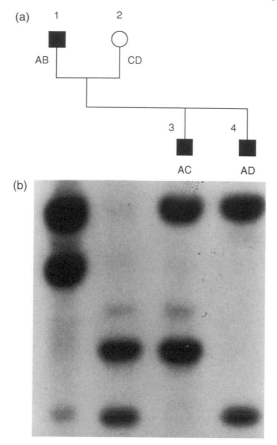

Fig. 2.5   (a) Part of a family pedigree where adult polycystic kidney disease occurs due to a defect at the PKD1 locus on chromosome 16p13.3; (b) Autoradiograph of a Southern blot of DNA from each family member after digestion with endonuclease PvuII and hybridization with the highly polymorphic probe 3′HVR. This probe is on 16p13.3, and shows 5% recombination with the PKD1 locus. In this family allele *A* co-segregates with the disease.

transferred to a nylon membrane by the capillary action of filter paper—this is the Southern blot (Southern 1975). The radioactive DNA probe is then incubated in solution with the nylon filter and binds to its complementary piece of DNA. Unbound probe is washed off and the filter exposed to x-ray film. When developed, this film (autoradiograph) shows a band or series of bands where the DNA probe has bound (Fig. 2.5). Since the probe is chosen to show up an RFLP, these band sized will differ between different individuals in the population. Figure 2.6 summarizes this process.

This is a time-consuming technique, and RFLPs often only detect two alleles in the population. As a consequence, families could frequently be uninformative for the marker. Linkage analysis could, and often did, take years with this system. Using CA repeats, however, linkage analysis can now take a matter of months, providing the family structure is correct and genetic heterogeneity is not a problem.

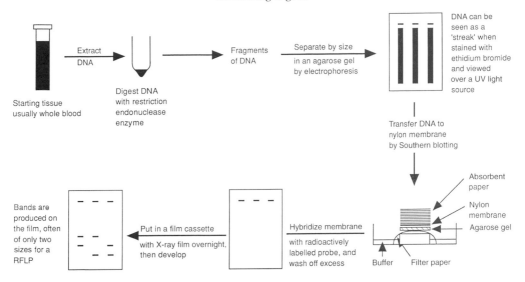

Fig. 2.6 A schematic diagram showing the processes involved in Southern blotting. The end results are bands on x-ray film which correspond to restriction fragment length polymorphisms (RFLPs).

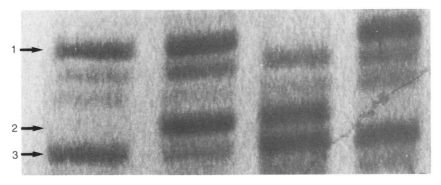

Fig. 2.7 An example of micro-satellites amplified by PCR in a family with adult polycystic kidney disease (part of a much larger pedigree). The micro-satellite in this case is SM7 (Harris *et al.* 1992), which shows about 1% recombination with the PKD1 locus. The first lane is DNA from the affected mother, lane 2 is from the unaffected father, then lanes 3 and 4 are affected children. The disease in this family is caused by a mutation at the PKD1 locus. The two darker bands for each individual represent the alleles, the fainter bands are so-called stutter bands. There are three alleles in this family (arrowed). The mother has alleles 1 and 3, the father 1 and 2. Each child has inherited allele 3 from the mother, which in this family is a marker for the disease gene.

Micro-satellites

As described in the first part of this chapter, micro-satellites are usually repeats of cytosine and adenosine bases scattered randomly throughout the genome, with no known function. They are highly polymorphic in the population; that is to say, the number of CA repeats at a given position in the genome will show considerable variation between different individuals. The development of PCR (Saiki *et al.* 1985) has meant that CA repeats can be visualized as bands on a gel or an x-ray film (Fig. 2.7), depending on whether non-radioactive or radioactive methods are used. PCR has been amply described elsewhere (Erlich *et al.* 1991), but the essential feature is that specific regions of DNA can be amplified a billion times providing the sequence of bases flanking that region is known. Thus, any CA repeat can be so amplified as long as the sequence either side has been characterized. Thanks to the work of James Weber in Omaha (Weber 1990) and Jean Weissenbach (at Genethon, Paris), there are now large numbers of markers available for PCR analysis, e.g. in June 1994, Genethon produced a genetic map of their micro-satellites which contained 2066 CA repeats for the human genome (Gyapay *et al.* 1994).

Examples of kidney disease where linkage analysis using markers have been successful include the autosomal recessive form of polycystic kidney disease to 6p21-cen (Zerres *et al.* 1994) and a second locus for autosomal dominant polycystic kidney disease at 4q21 (Kimberling *et al.* 1994; Peters *et al.* 1994).

Finding the gene

Once the position of a gene responsible for a disease has been established, the difficult process of isolating that gene begins. To narrow the region of the chromosome on which the gene must lie, two approaches are taken: (1) fine mapping using close recombinants in families and (2) physical mapping.

Fine mapping

Fine mapping involves investigating all families with the disorder that can be ascertained, using known markers on that region of the chromosome. Using recombination events, the closest markers that co-segregate with the disease gene, both distally and proximally, are found. The gene can then only lie between these points. The closer the markers are to the gene, the less likely

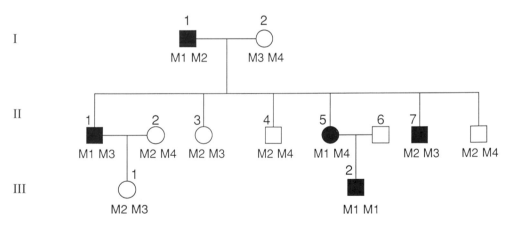

Fig. 2.8 A hypothetical pedigree showing transmission of an autosomal dominant disease, and its co-segregation with a marker (*M*), with alleles 1–4. No unaffected individuals have inherited marker M1 from the father, while three out of four affected individuals have. In seven out of eight cases, the marker M1 is linked to the disease locus. In individual II7, there has been a recombination between the marker and the disease locus. If this frequency of recombination was maintained in other families, that particular marker would show 12.5% recombination with the disease locus.

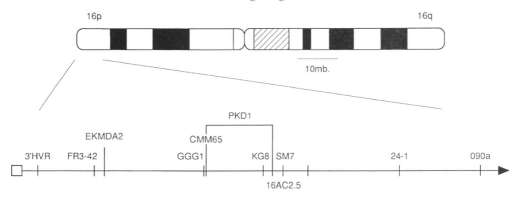

Fig. 2.9 Diagram of chromosome 16, showing the region around the PKD1 locus, with various markers indicated (modified from Germino *et al.* 1992).

recombination is to occur, so that this process reaches a point after which it becomes self-defeating. Fresh markers are often generated by laboratories working on the disease for use in recombinant and physical mapping. Figure 2.8 shows what happens when recombination occurs in a family. A marker, M1, which co-segregates with the gene for most family members, is replaced in one affected individual by M2. A recombination event at meiosis has separated the disease gene from the marker. How frequently this is found to occur in family studies shows the recombination frequency between gene and marker and this corresponds, approximately, to physical distance. One million base pairs is (roughly) equivalent to 1% recombination. Autosomal dominant polycystic kidney disease is again an excellent example of a disease where the genetic interval was reduced using newly generated probes and close recombinant events. Initial linkage studies (Reeders *et al.* 1985) used a very informative probe at the alpha-globin locus, 3'HVR. This showed 5% recombination with the PKD1 locus in family studies, and was shown to be distal to the PKD1 locus. Breuning *et al.* then identified a probe, 24-1, which was 4 recombination units proximal to the PKD1 locus (Breuning *et al.* 1987). More and more markers were generated by different laboratories and these were utilized in linkage analysis to build up a detailed map of the relevant area of chromosome 16p 13.3 (Fig. 2.9). Recombination events between these markers and the PKD1 gene eventually enabled the area in which the gene could lie to be narrowed to 750 kb (Germino *et al.* 1992).

Physical mapping and chromosome walking

Genetic distance often does not correspond to physical distance, as recombination can be more or less frequent than expected on different parts of different chromosomes. It is therefore important to determine how far apart flanking markers are in terms of physical distance. Strategies can then be designed to isolate and examine the stretch of DNA which must include the gene under investigation. Two very useful techniques in this regard are pulsed field gel electrophoresis (PFGE) and yeast artificial chromosomes (YACs).

Pulsed field gel electrophoresis (PFGE)

PFGE is an electrophoretic technique designed to separate very large pieces of DNA—up to several Mb—which conventional electrophoresis is incapable of achieving. There are various designs of apparatus, but essential to all of them is a method of changing the diretion of the current. Whereas ordinary electrophoresis applies current in a straight line, PFGE causes the current to change direction at short intervals (the 'pulses'). This constantly changes the way in which the DNA molecules are moving. The speed at which a molecule changes direction is dependent on its molecular weight, unlike conventional electrophoresis where large DNA molecules have a mobility independent of molecular weight. DNA is not extracted from whole blood as it is for Southern blotting, as this would shear the large fragments. Lymphocytes are separated from erythrocytes on a Ficoll gradient, removed by pipette, and added to a solution of low melting point agarose. The mix is placed in small plastic moulds called 'block formers', in which the agarose sets into small blocks containing a known amount of cells. These cells are then ready for manipulation prior to PFGE.

The pre-treatment given to the blocks of cells depends on the questions being asked. For a size separation, to find if two markers are physically near each other, the DNA in the block must be digested into fragments by endonuclease enzymes. For PFGE, enzymes known as 'rare cutters' are used. These cut infrequently in the genome, either because they have a long recognition sequence, such as GGCCNNNNNGGCC (where N = any base) for the enzyme Sfi1, or they recognize GC-rich sequences, that do not occur very often in DNA, e.g. the enzyme Not1 (GCGGCCGC).

Once the DNA has been digested, the blocks are sealed in wells in an agarose gel and the current is switched on for the desired time period, which can vary from 24 hours to several days depending on the size of the fragments under investigation. The DNA in the gel is transferred to a nylon membrane by Southern blotting, and this filter is hybridized to a series of DNA probes for the region being investigated. If different probes produce bands in the same place on an autoradiograph, they may be physically linked within the size of that band. If different-sized bands are shown up, the markers are further apart. The fact that two probes produe a band in the same place on the film does not mean they are on the same piece of DNA, they could be binding to different pieces of roughly the same size. To determine which situation exists, the DNA is digested with other rare cutters and is also partially digested. By these means, it can be seen whether the two probes are in fact physically linked to fragment sizes resolvable by PFGE. If they are, the DNA can be cloned into a YAC or a cosmid library for further investigation. If not, then other probes in the region can also be tested and a physical map drawn up of all known markers in that part of the chromosome. If there are not many markers known for that particular part of the genome, more need to be developed (see below).

Cloning

A genomic library of the region of interest can be made either when the flanking markers are close enough to be resolved onto a DNA fragment on a pulsed field gel, or much before that stage. Such libraries can be produced in many ways, e.g. from somatic cell hybrids of human and hamster cells containing only the chromosome of interest (or even only part of it) as its human component, or from micro-dissected pieces of chromosome. Libraries are simply pieces of DNA cut up with restriction enzymes and inserted into 'vectors'. These are usually artificially manipulated organisms which occur naturally, such as phage (a bacterial virus), plasmids (small circular pieces of DNA that occur in bacteria), or cosmids (combinations of elements from phage and plasmids). All of them can be cut with endonucleases and foreign DNA can be inserted between the cut ends. These vectors can self-replicate and be cultured (often inside bacteria). YACs are rather different, being derived from yeast chromosomes (Fig. 2.10). The advantage of starting with a

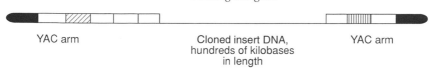

YAC arm   Cloned insert DNA,   YAC arm
hundreds of kilobases
in length

Fig. 2.10 Schematic diagram of a YAC (not to scale), showing basic components of the yeast chromosome arms. Dark areas are yeast telomeres, stippled region is a yeast centromere, shaded areas are yeast marker genes.

fragment of DNA resolvable on PFGE and known to contain flanking markers is that it can be cloned into a YAC, and it is possible to end up with a clone whith you know contains the gene because it hybridizes with markers on either side of it. YAC clones are prone to rearrangement and chimaerism (the combining with DNA from other parts of the genome before cloning) and this has to be guarded against. Once it is established that the gene is cloned into a YAC, there is still a great deal of work to be done. YACs can contain over 1 Mb of human DNA (1 million base pairs) and finding a gene in such a large piece of DNA is not easy. If a chromosomal translocation has been discovered for the disease, cloning may be much easier, since PFGE might reveal a different-sized fragment for the translocated chromosome compared to the normal. This so-called junction fragment could contain part of the gene and might be small enough to clone into a cosmid library, inserts from which could be removed and sequenced.

Chromosome walking and jumping

Either using a large insert within a YAC or a cosmid library of the genomic region of interest, information can be gathered about the DNA by either 'walking' or 'jumping' along the chromosome. Chromosome 'walking' involves using a clone from the library which lies within the area being investigated to pull out an overlapping clone from the library by homologous binding. The two clones are sequenced and that part of the second clone not homologous to the first must represent an adjoining piece of DNA.

This process can be repeated a large number of times to build up a sequence of the region, but it is a very time-consuming process. It is possible to combine 'walking' with 'jumping', a technique invented by Francis Collins and well-described by him (Collins 1988). Jumping libraries link pieces of DNA tens of thousands of bases apart on the genome and by both walking and jumping, areas of interest such as particular clusters of bases indicating the possible position of a gene can be examined. A further advantage in making a cosmid library from a YAC is that you are certain of walking in one direction if the starting point is one end of the YAC plus the first piece of inserted human DNA. Using processes of walking and jumping, many disease genes have been discovered, perhaps most notably cystic fibrosis (Rommens *et al.* 1989). There are, however, other methods of looking for genes within a given sequence of genomic DNA.

Isolating genes from complex mixtures

Long stretches of genomic DNA are likely to contain mostly non-coding, intervening sequences, which represent areas of no interest if a gene is being searched for. In fact, they can sometimes be 'unwalkable' through, e.g. because of a high GC content, hence the need to jump over certain areas. There are methods for isolating coding regions of DNA from genomic libraries, e.g. by the use of an 'exon-trapping' vector (Buckler *et al.* 1991), or by end ligation coincident cloning

(Brookes *et al.* 1994), or by 'prep-ISH' (Hozier *et al.* 1994). For the first two techniques, there is a need to start with genomic DNA from the region where the gene is known to be located. These can be libraries from that chromosome, or libraries from dissected parts of the chromosome, or cosmid contigs for a given region of the chromosome (a contig is a length of DNA for a given piece of chromosome, cloned into overlapping cosmids). All these sources share the common property of containing much more non-coding than coding DNA. To isolate genes which might be contained in such DNA, any of the aforementioned techniques can be used.

Exon trapping

For exon trapping, a special vector has been designed which contains splice donor and acceptor sites (Buckler *et al.* 1991). Genomic DNA is cloned into this vector and the clones are transfected into COS—7 cells (cultured African green-monkey kidney cells). Those clones which contain an exon amongst the human DNA that has been cloned into them are acted upon by the COS cell splicing mechanism and the intronic material is cut out, leaving only the exon. The COS cells then act on this DNA to make RNA, which is isolated from the cell. cDNA is made from the RNA using reverse transcriptase, and the cloned exon is amplified from this mixture by PCR, using the vector sequences known to lie either side of the exon. Clearly, this is not a simple procedure to explain. In essence, it is a mechanism for cloning genomic fragments, but ending up only with pieces of coding DNA (exons).

End ligation coincident sequence cloning

End ligation coincident sequence cloning is an ingenious system which utilizes primer sets that are biotinylated, to separate molecules which are homologous between complex genomic and cDNA mixtures. Magnetic beads with streptavidin capture these sequences, which can then be amplified by PCR. For more detailed information, readers are directed to the paper by Brookes *et al.* (1994).

Prep-ISH

Prep-ISH is a recently devised method for isolating coding regions of DNA from a particular region of a chromosome (Hozier *et al.* 1994). The complex mixture in this process is not genomic DNA but a mixture of cDNA (derived from messenger RNA, so only containing coding material). The cDNA can be derived from a cDNA library, or made from specific tissue mRNA which is reverse transcribed but is not cloned. The cDNA has special primers ligated to it for PCR amplification later in the process. When the cDNA is prepared, metaphase chromosome spreads are made on glass slides and the cDNA mixture is hybridized with these spreads. The piece of chromosome of interest, e.g. that region where a gene has been located to by linkage, is microdissected from the slide and any cDNA which has been hybridized is amplified up by PCR. The great advantage of this approach is that it needs no cloning steps and is therefore extremely rapid. Amplified fragments can be checked to see that they come from the correct region of the chromosome by using FISH (see below).

The methods described above are only three of many which have been designed to use genomic/cDNA mixtures to isolate genes or exons from given regions of the genome. The difficulties encountered in discovering a gene are well-illustrated by the case of adult polycystic kidney disease type 1, where over 20 genes were isolated from a 750 kb region without the gene responsible for the disorder being discovered (Germino *et al.* 1992). Such work is never wasted, however, since it produces information both on other genes in that region and gives valuable data on the area of the chromosome being studied.

Identifying genes and finding mutations

If a gene is located via a translocation event, it is highly likely that the gene which is disrupted is implicated in the disorder being investigated. If the gene is discovered by any of the other methods described above, it is often not easy to prove that the gene is responsible for the phenotype. The only way to do this is to demonstrate mutations in the gene in individuals with the disorder and be certain that these mutations are causative, rather than just polymorphisms that occur in the population, or rare changes which are not in fact deleterious. This is often not a simple matter, especially if the changes are missense alterations, where a single base change can produce a different amino acid at that codon. If the amino acid in question is conserved in other species and there is a charge change which might be expected to have a functional effect, these are strong predictors towards the mutation being disease related. Such an analysis can be misleading, however. Leumink *et al.* (1994), found a leucine to proline change in an individual with Alport's syndrome. Such a change would be strongly suggestive of pathogenesis, but further investigation in another family showed an unaffected father who carried this substitution while his affected son did not. Base changes, therefore, do not necessarily indicate a disease causing mutation and it is important to remember this when considering some of the methods for detecting mutations described below.

Deletion detection

In some genetic disorders it is immediately clear that the gene being investigated is that responsible for the disease state since large deletions are found in many individuals who are not affected. X-linked Alport's syndrome is an example of this (Barker *et al.* 1990). Such deletions can be seen on Southern blots of affected individuals, where bands normally seen are absent on the autoradiographs, as this is an X-linked disorder and males have only one copy of the gene. In autosomal dominant disorders with deletions, or in carriers of X-linked disorders, the situation is less clearcut since the normal copy of the gene can mask the deletions. It is possible to see altered-sized fragments from the gene with the deletion in such cases, either using conventional Southern blotting or pulsed field electrophoresis.

Exon scanning

Once a gene has been shown to be responsible for a disorder, by discovering a mutation/ mutations which occur in that gene only in affected individuals and not in the general population, then the coding region of the gene is analysed and if it is not a large gene, the genomic sequence can also be sequenced relatively quickly. Once the exon structure is known, new mutations can be searched for by exon scanning, i.e. looking for changes in the exon sequences. Such changes may or may not be disease-producing mutations, but the first step is to identify their location then sequence the exon in question to discover what the change actually is. There are two commonly used methods for exon scanning: single strand conformational polymorphism analysis (SSCP) and denaturing gradient gel electrophoresis (DGGE). The former is more widely used although it detects less mutations because it is technically more simple. In both techniques, specific primers are used to amplify different exons in the gene. SSCP utilizes the fact that single strands of amplified exon take up a certain conformational structure when run on a polyacrylamide gel. If there is a missence mutation, this conformation can alter and a different-sized band will be seen on electrophoresis. Not all changes will produce such a band shift, but it is a rapid way of screening the exons to see if affected individuals produce a different pattern to normals. The exons then have to be sequenced to discover the reason for the change and whether it is likely to cause the disease in that individual.

DGGE use the changes in melting temperature of an amplified two stranded PCR product which can occur when a mutation is present. In this technique, denaturing gels with a gradient of urea are used, at raised temperatures. Amplified exonic DNA is loaded on double stranded. This DNA migrates through the gel until it reaches a urea concentration where it separates and stops moving. Mutations in the exon will produce a different band pattern compared to the normal population and once again, the exon can be sequenced to determine the nature of the mutation.

Cytogenetic techniques

Molecular cytogenetics is becoming widely used in detection of deletion mutations, especially in dominant disorders such as Di George syndrome (Desmaze *et al.* 1993), or where carrier status in X-linked disease is uncertain, e.g. Duchenne muscular dystrophy (Ried *et al.* 1990). Fluorescent-labelled probes are used to show an absence of signal in affected cases. Fluorescent *in situ* hybridization (FISH) is likely to become more and more important in genetic analysis as the limits of resolution are increased.

The methods above are by no means exhaustive, but the details given are designed to show that many techniques are used in the molecular analysis of genetic diseases and also to give an idea why sometimes genes take years to be discovered, while on other occasions the process is much more rapid. It is always worth the extra effort of conducting a cytogenetic analysis in genetic disorders, since chromosomal abnormalities can be the best indicators of position for a disease gene and if you are lucky, they can actually pinpoint the gene itself.

References

Barker, D., Hostikka, S. K., Zhou, J., *et al.* (1990). Identification of mutations in the COL4A5 collagen gene in Alport's syndrome. *Science*, **248**, 1224–6.

Breuning, M. H., Reeders, S. T., Brunner, H., Ijdo, J. W., Saris, J. J., Verwest, A., *et al.* (1987). Improved early diagnosis of adult polycystic disease with flanking DNA markers. *Lancet*, **ii**, 1359–61.

Brookes, A. J., Slorach, E. M., Morrison, K., Qureshi, S., Davies, K., and Porteus, D. J. (1994). Cloning the shared components of complex DNA resources. *Hum. Mol. Gen.*, **3**, 2011–17.

Buckler, A. J., Chang, D. D., Graw, S. L., Brook, J. D., Haber, D. A., Sharp, P. A., *et al.* (1991). Exon amplification: a strategy to isolate mammalian genes based on RNA splicing. *Proc. Natl. Acad. Sci. USA*, **88**, 4005–9.

Collins, F. S. (1988). Chromosome jumping. In: *Genome analysis: a practical approach* (ed. K. Davies), pp. 73–94. IRL Press. ISBN 8S221 110 5.

Desmaze, C., Scambler, P., Prieur, M., Halford, S., Sidi, D., Le Deist, F., *et al.* (1993). Routine diagnosis of Di George syndrome by flourescent *in situ* hybridisation. *Hum. Genet.*, **90**, 663–5.

Erlich, H. A., Gelfad, D., and Sninsky, J. J. (1991). Recent advances in the polymerase chain reaction. *Science*, **252**, 1643–51.

Germino, G. G., Weinstat-Saslow, D., Himmelbauer, H., Gillespie, G. A. J., Somlo, S., Wirth, B., *et al.* (1992). The gene for autosomal dominant polycystic kidney disease lies in a 750 kb CpG-rich region. *Genomics*, **13**, 144–51.

Gyapay, G., Morissette, J., Vignal, A., Dib, C., Fizames, C., Millasseau, P., *et al.* (1994). The 1993–1994 Genethon human genetic linkage map. *Nature Genetics*, **7**, 246–339.

Harris, P. C., Barton, N. J., Higgs, D. R., Reeders, S. T., and Wilkie, A. O. M. (1990). A long-range restriction map between the a-globin complex and a marker closely linked to the polycystic kidney disease (PKD1) locus. *Genomics*, **7**, 195–206.

Hozier, J., Graham, R., Westfall, T., Siebert, P., and Davis, L. (1994). Preparative *in situ* hybridization: selection of chromosome region-specific libraries on mitotic chromosomes. *Genomics*, **19**, 441–7.

Kimberling, W. J., Kumar, S., Gabow, P. A. Kenyon, J. B., Connolly, C. J., and Somlo, S. (1993). Autosomal dominant polycystic kidney disease: localication of the second gene to chromosome 4q13–q23. *Genomics*, **18**, 467–72.

Knudson, A. G. (1971). Mutation and cancer: statistical study of retinoblastoma. *Proc. Natl. Acad. Sci.*, **68**, 820–3.

Ledbetter, D. H., Rich, D. C., O'Connell, P., Leppert M., and Carey, J. C. (1989). Precise localization of NF1 to 17q11.2 by balanced translocation. *Am. J. Hum. Genet.*, **44**, 20–4.

Lemmink, H. H., Mochizuki, T., Lambertus, P. W., van den Heuvel, J., Schrîder, C. H., Barrientos, A., *et al.* (1994). Mutations in the type IV collagen alpha 3 (COL4A3) gene in autosomal recessive Alport's syndrome. *Hum. Mol. Gen.*, **3**, 1269–73.

Paris Conference (1971). *Standardization in human cytogenetics: Birth defects.* Original article, Series 8 (No. 7). The National Foundation–March of Dimes, New York, USA.

Peters, D. J. M., Spruit, L., Saris, J. J., Ravine, D., Sandkuijl, L. A., Fossdal, R., *et al.* (1993). Chromosome 4 localization of a second gene for autosomal dominant polycystic kidney disease. *Nature Genet*, **5**, 359–62.

Reeders, S. T., Breuning, M. H., Davies, K. E., Nicholls, R. D., Jarman, A. P., Higgs, D. R., *et al.* (1985). A highly polymorphic DNA marker linked to adult polycystic kidney disease on chromosome 16. *Nature*, **317**, 542–4.

Ried, T., Mahler, V., Vogt, P., Blonden, L., van Ommen, G. J. B., Cremer, T., *et al.* (1990). Direct carrier detection by *in situ* suppression hybridization with cosmid clones of the Duchenne/Becker muscular dystrophy locus. *Hum. Gen.*, **85**, 581–6.

Rommens, J. M., Iannuzzi, M. C., Kerem, B-S., Drumm, M. L., Melmer, G., Dean, M., *et al.* (1989). *Science*, **245**, 1059–65.

Saiki, R. K., Scharf, S., Faloona, F., Mullis, K. B., Horn G. T., Erlich, H. A., *et al.* (1985). Enzymatic amplification of beta-blobin genomic sequences and restriction site analysis for diagnosis of sickle cell anaemia. *Science*, **230**, 1350–4.

Schmidt, M. A., Michels, V. V., and Dewald, G. W. (1987). Case of neurofibromatosis with rearrangements of chromosome 17 involving 17q11.2. *Am. J. Med. Genet.*, **28**, 771–5.

Southern, E. M. (1975). Detection of specific sequences among DNA fragments separated by gel electrophoresis. *J. Mol. Biol.*, **98**, 503–8.

The European Polycystic Kidney Disease Consortium (1994). The polycystic kidney disease 1 gene encodes a 14 kb transcript and lies within a duplicated region on chromosome 16. *Cell*, **77**, 881–94.

Weber, J. L. (1990). Informativeness of human (dC-dA)n (dG-dT)n polymorphisms. *Genomics*, **7**, 524–30.

Zerres, K., Mucher, G., Bachner, L., Deschennes, G., Eggermann, T., Kaarianen H., *et al.* (1994). Mapping of the gene for autosomal recessive polycystic kidney disease (ARPKD) to chromosome 6p21-cen. *Nature Gen.*, **7**, 429–32.

Bibliography and suggested further reading

Barakat, A. Y., Der Kaloustian, V. M., Mufarrij, A. A., and Birbari, A. E. (1986). *The kidney in genetic disease.* Churchill Livingstone, New York, USA.

Erlich, H. A. (1989). *PCR technology.* Stockton Press, New york, USA.

Gelehrter, T. D. and Collins, F. S. (1990). *Principles of medical genetics.* Williams and Wilkins, Baltimore, USA.

Humphries, S. E. and Malcolm, S. (1994). *From genotype to phenotype.* BIOS Scientific, Oxford, UK.

Lewin, B. (1994). *Genes V.* Oxford University Press, Oxford, UK.

McConkey, E. H. (1993). *Human genetics. The molecular revolution.* Jones and Barlett, London, UK.

McKusick, V. A. (1988). *Mendelian inheritance in man.* Jon Hopkins Press, Baltimore, USA.

Weatherall, D. J. (1991). *The new genetics and clinical practice* (3rd edn). Oxford University Press, Oxford, UK.

3

Computers and genetic diseases

Frances V. Elmslie and Robin M. Winter

Introduction

Computers have become essential tools in the day-to-day life of the clinical geneticist. Research into genetic disorders has expanded rapidly in the last few years and it has become impossible to keep up to date with new genetic information without the aid of centralized databases. In addition, the calculations involved in mapping and isolating genes are complex and require the aid of a computer. As more diseases are tackled so the computer scientists have risen to the challenge of producing an increasing range of software capable of analysing these problems. In this chapter we will give a broad overview of the ways in which computers are used, together with specific examples of recent, successful applications of the programs described.

Databases

Computerized databases are the ideal media for the classification and dissemination of new genetic data. These data include information on the map position of genes affecting the kidney and renal tract as well as (increasingly) information about the nature of the genes themselves and about specific mutations. There has also been a rapid increase in the knowledge of multiple malformation syndromes affecting the kidney and renal tract, and information on these can now best be retrieved by using computer databases.

One of the purposes of the Human Genome Project has been to facilitate the sharing of data, resources, and technology to enable researchers to work more rapidly, efficiently, and cost-effectively. Although databases which are regularly updated with the most recent genetic information have been widely available for a number of years, information sharing and services have been vastly improved by the development of World Wide Web (WWW) protocols. The presentation of data has been simplified and transfer of information is quicker and easier across the Internet. The majority of the genetic databases used routinely by the genetic community are now accessible via the WWW.

Online McKusick's Inheritance in Man (OMIM)

Online McKusick's Inheritance in Man (OMIM) is a database of all known human genetic loci comprising a detailed abstract for each locus and comprehensive references (Fig. 3.1). Where specific genes have been cloned, details of known mutations are given. The user can move between displays, giving the map location of the gene and the detailed abstract and references. There is also cross-linking to GDB (GDB—human genome database gene-mapping information: an international collaboration hosted at the Johns Hopkins University School of Medicine,

Location	Symbol	Title	MIM numbers
16pter-p13.3	HBAC, ABC	ALPHA GLOBIN GENE CLUSTER	
16pter-p13.3	HBA1	Haemoglobin alpha-1	141800
16pter-p13.3	HBA2	Haemoglobin alpha-2	141850
16pter-p13.3	HBQ1	Haemoglobin theta-1	142240
16pter-p13.3	HBZ, HBZ2	Haemoglobin zeta (formerly zeta-2)	142310
16pter-p13.3	HBHR, ATR	Alpha-thalassemia/mental retardation	141750
16pter-p11	PDE1B	Phosphodiesterase-1B	171891
16p13.31-p13	PKD1, APK	Polycystic kidney disease-1 (autoso)	173900
16p13.3	CATM	Cataract, congenital, with micropht	156850
16p13.3	PGP	Phosphoglycolate phosphatase	172280
16p13.3	PRM1	Sperm protamine P1	182880
16p13.3	PRM2	Sperm protamine P2	182890
16p13.3	RSTS, RTS	Rubinstein–Taybi syndrome	180849

etc.

$\Longrightarrow$ marks the row for 16p13.31-p13 PKD1, APK.

Fig. 3.1 OMIM—example of gene map.

(a)

Enter question 1 in the window below
----

polycystic AND renal

(b)
----
26 documents contain one or more words from your question

#1: [Weight = 100, 2 words; polycystic renal]
*173900 POLYCYSTIC KIDNEYS [ADULT POLYCYSTIC KIDNEY DISEASE; ADKD; PKD; PKD1;
POTTER TYPE III POLYCYSTIC KIDNEY DISEASE]

#2: [Weight = 85, 2 words; polycystic renal]
*263200 POLYCYSTIC KIDNEY DISEASE, INFANTILE, TYPE I [CYSTIC KIDNEY DISEASE, TYPE I;
AUTOSOMAL RECESSIVE POLYCYSTIC KIDNEY DISEASE; ARPKD; PKD3; HEPATIC FIBROSIS,
CONGENITAL, INCLUDED; CAROLI DISEASE, INCLUDED; RENAL-HEPATIC-PANCREATIC
DYSPLASIA, INCLUDED]
etc.

Fig. 3.2 (a) OMIM—example input; (b) OMIM—example output.

Baltimore). The database can be searched by typing in combinations of key words using Boolean operators (AND/OR/NOT) to formulate search queries (Fig. 3.2). OMIM and GDB are useful not only to obtain information about specific genes and mutations but also when searching for possible candidate genes, having localized a disease gene by linkage studies (Ballabio 1993).

The genome database (GDB)

The Genome Database was set up in 1990 in order to make mapping data more freely accessible to the scientific community. It has been through a number of changes since its inception and version 6.0 is now in operation. The database contains up-to-date information on the mapping of genes and marker loci and aims to integrate data from different sources and alternative methods of mapping. It is interactive—data may be entered directly by the user through the Web interface. Much of the data is already displayed graphically, and it is envisaged that the amount of data available as a graphical image will increase in future releases of GDB.

The London Dysmorphology Database (LDDB)

The London Dysmorphology Database (LDDB) is a computer database of over 2750 non-chromosomal, multiple congenital anomaly syndromes that can be used both as an aid to diagnosis for the clinician and as a reference source. Information in the database is constantly updated and over 1000 journals are now regularly reviewed to ascertain appropriate reports. The database is available for PC-compatible microcomputers (Winter and Baraitser 1996).

Malformation syndromes are indexed by a master list of clinical abnormalities that have been given a three-level code. For example:

(1) Urinary system;
  (2) Kidneys, general abnormalities;
    (3) Renal agenesis;
        Multiple renal cysts;
        Single renal cysts;
        Ectopic/supernumerary kidneys;
        Horseshoe kidneys;
        Hydronephrosis;
        Large kidneys, etc.

An example of the features attached to an individual syndrome is given in Fig. 3.3.

Syndromes can be searched for by using a combination of features at any level of the code, e.g.:

Brain, general abnormalities (structural) AND Multiple renal cysts

Several features can be used for a search and more sophisticated searches can be constructed (e.g. by asking for all syndromes with X out of Y features). An example of a search is shown in Fig. 3.4. Syndromes can also be searched for by a number of other criteria, for example, chromosome location, inheritance, and McKusick number. A detailed abstract and comprehensive reference list is available for each syndrome and clinical photographs and radiographs, stored on CD-ROM, are part of the database. A similar system, using photos stored on videodisc, is also available (POSSUM).

MECKEL–GRUBER SYNDROME (DYSENCEPHALIA
SPLANCHNOCYSTICA)
[Features]
* Cerebellar abnormalities (structural)
* Cerebral atrophy/myelin abnormality
* Dandy–Walker malformation
* Holoprosencephaly/arhinencephaly
* Multiple renal cysts
* Post-axial polydactyly of fingers
* Posterior encephalocele/meningocele
Abnormal liver (including function)
Anal atresia/stenosis
Biliary atresia/stenosis
Cardiac situs inversus/dextrocardia
Cleft palate
Cleft upper lip (non-midline)
Club foot, varus
etc.

Fig. 3.3 LDDB—syndrome feature list. (Matching search criteria from Fig. 3.3 are starred.)

(a) Feature list:

Post-axial polydactyly of fingers;
Multiple renal cysts;
Brain, general abnormalities;

(b) Selected syndromes:

CARPENTER–HUNTER—MICROMELIA; POLYSYNDACTYLY; ENCEPHALOCELE
DONNAI (1988)—MECKEL-LIKE SYNDROME
JEUNE (ASPHYXIATING THORACIC DYSTROPHY)
JOUBERT—CEREBELLAR VERMIS APLASIA PLUS OTHER ANOMALIES
KILLIAN/PALLISTER MOSAIC SYNDROME
LURIE (1991)—CEREBRO–RENO–DIGITAL SYNDROME
MECKEL–GRUBER SYNDROME (DYSENCEPHALIA SPLANCHNOCYSTICA)
MOHR–MAJEWSKI SYNDROME
ORAL–FACIAL–DIGITAL SYNDROME, TYPE I
REUSS (1989)—CYSTIC KIDNEYS; VENTRICULOMEGALY
SHORT RIB SYNDROME, BEEMER–LANGER TYPE
SHORT RIB–POLYDACTYLY SYNDROME TYPE 2 (MAJEWSKI)
SMITH–LEMLI–OPITZ SYNDROME TYPE II (SEVERE LETHAL FORM)

Fig. 3.4   (a) LDDB—syndrome search input; (b) LDDB—syndrome search output.

The use of computers in gene mapping

Linkage analysis

Two main approaches exist for the identification of disease genes: functional cloning and positional cloning. Functional cloning requires knowledge about the underlying protein defect. The gene encoding that protein is analysed for mutations in affected individuals. Positional cloning is an alternative approach. The first step in this approach is to identify on which chromosome the disease-causing gene lies. The exact position on the chromosome is gradually narrowed down; genes in the region are sought and examined for mutations until the gene itself is identified.

In a minority of cases, clues to the chromosomal location of disease–causing genes–may be given by chromosomal abnormalities present in individuals with the disease. In the absence of such abnormalities, the first step in positional cloning is linkage analysis.

In order to perform linkage analysis, suitable families must first be ascertained. Whether each individual is affected or unaffected by the disease being studied must be determined. Individuals in a family are typed using polymorphic DNA markers to determine which alleles are present at different marker loci. DNA markers include restriction fragment length polymorphisms (RFLP) in known genes or random DNA sequences and segments of repetitive DNA known as micro-satellites. The alleles inherited by affected and unaffected members over several generations of a family are sought.

When two gene loci are located on different chromosomes or are distant on the same chromosome, alleles at each locus are passed on independently. If an individual is heterozygous at one locus with alleles Aa and another with alleles Bb, then 50% of the gametes will contain alleles AB or ab and 50% Ab or aB. If the individual has inherited alleles A and B from one parent and a and b from the other then gametes with alleles AB or ab would be interpreted as non-recombinants and those with alleles Ab or aB as recombinants. There would be no linkage between these loci. However, when genes lie close together on a chromosome, recombination at meiosis is less likely to occur between them, and a deviation from the expected 1:1 ratio of recombinant to non-recombinant gametes is found. In this case the loci are said to be *linked*. Genetic linkage can be exploited to assign genes to specific chromosomes and to determine their distance from other genes. If genetic markers are positioned at regular intervals along each chromosome then a random linkage search can be used to locate a disease gene.

The recombination fraction (θ) is defined as the proportion of recombinants in the total number of offspring and gives an indirect measure of the distance between two loci (Ott 1991*a*). For a given pedigree:

$$\theta = \text{number of recombinants}/\left(\text{number of recombinants} + \text{number of non-recombinants}\right).$$

$\theta = 0.5$ implies that recombination is occurring randomly between two loci and the genes are unlinked, whereas if the two loci are linked $\theta < 0.5$. The recombination fraction varies between male and female meioses and results are often expressed allowing for male and female recombination rates (θ_m and θ_f respectively). When the pedigree is simple, θ can be estimated directly (Fig. 3.5)

In order to calculate the recombination fraction, one parent must be doubly heterozygous at the disease and marker loci, e.g. affected and C/H (Fig. 3.5). If they are not (e.g. C/C), it is impossible to determine which marker allele is segregating with the disease and the mating is said to be *uninformative* for linkage. If the linkage phase is unknown, that is, it is not known which marker allele has been inherited with the disease gene from a parent, it is possible to infer phase from the first offspring of the pedigree. If this individual is affected, it could be assumed that the allele inherited from the affected parent is the one segregating with the disease, and similarly, if they are unaffected, the allele present segregates with the wildtype gene. However, the first meiosis may represent a recombinant and in this case the inferred phase will be incorrect. Allowance for this must be made in calculations, so that both possibilities for the phase are considered.

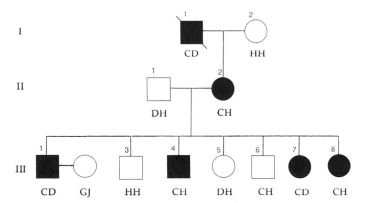

Fig. 3.5 Example pedigree modified from Reeders *et al.* (1985). In this family the disease trait (autosomal dominant polycystic kidney disease, for example) is segregating with allele C of a polymorphic marker. Individual III.6 has allele C but is unaffected. Assuming he is not a non-expressing gene carrier, he must represent a recombinant. The rest of the family are non recombinants. An estimate of $\theta = 1/1 + 6 = 0.14$.

The likelihood of observing a particular pedigree for a given recombination fraction can be calculated. The ratio of this likelihood where two loci are assumed to be linked ($\theta < 0.5$) against the case where the loci are assumed not to be linked ($\theta = 0.5$) is then calculated. The $\log_{10}$ of this likelihood (or odds) ratio is calculated for various values of θ and is known as the lod (**log od**ds) score (Z). Thus:

Z (θ) = $\log_{10}$ (probability of observing this family if loci are linked with a recombination fraction of θ/probability of observing this family if loci are unlinked ($\theta = 0.5$))

i.e. $Z(\theta) = \log_{10}\left(L(\theta)/L(0.5)\right)$

The value of θ that gives the highest lod score is the maximum likelihood estimate of the recombination fraction. Lod scores from different families can be added together for each value of θ.

A lod score is taken to be significant if it is >3, i.e. there is a 1000:1 chance that the gene is linked to the marker being tested. However, for any two autosomal loci, there is an a priori probability of 50:1 that they are linked. With a lod score of 3, this modifies the odds of linkage to 20:1 which is equivalent to statistical significance of 5%. Linkage is said to be excluded when the lod score is <−2 (odds against linkage 100:1).

A computer becomes essential when calculating lod scores in extended families, especially where there is incomplete marker data and for diseases that have a delayed onset or reduced penetrance. If a disease has reduced penetrance it is probable that some individuals in a family are clinically unaffected but do have the mutant gene. In calculations they may falsely appear to be recombinants. The LINKAGE and LIPED computer packages allow for reduced penetrance and the degree of penetrance can be altered according to what is known about the penetrance of the disease. In addition, linkage programs will allow for families in which the phase is unknown, the existence of consanguinity, or the absence of information on members of the pedigree.

Data must be entered into one of the linkage analysis computer programs such as LIPED (Ott 1976) or the LINKAGE package (Lathrop *et al.* 1984), either directly or using a linkage database system such as LINKSYS (Attwood and Bryant 1988), a program designed to manage the genealogical data. LINKSYS organizes data into three files, FAMILY, LOCUSLIB, and PHENOLIB, as follows:

(1) FAMILY:
  Family relationships;
  Sex of each individual;
  Whether affected or unaffected by the disease;
  Alleles present at particular loci being tested (genotype).
A separate file must be created for each family.
(2) LOCUSLIB:
  Locus name;
  Chromosomal location;
  Number and name of alleles at the locus;
  Population frequency of alleles.
(3) PHENOLIB:
  Information about the phenotype for each possible genotype at each locus. This includes by inference the mode of inheritance of the disease locus.

Output from the database can be generated in the form of a pedigree file which contains information about the phenotypes and relationships of individuals in a family and a parameter file

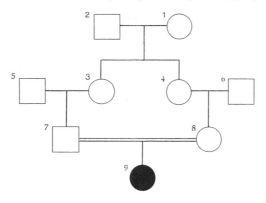

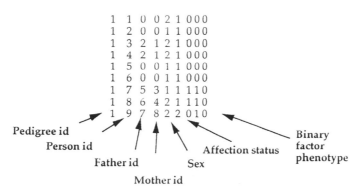

Fig. 3.6 LINKAGE example of consanguineous pedigree with corresponding pedigree file. Sex: 1 = male, 2 = female. Affection status: 1 = unaffected, 2 = affected.

containing information about the the loci to be analysed. These are the standard input files used by the LINKAGE package. An example of a pedigree file is give in Fig. 3.6 and of a parameter file in Fig. 3.7.

There are two main approaches to linkage analysis: two point and multipoint (Ott 1987). In two–point linkage analysis the disease locus is analysed with one particular marker locus. For each value of θ, a lod score is calculated for each family and combined. An example of a lod score table is given in Fig. 3.8. Calculation of two–point lod scores by hand is possible although laborious; however, a computer becomes essential when performing multipoint linkage analysis. More information is yielded from a multipoint linkage analysis because several different markers are compared with the disease trait simultaneously. Information about the position of the loci relative to each other can also be extracted.

Suppose that information is available for three linked loci, A, B, and C, in the same families, but the relative positions of the loci on the chromosome are unknown. The three recombination fractions between these loci are θ_{AB}, θ_{BC}, and θ_{AC}. Using pairwise linkage analysis, a lod score would be calculated by analysing pairs of loci in turn and estimating the recombination fraction

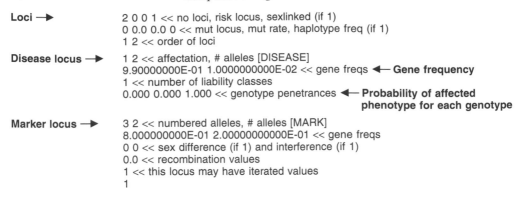

Fig. 3.7   LINKAGE—parameter file.

LOD TABLE REPORT

File: stream.out   Screen: 1 of 1

Order	0.0	0.01	0.05	0.1	0.2	0.3	0.4
1 = 2	0.57	0.55	0.47	0.38	0.22	0.11	0.04

Fig. 3.8   LINKAGE—lod score table.

for which the lod score is greatest. The gene order can be inferred by comparison of the estimated recombination rates. Using multipoint linkage analysis, the probabilities of three different recombination rates are estimated: (i) recombination between AB and BC; (ii) recombination between AB and no recombination between BC; (iii) no recombination between AB and recombination between BC. These three probabilities are denoted p_1, p_2, and p_3 respectively. $\theta_{AB} = p_1 + p_2$, $\theta_{BC} = p_1 + p_3$ and $\theta_{AC} = p_2 + p_3$. The estimates give the most likely gene order. It is usual practice to start by carrying out two-point linkage analysis between the disease trait and a number of marker loci scattered over the genome. When initial results appear to show linkage to specific markers, the density of markers tested in a particular region can be increased and multipoint linkage analysis can be carried out. If the order of marker loci along a chromosome is known, and data is available on the relative distances between them, then the likelihood of specific positions of a disease locus on this map can be calculated. These location scores can be used to plot a likelihood graph (Fig. 3.9).

A number of different computer programs exist for performing linkage analysis. Each has particular strengths, and certain programs are designed less for mapping disease gene loci than for creating large-scale maps of markers.

LIPED is a program for computing two-point lod scores. It is able to handle diseases that display age-dependent penetrance and will take account of differences in susceptibility to a disease, for example, according to sex. In addition, LIPED will produce sex differential lod scores. LINKAGE consists of four different programs: MLINK, LODSCORE, ILINK, AND LINKMAP. MLINK will construct two-point lod score tables and LODSCORE gives an estimation of the value of θ at which the lod score is highest. An example of an MLINK lod score table is given in Fig. 3.8. Multipoint gene order maps can be constructed using ILINK. LINKMAP will place a disease locus on a fixed marker map and generate location scores. An example of a graph drawn from the LINKMAP output, obtained using markers on chromosome

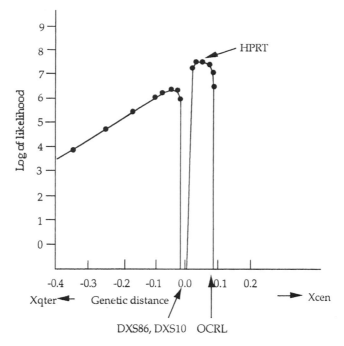

Fig. 3.9 LINKMAP analysis of markers HPRT, DXS10, DXS86, and OCRL (oculocerebrorenal syndrome) (Reilly *et al.* 1990, with permission).

$X_q 24-_q 26$ in mapping Lowe oculocerebrorenal syndrome, is given in Fig. 3.9. CRIMap (Green) is an alternative package designed to tackle large-scale problems. It is able to handle extended pedigrees and will produce large, multilocus linkage maps. However, the main limitation to its use in mapping disease loci is that it copes best with diseases that are fully penetrant, and makes less efficient use of partially informative individuals than either LIPED or LINKAGE. MAPMAKER (Lander *et al.* 1987) is not a general purpose linkage program, but is designed to create multipoint marker maps, for example from the CEPH (Centre d'Etude du Polymorphisme Humain) families. All these programs are IBM PC compatible. However, for large pedigrees with multiple markers and incomplete data, it can sometimes only be feasible to use more powerful machines, such as mainframes.

Autosomal dominant polycystic kidney disease (ADPKD) provides one example of mapping by linkage analysis. ADPKD was first reported to be linked to the DNA marker 3'HVR on the short arm of chromosome 16 (16p13.3) in 1985 (Reeders *et al.* 1985). Nine families, four British and five Dutch, representing the most typical clinical form of the disease, were enrolled. Blood was obtained from 183 family members. 3'HVR is a tandem repeat sequence lying close to the α– globin cluster near the telomere of chromosome 16p; polymorphism at this locus is attributed to variability in the number of repeats present. Eleven alleles, named A-L, were present and seven recombinants were observed from 127 meioses. Only three individuals were found to be uninformative, demonstrating the high polymorphism of the marker 3'HVR. Data was analysed using LIPED 3. An age of onset correction was used in the calculation of the lod score. The maximum lod score obtained was 7.31 at $\theta_m = 0.07$ and 16.41 at $\theta_f = 0.04$. The maximum combined lod score was 25.85 at $\theta = 0.05$. There was therefore unequivocal evidence for linkage of the disease trait to the marker 3'HVR, and the locus was designated PKD1. The authors suggested that such close linkage was indicative that a single locus was responsible for causing the disease, but that further studies were required to assess genetic heterogeneity.

A study of 28 northern European families (Reeders *et al.* 1987) found no evidence for a second locus for ADPKD. Two other reports from Wales and northern Italy also confirmed linkage between ADPKD and the α–globin cluster (Mandich *et al.* 1990; Lazarou *et al.* 1987).

Evidence of genetic heterogeneity soon emerged when two families, both of Italian origin, were found to be unlinked to 16p (Kimberling *et al.* 1988; Romeo *et al.* 1988). Genetic heterogeneity exists when two (or more) cases share the same clinical picture but are caused by mutations in different genes. In order to determine whether heterogeneity existed in any particular group of families being studied, the computer program, HOMOG (Ott 1991*b*), was used. The PKD1 gene on chromosome 16 was identified in 1994 by the demonstration of a chromosomal translocation which disrupted the gene (European Polycystic Kidney Disease Consortium 1994). The gene encodes a 14 kb transcript, distributed among 46 exons, which span 52 kb. The predicted protein, named polycystin, is an integral membrane protein involved in cell–cell/matrix interactions (Hughes *et al.* 1995). Eighteen different mutations have now been described in families with PKD1 (Turco *et al.* 1996), although characterization of mutations has been hampered by the fact that the majority of the region containing the PKD1 transcript is reiterated several times on the same chromosome.

Testing for heterogeneity

HOMOG is based on the admixture test devised by Smith (1963). It tests three hypotheses, H1, H2, and H0, against each other. H1 is the hypothesis that only one group of families exists, all linked to a particular locus; H2, that two groups exist, one linked and one unlinked to the locus; and H0, that linkage is absent in all families. In addition, it estimates the proportion of families showing linkage to the markers, the posterior probability that any particular family is in the linked group and the recombination rate between the marker and the disease. The hypotheses are compared using a Chi-squared test. For both Italian families mentioned above, significant evidence for heterogeneity was obtained when compared with the group of families of Reeders *et al.* 1985. The use of HOMOG in a number of different studies gave an estimate that 85% of ADPKD families were linked to chromosome 16 (Peters *et al.* 1992), and in the remainder, another gene or genes (designated PKD2) elsewhere in the genome was responsible for causing the disease. PKD2 has been mapped to chromosome 4 (Peters *et al.* 1993). All eight families studied had been found to be unlinked to chromosome 16p, and no further evidence for heterogeneity was found. The PKD2 gene has recently been cloned. It encodes a novel integral membrane protein, the amino acid sequence of which shows similarity to polycystin (Mochizuki *et al.* 1996). Recent evidence suggests that there may be a third, as yet unmapped, locus for ADPKD (Bogdanova *et al.* 1995; de Almeida *et al.* 1995).

Calculating genetic risk

Part of the work of the clinical geneticist involves assessment of risk in the offspring or relative of an individual with a disease. Now that the position of many genes is known without knowledge of the actual gene defect, the individuals at risk may be typed using polymorphic markers and the marker information incorporated into the calculation. For an X-linked disorder such as Lowe syndrome, there is a high incidence of new mutation, another factor that must be incorporated into the calculation. For example, individual III.1 in the pedigree shown in Fig. 3.10 has a brother with Lowe syndrome. She wishes to know her risk of being a carrier of the disease. There are two possibilities: either her mother is a carrier, in which case her risk of being a carrier = 1/2; or her brother represents a new mutation, in which case she has a very low risk of being a carrier. The calculation is shown in Fig. 3.11. The example given here is straightforward, but for larger pedigrees and when marker data is available, the calculations become more complex and the use of a computer saves time and minimizes the risk of error. The MLINK computer program in the LINKAGE package has a facility for the calculation of genetic risks, and other packages have been developed specifically for the purpose of estimating genetic risk.

Homozygosity mapping (Lander and Botstein 1987)

Mapping autosomal recessive disorders is more difficult than mapping autosomal dominant or X-linked disorders. Autosomal recessive disorders are individually rare and the tendency to

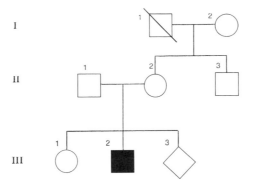

Fig. 3.10   Hypothetical pedigree of family, including a boy (III.2) with Lowe's syndrome.

(1) Risk of individual I.2 being a carrier
     (Ignoring II.2 and offspring)

	Carrier	Non-carrier
Prior probability	4μ	$1 - 4\mu$
Conditional probability	1/2	1
Joint probability	2μ	$1 - 4\mu \approx 1$
Posterior probability	$2\mu/1 + 2\mu \approx 2\mu$	

(2) Risk of individual II.2 being a carrier

Prior probability	$\mu + 2\mu = 3\mu$	$1 - 3\mu$
Conditional probability	1/2	μ
Joint probability	$3\mu/2$	$\mu - 3\mu^2 \approx \mu$
Posterior probability	$(3/2)/(1 + 3/2) = 3/5$	

(3) Risk of individual III.1 being a carrier = $1/2 \times 3/5 = 3/10$

Fig. 3.11   Risk calculation based on pedigree in Fig. 3.10. The mutation rate is given by μ. There is an a priori risk for any female of 4μ that she is a carrier of an X-linked disease, and therefore of not being carrier of $1-4\mu$. The conditional probability takes account of the presence of unaffected males in the pedigree.

small family sizes means that there is often no more than a single affected individual in a pedigree. The occurrence of consanguineous marriage can be exploited in mapping some autosomal recessive diseases, especially in those populations that are isolated or in which consangineous marriage is common. More information can be obtained from small families in this way than from a similar family in which there is no consanguinity, and a smaller number of families is required.

The method involves detection of the disease locus by virtue of the fact that the regions adjacent are likely to be homozygous by descent from a common ancestor. A child has a coefficient of inbreeding, F, defined as the probability that alleles at a given locus will be homozygous by descent. For a first-cousin marriage, $F = 1/16$; for an uncle–niece marriage, $F = 1/8$. For an autosomal recessive disease, the disease alleles have a specific frequency in the population (q) and are in Hardy–Weinberg equilibrium. If a child is affected, the relative probability that this is due to homozygosity by descent is given by $\alpha = Fq/Fq + (1-F)q^2$., i.e. α of all inbred offspring will be homozygous by descent at the disease locus and affected, while $1-\alpha$ will not be homozygous by descent but will be affected because of alleles that do not come from a common ancestor. The power of this approach is greatest when the disease allele is rare in the population, and when the marker used is so polymorphic that homozygosity for any allele has a high chance of representing homozygosity by descent.

Although calculations in consanguineous pedigrees are possible in conventional linkage programs, they take a great deal of computational time. Computer programs are being specifically designed to tackle these problems and are able to provide a more rapid solution.

Homozygosity mapping was used in the mapping of cystinuria to the short arm of chromosome 2 (2p) in 1994 (Pras *et al.* 1994). Cystinuria is an autosomal recessive disorder of amino acid transport and is the most common cause of hereditary renal stones worldwide. Amongst Libyan Jews, the carrier frequency of the gene may be as high as 1 in 25, and amongst the American population it is 1 in 60. The study of consanguineous families in specific racial groups minimizes the risk of intrafamilial heterogeneity since the affected offspring are most likely to be homozygous by descent for a single ancestral mutation. Three types of cystinuria have been described: type 1 heterozygotes show normal aminoaciduria, type II and III heterozygotes show cystine lysinuria. In contrast to homozygotes for types I and II, homozygotes for type II show an increase in cystine plasma levels after oral cystine administration. It was previously thought that the three types are due to allelism of the same gene (Calonge *et al.* 1994).

From the six consanguineous families there were 13 affected offspring. In one particular family there were two first-cousin marriages, one with three affected offspring, the other with two. At one marker tested, D2S391, all the affected family members were homozygous for allele 4 whereas none of the unaffected were. Overall, nine consanguineous affected offspring were homozygous at D2S391, 11 were homozygous at D2S119, 10 at D2S288, and six at D2S177, possibly giving an indication that D2S119 was closer to the disease locus than D2S391, D2S288, or D2S177.

Linkage analysis was performed using the LINKAGE package, assuming recessive inheritance, 100% penetrance in both sexes, and a gene frequency of 0.01. Two-point lod scores were generated using MLINK. Marker D2S119 yielded the highest two-point lod score of 8.23 at a θ of between 0.10 and 0.15, indicating that it was the closest marker to the disease locus. In addition to these calculations the investigators studied the recombinant haplotypes in their families in order to better localize the disease gene. There were a total of 11 informative recombination events in their families. Only one recombination was observed at D2S119 and this individual was non-recombinant at D2S177. The disease locus could therefore be localized further to lie between D2S119 and D2S177. Multipoint linkage analysis using LINKMAP was consistent with these findings.

Simultaneously with the mapping of cystinuria to chromosome 2p, another group demonstrated mutations in SCLA3 (previously known as rBAT) in patients with cystinuria (Calonge *et al.* 1994). Six missense mutations were found, accounting for 30% of the cystinuria chromosomes studied. SCLA3 encodes a transport protein for cystine, dibasic, and neutral amino acids. The gene is expressed in the brush border plasma membrane of both the proximal straight tubules of the nephron and the small intestine. Additional mutations in SCLA3 have been described (Gasparini *et al.* 1995; Pras *et al.* 1995). Evidence for genetic heterogeneity has also emerged. Mutations have been demonstrated in individuals with type 1 cystinuria and not in those with type II and III (Gasparini *et al.* 1995). Furthermore, linkage analysis performed using the marker D2S119 in 22 families with type 1 and/or type III cystinuria showed evidence for linkage with heterogeneity. Families with the intermediate phenotype type I/III and those with type III were shown not to be linked to D2S119 whilst those with type I showed homogeneous linkage (Calonge *et al.* 1995).

Pedigree drawing programs

A number of pedigree drawing programs are now available. Some of these simply provide a quick and easy method for producing clear, uniformly drawn pedigrees, such as PediPlot (Baggesen and Baggesen 1989), Plot2000 (Wolak and Sarfarazi 1986) for DOS machines, and Pedigree/Draw for Apple Macintosh (Mamelka *et al.* 1987). In PediPlot, information about individuals in a family is entered initially, together with details of their relationship to one another. The family is plotted on the basis of the information entered. This can be altered by adding additional family members or by altering the individual information. PEDRAW (Curtis 1990) is a pedigree drawing program designed to use the same input files as the LINKAGE programs or DOLINK. CYRILLIC (Chapman 1993), in addition to producing pedigree drawings, also acts as a visual interface to the linkage computer programs and a database, allowing information to be entered about disease and marker loci which can be transferred to a linkage analysis program (in particular MLINK). In CYRILLIC, the pedigree is drawn as the information is entered so that the display on the screen is the evolving pedigree drawing. Information on individuals can be changed at any time by amending the individual data, and the amount of information on display can be altered to encompass all or none of the information entered about the family. CYRILLIC has been specifically designed for use by clinical geneticists for whom the pedigree forms the basis of all information recorded about a family. Genetic risk for any particular individual in the pedigree can be estimated by identifying that individual as the proband. The input file to MLINK is amended to force calculation of the risk for that person.

Conclusion

It is clear that computers have a role in the every day life of the clinical geneticist. They have become both invaluable sources of information, far exceeding the capacity of the largest textbook, and indispensible tools to aid research into genetic disease as well as the process of genetic counselling.

References

Attwood, J. and Bryant, S. (1988). A computer program to make linkage analysis with LIPED and LINKAGE easier and less prone to input errors. *Annals of Human Genetics*, **52**, 259.

Baggesen, K. and Baggesen, N. (1989). Pediplot: a computer program for drawing pedigrees. *Annals of Genetics*, **32**, 126–8.

Ballabio, A. (1993). The rise and fall of positional cloning? *Nature Genetics*, **3**, 277–9.

Bogdanova, N., Dworniczak, B., Dragova, D., Todorov, V., Dimitrakov, D., Kalinov, K., *et al.* (1995). Genetic heterogeneity of polycystic kidney disease in Bulgaria, *Human Genetics*, **95**, 645–50.

Calonge, M. J., Gasparini, P., Chillaron, J., Chillon, M., Gallucci, M., Rousand, F., *et al.* (1994). Cystinuria caused by mutations in rBAT, a gene involved in the transport of cystine. *Nature Genetics*, **6**, 420–5.

Calonge, M.J., Volpini, V., Bisceglia, L., Rousaud, F., de Sanctis, L., Beccia, E., *et al.* (1995). Genetic heterogeneity in cystinuria: the SLC3A1 gene is linked to type I but not to type III cystinuria. *Proceedings of the National Academy of Science of USA*, **92**, 9667–71.

Chapman, C. J. (1990). A visual interface to computer programs for linkage analysis. *American Journal of Medical Genetics*, **36**, 155–60.

Chapman, C. J. (1993). *CYRILLIC*. Cherwell Scientific Publishing Limited, Oxford.

Curtis, D. (1990). A program to draw pedigrees using LINKAGE or LINKSYS data files. *Annals of Human Genetics*, **54**, 365–7.

de Almeida, S., de Almeida, E., Peters, D., Pinto, J. R., Tavora, I., Lavinha, J., *et al.* (1995). Autosomal dominant polycystic kidney disease: evidence for the existence of a third locus in a Portuguese family *Human Genetics*, **96**, 83–8.

European Polycystic Kidney Disease Consortium (1994). The polycystic kidney disease 1 gene encodes a 14 kb transcript and lies within a duplicated region on chromosome 16. *Cell*, **77**, 881–94.

Gasparini, P., Calonge, M. J., Bisceglia, L., Purroy, J., Dianzani, I., Notarangelo, A., *et al.* (1995). Molecular genetics of cystinuria: identification of four new mutations and seven polymorphisms, and evidence for genetic heterogeneity. *American Journal of Human Genetics*, **57**, 781–8.

Hughes, J., Ward, C. J., Peral, B., Aspinwall, R., Clark, K., SanMillan, J. L., *et al.* (1995). The polycystic kidney disease 1 (PKD1) gene encodes a novel protein with multiple cell recognition domains. *Nature Genetics*, **10**, 151–60.

Kimberling, W. J., Fain, P. R., Kenyon, J. B., Goldgar, D., Sujansky, E., and Gabow, P. A. (1988). Linkage heterogeneity of autosomal dominant polycystic kidney disease. *New England Journal of Medicine*, **319**, 913–17.

Lander, E. S. and Botstein, D. (1987). Homozygosity mapping: a way to map human recessive traits with the DNA of inbred children. *Science*, **236**, 1567–70.

Lander, E. S., Green, P., Abrahamson, J., Barlow, A., Daly, M. J., Lincoln, S. E., *et al.* (1987). MAPMAKER: an interactive computer package for constructing genetic linkage maps of experimental and natural populations. *Genomics*, **1**, 174–81.

Lathrop, G. M., Lalouel, J. M., Julier, C., and Ott, J. (1984). Strategies for multilocus linkage analysis in humans. *Proceedings of the National Academy of Sciences of USA*, **81**, 3443–6.

Lazarou, L. P., Davies, F., Sarfarazi, M., Coles, G. A., and Harper, P. S. (1987). Adult polycystic disease and linked RFLPs at the α globin locus: a genetic study in the South Wales population. *Journal of Medical Genetics*, **24**, 466–73.

McKusick, V. A. (1994). *OMIM (ONLINE MENDELIAN INHERITANCE IN MAN): Catalogs of autosomal dominant, autosomal recessive, X-linked, Y-linked, and mitochondrial phenotypes*. The Johns Hopkins University Press, Baltimore.

Mamelka, P. M., Dyke, B., and MacCluer, J. W. (1987). *Pedigree/Draw for the Apple Macintosh*. Department of Genetics, Southwest Foundation for Biomedical Research, San Antonio, Texas, USA.

Mandich, P., Restagno, G., Novelli, G., Bellone, E., Potenza, L. (1990). Autosomal dominant polycystic kidney disease: a linkage evaluation of heterogeneity in Italy. *American Journal of Medical Genetics*, **35**, 579–81.

Mochizuki, T., Wu, G., Hayashi, T., Xenophontos, S. L., Veldhuisen, B., Saris, J. J., *et al.* (1996). PKD2, a gene for polycystic kidney disease that encodes an integral membrane protein. *Science*, **272**, 1339–42.

Mueller, R. F. and Bishop, D. T. (1993). Autozygosity mapping, complex consanguinity, and autosomal recessive disorders. *Journal of Medical Genetics*, **30**, 798–9. (Letter).

Ott, J. (1976), A computer program for linkage analysis of general human pedigrees. *American Journal of Human Genetics*, **28**, 528–9.

Ott, J. (1987). A short guide to linkage analysis. In: *Genome analysis: a practical approach* (ed. K. Davies), pp. 19–32. IRL Press, Oxford.

Ott, J. (1991*a*). Basic genetics and cytogenetics. In: *Analysis of human genetic linkage* (Revised edn.), pp. 1–22. The Johns Hopkins University Press, Baltimore.

Ott, J. (1991*b*). The variability of the recombination fraction. In: *Analysis of human genetic linkage* (Revised edn.), pp. 194–216. The Johns Hopkins University Press, Baltimore.

Peters, D. J. M. and Sandkuijl, L. A. (1992). Genetic heterogeneity of polycystic kidney disease in Europe. *Contributions in Nephrology*, **97**, 128–39.

Peters, D. J. M., Spruit, L., Saris, J. J., Ravine, D., Sandkuijl, L. A., Fossdal, R., *et al.* (1993). Chromosome 4 localization of a second gene for autosomal dominant polycystic kidney disease. *Nature Genetics*, **5**, 359–62.

Pras, E., Arber, N., Aksentijevich, I., Katz, G., Shapiro, J. M., Prosen, L., *et al.* (1994). Localization of a gene causing cystinuria to chromosome 2p. *Nature Genetics*, **6**, 415–19.

Pras, E., Raben, N., Golomb, E., Arber, N., Aksentijevich, I., Schapiro, J. M., *et al.* (1995). Mutations in the SLC3A1 transporter gene in cystinuria. *American Journal of Human Genetics*, **56**, 1297–303.

Reeders, S. T., Breuning, M. H., Davies, K. E., Nicholls, R. D., Jarman, A. P., Higgs, D. R., *et al.* (1985). A highly polymorphic DNA marker linked to adult polycystic kidney disease on chromosome 16. *Nature*, **317**, 542–4.

Reeders, S. T., Breuning, M. H., Ryynanen, M. A., Wright, A. F., Davies, K. E., King, A. W., *et al.* (1987). A study of genetic linkage heterogeneity in adult polycystic kidney disease. *Human Genetics*, **76**, 348–51.

Reilly, D. S., Lewis, R. A., and Nussbaum, R. L. (1990). Genetic and physical mapping of Xq24q26 markers flanking the Lowe oculocerebrorenal syndrome. *Genomics*, **8**, 62–70.

Romeo, G., Costa, G., Catizone, L., Germino, G. G., Weatherall, D. J., Devoto, M., *et al.* (1988). A second genetic locus for autosomal dominant polycystic kidney disease. *Lancet*, **2**, 8–10.

Smith, C. A. B. (1963). Testing for heterogeneity of recombination fraction values in human genetics. *Annals of Human Genetics*, **27**, 289–304.

Turco, A. E., Rossetti, S., Bresin, E., Corra, S., Englisch, S., Gammaro, L., *et al.* (1996). Novel mutations in the PKD1 gene in European patients with autosomal dominant polycystic kidney disease (ADPKD). *American Journal of Human Genetics*, **59**, A290.

Winter, R. M. (1990). Computing and clinical genetics. In: *Computers in obstetrics and gynaecology* (ed. K. J. Dalton and T. Chard), pp. 209–16. Elsevier Science Publishers B. V., Oxford.

Winter, R. M. and Baraitser M. (1996). *The London dysmorphology database*. Oxford University Press, Oxford.

Wolak, G. R. and Sarfarazi, M. (1986). *PLOT2000. A pedigree plotting program*. Section of Medical Genetics, University Hospital of Wales.

4

Genetic counselling

Michael H. Patton

Introduction

Medical genetics is a relatively new discipline and one which has expanded extremely rapidly over the last decade. The initial development of knowledge was slow. In 1865, George Mendel developed the basic laws of Mendelian inheritance, but his work remained in obscurity until it was 'rediscovered' and presented to the scientific world. In 1901, Sir Archibald Garrod described the condition alkaptonuria (homogentisic acid oxidase deficiency) and coined the term 'inborn error of metabolism' to describe conditions that were both inherited and biochemical in their aetiology. In 1903, Walter Sutton and Theodor Boveri independently recognized the threadlike structures in the nucleus were connected with the transmission of inherited characteristics, and used the term 'chromosomes' to describe them.

It was only in the mid-1950s that clinically relevant knowledge began to develop. Although chromosomes had been described about fifty years previously, their relevance to disorders such as mental handicap was not appreciated until 1956 when Tjio and Levan (1956) showed that humans had 46 chromosomes. From this followed the discovery of trisomy 21 in Down's syndrome (Lejeune *et al.* 1959), trisomy 18 in Edwards' syndrome, and trisomy 13 in Patau's syndrome. Chromosome disorders were recognized to be important causes of mental handicap, malformations, and reproductive loss.

It has only been in the last 15 years that genetic knowledge has increased exponentially, because of the development of gene mapping. This has been an international endeavour using techniques such as *in situ* hybridization, linkage studies, somatic hybrids, and the fortuitous identification of chromosome rearrangements with human diseases. Data from these studies have been compiled and correlated at human gene mapping conferences which in turn have provided computerized databases for the scientific community. On a geographical map it is easier to place small settlements accurately when the borders and coastlines have been defined, and as more details are mapped so it becomes progressively easier to define the relationship between geographical features. In the same way, the more markers or gene loci that are mapped the easier it becomes to complete the details of the genome map. At the present time, over 2000 gene loci have been mapped out of the estimated 50–100 000 structural gene loci in the human genome (McKusick 1992).

The clinical delineation of inherited disorders has also progressed. The most comprehensive description of single gene disorders is given in *Mendelian inheritance in man* (McKusick 1992), which now lists 5500 individual entries in its 10th edition. In addition to this, regularly updated, computerized databases are available for malformation syndromes (Winter and Baraitser 1993) as many new syndromes are described.

It is important to transfer this growth of knowledge into clinical practice, and especially to make the technology available to those whom it will affect most, namely the families with inherited diseases. In the UK this has led to the development of regional genetic centers which provide information and support to families through genetic counselling.

Development of genetic services

The first genetic clinics in the UK were developed in academic departments where clinical service often had to take second place to research. The rapid increase in knowledge and subsequent increase in referrals have changed this approach. There is now a network of clinics built up through regional centres. These centres are based in teaching hospitals and cover defined geographical areas with populations of 1–3 million. Ideally, they will still be closely linked to academic units so that they may both benefit from research and contribute to it. The aim should also be to integrate the clinical and laboratory services so there is high-quality clinical interpretation of laboratory results and also the appropriate counselling available for individuals who have had genetic tests.

The regional centres have developed within defined geographical areas and within a comprehensive health care system. This has a number of advantages. It allows for a manageable genetic register system, and has meant that policies for genetic screening can be systematically evaluated. Genetic registers are more than diagnostic indexes. They provide a systematic method of storing clinical and genetic information on families with inherited disease and of providing support and follow-up for those families. As the follow-up may be in the form of clinic appointments or further diagnostic tests, it is easy for both parties to organize this on a local basis. There is also evidence that a network of local regional registers is far more likely to identify the majority of families than a national register.

Many genetic centres in the UK have tried to decentralize their role within the regions by providing local clinics in district hospitals. This works extremely well as the clinics do not usually require more than a clinic room. The laboratory samples for genetic analysis can be transported directly back to the laboratory in the genetic centre by the clinician. Such an approach may be very helpful in developing collaboration between a renal unit and the genetic service if the two are located in different hospitals.

Historically, many genetic centres have grown out of paediatric departments, and there has been a tendency to see genetics as being more relevant to childhood disease than adult disease. The trend is now towards an increasing number of adult referrals. In the author's own department there are now more adult than paediatric referrals. This reflects the changing perception of genetics. It may pose a problem in providing clinic facilities as the clinics will show a considerable mix in ages. It is probably better to use the quiet corner of an adult clinic than try to examine adults on paediatric beds.

Genetic counselling

The word 'counselling' has been widely used and often misused over the last decade, and so it is appropriate to start with a definition of genetic counselling which has been widely accepted:

Genetic counselling is the process by which patients or relatives at risk of a disorder that may be hereditary are advised of the consequences of the disorder, the probability of developing and transmitting it, and of the ways this may be prevented or ameliorated. (Harper 1988)

Three key words sum up the essence of the counselling process:

1. *Information.* The patient, more correctly known as the consultand or proband, is provided with factual knowledge so that they can reach their own fully informed decision.
2. *Non-directive.* Patients are not given advice or encouraged to pursue a particular course of action until they have become fully informed. They may be encouraged to make their own decision and be supported in that decision. If this sounds contrary to the usual medical model, it should be remembered that many of the decisions are not related directly to treatment but involve personal choices with which the patient will have to live.
3. *Non-judgemental.* The counsellor's role is to provide objective information and sympathetic support, regardless of whether the patient's decision seems foolish or is contrary to the counsellor's own ethical views.

Such aims may seem idealistic, but it is important that the patient should be in control of the new genetic technologies. Much 'high-technology medicine' is perceived as frightening because the patient no longer feels in control. It is particularly important that this should not happen in medical genetics, because it is a powerful technology that can produce enormous benefits but can also potentially be misused.

Most referrals to genetic clinics will be made through a general practitioner or specialist. Occasionally, self-referrals are made, but these are often in the form of a preliminary enquiry. The first stage in the counselling process is to gather the relevant background information for the clinic visit. In this respect, genetic referrals differ from those made to a general medical clinic as the consultand may well have no symptoms or signs, and the relevant clinic information refers to other family members who may be unable to attend the clinic or may have died. Collecting such information may be greatly assisted if the referral letter includes background details or the patient can reply to a questionnaire sent out with the appointment letter. Some centres will send a nurse out to make a home visit before the clinic. Such a visit can be of great help but is relatively expensive in both time and cost.

A number of specific problems may arise in obtaining clinical information on other affected family members. Hospital records are often only kept for several years because of lack of storage space. Some hospitals do microfiche records and, given time, can access these. An alternative approach is through the relative's general practitioner who will have copies of any key correspondence in his files. After death, most records will be destroyed but copies of post-mortem reports or death certificates may be available for many years.

Archival pathological material may still be available, e.g. renal biopsies, and these can be used in some circumstances for DNA diagnoses. Techniques such as polymerase chain reaction may be used when samples are poorly stored or have been preserved in formaldehyde. Chromosome records are usually available from the early 1960s, but even when slides have also been kept, it will be difficult to reanalyse these with the newer fluorescent *in situ* probes.

The appointment for genetic counselling should be in a quiet room, free from interruptions. The atmosphere should be friendly and relaxed with privacy and confidentiality guaranteed. It is desirable to convey an impression, however false, of unlimited time. Most centres will give 30 minutes to one hour for a counselling appointment.

The pedigree will be drawn up in the clinic or completed if preliminary details have already been ascertained. The nomenclature used is given in Chapter 2. In reality, drawing up a pedigree is not simply a mechanical process but also a means of taking a formal history and exploring the consultand's anxieties and the family members' reactions to the genetic illness. (It should also be routine to examine the family members attending the clinic.) Not infrequently, early signs or minor dysmorphic features suggesting variable expression may be elicited. If no abnormalities are found, it may contribute to the patient's ultimate reassurance, after all investigations have been negative.

The key to accurate genetic counselling is accurate diagnosis. This is particularly important because of the complexity of genetic disorders and the phenomena of genetic heterogeneity. Genetic heterogeneity means that:

(1) different genetic disorders may share a similar phenotype (phenotypic heterogeneity), e.g. dislocated lenses and tall stature are found in both Marfan's syndrome and homocystinuria but the former is autosomal dominant and the latter autosomal recessive;

(2) a genetic disorder may be caused by mutations in different loci (locus heterogeneity), e.g. tuberose sclerosis has loci on 1, 9, 16;

(3) different mutations at the same locus may produce clinically similar or dissimilar phenotypes (allelic heterogeneity), e.g. if genetic diagnosis is going to be based on mutation analysis it will be important to know which mutation is present in the family.

Having made a diagnosis or confirmed the diagnosis of the referring physician, the geneticist can discuss clinical features and prognosis. It is obviously important for the geneticist to acknowledge their limitations and accept that discussion of management and treatment is usually best left to other specialists, but often the geneticist will have special insights about the psychological and inherited aspects, which will be of benefit to the consultand. With rare syndromes it may be that the geneticist has actually acquired greater expertise than other specialists.

The next stage is to discuss the patterns of inheritance and the likelihood of the disorder being passed on. The educational background and age of the consultand is very important. The educational level may range from molecular biologists who wish to discuss mutation analysis through to elderly relatives who believe the disorder is due to 'bad blood' in the family. Most consultands will appreciate a short introduction to the concepts of genes and chromosomes, illustrated with a few well-chosen photographs. It is particularly important to distinguish between genes and chromosomes when explaining linkage studies.

When discussing the likelihood of recurrence, it is commonplace to talk about 'risks'. This, however, may be inappropriate since the aim of genetic counselling is to let individuals make informed decisions rather than 'take risks'. It is therefore more appropriate to discuss the probability or chance of recurrence. It is also important to discuss the probability in both figures and descriptive terms. Many people are not used to making personal decisions using statistics and will appreciate some guidance in general terms about whether a 5% recurrence is perceived as a high or low figure. Another reason for not simply providing statistical recurrence figures is that many individuals misunderstand percentages and particularly odds. It is not infrequent for an individual to be told he has a 1 in 20 chance but to come out saying he was told it was 20 to 1 odds of getting the disorder. It is also important to identify the perception the consultand may have. An individual whose brother has died from a subarachnoid haemorrhage may not be so interested in the chances of getting cysts in the kidneys, but will want to know what his chances of having a subarachnoid haemorrhage are and what he can do to prevent it. In disorders with variable expressivity, such questions are much more difficult to answer, and are not simply the mendelian odds of inheritance.

Having discussed the patterns of inheritance and recurrence, the options of genetic testing can be considered. For many of the severe handicapping disorders of childhood this discussion will centre around the approaches to prenatal diagnosis, with consideration of testing preconceptually to ensure that linkage studies are possible or that a specific mutation can be identified. Prenatal diagnosis should be discussed as an option on which the couple themselves can decide rather than the obvious outcome of genetic counselling. For many adult disorders, the possibility of pre-symptomatic testing is becoming more important. Where presymptomatic testing will lead to early and effective treatment, there will appear to be little difficulty in accepting this approach, but the benefits are not usually so clear-cut. For a number of psychological and other reasons there may be disadvantages about presymptomatic testing, and genetic counselling is a useful step in exploring the potential advantages and disadvantages for the individual.

It will be seen from this description that genetic counselling is frequently part of the medical process of diagnosis and conveying accurate information. This is very different from the perception of counselling which provides a long-term, supporting relationship. For the majority of individuals this support may be provided by the primary care team or the renal specialist. In some circumstances, e.g. where there is a genetic register, the genetics staff will provide long-term support. Where the knowledge of genetic implications has led to psychiatric morbidity, it will be important to recognize the need for professional psychiatric help.

Psychological and ethical issues

Misunderstanding the referral

The doctor making a referral to, or working in collaboration with, a genetic clinic should be clear about the process involved in genetic counselling and the reason for referral. Comments such as 'Why don't you go and see Dr X for a chat?' are patronizing to both patient and geneticist. In such circumstances the patient has no clear idea why he is going to a genetic clinic, and he may be indignant about being re-examined and having further blood samples taken. Similarly, to be told that the geneticist will 'sort you out' can be misinterpreted to suggest the geneticist will certainly advise termination if not sterilization, and if interpreted as such, will lead to the patient's failure to attend.

Timing of referral

When the patient has been diagnosed with serious inherited disease for the first time, there is a natural tendency to try to deal with all aspects, including the genetic aspects, at this stage. Often this is the worst time to provide genetic information since anxiety tends to reduce the amount of information learnt. It may be sufficient for a preliminary introduction to the genetics service and to have the appointment postponed for a month or two. Similarly, if a patient has died from an inherited disease it is better to postpone formal genetic counselling until the family have gone through the stages of grief. Further intervention should aim to provide bereavement counselling and not to provide genetic information until the family are ready to receive it.

Decision-making

It might be assumed that if a consultand has all the relevant information, it will be easy to make a decision. This viewpoint overlooks the personal and often unquantifiable factors that have to be resolved by the individual and their family. It may be worth stressing to the consultand that not only should their decision 'look right', it must also 'feel right'.

There are some situations that may block decision-making. Decisions made during pregnancy are often most difficult and will become more difficult if undue pressure is exerted to give a decision quickly. There are relatively few situations where a delay of 48 hours is going to be crucial, and highly charged emotional decisions made at leisure are less likely to be regretted later.

Another situation where decisions may be blocked is when the consultand defers a decision, awaiting further tests or in the hope that research might allow better tests in the future. Up to a point such an approach is realistic but it can become a mechanism for avoiding making any decision. When recognized as such, the counselling should be aimed at understanding the blocks to decision-making, and that in practice, decisions can only be made with the best information available at the time.

A situation that may be particularly difficult for genetic counsellors is when different members of the extended family disagree about genetic testing. It may be difficult to resolve whether one's responsibility to the individual or one's responsibility to the family should take precedence in general terms, but usually if the approach to other family members is through the consultand, most problems can be avoided. A more difficult situation for the counsellor is when the husband and wife disagree about choosing a particular reproductive option. A wise counsellor will present the options objectively, avoid taking sides, and suggest that the couple should discuss the matter further themselves before reaching a decision. On most occasions the decision will be agreed, but, unfortunately, difficult genetic decisions can lead to marital separation. In such circumstances, an outside agency such as a marriage counsellor may be better able to help than a genetic counsellor.

Presymptomatic testing for adult disease has produced new problems, which were first explored with the experience of testing for Huntington's disease (Meissen *et al.* 1988; Morris *et al.* 1989). In this disorder there was no specific treatment available to those who undertook presymptomatic testing and found they had inherited the gene mutation, but their gain was the personal knowledge they had acquired. This allowed individuals to plan their lives and, most importantly, relieved them of the uncertainty which had often made their lives extremely difficult. It has become a model for exploring the use of presymptomatic genetic diagnosis, although hopefully, with renal disorders, early diagnosis will also be associated with early treatment.

It has become important that an individual should give fully informed consent for presymptomatic testing after discussing the relative advantages and disadvantages of the test. This is often overlooked when the test may be an ultrasound scan rather than a 'gene test'. It has raised concerns about testing in children when there is no immediate gain to the child (Clarke 1994; Marteau 1994). It has also been realized that presymptomatic testing could raise new concerns about discrimination in employment or difficulties in gaining acceptable premiums for life or health insurance. These issues need wider public discussion and may, in some cases, require legalisative change.

Cultural differences

Attitudes to inherited disease and genetic testing, especially in pregnancy, will vary considerably from culture to culture. The system of providing genetic services through regional genetic centres has worked well in the UK. In the USA, a number of private companies have been set up especially to provide genetic testing in the population (Motulsky 1994). At present it is unclear how far commercial pressures may drive genetic testing, but from the above discussion it will be appreciated that genetic testing involves more than simply taking an extra blood sample along with the routine biochemistry.

References

Clarke, A. (1994). The genetic testing of children. Report of a working party of the Clinical Genetics Society (UK). *Journal of Medical Genetics*, 31, 785–98.

Harper, P. S. (1988). *Practical genetic counselling* (3rd edn). Wright, London.

Lejeune, J., Gautier, M., and Turpin, R. (1959). Etude des chromosomes somatiques de neuf enfants mongoliens. *Comp. Rend. Acad. Sci.*, 248, 1721–2.

McKusick, V. A. (1992). *Mendelian inheritance in man* (10th edn). Johns Hopkins University Press, Baltimore.

Marteau, T. M. (1994). The genetic testing of children. *Journal of Medical Genetics*, 31, 743.

Meissen, G. J., Myers, R. H., Mastromauro, C. A., *et al.* (1988). Predictive testing for Huntington's disease with the use of a linked DNA marker. *New England Journal of Medicine*, 43, 689–94.

Morris, M. J., Tyler, A., Lazarou, L., Meredith, L., and Harper, P. S. (1989). Problems in genetic prediction for Huntington's disease. *Lancet*, ii, 601–3.

Motulsky, A. O. (1994). Predictive genetic testing. *American Journal of Human Genetics*, 55, 603–5.

Tijo, J. H. and Levan, A. (1956). The chromosome number in man. *Hereditas*, 42, 1–6.

Winter, R. and Baraitser, M. (1993). *London dysmorphology database*. Oxford University Press, Oxford.

5

Prenatal diagnosis

Martin d'A. Crawfurd

Introduction

Clearly, genetically determined renal disorders are not sufficiently common to warrant routine prenatal screening, although more common developmental anomalies may be detected routinely. Definitive prenatal diagnosis in high-risk pregnancies is based on the techniques of prenatal diagnosis in use for genetic disorders in general. This subject has been extensively reviewed, as for example in a recent monograph (Brock *et al.* 1992). The techniques specifically relevant to renal genetic disorders fall into two main categories: fetal sampling procedures combined with cytogenetic, biochemical, or molecular genetic analyses; and imaging techniques. Recent advances that use various techniques of fetal cell enrichment combined with PCR-based DNA analyses for the analyses of fetal cells isolated from the maternal circulation raise hopes that this may prove feasible in future (Adinolfi 1992; Busch *et al.* 1994; Lo *et al.* 1994).

High-risk pregnancies are those in which there is a known risk of the fetus being affected by a mendelian inheritant disorder or where there is an increased risk of a developmental disorder, usually from the birth of a previous affected child. Mendelian disorders may be inherited in autosomal dominant or recessive or an X-linked manner.

There may be an increased risk of autosomal dominant disorder where either parent is known, on clinical or investigative grounds, to carry a gene for such a disorder, or where either parent is at risk of carrying such a gene because of antecedent family history. In the latter situation, if the at-risk parent can clearly be shown not to carry the gene, prenatal diagnosis becomes unnecessary.

The fetus is at risk of having an autosomal recessive disorder if the parents have had a previous affected child, if the parents are consanguineous and there is a family history of the disorder on at least one side, or if a positive family history or screening has led to carrier tests revealing both parents to be carriers.

An X-linked recessive disorder may be a risk if the mother is a known or likely carrier on pedigree or investigative grounds.

Developmental defects may be inherited in a mendelian manner, in which case the above criteria for risk apply. It may be due to chromosomal anomaly which may be suspected from a routine ultrasound scan or be detected on routine cytogenetic analyses of chorionic villus or amniotic fluid cells, or a risk may arise from a known parental chromosomal rearrangement. The simple autosomal trisomies, apart from Down's syndrome in which renal anomaly is rare, show only a weak association with maternal age and a very low recurrence risk.

Most of the common major congenital malformations and several rare malformation syndromes are of sporadic occurrence and show a low recurrence risk for sibs, mostly between 1% and 5%. Nevertheless, such recurrence risks are high enough to justify prenatal diagnosis, where practical, when there has already been an affected child.

Increasing use of prenatal fetal sonography, and of amniocentesis or chorionic villus samples, is leading to the frequent detection of the more common anomalies in low-risk cases.

Counselling for prenatal diagnosis of genetic renal disorder

Any woman contemplating pregnancy and known to be at risk for genetic renal disorder should be offered counselling regarding prenatal diagnosis for herself, and if she so wishes, her partner. Such counselling, whether given by an obstetrician, renal physician, or a clinical geneticist, needs to cover the level of risk, the prognosis for the disorder in question including its likely response to treatment, and a discussion on the advantages and disadvantages of alternative methods of prenatal diagnosis including the risk they pose of pregnancy loss. In most cases the object of prenatal diagnosis is to offer termination of pregnancy if the fetus is shown to be affected. In a few developmental disorders with urinary tract obstruction, the object may be to offer intrauterine relief of obstruction, and in such cases the likelihood of a successful outcome needs to be frankly discussed with the patient. Exceptionally, a woman who would not accept termination may nevertheless wish to know if her fetus is affected. Such a request should be considered sympathetically, although in NHS practice resources may not run to meeting such requests, and in private practice it may be necessary to check whether or not medical insurance covers it.

Ideally, such counselling should be undertaken before conception, but in many cases the patient will only present after the onset of pregnancy when it may be necessary to arrange counselling fairly urgently.

Further counselling may well be necessary after prenatal diagnosis has been undertaken, especially when the fetus is shown to be affected. This is particularly important if the patient has not had prior counselling. Such post-diagnostic counselling may include genetic counselling regarding future pregnancies, or this may be postponed to a later date, especially if termination has been decided on.

Finally, if the pregnancy is terminated the parents may need bereavement counselling afterwards.

Methods of prenatal diagnosis

Fetal sampling methods

Chorionic villus sampling is the preferred method for DNA analyses, as might be required for the prenatal diagnosis of Alport's disease (see Chapter 11.1) or adult polycystic kidney disease (see Chapter 8). It provides an adequate sample of fetal tissue for direct extraction and analyses of DNA without initial cell culture by 11–12 weeks pregnancy (as counted from LMP) (Silverman and Wapner 1992). It should not be attempted prior to 11 weeks because of the risk of fetal abnormality (Olney *et al.* 1994). A brief review of the techniques of DNA analyses is given by Malcolm (1992). At present, prenatal diagnosis using DNA analyses is feasible in only a limited number of urinary tract disorders. However, the recent spate of reports of gene isolation, or at least informative linkage, ensures that before long many more will be diagnosable.

Amniocentesis is traditionally undertaken at about 16 weeks and it is a relatively safe procedure (0.5–1% fetal loss) and has no adverse affect on live-born offspring (Baird *et al.* 1994). Recently, obstetricians have experimented with early amniocentesis at 10–14 weeks. Early amniocentesis has the advantage of earlier diagnosis but carries a greater risk of pregnancy loss than does 16-week amniocentesis or chorionic villus sampling, 2.5–5.3% compared to 0.5–1% and 2.3% respectively. However, most losses occur before 13 weeks and may also be related to operator inexperience. (Bombard *et al.* 1994; Eiben *et al.* 1994; Nicolaides *et al.* 1994; Saura *et al.* 1994; The Canadian Early and Mid-Trimester Amniocentesis (CEMAT) Group 1998). The cells isolated from the amniotic fluid can be cultured to provide sufficient for cytogenetic or biochemical, especially enzyme, analyses; and the supernatant fluid can be used for measurement of alpha-fetalprotein or other constituents or metabolites. The technique is well-established and relatively safe but does carry the risk of maternal cell contamination (MacLachlain 1992). Cytogenetic analysis might, for example, be required to confirm a suspicion of trisomy 13 as the cause of cystic kidneys and other developmental defects detected on ultrasound analysis. Amniotic fluid cell enzyme assay may be needed for the prenatal diagnosis of an inborn error of metabolism with renal involvement, such as Fabry's disease. Alpha-fetoprotein assay in either maternal serum or amniotic fluid gives raised values in Finnish-type congenital nephrotic syndrome (Ryynanen *et al.* 1983).

Fetal blood or tissue sampling may occasionally be indicated for confirmation of ambiguous cytogenetic findings or where there has been a failure of cell growth. It may also be indicated where ultrasound has detected obstructive uropathy in order to exclude a chromosomal basis (Nicolini and Rodeck 1992), or for measurement of an enzyme not expressed in peripheral blood cells.

Imaging methods

Fetal ultrasonography has proved to be an invaluable tool for the detection of developmental anomalies (Cambell and Pearce 1983), including those of the urinary tract. The sensitivity of the method is operator dependent and is higher in known risk cases and on routine screening (Chitty *et al.* 1991). The methodology has been recently reviewed (Docker 1992). Several groups have reported series of cases of fetal urinary tract anomaly detected by prenatal sonography (Thomas *et al.* 1986; Helin and Persson 1986; Quinlan *et al.* 1986; Smith *et al.* 1987; Scott and Renwick 1988; Bronshtein *et al.* 1990; Chitty *et al.* 1991; Luck 1992). From these studies it is clear that prenatal fetal ultrasonography is a valuable diagnostic technique but that the interpretation of ultrasound images can present considerable difficulties so the correct diagnosis or even recognition of abnormality is by no means straightforward, as for example in the diagnosis of renal agenesis. The technique carries appreciable false positive and negative rates. A useful development of sonography is the use of a transvaginal probe which permits urinary tract diagnosis in the first trimester (Bronshtein *et al.* 1990).

Detectable urinary tract anomalies include renal agenesis; duplication anomalies; horseshoe kidney; hydronephrosis and obstruction due to pelviureteric obstruction or to urethral valves, stenosis, or atresia; renal cysts due to infantile polycystic kidney disease, fetal onset of adult polycystic kidney disease, dysplastic kidneys, trisomy 13, Meckel's syndrome, and other causes; reflux; and bladder exstrophy. The detection of abnormality does not necessarily imply that termination is indicated. Some anomalies are symptomless, such as unilateral renal agenesis, horseshoe kidney, or duplication anomaly; others may be compatible with a long, symptom-free course and eventual treatment of renal failure, such as adult polycystic kidney disease; and yet others are inevitably lethal either *in utero* or in infancy, such as trisomy 13. Selected cases of urinary tract obstruction are amenable to intrauterine relief of obstruction by vesicoamniotic shunt.

In addition to specific urinary tract abnormalities, oligohydramnios and/or an empty bladder may be valuable indicators of urinary tract abnormality.

More sophisticated imaging techniques have not as yet become established in fetal urinary tract diagnosis. X-ray methods, although of value in the diagnosis of skeletal dysplasias in later pregnancy, have little to offer in urinary tract diagnosis. Conventional magnetic resonance imaging (MRI), although a safe method, is liable to artefact from fetal movement, especially before the end of the second trimester. After fetal sedation, motional artefact is reduced but not eliminated, and the kidneys especially remain difficult to visualize. At best, MRI does little more than confirm earlier ultrasound diagnosis (Johnson 1992). A modification of MRI, echo–planar imaging requires much shorter time intervals to obtain an image and, therefore, minimizes motional distortion. However, it is too early to assess the role of this technique in the diagnosis of fetal anomaly, either on the urinary tract or other organs (Johnson 1992).

Specific diagnoses

Specific diagnoses of fetal abnormality, made by the methods discussed above, are mentioned where relevant elsewhere in the text. They will not be discussed in detail here but are listed in Table 5.1. The conditions listed fall into three groups: chromosomal disorders; mendelian

Table 5.1   Specific diagnoses of fetal abnormality

Disorder or anomaly (MIM no.)	Urinary tract anomaly	Mode of inheritance	Method of prenatal diagnosis	Reference
Chromosomal				
Down's syndrome [47, +21]	Rare, approx. 6/1000 LB cases	CHR-TR	KAR; AFC, CVS	Fabia & Drolette 1970
Trisomy 13 [47, +13]	Cortical microcysts or mild cystic renal dysplasia consistently, and nodular renal blastema in half of all cases	CHR-TR	(1) Renal cysts on US (2) KAR; AFC, CVS	Schinzel 1979
Trisomy 18 [47, +18]	Horseshoe or unilateral fused kidney, and other renal anomalies in approximately 60% of all cases	CHR-TR	(1) Horseshoe kidney on US (2) KAR; AFC, CVS	Hamerton 1971
Turner's syndrome [45, X]	Horseshoe kidney or duplication defect in 60–70% of cases	CHR-MON	(1) US (2) KAR; AFC, CVS	Hung & Lo Presti 1965
Wolf–Hirschhorn syndrome [del(4p)]	Hypospadias and cryptorchidism in 93% of all cases	CHR-DEL	KAR; AFC, CVS	Vinals et al. 1994
Various 13q deletions with or without ring chromosome formation	Hypo-(or epi) Spadias, bifid scrotum, renal hypoplasia and/or hydronephrosis in a half of all cases	CHR-DEL	KAR; AFC, CVS	Niebuhr 1977
Miller–Dieker syndrome [del(17p13.3)]	Renal agenesis or cystic dysplasia	CHR-REAR	KAR; AFC, CVS	Dobyns et al. 1983
Carp-mouth syndrome [del(18q)]	Micropenis, hypoplastic scrotum, and ectopic testes in less than a half of all cases.	CHR-DEL	KAR; AFC, CVS	Rethore 1977

Table 5.1 *Continued*

Disorder or anomaly (MIM no.)	Urinary tract anomaly	Mode of inheritance	Method of prenatal diagnosis	Reference
WAGR complex [del(11p13)]	Wilms' tumour and genito-urinary anomaly	CHR-DEL	(1) KAR; AFC, CVS (2) DNA-M	Martinez-Mora *et al.* 1989
Cat eye syndrome [trisomy proximal 22q]	Renal agenesis, hypoplasia, ectopia, duplication or obstruction, and horseshoe kidney in many cases	CHR-TR	KAR; AFC, CVS	Pierson *et al.* 1975
Trisomy 7 [47, +7]	Renal cystic dysplasia in all non-mosaic cases	CHR-TR	KAR; AFC, CVS	Verp *et al.* 1987
Mendelian				
Adult polycystic kidney disease (PKD 1) (173900)	Tubular epithelial hyperplasia leading to variable-sized cysts of Bowman's capsule, tubules, and collecting ducts of individual nephrons	AD	(1) US occasionally possible (2) DNA-L (16p markers) (Note: prenatal diagnosis of PKD 2 not yet feasible)	Journel *et al.* 1989; Turco *et al.* 1992
Albright's hereditary osteodystrophy (103580)	Failure of renal phosphate excretion in response to parathormone due to a defect in a subunit of Gs protein	AD	(DNA-M)	Weinstein *et al.* 1992
Alport's disease (301050)	Glomerular basement membrane thickening and splitting leading to chronic glomerulonephritis due to a defect in 5(iv) collagen chain	XR	(DNA-L) (DNA-M)	Barker *et al.* 1990; Barker *et al.* 1991
Asphyxiating thoracic dystrophy (Jeune's syndrome) (208500)	Cystic renal disease (Potter type 4) leading to renal failure	AR	US for skeletal changes	Elejalde *et al.* 1985
Bardet–Biedl syndrome (209900)	Mixed tubular and interstitial nephritis with glomerulosclerosis and cystic change	AR	US for echodense fetal kidneys and polydactyly	Gershoni-Baruch *et al.* 1992
Bartter's syndrome (familial hypokalaemic alkalosis) (241200)	Juxtaglomerular hyperplasia with distal tubular defect in sodium and chloride transport (Chapter 28)	AR	FBS, METAB (for aldosterone) AFS, METAB	Shalev *et al.* 1994
Branchio–oto–renal dysplasia (BOR syndrome) (113650)	Renal aplasia, dysplasia, and pelviureteric duplication defects	AD	US (DNA-L)	Greenberg *et al.* 1988; Wang *et al.* 1994
Cryptophthalmos syndrome (219000)	Renal agenesis or dysplasia	AR	US for microphthalmia or renal abnormality	Ramsing *et al.* 1990
Cystinosis, infantile nephropathic type (219800)	Renal Fanconi syndrome associated with generalized tissue deposition of cystine crystals	AR	CVS, METAB by uptake of ^{35}S labelled cystine	Smith *et al.* 1987

Table 5.1 *Continued*

Disorder or anomaly (MIM no.)	Urinary tract anomaly	Mode of inheritance	Method of prenatal diagnosis	Reference
2,8-Dihydroxyadeninuria	2,8-dihydroxyadenine renal stones due to adenine phosphoribosyltransferase deficiency	Incomplete AR	(ENZ) (DNA-M)	Kamatini *et al.* 1990
Ectrodactyly-epidermal dysplasia–clefting (EEC) syndrome (129900)	Renal anomalies, usually obstructive, in a half of all cases	AD	US	Kohler *et al.* 1989
Fabry's disease (angiokeratoma corporis diffusum) (301500)	Renal deposition of ceramide with loss of tubular function, glomerulosclerosis, and renal failure due to galactosidase deficiency	XR	ENZ	Kleijer *et al.* 1987
Fryn's syndrome (229850)	Cystic dysplastic kidneys and/or renal agenesis	AR	US	Pellissier *et al.* 1992
Galactosaemia (230400)	Fanconi-like tubular defect due to deficiency of galactose-1-phosphate uridy transferase	AR	ENZ	Holton *et al.* 1989
Glycogen storage disease type 1A (von Gierke's disease) (232200)	Fanconi-like tubular defect due to deficiency of glucose-6-phosphatase.	AR	FLB, ENZ	Golbus *et al.* 1988
Hydronephrosis (143400)	Pelvi-ureteric obstruction	AD (Genetically heterogeneous)	US	Thomas *et al.* 1986
Hyperoxaluria type 1 (259900)	Calcium oxalate deposition with 2ry renal obstruction and infection from nephrolithiasis	AR	FLB, ENZ DNA-L	Danpure *et al.* 1989; Rumsby *et al.* 1994
Infantile polycystic kidney disease (263200)	Collecting duct cysts arranged in a radial pattern	AR	US MRI	Nishi *et al.* 1991; Tsuda *et al.* 1994
Joubert's syndrome (243910)	Cortical renal cysts in those patients who also have retinal dystrophy	AR	US	Ivarsson *et al.* 1993
Lowe's oculocerebrorenal syndrome (309000)	Fanconi-like tubular defect with failure of ammonia production	XR	DNA-L	Gazit *et al.* 1990
Meckel–Gruber syndrome (249000)	Cortical and medullary renal cysts	AR	US Fetoscopy	Pachi *et al.* 1989; Dumez *et al.* 1994
Nial-patella syndrome (Osteo-onycho-dystrophy (161200)	Glomerulonephropathy in nephropathic form only	AD	(FKB-histology)	Drut *et al.* 1992 (but comments of Gubler & Levy 1993)
Nephrogenic diabetes insipidus (304800)	Renal tubular resistance to vasopressin due to defect in vasopression type 2 receptor	XR with partial heterozygote expression	(DNA-L)	Knoers *et al.* 1988
Nephrotic syndrome, congenital, Finnish type (256300)	Fatty degeneration of renal tubular cells and proliferative glomerular changes with loss of epithelial foot processes and basement membrane splitting	AR	AFS-METAB for trehalase	Morin 1984

Table 5.1 *Continued*

Disorder or anomaly (MIM no.)	Urinary tract anomaly	Mode of inheritance	Method of prenatal diagnosis	Reference
Oroticaciduria I & II (258900 & 258920)	Ureteral and urethral obstruction by orotic acid crystals	AR	AFS-METAB for pyrimidines	Ohba *et al.* 1993
Opitz (BBB) syndrome (145410)	Hypospadias	AD	US	Hogdall *et al.* 1989
Perlman syndrome (familial diffuse nephroblastomatosis) 267000)	Bilateral renal hamartomas	AR	US	Ambrosino *et al.* 1990
Robert's syndrome (268300)	Large phallus, occasional horseshoe or polycystic kidney	AR	US	Stioui *et al.* 1992
Robinow syndrome (180700)	Micropenis and cryptorchidism, occasional cystic kidneys	AD	US	Loverro *et al.* 1990
Smith–Lemli–Opitz syndrome (270400)	Hypospadias and cryptorchidism	AR	US	Curry *et al.* 1987
Tuberous schlerosis, I & II (191100)	Angiomyolipomas and cysts of the kidney	AD with genetic heterogeneity	US (fetal echocardiography) MRI	Platt *et al.* 1987; Werner *et al.* 1994
Tyrosineanmia type I (fumarylacetoacetase deficiency) (276700)	Faeconi-like syndrome with swelling and degeneration of tubule cells	AR	AFS-METAB AFC, ENZ CVS (DNA-L) DNA-M	Kittingen & Brodtkorb, 1986; Jakobs *et al.* 1988; Rootwelt *et al.* 1990; Ploos van Amstel *et al.* 1994
Von Hippel–Lindau disease (193300)	Angiomatous cysts of kidneys which may progress to renal cell carcinoma	AD with variable expression	(DNA-L)	Maher *et al.* 1992
Xanthinuria (Xanthine oxidase deficiency (278300)	Xanthine renal stones	AR	AFC, ENZ CVS,	Desjacques *et al.* 1985
Zellweger (cerebro–hepato–renal) syndrome (214100)	Renal cortical (Potter type 4) cysts	AR with genetic heterogeneity	AFC, ENZ CVS	Schutgens *et al.* 1989
Non-or doubtfully mendelian Bladder exstrophy	Developmental anomaly	NON-MEN rare sib occurence	US	Jaffe *et al.* 1990
Fused (horseshoe) or ectopic kidney	Maldevelopment or malposition	NON-MEN	US	Colley & Hooker 1989
Multicystic dysplastic kidneys	Renal cysts, fibrosis and disorganised structure	NON-MEN	US and needle aspiration of cyst fluid	Nicolini *et al.* 1991
Prune belly syndrome (100100)	Variable from vesico-ureteral reflux through hydronephrosis to renal dysplasia, often associated with posterior urethral valves	NON-MEN male limited, probably multifactorial	US	Meizner *et al.* 1985

Table 5.1   *Continued*

Disorder or anomaly (MIM no.)	Urinary tract anomaly	Mode of inheritance	Method of prenatal diagnosis	Reference
Renal agenesis or adysplasia (191830)	Unilateral or bilateral agenesis or dysplasia, or unilateral agenesis and contralateral dysplasia, + Mullerian duct anomalies	AD with variable expression in some families	US	Kuller *et al.* 1994
Ureterocele (191650)	Cystic dilation of intravesical portion of ureter	?AD cases	US	Fitzsimmons *et al.* 1986
VACTERL association (a variant of VATER association (192350)	Renal anomalies, present in a half of all cases, include agenesis or hypoplasia, and dysplasia	NON-MEN	US	Claiborne *et al.* 1986
Vesicoureteral reflux (193000)	Abnormal insertion of ureters into the bladder leading to reflux, infection, and nephropathy, sometimes with renal scarring	AD with incomplete penetrance or multifactorial	US	Reznik *et al.* 1988

disorders, for which a MIM number is appended (McKusick's *Mendelial inheritance in man*, 11th edition, 1994); and non-mendelian disorders, mostly developmental.

The table lists, in the first column, disorders and developmental anomalies involving the urinary tract, with a MIM number where relevant. In the second column, characteristics of the renal or urinary tract anomaly found in the condition is stated. The third column gives the mode of inheritance: AD for autosomal dominant; AR for autosomal recessive; XR for X-linked recessive; CHR-TR, -MON, -DEL, -REAR for chromosomal trisomy, monosomy, deletion, or rearrangement; and/or NON-MEN for non-mendelian and non-chromosomal. Further comments where relevant are added, such as late onset or variable expression. Where there is genetic locus heterogeneity this is also mentioned. The statement that a condition is non-mendelian may, however, disguise new mutations of a gene which if not lethal would be dominant, or a molecular deletion.

Methods of prenatal diagnosis are given in the fourth column. KAR indicates karyotype analyses for chromosomal disorders; ENZ, enzyme analysis, usually on cultured amniotic fluid cells or chorionic villus sample unless otherwise indicated; METAB for assay of a metabolite in amniotic fluid supernatant; DNA-L for DNA analyses using linked probes or DNA-M for DNA diagnosis by detection of specific mutations, deletions, or amplified repeats; and US for ultrasound. AFC indicates amniotic fluid cells and AFA as amniotic fluid supernatant; CVS indicates chorionic villus sample; FB as fetal blood sample; FLB, fetal liver biopsy; and FKB, fetal kidney biopsy. Where the method of prenatal diagnosis is enclosed in brackets this indicates that although the methodology for prenatal diagnosis is available, an actual diagnosis has not been reported.

In the reference column, a single reference is given which in most cases is reported as prenatal diagnosis by the method indicated, but in the case of chromosomal disorders is mainly the description of a urinary tract finding.

Bibliography

Adinolfi, M. C. (1992). Fetal nucleated cells in the maternal circulation. In: *Prenatal diagnosis and screening* (ed. D. J. H. Brock, C. H. Rodeck, and M. A. Ferguson-Smith, pp. 651–60. Churchill-Livingstone, Edinburgh.

Ambrosino, M. M., Hernanz-Schulman, M., Horii S. C., *et al.* (1990). prenatal diagnosis of nephroblastomatosis in two siblings. *J. Ultrasound in Medicine*, 9, 49–51.

Baird, P. A., Yee, I. M. L., and Sadovnick, A. D. (1994). Population-based study of long-term outcome after amniocentesis. *Lancet*, 344, 1134–6.

Barker, D. F., Hostikka, S. L., Zhou, J., Chow, L. T., Oliphant, A. R., Gerken, S. C., *et al.* (1990). Identification of mutations in the COL 4A5 collagen gene in Alport's syndrome. *Science*, 248, 1224–7.

Barker, D. F., Fain, P. R., Goldgar, D. E., Dietz-Band, J. N., Turco, A. E., Kashtan, C. E., *et al.* (1991). IIigh-density genetic and physical mapping of DNA markers near the X-linked Alport syndrome locus: definition and use of flanking polymorphic markers. *Hum. Genet.*, 88, 189–94.

Bombard, A. T., Carter, S. M., and Nitowsky, H. M. (1994). Early amniocentesis versus chorionic villus sampling for fetal karyotyping. *Lancet*, 344, 826. (Letter).

Brock, D. J. H., Rodeck, C. H., and Ferguson-Smith, M. A. (ed.) (1992). *Prenatal diagnosis and screening*. Churchill Livingstone, Edinburgh.

Bronshtein, M., Yoffe, N., Brandes, J. M., and Blumenfeld, Z. (1990). First and early second-trimester diagnosis of fetal urinary tract anomalies using vaginal sonography. *Prenat. Diagnosis*, 10, 653–66.

Bronshtein, M., Bar-Hava, I., and Blumenfeld, Z. (1992). Clues and pitfalls in the early prenatal diagnosis of 'late-onset' infantile polycystic kidney. *Prenat. Diagnosis*, 12, 293–8.

Busch, J., Huber, P., Pfluger, E., Miltenyi, St., Holtz, J., and Radbruch, A. (1994). Enrichment of fetal cells from maternal blood by high-gradient magnetic cell sorting (double MACS) for PCR-based genetic analysis *Prenat. Diagnosis*, 14, 1129–40.

Campbell, S. and Pearce, J. M. (1983). The prenatal diagnosis of fetal structural anomalies by ultrasound. *Clin. Obstet. Gynaecol.*, 10, 475–506.

Cheng, H. H. and Nicolaides, K. H. (1992). Renal and urinary tract abnormalities. In: *Prenatal diagnosis and screening* (ed. D. J. H. Brock, C. H. Rodeck, and M. A. Ferguson-Smith), pp. 257–70. Churchill-Livingstone, Edinburgh.

Chitty, L. S., Hunt, G. H., Moore, I., and Lobb, M. O. (1991). Effectiveness of routine ultrasonography in detecting fetal structural abnormalities in a low-risk population. *BMJ*, 303, 1165.

Claiborne, A. K., Blocker, S. H., Martin, C. M., and McAllister, W. H. (1986). Prenatal and postnatal sonographic delineation of gastrointestinal abnormalities in a case of the VATER syndrome. *J. Ultrasound in Medicine*, 5, 45–7.

Colley, N. and Hooker, J. G. (1989). Prenatal diagnosis of pelvic kidney. *Prenat. Diagnosis*, 9, 361–3.

Curry, C. J. R., Carey, J. C., Holland, J. S., Chopra, D., Fineman, R., Golabi, M., *et al.* (1987). Smith–Lemli–Opitz syndrome type II. Multiple congenital anomalies with male pseudohermaphroditism and frequent early lethality. *Am. J. Med. Genet.*, 26, 45–57.

Danpure, C. J., Cooper, P. J., Jennings, P. R., Wise, P. J., Penketh, R. J., and Rodeck, C. H. (1989). Enzymatic prenatal diagnosis of primary hyperoxaluria type1: potential and limitations. *J. Inher. Metab. Dis.*, 12, (Suppl. 2), 286–8.

Desjacques, P., Mousson, B., Vianey-Liaud, C., Boulieu, R., Bory, C., and Baltassat, P. (1985). Combined deficiency of xanthine oxidase and sulphate oxidase: diagnosis of a new case followed by an antenatal diagnosis. *J. Inher. Metab. Dis.*, 8, (Suppl. 2), 117–18.

Dobyns, W. B., Stratton, R. F., Parke, J. T., Greenberg, F., Nussbaum, R. L., and Ledbetter, D. H. (1983). The Miller–Dieker syndrome: lissencephaly and monosomy 17p. *J. Pediatr.*, 102, 552–8.

Docker, M. F. (1992). Ultrasound imaging techniques. In: *Prenatal diagnosis and screening* (ed. D. J. H. Brock, C. H. Rodeck, and M. A. Ferguson-Smith), pp. 69–81. Churchill-Livingstone, Edinburgh.

Drut, R. M., Chandra, S., Latorraca, R., and Gilbert-Barness, E. (1992). Nail patella syndrome in a spontaneously aborted 18-week fetus: ultrastructural and immunofluorescent study of the kidneys. *Am. J. Med. Genet.*, **43**, 693–6.

Dumez, Y., Dommergues, M., Gubler, M-C., Bunduki, V., Narcy, F., Le Merrer, M., *et al.* (1986). Meckel–Gruber syndrome: prenatal diagnosis at 10 menstrual weeks using embryoscopy. *Prenat. Diagnosis*, **14**, 141–4.

Eiden, B., Osthelder, B., Hammans, W., and Goebel, R. (1994). Safety of early amniocentesis versus CVS. *Lancet*, **344**, 1303–4. (Letter).

Elejalde, B. R., de Elejalde, M. M., and Pansch, D. (1985). Prenatal diagnosis of Jeune's syndrome. *Am. J. Med. Genet.*, **21**, 433–8.

Fabia, J. and Drolette, M. (1970). Malformations and leukaemia in children with Down's syndrome. *Pediatrics*, **45**, 60–70.

Fitzsimmons, P. J., Frost, R. A., Millward, S., De Maria, J., and Toi, A. (1986). Prenatal and immediate postnatal ultrasonographic diagnosis of ureterocele. *J Canad. Assoc. Radiol.*, **37**, 189–91.

Gazit, E., Brand, N., Harel, Y., Lotan, D., and Barkai, G. (1990). Prenatal diagnosis of Lowe's syndrome: a case report with evidence of *de novo* mutation. *Prenat. Diagnosis*, **10**, 257–60.

Gershoni-Baruch, R., Nachlieli, T., Leibo, R., Degani, S., and Weisman, I. (1992). Cystic kidney dysplasia and polydactyly in 3 sibs with Bardet–Biedl syndrome. *Am. J. Med. Genet.*, **44**, 269–73.

Golbus, M. S., Simpson, T. J., Koresawa, M., Appelman, Z., and Alpers, C. E. (1988). The prenatal determination of glucose-6-phosphatase activity by fetal liver biopsy. *Prenat. Diagnosis*, **8**, 401–4.

Greenberg, C. R., Trevenen, C. L., and Evans, J. A. (1988). The BOR syndrome and renal agenesis— prenatal diagnosis and further clinical delineation. *Prenat. Diagnosis*, **8**, 103–8.

Gubler, M-C. and Levy, M. (1993). Prenatal diagnosis of nail-patella syndrome by intrauterine kidney biopsy. *Am. J. Med. Genet.*, **47**, 122–3.

Hamerton, J. L. (1971). *Human cytogenetics*, Vol II. *Clinical cytogenetics*. p 32. Academic Press, New York and London.

Hatton *et al.* (1989) ••

Helin, I. and Persson, P-H. (1986). Prenatal diagnosis of urinary tract abnormalities by ultrasound. *Pediatrics*, **78**, 879–83.

Hogdall, C., Siegel-Bartelt, J., Toi, A., and Ritchie, S. (1989). Prenatal diagnosis of Opitz (BBB) syndrome in the second trimester by ultrasound detection of hypospadias and hypertelorism. *Prenat. Diagnosis*, **9**, 783–93.

Holton, J. B., Allen, J. T., and Gillett, M. G. (1989). Prenatal diagnosis of disorders of galactose metabolism. *J. Inher. Metab. Dis.*, **12**, (Suppl. 1), 202–6.

Hung, W. and Lopressi, J. M. (1965). Urinary tract anomalies in gonadal dysgenesis. *Am. J. Roentgenol., Radium Ther. Nucl. Med., [NS]*, **395**, 439–41.

Ivarsson, S-A., Bjerre, I., Brun, A., Ljungberg, O., Maly, E., and Taylor, A. (1993). Joubert's syndrome associated with Leber amaurosis and multicystic kidneys. *Am. J. Med. Genet.*, **45**, 542–7.

Jaffe, R., Shoenfeld, A., and Ovadia, J. (1990). Sonographic findings in the prenatal diagnosis of bladder exstrophy. *Am. J. Obstet. Gynecol.*, **162**, 675–8.

Jakobs, C., Dorland, L., Wikekierink, B., Kok, R. M., de Jong, Ad P. J. M., and Wadman, S. K. (1988). Stable isotope dilution analysis of succinylacetone using electron capture negative ion mass fragmentography: an accurate approach to the pre-and neonatal diagnosis of hereditary tyrosinemia type I. *Clin. Chim. Acta*, **223**, 223–32.

Johnson, I. R. (1992). Radiological and magnetic visualization techniques. In: *Prenatal diagnosis and screening* (ed. D. J. H. Brock, C. H. Rodeck, and M. A. Ferguson-Smith), PP. 55–67. Churchill-Livingstone, Edinburgh.

Journel, H., Guyot, C., Balkeoch, P., Quenener, A., and Jouan, H. (1989). Unexpected ultrasonographic prenatal diagnosis of autosomal dominant polycystic kidney disease. *Prenat. Diagnosis*, 9, 663–71.

Kamatani, N., Kuroshima, S., Yamanaka, H., Nakashe, S., Take, H., and Hakoda. M. (1990). Identification of a compound heterozygote for adenine phosphoribosyltransferase deficiency (APRT*J/APRT*Q O) leading to 2,8 dihydroxyadenine urolithiasis. *Hum. Genet.*, 85, 500–4.

Kleijer, W. J., Hussaarts-Odijk, L. M., Sachs, E. S., *et al.* (1987). Prenatal diagnosis of Fabry's disease by direct analysis of chorionic villi. *Prenat. Diagnosis*, 7, 283–7.

Knoers, N., van der Heyden, H., van Oost, B. A., Monnens, L., Willems, J., and Ropers, H. H. (1989). Three-point linkage analysis using multiple DNA polymorphic markers in families with X-linked nephrogenic diabetes insipidus. *Genomics*, 4, 434–7.

Kohler, R., Sousa, P., and Jorge, C. S. (1989). Prenatal diagnosis of the ectrodactyly, ectodermal dysplasia, cleft palate (EEC) syndrome. *J. Ultrasound in Medicine*, 8, 337–9.

Krittingen, E. A. and Brodtkorb, E. (1986). The pre- and post-natal diagnosis of tyrosinaemia type I and the detection of the carrier state by assay of fumarylacetoacetase. *Scand. J. Clin. Lab. Invest.*, 46 (Suppl. 184), 35–40.

Kuller, J. A., Coulson, C. C., McCoy, M. C., Altman, G. C., Thorp, J. M. Jr., and Katz, V. L. (1994). Prenatal diagnosis of renal agenesis in a twin gestation. *Prenat. Diagnosis*, 14, 1090–2.

Lo, Y-M, Morey, A. L., Wainscoat, J. S., and Fleming, K. A. (1994). Culture of fetal erythroid cells from maternal peripheral blood. *Lancet*, 344, 264–5. (Letter).

Loverro, G., Guanti, G., Caruso, G., and Selvaggi, L. (1990). Robinow's syndrome: prenatal diagnosis. *Prenat. Diagnosis*, 10, 121–6.

Luck, C. A. (1992). Value of routine ultrasound scanning at 19 weeks; a four-year study of 8849 deliveries. *BMJ*, 304, 1474–8.

McKusick, V. A. (1994). *Mendelian inheritance in man* (11th edn). Johns Hopkins University Press, Baltimore.

MacLachlan, N. A. (1992). Amniocentesis. In: *Prenatal diagnosis and screening* (ed. D. J. H. Brock, C. H. Rodeck, and M. A. Ferguson-Smith), pp. 13–24. Churchill-Livingstone, Edinburgh.

Maher, E. R., Bentley, E., Payne, S. J., *et al.* (1992). Presymptomatic diagnosis of von Hippel–Lindau disease with flanking DNA markers. *J. Med. Genet.*, 29, 902–5.

Malcolm, S. (1992). Molecular genetics. In: *Prenatal diagnosis and screening* (ed. D. J. H. Brock, C. H. Rodeck, and M. A. Ferguson-Smith), pp. 147–58. Churchill-Livingstone, Edinburgh.

Martinez-Mora, J., Audi, L., Toran, N., Isnard, R., Castellvi, A., Iribarne, M. P., *et al.* (1989). Ambiguous genitalia, gonadoblastoma, aniridia, and mental retardation with deletion of chromosome 11. *J. Urol.*, 142, 1298–300.

Meizner, I., Bar-Ziv, J., and Katz, M. (1985). Prenatal ultrasonic diagnosis of the extreme form of prune belly syndrome. *J. Clin. Ultrasound*, 13, 581–3.

Meizner, I., Bar-Ziv, J., Bark, Y., and Abeliovich, D. (1986). Prenatal ultrasonic diagnosis of radial ray aplasia and renal anomalies (acro-renal syndrome). *Prenat. Diagnosis*, 6, 223–5.

Morin, P. R. (1984). Prenatal detection of the congenital nephrotic syndrome (Finnish type) by trehalase assay in amniotic fluid. *Prenat. Diagnosis*, 4, 257–60.

Nicolaides, K., Brizot, M., de L., Patel, F., and Snijders. R. (1994). Comparison of chorionic villus sampling and amniocentesis for fetal karyotyping at 10–13 weeks gestation. *Lancet*, 344, 435–9.

Nicolini, U., Fisk, N. M., Rodeck, C. H., and Beacham, J. (1992). Fetal urine biochemistry: an index of renal maturation and dysfunction. *Br. J. Obstet. Gynaecol.*, 99, 46–50.

Nicolini, U. and Rodeck, C. H. (1992). Fetal blood and tissue sampling. In: *Prenatal diagnosis and screening* (ed. D. J. H. Brock, C. H. Rodeck, and M. A. Ferguson-Smith), pp. 35–51. Churchill-Livingstone, Edinburgh.

Niebuhr, E. (1977). Partial trisomies and deletions of chromosome 13. In: *New chromosomal syndromes* (ed. J. J. Yunis), pp. 273–99. Academic Press, New York.

Nishi, T., Iwasaki, M., Yamoto, M., and Nakano, R (1991). Prenatal diagnosis of autosomal recessive polycystic kidney disease by ultrasonography and magnetic resonance imaging. *Acta Obstet. Gynecol. Scand*, **70**, 615–70.

Ohba, S., Kidonchi, K., Toyama, J., Oda, T., Tsuboi, T., Ichiki, T., *et al.* (1993). Quantitative analysis of amniotic fluid pyrimidines for the prenatal diagnosis of hereditary oroticacidurias. *J. Inter. Metab. Dis.*, **16**, 872–5.

Olney, R. S., Khoury, M. J., Botto, L. D., and Mastroiacovo, P. (1994). Limb defects and gestational age at chorionic villus sampling. *Lancet*, **344**, 476.

Pachi, A., Giancotti, A., Torcia, F., DeProsperi, V., and Maggi, E. (1989). Meckel–Gruber syndrome: ultrasonographic diagnosis at 13 weeks gestational age in an at-risk case. *Prenat. Diagnosis*, **9**, 187–90.

Pearce, J. M. (1989). The biophysical diagnosis of fetal abnormalities. In: *Obstetrics* (ed. A. Turnbull and G. Chamberlain), pp. 303–7. Churchill-Livingstone, Edinburgh.

Pellissier, M. C., Philip, N., Potier, A., Scheiner, C., Ayme, S., Mattei, J. F., *et al.* (1994). Prenatal diagnosis of Fryn's syndrome. *Prenat. Diagnosis*, **12**, 299–303.

Pierson, M., Gilgenkrantz, S., and Saborio, M. (1975). Syndrome dit de l'oeil de chat avec nanisme hypophysaire et développement mental normal. *Arch Fr. Pediatr.*, **32**, 835–48.

Platt, L. D., Devore, G. R., Horenstein, J., Pavlova, Z., Kovacs, B. and Falk, R. E. (1987). Prenaral Diagnosis of tuberous sclerosis; the use of feral echocardiography. *Prenat. Diagnosis*, **I**, 407–11.

Ploos van Amstel, J. K., Jansen, R. D. M., Verjaal, M., Van den Berg, I. E. T., and Berger, R. (1994). Prenatal diagnosis of type I hereditary tyrosinaemia. *Lancet*, **344**, 336. (Letter).

Quinlan R. W., Cruz, A. C., and Huddelston, J. F. (1986). Sonographic detection of fetal urinary tract anomalies. *Obstet. Gynecol.*, **67**, 558–65.

Ramsing, M., Rehder, H., Holzgreve, W., Meinecke, P., and Leng, W. (1990). Fraser syndrome (cryptophthalmos with syndactyly) in the fetus and newborn. *Clin. Genet.*, **37**, 84–96.

Rethore, M. O. (1977). Deletions and ring chromosomes. In: *Handbook of clinical neurology*. Vol. 26–7. *Congenital malformation of the brain and skull* (ed. J. P. Vinken and G. W. Bruyn), pp. 549–620. North Holland, Amsterdam.

Reznik, V. M., Kaplan, G. W., Murphy, J. L., Packer, M. G., Boychuk, D., Griswold, W. R., *et al.* (1988). Follow-up of infants with bilateral renal disease detected *in utero*. *Am J. Dis. Child.*, **142**, 453.

Rootwelt, H., Kvittingen, E. A., Agsteribbe, E., Hartog, M. V., van Faassen, H., and Berger, R. (1990). The fumarylacetoacetase gene: characterization of restriction fragment length polymorphisms and identification of haplotypes—possibility for prenatal diagnosis in families with compound genotypes for the tyrosinemia and 'pseudodeficiency' genes. 5th International Congress on Inborn Errors of Metabolism. Asilomar, California, 1–5 June 1990.

Rumsby, G., Uttley, W. S., and Kirk, J. M. (1994). First trimester diagnosis of primary hyperoxaluria type I. *Lancet*, **344**, 1018.

Ryynanen M., Seppalaa, M., and Kuusela P., *et al.* (1983). Antenatal screening for congenital nephrosis in Finland by maternal serum alpha fetoprotein. *Br. J. Obstet. Gynaecol.*, **90**, 437–42.

Saura, R., Roux D., Taine, L., Maugey, B., Lavlon, D., Laplace, J. P., *et al.* (1994). Early amniocentesis versus chorionic villus sampling for fetal karyotyping. *Lancet*, **344**, 825–6. (Letter).

Schinzel, A. (1979). Autosomale Chromosomenaberationen. *Arch. Genet.*, **52**, 1–204.

Schutgens, R. B. H., Schrakamp, G., Wanders, R. J. A., *et al.* (1989). Prenatal and perinatal diagnosis of peroxisomal disorders. *J. Inher. Metab. Dis.*, **12**, (Suppl. 1), 118–34.

Scott, J. E. S. and Renwick, M. (1988). Antenatal diagnosis of congenital abnormalities in the urinary tract. *Br. J. Urol.*, **62**, 295–300.

Shalev, H., Ohaly, M., Meizner, I., and Carmi, R. (1994). Prenatal diagnosis of Bartter syndrome. *Prenat. Diagnosis*, **14**, 996–8.

Silverman, N. S. and Wapner, R. J. (1992). Chorionic villus sampling. In: *Prenatal diagnosis and screening* (ed. D. J. H. Brock, C. H. Rodeck, and M. A. Ferguson-Smith), pp. 25–38. Churchill-Livingstone, Edinburgh.

Smith, D., Egginton, J. A., and Brookfield, D. S. K. (1987). Detection of abnormality of fetal urinary tract as a predictor of renal tract disease. *BMJ*, **294**, 27–8.

Smith, M. L., Pellett, D. L., Cass, M. M. J., Kennaway, N. G., Buist, N. R. M., Buckmaster, J., *et al.* (1987). Prenatal diagnosis of cystinosis utilizing chorionic villus sampling. *Prenat. Diagnosis*, **7**, 23–6.

Stioui, S., Privitera, O., Brambati, B., Zuliani, G., Lalotta, F., and Simoni, F. (1992). First-trimester prenatal diagnosis of Robert's syndrome. *Prenat. Diagnosis*, **12**, 145–9.

The Canadian Early and Mid-Trimester Amniocentesis Trial (CEMAT) Group (1998) Randomised trial to asscss safety and fetal outcome of early and midtrimester amniocentesis. *Lancet*, **350**, 242–7.

Thomas, D. F. M., Irving, H. C., and Arthur, R. J. (1986). Prenatal diagnosis: how useful is it? *Br. J. Urol.*, **57**, 784–7.

Tsuda, H., Matsumoto, M., Imanaka, M., and Ogita, S. (1994). Measurement of fetal urine production in mild infantile polycystic kidney disease—a case report. *Prenat. Diagnosis*, **14**, 1083–5.

Tureo, A., Peissel, B., Quaia, P., *et al.* (1992). Prenatal diagnosis of autosomal dominant polycystic kidney disease using flanking DNA markers and the polymerase chain reaction. *Prenat. Diagnosis*, **12**, 513–24.

Verp, M. S., Amarose, A. P., Esterly, J. R., and Moawad, A. H. (1987). Mosaic trisomy 7 and renal dysplasia. *Am. J. Med. Genet.*, **26**, 139–43.

Vinals, F., Sepulveda, W., and Selman, E. (1994). Prenatal detection of congenital hypospadias in the Wolf–Hirschhorn (4p-) syndrome. *Prenat. Diagnosis*, **14**, 1166–9.

Wang, Y., Treat, K., Schroer, R. J., Le Paslier, D., O'Brien, J. E., Callen, D. F., *et al.* (1994). Isolation of 2Mb YAC contig encompassing the branchio-oto-renal (BOR) syndrome locus in 8q 13.3. *Am. J. Hum. Genet.*, **55**(3), p. A273. (Abstract no. 1601).

Weinstein, L. S., Gejman, P. V., De Mazancourt, P., American, N., and Spiegel, A. M. (1992). A heterozygous 4 bp deletion mutation in the Gs gene (GNAS1) in a patient with Albright hereditary osteodystrophy. *Genomics*, **13**, 1319–21.

Werner, H. Jr., Mirlesse, V., Jacquemard, F., *et al.* (1994). Prenatal diagnosis of tuberous sclerosis. Use of magnetic resonance imaging and its implications for prognosis. *Prenat. Diagnosis*, **14**, 1151–4.

6

Growth, development, and management of renal disease in children

Heather Maxwell

Introduction

One of the goals of management of children with chronic renal disease is to ensure continued growth and development. Short stature, however, is a significant problem, and for many children it is the only visible sign of disease.

This chapter addresses growth and development in children with renal disease. Growth in specific renal conditions will be mentioned in the relevant chapters; more general issues will be dealt with here. The effect of renal disease on growth is influenced by a number of factors, the most important of which are age and type of renal disease.

Short stature is a particular problem for children with congenital renal disease who are more severely affected than children with acquired renal disease occurring later in childhood (Betts and Magrath 1974). Subsequent growth depends on pubertal stage and treatment modality (Potter and Greifer 1978; Schaefer *et al.* 1990). The type of renal disease is also important; children with inherited tubular problems are often very stunted (Potter and Greifer 1978). For many, but not all conditions, growth declines as renal function deteriorates (Betts and Magrath 1974), but with good supportive management normal growth rates can be maintained (Polito *et al.* 1987). In any one child there are multiple factors operating, and their relative importance is often difficult, if not impossible, to determine.

Firstly, it is important to recognize poor growth and there are a number of points which need to be considered when assessing growth. Secondly, height and growth vary with age, therefore it is important to standardize measurements when comparing groups or quantifying the effects of an intervention.

As can be seen from Fig. 6.1, the rate of growth varies throughout childhood (Tanner *et al.* 1966). At the time of birth, mean length is 50 cm and height velocity (HV) is at its greatest; HV slows down thereafter but is still considerable during the first two years. Mean HV is 26 cm in the first year of life, with a further 10 cm being added during the second year. By the age of two years, a child has reached half of its final adult height, so that one-third of postnatal growth has occurred in the first two years. Rate of growth is relatively constant during mid-childhood, gradually slowing down to a nadir of 5 cm/year before puberty. The pubertal growth spurt occurs on average after the age of 10 in girls, and after 12 in boys, and during the pubertal years approximately 30 cm are added to final adult height.

Growth in the first one to two years is dependent mainly on nutrition, with the influence of growth hormone becoming important thereafter. Growth hormone secretion increases during the pubertal growth spurt, under the influence of sex steroids.

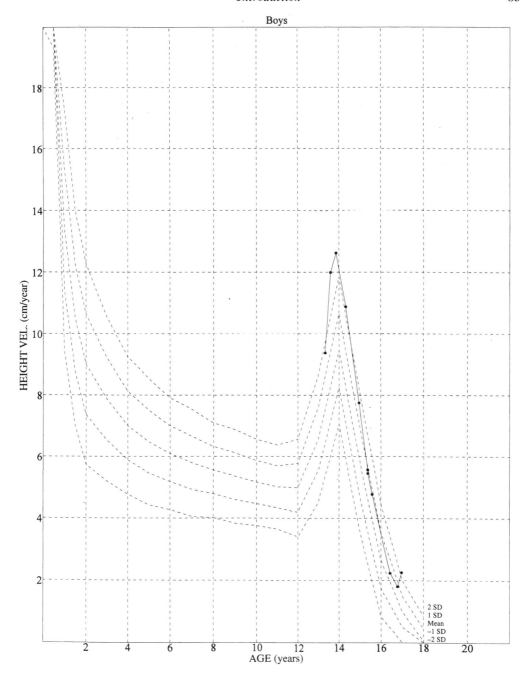

Fig. 6.1 Height velocity chart of a boy who received a renal transplant at the age of 12.9 years (Tanner *et al.* 1966).

When assessing growth in children, it is necessary to consider both the statural height already attained and the rate of growth at the time of study. Short stature is assumed when the height is below the 3rd centile for age and sex, although by this definition 3% of normal children are included. However, to maintain a position on the 3rd centile requires a normal HV; when HV decreases then the child falls away from the centiles. To return to the normal range requires a HV greater than expected for age, so-called catch-up growth.

Growth is expressed as cm per year; however, as growth is seasonal, and affected by intercurrent illness or stress, it is important to leave a suitable interval between measurements to allow accurate estimation of annualized HV. This is particularly so for children who are growing poorly. A minimum interval of six months should be used. Height should be measured at the same time of day by trained personnel using suitably accurate equipment, such as a wall-mounted stadiometer. In the first two years of life recumbent length is measured. During this time the occipito–frontal head circumference (OFC) has been shown to be a good measure of brain growth (Proyer and Thelander 1968; Winick and Rosso 1969).

For comparison of height and HV data, standard deviation scores (SDS) are used in preference to centiles.

$$\text{Height SDS}\left(\text{HtSDS}\right) = \frac{\text{Patient's height} - \text{mean height for age and sex}}{\text{standard deviation for age and sex}}$$

A HtSDS of zero approximates to the 50th centile and a HtSDS of −2 is equivalent to a height on the 3rd centile. HVSDS is calculated in a similar fashion.

Another factor which has to be taken into consideration during the assessment of growth is the bone age. Bone age reflects skeletal maturation and is an indicator of growth potential. A delayed bone age implies that the child may continue to grow for a relatively longer period of time.

Genetic factors influence height and the parent's height must be considered in the assessment of a child's height.

Patterns of growth in renal disease

Infancy

Children with congenital renal disease and those with problems commencing in infancy are most at risk of short stature (Betts and Magrath 1974). As described above, growth is fastest in infancy; ill health at this time results in a rapid loss of stature. Antenatal diagnosis of renal problems has allowed these infants to be followed from birth; growth is most affected in the first six months of life, when height SDS can decline by as much as 0.6 SD each month (Rizzoni *et al.* 1984). The children described in this report had a normal birth weight and length. Birth weight is usually normal, but a number of children with renal dysplasia are small at birth (Rees *et al.* 1989). Data on birth length are more scarce.

Similar observations of poor growth in infancy in renal disease have been reported by a number of groups (Jones *et al.* 1982; Kleinknecht *et al.* 1983; Rizzoni *et al.* 1984; Warady *et al.* 1988; Rees *et al.* 1989; Abitol *et al.* 1993). Comparing these reports, height SDS at presentation is negatively correlated with age; mean HtSDS for those presenting in the first month was −0.6 SD (Warady *et al.* 1988), while those presenting at one year had a mean HtSDS of −2.9 (Rees *et al.* 1989). Early diagnosis and treatment are essential.

Growth in infancy is highly dependent on nutrition (Betts and Magrath 1974), and provision of adequate calories can improve growth (Strife *et al.* 1986). Many of these infants have tubular dysfunction, and correction of electrolyte, base, and fluid loss results in a marked improvement in growth (Rees *et al.* 1989). These factors are discussed in detail below. In this age group, catch-up growth can be achieved in some infants with good conservative management and intensive nutritional support (Rees *et al.* 1989).

In addition to poor growth, end stage renal disease (ESRD) in infancy has been described as causing an encephalopathy, manifest by reduced cognitive ability, microcephaly, and reduced motor function (Rotundo *et al.* 1982; McGraw and Haka-Ikse 1985; Polinsky *et al.* 1987). Renal replacement therapy can alleviate this, with slight improvement occurring on peritoneal dialysis (Warady *et al.* 1988), and more marked improvement seen following renal transplantation (Nevins 1987; So *et al.* 1987; Davis *et al.* 1990; Najarian *et al.* 1990).

Midchildhood

After the first two years of life, children with chronic renal failure (CRF) grow at a normal rate, so that the child remains below but parallel to the 3rd centile. Catch-up growth is rare. Rees *et al.* (1989) found that after infancy, intensive conservative management resulted in only a slow improvement in growth. At presentation to the clinic, 61% of the children described were below the normal range for height; at the end of the study period, 53% remained below the 3rd centile.

In keeping with other reports, there was no correlation between growth in CRF and absolute glomeular filtration rate (GFR). Children with congenital renal problems tend to grow along the centiles at this stage (Betts and Magrath 1974; Claris-Appiani *et al.* 1989), and growth rate remains relatively normal until either ESRD or puberty is reached. Growth on dialysis is less than that observed during conservative management (Kleinknecht *et al.* 1980). Children with a later onset of renal problems often show a slowing down of growth in the initial stages of the illness, then grow along a lower centile when their condition is more stable.

Puberty

Puberty is associated with development of secondary sexual characteristics and an increase in growth rate. The onset of the pubertal growth spurt, which is taken as the time of minimum HV prior to the growth spurt, is delayed by an average of approximately two and a half years in both sexes (Schaefer *et al.* 1990). Interestingly the absolute height at which this occurs is similar to that in normal controls, but the peak velocity achieved during puberty is reduced to approximately 75% of that of controls. In addition, the duration of the pubertal growth spurt is attenuated; on average it is reduced by one year in boys and by one and a half years in girls. These factors combine to result in a reduction in expected height gain from the onset of puberty, from 30 to 17 cm in boys and from 29 to 14 cm in girls (Schaefer *et al.* 1990). Bone age at the end of puberty was less than expected; little growth occurred after a mean bone age of 15.6 years in boys and 14.7 in girls in this study. Growth potential is lost during puberty.

Much of the data regarding pubertal growth and development is from studies which combine children on different treatment modalities. In the study described above, the majority of children were on either conservative management or dialysis at the onset of puberty, with most being transplanted by the end of puberty. This course is not unusual in children with renal disease, so that data on the effects of treatment modality are hard to come by. Broyer *et al.* (1974) described 17 children on haemodialysis, of whom 10 were of a pubertal age; the pubertal growth spurt was absent or severely depressed in all 10 children. There is an ongoing multinational study of growth

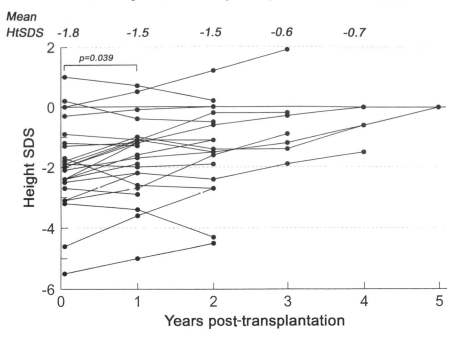

Fig. 6.2   HtSDS at yearly intervals after renal transplantation in 24 children of pubertal age (girls ≥10 years, boys ≥11 years).

and development during puberty in renal disease which hopefully will be able to provide this data (Scharer 1990).

Traditionally, growth during puberty in children with renal transplants has been described as poor, with some authors reporting little growth in those with a bone age over 12 years (Grushkin and Fine 1973; Rees *et al*. 1988). Since the introduction of cyclosporin A and the subsequent reduction in steroid dosage, we are seeing normal patterns of pubertal growth in some of our patients (Fig 6.1). HtSDS at yearly intervals following renal transplantation in children of pubertal age are shown in Fig. 6.2.

Sexual maturation is also delayed by approximately two and a half years in renal disease (Scharer 1990). Progression through puberty is generally normal, although temporary maturational delay has been reported (Schaefer and Mehls 1994). Secretion of luteinizing hormone is reduced in uraemic adolescents and adults, but normal in transplant patients (Rodger *et al*. 1985; Scharer 1990). The effects of uremia in childhood on future fertility are not known. Preliminary data suggest that sperm counts are reduced in men with renal transplants who developed ESRD in childhood (Scharer *et al*. 1989; Schaefer *et al*. 1991c). In contrast, testicular atrophy occurring in adult men who develop ESRD is reversed by successful renal transplantation (Phadke *et al*. 1970; Rodger *et al*. 1985).

Final adult height

The ultimate test of the management of growth is final adult height. There are only a few studies which provide this information. Changes in treatment protocols over the last two decades, and an increase in the proportion of younger patients now surviving, limit the applicability of such data to the present time. The European Dialysis and Transplantation (EDTA) Registry report a mean adult HtSDS of −2.0 for boys and −1.3 for girls in children commenced on renal replacement therapy before the age of 15 years, who were alive in 1984 (Rizzoni *et al.* 1986*a*). This report excluded patients with cystinosis and oxalosis, who are more severely stunted. Patients starting on renal replacement therapy before the age of 10 were shorter than those who started aged between 10 and 15. Patients who remained on dialysis were shorter than those who received renal transplants.

Final adult height SDS was less severely reduced at −0.8 in 22 patients who remained on conservative management throughout puberty (Schaefer *et al.* 1989).

More recent EDTA data gives a mean HtSDS, for children of *all* ages on dialysis, of −4.2 in boys and −3.8 in girls (Rizzoni *et al.* 1991). The equivalent figures for children with renal transplants were −2.7 and −2.3 respectively. The increase in the number of infants with congenital problems, who are often very short, may mask improvements in management of growth in the last few years.

Aetiology of renal disease

The cause of short stature in renal disease is most commonly multifactorial. Poor growth complicates CRF, renal tubular problems with or without reduced clearance, renal transplantation, and the use of corticosteroids, with different combinations of factors present in different settings. There are certain conditions where it is possible to study the isolated effect of one variable, e.g. acidosis in renal tubular acidosis. Conditions such as this are considered below. More often there are many factors at play, and the relative importance of each is difficult, if not impossible, to assess. As mentioned earlier, age at onset is an important factor, so that conditions which present in infancy are more likely to be a problem than those which present in later life. It is often difficult to differentiate the effects of the condition itself from the effects due to ill health at a time of rapid growth.

Children with infantile cystinosis are a particular problem (da Silva *et al.* 1985). These children lose height before there is a fall in GFR. In congenital or infantile nephrotic syndrome, poor growth is unrelated to GFR, and is probably due to poor nutrition secondary to loss of protein, abdominal distension, gut oedema, the use of corticosteroids, and to recurrent sepsis (Hallman *et al.* 1973; Adhikari *et al.* 1992). In older children with steroid-sensitive nephrotic syndrome, growth is related to steroid dosage, but catch-up growth occurs when steroids are withdrawn. Final height is usually normal in patients who have had steroid-sensitive nephrotic syndrome in childhood (Foote *et al.* 1985). The children most at risk of growth failure are those with focal segmental glomerulosclerosis who continue to have proteinuria and who usually progress to renal failure (Polito *et al.* 1988).

Aetiology of poor growth in renal disease

Nutrition

Currently, much emphasis is put on the role of inadequate nutrition as a cause of poor growth in children, and in particular, infants with renal disease. Uraemic rats eat less than *ad libitum*-fed controls and gain less weight than pair-fed controls, suggesting not only reduced appetite but also poor utilization of energy (Chantler *et al.* 1974). Calorie supplementation improves but does not normalize growth in uraemic rats (Adelman and Holliday 1974; Holliday 1975).

In children with CRF, energy intake has variously been described as being correlated with, (Simmons *et al.* 1971; Betts and Magrath 1974; Arnold *et al.* 1983) and not being correlated with, growth (Broyer *et al.* 1974; Betts *et al.* 1977; Wass *et al.* 1977). Betts and Magrath (1974) were able to relate reduced calorie intake with poor growth in CRF; less than 80% of the recommended daily allowance (RDA) for age for energy intake was associated with a growth rate of less than 75% of that expected for age. Similarly, Simmons *et al.* (1971) showed that in children on haemodialysis, only those with a calorie intake of greater than 70% of normal had normal growth, but Broyer *et al.* (1974) were unable to confirm this in their haemodialysis population. Likewise, calorie supplementation has been shown to improve growth in some groups of children, but not others (Simmons *et al.* 1971; Arnold *et al.* 1983). However, Betts *et al.*, in a prospective study did not find an improvement in growth with calorie supplements, although energy intake was only increased by 8.4%. Arnold *et al.*, in a two-year study, were able to correlate growth rate and energy intake during the first observational year. With calorie supplementation in the second year, growth rate increased towards that expected for age, but no catch-up occurred, and there was no longer any correlation between growth and energy intake. In this study, intake increased from 73% to 103% of RDA (Arnold *et al.* 1983). Sufficient energy intake appears to be permissive for normal growth but does not necessarily accelerate growth. In view of the evidence of poor utilization of energy in uraemia, perhaps even higher intakes are needed.

There is evidence that growth can be increased by energy supplementation in infants with CRF. Rees was able to show that catch-up growth can occur in children who present to a paediatric nephrologist before the age of two (Rees *et al.* 1989). Enteral feeding of 26 infants and young children with congenital renal disease in a single centre resulted in an improvement in length SDS from −2.9 and −2.0 after two years (Ledermann *et al.* 1994). A multicentre study by the North West Pacific Study Group, however, has given disappointing results; catch-up growth occurred in some but not all infants (Abitol *et al.* 1993). The management of these small children remains a challenge. Poor response to conservative management in some infants has resulted in a trial of the use of recombinant human growth hormone (rhGH) in this age group (Maxwell and Rees 1996*a*) (see below).

The reasons for poor intake are anorexia, vomiting, altered taste sensation, and sometimes inability to ingest adequate calories because of the large volumes of fluid ingested in some infants who are unable to conserve salt and water. If adequate nutrition cannot be achieved via the oral route then nasogastric or gastrostomy feeding should be instituted. Recurrent episodes of infection or repeated operations which interrupt feeding programmes can result in periods of poor growth.

Adequate calories are necessary for growth and anabolism; inadequate intake results in increased use of protein as an energy source. Inadequate protein intake as a cause of poor growth is uncommon these days but was frequently seen in the past (Chantler 1984). Trials of dietary protein restriction show that growth and weight gain are not affected by restriction of protein to World Health Organization (WHO) safe levels (0.8–1.1 g/kg/day) (Wingen *et al.* 1991).

Acidosis

The importance of normal acid-base balance to growth is apparent from the study of children with renal tubular acidosis (RTA). Both proximal and distal tubular acidosis present with growth failure (Nash *et al.* 1972). Each of the nine children with proximal RTA described by Nash presented within the first 18 months of life with failure to thrive and vomiting. Four children with distal RTA also presented with poor growth but in addition had symptoms related to polyuria and polydipsia. In both groups there was a sharp increase in HV upon starting alkali therapy. Thereafter growth continued at a slower but improved rate. Normal height was achieved in all patients, with three approaching the 50th centile. HV decreased in one patient in whom the parents temporarily stopped treatment. McSherry (1978) analysed 10 children with distal RTA: six had a height below the normal range; four were small but within the normal range. Of the latter four patients, two were newly diagnosed neonates and two had previously been shown to be non-acidotic. In the group as a whole, height was inversely correlated with duration of acidosis. On starting alkali therapy, HV increased two to threefold and all children achieved a height within the normal range. Mean height was greater than that predicted from parental heights.

Whilst the evidence in renal tubular acidosis is impressive, direct evidence that acidosis is an important cause of poor growth in CRF is lacking. Poor growth and acidosis have been shown to be correlated in some studies (West and Smith 1956), but it is not clear whether this is a causal association. Correction of acidosis *per se* has not been demonstrated to improve growth in CRF.

The mechanism of poor growth in metabolic acidosis and improved growth with alkali therapy is not entirely clear. It may be a direct effect of acidosis, or related to increased excretion of sodium, potassium, and calcium which occurs during metabolic acidosis. A recent abstract, however, suggests that the mechanism may be due to an effect on growth hormone secretion (Caldas and Fontoura 1994). GH secretion in children with CRF and RTA was studied in the acidotic and non-acidotic states; mean and peak spontaneous and provoked GH secretion was reduced in both groups during acidosis. IGF-I levels were also reduced during metabolic acidosis. GH secretion and IGF-I were no different from controls in the non-acidotic state. Further research in this area is awaited with interest.

Water and electrolyte

Isolated tubular defects resulting in loss of electrolytes are associated with a reduced growth rate; HV increases when these deficiencies are corrected. Such conditions point to the importance of water and certain electrolytes for growth. Children with Bartter's syndrome are short; replacement of sodium and potassium improves growth (Simopoulos 1979). Some of these children have a normal adult height, while others remain stunted. Similarly, in familial chloridorrhoea, a syndrome in which there is excessive loss of chloride in the stool, sodium chloride replacement results in improved growth (Roy and Arant 1981). A salt-depleted diet in rats is associated with poor growth (Wassner 1991). Approximately 50% of patients with nephrogenic diabetes insipidus are stunted. Increased fluid intake increases growth (Vest *et al.* 1963).

Salt and water loss frequently complicates CRF of dysplastic or obstructive origin. As with acidosis, the contribution which correction of these deficiencies makes to improved growth in CRF is difficult to quantify.

Renal osteodystrophy

Traditionally, renal osteodystrophy has been assumed to be an important cause of growth failure in renal disease (Stickler and Bergen 1973). With florid renal bone disease, complete cessation of growth can occur with destruction of the growth plate, or slipping of the epiphyses, but this is now an uncommon problem (Malluche and Faugere 1989).

An early report suggested that 1,25 dihydroxy vitamin D could increase growth velocity (Chan *et al.* 1981), but this has not been substantiated by larger studies (Chesney 1985). Six out of 11 children in the initial report showed an improvement in growth; many of these children had marked x-ray changes of renal bone disease prior to starting vitamin D therapy (Chan *et al.* 1981). Treatment of uraemic rats with vitamin D increases, but does not normalize, growth velocity (Mehls *et al.* 1978). Improved growth seems to be limited to those with marked bone disease. However, normal growth can occur in the presence of x-ray changes of renal osteodystrophy. The role of secondary hyperparathyroidism in poor growth is also unresolved; there is a suggestion of improved growth with suppression of parathyroid hormone secretion, but this has not been confirmed (Tamanaha *et al.* 1987).

Anaemia

There is a theoretical role for anaemia in poor growth of renal disease: anaemia is associated with decreased appetite and recurrent infections; conditions with marked anaemia, e.g. thalassaemia, are associated with poor growth (in the absence of iron overload), with recurrent transfusions improving growth. Poor oxygenation could be a rate-limiting step in cell proliferation. It has been difficult to look at the effects of anaemia in isolation; however, the widespread availability of recombinant human erythropoietin has allowed the problem to be addressed from a different angle. Does correction of anaemia improve growth? Initial reports were encouraging (Seidel *et al.* 1991), but a large, multicentre trial study has shown no beneficial effect on growth (Schaefer *et al.* 1991*a*).

Endocrine factors

Levels of growth hormone (GH) and insulin-like growth factor-I (IGF-I) are normal or raised in CRF and have only recently been implicated in short stature of renal disease (Samaan and Freeman 1970; Rees *et al.* 1990). GH is secreted in a nocturnal pulsatile fashion from the pituitary gland in response to episodic secretion of GH releasing hormone from the hypothalamus. Somatostatin from the hypothalamus acts to suppress the secretion of GH. Approximately 50% of circulating GH is bound to a binding protein—growth hormone binding protein (GHBP), which has identity with the GH receptor (Baumann 1989). GH acts on the liver to cause the secretion of IGF-I (Schoenle *et al.* 1982). This peptide is highly protein bound; six binding proteins have been identified in man (IGFBPs 1–6). The main carrier protein is IGFBP-3 which acts as a reservoir for IGF-I (Rosenfeld *et al.* 1994). Many of the anabolic actions of GH are mediated by IGF-I, but GH also acts directly at the growth end-place to stimulate growth (Isaksson *et al.* 1982), and thirdly it stimulates the local production of IGF-I (Nilsson *et al.* 1990). The relative contributions of circulating and locally produced IGF-I to growth are not known.

In CRF, control of secretion of GH is abnormal; stimulation of GH secretion results in overproduction (Tonshoff *et al.* 1990*b*). Overnight profiles of GH secretion show increased pulse amplitude and baseline GH (Schaefer *et al.* 1991*b*). The kidney is involved in clearing GH from the circulation, and this in part may explain the high baseline levels. GHBP is reduced in CRF (Maxwell *et al.* 1991), suggesting a reduction in GH receptors and a state of GH resistance.

Another possible mechanism of growth failure in renal disease may be a reduction in IGF-I bioactivity (Saenger 1974). Circulating IGF-I is normal when measured by RIA, but low when measured by bioassay. IGF-I is lower in dialysis-dependent patients than during the stages of conservative management of renal disease (Phillips and Kopple 1981).

Reduced IGF-I bioactivity has been reported to be due to increased amounts of IGFBP-3 (Blum *et al.* 1991). It has been postulated that fragments of IGFBP-3 which are normally cleared by the kidney accumulate in renal disease, and bind to and reduce free IGF-I. We and others, however, have not been able to confirm increased levels of IGFBP-3 in either CRF or following renal transplantation (Maxwell *et al.* 1995*a*). The fragment pattern in CRF was no different to controls. Preliminary studies in renal transplantation suggest that a greater proportion of IGFBP-3 is present as fragments, with a reduction in the percentage of intact protein (Unterman and Phillips 1985). The reason for this is not clear, but it is interesting to speculate that these fragments may be the steroid inhibitor of IGF-I bioactivity. Whilst this work is preliminary, the normal levels of IGFBP-3 in CRF do not support the theory that IGFBP-3 is a major inhibitor of growth in CRF.

Whatever the mechanism, rhGH increases HV in children with renal disease (see below). The control of several hormones is disturbed in CRF, and their circulating levels increased. The significance of these changes to poor growth are not clear, and their discussion is beyond the scope of this chapter. Other endocrine changes in renal disease have recently been reviewed (Schaefer *et al.* 1994).

Exogenous steroid therapy

Corticosteroids interfere with growth through a number of mechanisms. Spontaneous growth hormone secretion is reduced by steroids (Pantelakis *et al.* 1972), even in children on alternate-day steroids (Rees *et al.* 1988). Steroids are thought to alter somatostatin tone (Wehrenberg *et al.* 1990). Increased GH secretion at the time of puberty is particularly susceptible to steroid suppression (Rees *et al.* 1988).

IGF-I bioactivity is reduced in patients on steroids (Unterman and Phillips 1985). Bioactivity falls within six hours of the steroid dose, but returns to normal within 24 hours. Steroids may also reduce local IGF-I production; *in vitro* high levels of cortisol decrease skeletal IGF-I synthesis by reducing IGF-I transcription (McCarthy *et al.* 1990).

Steroids also interfere with collagen synthesis (Hyams *et al.* 1986). Type-I procollagen is a by-product of collagen synthesis; levels are reduced in children with inflammatory bowel disease on daily steroids, but not in those on alternate-day or no steroids. The relative importance of these mechanisms to poor growth during steroid therapy remains speculative.

Psychosocial

Emotional deprivation is a recognized cause of poor growth. Children suffering emotional deprivation have been shown to gain weight and grow when admitted to hospital (Green *et al.* 1984). The extra demands of a child with a chronic illness may be too great for a family already stressed by financial, housing, or other worries, and the child may not receive the care and attention that they need. Rizzoni *et al.* (1986*b*) described an association between growth and psychological and socio-economic status. Parents may find it difficult to bond with an infant with severe congenital abnormalities, in whom survival is not assured, developing an ambivalence towards a child whom they have not expected to survive.

The paediatric nephrology team must consist of members who can deal with the medical and nursing difficulties of dealing with children with chronic renal disease, but also members who can help deal with both the physical and logistical difficulties of caring for a sick child and with the financial and emotional needs of these families.

It is interesting that a small but significant increase in HV was seen in the placebo arm of a double-blind controlled study of the use of growth hormone in CRF (Hokken-Koelega *et al.* 1991).

Management of renal disease in children and its relevance to poor growth

Conservative management

Approximately 60% of children with CRF have a height which falls below the 3rd percentile (Rees *et al.* 1989). Renal dysphasia with or without obstruction and reflux is the most common cause of end-stage renal disease in childhood, with growth often being affected in the first year of life. Intensive nutritional support, orally, nasogastrically, or by gastrostomy feeding is imperative, particularly in the first year of life (Ledermann *et al.* 1994). After this age the effects of nutritional support are difficult to disentangle from other aspects of treatment. Calorie supplementation does not consistently result in improved growth (Betts *et al.* 1977), but poor growth can be demonstrated in children with diets deficient in calories (Simmons *et al.* 1971; Betts and Magrath 1974). As improved growth is not seen in every infant fed enterally, the use of recombinant human growth hormone (rhGH) is being evaluated in children of this age group (Maxwell and Rees 1996*a*).

Correction of acidosis, fluid and electrolyte abnormalities, and avoidance of secondary hyperparathyroidism and renal osteodystrophy by controlling serum phosphate level, and by the early use of activated vitamin D, are important aspects of management. Good conservative management allows normal growth, but catch-up growth is rare after infancy (Rees *et al.* 1989). RhGH improves HV in this age group (Rees *et al.* 1990); see below.

Dialysis

Despite correcting some of the metabolic abnormalities associated with renal failure, haemodialysis does not improve growth (Broyer *et al.* 1974). Broyer reported normal growth in four out of 17 children, with a variable reduction being seen in the remainder. Catch-up growth was not seen. Kleinknecht *et al.* (1980) reported mean HtSDS to decrease by 0.4 SD per year in children on haemodialysis. Children who grew better could not be distinguished by residual renal function or dialysis prescription. As with children managed conservatively (Arnold *et al.* 1983), energy was permissive for growth on dialysis, but did not induce catch-up growth (Simmons *et al.* 1971). Growth studies of children on dialysis tend to be complicated by high rates of withdrawal due to transplantation.

Growth during the first year of peritoneal dialysis (PD) is reported as being stable, and an improvement on that observed on haemodialysis (Fennell *et al.* 1984; Potter *et al.* 1986), but on more prolonged follow-up, growth rate on continuous ambulatory peritoneal dialysis (CAPD) declines (Fine and Mehls 1986).

The use of PD is becoming more common; of children under 15 on dialysis in the UK, 68% are on peritoneal dialysis, and 32% on haemodialysis (British Association for Paediatric Nephrology 1995). Home CAPD or continuous cycling peritoneal dialysis (CCPD) is the treatment of choice for chronic dialysis. It is possible in the majority of families, and allows the child to attend school regularly and to perform other normal childhood activities. Haemodialysis is disruptive in terms of schooling, access can be difficult, and fear of needle punctures a particular problem.

There are occasions, however, when haemodialysis is the only or preferred option. Poor social circumstances, persistent fluid overload, gastrointestinal abnormalities, or previous gut surgery may reduce the feasibility of PD.

PD is the treatment of choice for chronic dialysis in infants, and can be used successfully in the first few weeks of life (Fine *et al.* 1987). Difficulties with vascular access and small circulating blood volume make haemodialysis at this age difficult. In some circumstances, acute haemodialysis may be necessary, for example following abdominal surgery, to avoid compression of the diaphragm or for rapid removal of fluid or toxins. The umbilical vessels can be used in the neonate, and priming of lines is essential to prevent more than 10% extracorporeal circulation (Nevins and Mauer 1992).

Growth in infants on PD receiving enteral feeds is variable (Strife *et al.* 1986; Warady *et al.* 1988). Four infants commenced on PD before one month of age, had a mean HtSDS of −1.3 at one year of age. Neurological development was within the normal range in three and one was mildly retarded. Gross motor development was retarded in all infants. Mean OFC SDS was −1.4, with one patient being below the normal range (Warady *et al.* 1988). Kohaut reported on nine infants commenced on PD within the first six weeks of life (Kohaut *et al.* 1987); mean HtSDS at the start of CAPD was −0.8; after one year, −1.7. Mean OFC did not change during CAPD; −0.4 before and −0.5 at the end of CAPD. Four of the surviving six infants who are transplanted are developmentally normal, two are delayed. However, Strife *et al.* (1986) and Brewer *et al.* (1986) report stable and improved growth in three and 14 infants respectively. These are all small studies, with patients who no doubt differ in their clinical condition. The goal for these infants is renal transplantation; intensive nutritional management, and CAPD if necessary, should be carried out in an attempt to maintain growth and development until transplantation is possible.

Renal transplantation

The preferred mode of renal replacement therapy in childhood is transplantation, and many centres aim for pre-emptive transplantation. At present, approximately 25% of children are transplanted without prior dialysis (Tejani *et al.* 1993). Whilst pre-emptive transplantation provides no benefit in terms of post-transplant growth, it prevents the child from having a period in their life when they are obviously different from their peers, and when their activities are restricted, whether by necessity or by self-consciousness. Dialysis increases the child's dependence on their carers, whether that be at home or in hospital.

In the UK in 1992, 8% of transplants performed in children under 15 years were from live related donors (LRD), in contrast to North America where 55% are from LRD (Tejani *et al.* 1993). In North America, five-year patient survival for LRD is 97% and 94% for cadaver grafts respectively. Five-year graft survival is 73% for LRD and 59% for cadaver kidneys (Stablein and Tejani 1993). Comparable data from the EDTA reveals almost identical results (Broyer *et al.* 1993).

Growth following renal transplantation is variable and appears to be influenced by several factors, principally steroid dose and schedule, graft function, and age at transplantation. Some groups report disappointing growth with catch-up being limited to children under the age of six or seven (Ingelfinger *et al.* 1981; Bosque *et al.* 1983; Tejani *et al.* 1993). Others report stable or improved growth with some achieving almost complete catch-up (van Diemen-Steenvorde *et al.* 1987; Rees *et al.* 1988; Klare *et al.* 1991). Impressive growth can occur (Fig. 6.3).

The growth suppressive effects of corticosteroids have long been recognized (Lam and Arneil 1968). The introduction of cyclosporin A has allowed the use of much lower doses of steroids

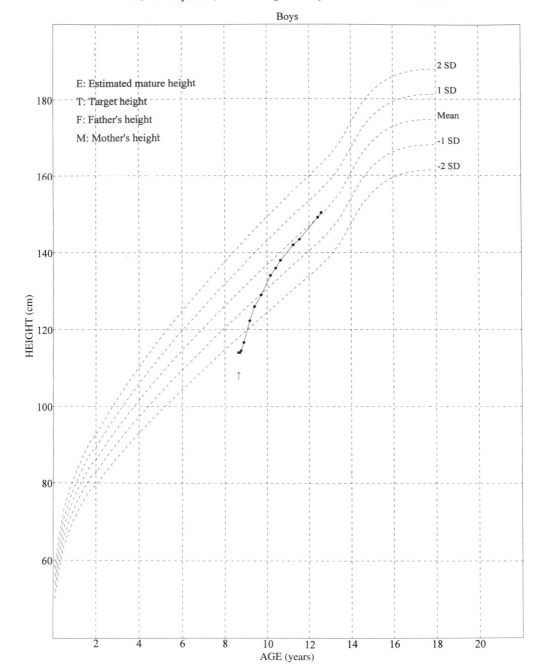

Fig. 6.3   Growth chart of a boy who received a renal transplant at the age of 8.7 years (Tanner *et al.*
1966).

(Offner *et al.* 1987), resulting in improved growth (Offner *et al.* 1987; Ettenger *et al.* 1991; Guest and Broyer 1991). Perhaps even more significantly, the use of the same total dose of prednisone in an alternate day regime compared to daily administration, results in improved growth (Broyer *et al.* 1992). In one study, children converted to alternate day steroids had a mean increase in HtSDS of 0.5 SD per year compared to a reduction of HtSDS by −0.1 in patients who continued on daily prednisone. All children received alternate day steroids for the second year and growth continued to improve (Broyer *et al.* 1992). A recent Dutch study has also found a positive effect of alternate day steroids on growth in the first two years after transplantation, and on final adult height (Hokken-Koelega *et al.* 1994*b,c*).

Even more impressive increases in HtSDS are seen when steroids are withdrawn completely; Klare *et al.* (1991) found an increase of 0.8 SD in the first post-transplant year, with almost complete catch-up occurring over the four years. Tejani *et al.* (1989) also found an increase in HtSDS on discontinuing steroids, but nine out of 23 had to restart prednisone after developing acute rejection episodes.

Renal function is another determinant of growth post-transplantation. In the North American paediatric renal transplant cooperative study, during a two-year period an increase in creatinine of 90 mcmol/l was associated with a decrease in HtSDS of −0.17 (Tejani *et al.* 1993). Pennisi *et al.* (1977) found a reduction in growth when GFR fell below 60 ml/min/1.73 m^2, and poor catch-up growth in the first two years after transplantation was associated with a GFR of less than 50 ml/min/1.73 m^2 (Hokken-Koelega *et al.* 1994*b*). Height velocity in the first post-transplant year in 44 children at our centre was correlated with GFR (Fig. 6.4).

Age at transplantation is also important; the greatest catch-up growth is seen in infants, with an improvement in HtSDS of 0.8 SD in the first year (Tejani *et al.* 1993). Catch-up growth is also reported in mid-childhood, but the improvement lessens with increasing age.

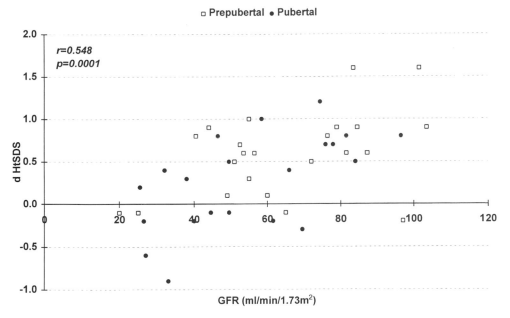

Fig. 6.4 Height velocity and GFR in the first post-transplant year in 44 consecutive children receiving renal transplants at one centre.

Most reports agree that growth during puberty is a problem. There is a reduction in GH secretion, with peak HV being negatively correlated with cumulative steroid dosage (Schaefer *et al.* 1991*b*). Some authors suggest that improvement in growth will only occur with a bone age of less than 12 years (Grushkin and Fine 1973; Fine and Ettenger 1988), but a pubertal growth spurt has been demonstrated in some patients, albeit of reduced amplitude (Najarian *et al.* 1990; Schaefer *et al.* 1991*b*). With the increasing use of low-dose, alternate-day steroids, some adolescents can achieve a very normal pubertal growth spurt (Fig. 6.1).

The management of infants with end-stage disease is more controversial. Transplantation at this age has been reported to carry a higher operative and post-operative morbidity and mortality, with reduced graft and patient survival being reported by some (Fine and Ettenger 1988), but not all centres (Nevins 1987; So *et al.* 1987; Davis *et al.* 1990; Najarian *et al.* 1990). Impressive results have been obtained from centres specializing in transplantation in infancy (Nevins 1987; So *et al.* 1987; Davis *et al.* 1990; Najarian *et al.* 1990). In these centres, patient and graft survival are no different to those in older children and adolescents. The best results are seen with the use of LRDs. It is clear that transplantation of small children should only be performed in specialized centres. Following transplantation, impressive catch-up growth is seen in infants (Tejani *et al.* 1993). Perhaps of greater importance is the improvement that is seen in indices of mental and motor development (Davis *et al.* 1990). There is also a marked improvement in OFC, suggesting increased brain growth (Winick and Rosso 1969).

Recombinant human growth hormone

Following the discovery that growth hormone improved growth in uraemic rats (Mehls and Ritz 1983), recombinant human growth hormone (rhGH) has been shown to improve growth in prepubertal children with CRF (Rees *et al.* 1990; Hokken-Koelega *et al.* 1991), in prepubertal and pubertal renal transplant patients (Rees *et al.* 1990; van Es 1991; Hokken-Koelega *et al.* 1994*a*) and in children on dialysis (Tonshoff *et al.* 1990*a*). We have recently published the results of a multicentre British study of the use of rhGH in renal disease (Maxwell and Rees 1994; 1996*b*). Height velocity in the first year of treatment doubled in children with CRF and renal transplants, with a smaller improvement being seen in those on dialysis. Children on peritoneal dialysis had a better response than those on haemodialysis. The greatest improvement in standardized height and HV was seen in eight infants and young children with CRF treated with rhGH for one year (Fig. 6.5).

There is as yet no available data of the effect of rhGH on final adult height in renal disease. Growth has been shown to be improved for up to three to five years, when compared with pre-treatment height velocities, but there is a waning effect of treatment (Fine *et al.* 1992; 1994).

There are potential concerns regarding the use of rhGH in renal disease. Patients with acromegaly have large kidneys which hyperfilter (Ikkos *et al.* 1956), and rhGH given to healthy adults results in an increase in renal plasma flow (RPF) and glomerular filtration rate (GFR) (Hirschberg *et al.* 1989). Transgenic mice secreting GH also show an increase in RPF and GFR, and go on to develop glomerulosclerosis (Doi *et al.* 1988). Renal failure does not develop in acromegaly however, in the absence of hypertension and diabetes (Gerschberg *et al.* 1957). RhGH and its mediator, IGF-I, have been shown to have short-term effects on renal function (Maxwell *et al.* 1995*b*; 1996), but no long-term sequelae have been reported (Fine *et al.* 1992; 1994).

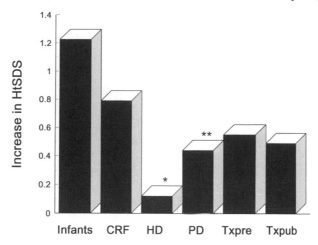

Fig. 6.5   Increase in HtSDS after one year of rhGH in eight infants (bone age <2 years) with CRF, 26 prepubertal children with CRF, six children on haemodialysis, nine on peritoneal dialysis, and 15 prepubertal and seven pubertal children with renal transplants. *p < 0.05 vs all other groups; **p < 0.05 vs CRF and infant groups.

Other potential concerns are the effect on the immune system. GH by definition is a mitogen, and has known interactions with the immune system (Bozzola *et al.* 1991). There is therefore a potential risk of increased rate of transplant rejection, infection, or of increased malignancy. Most studies do not report an increase in the incidence of rejection episodes, however there are individual case reports to the contrary (Tyden *et al.* 1990; Schwartz and Warady 1992). Indeed, the large, multicentre European study has found an increase in the incidence of rejection episodes only in those patients with a history of previous rejection episodes prior to rhGH treatment (Broyer *et al.* 1994; Pharmacia communication). No increased risk of malignancy or infection has been reported in renal patients on rhGH (Tonshoff *et al.* 1990a; van Es 1991; Fine *et al.* 1992, 1994; Hokken-Koelega *et al.* 1994a; Maxwell and Rees 1994, 1996b). We have looked at the effects of rhGH on lymphocyte subsets and markers of T cell activation (Maxwell *et al.* 1993), and found no changes in the children with renal transplants, and a slight but significant decrease in T helper cells in children with CRF, the significance of which is unclear.

Further follow-up of children with renal disease on rhGH will be needed to determine long-term safety and effect on final adult height. The Dutch group have reported impressive improvements in height in pubertal children with renal transplants, who often grow poorly, as described above (Hokken-Koelega *et al.* 1994a). It is difficult to disentangle the effects of the pubertal growth spurt from the effect of treatment. Good growth during puberty is seen in some children with renal transplants who are not on growth hormone. It is important to remember that children with renal disease may continue to go on growing for longer than usual, and that rhGH may be of potential, but not proven, benefit at this age.

There are rare reports of an association between benign intracranial hypertension and rhGH in children with renal disease (Malozowski *et al.* 1993). Deteriorating renal osteodystrophy, glucose intolerance, and worsening of an idiopathic scoliosis during rhGH treatment have also been reported (Maxwell and Rees 1996b).

Transfer to an adult nephrologist

Timing of transfer to an adult unit varies from centre to centre and is determined by a number of factors. These include the availability of local services, primary disease and related problems, social circumstances, pubertal stage, as well as mental development and degree of independence.

Many paediatric nephrologists will transfer patients to adult colleagues once the child has gone through puberty, or when growth and puberty are very nearly complete. This is likely to be at or around the time of leaving school and starting further education or employment.

Some children will have attended the same paediatric nephrology unit for most of their lives and may see other specialists at the same hospital. These families become very dependent on the unit and find it difficult to move on. Some children may not have achieved independence at this age, particularly those who have spent many of their childhood years in hospital. Transfer from the paediatric unit can be frightening for these children.

Non-compliance can be a particular problem during the adolescent years and is perhaps more easily dealt with in a paediatric setting where time and resources may be less stretched. Independence can be encouraged at the same time as maintaining a degree of supervision and support.

Each patient needs to be considered separately. The handover should not be rushed but should be gradual, giving the child and the family some time to get used to the idea. It should not be forgotten that children with renal disease can continue to grow for longer than usual, and that attention to growth and pubertal development are important.

References

Abitol, C. L., Zilleruelo, G., Montane, B., and Strauss, J. (1993). Growth of uraemic infants on forced feeding regimens. *Pediatr. Nephrol.*, **7**, 173–7.

Adelman, R. D. and Holliday, M. A. (1974). Improved growth in dwarf uraemic rats with calorie supplementation. *Pediatr. Res.*, **8**, 378. (Abstract).

Adhikari, M., Manikkam, N. E. G., and Coovadia, H. M. (1992). Effects of repeated courses of daily steroids and of persistent proteinuria on linear growth in children with nephrotic syndrome. *Pediatr. Nephrol.*, **6**, 4–9.

Arnold, W. C., Danford, D., and Holliday, M. A. (1983). Effects of calorie supplementation on growth in children with uraemia. *Kidney Int.*, **24**, 205–9.

Baumann, G. (1989). Circulating binding proteins for human growth hormone. In: *Advances in growth hormone and growth factor research* (ed. E. E. Muller, D. Cocchi, and V. Locatelli), pp. 69–83. Pythagora Press, Rome; Springer, Berlin, Heidelberg, New York.

Betts, P. R. and Magrath, G. (1974). Growth pattern and dietary intake of children with chronic renal insufficiency. *BMJ*, **1**, 189–93.

Betts, P. R., Magrath, G., and White, R. H. R. (1977). Role of dietary energy supplementation in growth of children with chronic renal insufficiency. *BMJ*, **1**, 416–18.

Blum, W. F., Ranke, M. B., Kietzmann, K., Tonshoff, B., and Mehls, O. (1991). Growth hormone resistance and inhibition of somatomedin activity by excess of insulin-like growth factor binding protein in uraemia. *Pediatr. Nephrol.*, **5**, 539–44.

Bosque, M., Munian, A., Bewick, M., Haycock, and Chantler, C. (1983). Growth after renal transplants. *Arch. Dis. Child.*, **58**, 110–14.

Bozzola, M., Valtorta, A., Moretta, A., and Schimpff, R. M. (1991). GH, GHRH and the immune system. *Growth Factors Curr. Med. Lit.*, **6**, 135–9.

Brewer, E. D., Holmes, S., and Tealey, J. (1986). Initiation and maintenance of growth in infants with end-stage renal disease managed with chronic peritoneal dialysis and nasogastric tube feedings. *Kidney Int.*, **29**, 230. (Abstract).

British Association for Paediatric Nephrology (BAPN) (1995). *The provision of services in the United Kingdom for children and adolescents with renal disease: report of a working party of BAPN, March 1995.* British Paediatric Association.

Broyer, M., Kleinknecht, C., Loirat, C., Marti-Henneberg, C., and Roy, M. P. (1974). Growth in children treated with long-term haemodialysis. *J. Pediatr.*, **84**, 642–9.

Broyer, M., Guest, G., and Gagnadoux, M. F. (1992). Growth rate in children receiving alternate-day steroid treament after kidney transplantation. *J. Pediatr.*, **120**, 721–5.

Broyer, M., Ehrich, Jones, E., and Selwood, N. (1993). Five-year survival of kidney transplantation in children: data from the European (EDTA-ERA) registry. *Kidney Int.*, **44**, S22–S25.

Broyer, M., Guest, G., Crosnier, H., Berard, E. on behalf of the Societe Francaise de Nephrologie Pediatrique (1994). Recombinant growth hormone in children after renal transplantation. *Lancet*, **343**, 539–40 (Letter).

Caldas, A. and Fontoura, M. (1994). Effects of chronic metabolic acidosis (CMA) in 24-hour growth hormone secretion. *Pediatr. Nephrol.*, **8**, C40.

Chan, J. C. M., Kodroff, M. B., and Landwehr, D. M. (1981). Effects of 1,25-dihydroxyvitamin-D3 on renal function, mineral balance, and growth in children with severe chronic renal failure. *Pediatrics*, **6**, 559–71.

Chantler, C., Lieberman, E., and Holliday, M. A. (1974). A rat model for the study of growth failure in uraemia. *Pediatr. Res.*, **8**, 109.

Chantler, C. (1984). Nutrtional assessment and management of children with renal insufficiency. In: *End-stage renal disease in children* (ed. R. N. Fine and A. B. Gruskin), pp. 193–208. WB Saunders, Philedelphia.

Chesney, R. W. (1985). Renal osteodystrophy in children. In: *Chronic renal disease: causes, complications and treatment* (ed. N. B. Cummings and S. Klahr), pp. 321–31. Plenum, New York.

Claris-Appiani, A., Bianchi, M. L., Bini, P., Ballabio, G., Caraceni, M. P., Funari, C., *et al.* (1989). Growth in young children with chronic renal failure. *Pediatr. Nephrol.*, **3**, 301–4.

da Silva, V. A., Zurbrugg, R. P., Lavanchy, P., Blumberg, A., and Suter, H. (1985). Long-term treatment of infantile nephropathic cystinosis with cysteamine. *N. Engl. J. Med.*, **313**, 1460–3.

Davis, I. D., Chang, P-N., and Nevins, T. E. (1990). Successful renal transplantation accelerates development in young uraemic children. *Pediatrics*, **86**, 594–600.

Doi, T., Striker, L. J., Quaife, C., Conti, F. G., Palmiter, R., Behringer, R., *et al.* (1988). Progressive glomerulosclerosis develops in transgenic mice chronically expressing growth hormone and growth hormone releasing factor but not in those expressing insulin-like growth factor-I. *Am. J. Pathol.*, **131**, 398–403.

Ettenger, R. B., Rosenthal, J. T., Marik, J., Grimm, P. C., Nelson, P., Malekzadeh, M. H., *et al.* (1991). Long-term results with cyclosporin immunosuppression in paediatric cadaver renal transplantation. *Transplant Proc.*, **23**, 1011–12.

Fennell, R. S., Orak, J. K., Hudson, T., Garin, E. H., Iravani, A., Van Deusen, W. J., *et al.* (1984). Growth in children with various therapies for end-stage renal disease. *Am. J. Dis. Child.*, **138**, 28–31.

Fine, R. N. and Mehls, O. (1986). CAPD/CCPD in children: four years' experience. *Kidney Int.*, **30**, S7–S10.

Fine, R. N., Salusky, I. B., and Ettenger, R. B. (1987). The therapeutic approach to the infant, child, and adolescent with end-stage disease. *Pediatr. Clin. North Am.*, **34**, 789–801.

Fine, R. N. and Ettenger, R. B. (1988). Renal transplantation in children. In: *Kidney transplantation: principles and practice* (3rd edn) (ed. P. J. Morris), pp. 635–91. WB Saunders, Philedelphia.

Fine, R. N., Yadin, O., Moulten, L., Nelson, P. A., Boechat, I., and Lippe, B. H. (1992). Extended recombinant human growth hormone treatment after renal transplantation in children. *J. Am. Soc. Nephrol.*, **2**, S274–S283.

Fine, R. N., Yadin, O., Moulton, L., Nelson, P. A., Boechat, M. I., and Lippe, B. N. (1994). Five years' experience with recombinant human growth hormone treatment of children with chronic renal failure. *J. Pediatr. Endocrinol.*, **7**, 1–2.

Foote, K. D., Brocklebank, J. T., and Meadow, S. R. (1985). Height attainment in children with steroid-sensitive nephrotic syndrome. *Lancet*, **ii**, 917–19.

Gerschberg, H., Heinemann, H. O., and Stumpf, H. H. (1957). Renal function studies and autopsy report in a patient with gigantism and acromegaly. *J. Clin. Endocrinol. Metab.*, **17**, 377–85.

Green, W. H., Campbell, M., and David, R. (1984). Psychosocial dwarfism: critical review of the evidence. *J. Am. Acad. Child. Psychiatry*, **23**, 39–48.

Grushkin, C. M. and Fine, R. N. (1973). Growth in children following renal transplantation. *Am. J. Dis. Child.*, **125**, 514–16.

Guest, G. and Broyer, M. (1991). Growth after renal transplantation: correlation with immunosuppressive therapy. *Pediatr. Nephrol.*, **5**, 143–6.

Hallman, N., Norio, R., and Rapola, J. (1973). Congenital nephrotic syndrome. *Nephron*, **11**, 101–10.

Hirschberg, R., Rabb, H., Begamo, R., and Kopple, J. D. (1989). The delayed effect of growth hormone on renal function in humans. *Kidney Int.*, **35**, 865–70.

Hokken-Koelega, A. C. S., Stijnen, T., de Muinck Keizer-Schrama, S. M. P. F., Wit, J. M., Wolff, E. D., de Jong, M. C. J. W., *et al.* (1991). Placebo-controlled, double-blind, cross-over trial of growth hormone treatment in prepubertal children with chronic renal failure. *Lancet*, **338**, 585–90.

Hokken-Koelega, A. C. S., Stijnen, T, de Ridder, M. A. J., de Muinck Keizer-Schrama, S. M. P. F., Wolff, E. D., de Jong, M. C. J. W., *et al.* (1994*a*). Growth hormone treatment in growth-retarded adolescents after renal transplant. *Lancet*, **343**, 1313–17.

Hokken-Koelega, A. C. S., van Zaal, M. A. E., de Ridder, M. A. J., Wolff, E. D., de Jong, R. C. J. W., Donckerwolcke, R. A., *et al.* (1994*b*). Growth after renal transplantation in prepubertal children: impact of various treatment modalities. *Paediatr. Res.*, **35**, 367–71.

Hokken-Koelega, A. C. S., van Zaal, M. A. E., van Bergen, W., de Ridder, M. A. J., Stijnen, T., Wolff, E. D., de Jong, R. C. J. W., *et al.* (1994*c*). Final height and its predictive factors after renal transplantation in childhood. *Paediatr. Res.*

Holliday, M. A. (1975). Calorie intake and growth in uraemia. *Kidney Int.*, **7**, S73–S78.

Hyams, J. S., Carey, D. E., Leichtner, A. M., and Goldberg, B. D. (1986). Type I procollagen as a biochemical marker of growth in children with inflammatory bowel disease. *J. Pediatr.*, **109**, 619–24.

Ikkos, D., Ljunggren, H., and Luft, R. (1956). Glomerular filtration rate and renal plasma flow in acromegaly. *Acta Endocrinol.*, **21**, 226–36.

Ingelfinger, J. R., Grupe, W. E., Harmon, W., Fernbach, S. K., and Levey, R. H. (1981). Growth acceleration following renal transplantation in children less than seven years of age. *J. Pediatr.*, **68**, 255–9.

Isaksson, O. G. P., Jansson, J. O., and Gause, J. A. M. (1982). Growth hormone stimulates longitudinal bone growth directly. *Science*, **216**, 1237–9.

Jones, R., Rigden, S. P. A., Barratt, T. M., and Chantler, C. (1982). The effect of chronic renal failure in infancy on growth, nutritional status and body composition. *Pediatr. Res.*, **16**, 784–91.

Klare, B., Strom, T. M., Hahn, H., Engelsberger, I., and Meusel, E. (1991). Remarkable long-term prognosis and excellent growth in kidney transplant children under cyclosporin montherapy. *Transplant Proc.*, **23**, 1013–17.

Kleinknecht, C., Broyer, M., Gagnadoux, M-F., Marti-Henneberg, C., Dartois, A-M., Kermanagh, C., *et al.* (1980). Growth in children treated with long-term dialysis. A study of 76 patients. *Adv. Nephrol.*, **9**, 133–63.

Kleinknecht, C., Broyer, M., Hout, D., Marti-Henneberg, C., and Datois, A-M. (1983). Growth and development of non-dialyzed children with chronic renal failure. *Kidney Int.*, **24**, S40–S47.

Kohaut, E. C., Whelchel, J., Waldo, F. B., and Diethelm, A. G. (1987). Aggressive therapy of infants with renal failure. *Pediatr. Nephrol.*, **1**, 150–3.

Lam, C. N. and Arneil, G. C. (1968). Long-term dwarfing effects of corticosteroid treatment for childhood nephrosis. *Arch. Dis. Child.*, **43**, 589–94.

Ledermann, S. E., Randall, M., Shaw, V., and Trompeter, R. S. (1994). Enteral nutrition in the infant and young child. *Pediatr. Nephrol.*, **8**, C35.

McCarthy, T. L., Centrella, M., and Canalis, E. (1990). Cortisol inhibits the synthesis of insulin-like growth factor-I in skeletal cells. *Endocrinology*, **126**, 1569–75.

McGraw, M. E. and Haka-Ikse, K. (1985). Neurologic-developmental sequelae of chronic renal failure in infancy. *J. Pediatr.*, **106**, 579–83.

McSherry, E. (1978). Acidosis and growth in non-uraemic renal disease. *Kidney Int.*, **14**, 349–54.

Malluche, H. M. and Faugere, M-C. (1989). Renal osteodystrophy. *N. Engl. J. Med.*, **5**, 317–19.

Malozowski, S., Tanner, L. A., Wysowski, D., and Flemming, G. A. (1993). Growth hormone, insulin-like growth factor-I, and benign intracranial hypertension. *N. Engl. J. Med.*, **329**, 665–6.

Maxwell, H., Maheshwari, H. G., Canosa, I., *et al.* (1991). Children with chronic renal failure have low serum growth hormone binding protein. *Pediatr. Nephrol.*, **5**, C53.

Maxwell, H., Amlot, P., and Rees, L. (1993). The effects of recombinant human growth hormone on lymphocyte subpopulations in children with chronic renal failure and renal transplants. *Paediatr. Nephrol.*, **7**, C52.

Maxwell, H. and Rees, L. on behalf of the British Association for Paediatric Nephrology (1994). The use of recombinant human growth hormone (rhGH) in renal disease: combined British data. *Pediatr. Nephrol.*, **8**, C40. (Abstract).

Maxwell, H., Jones, J., Rees, L., and Flyvbjerg, A. (1995*a*). Insulin-like growth factor binding protein-3 (IGFBP-3) in renal disease: the effects of recombinant human growth hormone. *Pediatr. Nephrol.*, **9**, C59.

Maxwell, H., Nair, D. R., Dalton, R. N., Rigden, S. P. A., and Rees, L. (1995*b*) Differential effects of recombinant human growth hormone on glomerular filtration rate and effective renal plasma flow in children with chronic renal failure. *Pediatr. Nephrol.*, **9**, 458–63.

Maxwell, H., Nair, D. R., Dalton, R. N., Rigden, S. P. A., and Rees, L. (1996). Recombinant human growth hormone and renal function in children with renal transplants. *J. Pediatr.*, **128**, 177–83.

Maxwell, H. and Rees, L. on behalf of the British Association for Paediatric Nephrology (1996*a*). Recombinant human growth hormone treatment in infants with chronic renal failure. *Arch. Dis. Child.*, **74**, 40–3.

Maxwell, H. and Rees, L. on behalf of the British Association for Paediatric Nephrology (1996*b*). The use of recombinant human growth hormone (rhGH) in renal disease: combined British data. (1996, submitted for publication.)

Mehls, O., Ritz, E., Gilli, G., Wangdak, T., and Krempien, B. (1978). Effect of vitamin D on growth in experimental uraemia. *Am. J. Clin. Nutr.*, **31**, 1927–31.

Mehls, O. and Ritz, E. (1983). Skeletal growth in experimental uraemia. *Kidney Int.*, **15** (Suppl.), S33–S62.

Najarian, J. S., Frey, D. J., Matas, A. J., Gillingham, K. J., So, S. K. S., Cook, M., *et al.* (1990). Renal transplantation in infants. *Ann. Surg.*, **212**, 353–65.

Nash, M. A., Torrado, A. D., Greifer, I., Spitzer, A., and Edelman, C. M. (1972). Renal tubular acidosis in infants and children. *J. Pediatr.*, **80**, 738–48.

Nevins, T. E. (1987). Transplantation in infants less than 1 year of age. *Pediatr. Nephrol.*, **1**, 154–6.

Nevins, T. E. and Mauer, S. M. (1992). Infant haemodialysis. In: *Dialysis therapy* (ed. A. R. Nissenson and R. N. Fine), pp. 349–52. Hanely and Belfus, Philadelphia.

Nilsson, A., Carlsson, B., Isgaard, J., Isaksson, O. G. P., and Rymo, L. (1990). Regulation by GH of insulin-like growth factor-I mRNA expression in rat epiphyseal growth plate as studied with *in situ* hybdridization. *J. Endocrinol.*, **125**, 67–74.

Offner, G., Hoyer, P. F., Juppner, H., Krohn, H. P., and Brodehl, J. (1987). Somatic growth after kidney transplantation. *Am. J. Dis. Child.*, **141**, 541–6.

Pantelakis, S. N., Sinaniotis, C. A., Sbirakis, S., Ikkos, D., and Doxiadis, S. A. (1972). Night and day growth hormone levels during treatment with corticosteroids and corticotrophin. *Arch. Dis. Child.*, **47**, 605–8.

Pennisi, A. J., Costin, G., Phillips, L. S., Uittenbogaart, C., Ettenger, R. B., Malekzadeh, M. H., *et al.* (1977). Linear growth in long-term renal allograft recipients. *Clin. Nephrol.*, **8**, 415–21.

Phadke, A., MacKinnon, K., and Dossetor, J. (1970). Male infertility in uraemia: restoration by renal allografts. *Can. Med. Assoc. J.*, **102**, 607–8.

Phillips, L. S. and Kopple, J. D. (1981). Circulating somatomedin activity and sulphate levels in adults with normal and impaired kidney function. *Metabolism*, **30**, 1091–5.

Polinsky, M. S., Kaiser, B. A., Stover, J. B., Frankenfield, M., and Baluarte, H. J. (1987). Neurologic development of children with severe chronic renal failure from infancy. *Pediatr. Nephrol.*, **1**, 157–65.

Polito, C., Greco, L., Totino, S. F., Oporto, M. R., La Manna, A., Strano, C. G., *et al.* (1987). Statural growth of children with chronic renal failure on conservative treatment. *Acta Paediatr. Scand.*, **76**, 97–102.

Polito, C., La Manna, A., Oliieri, A. N., and Di Toro, R. (1988). Proteinuria and statural growth . *Child Urol. Nephrol.*, **9**, 286–9.

Potter, D. E. and Greifer, I. (1978). Statural growth of children with renal disease. *Kidney Int.*, **14**, 334–9.

Potter, D. E., Luis, E. S., Wipfler, J. E., and Portale, A. A. (1986). Comparison of continuous ambulatory peritoneal dialysis and haemodialysis in children. *Kidney Int.*, **30**, S11–S14.

Proyer, H. and Thelander, H. (1968). Abnormally small head size and intellect in children. *J. Pediatr.*, **73**, 593–8.

Rees, L., Greene, S. A., Adlard, P., Jones, J., Haycock, G. B., Rigden, S. P. A., *et al.* (1988). Growth and endocrine function after renal transplantation. *Arch. Dis. Child.*, **63**, 1326–32.

Rees, L., Rigden, S. P. A., and Ward, G. M. (1989). Chronic renal failure and growth. *Arch. Dis. Child.*, **64**, 573–7.

Rees, L., Rigden, S. P. A., Ward, G., and Preece, M. A. (1990). Treatment of short stature in renal disease with recombinant human growth hormone. *Arch. Dis. Child.*, **65**, 856–60.

Rizzoni, G., Basso, T., and Setari, M. (1984). Growth in children with chronic renal failure on conservative management. *Kidney Int.*, **26**, 52–8.

Rizzoni, G., Broyer, M., Brunner, F. P., Brynger, and Challah, S. (1986*a*). Combined report on regular haemodialysis and transplantation in Europe, 1985. *Proc. EDTA*, **23**, 55–83.

Rizzoni, G., Broyer, M., Guest, G., Fine, R. N., and Holliday, M. A. (1986*b*) Growth retardation in children with chronic renal disease: scope of the problem. *Am. J. Kid. Dis.*, **7**, 256–61.

Rizzoni, G., Ehrich, J. H. H., Brunner, F. P., Geerlings, W., Fassbinder, W., Landais, P., *et al.* (1991). Combined report on regular dialysis and transplantation of children in Europe, 1990. *Nephrol. Dial. Transplant.*, **6**, 31–42.

Rodger, R. S. C., Morrison, L., Dewar, J. H., Wilkinson, R., Ward, M. K., and Kerr, D. N. S. (1985). Loss of pulsatile luteinising hormone secretion in men with chronic renal failure. *BMJ*, **291**, 1598–600.

Rosenfeld, R. G., Pham, H., Cohen, P., Fielder, P., Gargosky, S. E., Muller, H., *et al.* (1994). Insulin-like growth factor binding proteins and their regulation. *Acta. Paediatr. Suppl.*, **399**, 154–8.

Rotundo, A., Nevins, T. E., Lipton, M., Lockman, L. A., Mauer, S. M., and Michael, A. F. (1982). Progressive encephalopathy in children with chronic renal insufficiency in infancy. *Kidney Int.*, **21**, 486–91.

Roy, S. and Arant, B. (1981). Hypokalaemic metabolic alkalosis in normotensive infants with elevated plasma renin activity and hyperaldosteronism: role of dietary chloride deficiency. *Pediatrics*, **67**, 423–9.

Saenger, P., Wiedeman, E., Schwartz, E., Korth-Schutz, S., Lewy, J., Riggio, R., *et al.* (1974). Somatomedin and growth after rneal transplantation. *Pediatr. Res.*, **8**, 163–9.

Samaan, N. and Freeman, R. (1970). Growth hormone levels in severe renal failure. *Metabolism*, **19**, 102–13.

Schaefer, F., Gilli, G., and Scharer, K. (1989). Pubertal growth and final height in chronic renal failure. In: *Growth and endocrine changes in adolescents and young adults with chronic renal failure. Paediatric and adolescent endocrinology* (ed. R. Scharer), pp. 59–69. Karger, Basel.

Schaefer, F., Seidel, C., Binding, A., Gasser, T., Largo, R. H., Prader, A., *et al.* (1990). Pubertal growth in chronic renal failure. *Pediatr. Res.*, **28**, 5–10.

Schaefer, F., Andre, J. L., Krug, C., *et al.* (1991a) Growth and skeletal maturation in dialysed children treated with rh-erythrpoietin—a multicentre study. *Pediatr. Nephrol.*, **5**, C6.

Schaefer, F., Hamill, G., Stanhope, R., Preece, M. A., and Scharer, K. (1991b). Pulsatile growth hormone secretion in peripubertal patients with chronic renal failure. *J. Pediatr.*, **119**, 568–77.

Schaefer, F., Walther, U., Ruder, H., Huber, W., Marr, J., and Scharer, K. (1991c). Reduced spermaturia in adolescent any young adult patients after rcnal transplantation. *Nephrol. Dial. Transplant.*, **6**, 840.

Schaefer, F. and Mehls, O. (1994). Endocrine, metabolic and growth disorders. In: *Paediatric nephrology* (3rd edn) (ed. M. A. Holliday, T. M. Barratt, and E. D. Avner), pp. 1241–86. Williams and Wilkins, Baltimore.

Scharer, K., Schaefer, F., Trott, F., Kassman, K., and Gilli, G. (1989). Pubertal development in children with chronic renal failure. In: *Growth and endocrine changes in adolescents and young adults with chronic renal failure. Paediatric and adolescent endocrinology* (ed. K. Scharer), pp. 151–68. Karger, Basel.

Scharer, K. on behalf of the Study Group on Pubertal Development in Chronic Renal Failure (1990). Growth and development of children with chronic renal failure. *Acta. Paed. Scand.*, **366** (Suppl.), 90–2.

Schoenle, E., Zapf, T., and Foresch, E. R. (1982). Insulin-like growth factor I stimulates growth in hypophysectomised rats. *Nature*, **296**, 252–3.

Schwartz, I. D. and Warady, B. A. (1992). Cadaveric renal allograft rejection after treatment with recombinant human growth hormone. *J. Pediatr.*, **121**, 664–5.

Seidel, C., Schaefer, F., Walther, U., and Scharer. K. (1991). The application of knemometry in renal disease: preliminary observations. *Pediatr. Nephrol.*, **5**, 467–71.

Simmons, J. M., Wilson, C. J., Potter, D. E., and Holliday, M. A. (1971). Relation of calorie deficiency to growth failure in children on haemodialysis and the growth response to calorie supplementation. *N. Engl. J. Med.*, **285**, 653–6.

Simopoulos, A. P. (1979). Growth characteristics in Bartter's syndrome. *Nephron.*, **23**, 130–5.

So, S. K. S., Chang, P.-N., Najarian, J. S., Mauer, S. M., Simmons, R. L., and Nevins, T. E. (1987). Growth and development in infants after renal transplantation. *J. Pediatr.*, **110**, 343–50.

Stablein, D. M. and Tejani, A. (1993). Five-year patient and graft survival in North American children: a report of the North American paediatric transplant cooperative study. *Kidney Int.*, **44**, S16–S21.

Stickler, G. B. and Bergen, B. J. (1973). A review: short stature in renal disease. *Pediatr. Res.*, **7**, 978–82.

Strife, C. F., Quinlan, M., Mears, K., Davey, M. L., and Clardy, C. (1986). Improved growth of three uraemic children by nocturnal nasogastric feedings. *Am. J. Dis. Child.*, **140**, 438–43.

Tamanaha, K., Mak, R. H. K., Rigden, S. P. A., *et al.* (1987). Long-term suppression of hyperparathyroidism by phosphate binders in uraemic children. *Pediatr. Nephrol.*, **1**, 145–9.

Tanner, J. M., Whitehouse, R. H., and Takaishi, M. (1966). Standards from birth to maturity for height, weight, height velocity and weight velocity: British children 1965. *Arch. Dis. Child.*, **41**, 613–35.

Tejani, A., Butt, K. M. H., Rajpoot, D., Gonzalez, R., Buyan, N., Pomrantz, A., *et al.* (1989). Strategies for optimizing growth in children with kidney transplants. *Transplantation*, **47**, 229–33.

Tejani, A., Fine, R., Alexander, S., Harmon, W., and Stablein, D. (1993). Factors predictive of sustained growth in children after renal transplantation. *J. Pediatr.*, **122**, 397–402.

Tonshoff, B., Mehls, O., Heinrich, U., Blum, W. F., Ranke, M. B., and Schauer, A. (1990*a*). Growth-stimulating effects of recombinant human growth hormone in children with end-stage disease. *J. Pediatr.*, **116**, 561–6.

Tonshoff, B., Schaefer, F., and Mehls, O. (1990*b*). Disturbance of growth hormone—insulin-like growth factor axis in uraemia. *Pediatr. Nephrol.*, **4**, 654–62.

Tyden, G., Berg, U., and Reinholt, F. (1990). Acute renal graft rejection after treatment with human growth hormone. *Lancet*, **336**, 1455–6.

Unterman, T. G. and Phillips L. S. (1985). Glucocorticoid effects on somatomedins and somatomedin inhibitors. *J. Clin. Endocrinol. Metab.*, **61**, 618–26.

van Diemen-Steenvorde, R., Donckerwolcke, R. A., Brackel, H., Wolff, E. D., and de Jong, M. C. J. W. (1987). Growth and sexual maturation in children after kidney transplantation. *J. Pediatr.*, **110**, 351–6.

van ES, A. on behalf of the European Study Group (1991). Growth hormone treatment in short children with chronic renal failure and after renal transplantation: combined data from European clinical trials. *Acta. Paediatr. Scand.*, **379** (Suppl.), 42–8.

Vest, M., Talbot, N. B., and Crawford, J. D. (1963). Hypocaloric dwarfism and hydronephrosis in nephrogenic diabetes insipidus. *Am. J. Dis. Child.*, **105**, 175–81.

Warady, B. A., Kriley, M., Lovell, H., Farrell, S. E., and Hellerstein, S. (1988). Growth and development of infants with end-stage renal disease receiving long-term peritoneal dialysis. *J. Pediatr.*, **112**, 714–19.

Wass, V. J., Barratt, T. M., Howarth, R. V., Marshall, W. A., Chantler, C., Ogg, C. S., *et al.* (1977). Home haemodialysis: report of the London children's home dialysis group. *Lancet*, **i**, 242–6.

Wassner, S. J. (1991). The effect of sodium repletion on growth and protein turnover in sodium-depleted rats. *Pediatr. Neprhol.*, **5**, 501–4.

West, C. D. and Smith, W. C. (1956). An attempt to elucidate the cause of growth retardation in renal disease. *Am. J. Dis. Child.*, **91**, 460–76.

Wehrenberg, W. B., Janowski, B. A., Piering, A. W., and Culler, F. L. (1990). Glucocorticoids: potent inhibitors and stimulators of growth hormone secretion. *Endocrinology*, **126**, 3200–3.

Wingen, A-M., Fabian-Bach, C., and Mehls, O. (1991). European study group for nutritional treatment of chronic renal failure in childhood. Low-protein diet in children with chronic renal failure—1-year results. *Pediatr. Nephrol.*, **5**, 496–500.

Winick, M. and Rosso, P. (1969). Head circumference and cellular growth of the brain in normal and marasmic children. *J. Pediatr.*, **74**, 774–8.

PART II
A systematic approach to inherited renal disorders

Section A
Structural disorders

7

Chromosomal and development anomalies

Martin d' A. Crawfurd

Chromosomal disorders

Although renal and lower urinary tract anomalies are seldom the presenting feature of chromosomal disorders, they frequently form part of a multisystem malformation due to chromosomal anomaly. The renal abnormalities seen in chromosomal disorders include fused kidneys, duplication defects, renal agenesis or hypoplasia, hydronephrosis and hydroureter, renal dysplasia or cystic disease and hypospadias, micropenis, and cryptorchidism.

The overall pattern of malformation in individual chromosomal disorders is usually sufficiently characteristic to enable a clinical diagnosis to be made. However, within the broad picture there is considerable variation from case to case, even for the whole chromosome trisomies and monosomies. Although certain renal anomalies are characteristic of many of the more common chromosomal disorders, the picture is otherwise remarkably non-specific and no one renal malformation is unique to any specific chromosome disorder. This lack of specificity in renal (or other systems) anomalies and chromosomal disorders is not at present fully understood; just as we do not understand the genetic basis for the overall phenotype in any one chromosomal disorder. In deletions and duplications even the smallest difference in break points between different cases will alter some of the genes involved and hence are likely to affect the phenotype, through deletion or duplication of different specific genes, or possibly different position effects. These mechanisms, however, cannot account for the differences between cases with identical whole chromosomal trisomies or monosomies. In such cases, one can speculate that polymorphic gene variations that have no effect in the normal individual nevertheless contribute to the phenotype in the abnormal. Alternatively, chance variations in precise timing of developmental steps in the embryo may result in phenotypic differences in those with a chromosomal abnormality. That the mechanisms involved will eventually become clearer is evident by the recent narrowing down of the region of chromosome 21 responsible for Down's syndrome.

Study of the renal anomalies in chromosomal disorders suggests that two distinct processes are involved. Firstly, there may be a developmental error or failure of growth arising during embryogenesis, as for example in horseshoe kidney or duplication defects. A second type of process is that of urinary tract obstruction, unilateral in the case of pelviureteric or ureterovesical obstruction confined to one side, or bilateral when due to urethral obstruction, as from posterior valves or when ureteric obstruction is bilateral. Obvious consequences are hydronephrosis and hydroureter, and the cortical cysts seen in trisomy 13 and other chromosomal anomalies that resemble those classified by Potter as type 4 and associated with incomplete obstruction (Osathanondh and Potter 1964). Renal agenesis and dysplasia can probably be due to either process. Many cases with either unilateral or bilateral renal agenesis may well be developmental. In many cases of multicystic dysplasia there is no detectable obstruction. In other cases, dysplasia is clearly associated with obstruction, as in prune-belly syndrome with posterior urethral valves. Dysplasia in one kidney may be associated with agenesis in the other, often referred to as renal adysplasia. If followed sonographically, a fetal dysplastic kidney may gradually shrink and eventually disappear.

Trisomy 21 (Down's syndrome)

Renal tract anomalies are uncommon in Down's syndrome, and not even mentioned in any of the standard descriptions of the disorder. Fabia and Drolette (1970) observed an incidence of urinary tract malformation in Down's syndrome of about six per 1000, mainly hydronephrosis or hydroureter, cystic kidney, renal agenesis or hypoplasia, and bladder obstruction. Deaton (1973) observed death from renal failure in three out of 1000 Down's children.

Trisomy 13 (Patau's syndrome)

Taylor (1968) reviewed 55 cases of trisomy 13 from the literature and 27 cases of her own. Just over a half of her cases had a renal tract anomaly. The abnormalities found included polycystic kidney in a third of her autopsied cases, with duplication anomalies, hydronephrosis, and hydroureter in lesser proportions. Horseshoe kidney, common in trisomy 18, is an infrequent finding in trisomy 13.

In a detailed pathological study of 12 cases, Moerman and colleagues (1988) found microcysts, primarily cortical, in all cases but increasing in size and number with length of gestation. In half of their cases, occasional foci of nodular renal blastoma were also present. Renal malformations are found in about half of all cases of partial trisomy 13 due to mosaicism or translocation (Niebuhr 1977).

Trisomy 18 (Edward's syndrome)

Horseshoe or unilateral fused kidney is the characteristic renal malformation in this disorder, constituting about a half of all renal malformations seen. Other renal malformations include duplication anomalies, renal agenesis, hydronephrosis, and cortical cysts. Renal malformations are found in around 60% of all cases of trisomy 18 (Hammerton 1971).

45, X syndrome (Turner's syndrome)

Renal malformation is seen in around 60% of cases of Turner's syndrome, including aborted fetuses (Byrne and Blanc 1985). As in trisomy 18, horseshoe kidney is the most commonly observed renal tract malformation, but double kidney or ureter, renal agenesis, hydronephrosis, and renal cysts are also seen.

Other sex chromosomal anomalies

Patients with Klinefelter's syndrome (47, XXY), triple X syndrome, and the XXY syndrome have all been found in neonatal surveys, and in all three syndromes both renal and lower urinary tract malformations are rare. Renal malformations are also rare in high sex chromosome polyploid syndromes (48, XXXY, XXYY, XXXX; 49, XXXXY, XXXYY or XXXXX) and in XX males. However, there is some evidence of an increased tendency to hypospadias and hypogenitalism in the high male sex chromosome polyploid syndromes.

Other autosomal trisomies

In trisomy 8, usually only seen in mosaic form, renal tract malformations, apart from hydronephrosis, are rare. Trisomy 9 is invariably mosaic and may be associated with renal malformations. Renal agenesis or dysgenesis with Potter's syndrome has been reported in near-term fetuses with trisomy 7.

Triploidy

Renal anomalies, including hydronephrosis and cystic dysplasia, are seen in triploidy (69, XXY; 69, XXX; and the rare 69, XYY).

Duplications

About a half of reported cases of duplication 3q and deletion 3p rearrangements are associated with duplicated ureter, hydronephrosis, or cortical renal cysts (Wilson *et al.* 1985).

Trisomy 4p is a well-established anomaly associated with micropenis and hypospadias, and occasionally renal malformation or atresia (Rethore 1977). Partial trisomy 4q is also usually associated with varied renal malformations (Merlob *et al.* 1989).

Hydronephrosis and cortical cysts have been reported in partial trisomy 5p (Kleczkowska *et al.* 1987; Gustavson *et al.* 1988).

A variety of renal malformations have been recorded in about a half of all cases of trisomy for the long arm of chromosome 10 (10q), including hydronephrosis, renal dysplasia or cysts, and hypoplasia (Moreno–Fuenmayor *et al.* 1975).

Trisomy 11q in males is invariably associated with micropenis, and in either sex, renal malformations may be seen, including renal agenesis and renal artery anomalies (Giraud *et al.* 1975). Most cases occur in unbalanced offspring of a parent with an 11;22 translocation.

Trisomy 20 mosaicism is a common finding in amniotic fluid cell cultures but is not detectable in the newborn. Trisomy for the short arm of chromosome 20 is a malformation disorder in which renal malformations are occasionally seen.

Partial trisomy or tetrasomy for the proximal long arm of chromosome 22 gives rise to 'cat-eye' syndrome of coloboma and imperforate anus and renal malformations. The latter include renal agenesis or hypoplasia, horseshoe kidney, duplication defects, ectopia, or hydronephrosis (Schinzel *et al.* 1981).

Deletions

Partial deletion of the short arm of chromosome 4, Wolf-Hirschhorn syndrome, is a well-recognized syndrome of delayed growth, microcephaly, severe mental deficiency, hypertelorism, cleft lip and palate, and in males, hypospadias and cryptorchidism, and occasional renal anomaly (Lurie *et al.* 1980). Renal cysts have been noted in at least two out of four reported cases with a chromosome 4 long-arm deletion involving q21–q25 (Rose *et al.* 1991).

Cri-du-chat syndrome, partial monosomy for the short arm of chromosome 5, was one of the earliest deletion syndromes to be described. Renal and urinary tract malformations are the exception, but diverse anomalies have been reported, including renal agenesis or hypoplasia, horseshoe kidney, non-functioning kidney, precalyceal ectasia, and hypospadias (Lejeune *et al.* 1964).

Krassikoff and Seckhon (1990) have drawn attention to the similarity between a case of their own with hydroureters and terminal deletion of 6q, other reported 6q deletions, and Fryn's syndrome. They discuss whether Fryn's syndrome might be due to microdeletion of 6q or whether the deletion might be a phenocopy.

The 9p—syndrome is associated with micropenis and hypospadias in males and occasionally with hydronephrosis (Alfi *et al.* 1976); and interstitial deletion within the long arm of 9q with hydroureter and dysplastic kidney (Ying *et al.* 1982).

Renal dysplasia is a feature of 10p deletion (Elstner *et al.* 1984).

Probably the most intensely studied of all deletions is the del (11)(p13) associated with Wilms' tumour, aniridia, genito-urinary abnormality, and mental retardation. Any combination of these features may occur in association with a microscopic or submicroscopic deletion of 11p13, presumably depending on which of several contiguous genes are deleted (Francke *et al.* 1979).

Partial deletion of chromosome 13 is one of the commoner deletions. The essential phenotype is microcephaly with hypertelorism, microphthalmia, and a prominent nasal bridge, with or without retinoblastoma and/or thumb aplasia or hypoplasia. Niebuhr (1977) reviewed 77 such cases and classified them into four types. Category 1 comprises ring chromosomes with a loss of only the two terminal bands and is associated with a phenotype with normal thumbs; category 2 consists of rings or deletions with more extensive deletion of distal q bands and a phenotype including thumb abnormalities; in category 3 there is retinoblastoma and a mid-long-arm deletion; and in Category 4, a less extensive mid-arm deletion with neither retinoblastoma nor thumb abnormality. The urinary tract abnormalities associated with the 13q—syndrome comprise hypo- or epispadias, cryptorchidism and renal anomaly, mainly renal hypoplasia or hydronephrosis. However, the frequencies of the different urinary tract anomalies vary markedly among the four categories, hypospadias being common in categories 1–3 but not 4, cryptorchidism common in 1 and 2 but not 3 and 4, and renal anomaly common in all but category 3.

The Miller–Dieker syndrome of lissencephaly is associated, in at least a majority of patients and perhaps all, with deletion of band p13.3 in the short arm of chromosome 17. Cystic renal dysplasia or polycystic kidneys, renal agenesis, and cryptorchidism have been reported in some patients (Greenberg *et al.* 1986).

A variety of renal anomalies have been reported in 7% of cases with a deletion in the long arm of chromosome 18. These include renal agenesis and horseshoe kidney (Lurie and Lazjuk 1972).

Developmental anomalies

Urinary tract congenital malformations are fairly common; Leck and colleagues (1968) estimated a birth incidence, excluding hypospadias, of 3/1000. Stephens (1983) has published a monograph on congenital malformations of the renal tract and Barakat and colleagues (1986) and Crawfurd (1988) reviews on urogenital abnormalities in genetic disease. Although published up to a decade ago, these works provide a clinical description of a field that could not be greatly improved on today. The genetics of these anomalies were reviewed by Carter (1984) and in Crawfurd (1988), but here of course recent molecular studies have advanced our knowledge considerably. The current position is summarized in the gene map of congenital malformations prepared by Wilkie and colleagues (1994). Of the 139 loci listed, 20 could be considered to have a major urinary tract component, and a few more could now be added.

Congenital malformations can be divided into two groups: first, the common malformations of a single organ or structure such as isolated neural tube defects, congenital heart disease, cleft lip or palate, and horseshoe kidney; and second but comparatively rare, the multiple malformation syndromes. The former group are developmental errors of a single tissue or organ which are usually of a sporadic occurrence. For the most part, little is known of their aetiology. They are not associated with any detectable chromosomal anomaly and are not inherited in any simple mendelian manner. Environmental factors must play a part, as for most of them there is a substantial rate of discordance for monozygotic twins, and for a few evidence for specific environmental factors (for example, the role of folic acid in neural tube defect). Most also show an increased incidence in relatives, consistent in at least some with a multifactorial genetic predisposition. However, in the case of bilateral renal agenesis, as pointed out by Carter *et al.* (1979), the incidence in sibs at 3.5% is too high, given the birth incidence, to be accounted for by a simple multifactorial mechanism.

With regard to the multiple malformation syndromes, some, as discussed above, are due to chromosomal anomalies. Several others are clearly determined by single genes or at least micro-deletions, and show mendelian inheritance. These of course include all those placed on the gene map. A few have a specific known environmental aetiology, such as the thalidomide syndrome, fetal alcohol syndrome, and fetal rubella syndrome. Yet others are of usually sporadic occurrence and of unknown aetiology.

The multiple malformation syndromes present diagnostic difficulties because there are a great many of them and most are rare, some exceedingly rare. Standard textbooks, published papers, and computerized databases are all valuable aids in the recognition of these rarer disorders. A more fundamental problem is that of defining a specific disorder. As diagnosis is based on the interpretation of clinical signs rather than any objective investigation in those disorders for which neither a chromosomal nor a molecular basis is known, it is unavoidably subjective. The problem also arises as to how much variation in clinical signs can be permitted within a single syndrome. In recent years, several eponymous syndromes have been split into a number of types. This splitting is not just academic as it may represent different gene loci giving rise to similar but not identical syndromes, and may eventually lead to objective, molecular methods of diagnosis, including prenatal diagnosis.

Another distinction which needs to be made is that between malformations due to developmental error and deformations or disruptions due to the mechanical effects of mechanisms external to the system affected. The effects of urinary tract obstruction, discussed above under Chromosomal disorders, are a good example of deformation. A further example is Potter's syndrome due to deformation of facial features and limbs by oligohydramnios secondary to absent or non-functioning kidneys. Disruption, as for example by amniotic bands, is less likely to involve the urinary tract, although in severe abdominal disruption the bladder can be involved.

Renal agenesis or hypoplasia and dysplasia

Isolated renal adysplasia

Renal agenesis in its bilateral form is a common cause of lethal Potter's syndrome, but unilateral agenesis is of itself symptomless. However, renal disease in a solitary kidney is common, usually some degree of dysplastic change with or without hypoplasia, a finding that has given rise to the term 'renal adysplasia'. The term also covers the observation of renal agenesis or hypoplasia and renal dysplasia in different members of the same family. Nakada *et al.* (1988) observed ipsilateral adrenal agenesis in two out of seven patients with unilateral renal agenesis.

Carter and colleagues' study (1979), mentioned above, was too early for the ultrasound investigation of relatives. More recent studies using ultrasound have revealed high incidences.

Roodhooft *et al.* (1984) found renal anomalies in 9% of parents of children with bilateral renal agenesis or dysplasia. Among the offspring of affected obligate heterozygotes for hereditary renal adysplasia, 15–20%, have bilateral severe renal adysplasia, leading to the conclusion that this is an autosomal dominant disorder with between 50–90% penetrance (McPherson *et al.* 1987), despite the fact that most bilateral cases are sporadic. In all new cases of bilateral renal agenesis/ dysplasia, the parents should have a renal ultrasound scan. If the parents show no abnormality, the 3.5% sib recurrence risk of Carter *et al.* (1979) can be counselled; but if either parent shows any sign of a renal abnormality, a higher 15–20% sib risk should be counselled. In either case, prenatal intravaginal ultrasound scanning should be offered.

A quite distinct disorder is the rare oligomeganephronic renal hypoplasia with scanty large nephrons leading to early renal failure and death, associated in two instances with tapeto-retinal degeneration (Janin-Mercier *et al.* 1985). Most reported cases have been sporadic but there is one report of affected sibs (Moerman *et al.* 1984).

Sirenomelia

Urinary tract anomaly occurs as part of the syndrome of caudal regression along with sirenomelia. The usual urinary tract defect is bilateral renal agenesis with resultant oligohydramnios and Potter's syndrome. Other findings include renal dysplasia, rudimentary kidneys, horseshoe kidney, cystic kidneys, and extraversion of bladder. There is a strong association with monozygotic, especially monoamniotic, twinning (Smith *et al.* 1976).

Renal adysplasia with associated malformations

Renal agenesis or dysplasia may be associated with non-urinary tract malformation in a variety of multiple malformation syndromes other than sirenomelia. These associations fall into four main groups: genital tract, limb, eye, or ear defects, or with some combination of these.

Syndromes with renal adysplasia and genital tract malformation include the Mayer–Rokitansky–Kuster syndrome of vaginal atresia with rudimentary uterus and skeletal, mainly vertebral, defects (Pavanello *et al.* 1988), MURCS association (Davee *et al.* 1992), and certain cases of female pseudohermaphroditism with urinary tract anomalies (Seaver *et al.* 1994). Each of these disorders is usually of sporadic occurrence, but the occasional reports of familial occurrence has led to the suggestion of a multifactorial genetic aetiology, or even of autosomal dominant inheritance with incomplete penetrance (Schimke and King 1980). The various renal–genital syndromes are listed in Table 7.1. It is by no means clear that these syndromes are in fact distinct rather than stages within a spectrum.

Several disorders combine renal anomalies, most renal agenesis or dysplasia, and ear anomalies, all showing either autosomal dominant or recessive inheritance. The ear anomalies are mainly external ear malformations with or without middle-ear defects. Several of these syndromes are private syndromes reported in a single family. They are included in Table 7.2.

Table 7.3 lists multiple congenital anomaly syndromes of which renal agenesis or dysplasia and eye anomalies are components. The fourth group of malformations associated with renal anomalies are those with limb defects, listed in Table 7.4. This particular association has been reviewed in a survey of over 1.5 million births in Hungary between 1975 and 1984. These yielded 75 cases of combined renal and limb anomaly, usually associated with further malformations. The commonest recognized pattern was the VACTERL association (Evans *et al.* 1992*a*).

There are also several syndromes which combined many of the above non-renal malformations with renal agenesis, dysplasia, or hypoplasia. Five such multisystem multiple congenital malformation syndromes are listed in Table 7.5.

Table 7.1 Syndromes of renal and genital tract malformation

Syndrome	Renal defects	Genital tract defects	Mode of inheritance	References
Mayer–Rokitansky–Kuster syndrome (McK. no. 277000)	Renal adysplasia	Vaginal atresia and rudimentary aterus with vertebral defects	Heterogeneous with most cases sporadic, but at least some A.R.	Pavanello *et al.* 1988
MURCS association	Renal agenesis and/or ectopy	Absence of vagina and hypoplasia of uterus with cervico-thoracic vertebral defects	Sporadic	Davee *et al.* 1992
Female pseudo-hermaphroditism	Renal ± bladder agenesis or hypoplasia, hydronephrosis ± megacystis	Masculinized external genitalia ± absent uterus, vagina, and/or Fallopian tubes; imperforate anus	Sporadic	Seaver *et al.* 1994
Hereditary renal (or urogenital) adysplasia (McK. no. 191830)	Renal adysplasia	Uterus didelphys or unicornuate uterus, vesico-ureteral anomaly, or in male seminal vesical or vas deferens defects	A.D.	Schimke and King 1980; McPherson *et al.* 1987

McK. no. = Catalogue number from V. A. McKusick's (1994) *Mendelian inheritance in man* (10th edn). Johns Hopkins University Press, Baltimore; A.R. = Autosomal recessive; A.D. = Autosomal dominant.

Table 7.2 Syndromes of renal tract and ear malformation

Syndrome	Renal defect	Ear and other defects	Mode of inheritance	References
Oto–renal syndrome	Renal hypoplasia and nephritis	Preauricular pits	A.D.	Lachiewicz et al. 1985
Branchio–oto–renal (BOR) syndrome (McK. no. 113650)	Renal adysplasia and duplication defects	Cupped pinnae, preauricular sinuses, mixed hearing loss with Mondini cochlear malformation and fixed stapes	A.D.	Hilson 1957; Fraser et al. 1978
Varadi–Papp syndrome, or polydactyly, cleft lip, hamartomas, renal, deafness, retardation syndrome (McK. no. 277170). Also considered as a variant of OFD–VI	Bi- or unilateral renal agenesis or hypoplasia	Conductive hearing loss with cleft lip, polydactyly, hamartomas, and mental retardation	A.R.	Mattei and Ayme 1983; Munke et al. 1990
Auricular–renal adysplasia –hypospadias syndrome	Bi- or unilateral renal agenesis and hypospadias	'Bat' or Potter's facies ears	A.D.	Hilson 1957
Oto-renal–genital syndrome	Bi- or unilateral renal agenesis or hypoplasia	Low-set lop ears, and external auditory meatal atresia, otic anomalies and deafness, with vaginal atresia	A.R.	Winter et al. 1968; Melnick 1980

McK. no. = Catalogue number from V. A. McKusick's (1994) *Mendelian inheritance in man* (10th edn). Johns Hopkins University Press, Baltimore; A.D. = Autosomal dominant; A.R. = Autosomal recessive; OFD-VI = Oro–facial digital syndrome, type VI.

Table 7.3 Syndromes of renal tract and eye malformation

Syndrome	Renal defect	Eye defect	Other malformations	Mode of inheritance	References
Cryptophthalmos (Fraser's) syndrome (McK. no. 219000)	Bi- or unilateral renal agenesis	Cryptophthalmos and hypertelorism, lacrimal duct anomaly	Middle and/or outer ear malformation, midline facial cleft, laryngeal stenosis, syndactyly, and Mullerian anomalies	A.R.	Thomas et al. 1986; Francannet et al. 1990
Lenz microphthalmia (McK. no. 309800)	Renal aplasia or hypoplasia, cryptorchidism and hypospadias in 50% of cases	Microphthalmia or anophthalmia	Skeletal and dental anomalies, mental retardation	X.R.	Traboulsi et al. 1988
Rieger's syndrome (McK. no. 180500)	Hypospadias in males	Microcornea, iris hypoplasia, and anterior synechiae	Hypodontia, umbilical hernia, or protrosion	A.D.	Jorgenson et al. 1978
Acro–renal–ocular syndrome (McK. no. 102490)	Renal ectopia	Coloboma, ptosis, or Duane anomaly	Thumb hypoplasia	A.D.	Halal et al. 1984
Oculo–reno–cerebellar (ORC) syndrome (McK. no. 257970)	Glomerulopathy	Tapetoretinal degeneration	Absence of the cerebellar granular layer	A.R.	Hunter et al. 1982

McK. no. = Catalogue number from V. A. McKusick's (1994) *Mendelian inheritance in man* (10ᵗʰ edn). John Hopkins University Press, Baltimore; A.R. = Autosomal recessive; A.D. = Autosomal dominant; X.R. = X-linked recessive.

Table 7.4 Syndromes of renal tract and limb malformation

Syndrome	Renal defect	Limb anomaly	Other malformations	Mode of inheritance	References
Acro–renal syndrome (McK. no. 102520)	Oligo meganephronic hypoplasia	Absence deformities of digits, especially ectrodactyly	—	A.R.	Houlston and Macdermot 1992; Miteny et al. 1992;
Acro–renal–mandibular syndrome	Renal agenesis or dysplasia	Limb reduction defects	Micrognathia	A. R.	Evans et al. 1992b
VATER/VACTERL association (McK. no. 192350)	Renal agenesis, hypoplasia, or dysplasia in over a half of cases	Radial dysplasia or other limb anomalies	Vertebral anomalies, cardiac defects, tracheo-oesophageal fistula	Sporadic	Corsello et al. 1992
Cerebro–renal–digital syndrome	Renal cystic dysplasia	Preaxial polydactyly	Facial anomalies, high palate, dolicocephaly, agenesis of cerebellar vernias, mental retardation	A.R.	Piantanida et al. 1993
Neuro–facial–digito–renal (NFDR) syndrome (McK. no. 256690)	Renal agenesis	Triphalangeal thumbs	Dysmorphic facies with bifid nose, short stature, abnormal EEG, mental retardation	A.R.	Freire-Maia et al. 1982
Townes–Brocks syndrome (McK. no. 107480)	Renal hypoplasia	Hypoplastic or triphalangeal thumbs and other distal limb anomalies	Sensori-neural deafness, imperforate anus	A.D.	Cameron et al. 1991

McK. no. = Catalogue number from V. A. McKusick's (1994) *Mendelian inheritance in man* (10th edn). Johns Hopkins University Press, Baltimore; A.R. = Autosomal recessive; A.D. = Autosomal dominant; EEG = Electroencephalogram.

Table 7.5 Syndromes of renal tract and multiple other system malformation

Syndrome	Renal defect	Other malformations	Mode of inheritance	References
Syndrome of Rüdiger *et al.* (McK. no. 268650)	Uretero-vesical junction stenosis	Bicornuate uterus, brachy dactyly, and lack of cartilage in pinna	?A.R.	Rüdiger *et al.* 1971
DK-phocomelia syndrome (McK. no. 223340)	Renal agenesis or ureteral malposition	Vaginal atresia and uterine hypoplasia, or in male penile hyperplasia	Sporadic	Cherstvoy *et al.* 1980
Smith–Lemli –Opitz II or Rutledge's syndrome (McK. no. 268670)	Renal hypoplasia	Sex reversal in males, postaxial polydactyly, low-set malformed ears	A.R.	Donnai *et al.* 1986
McKusick– Kaufman syndrome (McK. no. 236700)	Hypospadias, hydronephrosis, ureteral stenosis, and polycystic kidney	Hydrometrocolpos, postaxial polydactyly and congenital heart disease	A.R.	Chitayat *et al.* 1987

McK. no. = Catalogue number from V. A. McKusick's (1994) *Mendelian inheritance in man* (10th edn). John Hopkins University Press, Baltimore. A.R. = Autosomal recessive.

Finally, there is a miscellaneous group of syndromes combining renal agenesis or dysplasia with other types of non-urinary tract malformations. These include central nervous system malformations with renal agenesis, cystic dysplasia, fusion, duplication, or ectopia in association with spina bifida observed in about 2% of the latter by Bamforth and Baird (1989), and with renal agenesis especially associated with upper thoracic (T5–T8) lesions (Hunt and Whitaker 1987); renal agenesis in the autosomal dominant Steinfeld syndrome of holoprosencephaly and visceral defects (Nothen *et al.* 1993); renal agenesis or hypoplasia in a syndrome of encephalocoele, radial defects, congenital heart and alimentary tract anomalies (Froster-Iskenius and Meinecke 1992). Renal agenesis, hypoplasia, ectopia, or horseshoe kidney are also seen in the autosomal recessive Fanconi's pancytopenia (Welshimer and Swift 1982); renal agenesis, horseshoe kidney, or a duplicated collecting system have all been reported in three out of 17 cases of the autosomal recessive cerebro–oculo–facio–skeletal (COFS) syndrome (Preus *et al.* 1977); in the incompletely dominant X-linked Goeminne syndrome of torticollis, keloids, cryptorchidism, infertility, and renal dysplasia the locus has been mapped to Xq28 (Zuffardi and Fraccaro 1982); cystic dysplastic kidneys have been described in the syndrome of polydactyly, campomelia, ambiguous genitalia, and cerebral malformation (Ades *et al.* 1994).

Fused kidneys

Fused or horseshoe kidney is relatively common with an estimated incidence of 1 : 400 (Glenn 1959), and is nearly always sporadic, although relatives are seldom investigated. Apart from isolated cases, fused kidney occurs in Turner's syndrome and Trisomy 18, and in the autosomal recessive facio–cardio–renal syndrome (Nevin *et al.* 1991), and has been reported in Jarcho–Levin syndrome (Karnes *et al.* 1991).

Congenital hydronephrosis

Congenital hydronephrosis may occur on its own, or in association with hydroureter, and occur on one side only or affect both kidneys. Bilateral hydronephrosis and hydroureter is generally assumed to be due to lower urinary tract obstruction. When occurring without hydroureter it is commonly due to pelviureteric obstruction, and in familial cases is thought to be aetiologically related to pelvicalicial duplication, paraureteric diverticulae' or vesicoureteral reflux (Atwell 1985). More recently, evidence for genetic heterogeneity of hereditary hydronephrosis with pelviureteric obstruction has been presented, and one locus assigned to chromosome 6p (Izquiredo *et al.* 1992). A subsequent report of multicystic dysplasia in a fetus with a de novo translocation 46, XX, t(6;19) (p23.1;q13.4) supports this assignment (Fryns *et al.* 1993*a*). Even unilateral hydronephrosis may be familial, or both uni- and bilateral cases may occur in the same family. One postulated mechanism of pelviureteric obstruction is an abnormal arrangement of muscular bundles at the junction (Antonakopoulos *et al.* 1985).

Congenital hydronephrosis due to either pelviureteric or lower urinary tract obstruction, most commonly posterior urethral valves, has been described in a variety of multiple congenital malformation syndromes. These include the autosomal recessive Johanson–Blizzard syndrome in which hydronephrosis and duplication defects may occur (Johanson and Blizzard 1971); uretero-pelvic junction obstruction in the sporadic Russell–Silver syndrome (Haslam *et al.* 1973); hydronephrosis and hydroureter with urethral valves, or vesicoureteral reflux with bladder dysfunction in the autosomal recessive urofacial or Ochoa syndrome (Teebi and Hassoon 1991); the probably autosomal recessive Schinzel–Giedion Syndrome (Al-Gazali *et al.* 1990); and the autosomal recessive Warburg (HARD +/−E) syndrome (Donnai and Farndon 1986).

Megacystis

An enlarged bladder, megacystis, may be secondary to lower urinary tract obstruction, or to bladder dysfunction as in the autosomal recessive megacystis–microcolon–intestinal hypoperistalsis syndrome (McNamara *et al.* 1994).

Duplication and ectopia

Duplication is the most common of the urinary tract malformations with a prevalance of 0.5% (Nation 1994). There have been several reports of familial occurrence of duplication defects or ectopia leading to a theory of autosomal dominant inheritance of duplication (Atwell *et al.* 1974). While this may be true for some of the comparitively rare familial cases, it cannot be true for duplication defects in general (Crawfurd 1988). However, duplication defects maybe a component of several multiple congenital malformation syndromes. Fraser *et al.* (1983) reported two families with an autosomal dominant syndrome comprising sensorineural hearing loss, external ear malformation or pre-auricular tags or pits, and urinary tract duplication, and which they designated as branchio–oto–ureteral (BOU) syndrome. Rich *et al.* (1987) reported a family in which a mother and son had the combination of facial dysmorphism, including low-set malformed ears, syndactyly or tapered digits, bilateral amastia and unilateral hydronephrosis and ureteral triplication. Duplication may involve the genital as well as the urinary tract, usually in the form of uterus didelphys, and this combination may rarely be familial (Fedder 1990).

Exstrophy and epispadias

A range of midline defects of the lower abdominal wall may be seen in the bladder exstrophy-epispadias complex. In its most severe form this results in the exceedingly rare cloacal exstrophy. Familial occurrence has been reported but is exceptional. Ives and colleagues (1980), in a study of a 102 index patients, found no recurrence among 162 sibs but Shapiro *et al.* (1984) found recurrence in three out of 215 children of index cases, in all five male but none of three female monozygotic co-twins, and in none of five dizygotic co-twins. An affected mother and son in one family and affected cousins in another have recently been reported (Messelink *et al.* 1994). Exstrophy is also a component of the exomphalos, exstrophy, imperforate anus, spinal defects (OEIS) complex (Carey *et al.* 1978).

Prune-belly syndrome

The characteristic absent abdominal wall musculature, urinary tract anomalies, and cryptorchidism of this predominantly male syndrome have been the subject of numerous hypotheses of pathogenesis, none of which wholly explain the findings (Grescovich and Nyberg 1988). There have also been several hypotheses regarding the role of genetic factors in its aetiology. The fact that the great majority of cases are sporadic and that more monozygotic twin pairs are discordant than concordant exclude a primarily genetic basis for most cases. It remains possible that there is a genetic basis for a small minority of cases that are familial, either single gene or polygenic.

Vesicoureteral reflux (see Chapter 9)

Vesicoureteral reflux in infants and young children is clinically important because of the high risk of renal scarring, which may lead to childhood hypertension and eventually renal failure. It is now accepted that scarring results from intrarenal reflux, whether associated with urinary tract infection or not, and is frequently of prenatal onset (Naljmaldan *et al.* 1990; Anderson and Rickwood 1991).

Although most cases of vesicoureteral reflux are sporadic there have been many reports of familial occurrence, and systematic surveys of sibs of index patients, using radionuclide cystography, have shown an incidence of reflux of up to a half with a higher incidence in boys under one year of age (Van den Abbeele *et al.* 1987; Aggarwal and Jones 1989; Kenda *et al.* 1991; Kenda and Fettich 1992). The pathogenesis is heterogeneous, involving medically treatable bladder instability (Scholtmeizer and Van Mastrigt 1991) or congenital malformation of the ureteric insertion into the bladder. The latter includes ectopic, especially lateral ectopic, insertion, short intravesical ureteric segment, or ureteric duplication. Atwell and colleagues (1977) have presented evidence that these different abnormalities may be associated.

Rare families have been reported with pedigrees suggestive of autosomal dominant inheritance (Chapman *et al.* 1985; Crawfurd 1988), or even X-linked (Middleton *et al.* 1975) of reflux. A segregation analysis of 88 families suggested a single major locus of less than 50% penetrance (Chapman *et al.* 1985). Others have argued for a multifactorial genetic basis for congenital reflux (De Vargas *et al.* 1978; Atwell and Allen 1980; Atwell 1985) with a 4% recurrence risk for reflux in first-degree relatives (Bois *et al.* 1975).

Several groups have reported postnatal follow-up of reflux diagnosed prenatally by ultrasound. In contrast to the majority of postnatally diagnosed cases, the prenatal ones tend to be more severe and predominantly male (Gordon *et al.* 1990).

Vesicoureteral reflux is not commonly seen as a component of multiple congenital anomaly syndromes. An exception is a syndrome of optic nerve colobomas, hypoplastic kidneys, and/or proteinuria and reflux reported in a father and three sons (Schimmenti *et al.* 1994).

Hypospadias

Hypospadias may be associated with chromosomal anomaly (as described previously), single gene defects, multifactorial genetic mechanisms, or environmental factors such as maternal progesterone administration in early pregnancy. In primary hypospadias the causal factor or factors are unknown.

It varies in severity from the mild glandular or coronal forms, as seen in the majority of cases, through varying degrees of penile hypospadias to the rare, severe penoscrotal or perineoscrotal form.

The overall incidence has been estimated as between 0.8 and 8.2 per thousand (Sweet *et al.* 1974; Leung *et al.* 1985). Recent studies have noted an increase in incidence in some geographical areas, for example in England and Wales (Matlai and Beral 1985), and Hungary where the increase is attributed to the wide use of hormone therapy (Czeizel 1985). Apportioning specific causes is more difficult. Aarskog (1970) found that about 6%, mainly XX/XY or X/XY mosaics, were secondary to chromosomal anomaly, and 6% secondary to maternal progesterone administration. Avellan (1975), in a Swedish study, concluded that 8.6% of cases were associated with other congenital malformations.

An increased familial incidence of primary hypospadias is well–documented with an incidence of about 4–10% among first-degree male relatives of affected boys (Bauer *et al.* 1979; Czeizel *et al.* 1979). Both multifactorial (Czeizel *et al.* 1979; Bauer *et al.* 1981) and single gene defects have been proposed to account for this familial occurrence. Reports of families with cases in several generations have led to the suggestion of autosomal dominant inheritance with reduced penetrance in at least four such families (Lowry and Kliman 1976; Cote *et al.* 1979; Dobrowolski *et al.* 1980). Other reports have suggested autosomal recessive inheritance (Sorensen 1953; Frydman *et al.* 1985; Tsur *et al.* 1987). A possible X-linked recessive inheritance of the association of hypospadias and spina bifida has also been postulated (Martinez-Frias 1994). Harris and Beaty (1993), who undertook a formal segregation analysis of 103 previously published pedigrees of Sorensen (1953), obtained inconclusive results and concluded that the causes in these familial cases are heterogeneous. Using two different methods of segregation analysis, one method pointed to autosomal dominant inheritance in preference to a recessive or a multifactorial model, and the other method indicated that dominant or recessive inheritance were equally likely but that non-mendelian sibship clustering fitted the data better.

Hypospadias is a feature of numerous multiple congenital anomaly syndromes. Apart from the XY/XX or X mosaic cases mentioned above, it may occur in XX males. In contrast to XX males lacking hypospadias, those with it do not carry detectable Y chromosome sequences (Numabe *et al.* 1992). In male pseudohermaphroditism type II with pseudovaginal perineoscrotal hypospadias there are normal levels of testerone but low levels of dihydrotestosterone due to 5 alphareductase deficiency (Imperato-McGinley *et al.* 1974); inheritance is autosomal recessive. In another recessive form of male pseudohermaphroditism with gynaecomastia in which masculinization occurs at puberty, and in which there may be perineal hypospadias, there is testicular deficiency of 17 ketoreductase activity (Saez *et al.* 1992).

The X-linked androgen insensitivity syndrome in its complete form results in phenotypic females with testictular feminization, but some patients with the incomplete form have a syndrome of hypogonadism with gynaecomastia and hypospadias known as Reifenstein's syndrome or male pseudohermaphroditism type I. The karyotype is 46,XY. Various defects in the androgen receptor gene at Xq11–q12 have been reported in patients with the complete form of androgen insensitivity: deletion of the steroid binding domain of the gene (Brown *et al.* 1988), aberrant MRNA splicing (Ris-Stalpers *et al.* 1990), and in Reifenstein's syndrome a point mutation within the DNA binding domain (Wooster *et al.* 1992). Androgen insensitivity has also been reported in severe pseudovaginal perineal–scrotal hypospadias with autosomal recessive inheritance (Opitz *et al.* 1972; Keenan 1980); and in one report in a case of Robinow's syndrome with ambiguous genitalia, glandular hypospadias, and persistent Mullerian ducts (Schonau *et al.* 1990).

A study of 10 patients with severe (penile or penoscrotal) hypospadias of unknown cause found evidence of neither 5 alphareductase deficiency nor partial androgen receptor defect in any of them (Gearhart *et al.* 1988), in contrast to earlier studies suggesting that androgen insensitivity may be involved in the less severe, common primary hypospadias (Svensson and Snochowski 1979; Keenan *et al.* 1984), and one more recent study of severe hypospadias (Schweikert *et al.* 1989).

Among syndromes in which hypospadias occurs is the autosomal dominant Opitz-G syndrome for midline defects, including hyperspadias, hypotelorism, oesophageal dysmobility with dysphagia, laryngo–tracheal clefts, mental retardation, renal or ureteral anomalies, cleft palate or bifid uvula, and congenital heart defects (Opitz 1987; Wilson and Oliver 1988). Hypospadias also occurs in the very similar BBB syndrome in which the same features occur but in which dysphagia is not a feature. The BBB syndrome may be identical in fact to Opitz G syndrome or may be distinct.

Other such syndromes include autosomal recessive 3-M syndrome in which one study found hypospadias in two out of three male cases (Winter *et al.* 1984); the recessive Smith–Lemli–Opitz syndrome (Joseph *et al.* 1987); recessive cryptophthalmos syndrome (Gupta and Saxena 1962; Boyd *et al.* 1988); dominant Rapp–Hodgkin ectodermal dysplasia (Wannarachne *et al.* 1972); dominant Rieger's syndrome (Jorgenson *et al.* 1978); recessive N syndrome (Hess *et al.* 1974); a probably recessive syndrome of radial and maxillary defects (Schmitt *et al.* 1982); the recessive brachio–skeletal–genital syndrome with penoscrotal hypospadias (Elsahy and Waters 1971); recessive Bowen syndrome (Bowen *et al.* 1964); the autosomal dominant syndrome of hypotelorism, submucosal cleft palate, and hypospadias (Schilbach and Rott 1988); the autosomal recessive syndrome of hypertelorism, hypospadias, tetralogy of Fallot (Farag and Teebi 1990); the sporadic triad of ectopic vas deferens, imperforate anus, and hypospadias (Hicks *et al.* 1989); a recessive syndrome of fronto–facio–nasal dysostosis with hypospadias and syndactyly (Richieri-Costa *et al.* 1989); an either autosomal or X-linked recessive syndrome with microcephaly, facial dysmorphism, mental retardation, joint laxity, nail dysplasia, and hypospadias (Goldblatt *et al.* 1987); and an isolated report of sensorineural deafness, synostosis, and hypospadias (Pfeiffer and Kapferer 1988).

Hypospadias is only an occasional finding in the autosomal domininant Shprintzen velofacio–cardial syndrome (Shprintzen *et al.* 1981), the dominant multiple lentigenes syndrome (Moynahan 1962), the recessive Dubowitz syndrome (Wilroy *et al.* 1978), the recessive Biemond II syndrome (Blumel and Kniker 1959), sacral agenesis (Crawfurd *et al.* 1992), and hand–foot–genital syndrome (Fryns *et al.* 1993*b*).

References

Aarskog, D. (1970). Clinical and cytogenetic studies in hypospadias. *Acta Paedr. Scand.*, **Suppl. 203**, 1–62.

Ades, L. C., Clapton, W. K., Morphett, A., Morris, L. L., and Haan, E. A. (1994). Polydactyly, campomelia, ambiguous genitalia, cystic dysplastic kidneys, and cerebral malformations in a fetus of consanguineous parents: a new multiple malformation syndrome, or a severe form of oral–facial digital syndrome type IV? *Am. J. Med. Genet.*, **49**, 211–17.

Aggarwal, V. K. and Jones, K. V. (1989). Vesicoureteric reflux: screening of first degree relatives. *Arch. Dis. Child.*, **64**, 1538–41.

Alfi, I., Donnell, G. N., Allerdice, P. W., and Derencsenyi, A. (1976). The 9p—syndrome. *Ann. Genet.*, **19**, 11–16.

Al-Gazali, L. I., Farndon, P., Burn, J., Flannery, D. B., Davison, C., and Mueller, R. F. (1990). The Schinzel–Giedion syndrome. *J. Med. Genet.*, **27**, 42–7.

Anderson, P. A. M. and Rickwood, A. M. K. (1991). Features of primary vesicoureteric reflux detected by prenatal sonography. *Br. J. Urol*, **67**, 267–71.

Antonakopoulos, G. N., Fuggle, W. J., Newman, J., Considine, J., and O'Brien, J. M. (1985). Idiopathic hydronephrosis: light microscopic features and pathogenesis. *Arch. Pathol. Lab Med.*, **109**, 1097–101.

Atwell, J. D. (1985). Familial pelvi-ureteric junction hydronephrosis and its association with a duplex pelvicalyceal system and vesicoureteric reflux. A family study. *Br. J. Urol.*, **57**, 365–9.

Atwell, J. D., Cook, P. L., Howell, C. J., Hyde, I., and Parker, B. C. (1974). Familial incidence of bifid and double ureters. *Arch. Dis. Child.*, **49**, 390–3.

Atwell, J. D., Cook, P. L., Strong, L., and Hyde, I. (1977). The interrelationship between vesicoureteric reflux, trigonal abnormalities, and a bifid pelvicalyceal collecting system: a family study. *Br. J. Urol.*, **49**, 97–107.

Atwell, J. D. and Allen, N. H. (1980). The interrelationship between paraureteric diverticula, vesicoureteral reflux, and duplication of the pelvicaliceal collecting system: a family study. *Br. J. Urol.*, **52**, 269–73.

Avellan, L. (1975). The incidence of hypospadias in Sweden. *Scand. J. Plast. Reconstr. Surg.*, **9**, 129–39.

Bamforth, S. J. and Baird, P. A. (1989). Spina bifida and hydrocephalus: a population study over a 35-year period. *Am. J. Hum. Genet.*, **44**, 225–32.

Barakat, A. Y., Seikaly, M. G., and Der Kaloustian, V. M. (1986). Urogenital abnormalities in genetic disease. *J. Urol.*, **136**, 778–85.

Bauer, S. B., Bull, M. J., and Retik, A. B. (1979). Hypospadias: a familial study. *J. Urol.*, **121**, 474–7.

Bauer, S. B., Retik, A. B., and Colodny, A. H. (1981). Genetic aspects of hypospadias. *Urol. Clin. N. Am.*, **8**, 559–64.

Blumel, J. and Kniker, W. T. (1959). Lawrence–Moon–Biedl syndrome: review of the literature and a report of five cases including a family group with three affected males. *Texas Rep. Biol. Med.*, **17**, 391–410.

Bois, E., Feingold, J., Benmaiz, H., and Briard, M. L. (1975). Congenital urinary tract malformations: epidemiologic and genetic aspects. *Clin. Genet.*, **8**, 37–47.

Bowen, P., Lee, C. N. S., Zellweger, H., and Lindenburg, R. (1964). A familial syndrome of multiple congenital defects. *Bull. John Hopkins Hosp.*, **114**, 402–14.

Boyd, P. A., Keeling, J. W., and Lindenbaum, R. H. (1988). Fraser syndrome (cryptophthalmos-syndactyly syndrome): a review of 11 cases with post-mortem findings. *Am. J. Med. Genet.*, **31**, 159–68.

Brown, T. R., Lubahn, D. B., Wilson, E. M., Joseph, D. R., French, F. S., and Migeon, C. J. (1988). Deletion of the steroid-binding domain of the human androgen receptor gene in one family with complete androgen insensitivity syndrome: evidence for further genetic heterogeneity in this syndrome. *Proc. Nat. Acad. Sci.*, **85**, 8151–5.

Byrne, J. and Blanc, W. A. (1985). Malformations and chromosome anomalies in spontaneously aborted fetuses with a single umbilical artery. *Am. J. Obstet., Gynecol.*, **151**, 340–2.

Cameron, T. H., Lachiewicz, A. M., and Aylesworth, A. S. (1991). Townes–Brocks syndrome in two mentally retarded youngsters. *Am. J. Med. Genet.*, **41**, 1–4.

Carey, J. C., Greenbaum, B., and Hall, B. D. (1978). The OEIS Complex (omphalocele, exstrophy, imperforate anus, spinal defects). *Birth Defects: Orig. Art. Ser.*, **14** (6B), 253–63.

Carter, C. O. (1984). The genetics of urinary tract malformations. *J. Genet. Hum.*, **32**, 23–9.

Carter, C. O., Evans, K., and Pescia, G. (1979). A family study of renal agenesis. *J. Med. Genet.*, **16**, 176–88.

Chapman, C. J., Bailey, R. R., Janus, G. D., Abbott, G. D., and Lynn, K. L. (1985). Vesicoureteric reflux: segregation analysis. *Am. J. Med. Genet.*, **20**, 577–84.

Cherstvoy, E., Lazjuk, G., Lurie, I., Ostrovskaya, T., and Shved, I. (1980). Syndrome of multiple congenital malformations including phocomelia, thrombocytopenia, encephalocele, and urogenital abnormalities. *Lancet*, **2**, 485.

Chitayat, D., Hahm, S. Y. E., Marion, R. W., Sachs, G. S., Goldman, D., Hutcheon, R. G., *et al.* (1987). Further delineation of the McKusick–Kaufman hydrometrocolpos-polydactyly syndrome. *Am. J. Dis. Child.*, **141**, 1133–6.

Corsello, G., Maresi, E., Corrao, A. M., Dimita, U., Locasio, M., Cammarata, M., *et al.* (1992). VATER/VACTERL association: clinical variability and expanding phenotype including laryngeal stenosis. *Am. J. Med. Genet.*, **44**, 813–15.

Cote, G. B., Petmezaki, S., and Bastakis, N. (1979). A gene for hypospadias in a child with presumed tetrasomy 18p. *Am. J. Med. Genet.*, **4**, 141–6.

Crawfurd, M. d'A (1988). Primary renal tract malformations. In: *The genetics of renal tract disorders*, pp. 525–99. Oxford University Press, Oxford.

Crawfurd, M. d'A., Cheshire, J., Wilson, T. M., and Woodhouse, C. R. J. (1992). The demonstration of monozygosity in twins discordant for sacral agenesis. *J. Med. Genet.*, **29**, 437–8.

Czeizel, A. (1985). Increasing trends in congenital malformations of male external genitalia. *Lancet*, **1**, 462–3.

Czeizel, A., Toth, J., and Erodi, E. (1979). Aetiological studies of hypospadias in Hungary. *Hum. Hered.*, **29**, 166–71.

Davee, M. A., Moore, C. A., Bull, M. J., and Hodes, M. E. (1992). Familial occurrence of renal and Mullerian duct hypoplasia, craniofacial anomalies, severe growth, and developmental delay. *Am. J. Med. Genet.*, **44**, 293–6.

Deaton, J. G. (1973). The mortality rate and causes of death among institutionalized mongols in Texas. *J. Ment. Defic. Res.*, **17**, 117–22.

De Vargas, A., Evans, K., Ransley, P., Rosenberg, A. R., Rothwell, D., Sherwood, T., *et al.* (1978). A family study of vesicoureteric reflux. *J. Med. Genet.*, **15**, 85–96.

Dobrowolski, Z., Kleczkowska, A., Bugajski, A., Galka, M., and Augustyn, M. (1980). Familial hypospadias in three generations. *Int. Urol., Nephrol.*, **12**, 217–20.

Donnai, D. and Farndon, P. A. (1986). Walker–Warburg syndrome (Warburg syndrome, HARD ± syndrome). *J. Med. Genet.*, **23**, 200–3.

Donnai, D., Young, I. D., Owen, W. G., Clark, S. A., Miller, P. F. W., and Knox, W. F. (1986). The lethal multiple congenital anomaly syndrome of polydactyly, sex reversal, renal hypoplasia, and unilobular lungs. *J. Med. Genet.*, **23**, 64–71.

Elsahy, N. I. and Waters, W. R. (1971). The brachio–skeletal genital syndrome: a new hereditary syndrome. *Plast. Recontructs. Surg.*, **48**, 542–50.

Elstner, C. L., Carey, J. C., Livingston, G., Moeschler, J., and Lubinsky, M. (1984). Further delineation of the 10p deletion syndrome. *Pediatrics*, **73**, 620–75.

Evans, J. A., Vitez, M., and Czeizel, A. (1992a). Patterns of acrorenal malformation associations. *Am. J. Med. Genet.*, **44**, 413–19.

Evans, J. A., Phillips, S., Reed, M., and Czeizel, A. (1992b). Acro–renal–mandibular syndrome: three new cases. *Proc. Greenwood Genet. Center*, **11**, 141.

Fabia, J. and Drolette, M. (1970). Malformations and leukaemia in children with Down's syndrome. *Pediatrics*, **45**, 60–70.

Farag, T. I. and Teebi, A. S. (1990). Autosomal recessive inheritance of a syndrome of hypertelorism, hypospadias, and tetralogy of Fallot. *Am. J. Med. Genet.*, **35**, 516–18.

Fedder, J. (1990). Uterus didelphys associated with duplex kidneys and ureters. *Acta Obstet. Gynecol. Scand.*, **69**, 665–6.

Francannet, C., Lefrancois, P., Dechelotte, P., Robert, E., Malpuech, G. and Robert, J. M. (1990). Fraser syndrome with renal agenesis in two consanguineous Turkish families. *Am. J. Med. Genet.*, **36**, 477–9.

Francke, U., Holmes, L. B., Atkins, L., and Ricardi, V. M. (1979). Aniridia–Wilms' tumor association: evidence for a specific deletion of 11p13. *Cytogenet. Cell Genet.*, **24**, 185–92.

Fraser, F. C., Ayme, S., Halal, F., and Sproule, J. (1983). Autosomal dominant duplication of the renal collecting system, hearing loss, and external ear anomalies: a new syndrome? *Am. J. Med. Genet.*, **14**, 473–8.

Freire-Maia, N., Pinheiro, M., and Opitz, J. M. (1982). The neurofaciodigitorenal (NFDR) syndrome. *Am. J. Med. Genet.*, **11**, 329–36.

Froster-Iskenius, U. and Meinecke, P. (1992). Encephalocele, radial defects, cardiac, gastrointestinal, anal, and renal anomalies: a new multiple congenital anomaly (MCA) syndrome? *Clinical Dysmorph.*, **1**, 37–41.

Frydman, M., Greiber, C., and Cohen, H. A. (1985). Uncomplicated familial hypospadias: evidence for autosomal recessive inheritance. *Am. J. Med. Genet.*, **21**, 51–5.

Fryns, J. P., Kleczkowska, A., Moerman, P. and Vandenberghe, K. (1993a). Hereditary hydronephrosis and the short arm of chromosome 6. *Hum. Genet.*, **91**, 515–16.

Fryns, J. P., Vogels, A., Decock, P., Vandenberghe, H. (1993b). The hand–foot–geital syndrome: on the variable expression in affected males. *Clin. Genet.*, **43**, 232–4.

Gearhart, J. P., Linhard, H. R., Berkovitz, G. D., Jeffs, R. D., and Brown, T. R. (1988). Androgen receptor levels and 5α-reductase activities in preputial skin and chordee tissue of boys with isolated hypospadias. *J. Urol.*, **140**, 1243–6.

Giraud, F., Mattei, J.-F., Mattei, M.-G., and Birnard, R. (1975). Trisomie partielle 11q et translocation familiale 11–22. *Humangenetik*, **28**, 343–7.

Glenn, J. F. (1959). Analysis of 51 patients with horseshoe kidney. *New Engl. J. Med.*, **261** 684–7.

Goldblatt, J., Wallis, C., and Viljoen, D. (1987). A new hypospadias—mental retardation syndrome in three brothers. *Am. J. Dis. Child.*, **141**, 1168–9.

Gordon, A. C., Thomas, D. F. M., Arthur, R. J., Irving, H. C., and Smith, S. E. W. (1990). Prenatally diagnosed reflux: a follow-up study. *Br. J. Urol.*, **65**, 407–12.

Greenberg, F., Stratton, R. F., Lockhart, L. H., Elder, F. F. B., Dobyns, W. B., and Ledbetter, D. H. (1986). Familial Miller–Dieker syndrome associated with pericentric inversion of chromosome 17. *Am. J. Med. Genet.*, **23**, 853–9.

Greskovich, F. J. III, and Nyberg, L. M. Jr. (1988). The prune-belly syndrome: a review of its etiology, defects, treatment, and prognosis. *J. Urol.*, **140**, 707–12.

Gupta, S. P. and Saxena, R. C. (1962). Cryptophthalmos. *Brit. J. Ophthal.*, **46**, 629–32.

Gustavson, K.-H., Lundberg, P. O., and Nicol, P. (1988). Familial partial trisomy 5p resulting from segregation of an insertional translocation. *Clin. Genet.*, **35**, 404–9.

Halal, F., Homsy, M., and Perreault, GH. (1984). Acro–renal–ocular syndrome: autosomal dominant thumb hypoplasia, renal ectopia, and eye defect. *Am. J. Med. Genet.*, **17**, 753–62.

Hamerton, J. L. (1971). Clinical cytogenetics. In: *Human cytogenetics, Vol. 2*, p. 32. Academic Press, New York.

Harris, E. L. and Beaty, T. H. (1993). Segregation analysis of hypospadias: a reanalysis of published pedigree data. *Am. J. Hum. Genet.*, **45**, 420–5.

Haslam, R. H. A., Berman, W., and Heller, R. M. (1973). Renal abnormalities in the Russell–Silver syndrome. *Pediatrics*, **51**, 216–22.

Herbert, A. A., Esterly, N. B., Holbrook, K. A., and Hall, J. C. (1987). The CHILD syndrome: histological and ultrastructural studies. *Arch. Dermatol.*, **123**, 503–9.

Hess, R. O., Kaveggia, E. G., and Opitz, J. M. (1974). The N syndrome: a 'new' multiple congenital anomaly–mental retardation syndrome. *Clin. Genet.*, **6**, 237–46.

Hicks, C. M., Skoog, S. J., and Done, S. (1989). Ectopic vas deferens, imperforate anus, and hypospadias: a new triad. *J. Urol.*, **141**, 586–8.

Hilson, D. (1957). Malformations of ears as sign of malformation of the genitourinary tract. *Br. Med. J.*, **2**, 785–9.

Houlston, R. and Macdermot, K. (1992). Acrorenal syndrome: further observations. *Clin. Dysmorph.*, **1**, 23–8.

Hunt, G. M. and Whitaker, R. H. (1987). The pattern of congenital renal anomalies associated with neural tube defects. *Develop. Med. Child Neurol.*, **29**, 91–5.

Hinter A. G. W., Jurenka, S., Thompson, D., and Evans, J. A. (1982). Absence of the cerebellar granular layer, mental retardation, tapetoretinal degeration, and progressive glomerulopathy: an autosomal recessive oculo–renal–cerebellar syndrome. *Am. J. Med. Genet.*, **11**, 383–95.

Imperato-McGinley, J., Guerrero, L, Gautier, T., and Peterson, R. E. (1974). Steroid 5 α-reductase deficiency in man: an inherited form of male pseudohermaphroditism. *Science*, **186**, 1213–15.

Ives, E., Coffey, R., and Carter, C. O. (1980). A family study of bladder exstrophy. *J. Med. Genet.*, **17**, 139–41.

Izquiredo, L., Porteous, M., Paramo, P. G., and Connor, J. M. (1992). Evidence for genetic heterogeneity in hereditary hydronephrosis caused by pelvic-ureteric junction obstruction, with one locus assigned to chromosome 6p. *Hum. Genet.*, **89**, 557–60.

Janin-Mercier, A., Palcoux, J. B., Gubler, M. C., de Latour, M., Dalens, H., and Fonck, Y. (1985). Oligomeganephronic renal hypoplasia with tapetoretinal degeneration. *Virchows Arc. [Pathol. Anat.]*, **407**, 477–83.

Johanson, A. and Blizzard, R. (1971). A syndrome of congenital aplasia of the alae nasi, deafness, hypothyroidism, dwarfism, absent permanent teeth, and malabsorption. *J. Pediatr*, **79**, 982–7.

Johnson, V. P. and Munson, D. P. (1990). A new syndrome of aphalangy, hemivertebrae, and urogenital–intestinal dysgenesis. *Clin. Genet.*, **38**, 346–52.

Jorgenson, R. J., Levin, L. S., Cross, H. E., Yoder, F., and Kelly, T. E. (1978). The Rieger syndrome. *Am. J. Med. Genet.*, **2**, 307–18.

Joseph, D. B., Uehling, D. T., Gilbert, E., and Laxova, R. (1987). Genitourinary abnormalities associated with the Smith–Lemli–Opitz syndrome. *J. Urol.*, **137**, 719–21.

Karnes, P. S., Day, D., Berry, S. A., and Pierpoint, M. E. M. (1991). Jarcho–Levin syndrome: four new cases and classification of subtypes. *Am J. Med. Genet.*, **40**, 264–70.

Keenan, B. S. (1980). Pseudovaginal perineoscrotal hypospadias: genetic heterogeneity. *Urol. Clin. N. Amer.*, **7**, 393–407.

Keenan, B. S., McNeel, R. L., and Gonzales, E. T. (1984). Abnormality of intracellular 5 α-dihydrotestosterone binding in simple hypospadias: studies on equilibrium steroid binding in sonicates of genital skin fibroblasts. *Ped. Res.*, **18**, 216–20.

Kenda, R. B., Kenig, T., and Budihna, N. (1991). Detecting vesico-ureteral reflux in asymptomatic siblings of chidren with reflux by direct radionuclide cystography. *Eur. J. Pediatr.*, **150**, 735–7.

Kenda, R. B. and Fettich, J. J. (1992). Vesicoureteric reflux and renal scars in asymptomatic siblings of children with reflux. *Arch. Dis. Child.*, **67**, 506–8.

Kleczkowska, A., Fryns, J. P., Moerman, P., Vandenberghe, K. and Vandenberghe, H. (1987). Trisomy of the short arm of chromosome 5: autopsy data in a malformed newborn with inv dup (5) (p13.1–p15.3). *Clin. Genet.*, **32**, 49–56.

Krassikoff, N. and Sekhon, G. S. (1990). Terminal deletion of 6q and Fryn's syndrome: A microdeletion/syndrome pair. *Am. J. Med., Genet.* **36**, 363–4.

Lachiewicz, A. M., Sibley, R., and Michael, A. F. (1985). Hereditary renal disease and preauricular pits: report of a kindred. *J. Pediatr.*, **106**, 948–50.

Leck, I., Record, R. G., McKeown, T., and Edwards, J. H. (1968). The incidence of malformations in Birmingham, England, 1950–1959. *Teratology*, **1**, 263–80.

Lejeune, J., Gautier, M., Lafourcade, J., Berger, R., and Turpin, R. (1964). Délétion partielle du bras court du chromosome 5. Cinquième cas de syndrome du cri du chat. *Ann. Genet.*, **7**, 7–12.

Leung, T. J., Baird, P. A., and McGillivray, B. (1985). Hypospadias in British Columbia. *Amer. J. Med. Genet.*, **21**, 39–48.

Lin, A. E., McPherson, E., Nwokoro, N. A., Clemens, M., Losken, H. W., and Mulvihill, J. J. (1993). Further delineation of Baller–Gerold syndrome. *Am. J. Med. Genet.*, **45**, 519–24.

Lin, H. J., Noiforchu, F., and Patell, S. (1993). Exstrophy of the cloaca in a 47, XXX child: review of genitourinary malformations in triple X patients. *Am. J. Med. Genet.*, **45**, 761–3.

Lowry, R. B. and Kliman, M. R. (1976). Hypospadias in successive generations—possible dominant gene inheritance. *Clin. Genet.*, **9**, 285–8.

Lurie, I. W. and Lazjuk, G. I. (1972). Partial monosomies 18. Review of cytogenetical and phenotypic variants. *Humangenetik*, **15**, 203–22.

Lurie, I. W., Lazjuk, G. I., Ussova, Y. I., Presman, E. B., and Gurevich, D. B. (1980). The Wolf–Hirschhorn syndrome. I. Genetics. *Clin. Genet.*, **17**, 375–84.

McNamara, H. M., Onwude, J. L., and Thornton, J. G. (1994). Megacystis–microcolon–intestinal hypoperistalsis syndrome: a case report supporting autosomal recessive inheritance. *Prenat. Diagnosis*, **14**, 153–4.

McPherson, E., Carey, J., Kramer, A., Hall, J. G., Pauli, R. M., Schimke, R. N., *et al.* (1987). Dominantly inherited renal adysplasia. *Amer. J. Med. Genet.*, **26**, 863–72.

Martinez-Frias, M. L. (1994). Spina bifida and hypospadias: a non-random association or an X-linked recessive condition? *Am. J. Med. Genet.*, **52**, 5–8.

Matlai, P. and Beral, V. (1985). Trends in congenital malformations of external genitalia. *Lancet*, **1**, 108.

Mattei, J.-F. and Ayme, S. (1983). Syndrome of polydactyly, cleft lip, lingual haemartomas, renal hypoplasia, hearing loss, and psychomotor retardation: variant of the Mohr syndrome or a new syndrome. *J. Med. Genet.*, **20**, 433–5.

Melnick, M. (1980). Hereditary hearing loss and ear dysplasia–renal dysplasia syndromes: syndrome delineation and possible pathogenesis. *Birth Defects Orig. Art. Series*, **16**(7), 59–72.

Merlob, P., Kohn, G., Litwin, A., Nissenkorn, I., Katznelson, M. B.-M., and Reisner, S. H. (1989). New chromosome aberration: duplication of a large part of chromosome 4q and partial deletion of chromosome 1q. *Am. J. Med. Genet.*, **32**, 22–6.

Messelink, E. J., Aronson, D. C., Knvist, M., Heij, H. A. and Vos, A. (1994). Four cases of bladder exstrophy in two families. *J. Med. Genet.*, **31**, 490–2.

Middleton, G. W., Howards, S. S., and Gillenwater, J. Y. (1975). Sex-linked familial reflux. *J. Urol.*, **114**, 36–9.

Milteny, M., Czeizel, A. E., Balogh, L., and Detre, Z. (1992). Autosomal recessive acrorenal syndrome. *Am. J. Med. Genet.*, **43**, 789–90.

Moerman, P., van Damme, B., Proesmans, W., Devlieger, H., Goddeeris, P., and Lauweryns, J. (1984). Oligomeganephronic renal hypoplasia in siblings. *J. Pediatr.*, **105**, 75–7.

Moerman, P., Fryns, J-P., van der Steen, K., Kleczkowska, A., and Lauweryns, J. (1988). The pathology of trisomy 13 syndrome: a study of 12 cases. *Hum. Genet.*, **80**, 349–56.

Moreno-Fuenmayor, H., Zachai, E. H., Mellman, W. J., and Anson, M. (1975). Familial partial trisomy of long arm of chromosome 10 (q 24–26). *Pediatrics*, **56**, 756–61.

Moynahan, L. J. (1962). Multiple symmetrical moles with psychic and somatic infantilism and genital hypoplasia. *Proc. Roy. Soc. Med.*, **55**, 959–60.

Münke, M., McDonald, D. M., Gonister, A., Gorlin, R. J. and Zachai, E. H. (1990). Oral–facial–digital syndrome type VI (Varadi syndrome): further clinical delineation. *Am. J. Med. Genet.*, **35**, 360–9.

Murr, M. M., Waziri, M. H., Schelper, R. L., and Abu-Youself, M. (1992). Case of multivertebral anomalies, cloacal dygenesis, and other anomalies presenting prenatally as cystic kidneys. *Am. J. Med. Genet.*, **42**, 761–5.

Nakada, T., Furuta, H., Kazam, T., and Katayama, T. (1988). Unilateral renal agenesis with or without ipsilateral adrenal agenesis. *J. Urol.*, **140**, 933–7.

Naljamaldin, A., Burge, D. M., and Atwell, J. D. (1990). Reflux nephropathy secondary to intrauterine vesicoureteric reflux. *J. Pediat. Surg.*, **25**, 387–90.

Nation, E. F. (1994). Duplication of kidney and ureter: a statistical study of 230 new cases. *J. Urol.*, **51**, 456–65.

Nevin, N. C., Hill, A. E., and Carson, D. J. (1991). Facio–cardio–renal (Eastman–Bixler) syndrome. *Am. J. Med. Genet.*, **40**, 31–3.

Niebuhr, E. (1977). Partial trisomies and deletions of chromosome 13. In: *New chromosomal syndromes* (ed. J. J. Yunis), pp. 273–99. Academic Press, New York.

Nothen, M. M., Knofle, G., Fodisch, H.-J., and Zerres, K. (1993). Steinfeld syndrome: report of a second family and further delineation of a rare autosomal dominant disorder. *Am. J. Med. Genet.*, **46**, 467–70.

Numabe, H., Nagafuchi, S., Nakahori, Y., Tamura, T., Kiuchi, H., Namiki, M., *et al.* (1992). DNA analyses of XX and XX-hypospadiac males. *Hum. Genet.*, **90**. 211–14.

Oley, C. A., Baraitser, M., and Grant, D. B. (1988). A reappraisal of the CHARGE association. *J. Med. Genet.*, **25**, 147–56.

Opitz, J. M. (1987). G syndrome (hypertelorism with esophageal abnormality and hypospadias, or hypospadias–dysphagia, or 'Opitz–Frias' or 'Opitz-G' syndrome)—perspective in 1987 and bibliography. *Am. J. Med. Genet.*, **28**, 275–85.

Opitz, J. M., Simpson, J. L., Sarto, G. E., New, M., and German, J. (1972). Pseudovaginal perineoscrotal hypospadias. *Clin. Genet.*, **3**, 1–26.

Osathanondh, V. and Potter, E. L. (1964). Pathogenesis of polycystic kidneys. *Arch. Pathol.*, **77**, 459–512.

Pavanello, R. de. C. M., Eiger, A., and Otto, P. A. (1988). Relationship between Mayer–Rokitansky–Kuster (MRK) anomaly and hereditary renal adysplasia (HRA). *Am. J. Med. Genet.*, **29**, 845–9.

Pfeiffer, R. A. and Kapferer, L. (1988). Sensorineural deafness, hypospadias, and synostosis of metacarpals and metatarsals 4 and 5: a previously apparently undescribed MCA/MR syndrome. *Am. J. Med. Genet.*, **31**, 5–10.

Piantanida, M., Tiberti, A., Plebani, A., Martelli, P., and Danesino, C. (1993). Cerebro–reno–digital syndrome in two sibs. *Am. J. Med. Genet.*, **47**, 420–2.

Preus, M., Kaplan. P., and Kirkham, T. H. (1977). Renal anomalies and oligohydramnios in the cerebro–occulofacial–skeletal syndrome. *Am. J. Dis. Child.*, **131**, 62–4.

Rethore, M. O. (1977). New chromosomal syndromes. In: *Chromosomes in biology and medicine* (ed. J. J. Yunis), pp. 119–83, Academic Press, New York.

Rich, M. A., Heimler, A., Waber, L., and Brock, W. A. (1987). Autosomal dominant transmission of ureteral triplication and bilateral amastia. *J. Urol.*, **137**, 102–5.

Richieri-Costa, A., Montagnoli, L., and Kamiya, T. Y. (1989). New syndrome: autosomal recessive acro–fronto–facio–nasal dysostosis associated with genitourinary anomalies. *Am. J. Med. Genet.*, 33, 121–4.

Ris-Stalpers, C., Kuiper, G. G. J. M., Faber, P. W., Schweikert, H. U., van Rooij, H. C. J., Zegers, N. D., *et al.* (1990). Aberrant splicing of androgen receptor mRNA results in synthesis of a nonfunctional receptor protein in a patient with androgen insensitivity. *Proc. Natl. Acad., Sci., USA*, 87, 7866–70.

Roodhooft, A. M., Birnholz, J. C., and Holmes, L. B. (1984). Familial nature of congenital absence and severe dysgenesis of both kidneys. *New Engl., J. Med.*, 310, 1341–5.

Rose, N. C., Schneider, A., McDonald-McGinn, D. M., Caserta, C., Emanuel, B. S., and Zackai, E. H. (1991). Interstitial deletion of 4 (q21q25) in a liveborn male. *Am. J. Med. Genet.*, 40, 77–9.

Rüdiger, R. A., Schmidt, W, Loose, D. A., and Passarge, E. (1971). Severe developmental failure with coarse facial features, distal limb hypoplasia, thickened palmar creases, bifid uvula, and ureteral stenosis: a previously unidentified familial disorder with renal outcome. *J. Pediatr.*, 79, 977–87.

Saez, J. M., Morera, A. M., De Peretti, E., and Bertrand, J. (1972). Further *in vivo* studies in male pseudohermaphroditism with gynecomastia due to a testicular 17-ketosteroid reductase defect (compared to a case of testicular feminization). *J. Clin. Endocr.*, 34, 598–600.

Schilbach, U. and Rott, H. D. (1988). Ocular hypotelorism, submucosal cleft palate, and hypospadias: a new autosomal dominant syndrome. *Am. J. Med. Genet.*, 31, 863–70.

Schimke, R. N. and King, C. R. (1980). Hereditary urogenital adysplasia. *Clin. Genet.*, 18, 417–20.

Schimmenti, L. A., Pierpont, M. E., Sharma, A. K., Vernier, R., Kashtan, C. E., Johnson, M. R., *et al.* (1994). Autosomal dominant optic nerve colobomas, renal anomalies and vesicoureteral reflux—a new syndrome. *Am. J. Hum. Genet.*, 55(3), Suppl. p.A92. Abstract 516.

Schinzel, A., Schmid, W., Fraccaro, M., Tiepolo, L., Zuffardi, O., Opitz, J. M., *et al.* (1981). The 'cat-eye syndrome': Dicentric small marker chromosome probably derived from a no. 22 (tetrasomy 22 pter q11) associated with a characteristic phenotype. Report of 11 patients and delineation of the clinical picture. *Hum. Genet.*, 57, 148–58.

Schmitt, E., Gillenwater, J. Y., and Kelley, T. E. (1982). An autosomal dominant syndrome of radial hypoplasia, triphalangeal thumbs, hypospadias, and maxillary diastema. *Am. J. Med. Genet.*, 13, 63–9.

Scholtmeizer, R. J. and Van Mastrigt, R. (1991). The effect of oxyphenonium bromide and oxybutinin hydrochloride on detrusor contractibility and reflux in children with vesicoureteral reflux and detrusor instability. *J. Urol.*, 146, 660–2.

Schonau, E., Pfeiffer, R. A., Schweikert, H. U., Bowing, B., and Schott, G. (1990). Robinow or 'fetal face syndrome' in a male infant with ambiguous genitalia and androgen receptor deficiency. *Eur. J. Pediatr.*, 149, 615–17.

Schweikert, H. U., Schlueter, M., and Romalo, G. (1989). Intracellular and nuclear binding of (3H) dihydrotestosterone in cultured genital skin fibroblasts of patients with severe hypospadias. *J. Clin. Invest.*, 83, 662–8.

Seaver, L. H., Grimes, J., and Erickson. R. P. (1994). Female pseudohermaphroditism with multiple caudal anomalies: absence of Y-specific DNA sequences as pathogenetic factors. *Am. J. Hum. Genet.*, 51, 16–21.

Shapiro, E., Lepor, H., and Jeffs, R. D. (1984). The inheritance of the exstrophy-epispadias complex. *J. Urol.*, 132, 308–10.

Shprintzen, R. J., Goldberg, R. B., Young, D., and Wolford, L. (1981). The velo–cardio–facial syndrome: a clinical and genetic analysis. *Pediatrics*, 67, 167–72.

Smith, D. W., Bartlett, C., and Harrah, L. M. (1976). Monozygotic twinning and the Duhamel Anomaly (imperforate anus to sirenomelia): a non-random association between two aberrations in morphogenesis. *Birth Defects Orig. Art. Series.* 12, 53–63.

Sorensen, H. R. (1953). *Hypospadias with special reference to aetiology.* Munksgaard, Copenhagen.

Stephens, F. D. (1983). *Congenital malformations of the urinary tract.* Praeger, New York.

Svenson, J. and Snochowski, M. (1979). Androgen receptor levels in preputial skin from boys with hypospadias. *J. Clin. Endocrinol. Metab.*, **49**, 340–5.

Sweet, R. A., Schrott, H. G., Kurland, R., and Culp, O. S. (1974). Study of the incidence of hypospadias in Rochester, Minnesota, 1940–1970, and a case–control comparison of possible etiologic factors. *Mayo Clinic Proc.*, **49**, 52–8.

Taylor, A. I. (1968). Autosomal trisomy syndromes: a detailed study of 27 cases of Edward's syndrome and 27 cases of Patau's syndrome. *J. Med. Genet.*, **5**, 227–52.

Teebi, A. S. and Hassoon, M. M. (1991). Urofacial syndrome associated with hydrocephalus due to aqueductal stenosis. *Am. J. Med. Genet.*, **40**, 199–200.

Thomas, I. T., Fcas, J. L., Felix, V., Sanchez de Leon, L., Helnondez, R. A., and Janes M. C. (1986). Isolated and syndromic crytophthalmos. *Am. J. Med. Genet.*, **25**, 85–98.

Thomas, I. T., Honore, G. M., Jewett, T., Velvis, H., Garber, P., and Ruiz, C. (1993). Holzgreve syndrome: recurrence in sibs. *Am. J. Med. Genet.*, **45**, 767–9.

Traboulsi, E. I., Lenz, W., Gonzalez-Ramos, M., Siegel, J., Macrae, W. G., and Maumenee, I. H. (1988). The Lenz microphthalmia syndrome. *Am. J. Ophthalmol.*, **105**, 40–5.

Tsur, M., Linder, N., and Cappis, S. (1987). Hypospadias in a consanguineous family. *Am. J. Hum. Genet.*, **27**, 487–9.

Van den Abbeele, A. D., Treves, S. T., Lebowitz, R. L., Baver, S., Davis, R. T., Retik, A., *et al.* (1987). Vesicoureteral reflux in asymptomatic siblings of patients with known reflux: radionuclide cystography. *Pediatrics*, **79**, 147–53.

Wannarachne, N., Hall, B. D., and Smith, A. W. (1972). Ectodermal dysplasia and multiple defects (Rapp–Hodgkins type). *J. Pediat.*, **81**, 1217–18.

Welshimer, K. and Swift, M. (1982). Congenital malformations and developmental disabilities in ataxia-telangiectasia, Fanconi anemia, and xeroderma pigmentosum families. *Am. J. Hum. Genet.*, **34**, 789–93.

Wilkie, A. O. M., Amberger, J. S., and McKusick, V. A. (1994). A gene map of congenital malformations. *J. Med. Genet.*, **31**, 507–17.

Wilroy. R. S. Jr., Tipton, R. E., and Summitt, R. L. (1978). The Dubowitz syndrome. *Am. J. Med. Genet.*, **2**, 275–84.

Wilson, G. N., Dasouki, M., and Barr, M. (1985). Further delineation of the dup (3q) syndrome. *Am. J. Med. Genet.*, **22**, 117–23.

Wilson, G. N. and Oliver, W. J. (1988). Further delineation of the G syndrome: a manageable genetic cause of infantile dysphagia. *J. Med. Genet.*, **25**, 157–63.

Winter, J. S. D., Kohn, G., Mellman, W. J., and Wagner, S. (1968). A familial syndrome of renal, genital, and middle-ear anomalies. *J Pediatr.*, **72**, 88–93.

Winter, R. M., Baraitser, M., Grant, D. B., Preece, M. A., and Hall, C. M. (1984). The 3-M syndrome. *J. Med. Genet.*, **21**, 124–8.

Wooster, R., Mangion. J., Eeles, R., Smith, S., Dowsett, M., Averill, D., *et al.* (1992). A germ line mutation in the androgen receptor gene in two brothers with breast cancer and Reifenstein syndrome. *Nature Genetics*, **2**, 132–4.

Ying, K. L., Curry, C. J. R., Rajani, K. B., Kassel, S. H., and Sparkes, R. S. (1982). *De novo* interstitial deletion in the long arm of chromosome 9: a new chromosome syndrome. *J. Med. Genet.*, **19**, 68–70.

Yunis, E., Ramirez, E., and Uribe, J. G. (1980). Full trisomy 7 and Potter's syndrome. *Hum. Genet.*, **54**, 13–18.

Zuffardi, O. and Fraccaro, M. (1982). Gene mapping and serendipity. The locus for torticollis, keloids, cryptorchidism, and renal dysplasia (31430, McKusick) is at Xq 28, distal to the G6PD locus. *Hum. Genet.*, **62**, 280–1.

8

Cystic diseases of the kidney

Patricia A. Gabow

Introduction

The renal cystic diseases encompass a wide array of disorders which vary in their modes of inheritance, their associated abnormalities, and the degree to which they impact the health of the individual. Renal cystic disease can be congenital, inherited, or acquired (Table 8.1) (Gilbert-Barness *et al.* 1990). The number of disorders which are accompanied by renal cysts suggests that they are a somewhat non-specific kidney response to a variety of genetic and non-genetic aberrations. Renal cysts can be an isolated abnormality or a part of systemic disease. Similarly, cysts can be an incidental finding discovered during abdominal imaging procedures, surgery, or autopsy or can contribute to significant morbidity and mortality.

A reasonable overall approach to this diverse group of abnormalities is to consider them in the general categories of congenital, hereditary, or acquired cystic diseases. However, the latter group of diseases are not the subject of this book. In assessing a patient within this conceptual framework, the physician uses data from personal and family history, physical examination, imaging information, renal function data, and occasionally histologic and genetic data. Often these data must be obtained on both the affected person as well as his or her parents. This database serves to define possible inheritance patterns as well as type and severity of renal and extrarenal manifestations.

Congenital renal cystic diseases

Congenital disorders can be inherited or have no component of hereditary. As the name implies, these disorders generally are identified *in utero* or at birth and are often part of a syndromic constellation of abnormalities (Table 8.1). As such, they most frequently are in the purview of the paediatrician and paediatric nephrologist. These disorders are dealt with in detail in Chapter 13.1 and in this chapter only autosomal recessive and autosomal dominant polycystic kidney disease (ARPKD and ADPKD) will be discussed in detail. The precise diagnosis of congenital renal cystic disorders requires a careful history regarding familial disease occurrence, a detailed assessment of the associated abnormalities, and renal imaging and renal function tests to assess structural and functional severity. Because some of these disorders result from chromosomal aberrations, cytogenetic studies may be required (see Chapter 13.1). In these syndromes the impact of the renal cystic disease component on the overall health of the fetus or the child varies considerably.

Table 8.1 Renal cystic diseases. (Adapted from Gilbert-Barness *et al.* 1990)

Congenital renal cystic diseases
    Chromosomal abnormalities
    Unknown etiology
Hereditary renal cystic diseases
    Autosomal recessive cystic diseases
        Autosomal recessive polycystic kidney disease
        Meckel's syndrome
        Fryn's syndrome
        Oro–facial–digital syndrome
        Zellweger syndrome
        Glutaric acidemia type II
    Autosomal dominant cystic diseases
        Autosomal dominant polycystic kidney disease
        Tuberous sclerosis
        Von-Hippel–Lindau syndrome
Acquired renal cystic diseases
    Simple cysts
    Hypokalaemic-induced cysts (primary aldosteronism)
    Acquired cystic disease

Hereditary renal cystic diseases

Autosomal recessive polycystic kidney disease

Epidemiology and genetics

Autosomal recessive polycystic kidney disease (ARPKD) is a renal and hepatic disease which can present from *in utero* to adolescence. It is uncommon with an occurrence that has been variably estimated from between 1/10 000 to 1/50 000 births (Potter 1972). This wide range of reported frequency reflects, at least in part, the difficulties in correctly diagnosing the aetiology of renal cystic disease in neonates. The distribution of ARPKD in different ethnic and racial groups has not been defined. As a recessive disorder, both parents of an affected child carry one copy of the defective gene but are not clinically affected; each of their offspring has a one-in-four chance of inheriting the defective gene from both parents and thus having the disease. The different ages of onset and the variability in phenotype gave rise to the suggestion that the disorder may not result from a single gene defect. However, the presence of phenotypic variability within a given family (Kaplan *et al.* 1988; 1989) leads to the conclusion that this is likely a single gene disorder (Kaplan and Kaplan 1990). Recently, the ARPKD gene has been shown to be on chromosome 6 (Zerres *et al.* 1994). In examining families with different disease severity, no genetic heterogeneity has been found supporting that a single gene defect can cause the phenotypic array seen in the disease (Guay-Woodford *et al.* 1995).

Pathogenesis

The understanding of the pathogenesis of the disorder has been advanced considerably by the availability of several recessive animal models of polycystic renal disease. The best studied has been the cpk murine model. As in ADPKD (see below), there appear to be contributions of altered secretion, cell proliferation, and abnormal basement membrane composition in renal cystogenesis in recessive polycystic kidney disease. In the cpk model it is clear that cystogenesis begins in fetal life with dilatations in the proximal tubule; as the disease progresses in neonatal life, the collecting ducts become the primary site of tubular dilatation (Avner *et al.* 1987). The cystogenic process in this model appears to be, at least in part, a failure of differentiation. Unlike ADPKD where there may be an increased effect of epidermal growth factor (EGF) (see below), in this murine model of ARPKD, the EGF effect appears to be decreased or lacking (Gattone and Calvet 1991). The addition of EGF in fact ameliorates cyst formation, suggesting a role for EGF in collecting duct differentiation and maturation (Gattone and Lowden 1992).

As in ADPKD, there appears to be a role for alterations in Na-K ATPase in cyst formation. Total kidney Na-K ATPase is increased in affected mice from fetal day 17 to postnatal day 12 compared to age-matched control mice (Avner *et al.* 1988). Moreover, in the metanephric organ culture model derived from these cpk mice, cyst induction occurs with increases in Na-K ATPase and is prevented by manoeuvres such as oubain administration which decrease Na-K ATPase (Avner *et al.* 1985). Also, Na-K ATPase has a predominant apical lateral location in collecting tubules of affected mice in early postnatal life versus its basolateral location in the collecting tubules of age-matched control mice (Avner *et al.* 1992). Of interest, this apical lateral distribution is one which is found in early collecting tubule development in control mice, adding support to a failure of differentiation in cystogenesis in cpk mice (Avner *et al.* 1992). It is clear how altered Na-K ATPase location could alter sodium directional transport and thereby contribute to cyst development and growth. In fact, altered directional transport has been demonstrated in human ADPKD epithelia in culture (Wilson *et al.* 1991). However, this mislocation of Na-K ATPase may not be a necessary component for cyst formation since this finding has not been confirmed in human ARPKD kidney tissue (Avner and Sweeney 1992).

The proliferative aspect of cystogenesis in the cpk mouse has been demonstrated in the proximal tubule in the later stages of cystogenesis (Avner *et al.* 1987). Moreover, increased expression of the protooncogenes, c-fos, c-myc, and c-Ki-ras, has been observed in cpk mice in comparison to controls, creating a potential link between a gene and cyst formation. C-myc expression decreases in the first three weeks of postnatal life in normal mice, but in cystic mice c-myc expression increases during this time period (Harding *et al.* 1992).

Although gross abnormalities of extracellular matrix have not been noted in the cpk mouse, collagen IV and laminin biosynthesis are increased in cultured kidney epithelium from affected mice compared to control kidney murine epithelium (Taub *et al.* 1990). The relationship of all of the abnormalities observed in the cpk mouse model and human ARPKD remains to be determined after the isolation of both the murine and human gene and gene products.

Pathology

Grossly, the kidneys are large with a dotted appearance to the external surface and a spongy appearance to the cut surfaces due to the radially oriented fusiform cysts. Microscopically, the renal lesion is cystic dilatations of the collecting tubules and ducts (Verani *et al.* 1989). Peritubular fibrosis can be seen (Verani *et al.* 1989). The cysts are lined by cuboidal or low columnar epithelium; unlike ADPKD, it seems that polypoid proliferation in the cyst lining is unusual. In addition, renal adenomas which represent another clinical manifestation of increased cell proliferation in ADPKD do not appear to be commonly noted in ARPKD. The liver often grossly appears normal without distinct cysts, but microscopically, the liver reveals hamartomatous bile duct proliferation, ductal dilatation (usually without frank cysts), and enlarged portal areas with surrounding fibrosis to some degree in virtually all patients. These histological findings result in the occasional use of liver and/or kidney biopsy to establish the diagnosis.

Methods of diagnosis and clinical manifestations

ARPKD was previously called infantile polycystic kidney disease since it was assumed that a polycystic renal disease that presented in childhood was the recessive type. It has since become clear that autosomal dominant renal cystic diseases, including autosomal dominant polycystic kidney disease (ADPKD) and tuberous sclerosis (TS), can present *in utero*, at birth, or in childhood (see below). These two entities as well as the other congenital disorders and simple cysts need to be differentiated in any fetus or child who presents with renal cystic disease (Wenzl *et al.* 1970; Yu and Sheth 1985; Cole *et al.* 1987; Kaariainen 1987; Pretorius *et al.* 1987; Fick *et al.* 1993). Some of the differentiating characteristics of ARPKD and ADPKD are detailed in Table 8.2. The differentiation of ARPKD from ADPKD is important for the genetic counselling of the family, determining the need for evaluation of the child for other manifestations and for prognosis. The single most reliable method at this time for distinguishing ARPKD and ADPKD is ultrasonography of both parents. Family history is not a sufficiently sensitive distinguishing parameter since two-thirds of parents with a child with very early onset ADPKD did not know they had ADPKD until after the birth of the affected child (Pretorius *et al.* 1987; Fick *et al.* 1993). A normal ultrasonogram in both parents strongly supports the diagnosis of ARPKD. However, it is well to remember that normal parental sonograms can occur if non-paternity is operative;

Table 8.2   Characteristics of ARPKD and ADPKD in children

Variable	ARPKD	ADPKD
Parent with renal cysts	No	Yes (100% if parent older than 30 years)
Presentation with nephromegaly *in utero* or infancy	Common	Occurs
Ultrasonography *in utero* or infancy	Large, hyperechoic kidneys, usually without cysts	Large, hyperechoic kidneys, cysts in ~30%
Incidental finding of renal cyst(s)	Rare	Common
Hepatomegaly in infancy or childhood	Common	Very rare, if ever
Hypertension	Almost every child	Almost all children who present < 1 year, ~30% of others
Hematuria	Common	Common
Decreased renal concentrating ability	Common, moderately severe	Occurs in children with many cysts, mild
Decreased GFR	Almost every child	Common in children who present <1 year, uncommon in others
ESRD in childhood	Common	Occurs in children who present <1 year, uncommon in others

normal parental ultrasonograms can also occasionally occur in ADPKD if the parents are less than 30 years of age since individuals with the ADPKD gene have an 11–24% chance of having a normal ultrasonogram before age 30 (Parfrey *et al.* 1990).

Ultrasonography of the parents is also important in differentiating ARPKD and TS, but careful evaluation for the nonrenal manifestations of TS in both the child and the parent is equally important (Tables 8.2 and 8.3). It is important to note that children, more commonly than adults with TS, appear to have renal cystic disease either alone or in combination with angiolipoma (Stillwell *et al.* 1987). As in ARPKD and ADPKD, enlarged kidneys, abdominal masses, pain, haematuria, and proteinuria can occur in TS (Stillwell *et al.* 1987; Roach 1992). These similarities have lead to the misdiagnosis of TS as polycystic kidney disease (Wenzl *et al.* 1970).

Table 8.3 Comparison of autosomal dominant polycystic kidney diseases

Characteristic	ADPKD	TS	VHL
Prevalence	1/200–1/1000	1/10000–1/100000	1/36000
Chromosome gene location	16 and 4 & another unknown site	9, 16	3
% of patients new mutations	<10%	60–70%	6.5–16%
Age of onset	Fetus to old age	Neonate to old age	Child to old age
ESRD	~50%	Occurs	No
Organs involved: Kidney			
cysts	Always	10–20%	Common
benign tumours	20%	50–80%	?
renal cell carcinoma	Unusual	Occurs	38–55%
Central nervous system			
vessels	~10%	No	No
brain	Rare cysts	Very common abnormalities	50–60% tumours
Eye	No	~80%	~60%
Heart	26% valve abnormalities	~60%	No
Lung	No	Rare	No
Liver	50–60% cysts	No	Rare, adenoma
Pancreas	Rare, cyst	No	Common, cysts and tumours
Adrenal	Rare, adenoma	No	7–19% pheochromocytoma
Bone	No	Yes, cysts	No
Skin	No	Common	No

Differentiation of ARPKD from simple renal cysts is generally less of a diagnostic dilemma than differentiating it from ADPKD since in ARPKD the kidneys are always enlarged even early in the course of the disease and often discrete cysts are not present; neither of which would be the case with simple cysts. In contrast, in ADPKD in childhood the kidneys may not be enlarged and the occurrence of a single or a few cysts is characteristic. Moreover, the presence of hypertension, renal insufficiency, and hepatic abnormalities in ARPKD would serve to differentiate it from simple cysts.

The difficulties that are encountered in correctly diagnosing renal cystic disease in neonates and very young children are underscored by the frequency of initial misdiagnosis in this age group. In a retrospective study of 48 patients who had been diagnosed with polycystic kidney disease in the first year of life and survived to at least one month of age, 18 could not be placed in a specific diagnostic category, two children with ARPKD had been misclassified initially, and four of the six children with ADPKD were initially diagnosed as having ARPKD (Cole *et al.* 1987). The need to consider other diagnostic possibilities is also underscored by this study since seven of the 48 patients had other renal diseases, including three children with glomerulocystic disease and two with TS (Cole *et al.* 1987). Because of these difficulties, some authors believe that definitive diagnosis of the type of cystic renal disease should not be made without a liver biopsy in a child from a family without a clear history of either ARPKD or ADPKD (Cole *et al.* 1987). In some rare cases, a renal biopsy may also be necessary.

Although ultrasonography does not reliably distinguish between ARPKD and ADPKD in an affected child, it is the main renal imaging modality utilized (Stapleton *et al.* 1983; Kaariainen *et al.* 1988). Early in the course of ARPKD, in the fetal or the neonatal period, the characteristic ultrasonographic appearance is one of enlarged kidneys with reniform shape, diffusely increased renal echogenicity with poor delineation of intrarenal structures. In the fetus, often oligohydramnios and a non-visualized bladder are identified; rarely, macrocysts less than 2 cm in size are detected (Kaplan and Kaplan 1990; Bronshtein *et al.* 1992). In older children, the increased echogenicity is often confined to the medulla but the macrocysts remain small. In fact, the presence of larger, discrete renal cysts is more suggestive of ADPKD. However, renal cysts are often not detected in early-onset ADPKD as well (Pretorius *et al.* 1987; Fick *et al.* 1993).

The ultrasonographic findings in ARPKD can be detected *in utero* as early as 14 weeks of gestation (Bronshtein *et al.* 1990). However, there are instances in which ultrasonography was interpreted as normal in the first trimester yet was abnormal in the third trimester (Reilly *et al.* 1979; Mahony *et al.* 1984; Bronshtein *et al.* 1992). Additionally, there is at least one report of a normal ultrasonography at 30 weeks with an affected child at birth (Romero *et al.* 1984). Thus, it is clear that although prenatal ultrasonography is indicated in fetuses who are at risk for ARPKD, a normal study does not completely exclude the disease.

Clinically, approximately 45% of ARPKD children present in the first month of life; another 45% present between one month and one year, and the remainder present after the first year of life (Kaplan *et al.* 1989). Those children who are diagnosed at birth usually present with either respiratory failure and/or abdominal masses. In these severely affected children the respiratory distress can result from the massively enlarged kidneys or from a pneumothorax and/or pulmonary hypoplasia which is an accompaniment of *in utero* renal dysfunction. Those children presenting later in the first year of life most often present with abdominal masses while those presenting at an older age often present with hepatomegaly and occasionally ascending cholangitis.

As a general rule, those children presenting earlier in life have more severe renal disease and those presenting later in life have more severe hepatic disease. In fact, on the basis of age of presentation and severity of renal and hepatic involvement, Blyth and Ockenden in 1971 suggested four subtypes of the disease: perinatal, neonatal, infantile, and juvenile (Blyth and Ockenden 1971). In this classification the perinatal type has 90% of the nephrons involved in the cystogenic process and, as a result, the fetuses or newborns present with abdominal masses and renal failure in the perinatal or neonatal period. Although all bile ducts are dilated, periportal fibrosis is minimal. In the neonatal type, 60% of the nephrons are involved and renal failure often occurs in the first year of life. As in the perinatal form, all the bile ducts appear to be involved and mild hepatic fibrosis is present. The infantile form has an even milder renal disease, but more hepatic involvement, and the children generally present with nephromegaly and hepatomegaly at three to six months of age. In these children only 25% of the nephrons appear cystic; moderate hepatic fibrosis and its sequelae occur. The juvenile form presents later in childhood or adolescence, usually with hepatomegaly and/or sequelae of hepatic disease.

In ARPKD, the renal disease is manifested by haematuria, non-nephrotic range proteinuria, decreased renal concentrating ability, hypertension, and renal insufficiency. Haematuria and proteinuria are present in about one-third of children (Cole *et al.* 1987). In one study, all ARPKD children who had blood pressure determinations at three months of age were hypertensive and this persisted at one year of age (Cole *et al.* 1987). The hypertension in these children can be difficult to control; in some children, therapy with as many as four medications may be required (Cole *et al.* 1987). The hepatic disease often is first manifested by hepatomegaly. Ascending cholangitis and the sequelae of portal hypertension, including haematemesis from variceal bleeding and splenomegaly, can also be presenting manifestations.

Management and outcome

Although no disease-specific treatments exist, it appears that appropriate management of the complications have improved the outcome of ARPKD children. The recognition of the risk of respiratory complications and the availability of ventilatory support appear to have improved the survival of those children who present *in utero* or at birth. Diagnosis and aggressive treatment of the hypertension also appear to be important in ameliorating the course of the renal disease (Cole *et al.* 1987). Portal hypertension becomes a significant problem in children who survive the neonatal period. In one study, 47% of children older than three months had splenomegaly (Kaplan *et al.* 1989). Management of the portal hypertension, including portacaval shunts, is necessary (Cole *et al.* 1987). A few children have been successfully treated with combined hepatic and renal transplantation (Kaiser *et al.* 1990).

In the study by Kaplan *et al.*, 24 ARPKD children seen between 1980 and 1986 at the Hospital for Sick Children at Great Ormond Street had survival rates of 79% at one year, 51% at 10 years, and 46% at 15 years. Among those children who are alive at one year of age, life table survival rates were 82% at 10 years and 79% at 15 years (Kaplan *et al.* 1989). In the study by Cole *et al.* of 17 ARPKD children who survived the first month of life, mean follow-up was 60.1 ± 47.9 months and their age was 6.1 ± 4.3 years at the time of follow-up evaluation (Cole *et al.* 1987). In these children, glomerular filtration rate (GFR) decreased in the first year of life; eight children had a GFR of >40 ml/min/1.73 m^2 at last follow-up; six children had a GFR of <40 ml/min/ 1.73 m^2, and five of them required dialysis or transplantation. The age of ESRD ranged from 8– 197 months. The development of portal hypertension and its sequelae were common; four children had splenomegaly develop, two had bleeding esophageal varices, and one required a portacaval shunt. Two patients died within the first year of life, one of pulmonary insufficiency and one of sepsis.

Autosomal dominant polycystic kidney diseases

There are three major autosomal dominant polycystic kidney diseases: tuberous sclerosis (TS), von Hippel–Lindau (VHL), and ADPKD. This group of disorders is of interest in that they share much more than autosomal dominant mode of inheritance and the occurrence of renal cysts (Table 8.3). Although TS and VHL are discussed in detail in Chapter 9, some comments of how these diseases, particularly TS, relate to ADPKD are worth some discussion. All three are systemic disorders albeit not with the same organ system involvement; all display considerable phenotypic variability, including ages of onset which range from childhood to old age (Malek *et al*. 1987; Chang *et al*. 1990; Choyke *et al*. 1990; Filling-Katz *et al*. 1991; Roach 1992). All, particularly TS and ADPKD, have stated high spontaneous mutation rates (Dalgaard 1957; Maher *et al*. 1990; Webb and Osborne 1992). The renal cysts in all display hyperproliferative epithelia, and renal cell proliferation occurs not only within the cysts but also within the renal parenchyma as adenoma or renal cell carcinoma (Evan *et al*. 1979; Gregoire *et al*. 1987; Solomon and Schwartz 1988). TS displays genetic heterogeneity (Fahsold *et al*. 1991; Haines *et al*. 1991) as does ADPKD, and in fact one of the TS genes is located on chromosome 16 in close proximity to the ADPKD1 gene (Kandt *et al*. 1992). The phenotypic manifestations are similar enough to result in the misdiagnosis of TS as ADPKD in some patients (Anderson and Tannen 1969; Durham 1987).

Autosomal dominant polycystic kidney disease

Autosomal dominant polycystic kidney disease is of interest to both the practising and academic physician because it is common, has interesting genetic and pathogenetic mechanisms, exhibits protean manifestations, and is a major cause of end-stage renal disease (ESRD), costing in excess of $200 million per year for treatment of the ESRD in the United States.

Epidemiology and genetics

Although ADPKD appears to have a worldwide distribution, there are no precise data on its prevalence in different countries. In Europe and the United States the disease occurs in approximately one in 200 to one in 1000 people (Higgins 1952; Dalgaard 1957; Danovitch 1981; Iglesias *et al*. 1983). Studies from Olmstead county in Minnesota determined that the age and sex adjusted yearly incidence in the United States is 1.38 in 100 000 from clinical data; this incidence figure almost doubles when patients diagnosed at autopsy are included (Iglesias *et al*. 1983). Although the disease has been said to be less common in Africa (Seedat *et al*. 1984) and among American blacks, there is little information on the subject.

As the name implies, ADPKD is a hereditary disorder with the defective gene located on an autosome (non-sex chromosome) and it is transmitted in a dominant fashion. With this type of inheritance males and females are equally likely to inherit the disease, and each offspring of an affected individual has a 50/50 chance of inheriting the chromosome with the abnormal gene and hence the disease. In 1985, our understanding of the genetics of ADPKD entered the modern era with the application of gene linkage techniques. With these techniques, polymorphic DNA probes whose chromosomes of origin are known were utilized to examine the DNA of ADPKD families. When certain probes are consistently transmitted with a disease, linkage of the disease gene and the probe must be present and thus the chromosome location of the putative gene can be determined. However, with this method neither the gene itself nor the gene product are identified. Initial gene linkage studies of 100 ADPKD families demonstrated linkage of the

ADPKD gene to chromosome 16 (Reeders *et al.* 1989). However, in 1988, a number of families were observed in which the ADPKD gene was not linked to chromosome 16 markers (Kimberling *et al.* 1988; Romeo *et al.* 1988). Thus, there must be at least two different ADPKD genes. In 1993, the location of the second ADPKD gene (ADPKD2) was determined to be on chromosome 4 (Kimberling *et al.* 1993). Families have now been identified who do not have their ADPKD gene on either chromosome 16 or chromosome 4; the site of this ADPKD3 gene has not been determined (Daoust *et al.* 1995).

Both the ADPKD1 and ADPKD2 genes have now been cloned (European Polycystic Kidney Disease Consortium 1994; Mochizuki *et al.* 1996). The ADPKD1 gene is very large and complex (European Polycystic Kidney Disease Consortium 1994). It is a 53 kilobase gene. The deduced protein, called polycystin, has multiple transmembrane domains. It has regions with leucine–rich repeats, C–type lectin, immunoglobulin repeats, and fibronectin-related domains. The proposed structure suggests that polycystin is involved in cell–cell or cell–matrix interaction (European Polycystic Kidney Disease Consortium 1994). In addition, the gene is repeated several times on chromosome 16. The ADPKD2 gene has some similarity to the ADPKD1 gene. It has a predicted 968 amino acid protein with six transmembrane spans and it appears to have some homology with the family of voltage-activated calcium channels (Mochizuki *et al.* 1996).

The ADPKD1 gene appears to account for 90% or more of the disease in people of European ancestry (Kimberling *et al.* 1990); the gene type distribution in other ethnic and racial groups has not yet been defined. The discovery of the location of the ADPKD1 and ADPKD2 genes has permitted the use of gene linkage techniques in presymtomatic and prenatal diagnosis (see below). The cloning of the ADPKD1 and ADPKD2 genes will eventually permit more direct testing which will not require testing of other family members to identify affected individuals (European Polycystic Kidney Disease Consortium 1994; Mochizuki *et al.* 1996).

The occurrence of genetic heterogeneity raises the question of whether the phenotypes or clinical presentations of the two genes differ. Certainly, before genetic heterogeneity was documented, clinicians were aware of the considerable phenotypic variability in the disease, particularly between families, but they had not divided the disease into distinct phenotypes. With the knowledge of genetic heterogeneity, at least part of the interfamily variability can now be explained by differences in genotype. In fact, current studies show that there is a difference in the age of onset and severity of the renal disease between the gene types (see below), but little other clinical information is available. The precise understanding of differences between these genes and the disorders they produce will require further study of the genes and their proteins.

Although genetic heterogeneity could explain interfamily variability, it could not explain intrafamily variability. Although Dalgaard noted similarity in the age of death and ESRD in members of a given family (Dalgaard 1957), more recent studies suggest discordance in the progression of renal dysfunction in 38% of family members (Milutinovic *et al.* 1992). However, yet another genetic twist might offer an explanation. Genetic anticipation may occur in this disease. The clinical characteristics of genetic anticipation include an apparently high spontaneous mutation rate, earlier and greater disease severity in successive generations, and congenital or neonatal onset of disease in offspring of parents with typical adult onset. ADPKD has these characteristics. Many studies, including those in recent years, document that only about 60% of ADPKD patients have a positive family history (Dalgaard 1957; Gabow *et al.* 1984). This could represent a true high spontaneous mutation rate or it could represent only an apparent high mutation rate with mild disease in the older generation escaping clinical diagnosis. The latter is suggested by the fact that even in a modern era, one-half of ADPKD patients are not diagnosed until they come to autopsy (Iglesias *et al.* 1983). In addition, there are numerous examples of children with ADPKD, who are diagnosed *in utero* or in the first year of life, whose parents have typical adult-onset disease (Cole *et al.* 1987; Pretorius *et al.* 1987; Kaariainen *et al.* 1988; Fick *et al.* 1993). In fact, two-thirds of the affected parents of early-onset children were not aware they had the disease until the child's disease prompted their evaluation (Pretorius *et al.* 1987; Fick *et al.* 1993). A recent study formally examined 220 ADPKD families for anticipation, utilizing the criteria of a child affected in the first year of life or the development of endstage renal disease 10 years earlier in offspring than parent, and found evidence of anticipation in 48% of the informative families (Fick *et al.* 1994). A pedigree of such a family is shown in Fig. 8.1.

Anticipation has been observed in other genetic diseases (Richards and Sutherland 1992), including myotonic dystrophy which is also a systemic autosomal dominant disease (Harley *et al.* 1992). In that disease, gene size increases due to greater numbers of specific triplet repeats; as the number of repeats increases phenotypic severity of the disease also occurs (Harley *et al.* 1992). It does not appear that this mechanism explains the apparent clinical anticipation in ADPKD.

Pathogenesis

Attempts to understand the pathogenesis of ADPKD have largely focused on elucidation of the mechanisms of renal cystogenesis. As in ARPKD, this has been accomplished utilizing patients'

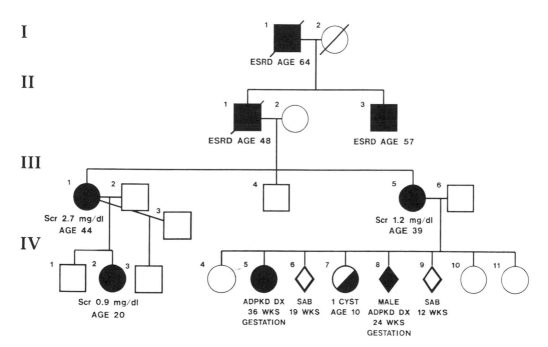

Fig. 8.1 Pedigree of a kindred with ADPKD demonstrating genetic anticipation. Circles denote female family members, squares male family members, solid squares affected members, half-solid symbols suspicious family members, and diamonds fetuses. A slant through a symbol denotes the family member is deceased. In this pedigree two types of genetic anticipation are shown. Subject II-1 entered ESRD at age 48, 16 years earlier than his affected father. In addition, subjects IV-5 and IV-8 presented with ADPKD *in utero*, in contrast to their mother with typical adult-onset ADPKD. (Used by permission: Fick *et al.* 1994.) Scr = serum creatinine concentration; ESRD = end-stage renal disease; wks = weeks; DX = diagnosed; SAB = spontaneous abortion.

renal histology, animal models, and cell culture techniques. Many of the basic mechanisms described above for ARPKD are likely to be similar in ADPKD. Early in the course of disease about 5% of the nephrons appear to be cystic (Grantham *et al.* 1987). It is not known if cysts only enlarge or if more nephrons develop cysts as the disease progresses. The cysts initially develop as outpouchings or diverticula from intact renal tubules (Osathanondh and Potter 1964; Heggö 1966; Baert 1978), but as cysts enlarge they appear to lose their connections with the tubule of origin (Grantham *et al.* 1987). Once this tubular connection is lost, cysts cannot enlarge by trapping glomerular filtrate within the cyst cavity. In fact, cyst enlargement appears to result from the concurrence of cell proliferation and secretion. The evidence for cellular proliferation comes from cell culture models of cyst formation, cell culture of cystic epithelia from kidneys of ADPKD patients, and histologic examination of cystic kidneys. Although Madin–Darby canine kidney (MDCK) cells originate from non-cystic renal cell lines, some MDCK cells will proliferate and form balls of cells or cyst-like structures when dispersed in a collagen gel (Grantham *et al.* 1989; Mangoo-Karim *et al.* 1989). This has been used as a model of cyst formation. The 'cysts' form when both secretion and proliferation occur; in contrast, balls of cells form under experimental conditions which do not favor secretion (Mangoo-Karim *et al.* 1989). Substances which increase cAMP increase secretion and promote 'cyst' enlargement (Mangoo-Karim *et al.* 1989). Renal cyst epithelia from human ADPKD kidneys grown in primary cell culture have been shown to exhibit increased proliferative potential with increased numbers of cell divisions in comparison to normal renal tubular epithelium (Wilson *et al.* 1992). In this setting, the cyst epithelium exhibits an amplified proliferative response to certain growth factors such as epidermal growth factor (EGF) (Wilson 1991). This is of particular interest since EGF has been found in the renal cyst fluid of ADPKD patients and receptors for EGF have been demonstrated on the apical (cyst lumen) side of the cells, enabling a cellular response to the cyst fluid EGF (Wilson 1991).

In a less dynamic fashion, increased proliferation in ADPKD is suggested by the occurrence of cellular hyperplasia within cysts with the formation of polyploid lesions (Evan *et al.* 1979; Grantham *et al.* 1987) and by the presence of renal adenomas in 21% of the kidneys of ADPKD patients (Gregoire *et al.* 1987). These adenoma or 'balls of cells' may represent proliferation without secretion as has been demonstrated in the MDCK model. As such, the importance of secretion in cystogenesis is underscored.

In vivo, cyst epithelium has substantial secretory capacity (Bennett *et al.* 1987; Everson *et al.* 1990). Cysts that have been drained percutaneously without destroying the epithelial viability with sclerosing agents reaccumulate the fluid within weeks. Moreover, there is some data to suggest that, as with the MDCK model, cysts *in vivo* respond to agents which increase cAMP (Everson *et al.* 1990). The robust nature of the secretory capacity of the renal cyst epithelium is shown by studies in which individual renal cysts were dissected from cystic kidneys; these cysts secrete when the lumen has natural cyst fluid but not when defined media is within the lumen, suggesting that cyst fluid contains secretogogues (Ye and Grantham 1993) just as it contains growth factors.

The mechanism of the secretion in renal cysts is not completely defined. Some investigators have demonstrated altered location of Na-K ATPase from the basolateral cell surface to the apical region of human ADPKD cyst epithelium (Wilson *et al.* 1991). Moreover, these same investigators have demonstrated that the altered location is accompanied by altered sodium transport from the basal to apical surface (Wilson *et al.* 1991). Clearly, such alteration in sodium transport could contribute to cyst fluid accumulation. However, this alteration cannot be an absolute essential to cyst growth since this altered location of Na-K ATPase has not been found in human autosomal recessive polycystic kidney disease (see above) (Avner and Sweeney 1992) nor in the chemically-induced models of cystic disease (Carone *et al.* 1992). A role for chloride secretion and for a chloride/bicarbonate exchanger in cyst fluid secretion has also been suggested from data from the MDCK cyst model (Mangoo-Karim *et al.* 1989; Macias *et al.* 1992; Tanner *et al.* 1992; Ye and Grantham 1993).

In addition to the alterations in growth and secretion which have been demonstrated in renal cystogenesis, the data from both models and human disease support a role for altered extracellular matrix. In chemically-induced animal models of renal cystic disease, basement membrane changes are concomitant events with cyst formation (Carone *et al.* 1989). Moreover, human renal cystic epithelium from ADPKD kidneys elaborates in tissue culture a very abnormal appearing basement membrane compared to the basement membrane elaborated by normal renal tubules (Wilson *et al.* 1986; 1992). Although there is no uniformity of the observed alterations in basement membrane composition in various types of cystic disease, the basement membrane from all models and types of polycystic kidney disease which have been examined have shown some alteration in basement membrane composition, suggesting a central role of this alteration in renal cystogenesis (Carone *et al.* 1988; Ebihara *et al.* 1988; Granot *et al.* 1990; Ojeda *et al.* 1990; Taub *et al.* 1990). As with proliferation, histologic data from kidneys of ADPKD patients support altered extracellular matrix. Very early in the course of ADPKD the basement membrane in the kidneys appears split and fragmented (Milutinovic and Agodoa 1983). As the disease progresses, the basement membrane surrounding the renal cysts becomes thickened and contains large amounts of amorphous interwoven fibrils (Cuppage *et al.* 1980; Wilson *et al.* 1992). This type of data as well as the type and array of systemic manifestations in ADPKD support a defect in extracellular matrix. Thus, current data suggest that cellular proliferation, altered secretion, and abnormal extracellular matrix are all part of the process of renal cystogenesis.

Although it is not clear which, if any, of the processes are the primary result of the genetic defect, some data from transgenic mice models in which proto-oncogenes are in the transgenes demonstrate that alterations in a growth gene can produce renal cyst formation (Delarue *et al.* 1991; Kelley *et al.* 1991; Trudel *et al.* 1991). However, the failure of all of these transgenic models but one to produce extrarenal effects (Wilkinson *et al.* 1993) raises questions about the central role of proliferation in a systemic disease like ADPKD. The primary gene defects will become clear with further understanding of the function of the ADPKD proteins.

Methods of diagnosis

The variability and lack of sensitivity and specificity of symptoms, signs, and routine laboratory findings make these unreliable methods for establishing the diagnosis of ADPKD either in at-risk family members or in the general population (Gabow *et al.* 1984). Since it appears that renal cysts are an invariable and early manifestation of ADPKD, renal imaging to detect renal cysts has become the mainstay of diagnosis. The preferred renal imaging modality is ultrasonography. It is sensitive, specific, requires no contrast or radiation exposure, and is relatively inexpensive.

Studies suggest that only 11–24% of persons from ADPKD1 families will have a normal ultrasonogram before 30 years of age (Bear *et al.* 1984, 1992; Churchill *et al.* 1984; Parfrey *et al.* 1990). Examination of children who carry the ADPKD1 gene demonstrates that 38% of those under age five years and 25% under age 18 will have a normal ultrasonogram (Gabow *et al.* 1997).

Gene linkage analysis techniques can also be utilized to establish the likelihood of the gene carrier status (Fig. 8.2). In order to determine the gene status of an individual at risk for ADPKD, at least two other affected family members must be tested to establish which type of the

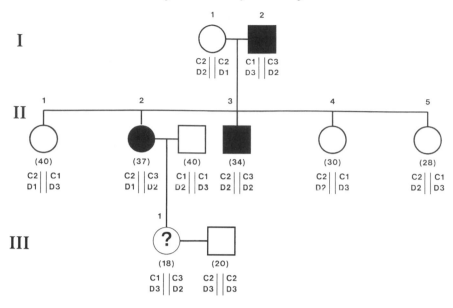

Fig. 8.2   Pedigree of a kindred with ADPKD1. Circles denote female family members, squares male family members, and solid symbols affected members. Ages are shown in parentheses. Subject III-1 wished to know her status before her marriage. Ultrasonography was negative. Two types of chromosome 16 p markers were used (C and D). The three possible alleles are indicated (1, 2 and 3). Markers C and D are assumed to flank the ADPKD1 gene, each within 5 centimorgans of the ADPKD1 gene locus. These types are depicted below each symbol. In this family the haplotype C3, D2 is transmitted with the ADPKD1 gene. Therefore, subject III-1 has an approximately 99% chance of being a gene carrier. (Used by permission: Gabow 1993.)

polymorphic probe is travelling with the ADPKD gene in that particular family. With the availability of multiple probes, including flanking probes, the likelihood of carrying the gene could be defined in most members of ADPKD1 families with 99% certainty (Reeders *et al.* 1989; Kimberling *et al.* 1991). The cloning of the ADPKD1 and ADPKD2 genes will eventually simplify gene carrier identification. However, for now, gene linkage analysis is still required in ADPKD1 and ADPKD2 families. Because of its current cost and the need to involve other family members, gene linkage analysis should be reserved for the relatively small subset of people who are gene carriers without detectable renal cysts and who are being considered for live related transplant donors (Hannig *et al.* 1991), whose family planning would be altered, who feel for other reasons they must know their status, or those whose clinical treatment would be changed if they were known to have the disease. An example of the latter situation would be someone who would be screened for aneurysms if they were known to have ADPKD. Random, non-clinically-directed screening is not advisable with either gene linkage tests or with renal imaging (Gabow *et al.* 1989). All testing should have the purpose of addressing the patient's desires or determining clinical intervention or prognosis. Screening must balance any benefits against the effects a positive diagnosis would have on insurability and even employability. All testing should be accompanied by counselling.

Prenatal testing can be performed to identify affected fetuses (Reeders *et al.* 1986; Ceccherini *et al.* 1989; Novelli *et al.* 1989; Turco *et al.* 1992). Ultrasonography will identify some fetuses who already have phenotypic evidence of ADPKD as early as 16 weeks of gestation. (Cohen and Haller 1987). Gene linkage analysis can also be utilized with fetal DNA being obtained either via amniocentesis (Reeders *et al.* 1986) or chorionic villous sampling (Gabow and Wilkins-Haug 1991; Turco *et al.* 1992). The latter has the advantage of permitting testing earlier in the gestation. Although the sensitivity of prenatal ultrasonography in this setting has not been defined, its advantages over gene linkage include its being less invasive and providing more information about the course of disease in the fetus, as these early-onset children tend to do less well (see below). In contrast, gene linkage is more sensitive, but knowledge of the fetus' gene status does not predict the disease course. In one study which utilized a questionnaire, 97% of 137 at-risk adults stated they would utilize gene linkage analysis to define their status and 88% of 141 affected subjects stated they would use the test to define the status of their children (Sujansky *et al.* 1990). However, of the 65% of affected persons who stated they would use prenatal testing, only 4% of affected subjects would terminate a pregnancy for ADPKD. In contrast, 25% of the same individuals would terminate a pregnancy for a very serious medical problem (Sujansky *et al.* 1990). It appears that having experienced this late-onset disease themselves leads affected individuals to not consider ADPKD very serious. In fact, prenatal diagnosis has not been utilized to any extent in either the United States or Europe (Zerres 1992).

Clinical manifestations and management

The clinical manifestations of ADPKD can be divided into renal and extrarenal and cystic and non-cystic (Table 8.4). The renal manifestations of the disease are myriad. Cyst growth and development are the prime manifestations. Early in the course of the diesase the renal cysts are few in number, with children occasionally having only unilateral cysts and even those children with bilateral cysts usually having less than 10 (Fick *et al.* 1994). However, by age 30 almost all affected subjects have multiple, bilateral renal cysts. The kidneys become progressively enlarged, often reaching enormous size by late in life. Kidneys as large as 40 cm and as heavy as 8 kg have been described. Many of the renal signs, symptoms, and complications, including pain, hypertension, decreased renal function, and decreased renal concentrating ability, appear to be related to the cysts' presence and the structural deformation they cause.

Pain is one of the most common symptoms of ADPKD, occurring in 50% of affected people (Gabow and Grantham 1993). Although there is no absolute relationship between renal size and pain, it is much more common in individuals with kidneys greater than 15 cm in size (Milutinovic *et al.* 1984). In a few patients the pain is disabling, requiring narcotic analgesics. In this subset of patients, cyst reduction procedures are helpful. If there are only a few large cysts present, cyst reduction can be accomplished by percutaneous cyst puncture (Bennett *et al.* 1987) and alcohol sclerosis. However, if there are many large cysts or many moderately-sized cysts, open surgical cyst reduction is preferred. In the patient who undergoes this procedure, 80% are pain free at 12 months (Elzinga *et al.* 1992). Laparoscopic cyst decompression has also been described (Elzinga *et al.* 1992). The impressive therapeutic response of pain to cyst reduction underscores the relationship between renal size and pain. It is worth noting that these procedures have not been shown to either improve or worsen renal function over time (Elzinga *et al.* 1992). However, acute renal failure following percutaneous cyst reduction has been reported in a patient on enalapril with very large kidneys and baseline decreased renal function (Chapman *et al.* 1991).

Hypertension is as common as pain. Like pain, hypertension is related to the severity of the renal structural lesion (Gabow *et al.* 1990). In both adults and children, those individuals who still have normal renal function and hypertension have larger kidneys reflecting more and larger cysts

Cystic diseases of the kidney

Table 8.4 Frequency of manifestations of autosomal dominant polycystic kidney disease (Used by permission: Gabow 1993)

Manifestation	Frequency
Extrarenal	
Gastrointestinal	
Hepatic cysts	Approximately 50%; increases with age
Cholangiocarcinoma	Rare
Congenital hepatic fibrosis	Rare
Pancreatic cysts	Approximately 7%
Colonic diverticula	Affects 80% of patients with ESRD
Cardiovascular	
Cardiac valvular abnormalities	26%
Intracranial aneurysms	5–10%
Thoracic and abdominal aortic aneurysms	Unknown
Genital	
Ovarian cysts	Unknown
Testicular cysts	Unknown
Seminal-vesicle cysts	Unknown
Miscellaneous	
Arachnoid cysts	5%
Pineal cysts	Rare
Splenic cysts	Rare
Renal	
Anatomical	
Renal cysts	100%
Renal adenomas	21%
Cyst calcification	Common
Functional	
Decreased renal concentrating ability	Affects potentially all adults
Decreased urinary citrate excretion	67% (10 of 15 subjects)
Impaired renal acidification	Unknown
Hormonal alterations	
Increased renin production	Probably affects all hypertensive adults
Preserved erythropoietin production	Probably affects all patients with ESRD
Complications	
Hypertension	Affects >80% of patients with ESRD*
Haematuria, hemorrhage, or both	50%
Acute and chronic pain	60%
Urinary tract infections–bladder, interstitium, cysts	Common
Nephrolithiasis	20–36%
Nephromegaly	100%
Renal failure	Affects 45% of patients by the age of 60

*This complication also affects 30% of children with polycystic kidney disease.

(Gabow *et al.* 1990; Fick *et al.* 1994). The relationship between structural deformation and hypertension appears to be via the renin–angiotensin–aldosterone system (RAAS). Certainly the cysts result in disruption of the intrarenal vasculature (Ettinger *et al.* 1969; Cornell 1970). This likely results in areas of renal ischaemia and consequent stimulation of the renin release. It has been shown that hypertensive ADPKD patients with normal renal function have higher plasma renin levels compared to essential hypertensive patients with similar renal function and comparable blood pressures (Chapman *et al.* 1990). Moreover, administration of captopril, a provocative manoeuvre aimed at unmasking the role of the RAAS, results in higher levels of renin in the ADPKD hypertensive patients compared to the essential hypertensive patients (Chapman *et al.* 1990). Since ADPKD is a bilateral renal disease, the intrarenal ischaemia is likely to be bilateral and hence ADPKD should more closely resemble bilateral renal artery stenosis rather than unilateral disease. In fact, as in bilateral renal artery stenosis, angiotensin converting enzyme inhibition has resulted in acute renal failure in some patients (Chapman *et al.* 1991). The patients with this complication have been those with baseline impairment of renal function and very large kidneys, presumably with the most severe intrarenal ischaemia (Chapman *et al.* 1991). In addition to these functional data regarding the RAAS, pathological studies have shown increased renin in ADPKD nephrectomy specimens and distribution outside the area of the juxtaglomerular apparatus with renin within the cyst and arteriolar walls (Graham and Lindop 1988).

Haematuria occurs in 30–50% of ADPKD patients and can be the presenting manifestation in 13–23% of adults (Kaehny and Everson 1991). The mean age of the first episode of gross haematuria is about 30 years of age (Gabow *et al.* 1992). Larger kidneys and the presence of hypertension are correlated with the occurrence of gross haematuria (Gabow *et al.* 1992). Haematuria is usually self-limited, lasting a week or less in 56% of patients (Gabow *et al.* 1992). Therefore, except in very rare circumstances, management should be conservative with bedrest, analgesics, and fluid.

Urinary tract infections are said to be common in ADPKD patients, but this conclusion is often not based on culture data. Nonetheless, documented infections do occur and the site can be the bladder, the renal parenchyma, or the cysts. It is important to distinguish between the latter two because their therapy differs. Both upper tract infections present with flank pain, fever, and chills. Although discrete areas of renal tenderness, positive blood cultures, and the absence of pyuria suggest cyst infection (Schwab *et al.* 1987), usually the diagnosis of a cyst infection is made when a patient with upper tract symptoms fails to respond to antibiotics usually used to treat pyelonephritis. This therapeutic failure occurs even though the organism may be sensitive because the antibiotics commonly used in pyelonephritis, such as ampicillin, the cephalosporins, and the aminoglycosides, fail to penetrate the cyst (Schwab *et al.* 1987). Antibiotics with good cyst penetration include trimethoprim-sulfamethoxazole, chloramphenicol, and ciprofloxacin (Schwab 1985; Gabow and Bennett 1991). There are few data on how long antibiotic treatment is required for cyst infection, but some patients may require two to three months of antibiotic therapy (Gabow and Bennett 1991). Current information suggests that no imaging study is helpful in diagnosing either the presence or site of renal cyst infection in most patients. However, if a discrete infected cyst is identified with renal imaging studies, the cyst can be drained percutaneously (Chapman *et al.* 1990). Very rarely, if ever, should surgical intervention be necessary for treatment of renal infection.

Nephrolithiasis occurs in 20–36% of ADPKD patients (Torres *et al.* 1988; Levine and Grantham 1992). This diagnosis must be considered in a patient with acute pain and haematuria.

The diagnosis may be difficult to establish because of the distorted renal anatomy. It must be distinguished from cyst haemorrhage. Computed tomography is likely to be the best renal imaging procedure for detecting renal stones (Levine and Grantham 1992). ADPKD patients are likely predisposed to stone disease because of the relative intrarenal stasis and obstruction caused by cyst compression as well as by metabolic factors. The most consistent metabolic abnormality is hypocitraturia (Torres *et al.* 1988). About 47% of patients have calcium oxalate stones and about 57% have uric acid stones (Torres *et al.* 1988). However, only 12% of the patients in one series with nephrolithiasis had hyperuricosuria and only 7% were hypercalciuric (Torres *et al.* 1988). Moreover, neither hyperuricaemia nor hyperuricosuria are more frequent in ADPKD patients than in unaffected family members when the confounding effects of gender, blood pressure, and renal function are considered (Kaehny *et al.* 1990).

Although renal failure is the most serious renal complication of ADPKD, it occurs in only about 50% of patients by about age 60 (Churchill *et al.* 1984; Parfrey *et al.* 1990; Bear *et al.* 1992; Gabow *et al.* 1992). The factors which have been reported in some studies to correlate with more severe renal disease are the ADPKD1 gene, being male, being black, the concurrence of sickle haemoglobin, earlier age of disease onset, hypertension, the numbers of episodes of gross haematuria, larger kidneys, and in males, urinary tract infections (Iglesias *et al.* 1983; Gretz *et al.* 1989; Gonzalo *et al.* 1990; Parfrey *et al.* 1990; Bear *et al.* 1992; Gabow *et al.* 1992, 1992; Yium *et al.* 1994). There are conflicting data regarding the effects of gender of the affected parent and pregnancy on the renal disease. One study has shown a more severe course of the renal disease when the gene is transmitted from the mother (Bear *et al.* 1992) while another longitudinal study has shown no difference (Gabow *et al.* 1992). Some studies demonstrated no difference in renal function in women related to parity (Milutinovic *et al.* 1983; Bear *et al.* 1992); however, another study utilizing longitudinal data suggested that women with three or more pregnancies have worse renal function than women with fewer pregnancies (Gabow *et al.* 1992). Both black males and black females with ADPKD start dialysis significantly earlier than their white counterparts. Also, black ESRD patients with ADPKD have a higher frequency of sickle-cell trait than other black ESRD patients. Moreover, ADPKD blacks with sickle hemoglobin appear to enter ESRD earlier than other black ADPKD patients (Yium *et al.* 1994). There are few data regarding the effect of race or ethnicity in other groups.

When renal failure occurs in ADPKD patients they should be considered candidates for transplantation, haemodialysis, and continuous ambulatory peritoneal dialysis (CAPD). ADPKD patients appear to do as well as other non-diabetic patients with these therapeutic modalities (Fitzpatrick *et al.* 1990; Singh and Hariharan 1991). Although the issue of nephrectomy in ADPKD patients has not been completely resolved, it does appear that there is about a 5% mortality for this procedure in these patients (Warholm *et al.* 1992). Therefore, it seems that this procedure may be best reserved for patients with a history of recent and recurrent renal infections and/or haematuria, patients whose renal size is causing significant morbidity, and patients with suspected renal malignancy.

As discussed below, ADPKD patients with ESRD appear to have a higher frequency of diverticular complications than other ESRD patients. Therefore, some centres screen for diverticular disease prior to transplantation. There are no data to determine if this decreases mortality and morbidity in ADPKD patients who undergo transplantation.

Although renal cell carcinoma has been reported in ADPKD patients (Regan *et al.* 1977; Tegtmeyer *et al.* 1978; Kumar *et al.* 1980; Ng and Suki 1980; Sogbein *et al.* 1981), there does not appear to be the high risk that is reported in acquired cystic disease (Torres *et al.* 1985). In fact, in some ADPKD patients, the cystic lesions regress with dialysis therapy (Thaysen and Thomsen

1982). The most common causes of death in ADPKD ESRD patients appear to be infections and cardivascular disease, similar to other ESRD patients (Lazarus *et al.* 1971; De Bono and Evans 1977; Iglesias *et al.* 1983; Fitzpatrick *et al.* 1990). However, as noted above, diverticular (Gabow 1990) and hepatic complications may be more frequent in ADPKD patients than in patients with other aetiology of ESRD.

The pathogenetic mechanisms for the renal failure in ADPKD have not been elucidated. However, pathological data suggest a prominent role for hypertension. Kidneys of ADPKD patients with early renal failure showed prominent vascular sclerosis, interstitial fibrosis, and tubular atrophy compatible with hypertensive renal damage (Zeier *et al.* 1992).

Although the impairment of glomerular function appears late in the disease course, at least some tubular functions are impaired early. A renal concentrating defect is present even in children with normal renal function who have greater than 10 renal cysts (Fick *et al.* 1994). In adults at any age the urinary osmolality is less in affected individuals with normal renal function than it is in unaffected family members (Gabow *et al.* 1989). This defect appears to relate in part to the severity of the structural lesion (Gabow *et al.* 1989). However, there is likely to also be a cellular component since ADPKD cyst epithelium grown in tissue culture does not exhibit an appropriate adenyl cyclase response to vasopressin (Wilson *et al.* 1986). Other functional and hormonal abnormalities also occur. A few studies have examined renal acidification in ADPKD patients. Some studies with small numbers of ADPKD patients have demonstrated an impaired renal ammonium excretion (Preuss *et al.* 1979; Pabico and McKenna 1992). However, ADPKD patients who are not in renal failure do not demonstrate systemic acidosis. Some studies have also shown a decreased urinary pH in ADPKD patients compared to controls (Torres *et al.* 1988). This is an area which requires further evaluation.

Both erythropoietin and renin secretion appear to be increased in certain phases of ADPKD. Prior to renal failure there is no evidence that renal erythropoietin production is increased since polycythaemia is only rarely reported (Forssell 1958; Brandt *et al.* 1963; Anderson and Walker 1969; Gabow *et al.* 1984). However, once ESRD occurs, erythropoietin levels are better maintained in ADPKD patients than in patients with ESRD from other causes (Maggiore *et al.* 1967; Chandra *et al.* 1985; Besarab *et al.* 1987; Pavlovic-Kentera *et al.* 1987). The reason for this apparent late, but not early, relative increase in erythropoietin is not clear, but it may relate to severity of cystic involvement since erythropoietin is made by cells adjacent to the cysts and erythropoietin is present in cyst fluid (Eckardt *et al.* 1989). In fact, the level in the fluid correlates with the increased serum levels, suggesting that the cysts may be the source of the erythropoietin in the ADPKD patient with ESRD (Eckardt *et al.* 1989). In contrast to erythropoietin, renin levels appear to be elevated early in the course of the disease, as discussed above.

The extrarenal manifestations of ADPKD are many and can have a significant impact on patient morbidity and mortality. The gastrointestinal tract is the most frequent site of extrarenal involvement. Hepatic cysts are present in about 50% of ADPKD patients overall, but age and severity of renal function impairment have a marked effect on the frequency of hepatic cysts (Milutinovic *et al.* 1980; Gabow *et al.* 1990). Hepatic cysts are very rare in ADPKD children but occur in 75% of ADPKD subjects over age 60. Renal insufficiency is more common in ADPKD subjects with hepatic cysts compared to subjects without hepatic cysts, independent of age (Milutinovic *et al.* 1980; Gabow *et al.* 1990). Gender also appears to be a major modulator of hepatic cystogenesis. Although men and women have the same frequency of the presence of any hepatic cysts, massive hepatic cystic disease appears to occur almost exclusively in women (Everson *et al.* 1988; Gabow *et al.* 1990). In addition, pregnancy markedly influences the frequency and severity of the hepatic cystic disease. ADPKD women with hepatic cysts are more likely to have been pregnant than women without hepatic cysts and hepatic cyst number and size are influenced by both the occurrence and the number of pregnancies (Gabow *et al.* 1990). This suggests a modulating effect of female steroid hormones on hepatic cyst formation. Liver function tests are normal even in the face of massive hepatomegaly except for those patients with the very unusual occurrence of bile duct obstruction from the extrinsic compression by a cyst(s) (Lin *et al.* 1968; Howard *et al.* 1976; Wittig *et al.* 1978; Ergun *et al.* 1980; Gabow *et al.* 1990). The sheer size of the liver secondary to hepatic cysts does result in disabling discomfort in some patients. These patients may respond to percutaneous cyst decompression with alcohol sclerosis when one or a few large cysts are present (Everson *et al.* 1990). Occasionally, more aggressive intervention with surgical fenestration and/or partial hepatectomy is required (Newman *et al.* 1990).

Although complications occur with hepatic cysts, they appear less common than complications of renal cysts. Bleeding into hepatic cysts and cyst infections occur. Patients with hepatic cyst infections have right upper quadrant pain, leukocytosis, and an increased sedimentation rate (Telenti *et al.* 1990). There is less information regarding antibiotic penetration of hepatic cysts than renal cysts, but the patients appear to require both antibiotic therapy and a drainage procedure for adequate treatment (Telenti *et al.* 1990). Very rarely, portal hypertension can occur as a consequence of hepatic cystic disease (DelGuercio *et al.* 1973; Jones *et al.* 1974; Iannuccilli and Yu 1981; Ratcliffe *et al.* 1984; van Erpecum *et al.* 1987). A few cases of congenital hepatic fibrosis have been described in ADPKD patients (Cobben *et al.* 1990). Similarly, rare patients with cholangiocarcinoma in a cyst have been reported (Willis 1943; Richmond 1956; Okuda *et al.* 1977; Imamura *et al.* 1984). The importance of hepatic complications is underscored by the observation that 10.5% of ADPKD patients undergoing haemodialysis died from hepatic complications (Grunfeld *et al.* 1985).

The other major gastrointestinal manifestation of ADPKD is colonic diverticula. In 1980, Scheff *et al.* reported an 83% occurrence of colonic diverticula in 12 ADPKD dialysis patients, which was significantly greater than the 32% occurrence in non-ADPKD dialysis patients and the 38% occurrence in age-matched, non-dialysis control patients. Not only was there a greater frequency of diverticula in the ADPKD dialysis patients but they were the only patient group to have the major complications of perforation and intra-abdominal abscess from the diverticula (Scheff *et al.* 1980). Similarly, a review of the literature of patients receiving renal replacement therapy who experience a diverticular complication show over-representation of ADPKD patients (Gabow 1990). It has not yet been shown in this increased frequency of diverticular occurs in the ADPKD population prior to ESRD.

Cardiovascular abnormalities are also common in ADPKD. There are two retrospective studies which include autopsy data. The first study by Leier *et al.* demonstrated an 18% occurrence of cardiac valve abnormalities with the aortic valve most commonly involved. Two of the seven patients with aortic root and annulus dilatation required valvular replacement (Leier *et al.* 1984). A second series derived from autopsies demonstrated a 29% occurrence of valvular abnormalities with the mitral valve being the most commonly involved (Zeier *et al.* 1988). There have also been two large prospective studies utilizing echocardiography. Hossack *et al.* studied 163 ADPKD patients, 130 family members who did not have renal cysts by ultrasonography, and 100 controls. The ADPKD patients had a greater frequency of palpitations, atypical chest pain, and clicks than the control patients (Hossack *et al.* 1988). Utilizing strict definitions for mitral valve prolapse, there was a 26% occurrence of mitral valve prolapse in the ADPKD patients compared to 12% in the family members and 2% in the control group. Aortic valve abnormalities were also observed. Timio *et al.* studied 228 ADPKD patients and 146 unaffected subjects in one large multigenerational family as well as controls. The results were quite similar to those of Hossack *et al.* with a 25% occurrence of mitral valve prolapse in the affected subjects, 20% in the unaffected family members, and 2% in the control subjects. Aortic regurgitant murmurs were found in 19% of the ADPKD patients, 17% of unaffected family members, and 5% of the controls (Timio *et al.* 1992). The high occurrence of valvular abnormalities, particularly mitral valve prolapse, in unaffected family members in both these studies raises questions about the aetiology of the valve defects in this disease. If this were a phenotypic manifestation of the ADPKD gene, one would not expect these findings. The Timio study was a longitudinal study over a decade and there was no marked increase in valvular abnormalities over time, but the prevalence of left ventricular hypertrophy as measured by echocardiography did increase over 10 years, being present in 24% of ADPKD patients at entry and 35% at 10 years (Timio *et al.* 1992). This cardiac end-organ effect of hypertension appears to begin early in the course of the disease in that young adults with ADPKD have higher, albeit normal, left ventricular mass in comparison to age-matched controls (Zeier *et al.* 1993).

One of the most catastrophic manifestations of ADPKD is a ruptured intracranial aneurysm. The association between ADPKD and intracranial aneurysms was first noted in 1904 (Dunger 1904); however, the reported frequency of the association has varied widely in subsequent reports from 0–40% (Suter 1949; Ask-Upmark and Ingvar 1950; Brown 1951; Bigelow 1953; Dalgaard 1957; Ditlefsen and Tonjum 1960; Wakabayashi *et al.* 1983). The reasons for this variability reflect in part the populations studied and the methods used for diagnosis. In recent years there have been three prospective studies performed which serve to establish the overall frequency of the association and to provide information regarding the utility of the different diagnostic techniques. One study of 92 asymptomatic ADPKD patients utilized either 4 vessel angiography and/or dynamic computed tomography with 2 mm cuts in both the coronal and axial planes. Two of the 21 patients who underwent only angiography demonstrated aneurysms; 11 of the 71 patients who first underwent CAT scans had areas suspicious for aneurysms. Seven of these then underwent angiography and all had vascular abnormalities in the area in question but only two had aneurysms. Thus, 4.3% of the patients in this study had aneurysms demonstrated (Chapman *et al.* 1992). Another interesting observation emerged in this study. Twenty-five per cent of the ADPKD patients developed a complication from angiography compared to 10% in controls. Moreover, the complications were more serious in the ADPKD patients, including complete occlusion of the internal carotid artery from spasm in two ADPKD patients (Chapman *et al.* 1992). This complication rate suggests altered vascular reactivity in ADPKD patients compared to controls. A second study of 96 asymptomatic patients utilized magnetic resonance imaging and computed tomography with 3 mm cuts in the axial plane. Although 14% of patients had areas suspicious for aneurysms or incomplete visualization, no patient had a definite aneurysm (Torres *et al.* 1990). A third study utilized magnetic resonance angiography in 85 asymptomatic patients and nine symptomatic patients; 10.5% demonstrated aneurysms (Huston *et al.* 1993). Together these studies suggest that either dynamic CAT scan with 2 mm cuts in two planes or magnetic resonance angiography are the best screening methods for intracranial aneurysms in this population. Moreover, the frequency of aneurysms in ADPKD suggests that it is not cost-effective to screen all ADPKD patients for aneurysms (Levey *et al.* 1983; Levey 1990). None of these prospective studies identified factors which would determine the ADPKD patients who are most at risk for this complication. However, other reports suggest that aneurysms may cluster within certain ADPKD families (Chauveau *et al.* 1992; Schievink *et al.* 1992; Chapman *et al.* 1993). Therefore, the current recommendation is to only screen ADPKD adults who have a positive family history for intracranial aneurysm but are not yet in renal failure; those whose occupation or hobbies place them or others in danger in the event of rupture, such as airline pilots; those who are undergoing surgical procedures in which haemodynamic instability with severe hypertension may occur; or those who absolutely require the information for peace of mind (Levey 1990; Torres *et al.* 1990).

There are limited data on the natural history of aneurysms in ADPKD patients. Although there has been no systematic follow-up of ADPKD patients with asymptomatic aneurysms, a second ruptured intracranial aneurysm has been reported in patients with a previous rupture (Chauveau *et al.* 1990). The outcome data of ADPKD patients with ruptured intracranial aneurysms is also limited. However, there is a suggestion of greater mortality and morbidity of ruptured aneurysms in ADPKD patients than in the general population (Schievink *et al.* 1992; Chapman *et al.* 1993; Huston *et al.* 1993). It is well to remember that not all acute intracranial catastrophes in ADPKD are the result of ruptured aneurysms; in fact, a majority of cerebral vascular accidents in ADPKD patients are due to hypertensive intracerebral haemorrhages or infarction (Zeier *et al.* 1988; Ryu 1990).

An array of miscellaneous abnormalities representling both cystic and non-cystic manifestations exist in ADPKD. The most common of these is hernia formation. Both umbilical and inguinal hernias appear more common in ADPKD patients than in unaffected family members. Ovarian cysts occur in ADPKD women but the exact frequency has not been determined. Arachnoid cysts in the brain have been reported in 5% of ADPKD patients compared to 1% of control patients (Torres *et al.* 1990). Pancreatic cysts have been reported in various studies to have a frequency from rare to 7% (Zeier *et al.* 1988). Other cysts, such as seminal vesical cysts and splenic cysts, have rarely been reported (Dalgaard 1957; Alpern *et al.* 1991). None of these infrequent extrarenal cysts have been reported to result in clinical problems.

References

Alpern, M. B., Dorfman, R. E., Gross, B. H., Gottlieb, C. A., and Sandler, M. A. (1991). Seminal vesicle cysts: Association with adult polycystic kidney disease. *Radiology*, **180**, 79–80.

Anderson, D. and Tannen, R. L. (1969). Tuberous sclerosis and chronic renal failure. *Am. J. Med.*, **47**, 163–8.

Anderson, E. T. and Walker, B. R. (1969). Polycystic kidney disease, polycythemia, and azotemia. *J.A.M.A.*, **208**, 2472–3.

Ask-Upmark, E. and Ingvar, D. (1950). A follow-up examination of 138 cases of subarachnoid hemorrhage. *Acta Med. Scand.*, **138**, 15–31.

Avner, E. D., Sweeney, W. E. Jr., Finegold, D. N., Piesco, N. P., and Ellis, D. (1985). Sodium-potassium ATPase activity mediates cyst formation in metanephric organ culture. *Kidney Int.*, **28**, 447–55.

Avner, E. D., Studnicki, F. E., Young, M. C., Sweeney, W. E. Jr., Piesco, N. P., Ellis, D., *et al.* (1987). Congenital murine polycystic kidney disease. I. The ontogeny of tubular cyst formation. *Pediatr. Nephrol.*, **1**, 587–96.

Avner, E. D., Sweeney, W. E. Jr., Young, M. C., and Ellis, D. (1988). Congenital murine polycystic kidney disease. II. Pathogenesis of tubular cyst formation. *Pediatr. Nephrol.*, **2**, 210–8.

Avner, E. D. and Sweeney, W. E. (1992). Epidermal growth factor receptor, but not NaKATPase, is mislocated to apical cell surfaces of collecting tubule cysts in human autosomal recessive polycystic kidney disease. *J. Am. Soc. Nephrol.*, **3**, 292. (Abstract).

Avner, E. D., Sweeney, W. E., and Nelson, W. J. (1992). Abnormal sodium pump distribution during renal tubulogenesis in congenital murine polycystic kidney disease. *Proc. Natl. Acad. Sci.*, **89**, 7447–51.

Baert, L. (1978). Hereditary polycystic kidney disease (adult form): A microdissection study of two cases at an early stage of the disease. *Kidney Int.*, 13, 519–25.

Bear, J. C., McManamon, P., Morgan, J., Payne, R. H., Lewis, H., Gault, M. H., *et al.* (1984). Age at clinical onset and at ultrasonographic detection of adult polycystic kidney disease: Data for genetic counselling. *Am. J. Med. Genet.*, 18, 45–53.

Bear, J. C., Parfrey, P. S., Morgan, J. M., Martin, C. J., and Cramer, B. C. (1992). Autosomal dominant polycystic kidney disease: New information for genetic counselling. *Am. J. Med. Genet.*, 43, 548–53.

Bennett, W. M., Elzinga, L., Golper, T. A., and Barry, J. M. (1987). Reduction of cyst volume for symptomatic management of autosomal dominant polycystic kidney disease. *J. Urol.*, 137, 620–2.

Besarab, A., Caro, J., Jarrell, B. E., Francos, G., and Erslev, A. J. (1987). Dynamics of erythropoiesis following renal transplantation. *Kidney Int.*, 32, 526–36.

Bigelow, N. H. (1953). The association of polycystic kidneys with intracranial aneurysms and other related disorders. *Am. J. Med. Sci.*, 225, 485–94.

Blyth, H. and Ockenden, B. G. (1971). Polycystic disease of kidneys and liver presenting in childhood. *J. Med. Genet.*, 8, 257–84.

Brandt, P. W. T., Dacie, J. V., Steiner, R. E., and Szur, L. (1963). Incidence of renal lesions in polycythaemia: A survey of 91 patients. *Br. Med. J.*, 2, 468–72.

Bronshtein, M., Yoffe, N., Brandes, J. M., and Blumenfeld, Z. (1990). First and early second-trimester diagnosis of fetal urinary tract anomalies using transvaginal sonography. *Prenat. Diag.*, 10, 653–66.

Bronshtein, M., Bar-Hava, I., and Blumenfeld, Z. (1992). Clues and pitfalls in the early prenatal diagnosis of 'late-onset' infantile polycystic kidney. *Prenat. Diag.*, 12, 293–8.

Brown, R. A. P. (1951). Polycystic disease of the kidneys and intracranial aneurysms. Theaetiology and interrelationship of these conditions: Review of recent literature and report of seven cases in which both conditions coexisted. *Glasgow Med. J.*, 32, 333–48.

Carone, F. A., Makino, H., and Kanwar, Y. S. (1988). Basement membrane antigens in renal polycystic disease. *Am. J. Pathol.*, 130, 466–71.

Carone, F. A., Hollenberg, P. F., Nakamura, S., Punyarit, P., Glogowski, W., and Flouret, G. (1989). Tubular basement membrane change occurs *pari passu* with the development of cyst formation. *Kidney Int.*, 35, 1034–40.

Carone, F. A., Nakamura, S., Punyarit, P., Kanwar, Y. S., and Nelson, W. J. (1992). Sequential tubular cell and basement membrane changes in polycystic kidney disease. *J. Am. Soc. Nephrol.*, 3, 244–53.

Ceccherini, I., Lituania, M., Cordone, M. S., Perfumo, F., Gusmano, R., Callea, F., *et al.* (1989). Autosomal dominant polycystic kidney disease: Prenatal diagnosis by DNA analysis and sonography at 14 weeks. *Prenat. Diag.*, 9, 751–8.

Chandra, M., Miller, M. E., Garcia, J. F., Mossey, R. T., and McVicar, M. (1985). Serum immunoreactive erythropoietin levels in patients with polycystic kidney disease as compared with other hemodialysis patients. *Nephron*, 39, 26–9.

Chang, R., Seizinger, B. R., and Dwyer, A. J. (1990). Von Hippel–Lindau disease: Radiologic screening for visceral manifestations. *Radiology*, 174, 815–20.

Chapman, A. B., Johnson, A., Gabow, P. A., and Schrier, R. W. (1990). The renin–angiotensin–aldosterone system and autosomal dominant polycystic kidney disease. *N. Engl. J. Med.*, 323, 1091–6.

Chapman, A. B., Thickman, D., and Gabow, P. A. (1990). Percutaneous cyst puncture in the treatment of cyst infection in autosomal dominant polycystic kidney disease. *Am. J. Kidney Dis.*, 16, 252–5.

Chapman, A. B., Gabow, P. A., and Schrier, R. W. (1991). Reversible renal failure associated with angiotensin-converting enzyme inhibitors in polycystic kidney disease. *Ann. Intern. Med.*, 115, 769–73.

Chapman, A. B., Rubinstein, D., Hughes, R., Stears, J. C., Earnest, M. P., Johnson, A. M., *et al.* (1992). Intracranial aneurysms in autosomal dominant polycystic kidney disease. *N. Engl. J. Med.*, 327, 916–20.

Chapman, A. B., Johnson, A. M., and Gabow, P. A. (1993). Intracranial aneurysms in patients with autosomal dominant polycystic kidney disease: How to diagnose and who to screen. *Am. J. Kidney Dis.*, 22, 526–31.

Chauveau, D., Sirieix, M-E., Schillinger, F., Legendre, C., and Grunfeld, J-P. (1990). Recurrent rupture of intracranial aneurysms in autosomal dominant polycystic kidney disease. *Br. Med. J.*, 301, 966–7.

Chauveau, D., Pirson, Y., Verellen-Dumoulin, C., and Grünfeld, J-P. (1992). Ruptured intracranial aneurysms in autosomal dominant polycystic kidney disease *J. Am. Soc. Nephrol.*, 3, 293. (Abstract).

Choyke, P. L., Filling-Katz, M. R., Shawker, T. H., Gorin, M. B., Travis, W. D., Chang, R., *et al.* (1990). von Hippel—Lindau disease: Radiologic screening for visceral manifestations. *Radiology*, 174, 815–20.

Churchill, D. N., Bear, J. C., Morgan, J., Payne, R. H., McManamon, P. J., and Gault, M. H. (1984). Prognosis of adult-onset polycystic kidney disease reevaluated. *Kidney Int.*, 26, 190–3.

Cobben, J. M., Breuning, M. H., Schoots, C., Ten Kate, L. P., and Zerres, K. (1990). Congenital hepatic fibrosis in autosomal-dominant polycystic kidney disease. *Kidney Int.*, 38, 880–5.

Cohen, H. L. and Haller, J. O. (1987). Diagnostic sonography of the fetal genitourinary tract. *Urol. Radiol.*, 9, 88–98.

Cole, B. R., Conley, S. B., and Stapleton, F. B. (1987). Polycystic kidney disease in the first year of life. *J. Pediatr.*, 111, 693–9.

Cornell, S. H. (1970). Angiography in polycystic disease of the kidneys. *J. Urol.*, 103, 24–6.

Cuppage, F. E., Huseman, R. A., Chapman, A., and Grantham, J. J. (1980). Ultrastructure and function of cysts from human adult polycystic kidneys. *Kidney Int.*, 17, 372–81.

Dalgaard, O. Z. (1957). Bilateral polycystic disease of the kidneys: A follow-up of 284 patients and their families. *Acta Med. Scand.*, (Suppl.) 328, 1–255.

Danovitch, G. M. (1981). Clinical features and pathophysiology of polycystic kidney disease in man. *Jpn. J. Nephrol.*, 23, 999–1001.

Daoust, M. C., Reynolds, D. M., Bichet, D. G., and Somlo, S. (1995). Evidence for a third genetic locus for autosomal dominant polycystic kidney disease. *Genomics*, 25, 733–6.

De Bono, D. P. and Evans, D. B. (1977). The management of polycystic kidney disease with special reference to dialysis and transplantation. *Q. J. Med.*, 46, 353–63.

Delarue, F., Virone, A., Hagege, J., Lacave, R., Peraldi, M-N., Adida, C., *et al.* (1991). Stable cell line of T-SV40 immortalized human glomerular visceral epithelial cells. *Kidney Int.*, 40, 906–12.

DelGuercio, A., Greco, J., Kim, K. E., Chinitz, J., and Swartz, C. (1973). Esophageal varices in adult patients with polycystic kidney and liver disease. *N. Engl. J. Med.*, 289, 678–9.

Ditlefsen, E. M. L. and Tonjum, A. M. (1960). Intracranial aneurysms and polycystic kidneys. *Acta Med. Scand.*, 168, 51–4.

Dunger, R. (1904). Zur Lehre von der Cystenniere, mit besonderer Berucksichtigung ihrer Hereditat. *Beitr. Path. Anat.*, 35, 445–509.

Durham, D. S. (1987). Tuberous sclerosis mimicking adult polycystic kidney disease. *Aust. N. Z. J. Med.*, 17, 71–3.

Ebihara, I., Killen, P. D., Laurie, G. W., Huang, T., Yamada, Y., Martin, G. R., *et al.* (1988). Altered mRNA expression of basement membrane components in a murine model of polycystic kidney disease. *Lab. Invest.*, 58, 262–9.

Eckardt, K-U., Mollmann, M., Neumann, R., Brunkhorst, R., Burger, H-U., Lonnemann, G., *et al.* (1989). Erythropoietin in polycystic kidneys. *J. Clin. Invest.*, 84, 1160–6.

Elzinga, L. W., Barry, J. M., Torres, V. E., Zincke, H., Wahner, H. W., Swan, S., *et al.* (1992). Cyst decompression surgery for autosomal dominant polycystic kidney disease. *J. Am. Soc. Nephrol.*, **2**, 1219–26.

Ergun, H., Wolf, B. H., and Hissong, S. L. (1980). Obstructive jaundice caused by polycystic liver disease. *Radiology*, **136**, 435–6.

Ettinger, A., Kahn, P. C., and Wise, H. M. Jr. (1969). The importance of selective renal angiography in the diagnosis of polycystic disease. *J. Urol.*, **102**, 156–61.

European Polycystic Kidney Disease Consortium (1994). The polycystic kidney disease 1 gene encodes a 14 kb transcript and lies within a duplicated region on chromosome 16. *Cell*, **77**, 881–94.

Evan, A. P., Gardner, K. D. Jr., and Bernstein, J. (1979). Polypoid and papillary epithelial hyperplasia: A potential cause of ductal obstruction in adult polycystic disease. *Kidney Int.*, **16**, 743–50.

Everson, G. T., Scherzinger, A., Berger-Leff, N., Reichen, J., Lezotte, D., Manco-Johnson, M., *et al.* (1988). Polycystic liver disease: Quantitation of parenchymal and cyst volumes from computed tomography images and clinical correlates of hepatic cysts. *Hepatology*, **8**, 1627–34.

Everson, G. T., Emmett, M., Brown, W. R., Redmond, P., and Thickman, D. (1990). Functional similarities of hepatic cystic and biliary epithelium: Studies of fluid constituents and *in vivo* secretion in response to secretin. *Hepatology*, **11**, 557–65.

Fahsold, R., Rott, H-D., and Lorenz, P. (1991). A third gene locus for tuberous sclerosis is closely linked to the phenylalanine hydroxylase gene locus. *Hum. Genet.*, **88**, 85–90.

Fick, G. M., Johnson, A. M., Strain, J. D., Kimberling, W. J., Kumar, S., Manco-Johnson, M. L., *et al.* (1993). Characteristics of very early-onset autosomal dominant polycystic kidney disease. *J. Am. Soc. Nephrol.*, **3**, 1863–70.

Fick, G. M., Duley, I. T., Johnson, A. M., Strain, J., Manco-Johnson, M. L., and Gabow, P. A. (1994). The spectrum of autosomal dominant polycystic kidney disease in children. *J. Am. Soc. Nephrol.*, **4**, 1654–60.

Fick, G. M., Johnson, A. M., and Gabow, P. A. (1994). Is there evidence for anticipation in autosomal dominant polycystic kidney disease? *Kidney Int.*, **45**, 1153–62.

Filling-Katz, M. R., Choyke, P. L., Oldfield, E., Charnas, L. Patronas, N. J., Glenn, G. M., *et al.* (1991). Central nervous system involvement in von Hippel–Lindau disease. *Neurology*, **41**, 41–6.

Fitzpatrick, P. M., Torres, V. E., Charboneau, J. W., Offord, K. P., Holley, K. E., and Zincke, H. (1990). Long-term outcome of renal transplantation in autosomal dominant polycystic kidney disease. *Am. J. Kidney Dis.*, **15**, 535–43.

Forssell, J. (1958). Nephrogenous polycythaemia. *Acta Med. Scand.*, **161**, 169–79.

Gabow, P. A., Iklé, D. W., and Holmes, J. H. (1984). Polycystic kidney disease: Prospective analysis of non-azotemic patients and family members. *Ann. Intern. Med.*, **101**, 238–47.

Gabow, P. A., Kaehny, W. D., Johnson, A. M., Duley, I. T., Manco-Johnson, M., Lezotte, D. C., *et al.* (1989). The clinical utility of renal concentrating capacity in polycystic kidney disease. *Kidney Int.*, **35**, 675–80.

Gabow, P. A., Grantham. J. J., Bennett, W., Childress, J. F., Cole, B., Conneally, P. M., *et al.* (1989). Gene testing in autosomal dominant polycystic kidney disease: Results of National Kidney Foundation workshop. *Am. J. Kidney Dis.*, **13**, 85–7.

Gabow, P. A. (1990). Autosomal dominant polycystic kidney disease—More than a renal disease. *Am. J. Kidney Dis.*, **16**, 403–13. (Review).

Gabow, P. A., Chapman, A. B., Johnson, A. M., Tangel, D. J., Duley, I. T., Kaehny, W. D., *et al.* (1990). Renal structure and hypertension in autosomal dominant polycystic kidney disease. *Kidney Int.*, **38**, 1177–80.

Gabow, P. A., Johnson, A. M., Kaehny, W. D., Manco-Johnson, M. L., Duley, I. T., and Everson, G. T. (1990). Risk factors for the development of hepatic cysts in autosomal dominant polycystic kidney disease. *Hepatology*, **11**, 1033–7.

Gabow, P. A. and Bennett, W. M. (1991). Renal manifestations: Complication management and long-term outcome of autosomal dominant polycystic kidney disease. *Semin. Nephrol.*, **11**, 643–52.

Gabow, P. A. and Wilkins-Haug, L. (1991). Prediction of likelihood of polycystic kidney disease in the fetus when a parent has autosomal dominant polycystic kidney disease. In: *International yearbook of nephrology 1992* (ed. V. E. Andreucci and L. G. Fine), pp. 199–207. Springer-Verlag, London.

Gabow, P. A., Duley, I., and Johnson, A. M. (1992). Clinical profiles of gross hematuria in autosomal dominant polycystic kidney disease. *Am. J. Kidney Dis.*, **20**, 140–3.

Gabow, P. A., Johnson, A. M., Kaehny W. D., Kimberling, W. J., Lezotte, D. C., Duley, I. T., *et al.* (1992). Factors affecting the progression of renal disease in autosomal-dominant polycystic kidney disease. *Kidney Int.*, **41**, 1311–19.

Gabow, P. A. (1993). Autosomal dominant polycystic kidney disease. *N. Engl. J. Med.*, **329**, 332–42.

Gabow, P. A. and Grantham, J. J. Polycystic kidney disease. In *Diseases of the kidney* (5th ed) (ed. R. W. Schrier and C. W. Gottschalk), pp. Little, Brown and Company; Boston, 1993, 535–69.

Gabow, P. A., Kimberling, W. J., Strain, J. D., Manco-Johnson, M. L., and Johnson, A. M. (1997). Utility of ultrasonography in the diagnosis of autosomal dominant polycystic kidney disease. *J. Am. Soc. Nephrol.*, **8**, 105–10.

Gattone, V. H. and Calvet, J. P. (1991). Murine infantile polycystic kidney disease: A role for reduced renal epidermal growth factor. *Am. J. Kidney Dis.*, **17**, 606–7.

Gattone, V. H. and Lowden, D. A. (1992). Epidermal growth factor ameliorates infantile polycystic kidney disease in mice. *J. Am. Soc. Nephrol.*, **3**, 295.

Gilbert-Barness, E. F., Opitz, J. M., and Barness, L. A. (1990). Heritable malformations of the kidney and urinary tract. In: *Inheritance of kidney and urinary tract diseases* (ed. A. Spitzer and E. D. Avner), pp. 327–400. Kluwer Academic Publishers, Boston.

Gonzalo, A., Rivera, M., Quereda, C., and Ortuno, J. (1990). Clinical features and prognosis of adult polycystic kidney disease. *Am. J. Nephrol.*, **10**, 470–4.

Graham, P. C. and Lindop, G. B. M. (1988). The anatomy of the renin-secreting cell in adult polycystic kidney disease. *Kidney Int.*, **33**, 1084–90.

Granot, Y., Van Putten, V., Przekwas, J., Gabow, P. A., and Schrier, R. W. (1990). Intra- and extracellular proteins in human normal and polycystic kidney epithelial cells. *Kidney Int.*, **37**, 1301–9.

Grantham, J. J., Geiser, J. L., and Evan, A. P. (1987). Cyst formation and growth in autosomal dominant polycystic kidney disease. *Kidney Int.*, **31**, 1145–52.

Grantham, J. J., Uchic, M., Cragoe, E. J. Jr., Kornhaus, J., Grantham, J. A., Donoso, V., *et al.* (1989). Chemical modification of cell proliferation and fluid secretion in renal cysts. *Kidney Int.*, **35**, 1379–89.

Gregoire, J. R., Torres, V. E., Holley, K. E., and Farrow, G. M. (1987). Renal epithelial hyperplastic and neoplastic proliferation in autosomal dominant polycystic kidney disease. *Am. J. Kidney Dis.*, **9**, 27–38.

Gretz, N., Zeier, M., Geberth, S., Strauch, M., and Ritz, E. (1989). Is gender a determinant for evolution of renal failure? A study in autosomal dominant polycystic kidney disease. *Am. J. Kidney Dis.*, **14**, 178–83.

Grunfeld, J. P., Albouze, G., Jungers, P., Landais, P., Dana, A., Droz, D., *et al.* (1985). Liver changes and complications in adult polycystic kidney disease. *Adv. Nephrol.*, **14**, 1–20.

Guay-Woodford, L. M., Muecher, G., Hopkins, S. D., Avner, E. D., Germino, G. G., Guillot, A. P., *et al.* (1995). The severe perinatal form of autosomal recessive polycystic kidney disease maps to chromosome 6p21.1–p12: Implications for genetic counseling. *Am. J. Hum. Genet.*, **56**, 1101–7.

Haines, J. L., Short, M. P., Kwiatkowski, D. J., Jewell, A., Andermann, E., Bejjani, B., *et al.* (1991). Localization of one gene for tuberous sclerosis within 9q32–9q34, and further evidence for heterogeneity. *Am. J. Hum. Genet.*, **49**, 764–72.

Hannig, V. L., Hopkins, J. R., Johnson, H. K., Phillips, J. A., and Reeders, S. T. (1991). Presymptomatic testing for adult-onset polycystic kidney disease in at-risk kidney transplant donors. *Am. J. Med. Genet.*, **40**, 425–8.

Harding, M. A., Gattone, V. H., Grantham, J. J., and Calvet, J. P. (1992). Localization of overexpressed c-myc mRNA in polycystic kidneys of the cpk mouse. *Kidney Int.*, **41**, 317–25.

Harley, H. G., Rundle, S. A., Reardon, W., Myring, J., Crow, S., Brook, J. D., *et al.* (1992). Unstable DNA sequence in myotonic dystrophy. *Lancet*, **339**, 1125–8.

Higgins, C. C. (1952). Bilateral polycystic kidney disease: Review of ninety-four cases. *Arch. Surg.*, **65**, 318–29.

Heggö, O. (1966). A microdissection study of cystic disease of the kidneys in adults. *J. Pathol. Bact.*, **91**, 311–5.

Hossack, K. F., Leddy, C. L., Johnson, A. M., Schrier, R. W., and Gabow, P. A. (1988). Echocardiographic findings in autosomal dominant polycystic kidney disease. *N. Engl. J. Med.*, **319**, 907–12.

Howard, R. J., Hanson, R. F., and Delaney, J. P. (1976). Jaundice associated with polycystic liver disease: Relief by surgical decompression of the cysts. *Arch. Surg.*, **111**, 816–17.

Huston, J. III., Torres, V. E., Sullivan, P. P., Offord, K. P., and Wiebers, D. O. (1993). Value of magnetic resonance angiography for the detection of intracrainal aneurysms in autosomal dominant polycystic kidney disease. *J. Am. Soc. Nephrol.*, **3**, 1871–7.

Iannuccilli, E. A. and Yu, P. P. (1981). Adult fibropolycystic liver disease and symptomatic portal hypertension. Only five cases of this rare combination have been reported. *R. I. Med. J.*, **64**, 551–4.

Iglesias, C. G., Torres, V. E., Offord, K. P., Holley, K. E., Beard, C. M., and Kurland, L. T. (1983). Epidemiology of adult polycystic kidney disease, Olmstead County, Minnesota, 1935–1980. *Am. J. Kidney Dis.*, **2**, 630–9.

Imamura, M., Miyashita, T., Tani, T., Naito, A., Tobe, T., and Takahashi, K. (1984). Cholangiocellular carcinoma associated with multiple liver cysts. *Am. J. Gastroenterol.*, **79**, 790–5.

Jones, W. L., Mountain, J. C., and Warren, K. W. (1974) Symptomatic non-parasitic cysts of the liver. *Br. J. Surg.*, **61**, 118–23.

Kaariainen, H. (1987). Polycystic kidney disease in children: A genetic and epidemiological study of 82 Finnish patients. *J. Med. Genet.*, **24**, 474–81.

Kaariainen, H., Jaaskelainen, J., Kivisaari, L., Koskimies, O., and Norio, R. (1988). Dominant and recessive polycystic kidney disease in children: Classification by intravenous pyelography, ultrasound, and computed tomography. *Pediatr. Radiol.*, **18**, 45–50.

Kaariainen, H., Koskimies, O., and Norio, R. (1988). Dominant and recessive polycystic kidney disease in children: Evaluation of clinical features and laboratory data. *Pediatr. Nephrol.*, **2**, 296–302.

Kaehny, W. D., Tangel, D. J., Johnson, A. M., Kimberling, W. J., Schrier, R. W., and Gabow, P. A. (1990). Uric acid handling in autosomal dominant polycystic kidney disease with normal filtration rates. *Am. J. Med.*, **89**, 49–52.

Kaehny, W. D. and Everson, G. T. (1991). Extrarenal manifestations of autosomal dominant polycystic kidney disease. *Semin. Nephrol.*, **11**, 661–70.

Kaiser, B., Dunn, S., Falkenstien, K., Mochon, M., Piccoli, D., and Baluarte, H. J. (1990). Successful combined liver/kidney transplantation in a child with congenital hepatic fibrosis and infantile polycystic kidney disease *J. Am. Soc. Nephrol.*, **1**, 761. (Abstract).

Kandt, R. S., Haines, J. L., Smith, M., Northrup, H., Gardner, R. J. M., Short, M. P., et al. (1992). Linkage of important gene locus for tuberous sclerosis to a chromosome 16 marker for polycystic kidney disease. *Nature Genet.*, **2**, 37–41.

Kaplan, B. S., Kaplan, P., de Chadarevian, J-P., Jequier, S., O'Regan, S., and Russo, P. (1988). Variable expression of autosomal recessive polycystic kidney disease and congenital hepatic fibrosis within a family. *Am. J. Med. Genet.*, **29**, 639–47.

Kaplan, B. S., Fay, J., Shah, V., Dillion, M. J., and Barratt, T. M. (1989). Autosomal recessive polycystic kidney disease. *Pediatr. Nephrol.*, **3**, 43–9.

Kaplan, B. S. and Kaplan, P. (1990). Autosomal recessive polycystic kidney disease. In: *Inheritance of kidney and urinary tract diseases* (ed. A. Spitzer and E. D. Avner), pp. 265–76. Kluwer Academic Publishers, Boston.

Kelley, K. A., Agarwal, N., Reeders, S., and Herrup, K. (1991). Renal cyst formation and multifocal neoplasia in transgenic mice carrying the simian virus 40 early region. *J. Am. Soc. Nephrol.*, **2**, 84–97.

Kimberling, W. J., Fain, P. R., Kenyon, J. B., Goldgar, D., Sujansky, E., and Gabow, P. A. (1988). Linkage heterogeneity of autosomal dominant polycystic kidney disease. *N. Engl. J. Med.*, **319**, 913–18.

Kimberling, W. J., Pieke, S. A., Kenyon, J. B., and Gabow, P. A. (1990). An estimate of the proportion of families with autosomal dominant polycystic kidney disease unlinked to chromosome 16 *Kidney Int.*, **37**, 249. (Abstract).

Kimberling, W. J, Pieke-Dahl, S. A., and Kumar, S. (1991). The genetics of cystic diseases of the kidney. *Semin. Nephrol.*, **11**, 596–606.

Kimberling, W. J., Kumar, S., Gabow, P. A., Kenyon, J. B., Connolly, C. J., and Somlo, S. (1993). Autosomal dominant polycystic kidney disease: Localization of the second gene to chromosome 4q13–q23. *Genomics*, **18**, 467–72.

Kumar, S., Cederbaum, A. I., and Pletka, P. G. (1980). Renal cell carcinoma in polycystic kidneys: Case report and review of literature. *J. Urol.*, **124**, 708–9.

Lazarus, J. M., Bailey, G. L., Hampers, C. L., and Merrill, J. P. (1971). Hemodialysis and transplantation in adults with polycystic renal disease. *J.A.M.A.*, **217**, 1821–4.

Leier, C. V., Baker, P. B., Kilman, J. W., and Wooley, C. F. (1984). Cardiovascular abnormalities associated with adult polycystic kidney disease. *Ann. Intern. Med.*, **100**, 683–8.

Levey, A. S., Pauker, S. G., and Kassirer, J. P. (1983). Occult intracranial aneurysms in polycystic kidney disease: When is cerebral arteriography indicated? *N. Engl. J. Med.*, **308**, 986–94.

Levey, A. S. (1990). Screening for occult intracranial aneurysms in polycystic kidney disease: Interim guidelines. *J. Am. Soc. Nephrol.*, **1**, 9–12. (Editorial).

Levine, E. and Grantham, J. J. (1992). Calcified renal stones and cyst calcifications in autosomal dominant polycystic and kidney disease: Clinical and CT study in 84 patients. *A.J.R.*, **159**, 77–81.

Lin, T. Y., Chen, C. C., and Wang, S. M. (1968). Treatment of non-parasitic disease of the liver. A new approach to therapy with polycystic liver. *Ann. Surg.*, **168**, 921–7.

Macias, W. L., McAteer, J. A., Tanner, G. A., Fritz, A. L., and Armstrong, W. M. (1992). NaCl transport by Madin–Darby canine kidney cyst epithelial cells. *Kidney Int.*, **42**, 308–19.

Maggiore, Q., Navalesi, R., Biagini, M., Balestri, P. L., and Giagnoni, P. (1967). Comparative studies on uraemic anaemia in polycystic kidney disease and in other renal diseases. *Proc. Eur. Dialysis Transplant Assoc.*, **4**, 264–6.

Maher, E. R., Yates, J. R. W., Harries, R., Benjamin, C., Harris, R., Moore, A. T., *et al.* (1990). Clinical features and natural history of Hippel–Lindau disease. *Quarterly J. Med.*, **77**, 1151–63.

Mahony, B. S., Callen, P. W., Filly, R. A., and Golbus, M. S. (1984). Progression of infantile polycystic kidney disease in early pregnancy. *J. Ultrasound Med.*, **3**, 277–9.

Malek, R. S., Omess, P. J., Benson, R. C. Jr., and Zincke, H. (1987). Renal cell carcinoma in von Hippel–Lindau syndrome. *Am. J. Med.*, **82**, 236–8.

Mangoo-Karim, R., Uchic, M., Lechene, C., and Grantham, J. J. (1989). Renal epithelial cyst formation and enlargement *in vitro*: Dependence on cAMP. *Proc. Natl. Acad. Sci. USA*, **86**, 6007–11.

Milutinovic, J., Fialkow, P. J., Rudd, T. G., Agodoa, L. Y., Phillips, L. A., and Bryant, J. I. (1980). Liver cysts in patients with autosomal dominant polycystic kidney disease. *Am. J. Med.*, **68**, 741–4.

Milutinovic, J. and Agodoa, L. Y. (1983). Potential causes and pathogenesis in autosomal dominant polycystic kidney disease. *Nephron*, **33**, 139–44.

Milutinovic, J., Fialkow, P. J., Agodoa, L. Y., Phillips, L. A., and Bryant, J. I. (1983). Fertility and pregnancy complications in women with autosomal dominant polycystic kidney disease. *Obstet. Gynecol.*, **61**, 566–70.

Milutinovic, J., Fialkow, P. J., Agodoa, L. Y., Phillips, L. A., Rudd, T. G., and Bryant, J. I. (1984). Autosomal dominant polycystic kidney disease: Symptoms and clinical findings. *Q. J. Med.*, **53**, 511–22.

Milutinovic, J., Rust, P. F., Fialkow, P. J., Agodoa, L. Y., Phillips, L. A., Rudd, T. G., *et al.* (1992). Intrafamilial phenotypic expression of autosomal dominant polycystic kidney disease. *Am. J. Kidney Dis.*, **19**, 465–72.

Mochizuki, T., Wu, G., Hayashi, T., Xenophontos, S. L., Veldhuisen, B., Saris, J. J., *et al.* (1996). PKD2, a gene for polycystic kidney disease that encodes an integral membrane protein. *Science*, **272**, 1339–42.

Newman, K. D., Torres, V. E., Rakela, J., and Nagorney, D. M. (1990). Treatment of highly symptomatic polycystic liver disease: Preliminary experience with a combined hepatic resection–fenestration procedure. *Ann. Surg.*, **212**, 30–7.

Ng, R. C. K. and Suki, W. N. (1980). Renal cell carcinoma occurring in a polycystic kidney of a transplant recipient. *J. Urol.*, **124**, 710–12.

Novelli, G., Frontali, M., Baldini, D., Bosman, C., Dallapiccola, B., Pachi, A., *et al.* (1989). Prenatal diagnosis of adult polycystic kidney disease with DNA markers on chromosome 16 and the genetic heterogeneity problem. *Prenat. Diag.*, **9**, 759–67.

Ojeda, J. L., Ros, M. A., Icardo, J. M., and Garcia-Porrero, J. A. (1990). Basement membrane alterations during development and regression of tubular cysts. *Kidney Int.*, **37**, 1270–80.

Okuda, K., Kubo, Y., Okazaki, N., Arishima, T., Hashimoto, M., Jinnouchi, S., *et al.* (1977). Clinical aspects of intrahepatic bile duct carcinoma including hilar carcinoma: A study of 57 autopsy-proven cases. *Cancer*, **39**, 232–46.

Osathanondh, V. and Potter, E. L. (1964). Pathogenesis of polycystic kidneys: Historical survey. *Arch. Pathol.*, **77**, 459–65.

Pabico, R. C. and McKenna, B. A. (1992). Renal tubular dysfunction in cystic disease of the kidney. *J. Am. Soc. Nephrol.*, **3**, 300. (Abstract).

Parfrey, P. S., Bear, J. C., Morgan, J., Cramer, B. C., McManamon, P. J., Gault, M. H., *et al.* (1990). The diagnosis and prognosis of autosomal dominant polycystic kidney disease. *N. Engl. J. Med.*, **323**, 1085–90.

Pavlovic-Kentera, V., Clemons, G. K., Djukanovic, L., and Biljanovic-Paunovic, L. (1987). Erythropoietin and anemia in chronic renal failure. *Exp. Hematol.*, **15**, 785–9.

Potter, E. L. (1972). *Normal and abnormal development of the kidney.* Chicago Year Book.

Pretorius, D. H., Lee, M. E., Manco-Johnson, M. L., Weingast, G. R., Sedman, A. B., and Gabow, P. A. (1987). Diagnosis of autosomal dominant polycystic disease *in utero* and in the young infant. *J. Ultrasound Med.*, **6**, 249–55.

Preuss, H., Geoly, K., Johnson, M., Chester, A., Kliger, A., and Schreiner, G. (1979). Tubular function in adult polycystic kidney disease. *Nephron*, **24**, 198–204.

Ratcliffe, P. J., Reeders, S., and Theaker, J. M. (1984). Bleeding oesophageal varices and hepatic dysfunction in adult polycystic kidney disease. *Br. Med. J.*, **288**, 1330–1.

Reeders, S. T., Gal, A., Propping, P., Waldherr, R., Davies, K. E., Zerres, K., *et al.* (1986). Prenatal diagnosis of autosomal dominant polycystic kidney disease with a DNA probe. *Lancet*, **2**, 6–8.

Reeders, S. T., Germino, G. G., and Gillespie, G. A. J. (1989). Recent advances in the genetics of renal cystic disease. *Mol. Biol. Med.*, **6**, 81–6.

Regan, R. J., Abercrombie, G. F., and Lee, H. A. (1977). Polycystic renal disease: Occurrence of malignant change and role of nephrectomy in potential transplant recipients. *Br. J. Urol.*, **49**, 85–91.

Reilly, K. B., Rubin, S. P., Blanke, B. G., and Yeh, M-N. (1979). Infantile polycystic kidney disease: A difficult antenatal diagnosis. *Am. J. Obstet. Gynecol.*, **133**, 580–2.

Richards, R. I. and Sutherland, G. R. (1992). Dynamic mutations: A new class of mutations causing human disease. *Cell*, **70**, 709–12. (Review).

Richmond, H. G. (1956). Carcinoma arising in congenital cysts of the liver. *J. Pathol. Bacteriol.*, **72**, 681–3.

Roach, E. S. (1992). Neurocutaneous syndromes. *Ped. Clin. N. Am.*, **39**, 591–620.

Romero, R., Cullen, M., Jeanty, P., Grannum, P., Reece, E. A., Venus, I., *et al.* (1984). The diagnosis of congenital renal anomalies with ultrasound. II. Infantile polycystic kidney disease. *Am. J. Obstet. Gynecol.*, **150**, 259–62.

Romeo, G., Devoto, M., Costa, G., Roncuzzi, L., Catizone, L., Zucchelli, P., *et al.* (1988). A second genetic locus for autosomal dominant polycystic kidney disease. *Lancet*, **2**, 8–10.

Ryu, S-J. (1990). Intracranial hemorrhage in patients with polycystic kidney disease. *Stroke*, **21**, 291–4.

Scheff, R. T., Zuckerman, G., Harter, H., Delmez, J., and Koehler, R. (1980). Diverticular disease in patients with chronic renal failure due to polycystic kidney disease. *Ann. Intern. Med.*, **92**, 202–4.

Schievink, W. I., Torres, V. E., Piepgras, D. G., and Wiebers, D. O. (1992). Saccular intracranial aneurysms in autosomal dominant polycystic kidney disease. *J. Am. Soc. Nephrol.*, **3**, 88–95.

Schwab, S. J. (1985). Efficacy of chloramphenicol in refractory cyst infections in autosomal dominant polycystic kidney disease. *Am. J. Kidney Dis.*, **5**, 258–61.

Schwab, S. J., Bander, S. J., and Klahr, S. (1987). Renal infection in autosomal dominant polycystic kidney disease. *Am. J. Med.*, **82**, 714–18.

Seedat, Y. K., Naicker S, Rawat, R., and Parsoo, I. (1984). Racial differences in the causes of end-stage renal failure in Natal. *S. Afr. Med. J.*, **65**, 956–8.

Singh, S. and Hariharan, S. (1991). Renal replacement therapy in autosomal dominant polycystic kidney disease. *Nephron*, **57**, 40–4.

Sogbein, S. K., Moors, D. E., and Jindal, S. L. (1981). A case of bilateral renal cell carcinoma in polycystic kidneys. *Can. J. Surg.*, **24**, 193–4.

Solomon, D. and Schwartz, A. (1988). Renal pathology in von Hippel–Lindau disease. *Hum. Path.*, **19**, 1072–9.

Stapleton, F. B., Magill, H. L., and Kelley, D. R. (1983). Infantile polycystic kidney disease: An imaging dilemma. *Urol. Radiol.*, **5**, 89–94.

Stillwell, T. J., Gomez, M. R., and Kelalis, P. P. (1987). Renal lesions in tuberous sclerosis. *J. Urol.*, **138**, 477–81.

Sujansky, E., Kreutzer, S. B., Johnson, A. M., Lezotte, D. C., Schrier, R. W., and Gabow, P. A. (1990). Attitudes of at-risk and affected individuals regarding presymptomatic testing for autosomal dominant polycystic kidney disease. *Am. J. Med. Genet.*, **35**, 510–15.

Suter, W. (1949). Das kongenitale aneurysma der basalen gehirnarterien und cystennieren. *Schweiz. Med. Wochenschr.*, **79**, 471–6.

Tanner, G. A., Maxwell, M. R., and McAteer, J. A. (1992). Fluid transport in a cultured cell model of kidney epithelial cyst enlargement. *J. Am. Soc. Nephrol.*, **2**, 1208–18.

Taub, M., Laurie, G. W., Martin, G. R., and Kleinman, H. K. (1990). Altered basement membrane protein biosynthesis by primary cultures of cpk/cpk mouse kidney. *Kidney Int.*, **37**, 1090–7.

Tegtmeyer, C. J., Cail, W., Wyker, A. W. Jr., and Gillenwater, J. Y. (1978). Angiographic diagnosis of renal tumors associated with polycystic disease. *Radiology*, **126**, 105–9.

Telenti, A., Torres, V. E., Gross, J. B. Jr., Van Scoy, R. E., Brown, M. L., and Hattery, R. R. (1990). Hepatic cyst infection in autosomal dominant polycystic kidney disease. *Mayo. Clin. Proc.*, **65**, 933–42.

Thaysen, J. H. and Thomsen, H. S. (1982). Involution of polycystic kidneys during replacement therapy of terminal renal failure. *Acta Med. Scand.*, **212**, 389–94.

Timio, M., Monarca, C., Pede, S., Gentili, S., Verdura, C., and Lolli, S. (1992). The spectrum of cardiovascular abnormalities in autosomal dominant polycystic kidney disease: A 10-year follow-up in a five-generation kindred. *Clin. Nephrol.*, **37**, 245–51.

Torres, V. E., Holley, K. E., and Offord, K. P. (1985). General features of autosomal dominant polycystic kidney disease: Epidemiology. In: *Problems in diagnosis and management of polycystic kidney disease* (ed. J. J. Grantham and K. D. Gardner), pp. 49–69. PKR Foundation, Kansas City.

Torres, V. E., Erickson, S. B., Smith, L. H., Wilson, D. M., Hattery, R. R., and Segura, J. W. (1988). The association of nephrolithiasis and autosomal dominant polycystic kidney disease. *Am. J. Kidney Dis.*, **11**, 318–25.

Torres, V. E., Wiebers, D. O., and Forbes, G. S. (1990). Cranial computed tomography and magnetic resonance imaging in autosomal dominant polycystic kidney disease. *J. Am. Soc. Nephrol.*, **1**, 84–90.

Trudel, M., D'Agati, V., and Costantini, F. (1991). c-myc as an inducer of polycystic kidney disease in transgenic mice. *Kidney Int.*, **39**, 665–71.

Turco, A., Peissel, B., Quaia, P., Morandi, R., Bovicelli, L., and Pignatti, P. F. (1992). Prenatal diagnosis of autosomal dominant polycystic kidney disease using flanking DNA markers and the polymerase chain reaction. *Prenat. Diag.*, **12**, 513–24.

van Erpecum, K. J., Janssens, A. R., Terpstra, J. L., Tjon, A., and Tham RTO. (1987). Highly symptomatic adult polycystic disease of the liver: A report of 15 cases. *J. Hepatol.*, **5**, 109–17.

Verani, R., Walker, P., and Silva, F. G. (1989). Renal cystic disease of infancy: Results of histochemical studies. *Pediatr. Nephrol.*, **3**, 37–42.

Wakabayashi, T., Fujita, S., Ohbora, Y., Suyama, T., Tamaki, N., and Matsumoto, S. (1983). Polycystic kidney disease and intracranial aneurysms: Early angiographic diagnosis and early operation for the unruptured aneurysm. *J. Neurosurg.*, **58**, 488–91.

Warholm, C., Rekola, S., and Roll, M. (1992). Fatal outcome of bilateral nephrectomy in a patient with polycystic kidney disease: Case report. *Scand. J. Urol. Nephrol.*, **26**, 201–3.

Webb, D. W. and Osborne, J. P. (1992). New research in tuberous sclerosis. *Br. Med. J.*, **304**, 1647–8.

Wenzl, J. E., Lagos, J. C., and Albers, D. D. (1970). Tuberous sclerosis presenting as polycystic kidneys and seizures in an infant. *J. Pediatr.*, **77**, 673–4.

Willis, R. A. (1943). Carcinoma arising in congenital cysts of the liver. *J. Pathol.*, **55**, 492–5.

Wilkinson, J. E., Woychik, R., Godfrey, V. L., and Moyer, J. (1993). The TG737 mouse: An animal model of ARPKD. In: *Proceedings of Fifth International Workshop on Polycystic Kidney Disease* (ed. P. A. Gabow and J. J. Grantham), p. 144. Polycystic Kidney Research Foundation, Kansas City.

Wilson, P. D., Schrier, R. W., Breckon, R. D., and Gabow, P. A. (1986). A new method for studying human polycystic kidney disease epithelia in culture. *Kidney Int.*, **30**, 371–8.

Wilson, P. D. (1991). Aberrant epithelial cell growth in autosomal dominant polycystic kidney disease. *Am. J. Kidney Dis.*, **17**, 634–7.

Wilson, P. D., Sherwood, A. C., Palla, K., Du, J., Watson, R., and Norman, J. T. (1991). Reversed polarity of Na+-K+-ATPase: Mislocation to apical plasma membranes in polycystic kidney disease epithelia. *Am. J. Physiol.*, **260**, F420–F430.

Wilson, P. D., Hreniuk, D., and Gabow, P. A. (1992). Abnormal extracellular matrix and excessive growth of human adult polycystic kidney disease epithelia. *J. Cell Physiol.*, **150**, 360–9.

Wittig, J. H., Burns, R., Longmire, W. P. Jr. (1978). Jaundice associated with polycystic liver disease. *Am. J. Surg.*, **136**, 383–6.

Ye, M. and Grantham, J. J. (1993). The secretion of fluid by renal cysts from patients with autosomal dominant polycystic kidney disease. *N. Engl. J. Med.*, **329**, 310–13.

Yium, J., Gabow, P., Johnson, A., Kimberling, W., and Martinez-Maldonado, M. (1994). Autosomal dominant polycystic kidney disease in blacks: Clinical course and effects of sickle-cell hemoglobin. *J. Am. Soc. Nephrol.*, **4**, 1670–4.

Yu, D. T. and Sheth, K. J. (1985). Cystic renal involvement in tuberous sclerosis. *Clin. Peds.*, **24**, 36–9.

Zeier, M., Geberth, S., Ritz, E., Jaeger, T., and Waldherr, R. (1988). Adult dominant polycystic kidney disease: Clinical problems. *Nephron*, **49**, 177–83. (Editorial).

Zeier, M., Fehrenbach, P., Geberth, S., Möhring, K., Waldherr, R., and Ritz, E. (1992). Renal histology in polycystic kidney disease with incipient and advanced renal failure. *Kidney Int.*, **42**, 1259–65.

Zeier, M., Geberth, S., Schmidt, K. G., Mandelbaum, A., and Ritz, E. (1993). Elevated blood pressure profile and left ventricular mass in children and young adults with autosomal dominant polycystic kidney disease. *J. Am. Soc. Nephrol.*, **3**, 1451–7.

Zerres, K. (1992). Polycystic kidney disease: Thoughts on the meaning of prevention. In: *Contributions to nephrology: polycystic kidney disease* (ed. G. M. Berlyne and S. Giovannetti), pp. 7–14. Karger, Basel.

Zerres, K., Mucher, G., Bachner, L., Deschennes, G., Eggermann, T., Kaariainen, H., *et al.* (1994). Mapping of the gene for autosomal recessive polycystic kidney disease (ARPKD) to chromosome 6p21-cen. *Nature Genet.*, **7**, 429–32.

9

Familial and genetic aspects of primary vesicoureteric reflux

Ross R. Bailey[†]

Introduction

Reflux nephropathy is the cause of about 10% of all cases of end-stage renal failure, and up to 50% of those presenting in childhood (Disney 1991; Bailey 1992; Bailey *et al.* 1993, 1994). Reflux nephropathy is therefore comparable in frequency to autosomal dominant adult polycystic kidney disease as a cause of end-stage renal failure. Reflux nephropathy is associated with the severer degrees of primary vesicoureteric reflux (Bailey 1973, 1992; Bailey *et al.* 1993). The latter is due to a congenital anomaly (McGovern *et al.* 1960; Hutch 1961), which in some instances is familial and inherited. This chapter will review the familial and genetic data so far reported in patients with primary vesicoureteric reflux or reflux nephropathy.

Family studies

Twins and triplets (Table 9.1)

Since Stephens *et al.* (1955) reported vesicoureteric reflux in a set of identical twins there have been several further reports (Mebust and Foret 1972; Pochaczevsky *et al.* 1974; Hampel *et al.* 1975; Redman 1976; De Vargas *et al.* 1978; Kerr and Pillai 1983; Winearls and Hind 1983).

In addition, vesicoureteric reflux has been reported in a set of triplet girls (Hayden and Koff 1984). The triplets (two monozygotic and one dizygotic) were 14 weeks old when investigated for urinary tract infections in the monozygotic pair; the latter already had reflux nephropathy at presentation. The asymptomatic dizygotic triplet had no evidence of renal parenchymal scarring.

Early family studies

Since the early 1960s, a number of authors have reported a familial aggregation of vesicoureteric reflux, but the mode of inheritance was unclear. Several investigators suggested that vesicoureteric reflux may be a multifactorial trait (Burger 1972; Mobley 1973; Burger and Burger 1974; Bois *et al.* 1975; De Vargas *et al.* 1978; Jerkins and Noe 1982), while others proposed an autosomal dominant gene with variable penetrance (Miller and Caspari 1972; Frye *et al.* 1974; Lewy and Belman 1975; Atwell *et al.* 1977; Heale *et al.* 1979; Bailey *et al.* 1984; Chapman *et al.* 1985). On the basis of single family studies, it has been suggested that it may be an X-linked

[†] Deceased.

Table 9.1   Published literature of familial vesicoureteric reflux

Reference	No. of families with more than one affected member	Suggested transmission
Stephens *et al.* 1955	1	
Mebust and Foret 1972	1	
Pochaczevsky *et al.* 1974	1	
Hampel *et al.* 1975	1	Identical twins
Kerr and Pillai 1975	1	
Redman 1976	1	
De Vargas *et al.* 1978	1	
Winearls and Hind 1983	1	
Hayden and Koff 1984	1	Triplets
Stephens and Lenaghan 1962	2	Familial tendency
Tobenkin 1964	1	Possible female sex-linked
Baker *et al.* 1965	9	NS
Ambrose 1969	2	NS
Mulcahy *et al.* 1970	3	NS
Simpson and German 1970	5	NS
Amar 1972	8	NS
Burger 1972	7	Polygenic multifactorial
Miller and Caspari 1972	10	Dominant gene with incomplete penetrance
Schmidt *et al.* 1972	9	NS
Mobley 1973	1	Polygenic multifactorial
Zel and Retik 1973	20	NS
Frye *et al.* 1974	1	Single gene inheritance with variable expression and occasional lack of penetrance
Bois *et al.* 1975	8	Polygenic inheritance and undefined environmental factors
Bredin *et al.* 1975	8	NS
Lewy and Belman 1975	1	Autosomal dominant with incomplete penetrance
Middleton *et al.* 1975	1	Sex-linked
Dwoskin 1976	40	NS
Atwell *et al.* 1977	10	Autosomal dominant with variable penetrance
De Vargas *et al.* 1978	39	Multifactorial
Bailey 1979	17	Autosomal dominant with variable penetrance
Heale *et al.* 1979	15	Autosomal dominant with variable penetrance
Jerkins and Noe 1982	NS	Polygenic inheritance with variable penetrance
Chapman *et al.* 1985	30	Autosomal dominant with random environmental effect
Noe 1992	*	?polygenic ?sex-linked ?dominant
Noe *et al.* 1992	24	autosomal dominant

NS = not stated; * = 354 siblings of 275 index patients studied −119 (35%) of the siblings with reflux.

Table 9.2 Review of the published literature of familial vesicoureteric reflux up until 1983 (Bailey *et al.* 1984)

---

27 reports—212 affected families
Suggested transmission:
   Autosomal dominant with incomplete penetrance: 5 reports—37 families
   Polygenic multifactorial: 4 reports—55 families
   Sex-linked: 2 reports—2 families
   Not stated: 16 reports—118 families

---

condition (Tobenkin 1964; Middleton *et al.* 1975). An editorial in 1975 reviewed the familial occurrence of vesicoureteric reflux, but noted no uniform inheritance pattern.

The distribution of affected individuals in most reported families, however, suggested a dominant gene. Bailey *et al.* (1984) reviewed all publications relating to familial vesicoureteric reflux and the findings are summarized in Table 9.2. The updated literature is included in Table 9.1.

Studies in this institution

Three studies undertaken in the author's institution have more clearly elucidated the inheritance of vesicoureteric reflux. Firstly, Heale *et al.* (1979) reported 15 families who had come to attention on casual enquiry of 213 patients with reflux nephropathy. Radiological abnormalities of the urinary tract were found in 67 (38%) of 175 relatives of the 15 propositi. In 12 of these 15 families there was an hereditary pattern, suggesting autosomal dominant inheritance with variable penetrance. Bailey (1979) then reported 56 further families and noted that in 17 (30%) of these there were one or more affected members. Finally, data from a total of 88 affected families were subjected to complex segregation analysis (Bailey *et al.* 1984; Chapman *et al.* 1985) using a mixed model (Lalouel and Morton 1981) and a computer program (POINTER). Eighteen families were ascertained through a proband with end-stage reflux nephropathy, two through a proband with severe renal failure, and 68 through a proband with reflux and normal renal function. In 30 of the 88 families additional affected members were found (Tables 9.3–9.5). Some of these are depicted in Fig. 9.1. Of the 242 relatives investigated, 48 were affected. Three generations were affected in six families and two generations in a further 15 families. In a few cases, apparently non-affected relatives were likely asymptomatic carriers of the gene as they had both affected offspring and an affected parent (Fig. 9.1, Family 6). In one family (Fig. 9.1, Family 7), both parents were affected but the only child was unaffected. This would be consistent with a dominant but not a recessive mode of inheritance. The details of the 32 transfers across a generation are included in Table 9.6 and compared with another series (Lewy and Belman 1975) from the literature.

Complex segregation analysis showed that a single major locus was the most important causal factor, with the mutant allele being dominant to the normal allele and having a gene frequency of about 0.16%. Detailed testing of the subjects with vesicoureteric reflux, reflux nephropathy, or end-stage renal failure showed no heterogeneity in the data, supporting the hypothesis that the major locus is responsible. The analysis indicated that the hypothesis of no genetic effect could be easily rejected, as could the recessive model. Polygenic inheritance fitted better, but the best model was that of a single dominant gene acting together with random environmental

Table 9.3   Summary of 88 families investigated by Chapman *et al.* 1985

Group	No. of families investigated	No. of family members investigated (excluding propositus)	No. of families affected	
			No.	%
Requiring renal replacement therapy	18	43	5	28
Renal failure	2	4	1	50
Normal renal function	68	195	24	35
Total	88	242	30	34

Table 9.4   Details of all 88 families investigated in Table 9.3

Group (no. of families)	Family members affected (No. /total)			
	siblings	offspring	parents	others
Requiring renal replacement therapy (18)	4/8	5/21	1/10	2/4
Renal failure (2)	1/1	0/3	0/0	0/0
Normal renal function (68)	9/43	12/108	4/26	10/18
Total no.	14/52	17/132	5/36	12/22
%	27	13	14	55

Table 9.5   Details of 30 families with one or more affected members with vesicoureteric reflux or reflux nephropathy

Group (total no. of families)	No. of affected families	Family members affected (no. /total)			
		siblings	offspring	parents	others
Requiring renal replacement therapy (18)	5	4/4	5/10	1/1	2/3
Renal failure (2)	1	1/1	0/0	0/0	0/0
Normal renal function (68)	24	9/26	12/38	4/10	10/15
Total	30	14/31	17/48	5/11	12/18

effect. According to the model and using information on the prevalence of end-stage reflux nephropathy, it was calculated that 45% of gene carriers would have vesicoureteric reflux and/or reflux nephropathy as adults and 15% would develop end-stage renal failure, compared with 0.05% and 0.001%, respectively, for those not carrying the gene. These studies suggested that the trait of vesicoureteric reflux is one of the commonest mendelian dominant traits known in man.

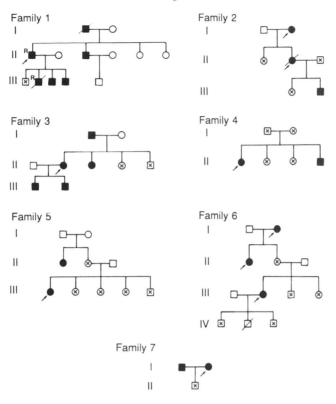

Fig. 9.1

Table 9.6 Pattern of transfer of vesicoureteric reflux in two consecutive generations

	Bailey *et al.* 1984	Literature review by Lewy and Belman 1975
Mother → daughter	13	8
Mother → son	8	3
Father → daughter	4	5
Father → son	7	1
Total	32	17

Other studies

Jerkins and Noe (1982) undertook a prospective study to identify the incidence of vesicoureteric reflux in the siblings of patients with primary reflux. Of 78 patients (60 female) with reflux, 104 white siblings, aged three months to 15 years, were screened with an awake voiding cystourethrogram and 34 (32%) were found to have reflux. Twenty-five of the latter (73%) had no history of urinary tract infection or voiding symptoms. The highest incidence of reflux was found in those siblings with reflux nephropathy. This study was extended (Noe 1992) to over 300 siblings and the pattern of the original findings was maintained.

Van den Abbeele *et al.* (1987) studied 60 asymptomatic siblings of patients known to have vesicoureteric reflux, using radionuclide cystography. Reflux was detected in 27 (45%) of the 60 siblings, which was unilateral in 15 and bilateral in 12. The authors recommended this imaging modality to screen siblings because of the lower gonadal dose of radiation.

Buonomo *et al.* (1993) found that 16 symptom-free siblings of children with vesicoureteric reflux had this condition and subsequently underwent DMSA scintigraphy. Six of these 16 children had scintigraphic evidence of renal parenchymal damage. Navarro *et al.* (1993) concluded that children with familial reflux nephropathy had more severe degrees of vesicoureteric reflux and reflux nephropathy, while males had a higher risk of renal insufficiency than a group of children with reflux but with no proven family history.

Genetics of vesicoureteric reflux

Early studies

The familial aggregation of vesicoureteric reflux and reflux nephropathy suggested an inherited basis. For this reason a search was started for possible genetic markers. An early study in this department (Bailey and Wallace 1978) showed that HLA-B12 was significantly more frequent in patients reaching end-stage reflux nephropathy compared with those entering two New Zealand dialysis-transplant programmes from all other causes. Sengar *et al.* (1978*a,b*) studied the histocompatibility antigens of 36 unrelated French Canadian children (34 girls) with a history of at least two urinary tract infections, and found HLA-AW32 to be present in six of 16 with vesicoureteric reflux, compared with none of 20 without reflux. These authors suggested that a gene(s) other than those governing the HLA was responsible for the genesis of reflux. However, these would be in close linkage with the major histocompatibility complex and may be in linkage disequilibrium with AW32. Another group of investigators suggested HLA-A3 may be more frequent in those with vesicoureteric reflux (MacDonald *et al.* 1976).

The frequency of 40 HLA antigen specificities was determined in 44 American patients with end-stage reflux nephropathy and compared with 526 blood donors (Torres *et al.* 1980). Higher than normal frequencies were observed for HLA-B12 in female patients and HLA-B15 in both sexes. In addition, there was an increase in the frequency of the combinations A9/B8, A9/BW15, A1/A9, and B8/BW15 in the male patients. It was concluded that the major histocompatibility antigens may be in linkage disequilibrium with the gene(s) determining the susceptibility to renal damage by vesicoureteric reflux, and that this linkage, or its clinical expression, may be influenced by variations in relation to the sex of the patients.

Bailey *et al.* (1984) extended their earlier study (Bailey and Wallace 1978) to 33 patients with end-stage reflux nephropathy and 108 patients with end-stage renal failure from all other causes and compared them with 179 blood donors. Comparisons of HLA antigen and HLA haplotype frequencies in patients and controls were made. Analysis of the HLA antigen frequency in the control subjects versus patients with end-stage reflux nephropathy showed that only for HLA-A9 was there a significantly higher incidence in the patients. When the patients were subdivided according to sex the trend persisted, but statistical significance was lost. The haplotypes which showed a difference between patients with end-stage reflux nephropathy and the controls were HLA-A9/B12 and HLA-A2/B8. However, neither combination was statistically significant. When patients with end-stage reflux nephropathy were compared with those with renal failure from all other causes the relative incidence of these two haplotypes was significantly more frequent in the former.

Recent developments

A gene responsible for vesicoureteric reflux may, in theory, be identified by linkage analysis in affected pedigrees. Candidate genes may also be screened by mutational analysis in affected individuals. Since reflux may be genetically heterogeneous, linkage analysis should ideally be done on a single, large affected pedigree. The major problem with such an analysis is the determination of the disease status of an individual, as reflux may spontaneously resolve by puberty, particularly when it is of a mild degree. Such an individual may be asymptomatic as an adult and have normal kidneys, making vesicoureteric reflux appear incompletely penetrant. The only way of unequivocally excluding reflux is by screening an individual in infancy using voiding cystourethrography, a test which is invasive, time-consuming, and unpleasant. It follows, therefore, that in a linkage study an asymptomatic adult cannot necessarily be classified as being unaffected.

The possibility that vesicoureteric reflux may be polygenic was rendered unlikely by the finding of Sanyanusin *et al.* (1995) in a family where reflux occurred as part of a syndrome associated with mutation of the *PAX2* gene. The authors identified frame-shift mutations in exons 2 and 5 of *PAX2* in several patients with coloboma–ureteric–renal syndrome, which included vesicoureteric reflux as part of the phenotype. These results suggested that mutation of a single gene, such as *PAX2* or similar genes, could be sufficient to cause primary vesicoureteric reflux.

PAX2 would appear to be a good candidate gene for mutations associated with developmental abnormalities of the ureteric bud and kidney. During development of the urinary tract, *PAX2* is expressed in the ureteric bud and in the differentiating nephrogenic mesenchyme (Eccles *et al.* 1992). *PAX2* is part of the family of nine paired-box genes (Strachan and Read 1994) and plays a critical role in the development of both the kidney and ureteric bud (Keller *et al.* 1994; Sanyanusin *et al.* 1995). The human *PAX2* gene is located on human chromosome 10q24–q25 and contains an octapeptide domain in addition to the paired box region. These domains allow it to bind DNA, hence it is thought to act as a transcriptional regulator.

To test the possibility that a *PAX2* mutation may cause primary vesicoureteric reflux, Eccles *et al.* (1996) have analysed the *PAX2* gene in eight unrelated pedigrees with reflux. Exons 2–12 of the *PAX2* gene were examined by single-stranded conformational polymorphism (SSCP) analysis in 23 clinically affected and 34 disease-free individuals from the eight families. No SSCP polymorphisms were detected in *PAX2*, suggesting that *PAX2* was not mutated in any of these patients. Three markers near the *PAX2* gene, including a dinucleotide repeat in intron 8 of *PAX2*, were also used for linkage analysis, but linkage could not be established. Although *PAX2* is a most promising candidate as a major gene for reflux, these findings have suggested that *PAX2* may not be involved in the aetiology of primary reflux. Recently, Winyard and Feather (1996) have suggested that *PAX8* may be a better candidate gene, since it has a similar expression in the kidney but not in the eye. Other candidate genes need to be identified and tested for, as well as further linkage studies.

Associations of vesicoureteric reflux with other conditions

Infants and children with vesicoureteric reflux have a higher incidence of nocturnal enuresis (Bacopoulos *et al.* 1987), as well as evidence of lower urinary tract dysfunction such as detrusor instability or detrusor-sphincter dyssynergia (van Gool *et al.* 1984). Hypospadias, undescended testicles, bifid pelvicalyceal collecting system (Atwell *et al.* 1977), ureteric duplication (Whitaker and Danks 1966), pelviureteric junction obstruction, and other urological conditions may also be associated with primary vesicoureteric reflux (Bois *et al.* 1975). Family studies of the parents and siblings of infants and children with bifid or double ureters have suggested that the inheritance of a duplex urinary tract is by an autosomal dominant gene of variable penetrance (Whitaker and Danks 1966).

Vesicoureteric reflux has also been reported in association with a range of other congenital disorders, including Hirschsprung's disease, anorectal abnormalities (e.g. short colon syndrome), the prune-belly syndrome (Gilbert and Opitz 1979; Cook and Stephens 1993), a syndrome of ectrodactyly, ectodermal dysplasia and cleft lip/palate (Tucker and Lipson 1990), coloboma–ureteral–renal syndrome (Schimmenti *et al.* 1995), and Robinow dwarfism (Bain *et al.* 1986). Chromosomal abnormalities of the short arms of chromosomes 8 or 10 have been reported in two studies where vesicoureteric reflux was associated with either developmental disabilities, skeletal anomalies, hypotonia, rectal atresia, horseshoe kidney, and malrotation of the intestine (Fisher *et al.* 1983) or with multicystic kidney, hearing loss, heart defects, growth retardation, and psycho-motor delay (Hon *et al.* 1995).

Perhaps studies of patients with these associated congenital anomalies may give a clue to the genetic abnormality resulting in primary vesicoureteric reflux.

Screening for primary vesicoureteric reflux

From the available evidence it is recommended that all neonates who have an affected parent or sibling with vesicoureteric reflux or reflux nephropathy should have the former excluded (Chapman *et al.* 1985; Van den Abbeele *et al.* 1987; Aggarwal and Verrier Jones 1989; Sahin *et al.* 1991; Bailey 1992; Kenda and Fettich 1992; Noe 1992; Peeden and Noe 1992; Uehling *et al.* 1992; Bailey *et al.* 1993). This is particularly important if the propositus has reflux nephropathy or renal failure.

It is now recommended that these pregnancies should be followed with prenatal ultrasonography. Any infant who is found to have a fetal renal pelvic dilatation of 4 mm or more should firstly have a renal ultrasound examination at five to seven days of age to exclude severe obstruction, and secondly a voiding cystourethrogram and repeat renal ultrasonography at about six weeks of age to exclude vesicoureteric reflux.

Vesicoureteric reflux should also be suspected in families with more than one member having hypertension, proteinuria, or renal failure at a young age, or women with severe or atypical pre-eclampsia.

Future studies

More candidate genes for vesicoureteric reflux need to be identified as well as studies of genetic linkage. Unfortunately this disorder has not been fashionable for those investigators with the appropriate expertise. This avenue of genetic research deserves greater attention.

An additional point of importance is that the prevalence of vesicoureteric reflux in black American and African children presenting with a urinary tract infection appears to be considerably less than in white children (Arant 1981). More studies are necessary on the prevalence of vesicoureteric reflux in children of different racial groups.

References

Aggarwal, V. K. and Verrier Jones, K. (1989). Vesicoureteric reflux: screening of first-degree relatives. *Archives of Disease in Childhood*, **64**, 1538–41.

Amar, A. D. (1972). Familial vesicoureteral reflux. *Journal of Urology*, **108**, 969–71.

Ambrose, S. S. (1969). Reflux pyelonephritis in adults secondary to congenital lesions of the ureteral orifice. *Journal of Urology*, **102**, 303–4.

Arant, B. S. (1991). Veiscoureteric reflux and renal injury. *American Journal of Kidney Disease*, **17**, 491–511.

Atwell, J. D., Cook, P. L., Strong, L., and Hyde, I. (1977). The interrelationship between vesicoureteric reflux, trigonal abnormalities and a bifid pelvi-calyceal collecting system: a family study. *British Journal of Urology*, **49**, 97–107.

Bacopoulos, C., Karpathios, T., Panagiotou, J., Nicolaidou, P., Androlakakis, P., and Messaritakis, J. (1987). Primary nocturnal enuresis in children with vesicoureteric reflux. *British Medical Journal*, **294**, 678–9.

Bailey, R. R. (1973). The relationship of vesicoureteric reflux to urinary tract infection and chronic pyelonephritis—reflux nephropathy. *Clinical Nephrology*, **1**, 132–41.

Bailey, R. R. (1979). An overview of reflux nephropathy. In: *Reflux nephropathy* (ed. J. Hodson and P. Kincaid-Smith), 1, pp. 3–13. Masson, New York.

Bailey, R. R. (1992). Vesicoureteric reflux and reflux nephropathy. In: *Oxford textbook of clinical nephrology* (ed. S. Cameron, A. M. Davison, J.-P. Grünfeld, D. Kerr, and E. Ritz), pp. 1983–2002. Oxford Medical Publications, Oxford.

Bailey, R. R. and Wallace, M. (1978). HLA-B12 as a genetic marker for vesicoureteral reflux? *British Medical Journal*, **1**, 48–9.

Bailey, R. R., Janus, E., McLoughlin, K., Lynn, K. L., and Abbott, G. D. (1984). Familial and genetic data in reflux nephropathy. In: *Reflux nephropathy update: 1983* (ed. C. J. Hodson, R. H. Heptinstall, and J. Winberg), pp. 40–51. Karger, Basel.

Bailey, R. R., Maling, T. M. J., and Swainson, C. P. (1993). Vesicoureteric reflux and reflux nephropathy. In: *Diseases of the kidney* (5th edn) (ed. R. W. Schrier and C. W. Gottschalk), pp. 689–727. Little, Brown and Co., Boston.

Bailey, R. R., Lynn, K. L., and Robson, R. A. (1994). End-stage reflux nephropathy. *Renal Failure*, **16**, 27–35.

Bain, M. D., Winter, R. M., and Burn, J. (1986). Robinow syndrome without mesomelic 'brachymelia': a report of five cases. *Journal of Medical Genetics*, **23**, 350–4.

Baker, R., Maxted W., McCrystal H., and Kelly, T. (1965). Unpredictable results associated with treatment of 133 children with ureterorenal reflux. *Journal of Urology*, **94**, 362–75.

Bois, E., Feingold, J., Benmaiz, H., and Briard, M. L. (1975). Congenital urinary tract malformations: epidemiologic and genetic aspects. *Clinical Genetics*, **8**, 37–47.

Bredin, H. C., Winchester, P., McGovern, J. H., and Degnan, M. (1975). Family study of vesicoureteral reflux. *Journal of Urology*, **113**, 623–5.

Buonomo, C., Treves, S. T., Jones, B., Summerville, D., Bauer, S., and Retik, A. (1993). Silent renal damage in symptom-free siblings of children with vesicoureteral reflux—assessment with technetium Tc-99m dimercapto-succinic acid scintigraphy. *Journal of Pediatrics*, **122**, 721–3.

Burger, R. H. (1972). A theory on the nature of transmission of congenital vesicoureteral reflux. *Journal of Urology*, **108**, 249–54.

Burger, R. H. and Burger, S. E. (1974). Genetic determinants of urologic disease. *Urologic Clinics of North America*, **1**, 419–40.

Chapman, C. J., Bailey, R. R., Janus E. D., Abbott G. D., and Lynn, K. L. (1985). Vesicoureteric reflux: segregation analysis. *American Journal of Medical Genetics*, **20**, 577–84.

Cook, W. A. and Stephens, F. D. (1993). Congenital urologic anomalies. In: *Diseases of the kidney* (ed. R. W. Schrier and C. W. Gottschalk), Vol. 1, pp. 637–55. Little, Brown and Co., Boston.

De Vargas, A., Evans, K., Ransley, P., Rosenberg, A. R., Rothwell, D., Sherwood, T., *et al.* (1978). A family study of vesicoureteric reflux. *Journal of Medical Genetics*, **15**, 85–96.

Disney, A. P. S. (1991). Reflux nephropathy in Australia and New Zealand: prevalence, incidence and management—1975–1989. In: *Second C. J. Hodson Symposium on Reflux Nephropathy* (ed. R. R. Bailey), pp. 53–6. Design Printing Serices, Christchurch.

Dwoskin, J. Y. (1976). Sibling uropathology. *Journal of Urology*, **115**, 726–7.

Eccles, M. R., Wallis, L. J., Fidler, A. E., Spurr, N. K., Goodfellow, P. J., and Reeve, A. E. (1992). Expression of the *PAX2* gene in human fetal kidney and Wilms' tumor. *Cell Growth Differentiation*, **3**, 279–90.

Eccles, M. R., Bailey, R. R., Abbott, G. D., and Sullivan, M. J. (1996). Unravelling the genetics of vesicoureteric reflux: a common familial disorder. *Human Molecular Genetics*, **5**, 1425–9.

Editorial (1975). Vesicoureteral reflux and its familial distribution. *British Medical Journal*, **2**, 726.

Frye, R. N., Patel, H. R., and Parsons, V. (1974). Familial renal tract abnormalities and cortical scarring. *Nephron*, **12**, 188–96.

Gilbert, E. and Opitz, J. (1979). Renal involvement in genetic-hereditary malformation syndromes. In: *Nephrology* (ed. J. Hamburger, J. Crosnier, and J. P. Grünfeld), p. 932. Wiley, New York.

Hampel, N., Levin, D. R., and Gersh, I. (1975). Bilateral vesicoureteric reflux with pyelonephritis in identical twins. *British Journal of Urology*, **47**, 535–7.

Hayden, L. J. and Koff, S. A. (1984). Vesicoureteral reflux in triplets. *Journal of Urology*, **132**, 516–17.

Heale, W. F., Shannon, F. T., Utley, W. L. F., and Rolleston, G. L. (1979) Familial and hereditary reflux nephropathy. In: *Reflux nephropathy* (ed. J. Hodson and P. Kincaid-Smith), pp. 48–52. Masson, New York.

Hon, E., Chapman, C., and Gunn, T. R. (1995). Family with partial monosomy 10p and trisomy 10p. *American Journal of Medical Genetics*, **56**, 136–40.

Hutch, J. A. (1961). Theory of maturation of the intravesical ureter. *Journal of Urology*, **86**, 534–8.

Jerkins, G. R. and Noe, H. N. (1982). Familial vesicoureteral reflux: a prospective study. *Journal of Urology*, **128**, 774–8.

Keller, S. A., Jones, J. M., Boyle, A., Barrow, L. L., Killen, P. D., Green, D. G., *et al.* (1994). Kidney and retinal defects (*Krd*), a transgene induced mutation with a deletion of mouse chromosome 19 that includes the *Pax-2* locus. *Genomics*, **23**, 309–20.

Kenda, R. B. and Fettich, J. J. (1992). Vesicoureteric reflux and renal scarring in asymptomatic siblings of children with reflux. *Archives of Disease in Childhood*, **67**, 506–8.

Kerr, D. N. S. and Pillai, P. M. (1983). Identical twins with identical vesicoureteric reflux: chronic pyelonephritis in one. *British Medical Journal*, **286**, 1245–6.

Lalouel, J. M. and Morton, N. E. (1981). Complex segregation analysis with pointers. *Human Heredity*, **31**, 312–21.

Lewy, P. R. and Belman, A. B. (1975). Familial occurrence of non-obstructive, non-infectious vesicoureteral reflux with renal scarring. *Journal of Pediatrics*, **86**, 851–6.

MacDonald, I. M., Dumble, L. J., and Kincaid-Smith, P. S. (1976). HLA-A3, vesicoureteric reflux and analgesic abuse. *1st International Symposium on HLA and Disease, Paris. Abstract book*, p. 255.

McGovern, J. H., Marshall, V. R., and Paquin, A. (1960). Vesicoureteral regurgitation in children. *Journal of Urology*, **83**, 122–49.

Mebust, W. K. and Foret, J. D. (1972). Vesicoureteral reflux in identical twins. *Journal of Urology*, **108**, 635–6.

Middleton, G. W., Howards, S. S., and Gillenwater, J. Y. (1975). Sex-linked familial reflux. *Journal of Urology*, **114**, 36–9.

Miller, H. C. and Caspari, E. W. (1972). Ureteral reflux as genetic trait. *Journal of American Medical Association*, **220**, 842–3.

Mobley, D. F. (1973). Familial vesicoureteral reflux. *Urology*, **2**, 514–18.

Mulcahy, J. J., Kelalis, P. P., Stickler, G. B., and Burke, E. C. (1970). Familial vesicoureteral reflux. *Journal of Urology*, **104**, 762–4.

Navarro, M., Espinosa, L., Muñoz, L., Izquierdo, E., and Alonso, A. (1993). Familial reflux nephropathy: severity of renal damage. *Pediatric Nephrology*, **7**, C17.

Noe, H. N. (1992). The long-term results of prospective sibling reflux screening. *Journal of Urology*, **148**, 1739–42.

Noe, H. N., Wyatt, R. J., Peeden, J. N. Jr., and Rivas, M. L. (1992). The transmission of vesicoureteral reflux from parent to child. *Journal of Urology*, **148**, 1869–71.

Peeden, J. N. Jr. and Noe, H. N. (1992). Is it practical to screen for familial vesicoureteral reflux within a private pediatric practice. *Pediatrics*, **89**, 758–60.

Pochaczevsky, R., Naysan, P., and Ratner, H. (1974). Congenital non-obstructive hydronephrosis and bilateral vesicoureteral reflux in identical twins. *American Journal of Roentgenology, Radium Therapy and Nuclear Medicine*, **120**, 398–401.

Redman, J. F. (1976). Vesicoureteral reflux in identical twins. *Journal of Urology*, **116**, 792–3.

Sahin, A., Ergen, A., Balbay, D., Basar, I., Ozen, H., and Remzi, D. (1991). Screening of asymptomatic siblings of patients with vesicoureteral reflux. *International Urology and Nephrology*, **23**, 437–40.

Sanyanusin, P., Schimmenti, L. A., McNoe, L. A., Ward, T. A., Pierpoint, E. M., Sullivan, M. J., *et al.* (1995). Mutation of the *PAX2* gene in a family with optic nerve colobomas, vesicoureteral reflux and renal anomalies. *Nature Genetics*, **9**, 358–63.

Schimmenti, L. A., Pierpont, M. E., Carpenter, B. L. M., Kashtan, C. E., Johnson, M. R., and Dobyns, W. B. (1995). Autosomal dominant optic nerve colobomas, vesicoureteral reflux, and renal anomalies. *American Journal of Medical Genetics*, **59**, 204–8.

Schmidt, J. D., Hawtrey, C. E., Flocks, R. H., and Culp, D. A. (1972). Vesicoureteral reflux. An inherited lesion. *Journal of American Medical Association*, **220**, 821–4.

Sengar, D. P. S., Rashid, A., and Wolfish, N. M. (1978*a*). Histocompatability antigens and urinary tract abnormalities. *British Medical Journal*, **1**, 1146.

Sengar, D. P. S., McLeish, W. A., Rashid, A., and Wolfish, N. M. (1978*b*). Histocompatibility antigens in urinary tract infection and vesicoureteral reflux: a preliminary communication. *Clinical Nephrology*, **10**, 166–9.

Simpson, J. L. and German, J. (1970). Familial urinary tract anomalies. *Journal of American Medical Association*, **212**, 2264–5.

Stephens, F. D., Joske, R. A., and Simmons, R. T. (1955). Megaureter with vesicoureteric reflux in twins. *Australia and New Zealand Journal of Surgery*, **24**, 192–4.

Stephens, F. D. and Lenaghan, D. (1962). The anatomical basis and dynamics of vesicoureteral reflux. *Journal of Urology*, **87**, 669–80.

Strachan, T. and Read, A. (1994). PAX genes. *Current Opinion in Genetics and Development*, **4**, 427–38.

Tobenkin, M. I. (1964). Hereditary vesicoureteral reflux. *Southern Medical Journal*, **57**, 139–47.

Torres, V. E., Moore, S. B., Kurtz, S. B., Offord, K. P., and Kelalis, P. P. (1980). In search of a marker for genetic susceptibility to reflux nephropathy. *Clinical Nephrology*, **14**, 217–22.

Tucker, K. and Lipson, A. (1990). Choanal atresia as a feature of ectrodactyly-ectodermal dysplasia-clefting (EEC) syndrome: a further case. *Journal of Medical Genetics*, **27**, 213.

Uehling, D. T., Vlach, R. E., Pauli, R. M., and Friedman, A. L. (1992). Vesicoureteric reflux in siblings. *British Journal of Urology*, **69**, 534–7.

Van den Abbeele, A. D., Treves, S. T., Lebowitz, R. L., Bauer, S., Davis, R. T., Retik, A., *et al.*

(1987). Vesicoureteral reflux in asymptomatic siblings of patients with known reflux: radionuclide cystography. *Pediatrics*, **79**, 147–53.

van Gool, J. D., Kuitjen, R. H., Donckerwolcke, R. A., Messer, A. P., and Vijverberg, M. (1984). Bladder–sphincter dysfunction, urinary infection and vesico-ureteral reflux with special reference to cognitive bladder training. In: *Reflux nephropathy update: 1983* (ed. C. J. Hodson, R. H. Heptinstall, and J. Winberg), pp. 190–210. Karger, Basel.

Whitaker, J. and Danks, D. M. (1966). A study of the inheritance of duplication of the kidneys and ureters. *Journal of Urology*, **95**, 176–8.

Wiggelinkhuizen, J. and Retief, P. J. M. (1977). Familial vesicoureteral reflux. *South African Medical Journal*, **51**, 964–8.

Winearls, C. G. and Hind, C. R. K. (1983). Identical twins with vesicoureteric reflux. *British Medical Journal*, **286**, 1978.

Winyard, P. and Feather, S. (1996). Genetics of human kidney malformations. *Nephrology, Dialysis and Transplantation*, **11**, 976–8.

Zel, G. and Retik, A. B. (1973). Familial vesicoureteral reflux. *Urology*, **2**, 249–51.

Further reading

Ross, J. H. (1994). The evaluation and management of vesicoureteral reflux. *Seminars in Nephrology*, **14**, 523–30.

Section B
Glomerular disorders

10

Congenital nephrotic syndrome

Marie-Claire Gubler

Introduction

The term 'congenital nephrotic syndrome' (CNS) is used to designate nephrotic syndrome (NS) which is present at birth or, by extension, detected within the first three months of life, whereas 'infantile nephrotic syndrome' applies to NS of later onset, up to one year of age. Most have a genetic basis and a poor outcome. The best example of CNS was initially observed and described in Finland by Hallman and Hjelt (1959) and is now called congenital nephrotic syndrome of Finnish type. Later, the histopathological study of renal biopsy specimens demonstrated the heterogeneity of NS occurring in the first year of life, and, especially, identified diffuse mesangial sclerosis (DMS) as another type of CNS (Habib and Bois 1973; Kaplan *et al.* 1974; Schneller *et al.* 1983; Sibley *et al.* 1985). For these reasons, precise diagnosis of the underlying glomerular lesion should be based on clinical, laboratory, and histological criteria. In such conditions, it is possible to recognize the rare cases of secondary and possibly curable CNS, related to syphilis, toxoplasmosis, cytomegalovirus, mercury exposure, or thrombotic microangiopathy.

In this chapter we shall review the various hereditary conditions which may be associated with NS at birth or within the first year of life, with special emphasis on diffuse mesangial sclerosis, a clinicopathologic entity which can occur as an isolated finding or be associated with male pseudohermaphroditism and/or Wilms' tumor (Habib *et al.* 1985). Recent and impressive progress in molecular genetics and biology have given or will soon give new insights into the molecular basis of these diseases. A good example is provided by the recent identification of the autosomal recessive forms of nephrosis (Fuchshuber *et al.* 1995).

Congenital nephrotic syndrome of Finnish type (CNF)

Epidemiology and genetics

Often called 'microcystic kidney', CNF is very common in Finland (Norio 1966; Hallman *et al.* 1973), but both familial and apparently sporadic cases have been described in various ethnic groups throughout the world (Habib and Bois 1973; Kaplan *et al.* 1974; Mahan *et al.* 1984; Sibley *et al.* 1985). Autosomal recessive transmission of the disease has been established: both sexes are equally affected and the proportion of affected children in sibships is close to 0.25 (Norio 1966). In the Finnish series, more than half of the parents of CNF patients were found to be related. There was no relationship between the birth order and the children affected within the sibship. There were no manifestations of the disease in heterozygous individuals. The gene frequency is about 1:200 in Finland and before the introduction of antenatal diagnosis and termination of affected fetuses, the estimated incidence of CNF in newborns was 1.2 per 10000, attaining 1 per

2600 within certain areas (Norio 1966; Ryynänen *et al.* 1983). Recently, in Finland, the CNF gene on the long arm of chromosome 19 was localized (Kestilä *et al.* 1994*b*). Linkage to the same locus has been confirmed in non-Finnish CNF families (Fuchshuber *et al.* 1996).

Clinical features

The clinical picture of CNF is uniformly severe with evidence of *in utero* onset of the disease. Babies are premature with a low birthweight for their age. The placenta is large, over 25% of the birthweight. Oedema may be present at birth or appears during the first week of life in half of the patients. According to Hallman *et al.*'s experience (1973), full nephrotic syndrome with oedema and ascites is always present before the age of three months. Blood pressure is normal. The patients have a distinctive facies, a snub nose and a calcaneoid position of the ankles, but no clear-cut malformations. Their nutritional status is poor and somatic development is retarded. They are highly susceptible to infections and vascular complications because of the severity of their nephrotic syndrome. Before the development of active treatment, they usually died within the first six months of life from infection, severe diarrhoea with electrolyte imbalance, or thromboembolic complications (Huttunen 1976). With appropriate supportive treatment, prolonged survival is now possible, but, in our experience, patients usually progress to end-stage renal failure (ESRF) between three and eight years of age.

Laboratory findings

Severe nephrotic syndrome resistant to all types of treatment is observed in all patients. Massive proteinuria is present from birth and is, initially, highly selective (Huttunen 1976). Haematuria is not a common feature. Profound hypoalbuminaemia and hypogammaglobulinaemia are constant. They are present before birth since Hallman *et al.* (1973) have reported alteration of serum proteins in blood samples from the umbilical cord. Blood urea nitrogen (BUN) is initially normal. Bilateral nephrectomy with supportive renal replacement therapy normalizes serum protein chemistry and improves the general condition of these patients (Mahan *et al.* 1984, Holmberg *et al.* 1991).

Pathology

Light microscopic studies of early renal biopsy specimens do not demonstrate major glomerular changes: glomeruli show only mild mesangial hypercellularity accompanied by an increase of PAS and silver-positive matrix (Fig. 10.1) (Habib and Bois 1973, Huttunen *et al.* 1980). Glomeruli from affected fetuses of 18–20 gestational weeks did not show any change compared to age-paired controls (Rapola *et al.* 1984). No specific deposits were detected by immunofluorescence studies. Extensive loss of foot processes was observed by electron microscopy in postnatal kidneys and in the most mature glomeruli of fetal kidneys (Fig. 10.2) (Rapola *et al.* 1984). Morphometric measurements have shown thinner lamina densa of the glomerular basement membrane (GBM) in CNF than in age-matched control kidneys, supporting the hypothesis of a basic defect in the synthesis of the lamina densa (Autio-Harmainen and Rapola 1983). Progressive increase in mesangial matrix and glomerular sclerosis develop with age and progression of the disease to ESRF. They have been related to the progressive and non-specific accumulation of basement material, laminin and type IV collagen, in the glomerular mesangium and the peripheral capillaries (Autio-Harmainen *et al.* 1985).

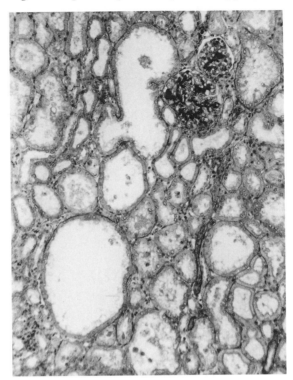

Fig. 10.1   Congenital nephrotic syndrome of Finnish type. Light microscopy. Moderate mesangial hypercellularity with increase in mesangial matrix associated with irregular microcystic dilatation of proximal tubules.

Irregular microcystic dilatations of proximal tubules are the most striking features (Fig. 10.1). However, they are not specific (see below) and are inconstantly found in renal biopsy specimens (75% of cases). They may be observed in the affected fetus, with a very focal distribution (Rapola *et al.* 1984). An interesting finding in the fetal kidneys is excessive alphafetoprotein loading of proximal tubules, an additional diagnostic marker for heavy prenatal proteinuria. Later in the course of the disease, interstitial fibrosis, lymphocytic and plasma cell infiltration, tubular atrophy, and periglomerular fibrosis develop in parallel with progressive sclerosis of the glomeruli.

On the whole, studies of renal biopsy specimens show renal changes 'consistent with' but not 'pathognomonic for' the diagnosis of CNF.

Pathogenesis

It has been suggested that the disease is the consequence of a genetically transmitted error in the structure of the glomerular capillary filter. Immunohistochemical studies for laminin, type IV collagen, and fibronectin have not revealed any early changes in CNF compared with age–paired controls (Rapola *et al.* 1984). Decrease of the anionic charge of the GBM and especially reduction in the amount of heparan sulphate proteoglycan, resulting in loss of the GBM charge selectivity and massive proteinuria, could be considered the basic pathogenic defect in CNF (Barratt 1990). Vernier *et al.* (1983) found a significant decrease in the number of negatively charged sites in the

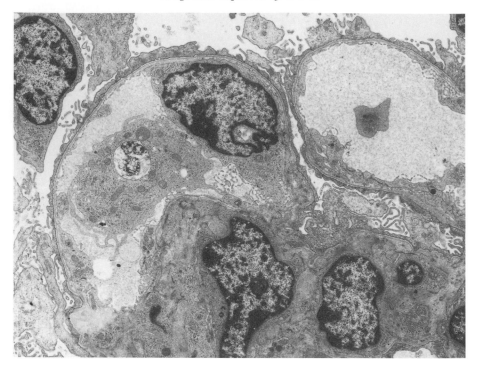

Fig. 10.2 Congenital nephrotic syndrome of Finnish type (two-month-old infant). Electron microscopy ×5000. Moderate mesangial hypercellularity, diffuse effacement of foot processes, and thin GBM (at least partially related to the young age of the patient).

GBM of patients with CNS, and Vermylen *et al.* (1989) showed significant increase in urinary excretion of heparan sulphate due to defective incorporation of glycosaminoglycan into the GBM. More recently, the number of anionic sites in the lamina rara externa was found to be normal in 11 patients with CNF (Ljungberg *et al.* 1992). In addition, in a study of the glycosaminoglycan content and composition of the GBM and the tubular basement membrane (TBM) of three patients affected with CNF, no difference was found in the urinary glycosaminoglycan excretion or the GBM immunohistochemical distribution of the core protein of GBM heparan sulphate proteoglycan between patients and normal controls (Van den Heuvel *et al.* 1992). Currently, the pathogenetic role of a gene defect involved in proteoglycan metabolism is unproven and the precise cause of CNF remains to be elucidated. Moreover, it has been shown that the defect is not in any of the gene coding for major components of basement membranes, including the gene of the basement membrane heparan sulphate proteoglycan core protein (Kestilä *et al.* 1994*a*). Rather, it involves a not yet identified gene located on the long arm of chromosome 19 (Kestilä *et al.* 1994*b*). It is clear that new information will come from the impending identification of the CNF gene.

Treatment

Corticosteroids and immunosuppressive drugs are uniformly ineffective. They may be dangerous in these patients, who are highly susceptible to infections. With conservative treatment, including daily or alternate-day albumin infusion, gammaglobulin replacement, nutrition with a high-protein and low-salt diet, vitamin and thyroxine substitution, and prevention of infections and thrombotic complications, prolonged survival may be possible. According to the nutritional status of the patients, diet may be provided by continuous or discontinuous enteral nutrition or by parenteral nutrition. Normal development and growth may be achieved with this regimen (Guillot *et al.* 1980; Broyer *et al.* 1988). However, Holmberg *et al.* (1991) report that the rate of intercurrent complications remains high, growth and development are retarded, and the treatment of choice is renal transplantation before ESRF (Mahan *et al.* 1984, Holmberg *et al.* 1991). The strategy proposed by the Finnish group is:

(1) early diagnosis and immediate institution of supportive treatment;
(2) bilateral nephrectomy and starting of continuous peritoneal dialysis (CCPD) when the patient reaches a weight of 8–9 kg;
(3) renal transplantation after three to six months on CCPD when a better nutritional status and a weight of 10 kg have been obtained.

Dramatic normalization of psychomotor development, catch-up growth, and disappearance of severe complications have been observed after successful transplantation. A few cases of recurrent nephrotic syndrome have also been observed after transplantation. Recently, Pomeranz *et al.* (1993), using combined captopril/indomethacin therapy in two CNF children, showed a remarkable effect on proteinuria and striking improvement in nutritional status and growth. This favourable result needs to be confirmed in a larger series.

Prenatal diagnosis and prevention

CNF becomes manifest during early fetal life, from the age of 15–16 gestational weeks. The initial symptom is fetal proteinuria, which leads to a more than 10-fold increase in the amniotic fluid alphafetoprotein (AFP) concentration. A parallel but less impressive increase in the maternal serum AFP level is associated. These changes in maternal serum and in amniotic fluid AFP are not specific but allow antenatal diagnosis of CNF in at-risk pregnancies (Kjessler 1977), with termination of the affected fetus (Aula *et al.* 1978). Maternal serum AFP measurement, performed from the age of 16 weeks' gestation, is the only method available for general screening of exposed populations (Ryynänen *et al.* 1983). In East Finland, as a result of prenatal screening, the prevalence of CNF at birth decreased from 1/2600 to 1/11086 (Heinonen *et al.* 1996). Prenatal diagnosis by linkage analysis, possible from the 12th week of gestation, is now feasible in families with a previously affected child.

Diffuse mesangial sclerosis (DMS)

This clinicopathological entity, which may be confused with CNF because of its early onset, differs by its rapid progression to ESRF and by the characteristic pattern of glomerular involvement. The same pattern of glomerular lesions is observed in the Drash syndrome, characterized by the association of nephropathy, male pseudohermaphroditism, and Wilms' tumour (see below).

Epidemiology and genetics

DMS seems to be a rare cause of congenital or infantile nephrotic syndrome. Since the first report in 1973, only about 30 cases of isolated DMS have been reported (Habib *et al.* 1993). However, the incidence of the disease is perhaps underestimated since records of the Pediatric Department of Necker—Enfants Malades show that 26 patients have been followed in the last 20 years. Family data strongly suggest that the disease is transmitted as an autosomal recessive trait.

Clinical and laboratory features

NS may be present at birth or may even be detected *in utero* on the finding of elevated maternal alphafetoprotein serum level (Spear *et al.* 1991). The antenatal discovery of large hyperechogenic kidneys mimicking polycystic kidneys may be the first symptom of the disease (Parchoux *et al.* 1988). More often than not, the patients are normal at birth and have a normal birth weight. NS develops progressively during the first year or the first two years of life after a period of increasing proteinuria. Renal insufficiency may be present from the onset of renal symptoms. Various extrarenal signs have been reported in a few patients: nystagmus, nystagmus with mental retardation, cataract, mental retardation with microcephaly and myocarditis, severe myopia with cardiac arrhythmia, muscular dystrophy, and facial dysmorphic features (review in Habib *et al.* 1993).

NS is usually less severe than in CNF and does not require specific supportive treatment. It is always resistant to corticosteroids and immunosuppressive drugs. The prognosis is poor, and all patients progress to ESRF in intervals ranging from days to five years, most often within a few months following the discovery of renal symptoms. The majority of patients are in ESRF before the age of three years (Habib *et al.* 1993). At this stage, hypertension is very frequent.

Moderate nephrotic syndrome and progressive decrease in glomerular filtration rate (GFR) are the only significant laboratory features.

Pathology

By light microscopy, in the early stages, the glomerular lesions are mainly characterized by a fibrillar increase in mesangial matrix with no mesangial cell proliferation (Fig. 10.3). The capillary walls are apparently normal but are lined by hypertrophied podocytes. The fully developed lesion of DMS is characterized by the combination of thickening of the glomerular basement membranes and massive enlargment of mesangial areas, leading to reduction in the patency of the capillary lumens (Fig. 10.4). The expanded mesangial matrix has a spongy appearance with mesangial cells embedded in a delicate, fine PAS and silver positive network. Rarely, subendothelial deposits may be seen. In advanced stages, this mesangial sclerosis contracts the tufts which look like a solidified mass in a urinary space which is often dilated (Figs 10.4 and 10.5). The sclerotic tuft is surrounded by a layer of hypertrophied and vacuolized podocytes, but crescents are unusual. These various stages may coexist in the same specimen with a corticomedullary gradient of involvement, the deepest glomeruli being the least affected. In the subcapsular zone there are small, simplified glomeruli with no more than three to four capillary loops scattered among undifferentiated tubules. In some cases the glomerular changes may be more homogeneous throughout the whole cortex. Almost always associated with the glomerulopathy, tubular lesions are impressive, especially in the deeper cortex, the tubules being considerably dilated and often containing hyaline casts.

By electron microscopy, there is mild hypertrophy of endothelial cells. Mesangial cells are markedly hypertrophic and surrounded by an abundant mesangial matrix which often contains

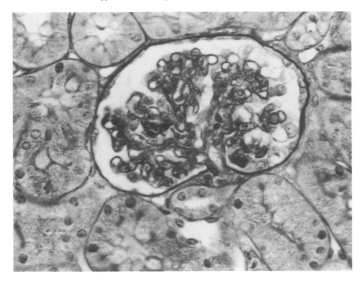

Fig. 10.3 Diffuse mesangial sclerosis. Light microscopy. Early stage of the lesion characterized by the marked increase in mesangial matrix and the presence of large vacuolated podocytes.

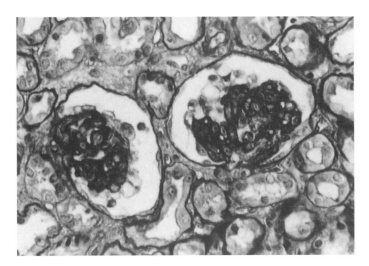

Fig. 10.4 Diffuse mesangial sclerosis. Light microscopy. Fully developed glomerular lesion characterized by massive enlargement of the mesangial areas associated with retraction of capillary loops. The adjacent glomerulus is completely contracted. In both glomeruli, podocytes are hypertrophied and vacuolized.

collagen fibrils. Segmental thickening of the GBM, due to the subepithelial apposition of thin layers of basal lamina separated by lucent areas, gives a wavy appearance to its external contour. The podocytes are markedly hypertrophied with irregular effacement of foot processes and focal detachment from the GBM; they contain many vacuoles.

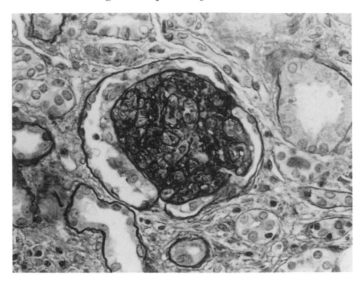

Fig. 10.5 Diffuse mesangial sclerosis. Light microscopy. Sclerotic glomeruli are characterized by the persistence of the periodic acid–Schiff positive network of extracellular matrix embedding endo-capillary cells. The tuft is surrounded by a crown of enlarged podocytes.

By immunofluorescence, mesangial deposits of IgM, C3, and C1q are present in the least affected glomeruli while deposits of IgM and C3 outline the periphery of the sclerosed glomeruli.

Pathogenesis

The pathogenesis of the isolated form of DMS is unknown. A primary defect involving the podocyte or one of the components of the glomerular extracellular matrix may be hypothesized. Changes in the WT1 gene have been described in isolated DMS, but they were found in two very young XX females who underwent early binephrectomy because of rapid progression to ESRF (Wühl *et al.* 1996) (see p. 186). We recently found WT1 mutations in one male and three females with isolated DMS whereas no mutation was detected in six others, suggesting that other genes could be involved in the pathogenesis of the disease (Jeanpierre *et al.* 1998).

Treatment and prevention

Treatment of the nephrotic syndrome due to DMS does not pose specific problems. However, the question of removing both kidneys at the time of transplantation is raised by the theorical risk of developing a Wilms' tumour (WT). Examination of 24 end-stage kidneys from 14 children with isolated DMS showed no WT. Nodules of nephroblastomatosis were found in only one kidney (Habib *et al.* 1993). No recurrence of the nephrotic syndrome has been observed after renal transplantation.

DMS is generally recognized to be transmitted as an autosomal recessive trait. The risk of occurrence in siblings is statistically 25%. The antenatal detection of affected fetuses is impossible since the gene is unknown and has not been localized. It is clear that normal amniotic fluid alphafetoprotein level cannot exclude the diagnosis of DMS in a fetus 'at risk'.

Because the same glomerular lesion is observed in the Drash syndrome, karyotyping and ultrasonographic study of the kidney should be performed in any phenotypic female presenting with DMS.

Diffuse mesangial sclerosis and Drash syndrome

In 1967, Denys *et al.*, and three years later Drash *et al.* (1970), reported the association of nephropathy, male pseudohermaphroditism (MPH), and WT. All the patients affected were infants presenting with heavy proteinuria with or without nephrotic syndrome, and progressing rapidly to ESRF (Habib *et al.* 1993). In 1985, incomplete forms of the syndrome were described and the glomerulopathy was identified as DMS (Habib *et al.* 1985).

Epidemiology and genetics

More than 60 cases of Drash syndrome have currently been reported (Gallo and Chemes 1987; Manivel *et al.* 1987; Jadresic *et al.* 1990; Coppes *et al.* 1993; Habib *et al.* 1993). Contrary to isolated DMS, Drash syndrome appears to be sporadic. Familial occurrence of the syndrome has been mentioned in only two kindreds: two siblings, 13 and seven months old, with DMS and WT (Zunin and Soave 1964) and two homozygous, 10-week-old twins with DMS and gonadal dysgenesis (Carter *et al.* 1980). Constitutional WT1 mutations have been described in the Denys–Drash syndrome.

Clinical and laboratory features–pathology

DMS is a constant feature of the Drash syndrome. It is associated with coexisting features of the triad in the complete form, and with only one of them in the incomplete forms of the syndrome.

As in isolated DMS, the nephropathy presenting as the nephrotic syndrome, often preceded by trivial proteinuria, is usually discovered within the first months of life, if not at birth. Hypertension is frequent. Progression to ESRF before the age of four years is the rule. No recurrence of the original disease has been observed after renal transplantation. The early onset of the nephropathy is opposed to the late appearance of proteinuria/NS as a possible sequela of nephronic reduction after surgical removal and treatment of Wilms' tumours (Welch and McAdams 1986).

Wilms' tumour may be the first manifestation of the disease, but in nearly half of the cases of Drash syndrome, it is detected after the development of the NS and even sometimes at autopsy. These data imply the need for a systematic ultrasonographic search for nephroblastoma in patients presenting with DMS. The tumour may be uni- or bilateral and is associated in a few cases with nodules of nephroblastomatosis (Coppes *et al.* 1993; Habib *et al.* 1993).

MPH, characterized by ambiguous genitalia or female phenotype with dysgenetic testis or streak gonads, is observed in all 46,XY patients. By contrast, all 46,XX children have a normal female phenotype, with normal ovaries, when information is available. The finding of a normal male phenotype seems to exclude the diagnosis of Drash syndrome.

Renal lesions are similar to those observed in isolated DMS. In the subcapsular cortex, the presence of numerous small, poorly developed glomeruli presenting with various degrees of glomerulosclerosis seems to be constant (Habib *et al.* 1985).

Pathogenesis

It is now clear that constitutional mutations in the WT gene, WT1, at chromosome 11q13 are observed in most Drash patients (Little and Wells 1997).

Wilms' tumour, or nephroblastoma, is an embryonic kidney tumour thought to arise through aberrant mesenchymal stem cell differentiation and loss of function of 'tumour' suppressor gene(s)' (Weinberg 1991). This tumour may be accompanied by congenital abnormalities as in Drash syndrome, or as in WAGR syndrome which associates a Wilms' tumour (W), aniridia (A), genito-urinary abnormalities (G), and mental retardation (R). Deletion analysis of individuals with WAGR syndrome has shown that a WT gene lies at chromosomal position 11p13. This led to the isolation of a candidate WT gene encoding a zinc-finger protein which is likely to be a transcription factor (Call *et al.* 1990; Gessler *et al.* 1990). The genomic organization of the human gene has been described (Gessler *et al.* 1992). Pritchard-Jones *et al.* (1990), using *in situ* messenger RNA hybridization techniques on human embryos, have shown that this candidate gene is expressed specifically in the condensed mesenchyme, renal vesicle, and podocytes of the developing kidney, the highest expression being achieved in the developing podocytes. The other main sites of expression are the genital ridge, fetal gonad, and mesothelium. The expression of the murine WT1 gene is also tissue and time restricted. Within the developing kidney it is consistent with the postulated role of the gene as a negative regulator of growth (Buckler *et al.* 1991). Mutation introduced by gene targeting into the murine WT1 gene results in embryonic lethality in homozygotes with a failure of urogenital development (Kreidberg *et al.* 1993). All of these findings establish a crucial role for WT1 in early kidney and gonadal development.

The demonstration that this candidate gene was indeed a Wilms' tumour gene was given by Haber *et al.* (1990). They found an internal deletion of 25 base pairs within this candidate gene in a case of sporadic WT. Huff *et al.* (1991) reported a constitutional intragenic deletion in a patient presenting with a bilateral WT. Furthermore, the fact that WT1 is expressed in the gonads suggests that the genital abnormalities often associated with WT are pleiotropic effects of mutations in the WT gene itself. This hypothesis has been confirmed by Pelletier *et al.* (1991*a*), who identified two constitutional mutations within the WT1 genes, one within exon 4 and one within exon 6, in two individuals with a combination of WT and genital abnormalities.

As far as Drash syndrome is concerned, no major rearrangements within the 11p13 region have been detected (Jadresic *et al.* 1991). However, Pelletier *et al.* (1991*b*) found *de novo* point mutations in the zinc-finger domain of one WT1 allele in 10 patients presenting with Drash syndrome. In nine of them, the heterozygous constitutional mutation was located in exon 9 and in one in exon 8, which encode, respectively, the third and second finger domains of the molecule. About 50 germline WT1 mutations have now been described (Baird *et al.* 1992; Bruening *et al.* 1992; Coppes *et al.* 1993; Little and Wells 1997). Most of them are missense point mutations affecting exons 9 or 8. They presumably lead to changes in the structural organization of the respective zinc fingers and to loss or alteration of their DNA binding function. By contrast, mutations observed in WAGR syndrome patients, who have a less severe genito-urinary phenotype than Drash patients, are heterozygous deletions in the WT1 gene. From these observations it could be suggested that WT1 mutations in Drash syndrome may act in a dominant-negative fashion (Hastie 1992; Little *et al.* 1993). When the WT developed in patients with Drash syndrome has been analysed, reduction to homozygosity of the constitutional mutation is usually observed (Coppes *et al.* 1993), an additional confirmation of the two-hit hypothesis proposed by

Knudson and Strong in the genesis of tumours (1972). One exception, reported by Little *et al.* (1993), suggests that the second mutation occurs in another part of the WT1 gene or at another WT locus.

It should be emphasized that no WT1 mutation within exons 8 and 9, but mutations in the donor splice site in intron 9 have been found in patients presenting with Frasier's syndrome (Poulat *et al.* 1993; Barbaux *et al.* 1997), also characterized by the association of a glomerulopathy with gonadal dysgenesis in females with a 46,XY genotype (Frasier *et al.* 1964; Hanning *et al.* 1985; Moorthy *et al.* 1987). These patients are at risk of developing gonadoblastoma and not nephroblastoma. The progressive glomerulopathy they present with occurs later in life than in the Drash syndrome, is not DMS but focal and segmental glomerulosclerosis and/or hyalinosis, and leads to ESRF between eight and 23 years of age.

Idiopathic nephrosis

Idiopathic nephrosis rarely occurs at birth and only sometimes during the first year of life. The clinical expression is usually less severe than in CNF. All the morphological variants of idiopathic nephrosis may be observed, including minimal change disease, diffuse mesangial proliferation, and focal and segmental glomerular sclerosis. Immunofluorescence is often negative but in some cases mesangial deposits of IgM and/or IgG are present. The identification of this form of NS is important from a therapeutic point of view since a proportion of patients may respond to steroid therapy and have a favourable course (Sibley *et al.* 1985). Some patients retain stable renal function for many years (Barratt 1992). However, most cases are steroid resistant and eventually progress to ESRF (Kleinknecht 1983). Steroid-resistant idiopathic nephrotic syndrome, especially occurring in the first year of life, may be familial (Kleinknecht *et al.* 1981). Recently, genome linkage analysis has been performed in a distinct group of familial steroid-resistant nephrotic syndrome characterized by the early occurrence of symptoms in siblings, the high incidence of inbreeding, the constant progression to ESRF within a few years, and the absence of recurrence after transplantation. Results allows assignment of a disease locus (SRN1) to a defined chromosomal region on 1q25-q31, thus confirming the existence of a distinct entity of autosomal recessive nephrosis (Fuchshuber *et al.* 1996).

Other hereditary diseases leading to early nephrotic syndrome

Congenital NS has been reported in one patient affected with nail–patella syndrome (see Chapter 11).

The Galloway syndrome is characterized by the association of microcephaly, mental retardation, hiatus hernia, and nephrotic syndrome (Galloway and Movat 1968). It seems to be transmitted as an autosomal recessive trait. The nephrotic syndrome is usually severe, steroid resistant, and present from the first days of life. Death occurs before the age of three years, often due to superimposed infectious complications (Hanning *et al.* 1985). Minimal glomerular changes with focal and segmental sclerosis/hyalinosis are usually observed on renal biopsy specimens whereas DMS has been described in a few patients (Cooperstone *et al.* 1993).

Early and progressive nephrotic syndrome leading to ESRF in the first years of life is one of the components of nephrosialidosis, a rare and severe autosomal recessive form of glucoproteinosis (Maroteaux *et al.* 1978). Congenital nephrotic syndrome is not a feature of other types of storage diseases.

Mattoo and Makhtar (1990) described a new form of familial glomerulopathy characterized by the early occurrence of steroid-resistant nephrotic syndrome with tubular dysfunction. Ultrastructural studies showed major structural changes of the GBM. The mode of transmission of the disease was not elucidated.

References

Aula, P., Rapola, J., Karjalainen, O., Lindgren, J., Hartikainen, A. L., and Seppala, M. (1978). Prenatal diagnosis of congenital nephrosis in 23 high-risk families. *American Journal of Diseases of Children*, **132**, 984–7.

Autio-Harmainen, H. and Rapola, J. (1983). The thickness of the glomerular basement membrane in congenital nephrotic syndrome of the Finnish type. *Nephron*, **34**, 48–50.

Autio-Harmainen, H., Karttunen, T., Risteli, J., and Rapola, J. (1985). Accumulation of laminin and type IV collagen in the kidney in congenital nephrotic syndrome. *Kidney International*, **27**, 662–6.

Baird, P. N., Santos, A., Groves, N., Jadresic, L., and Cowell, J. K. (1992). Constitutional mutations in the WT1 gene in patients with Denys–Drash syndrome. *Human Molecular Genetics*, **1**, 301–5.

Barbaux, S., Niaudet, P., Gubler, M. C., Grünfeld, J. P., Jaubert, F., Kuttenn, F. *et al.* (1997). Donor splice-site mutations in WT1 are responsible for Frasier syndrome. *Nature Genetics*, **17**, 467–70.

Barratt, T. M. (1992) Congenital nephrotic syndrome. In: *Oxford textbook of clinical nephrology* (ed. S. Cameron, A. M. Davidson, J. P. Grünfeld, D. Kerr, and E. Ritz), Vol. 3, pp. 2218–20. Oxford University Press, Oxford.

Broyer, M., Narcy, P., Rault, G., Dartois, A. M., and Ricour, C. (1988). Nutritional therapy in nephropathic children. In: *Nutritional support for sick children*. Contributions to '*Infusion therapy and clinical nutrition*', vol. 19, pp. 61–7. Karger, Basel.

Bruening, W., Bardeesy, N., Silverman, B. L., Cohn, R. A., Machin, G. A., Aronson A. J., *et al.* (1992). Germline intronic and exonic mutations in the Wilms' tumour gene (WT1) affecting urogenital development. *Nature Genetics*, **1**, 144–8.

Buckler, A. J., Pelletier, J., Haber, D. A., Glaser, T., and Housman, D. E. (1991). Isolation characterization, and expression of the murine Wilms' tumor gene (WT1) during kidney development. *Molecular and Cellular Biology*, **11**, 1707–12.

Call, K. M., Glaser, T., Ito, C. Y., Buckler, A. J., Pelletier, J., Haber, D. A., *et al.* (1990). Isolation and characterization of a zinc-finger polypeptide gene at the human chromosome 11 Wilms' tumor locus. *Cell*, **60**, 509–20.

Carter, J. E., Dimmick, J. E., and Lirenman, D. S. (1980). Congenital nephrosis with gonadal dysgenesis in twins. *Pediatric Research*, **14**, 1044.(Abstract).

Cooperstone, B. G., Friedman, A., and Kaplan, B. S. (1993). Galloway-Movat syndrome of abnormal gyral patterns and glomerulopathy. *American Journal of Medical Genetics*, **47**, 250–4.

Coppes, M. J., Campbell, C. E., and Williams, B. R. G. (1993). The role of WT1 in Wilms' tumorigenesis. *FASEB Journal*, **7**, 886–95.

Denys, P., Malvaux, P., Van den Berghe, H., Tanghe, W., and Proesmans, W. (1967). Association d'un syndrome anatomopathologique de pseudo-hermaphrodisme masculin, d'une tumeur de Wilms, d'une néphropathie parenchymateuse et d'un mosaicisme XX/XY. *Archives Françaises de Pediatrie*, **24**, 729–39.

Drash, A., Sherman, F., Hartmann, W., and Blizzard, R. M. (1970). A syndrome of pseudohermaphroditism, Wilms' tumor, hypertension and degenerative renal disease. *Journal of Pediatrics*, **76**, 585–93.

Frasier, S. D., Andres, G. A., Cooney, D. R., and MacDonald, M. (1983). Gonadoblastoma associated with pure gonadal dysgenesis: gonadoblastoma, Wilms' tumor and nephron disease. *Laboratory Investigation*, **48**, 4P. (Abstract).

Fuchshuber, A., Jean, G., Gribouval, O., Gubler, M. C., Beckmann, J. S., Niaudet, P., *et al.* (1995).

Mapping a gene (SNR1) to chromosome 1q25–q31 in idiopathic nephrotic syndrome confirms a distinct entity of autosomal recessive nephrosis. *Human Molecular Genetics*, **4**, 2155–8.

Fuchshuber, A., Niaudet, P., Gribouval, O., Jean, G., Gubler, M. C., Broyer, M., *et al.* (1996). Congenital nephrotic syndrome of the Finnish type: linkage to the locus in a non-Finnish population. *Pediatric Nephrology*, **10**, 135–8.

Gallo, G. B. and Chemes, H. E. (1987). The association of Wilms' tumor, male pseudohermaphroditism and diffuse glomerular disease (Drash syndrome): report of 8 cases with clinical and morphologic findings and review of the literature. *Pediatric Pathology*, **7**, 175–89.

Galloway, W. H. and Movat, A. P. (1968). Congenital microcephaly with hiatus hernia and nephrotic syndrome in two sibs. *Journal of Medical Genetics*, **5**, 319–21.

Gessler, M., Pouska, A., Cavenee, W., Neve, R. L., Orkin, S. H., and Bruns, G. A. P. (1990). Homozygous deletion in Wilms' tumours of a zine-finger gene identified by chromosome jumping. *Nature*, **343**, 774–8.

Gessler, M., König, A. and Bruns, G. A. P. (1992). The genomic organization and expression of the WT1 gene. *Genomics*, **12**, 807–13.

Guillot, M., Broyer, M., Cathelineau, M., Boulègue, D., Dartois, A. M., Folio, D., *et at.* (1980). Nutrition entérale à débit constant en néphrologie pédiatrique. Résultats à long terme de son utilisation dans les néphroses congénitales, les cystinoses graves et les insuffisances rénales. *Archives Françaises de Pédiatrie*, **37**, 497–505.

Haber, D. A., Buckler, A. J., Glaser, T., Call, K. M., Pelletier, J., Sohn, R. L., *et al.* (1990). An internal deletion within an llp13 zinc-finger gene contributes to the development of Wilms' tumor. *Cell*, **61**, 1257–69.

Habib, R. and Bois, E. (1973). Hétérogénéité des syndromes néphrotiques à début précoce du nourrisson (Syndrome néphrotique 'infantile'). *Helvetica Paediatrica Acta*, **28**, 91–107.

Habib, R., Loirat, C., Gubler, M. C., Niaudet, P., Bensman, A., Levy, M., *et al.* (1985). The nephropathy associated with male pseudohermaphroditism and Wilms' tumor (Drash syndrome): a distinctive glomerular lesion, report of 10 cases. *Clinical Nephrology*, **24**, 269–78.

Habib, R., Gubler, M. C., Antignac, C., and Gagnadoux, M. F. (1993). Diffuse mesangial sclerosis: A congenital glomerulopathy with nephrotic syndrome. *Advances in Nephrology*, **22**, 43–56.

Hallman, N. and Hjelt, L. (1959). Congenital nephrotic syndrome. *Journal of Pediatrics*, **55**, 152–7.

Hallman, N., Norio, R., and Rapola, J. (1973). Congenital nephrotic syndrome. *Nephron*, **11**, 101–10.

Hanning, R. V., Chesney, R. W., Moorthy, A. V., and Gilbert, E. F. (1985). A syndrome of chronic renal failure and XY gonadal dysgenesis in young phenotypic females without genital ambiguity. *American Journal of Kidney Disease*, **6**, 40–8.

Hastie, N. D. (1992). Dominant negative mutations in the Wilms' tumour (WT1) gene cause Denys–Drash syndrome, proof that a tumour-suppressor gene plays a crucial role in normal genitourinary development. *Human Molecular Genetics*, **1**, 293–5.

Heinonen, S., Ryynänen, M., Kirkinen, P., Penttilä, I., Syrjänen, K., Seppälä, M., *et al.* (1996). Prenatal screening for congenital nephrosis in East Finland: Results and impact on the birth prevalence of the disease. *Prenatal Diagnosis*, **16**, 207–13.

Holmberg, C., Jalanko, H., Koskimies, O., Leijala, M., Salmela, K., Eklund, B., *et al.* (1991). Renal transplantation in small children with congenital nephrotic syndrome of the Finnish type. *Transplantation Proceedings*, **23**, 1378–9.

Huff, V., Miwa, H., Haber, D. A., Call, K. M., Houman, D., Strong, L. C., *et al.* (1991). Evidence for WT1 as a Wilms' tumor (WT) gene: intragenic deletion in bilateral WT. *American Journal of Human Genetics*, **48**, 997–1003.

Huttunen, N. P. (1976). Congenital nephrotic syndrome of Finnish type. *Archives of Disease in Childhood*, **51**, 344–8.

Huttunen, R. P., Rapola, J., Vilska, J., and Hallman, N. (1980). Renal pathology of congenital nephrotic syndrome of Finnish type. A quantitative light microscopic study on 50 patients. *International Journal of Pediatric Nephrology*, **1**, 10–16.

Jadresic, L., Leake, J., Gordon, I., Dillon, M. J., Grant, D. B., and Pritchard, J. (1990). Clinicopathologic review of twelve children with nephropathy, Wilms' tumor and genital abnormalities (Drash syndrome). *Journal of Pediatrics*, **117**, 717–25.

Jadresic, L., Wadey, R. B., Buckle, B., Barrat, T. M., Mitchell, C. D., and Cowell, J. K. (1991). Molecular analysis of chromosome region 11p13 in patients with Drash syndrome. *Human Genetics*, **86**, 497–501.

Jeanpierre, C., Denamur, E., Henry, I., Cabanis, M. O., Luce, S., Cécille, A., *et al.* (1998, soumis). Identification of constitutional WT1 mutations in patients with isolated diffuse mesangial sclerosis (IDMS) and analysis of genotype-phenotype correlations using a computerized mutation database.

Kaplan, B. S., Bureau, M. A. and Drummond, K. N. (1974). The nephrotic syndrome in the first year of life: Is a pathologic classification possible? *Journal of Pediatrics*, **85**, 615–21.

Kestilä, M., Männikkö, M., Holmberg, C., Korpela, K., Savolainen, E. R., Peltoncn, L., *et al.* (1994*a*). Exclusion of eight genes as mutated loci in congenital nephrotic syndrome of the Finnish type. *Kidney International*, **45**, 986–90.

Kestilä, M., Männikkö, M., Holmberg, C., Gyapay, G., Weissenbach, J., Savolainen, E. R., *et al.* (1994*b*). Congenital nephrotic syndrome of the Finnish type maps to the long arm of chromosome 19. *American Journal of Human Genetics*, **54**, 575.

Kjessler, B., Hultquist, G., Johansson, S. G. O., Sherman, M. S., and Gustavson, K. H. (1977). Antenatal diagnosis of congenital nephrosis of Finnish type. *Acta Obstetrica Gynecologyca Scandinavica*, **69** (Suppl.), 59–77.

Kleinknecht, C. (1983). Syndromes néphrotiques familiaux. In: *Néphrologie pédiatrique* (ed. P. Royer, R. Habib, H. Mathieu, and M. Broyer), pp. 53–61. Flammarion Medecine-Sciences.

Kleinknecht, C., Lenoir, G., Broyer, M., and Habib, R. (1981). Coexistence of antenatal, infantile, and juvenile nephrotic syndrome in a single family. *Journal of Pediatrics*, **98**, 938–40.

Knudson, A. G. and Strong, L. C. (1972). Mutation and cancer: a model for Wilms 'tumor of the kidney. *Journal of the National Cancer Institute*, **48**, 313–24.

Kreidberg, J. A., Sariola, H., Loring J. M., Maeda, M., Pelletier, J., Housman, D., *et al.* (1993). WT-1 is required for early kidney development. *Cell*, **74**, 679–91.

Little M. H., Williamson, K. A., Mannens, M., Kelsey, A., Gosden, C., Hastie N. D., *et al.* (1993). Evidence that WT1 mutations in Denys–Drash syndrome patients may act in a dominant-negative fashion. *Human Molecular Genetics*, **2**, 259–64.

Little, M. and Wells, C. (1997). A clinical overview of WT1 gene mutations. *Human Mutations*, **9**, 209–25.

Ljungberg, P., Jalanko, H., Rapola, J., Holmberg, C., and Holthöfer, H. (1992). Glomerular anionic charge in congenital nephrotic syndrome of the Finnish type. *Pediatric Nephrology*, **5**, C105.

Mahan, J. D., Mauer, S. M., Sibley, R. K., and Vernier, R. C. (1984). Congenital nephrotic syndrome: the evolution of medical management and results of renal transplantation. *Journal of Pediatrics*, **105**, 548–57.

Manivel, J. C., Sibley, R. K., and Dehner, L. P. (1987). Complete and incomplete Drash syndrome: a clinical pathologic study of 5 cases of a dysontogenetic neoplastic complex. *Human Pathology*, **18**, 80–9.

Maroteaux, P., Humbel, R., Strecker, G., Michalski, J. C., and Mande, R. (1978). Un nouveau type de sialidose avec atteinte rénale: la néphrosialidose. *Archives Françaises de Pédiatrie*, **35**, 819–929.

Mattoo, T. K. and Akhtar, M. (1990). Familial glomerulopathy with proximal tubular dysfunction: a new syndrome? *Pediatric Nephrology*, **4**, 223–7.

Moorthy, A. V., Chesnay, R. W., and Lubinsky, M. (1987). Chronic renal failure and XY gonadal dysgenesis: Frasier's syndrome, a commentary on reported cases. *American Journal of Medical Genetic* **3** (Suppl.), 297–302.

Norio, R. (1966). Heredity in the congenital nephrotic syndrome: a genetic study of 57 Finnish families with a review of reported cases. *Annales Paediatrica Fennica*, **12** (Suppl. 27), 1–94.

Parchoux, B., Bourgeois, J., Gilly, J., Barral, G., Guibaud, P., and Larbre, F. (1988). Gros reins *in utero* et insuffisance rénale néonatale par sclérose mésangiale diffuse. *Pédiatrie*, **43**, 219–22.

Pelletier, J., Bruening, W., Kashtan, C. E., Mauer, S. M., Manivel, J. C., Striegel, J. E., *et al.* (1991*a*). Germline mutations in the Wilms' tumor suppressor gene are associated with abnormal urogenital development in Denys–Drash syndrome. *Cell*, **67**, 437–47.

Pelletier, J., Bruening, W., Li, F. P., Haber, D. A., Glaser, T., and Housman, D. E. (1991*b*). WT1 mutations contribute to abnormal genital system development and hereditary Wilms' tumor. *Nature*, **353**, 431–4.

Pomeranz, A., Korzets, Z., Wolach, B., and Bernheim, J. (1993). Finnish congenital nephrotic syndrome (FCNS) managed successfully by combined captopril/indomethacin therapy. *Nephrology Dialysis and Transplantation*, **8**, 927–8.

Poulat, F., Morin, D., König A., Brun, P., Giltay, J., Sultan, C., *et al.* (1993). Distinct molecular origins in Denys–Drash and Frasier's syndrome. *Human Genetics*, **91**, 285–6.

Pritchard-Jones, K., Fleming, S., Davidson, D., Bickmore, W., Porteous, D., Gosden, C., *et al.* (1990). The candidate Wilms' tumor gene is involved in genito-urinary development. *Nature*, **346**, 194–7.

Rapola, J., Sariola, H., and Ekblom, P. (1984). Pathology of fetal congenital nephrosis: Immunohistochemical and ultrastructural studies. *Kidney International*, **25**, 701–7.

Ryynänen, M., Seppälä, M., Kuusela, P., Rapola, J., Aula, P., Seppä, A., *et al.* (1983). Antenatal screening for congenital nephrosis in Finland by maternal serum α-fetoprotein. *British Journal of Obstetrics and Gynaecology*, **90**, 437–42.

Schneller, P., Braga, S. E., Moser, H., Zimmermann, A., and Oetliker, O. (1983). Congenital nephrotic syndrome: Clinicopathological heterogeneity and prenatal diagnosis. *Clinical Nephrology*, **19**, 243–9.

Sibley, R. K., Mahan, J., Mauer, S. M., and Vernier, R. L. (1985). A clinicopathologic study of forty-eight infants with nephrotic syndrome. *Kidney International*, **27**, 544–52.

Spear, G. S., Steinhaus, K. A., and Quddusi, A. (1991). Diffuse mesangial sclerosis in a fetus. *Clinical Nephrology*, **36**, 46–8.

Van den Heuvel, L. P. W. J., Van den Born, J., Jalanko, H., Schröder, C. H., Veerkamp, J. H., Assmann, K. J. M., *et al.* (1992). The glycosaminoglycan content of renal basement membranes in the congenital nephrotic syndrome of the Finnish type. *Pediatric Nephrology*, **6**, 10–15.

Vermylen, C., Levin, M., Mossman, J., and Barratt, J. M. (1989). Glomerular and urinary heparan sulfate in congenital nephrotic syndrome. *Pediatric Nephrology*, **3**, 122–9.

Vernier, R. L., Klein, D. J., Sisson, S. P., Mahan, J. D., Oegena, T. R., and Brown, D. M. (1983). Heparan sulfate-rich anionic sites in the human glomerular basement membrane. Decreased concentration in congenital nephrotic syndrome. *New England Journal of Medicine*, **309**, 1001–9.

Weinberg, R. A. (1991). Tumor suppressor genes. *Science*, **254**, 1138–46.

Welch, T. R. and McAdams, A. J. (1986). Focal glomerulosclerosis as a late sequela of Wilms' tumor. *Journal of Pediatrics*, **108**, 105–9.

Wühl, E., Schumacher, V., Altrogge, H., Bonzel, K. E., Bulla, M., de Santo, G., *et al.* (1996). Mutations in the WT1 gene in congenital and infantile nephrotic syndrome with or without Wilms' tumor/pseudohermaphroditism (Denys–Drash syndrome). *Pediatric Nephrology*, **10**, C159. (Abstract).

Zunin, C. and Soave, F. (1964). Association of nephrotic syndrome and nephroblastoma in siblings. *Annales Paediatrici*, **203**, 29–38.

11.1

Disorders of the basement membrane: hereditary nephritis

Frances A. Flinter

Alport's syndrome

Alport's syndrome is a predominantly X-linked hereditary glomerulonephropathy which is associated with sensorineural deafness and characteristic eye lesions. The gene frequency of Alport's syndrome is about 1 in 5000, and the disease accounts for about 0.6% of all patients who start renal replacement therapy in Europe (Atkin *et al.* 1988*a*). The recent cloning of a gene involved in at least 40% of cases means that accurate carrier detection and prenatal diagnosis are becoming available, and should soon be followed by an improved understanding of the pathology of the disease at a molecular level.

Professor A. C. Alport (1880–1959)

Arthur Cecil Alport was a South African physician who qualified in medicine at the University of Edinburgh in 1905, and then returned to Johannesburg where he practised in partnership with his brother-in-law. During this time he owned a small gold mine, which, to his disappointment, proved to be unproductive.

In 1914, Alport joined the Royal Army Medical Corps and served in South West Africa, Macedonia, and Salonika. He gained extensive experience in tropical diseases and wrote a book called *Malaria and its treatment*.

In 1918, he was appointed Specialist in Tropical Medicine at the Ministry of Pensions in London, and in 1922 he became assistant director of the medical unit at St Mary's Hospital, Paddington.

In 1927, he became interested in a family living in London in which several members had hereditary nephritis. A. E. Garrod assisted him with biochemical studies of their urine and Alexander Fleming performed bacteriological investigations. Alport's detailed report about the family was published in the *British Medical Journal* in 1927 (Alport 1927).

In 1937, he took up the Chair of Medicine in Cairo; but he became very disillusioned with the corrupt practices which he found and resigned six years later.

Alport died in London in 1959 and was survived by his son, Lord Alport, who served as Minister of Commonwealth Relations in the MacMillan government (Obituaries *British Medical Journal* 1959; *Lancet* 1959).

Historical review of hereditary nephritis

It has been recognized for more than a century that renal disease can be inherited (Dickinson 1875), and the family which Alport described in 1927 had already been reported several times during the previous 25 years.

In 1902, Guthrie described an English family in which 12 of 15 members from two generations had 'idiopathic' haematuria. In all the patients the haematuria became worse intermittently, usually in association with fever. Most of these patients also had proteinuria (Guthrie 1902).

The same family was reviewed several times over the next 20 years (Hurst [anglicized from Hertz] 1923; Kendall and Hertz 1912). Some affected individuals died from uraemia, and Hurst noted that three siblings were deaf. In 1924, Eason drew attention to the marked contrast in severity of the disease between males and females, with early death typical in males (Eason *et al.* 1924).

When Alport described the family three years later, the pedigree extended over three generations. He noted that most individuals with haematuria also had 'nerve' deafness, and he was the first person to recognize this combination as a specific clinical syndrome. He reported that haematuria was the commonest presenting symptom; and that although affected males died young, women with haematuria and deafness usually lived to old age.

Between 1929 and 1959, 15 families with similar signs and symptoms from many different countries were described (Flinter *et al.* 1989), and in 1961 Williamson added two more families and suggested the eponym 'Alport's syndrome' (Williamson 1961). During the 1960s and early 1970s a further 150 families were described from around the world (Flinter *et al.* 1989). The use of the eponym was no longer restricted to cases of hereditary nephritis occurring in association with sensorineural deafness, and a clinically heterogeneous group emerged. Patients with benign familial haematuria were included (Tina *et al.* 1982), and several other distinct types of hereditary nephritis without deafness were also called Alport's syndrome (Gubler *et al.* 1981; Waldherr 1982; Grünfeld 1985; Hasstedt *et al.* 1986; Grünfeld *et al.* 1987; Crawfurd 1988). Only a few authors applied strict diagnostic criteria before using the eponym (Flinter *et al.* 1987; Rambausek *et al.* 1987; Flinter 1989) in order to define a subgroup which demonstrated clinical homogeneity. This discrete subgroup of patients with 'classic' Alport's syndrome was subsequently used for DNA linkage studies, and the gene was mapped to the long arm of the X chromosome in 1988.

Classic Alport's syndrome

Diagnostic criteria used to ascertain patients with 'classic', X-linked Alport's syndrome

In 1988, a set of four strict diagnostic criteria was described which enables the identification of families which are apparently affected by the same hereditary nephritis as Alport's original family (Flinter *et al.* 1988). Any patient presenting with unexplained haematuria and his/her close relatives are studied with reference to each of the four clinical criteria listed below;

(1) positive family history of haematuria, chronic renal failure, or both;
(2) electron microscopic evidence on renal biopsy of alteration of the glomerular basement membrane (see below);
(3) characteristic ophthalmic signs, i.e. lenticonus, macular flecks;
(4) high-tone, sensorineural deafness.

Any family in which various members, between them, fulfil at least three of the four criteria may be diagnosed as having classic Alport's syndrome, and presumed to have an X-linked disease. In some families, all the clinical features may coexist in the proband, particularly if he is an adult male. These criteria will be considered separately in some detail.

1. Positive family history

Several authors have emphasized the importance of obtaining an accurate and detailed family history from any patient who may have glomerulonephritis (Graham 1959; Waldherr 1982; Yoshikawa *et al.* 1982; Grünfeld *et al.* 1985; Rambausek *et al.* 1987). In one German study, only 20% of patients with familial glomerulonephritis were aware of renal disease in their relatives, and the majority of affected relatives were diagnosed *de novo* after systematic examination and investigation (Rambausek *et al.* 1987). This study provides an indication of the proportion of patients with familial glomerulonephritis who have 'classic' Alport's syndrome:

Familial glomerulonephritis in Heidelberg.   Between 1970 and 1984, glomerulonephritis was diagnosed in 860 patients in Heidelberg. Of these, 86 (10%) had at least one first-degree relative with glomerulonephritis. These 86 patients originated from 45 families, and a total of 1674 family members was screened. One hundred and seventy two were found to have glomerulonephritis, of whom 101 could be classified. Of the 101 patients, 50% had 'classic' Alport's syndrome; 22% had atypical hereditary nephritis; 18% had familial IgA nephropathy; 2% had focal segmental glomerulosclerosis with Wolff–Parkinson–White syndrome; and 8% had benign familial haematuria. Overall, 10% of cases of glomerulonephritis were found to be familial, and of these, half had 'classic' Alport's syndrome (Rambausek *et al.* 1987).

From a practical point of view, it is essential to obtain a detailed family history from anyone presenting with unexplained haematuria. As well as unearthing obvious cases of renal disease amongst relatives, suspicions may be raised by early deaths in adult males in previous generations, deaths ascribed to 'Bright's disease', and deaths occurring during pregnancy or delivery. It may be worth requesting medical records of relatives who may have renal disease, or whose cause of death is unclear.

Documentation of hearing problems and histology reports of renal biopsies are particularly useful. It is surprising how often family histories are not recorded, with the result that the familial nature of a patient's glomerulonephritis may be missed altogether. The author has seen a family in which an undiagnosed young adult male received a live donor transplant from his sister several years before she gave birth to a daughter who subsequently presented with haematuria and was found to have Alport's syndrome. This means that the child's mother must also have the Alport gene, and now only has one kidney.

In addition to taking a family history, it may also be appropriate to examine first- and even second-degree relatives. For example, a child with unexplained haematuria but no other clinical signs was diagnosed after his mother was screened and found to have microscopic haematuria, high-tone sensorineural deafness, and characteristic eye signs (q.v.).

2. Pathological evidence of Alport's syndrome

The renal pathological lesions in Alport's syndrome were considered to be non-specific for many years (Castleman and Kibbee 1957; Krickstein *et al.* 1966; Grünfeld 1985). Light microscopy is of little value in establishing the diagnosis of Alport's syndrome because of the non-specific nature of the glomerular lesions. In affected children up to the age of 10 years, the kidney appears normal by light microscopy. Thereafter non-specific segmental sclerosis and obsolescence are seen, together with tubular atrophy (Krickstein *et al.* 1966), interstitial fibrosis, and infiltration by lymphocytes and plasma cells with clusters of foam cells (Goldbloom *et al.* 1957; Neustein *et al.* 1972). The foam cells are often arranged in rows between the tubules, but may be grouped in irregular clusters. All the interstitial changes are non-specific, however, and foam cells may also be found in other kidney diseases (Whalen *et al.* 1961).

Despite the limitations of light microscopy, some important clues may be obtained which suggest the diagnosis. These include the presence of fetal-like glomeruli (which are extremely rare in normal kidneys after the age of 8 years), alterations of the glomerular basement membrane (GBM), and reduction in size of the capillary loops (Rumpelt 1987). Obvious thickening of the GBM under the light microscope is a relatively late phenomenon (Kaufman *et al.* 1970). The size of the glomerular capillaries appears to be reduced on light microscopic examination (Rumpelt 1987), and immunofluorescence studies using labelled immunoglobulin and complement molecules are usually negative (Gubler *et al.* 1981). With experience gained from electron microscopy, pathologists acquired the ability to recognize thickening of the glomerular capillary walls by light microscopy (Habib *et al.* 1982).

Electron microscopy.   In 1972–73, three separate groups of pathologists drew attention to various definite ultrastructural lesions of the GBM in hereditary nephritis (Hinglais *et al.* 1972; Spear and Slusser 1972; Churg and Sherman 1973).

The GBM may appear thin, particularly in children, due to a reduction in the diameter of the lamina densa, which may range between 50 and 150 nm compared with 200 and 350 nm in age-matched controls; while the texture of the GBM remains normal (Hill *et al.* 1974; Gubler *et al.* 1981; Yoshikawa *et al.* 1981). In the same biopsy specimen there may be areas where the GBM splits and the lamina densa becomes thicker, reaching a diameter of 300–510 nm (Rumpelt 1987). Instead of a homogeneous band, there is a network of small, anastomosing strands measuring about 100 nm in thickness. Lucent areas within the lamina densa contain small, dark particles of various sizes (average 50 nm diameter).

The ultrastructural pattern can be very complex. Grünfeld reports that the GBM lesions can be patchy, alternating with segments of normal thickness, particularly in children and adult females (Grünfeld 1985); and serial renal biopsies reveal that the lesions may be absent on the first biopsy and appear subsequently (Beathard and Granholm 1977), or become more extensive (Hinglais *et al.* 1972). Rumpelt (1980) noted that splitting increases with time, while the number of thin segments seems to decline.

Many authors have discussed whether the GBM changes are diagnostic or just typical of Alport's syndrome. Both GBM thickening and splitting are highly suggestive of the condition when the changes are diffuse and when immunofluorescence studies are negative (Hinglais *et al.* 1972; Gubler *et al.* 1981; Yoshikawa *et al.* 1981; Habib *et al.* 1982). Segmental areas of GBM splitting may be found in other renal disease, however (Hill *et al.* 1974; Gubler *et al.* 1980), and it may occur in basement membranes lining atrophic renal tubules, irrespective of the underlying kidney disorder.

In conclusion, although the various individual lesions are non-specific, the simultaneous occurrence of extensive thickening and splitting of the GBM with the inclusion of electron-lucent areas containing dense granulations appears to be characteristic of Alport's syndrome, and these features will only be detected if the renal biopsy is examined under the electron microscope.

α3(IV) antigenicity in Alport's syndrome.   In the late 1970s it was noted that patients with hereditary nephritis and the characteristic GBM changes described above lacked (or masked) one or more of the normal GBM antigens (McCoy *et al.* 1976; Olson *et al.* 1980). The indirect immunofluorescence technique was used to demonstrate that there was no binding of anti-GBM antibodies to the glomeruli of patients with Alport's syndrome, suggesting that the absent GBM antigen is related to the antigens against which antibodies are targeted in Goodpasture's syndrome. It was also known that patients with Alport's syndrome who receive a renal transplant have a small risk (3–5%) of developing circulating anti-GBM antibodies in response to the novel GBM antigens present in the donor kidney, thereby inducing glomerulonephritis in the transplant (Wilson 1980).

The significance of the lack of one or more GBM antigens found in some patients with Alport's syndrome remained controversial for several years. It was shown to be a variable finding (Jenis *et al.* 1981), and it was unclear how useful immunofluorescent studies of renal tissue with Goodpasture anti-GBM antisera would be in clinical practice (Savage *et al.* 1986).

Most type IV collagen molecules are heterotrimers consisting predominantly of α1 and α2 chains in a 2 : 1 ratio. In the late 1980s two additional chains were indentified which can also form part of the triple helix and these were designated the α3 and α4 chains (Butkowski *et al.* 1987; Saus *et al.* 1988). The α3(IV) chain was of particular interest due to the finding that the Goodpasture antigen is located in the NCI domain of this chain (Butkowski *et al.* 1989); however, the genes coding for the α3 and α4 chains of type IV collagen mapped to chromosome 2 (Morrison *et al.* 1991). Clinical and genetic evidence pointed strongly toward a causative gene on the X chromosome, and in 1990 a fifth type IV collagen chain, α5(IV), was found, this time coded for by a gene on the X chromosome (Hostikka *et al.* 1990).

It is now believed that mutations in the gene coding for α5(IV) collagen (i.e. the COL4A5 gene) mean that the α5(IV) collagen chain is altered or absent. When a patient with a COL4A5 mutation is transplanted, the α5(IV) collagen expressed in the donor kidney presents a novel antigen against which antibodies may be made. These antibodies bind to the NCI domain of α5(IV) (causing anti-GBM antibody nephritis), and may cross-react with the NCI domain of other collagen chains, including α3(IV), as there is considerable homology between all six of the type IV collagen chains. As described above, antibodies to the NCI domain of α3(IV) from patients with Goodpasture's syndrome fail to bind to the basement membranes of native kidneys in some Alport's patients. It has been suggested that mutations in COL4A5 causing the synthesis of an abnormal α5(IV) collagen chain may lead to the failure of stable incorporation of α3(IV) chains into the GBM, so that the antigenicity of α3(IV) is masked (Morrison *et al.* 1991).

3. Ocular manifestations of Alport's syndrome

Ocular disorders, occurring in association with renal disease and deafness, were originally described by Sohar (1954), and many families with this triad of clinical signs have been reported subsequently (Govan 1983). A few families have been reported in which the nephropathy is associated with eye anomalies but normal hearing, but this is unusual (Grünfeld 1985; Flinter 1989).

The ocular manifestations of Alport's syndrome mainly involve the lens, and bilateral anterior lenticonus is the most specific abnormality (Fig. 11.1.1). True anterior lenticonus has been confused with anterior pyramidal opacities, which may be associated with microcornea and anterior chamber cleavage anomalies (Sand and Abraham 1962). The literature on lenticonus in Alport's syndrome has been extensively reviewed by Govan (1983) and Nielsen (1978). Nielsen wrote that during the previous 13 years all reported cases of lenticonus which had been investigated were found to have evidence of nephritis, and concluded that anterior lenticonus was diagnostic of Alport's syndrome. Govan's study of a further 16 patients with Alport's syndrome confirmed these findings.

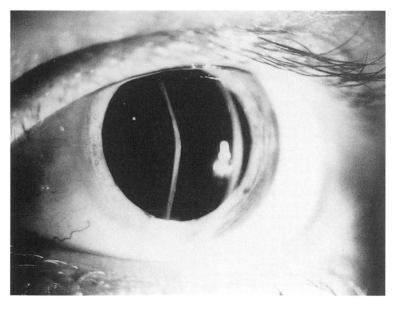

Fig. 11.1.1   Anterior lenticonus.

Anterior lenticonus is usually associated with a gradual deterioration of vision and the development of axial myopia. Several patients in Govan's study could date the onset of their myopia and often stated that it was progressive (Govan 1983); however, a well-documented increase in the lenticonus has been reported only rarely (Ursui *et al.* 1978).

Anterior lenticonus may progress to anterior capsular cataract, and surgical intervention is occasionally required.

Posterior lenticonus is noted occasionally in Alport's syndrome (Govan 1983); and spherophakia has also been reported; however, the latter may just represent marked anterior lenticonus.

Many lens opacities have been described in association with Alport's syndrome but none appears to be specific. Up to 75% of patients under 40 years develop posterior subcapsular lens opacities after renal transplantation (Govan 1983), and there are only isolated reports of lens opacities developing in patients on haemodialysis who were not receiving steroids (Polak 1980).

Macular flecks are a second characteristic feature of Alport's syndrome, and were reported initially by Castleman and Kibbee (1957). Scattered white flecks may be seen in the perifoveal region, and these do not appear to have a significant effect on vision. Flecks in the mid-periphery are less frequent, and fluorescein angiography of the macular region is always normal. Macular flecks have been detected in patients whose renal function was normal at the time of examination, but deteriorated many years later (Perrin *et al.* 1980).

Govan (1983) concludes that the diagnosis of Alport's syndrome can be made on the presence of one or more of three characteristic features:

(1) anterior lenticonus (Fig. 11.1.1);
(2) macular flecks (Fig. 11.1.2);
(3) peripheral coalescing flecks (Fig. 11.1.3).

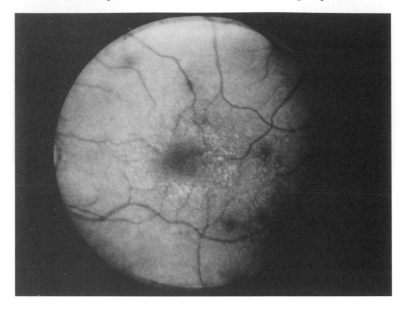

Fig. 11.1.2 White, macular flecks.

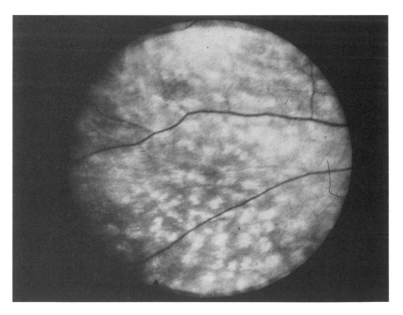

Fig. 11.1.3 White, peripheral coalescing flecks.

It is worth referring any member of a family which is suspected of which having Alport's syndrome for formal ophthalmological examination using a slit lamp ophthalmoscope. In the case of a child, it is highly unlikely that any abnormality will be detected, but the child's parents may have the diagnostic signs. When screening parents, therefore, as well as testing their urine and performing audiograms, their eyes should also be examined carefully. The absence of the above

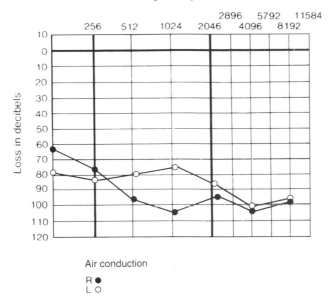

Fig. 11.1.4   Audiogram demonstrating high-tone sensorineural deafness.

features, however, does not exclude the diagnosis, as they are only found in 75% of affected males, 33% of affected females, and very rarely in childhood.

4. High-tone sensorineural deafness

The development of sensorineural deafness is one of the most useful clinical signs in a patient with haematuria, and will suggest the diagnosis of Alport's syndrome even in the absence of a renal biopsy or a positive family history of renal disease. The hearing loss is usually bilateral and may cause either clinically evident deafness or a milder defect which is only revealed by formal audiometric testing. It is important to perform an audiogram on any patient presenting with unexplained haematuria as subclinical hearing impairment may otherwise be missed (Fig. 11.1.4).

The hearing defect can be detected before the age of 10 years in many cases (Gubler *et al.* 1981), particularly in boys. In children, serial audiograms may show progressive hearing loss (Gregg and Becker 1963; Flinter 1990), necessitating a hearing aid (Gubler *et al.* 1981). In adults, the hearing impairment tends not to progress (Grünfeld 1985) and most patients retain some hearing capacity (Iverson 1974). Hearing improvement has been described occasionally after successful renal transplantation (McDonald *et al.* 1978), but this change may be non-specific because deafness attributable to uraemia may also improve after transplantation (Mitschke *et al.* 1977).

The pathological lesions responsible for the hearing loss are not well-delineated. Crawfurd and Toghill (1968) examined the temporal bones from a boy who died of Alport's syndrome and found atrophy of the organ of Corti and foam cells in the saccus endolymphaticus. Other abnormalities described include collagen changes in the organ of Corti (Lachheim *et al.* 1968) and a predominance of sensory cell degeneration (Johnsson and Arenberg 1981). The cochlear abnormalities are characterized by atrophy of the stria vascularis, and electron microscopic studies have shown a multilayered basement membrane of the vas spirale (Weidauer and Arnold 1975). This is consistent with the abnormalities found in the GBM and also the lens capsule.

Clinical course of males with 'classic' Alport's syndrome

The typical clinical course of a male who has Alport's syndrome can be divided into five-year sections:

(1) haematuria by five years (intermittently macroscopic during intercurrent infections);
(2) sensorineural deafness, often becoming apparent around 10 years;
(3) blood pressure begins to rise around 15 years;
(4) renal function deteriorating by 20 years;
(5) CRF by 25 years. Ophthalmic signs often detectable by 25 years.

Obviously, these figures are only a rough guide to any individual's course and there can be considerable inter- and intrafamilial variation, but they can provide a useful *aide-mémoire* (Flinter 1997).

Macroscopic haematuria is the commonest presenting sign in males (67% present in this way, at an average age of 3.5 years). A further 10% of males present when microscopic haematuria is detected coincidentally during routine urinalysis, and 4% are detected after screening performed because of a positive family history of Alport's syndrome. In 2.5% of males, presentation is with hypertension. Five per cent of affected males present with the nephrotic syndrome; and, al-

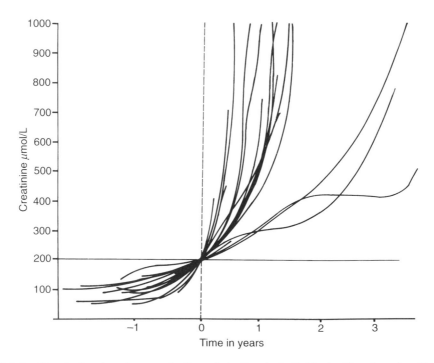

Fig. 11.1.5 Graph showing the speed of renal decline in individual affected males. Each curve represents the serial serum creatinines of one patient, and the curves have been superimposed to pivot around a fixed point at which the creatinine = 200 μmol/L.

though the proteinuria and oedema may resolve after conventional treatment, microscopic hae-maturia persists. Ten per cent of males present with symptoms attributable to chronic renal failure (Flinter 1990; Flinter and Chantler 1990). Males with haematuria due to Alport's syn-drome all develop proteinuria subsequently. The author has never seen a case in which the onset of proteinuria preceded the development of haematuria.

The average age at which hypertension is detected in males is 17 years (range 10–35 years), and the serum creatinine typically begins to rise at 18 years (range 10–35 years).

The average time interval between the serum creatinine rising above 200 μmol/L and the patient developing endstage chronic renal failure is 16 months (Fig. 11.1.5). Rigorous control of the blood pressure during the 'teens may prolong the useful function of the native kidneys. By the age of 25 years, only 6% of affected males still have a normal serum creatinine, and it is most unusual for affected males to retain normal renal function beyond the age of 30 years (Flinter 1990; Flinter and Chantler 1990).

In one study, 72% of affected males had lenticonus, macular flecks, or both (Flinter and Chantler 1990); however, some of the males with normal eyes were still children, and it is now known that the eye signs are rarely detected during childhood. The prevalence of eye signs in affected adult males is therefore probably even higher than 72%. The youngest patient in whom the characteristic eye signs have been seen (lenticonus in this case) was 13 years. The eye signs usually become apparent at about the time the kidneys fail, and it is probably not worth looking for them routinely in children under the age of 12 years.

Most males develop high-tone sensorineural deafness (a prevalence of 83% is once again an underestimate as children were included). The average deficit is −66 dB, and annual audiograms in all affected males from the age of five years may be indicated (Flinter 1990; Flinter and Chantler 1990).

Clinical course in females

This is very much more variable, and although a few females may be as severely affected as males, many remain asymptomatic (with microscopic haematuria) throughout a normal lifespan (Flinter 1997). This considerable range may be explained by Lyonization, the process by which one X chromosome is randomly and independently inactivated in every cell in the body.

Haematuria is the commonest presenting sign in females with Alport's syndrome. Thirty six per cent of cases present with macroscopic haematuria, at an average age of nine years (range 1–40 years). A further 8% are found coincidentally to have microscopic haematuria on routine urinalysis, and 32% are detected after screening performed because of the known positive family history. By 20 years of age, our experience has been that every female with Alport's syndrome has microscopic haematuria (Ferguson and Rance 1972; Flinter and Chantler 1990), although some earlier literature reports suggest a gene penetrance in females of only 85%, implying that 15% of carrier females may have normal urinalysis.

Five per cent of females present with hypertension, 8% with pre-eclamptic toxaemia, and 6% with symptoms attributable to uraemia. About two-thirds of women with haematuria subse-quently develop proteinuria as well, but the nephrotic syndrome is extremely rare. One-third of affected females become hypertensive (at an average age of 32 years; range 17–55 years), and a minority develop chronic renal failure.

In a previous study (Flinter and Chantler 1990), the authors reported a 15% prevalence of chronic renal failure in affected females; however, this figure may be an overestimate of the actual risk because of ascertainment bias, and a risk figure of 5–10% is probably more appropriate to quote in clinical practice. Of those females with chronic renal failure, the average age at which the serum creatinine began to rise was 31 years (range 10–48 years) and, on average, it took 8.6 years for females with declining renal function to develop end-stage chronic renal failure requiring renal replacement therapy (Flinter 1989; Flinter and Chantler 1990).

Just over one-third of females has evidence of the characteristic eye signs seen in Alport's syndrome, and 57% develop sensorineural deafness with an average loss of −50 dB.

Extrarenal abnormalities which may be associated with Alport's syndrome

Several extrarenal abnormalities, in addition to deafness and ocular signs, have been described in Alport's syndrome, but the significance of some of these associations is unclear.

Hyperprolinaemia and hyperaminoaciduria have been reported in a few families with familial nephritis (including Alport's syndrome) (Kopelman *et al.* 1964; Gubler *et al.* 1981), but the association may be coincidental (Iverson 1974; Gubler *et al.* 1981).

Macrothrombocytopaenia (thrombocytopaenia and giant platelets) occurring in association with hereditary nephritis was reported first by Epstein *et al.* (1972), and some authors believe that this is significant (Brivet *et al.* 1981). Analysis of reported pedigrees shows that in at least three families the platelet disease and renal disease may occur separately, however, suggesting that it is purely coincidental that the two conditions have occurred together in some individuals (Eckstein *et al.* 1975; Peterson *et al.* 1985; Flinter and Chantler 1990).

Antithyroid antibody abnormalities occurring in association with Alport's syndrome may also be coincidental, since the two conditions may segregate independently within the same family (Miyoshi *et al.* 1975).

Oesophageal, tracheobronchial, and genital leiomyomatosis with vulval and clitoral enlargement is one condition which definitely does occur in association with Alport's syndrome in a minority of families (Johnston *et al.* 1953; Grünfeld *et al.* 1987; Conchat *et al.* 1988). This is a very rare condition which was first reported and recently reviewed by Garcia-Torres and Orozco (1993), and this particular phenotype has been correlated with specific mutations at the 5′ end of COL4A5 (the Alport gene) that extend across into the beginning of the COL4A6 gene which is immediately adjacent (q.v.).

The genetics of Alport's syndrome

In 1990, the gene involved in 'classic' Alport's syndrome was cloned and found to be located on the long arm of the X chromosome at Xq22 (Hostikka *et al.* 1990; Myers *et al.* 1990). The Alport gene (COL4A5) codes for a novel chain of type IV collagen, known as α5 (IV). This discovery finally resolved 60 years of controversy and debate regarding the pattern of inheritance of most cases of Alport's syndrome.

Historically, the basic problem had been the failure of successive investigators to adopt a strict clinical definition to enable identification of a particular type of hereditary nephritis similar to the disease which affected Alport's original family. A variety of different hereditary nephritides, including some without any extrarenal manifestations, was labelled 'Alport's syndrome', and many papers with complicated clinical and genetic analyses were published (for review see Flinter 1989; Flinter and Chantler 1990). In retrospect, it is not surprising that genetic analysis of such a clinically heterogeneous group proved so difficult, and gave rise to several quite imaginative and unusual genetic theories (Perkoff *et al.* 1951, 1958, 1960; Stephens *et al.* 1951; Morton 1957; Graham 1960; Shaw and Glover 1961; MacNeill and Shaw 1973; Mayo 1973).

The considerable contrast in the severity of Alport's syndrome between males and females had led many observers to suspect that at least some cases of Alport's syndrome are X-linked, long before the gene was cloned (O' Neill *et al.* 1978; Hasstedt and Atkin 1983). Additional evidence for the X-linked theory came from segregation analyses of the phenotype of offspring born to affected individuals. Once haematuria, rather than pyuria, was adopted as the primary evidence for the presence of the Alport gene (O'Neill *et al.* 1978), all cases of male-to-male transmission were eliminated and all the daughters of affected men were found to be gene carriers (Flinter *et al.* 1988; Flinter and Chantler 1990).

Gene linkage studies performed in the 1980s to track the inheritance of X-linked markers from one generation to the next in families with Alport's syndrome all pointed towards gene localization on the long arm of the X chromosome (Atkin *et al.* 1988*a*; Brunner *et al.* 1988; Flinter *et al.* 1989).

Biochemical and immunohistochemical information, together with knowledge of the ultrastructural defects of the GBM in patients with Alport's syndrome, led researchers to look for an X-linked gene coding for a collagen molecule.

Type IV collagen is the main structural component of basement membranes and it was isolated in 1971 (Kefalides 1971). The primary structure of type IV collagen was elucidated in the 1980s, and it was shown to consist primarily of two types of polypeptide chains, the α1 and α2 chains (known as α1(IV) and α2(IV)), which are incorporated in a 2:1 ratio. These chains, which are highly homologous, associate to form a triple-helical heterotrimeric molecule (Soininen *et al.* 1987; Hostikka and Tryggvason 1988).

Other components, including laminin, proteoglycans, and entactin, are bound into this complex network of polypeptide chains to form the GBM.

The genes for the α1 and α2 chains of type IV collagen (COL4A1 and COL4A2) mapped to chromosome 13, and therefore were excluded as candidate genes for Alport's syndrome (Griffin *et al.* 1987). Subsequently, the genes coding for the rarer α3 and α4 collagen chains (COL4A3 and COL4A4) were also isolated from basement membranes and were mapped to chromosome 2 (Morrison *et al.* 1991). This was a particularly interesting finding as α3(IV) was shown to be the collagen chain against which antibodies develop in Goodpasture's syndrome (q.v.).

Cloning the COL4A5 gene

The strategy adopted to discover an X-linked collagen gene exploited the knowledge that all four type IV collagen chains identified previously contained sequences which had been completely conserved between species during evolution (Tryggvason 1992; Flinter 1993). These sequences were presumed to be crucial for any type IV collagen chain. A cDNA library from human placenta (which is rich in basement membranes) was screened with synthetic oligonucleotides coding for conserved sequences. Only six out of 700 positive clones did not code for the α1(IV) or α2(IV) chains. These clones were sequenced and found to code for a novel type IV collagen chain which was called COL4A5 (Hostikka *et al.* 1990). Immunohistochemical staining demonstrated that the location of the α5(IV) chain was restricted almost exclusively to the GBM; and the gene mapped to Xq22.2 (Hostikka *et al.* 1990), the area implicated in linkage studies. A second group reported the cloning and localization of COL4A5 independently at the same time (Myers *et al.* 1990).

The exon–intron structure of the gene was elucidated by restriction enzyme mapping, nucleotide sequencing, and heteroduplex analyses (Barker *et al.* 1990; Zhou *et al.* 1991*a*); and a detailed and extensive 2.4 Mb long-range restriction map was constructed around it (Vetrie *et al.* 1992*a*).

The COL4A5 gene contains 51 exons, covering 240–310 kb of genomic DNA which produces a 6.5 kb transcript. It is one of the largest collagen genes characterized to date (the initial publications numbered exons starting from the 3′ end, as more sequence data were available from that end; but the order has now reverted to the normal convention of numbering from the 5′ end of the gene).

Once cDNA probes from the COL4A5 gene became available in 1990, several groups started screening DNA from their patients. A variety of mutations within the gene was reported in several unrelated affected individuals, and shown to segregate with the disease through the pedigrees, providing the final proof that COL4A5 is indeed the gene involved in Alport's syndrome (Barker *et al.* 1990; Boye *et al.* 1991; Zhou *et al.* 1991*b*).

In 1991, at an international workshop in Oulu, Finland, an International Alport Syndrome Consortium was established, chaired by Professor Karl Tryggvason. More recently, in 1994, the European Community agreed to fund a Concerted Action programme on Alport's syndrome. The main aims of these groups, which are closely linked, are to facilitate research in this area by providing a forum through which participating research groups can share resources and data, and to pool results for speedier analysis (Flinter and Bobrow 1992).

To date, more than 200 mutations have been reported, and most are unique to a particular pedigree at the molecular level. All research groups are finding that about 10–15% of DNA samples from Alport's syndrome patients have altered restriction fragment patterns detected by Southern blot analysis. These mutations are, therefore, comparatively straightforward to detect. Further characterization of these mutations using pulsed field gel electrophoresis (PFGE) and polymerase chain reaction (PCR) amplification of individual exons reveals that they include a variety of deletions, insertions, and duplications, as well as point mutations at restriction sites (Flinter 1997).

The largest deletion identified so far involves the loss of 450 kb of DNA, only about 10 kb of which lies within the gene, the rest of the deletion extending out beyond the 3′ end of COL4A5 (Boye *et al.* 1991; Vetrie *et al.* 1992*b*). Another patient is deleted for 50 of the 51 exons, having only exon 1 (Boye, unpublished data).

The smallest mutations defined are point mutations, such as a single base mutation coverting a conserved cysteine to serine (Zhou *et al.* 1991*b*); and when such an event occurs at a restriction enzyme recognition site, it is easily demonstrable by Southern blotting. Thus it is not just the size of a mutation which determines the ease with which it may be detected.

Unfortunately, most mutations (i.e. the remaining 85–90%) are not detectable on Southern blotting, and the identification of these requires more subtle methods and takes much longer. A variety of techniques is being employed currently, including denaturing gradient gel electrophoresis (DGGE), single-strand conformational polymorphism (SSCP) analysis, chemical cleavage of mismatch (CCM), and RNAse cleavage (Boye *et al.* 1992). These techniques allow a comparison of patient and control DNA to highlight any base mismatches, which can be characterized in more detail subsequently. In the future, the use of automated DNA sequencing may reduce the time and expense of mutation screening considerably.

Practical applications of mutation screening

The mapping and cloning of genes generates publicity, but is only the first step towards understanding a gene's function. Once a specific mutation has been defined in a particular pedigree, however, presymptomatic diagnosis for males at risk, precise carrier detection for females, and prenatal diagnosis (by chorion villus biopsy) become available for that individual family, with results available in one to three weeks, depending on the complexity of the tests involved. For example, a mutation which alters the DNA so that an abnormal band is seen in Southern blotting is comparatively easy to screen for in relevant family members. A mutation which leads to a band disappearing, however, is much harder to screen for in females because the normal X chromosome will contribute a normal band, and so the deleted band may only become apparent if dosage studies are performed. The European Concerted Action on Alport's Syndrome aims to pool information on every mutation defined, together with a clinical profile of each patient so that critical domains of the gene and its product, and any genotype/phenotype correlations, may be identified. There may be a range of effects of disordered gene function, with different mutations altering the strength of the collagen IV network in various ways, for example.

Antiglomerular basement membrane antibody nephritis

One theory postulated by Kashtan (Minneapolis) is that major rearrangements within the COL4A5 gene might be more likely to lead to anti-GBM nephritis (of which there are 22 cases in the world literature: Cameron 1991; Kashtan 1993). Data are now emerging which support this hypothesis. The risk of anti-GBM antibody nephritis in transplanted Alport's patients generally is 3–5%. However, in patients with a large deletion in COL4A5 the risk is much higher—40–50%—and the grafts are lost rapidly, despite intervention. Unfortunately, the problem generally recurs in subsequent grafts, and patients who are known at the time of transplant to have a large deletion in COL4A5 can be forewarned that their chance of having a successful transplant is only about 50%.

It is also becoming apparent that large deletions in COL4A5 are associated with earlier development of chronic renal failure (frequently less than 20 years), and a high incidence of both sensorineural deafness and the characteristic eye signs.

A second type IV collagen gene on the X chromosome—the COL4A6 gene

The fact that several collagen genes were known to exist in pairs, e.g. COL4A1 and COL4A2 on chromosome 13, and COL4A3 and COL4A4 on chromosome 2, led to speculation that there might be another type IV collagen gene adjacent to COL4A5 on the X chromosome (Griffin *et al.* 1987; Cutting *et al.* 1988; Morrison *et al.* 1991). Long-range mapping of the COL4A5 gene using overlapping cDNA clones and pulsed field gel electrophoresis had proved useful in the characterization of mutations in patients with Alport's syndrome. It also provided further clues in the search for another type IV collagen gene in close proximity to COL4A5, because of the discovery of CpG islands in the DNA flanking the COL4A5 locus (Vetrie *et al.* 1992*c*). Such clusters of sites have been shown to be related to CG-rich, methylation-sensitive tracts of DNA near gene promoters (Bird 1986). A CpG island about 180–225 kb 5′ to the COL4A5 gene was identified and another CpG island was defined 40–50 kb from the 3′ end of the COL4A5 locus. The COL4A6 gene, encoding a new type IV collagen, was found upstream of COL4A5 in 1993 (Zhou *et al.* 1993*a,b*). The exon/intron structure, the location of cysteine residues within the N-terminal region, and the collagen interruptions indicate that COL4A6 is homologous to COL4A2, as predicted. It seems, therefore, that the type IV collagen chains can be divided into two structural families: the α1(IV)-like family: α1(IV), α3(IV), and α5(IV); and the α2(IV)-like family: α2(IV), α4(IV), and α6(IV). Further research will establish whether these families have distinct functional differences.

The discovery of the novel COL4A6 gene provided a second candidate gene for Alport's syndrome, and mutation screening with novel cDNA probes using patient DNA was performed. So far, however, no patients with Alport's syndrome have been found to have an isolated mutation in COL4A6 with an intact COL4A5.

One convincing genotype/phenotype correlation which has emerged is that between mutations involving both COL4A5 and COL4A6 and the association of oesophageal leiomyomatosis with Alport's syndrome. There is a cluster of 14 such families in France, and they have been extensively studied at the molecular level (Antignac *et al.* 1993*a,b*). All these patients appear to have deletions at the 5′ end of COL4A5 which extend out beyond COL4A5, across the gap between COL4A5 and COL4A6, and into COL4A6, including a deletion of the first two exons of the latter.

Where are the missing mutations?

In about half the families with 'classic' X-linked Alport's syndrome, no mutation has been found in COL4A5 or COL4A6, and there are several possible locations for the missing mutations. Some may line within COL4A5 itself, as without sequencing the whole gene (a massive undertaking in a 250 kb gene) some mutations will not be detected. In addition, current mutaiton detection strategies screen only the coding regions, and not the introns or the regulatory regions of COL4A5. Also, certain types of mutations such as large gene duplications or inversions are not detected by standard molecular approaches. Finally, there may be another gene associated with Alport's syndrome, closely linked to COL4A5 on the X-chromosome.

Other forms of hereditary nephritis

The diagnostic criteria listed at the beginning of this chapter enable the identification of families with X-linked hereditary nephritis for which the eponym 'Alport's syndrome' is appropriate. The majority of families being investigated for hereditary nephritis will eventually fulfil a sufficient number of these criteria to be formally diagnosed, once parents and other close relatives have been studied appropriately clinically including urinanalysis audiometry and formal ophthalmological review. In a few families, the sole living affected individual may be too young for the absence of eye signs or deafness to be of any significance, and definitive diagnosis may be impossible for a few years, particularly if the propositus represents a new gene mutation and has unaffected parents. In these cases the demonstration of a mutation in the COL4A5 gene would be diagnostic, but in the absence of this it is recommended that regular audiograms and eye examinations are considered, until mutation analysis within the Alport gene becomes more widely available.

A minority of families with hereditary nephritis fails to fulfil the diagnostic criteria for classic Alport's syndrome even when the proband is adult, despite careful examination of close relatives. These families appear to have a distinct, autosomally inherited nephritis which is never associated with the characteristic eye signs, and rarely associated with deafness.

A review of the literature on 'Alport's syndrome' can be very confusing, because for years the eponym was applied to a variety of hereditary nephritides which are clinically very heterogeneous.

Autosomal dominant progressive hereditary nephritis without deafness

There are over 30 pedigrees published in the literature which show male-to-male transmission of a renal disease which is called 'Alport's syndrome', but the diagnostic criteria used vary considerably, and none would fulfil the criteria listed above (Flinter *et al.* 1987, 1988; Crawfurd 1988). In particular, none of the affected individuals has any evidence in the eyes of lenticonus or macular flecks (Govan 1983), but a variety of non-specific eye abnormalities (e.g. cataract) is described (Reyersbach and Butler 1954; Shaw and Glover 1961). The histological evidence for Alport's syndrome is also weak in these pedigrees as most of the abnormalities described are patchy and non-specific changes of the GBM.

Autosomal dominant hereditary nephritis certainly does exist, but it is considerably less common than classic, X-linked, Alport's syndrome, and clinically distinct. A better name for this condition is 'autosomal dominant hereditary nephritis without deafness'.

Autosomal dominant hereditary nephritis affects males and females with equal severity, as would be expected. Macroscopic haematuria is rare, and renal disease is usually diagnosed in adult life after the detection of microscopic haematuria, proteinuria (sometimes leading to the nephrotic syndrome), or elevated blood pressure prompts evaluation. There are no associated ocular or auditory defects. The clinical course is variable, but an equal proportion of males and females eventually develop chronic renal failure, often in middle age (Goldman and Haberfelde 1959; Pashayan *et al.* 1971; Richmond *et al.* 1981; Yoshikawa *et al.* 1982).

The basic defect in autosomal dominant hereditary nephritis without deafness is unknown. Teisberg *et al.* (1973) presented evidence suggestive of an inherited defect in immune function: sera from their patients were unable to lyse the third component of complement *in vitro*.

Careful clinical re-evaluation of many families previously thought to have autosomal dominant hereditary nephritis without deafness has led to some of them being reclassified as Alport's syndrome after the detection of the characteristic extrarenal abnormalities, and in some of these families COl4A5 mutations have now been described. The small number of families which remains in the former category is being analysed in gene linkage studies with anonymous DNA probes, and preliminary data suggest that they may be linked to markers on chromosome 2, the site of the COL4A3 and COL4A4 genes.

Autosomal recessive progressive hereditary nephritis

A few families have been reported which demonstrate an autosomal recessive form of Alport's syndrome. In some of these families the nephritis is atypical (Grünfeld *et al.* 1973), and in others it is possible that the mother is in fact a carrier of an X-linked gene (Wood and Knight 1966; Gaboardi *et al.* 1974; Habib *et al.* 1982), but several also have healthy consanguineous parents who have had multiple affected children of both sexes. The children develop chronic renal failure at an early age (chronic renal failure in a female child with X-linked Alport's syndrome would be exceptionally unusual). In some cases both parents have abnormal urinalysis (microscopic haematuria), but in others the parents are completely unaffected. Three North African families studied recently were found to have renal disease which was linked to the COL4A3 gene on chromosome 2, but deafness and ocular changes were found in only one of the three families (Antignac *et al.* 1993*b*; Chan *et al.* 1993). Two separate mutations within the COL4A3 gene in two unrelated patients with nephritis and deafness (but normal eyes) provide the most convincing evidence to date of the existence of an autosomal recessive hereditary nephritis with deafness on chromosome 2 which might mimic Alport's syndrome (Mochizuki *et al.* 1994), and in other families mutations in COL4A4 may also be involved.

Autosomal dominant thin membrane disease

This benign disease, also known as 'benign recurrent haematuria', has been separated from other causes of renal haematuria by its characteristic findings on electron microscopy (Glassock 1989; Tiebosch *et al.* 1989). At a clinical level it may be difficult to distinguish from the progressive glomerulonephritides, but taking a detailed family history may provide some clues.

The typical presentation of patients with thin membrane disease is the coincidental detection of asymptomatic, microscopic haematuria (macroscopic haematuria being uncommon).

Seventy per cent of patients at presentation do not have any detectable abnormal protein excretion, and the degree of proteinuria at any stage is variable and of little prognostic significance. There are no extrarenal manifestations, and, in particular, hearing is normal.

The only specific diagnostic test is renal biopsy, although this may be unnecessary if results are already available from close relatives affected with the same condition. Light microscopic examination is normal, and careful review under the electron microscope is required. Under electron microscopy, the capillary GBM thickness is decreased to 265 nm or less (normal = 375 ± 75 nm for males, and 325 ± 40 nm for females). Immunofluorescence may reveal diffuse mesangial C3 deposition in some patients (Tiebosch *et al.* 1989).

Thin-basement membrane nephropathy is inherited as an autosomal dominant condition, and screening of close relatives is indicated—indeed, it may even assist in obtaining a diagnosis. If the extended pedigree reveals adult men with persistent microscopic haematuria, normal blood pressure and renal function, and normal hearing, then Alport's syndrome can be excluded, and the main differential diagnosis is IgA nephropathy.

In the prospective study of Tiebosch *et al.* (1989) following patients with apparently idiopathic renal haematuria, normal blood pressure, and renal function, 23% were found to have thin-membrane disease, 34% had IgA nephropathy, and 43% had either entirely normal renal tissue or other glomerular or tubulointerstitial diseases. Thin-membrane disease was rarely the final diagnosis if presentation was with macroscopic haematuria. Caution is required, however, as a thin GBM can also be found in progressive hereditary nephritis, particularly early on in the disease, and this lesion should not be considered as a guarantee of a benign long-term prognosis.

The prognosis of thin-membrane disease is good, and few cases are described in whom renal failure has developed (Dische *et al.* 1985; Coleman *et al.* 1986; Abe *et al.* 1987; Glassock 1989; Tiebosch *et al.* 1989). The detection of a mutation in COL4A4 co-segregating with apparently benign familial haematuria in a Dutch family has led to the suggestion that benign familial haematuria may represent the heterozygous (i.e. carrier) state of autosomal recessive Alport's syndrome (Lemmink *et al.* 1996).

Conclusion

Sometimes it is difficult to distinguish clinically between classic, X-linked Alport's syndrome, autosomal dominant progressive nephritis without deafness, autosomal recessive progressive nephritis, and thin-basement membrane disease. Obtaining a detailed family history is sometimes the most useful investigation, particularly if older affected relatives can be identified. The existence of parental consanguinity should not lead to an automatic assumption of autosomal recessive inheritance, and the mother of the proband should be examined very carefully for evidence that she might carry an X-linked gene. In some circumstances, more useful clinical information may be obtained by arranging audiometry and formal ophthalmological review of the adult relatives than of the proband if the latter is still a child.

The detection of the characteristic eye signs which are specific to Alport's syndrome confirms the diagnosis, but their absence does not refute it. Similarly, high-tone sensorineural deafness makes Alport's syndrome highly likely, but normal hearing is compatible with any of the three diagnoses and deafness may coexist with other hereditary nephritides. Examination of a renal biopsy under the electron microscope may be very helpful, but can be disappointing, and even misleading in children in whom the characteristic GBM changes have not yet had time to develop. Rarely, repeat biopsies may be required in order to establish whether a particular disease is evolving.

The ultimate arbiter will be the molecular biologists, but currently their powers are restricted. The COL4A5 Alport gene is now well-defined, and mutations within it can now be identified in some patients, confirming the diagnosis in those cases. At the moment, failure to demonstrate a mutation in COL4A5 does not exclude the diagnosis of Alport's syndrome, but it remains to be seen whether the remaining mutations lie in COL4A5 (or associated regulatory regions) or within another gene(s) nearby. The possibility that cases of autosomal dominant and autosomal recessive nephritis may be explained by mutations in COL4A3 and COL4A4 is exciting, as is the potential overlap between carriers of autosomal recessive hereditary nephritis and the condition of benign familial haematuria.

References

Abe, S., Amagasaki, Y., and Iyori, S. (1987). Thin-basement membrane syndrome in adults. *Journal of Clinical pathology*, **40**, 318.

Alport, A. C. (1927). Hereditary familial congenital haemorrhagic nephritis. *British Medical Journal*, **1**, 504–6.

Antignac, C., Dahan, K., Heidet, L., Zhou, J., and Gubler, M. C. (1993*a*). Alport syndrome (AS) and diffuse esophageal leiomyomatosis (DL). (Abstract). Second International Workshop on Alport Syndrome, New Haven, USA. p. 1.

Antignac, C., Knebelmann, B., Deschenes G., and Gubler, M. C. (1993*b*). Recessive forms of Alport syndrome. (Abstract). Second International Workshop on Alport Syndrome, New Haven, USA. p. 2.

Atkin, C. L., Gregory, M. C., and Border, W. A. (1988*a*). Alport syndrome. In: *Diseases of the kidney* (ed. R. W. Schrier and C. W. Gottshcalk), pp. 617–41. Little, Brown and Co., Boston.

Atkin, C. L., Hasstedt, S. J., Menlove, L., Cannon, L., Kirschner, N., Schwartz, C., *et al.* (1988*b*). Mapping of Alport syndrome to the long arm of the X chromosome. *American Journal of Human Genetics*, **42**, 249–55.

Barker, D. F., Hostikka, S. L., Zhou, J., Chow, L. T., Oliphant, A. R., Gerken, S. C., *et al.* (1990). Identification of mutations in the COL4A5 collagen gene in Alport syndrome. *Science*, **248**, 1224–7.

Beathard, G. A. and Granholm, N. A. (1977). Development of the characteristic ultrastructural lesion of hereditary nephritis during the course of the disease. *American Journal of Medicine*, **62**, 751–6.

Bird, A. P. (1986). CpG-rich islands and the function of DNA methylation. *Nature*, **321**, 209–13.

Boye, E., Vetrie, D., Flinter, F. A., Buckle, B., Pihlajaniemi, T., Hamalainen, E-R., *et al.* (1991). Major rearrangements in the α5 (IV) collagen gene in three patients with Alport's syndrome. *Genomics*, **11**, 1125–32.

Boye, E., Vetrie, D., Roberts, R., Flinter, F., Bobrow, M., and Harris, A. (1992). A multistrategy approach to the detection of mutations in Alport's syndrome. *American Journal of Human Genetics*, **51**, A820.

British Medical Journal (1959). **1**, 1191.

Brivet, F., Girot, R., Barbanel, C., Gazengel, C., Maier, M., and Crosnier, J. (1981). Hereditary nephritis associated with May–Hegglin anomaly. *Nephron*, **29**, 59–62.

Brunner, H., Schröder, C., van Bennekom, C., Lamberman, E., Tuerlings, J., Menzel, D., *et al.* (1988). Localisation of the gene for X-linked Alport syndrome. *Kidney International*, **34** , 507–10.

Butkowski, R. J., Langeveld, J. P. M., Wieslander, J., Hamilton, J., and Hudson, B. G. (1987).

Localization of the Goodpasture epitope to a novel chain of basement membrane collagen. *Journal of Biological Chemistry*, **262**, 7874–7.

Butkowski, R. J., Wieslander, J., Kleppel, M., Michael, A. F., and Fish, A. J. (1989). Basement membrane collagen in the kidney: regional localisation of novel chains related to collagen IV. *Kidney International*, **35**, 1195–202.

Cameron, J. S. (1991). Recurrent primary disease and *de novo* nephritis following renal transplantation. *Pediatric Nephrology*, **5**, 412–21.

Castleman, B. and Kibbee, B. U. (1957). Case records of the Massachusetts General Hospital. *New England Journal of Medicine*, **257**, 1231–7.

Chan, B. J., Antignac, C., Gubler, M.-C., *et al.* (1993). A new locus for Alport syndrome: linkage of autosomal recessive Alport syndrome to the gene encoding the α3 chain of type IV collagen. (Abstract). Second International Workshop on Alport Syndrome, New Haven, USA. p. 3.

Churg, J. and Sherman, R. L. (1973). Pathologic characteristics of hereditary nephritis. *Archives of Pathology*, **95**, 374–9.

Coleman, M., Haynes, W. D., Oumopooulos, P., *et al.* (1986). Glomerular basement membrane abnormalities associated with apparently idiopathic haematuria: ultrastructural morphometric studies. *Human Pathology*, **17**, 1022.

Conchat, P., Guilbaud, P., Garcia-Torres, R., Roussel, B., Guarner, V., and Larbre, F. (1988). Diffuse leiomyomatosis in Alport syndrome. *Journal of Paediatrics*, **113**, 339–43.

Crawfurd, M. d'A. (1988). Hereditary nephritis with deafness (Alport's disease). In: *The genetics of renal tract disorders*. Oxford Monographs on Medical Genetics No. 14, p. 351. Oxford University Press, Oxford.

Crawfurd, M. d'A. and Toghill, P. J. (1968). Alport's syndrome of hereditary nephritis and deafness. *Quarterly Journal of Medicine*, **37**, 563–76.

Cutting, G. R., Kazazian, H. H., Altonarakis, S. E., Killen, P. D., Yamada, Y., and Francomano, C. A. (1988). Macrorestriction mapping of COL4A1 and COL4A2 collagen genes on human chromosome 13q34. *Genomics*, **3**, 256–63.

Dickinson, W. H. (1875). Diseases of the kidney characterized by albuminuria. In: *A system of medicine* (ed. T. C. Allbut), p. 352. Macmillan, New York.

Dische, F. E., Weston, M. J., and Parsons, N. (1985). Abnormally thin basement membranes associated with hematuria, proteinuria or renal failure in adults. *American Journal of Nephrology*, **5**, 103.

Eason, J., Smith, G. L. M., and Buchanan, G. (1924). Hereditary and familial nephritis. *Lancet*, **ii**, 639–46.

Eckstein, J. D., Filip, D. J., and Watts, J. C. (1975). Hereditary thrombocytopaenia, deafness and renal disease. *Annals of Internal Medicine*, **82**, 639–45.

Epstein, C. J., Sahud, M. A., Piel, C. F., Goodman, J. R., Bernfield, M. R., Kushner, J. H., *et al.* (1972). Hereditary macrothrombocytopathia, nephritis and deafness. *American Journal of Medicine*, **52**, 299–310.

Ferguson, A. C. and Rance, C. P. (1972). Hereditary nephropathy with nerve deafness (Alport's syndrome). *American Journal of Diseases of Children*, **124** , 84–8.

Flinter, F. A. (1989). A clinical and genetic study of Alport's syndrome. MD thesis. University of London.

Flinter, F. A. (1990). Alport's syndrome. A clinical and genetic study. In: *Recent advances in hereditary nephritis*. Contributions to Nephrology Series 80 (ed. A. Sessa and G. Battini). pp. 9–16. Karger, Basel.

Flinter, F. A. (1993). Molecular genetics of Alport's syndrome. *Quarterly Journal of Medicine*, **86**, 289–92.

Flinter, F. A. (1997) Alport's syndrome. *Journal of Medical Genetics*, **34**, 326–30.

Flinter, F. A., Bobrow, M., and Chantler, C. (1987). Alport's syndrome or hereditary nephritis? *Pediatric Nephrology*, **1**, 438–40.

Flinter, F. A., Cameron, J. S., Chantler, C., Houston, I., and Bobrow, M. (1988). Genetics of classic Alport's syndrome. *Lancet*, **ii**, 1005–7.

Flinter, F. A., Abbs, S., and Bobrow, M. (1989). Localization of the gene for classic Alport syndrome. *Genomics*, **4**, 335–8.

Flinter, F. A. and Chantler, C. (1990). The inheritance of Alport's syndrome. In: *Inheritance of kidney and urinary tract diseases* (ed. A. Spitzer and E. D. Avner). pp. 107–20. Kluwer Academic Publications, London, Boston.

Flinter, F. and Bobrow, M. (1992). The molecular genetics of Alport syndrome: report of two workshops. *Journal of Medical Genetics*, **29**, 352–3.

Gaboardi, F., Edefonti, A., Imbasciati, E., *et al.* (1974). Alport's syndrome (progressive hereditary nephritis). *Clinical Nephrology*, **2**, 143–56.

Garcia-Torres, R. and Orozco, L. (1993). Alport–leiomyomatosis syndrome: An update. *American Journal of Kidney Disease*, **22**, 641–8.

Glassock, R. J. (1989). Through thick and thin. *New England Journal of Medicine*, **320**, 51. (Editorial).

Goldbloom, R. B., Fraser, F. C., Waugh, D., Aronovitch, M., and Wigglesworth, F. W. (1957). Hereditary renal disease associated with nerve deafness and ocular lesions. *Pediatrics*, **20**, 241–52.

Goldman, R. and Haberfelde, G. C. (1959). Hereditary nephritis: report of a kindred. *New England Journal of Medicine*, **261**, 734–8.

Govan, J. A. A. (1983). Ocular manifestations of Alport's syndrome: a hereditary disorder of basement membrane? *British Journal of Ophthalmology*, **67**, 493–503.

Graham, J. B. (1959). Hereditary chronic kidney disease: an alternative to partial sex-linkage in the Utah kindred. *American Journal of Human Genetics*, **11**, 333–8.

Graham, J. B. (1960). Chronic hereditary nephritis: not shown to be partially sex-linked. *American Journal of Human Genetics*, **12**, 382–4.

Gregg, J. B. and Becker, S. F. (1963). Concomitant progressive deafness, chronic nephritis and ocular lens disease. *Archives of Ophthalmology*, **69**, 293–9.

Griffin, C. A., Emanuel, B. S., Hansen, J. R., Canavee, W. K., and Myers, J. C. (1987). Human collagen genes encoding basement membrane alphal (IV) and alpha2 (IV) chains map to the distal long arm of chromosome 13. *Proceedings of the National Academy of Sciences, USA*, **84**, 512–16.

Grünfeld, J-P. (1985). The clinical spectrum of hereditary nephritis. *Kidney International*, **27**, 83–92.

Grünfeld, J-P., Bois, E-P., and Hinglais, N. (1973). Progressive and non-progressive hereditary chronic nephritis. *Kidney International*, **4**, 216–28.

Grünfeld, J-P., Noel, L-H., Hafez, S., and Droz, D. (1985). Renal prognosis in women with hereditary nephritis. *Clinical Nephrology*, **23**, 267–71.

Grünfeld, J. P., Grateau, G., Noel, L-H., Charbonneau, R., Gubler, M. C., Savage, G. O. S., *et al.* (1987). Variants of Alport's syndrome. *Pediatric Nephrology*, **1**, 419–21.

Gubler, M. C., Lévy, M., Naizot, C., and Habib, R. (1980). Glomerular besement membrane changes in hereditary glomerular diseases. *Renal Physiology*, **3**, 405–13.

Gubler, M., Lévy, M., Broyer, M., Naizot, C., Gonzales, G., Perrin, D., *et al.* (1981). Alport's syndrome: a report of 58 cases and a review of the literature. *American Journal of Medicine*, **70**, 493–505.

Guthrie, L. G. (1902). 'Idiopathic' or congenital hereditary and family haematuria. *Lancet*, **i**, 1243–6.

Habib, R., Gubler, M. C., Hinglais, N., Noël, L. H., Droz, D., Lévy, M., *et al.* (1982). Alport's syndrome: experience at Hopital Necker. *Kidney International*, **21**, S11, S20–8.

Hasstedt, S. J. and Atkin, C. L. (1983). X-linked inheritance of Alport syndrome: family P revisited. *American Journal of Human Genetics*, **35**, 1241–51.

Hasstedt, S. J., Atkin, C. L., and San Juan, A. C. (1986). Genetic heterogeneity among kindreds with Alport's syndrome. *American Journal of Human Genetics*, **38**, 940–53.

Hill, G. S., Jenis, E. H., and Goodloe, S. (1974). The non-specificity of the ultrastructural alterations in hereditary nephritis with additional observations on benign familial haematuria. *Laboratory Investigations*, **31**, 516–32.

Hinglais, N., Grünfeld, J.-P., and Bois, E. (1972). Characteristic ultrastructural lesion of the glomerular basement membrane in progressive nephritis (Alport's syndrome). *Laboratory Investigations*, **27**, 473–87.

Hostikka, S. L. and Tryggvason, K. (1988). The complete primary structure of the α2 chain of human type IV collagen and comparison with the α1 (VI) chain. *Journal of Biological Chemistry*, **263**, 19488–93.

Hostikka, S. L., Eddy, R. L., Byers, M. G., Höyhtyä, M., Shows, T. B., and Tryggvason, K. (1990). Identification of a distinct type IV collagen α chain with restricted kidney distribution and assignment of its gene to the locus of X chromosome-linked Alport syndrome. *Proceedings of the National Academy of Sciences, USA*, **87**, 1606–10.

Hurst, A. F. (1923). Hereditary familial congenital nephritis occurring in 16 individuals in 3 generations. *Guy's Hospital Reports*, **73**, 368–70.

Iverson, U. M. (1974). Hereditary nephropathy with hearing loss: 'Alport's syndrome'. *Acta Paediatrica Scandinavia*, Suppl. **245**, 1–23.

Jenis, E. H., Valeski, J. E., and Calcagno, P. L. (1981). Variability of anti-glomerular basement membrane binding in hereditary nephritis. *Clinical Nephrology*, **15**, 111–14.

Johnsson, L. G. and Arenberg, I. K. (1981). Cochlear abnormalities in Alport's syndrome. *Archives of Otolaryngology*, **107**, 340–9.

Johnston, J. B., Theron, Clagett, O., and McDonald, J. R. (1953). Smooth-muscle tumours of the oesophagus. *Thorax*, **8**, 251–65.

Kashtan, C. (1993). Clinical aspects of post-transplant anti-glomerular basement membrane nephritis in patients with Alport syndrome. (Abstract). Second International Workshop on Alport Syndrome, New Haven, USA. p. 9.

Kaufman, D. B., McIntosh, R. M., Smith, F. G. Jr., and Vernier, R. L. (1970). Diffuse familial nephropathy: a clinicopathological study. *Journal of Pediatrics*, **77**, 37–47.

Kefalides, N. A. (1971). Isolation of a collagen from basement membranes containing three identical α-chains. *Biochemistry and Biophysics Research Communications*, **45**, 226–34.

Kendall, G. and Hertz, A. F. (1912). Hereditary familial congenital haemorrhagic nephritis. *Guy's Hospital Reports*, **66**, 137–41.

Kopelman, H., Asatoor, A. M., and Milne, M. D. (1964). Hyperprolinaemia and hereditary nephritis. *Lancet*, **ii**, 1075–9.

Krickstein, H. I., Gloor, F. J., and Balogh, K. Jr. (1966). Renal pathology in hereditary nephritis with nerve deafness. *Archives of Pathology*, **82**, 506–17.

Lachheim, L., Kemnitz, P., Büttner, H., Thal, W., and Witkowski, R. (1968). Erbliche Nephritis mit Innenhorschwerhörigkeit (Alport Syndrom). *Deutsche Medizinische Wochenschrift*, **93**, 1891–6.

Lancet (1959). **i**, 947.

Lemminck, H. H., Nillesen, W. N., Mochizuki, T., Schröder, C. H., Brunner, H. G., van Oost, B. A., *et al.* (1996). Benign familial hematuria due to a mutation of the type IV collagen alpha chain. *Journal of Clinical Investigation*, **98**, 1114–18.

McCoy, R. C., Johnson, H. K., Stone, W. J., and Wilson, C. B. (1976). Variation in glomerular basement membrane antigens in hereditary nephritis. *Laboratory Investigation*, **34**, 325. (Abstract).

McDonald, T. J., Zincke, H., Anderson, C. F., and Ott, N. T. (1978). Reversal of deafness after renal transplantation in Alport's syndrome. *Laryngoscope*, **88**, 38–42.

MacNeil, E. and Shaw, R. F. (1973). Segregation ratio in Alport's syndrome. *Journal of Medical Genetics*, **10**, 23–6.

Mayo, O. (1973). Alport's syndrome. *Journal of Medical Genetics*, **10**, 396–7.

Mitschke, H., Schmidt, P., Zazgornik, J., Kopsa, H., and Pils, P. (1977). Effect of renal transplantation on uraemic deafness: a long-term study. *Audiology*, **16**, 530–4.

Miyoshi, K., Suzuki, M., Ohno, F., Yamano, T., Yagi, F., and Khono, H. (1975). Antithyroid antibodies in Alport's syndrome. *Lancet*, **ii**, 480–2.

Mochizuki, T., Lemmick, H. H., Mariyama, M., Antignac, C., Gubler, M.-C., Pirson, Y., *et al.* (1994). Identification of mutations in the α3 (IV) and α4 (IV) collagen genes in autosomal recessive Alport syndrome. *Nature Genetics*, **8**, 77–82.

Morrison, K. E., Mariyama, M., Yang-Feng, T. L., and Reeders, S. T. (1991). Sequence and localization of a partial cDNA encoding the human α3 chain of type IV collagen. *American Journal of Human Genetics*, **49**, 545–54.

Morton, N. E. (1957). Further scoring types in sequential linkage tests with a critical review of autosomal and partial sex-linkage in man. *American Journal of Human Genetics*, **9**, 55–75.

Myers, J. C., Jones, T. A., Pohjolainen, E. R., Kadni, A. S., Goddard, A. D., Sheer, D., *et al.* (1990). Molecular cloning of α5 (IV) collagen and assignment of the gene to the region of the X-chromosome containing the Alport syndrome locus. *American Journal of Human Genetics*, **46**, 1024–33.

Neustein, H. B., O'Brien, J. S., Rossner, R. J., and Fillerup, D. L. (1972). Chronic nephritis and renal foam cells. *Archives of Pathology*, **93**, 503–9.

Nielsen, C. E. (1978). Anterior lenticonus and Alport's syndrome. *Acta Opththalmologica*, **56**, 518–30.

Olson, D. L., Anand, S. K., Landing, B. H., Heuser, E., Grushkin, C. M., and Lieberman, E. (1980). Diagnosis of hereditary nephritis by failure of glomeruli to bind anti-glomerular basement membrane antibodies. *Pediatrics*, **96**, 697–9.

O'Neill, W.M. Jr., Atkin, C. L., and Bloomer, H. A. (1978). Hereditary nephritis. A re-examination of its clinical and genetic features. *Annals of Internal Medicine*, **88**, 176–82.

Pashayan, H., Fraser, F. C., and Goldbloom, R. B. (1971). A family showing hereditary nephropathy. *American Journal of Human Genetics*, **23**, 555–67.

Perkoff, G. T., Stephens, F. E., Dolowitz, D. A., and Tyler, F. H. (1951). A clinical study of hereditary interestitial pyelonephritis. *Archives of Internal Medicine*, **88**, 191–200.

Perkoff, G. T., Nugent, C. A., Dolowitz, D. A., Stephens, F. E., Carnes, W. H., and Tyler, F. H. (1958). A follow-up study of hereditary chronic nephritis. *Archives of Internal Medicine*, **102**, 733–46.

Perkoff, G. T., Stephens, F. E., and Tyler, F. H. (1960). Chronic hereditary nephritis and Y-chromosome linkage: reply to Graham. *American Journal of Human Genetics*, **12**, 381–2.

Perrin, D., Jungers, P., Grunfeld, J-P., Delons, S., Noel, L. H., and Zenatti, C. (1980). Perimacular changes in Alport's syndrome. *Clinical Nephrology*, **13**, 163–7.

Peterson, L. C., Venkateswara Rao, K., Crosson, J. T., and White, J. G. (1985). Fechtner syndrome—a variant of Alport's syndrome with leucocyte inclusions and macrothrombocytopenia. *Blood*, **65**, 397–406.

Polak, B. C. P. (1980). Ophthalmological complications of haemodialysis and kidney transplant. *Documenta Ophthalmologica*, **49**, 1–96.

Rambausek, M., Hartz, G., Waldherr, R., Andrassy, K., and Ritz, E. (1987). Familial glomerulonephritis. *Pediatric Nephrology*, **1**, 416–18.

Reyersbach, G. C. and Butler, A. M. (1954). Congenital hereditary hematuria. *New England Journal of Medicine*, **251**, 377–80.

Richmond, J. M., Whitworth, J. A., and Kincaid-Smith, P. S. (1981). Familial interstitial nephritis. *Clinical Nephrology*, **16**, 109–13.

Rumpelt, H. J. (1980). Hereditary nephropathy (Alport's syndrome): correlation of clinical data with glomerular basement membrane alterations. *Clinical Nephrology*, **13**, 203–7.

Rumpelt, H-J. (1987). Alport's syndrome: specificity and pathogenesis of glomerular basement membrane alterations. *Pediatric Nephrology*, **1**, 422–7.

Sand, B. J. and Abraham, S. V. (1962). Anterior lenticonus. *American Journal of Ophthalmology*, **53**, 636–9.

Saus, J., Wieslander, J., Langeveld, J. P. M., Quinones, S., and Hudson, B. G. (1988). Identification of the Goodpasture antigen as the α3 chain of collagen IV. *Journal of Biological Chemistry*, **263**, 13374–80.

Savage, C. O. S., Reed, A., and Kershaw, M. (1986). Use of a monoclonal antibody in differential diagnosis of children with haematuria and hereditary nephritis. *Lancet*, **1**, 459–61.

Shaw, R. F. and Glover, R. A. (1961). Abnormal segregation in hereditary renal disease with deafness. *American Journal of Human Genetics*, **13**, 89–97.

Sohar, E. (1954). A heredo-familial syndrome characterized by renal disease, inner ear deafness and ocular changes. *Harefuah*, **27**, 161.

Soininen, R., Haka-Risku, T., Prockop, D. J., and Tryggvason, K. (1987). Complete primary structure of the α1 chain of human basement membrane (type IV) collagen. *FEBS Letters*, **225**, 188–94.

Spear, G. S. and Slusser, R. J. (1972). Alport's syndrome. Emphasizing electron microscopic studies of the glomerulus. *American Journal of Pathology*, **69**, 213–20.

Stephens, F. E., Perkoff, G. T., Dolowitz, D. A., and Tyler, F. H. (1951). Partially sex-linked dominant inheritance of interstitial pyelonephritis. *American Journal of Human Genetics*, **3**, 303–13.

Teisberg, P., Grottum, K. A., Myhre, E., and Flatmark, A. L. (1973). *In vivo* activation of complement in hereditary nephropathy. *Lancet*, ii, 356–8.

Tiebosch A. T. M. G., Frederik, P. M., van breda Vreisman, P., *et al.* (1989). Thin-basement membrane nephropathy in adults with persistent haematuria. *New England Journal of Medicine*, **320**, 14.

Tina, L., Jenis, E., Jose, P., Mendani, C., Papadopoulos, Z., and Calcagno, P. (1982). The glomerular basement membrane in benign familial haematuria. *Clinical Nephrology*, **17**, 1–4.

Tryggvason, K. (1992). Trends in molecular medicine: Cloning of Alport syndrome gene. *Annals of Medicine*, **23**, 237–9.

Ursui, J., Kogo, S., and Kitahara, H. (1978). Alport's syndrome. *Folia Ophthalmologica Japan*, **29**, 1012–18.

Vetrie, D., Flinter, F., Bobrow, M., and Harris, A. (1992*a*). Long-range mapping of the gene for the human α5 (IV) collagen chain at Xq22–23. *Genomics*, **12**, 130–8.

Vetrie, D., Boye, E., Flinter, F. A., Bobrow, M., and Harris, A. (1992*b*). DNA rearrangements in the α5 (IV) collagen gene of individuals with Alport's syndrome (AS): further refinement using pulsed field electrophoresis. *Genomics*, **14**, 624–33.

Vetrie, D., Flinter, F., Bobrow, M., and Harris, A. (1992*c*). Construction of a yeast artificial chromosome contig encompassing the human α5 (IV) collagen gene. *Genomics*, **14**, 634–42.

Waldherr, R. (1982). Familial glomerular disease. *Contributions to Nephrology*, **33**, 104–21.

Weidauer, H. and Arnold, W. (1975). Consideration to the aetiology of Alport's syndrome. *Archives of Otorhinolaryngology*, **210**, 361.

Whalen, R. E., Huang, S., Peschele, E., and McIntosh, H. D. (1961). Hereditary nephropathy, deafness and renal foam cells. *American Journal of Medicine*, **31**, 171–86.

Williamson, D. A. J. (1961). Alport's syndrome of hereditary nephritis with deafness. *Lancet*, ii, 1321–3.

Wood, J. and Knight, L. W. (1966). A family with Alport's syndrome of hereditary nephritis and deafness. *Australasian Annals of Medicine*, **15**, 227.

Yoshikawa, N., Cameron, A. H., and White, H. R. (1981). The glomerular basal lamina in hereditary nephritis. *Journal of Pathology*, **135**, 199–209.

Yoshikawa, N., White, R. H. R., and Cameron, A. H. (1982). Familial hematuria: clinico-pathological correlations. *Clinical Nephrology*, **17**, 172–82.

Zhou, J., Hostikka, S. L., Chow, L. T., and Tryggvason, K. (1991*a*). Characterization of the 3′ half of the human type IV collagen α5 gene that is affected in the Alport syndrome. *Genomics*, **9**, 1–9.

Zhou, J., Barker, D. F., Hostikka, S. L., Gregory, M. C., Atkin, C. L., and Tryggvason, K. (1991*b*). Single base mutation in α5 (IV) collagen chain converting a conserved cysteine to serine in Alport syndrome. *Genomics*, **9**, 10–18.

Zhou, J., Smeets, H., de Paepe, A., *et al.* (1993*a*). The α5 and α6 chains of type IV collagen are both mutated in the patients with X-linked Alport syndrome and leiomyomatosis. (Abstract). Second International Workshop on Alport Syndrome, New Haven, USA. p. 35.

Zhou, J., Mochizuki, T., Vetrie, D., *et al.* (1993*b*). Isolation of a novel type IV collagen gene, α6 (IV), and the genomic organization of COL4A5/COL4A6. (Abstract). Second International Workshop on Alport Syndrome, New Haven, USA. p. 34.

11.2

Disorders of the basement membrane: thin glomerular basement membrane syndrome, nail–patella syndrome, and collagen type III glomerulopathy

Marie-Claire Gubler

Thin glomerular basement membrane syndrome

Thin glomerular basement membrane (GBM) is an ultrastructural anomaly, observed in several clinical conditions, characterized by the occurrence of microscopic haematuria. The lesion is freuqently associated with the benign course of the haematuric disease and the terms 'thin glomerular basement membrane disease' (Basta-Jovanovic *et al.* 1990; Yamazaki *et al.* 1993) or 'thin (glomerular basement) membrane nephropathy' (Aarons *et al.* 1989, Dische *et al.* 1989, 1990, Perry *et al.* 1989, Tiesbosch *et al.* 1989, Bailey 1990, Lang *et al.* 1990) have often been used to designate 'familial benign haematuria'. However, these terms are misleading since the finding of thin GBM is not the guarantee of a benign disease, the same ultrastructural lesion being sometimes observed in nephritis with a progressive course. Another difficulty resides in the absence of a widely accepted definition of the inferior limit of normal GBM and consequently of the thin GBM.

Normal thickness of the GBM. Definition and incidence of thin basement membrane

The normal thickness of human GBM has been estimated by different investigators (Table 11.2.1) using different morphometric techniques and mathematical analysis. In fetuses and at birth, the GBM thickness is about 100–150 nm (Vernier *et al.* 1962; Vogler *et al.* 1987). It increases progressively during the first years of life to reach 200 nm at one year (Vogler *et al.* 1987) and 300 nm by 10 years (Kobayashi *et al.* 1980; Milanesi *et al.* 1984; Vogler *et al.* 1987; Morita *et al.* 1988). In adults, normal GBM thickness ranges from 320 ± 35 nm (Aarons *et al.* 1989) to 395 $\pm$ 65 nm (Dische *et al.* 1990). These differences could be due to different techniques of tissue fixation and embedding. According to Jörgensen and Bentzon (1968), no dependence could be demonstrated between the results of the measurements and the age and sex of adult patients. Conversely, in other studies, the GBM thickness was found to continue to increase throughout life (Shindo *et al.* 1988) and to be significantly greater in males than in females (Steffes *et al.* 1983; Shindo *et al.* 1988).

The diagnosis of 'thin GBM' may be based on the finding by eye of extensive attenuation of the GBM as the main ultrastructural change, a finding secondarily confirmed by serial GBM measurements (Gubler *et al.* 1990). Another approach has been to evaluate the frequency of attenuated GBM segments and to classify as thin GBM, those patients with more than 10% of

Table 11.2.1   Normal thickness of the GBM (as reported in the literature)

Vernier and Birch-Anderson (1962)	Fetus and children <3 yrs	100 ↗ 300 nm
Kobayashi *et al.* (1980)	Children 1–12 yrs	270 ↗ 340 nm
Morita *et al.* (1973)	Children 1–13 yrs	200 ↗ 310 nm
Lang *et al.* (1990)	Children 1–16 yrs	180 ↗ 330 nm (NS-IgA)
Shindo *et al.* (1988)	Children and adults	295–392 nm (H)
		314–462 nm (NS)
Basta-Jovanovic *et al.* (1990)	Children and adults	287–317 nm (NS)
Osawa *et al.* (1966)	Adults	315 ± 98 nm
Jorgensen and Bentzon (1968)	Adults	329 nm
Steffes *et al.* (1983)	Adults	326 nm (females)
		373 nm (males)
Aarons *et al.* (1989)	Adults	320 ± 35 nm
Dische *et al.* (1990)	Adults	330–460 nm

NS = idiopathic nephrotic syndome; IgA = IgA nephropathy; H = recurrent hematuira.

measurements less than 200 nm (Milanesi *et al.* 1984). Most often, the diagnosis of thin GBM has been based on the value of arithmetic or harmonic means obtained from serial measurements of GBM thickness. The discriminating point between normal and low GBM thickness values varied according to normal standards in different groups: it was 250 nm for Steffes *et al.* (1983) and Tiebosch *et al.* (1989), and 330 nm for Dische *et al.* (1985). These discrepancies underline the difficulties and the limits of the diagnosis of thin GBM, and the necessity for each laboratory to establish its own standard.

The true incidence of the thin GBM lesion is not fully appreciated. However, recent data obtained from systematic ultrastructural evaluation of the GBM indicate that it is more frequent than previously thought. Thin GBMs have been found in 9.2% and 11% of non-transplant renal biopsies in the series of Dische *et al.* (1990) and Aarons *et al.* (1989) respectively, in the absence of any detected clinical manifestation. According to Dische *et al.* (1990), the incidence of this abnormality in the general population lies between 5.2 and 9.2%. This high incidence accurately raises the question of the significance of borderline changes in GBM thickness: do they represent physiological variants or pathological changes possibly responsible for hematuria? Thin GBM is the common lesion detected in most series of haematuric children (Trachtman *et al.* 1984; Lang *et al.* 1990; Schröder *et al.* 1990), but not in our patients where it is five times less frequent than IgA nephropathy (Gubler *et al.* 1990). The incidence in adult haematuric patients seems to be similar to that of IgA nephropathy (Dische *et al.* 1985; Perry *et al.* 1989; Tiebosch *et al.* 1989).

Pathology

By *light microscopy*, the renal tissue is normal, except for the occasional presence of red blood cells within tubular lumens. A minor degree of mesangial thickening may be seen. Conventional *immunofluorescence* is classically negative (Abe *et al.* 1987) but small granular deposits of C3 and/ or IgG, IgM, and C1q irregularly distributed on the tuft are detected in about half of the patients (Gubler *et al.* 1990; Saxena *et al.* 1990) These non-specific findings are often associated with vascular deposits of C3.

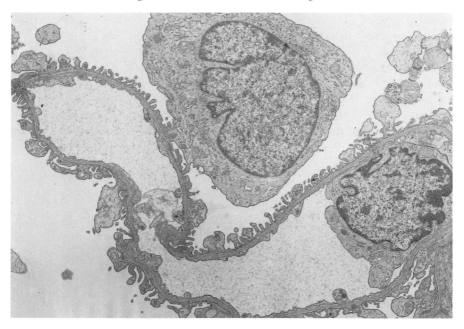

Fig. 11.2.1 Thin glomerular basement membrane syndrome. Electron microscopy ×4800. Uranyl acetate, lead citrate. Diffuse thinning of the GBM.

Immunohistochemical analysis of the collagenous composition of the GBM performed with anti-GBM serum from patients affected with the Goodpasture syndrome (Aarons *et al.* 1989; Schröder *et al.* 1990; Savige 1991), with the monoclonal antibody MCA-P1 which recognizes the Goodpasture epitope localized in the NC1 domain to the α3 chain of type IV collagen (Dische *et al.* 1989; Gubler *et al.* 1990) or with antibodies to the different chains of type IV collagen (Gubler *et al.* 1993; Petterson *et al.* 1990), gave normal results in most patients tested.

Diffuse and extreme attenuation of the GBM is the only lesion detected at the *ultrastructural level* (Fig. 11.2.1). Thinning of the GBM is usually regular and diffuse but, in some cases, GBM attenuation is patchy and strict GBM measurements may be necessary for diagnosis (Aarons *et al.* 1989). The structure and contours of the GBM are normal. In all cases the thickness of the lamina densa is strikingly reduced. There is a wide discrepancy among investigators concerning the definition of thin GBM. In the first paper by Rogers *et al.* (1973), the average thickness of the GBM was 150 nm. GBM thickness was between 100 and 200 nm in most paediatric series (Tina *et al.* 1982; Yoshikawa *et al.* 1984; Gubler *et al.* 1990). In adult series, the mean GBM thickness values leading to the diagnosis of thin GBM varied from 206 nm to 319 nm (Dische *et al.* 1985; Aarons *et al.* 1989; Perry *et al.* 1989). Overlaps between 'abnormal' values and normal values measured in controls were observed in some of these last series.

Clinical features

Persistent microscopic haematuria is the classical symptom in patients with thin GBM. It is often detected in childhood (Gubler *et al.* 1990; Kobayashi *et al.* 1980; Piel *et al.* 1982; Tina *et al.* 1982; Yoshikawa *et al.* 1984). Recurrent episodes of gross haematuria have been reported in some cases

(Kobayashi *et al.* 1980; Trachtman *et al.* 1984; Aarons *et al.* 1989; Perry *et al.* 1989; Lang *et al.* 1990). Proteinuria is usually absent but was the main problem in a few patients (Dische *et al.* 1985; Tiebosch *et al.* 1989). Hypertension, renal failure, and/or progression to end-stage renal failure (ESRF) have rarely been observed (Yum *et al.* 1983; Aarons *et al.* 1989; Tiebosch *et al.* 1989; Gubler *et al.* 1990). Extrarenal symptoms are usually absent, but deafness affecting the proband or one haematuric relative has occasionally been described (Piel *et al.* 1982; Aarons *et al.* 1989; Gubler *et al.* 1990, 1993). Thus, it is clear that the clinical syndrome associated with thin GBM is heterogeneous, suggesting that the lesion may have different aetiologic origins.

Aetiology

Familial benign haematuria

Familial benign haematuria (FBH) is characterized by the familial occurrence of persistent microscopic haematuria, usually detected in childhood. Episodes of gross haematuria have been reported but are quite rare. Haematuria remains isolated throughout life and, by definition, never progresses to ESRF. Diffuse attenuation of the GBM is usually considered the hallmark of the condition but is not specific (Hill *et al.* 1974; Piel *et al.* 1982; Abe *et al.* 1987; Aarons *et al.* 1989; Gubler *et al.* 1990). The family initially reported by Rogers *et al.* (1973) is quite representative of the condition: eight members with isolated persistent haematuria have been identified in four generations. Five of them, ranging from ages 19 to 51, have been biopsied and all of them showed thin GBM without any other glomerular change.

FBH is usually considered to be transmitted as an autosomal dominant trait. However, reliable data on the mode of transmission are scarce. In the families extensively studied by Rogers *et al.* (1973) and Bailey (1990), the disease is clearly inherited as a dominant trait, but the autosomal inheritance is not demonstrated in the absence of father-to-son transmission. We observed male-to-male transmission in two out of 10 families with FBH. Also, Aarons *et al.* (1989) and Schröder *et al.* (1990) gave convincing evidence of the autosomal dominant transmission of the condition in some of their kindreds.

The incidence of this haematuric disorder has not been clearly evaluated. The basic biochemical defect has not been characterized. The antigenicity of the GBM has always been found normal. Considering FBH with thin GBM as a variant of Alport's syndrome, a primary defect in the autosomal genes COL4A1-COL4A4 coding for the $\alpha1$–$\alpha4$ chains or type IV collagen could have been hypothesized. No linkage to COL4A1 or COL4A2 has been detected in the families studied by Savige (1991) and no association between 'thin basement membrane disease' and COL4A3-COL4A4 has been found in the families tested by Yamzaki *et al.* (1993). However, unpublished results from our laboratory and the demonstration of COL4A4 mutations in one kindred with 'familial benign haematuria' (Lemmink *et al.* 1996) strongly suggest that some patients presenting with 'familial benign haematuria' are actually heterozygotes for the autosomal recessive form of Alport's syndrome.

The prognosis of the condition is quite good. The diagnosis of benign disease may be difficult to establish however, since it is based on a series of negative findings (absence of proteinuria, renal failure, or extrarenal symptoms), on the finding of a non-specific ultrastructural lesion, the thin GBM, and above all on the results of family investigations demonstrating the absence of progression in the adult males. The diagnosis has to be reconsidered if any new symptom is observed secondarily during the follow-up period.

Sporadic benign haematuria

Sporadic cases of benign haematuria with thin GBM have been reported by different groups (Kobayashi *et al.* 1980; Piel *et al.* 1982; Trachtman *et al.* 1984; Yoshikawa *et al.* 1984; Gubler *et al.* 1990). They are rare in the series of haematuric children reported by Schröder (1990) who detected a family history in most children with thin GBM. Contrary to the findings of Tina *et al.* (1982), he did not observe any difference in the GBM thickness between sporadic and familial benign haematuria. The relationship of sporadic benign haematuria with FBH has not been elucidated, one possibility being that it represents new mutations for FBH. When detected in young children or in females, isolated haematuria with thin GBM could also reveal a new mutation for Alport's syndrome.

Progressive hereditary haematuric nephritis without deafness (or type IV Alport's syndrome)

This syndrome is characterized by the existence of renal impairment with haematuria resembling adult-type Alport's syndrome but progressing to end-stage renal failure without sensorineural hearing loss or any other extrarenal symptom. Thin GBM with normal antigenicity is frequently observed in patients with this condition (Gubler *et al.* 1993). It seems apparent that some of the patients reported as having thin basement membrane nephropathy, and who developed proteinuria with or without progressive renal failure or were found to have a family history of nephritis, are probably affected with this syndrome (Yum *et al.* 1983; Dische *et al.* 1985; Aarons *et al.* 1989; Perry *et al.* 1989; Tiebosch *et al.* 1989). Mutations in the COL4A5 gene coding for the $\alpha 5$ chain of type IV collagen have been described by Gregory *et al.* (1991) in three related families, demonstrating that this syndrome is actually a variant of Alport's syndrome.

Alport's syndrome

Typical cases of Alport's syndrome are characterized by irregular and marked thickening of the GBM with splitting and splintering of the lamina densa. However, especially in children, GBM thickening is segmental, and, a second anomaly, thinning of the GBM is associated and may be predominant (Rumpelt 1980; Gubler *et al.* 1981; Piel *et al.* 1982; Yoshikawa *et al.* 1988). Moreover, in some kindreds with the most typical clinical history of Alport's syndrome, the only lesion, whatever the age of patients, is thin GBM (Piel *et al.* 1982; Yoshikawa *et al.* 1988; Gubler *et al.* 1990; Pettersson *et al.* 1990). Progression to ESRF is due to retraction and collapse of capillary loops (Fig. 11.2.2). The antigenicity of the GBM has been evaluated in only a few patients: it was found normal in most, but patchy distribution of the $\alpha 3$ chain of type IV collagen was observed in three female patients (Gubler *et al.* 1990; Pettersson *et al.* 1990).

Diagnosis and prognosis

The diagnosis of thin GBM is based on careful examination and measurements of the GBM. But the prognosis of the lesion depends on the benign or progressive nature of the underlying disorder. It may be easy to recognize FBH when several males of the kindred, in successive generations, are affected with isolated microscopic haematuria. Conversely, when haematuric patients are very young and/or when only females are haematuric, the situation is quite different because no specific markers are available for distinguishing between patients affected with a very benign disease and patients who will progress to renal failure. The same is true for young or female patients presenting with apparently sporadic haematuria with thin GBM. Before predict-

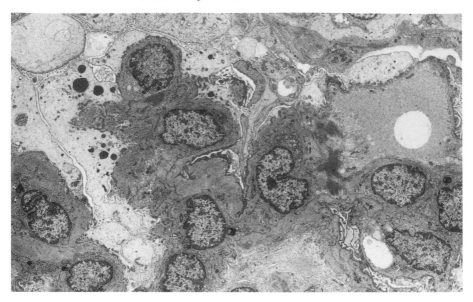

Fig. 11.2.2   Thin glomerular basement membrane syndrome. Electron microscopy ×3000. Uranyl acetate, lead citrate. Retraction and collapsus of a capillary loop. Adjacent capillary loops are lined by a thin GBM.

ing a benign course, the precise nature of the disease has to be identified by clinical and familial investigations and long-term surveillance.

Hereditary osteo-onychodysplasia (nail–patella syndrome)

Hereditary osteo-onychodysplasia (HOOD) or nail–patella syndrome (NPS) is a rare, autosomal dominant disorder characterized by the association of nail dysplasia and bone abnormalities. Renal involvement is an inconstant finding. This curious association, as well as the presence of fibrillar collagen within the GBM, have suggested that HOOD could be an inherited connective tissue disorder. Recently, similar collagen accumulation within the GBM has been described in patients presenting with familial progressive glomerulopathy without nail and bone involvement (Arakawa and Yamanaka 1991; Gubler *et al.* 1993). These findings raise the question of a variant of the disease or of a new type of glomerulopathy.

Clinical symptoms

Dysmorphic features

The dysmorphic features were first described by Little (1897) who observed a family of 18 members in whom nails and patellas were absent. Several reports followed leading to the identification of the characteristic quartet of nail hypoplasia, absent patellas, radial head dislocation, and iliac horn. Involvement is bilateral and symmertrical and may be recognized at birth in most patients.

Nail involvement is almost constant and usually visible from birth. In the review of the literature presented by Meyrier *et al.* (1990), it was absent in only six out of 147 patients, despite the presence of other elements of the tetrad. The nails were hypoplastic or absent in the 44

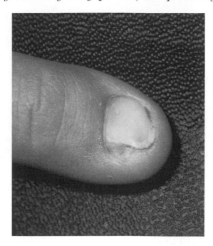

Fig. 11.2.3   Dystrophy involving the ulnar side of the thumb nail.

patients studied by Guidera *et al.* (1991) in a multicentre analysis. Nail involvement predominates on the hands where the thumb and the index and the ulnar side of each involved nail are more severely affected (Fig. 11.2.3). The toenails were normal in all patients of the series of Guidera *et al.* (1991). Lesions range from hemidysplasia to total nail aplasia. Frequent features are longitudinal pterygion, nail splitting, and absence or triangular appearance of the lunulae (Daniel *et al.* 1980).

The *knees* are abnormal in 95% (Meyrier *et al.* 1990) to 100% (Guidera *et al.* 1991) of cases. The patellae are hypoplastic or even absent. The small patellae have a tendency to dislocate laterally, producing difficulties in learning to walk in children and in walking downstairs in adults (Lucas *et al.* 1966). The dysplasia may also involve other structures of the knee, including femoral condyles and tibial epiphysis anomalies, with irregularity of the articular surface leading to genu valgum deformities and flexion contracture. The functional disability is usually limited and the most frequent complications are knee pains, recurring patella dislocations, and early onset of arthrosis.

Elbow dysplasia is observed in 94% of cases, according to Meyrier *et al.* (1990). The radial head is frequently small with subluxation or dislocation in a posterolateral position. Associated anomalies include deformities of the distal humeral extremity, hypoplasia of the olecranon, and elongation of the radial neck. These anomalies may lead to mild to severe limitation of extension, pronation, and supination of the forearm, especially in cases of webbing of the skin at the anterior aspect of the elbow joint.

Iliac horns, pathognomonic for the disease, usually discovered on routine IVP, are observed in about 70% of cases (Fig. 11.2.4). They are asymptomatic, bilateral, symmetrical bony formations arising from the posterior aspect of the ilium (Lucas *et al.* 1966). In some cases they may be detected clinically by palpation through the buttock muscles. They are frequently associated with other pelvic anomalies.

In addition to the components of the tetrad, various other bone abnormalities have been described. In the paediatric population studied by Guidera *et al.* (1991), the major initial abnormality affected *the foot and the ankles*: 25 out of 44 patients had unilateral or bilateral clubfoot; equinus, pes planus calcaneo valgus deformities were also observed. Scoliosis, sometimes requiring surgical treatment, is not infrequent (Lucas *et al.* 1966; Guidera *et al.* 1991).

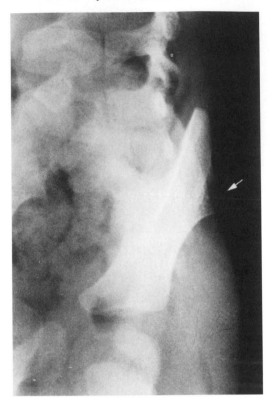

Fig. 11.2.4   X-ray of the pelvis. The lateral incidence shows the iliac horn extending posteriorly from the body of the ilium. (From Dr J. C. Leonard.)

According to the severity of the dysmorphic syndrome, HOOD may be discovered at various ages but the notion of family history strongly contributes to its early recognition. Mild forms of the disease may remain undetected over decades.

Renal involvement

Clinical renal involvement is not a constant feature of the syndrome. It was first reported in 1950 (Brixey and Burke; Hawkins and Smith) and seems to occur in about 30–40% of cases (Carbonara and Alpert 1964; Simila *et al.* 1970). Only four of the patients reported by Guidera *et al.* (1991) had renal abnormalities. Both sexes are equally affected but clinical expression of renal involvement varies among families: it is frequent and severe in some kindreds whereas it may be totally absent in others (Looij *et al.* 1988; Lommen *et al.* 1989). In addition, in HOOD families with nephropathy some affected members may be free of any renal symptom.

Proteinuria, sometimes associated with microscopic haematuria, is the most frequent presenting feature. Nephrotic syndrome was observed in three out of 122 patients reviewed by Meyrier *et al.* (1990). Progression to ESRF occurs in about 30% of patients with renal symptoms. Cases of rapid evolution to renal failure have been observed in the paediatric population.

A curious feature of the disease is the total unpredictability of renal prognosis. For example, a neonate belonging to a severely affected family, presenting with typical deformities and nephrotic syndrome at birth, developed a complete remission within two weeks (Simila *et al.* 1970). We had the opportunity to observe identical twin brothers affected with HOOD: one of them developed ESRF at 15 years of age whereas his brother had only intermittent proteinuria at 27. This suggests that non-genetic factors, which remain to be identified, may be implicated in the rapid progression of the glomerulopathy in some patients. Various types of superimposed nephritis, Goodpasture syndrome (Curtis *et al.* 1976), membranous nephropathy (Mackay *et al.* 1985), necrotizing angiitis (Croock *et al.* 1987), and IgA nephropathy (Meyrier *et al.* 1990) have been observed in HOOD patients. In addition to glomerular involvement, minor and usually silent urologic abnormalities have been detected in some patients. It is not demonstrated that their incidence is higher than in a control population.

Pathology

Light microscopy is poorly contributive. Renal tissue may be normal. Non-specific focal and segmental glomerular sclerosis and/or hyalinosis develop with the progression of renal failure. *Immunofluorescence* is negative or shows focal and non-specific deposits of IgM and C3.

The pathognomonic lesion has been identified by *electron microscopy*. Del Pozo and Lapp (1970) observed a prominent thickening of the GBM with the presence of irregular, sharply-defined, electron-lucent areas within the lamina densa. They suggested that the primary lesion could be in the GBM. The following year, Ben Bassat *et al.* (1971) identified clusters of fibrillar collagen irregularly distributed within thick GBM segments and the mesangial matrix and more precisely within areas of rarefaction. Further studies showed that with standard staining techniques the GBM and the mesangial matrix often have the 'moth-eaten' appearance initially described by del Pozo *et al.* (1970) (Fig. 11.2.5) due to lack of staining of the abnormal collagen; and that double staining with uranyl acetate and phosphotungstic acid is often necessary to disclose the collagen bundles (Fig. 11.2.6). Collagen bundles have a fibrillar structure similar to that of interstitial collagen, with a major periodicity of 40–60 nm. In some instances no periodic-

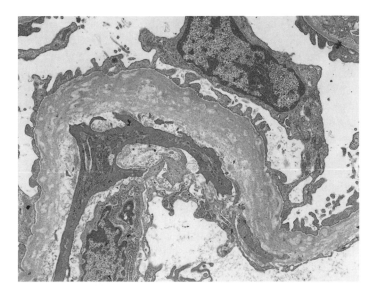

Fig. 11.2.5 Nail—patella syndrome. Electron microscopy ×6300. Uranyl acetate, lead citrate. Marked thickening of the GBM which has a moth-eaten appearance.

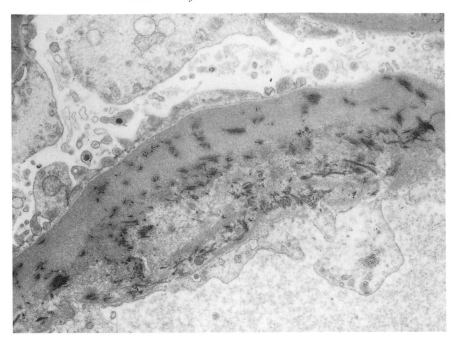

Fig. 11.2.6 Nail–patella syndrome. Electron microscopy ×10 000. Phosphotungstic acid staining. Presence of bundles of fibrillar collagen with the thick GBM.

ity can be detected. The width of individual fibrils varies considerably. These collagen fibrils are usually located within the lamina densa, sometimes within the laminae rarae interna and/or externa (Ben Bassat *et al.* 1971; Hoyer *et al.* 1972; Bennet *et al.* 1973; Morita *et al.* 1973; Gubler *et al.* 1980; Taguchi *et al.* 1988). They are considered to be a constant marker of the disease, observed even in a HOOD patient without any renal symptom. However, we could not detect any GBM collagen fibre in the first biopsy specimen from a child affected with HOOD and presenting with infantile nephrotic syndrome. The lesions were evident on the second renal specimen obtained three years later. By contrast, in the two-year-old child reported by Browning *et al.* (1988), diffuse thickening of the GBM was associated with focal subendothelial accumulation of fibrillar collagen. In our experience, bundles of fibrillar collagen within the mesangial matrix are always associated with GBM lesions. No tubular basement membrane involvement has been described.

There is a curious lack of correlation between the severity and the extension of ultrastructural GBM lesions on the one hand, and the patient's age, the severity of proteinuria, or even the degree of renal failure on the other. Typical lesions have been found in patients who were not proteinuric (Bennet *et al.* 1973; Morita *et al.* 1973).

Skin lesions have been detected in one patient with HOOD and vascular dilatations; significant dermal vessel basal lamina reduplication was associated with epidermal basement membrane thickening and splitting (Burkhart *et al.* 1980). We did not observe such lesions in the two patients studied.

Immunohistochemical studies of the GBM, using the monoclonal MCAP1 antibody which recognizes the NC1 domain of the a3 chain of type IV collagen, showed normal GBM labelling in one patient and no labelling in two others (Sutcliffe *et al.* 1989). We did not observe these anomalies in the renal specimens of the two patients studied: the glomerular distribution of type IV collagen chains was normal and the changes involved types III and VI collagen. They were characterized by the abnormal presence of type III collagen within glomeruli associated with an abnormal distribution of type VI collagen, confirming the abnormal biochemical composition of the glomerular extracellular matrix.

Incidence and genetic transmission

Nail–patella syndrome has been reported in kindreds of all geographic and ethnic origins (Meyrier *et al.* 1990). Its actual incidence is considered to be 22 per million in England and 4.5 per million in the United States (Dombros and Katz 1982; Guidera *et al.* 1991).

The syndrome is transmitted as an autosomal dominant trait. The gene is closely linked to those coding for ABO blood groups and for adenylate kinase (Renwick and Lawler 1955; Schleutermann *et al.* 1969). The three genes are located at the distal end of the long arm of chromosome 9 (9q34) (Fergusson-Smith *et al.* 1976). Recently, COL5A1, the gene coding for the a1 chain of collagen V has been mapped to the q34.2-q34.3 region of chromosome 9. This location made the COL5A1 a candidate gene for HOOD (Greenspan *et al.* 1992). COL5A1 heterozygous deletion and fibroblast underexpression of the α1 chain of type V collagen have been observed in a girl presenting with dysplastic nails, similar to those in the nail–patella syndrome, but normal patella, associated with skin and bone lesions similar to those found in the Goltz syndrome (Ghiggeri *et al.* 1993). It was suggested by the authors that the nail–patella syndrome could be attribuable to mutations inside the COL5A1 gene rather than to a deletion of it. However, COL5A1 has been excluded as a possible gene for the nail–patella syndrome (Campeau *et al.* 1995; Greenspan *et al.* 1995). Recently, the HOOD locus has been finely mapped within a 1–2 cM interval and two candidate genes are currently under investigation (McIntosh *et al.* 1997).

Taking into account the absence of nephropathy in some kindreds, Lommen *et al.* (1989) suggested that there are two allelic mutations of the HOOD locus, one causing HOOD without nephropathy and one associated with the possible occurrence of nephropathy. The risks for affected parents of having a child with nephropathy, eventually leading to ESRF, should be different in these two types of families.

Diagnosis and treatment

As seen above, clinical diagnosis of nail–patella syndrome is based on the identification of the elements of the classic tetrad. At the ultrastructural level, the finding of collagen fibres within the GBM of non-sclerotic glomeruli is quite diagnostic for the condition. One interesting exception has been the detection of almost similar lesions in a few patients without the extrarenal anomalies of the HOOD series (see below). In addition, fibrillar collagen, or type III collagen detected by immunohistochemistry (Yoshioka *et al.* 1989), may be focally observed within the mesangium in various types of glomerulonephritis.

Evolution of renal symptoms is unpredictable. No specific treatment is available. No recurrence of GBM lesions and no anti-GBM glomerulonephritis have so far been reported after kidney transplantation (Uranga *et al.* 1973; Chan *et al.* 1988).

Collagen type III glomerulopathy

Within recent years, massive accumulation of collagen fibres within the glomerular tuft has been reported in 27 patients presenting with proteinuria unassociated with extrarenal symptoms

(Sabnis *et al.* 1980; Dombros and Katz 1982; Salcedo 1984; Gubler *et al.* 1990; Ikeda *et al.* 1990; Arakawa and Yamanaka 1991; Imbasciati *et al.* 1991; Vogh *et al.* 1995; Tamura *et al.* 1996). The glomerulopathy has been termed 'primary glomerular fibrosis', 'collagen type III glomerulopathy', or 'collagenofibrotic glomerulonephropathy'. The glomerular lesions were initially considered as incomplete, purely renal forms of HOOD (Sabnis *et al.* 1980). However, analysis of morphological, clinical, and genetic data strongly suggests that they represent a new type (or new types) of glomerulopathy.

Clinical symptoms

Collagen type III glomerulopathy has been observed in both sexes and in patients aged from 1–70 years. Persistent proteinuria is often the presenting symptom. Microscopic haematuria and hypertension are inconstant. Stable renal function or slow progression to renal failure is observed in most adult patients whereas a protracted course to ESRF is described in most children (Salcedo 1984; Gubler *et al.* 1993). Anaemia is a frequent finding, and respiratory involvement or superimposed haemolytic uraemic syndrome have been observed in some paediatric patients (Gubler *et al.* 1993). Association with factor H deficiency has been reported in one patient (Vogh *et al.* 1995).

Pathology

By *light microscopy*, morphological lesions are very peculiar, mimicking thrombotic microangiopathy of the glomerular type: the glomerular tuft is markedly enlarged due to both expansion of the mesangial matrix without cell proliferation and generalized widening of the subendothelial aspect of the GBM. *Immunofluorescence* is usually negative or shows non-specific focal deposits of immunoglobulins and/or complement factors. *Electron microscopic* examination, after phosphotungstic acid staining, reveals the presence of bundles of collagen fibres accumulated within the expended mesangium and the subendothelial space of the GBM. Conversely to changes observed in the nail–patella syndrome, the lamina densa is usually normal. Antibodies to type III collagen strongly stain the glomerular tuft.

Genetic data

Family investigations have been negative in most adult patients reported to date. However, positive family history of nephritis was found in four patients and was consistent with an autosomal dominant transmission in two (Sabnis *et al.* 1980; Dombros *et al.* 1984) and with an autosomal recessive transmission in two others (Tamura *et al.* 1996). Parental consanguinity, involvement of several sibs of both sexes, and absence of renal and extrarenal symptoms in parents strongly support the hypothesis of autosomal recessive transmission of the disease in the paediatric series (Salcedo 1984; Gubler *et al.* 1993).

Interestingly, all patients investigated have been shown to have extremely high serum levels of procollagen III peptide, the N-terminal sequence of the precursor procollagen molecule (Tamura *et al.* 1996). This precursor is cleaved and the increased concentration of the peptide in the serum is a marker of stimulated type III collagen synthesis in a variety of renal or extrarenal diseases. However, because of the very high level observed in patients with collagen type III glomerulopathy, determination of type III collagen peptide could be used as a non-invasive indicator of the disease in relatives of affected patients. It could also be useful in the investigation of atypical cases of glomerulopathies mimicking thrombotic microangiopathy or membranoproliferative glomerulonephritis.

References

Aarons, I., Smith, P. S., Davies, R. A, Woodroffe, A. J., and Clarkson, A. R. (1989). Thin membrane nephropathy: A clinicopathological study. *Clinical Nephrology*, **32**, 151–8.

Abe, S., Amagasaki, Y., Konishi, K., Kato, E., Sakaguchi, H., and Shimoyama, K. (1987). Thin basement membrane syndrome in adults. *Journal of Clinical Pathology*, **40**, 318–22.

Arakawa, M. and Yamanaka, N. (ed.) (1991). *Collagenofibrinotic glomerulonephropathy*. Nishimura, Nigata; Smith-Gordon, London.

Bailey, R. R. (1990). Familial haematuria due to thin basement membrane nephropathy. *New Zealand Medical Journal*, **103**, 312–13.

Basta-Jovanovic, G., Venkatasehan V. S., Gil, J., Kim, D. U., Dikman, S. H., and Churg, J. (1990). Morphometric analysis of glomerular basement membranes in thin basement membrane disease. *Clinical Nephrology*, **33**, 110–14.

Ben Bassat, M., Cohen, L., and Rosenfield, J. (1971). The glomerular basement membrane in the nail–patella syndrome. *Archives of Pathology*, **92**, 350–5.

Bennet, W. M., Musgrave, J. E., Campbell, R. A., Elliot, D., Cox, R., Brooks, R. E., *et al.* (1973). The nephropathy of the nail–patella syndrome. Clinicopathologic analysis of 11 kindreds. *American Journal of Medicine*, **54**, 304–19.

Brixey, A. M. and Burke, R. M. (1950). Arthro-onychodysplasia. *American Journal of Medicine*, **8**, 738–44.

Browning, M. C., Weidner, N., and Lorentz, W. B. Jr. (1988). Renal histopathology of the nail–patella syndrome in a two-year-old boy. *Clinical Nephrology*, **29**, 210–13.

Burkhart, C. G., Bhumbra, R., and Iannone, A. M. (1980). Nail–patella syndrome. A distinctive clinical and electron microscopic presentation. *Journal of the American Academy of Dermatology*, **3**, 251–6.

Campeau, E., Watkins, D., Rouleau, G. A., Babul, R., Buchanan, J. A., Meschino, W., *et al.* (1995). Linkage analysis of the nail–patella syndrome. *American Journal of Human Genetics*, **56**, 243–7.

Carbonara, P. and Alpert, M. (1964). Hereditary osteo-onychodysplasia. *American Journal of Medicine*, **248**, 138–51.

Chan, R. C. K., Chan, K. W., Cheng, I. K. P., and Chan, M. K. (1988). Living-related renal transplantation in a patient with nail–patella syndrome. *Nephron*, **50**, 164–6.

Croock, A. D., Bashar Kahaleh, M., and Powers, J. M. (1987). Vasculitis and renal disease in nail–patella syndrome: Case report and literature review. *Annals of Rheumatic Diseases*, **46**, 562–5.

Curtis, J. J., Athena, D. B., Leach, R. P., Galla, J. H., Lucas, B. A., and Luke, R. G. (1976). Goodpasture's syndrome in a patient with the nail–patella syndrome. *American Journal of Medicine*, **61**, 401–6.

Daniel, C. R., Osment, L. S., and Noojin, R. O. (1980). Triangular lunulae. A clue to nail–patella syndrome. *Archives of Dermatology*, **116**, 448–9.

Del Pozo, E. and Lapp, H. (1970). Ultrastructure of the kidney in the nephropathy of the nail–patella syndrome. *American Journal of Clinical Pathology*, **54**, 845–51.

Dische, F. E., Weston, M. J., and Parsons, V. (1985). Abnormally thin glomerular basement membranes associated with hematuria, proteinuria or renal failure. *American Journal of Nephrology*, **5**, 103–9.

Dische, F. E., Brooke, I. P., Cashman, S. I., Severn, A., Taube, D., Parsons, V., *et al.* (1989). Reactivity of monoclonal antibody P1 with glomerular basement membrane in thin-membrane nephropathy. *Nephrology, Dialysis, Transplantation*, **4**, 611–17.

Dische, F. E., Anderson, V. E. R., Keane, S. J., Taube, D., Bewick, M., and Parsons, V. (1990). Incidence of thin membrane nephropathy: morphometric investigation of a population sample. *Journal of Clinical Pathology*, **43**, 457–60.

Dombros, N. and Katz, A. (1982). Nail–patella-like lesions in the absence of skeletal abnormalities. *American Journal of Kidney Diseases*, **1**, 237–40.

Fergusson-Smith, M. A., Aitken, D. A., Turleau, C., and De Grouchy, J. (1976). Localisation of the human ABO: NP1: AK1 linkage group by regional assignment of AK1 to 9 q34. *Human Genetics*, **34**, 35–43.

Ghiggeri, G. M., Caridi, G., Altieri, P., Pezzolo, A., Gimelli, G., and Zuffardi, O. (1993). Are the nail–patella syndrome and the autosomal Goltz-like syndrome the phenotypic expressions of different alleles at the COL5A1 locus? *Human Genetics*, **91**, 175–7.

Greenspan, D. S., Byers, M. G., Eddy, R. L., Cheng, W., Jani-Sait, S., and Shows, T. B. (1992). Human collagen gene COL5A1 maps to the q34.2–q34.3 region of chromosome 9, near the locus for nail–patella syndrome. *Genomics*, **12**, 836–7.

Greenspan, D. S., Northrup, H., Au, K. S., McAllister, K. A., Francomano, C. A., Wenstrup, R. J., *et al.* (1995). COL5A1: Fine genetic mapping and exclusion as candidate gene in families with nail–patella syndrome, tuberous sclerosis 1, hereditary hemorrhagic telangiectasia, and Ehlers–Danlos syndrome type II. *Genomics*, **25**, 737–9.

Gregory, M. C., Skinner, B., Atkin, C. L., and Barker, D. F. (1991). A novel mutation in COL4A5 relates three families with type IV Alport syndrome. *Journal of the American Society of Nephrology*, **2**, 254.

Gubler, M. C., Levy, M., and Naizot, C. (1980). Glomerular basement membrane changes in hereditary glomerular diseases. *Renal Physiology*, **3**, 405–13.

Gubler, M. C., Levy, M., Broyer, M., Naizot, C., Gonzales, G., Perrin, D., *et al.* (1981). Alport's syndrome: a report of 58 cases and a review of the literature. *Amercian Journal of Medicine*, **70**, 493–505.

Gubler, M. C., Beaufils, H., Noël, L. H., and Habib, R. (1990). Significance of thin glomerular basement membranes in hematuric children. *Contribution to Nephrology*, **80**, 141–56.

Gubler, M. C., Antignac, C., and Deschênes, G., (1993). Genetic, clinical and morphologic heterogeneity in Alport's syndrome. *Advances in Nephrology*, **22**, 14–35.

Gubler, M. C., Dommergues, J. P., Foulard, M., Bensman, A., Leroy, J. P., Broyer, M., *et al.* (1993). Collagen type III glomerulopathy: a new type of hereditary nephropathy. *Pediatric Nephrology*, **7**, 354–60.

Guidera, K. J., Satterwhite, Y., Ogden, J. A., Pugh, L., and Ganey, T. (1991). Nail–patella syndrome: A review of 44 orthopaedic patients. *Journal of Pediatric Orthopedics*, **11**, 737–42.

Hawkins, C. F. and Smith, O. E. (1950). Renal dysplasia in a family with multiple hereditary abnormalities, including iliac horns. *Lancet*, **1**, 803–11.

Hill, G. S., Jenis, E. H., and Goodloe, S. (1974). The non-specificity of the ultrastructural alterations in herediatary nephritis. *Laboratory Investigation*, **31**, 516–32.

Hoyer, J. R., Michael, A. F., and Vernier, R. L. (1972). Renal disease in nail–patella syndrome: Clinical and morphologic studies. *Kidney International*, **2**, 231–8.

Ikeda, K., Yokoyama, H., Tomosugi, N., Kida, H., Ooshima, A., and Kobayashi, K. (1990). Primary glomerular fibrosis: a new nephropathy caused by diffuse intraglomerular increase in atypical type III collagen fibers. *Clinical Nephrology*, **33**, 155–9.

Imbasciati, E., Gherardi, G., Morozumi, K., Gudat, F., Epper, R., Basler, V., *et al.* (1991). Collagen type III glomerulopathy: A new idiopathic glomerular disease. *American Journal of Nephrology*, **11**, 422–9.

Jorgensen, F. and Bentzon, W. (1968). The ultrastructure of the normal human glomerulus. Thickness of glomerular basement membrane. *Laboratory Investigation*, **18**, 42–8.

Kobayashi, O., Wada, H., Okawa, K., and Maeda, H. (1980). Renal glomerula changes of non-familial and familial benign hematuria. *International Journal of Pediatric Nephrology*, **1**, 86–92.

Lang, S., Stevenson, B., and Risdon, R. A. (1990). Thin basement membrane nephropathy as a cause of recurrent haematuria in childhood. *Histopathology*, **16**, 331–7.

Lemminck, H. H., Nillesen, W. M., Mochizuki, T., Schröder, C. H., van Oost, B. A., Monnens, L. A. H., *et al.* (1996). *Journal of Clinical Investigation*, **98**, 1114–18.

Little, E. M. (1897). Congenital absence or delayed development of the patella. *Lancet*, **2**, 781–4.

Lommen, E. J. P., Hamel, B. C. J., and Te Slaa, R. L. (1989). Nephropathy in hereditary osteo-onychodysplasia (HOOD): variable expression or genetic heterogeneity? In: *Genetics of kidney disorders* (ed. A. R. Liss), pp. 157–60.

Looij, B. J., Te Slaa, R. L., Hogewind, B. L., and van de Kamp, J. J. P. (1988). Genetic counselling in hereditary osteo-onychodysplasia with nephropathy. *Journal of Medical Genetics*, **25**, 682–6.

Lucas, G. L. and Opitz, J. M. (1966). The nail–patella syndrome. Clinical and genetic aspects of 5 kindreds with 38 affected family members. *Journal of Pediatrics*, **68**, 273–88.

Mackay, I. G., Doig, A., and Thomson, D. (1985). Membranous nephropathy in a patient with nail–patella syndrome nephropathy. *Scottish Medical Journal*, **30**, 47 9.

McIntosh, I., Clough, M. V., Schäffer, A. A., Puffenberger, E. Q., Horton, V. K., Peters, K., *et al.* (1997). Fine mapping of the nail-patella syndrome locus at 9q34. *American Journal of Human Genetics*, **60**, 133–42.

McLay, A. L. C., Jackson, R., Meyboom, F., and Boulton Jones, J. M. (1992). Glomeular basement membrane thinning in adults: clinicopathological correlations of a new diagnosis approach. *Nephrology Dialysis Transplantation*, **7**, 191–9.

Meyrier, A., Rizzo, R., and Gubler, M. C. (1990). The nail–patella syndrome. A review. *Journal of Nephrology*, **2**, 133–40.

Milanesi, C., Rizzoni, G., Braggion, F., and Galdiolo, D. (1984). Electron microscopy for measurement of glomerular basement membrane width in children with benign familial hematuria. *Applied Pathology*, **2**, 199–204.

Morita, M., White, R. H. R., Raafat, F., Barnes, J. M., and Standring, D. M. (1988). Glomerular basement membrane thickness in children. A morphologic study. *Pediatric Nephrology*, **2**, 190–5.

Morita, T., Laughlin, L. O., Kawano, K., Kimmelstiel, P., Suzuki, Y., and Churg, J. (1973). Nail–patella syndrome. Light and electron microscopic studies of the kidney. *Archives of Internal Medicine*, **131**, 271–7.

Osawa, G., Kimmelstiel, P., and Seiling, V. (1966). Thickness of glomerular basement membranes. *The American Journal of Clinical Pathology*, **45**, 7–20.

Perry, G. J., George, C. R. P., Field, M. J., Collett P. V., Kalowski, S., Wyndham, R. N., *et al.* (1989). Thin-membrane nephropathy, a common cause of glomerular haematuria. *Medical Journal of Australia*, **151**, 636–42.

Petterson, E., Törnroth, T., and Wieslander, J. (1990). Abnormally thin glomerular basement membrane and the Goodpasture epitope. *Clinical Nephrology*, **33**, 105–9.

Piel, C. F., Blava, C. G., and Goodman, J. R. (1982). Glomerular basement membrane attenuations in familial nephritis and 'benign' hematuria. *Journal of Pediatrics*, **101**, 358–65.

Renwick, J. H. and Lawler, S. D. (1955). Genetical linkage between the ABO and nail–patella loci. *Annals of Human Genetics*, **19**, 312–31.

Rogers, P. W., Kurtzman, N. A., Bunn, S. M., and White, M. G. (1973). Familial benign essential hematuria. *Archives of Internal of Medicine*, **131**, 257–62.

Rumpelt, H. J. (1980). Hereditary nephropathy (Alport syndrome): correlations of clinical data with glomerular basement membrane alterations. *Clinical Nephrology*, **13**, 203–7.

Sabnis, S. G., Antonovych, T. T., Argy, W. P., Rakowski, T. A., Gandy, D. R., and Salcedo, J. R. (1980). Nail–patella syndrome. *Clinical Nephrology*, **14**, 148–53.

Salcedo, J. R. (1984). An autosomal recessive disorder with glomerular basement membrane abnormalities similar to those seen in the nail–patella syndrome. Report of a kindred. *American Journal of Medical Genetics*, **19**, 579–84.

Savige, J. (1991). Hereditary abnormalities of renal basement membranes. *Pathology*, **23**, 350–5.

Saxena *et al.* (1990).

Schleutermann, D. A., Bias, W. D., Murdoch, J. L., and Mc Kusik, V. A. (1969). Linkage of the loci for the nail–patella syndrome and adenylate kinase. *American Journal of Human Genetics*, **21**, 606–30.

Schröder, C. H., Bontemps, C. M., Assmann, K. J. M., Schuurmans Stekhoven, J. H., Foidart, J. M., Monnens L. A. H., *et al.* (1990). Renal biopsy and family studies in 65 children with isolated hematuria. *Acta Paediatrica Scandinavica*, **79**, 630–6.

Shindo, S., Yoshimoto, M., Kuriya, N., and Berstein, J. (1988). Glomerular basement membrane thickness in recurrent and persistent hematuria and nephrotic syndrome: correlation with sex and age. *Pediatric Nephrology*, **2**, 196–9.

Simila, S., Vesa, L., and Wasz-Hockert, O. (1970). Hereditary onycho-osteodysplasia (The nail–patella syndrome) with nephrosis-like renal disease in a newborn boy. *Pediatrics*, **46**, 61–5.

Steffes, M. W., Barbosa, J., Basgen, J. M., Sutherland, D. E. R., Najarian, J. S., and Mauer, S. M. (1983). Quantitative glomerular morphology of the normal human kidney. *Laboratory Investigation*, **49**, 82–6.

Sutcliffe *et al.* (1989).

Taguchi, T., Takebayashi, S., Nishimura, M., and Tsuru, N. (1988). Nephropathy of nail–patella syndrome. *Ultrastructural Pathology*, **12**, 175–83.

Tamura, H., Matsuda, A., Kidoguchi, N., Matsumura, O., Mitarai, T., and Isoda, K. (1996). A family with two sisters with collagenofibrotic glomerulonephropathy. *American Journal of Kidney Diseases*, **27**, 588–95.

Tiebosch, A. T. M. G., Frederik, P. M., van Breda Vriesman, P. J. C., Mooy, J. M. V., van Rie, H., van de Wiel, T. W. M., *et al.* (1989). Thin basement-membrane nephropathy in adults with persistent hematuria. *New England Journal of Medicine*, **320**, 14–8.

Tina, L., Jenis, E., Jose, P., Medani, C., Papadopoulo, Z., and Calcagno, P. (1982). The glomerular basement membrane in benign familial hematuria. *Clinical Nephrology*, **17**, 1–4.

Trachtman, H., Weiss, R. A., Benett, B., and Griefer, I. (1984). Isolated hematuria in children: indications for a renal biopsy. *Kidney International*, **25**, 94–9.

Uranga, V. M., Simmons, R. L., Hoyer, J. R., Kjellstrand, C. M., Buselmeier, T. J., and Najarian, J. S. (1973). Renal transplantation for the nail–patella syndorme. *American Journal of Surgery*, **125**, 777–9.

Vernier, R. L. and Birch-Anderson, A. (1962). Studies of the human fetal kidney. I. Development of the glomerulus. *Journal of Pediatrics*, **60**, 754–68.

Vogh, B. A., Wyatt, R. J., Burke, B. A., Simonton, S. C., and Kashtan, C. E. (1995). Inherited factor H deficiency and collagen type III glomerulopathy. *Pediatric Nephrology*, **9**, 11–15.

Vogler, C., McAdams, A., and Homan, S. H. (1987). Glomerular basement membrane and lamina densa in infants and children: An ultrastructural evaluation. *Pediatric Pathology*, **7**, 527–34.

Yamazaki, H., Nakagawa, Y., Saito, A., Nishi, S., Sakatsume, M., Meguro, H., *et al.* (1993). Linkage analysis of thin basement membrane disease and type IV collagen $\alpha 3$ and $\alpha 4$ chain genes. *Journal of the American Society of Nephrology*, **4**, 827.

Yoshikawa, N., Hashimoto, H., Katayama, Y., Yamada, Y., Matsuo, T., and Okada, S. (1984). The thin glomerular basement membrane in children with hematuria. *Journal of Pathology*, **142**, 253–7.

Yoshikawa, N., Ito, H., Matsuyama, S., Hazikano, ••, Okada, S., and Matsuo, T. (1988). Hereditary nephritis in children with and without characteristic glomerular basement membrane alterations. *Clinical Nephrology*, **30**, 122–7.

Yoshioka, K., Takemura, T., and Tohda, M. (1989). Glomerular localization of type III collagen in human kidney disease. *Kidney International*, **35**, 1203–11.

Yum, M. and Bergstein, J. M. (1983). Basement membrane nephropathy: A new classification for Alport's syndrome and asymptomatic hematuria based on ultrasutructural findings. *Human Pathology*, **14**, 956–1003.

12

Genetic aspects of primary glomerular diseases and haemolytic–uraemic syndrome

Micheline Lévy and Philippe Lesavre

Introduction

In the past, it was generally assumed that haemolytic–uraemic syndrome and primary glomerular diseases were randomly distributed in the population and, in most large series, there was no mention of affected relatives.

Although systematic examination of patients' relatives remains an uncommon approach in nephrology, a few authors pointed out occasional families having two (or more) affected relatives. Such an investigation in a series of 860 patients with primary chronic glomerulonephritis identified, besides families with Alport's syndrome, a relatively small number of patients with affected relatives (six with IgA nephropathy and one with nephrotic syndrome with focal glomerular sclerosis) (Rambausek *et al.* 1987). It should be emphasized, however, that the occurrence of multiple cases in a family does not necessarily imply a role of genetic factors since multiple cases may simply occur by chance, or be due to exposure to the same environmental factors. The first step, therefore, should consist of showing by epidemiologic and statistical methods that a disease clusters more frequently than expected by chance in some families (familial agregation). Subsequently, a variety of genetic methods are classically used to separate genetic and environmental factors (King *et al.* 1984).

The rarity of multiplex families, the complexity of the renal diseases, and, above all, the lack of knowledge of pathogenetic mechanisms in each make such genetic studies at the family level difficult. Nevertheless, the implication of genetic factors became more likely. Support for these ideas was provided by different distribution of the diseases in ethnically different populations and data derived from the systematic search for associations with gene markers at the population level (association studies). Besides HLA (class I and essentially class II) alleles (Fig. 12.1) which have been extensively studied, other 'candidate genes' thought to have a function that could itself be involved in the disease have received attention. Complement components have been widely studied, immunoglobulin, T cell receptor, and tumour necrosis factor genes less frequently (Figs 12.1 and 12.2; Table 12.1). In the future it will probably be important to gain indications on the role of other candidate genes such as, for example, the other cytokine genes and/or their related receptors and inhibitors (Rees 1994).

Combined data have suggested that glomerular diseases and haemolytic–uraemic syndrome might be multifactorial (as are hypertension, diabetes, cancer, autoimmune diseases, etc.), meaning that a number of interacting factors, environmental and genetic, would contribute to the susceptibility of the individual. There may not exist a 'disease gene' in the sense of a rare mutated allele as implicated in monogenic diseases, but rather several common genetic risk factors (ie polymorphisms, each one normal if considered alone and each having independently a minor effect.

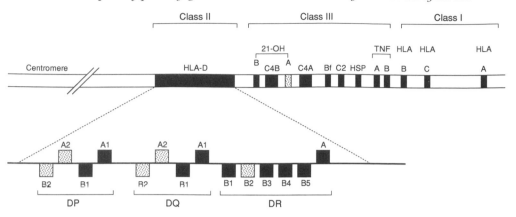

Fig. 12.1   Schematic map of the human MHC. Black boxes represent functional genes. Dotted boxes represent pseudogenes or genes whose product has not been characterized. Class I genes (HLA-A, B, C) encode α chains which combine with β 2 microglobuline. Class III genes include genes encoding complement components, e.g. C2, factor B (Bf), C4A, and C4B, as well as tumour necrosis factor (TNF), heat-shock protein-70 (HSP), and 21-hydroxylase (21-0H). In the C4 region, the number of genes depend on the haplotype. The class II genes are subdivided into three main regions, DR, DP, and DQ. Class II molecules consist of two associated chains, α and β, encoded by separated A and B genes. In the HLA-DR region, the number of genes depends on the haplotype. All DR haplotypes contain a single DRA gene and the number of β chains varies. Usually, one or two of the β chains are expressed. The HLAII region also contains TAP and LMP genes.

It should be emphasized that recent advances in genetic epidemiology have clearly shown the possibility of a heterogeneous determinism of many diseases. The coexistence of different familial distributions demonstrated through the use of segregation and linkage analyses have led to the conclusion that some diseases might be the result of a mixture of different aetiologic entities, corresponding to: sporadic cases (i.e. those that appear randomly), and/or a multifactorial form related to both environmental and genetic factors, and/or a mendelian form related to the presence of one (or several) mutation(s) that predetermine the development of the disease. For example, in breast cancer it has been shown that one distribution corresponds to sporadic cases, representing 95% of the cases, and another to a low-frequency mutation with autosomal dominant transmission. In Alzheimer's disease, besides the three autosomal dominant forms that have been described, there is a multifactorial form, apolipoprotein E being a genetic risk factor. It has been recently demonstrated that a subset of patients with mendelian transmission is also the case in idiopathic nephrotic syndrome and in haemolytic–uraemic syndrome. In both diseases, a very small number of cases, with well-defined clinical characteristics, correspond to a mutation with recessive autosomal transmission. Moreover, attention has recently been given to uncommon morphological patterns, not fitting established classifications of glomerular diseases. These newly recognized, non-immune-mediated glomerular diseases, i.e. collagen type III glomerulopathy, lipoprotein glomerulopathy, and glomerulopathy associated with predominant fibronectin deposits, appear to be inherited in an autosomal recessive pattern for the first two and in a dominant pattern for the third.

The DNA-based strategies of disease analysis and technical approaches, adopted in monogenic diseases to explore the human genome through the use of highly polymorphic genetic markers, are now applied to the complex diseases. In reality, the choice of a strategy (systematic screening

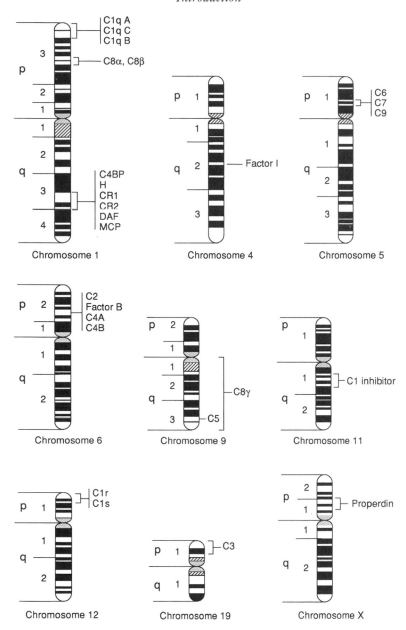

Fig. 12.2 Chromosome localization of the human complement genes. The localization of factor D is unknown. DAF-decay accelerating factors; MCP-membrane cofactor protein; CR1 and CR2-complement receptors; C4BP-C4 binding protein.

of the whole genome, candidate gene approach) and of statistics is not trivial as it may be difficult to realize what situation one is in.

The concept that genetic background may affect progression of disease emerged later (He *et al.* 1996). Various studies have implicated the polymorphism of the genetic markers, especially HLA

Table 12.1   Localization of the genes on the human genome

	Location*
IMMUNOGLOBULINS	
Heavy chain gene cluster	14q32–q33
Kappa light chain gene cluster	2p12
Lambda light chain gene cluster	22q11.q12
T CELL ANTIGEN RECEPTORS	
Alpha and delta polypeptides	14q11.2
Beta polypeptide	7q35
Gamma polypeptide	7p14.2–p13
COMPLEMENT COMPONENTS	
Classical pathway	
C1qA, C1qB (C1qC?)	1p36.3–p34.1
C1r, C1s (closely linked)	12p13
C4A	6p21.3
C4B	6p21.3
C2	6p21.3
C1 inhibitor	11q–q13.1
Alternate pathway	
Factor B	6p21.3
Factor D	?
Properdin	Xp11.4–p11.23
C3, factors I and H	
C3	19p13.3–p13.2
Factor I	4q25
Factor H (in RCA cluster**)	1q32
Terminal components	
C5	9q34.1
C6, C7, C9 (closely linked)	5p13
C8A, C8B	1p32
C8C	9q
CYTOKINES	
Tumour necrosis factor	6p21.3

*= chromosome site; p = short arm; q = long arm; number = band.
**Regulators of the complement activation (RCA) include complement receptors 1 and 2, factor H, C4 binding protein, membrane cofactor protein, decay accelerating factor.

alleles, and more recently angiotensin converting enzyme gene in the progressive deterioration in renal function.

An overview of HLA and complement component studies

HLA alleles

Hundreds of association studies since the mid 1970s have compared genetic marker frequencies in diverse diseases, including glomerular disease and haemolytic–uraemic syndrome. A statistically significant difference in the frequency of the marker when comparing unrelated patients to unrelated healthy controls of the same homogenous ethnic origin leads to the conclusion that there is an association between the marker locus and the disease locus. Nevertheless, association studies have statistical limitations (Kidd 1993; MacGregor and Silman 1993). Even if the findings have been 'replicated', which is not always the case, the problem of interpretation remains.

An HLA and disease association is not directly helpful in analysing disease pathogenesis unless the functional relevance of the major histocompatibility complex (MHC) molecule is understood. HLA molecules have a major role in presentation to T lymphocytes of bound peptides derived largely from the antigen presenting cell. Class II genes are highly polymorphic with the greatest polymorphism in the first domain which interacts with the antigenic peptide and the T cell receptor and is thus critical to the function of the molecule.

It is tempting to suggest that HLA alleles showing strong positive associations are directly involved in disease pathogenesis through their binding and presenting antigenic peptides to T cells. It may also be not only a single HLA allele but a particular set of HLA alleles that confer susceptibility to autoimmunity and autoimmune diseases. Lastly, there is also a basis for hypothesizing that the genes themselves are not responsible but are serving as linked genetic markers to the true disease gene, located in or near the MHC.

One major difficulty in interpretation is due to the discordant results frequently noted in different populations. Therefore, many explanations are currently proposed:

● a common, as yet unidentified, determinant shared by these alleles;
● different susceptibility genes operating in the different ethnic groups;
● differences in the disease itself in different populations;
● existence of more than one disease mechanism.

The patterns of linkage disequilibrium (a phenomenon whereby certain alleles at one locus consistently occur with certain alleles at another locus on the same chromosome) need to be considered when assessing the possible contributions of individual markers to genetic susceptibility.

Demonstration of HLA class I and class II associations was initially based on serological studies. More recently, the investigations used typing by restriction fragment length polymorphism (RFLP) analysis, and subsequently hybridization with sequence-specific oligonucleotide (SSO) probes applied to polymerase chain reaction (PCR) amplified DNA. It is now possible to translate DNA sequence information inferred from molecular typing into aminoacid sequences for the HLA molecules.

Complement components

Homozygous deficiencies

Inherited deficiencies of all complement components are being recognized with different frequencies in various populations (Table 12.2). Epidemiological studies showed that it was possible to have complement deficiency and remain healthy. C2 deficiency although still very rare, is the most common homozygous complement deficiency in Caucasoids (1:10000 to 1:300000) whereas deficiency of C9, rare in Caucasoids, is by far the most common homozygous complement deficiency in the Japanese population (1:1000) (Morgan and Walport 1991).

Complement deficiencies are inherited as autosomal recessive disorders (the two exceptions being properdin deficiency inherited as an X-linked recessive disorder and hereditary angioedema due to C1 inhibitor deficiency inherited as an autosomal dominant disorder). As shown by

Table 12.2   Homozygous complement deficiencies and reported associated diseases

Component	Relative frequency of deficiency	Diseases
Classical pathway		
C1q	Common	Lupus*** in majority; pyogenic infections; rare GN (MCGN)
C1r/C1s	Rare	Lupus in majority; pyogenic infections; rare GN (MCGN)
C4	Rare	Lupus in majority; pyogenic infections; rare GN (IgAN) and SHP
C2	The most common in Caucasoids	25% healthy; sometimes pyogenic infections; rare GN (MN, MPGN, MCGN, and SHP)
C1 inhibitor*	Common	HAE in all; rarely associated lupus or GN (MCGN, MPGN)
Alternative pathway		
Factor D	1 case	*Neisseria* infections****
Properdin	Common	*Neisseria* infections (in males only)
Factor B	None	
C3, factors H and I		
C3	Rare	Pyogenic infections in majority; rare lupus or GN (MCGN, MPGN, IgAN)
Factor H**	Rare	Pyogenic infections; rare GN (MPGN) and HUS
Factor I**	Rare	Pyogenic infections
Terminal pathway		
C5	Rare	*Neisseria* infections; rare lupus
C6	The 2nd most common in Caucasoids	25% healthy; *Neisseria* infections; rare lupus
C7	The 2nd most common in Japanese	25% healthy; *Neisseria* infections; rare lupus
C8	Common	25% healthy; *Neisseria* infections; rare lupus
C9	The most common in Japanese;	most healthy; rare *Neisseria* infections
	Rare in Caucasoids	*Neisseria* infections

*Deficiency of C1 inhibitor results in acquired deficiency of classical components and continuous activation of C4.

**Deficiency of either factor H or factor I results in acquired C3 deficiency.

***Lupus includes SLE, lupus-like diseases, and discoid lupus.

****Neisserial infections include systemic gonococcal and most often meningococcal diseases.

HAE = hereditary angioedema; CN = glomerulonephritis; MN = membranous nephropathy; IgAN = IgA nephropathy; MCGN = mesangiocapillary glomerulonephritis; MPGN = membranoproliferative glomerulonephritis; SHP = Schönlein Henoch purpura; HUS = haemolytic–uraemic syndrome.

molecular biology, gene defects correspond to various common mechanisms of molecular pathology (point mutations, splice junction mutations and deletions, etc.) (Walport 1993; Lokki and Colten 1996).

The type of disease varies according to the identity of the missing protein (Table 12.2) (Morgan and Walport 1991; Mathieson and Peters 1993; McLean 1993). In brief, deficiencies of the complement proteins of the classical pathway are associated with a high prevalence of autoimmune diseases, in particular systemic lupus erythematosus (SLE) or lupus-like disease, and with susceptibility to systemic infection with pyogenic organisms such as *Streptococcus* or *Staphylococcus* while those of the membrane attack complex are associated with susceptibility to *Neisseria* infection, particularly with *Neisseria meningitidis*.

Complement component deficiencies have been extensively studied in SLE. There appears to be a hierarchy of SLE prevalence and severity according to the position of the protein in the activation pathway. Lupus tends to be more severe with C1 and C4 deficiency, whereas patients with C2 deficiency generally suffer from disease of severity similar to that seen in complement-sufficient patients. Moreover, deficiency of C1q, C1r/C1s, and C4 are each associated with a very high prevalence of lupus (>75%) whereas deficiency of C2 is associated with a lower prevalence of disease (about 33%). Occasional SLE patients have deficiencies of late-acting components, but this is unusual. Complement deficiencies are rare defects that only explain a minority of SLE cases. The explanation put forward is that the immune complexes are inefficiently disposed of, and therefore allowed to accumulate in the tissues, especially the kidney, where they lead to inflammation, tissue damage, release of autoantigens, production of autoantibodies, and generation of more immune complexes. The higher incidence of SLE with C4 than C2 deficiency highlights the physiological role of C4 in binding to immune complexes, independent of its part in activating C3. Alternative explanations include a failure of the complement system to neutralize viruses or another undefined role for complement in immune regulation.

By contrast, only a few patients with glomerular diseases or haemolytic–uraemic syndrome have been shown to have homozygous complement deficiencies (Praz *et al.* 1984). Most frequently involved were components of the classical pathway. Glomerulonephritis may also be associated with regulator protein deficiencies, such as factor H or C1 inhibitor. Reports concerning deficiencies involving components of the terminal pathway are rare (Coleman *et al.* 1983).

It is important to insist that there is no constant association of a missing protein with a particular disease. For example, homozygous deficiency of factor H has been reported in 16 subjects belonging to eight families. Among these individuals, three suffered from meningococcal infections, nine had had glomerulonephritis, two had a haemolytic–uraemic syndrome, one had asthma, one who was C2 deficient as well suffered from SLE, and one suffered from subacute cutaneous lupus erythematosus and had had meningococcal meningitis. It addition, three were healthy (Fijen *et al.* 1996).

Polymorphism and partial deficiencies

The existence of polymorphism for complement proteins has led to speculation that some allotypes favour the occurrence of either a given glomerular disease or SLE. C3 (31 allotypes), factor B (26 allotypes), and, above all, C4 (40 allotypes) have been commonly studied.

C4 is encoded by two closely linked polymorphic genes, C4A and C4B, located within the MHC class III region (Fig. 12.1). Both genes have a surprisingly high incidence of non-functioning, or null allotypes (so-called quantity zero, or C4*Q0). Complete C4 deficiency, requiring the inheritance of null alleles at both loci, is rare. By contrast, single null alleles are common at both loci, resulting in the frequent detection of individuals with heterozygous deficiency of one or both isotypes. Only 60% of the population have four functioning genes, making partial deficiency of C4 the most common immune deficiency in man.

A number of reports examined the frequency of these null C4 alleles, especially in SLE and in glomerular diseases. The strong link between homozygous deficiency and these diseases led to the hypothesis that partial inherited complement deficiency, especially of C4A, might also cause increased susceptibility. One attractive hypothesis is that C4A allotypes have a greater capacity than do C4B to attach to amino groups such as those found on immune complexes. Absence of C4A could lead to prolonged intravascular survival of immune complexes and a greater risk of inflammation of target organs. At present, the exact role of C4A deficiency remains speculative.

Minimal-change nephrotic syndrome—focal and segmental glomerular sclerosis

Minimal-change nephrotic syndrome is characterized histopathologically by the absence of major structural change. Although there are extensively studied immunological modifications, its pathogenesis remains unknown.

The disease exists widely in children throughout the world, is the cause in 75% of cases of nephrotic syndrome in children, and usually responds to steroid therapy. In contrast, nephrotic syndrome with focal segmental glomerular sclerosis is often steroid resistant and often progresses to renal failure. The relationship between the two remains controversial. One wonders whether they represent aetiologically distinct processes or reflect different aspects of a single disease. The problem is further complicated by the fact that focal segmental glomerular sclerosis, shown to be a reaction of the glomerulus to many injuries, may be detected in patients presenting with nephrotic-range proteinuria without hypoalbuminaemia.

All series in the USA and South Africa showed that black nephrotic patients (children and adults) are at greater risk for the development of focal and segmental glomerular sclerosis (D'Agati 1994). In a logistic regression analysis, race remained the only significant predictor of focal and segmental glomerular sclerosis, with black adult patients four times as susceptible as white patients (Korbet *et al.* 1996). The increased propensity to focal and segmental glomerular sclerosis may relate to larger glomerular volume in blacks than whites or to a genetically control-led difference in the propensity for extracellular matrix production (D'Agati 1994). It has also been shown that the frequency of focal and segmental glomerular sclerosis is higher in Hispanic children as well (Cortes and Tejani 1996).

The occurrence of nephrotic syndrome with focal and segmental glomerular sclerosis, inherited in a recessive manner in transgenic mice, offers new opportunities in understanding the disease. Mice carrying a retroviral insert in both alleles of the MpV17 gene develop nephrotic syndrome at a young age and die later as a consequence of renal failure (Weiher 1993). Schenkel *et al.* (1995) have analysed several cases of familial glomerulosclerosis and did not find alterations of the respective Mpv 17 genes. Besides, mutant mice lacking laminin β2 rerealed proteinuria, lack of glomerular alterations, fusion of foot processes, resembling minimal-change rephrotic syndrome (Noakes *et al.* 1995).

Multiplex families—demonstration of familial aggregation

The possible occurrence of nephrotic syndrome in siblings has been known since 1951 (Fanconi *et al.* 1951) and familial aggregation of nephrotic syndrome was subsequently demonstrated in two studies. In the European survey of 1877 nephrotic children (excluding Finnish-type congenital nephrosis, clearly an autosomal recessive disease), a familial incidence was found in 3.35% of the cases (63 families), an incidence higher than that of nephrotic syndrome in the general population (White *et al.* 1973). In most families, two or three sibs were affected. There were also four families with members affected over two generations. Further studies of 15 pairs of sibs showed a high degree of concordance of age at onset, renal morphology, and outcome [Moncrieff *et al.* 1973].

In the second study, pedigree information was obtained from 70 consecutive patients in the United States (Bader *et al.* 1974). Sixteen patients were found to have affected relatives. The recurrence risk in sibs of affected patients was 6%, higher than the incidence in the general population. Family data analysed through segregation analysis were compatible with polygenic inheritance, i.e. the joint action of many genes with small additive effects. In contrast to the European data, the clinical course and the histopathological classification in affected sibs were not necessarily similar.

Subsequently, reports of families with multiple cases of nephrotic syndrome, particularly with steroid-sensitive nephrotic syndrome (Kim *et al.* 1991), have been rare possibly because paediatricians no longer report their cases. Nephrosis has also been reported to occur in sibs affected by various other disease such as T cell deficiency (Tabin *et al.* 1983), brain malformations (Palm *et al.* 1986), or nerve deafness and hypoparathyroidism (Barakat *et al.* 1977). The possibility of distinct hereditary syndromes has to be considered.

As for familial focal and segmental glomerular sclerosis, there are some 20 reports of either affected siblings, suggesting an autosomal recessive transmission, or affected relatives over two or even three generations, suggesting an autosomal dominant transmission (Tejani *et al.* 1983, McCurdy *et al.* 1987, Mathis *et al.* 1992, Conlon *et al.* 1995, Goodman *et al.* 1995, Faubert and Porush 1997). As outlined by Conlon *et al.*, the pattern of inheritance is less clear in some families. Clinical presentation (nephrotic syndrome or proteinuria) and kidney lesions (minimal changes or focal and segmental glomerular sclerosis) may coexist in a given family. Because of their clinical and histological heterogeneity as well as their various patterns of inheritance, these observations are difficult to classify.

HLA class I and II alleles: association studies

Most studies seem to conclude to different genetic background in steroid-sensitive and in steroid-resistant nephrotic syndrome. Idiopathic nephrotic syndrome was initially linked to HLA-B8, B12, and B18. Then in the 1980s, the most significant associations were found with HLA-DR, DR7 in France, Spain, Australia, and Germany, and DR8 in Japan. Some groups, however, failed to demonstrate any association.

An increased HLA-DR4 frequency was shown in both white and black nephrotic patients with focal and segmental glomerular sclerosis in the United States. Most developed end-stage renal failure. The association was especially apparent in those with adult-onset disease (Glicklich *et al.* 1988).

Subsequent studies tried to evaluate the importance of the DQ chain. Using serology, an increase in DQw2 was noted in Caucasoid children in the United States with steroid-sensitive nephrotic syndrome (Lagueruela *et al.* 1990). In these children, but not in steroid-resistant patients, one or two extended haplotypes with B8 (HLA-A1, B8, DR3, DRW52, SCO1) or B44 (HLA-B44, DR7, DRW53, FC31) were also evidenced. Using RFLPs in a series of Caucasoid British children with steroid-sensitive nephrotic syndrome, the association with the β chains of DR7 and HLA-DQw2 was confirmed (Clark *et al.* 1990).

In separate studies using DNA analysis (RFLP and PCR-SSO methods), HLA class II allele frequencies were studied in both French and German patients with steroid-sensitive and resistant nephrotic syndrome (Abbal *et al.* 1992; Konrad *et al.* 1994). The conclusions in steroid-sensitive patients are the following: the association with HLA-DR7 and -DQ2 is due to their respective splits(DRB1*07 and DQB1 *0201); there is an increased frequency of DQA3 (DQA1*0201); the relative risk is higher in patients who carry both the DR3 and DR7 alleles. In contrast, steroid-resistant patients do not exhibit strong association with class II alleles.

Further studies of the same group extended typing to a larger number of patients (Bouissou *et al.* 1995). The authors insisted on the relation between the clinical course (i.e relapses, prolonged course, and steroid-dependence) and HLA associations. In view of these findings, they suggest that HLA alleles are implicated in the clinical course of nephrotic syndrome in children.

The familial steroid-resistant nephrotic syndrome: an entity of autosomal recessive nephrosis

The recurrence of the disease after renal transplantation in most cases of idiopathic nephrotic syndrome is currently explained by the presence of some circulating factors increasing the glomerular permeability. In contrast, the absence of relapses in others suggests a primary defect in molecular structure of the glomerulus, probably of the glomerular basement membrane (GBM) in these patients.

Based on this distinction, Fuchschuber *et al.* (1995) investigated a group of patients with the following characteristic features: familial occurrence, age of onset in early childhood, resistance to steroid therapy, progression to end-stage renal failure within a few years, and absence of recurrence after renal transplantation. Using linkage analysis with informative micro-satellite markers, they assigned a disease locus (SNR1) to a defined chromosomal region on 1q25–31, thus confirming the existence of a distinct entity of autosomal recessive nephrosis.

Anti-glomerular basement membrane antibody disease

Anti-glomerular basement membrane antibody disease is a relatively rare form of glomerulonephritis, most often severe, and when accompanied by pulmonary haemorrhage is termed Goodpasture's syndrome. The disease is defined by the presence of autoantibodies to particular target antigen of the GBM, characterized as the NC1 domain of the α3 chain of type IV collagen. The gene has been cloned and localized on chromosome 2.

Multiplex families are extremely rare (two pairs of twins, three pairs of siblings, and two pairs of cousins) and evidence for a genetic basis is based on the association of the disease with HLA alleles.

Association studies

HLA Class II alleles

In 1978, serological studies showed a large increase in the frequency of HLA-DR2 in Caucasoid patients from the United Kingdom (88% of patients versus 32% of controls, relative risk 15.9) (Rees *et al.* 1978). Subsequently, genotyping with RFLP in series of Caucasoid patients from Australia narrowed the association to the DRw15, a split of DR2 (Dunckley *et al.* 1991). Another study using molecular analysis SSO probe hybridization in patients in the United States showed that most patients were DR2, and that all DR2 patients were restricted to DRB1*1501 and DQB1*0602 alleles. There was an additional association with the DRB1*0301/DQB1*0201 haplotype (Huey *et al.* 1993).

Further molecular studies using RFLPs together with SSO typing in the United Kingdom showed a greatly increased frequency of DRw15 (75.5% of patients versus 31% of controls), due exclusively to an excess of haplotypes bearing DRw15 (DRB1*1501 and *1502) as part of the common Caucasoid haplotype also containing DQw6 (DQA1*01 and DQB*106) (Burns *et al.* 1995). These alleles are in very strong linkage disequilibrium and theoretically the increased susceptibility could be due to any of them or to genes at other undefined loci on the same haplotype. As described in other situations, such data may be in favour of haplotype effects.

Another hypothesis has been put forward by the authors who noted that the frequency of DR4 was also increased, especially in patients without DRw15, whereas the frequency of DR1 alleles was significantly reduced. It was tempting for them to imagine that knowledge of the epitope(s) forming the specificity for the autoantibody and knowledge of the aminoacid sequences of the various susceptible HLA will help in understanding the role of the HLA molecule in the aetiology of the nephritis. Comparing the aminoacid sequences of expressed DRβ chains, they showed that the HLA-DRw15 and DR4 molecules associated with Goodpasture's disease shared four polymorphic aminoacids, none being shared with DR1. The authors suggested the possibility that it was this particular motif, lying on the floor of the antigen binding groove, that was more strongly associated with Goodpasture's disease (detected in 91.8% of patients tested) than any individual DR allele. They recently identified the processed autoantigen-derived peptides bound to HLA-DR15 (Phelps *et al.* 1996, Fisher *et al.* 1997). This identification clarifies for the first time the relation between self-antigen-derived peptide presentation, class II type, and autoreactivity.

Membranous nephropathy

Membranous nephropathy is one of the major causes of the adult nephrotic syndrome, leading to end-stage renal failure in 20–40% of the cases. It has a well-defined histopathologic appearance (subepithelial deposits) which is not necessarily the result of a single aetiology since associations with numerous extrarenal disorders, such as infection, autoimmune disease, tumour, and drug reaction, are well-known. The category 'idiopathic' is therefore a diagnosis of exclusion and it is not impossible that even idiopathic membranous nephropathy represents different diseases with heterogeneous causes. Membranous nephropathy is generally cited as the prototype of immune complex glomerular diseases. Although the mechanisms of subepithelial deposit formation are well-understood in experimental models, the pathophysiology in the human remains mysterious.

Contrasting with the large number of isolated cases reported in most countries, families with multiple cases are extremely rare (less than 10 families). Reported patients are most often pairs of brothers, with the exception of one brother–sister pair and two father–son pairs (Elshibabi *et al.* 1993, Maccario *et al.* 1995).

At present, the only indicators of possible genetic predisposition are association studies which have pointed to associations with HLA alleles.

Association studies

HLA class II alleles

In 1979, a strong association between membranous nephropathy and HLA-DR3 was observed in patients in the United Kingdom (75% of patients versus 20% of controls; relative risk 12)

(Klouda *et al.* 1979). There has been overall agreement that DR3 is the major allelic association in Northern European Caucasoids, but the association seems far less clear in other Caucasoid populations, especially in the United States.

In Caucasoids, it was unclear whether the association with the haplotype A1-B8, DR3 was due to an HLA-DR or DQ locus linked to HLA class II. A proposal, based on comparison of molecular mapping of the class II region in HLA-A1, B8, DR3 patients, and healthy controls, is that the vicinity of DP could have implications for genetic susceptibility (Sacks *et al.* 1993).

A molecular study of UK patients and their families concluded that HLA-DR3 is the prime marker of disease susceptibility within the major histocompatibility complex (Dyer *et al.* 1992). A large study using PCR-SSO compared northern European (British) with southern Caucasoid (Greek) patients (Vaughan *et al.* 1995). It was shown that DRB1*0301 rather than DRB3*0101 is the primary association in British patients whereas, in Greek patients, the association with DRB1*0301 is weaker. The data do not support a major role for DQ although the high frequency of DQA1*0501 noted in Greek patients may be of importance. It is also concluded that the HLA-A1-B8-DR3 haplotype does not extend to DPB.

Results differ in Japanese patients since there is a strong association with class II, but the antigen is DR2 (Hiki *et al.* 1984). DRB1*1501-DQA1*0102-DQB1*0602 appears to be the primary association (Vaughan *et al.* 1992). Another analysis by RFLP of HLA class II genes in Japanese patients also suggests that there might be a definite association with specific DQ gene (Ogahara *et al.* 1992). The apparent contradiction between the HLA associations in Caucasoid and Japanese patients leads to speculation as to whether the aetiopathogenesis of the disease is the same in the two populations.

C4, T cell receptor, immunoglobulin, tumour necrosis factor

A strong, positive association between C4 gene deletion and membranous nephropathy was found in Caucasoid patients. By contrast, there was no association in Japanese patients (Sacks *et al.* 1992). The increase in the frequency in allele 5.5 homozygotes was interpreted as being due to an increased frequency of the haplotype A1-B8-TNF β5.5-DR3 (Medcraft *et al.* 1993).

The association with T cell receptor constant β chain and immunoglobulin heavy chain switch region polymorphism was shown in one study concerning British patients (Demaine *et al.* 1988).

Membranoproliferative glomerulonephritis

All authors have subtyped membranoproliferative glomerulonephritis, on the basis of morphologic lesions, into types I, II, and III. Type I, the most common, is characterized by subendothelial deposits, type II by intramembranous dense deposits, and type III by both subendothelial and subepithelial deposits.

Type I and type III are probably variants of the same disease in which glomerular deposition of immune complexes that activate the classical pathway of complement seems to play a key role. The antigen(s) responsible is (are) unknown.

By contrast, deposits of immune complexes are absent in membranoproliferative type II which is associated with alternative pathway complement activation. This activation is usually caused by C3 nephritic factor, IgG antibodies which stabilize the alternative C3 convertase. The association between C3 nephritic factor-induced hypocomplementaemia and the development of nephritis is still obscure. The other striking association is with partial lipodystrophy (Mathieson and Peters 1993).

Multiplex families

Few multiplex families with membranoproliferative glomerulonephritis type I have been reported. Berry *et al.* (1981). Abderrahim *et al.* (1990), and Bakkaloglu *et al.* (1995) reported families with two or more sibs affected, thus suggesting an autosomal recessive inheritance. By contrast, Stutchfield *et al.* (1986) described a kindred in which three half-brothers, each with a different father and a nephew of theirs had a proven or presumed variant of membranoproliferative type I. The authors interpreted this family as evidence of an X-linked recessive inheritance. Finally, an autosomal mode of transmission has been suggested in another family in which a mother and her infant showed hypocomplementaemic membranoproliferative glomerulonephritis (Linshaw *et al.* 1987). It should be noted that there is often a confusion with families presenting newly recognized, non-immune complex mediated chronic glomerulonephritis presented below.

Of note is the familial incidence of C3 nephritic factor found in one patient with membranoproliferative glomerulonephritis type I and two of his siblings. Other relatives, including their dead father, suffered from a renal illness (Lopez-Trascasa *et al.* 1991).

As for type II, the reports of multiplex families are extremely rare. Atypical dense intramembranous deposit disease has been described in two brothers of a consanguineous marriage with H deficiency (Levy *et al.* 1986).

Complement component deficiencies

Type I membranoproliferative glomerulonephritis has been described in young Finnish Landrace lambs (Angus *et al.* 1980), in dogs which are C3 deficient (Cork *et al.* 1991), and in humans with various hereditary deficiencies of complement components (but no other systemic disease), thus leading to the hypothesis that such complement component deficiencies predispose to immune complex glomerulonephritis. In 1983, Coleman *et al.* showed that partial complement deficiencies were more frequent in patients with membranoproliferative glomerulonephritis type I and III than among normal subjects or patients with other glomerulonephritis. By contrast, no complement deficiency was detected in patients with type II.

Type I has been described in several patients with C1q deficiency (Berkel and Loos 1983), C2 (Loirat *et al.* 1980), C3 (Berger *et al.* 1983; Borzy and Houghton 1985), C1 inhibitor (van Bommel *et al.* 1995), and CR1 (Ohi *et al.* 1986) deficiencies.

The first animal model for type II membranoproliferative glomerulonephritis was described in piglets with hereditary factor H deficiency (Hogasen *et al.* 1995). As previously mentioned, two brothers with hereditary factor H deficiency and type II membranoproliferative glomerulonephritis have been described (Levy *et al.* 1986).

Association studies

HLA alleles

One group in the USA (Welch *et al.* 1986) suggested that haplotype HLA-A1, B8, SC01, DR3 was associated with susceptibility to types I and III, as well as to systemic lupus erythematosus. The same group attempted to define the limits of the HLA haplotype (Bishof *et al.* 1993). They found that in patients and normal controls, all HLA-A1, B8, SC01, DR3 haplotypes were DQw2, whereas there were no significant differences in DP distribution in patients or controls. They suggested, therefore, that the loci important to disease susceptibility were more likely to occur telomeric to DP.

C3 allotypes in patients with C3 nephritic factor

C3 polymorphism was studied in 26 patients with C3 nephritic factor (18 with type II membranoproliferative glomerulonephritis alone, two with partial lipodystrophy, and six with both) (Finn and Mathieson 1993). These patients have an increased frequency of C3F.

IgA nephropathy

IgA nephropathy has been reported to be the most frequent cause of glomerulonephritis among patients who undergo renal biopsy. It accounts for 29% in Asia, 12% in Australia, and 11% in Europe, but it is uncommon in North America (5%) (Schena 1995). IgA nephropathy is rare in American blacks (Pontier and Patel 1994). Variations in prevalence among well-defined ethnic groups could be an argument in favour of shared factors, genetic and/or environmental, playing a role in aetiology. As noted by many authors, the differences between countries may also reflect differences in national biopsy strategies since the disease can only be defined by immunofluorescence study of the kidney revealing the presence of IgA containing mesangial deposits.

Despite considerable research effort, its immunopathogenesis in the human remains an enigma. It has been suggested that the IgA mesangial deposition would not cover a single entity, but would be secondary to several different pathogenetic mechanisms.

Among the large number of experimental models, one emphasizing the possible importance of genetic background has been developped by Genin *et al.* (1985) who showed that high IgA responder mice develop significantly increased IgA mesangial deposits after oral immunization, compared with a low-responder strain.

Family studies

Multiplex families

Soon after the identification of the disease in the 1970s, several of the first large studies on IgA nephropathy already indicated a history of renal disease in the patients' relatives. Subsequently, some 30 families with two relatives having biopsy-confirmed IgA nephropathy have been reported (Levy and Lesavre 1992). A retrospective study, conducted by French nephrologists, revealed 35 families with two (or more) affected members, suggesting that multiplex families are more frequent than previously thought (Levy and Lesavre 1992). Sibs, and particularly brothers, were the most frequently affected, but the parent–offspring combination was also noted. The male preponderance and the progression to end-stage renal failure noted in 30% of cases are identical to the data obtained in isolated cases. Half of the patients were younger than 16 years at onset. The long interval, up to 15–20 years, frequently observed between the apparent onset of the disease in family members, favours a genetic predisposition rather than the influence of environmental factors. Interestingly, both IgA nephropathy and anaphylactoid purpura (with or without renal involvement) occurred in several families. The frequency of families with multiple cases is unknown since few renal units systematically monitor the urine of family members and, even if microscopic haematuria were detected, few would recommend renal biopsy.

It must be underlined that familial aggregation in IgA nephropathy has never been demonstrated. Nevertheless, familial aggregation of urinary abnormalities has been demonstrated by

Schena *et al.* (1995) who compared the prevalence of urinary abnormalities among the 269 first-degree relatives of affected individuals from 48 families with that in a large number of young people from the general population (8255 students). Urinary abnormalities were found in 22.6% of relatives versus 4.3% in the general population.

Extended pedigrees

Besides these multiplex families, an extended Kentucky pedigree comprises 14 patients with IgA nephropathy, 17 relatives with clinical glomerulonephritis, and six other relatives for whom chronic nephritis was indicated on the death certificates. Having observed that patients' birth-places and those of their parents, grandparents, and great-grandparents were clustered in the far eastern portion of Kentucky, the authors suggested that the patients' ancestors would be settlers who entered the region at the end of the eighteenth century. In their opinion, gene(s) causing susceptibility to IgA nephropathy would have been carried by one or several of the original settlers (a founder effect) (Wyatt *et al.* 1987).

Intriguing data are provided by extended pedigrees in ethnically diverse populations. A high prevalence of glomerulonephritis and marked familial clustering have been reported in Zuni Indians (Hoy *et al.* 1989), Australian Aborigines (O'Connell *et al.* 1987), and in northern Italy (Scolari *et al.* 1992). Although IgA nephropathy was the most commonly encountered in these pedigrees, it was not the only glomerular disease in the affected members. The coexistence of different histopathological forms of primary glomerulonephritis, most often mesangial glomerulonephritis, is tentatively explained by inherited susceptibility to develop glomerulonephritis and variable response to presumptive environmental stimuli.

Immune response abnormalities in asymptomatic relatives

Following the observation of increased serum IgA levels in healthy family members, several studies have demonstrated abnormalities involving the regulation of IgA synthesis in relatives. For example, a study conducted by Italian workers showed one (high levels of IgA, polymeric IgA, IgA rheumatoid factor, or circulating IgA1/IgM or IgA1/IgG immune complexes) or more abnormalities of the IgA system in 66% of relatives of nine unrelated pedigrees (Schena *et al.* 1995). Not all abnormalities in patients were present in relatives. Nor did the immunological abnormalities correlate in any way with the presence of microhaematuria. They also investigated the *in vitro* immunoglobulin synthesis by peripheral blood mononuclear cells in patients and relatives. High pokeweed mitogen-induced cell production of IgA, IgA1, and IgM, polymeric IgA, and IgA rheumatoid factor was found in 64% of relatives. The production increased both in relatives with urinary abnormalities and in those with normal urinalyses.

Further studies of the same group suggested that these immunologic abnormalities of the IgA system might depend on an altered pattern of cytokine production. They showed hyperproduction of IL-2 whereas Il-4, IL-6, and IFN-γ production were normal, in patients and their microhaematuric relatives. Production increased considerably after phytohaemagglutinin stimulation. Conversely, cytokine synthesis in relatives with normal urinalyses did not differ from normal.

Familial hypertension

Various studies showed an increased incidence of hypertension in parents of patients with IgA nephropathy, suggesting familial predisposition to hypertension (Schmidt *et al.* 1990; Autuly *et al.* 1991). Ho *et al.* (1996) showed a higher blood pressure in the first-degree relatives of hypertensive IgA probands compared with relatives of normotensive probands. They demonstrated a strong correlation of Vmax/Km ratio of sodium–lithium countertransport between the IgA probands and their first-degree relatives and suggested that an inherited abnormality of this sodium–lithium countertransport parameter present before IgA nephropathy could help to identify patients who are at greater risk of developing hypertension.

Association studies

Genetic studies have been hampered by the diversity underlying IgA nephropathy and no clear, consistent or uniform association of disease susceptibility to gene markers has been identified.

HLA class I and class II alleles

HLA alleles in patients with IgA nephropathy were widely studied with classic serologic methods during the 1970s and 1980s. An association with HLA-B35 was initially observed in France, the United States, and Australia. Other reports showed increased frequencies of HLA-B12 in the United States, HLA-B37 in Japan, HLA-DR1 in England, and HLA-DR4 in France. Many other reports (from the United States, Japan, Singapore, Hungary, the Netherlands, Germany, France, Italy, Spain, England, and Finland) showed no statistical differences between patients and healthy controls. Finally, none of the reports in the 1990s has confirmed any association with serologically defined HLA in Caucasoid patients in the United Kingdom (Li *et al*. 1991), France (Berthoux *et al*. 1993), Great Britain, Finland, and Italy (Moore 1993), Germany (Rambausek *et al*. 1993), the USA (Luger *et al*. 1994), and in Chinese patients in Taiwan (Huang *et al*. 1989). By contrast, IgA nephropathy has been consistently associated with HLA-DR4 in Japanese patients (Hiki *et al*. 1991). The implication of HLA DR4 in the evolution of the disease in Japanese patients is, however, controversial. HLA-B35 has been described as a poor prognosis marker by French authors (Berthoux *et al*. 1993).

In view of the similar frequencies of HLA-DR in Caucasoid patients and controls and because of the marked linkage disequilibrium between DR and DQ, various authors oriented further molecular biological research in the direction of the DP and DQ loci. All studies indicate that the DP genes do not appear to contribute to susceptibility to IgA nephropathy (Luger *et al*. 1994).

No strong or consistent association of DQ alleles was found in Caucasoid patients from the United States (Luger *et al*. 1994), Australia (Knight *et al*. 1995), or France (Raguénès *et al*. 1995). In patients in Germany, there were no abnormal frequencies of DR and DQ by RFLP typing, with the exception of an increased frequency of DQA1 (Rambausek *et al*. 1993).

Using a more discriminatory methodology than their group previously applied to British patients, Fenessy *et al*. (1996) were unable to confirm their findings of an association of IgA nephropathy with DQB in British Caucasoid subjects. Extending their studies to Caucasoid populations from northern (Finnish) and southern (Italian) Europe, they found no consistent association of DQ alleles between the populations studied. They showed a decreased frequency of DQB1*0201 in British patients, a decreased frequency of DQB1*0602 in Finnish patients, whereas there was no association between DQ markers and IgA nephropathy in Italian patients.

Results in Asian populations appear different. In Chinese patients from Taiwan, Li *et al*. (1994) found a higher frequency of homozygous DQβ3b (DQw7) when compared to controls. In Japanese patients, an increased frequency of DQB (DQw4/8/9) and D-DR4 was found in one series (Abe *et al*. 1993) and an increase of DQA1*0301 in another (Jin *et al*. 1996).

These findings seem to indicate that there is no single DQ allele predisposing to IgA nephropathy in these populations. As suggested by Fenessy *et al*. (1996), different susceptibility genes may operate in different populations and may account for the variations in prevalence in different geographical locations. In addition, one may suggest that IgA nephropathy is a heterogeneous disease, with entities determined by different susceptibility genes.

HLA class III alleles

IgA nephropathy has been described in occasional patients with C1q (Topaloglu *et al.* 1996), C3 (Imai *et al.* 1991), and C1 inhibitor (Srinivasan and Beck 1993) deficiencies.

There have been several reports suggesting the association of IgA nephropathy with C4 deficiency, especially C4B deficiency. In 1991, Wyatt *et al.*, re-evaluating published series concluded that, compared to local controls, there is no increase in the frequency of C4B deficiency in patients in Kentucky and the US mid-south or in Italy and Spain. Moreover, the heterogeneity of the C4B deficiency studied at the DNA level was considered to be an argument against a linkage between this deficiency and a locus coding for a susceptibility gene (Welch *et al.* 1989). Similarly, C4A deficiency was not shown to be significantly associated with IgA nephropathy in any reported population (Berthoux *et al.* 1993).

More recently, in one series of 93 patients in southern Sweden, the distribution of C4 phenotypes did not differ from the distribution in the normal population (Wopenka *et al.* 1996). But there were three patients who had homozygous C4A deficiency. Because these patients belonged to a group of patients with end-stage renal failure, the Swedish authors suggested that homozygous C4A predisposes to poor prognosis.

In Japanese patients with IgA nephropathy and Henoch Schönlein purpura nephritis, there was an increased frequency of hemizygous deletion of C4 gene (Abe *et al.* 1993). In another Japanese series, C4 gene deletions were found in four out of 22 cases of IgA nephropathy and in five out of 27 cases of Henoch Schönlein nephropathy (Jin *et al.* 1996). Molecular analysis of the deletion showed that all cases were complement 4 locus II gene deletion, and the deleted gene could be either C4A or C4B.

The associations with the polymorphisms of factor B (BfF), C3 (C3F), and C7 (C7 5) are weak and suggest that allelic variations at these loci are not of primary importance in determining susceptibility to the disease (Levy and Lesavre 1992; Rambausek *et al.* 1993; Finn *et al.* 1994).

T cell receptor

Discrepant results have been reported in different Caucasoid populations (Martinetti *et al.* 1992; Rambausek *et al.* 1993). In a series of Japanese patients, the genotype frequency of T cell receptor beta-chain was not different between healthy and IgA patients (Nagasawa *et al.* 1995).

d. Immunoglobulin

Various studies were oriented towards immunoglobulin heavy chain allotypes. It was suggested that alleles of the IgA2 heavy chains might be implicated in the aetiology of IgA nephropathy and that the presence of the A2m (1) allotype would protect black subjects. A final study disproved this hypothesis (Crowley-Nowick *et al.* 1990).

The Gm and Km phenotype distribution did not show significant difference between patients and controls from Italy (Martinetti *et al.* 1992) and the USA (Luger *et al.* 1994).

The preferential IgA1 expression prompted investigators to study RFLP fragments of the IgA1 and IgA2 switch region (Sα1 and Sα2). In a French series comprising 41 patients, the alleles present in the control population were detected in patients with analogous frequencies, but a larger polymorphism was found in patients since two new alleles in the Sα1 and six new alleles in the Sα2 region were found (Levy and Lesavre 1992). In a large series of German patients, the proportion of homozygotes for the 7.4 kb Sα1 allele was significantly increased (Rambausek *et al.*

1993). The biological significance of these findings is unknown. Comparing the genotypic frequency of the switch region of the IgM (Sμ) and IgA1 (Sα1) heavy chain in Japanese children with IgA nephropathy and in normal controls, Japanese authors suggested that these regions may not influence susceptibility to IgA nephropathy but may influence the pathological expression. There was a decreased frequency of the 2.6/2/1 (Sμ) heterozygous phenotype in patients showing diffuse mesangial proliferation (Shimomura *et al.* 1995). Finally, no association was observed in a series of Australian patients (Knight *et al.* 1995).

In addition, abnormal carbohydrate composition within the IgA1 molecule has been described (Allen *et al.* 1997). The altered IgA1-O galactolysation may be related to a reduced activity of an intracellular enzyme. Although potentially important in familial forms, this defect has not yet been studied in relatives.

Polymorphism of the angiotensin-converting enzyme as a factor of progression

Following experimental and clinical reports showing that an activated renin system is involved in the pathogenesis of glomerular damage and that there is an individual variability in angiotensin-converting enzyme linked to an insertion/deletion (I/D) polymorphism in the gene, different authors tested whether there was a link between the genotype of the angiotensin-converting enzyme and IgA nephropathy. None of the studies performed in British (Harden *et al.* 1995), Japanese (Yorioka *et al.* 1995; Yoshida *et al.* 1995), German, Australian, Italian, Austrian (Schmidt *et al.* 1995), and American Caucasoid (Hunley *et al.* 1996) patients was able to demonstrate a different genotype distribution between controls and patients, which suggests that the angiotensin-converting enzyme genotype does not influence the likehood of developing IgA nephropathy.

Four studies (Harden *et al.* 1995; Yorioka *et al.* 1995; Yoshida *et al.* 1995; Hunley *et al.* 1996) suggested that the DD genotype was a risk factor for progression to chronic renal failure in genetically distinct and geographically remote populations. One study (Schmidt *et al.* 1995) found no difference between patients with stable renal function and patients with end-stage renal failure.

Two other gene polymorphisms of the renin angiotensin system, angiotensinogen or angiotensin type 1 receptor gene polymorphism, were studied. Neither was associated with progressive renal deterioration (Hunley *et al.* 1996).

Newly recognized, non-immune complex mediated chronic glomerulonephritis

Collagen III glomerulopathy (or primary glomerular fibrosis, collagenofibrotic glomerulopathy) (See Chapter 11.2)

Until now, approximately 30 patients, adults and children, have been reported. Routine immunofluorescent studies are essentially negative, but there is mesangial and subendothelial staining for type III collagen. The occurrence of the disease in three sibling pairs suggests autosomal recessive inheritance (Salcedo 1984; Gubler *et al.* 1993; Mizuiri *et al.* 1993; Tamura *et al.* 1996). Consanguineous marriages of the parents were present in two families. In addition, the association of inherited factor H deficiency with this type of glomerulopathy was reported in a small boy (Vogt *et al.* 1995).

At the ultrastructural level, the presence of fibrillar collagen within the GBM is currently considered as the hallmark of nail–patella nephropathy. The mode of transmission clearly demonstrates that the disease is not a variant of nail–patella syndrome which is transmitted as an autosomal dominant trait.

Lipoprotein glomerulopathy

This disease, frequently reported in the Japanese, is characterized by an obstruction of the capillary loop by lipids. The occurrence of the disease in siblings suggests an autosomal recessive inheritance (Saito *et al.* 1989). It has been suggested by Japanese authors that the lipid storage was due to excess apo E associated with heterozygous E2/3 apo E isoform. A missense mutation (apo E- Sendai) in apolipoprotein E gene was detected in three Japanese patients (Oikawa *et al.* 1997). The apparently increased prevalence of the disease in Japan could be explained by a founder effect (Karet and Lifton 1997). Recurrence in a transplanted kidney has been reported (Djamali *et al.* 1996). The role of apo E in a Caucasoid patient appeared, however, controversial (Meyrier *et al.* 1995).

Glomerulopathy associated with predominant fibronectin deposits

Several cases of fibrillary glomerulonephritis characterized by massive deposition of fibronectin, in the absence of immunoglobulin or complement, have been recently documented (Assmann *et al.* 1995; Strom *et al.* 1995). This glomerulopathy is frequently familial and its occurrence in successive generations suggests an autosomal mode of inheritance. Genes for fibronectin, villin and desmin were excluded as causative genes. Recurrence in a transplanted kidney has been reported (Gemperlé *et al.* 1996).

Haemolytic–uraemic syndrome

Haemolytic–uraemic syndrome is the most common cause of acute renal failure in infants and children in many countries, e.g. Argentina. By contrast, it is rare in blacks (Jernigan and Waldo 1994) and uncommon in Japan.

The sudden onset of the clinical triad (haemolytic anaemia with fragmented erythrocytes, thrombocytopenia, and acute renal failure) and the predominant occurrence of the disease in infants, following prodromal diarrhoea and summer epidemics, long suggested an infectious aetiology. It was shown that numerous viral and bacterial agents associated with diarrhoea were implicated in the haemolytic–uraemic syndrome. The most striking progress in understanding of the disease was demonstration of verotoxin-producing *Escherichia coli* in many of the 'typical' cases in European and North American children (Karmali *et al.* 1983). Only 2–7% of patients infected with verotoxin-producing *Escherichia coli* will develop haemolytic–uraemic syndrome. This implies that there are important host factors which determine whether a given patient will develop the disease.

The observation of 'atypical' (gradual onset, no prodromal phase, no seasonal occurrence, possible relapses) and the occurrence of haemolytic–uraemic syndrome in adults following medical treatments (oral contraception, for example) or after pregnancy indicated that the disease could have other aetiologies, and probably various mechanisms. The clinical and prognostic differences between the two forms were supported by the difference in the glomerular lesions, glomerular microangiopathy in the typical form and arterial microangiopathy with ischaemic glomeruli in the atypical form.

Multiplex families

One year after the definition of the syndrome in 1955, familial occurrence was reported in two five-month-old brothers in whom onset of haemolytic–uraemic syndrome was separated by one year. Both infants died (Fison 1956).

Reviewing in 1975 the multiplex families reported in the literature, Kaplan *et al.* were able to distinguish two groups. Group 1 consisted of siblings in whom the onset occurred within days or weeks of each other, and usually followed a 'typical' prodrome of diarrhoea. Families often, but not always, lived in regions in which haemolytic–uraemic syndrome was considered to be endemic. Group 2 consisted of siblings in whom onset was separated by more than one year. Few had a prodrome of diarrhoea and most lived in areas in which the disease occurs infrequently. Prognosis was good in group 1 and poor in group 2. The authors suggested that patients in group 1 had acquired haemolytic–uraemic syndrome as a result of a pathogenic agent in the common environment, whereas patients in group 2 seemed to have genetic predisposition to haemolytic–uraemic syndrome that would be transmitted in an autosomal recessive mode. In addition, they noted a few families in which atypical haemolytic–uraemic syndrome appeared to have been inherited in an autosomal dominant mode, sometimes at different ages in the family.

The complexity of the problem is increased by the possible coexistence of haemolytic–uraemic syndrome and thrombotic thrombocytopenic purpura (a multi-organ vascular disease) in a given family. In addition, the disease may be idiopathic in one individual but follow pregnancy or use of oral contraceptives in a relative.

Multiplex families are rare. In a large Argentinian series of 631 patients, 19 (3%) were familial cases, of which nine patients (four families) were concomitant, six (three families) non-concomitant, and four (one family) recurrent (Voyer *et al.* 1996). In a French series of 161 children, among the 147 patients with postinfectious typical cases there were three pairs of twins in whom onset occurred a few days apart and among the 14 atypical cases two pairs of sibs, all infants at onset, who developed the disease three and six years apart (Loirat *et al.* 1993). In a British series of 176 patients, 21 were classified as diarrhoeal-negative cases and of these, one patient had two affected siblings (Fitzpatrick *et al.* 1992).

Multiplex families with typical haemolytic–uraemic syndrome

Voyer *et al.* (1996) suggested that genetic determinants play a role in the typical familial cases. It will be necessary to assess the relative contribution of environmental and genetic factors in these cases and to demonstrate whether the processes (aetiopathogenetic, genetic) implicated in the numerous isolated cases differ or not from those implicated in the rare families with multiple cases.

Two studies point to an association between postinfectious cases and HLA-B40 (van de Kar *et al.* 1991; Sheth *et al.* 1994), whereas another shows that HLA-DR3 protects against thrombotic thrombocytopenic purpura/adult haemolytic–uraemic syndrome (Joseph *et al.* 1994).

Multiplex families with atypical haemolytic–uraemic syndrome

In 1992, Kaplan and Kaplan reviewed 43 families collected in the literature with two to six siblings affected, suggesting autosomal recessive transmission. Both sexes were equally affected and parents were unaffected. The interval between onset ranged from 11 months to 10 years. Onset of disease occurred frequently at similar ages in the sibship, but the ages varied among families from two weeks to 35 years. There are families in which only children were affected, others with both children and adults, and finally some with only adults affected (Berns *et al.* 1992). Some patients have recurrent episodes (Mattoo *et al.* 1989; Kaplan and Kaplan 1992).

On the other hand, some 15 families with apparent autosomal transmission have been reported (Berns *et al.* 1992; Kaplan and Kaplan 1992). Two to six members over two and three generations were affected, with an equal sex ratio. Most patients were adults, although children were also affected. There were most often marked differences in clinical expression (haemolytic–uraemic syndrome, thrombotic thrombocytopenic purpura) within and among families.

It was logical to investigate some factors which might be functionally related to the prominent vascular lesions and interpreted as related to anomalies of the endothelium and platelet interactions. Failure of vascular prostacyclin synthesis was found in patients and their healthy relatives (Remuzzi *et al.* 1979; Turi *et al.* 1986). A role for abnormalities of von Willebrand factor in the pathogenesis of non-familial and familial forms has also been proposed (Berns *et al.* 1992).

It has been suggested that a defect in complement factors may predispose to haemolytic–uraemic syndrome. Persistent depression of C3 (Carreras *et al.* 1981), presence of a rare variant of C3 (Wyatt *et al.* 1985), and deficiency in H factor (Thompson and Winterborn 1981; Pichette *et al.* 1994) were noted in occasional patients.

The rarity of these families and their aetiological and clinical heterogeneity obviously make genetic studies difficult. It remains to demonstrate by segregation and linkage analysis whether these families represent different mendelian subentities.

Haemolytic–uraemic syndrome due to a congenital defect in intracellular cobalamin metabolism: an autosomal recessive entity

A small subgroup with a mendelian inheritance has been isolated. Haemolytic–uraemic syndrome may be part of the phenotypic spectrum of an intracellular disorder of vitamin B_{12}, named CblC defect, an autosomal recessive disorder (Russo *et al.* 1992; Chenel *et al.* 1993). CblC defect had been evidenced in some 40 children with failure to thrive, neurologic manifestations, a characteristic macular degeneration, and methylmalonic aciduria and homocystinuria. Among these, one-fourth had presented with a particularly severe and lethal form with widespread multisystemic manifestations, including haemolytic–uraemic syndrome, occurring in the first days of life. Diagnosis of the defect has important implications for rapid treatment (hydroxycobalamine, folinic acid, and betaine), family counselling, and prenatal diagnosis (Zammarchi *et al.* 1990).

References

Abbal, M., Haeffner, A., Bouissou, F., Mytilineos, J., Ohayon, E., Schärer, K., *et al.* (1992). HLA and the idiopathic nephrotic syndrome. In: *HLA 1991. Proceedings of the Eleventh International Histocompatibility Workshop and Conference* (ed. K. Tsuji, M. Aizawa, and T. Sazuki), pp. 755–8. Oxford University Press, Oxford.

Abderrahim, E., Kheder, A., Ben Maiz, H., Ben Moussa, F., and Ben Ayed, H. (1990). Glomérulonéphrite membranoproliférative chez deux frères. *Néphrologie*, 11, 227–9.

Abe, J., Kohsaka, T., Tanaka, M., and Kobayashi, N. (1993). Genetic study on HLA class II and class III region in the disease associated with IgA nephropathy. *Nephron*, 65, 17–22.

Allen, A. C., Topham, P. S., Harper, S. J., and Feehally, J. (1997). Leucocyte β1,3 galactosyltransferase activity in IgA nephropathy. *Nephrology Dialysis Transplantation*, 12, 701–6.

Angus, K. W., Gardiner, A. C., Mitchell, B., and Thomson, D. (1980). Mesangiocapillary glomcrulonephritis in lambs: the ultrastructure and immunopathology of diffuse glomerulonephritis in newly born Finnish Landrace lambs. *Journal of Pathology*, **131**, 65–74.

Assmann, K. J. M., Koene, R. A. P., and Wetzels, J. F. M. (1995). Familial glomerulonephritis characterized by massive deposits of fibronectin. *American Journal of Kidney Diseases*, **25**, 781–91.

Autuly, V., Laruelle, E., Benziane, A., Ang, K. S., Cam, G., Ramée, M. P., *et al.* (1991). Increased genetic risk of hypertension in immunoglobulin A nephropathy but not in membranous nephropathy. *Journal of Hypertension*, **9** (Suppl. 6), S220–S221.

Bader, P. I., Grove, J., Nance, W. E., and Trygstad, C. (1974). Inheritance of idiopathic nephrotic syndrome. *Birth Defects*, **10**, 73–9.

Bakkaloglu, A., Söylemezoglu, O., Tinaztepe, K., Saatci, Ü., and Söylemezoglu, F. (1995). Familial membranoproliferative glomerulonephritis. *Nephrology Dialysis Transplantation*, **10**, 21–4.

Barakat, A. Y., D'Albora, J. B., Martin, M. M., and Jose, P. A. (1977). Familial nephrosis, nerve deafness, and hypoparathyroidism. *Journal of Pediatrics*, **91**, 61–4.

Berger, M., Balow, J. E., Wilson, C. B., and Frank, M. M. (1983). Circulating immune complexes and glomerulonephritis in a patient with congenital absence of the third component of complement. *New England Journal of Medicine*, **308**, 1009–12.

Berkel, A. I. and Loos, M. (1983). Klinische Befunde bein Kindern mit selektiven Mangel an C1q, einer Untereiheit der esrsten Komplementkomponente. *Monatsscriften Kinderheilkd*, **131**, 161–5.

Berns, J. S., Kaplan, B. S., Mackow, R. C., and Hefter, L. G. (1992). Inherited hemolytic–uremic syndrome in adults. *American Journal of Kidney Diseases*, **19**, 331–4.

Berry, P. L., McEnery, P. T., McAdams, A. J., and West, C. D. (1981). Membranoproliferative glomerulonephritis in two sibships. *Clinical Nephrology*, **16**, 101–6.

Berthoux, F. C., Alamartine, E., Laurent, B., Berthoux, P., Vacherot, C., Lambert, C., *et al.* (1993). Primary IgA glomerulonephritis and major histocompatibility complex revisited. In: *IgA nephropathy: the 25th year*, Vol. 104, (ed. M. C. Béné, G. C. Faure, and M. Kessler), pp. 54–60. Contribution to Nephrology, Karger, Basel.

Bishof, N. A., Welch, T. R., Beischel, L. S., Carson, D., and Donnelly, P. A. (1993). DP polymorphism in HLA-A1, -B8, -DR3 extended haplotypes associated with membranoproliferative glomerulonephritis and systemic lupus erythematosus. *Pediatric Nephrology*, **7**, 243–6.

Borzy, M. S. and Houghton, D. (1985). Mixed-pattern deposit glomerulonephritis in a child with inherited deficiency of the third component of complement. *American Journal of Kidney Diseases*, **5**, 54–9.

Bouissou, F., Meissner, I., Konrad, M., Sommer, E., Mytilineos, J., Ohayon, E., *et al.* (1995). Clinical implications from studies of HLA antigens in idiopathic nephrotic syndrome in children. *Clinical Nephrology*, **44**, 279–83.

Burns, A. P., Fisher, M., Li, P., Pusey, C. D., and Rees, A. J. (1995). Molecular analysis of HLA class II genes in Goodpasture's disease. *Quarterly Journal of Medicine*, **88**, 93–100.

Carreras, L., Romero, R., Resequens, C., Oliver, A. J., Carrera, M., Clavo, M., *et al.* (1981). Familial hypocomplementemic hemolytic–uraemic syndrome with HLA-A3, B7 haplotype. *Journal of the American Medical Association*, **245**, 602–4.

Chenel, C., Wood, C., Gourrier, E., Zittoun, J., Casadevall, I., and Ogier, H. (1993). Syndrome hémolytique et urémique néonatal, acidurie méthylmalonique et homocystinurie par déficit intracellulaire de la vitamine B$_{12}$. Intérêt du diagnostic étiologique. *Archives Françaises de Pediatrie*, **50**, 749–54.

Clark, A. G. B., Vaughan, R. W., Stephens, H. A. F., Chantler, C., Williams, D. G., and Welsh, K. I. (1990). Genes encoding the β-chains of HLA-DR7 and HLA-DQw2 define major susceptibility determinants for idiopathic nephrotic syndrome. *Clinical Science*, **78**, 391–7.

Coleman, T. H., Forristal, J., Kosaka, T., and West, C. D. (1983). Inherited complement component deficiencies in membranoproliferative glomerulonephritis. *Kidney International*, **24**, 681–90.

Conlon, P. J., Butterfly, D., Albers, F., Rodby, R., Gunnells, J. C., and Howell, D. N. (1995). Clinical and pathologic features of familial focal segmental glomerulosclerosis. *American Journal of Kidney Diseases*, **26**, 34–40.

Cork, L. C., Morris, J. M., Olson, J. L., Krakowa, S., Swift, A. J., and Winkelstein, J. A. (1991). Membranoproliferative glomerulonephritis in dogs with a genetically determined deficiency of the third component of complement. *Clinical Immunology Immunopathology*, **60**, 455–70.

Cortes, L. and Tejani, A. (1996). Dilemma of focal segmental glomerular sclerosis. *Kidney International*, **49** (Suppl. 53), S57–S63.

Crowley-Nowick, P. A., Julian, B. A., Wyatt, R. J., Waldo, F. B., Galla, J. H., Walla, B., *et al.* (1990). IgA2 allotyping in Blacks with IgA nephropathy. *Journal of the American Society of Nephrology*, **1**, 306. (Abstract 8).

D'Agati, V. (1994). The many masks of focal segmental glomerulosclerosis. *Kidney International*, **46**, 1223–41.

Demaine, A. G., Vaughan R. W., Taube, D. H., and Welsh, K. I. (1988). Association of membranous nephropathy with T-cell receptor constant β chain and immunoglobulin heavy chain switch region polymorphisms. *Immunogenetics*, **27**, 19–23.

Djamali, A., Cristol, J. P., Turc-Baron, C., Beucler, I., Baldet, P., and Mourad, G. (1996). Lipoprotein glomerulopathy: a new French case with recurrence on the transplant. *Presse médicale*, **27**, 622–30.

Dunckley, H., Chapman, J. R., Burke, J., Charlesworth, J., Hays, J., Haywood, E., *et al.* (1991). HLA-DR and -DQ genotyping in anti-GBM disease. *Disease Markers*, **9**, 249–56.

Dyer, P. A., Short, C. D., Clarke, E. A., and Mallick, N. P. (1992). HLA antigen and gene polymorphisms and haplotypes established by family studies in membranous nephropathy. *Nephrology Dialysis and Transplantation* **1** (Suppl.), 42–7.

Elshibabi, I., Kaye, C. I., and Brzowski, A. (1993). Membranous nephropathy in two human leukocyte antigen-identical brothers. *Journal of Pediatrics*, **123**, 940–2.

Fanconi, G., Kousmine, C., and Frischknecht, W. (1951). Constitutional factors in the pathogenesis of the nephrotic syndrome. *Helvetica Paediatrica Acta*, **6**, 199–218.

Faubert, P. F. and Porush, J. G. (1997). Familial focal segmental glomerulosclerosis: nine cases in four families and review of the literature. *American Journal of Kidney Diseases*, **30**, 265–70.

Fenessy, M., Hitman, G. A., Moore, R. H., Metcalfe, K., Medcraft, J. Sincio, R. A., *et al.* (1996). HLA-DQ genes polymorphism in primary IgA nephropathy in three European populations. *Kidney International*, **49**, 477–80.

Fijen, C. A., Kuisjper, E. J., Te Bulte, M., van de Heuvel, M. M., Sim, R. B., Daha, M. R., *et al.*, (1996). Heterozygous and homozygous factor H deficiency states in a Dutch family. *Clinical and experimental Immunology*, **105**, 511–6.

Finn, J. E. and Mathieson, P. W. (1993). Molecular analysis of C3 allotypes in patients with nephritic factor. *Clinical Experimental Immunology*, **91**, 410–14.

Finn, J. E., Li, P. K., Lai, K. N., and Mathieson, P. W. (1994). Molecular analysis of C3 allotypes in Chinese patients with immunoglobulin A nephropathy. *American Journal of Kidney Diseases*, **23**, 543–6.

Fisher, M., Pusey, C. D., Vaughan, R. W., and Rees, A. J. (1997). Susceptibility to anti-glomerular basement membrane disease is strongly associated with HLA-DRB1 genes. *Kidney International*, **31**, 22–229.

Fison, T. N. (1956). Acute glomerulonephritis in infancy. *Archives of Diseases in Childhood*, **3**, 101–9.

Fitzpatrick, M. M., Dillon, M. J., Barratt, T. M., and Trompeter, R. S. (1992). Atypical haemolytic–uraemic syndrome. In: *Haemolytic–uraemic syndrome and thrombopenic thrombocytopenic purpura* (ed. B. S. Kaplan, R. S. Trompeter, and J. L. Moake), pp. 163–78. Marcel Dekker, Inc., New York.

Fuchschuber, A., Jean, G., Gribouval, O., Gubler, M-C., Broyer, M., Beckmann, J. S., *et al.* (1995). Mapping a gene (SRN1) to chromosome 1q25–q31 in idiopathic nephrotic syndrome confirms a distinct entity of autosomal recessive nephrosis. *Human Molecular Genetics*, **11**, 2155–8.

Gemperle, O., Neuweiler, J., Reutter, F. W., Hildebrandt, F., and Krapf, R. (1996) Familial glomerulopathy with giant fibrillar (fibronectin-positive) deposits: 15-year follow-up in a large kindred. *American Journal of Kidney diseases*, **28**, 668–75.

Genin, C., Sabatier, J. C., and Berthoux, F. (1985). IgA mesangial deposition in C3H/Hej mice after oral immunization. *Proceedings of the European Dialysis and Transplantation Association*, **21**, 703–8.

Glicklich, D., Haskell, L., Senitzer, D., and Weiss, R. A. (1988). Possible genetic predisposition to idiopathic focal segmental glomerulosclerosis. *American Journal of Kidney Diseases*, **12**, 26–30.

Goodman, D. J., Clarke, B., Hope, R. N., Miach, P. J., and Dawborn, J. K. (1995). Familial focal glomerulosclerosis: a genetic linkage to the HLA locus? *American Journal of Nephrology*, **15**, 442–5.

Gubler, M. C., Dommergues, J. P., Foulard, M., Bensman, A., Leroy, J. P., Broyer, M., *et al.* (1993). Collagen type III glomerulopathy: a new type of hereditary nephropathy. *Pediatric Nephrology*, **7**, 354–60.

Harden, P. N., Geddes, C., Rowe, P. A., McIlroy, J. H., Boulton-Jones, M., Rodger, R. S. C., *et al.* (1995). Polymorphisms in angiotensin-converting enzyme gene and progression of IgA nephropathy. *Lancet*, **345**, 1540–2.

He, C. J., Esposito, C., Phillips, C., Zalups, R. K., Henderson, D. A., Striker G. E., *et al.* (1996). Dissociation of glomerular hypertrophy, cell proliferation, and glomerulosclerosis in mouse strains heterozygous for a mutation (Os) which induces a 50% reduction in nephron number. *Journal of Clinical Investigation*, **97**, 1242–49.

Hiki, Y., Kobayashi, Y., Itoh, I., and Kashiwagi, N. (1984). Strong association of HLA-DR2 and MTI with idiopathic membranous nephropathy. *Kidney International*, **25**, 953–7.

Hiki, Y., Kobayashi, Y., Ookubo, M., Obata, F., and Kashiwagi, N. (1991). Association of HLA-DQw4 with IgA nephropathy in the Japanese population. *Nephron*, **58**, 109–11.

Ho, K. L., Rutherford, P. A., Thomas, T. H., and Wilkinson, R. (1996). Abnormal sodium–lithium countertransport kinetics in immunoglobulin A nephropathy patients and their families: association with hypertension. *American Journal of Kidney Diseases*, **27**, 334–40.

Hogasen, K., Janse, J. H., Mollnes, T. E., Hovdenes, J., and Harboe, M. (1995). Hereditary porcine membranoproliferative glomerulonephritis type II is caused by factor H deficiency. *Journal of Clinical Investigation*, **95**, 1054–61.

Hoy, W., Smith, S. M., Hughson, M. D., . . . (1989). Mesangioproliferative glomerulonephritis in Southwestern American Indians. *Transplantation Proceedings*, **113**, 158–63.

Huang, C. C., Hu, S. A., Lin, J. L., and Wu, J. H. (1989). HLA and Chinese IgA nephropathy in Taiwan. *Tissue Antigens*, **33**, 45–7.

Huey, B., McCormick, K., Capper, J., Ratliff, C., Colombe, B. W., Garovoy, M. R., *et al.* (1993). Associations of HLA-DR and HLA-DQ types with anti-GBM nephritis with sequence-specific oligonucleotide probe hybridization. *Kidney International*, **44**, 307–12.

Hunley, T. E., Julian, B. A., Phillips III, J. A., Summar, M. L., Yoshida, H., Horn, R. G., *et al.* (1996). Angiotensin converting enzyme gene polymorphism: potential silencer motif and impact on progression in IgA nephropathy. *Kidney International*, **49**, 571–7.

Imai, K., Nakajima, K., Eguchi, K., Miyazaki, M., Endoh, M., Tomino, Y., *et al.* (1991). Homozygous C3 deficiency associated with IgA nephropathy. *Nephron*, **59**, 148–52.

Jenkins, D. (1990). Linkage disequibrium prevents precise definition of susceptibility determinants for idiopathic nephrotic syndrome. *Clinical Science*, **79**, 669–70.

Jernigan, S. M. and Waldo, F. B. (1994). Racial incidence of haemolytic–uraemic syndrome. *Pediatric Nephrology*, **8**, 545–7.

Jin, K. J., Kohsaka, T., Koo, J. W., Ha, I. S., Cheong, H. I., and Choi, Y. (1996). Complement 4 locus II gene deletion and DQA1*0301 gene: genetic risk factors for IgA nephropathy and Henoch-Schönlein nephritis. *Nephron*, **73**, 390–5.

Joseph, J., Smith, K. J., Hadley, T. J., Djulbegovic, B., Troup, G. M., Oldfather, J., *et al.* (1994). HLA-DR3 protects against thrombotic thrombocytopenic purpura/adult haemolytic–uraemic syndrome. *American Journal of Hematology*, **47**, 189–93.

Kaplan, B. S., Chesney, R. W., and Drummond, K. N. (1975). Haemolytic–uraemic syndrome in families. *New England Journal of Medicine*, **202**, 1090–3.

Kaplan, B. S. and Kaplan, P. (1992). Haemolytic–uraemic syndrome in families. In: *Haemolytic–uraemic syndrome and thrombopenic thrombocytopenic purpura* (ed. B. S. Kaplan, R. S. Trompeter, and J. L. Moake), pp. 213–25. Marcel Dekker, Inc., New York.

Karet, F. E. and Lifton, R. P. (1997). Lipoprotein glomerulopathy: a new role for apolipoprotein E? *Journal of the American Society of Nephrology*, 8, 840–3.

Karmali, M. A., Petric, M., and Lim, C. (1983). Sporadic cases of haemolytic–uraemic syndrome associated with faecal cytotoxin and cytotoxin-producing *Escherichia coli* in stools. *Lancet*, 1, 619–20.

Kidd, K. K. (1993). Associations of disease with genetic markers: déjà vu all over again. *American Journal of Medical Genetics*, 48, 71–3.

Kim, P. K., Pai, K. S., Hawang, C. H., Park, M. S., Jeong, H. J., and Choi, I. J. (1991). Familial nephrotic syndrome and HLA-DR5. *Childhood Nephology Urology*, 11, 55–60.

King M. C., Lee, G. M., Spinner, N. B., Thomson, G., and Wrensch, M. R. (1984). Genetic epidemiology. *Annual Review of Public Health*, 5, 1–52.

Klouda, P. T., Manos, J., Acheson, E. J., Dyer, P. A., Golby, F. S., Harris, R., *et al.* (1979). Strong association between idiopathic membranous nephropathy and HLA-Dw3. *Lancet*, ii, 770–1.

Knight, J. F., Falk, M. C., Ng, G., Fanning, G. C., Artlett, C. M., and Roy, L. P. (1995). IgA Nephropathy: immunogenetic studies of Australian patients. In: *IgA Nephropathy: pathogenesis and treatment* (ed. A. R. Clarkson and A. J. Woodroffe), vol. 111, pp. 18–23. Contributions to Nephrology, Karger, Basel.

Konrad, M., Mytilineos, J., Bouissou, F., Scherer, S., Gulli, M. P., Meissner, I., *et al.* (1994). HLA class II asociations with idiopathic nephrotic syndrome in children. *Tissue Antigens*, 43, 275–80.

Korbet, S. L., Genchi, R. M., Borok, R. Z., and Schwartz, M. M. (1996). The racial prevalence of glomerular lesions in nephrotic adults. *American Journal of Kidney Diseases*, 27, 647–51.

Lagueruela, C. C., Buettner, T. L., Cole, B. R., Kissane, J. M., and Robson, A. M. (1990). HLA extended haplotypes in steroid-sensitive nephrotic syndrome of childhood. *Kidney International*, 38, 145–50.

Levy M. (1993). Multiplex families in IgA nephropathy. In: *IgA nephropathy: the 25th year* (ed. M. C. Béné, G. C. Faure, and M. Kessler), vol. 104, pp. 46–53. Contributions to Nephrology, Karger, Basel.

Levy, M., Halbwachs-Mecarelli, L., Gubler, M. C., Kohout, G., Bensenouci, A., Niaudet, P., *et al.* (1986). H deficiency in two brothers with atypical dense intramembranous deposit disease. *Kidney International*, 30, 949–56.

Levy, M. and Lesavre, P. (1992). Genetic factors in IgA nephropathy. In: *Advances in nephrology* (ed. J. P. Grünfeld, J. F. Bach, H. Kreis, and M. H. Maxwell), Vol. 21, pp. 23–51. Mosby Year Book, St Louis.

Lhotta, K., Thoenes, W., Glatz, J., Hintner, H., Kronenberg, E., Joannidis, M., *et al.* (1993). Hereditary complete deficiency of the fourth component of complement: effects on the kidney. *Clinical Nephrology*, 39, 117–24.

Lhotta, K., Neunhäusere, M., Sölder, B., Uring-Lambert, B., Würzner, R., Rumpelt, H. J., *et al.* (1996). Recurrent hematuria: a novel clinical presentation of hereditary complete complement C4 deficiency. *American Journal of Kidney Diseases*, 27, 424–7.

Li, P. K-T., Poon, A. S. Y., and Lai, K. N. (1994). Molecular genetics of MHC class II alleles in Chinese patients with IgA nephropathy. *Kidney International*, 46, 185–90.

Linshaw, M. A., Stapleton, F. B., Cuppage, F. E., Forristal, J., West, C. D., Schreiber, R. D., *et al.* (1987). Hypocomplementemic glomerulonephritis in an infant and mother. *American Journal of Nephrology*, 7, 470–7.

Loirat, C., Levy, M., Peltier, A. P., Broyer, M., Checoury, A., and Mathieu, H. (1980). Deficiency of the second component of complement. Its occurrence with membranoproliferative glomerulonephritis. *Archives of Pathology and Laboratory Medicine*, 104, 467–72.

Loirat, C., Baudouin, V., Sonsino, E., Mariani-Kurdjiian, P., and Elion, J. (1993). Haemolytic–uraemic syndrome in the child. *Advances in Nephrology*, **22**, 141–68.

Lokki, M.-L. and Colten, H. R. (1995). Genetic deficiencies of complement. *Annals of Medicine*, **27**, 451–9.

Lopez-Trascasa, M., Martin-Villa, J. M., Vicario, J. L., Marin, M. A., Martinez-Ara, J., Garcia-Messeguer, M. C., *et al.* (1991). Familial incidence of C3 nephritic factor. *Nephron*, **59**, 261–5.

Luger, A. M., Komathireddy, G., Walker, R. E. W., Pandey, J. P., and Hoffman, R. W. (1994). Molecular and serologic analyses of HLA genes and immunglobulin allotypes in IgA nephropathy. *Autoimmunity*, **19**, 1–5.

Maccario, M., Segagni, S., Efficace, E., Piazza, V., Poggio, F., Villa, G., *et al.* (1995). Idiopathic membranous nephropathy in two siblings. *Nephrology Dialysis Transplantation*, **10**, 108–10.

McCurdy, F. A., Butera, P. J., and Wilson, R. (1987). The familial occurrence of focal segmental glomerular sclerosis. *American Journal of Kidney Diseases*, **10**, 467–9.

MacGregor, A. J. and Silman, A. J. (1993). Epidemiological approaches to the immunogenetics of autoimmune rheumatic disease. *Annals of the Rheumatic Diseases*, **52**, 310–13.

McLean, R. H. (1993). Complement and glomerulonephritis–an update. *Pediatric Nephrology*, **7**, 226–32.

Martinetti, M., Cuccia, M., Amoroso, A., Boreli, I., Capello, N., Daielli, C., *et al.* (1992). Idiopathic mesangial IgA nephropathy: an immunogenetic study. In: *Proceedings of the Eleventh International Histocompatibility Workshop and Conference* (ed. K. Tsuji, M. Aizawa, and T. Sasazuki), pp. 749–55. Oxford Science Publications.

Mathieson, P. W. and Peters, D. K. (1993). Deficiency and depletion of complement in the pathogenesis of nephritis and vasculitis. *Kidney International*, **44** (Suppl. 42), S13–S18.

Mathis, B., Calabrese, K. E., and Slick, G. L. (1992). Familial glomerular disease with asymptomatic proteinuria and nephrotic syndrome: a new clinical entity. *JAOA*, **92**, 875–84.

Mattoo, T. K., Mahmood, M. A., Al-Harbi, M. S., and Mikail, I. (1989). Familial recurrent haemolytic–uraemic syndrome. *Journal of Pediatrics*, **114**, 814–16.

Medcrafte, J., Hitman, G. A., Sachs, J. A., Whixhelow, C. E., Raafat, I., and Moore, R. H. (1993). Autoimmune renal disease and tumour necrosis factor beta gene polymorphism. *Cinical Nephrology*, **40**, 63–8.

Meyrier, A., Dairou, F., Callard, P., and Mougenot, B. (1995). Lipoprotein nephropathy: first case in a white European. *Nephrology Dialysis Transplantation*, **10**, 546–8.

Mizuiri, S., Hasegawa, A., Kikuchi, A., Amagasaki, Y., Nakamura, N., and Sakaguchi, H. (1993). A case of collagenofibrotic glomerulonephropathy associated with hepatic perisinusoidal fibrosis. *Nephron*, **63**, 183–7.

Moncrieff, M. W., White, R. H. R., Winterborn, M. H., Glasgow, E. F., Cameron, J. S., and Ogg, C. S. (1973). The familial nephrotic syndrome. II. A clinicopathological study. *Clinical Nephrology*, **1**, 220–9.

Moore, R. (1993). Major histocompatibility complex gene polymorphism in primary IgA nephropathy. *Kidney International*, **43** (Suppl. 39), S9–S12.

Morgan, B. P. and Walport, M. J. (1991). Complement deficiency and disease. *Immunology Today*, **12**, 301–6.

Nagasawa, R., Matsumura, O., Mayruyma, N., Mitarai, T., and Isoda, K. (1995). T-cell receptor beta-chain gene polymorphism and the prognosis of IgA nephropathy in Japanese patients. *Nephron*, **70**, 502–3.

Noakes, P. G., Miner, J. H., Gautam, M., Cunningham, J. M., Snes, J. R., and Merlie, J. P. (1995). The renal glomerulus of mice lacking s-laminin/laminin β2: nephrosis despite molecular compensation by laminin β1. *Nature Genetics*, **10**, 400–6.

O' Connell, P. J., Ibels, L. S., Thomas, M. A., Harris, M., and Eckstein, R. P. (1987). Familial IgA nephropathy: a study in an Autraslian Aboriginal family. *Australian and New Zealand Journal of Medicine*, **17**, 27–33.

Ogahara, S., Naito, S., Abe, K., Michinaga, I., and Arakawa, K. (1992). Analysis of HLA class II genes in Japanese patients with idiopathic membranous glomerulonephritis. *Kidney International*, **41**, 175–82.

Ohi, H., Ikezawa, T., Wanatabe, S., Seki, M., Mizutani, Y., Nawa, N., *et al.* (1986). Two cases of mesangiocapillary glomerulonephritis with CR1 deficiency. *Nephron*, **43**, 307.

Oikawa, S., Matsunaga, A., Saito, T., Sato, H., Seki, T., Hoshi, K., *et al.* (1997). Apolipoprotein E Sendai (Arginine 145 → Proline): a new variant associated with lipoprotein glomerulopathy. *Journal of the American Society of Nephrology*, **8**, 820–3.

Palm, L., Hägerstrand, I., Kristoffersson, U., Blennow, G., Brun, A., and Jörgensen, C. (1986). Nephrosis and disturbances of neuronal migration in male siblings–a new hereditary disorder? *Archives of Disease in Childhood*, **61**, 545–8.

Phelps, R. G., Turner, A. N., and Rees, A. J. (1996). Direct identification of naturally processed autoantigen-derived peptides bound to HLA-DR15. *Journal of Biochemical Chemistry*, **271**, 18549 53.

Pichette, V., Quérin, S., Schürch, W., Brun, G., Lehner-Netsch, J., and Delage, J. M. (1994). Familial haemolytic–uraemic syndrome and homozygous factor H deficiency. *American Journal of Kidney Disease*, **24**, 936–41.

Pontier, P. J. and Patel. T. G. (1994). Racial differences in the prevalence and presentation of glomerular diseases in adults. *Clinical Nephrology*, **42**, 79–84.

Praz, F., Halbwachs, L., and Lesavre, P. (1984). Genetic aspects of complement and glomerulonephritis. *Advances in Nephrology*, **13**, 271–96.

Raguénès, O., Mercier, B., Clèdes, J., Whebe, B., and Férec C. (1995). HLA class II typing and idiopathic IgA nephropathy: DQB*0301, a possible marker of unfavorable outcome. *Tissue Antigens*, **45**, 246–9.

Rambausek, M., Hartz, G., Waldherr, R., Andrassy, K., and Ritz, E. (1987). Familial glomerulonephritis. *Pediatric Nephrology*, **1**, 416–18.

Rambausek, M. H., Waldherr, R., and Ritz, E. (1993). Immunogenetic findings in glomerulonephritis. *Kidney International*, **43** (Suppl. 39), S3–S8.

Rees, A. J. (1994). The immunogenetics of glomerulonephritis. *Kidney International*, **45**, 377–83.

Rees, A. J., Peters, D. K., Compston, D. A. S., and Batchelor, J. R. (1978). Strong association between HLA-DRw2 and antibody-mediated Goodpasture's syndrome. *Lancet*, **1**, 966–8.

Remuzzi, G., Marchesi, D., Misiani, R., Mecca, G., de Gaetano, G., and Donati, M. B. (1979). Familial deficiency of a plasma factor stimulating vascular prostacyclin activity. *Thrombosis Research*, **16**, 517–25.

Russo, P., Doyon, J., Sonsino, E., Ogier, H., and Saudubray, J-M. (1992). Congenital anomaly of vitamin B_{12} metabolism–an analysis of three cases. *Human Pathology*, **23**, 504–12.

Sacks, S. H., Nomura, S., Warner, C., Naito, S., Ogahara, S., Vaughan, R., *et al.* (1992). Analysis of complement C4 loci in Caucasoids and Japanese with idiopathic membranous nephropathy. *Kidney International*, **42**, 882–7.

Sacks, S. H., Warner, C., Campbell, R. D., and Dunham, I. (1993). Molecular mapping of the HLA class II region in HLA-DR3 associated membranous nephropathy. *Kidney International*, **43** (Suppl. 39), S13–S19.

Saito, T., Sato, H., Kudo, K., Oikawa, S., Shibata, T., Hara, Y., *et al.* (1989). Glomerular lipoprotein thrombi in a patient with hyperlipoproteinemia. *American Journal of Kidney Diseases*, **13**, 148–53.

Salcedo, J. R. (1984). An autosomal recessive disorder with glomerular basement membrane abnormalities similar to those seen in the nail–patella syndrome. Report of a kindred. *American Journal of Medical Genetics*, **19**, 579–84.

Schena, F. P. (1995). Immunogenetic aspects of primary IgA nephropathy. *Kidney International*, **48**, 1998–2013.

Schenkel, J., Zwacka, R., Rutenberg, C., Reuter, A., Waldherr, R., and Wieher, H. (1995). Functional rescue of the glomerulosclerosis phenotype in Mpv17 mice by transgenesis with the human Mpv17 homologue. *Kidney International*, **48**, 80–4.

Schmidt, M., Meyers, S., Wegner, R., and Ritz, E. (1990). Increased genetic risk of hypertension in glomerulonephritis? *Journal of Hypertension*, 8, 573–7.

Schmidt, S., Stier, E., Hartung, R., Stein, G., Bahnisch, J., Woodroffe, A., *et al.* (1995). No association of converting enzyme insertion/deletion polymorphism with immunoglobulin A glomerulonephritis. *American Journal of Kidney Diseases*, 26, 727–31.

Scolari, F., Amoroso, A., Savoldi, S., Prati, E., Scaini, P., Manganoni, A., *et al.* (1992). Familial occurrence of primary glomerulonephritis: evidence for a role of genetic factors. *Nephrology Dialysis Transplantation*, 7, 587–96.

Sheth, K., Gill, J. C., Leichter, H. E., Havens, P. L., and Hunter, J. B. (1994). Increased incidence of HLA-B40 group antigens in children with haemolytic–uraemic syndrome. *Nephron*, 68, 433–6.

Shimomura, M., Yoshikawa, N., Iijima, K., Nakamura, H., Miyazaki, M., and Sakai, H. (1995). Polymorphism of immunoglobulin heavy chain switch region gene in children with severe IgA nephropathy. *Clinical Nephrology*, 43, 211–15.

Srinivasan, J. and Beck, P. (1993). IgA nephropathy in hereditary angioedema. *Postgraduate Medical Journal*, 69, 95–9.

Strom, E. H., Banfi, G., Krapf, R., Abt, A. B., Mazzuco, G., Monga, G., *et al.* (1995). Glomerulopathy associated with predominant fibronectin deposits: a newly recognized hereditary disease. *Kidney International*, 48, 163–70.

Stutchfield, P. R., White, R. H. R., Cameron, A. H., Thomson, R. A., Maskintosh, P., and Wells, L. (1986). X-linked mesangiocapillary glomerulonephritis. *Clinical Nephrology*, 26, 150–6.

Tabin, R., Guignard, J-P., Gautier, E., Dubrit, M., Jeannet, M., Golaz, J., *et al.* (1983). Corticoresistant nephrotic syndrome associated with T-cell deficiency in two sisters. *Pediatrics*, 71, 93–6.

Tamura, H., Matsuda, A., Kidoguchi, N., Matsumura, O., Mitarai, T., and Isoda, K. (1996). A family with two sisters with collagenofibrotic glomerulonephropathy. *American Journal of Kidney Diseases*, 27, 588–95.

Tejani, A., Nicastri, A., Phadke, K., Sen, D., Adamson, O., Dunn, I., *et al.* (1983). Familial focal segmental glomerulosclerosis. *International Journal of Pediatric Nephrology*, 4, 231–4.

Thompson, R. A. and Winterborn, M. H. (1981). Hypocomplementaemia due to a genetic deficiency of β1H globulin. *Clinical Experimental Immunology*, 46, 110–19.

Topaloglu, R., Bakkaloglu, A., Slingsby, J. H., Mihatsch, J., Pascual, M., Norsworthy, P., *et al.* (1996). Molecular basis of hereditary C1q deficiency associated with SLE and IgA nephropathy in a Turkish family. *Kidney International*, 50, 635–42.

Turi, S., Beattie, T. J., Belch, J. J. F., and Murphy, A. V. (1986). Disturbances of prostacyclin metabolism in children with haemolytic–uraemic syndrome and in first-degree relatives. *Clinical Nephrology*, 25, 193–8.

van Bommel, E. F. H., Ouwehand, A. J., Mulder, A. H., and Weimar, W. (1995). Mesangiocapillary glomerulonephritis associated with hereditary angioedema. *Nephron*, 69, 178–9.

van de Kar, N., Reekers, P., van Acker, K., Donckerwolke, R., Ploos van Amstel, S., Proesmans, W., *et al.* (1991). Association between the epidemic form of haemolytic–uraemic syndrome and HLA-B40 in the Netherlands and Flander. *Nephron*, 59, 170.

Vaughan, R. W., Demaine, A. G., and Welsh, K. I. (1989). A DQA1 allele is strongly associated with idiopathic membranous nephropathy. *Tissue Antigens*, 34, 261–9.

Vaughan, R. W., Ogahara, S., Acquart, S., Pleindoux, M. J., Berthoux, P., Berthoux, F. C., *et al.* (1992). Idiopathic membranous nephropathy. In: *HLA 1991. Proceedings of the Eleventh International Histocompatibility Workshop and Conference* (ed. K. Tsuji, M. Aizawa, and T. Sasazuki), pp. 745–8. Oxford University Press, Oxford.

Vaughan, R. W., Tighe, M. R., Bok, K., Alexopoulos, S., Padakis, J., Lanchbury, J. S. S., *et al.* (1995). An analysis of HLA class II gene polymorphism in British and Greek idiopathic membranous nephropathy patients. *European Journal of Immunogenetics*, 22, 179–86.

Vogt, B. A., Wyat, R. J., Burke, B. A., Simonton, S. C., and Kashtan, C. E. (1995). Inherited factor H deficiency and collagen type III glomerulopathy. *Pediatric Nephrology*, 9, 11–15.

Voyer, L. E., Wainsztein, R. E., Quadri, B. E., and Corti, S. E. (1996). Haemolytic–uraemic syndrome in families–an Argentinian experience. *Pediatric Nephrology*, **10**, 70–2.

Walport, M. J. (1993). Inherited complement deficiency–clues to the physiological activity of complement *in vivo*. *Quarterly Journal of Medicine*, **86**, 355–8.

Weiher, H. (1993). Glomerular sclerosis in transgenic mice: the Mpv-17 gene and its human homologue. In: *Advances in nephrology* (ed. J. P. Grünfeld, J. F. Bach, H. Kreis, and M. H. Maxwell), vol. 22, pp. 37–42, Mosby Year Book, St Louis.

Welch, T. R., Beischel, L., Balarkrishnan, K., Quinlan, M., and West, C. D. (1986). Major histocompatibility complex extended haplotypes in membranoproliferative glomerulonephritis. *New England Journal of Medicine*, **314**, 1476–81.

Welch, T. R., Beischel, L. S., and Choi, E. M. (1989). Molecular genetics of C4B deficiency in IgA nephropathy. *Human Immunology*, **26**, 353–63.

White, R. H. R. (1973). The familial nephrotic syndrome. I. A European survey. *Clinical Nephrology*, **1**, 215–19.

Wopenka, U., Thyselle, H., Sjöhom, A. G., and Truedsson, L. (1996). C4 phenotypes in IgA nephropathy: disease progression associated with C4A deficiency but not with C4 isotype concentrations. *Clinical Nephrology*, **45**, 141–5.

Wyatt, R. J., Jones, D., Stapleton, F. B., Roy III, S., Odom, T. W., and McLean, R. H. (1985). Recurrent haemolytic–uraemic syndrome with the hypomorphic fast allele of the third component of complement. *The Journal of Pediatrics*, **107**, 564–6.

Wyatt, R. J., Rivas, M. L., Julian, B. A., Quiggins, P. A., Woodford, S. Y., McMorrow, R. G., *et al.* (1987). Regionalization in hereditary IgA nephropathy. *American Journal of Human Genetics*, **41**, 36–50.

Wyatt, R. J., Julian, B. A., and Rivas, M. L., (1991). Role for specific complement phenotype and deficiencies in the clinical expression of IgA nephropathy. *American Journal of Medical Sciences*, **301**, 115–23.

Yorioka, T., Suehiro, T., Yasuoka, N., Hashimoto, K., and Jkawada, M. (1995). Polymorphism of the angiotensin-converting enzyme gene and clinical aspects of IgA nephropathy. *Clinical Nephrology*, **44**, 80–5.

Yoshida, H., Mitarai, T., Kawamura, T., Kitajima, T., Miyazaki, Y., Nagasawa, R., *et al.* (1995). Role of the deletion of the angiotensin converting enzyme gene in the progression and therapeutic responsiveness of IgA nephropathy. *Journal of Clinical Investigation*, **96**, 2162–9.

Zammarchi, E., Cippi, A., Falorni, S., Pasquini, E., Cooper, B. A., and Rosenblatt, D. S. (1990). Cblc disease: case report and monitoring of a pregnancy at risk by chorionic villus sampling. *Journal of Investigative Medicine*, **13**, 139–42.

Section C
Tubular and tubulointerstitial disorders

13.1

Aminoacidurias and the Fanconi syndrome

George B. Haycock

Introduction

About two-thirds of the volume of the glomerular filtrate is reabsorbed isotonically in the proximal tubule. The energy driving this process is generated from ATP by the action of Na, K-ATPase in the basolateral membrane of the tubular cell, resulting in transport of three sodium (Na) ions out of the cell in exchange for two potassium (K) ions. The resulting low intracellular Na concentration creates and maintains a steep electrochemical Na gradient from the bubular fluid to the cell interior across the brush border of the apical membrane. The brush border contains a number of transport proteins, each of which facilitates diffusive entry of Na and a specific cotransportate into the cell. Sodium is therefore transported from the luminal fluid to the peritubular fluid in two stages, of which the second (extrusion from the cell) is directly coupled to energy metabolism but also indirectly powers the entry step of both Na and its cotransportates; this latter process is called *secondary active transport*. Substances reabsorbed with Na in this way include inorganic phosphate (Hoffman *et al.* 1976), glucose (Kinne *et al.* 1975), and amino acids (Frömter 1982) (Fig. 13.1.1). Some Na enters the cell from the lumen by exchange with hydrogen ions (H^+) via the *antiporter* (Seifter and Aronson 1986), also by secondary active transport. The resulting acidification of the tubular fluid, augmented by active, electrogenic H^+ secretion, is important in bicarbonate reabsorption (Fig. 13.1.2). By simultaneously measuring glomerular filtration rate, the plasma concentration rate of a transported substance (S), and the urinary excretion rate of S, the characteristics of the tubular reabsorption of S can be expressed as a series of *titration curves* as shown in Fig. 13.1.3.

Defects of proximal tubular reabsorption fall into two main classes. The first of these comprises specific, usually inherited, defects of a single transport function: examples include familial X-linked hypophosphataemic rickets and renal glycosuria, each of which is believed to be due to a mutation leading to absence or functional abnormality of the apical Na-phosphate and Na-glucose transporters, respectively. The second class is generalized disease of the tubule leading to defective reabsorption of most or all of these substances, the renal Fanconi syndrome. Chapter 13.1 deals with aminoacidurias and the Fanconi syndrome.

Aminoacidurias

Amino acids are freely filtered at the glomerulus and reabsorbed by a set of transport systems that conform to the model schematized in Figs 13.1.1 and 13.1.3. The array of amino acid transporters in the apical membrane is very complex. There appear to be two subclasses of them: specific

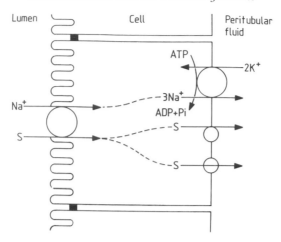

Fig. 13.1.1 Generalized scheme for sodium-coupled reabsorption of a solute, S, in the proximal tubule. The energy-consuming process is transport of Na out of the cell across the basolateral membrane by the Na, K-ATPase transport system (top right in diagram). See text for further explanation.

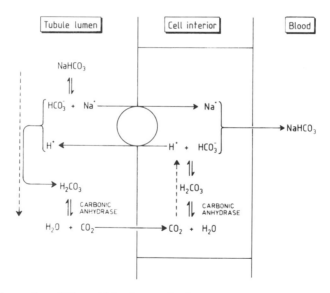

Fig. 13.1.2 Reabsorption of filtered bicarbonate in the proximal tubule. Hydrogen ions (H^+) enter the lumen by countertransport with sodium (top left) and by electrogenic H^+ transport (not shown in diagram). The resulting carbonic acid is dehydrated to CO_2 and water by carbonic anhydrase in the tubular fluid. The highly diffusible CO_2 enters the cell down its concentration gradient, where it is rehydrated to carbonic acid, again under the influence of carbonic anhydrase. Ionization of this carbonic acid yields more H^+ for secretion and bicarbonate to restore to the blood.

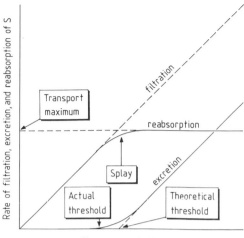

Fig. 13.1.3 Titration curves describing the rate of filtration, tubular reabsorption, and excretion of a solute, S, by saturable active transport at different plasma concentrations. The transport maximum for S is abbreviated to TmS, and the theoretical threshold for S is TmS/GFR.

Table 13.1.1 Classification of renal aminoacidurias

A. Cystine and dibasic amino acids
    Classical cystinuria
    Isolated hypercystinuria
    Dibasic aminoacidurias
        Type 1
        Type 2
    Lysinuria

B. Neutral amino acids
    Hartnup disease
    Methionine malabsorption
    Histidinuria

C. Glycine and imino acids
    Iminoglycinuria
    Glycinuria

D. Dicarboxylic amino acids
    Dicarboxylic aminoaciduria

transporters for each individual compound and a less substrate-specific set of proteins, each of which carries members of a group of amino acids. Tubular reabsorption of amino acids is normally almost complete, ranging from 97–99.9% of the filtered load, except for histidine which is only 90–95% reabsorbed (Brodehl and Gellison 1968). It is clear from examination of Fig. 13.1.3 that increased urinary excretion of an amino acid might occur either at a normal plasma concentration, implying defective tubular reabsorption, or in the presence of normal tubular transport if its plasma concentration is increased above the renal threshold. Aminoacidurias due to the first of these mechanisms are called *renal aminoacidurias*, while those due to the second are known as *non-renal* or *overflow aminoacidurias* and are not considered further here. The main renal aminoacidurias are listed by group in Table 13.1.1. All are rare or very rare except cystinuria.

Cystinuria (See Chapter 23)

The renal defect

Classical cystinuria is due to a recessively inherited defect of the group carrier that facilitates entry of cysteine and the dibasic amino acids arginine, lysine, and ornithine into the proximal tubular cell (Dent and Rose 1951). Cystine, a dimer of cysteine, has structural similarities to the dibasic amino acids which presumably explains why they are recognized by the same transport protein. Infusion of lysine into normal individuals, but not patients with cystinuria, causes the excretion of cystine, arginine, and ornithine to increase (Robson and Rose 1957), as would be predicted if they are competing for a common transporter which is absent in the disease. Urinary excretion of all four acids is grossly increased but cystine alone is responsible for the only clinical manifestation of the disease, which is recurrent cystine urolithiasis. The urinary excretion rate of cystine may actually exceed its rate of glomerular filtration (Crawhall *et al.* 1967; Lester and Cusworth 1973), implying net tubular secretion. This is probably due to passive leaking of cystine from cell to lumen; some cyst(e)ine is taken up from the peritubular fluid across the basolateral membrane, probably for the cell's own 'housekeeping' needs, and addition of part of this to the filtered load would account for the observation.

The intestinal defect

Intestinal absorption of cystine and dibasic amino acids is impaired in some patients with cystinuria (Milne *et al.* 1961; Asatoor *et al.* 1962) (see below, under Genetics). However, neither the urinary wasting nor the intestinal malabsorption of these substances is nutritionally significant, probably because enough of them is absorbed as dipeptides and oligopeptides to meet nutritional needs (Hellier *et al.* 1970). This interpretation is supported by the observation that, in patients with cystinuria, urinary cystine excretion increases following protein feeding but not oral administration of cystine itself (Brand *et al.* 1935).

Genetics

At least three subtypes of classical cystinuria can be distinguished (Rosenberg *et al.* 1966). Type 1 shows absent intestinal uptake of cystine and dibasic amino acids and normal amino acid excretion in heterozygotes. Types 2 and 3 are characterized by greater than normal urinary excretion of cystine and dibasic amino acids in heterozygotes, though much less than occurs in homozygotes. Patients with type 2 have some intestinal uptake of cystine, although less than normal, but none of dibasic amino acids, while those with type 3 have normal or near normal intestinal absorption of both. There is no clinical need to distinguish among the three types, however, as mixed heterozygotes behave as typical stone-forming homozygotes. It is likely that this heterogeneity is due to different mutations affecting the gene that codes for the cystine/dibasic amino acid transporter.

Clinical features

The incidence and prevalence of cystinuria are unknown, mainly because there is an unknown number of affected individuals who do not form stones. Estimates based on screening population samples vary from 1:100000 (Bostram and Hambraeus 1964) to 1:1100 (Thalhammer 1975). The latter figure was based on a sample of 70000 newborns screened in Vienna and, even if true for the population from which that sample was drawn, cannot be extrapolated to other populations. The symptoms of cystinuria are those of recurrent stone formation: renal colic, haematuria, infections, or the passage of stones in the urine. Urethral obstruction occurs occasionally, usually in males. Chronic renal failure may develop if stone formation is bilateral and if treatment, including measures to prevent recurrence, is inadequate. Cystine calculi may present at any age but most commonly do so in childhood or early adult life. They are radio-opaque, although typically less so than stones with a high calcium content, and often possess a uniform, 'ground glass' appearance on X-rays. They may be single or multiple, unilateral or bilateral, and range in size from gravel to complete staghorn casts of the pelvicalyceal systems.

Diagnosis

A simple, semiquantitative colorimetric screening test (the cyanide–nitroprusside test) is available. If this is positive, the diagnosis should be confirmed by measurement of the 24-hour excretion rate of cystine and dibasic amino acids because homocysteine gives a false positive cyanide–nitroprusside test and some heterozygotes for types 2 and 3 cystinuria may also give a positive reaction. Normal individuals excrete less than 10 nmol cystine/mol creatinine (often expressed as <20 nmol $^1/_2$-cystine, i.e. cysteine). Patients homozygous for cystinuria excrete at least 10 times this amount.

Treatment

Apart from its concentration in solution, the main factor determining the tendency of cystine to precipitate and form stones is pH. In the physiological urine pH range of 4.5–7.5, the upper limit of solubility is 1.0–1.25 mmol/l; however, solubility rises steeply at pH >7.5. The initial strategy to prevent stone formation is therefore to dilute and alkalinize the urine by means of high water intake and oral alkali administration. A rough guide to the amount of water to be prescribed can be derived from the 24-hour urinary cystine excretion rate, 1 litre of water being given for every 1 mmol urinary cystine. This is difficult to achieve, especially at night, and may require ingestion of 4–10 litres daily. Alkali should be given in several divided daily doses to maintain urine pH continuously above 7.5 and preferably 8. Many patients find it difficult or impossible to comply with this regimen. Nevertheless, if adhered to it is safe and effective and it should be the treatment of first choice. If water and alkali are ineffective, D-penicillamine (Crawhall *et al.* 1963) can be given by mouth in an initial dose of 30 mg/kg/day to a maximum of 2 g/day in adults. D-penicillamine reacts with cystine to form a mixed D-penicillamine/cysteine disulphide which is much more soluble than cystine. The drug is effective but unfortunately causes many side-effects including proteinuria, rashes and arthralgia, bone marrow suppression, epidermolysis, and loss of the sensation of taste. It antagonizes the effects of pyridoxine (Jaffe *et al.* 1964) and supplements of this vitamin in a dose of 10 mg daily should be given to patients on D-penicillamine. Other sulphydryl compounds such as mercaptopropionyl glycine (Hautmann *et al.* 1977) act similarly but unfortunately are attended by similar side-effects. A low Na diet has been found to reduce cystine excretion significantly in limited studies (Jaeger *et al.* 1986). The practical therapeutic potential of this approach remains to be assessed in adequate trials; presumably it would need to be accompanied by alkali therapy in the form of a K-based preparation.

When stones have formed they should be treated on their merits by a urologist experienced in the management of urolithiasis and with access to all modern modalities of treatment, including surgery, lithotripsy, and percutaneous nephrolithotomy.

Isolated hypercystinuria

Two siblings have been described with abnormally high urinary excretion of cystine without dibasic aminoaciduria (Brodehl *et al.* 1967). They did not form stones. The significance of this observation is its demonstration of a tubular cystine transporter distinct from that which carries cystine and dibasic amino acids.

Dibasic aminoaciduria

Two forms of dibasic aminoaciduria without cystinuria have been recognized.

1. Lysinuric protein intolerance

In this serious disease, dibasic aminoaciduria is accompanied by severe intestinal malabsorption of arginine, lysine, and ornithine (Perheentupa and Visakorpi 1965). Protein feeding induces hyperammonaemia, vomiting, acidosis, and neurological manifestations including coma. These symptoms are thought to be caused by intracellular depletion of arginine and ornithine, important components of the urea cycle. Moderate protein restriction with dietary supplements of citrulline, which can be converted to arginine and ornithine, and small amounts of lysine is currently the treatment of choice (Rajantie *et al.* 1980).

2. Dibasic aminoaciduria without hyperammonaemia

Numerous asymptomatic members of a single pedigree were found to have dibasic aminoaciduria without cystinuria (Whelan and Scriver 1968). The benign nature of the disease, in contrast to lysinuric protein intolerance, may be due to absence of gastrointestinal involvement.

Lysinuria

One severely mentally handicapped child with isolated lysinuria and a defect of intestinal lysine absorption has been described (Omura *et al.* 1976). This case further attests to the multiplicity of tubular transporters for cystine and dibasic amino acids.

Hartnup disease

This uncommon condition is due to incomplete tubular reabsorption of all the neutral amino acids (alanine, asparagine, glutamine, histidine, isoleucine, leucine, methionine, phenylalanine, serine, threonine, tryptophan, tyrosine, and valine). Like classical cystinuria, this is presumably due to deficiency in a group amino acid transporter. Other amino acids are reabsorbed normally. Affected patients also have impaired intestinal absorption of the same amino acids (Milne *et al.* 1960). The condition is named after the English family in which it was first described.

Genetics

Hartnup disease is inherited as an autosomal recessive, with an estimated incidence of 1 : 20 000 (Levy 1973).

Clinical features

Signs and symptoms of Hartnup disease include an erythematous, photosensitive, scaly rash that is identical to pellagra, cerebellar ataxia, intermittent confusional states, and occasional mental retardation. These are all due to deficiency of nicotinamide, of which tryptophan is a dietary precursor.

Diagnosis

Chromatographic analysis of urinary amino acid excretion is diagnostic. Hartnup disease must be carefully distinguished from the Fanconi syndrome, in which the aminoaciduria is generalized, and from other, more specific, neutral aminoacidurias.

Treatment

Supplementation with nicotinic acid is curative (Halvorsen and Halvorsen 1963). Supplements should be continued for life, even in asymptomatic patients, since the possible adverse long-term effects of marginal deficiency of this vitamin are unknown.

Specific neutral aminoacidurias

Methionine malabsorption with methioninuria (oasthouse syndrome) has been described in two (unrelated) children (Smith and Strang 1958; Hooft *et al.* 1965). Unabsorbed methionine is degraded by intestinal bacteria to α-hydroxybutyric acid which is then absorbed into the bloodstream and excreted in the urine, imparting to it an offensive odour that accounts for its alternative name. The clinical features are white hair, oedema, mental retardation, and seizures. A low methionine diet led to disappearance of the characteristic odour from the urine and marked clinical improvement, suggesting that accumulation of α-hydroxybutyric acid is responsible for the adverse effects of the disease.

Two mentally retarded brothers have been described with isolated *histidinuria* and an associated intestinal malabsorption of histidine. The parents had a mild impairment of intestinal histidine absorption but no histidinuria, suggesting recessive inheritance.

Disorders of renal glycine and imino acid transport

A number of individuals have now been described with *iminoglycinuria* (Joseph *et al.* 1958; Procopis and Turner 1971), i.e. increased urinary excretion of proline, hydroxyproline, and glycine. It is probably benign, most affected persons being clinically normal. The fact that the first patient described with iminoglycinuria had neurological disease is probably coincidental (children with mental retardation and seizures are preferentially likely to be investigated for metabolic disorders). As with classical cystinuria there is allelic variation in that some subjects have intestinal involvement and some do not, while heterozygotes in some pedigrees but not others excrete increased amounts of glycine. The estimated incidence is 1 : 20 000 (Levy 1973).

Isolated *glycinuria* has been described in asymptomatic patients in whom it appears to behave as a dominantly inherited characteristic (de Vries *et al.* 1957). In a single family, glycinuria was associated with calcium oxalate stone formation, but the nature of this association is obscure. As mentioned in the previous paragraph, some obligate heterozygotes for iminoglycinuria have isolated glycinuria, and it may be that others identified as 'dominant' glycinuria are in fact heterozygotes for iminoglycinuria in families in which homozygosity has not occurred.

Glucoglycinuria, the combination of renal glycosuria and glycinuria without iminoglycinuria, has been described in 13 members of a large pedigree (Käser *et al.* 1962) in which it behaved in a dominant fashion (but the same reservation may apply as in isolated glycinuria, see previous paragraph). All members of the family who were tested had either glycosuria and glycinuria or neither, indicating either a common transport defect or two defects that are genetically very closely linked.

Dicarboxylic aminoaciduria

Two unrelated patients have been described with greatly increased urinary excretion of aspartic and glutamic acids (Teijama *et al.* 1974; Melancon *et al.* 1977). One was male and one female, and the parents of both showed no aminoaciduria, which suggests recessive inheritance. One patient was mentally retarded and hypothyroid while the other was normal. The relation of the aminoaciduria to the abnormalities in the retarded patient is unknown.

The Fanconi syndrome

Many diseases cause defective proximal tubular transport of most or all of the solutes normally reabsorbed there. The result is the Fanconi syndrome (De Toni-Debré–Fanconi syndrome). The substances excreted in excess are numerous and are listed in Table 13.1.2.

Pathogenesis

Several explanations for the Fanconi syndrome are theoretically possible. They include:

(1) generalized disturbance of apical membrane function, with consequent impairment of brush-border membrane transporters;
(2) leakiness of the apical membrane with back-diffusion of reabsorbed solutes;

Table 13.1.2 Substances excreted to excess in the urine in the Fanconi syndrome

Amino acids (all)
Glucose
Phosphate
Bicarbonate
Uric acid
Calcium
Magnesium
Citrate
Sodium
Potassium
Low molecular-weight proteins

(3) defective Na extrusion at the basolateral membrane, attenuating the lumen-to-cell interior Na gradient that energizes solute entry;

(4) leakiness of the basolateral membrane with excessive Na entry from the peritubular side;

(5) defective energy generation or coupling of energy production to Na-K exchange.

Little evidence is available in human patients as to which of these is responsible, or indeed whether the same mechanism is operating in patients with the Fanconi syndrome due to different underlying diseases. One patient has been described with total lack of the proximal, tubular, brush-border membrane and (not surprisingly) very severe Fanconi syndrome (Manz *et al.* 1984). In two extensively studied animal models of the syndrome, induced by maleic acid (Berliner *et al.* 1950) and cadmium (Bonnell *et al.* 1960) respectively, the evidence favours interference with the supply of energy to Na, K-ATPase (Schärer *et al.* 1972; Gonick *et al.* 1980; Pacanis *et al.* 1981). It is likely, though unproven, that the Fanconi syndromes due to inborn errors of metabolism and the accumulation of abnormal substances within the proximal tubular cells are due to a similar process.

The cause of hypokalaemia in the Fanconi syndrome

The impaired proximal tubular Na reabsorption that is a central feature of the Fanconi syndrome has two consequences that combine to cause secondary K loss. The first is a tendency to renal salt wasting (Houston *et al.* 1968), leading to chronic, extracellular fluid volume contraction and stimulation of the renin–angiotensin–aldosterone system. The second is increased Na delivery to distal nephron segments, including the cortical collecting duct which is the principal site of K secretion (Sebastian *et al.* 1971). The driving force for K secretion is the lumen-negative voltage generated by Na reabsorption. This is both load dependent, and therefore stimulated by increased distal Na delivery, and aldosterone sensitive, and therefore further increased by hyperaldosteronism. A third possible factor is the increased distal delivery of bicarbonate, a less permeant anion than the chloride which normally accompanies Na in the distal nephron (Giebisch and Stanton 1979). K wasting may be gross, amounting in some cases to a fractional K excretion greater than 1, i.e. more K is excreted than is filtered at the glomerulus (Brodehl *et al.* 1965).

Causes

The causes of the Fanconi syndrome can be divided into three main groups:

(1) idiopathic or primary Fanconi syndrome;

(2) inborn errors of metabolism;

(3) acquired diseases.

These are listed in Table 13.1.3.

Clinical features

The clinical presentation of the Fanconi syndrome depends partly on its cause and on the age of onset.

Onset in infancy and childhood

Most infants and children with the Fanconi syndrome have inborn errors of metabolism. By far the commonest of these is cystinosis, which is described in more detail in Chapter 17. Typically,

Table 13.1.3   Causes of the Fanconi syndrome

A. Hereditary causes
    Primary familial Fanconi syndrome
    Inborn errors of metabolism
        Cystinosis
        Lowe's syndrome
        Hereditary fructose intolerance
        Galactosaemia
        Tyrosinaemia type 1 (tyrosinosis)
        Glycogen storage disease
        Wilson's disease

B. Acquired diseases
    Multiple myeloma
    Other paraproteinaemias
    Amyloidosis
    Sjögren's syndrome
    Interstitial nephritis
    Drugs
        Outdated tetracycline
        Sodium valproate
        Aminoglycosides
    Heavy metals
        Cadmium
        Lead
        Mercury
        Cis-platinum
    Other poisons
        Toluene (solvent inhalation)
        Paraquat
    Balkan nephropathy
    Vitamin D deficiency rickets
    Vitamin D dependency rickets

children with cystinosis present at about six months of age with failure to thrive, anorexia and vomiting, polyuria and polydipsia, rickets, and metabolic acidosis. Growth failure is severe even while glomerular filtration rate is normal or only slightly reduced. Examination of blood and urine samples reveals typical findings of the Fanconi syndrome (see below). The evolution of the tubulopathy of Lowe's syndrome (Lowe *et al.* 1950) is similar to that of cystinosis but more variable in severity. In both cystinosis and Lowe's syndrome the Fanconi syndrome becomes spontaneously less severe as progressive glomerular insufficiency supervenes in later childhood (the evolution of cystinosis is currently being modified by cysteamine treatment, which slows the progression of renal insufficiency). The Fanconi syndrome seen in hereditary fructose intolerance and galactosaemia resolves when the diagnosis is made and the offending food (fructose or galactose) is removed from the diet. However, it may recur if these sugars are reintroduced into the diet, within minutes or hours in the case of fructose intolerance and days in that of galactosaemia. Similarly, the Fanconi syndrome of type 1 tyrosinaemia is reversible following the introduction of a diet low in phenylalanine and tyrosine (Halvorsen *et al.* 1966).

Unfortunately, affected individuals usually succumb eventually to non-renal manifestations of the disease.

The Fanconi syndrome is a feature of Wilson's disease, although eclipsed in importance by liver and neurological involvement. It appears much later than in cystinosis, typically during the second decade, and is commonly identified during investigation of a patient presenting with unexplained liver or nervous system disease. It is completely reversible on treatment with D-penicillamine (Elsas *et al.* 1971).

Onset in adult life

Acquired renal diseases account for most adults presenting with the Fanconi syndrome. The commonest of these is multiple myeloma (Wallis and Engle 1957). The tubulopathy associated with myeloma is gradual in onset, the first detectable features usually being asymptomatic glycosuria and/or aminoaciduria. Progression to a full-blown Fanconi syndrome occurs over months or years. Other paraproteinaemias, such as light chain nephropathy and amyloidosis, may behave in a similar manner. In patients in whom growth is already complete, failure to thrive is by definition not a feature. Polyuria, dehydration, muscle weakness due to electrolyte depletion (especially K), and progressive osteomalacic bone disease are the predominant signs and symptoms.

Autoimmune (interstitial nephritis) or alloimmune (graft rejection) injury to the kidney may cause the Fanconi syndrome, although acute deterioration of glomerular function is usually more prominent. In these conditions the syndrome is usually a biochemical finding without clinical manifestations, promptly reversed by immunosuppressive therapy.

Toxic nephropathies often show features of the Fanconi syndrome, whether due to drugs or environmental hazards such as cadmium and lead. The severity of the disease and the degree to which it is reversible depend on the dose and duration of exposure to the relevant poison and the availability of antidotes (e.g. chelating agents in heavy-metal poisoning). Chronic intoxications may cause permanent damage that is not reversed when the toxic agent is withdrawn.

Diagnosis

The diagnosis of the Fanconi syndrome is established by the presence of characteristic blood and urine abnormalities. Generalized *aminoaciduria* is present; chromatographic analysis of the pattern of amino acid excretion is essential to avoid confusion with more specific aminoacidurias such as Hartnup disease. Renal *glycosuria* (i.e. glycosuria at normal blood glucose concentrations) is found. *Hypophosphataemic rickets* is an important feature. As in familial X-linked hypophosphataemic rickets, phosphaturia is present at plasma concentrations at which the urine would normally be phosphate free. This is best documented by calculating the *theoretical phosphate threshold*, abbreviated as TmP/GFR (see Fig. 13.1.3). TmP/GFR is calculated as:

$$\text{TmP/GFR} = P_P \times \left(\frac{U_P \times P_C}{U_C} \right)$$

where U and P are urine and plasma concentrations respectively and the subscripts P and C are phosphate and creatinine.

Proximal renal tubular acidosis (PRTA) is defined as hyperchloraemic metabolic acidosis with normal ability to acidify the urine. The cause is proximal tubular bicarbonate wasting due to a low renal bicarbonate threshold. Characteristic findings include the ability to lower urinary pH to <5.4 under acid loading, and massive bicarbonate wasting at normal plasma bicarbonate concentrations. The simplest (and kindest) way to confirm the diagnosis of PRTA is to administer bicarbonate, either orally or intravenously, until the plasma bicarbonate is normal (24–27 mmol/L depending on age), and then to measure the fractional excretion of filtered bicarbonate (FE_{BIC}):

$$FE_{BIC}(\%) = \frac{U:P_{BIC}}{U:P_C} \times 100$$

where $U:P$ represents the urine-to-plasma concentration ratio and the subscripts BIC and C are bicarbonate and creatinine respectively. Alternatively:

$$FE_{BIC}(\%) = \frac{U_{BIC} \times P_C}{U_C \times P_{BIC}} \times 100$$

In normal subjects and those with classical (distal) RTA the value is <3%; in PRTA it is much higher, typically 5–15%. *Hypokalaemia* can be shown to be of renal origin merely by finding measurable amounts of K in the urine when the plasma concentration is below the normal range. *Hypouricaemia*, *hypercalciuria*, and variable *polyuria* and *polydipsia* are also present.

Treatment

General

Not all the biochemical abnormalities of the Fanconi syndrome require treatment. For example, the aminoaciduria and glycosuria are not of nutritional significance and need no specific attention. Hypophosphataemia should be treated with oral supplements of neutral phosphate in an initial dose of 10–50 mg/kg/day, adjusted according to response. The limiting factor is usually diarrhoea. If rickets or osteomalacia is present, a vitamin D preparation such as 1,25-dihydroxycholecalciferol in a dose of 5–10 ng/kg/day should be added. If vitamin D is used, it is essential to monitor the plasma calcium concentration (<2.6 mmol/L) and the urinary calcium excretion rate (<0.1 mmol/kg/day or urine calcium:creatinine ratio <0.7 mmol/mmol). If either of these rises above the normal range the dose should be reduced or the vitamin withdrawn. Acidosis is treated with oral alkali, bicarbonate, or equivalent such as citrate. Because of the low renal bicarbonate threshold, large amounts may be needed, up to 10 mmol/kg/day, given in frequent divided doses (three to five times daily). Because potassium supplementation is also necessary in most cases, it is appropriate to give the alkali wholly or partly as the potassium salt, e.g. potassium citrate or a mixture of sodium and potassium citrate (Scholl's solution). Although urinary salt wasting of some degree is usually present in the Fanconi syndrome, it is probably counter-productive to give formal salt supplements because the resulting volume expansion may actually increase the urinary losses of other solutes (Arant *et al.* 1976). It is sufficient to allow unrestricted access to dietary salt; salt depletion causes salt craving, and affected patients will spontaneously increase their salt intake by an appropriate amount. Likewise, access to drinking water should be unrestricted but it is generally unnecessary to prescribe a high water intake as such.

Prostaglandin synthetase inhibitors such as indomethacin ameliorate many of the features of the Fanconi syndrome, at least when it is due to cystinosis, by increasing fractional reabsorption of glomerular filtrate in the proximal tubule (Haycock *et al.* 1982). Symptomatic relief, especially of polyuria and polydipsia, can be considerable. The role of these drugs, if any, in the Fanconi syndrome due to other causes has not been established.

Specific

When the Fanconi syndrome is due to a treatable metabolic cause, such as fructosaemia, galactosaemia, tyrosinaemia type 1 (dietary manipulation), or Wilson's disease (chelation), treatment will lead to improvement or disappearance of the renal disease. It is, by now, clear that the early institution of cysteamine or phosphocysteamine treatment in cystinosis can delay progression of the Fanconi syndrome, although how completely is still not established; and these drugs are sufficiently unpleasant to take that compliance often limits effectiveness.

References

Arant, B. S., Greifer, I., Edelmann, C. M. Jr., and Spitzer, A. (1976). Effect of chronic salt and water loading on the tubular defects of a child with Fanconi syndrome (cystinosis). *Pediatrics*, **58**, 370–7.

Asatoor, A. M., Lacey, B. W., London, B. R., and Milne, M. D. (1962). Amino acid metabolism in cystinuria. *Clinical Science*, **23**, 285–304.

Berliner, R. W., Kennedy, T. J., and Hilton, J. G. (1950). Effect of maleic acid on renal function. *Proceedings of the Society for Experimental Medicine and Biology*, **75**, 791–4.

Bonnell, J. A., Ross, J. H., and King, E. (1960). Renal lesions in experimental cadmium poisoning. *British Journal of Industrial Medicine*, **17**, 69–80.

Bostrom, H. and Hambraeus, L. (1964). Cystinuria in Sweden. VII. Clinical, histopathological, and medico-sociological aspects of the disease. *Acta Medica Scandinavica*, **175** (Suppl. 411), 1–128.

Brand, E., Cahill, G. H., and Harris, M. M. (1935). Cystinuria. II. The metabolism of cysteine, methionine and glutathione. *Journal of Biological Chemistry*, **109**, 69–83.

Brodehl, J., Hagge, W., and Gellison, K. (1965). Die Veränderungen der Nierenfunktion bei der Cystinose. Teil I: Die Inulin-, PAH- und Elektrolyt-Clearance in verscheidenen Stadien der Erkrankung. *Annales Paediatrici (Basel)*, **205**, 131–54.

Brodehl, J., Gellison, K., and Kowalewski, S. (1967). Isolated cystinuria (without lysine–ornithine–argininuria) in a family with hypocalcemic tetany. *Klinische Wochenschrift*, **45**, 38–40.

Brodehl, J. and Gellison, K. (1968). Endogenous renal transport of free amino acids in infancy and childhood. *Pediatrics*, **42**, 395–404.

Crawhall, J. C., Scowen, E. F., and Watts, R. W. E. (1963). Effects of penicillamine on cystinuria. *British Medical Journal*, **1**, 585–90.

Crawhall, J. C., Scowen, E. F., Thompson, C. J., and Watts, R. W. E. (1967). The renal clearance of amino acids in cystinuria. *Journal of Clinical Investigation*, **46**, 1162–70.

Dent, C. E. and Rose, G. A. (1951). Amino acid metabolism in cystinuria. *Quarterly Journal of Medicine*, **20**, 205–18.

de Vries, A., Kochwa, S., Lazebnik, J., Frank, M., and Djaldetti, M. (1957). Glycinuria, a hereditary disorder associated with nephrolithiasis. *American Journal of Medicine*, **23**, 408–15.

Elsas, L. J., Hayslett, J. P., Spargo, B. H., Durant, J. L., and Rosenberg, L. E. (1971). Wilson's disease with reversible renal tubular dysfunction. *Annals of Internal Medicine*, **75**, 427–33.

Frömter, E. (1982). Electrophysiological analysis of rat renal sugar and amino acid transport. I. Basic phenomena. *Pflügers Archiv.*, **393**, 179–89.

Giebisch, G. and Stanton, B. (1979). Potassium transport in the nephron. *Annual Reviews of Physiology*, **41**, 241–56.

Gonick, H. C., Indraprasit, S., Rosen, V. J., Neustein, H., van de Velde, R., and Raghaven, S. R. V. (1980). Experimental Fanconi syndrome. III. Effect of cadmium on renal tubular function, the ATP-Na-K-ATPase transport system, and the renal tubular ultrastructure. *Mineral and Electrolyte Metabolism*, **3**, 21–35.

Halvorsen, K. and Halvorsen, S. (1963). Hartnup disease. *Pediatrics*, **31**, 29–38.

Halvorsen, S., Pande, H., Loken, A. C., and Gjessing, L. R. (1966). Tyrosinosis. A study of 6 cases. *Archives of Disease in Childhood*, **41**, 238–49.

Hautmann, R., Terhorst, B., Stuhlsatz, H. W., and Lutzeyer, W. (1977). Mercaptopropionylglycine: a progress in cystine stone therapy. *Journal of Urology*, **117**, 628–30.

Haycock, G. B., Al-Dahhan, J., Mak, R. H. K., and Chantler, C. (1982). The effect of indomethacin on clinical progress and renal function in children with cystinosis. *Archives of Disease in Childhood*, **57**, 934–9.

Hellier, M. D., Perrett, D., and Holdsworth, L. E. (1970). Dipeptide absorption in cystinuria. *British Medical Journal*, **4**, 782–3.

Hoffmann, N., Thees, M., and Kinne, R. (1976). Phosphate transport by isolated renal brush border vesicles. *Pflügers Archiv.*, **362**, 147–56.

Hooft, C., Timmermans, J., Snoeck, J., Antener, I., Oyaert, W., and van den Hende, C. (1965). Methionine malabsorption syndrome. *Annals of Pediatrics*, **205**, 73–84.

Houston, I. B., Boichis, H., and Edelmann, C. M. Jr. (1968). Fanconi syndrome with renal sodium wasting and metabolic alkalosis. *American Journal of Medicine*, **44**, 638–46.

Jaeger, P., Portmann, L., Saunders, A., Rosenberg, L. E., and Thier, S. O. (1986). Anticystinuric effects of glutamine and of dietary sodium restriction. *New England Journal of Medicine*, **315**, 1120–3.

Jaffe, I. A., Altmann, K., and Merryman, P. (1964). The antipyridoxine effect of penicillamine in man. *Journal of Clinical Investigation*, **43**, 1869–73.

Joseph, R., Ribierre, M., Job, J-C., and Girault, M. (1958). Maladie familiale asociant des convulsions à début très précoce, une albuminorachie et une hyperaminoacidurie. *Archives Françaises de Pédiatrie*, **15**, 374–87.

Käser, H., Cottier, P., and Antener, I. (1962). Glucoglycinuria, a new familial syndrome. *Journal of Pediatrics*, **61**, 386–94.

Kinne, R., Murer, H., and Kinne-Saffran, E. (1975). Sugar transport by renal plasma membrane vesicles. Characterisation of the systems in the brush-border microvilli and basal-lateral membranes. *Journal of Membrane Biology*, **21**, 375–95.

Lester, F. T. and Cusworth, D. C. (1973). Lysine infusion in cystinuria: theoretical renal thresholds for lysine. *Clinical Science*, **44**, 99–111.

Levy, H. L. (1973). Genetic screening. In: *Progress in human genetics* (ed. H. Herns and K. Hirschorn), vol. 4, pp. 1–104. Plenum Press, New York.

Lowe, C. U., Terrey, M., and McLachlan, E. (1950). Organic aciduria, decreased renal ammonia production, hydrophthalmus, and mental retardation. *American Journal of Diseases of Children*, **83**, 164–84.

Manz, F., Waldherr, R., Fritz, H. P., Lutz, P., Nützenadel, W., Reitter, B., *et al.* (1984). Idiopathic de Toni–Debré–Fanconi syndrome with absence of proximal tubular brush border. *Clinical Nephrology*, **22**, 149–57.

Melancon, S. B., Dallaire, L., Lemieux, B., Robitaille, P., and Potier, M. (1977). Dicarboxylic aminoaciduria: an inborn error of amino acid conservation. *Journal of Pediatrics*, **91**, 422–7.

Milne, M. D., Crawford, M. A., Girao, C. B., and Loughbridge, L. (1960). The metabolic disorder in Hartnup disease. *Quarterly Journal of Medicine*, **29**, 407–21.

Milne, M. D., Asatoor, A. M., Edwards, K. D. G., and Loughridge, L. W. (1961). The intestinal absorption defect in cystinuria. *Gut*, **2**, 323–37.

Omura, K., *et al.* (1976). Lysine malabsorption syndrome: a new type transport defect. *Pediatrics*, **57**, 102–5.

Pacanis, A., Strzelecki, T., and Rogulski, J. (1981). Effects of maleate on the content of CoA and its derivatives in rat kidney mitochondria. *Journal of Biological Chemistry*, **256**, 13035–8.

Perheentupa, J. and Visakorpi, J. K. (1965). Protein intolerance with deficiency transport of basic amino acids: another inborn error of metabolism. *Lancet*, **2**, 813–16.

Procopis, P. G. and Turner, B. (1971). Iminoaciduria: a benign renal tubular defect. *Journal of Pediatrics*, **79**, 419–22.

Rajantie, J., Simell, O., Rapola, J., and Perheentupa, J. (1980). Lysinuric protein intolerance: a two-year trial of dietary supplementation therapy with citrulline and lysine. *Journal of Pediatrics*, **97**, 927–32.

Robson, E. B. and Rose, G. A. (1957). The effects of intravenous lysine on the renal clearances of cystine, arginine, and ornithine in normal subjects, in patients with cystinuria and their relatives. *Clinical Science*, **16**, 75–91.

Rosenberg, L. E., Downing, S., Durant, J. L., and Segal, S. (1966). Cystinuria: biochemical evidence for three genetically distinct diseases. *Journal of Clinical Investigation*, **45**, 365–71.

Schärer K., Yoshida, T., Voyer, L., Berlan, S., Pietra, G., and Metcoff, J. (1972). Impaired renal gluconeogenesis and energy metabolism in maleic acid induced-nephropathy in rats. *Research in Experimental Medicine*, **157**, 136–52.

Sebastian, A., McSherry, E., and Morris, R. C. (1971). On the mechanism of renal potassium wasting in renal tubular acidosis associated with the Fanconi syndrome (type 2 RTA). *Journal of Clinical Investigation*, **50**, 231–3.

Seifter, J. L. and Aronson, P. S. (1986). Properties and physiologic roles of the plasma membrane sodium-hydrogen exchanger. *Journal of Clinical Investigation*, **78**, 859–64.

Smith, A. J. and Strang, L. B. (1958). An inborn error of metabolism with the urinary excretion of alpha-hydroxybutyric acid and phenylpyruvic acid. *Archives of Disease in Childhood*, **33**, 109–13.

Teijema, H. L., van Gelderen, H. H., Geisberts, M. A. H., and Laurent de Angulo, M. S. L. (1974). Dicarboxylic aminoaciduria: an inborn error of glutamate and aspartate transport with metabolic implications, in combination with a hyperprolinemia. *Metabolism*, **23**, 115–23.

Thalhammer, O. (1975). Frequency of inborn errors of metabolism, especially PKU, in some representative screening centers around the world: a collaborative study. *Humangenetik*, **30**, 273–86.

Wallis, L. A. and Engle, R. L. (1957). The adult Fanconi syndrome. II. Review of eighteen cases. *American Journal of Medicine*, **22**, 13–23.

Whelan, D. T. and Scriver, C. R. (1968). Hyperdibasic-aminoaciduria: an inherited disorder of amino acid transport. *Pediatric Research*, **2**, 525–39.

13.2

Nephrogenic diabetes insipidus

Daniel G. Bichet

Introduction

Diabetes insipidus is a disorder characterized by the excretion of abnormally large volumes (>30 ml/kg of body weight/day, for adult subjects) of dilute urine (<250 osmoles per kilogram). Three basic defects can be involved. The most common, a deficient secretion of the antidiuretic hormone arginine-vasopressin (AVP), is referred to as neurogenic (or central, or hypothalamic) diabetes insipidus. Diabetes insipidus can also result from renal insensitivity to the antidiuretic effect of AVP which is referred to as nephrogenic diabetes insipidus. Finally, excessive water intake can result in polyuria, which is referred to as primary polydipsia.

The identification, characterization, and mutational analysis of two different genes, namely, the arginine-vasopressin receptor 2 gene (*AVPR2*), and the vasopressin-sensitive water channel gene (aquaporin-2, *AQP2*), provide the basis for the understanding of two different hereditary forms of nephrogenic diabetes insipidus, X-linked nephrogenic diabetes insipidus, and autosomal recessive nephrogenic diabetes insipidus. These advances provide diagnostic tools for physicians caring for these patients.

Genes involved in nephrogenic diabetes insipidus

The first step in the action of the antidiuretic hormone, arginine-vasopressin (AVP), on water excretion is its binding to arginine-vasopressin type 2 receptors (V_2 receptors) on the basolateral membrane of the collecting duct cells (Fig. 13.2.1). The human V_2 receptor gene, *AVPR2*, is located in chromosome region Xq28 and has three exons and two small introns (Birnbaumer *et al.* 1992; Seibold *et al.* 1992). The sequence of the cDNA predicts a polypeptide of 371 amino acids with a structure typical of guanine-nucleotide (G) protein-coupled receptors with seven transmembrane, four extracellular, and four cytoplasmic domains (Watson and Arkinstall 1994; see also Fig. 13.2.2). The activation of the V_2 receptor on renal collecting tubules stimulates adenylyl cyclase via the stimulatory G protein (G_s) and promotes the cyclic AMP-mediated incorporation of water pores into the luminal surface of these cells (Fig. 13.2.1). This is the molecular basis of the vasopressin-induced increase in the osmotic water permeability of the apical membrane of the collecting tubule.

The gene that codes for the water channel of the apical membrane of the kidney-collecting tubule has been designated aquaporin-2 (*AQP2*) and was cloned by homology to the rat aquaporin of collecting duct (Fushimi *et al.* 1993; Deen *et al.* 1994a; Sasaki *et al.* 1994). The human *AQP2* gene is located in chromosome region 12q13 and has four exons and three introns (Deen *et al.* 1994a,b; Sasaki *et al.* 1994). It is predicted to code for a polypeptide of 271 amino acids which is organized into two repeats oriented at 180° to each other, and which has six

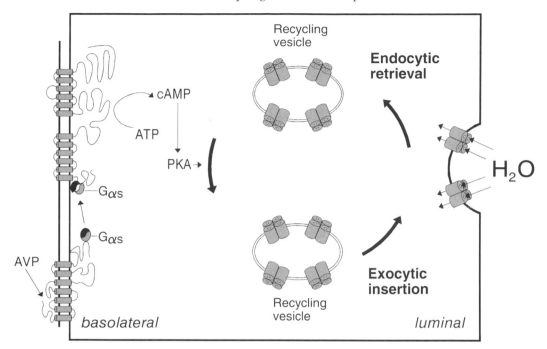

Fig. 13.2.1 Diagrammatic view of the intracellular action of the antidiuretic hormone, arginine vasopressin (AVP). The hormone is bound to the vasopressin V2 receptor (a G-protein-linked receptor with seven transmembrane, four extracellular, and four intracellular domains) on the basolateral membrane. AVP activates adenylate-cyclase increasing the intracellular concentration of cyclic AMP (cAMP). The topology of adenylyl cyclase is characterized by two tandem repeats of six hydrophobic putative transmembrane domains separated by a large cytoplasmic loop and terminating in a large intracellular tail. Cyclic AMP generation follows receptor-linked activation of the heterometric G protein Gs and interaction of the free Gαs-chain with the adenylyl cyclase catalyst. A cyclic AMP-dependent protein kinase (PKA) is the target of the cAMP generated. Cytoplasmic vesicles carrying the water channel proteins (represented as homotetrameric complexes; Agre *et al.* 1993) are fused to the luminal membrane in response to vasopressin, thereby increasing the water permeability of this membrane. When vasopressin is not available, water channels are retrieved by an endocytic process and water permeability returns to its original low rate.

membrane-spanning domains, both terminal ends located intracellularly, and conserved Asn-Pro-Ala boxes (Fig. 13.2.3). These features are characteristic of the major intrinsic protein family (Sasaki *et al.* 1994). There is 48% amino acid sequence identity between *AQP2* and the human channel-forming integral protein of 28 kDa (*CHIP28* or aquaporin-1), a water channel in erythrocytes and the kidney proximal and descending tubules (Agre *et al.* 1993).

X-linked nephrogenic diabetes insipidus

X-linked nephrogenic diabetes insipidus (NDI, designated 304800 in *Mendelian inheritance in man* (McKusick 1990), is a rare disease in which the urine of affected male patients is not concentrated after the administration of AVP.

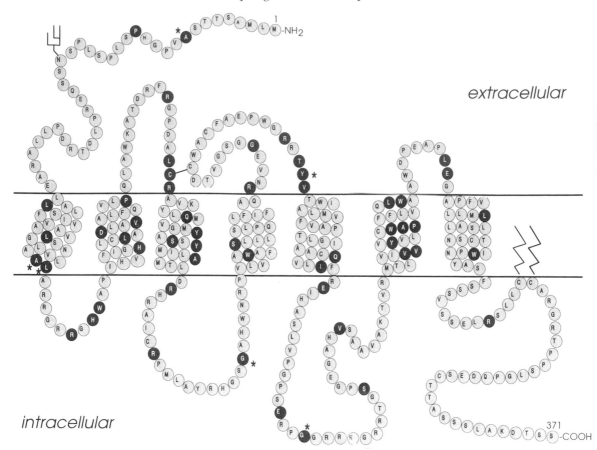

Fig. 13.2.2 Schematic representation of the V_2 receptor showing its proposed topology and identification of 60 *AVPR2* mutations which include 31 missense, 10 nonsense, 16 frameshift, 2 inframe deletion, and 1 splice-site mutations. Also, we have found three large deletions which are incompletely characterized, and are not included in the figure. Predicted amino acids are given in the one-letter code. Solid symbols indicate the predicted location of the mutations; an asterisk indicates different mutations in the same codon. The names of the mutations were assigned following the conventional nomenclature (Beaudet and Tsui 1993). The extracellular (E_I to E_{IV}), cytoplasmic (C_I to C_V) and transmembrane domains (TM_I to TM_{VII}) are labelled according to Sharif and Hanley (1992). E_I: 98del28, 98ins28, 113delCT. TM_I: L44F, L44P, L53R, A61V, L62P. TM_I and C_I: 253del35, 255del9. C_I: 274insG, W71X. TM_{II}: H80R, L83P, D85N, V88M, P95L. E_{II}: R106C, 402delCT, C112R, R113W. TM_{III}: Q119X, Y124X, S126F, Y128S, A132D. C_{II}: R137H, R143P, 528del7, 528delG. TM_{IV}: W164S, S167L, S167T. E_{III}: R181C, G185C, R202C, T204N, 684delTA, Y205C, V206D. TM_V: Q225X, 753insC. C_{III}: E231X, 763delA, E242X, 804insG, 804delG, 834delA, 855delG. TM_{VI}: V277A, ΔV278, Y280C, W284X, A285P, P286R, P268L, L292P, W293X. E_{IV}: 977delG, 980A$\rightarrow$G. TM_{VII}: L312X, W323R. C_{IV}: R337X. For a complete description of the mutations, see references quoted in the text.

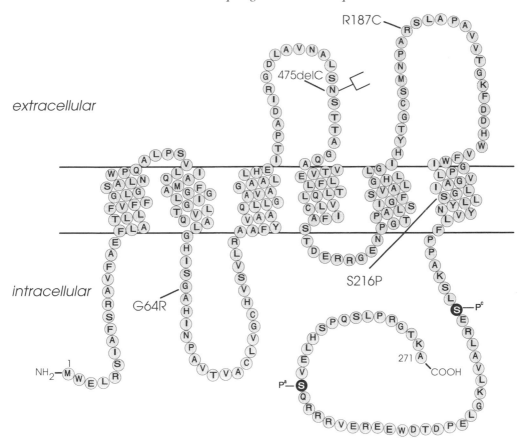

Fig. 13.2.3 Schematic representation of the aquaporin-2 protein showing its proposed topology and the position of 4 *AQP2* mutations (Deen *et al.* 1994; van Lieburg *et al.* 1994).

Clinical characteristics

The 'historical' clinical characteristics include hypernatraemia, hyperthermia, mental retardation, and repeated episodes of dehydration in early infancy (Forssman 1942; Waring *et al.* 1945; Williams and Henry 1947; Crawford and Bode 1975). Mental retardation, a consequence of repeated episodes of dehydration, was prevalent in the Crawford and Bode study (1975), in which only nine of 82 patients (11%) had normal intelligence. Early recognition and treatment of X-linked nephrogenic diabetes insipidus with an abundant intake of water allows a normal lifespan with normal physical and mental development (Niaudet *et al.* 1984; and personal observations). Two characteristics suggestive of X-linked NDI are the familial occurrence and the confinement of mental retardation to male patients. It is therefore tempting to assume that the family described in 1892 by McIlraith (1892) and discussed by Reeves and Andreoli (1989) was an X-linked NDI family. Lacombe (1841) and Weil (1884) described a familial form of diabetes insipidus with an autosomal type of transmission and without any associated mental retardation. The descendants of the family originally described by Weil were later found to have autosomal dominant neurogenic diabetes insipidus (Weil 1908; Camerer 1935; Dölle 1951), a now well-characterized entity secondary to mutations in the prepro–arginine–vasopressin–neurophysin II gene (*prepro-AVP-NPII*) (Ito *et al.* 1991; Bahnsen *et al.* 1992; Krishnamani *et al.* 1993; McLeod *et al.* 1993; Miller 1993; Yuasa *et al.* 1993; Repaske and Browning 1994). Patients with autosomal dominant neurogenic diabetes insipidus retain some limited capacity to secrete AVP during severe dehydration, and the polyuro-polydipsic symptoms usually appear after the first year of life (Pedersen *et al.* 1985) when the infant's demand for water is more likely to be understood by adults.

The early symptomatology of the nephrogenic disorder and its severity in infancy is clearly described by Crawford and Bode (1975). The first manifestations of the disease can be recognized during the first week of life. The infants are irritable, cry almost constantly, and, although eager to suck, will vomit milk soon after ingestion unless prefed with water. The histories given by the mothers often include persistent constipation, erratic, unexplained fever, and failure to gain weight. Even though the patients characteristically show no visible evidence of perspiration, increased water loss during fever or in warm weather exaggerates the symptoms. Unless the condition is recognized early, children will experience frequent bouts of hypertonic dehydration, sometimes complicated by convulsions or death; mental retardation is frequently a consequence of these episodes. The intake of large quantities of water, combined with the patient's voluntary restriction of dietary salt and protein intake, lead to hypocaloric dwarfism beginning in infancy. Affected children frequently develop lower urinary tract dilatation and obstruction, probably secondary to the large volume of urine produced (Streitz and Streitz 1988). Dilatation of the lower urinary tract is also seen in primary polydipsic patients and in patients with neurogenic diabetes insipidus (Boyd *et al.* 1980; Gauthier *et al.* 1981). Chronic renal insufficiency may occur by the end of the first decade of life and could be the result of episodes of dehydration with thrombosis of the glomerular tufts (Crawford and Bode 1975).

Genetics and history: the Hopewell hypothesis

Four 'classical' families with X-linked nephrogenic diabetes insipidus have been described (Forssman 1942, 1975; Williams and Henry 1947; Cannon 1955). Bode and Crawford (1969) studied a large, extended kindred with X-linked nephrogenic diabetes insipidus and described the history and folklore of 'the water drinker's curse':

A Gypsy woman and her son were travelling the road and became thirsty. Pausing at the well in front of the next house, the Gypsy requested water for her son: the housewife refused, whereupon the Gypsy woman cast upon her a curse. Henceforth, the story goes, all the women's sons would be afflicted with a craving for water. The curse would be passed on by her daughters and visited upon their sons for generations to come.

On the basis of their genealogical reconstructions, Bode and Crawford proposed 'the Hopewell hypothesis'; that is, most cases of X-linked NDI in North America could be traced to descendants of Ulster Scots who arrived in Nova Scotia in 1761 on the ship *Hopewell*.

We have re-examined the Hopewell hypothesis by genealogical, haplotype, and mutational analysis of many North American families with X-linked NDI (Bichet *et al.* 1992, 1993, 1994). We have demonstrated the independent origin of NDI among these families. The W71X mutation (the Hopewell mutation) was identified in 64 individuals, the largest known number of NDI patients and carriers in North America who share a V_2 receptor mutation (*vide infra*) identical by descent. Most of the patients with this mutation reside predominantly in two villages with a total population size of about 2500; a prevalence of 24/1000 males was calculated in these well-defined communities as compared to a prevalence of 4/1 000 000 males in the province of Quebec (Bichet *et al.* 1992).

Mutations in the V₂ receptor gene (*AVPR2*) are the molecular basis of X-linked NDI

In 1989, we observed that the administration of 1-desamino[8-D-arginine] vasopressin (*dDAVP*), a V₂ receptor agonist, increased plasma cyclic AMP concentrations in normal subjects but had no effect in 14 male patients with X-linked NDI (Bichet *et al.* 1989). Intermediate responses were observed in obligate carriers of the disease, possibly corresponding to half of the normal receptor response. Based on these results, we predicted that the defective gene in these patients with X-linked NDI was likely to code for a defective V₂ receptor (Bichet *et al.* 1989). Since that time, a number of experimental results have confirmed our hypothesis:

(1) the NDI locus was mapped to the distal region of the long arm of the X chromosome, Xq28 (Kambouris *et al.* 1988; Knoers *et al.* 1989; Bichet *et al.* 1992; van Den Ouweland 1992*b*);
(2) the V₂ receptor was identified as a candidate gene for NDI (Jans *et al.* 1990);
(3) the human V₂ receptor was cloned (Birnbaumer *et al.* 1992);
(4) 60 putative disease-causing mutations have been identified in the V₂ receptor in 95 unrelated X-linked NDI families (Pan *et al.* 1992, 1994; Rosenthal *et al.* 1992; van Den Ouweland 1992*a*; Bichet *et al.* 1993, 1994; Holtzman *et al.* 1993*a,b*, 1994; Merendino *et al.* 1993; Tsukaguchi *et al.* 1993; Faà *et al.* 1994; Friedman *et al.* 1994; Knoers *et al.* 1994; Wenkert *et al.* 1994; Wildin *et al.* 1994; Yuasa *et al.* 1994; Oksche *et al.* 1995).

It can be estimated that approximately one-third of the new cases of affected males will be due to new mutations and, indeed, several *de novo* mutations have now been documented (Pan *et al.* 1992; Bichet *et al.* 1994; Knoers *et al.* 1994; Wildin *et al.* 1994).

There is evidence of hot spots for mutations within the V₂ receptor. Firstly, 11 mutations were observed in more than one independent NDI family and, secondly, the same recurrent mutation occurred on different haplotypes defined by markers within or close to the *AVPR2* gene (Bichet *et al.* 1994; Knoers *et al.* 1994). Sixty-four per cent of these recurrent mutations were single nucleotide substitutions at a CpG dinucleotide which are known mutation hot spots (Cooper and Krawczak 1993). In addition, over two-thirds of the several small deletion or insertion mutations (from 1 to 35 bp) involved direct or complementary repeats or runs of up to six guanines. These deletions or insertions most probably resulted from DNA strand slippage and mispairing during replication (Krawczak and Cooper 1991; Sinden and Wells 1992; Kooper and Krawczak 1993; Eng *et al.* 1993).

It is of some interest that the mutations are scattered throughout the V₂ receptor sequence, being found in all domains including the extracellular and intracellular tails, each of the seven transmembrane spanning regions, and each of the extracellular and intracellular loops (Fig. 13.2.2). Study of the naturally occurring mutations will be extremely helpful in pinpointing critical functional regions of the molecule. Mutations leading to significantly truncated polypeptides will yield non-functional receptors—in most cases the protein will not be efficiently targeted to the plasma membrane. Missense mutations could cause misfolding of the protein and trapping in the endoplasmic reticulum, or could alter formation of the binding pocket or disrupt the contact sites with the G$_s$ protein. In a few cases, the functional consequences of particular mutations have already been assessed by expression of V₂ receptor cDNA in cultured mammalian cells. For example, it was shown that the R137H mutant receptor expressed in kidney cells exhibited a normal binding affinity for AVP but failed to stimulate the G_s/adenylyl cyclase system (Rosenthal *et al.* 1993). The R113W mutant protein exhibited a combination of functional defects, including a lowered affinity for vasopressin, a diminished ability to stimulate adenylyl cyclase, together with a diminished ability to reach the cell surface (Birnbaumer *et al.* 1994). No adenylyl cyclase activity was detected in COS cells transfected with cDNAs having either a nonsense mutation (Q119X), frameshift mutations (763delA or 855delG), or missense mutations (Y128S, R181C, P286R) (Pan *et al.* 1994). In addition, functional analysis of *AVPR2* mutations provided evidence that the 810del12 mutation is not the cause of NDI in a patient who had this mutation as well as the R181C mutation (Pan *et al.* 1994). The R181C mutant receptor had less than half of the normal adenylyl cyclase activity, and although it was expressed at the same level as the normal V_2 receptor, the EC_{50} for adenylyl cyclase stimulation was increased, presumably due to its altered structure. The A61V mutation did not affect vasopressin binding or stimulation of adenylyl cyclase activity. It was concluded that this mutation is not the cause of the nephrogenic diabetes insipidus in this patient but rather is a rare polymorphism. In patients with indisputable nephrogenic diabetes (as assessed with precise phenotypic testing) and no mutations in *AVPR2*, several hypotheses could be considered:

(1) the mutation could have been 'missed' by the technique(s) used;
(2) a mutation could affect the promoter region of the *AVPR2* gene;
(3) in isolated cases, or patient with non-X-linked inheritance, mutations in *AQP2* are now described (Deen *et al.* 1994*a*, van Lieburg *et al.* 1994);
(4) finally, other unknown genes important for vasopressin-regulated water transport across the kidney-collecting tubule could be involved.

Carrier detection and perinatal testing

We are encouraging physicians following other families with X-linked NDI to recommend mutational analysis well before the birth of an at-risk male infant since early diagnosis and treatment of male infants affected with NDI can avert the physical and mental retardation associated with the episodes of dehydration. We are investigating new families through two approaches: mutational analysis of the *AVPR2* gene by sequencing of the entire gene, and Xq28 analysis. In our experience (Bichet, unpublished data), a mutation has been identified in every patient with a clinical diagnosis of X-linked NDI and abnormal renal and extrarenal V_2 receptor responses (Bichet *et al.* 1988). We have done prenatal testing (Bichet *et al.* 1992) and diagnosis within 48 hours after birth by obtaining blood from the cord immediately after delivery and before placental extraction.

Diagnosis

If the mutational analysis of a specific family is already known and segregates with the observed phenotype, the molecular diagnosis of affected male infants should be done during the first week of life and only confirmed with measurements of urinary osmolality and plasma sodium concentration. Later on, at six months of age or later, dDAVP administration (1 µg s.c.) can confirm the collecting duct resistance to exogenous AVP. Short dehydration tests are technically difficult in very young infants and great care should be taken to avoid any severe hypertonic state, arbitrarily defined as a plasma sodium >150 mEq/L. In my experience, the phenotypic characteristics are so obvious (a male with polyuria polydipsia, PNa ≈ 150 mEq/L with a urinary osmolality

<200 mmol/kg/H$_2$O unchanged after dDAVP administration) that these short dehydration tests are unnecessary. Normal values for urinary volume rate (relative to body mass) and urinary osmolality in children are indicated in Table 13.2.1. Normal values of the renal concentrating capacity in the fetus and newborn and maximum urinary osmolality values obtained after dDAVP administration are indicated in Table 13.2.2.

The family history of X-linked NDI usually discloses affected male patients and/or males who

Table 13.2.1 Urinary volume rate (relative to body mass) and urinary osmolality in children

Age	Urinary volume rate mL D^{-1} kg^{-1} (mean ± SD)	Osmolality mmol/kg (mean ± SD)
1st day	8.5 ± 3.5	—
7th day	76 ± 17	—
0–6 months	34 ± 6	462 ± 85
6 months to 1 year	29 ± 12	880 ± 283
1–2 years	25 ± 7	1004 ± 297
2–3 years	33 ± 9	812 ± 215
3–4 years	34 ± 7	808 ± 249
4–5 years	29 ± 10	735 ± 165
5–7 years	25 ± 7	726 ± 338
7–11 years	25 ± 7	711 ± 56
11–14 years	19 ± 3	824 ± 76

From (1981). Units of measurements, body fluids, composition of the body, nutriton. In: *Geigy scientific tables* (8th edn) (ed. C. Lentner), vol. 1, p. 55. Medical Educational Division, Ciba-Geigy Corporation, West Caldwell, New Jersey 07006, USA, with permission.

Table 13.2.2 Normal values of renal concentrating capacity in the fetus and newborn

U$_{osm}$:	
Urine before birth	137 (97–232) mmol/kg
First urine after birth	317 (151–480) mmol/kg
First 48 hours after birth	420 (288–536) mmol/kg
U$_{osm}$/P$_{osm}$:	
First 3 hours after birth	0.98 (0.49–1.49)
Maximum urinary osmolality (deamino-arginine vasopressin test):	
1–3 weeks	385 (350–430) mmol/kg
4–6 weeks	565 (480–630) mmol/kg

From (1981). Units of measurements, body fluids, composition of the body, nutrition. In: *Geigy scientific tables* (8th edn) (ed. C. Lenter), vol. 1, p. 106. Medical Educational Division, Cida-Geigy Corporation, West Caldwell, New Jersey 07006 USA, with permission.

died early in life with polyuric and polydipsic symptoms. However, several generations may have passed since the birth of the last affected male and a 'sporadic' case may then be diagnosed. In addition, a significant proportion of X-linked NDI families bear *de novo* mutations and the proband may be the first affected male (Pan *et al.* 1992; Bichet *et al.* 1994; Knoers *et al.* 1994; Wildin *et al.* 1994). As a consequence, the absence of family history of X-linked NDI does not rule out the disease, and DNA of sporadic patients and their mothers should be analysed for *AVPR2* mutations.

Treatment

The treatment of congenital nephrogenic diabetes insipidus has been recently reviewed (Knoers and Monnens 1992). An abundant, unrestricted water intake should always be provided and affected male patients should be carefully followed during their first years of life (Niaudet *et al.* 1984). Water should be offered every two hours day and night, and temperature, appetite, and growth should be monitored. The parents of these children easily accept setting their alarm clock every two hours during the night! Hospital admision may be necessary to allow continuous gastric feeding. A low osmolar and sodium diet, hydrochlorothiazide (1–2 mg/kg/day) and indomethacin (0.75–1.5 mg/kg) substantially reduce water excretion (Blalock *et al.* 1977; Alon and Chan 1985; Libber *et al.* 1986) and are helpful in the treatment of children. Many adult patients receive no treatment.

Autosomal recessive nephrogenic diabetes insipidus and mutations in the *AQP2* gene

On the basis of (1) phenotypic characteristics of both males and females affected with NDI, and (2) on dDAVP infusion studies, a non-X-linked form of NDI with a postreceptor defect was suggested (Brenner *et al.* 1988; Knoers and Monnens 1991; Langley *et al.* 1991; Lonergan *et al.* 1993). In contrast to male patients affected with X-linked NDI (Bichet *et al.* 1988, 1989), the plasma concentrations of factor VIII and von Willebrand factor rose normally, two- threefold, whereas urinary osmolality remained low in two male and two female NDI patients after dDAVP infusion (Brenner *et al.* 1988). X-linked NDI was excluded for two sisters with vasopressin-resistant hypotonicity because they inheritied different alleles of an Xq28 marker from their mother; autosomal recessive inheritance was suggested on the basis of the gender of the patients, parental consanguinity, and normal urine concentration in the parents (Langley *et al.* 1991). Two male patients were described with normal stimulation of plasma cyclic-AMP after dDAVP administration in whom no *AVPR2* mutation was identified (Lonergan *et al.* 1993). A patient who presented shortly after birth with typical features of NDI but showed normal coagulation, fibrinolytic, and vasodilatory responses to dDAVP has recently been shown to be a compound heterozygote for two missense mutations (R187C and S217P) in the *AQP2* gene (Knoers *et al.* 1991; Deen *et al.* 1994; Fig. 13.2.3). Three NDI patients from consanguineous matings were found to be homozygous for missense mutations (R187C or G64R) or a frameshift mutation (369delC) in the *AQP2* gene. Functional expression studies showed that *Xenopus* oocytes injected with mutant cRNA had abnormal coefficients of water permeability while *Xenopus* oocytes injected with both mutant and normal cRNAs had coefficients of water permeability similar to that of normal constructs alone (Deen *et al.* 1994; van Lieburg *et al.* 1994). These findings provide conclusive evidence that NDI can be caused by homozygosity for mutations in the *AQP2* gene. The observation of increased frequency of consanguinity between normal parents of

Table 13.2.3 Differential diagnosis of congenital NDI

1. Provide an abundant, unrestricted water intake in very young infants with a presumptive diagnosis of congenital NDI.

2. Obtain a family history. If classical X-linked inheritance and affected males with vasopressin resistance are already known, proceed to a minimal phenotypic evaluation and to a mutational analysis of the *AVPR2* gene.

3. Phenotypic criteria: plasma osmolality $\geq$300 mmol/kg, plasma sodium $\geq$147 mEq/L, urinary osmolality <200 mmol/kg unchanged after 1 μg s.c. of dDAVP (collect and measure U_{osm} every 30 min. during 120 min. after dDAVP administration).

4. In the absence of family history, suspect a *de novo AVPR2* mutation (abnormal *AVPR2* sequencing result) or a (rare) non-X-linked diabetes insipidus case (normal *AVPR2* gene, possibly of mutation(s) in *AQP2*).

5. Dehydration tests and Pitressin administration are unwarranted.

affected children with *AQP2* mutations is consitent with autosomal recessive inheritance of a rare genetic disease. The clinical characteristics, in particular the early dehydration episodes, seem to be identical in X-linked and autosomal recessive nephrogenic diabetes insipidus. The treatment of both entities in similar.

Recommendations

For a full account of the recommendations in the differential diagnosis of congenitial NDI, see Table 13.2.3.

Acknowledgements

I would like to thank Michèle Lonergan, Marie-Françoise Arthus, Geoffrey Hendy, Mary Fujiwara, Kenneth Morgan, Walter Rosental, and Mariel Birnbaumer for their important contributions to these studies and Danielle Binette for her help in preparing the manuscript.

References

Agre, P., *et al.* (1993). Aquaporin CHIP: the archetypal molecular water channel. *American Journal of Physiology*, **265**, F463–76.

Alon, U. and Chan, J. C. (1985). Hydrochlorothiazide-amiloride in the treatment of congenital nephrogenic diabetes insipidus. *American Journal of Nephrology*, **5**, 9–13.

Bahnsen, U., *et al.* (1992). A missense mutation in the vasopressin–neurophysin precursor gene cosegregates with human autosomal dominant neurohypophyseal diabetes insipidus. *EMBO Journal (Oxford)*, **11**, 189–23.

Beaudet, A. L. and Tsui, L. C. (1993). Special feature: a suggested nomenclature for designating mutations. *Hum. Mutat.*, **2**, 245–8.

Bichet, D. G., *et al.* (1988). Hemodynamic and coagulation responses to 1-desamino[8-D-arginine]vasopressin in patients with congenital nephrogenic diabetes insipidus. *New England Journal of Medicine*, **318**, 881–7.

Bichet, D. G., *et al.* (1989). Epinephrine and dDAVP administration in patients with congenital nephrogenic diabetes insipidus. Evidence for a pre-cyclic AMP V₂ receptor defective mechanism. *Kidney International*, **36**, 859–66.

Bichet, D. G., *et al.* (1992). X-linked nephrogenic diabetes insipidus: from the ship *Hopewell* to RFLP studies. *American Journal of Human Genetics*, **51**, 1089–102.

Bichet, D. G., *et al.* (1993). X-linked nephrogenic diabetes insipidus mutations in North America and the Hopewell hypothesis. *Journal of Clinical Investigation*, **92**, 1262–8.

Bichet, D. G., *et al.* (1994). Nature and recurrence of *AVPR2* mutations in X-linked nephrogenic diabetes insipidus. *American Journal of Human Genetics*, **55**, 278–86.

Birnbaumer, M., *et al.* (1992). Molecular cloning of the receptor for human antidiuretic hormone. *Nature*, **357**, 333–5.

Birnbaumer, M., *et al.* (1994). An extracellular CNDI mutation of the vasopressin receptor reduces cell surface expression, affinity for ligand and coupling to the G$_s$/adenylyl cyclase system. *Molecular Endocrinology*, **8**, 886–94.

Blalock, T. J., *et al.* (1977). Role of diet in the management of vasopressin-responsive and -resistant diabetes insipidus. *American Journal of Clinical Nutrition*, **30**, 1070–6.

Bode, H. H. and Crawford, J. D. (1969). Nephrogenic diabetes insipidus in North America. The Hopewell hypothesis. *New England Journal of Medicine*, **280**, 750–4.

Boyd, S. D., *et al.* (1980). Diabetes insipidus and nonobstructive dilation of urinary tract. *Urology*, **26**, 266–9.

Brenner, B., *et al.* (1988). Normal response of factor VIII and von Willebrand factor to 1-deamino-8D-arginine vasopressin in nephrogenic diabetes insipidus. *Journal of Clinical Endocrinology and Metabolism*, **67**, 191–3.

Camerer, J. W. (1935). Eine Ergänzung des Weilschen Diabetes-insipidus-Stammbaumes. *Archiv für Rassen- und Gesellschaftshygiene Biologie*, **28**, 382.

Cannon, J. F. (1955). Diabetes insipidus clinical and experimental studies with consideration of genetic relationships. *Archives of Internal Medicine*, **96**, 215–72.

Cooper, D. N. and Krawczak, M. (1993). *Human gene mutation*. BIOS Scientific Publishers, Oxford.

Crawford, J. D. and Bode, H. H. (1975). Disorders of the posterior pituitary in children. In: *Endocrine and genetic diseases of childhood and adolescence* (2nd edn) (ed. L. I. Gardner), pp. 126–58. W. B. Saunders, Philadelphia.

Deen, P. M. T., *et al.* (1994a). Requirement of human renal water channel aquaporin-2 for vasopressin-dependent concentration of urine. *Science*, **264**, 92–5.

Deen, P. M. T., *et al.* (1994b). Assignment of the human gene for the water channel of renal collecting duct aquaporin 2 (AQP2) to chromosome 12 region q12 → q13. *Cytogenetics and Cell Genetics*, **66**, 260–2.

Dölle, W. (1951). Eine weitere Ergänzung des Weilschen Diabetes-insipidus-Stammbaumes. *Zeitschrift für Menschliche Vererbungs- und Konstitutionslehre*, **30**, 372–4.

Eng, C. M. *et al.* (1993). Nature and frequency of mutations in the α-galactosidase A gene that cause Fabry disease. *American Journal of Human Genetics*, **53**, 1186–97.

Faà, V., *et al.* (1994). Mutations in the vasopressin V2-receptor gene in three families of Italian descent with nephrogenic diabetes insipidus. *Human Molecular Genetics*, **3**, 1685–6.

Forssman, H. (1942). On the mode of heriditary transmission in diabetes insipidus. *Nordisk Medicin*, **16**, 3211–3.

Forssman, H. (1975). Modern medical history. The recognition of nephrogenic diabetes insipidus. *Acta Medica Scandinavica*, **197**, 1–6.

Friedman, E., *et al.* (1994). Nephrogenic diabetes insipidus: An X chromosome-linked dominant inheritance pattern with a vasopressin type 2 receptor gene that is structurally normal. *Proceedings of the National Academy of Sciences USA*, **91**, 8457–61.

Fushimi, K., *et al.* (1993). Cloning and expression of apical membrane water channel of rat kidney-collecting tubule. *Nature*, **361**, 549–52.

Gautier, B., *et al.* (1981). Mégauretère, mégavessie et diabète insipide familial. *Semaine des Hôpitaux de Paris*, **57**, 60–1.

Holtzman, E. J., *et al.* (1993*a*). Brief report: a molecular defect in the vasopressin V2-receptor gene causing nephrogenic diabetes insipidus. *New England Journal of Medicine*, **328**, 1534–7.

Holtzman, E. J., *et al.* (1993*b*). A null mutation in the vasopressin V2 receptor gene (*AVPR2*) associated with nephrogenic diabetes insipidus in the Hopewell kindred. *Human Molecular Genetics*, **2**, 1201–4.

Holtzman, E. J., *et al.* (1994). Mutations in the vasopressin V2 receptor gene in two families with nephrogenic diabetes insipidus. *Journal of the American Society of Nephrology*, **5**, 169–76.

Ito, M., *et al.* (1991). A single-base substitution in the coding region for neurophysin II associated with familial central diabetes insipidus. *Journal of Clinical Investigation*, **87**, 725–8.

Jans, D. A., *et al.* (1990). Derivatives of somatic cell hybrids which carry the human gene locus for nephrogenic diabetes insipidus (NDI) express functional vasopressin renal V$_2$-type receptors. *Journal of Biological Chemistry*, **265**, 15379–82.

Kambouris, M., *et al.* (1988). Localization of the gene for X-linked nephrogenic diabetes insipidus to Xq28. *American Journal of Medical Genetics (New York)*, **29**, 239–46.

Knoers, N., *et al.* (1989). Three-point linkage analysis using multiple DNA polymorphic markers in families with X-linked nephrogenic diabetes insipidus. *Genomics*, **4**, 434–7.

Knoers, N. and Monnens, A. H. (1991). A variant of nephrogenic diabetes insipidus: V$_2$ receptor abnormality restricted to the kidney. *European Journal of Pediatrics (Berlin)*, **150**, 370–3.

Knoers, N. and Monnens, L. A. H. (1992). Nephrogenic diabetes insipidus: clinical symptoms, pathogenesis, genetics and treatment. *Pediatrics Nephrology*, **6**, 476–82.

Knoers, N. V. A. M., *et al.* (1994). Inheritance of mutations in the V$_2$ receptor gene in thirteen families with nephrogenic diabetes insipidus. *Kidney International*, **46**, 170–6.

Krawczak, M. and Cooper, D. N. (1991). Gene deletions causing human genetic disease: mechanisms of mutagenesis and the role of the local sequence environment. *Human Genetics*, **86**, 425–41.

Krishnamani, M. R. S., Phillips III, J. A., and Copeland, K. C. (1993). Detection of a novel arginine vasopressin defect by dideoxy fingerprinting. *Journal of Clinical Endocrinology and Metabolism*, **77**, 596–8.

Lacombe, U. L. (1841). *De la polydipsie*. Thesis of Medicine, No. 99, pp. 1–87. Imprimerie et Fonderie de Rignoux, Paris.

Langley, J. M., *et al.* (1991). Autosomal recessive inheritance of vasopressin-resistant diabetes insipidus. *American Journal of Medical Genetics (New York)*, **38**, 90–4.

Libber, S., Harrison, H., and Spector, D. (1986). Treatment of nephrogenic diabetes insipidus with prostaglandin synthesis inhibitors. *Journal of Pediatrics*, **108**, 305–11.

Lonergan, M., *et al.* (1993). Non-X-linked nephrogenic diabetes insipidus: phenotype and genotype features. *Journal of the American Society of Nephrology*, **4**, 264A.

McIlraith, C. H. (1892). Notes on some cases of diabetes insipidus with marked family and hereditary tendencies. *Lancet*, **2**, 767–8.

McKusick, V. A. (ed.) (1990). Diabetes insipidus renal type I. In: *Mendelian inheritance in man* (9th edn), pp. 1585–90. Johns Hopkins University Press, Baltimore.

McLeod, J. F., *et al.* (1993). Familial neurohypophyseal diabetes insipidus associated with a signal peptide mutation. *Journal of Clinical Endocrinology and Metabolism*, **77**, 599A–599G.

Merendino, J. J., *et al.* (1993). Brief report: a mutation in the vasopressin V2-receptor gene in a kindred with X-linked nephrogenic diabetes insipidus. *New England Journal of Medicine*, **328**, 1538–41.

Miller, W. L. (1993). Molecular genetics of familial central diabetes insipidus (Editorial). *Journal of Clinical Endocrinology Metabolism*, **77**, 592–5.

Niaudet, P., *et al.* (1984). Nephrogenic diabetes insipidus: Clinical and pathophysiological aspects. In: *Advances in nephrology* (ed. J. P. Grünfeld and M. H. Maxwell), vol. 13, pp. 247–60. Year Book Medical Publishers, Chicago.

Oksche, A., *et al.* (1995). Two novel mutations in the vasopressin V2 receptor gene in patients with congenital nephrogenic diabetes insipidus. *Biochemical and Biophysical Research Communications.* In press.

Pan, Y., *et al.* (1992). Mutations in the V2 vasopressin receptor gene are associated with X-linked nephrogenic diabetes insipidus. *Nature Genetics,* **2,** 103–6.

Pan, Y., *et al.* (1994). The effect of eight V2 vasopressin receptor mutations on stimulation of adenylyl cyclase and binding to vasopressin. *Journal of Biological Chemistry,* **269,** 31933–7.

Pedersen, E. B., *et al.* (1985). Familial cranial diabetes insipidus: a report of five families: genetic, diagnostic and therapeutic aspects. *Quarterly Journal of Medicine New Series,* **57,** 883–96.

Reeves, W. B. and Andreoli, T. E. (1989). Nephrogenic diabetes insipidus. In: *The metabolic basis of inherited disease* (ed. C. R. Scriver, A. L. Beaudet, W. S. Sly, and D. Valle), pp. 1985–2011. McGraw-Hill, New York.

Repaske, R. D. and Browning, M. E. (1994). A *de novo* mutation in the coding sequence for neurophysin-II (Pro^{24} → Leu) is associated with onset and transmission of autosomal dominant neurohypophyseal diabetes insipidus. *Journal of Clinical Endocrinology and Metabolism,* **79,** 421–7.

Rosenthal, W., *et al.* (1992). Molecular identification of the gene responsible for congenital nephrogenic diabetes insipidus. *Nature,* **359,** 233–5.

Rosenthal, W., *et al.* (1993). Nephrogenic diabetes insipidus: a V2 vasopresin receptor unable to stimulate adenylyl cyclase. *Journal of Biological Chemistry,* **268,** 13030–3.

Sasaki, S., *et al.* (1994). Cloning, characterization, and chromosomal mapping of human aquaporin of collecting duct. *Journal of Clinical Investigation,* **93,** 1250–56.

Seibold, A., Brabet, P., Rosenthal, W., and Birnbaumer, M. (1992) Structure and chromosomal localization of the human antidiuretic hormone receptor gene. *Americal Journal of Human Genetics,* **51,** 1078–83.

Sharif, M. and Hanley, M. R. (1992). Peptide receptors: stepping up the pressure. *Nature,* **357,** 279–80.

Sinden, R. R. and Wells, R. D. (1992). DNA structure, mutations, and human genetic disease. *Current Opinion in Biotechnology,* **3,** 612–22.

Streitz, J. M. Jr. and Streitz, J. M. (1988). Polyuric urinary tract dilatation with renal damage. *The Journal of Urology,* **139,** 784–5.

Tsukaguchi, H., *et al.* (1993). Two novel mutations in the vasopressin V$_2$ receptor gene in unrelated Japanese kindreds with nephrogenic diabetes insipidus. *Biochemical Biophysical Research Communications,* **197,** 1000–10.

van Den Ouweland, A. M. W., *et al.* (1992*a*). Mutations in the vasopressin type 2 receptor gene (*AVPR2*) associated with nephrogenic diabetes insipidus. *Nature Genetics,* **2,** 99–102.

van Den Ouweland, A. M. W., *et al.* (1992*b*). Colocalization of the gene for nephrogenic diabetes insipidus (NDI) and the vasopressin type 2 receptor gene (*AVPR2*) in the Xq28 region. *Genomics,* **13,** 1350–2.

van Lieburg, A. F., *et al.* (1994). Patients with autosomal nephrogenic diabetes insipidus: homozygous for mutations in the aquaporin 2 water channel gene. *Americal Journal of Human Genetics,* **55,** 648–52.

Waring, A. J., *et al.* (1945). A congenital defect of water metabolism. *American Journal of Diseases of Children (Chicago),* **69,** 323–4.

Watson, S. and Arkinstall, S. (ed.) (1994). *The G-protein-linked receptor facts book,* p. 427. Academic Press Limited, Hartcourt Brace & Company, London.

Weil, A. (1884). Ueber die hereditare form des diabetes insipidus. *Archives fur Pathologische Anatomie und Physiologie and fur Klinische Medicine (Virchow's Archives),* **95,** 70–95.

Weil, A. (1908). Ueber die hereditare form des diabetes insipidus. *Deutches Archiv fur Klinische Medizin,* **93,** 180–290.

Wenkert, D., *et al.* (1994). Novel mutations in the V2 vasopressin receptor gene of patients with X-linked nephrogenic diabetes insipidus. *Human Molecular Genetics,* **3,** 1429–30.

Wildin, R. S., *et al.* (1994). Heterogeneous *AVPR2* gene mutations in congenital nephrogenic diabetes insipidus. *American Journal of Human Genetics*, **55**, 266–77.

Williams, R. M. and Henry, C. (1947). Nephrogenic diabetes insipidus transmitted by females and appearing during infancy in males. *Annals of Internal Medicine*, **27**, 84–95.

Yuasa, H., *et al.* (1993). Glu-47, which forms a salt bridge between neurophysin-II and arginine vasopressin, is deleted in patients with familial central diabetes insipidus. *Journal of Clinical Endocrinology and Metabolism*, **77**, 600–4.

Yuasa, H., *et al.* (1994). Novel mutations in the V2 vasopressin receptor gene in two pedigrees with congenital nephrogenic diabetes insipidus. *Journal of Clinical Endocrinology and Metabolism*, **79**, 361–5.

13.3

Renal tubular acidosis

T. G. Feest

Introduction

The importance of the kidney as a means of excreting acid was first noted by Von Jaksch in 1888 when he observed the increased blood acidity in renal failure. As the number of functioning nephrons is reduced, whatever the disease process, the ability of the kidney to excrete acid and regulate plasma bicarbonate concentration decreases. When glomerular filtration has reduced below about 20 ml/min, systemic acidosis frequently occurs. Such 'uraemic' acidosis is at least in part due to the retention of organic anions, with a subsequent increase in the anion gap (the difference between the sum of plasma sodium and potassium and the sum of plasma chloride and bicarbonate). In some renal conditions there are selective abnormalities of renal tubular function which lead to failure of the kidney to control acid base balance, despite maintenance of normal or relatively normal glomerular filtration. In these conditions there is no increase in unmeasured anion but an increase in plasma chloride which mirrors the fall in plasma bicarbonate. There is thus no increase in the anion gap (Wrong and Davies 1959). It is these conditions which are commonly called 'renal tubular acidosis'.

This chapter will review the renal tubular regulation of acid base balance, consider the various types of defect of this regulation, and will then concentrate on the diagnosis, presentation, and treatment of these disorders with emphasis on the most common clinical defect, distal renal tubular acidosis.

Renal regulation of acid base balance

The pH of the plasma under normal conditions is regulated at a value close to 7.4 by the combined continuous action of the lungs and the kidneys. The plasma pH is dependent on the concentration of bicarbonate ion and carbon dioxide within the plasma, as formulated in the Henderson–Hasselbalch equation:

$$pH = 6.1 + \log \frac{\left[HCO_3^- \right]}{\left[H_2CO_3 \right]}$$

Plasma carbon dioxide tension is controlled within narrow limits by the lungs, and the kidneys are concerned with control of plasma bicarbonate concentration. The kidneys maintain plasma bicarbonate in two ways: (1) by reclamation of bicarbonate from the glomerular filtrate, and (2) by generation of new bicarbonate (Pitts and Lottspeich 1946; Rector *et al.* 1965) (Fig. 13.3.1). This latter process is necessary because the acid products of metabolic activity, especially H_2SO_4,

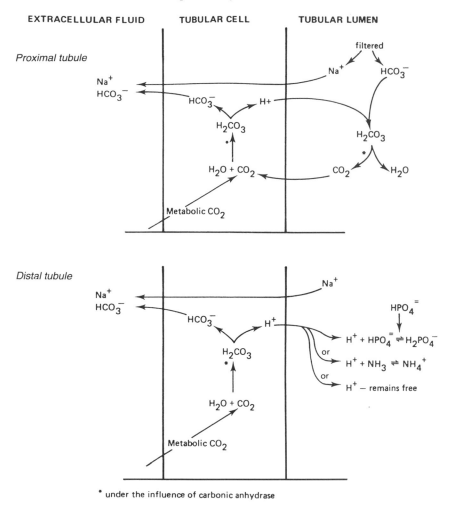

Fig. 13.3.1 Proximal and distal tubular secretion of hydrogen ion.

derived largely from metabolism of proteins and phospholipids, are released into the extracellular fluid causing decomposition of bicarbonate to water and carbon dioxide.

The kidney uses the same basic mechanism to achieve both reclamation of filtered bicarbonate in the proximal tubule and bicarbonate generation in the distal tubule (Fig. 13.3.1) (Rector *et al.* 1965). Both are achieved by generation of the bicarbonate ion from carbon dioxide and water, within the tubular cell under the influence of carbonic anhydrase:

$$H_2O + CO_2 = H_2CO_3 = HCO_3^- + H^+$$

$$|$$

$$\text{Carbonic anhydrase}$$

The hydrogen ion thus generated is secreted into the tubular lumen and the bicarbonate ion enters the extracellular fluid.

The proximal tubule—bicarbonate reclamation

In the proximal tubule the hydrogen ion secreted combines with filtered bicarbonate to form carbonic acid. Under the influence of the carbonic anydrase, which is plentiful on the luminal side of the proximal tubular brush border, this carbonic acid is converted to water and carbon dioxide. The carbon dioxide is absorbed and used to generate hydrogen ion and bicarbonate ion, the latter being transported across the basolateral membrane into the circulation (Fig. 13.3.1). Thus the secretion of hydrogen ion is accompanied by the reclamation of filtered bicarbonate, although the bicarbonate ions filtered through the glomerulus are not those which are released into the extracellular fluid, hence the term 'reclamation' rather than 'reabsorption' (Seldin 1976).

Very little bicarbonate leaks into normal urine at a pH below 6.0 (Wolf 1947), so one may calculate that an individual with a normal glomerular filtration rate and a plasma bicarbonate of 25 mmol/L reclaims 2500 mmol/day of bicarbonate. With this process there is no build up of proximal tubular luminal free hydrogen ion and therefore very little change of pH as the filtrate passes through the proximal tubules (Rector *et al.* 1965). In rats, about 90% of filtered bicarbonate is reclaimed in the proximal tubule (Gottschalk *et al.* 1960; Rector 1964), the pH of the tubular fluid leaving the proximal tubule being about 6.7, and the concentration of bicarbonate about 7 mmol/L.

In systemic acidosis, when the plasma bicarbonate is reduced the rat is able to lower proximal tubular bicarbonate concentrations as low as 1 mmol/L (Gottschalk *et al.* 1960). It is thought that proximal tubular bicarbonate reclamation in man is similar.

Proximal tubular reclamation of bicarbonate is achieved by an active cellular transport mechanism, involving a sodium/hydrogen ion antiporter on the luminal border, secreting hydrogen ion into the tubule, and a sodium/bicarbonate cotransport mechanism on the basolateral border 'reclaiming' bicarbonate (Aronson 1983). Many factors influence this process (Cogan and Alpern 1984). It can be further stimulated by increasing plasma carbon dioxide tension (Brazeau and Gilman 1953), and also increases as glomerular filtration rises. It is inhibited by parathyroid hormone (Bichara *et al.* 1986). Reclamation of bicarbonate is virtually complete with plasma concentrations below 25 mmol/L, but above this level bicarbonate spills out into the urine (Pitts and Lottspeich 1946). Significant urinary leak of bicarbonate at plasma concentrations below 25 mmol/L in an adult and 22 mmol/L in a child (Edelmann *et al.* 1967; Broyer *et al.* 1969) suggests a defect of proximal tubular bicarbonate reclamation (Rector *et al.* 1960). This is the lesion of proximal renal tubular acidosis.

The distal tubule—hydrogen ion excretion

Bicarbonate ion reclamation by the proximal tubule does not achieve the net urinary excretion of hydrogen ion which is necessary to compensate for the normal adult daily metabolic production in the body of 40–90 mmol of fixed acid, formed from oxidation of sulphur and phosphorous in dietary protein. In infants this is around 2 mmol/kg/day but decreases with age to around 1 mmol/kg/day in adults. Net renal excretion of hydrogen ion arises from generation and secretion of hydrogen ion within the distal tubular cells with simultaneous release of bicarbonate into the circulation, in a similar way to that in the proximal tubular cells (Fig. 13.3.1). However, within the distal tubular lumen the situation differs from the proximal tubule. There are very small amounts of bicarbonate present with which the secreted hydrogen ion may combine to form carbonic acid, and the distal luminal brush border contains little or no carbonic anhydrase so that any carbonic acid formed is not rapidly dehydrated.

The majority of hydrogen ion secreted within the distal tubule therefore must combine with buffers present, such as phosphate, urate, or creatinine, or combine with ammonia to form an ammonium radical, or remain free in the tubular fluid thus lowering the urine pH (Fig. 13.3.1). Normal kidneys can secrete a urine as acid as pH 4.5, at which level the hydrogen ion of the urine is 800 times that of plasma (Pitts *et al.* 1948). Even at this low pH, the urine contains negligible amounts of free hydrogen ion—about 0.03 mmol/L. Thus free hydrogen ion contributes little to the normal urine acid excretion of up to 90 mmol of hydrogen ion per day (Wrong and Davies 1959).

The importance of lowering pH is that by so doing the kidney can make use of the buffering capacities of phosphate (pk 6.85), creatinine (pk 4.97), and other organic acids present in the urine. The amount of hydrogen ion secreted in the urine combined with buffer can be estimated by titrating urine with alkali to the pH of plasma (7.4) and is commonly termed 'titratable acid secretion'. The importance of each buffer varies with pH, such that at urine pH 6.8 phosphate contributes up to 90% of buffering capacity, whereas below pH 5 about 20% of buffering is attributable to creatinine, 50% or less to phosphate, and 30% to other acids including urate. It is the loss of the ability to secrete titratable acid which is of major importance in distal renal tubular acidosis.

Mechanisms and abnormalities of distal acidification

Acid is secreted in the cortical and medullary collecting tubules. Both the intercalated A cells (Kurtzman 1990; Schuster 1990) and the principal tubular cells (Laski 1987) are involved, although it is thought that the alpha intercalated A cells have the primary role. At least five mechanisms appear to be involved in acid secretion (Fig. 13.3.2).

(1) An H+ATPase which is able to secrete protons against an electrochemical gradient (Stone and Xie 1988). This is plentiful on the apical border of intercalated A calls. This enzyme has been absent on immunohistology of renal biopsy material in some patients with hypokalaemic distal RTA associated with Sjögren's syndrome (Bastani 1995);

(2) an H+/K+-ATPase present in both principal cells and intercalated A cells;

(3) bicarbonate/chloride anion exchange on the basolateral membrane of the intercalated A cells (Preisig and Alpern 1991; Verlander *et al.* 1991). Band 3 protein catalyses bicarbonate secretion in exchange for chloride through the serosal membrane (Schuster *et al.* 1986, Wagner 1987). If this mechanism fails the intracellular pH will rise and hydrogen ion will not be available for secretion. A variety of genetic variants of band 3 protein leading to functional abnormalities of this anion exchange protein have been described in families with autosomal dominant distal RTA (Bruce *et al.* 1997);

(4) Hydrogen ion secretion in the distal tubule is highly sensitive to changes in the lumen negative transepithelial electrical gradient. This is due to active sodium transport. Increased sodium reabsorption encourages the secretion of positively charged ions such as potassium or hydrogen. Sodium reabsorption in this segment is driven by aldosterone. If sodium reabsorption in this segment is inhibited, for example by amiloride or by lack of aldosterone, there will be reduced hydrogen ion and potassium secretion (Batlle 1986). By contrast, increased delivery of sodium salts stimulates sodium reabsorption in this segment, with an increased transepithelial potential difference and increased excretion of potassium and hydrogen ions. This can be stimulated by infusion of sodium salts such as sodium sulphate, or by frusemide (Rastogi *et al.* 1984).

(5) the normal collecting tubule apical membrane is able to maintain a high hydrogen ion gradient across it. A defect in the membrane would allow increased passive back diffusion of hydrogen ion, leading to acidosis.

Renal tubular acidosis

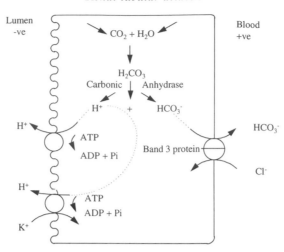

Fig. 13.3.2 The intercalated A cell. Diagram of mechanisms for H^+ and HCO_3^- transport.

There is no clear single tubular defect responsible in distal RTA (Morris and Ives 1991) and it is likely that different mechanisms apply in different conditions leading to the variablity of the clinical syndrome seen (Kurtzman 1990). Thus, there are different abnormalities of band 3 protein in different families with autosomal dominant RTA. In this condition significant hypokalaemia is extremely rare. In hypokalaemic auto-immune RTA the H^+-ATPase may be damaged. In other circumstances there could be a defect in the H/K/ATPase with a failure of hydrogen ion for potassium ion exchange which would cause hypokalaemic RTA. Impaired sodium transport in the collecting tubule would reduce luminal negative potential and would reduce proton secretion, inhibiting both potassium and hydrogen ion secretion, causing hyperkalaemic RTA.

Thus the syndrome of distal renal tubular acidosis is a true clinical syndrome which may arise from a variety of defects.

Generation of urinary pCO_2

Pitts and Lotspeich (1942) demonstrated that alkaline urines contain carbon dioxide at tensions higher than those of plasma. In states of alkali loading with alkaline urine bicarbonate is present in distal tubular urine. Any hydrogen ion secreted will form carbonic acid which will be only slowly dehydrated to release carbon dioxide, as no carbonic anhydrase is present on the luminal surface of the distal nephron (Hausler 1958; Rector 1964).

The lower urinary tract is relatively impermeable to carbon dioxide and thus urinary PCO_2 rises to levels above that of plasma. Halperin *et al.* (1974) suggested that the urinary minus blood PCO_2 during bicarbonate loading is a measure of distal tubular hydrogen ion secreting ability. In these circumstances, urine pH is above 7.4 and the distal tubule does not have to secrete hydrogen ion against a hydrogen ion gradient. Thus any backleak of hydrogen ion or inability to secrete against a gradient will be eliminated, and the formation of CO_2 is directly related to the rate of excretion of hydrogen ion. The urinary minus blood pCO_2 could therefore be used as a measure of maximum hydrogen ion secreting ability. It has been suggested that this test should be used to determine the presence of a distal tubular acidification defect rather than minimal urine pH.

There are many other factors which influence urinary minus blood pCO_2, especially the renal countercurrent system (DuBose 1982; Donkerwolcke *et al.* 1983; DuBose and Caflish 1985; Wrong 1991). Normally there is a rise in pCO_2 in the collecting tubule due to trapping in the medullary countercurrent system. This is reduced if the countercurrent mechanism is damaged, as is common in distal renal tubular acidosis (DRTA). Thus maximal hydrogen ion secretion is only one of the factors influencing urinary minus blood pCO_2, and urinary minus blood pCO_2 is not a specific test of hydrogen ion excretion ability.

Ammonia and acid base balance

The kidney is also able to secrete hydrogen ion by ammoniagenesis. Ammonia is a highly fat-soluble substance produced in the proximal tubule and easily crosses the cell membrane by non-ionic diffusion. Ammonia progresses from its site of synthesis in the proximal tubule to the lumen of the collecting tubules by a series of specialized, complex processes involving proximal tubular secretion, loop of Henle reabsorption, accumulation in the medullary interstitutium, and final secretion into the collecting tubule (Good and Knepper 1985). Once in the collecting tubular lumen, it combines with free hydrogen ions to form the positively charged ammonium radical, which does not readily diffuse out of the lumen (Milne *et al.* 1958).

The pK of the ammonium ion is 9.3, so in urine this is effectively an irreversible process, as urine pH never approaches this level. This is a very effective mechanism for acid excretion without lowering urine pH significantly.

Glutamine is the principle precursor of ammonia (Pitts *et al.* 1963; Orloff and Berliner 1966). Ammonia is formed by deamination of glutamine by glutaminase. The kidney is able to increase ammonium excretion acutely in response to an acid load (Wrong and Davies 1959) and can increase it even further during chronic acidosis (Gamble *et al.* 1925; Sartorius *et al.* 1949). This long-term adaptation to chronic acidosis is partly by enzyme induction (Rector *et al.* 1954), but there are many other complex mechanisms involved. There is redirection of glutamine from the splanchnic bed and ureagenesis to the kidneys for ammoniagenesis and bicarbonate generation (Tamarppoo *et al.* 1990), increased muscle glutamine synthesis and release (Lemieux *et al.* 1980; Welbourne 1986), and increased renal mitochondrial uptake of glutamine by a specific transport mechanism (Adam and Simpson 1974).

The importance of ammoniagenesis in protecting against acidosis was recognized by Henderson and Palmer in 1915. Reduced excretion of ammonium in chronic renal failure is one of the major causes of acidosis. In this situation, individual nephrons probably excrete increased amounts of ammonium, but the overall nephron loss leads to an ammonium deficit (Simpson 1971).

The ability to compensate for tubular acidification defects by excreting ammonium has been shown to be a critical factor in determining whether or not individuals develop systemic acidosis (Wrong and Davies 1959; Buckalew *et al.* 1968; Feest and Wrong 1982). Ammonium excretion is of such importance that Carlisle *et al.* (1991) suggested that low ammonium excretion disease is a form of renal tubular acidosis.

Urinary ammonium is measured in very few laboratories although there are many accurate standard laboratory techniques which could easily be applied to urine (Wrong 1991). It has been suggested that measurement of the urinary anion gap may enable reasonable calculation of ammonium excretion (Halperin *et al.* 1988) although it has been demonstrated that this may lead to errors by a factor of at least twofold (Wrong 1988). Overall, therefore although renal ammoniagenesis and ammonium excretion may be critical factors in determining systemic acidosis in a variety of conditions with renal tubular dysfunction, especially when associated with interstitial nephritis (Carlisle *et al.* 1991; Wrong 1991), there are no renal tubular syndromes specifically associated with poor ammoniagenesis.

Types of renal tubular acidosis

From this description of the renal tubular regulation of acid base balance it is clear that several tubular defects could give rise to renal tubular acidosis (RTA). The term 'RTA' is usually given to a collection of transport defects in the renal tubules leading to failure of excretion of hydrogen ion or reclamation of bicarbonate or both. The subsequent degree of acidosis, particularly in distal renal tubular defects, will largely depend on the ability of the kidney to generate ammonia to help excrete hydrogen ion. In some patients with distal defects this ability is such that in normal circumstances acidosis does not occur, although patients may have many of the other clinical features of the distal renal tubular defect. There may be several different cellular defects giving rise to either proximal or distal tubular acidosis, but the clinical syndromes produced depend not on the precise nature of the defect but on whether the defect is proximal or distal. Various eponyms or numbers have been given to types of renal tubular acidosis, but it is simplest and most clinically relevant to classify them, as follows, on an anatomical/descriptive basis. In clinical practice four main types have been recognized:

1. *Proximal renal tubular acidosis.* The acidosis is caused by renal bicarbonate wasting due to a diminished ability to reclaim bicarbonate in the proximal renal tubules. As plasma bicarbonate falls and thus the filtered load of bicarbonate drops below the reclamation threshold of the proximal tubule, the tubules are then able to reclaim the reduced amounts of filtered bicarbonate. The distal tubules are thus presented with a urine, as in normal patients, with a low bicarbonate content. They are then able to acidify the urine normally (Soriano *et al.* 1967). Acidosis in such patients is very resistant to correction with large doses of alkali, for as the plasma bicarbonate rises, the filtered load of bicarbonate rises above the tubular reclamation threshold and bicarbonate spills into the urine. The lesion is usually found in association with a wide range of other tubular abnormalities (Sebastian *et al.* 1971), and is often referred to as 'Type II' RTA (Table 13.3.1).

2. *Distal renal tubular acidosis.* In this lesion there is an inability to lower urine pH normally, and thus an inability to utilize urinary buffers in the excretion of acid. The majority of cases are either familial or are associated with autoimmune disorders, although there is a wide range of rarer causes (Table 13.3.2). The plasma bicarbonate is frequently very low in this condition, even down to 4 or 5 mmol/L. It is readily corrected by relatively small doses of sodium bicarbonate in a range of 50–90 mmol/day which is equivalent to the average daily urinary titratable acid excretion. This is the most common form of renal tubular acidosis, especially in adults. It is accompanied by a distinct clinical syndrome. Much of the clinical part of this chapter will be devoted to this condition. It has also been known as 'classic' or 'Type I' RTA.

3. *Hyperkalaemic renal tubular acidosis.* This was first described by Sebastian and Morris in 1977. In this condition acidosis is accompanied by a raised plasma potassium and low renal potassium clearance, and the kidney can usually produce an acid urine. There is a small but not significant reduction in bicarbonate reclamation. Acidosis may be largely due to impaired renal ammonia-genesis (Batlle 1981) which may be a result of hyperkalaemia. It is associated

Table 13.3.1 Proximal renal tubular acidosis—clinical associations

Not Associated with multiple dysfunctions of the proximal tubule

Primary	— Infantile (transient or persistent)
	— Adult
Familial	— Autosomal dominant
	— Autosomal recessive
Drug induced	— Sulfanilamide, acetazolamide

Associated with multiple dysfunction of the proximal tubule

Primary	— Sporadic
	— Genetically transmitted
Genetically transmitted systemic disease	— Cystinosis, Wilson's disease, Lowe's syndrome, tyrosinosis, hereditary fructose intolerance, galactosaemia
Metabolic disorders	— Vitamin D deficiency, hyperparathyroidism
	— Hypercalciuric rickets (children)
	— Pseudo-vitamin D deficiency rickets (children)
Medullary cystic disease	
Miscellaneous	— Multiple myelomatosis, amyloidosis
Renal transplantation	
Drugs	— Outdated tetracycline, 6 mercaptopurine, cadmium

Table 13.3.2 Clinical types of distal renal tubular acidification defect (DRTAD)

Primary	— Familial — autosomal dominant
	— recessive with neural deafness
	— Transient infantile
	— Sporadic
Secondary to	— Associated with autoimmune disorders
	— Hypercalcaemia
	— Nephrocalcinosis
	— Toxins — amphotericin B (McCurdy and Elkinton 1968)
	— analgesics (Steele and Edwards 1971)
	— lithium (Perez *et al.* 1975)
	— toluene (Taher *et al.* 1974)
	— glue-sniffing (Moss *et al.* 1980)
	— methicillin (Cogan and Arieff 1978)
	— Medullary sponge kidney
	— Obstructive uropathy
	— Renal transplantation
	— Acute tubular necrosis
	— ? Pyelonephritis
Associated with genetic disorders	— Ehlers-Danlos syndrome
	— Elliptocytosis
	— Marfan's syndrome
	— Sickle cell anaemia
	— Familial hypercalcuria
	— Recessive osteopetrosis and carbonic anhydrase II deficiency
	— Dent's disease

with aldosterone deficiency, may be secondary to hyporeninism, and sometimes is seen with resistance to the renal tubular effects of aldosterone (DuBose and Caflish 1985). This syndrome has also been called Type IV RTA. It is often seen in patients with chronic renal parenchymal damage and is most common in children (Rodriguez-Soriano and Vallo 1988). It is not associated with bone disease or nephrocalcinosis.

4. *Mixed types of renal tubular acidosis.* There have been several reports of mixed patterns of RTA. A mixture of proximal and distal defects, frequently seen in children, was labelled as Type III RTA by McSherry *et al.* (1972). In the majority of these cases the proximal lesion was transient. A mixture of distal and hyperkalaemic RTA was identified by Donkerwolcke *et al.* (1979) and as a complication of obstruction uropathy by Battle *et al.* (1981). There are clearly numerous possibilities for the proliferation of numbered types of RTA depending on the mix of the three basic types. This is simply confusing and it is preferable to retain a descriptive/anatomical nomenclature for these cases.

Diagnosis of RTA

Table 13.3.3 lists the features which help to differentiate between the different forms of RTA.

Patients with proximal RTA by definition must have a reduced plasma bicarbonate and be acidotic. The bicarbonate threshold in this situation does not usually fall below 15 mmol/L. Urine will be normal to a pH below 5.32. There will frequently be other tubular defects, such as tubular glycosuria, amino-aciduria, phosphate loss, and tubular protein loss.

Inability to lower the urine pH normally has been the traditional method of defining and diagnosing distal RTA. As has been discussed, urinary minus blood pCO_2 has been suggested as a diagnostic method of defining a distal tubular acidification defect (DRTAD) due to a limited maximal rate of hydrogen ion secretion. This may be abnormal even when urine pH is reduced normally. However, as problems with the renal counter-current system can significantly affect urinary minus blood pCO_2, this abnormality is not specific to DRTAD. Its presence in many people with DRTAD may be partly related to the fact that they nearly all have reduced urine concentrating ability (Feest and Wrong 1982). It is not appropriate therefore to use this test as a defining or diagnostic feature for DRTAD. There has been much argument about the use of this test to define DRTAD as either gradient or rate limited. Such a separation is theoretically interesting but not clearly defined in clinical practice, and at present is of little clinical value. It seems most appropriate to continue to regard inability to acidify urine normally as the defining and diagnostic feature of this condition.

Ammoniagenesis and ammonium excretion are clearly important in preventing acidosis but are not necessarily depressed in DRTAD. It may be important to investigate ammonia-genesis in affected patients, but not as a diagnostic feature of DRTAD.

Patients with DRTAD may not be acidotic, alternatively they may have severe acidosis with plasma bicarbonate as low as 4 or 5 mmol/L. They will not be able to reduce urine pH during spontaneous or induced acidosis below 5.32. It is unusual for other significant tubular defects to be present. Depending on the length of time the condition has been present there may be nephrocalcinosis or lithiasis, and if there has been severe acidosis there may be bone disease. Adult female patients have a high incidence of concomitant autoimmune disorders.

If patients are not spontaneously acidotic, the gold standard for diagnosing DRTAD is an acid load test aiming to reduce urine pH to below 5.32. The most commonly used test is the short acidification test of Wrong and Davies (1959). Orally, 0.1 G/kg of ammonium chloride is administered and urine pH monitored over the next four hours. It should fall below 5.32. Ammonium chloride induces significant nausea and vomiting and needs to be taken in capsule form over a

Table 13.3.3   Differential features of types of RTA

	Proximal	Distal	Hyperkalaemic
Minimum urine pH	< 5.32	> 5.32	< 5.32
Plasma bicarbonate	Reduced	Very low—normal	Reduced
Plasma potassium	Usually reduced	Often reduced	Raised
Other tubular defects	Usual	Rarely signficant	Rare
Ammoniagenesis	Normal	Variable	Reduced
Glomerular filtration	Usually reduced	Normal or mild reduction	May be severely reduced
Response to alkali	Poor	Good	Good
(Dose mmol HCO_3/kg/day)	3–10	1–3	1–2
Nephrocalcinosis	Rare	Frequent	Absent
Bone disease	Rare	Frequent if acidotic	Absent

period of 30 minutes together with some food and drink. The test is not valid if vomiting occurs. If urine pH has not fallen below 5.3 within three hours it is wise to check plasma bicarbonate to ensure that a degree of acidosis has occurred before diagnosing an acidification defect. If patients are significantly hyperkalaemic, it can be difficult to overcome the metabolic alkalosis induced by this. In difficult cases it may be necessary to perform the three-day acid-load test (Elkinton *et al.* 1960).

Both these acid-loading tests require time and care to perform, and ammonium chloride is unpleasant to take. For this reason alternative tests have been sought, particularly for use in children. It is always worthwhile testing one or two random early-morning urine samples as many normal patients will spontaneously produce an acid urine. Chafe and Gault (1994), in a study of 110 people, found 10 with abnormal acidification. They showed that nine of the patients with abnormal acidification had a pH of 6.1 or above on two early-morning fasting urine samples, giving a sensitivity of 90%. Only four of the 100 normal individuals in this series failed to have one of two fasting urine samples with a pH below 6.1, giving a specificity of 96%. With further investigation and slight lowering of the threshold level this could form a useful screening test to select those patients in whom acidification tests are worthwhile.

A single dose of frusemide also produces a highly acid urine (Rastogi *et al.* 1984; Batlle 1986), a test which may prove more acceptable to patients than ammonium chloride. This test needs further evaluation before being widely accepted.

It may be a useful addition to assess urine ammonium excretion. This may be crudely achieved by measuring the urine anion gap (Goldstein *et al.* 1986), working on the rough equation: $Na^+ + K^+ + NH4^+ = Chloride^- + 80$. '80' represents the relatively consistent excess of sulphate, phospate, and other organic anions in the urine over cations such as calcium and magnesium.

A patient with normal ammonia-genesis should be able to generate at least 80 mmol/day of ammonium in response to acidosis. Acidotic patients in whom the sum of the sodium + potassium urine cations is greater than the chloride concentration are excreting less than 80 mmol of ammonia per day and may have an ammonium excretion defect. This could simply represent diminished glomerular filtration rate. This method of assessing urinury ammonium is inaccurate, and better assessment can be made by relatively straightforward specific tests of ammonium secretion (Wrong 1988).

Proximal renal tubular acidosis

The pathogenesis of this syndrome is unknown. It is usually part of a generalized Fanconi syndrome with other proximal tubular disorders such as glycosuria, hyperphosphaturia, hyper-aminoaciduria, and hyperuricosuria. It occurs rarely as an isolated lesion (Edelmann 1985). Although it is tempting to suspect an abnormality of carbonic anhydrase II, there is no evidence for this as patients with a genetic absence of renal carbonic anhydrase II develop distal rather than proximal tubular acidosis (Sly *et al.* 1985). The causes and associations of this condition are listed in table 1.

Isolated proximal tubular acidosis

This may be familial or non-familial. A non-familial isolated transient proximal acidosis has been described in infants (Edelmann *et al.* 1965; Nash *et al.* 1972), with a male predominance. Hypercalcuria and nephrocalcinosis did not occur. Morris (1966) showed that this lesion was also present in many infants with a transient form of distal renal tubular acidosis. An isolated lesion has also been reported in adults (York and Yendt 1966). Renal potassium loss frequently occurs but is rarely symptomatic. This is stimulated by increased delivery of sodium bicarbonate to the distal tubule and by hyperaldosterone caused by the sodium and volume depletion which often accompany the condition.

Despite severe acidosis, the only significant clinical effect of this abnormality seems to be mild growth retardation in growing children, which responds well to bicarbonate therapy.

A familial isolated proximal tubular acidosis was reported by Brenes *et al.* (1977) in nine members of a family through two generations. The lesion was persistent with autosomal dominant inheritance. Despite severe, persistent acidosis, the only significant clinical effect seemed to be mild growth retardation which appears to respond to bicarbonate therapy. There are also reports of persistent proximal acidosis as an isolated renal lesion (Winsnes *et al.* 1979; Igarashi *et al.* 1994) which was thought to be of recessive inheritance. Although the renal lesion was isolated these cases had multiple other anomalies, including mental retardation, corneal opacities, cataracts and glaucoma, and enamel tooth defects.

A proximal renal tubular acidosis may also be seen as an isolated lesion induced by acetazolamide or sulphanilomide.

Proximal tubular acidosis associated with other renal disorders

Proximal tubular acidosis is nearly always seen as part of a generalized Fanconi syndrome for which there are many causes (Table 13.3.1). The dominant clinical features are usually those of the many diseases which accompany the condition. The nephrolothiasis, nephrocalcinosis, and bone disease seen in distal RTA do not usually occur as a result of proximal RTA.

An association with recurrent kidney stones was identified by Backman *et al.* (1980) who, in a study of 318 recurrent stone-formers, found 34 patients with phosphate stones and mild defects of bicarbonate reclamation. Although this may have been secondary to the stone disease, it does raise the question of whether mild persistent proximal RTA could predispose to phosphate stone formation.

The absence of bone lesions in proximal RTA suggests that acidosis itself does not necessarily predispose to bone disease. Where rickets or osteomalacia have occurred in proximal RTA, it has usually been as a result of hypophosphataemia associated with Fanconi syndrome. However,

York and Yendt (1966) described an adult with an isolated proximal tubular acidosis and osteomalacia. There is experimental evidence that acute but not chronic acidosis impairs conversion of 25-(OH) vitamin D to 1,25-(OH)$_2$ vitamin D, but this has not been demonstrated in human chronic metabolic acidosis (Cunningham *et al.* 1984), although correction of acidosis does correct the bone lesion in the majority of patients with distal RTA (see below). The reason for growth retardation in proximal RTA is unknown.

Therapy of proximal RTA

Sodium bicarbonate is used to correct acidosis, but doses up to 10 mmol/kg/day may be needed (Sebastian and Morris 1979). Large doses are needed as when plasma bicarbonate rises towards normal there is an increased filtered load of bicarbonate which the defective proximal tubule is unable to handle. This leads to an increased bicarbonate load in the distal tubule which exceeds its capacity to reclaim bicarbonate and bicarbonate escapes into urine. As treatment increases distal tubular sodium delivery, hypokalaemia may become worse. In patients with severe hypokalaemia, up to 50% of the bicarbonate may be given as a potassium salt. Potassium supplementation is not usually necessary in the isolated lesion. Administration of thiazide diuretics may be helpful. They reduce plasma volume and thus filtered load of bicarbonate and so reduce the bicarbonate supplementation needed (Rampini *et al.* 1968; Callis *et al.* 1970). Doses of up to 2 mg/kg/day of hydrochlorothiazide may be necessary in the first instance. The reduction of urinary calcium and phosphate excretion induced by thiazides may also be helpful in those with multiple tubular lesions and osteomalacia. Thiazides will increase potassium loss and potassium supplements are always needed when they are administered.

As has been emphasized, rickets and osteomalacia occurring in proximal RTA are a result of concomitant hypophosphataemia and possible calcium loss caused by the Fanconi syndrome. Treatment needs to be with phosphate supplements and possible supplementation with vitamin D. Correction of acidosis alone with not heal the bones.

Distal renal tubular acidosis

This is the most common and clinically important form of RTA. The clinical syndrome which occurs is the result of a DRTAD. The defining feature of this syndrome should still be regarded as the inability to lower urine pH below 5.3 in the presence of relatively normal glomerular function. Many patients with DRTAD are unable to reduce their urine pH below 6, in contrast to normals who may reduce as low as 4.5. This is the classical syndrome described in the early literature on RTA with the major clinical feature of nephrocalcinosis and renal stones, osteomalacia or rickets, renal potassium and sodium losing, and a urine concentration defect.

The majority of patients have hyperchloraemic acidosis, but about one-third are not acidotic in normal circumstances. Renal excretion of hydrogen ion is adequate to cope with a basal metabolic load of acid, largely due to retention of ammonia-genesis. These patients have been described as having 'the incomplete syndrome' of DRTAD. They have two of the major features of the complete syndrome, i.e. nephrocalcinosis and potassium depletion, but they do not develop osteomalacia or rickets (Feest and Wrong 1982). Study of urinary acidification with an acid load, usually by means of the short ammonium chloride test (Wrong and Davies 1959) or a prolonged three-day acid load (Elkinton *et al.* 1960), will confirm the presence of DRTAD in such cases.

DRTAD is usually classified as either primary (idiopathic) or secondary. There are many known causes and associated conditions (Table 3.3.2). It is important to seek a primary cause for DRTAD when it has been diagnosed. Hypercalcuria is not usually recognized as a cause, although two large kindreds have been described with a familial ideopathic hypercalcuria predisposing to DRTAD in a few cases (Buckalew *et al.* 1974, Hamed *et al.* 1979). Both hypercalcaemia and hypercalcuria can cause nephrocalcinosis and many conditions which cause nephrocalcinosis (medullary sponge kidney, analgesic nephropathy, primary oxaluria) are often associated with DRTAD (Wrong and Feest 1976). Any condition causing significant nephrocalcinosis is a potential cause of DRTAD. Careful history-taking is essential as hypercalcaemia, a frequent cause of nephrocalcinosis, is easily overlooked. The DRTAD may persist long after hypercalcaemia has regressed or been treated.

Pyelonephritis with mild renal damage does not seem to cause DRTAD (Lathem 1958) but may do so when there is severe structural renal damage and depressed glomerular filtration (Cochran *et al.* 1968). Urinary tract infections are common in DRTAD but are usually secondary to nephrocalcinosis and renal stones.

Primary DRTAD

These patients fall into familial, transient infantile, and sporadic groups. Clearly the sporadic cases may have a primary cause which has been undiagnosed.

Familial DRTAD

Familial DRTAD is the most common form of the condition in children. It is usually inherited as an autosomal dominant which is widely distributed, affecting Caucasian, Asiatic, and African families (Seedat 1964; Seldin and Wilson 1972). There is an equal-sex incidence and complete and incomplete cases may occur in the same family (Seedat 1964; Gyory and Edwards 1968), indicating that both the incomplete and complete forms of the disorder are manifestations of the same underlying defect. In family studies it is therefore important that acidification tests should be performed in non-acidotic members of the family before they are considered as not having DRTAD. The familial defect appears to be present from birth as no familial case has ever been shown to have had a normal urine acidification test at any time before diagnosis. Manifestations in early childhood may be overlooked as they are non-specific, including vomiting, constipation, polyuria, dehydration, and failure to thrive. Rickets may present in severe cases, but frequently the only clinical abnormality beyond infancy is a degree of growth retardation (Nash *et al.* 1972).

Thera are other familial conditions associated with DRTAD. The families with ideopathic hypercalcuria, inherited in a dominant pattern, reported by Buckalew *et al.* (1974) and Hamed *et al.* (1979), have already been mentioned. Recessive transmission associated with hereditary nerve deafness was first described by Nance and Sweeney in 1971. A recessive syndrome of distal tubular acidosis, osteopetrosis, and cerebral calcification was described by Zackai *et al.* (1972) and later shown to be due to deficiency of carbonic anhydrase II (Sly *et al.* 1985). More recently, an X-linked recessive condition, carried on the short arm of the X chromosome, was described by Wrong *et al.* (1994). Christened 'Dent's disease', this is a familial proximal renal tubular syndrome with low molecular weight proteinuria, hypercalcuria, and nephrocalcinosis and bone disease, in which distal renal tubular acidosis may also occur. Some patients progress into renal failure even in the absence of nephrocalcinosis and renal obstruction.

Distal RTA may also have familial incidence when it is associated with other inherited conditions such as sickle-cell disease (Ho Ping Kong and Alleyn 1968), Ehlers–Danlos syndrome (Levine and Michael 1967), and elliptocytosis (Baehner *et al.* 1968).

Transient infantile DRTAD

The initial reports of RTA were of infants and young children (Lightwood 1935; Butler *et al.* 1936) who appear to have had a different disorder from that seen today. They presented as infants with severe dehydration and failure to thrive. Follow-up has demonstrated that the underlying DRTAD recovered (Buchanan and Komrower 1958) and that acidosis did not return when therapy ceased (Lightwood *et al.* 1953). The disease has been rarely seen since 1950 and it may have been caused by some extrinsic factor leading to hypercalcaemia which was often present (Stapleton 1949, Carre *et al.* 1954), possibly due to fortification of milk with vitamin D (Soriano and Edelmann 1969) which was then common.

Secondary DRTAD

Distal acidosis may occur as a secondary condition in a wide number of systemic or generalized renal disorders (Table 13.3.2). By far the most frequent association is with autoimmune disorders.

Immune-related DRTAD

This is almost exclusively confined to women. DRTAD is associated with a wide range of autoimmune disorders (Wrong and Feest 1980; Morris 1981). The most common associations are with thyroid disease, rheumatoid-type polyarthritis, cutaneous vasculitis, and Sjogren's syndrome; and DRTAD has also been demonstrated in patients with systemic lupus without evidence of significant glomerular involvement in the disease. One of the serum immunoglobulin fractions is nearly always raised in these patients, IgG in 75%, IgA in 36%, and IgM in 13% (Wrong *et al.* 1993). Antibody to renal collecting duct-intercalated cells was found in only three of 10 tested patients (Wrong *et al.* 1993). A wide range of autoantibodies is found in these patients, but no antibody specifically relating to immune-related DRTAD has been identified. The DRTAD may follow or antedate clinical manifestations of the accompanying immune disorder although the immunoglobulin and auto-antibody abnormalities are present at the time of diagnosis. These patients often have a severe acidification defect, may have a mild proximal bicarbonate leak, and have significant potassium losing as well as acidification problems (Wrong *et al.* 1993). Renal histology has been variable but frequently shows an interstitial nephritis with infiltration by lymphocytes and macrophages. Immunofluorescent studies have usually been negative (Shioji *et al.* 1970; Feest *et al.* 1978a; Matsumara *et al.* 1988; Wrong *et al.* 1993).

Patients with immune-related DRTAD tend to have more generalized renal damage than familial cases. Mean creatinine clearance is around 60 ml/min compared with 80 ml/min in familial patients (Wrong *et al.* 1993).

Other secondary DRTAD

Other secondary types of DRTAD are listed in Table 13.3.2. It can be difficult to determine whether nephrocalcinosis present is secondary to the DRTAD or a possible cause of the acidification problem. As many types of nephrocalcinosis can lead to DRTAD it is most important to obtain histories of possible previous hypercalcaemia, hypercalcuria, or other factors which could predispose to nephrocalcinosis. Up to 20% of patients with medullary sponge kidney have been reported to have acidification defects (Feest 1979), and as this condition cannot always be distinguished by intravenous urography from nephrocalcinosis due to other causes this may account for a significant number of the 'idiopathic' cases.

Renal tubular acidosis

Factors determining systemic acidosis in DRTAD

A reduced ability to lower urine pH leads to reduced utilizations of urinary buffers and reduced excretion of titrable acid. The ability to excrete acid will depend on the minimum pH achieved. At pH 6.9, urine contains little titrable acid as only 30% of urinary phosphate is acting as a hydrogen ion acceptor. Urine with a pH of 6 makes full use of available phosphate buffers, and in urine at pH 5 urate and creatinine are utilized as buffers.

Ability to excrete ammonium will also determine total acid excretion. In most forms of renal disease this is reduced in proportion to reduction in glomerular filtration (Wrong and Davies 1959; Simpson 1971), probably because both variables are functions of surviving nephron mass. In DRTAD, glomerular filtration is frequently moderately impaired and it has been demonstrated that, with a few exceptions, the relationship between glomerular filtration rate and stimulated ammonium excretion DRTAD follows the same regression line as in other forms of renal disease, although with a wider scatter (Fig. 13.3.3) (Feest and Wrong 1982). Minimum urine pH and stimulated ammonium excretion rate are the major factors determining whether or not individual patients become acidotic (Fig. 13.3.4). These two factors account for 66% of the variability of plasma bicarbonate. The remaining variability is probably due to individual variations such as diet and metabolic activity. A few patients compensate for their acidification defect by massively increasing renal ammonia production.

Clinical features of DRTAD

The common clinical features of DRTAD are listed in Table 13.3.4. Patients may remain asymptomatic for many years after the onset of the lesion. As an increasing number of patients are

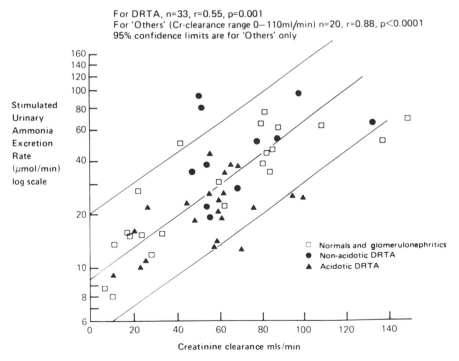

Fig. 13.3.3 Relationship of creatinine clearance and urinary ammonia excretion.

now diagnosed during family studies or investigation of people with autoimmune disorders, the overall recognition of asymptomatic patients is rising. Treatment of these patients should be effective in preventing complications. The percentage incidence of the various manifestations in Table 13.3.4 are from a series of 56 patients who have developed symptoms attributable to DRTAD before diagnosis (Feest and Wrong 1982).

Nephrocalcinosis and renal stone formation

Renal colic occurred in over 60% of symptomatic patients and was frequently accompanied by haematuria. It was the single most common symptom, and affects men twice as frequently as women. It occurred in complete and incomplete cases. Radiological nephrocalcinosis was present in over 80% of patients with all types of DRTAD. In addition, many patients have histological nephrocalcinosis when X-rays appeared normal (Feest *et al.* 1978*b*). Renal stones in this condition are nearly always predominantly calcium phosphate (Bauld *et al.* 1958; Backman *et al.* 1980; Feest and Wrong, 1982), in contrast with most other forms of renal stones which are predominantly calcium oxalate.

The cause of nephrocalcinosis and stone formation is uncertain, but there are many factors which contribute. The higher urinary pH will tend to decrease the solubility of calcium phosphate as the pK of phosphate is 6.85. Relative hypercalciuria as a result of systemic acidosis causing mobilization of bone mineral as buffer has been widely reported in this condition. Absolute hypercalcuria is uncommon (Fig. 13.3.5) (Feest and Wrong 1982) but occurs in both acidotic and non–acidotic patients. Treatment with alkali can produce a significant fall in urinary calcium in many patients, especially those with a calcium excretion in the higher range (Fig. 13.3.6). This mild hypercalcuria may be a contributory factor to nephrocalcinosis and stone formation. Large renal stones are relatively uncommon. Stag horn calculi seem only to occur in

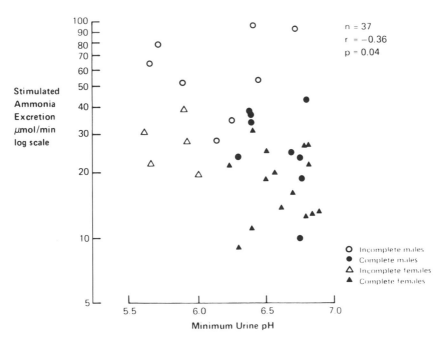

Fig. 13.3.4 Relationship between minimum urine pH and stimulated urine ammonia excretion in DRTA.

Table 13.3.4 The syndrome of DRTAD

	% incidence	Comments
Symptomatic clinical features		
Nephrocalcinosis	83	More common in
Renal stones	50	males
Osteomalacia/rickets	32	
Muscle weakness	27	Rare in familial DRTAD
Urinary tract infection	38	More common in females
Hypertension	11	
Renal salt wasting		
Poor growth		
Laboratory findings		
Acidosis	70	
Hypokalaemia	57	
Urine concentration defects	90	
Erythrocytosis	3	
Creatinine clearance below 85 ml/min	90	
Sterile pyuria		Always present with nephrocalcinosis

those patients, mostly women, with recurrent pyelonephritis. Pyelonephritis does not seem to be related to straightforward nephrocalcinosis.

Hypocitraturia is probably one of the major factors inducing stones and nephrocalcinosis in this condition. It is present in the majority of patients (Dedmon and Wrong 1962; Royer *et al.* 1962). Hypocitraturia is sufficiently frequent to have been used as a screening test for DRTAD in family studies (Norman *et al.* 1978). Citrate forms negatively charged soluble complexes with calcium (Harrison 1956) and is present in urine in sufficient quantities to be a significant inhibitor of calcium salt precipitation. Thus hypocitraturia may predispose to nephrocalcinosis and stone formation. Much of urinary citrate is derived from renal tubular cells. Citrate excretion is inhibited by intracellular acidosis and potassium excretion. Cytoplasmic acidosis promotes citrate entry into the mitochondria with subsequent stimulation of citrate absorption from the tubular lumen (Harrison 1956; Crawford *et al.* 1958; Simpson 1983). However, correction of acidosis and hyperkalaemia does not fully correct hypocitraturia in DRTAD in relation to urine pH (Dedmon and Wrong 1962). For this reason sodium citrate and potassium citrate are often used in therapy of DRTAD to try to increase urinary citrate and reduce the probability of stones and nephrocalcinosis.

All these abnormalities discussed may theoretically lead to urinary stone formation, but it should be noted that histological studies suggest that calcium deposition in the renal substance is the initial process in the nephrocalcinosis of the DRTAD. Mechanisms which would lead to interstitial nephrocalcinosis rather than tubular crystal formation are unknown.

Bone disease, calcium, and phosphorous

The bone lesion seen in DRTAD is osteomalacia, which may manifest itself as rickets in growing children. The lesion is related to acidosis, as it is not seen in patients with incomplete DRTAD, and correction of acidosis with alkali leads to healing of the bone disease (Richards *et al.* 1972). Persistent acidosis induces selective resorption of bone mineral which increases extracellular-

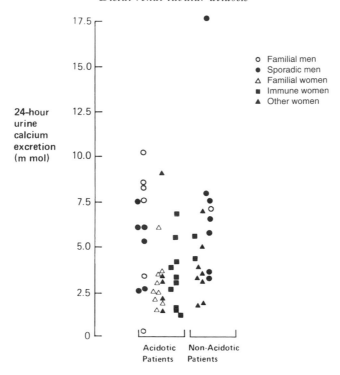

Fig. 13.3.5 Urine calcium excretion in DRTA.

fluid buffer capacity (Lemann *et al.* 1996; Bushisky and Lechleider 1987) which is independent of parathyroid activity (Barzel 1975). Mild elevation of serum parathyroid hormone has been occasionally reported in DRTAD (Firpo *et al.* 1972; Lee *et al.* 1976). Bone biopsies have shown mild osteitis fibrosa but the dominant lesion is that of osteomalacia (Feest and Wrong 1982). The mechanism by which chronic metabolic acidosis causes osteomalacia is unknown. In rats it causes osteopenia but not osteomalacia (Jaffe *et al.* 1932; Kraut *et al.* 1986). There has been speculation that acidosis may alter metabolism of vitamin D but this does not appear to be the case in humans (Cunningham *et al.* 1984). There is evidence that patients with DRTAD have poor intestinal calcium absorption which improves with alkali therapy (Preminger *et al.* 1987). This, coupled with the release of calcium salts from bone to act as buffers, leading to relative hypercalciuria, may put patients in negative calcium balance. However, this of itself should not induce osteomalacia. Low plasma phosphate is also a very potent cause of osteomalacia but is rarely found in DRTAD. There is a possible parallel in the osteomalacia seen in patients with chronic renal failure which does seem to be related to acidosis (Cochran and Nordin 1969) and reponds to correction of acidosis (Cochran and Wilkinson, 1975). Overall, the cause of osteomalacia in DRTAD still remains uncertain.

Sodium and potassium metabolism

Sodium loss is common in DRTAD but rarely of sufficient severity to cause many clinical symptoms unless intercurrent disease, such as diarrhoea and vomiting, induces further sodium or fluid depletion. Polyuria and thirst as a result of the sodium leak found in the majority of patients

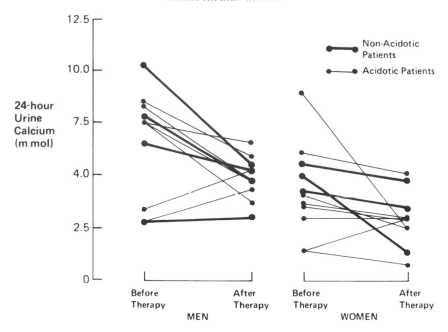

Fig. 13.3.6   The effect of bicarbonate therapy on urine calcium excretion in DRTA.

are difficult symptoms to assess but are probably present in up to 50% of patients. Such defects are commonly found in patients with nephrocalcinosis of any cause (Wrong and Feest 1976), but are seen in DRTAD in the absence of nephrocalcinosis.

Hypokalaemia occurs in over 50% of symptomatic patients (Feest and Wrong 1982; Caruana and Buckalew 1988), many of whom develop muscle weakness and paralysis. It is more frequent in acidotic patients but is much less common in familial patients despite the fact that they have severe acidification defects and are usually acidotic (Fig. 13.3.7). This may be due to a different underlying mechanism for the development of DRTAD, or due to concomitant tubular damage in non-familial patients. There is a severe potassium-losing status associated with autoimmune disorders without DRTAD (Wrong *et al.* 1993), and it does appear that immune-related DRTAD patients frequently have a more severe potassium loss than familial patients.

There are probably several mechanisms for potassium loss. In a disorder inhibiting the H+/ K+/ATPase rather than the hydrogen ion antiporter, one would expect acidosis to be accompanied by urinary potassium loss. Acidosis itself may also lead to potassium loss by decreasing proximal nephron sodium absorption. The resulting increase in sodium delivery to the distal nephron will stimulate potassium and hydrogen ion exchange for sodium, which in DRTAD will be largely potassium exchange leading to hypokalaemia. In addition, any sodium depletion will lead to secondary hyperaldosteronism with further distal tubular secretion of potassium in exchange for sodium. Hyperaldosteronism is sometimes present in DRTAD, but potassium depletion may occur in its absence (Gill *et al.* 1967).

Correction of acidosis with sodium bicarbonate reverses the negative potassium balance in up to 95% of patients with DRTAD. This is in part due to the sodium supplement and increased delivery of sodium to the distal nephron. A small proportion continue to lose potassium, indicating a persistent defect in distal resorption of potassium. These patients need potassium supplements.

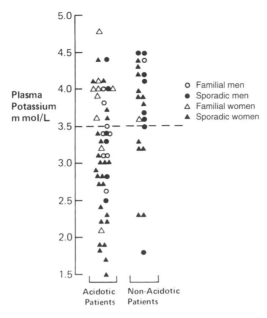

Fig. 13.3.7 Plasma potassium levels in 69 patients with DRTA.

Other clinical features

Urinary tract infection occurs in up to 40% of patients, predominantly women. A few patients have severe recurrent infections which occasionally lead to stag horn calculi. Despite the salt-losing tendency, hypertension may be seen in up to 10% of patients with DRTAD. There is also a low incidence of true erythrocytosis due to increased erythropoietin production, a feature which is also seen in other conditions with nephrocalcinosis (Feest *et al.* 1978*b*).

Mild proximal tubular dysfunction is occasionally seen but in the majority of cases does not lead to symptoms. Mild aminoaciduria can be caused by acidosis or hypokalaemia and responds to alkali therapy (Denton *et al.* 1951). Tubular proteinuria responding to alkalis has also been reported (Saito 1970). There is, however, widespread experience that very mild proteinuria may persist after correction of acidosis in up to 50% of patients. Overt albuminuria and glycosuria are rare.

Glomerular function

By definition, glomular function is relatively well-preserved in patients with DRTAD. In the majority of patients, however, some glomular damage is present with blood urea being raised in up to 25% of patients and creatinine clearance being reduced below 85 ml/min in 90%. Severe depression of glomerular function, especially in familial cases, seems to be related to nephrocalcinosis and may perhaps occur as a result of chronic inflammation and recurrent episodes of urinary obstruction and infection. Chronic potassium depletion may also be a factor.

Glomerular function may be reduced even in the absence of nephrocalcinosis, infection, or potassium depletion. It is more severely reduced in immune-related patients than in familial patients (Wrong *et al.* 1993), and is probably due to the immunologically immediated chronic interstitial nephritis which is present. Severe renal dysfunction leading to dialysis is extremely rare in DRTAD unless it is a manifestation of an underlying primary disease such as systemic lupus. It can occasionally occur as a result of recurrent urinary tract obstruction and infection.

Treatment and prognosis of DRTAD

The treatment of DRTAD is to give enough oral alkali to correct acidosis, reduce urine calcium excretion, and increase urine citrate excretion. Sodium bicarbonate in a dose of 0.5–3.0 mmol/kg/day is usually adequate in adults but larger doses may be needed in infants. Correction of acidosis alone is sufficient to heal bone disease when present (Feest and Wrong 1982) and will also correct the retarded growth seen in children (McSherry and Morris 1978). In the majority of cases alkali therapy will also correct hypokalaemia, although between 5–10% of patients will need a potassium supplement after acidosis is corrected. This can conveniently be given in the form of potassium citrate, bicarbonate, or chloride, usually between 0.5 and 1.0/kg/day. Some physicians prefer always to give a part of the alkali in the form of sodium or potassium citrate in an effort to further increase citrate excretion.

Nephrocalcinosis and stone formation with the potential risk of infection, obstruction, and possible long-term renal decline are the most troublesome complications of DRTAD. The appearance of nephrocalcinosis is variable. Untreated acidotic familial patients may reach adult life without this complication. It is therefore difficult to be certain about the protective effect of alkalis but the general concensus is that they are of value. Nephrocalcinosis, once formed, seldom disappears. There is evidence that administration of alkali slows or stops a further development of nephrocalcinosis, even in non-acidotic patients (Feest and Wrong 1982), and also reduces the rate of stone formation (Preminger *et al.* 1985).

Alkali therapy is general considered to be helpful in preventing nephrocalcinosis in non-acidotic patients but the dose is difficult to monitor. As a general principle, it is appropriate to measure urine calcium excretion in all patients before and after administration of alkali. If there has been no fall in urine calcium excretion after administration, the alkali dosage could be cautiously increased further to see if urine calcium excretion can be reduced.

As nephrocalcinosis and renal stones are the main cause of morbidity and mortality in DRTAD, other therapeutic measures have been attempted. Efforts to reduce urinary calcium excretion with thiazide diuretics are potentially dangerous as this can increase potassium depletion. Low calcium diet and sodium phosphate are contraindicated as many patients with DRTAD have urine oxalate excretion in the upper part of the normal range, and these treatments could increase this further (Feest and Wrong 1982). Oral pyridoxine has also been administered to patients with relatively high urine oxalate excretion rates. Attempts have also been made to increase calcium salt solubility in urine by increasing urinary magnesium, but most patients are unable to tolerate magnesium salts due to the intestinal complications: magnesium glycerophosphate may be the most acceptable.

An essential part of treatment is careful follow-up with frequent checks for urinary infection and obstruction. Any intervening urinary infections should be treated aggressively. Many patients have needed urological surgery to relieve obstruction. Lithotripsy is not appropriate treatment for nephrocalcinosis. Its safety and value in patients with large renal stones in this condition has not been assessed.

Prognosis

The prognosis of treated patients is excellent. Death or renal failure directly attributable to DRTAD is extremely rare in the absence of untreated ureteric obstruction. In secondary DRTAD there may be appreciable morbidity related to the primary condition, especially in autoimmune disorders.

Dent's disease (X-linked recessive nephrolithiasis)

This condition is a familial proximal renal tubular syndrome with low molecular weight proteinuria, hypercalciuria, nephrocalcinosis, osteomalacia or rickets, and progressive renal failure. It exhibits an X-linked recessive inheritance pattern, although female carriers frequently show mild features such as tubular proteinuria, and may rarely develop renal stones and renal failure (Wrong *et al.* 1994). Unlike distal RTA, in this condition bone disease may occur in the absence of systemic acidosis. Families have been described in many countries including the UK (Wrong *et al.* 1994) and USA (Frymoyer *et al.* 1991). Distal renal tubular acidosis has also been described in some patients, but only occurs in patients with nephrocalcinosis and may be a secondary phenomenon. There is frequent steady progression to end stage renal failure by middle life, even in the absence of recurrent ureteric obstruction or urinary infection. The responsible gene has been mapped to the short arm of the X chromosome at Xp11.22 (Pook *et al.* 1993; Scheinman *et al.* 1993). The gene is CLCN5, which codes for a transmembrane protein which is part of a voltage gated chloride channel (Lloyd *et al.* 1996). In one family a micro-deletion was found, in others differing mutations have been identified. It is not clear why an abnormality in a single chloride channel should give rise to such widespread tubular lesions, involving both the proximal tubule (proteinuria), and distal tubule (hypercalciuria).

Hyperkalaemic renal tubular acidosis

These patients have sustained hyperkalaemia, normal ability to acidify urine, and decreased ammonium excretion out of proportion to their glomerular filtration rate. In the majority of patients the condition is related to reduced circulating levels of aldosterone or poor renal tubular response to this hormone. However, aldosterone deficiency alone does not cause acidosis (Perez *et al.* 1976) and it is thought that most patients with this form of RTA have a combination of hypoaldosteronism and moderate renal damage. Hyperkalaemia itself may also stimulate metabolic acidosis by inhibiting ammoniagenesis (Hulter *et al.* 1983).

In clinical terms, this condition commonly occurs in patients with a combination of hyperaldosteronism and moderate renal damage, the aldosteronism deficiency being due to deficient renin production (Schambelan *et al.* 1972; Perez *et al.* 1974), a combination often seen in chronic interstitial nephritis and diabetic nephropathy. Other situations in which there is reduced sodium for potassium exchange in the distal tubule may also predispose to hyperkalaemic renal acidosis, particularly volume contraction when there is very little sodium delivery to the distal tubule thus reducing the opportunity for sodium exchange for potassium or hydrogen ion, and potassium-retaining drugs which directly inhibit these mechanisms.

Hyperkalaemic RTA may also rarely be a manifestation or reduce renal responsiveness to aldosterone with secondary high plasma levels of renin and aldosterone (Batlle *et al.* 1981).

Patients with hyperkalaemic RTA do not usually have any evidence of proximal tubular dysfunction. Plasma bicarbonate can easily be maintained at normal levels with bicarbonate supplements. There is then a very small leak of filtered bicarbonate into the urine. A major contributory factor to acidosis is impaired ammonia excretion (Perez *et al.* 1976; Hulter *et al.* 1977), which is always below normal for urine pH, degree of systemic acidosis, or creatinine clearance. The hyperkalaemia itself is a major factor in suppressing ammonium excretion. If hyperkalaemia is corrected by cation exchange resins or administration of aldosterone, ammonium excretion improves and acidosis is largely corrected (Szylman *et al.* 1976).

Treatment is largely by use of fludrocortisone which may be needed in doses in excess of the physiological replacement (Sebastian and Morris 1977). In such cases, alkalis and cation exchange resins may be also used to lower plasma potassium and correct acidosis.

Acknowledgement

I wish to acknowledge the continuing support of Professor Oliver Wrong who first stimulated my interest in these conditions 20 years ago, and gave me access to many patients and a wealth of information.

Bibliography

Adam, W. and Simpson, D. P. (1974). Glutamine transport in rat kidney mitochondria in metabolic acidosis. *Journal of Clinical Investigations*, **54**, 165–74.

Aronson, P. S. (1983). Mechanisms of active H^+ secretion in the proximal tubule. *American Journal of Physiology*, **245**, F647–59.

Backman, U., Danielson, B. G., Johansson, G., Ljunghall, S., and Wikstrom, B. (1980). Incidence and clinical importance of renal tubular defects in recurrent renal stone formers. *Nephron*, **25**, 96–101.

Baehner, R. L., Gilchrist, G. S., and Anderson, E. J. (1968). Hereditary elliptocytosis and primary renal tubular acidosis in a single family. *American Journal of Diseases of Children*, **115**, 414–19.

Barzel, U. S. (1975). The effect of chronic ammonium chloride ingestion on parathyroid hormone function. *Nephron*, **14**, 339–46.

Bastani, B., Haragsim, I., Gluck, S., and Siamopoulos, K. C. (1995). Lack of H-ATPase in distal nephron causing hypokalemic distal RTA in a patient with Sjogren's syndrome. *Nephrology Dialysis Transplantation*, **10**, 908–13.

Batlle, D. C. (1981). Hyperkalemic hyperchloremic metabolic acidosis associated with selective aldosterone deficiency and distal renal tubular acidosis. *Seminars in Nephrology*, **1**, 260–74.

Batlle, D. C. (1986). Segmental characterization of defects in collecting tubule acidification. *Kidney International*, **30**, 546–54.

Batlle, D. C., Arruda, J. A. L., and Kurtzman, N. A. (1981). Hyperkalemic distal renal tubular acidosis associated with obstructive uropathy. *New England Journal of Medicine*, **304**, 373–80.

Bauld, W. S., Macdonald, S. A., and Hill, M. C. (1958). Effect of renal tubular acidosis on calcium excretion. *British Journal of Urology*, **30**, 285–91.

Bichara, M., Mercier, O., Paillard, M., and Leviel, F. (1986). Effects of parathyroid hormone on urinary acidification. *American Journal of Physiology*, **251**, F444–53.

Brazeau, P. and Gilman, A. (1953). Effect of plasma CO2 tension on renal tubular reabsorption of bicarbonate. *American Journal Physiology*, **175**, 33–8.

Brenes, L. G., Brenes, J. M., and Hernandez, M. M. (1977). Familial proximal renal tubular acidosis. A distinct clinical entity. *American Journal Medicine*, **63**, 244–52.

Broyer, M., Proesmans, W., and Royer, P. (1969). La titration des bicarbonates chez l'enfant normal et au cours des diverse nephropathies. *Revue Francaise d'Etudes Cliniques et Bioliques*, **6**, 556–67.

Bruce, L. J., Cope, D. L., Jones, G. K., Schofield, A. E., Burley, M., Povey, S., Unwin, R. J., Wrong, O., and Tanner, M. J. A. (1997) Familial renal tubular acidosis is associated with mutations in the red cell anion exchanger (band3:AE1) gene. *Journal of Clinical Investigation*, **100**, 1693–707.

Buchanan, E. U. and Komrower, G. M. (1958). The prognosis of idiopathic renal acidosis in infancy with observations on urine acidification and ammonia production in children. *Archives of Diseases in Childhood*, **33**, 532–5.

Buckalew, V. M., McCurdy, D. K., Ludwig, G. D., Chaykin, L. B., and Elkinton, J. R. (1968). Incomplete renal tubular acidosis. *American Journal of Medicine*, **45**, 32–42.

Buckalew, V. M., Purvis, P. L., Shulman, M. G., Herndon, C. N., and Rudman, D. (1974). Hereditary renal tubular acidosis. *Medicine*, **53**, 229–54.

Bushinsky, D. A. and Lechleider, R. J. (1987). Mechanism of proton induced bone calcium release: calcium carbonate dissolution. *American Journal of Physiology*, **253**, F998–1005.

Butler, A. M., Wilson, J. L., and Farber, S. (1936). Dehydration and acidosis with calcification at renal tubules. *Journal of Paediatrics*, **8**, 489–99.

Callis, L., Castello, F., Fortuny, G., Vallo, A., and Ballabriga, A. (1970). Effect of hydrochlorothiazide on rickets and on renal tubular acidosis in two patients with cystinosis. *Helvetica Paediatrica Acta*, **25**, 602–19.

Carlisle, E. J. F., Donnelly, S. M., and Halperin, M. L. (1991). Renal tubular acidosis (RTA): Recognize the ammonium defect and pHorget the urine pH. *Paediatric Nephrology*, **5**, 242–8.

Carre, I. J., Wood, B. S. B., and Smallwood, W. L. (1954). Idiopathic renal acidosis in infancy. *Archives of Diseases in Childhood*, **29**, 326–33.

Caruana, R. J. and Buckalew, V. M. (1988). The syndrome of distal (type I) renal tubular acidosis. *Medicine*, **67**, 84–99.

Chafe, L. and Gault, M. H. (1994). First morning urine pH in the diagnosis of renal tubular acidosis with nephrolithiasis. *Clinical Nephrology*, **41**, 159–62.

Cochran, M., Peacock, M., Smith, D. A., and Nordin, B. E. C. (1968). Renal tubular acidosis of pyelonephritis with renal stone disease. *British Medical Journal*, **2**, 721–9.

Cochran, M. and Nordin, B. E. C. (1969). Role of acidosis in renal osteomalacia. *British Medical Journal*, **2**, 276–9.

Cochran, M. and Wilkinson, R. (1975). Effect of correction of metabolic acidosis on bone mineralisation rates of patients with osteomalacia. *Nephron*, **15**, 98–110.

Cogan, M. C. and Arieff, A. I. (1978). Sodium wasting, acidosis, and hyperkalemia induced by methicillin interstitial nephritis. *American Journal of Medicine*, **64**, 500–7.

Cogan, M. G. and Alpern, R. J. (1984). Regulation of proximal bicarbonate reabsorption. *American Journal of Physiology*, **247**, F387–95.

Crawford, M. A., Milne, M. D., and Scribner, B. H. (1959). The effects of changes in acid-base balance on urinary citrate in the rate. *Journal of Physiology*, **149**, 413–23.

Cunningham, J., Bikle, D. D., and Avioli, L. V. (1984). Acute, but not chronic, metabolic acidosis disturbs 25-hydroxyvitamin D_3 metabolism. *Kidney International*, **25**, 47–52.

Dedmon, R. E. and Wrong, O. M. (1962). The excretion of organic anion in renal tubular acidosis with particular reference to citrate. *Clinical Science*, **22**, 19–32.

Denton, D. A., Wynn, V., McDonald, I. R., and Simon, S. (1951). Renal regulation of the extracellular fluid. II. Renal physiology in electrolyte balance. *Acta Medica Scandinavica*, Suppl. **261**, 1–202.

Donkerwolcke, R. A., Valk, C., van Wijngaarden-Penterman, M. J. G., and van Stekelenburg, G. J. (1979). A case of transient renal tubular acidosis type 1,4, hybrid RTA. *Paediatric Research*, **13**, 1177–8.

Donkerwolcke, R. A., Valk, C., van Wijngaarden-Penterman, M. J. G., and van Stekelenburg, G. J. (1983). The diagnostic value of the urine to blood carbon dioxide tension gradient for the assessment of distal tubular hydrogen secretion in paediatric patients with renal tubular disorders. *Clinical Nephrology*, **19**, 254–8.

DuBose, T. D. Jr. (1982). Hydrogen ion secretion by the collecting duct is a determinant of the urine to blood pCO_2 gradient in alkaline urine. *Journal of Clinical Investigations*, **69**, 145–56.

DuBose, T. D. Jr. and Caflish, C. R. (1985). Validation of the difference in urine to blood carbon dioxide tension during experimental models of distale renal tubular acidosis. *Journal of Clinical Investigations*, **75**, 1116–23.

Edelmann, C. M. Jr. (1985). Isolated proximal (type 2) renal tubular acidosis. In: *Renal tubular disorders* (ed. H. C. Gonick and V. M. Buckalew Jr.), pp. 261–79. Marcel Drekker, New York.

Edelmann, C. M. Jr., Rodriguez-Soriano, J., Boichis, H., and Stark, H. (1965). An isolated defect in renal bicarbonate reabsorption as a cause of hyperchloremic acidosis. *Journal of Paediatrics*, **67**, 946–7.

Edelmann, C. M. Jr., Rodriguez-Soriano, J., Boichis, H., Gruskin, A. B., and Acosta, M. I. (1967).

Renal bicarbonate reabsorption and hydrogen ion excretion in normal infants. *Journal of Clinical Investigations*, **46**, 1309–17.

Elkinton, J. R., Huth, E. J., Webster, G. D., and McCance, R. A. (1960). The renal excretion of hydrogen ion in renal tubular acidosis. I. The quantitative assessment of the response to ammonium chloride as an acid load. *American Journal of Medicine*, **29**, 554–75.

Feest, T. G. (1977). Medullary sponge kidney: abnormalities of renal tubular and glomerular function and their relationship to clinical features. *Proceedings of the European Dialysis and Transplant Association*, **14**, 511–17.

Feest, T. G., Lockwood, C. M., Morley, A. R., and Uff, J. S. (1978*a*). Renal immunopathology in distal renal tubular acidosis. *Clinical Nephrology*, **10**, 187–98.

Feest, T. G., Proctor, S., Brown, R., and Wrong, O. M. (1978*b*). Nephrocalcinosis: another cause of renal erythrocytosis. *British Medical Journal*, **2**, 605–6.

Feest, T. G. and Wrong, O. M. (1982). Renal tubular acidosis. In: *Recent advances in renal medicine* (ed. N. F. Jones and D. K. Peters), vol. 2, pp. 243–71. Churchill Livingstone, Edinburgh.

Firpo, J. J., Canterbury, J. M., Segil, L., and Coe, F. L. (1972). Mechanism of hyperparathyroidism in distal renal tubular acidosis. *Clinical Research*, **20**, 636.

Frymoyer, P. A., Scheinman, S. J., Dunham, P. B., Jones, D. B., Hueber, P., Schroeder, E. T. (1991). X-linked recessive nephrolithiasis with renal failure. *New England Journal of Medicine*, **326**, 1029–30.

Gamble, J. L., Blackfan, K. D., and Hamilton, B. (1925). A study of the diuretic action of acid-producing salts. *Journal of Clinical Investigations*, **1**, 359–88.

Gill, J. R., Bell, N. H., and Bartter, F. C. (1967). Impaired conservation of sodium and potassium in renal acidosis and its correction by buffer anions. *Clinical Science*, **33**, 577–92.

Goldstein, M. B., Bear, R., Richardson, R. M. A., Mardsen, P. A., and Halperin, M. L. (1986). The urine anion gap: A clinically useful index of acid excretion. *American Journal of Medical Sciences*, **292**, 198–202.

Good, D. W. and Knepper, M. A. (1985). Ammonia transport in the mamalian kidney. *American Journal of Physiology*, **248**, F459–71.

Gottschalk, C. W., Lassiter, W. E., and Mylle, M. (1960). Localization of urine acidification in the mammalian kidney. *American Journal of Physiology*, **198**, 581–5.

Gyory, A. Z. and Edwards, K. D. G. (1968). Renal tubular acidosis. *American Journal of Medicine*, **45**, 43–62.

Halperin, M. L., Goldstein, M. B., Haig, A., Johnson, M. D., and Stinebaugh, B. J. (1974). Studies on the pathogenesis of type I (distal) renal tubular acidosis as revealed by urinary pCO_2 tensions. *Journal of Clinical Investigations*, **53**, 669–77.

Halperin, M. L., Richardson, R. M. A., Bear, R. A., Magner, P. O., Kamel, K., and Ethier, J. H. (1988). Urine ammonium: the key to the diagnosis of distal renal tubular acidosis. *Nephron*, **50**, 1–4.

Hamed, I. A., Czerwinski, A. W., Coats, B., Kaufman, C., and Altmiller, D. H. (1979). Familial absorptive hypercalcuria and renal tubular acidosis. *American Journal of Medicine*, **67**, 385–91.

Harrison, H. E. (1956). The interrelation of citrate and calcium metabolism. *American Journal of Medicine*, **20**, 1–3.

Hausler, G. (1958). Zur Technik und Spezifitat des histochemischen Carboan-hydrasenachiveises im Modellversuch und in Gewebsschnitten von Rattennieren. Zeitschrift fur Zellforschung und Mikroskopische Anatomie. *Abteilung Histochemie*, **1**, 29–47.

Henderson, L. J. and Palmer, W. W. (1915). On the several factors of acid excretion in nephritis. *Journal of Biological Chemistry*, **21**, 37–55.

Ho Ping Kong, H. and Alleyne, G. A. O. (1968). Defect in urinary acidification in adults with sickle-cell anaemia. *Lancet*, **2**, 954–5.

Hulter, H., Ilnicki, L., Harbottle, J., and Sebastian, A. (1977). Impaired renal H+ secretion and NH_3 production in mineralocorticoid deficient glucocorticoid-replete dogs. *American Journal of Physiology*, **232**, F136–F146.

Hulter, H. N., Toto, R. D., Ilnicki, L. P., and Sebastian, A. (1983). Chronic hyperkalaemic renal tubular acidosis induced by KCI loading. *American Journal of Physiology*, **244**, F255–64.

Igarashi, T., Ishii, T., Watanabe, K., Hayakawa, H., Horio, K., Sone, Y., *et al.* (1994). Persistent isolated proximal renal tubular acidosis—a systemic disease with a distinct clinical entity. *Paediatric Nephrology*, **8**, 70–1.

Jaffe, H. L., Bodansky, A., and Chandler, J. P. (1932). Ammonium chloride decalcification as modified by calcium intake: the relation between generalised osteoporosis and osteitis fibrosa. *Journal of Experimental Medicine*, **56**, 823–34.

Jaksch, R. von. (1988). Uber die Alkalescenz des Blutes bei Krankheiten. Zeitchrift fur *klinische Medicin*, **13**, 350–62.

Kraut, J. A., Mishler, D. R., Singer, F. R., and Goodman, W. G. (1986). The effects of metabolic acidosis on bone formation and bone resorption in the rat. *Kidney International*, **30**, 694–700.

Kurtzman, N. A. (1990). Disorders of distal acidification. *Kidney International*, **38**, 720–7.

Laski, M. E. (1987). Total CO_2 flux in isolated tubules during carbonic anhydrase inhibition: Unique effects of ouabain and amiloride. *American Journal of Physiology*, **252**, F322–F330.

Lathem, W. (1958). Hyperchloremic acidosis in chronic pyelonephritis. *New England Journal of Medicine*, **258**, 1031–6.

Lee, D. N. B., Drinkard, J. P., Gonick, H. C., Coulson, W. F., and Cracchiolo, A. (1976). Pathogenesis of renal calculi in distal renal tubular acidosis. *Clinical Orthopaedics*, **121**, 234–42.

Lemann, J., Litzow, J. R., and Lennon, E. J. (1967). Studies of the mechanism by which chronic metabolic acidosis augments urinary calcium excretion in man. *Journal of Clinical Investigation*, **46**, 1318–28.

Lemieux, G., Watford, M., Vinay, P., and Gougoux, A. (1980). Metabolic changes in skeletal muscle during chronic metabolic acidosis. *International Journal of Biochemistry*, **12**, 75–83.

Levine, A. S. and Michael, A. F. (1967). Ehlers–Danlos syndrome with renal tubular acidosis and medullary sponge kidneys. *Journal of Paediatrics*, **71**, 107–13.

Lightwood, R. (1935). Communiction to the British Paediatric Association. *Archives of Disease in Childhood*, **10**, 205–6.

Lightwood, R., Payne, W. W., and Black, J. A. (1953). Infantile renal acidosis. *Paediatrics*, **12**, 628–44.

Lightwood, R. and Butler, N. (1963). Decline in primary infantile renal acidosis. Aetiological implications. *British Medical Journal*, **1**, 855–7.

Lloyd, S. E., Pearce, S. H. S., Fisher, S. E., Steinmeyer, K., Schwappach, B., Scheinman, S. J., *et al.* (1996) A common molecular basis for three inherited kidney stone diseases. *Nature*, **379**, 445–9.

Matsumara, R., Kondo, Y., Sugiyama, T., Sueshi, M., Koike, T., Takabayashi, K., *et al.* (1988). Immunohistochemical identification of infiltrating mononuclear cells in tubulointerstital nephritis associated with Sjogren's syndrome. *Clinical Nephrology*, **30**, 335–40.

McCurdy, D. K., Cornwell, G. G., and De Pratti, V. J. (1967). Hyperglobulinemic renal tubular acidosis. *Annals of Internal Medicine*, **67**, 110–17.

McCurdy, D. K. and Elkinton, J. R. (1968). Renal tubular acidosis due to amphotericin B. *New England Journal of Medicine*, **276**, 124–30.

McSherry, E., Sebastian, A., and Morris, R. C. (1972). Renal tubular acidosis (RTA) in infants: the several kinds, including bicarbonate wasting, classic renal tubular acidosis. *Journal of Clinical Investigation*, **51**, 499–514.

McSherry, E. and Morris, R. C. (1978). Attainment and maintenance of normal stature with alkali therapy in infants and children with classic renal tubular acidosis. *Journal of Clinical Investigation*, **61**, 509–27.

Milne, M. D., Scribner, B. H., and Crawford, M. A. (1958). Non-ionic diffsion and the excretion of weak acids and bases. *American Journal of Medicine*, **24**, 709–29.

Morris, R. C. (1966). Evidence for an acidification defect of the proximal renal tubule in experimental and clinical renal disease. *Journal of Clinical Investigation*, **45**, 1048–9.

Morris, R. C., Sebastian, A., and McSherry, E. (1972). Renal acidosis. *Kidney International*, **1**, 322–40.

Morris, R. C. Jr. (1981). Renal tubular acidosis. *New England Journal of Medicine*, **304**, 418–20.

Morris, R. C. and Ives, H. E. (1991). Inherited disorders of the renal tubule. In: *The kidney* (5th edn) (ed. B. M. Brenner and F. C. Rector), pp. 596–659. Saunders, Philadelphia.

Moss, A. H., Kaehny, W. D., Goodmand, S. I., Haut, L. L., and Haussler, M. R. (1980). Fanconi's syndrome and distal renal tubular acidosis after glue sniffing. *Annals of Internal Medicine*, **92**, 69–70.

Nance, W. E. and Sweeney, A. (1971). Evidence for autosomal recessive inheritance of the syndrome of renal tubular acidosis with deafness. *Birth Defects*, **7**, 70–3.

Nash, M. A., Torrado, A., Greifer, I., Spitzer, A., and Edelmann, C. M. Jr. (1972). Renal tubular acidosis in infants and children. Clinical course, response to treatment and prognosis. *Journal of Paediatrics*, **80**, 738–48.

Norman, M. E., Feldman, N. I., Cohn, R. M., Roth, K. S., and McCurdy, D. K. (1978). Urinary citrate excretion in the diagnosis of renal tubular acidosis. *Journal of Paediatrics*, **9**, 394–400.

Orloff, J. and Berliner, R. W. (1956). The mechanism of ammonia excretion in the dog. *Journal of Clinical Investigation*, **35**, 223–35.

Perez, G. O., Oster, J. R., and Vaamonde, C. A. (1974). Renal acidosis and renal potassium handling in selective hypoaldosteronism. *American Journal of Medicine*, **57**, 809–16.

Perez, G. O., Oster, J. R., and Vaamonde, C. A. (1975). Incomplete syndrome of renal tubular acidosis induced by lithium carbonate. *Journal of Laboratory and Clinical Medicine*, **86**, 386–94.

Perez, G. O., Oster, J. R., and Vaamonde, C. (1976). Renal acidification in patients with mineralo-corticoid deficiency. *Nephron*, **17**, 461–73.

Pitts, R. F. and Lotspeich, W. D. (1946). Bicarbonate and the renal regular of acid-base balance. *American Journal of Physiology*, **147**, 138–54.

Pitts, R. F., Lotspeich, W. D., Schiess, W. A., and Ayer, R. L. (1948). The renal regulation of acid-base balance in man. II The nature of the mechanism of acidifying the urine. *Journal of Clinical Investigation*, **27**, 48–56.

Pitts, R. F., de Haas, T., and Klein, J. (1963). Relation of renal amino and amide nitrogen excretion to ammonia production. *American Journal of Physiology*, **204**, 187–91.

Pook, M. A., Wrong, O., Wooding, C., Norden, A. G. W., Feest, T. G., and Thakker, R. V. (1993). Dent's disease, a renal Fanconi syndrome with nephrocalcinosis and kidney stones, is associated with a microdeletion involving DXS255 and maps to Xp11.22. *Human Molecular Genetics*, **2**, 2129–34.

Preisig, P. A. and Alpern, R. J. (1991). Basolateral membrane H/HCO$_3$ transport in renal tubules. *Kidney International*, **39**, 1077–86.

Preminger, G. M., Sakhale, K., Skurda, C., and Pak, C. Y. C. (1985). Prevention of recurrent calcium stone formation with potassium citrate therapy in patients with distal renal tubular acidosis. *Journal of Urology*, **134**, 20–3.

Preminger, G. M., Sakhale, K., and Pak, C. Y. C. (1987). Hypercalcuria and altered intestinal calcium absorption occurring independently of vitamin D in incomplete distal renal tubular acidosis. *Metabolism*, **36**, 176–9.

Rampini, S., Fanconi, A., Illig, R., and Prader, A. (1968). Effect of hydrochlorothiazide on proximal renal tubular acidosis in a patient with idiopathic De Toni–Debre–Fanconi syndrome. *Helvetica Paediatrica Acta*, **23**, 13–21.

Rastogi, S. P., Crawford, C., Wheeler, R., Flanigan, W., and Arruda, J. A. L. (1984). Effect of frusemide on urinary acidification in distal renal tubular acidosis. *Journal of Laboratory Clinical Medicine*, **104**, 271–82.

Rector, F. C., Seldin, D. W., and Copenhaver, J. C. (1954). The mechanism of ammonia excretion during ammonium chloride acidosis. *Journal of Clinical Investigation*, **34**, 20–6.

Rector, F. C., Seldin, D. W., Roberts, H. D., and Smith, J. S. (1960). The role of plasma CO2 tension and carbonic anhydrase activity in the renal absorption of bicarbonate. *Journal of Clinical Investigation*, **39**, 1706–21.

Rector, F. C. (1964). Micropuncture studies on the mechanism of urinary acidification. In: *Renal metabolism and epidemiology of some renal disease*, p. 9. National Kidney Foundation, New York.

Rector, F. C., Carter, N. W., and Seldin, D. W. (1965). The mechanism of bicarbonate reabsorption in the proximal and distal tubules of the kidney. *Journal of Clinical Investigation*, **44**, 278–90.

Richards, P., Chamberlain, M. J., and Wrong, O. M. (1972). Treatment of osteomalacia of renal tubular acidosis by bicarbonate alone. *Lancet*, **2**, 994–7.

Rodriguez-Soriano, J. and Vallo, A. (1988). Renal tubular hyperkalaemia in childhood. *Paediatric Nephrology*, **2**, 498–500.

Rodriguez-Soriano, J. and Vallo, A. (1990). Renal tubular acidosis. *Paediatric Nephrology*, **4**, 268–75.

Royer, P., Lestradet, H., Nordmann, R., Mathieu, H., and Rodriquez-Soriano, J. (1962). Etudes sur quatre cas d'acidose tubulaire chronique idiopathique avec hypocitraturie. *Semaine Hopital Paris*, **38**, 808–29.

Sabatini, S. and Kurtzman, N. A. (1990). Enzyme activity in obstructive uropathy: The biochemical basis for salt wastage and the acidification defect. *Kidney International*, **37**, 79–84.

Saito, H., Furuyama, T., Shioji, R., Onodera, S., and Sasaki, Y. (1970). Polyacrylamide gel electrophoretic and immunochamical studies on urinary proteins in Sjögren's syndrome, with special reference to tubular proteinuria. *Tohoku Journal of Experimental Medicine*, **101**, 205–14.

Sartorius, O. W., Roemmelt, J. C., and Pitts, R. F. (1949). The renal regulation of acid–base balance in man. IV. The nature of the renal compensation in ammonium chloride acidosis. *Journal Clinical Investigation*, **28**, 423–39.

Schambelan, M. Stockigt, J. R., and Biglieri, E. G. (1972). Isolated hypoaldosteronism in adults. *New England Journal of Medicine*, **287**, 573–8.

Scheinman, S. I., Pook, M. A., Wooding, C., Pang, J. T., Frymoyer, P. A., and Thakker, R. V. (1993). Mapping the gene causing X-linked recessive nephrolithiasis to Xp11.22 by linkage studies. *Journal of Clinical Investigation*, **91**, 2351–7.

Schuster, V. L. (1990). Bicarbonate reabsorption and secretion in the cortical and outer medullary collecting tubule. *Seminars in Nephrology*, **10**, 139–47.

Schuster, V. L., Bonsib, S. M., and Jennings, M. L. (1986). Two types of collecting duct mitochondria-rich (intercalated) cells: lectin and band 3 cytochemistry. *American Journal of Physiology*, **251**, C347–55.

Sebastian, A., McSherry, E., and Morris, R. C. (1971). Renal potassium wasting in renal tubular acidosis (RTA): its occurrence in types 1 and 2 RTA despite sustained correction of systemic acidosis. *Journal Clinical Investigation*, **50**, 667–8.

Sebastian, A. and Morris, R. C. (1977). Renal tubular acidosis. *Clinical Nephrology*, **7**, 216–36.

Sebastian, A. and Morris, R. C. (1979). Renal tubular acidosis. In: *Strauss and Welt's Disease of the Kidney* (3rd edn) (ed. L. E. Early and C. W. Gottschalk), pp. 1029–54. Little, Brown, Boston.

Seedat, Y. K. (1964). Some observations of renal tubular acidosis—a family study. *South African Medical Journal*, **38**, 606–10.

Seldin, D. W. (1976). Metabolic alkalosis. In: *The kidney* (ed. B. M. Brenner and F. C. Rector), p. 661. WB Saunders & Co., Philadelphia.

Seldin, D. W. and Wilson, J. D. (1972). Renal tubular acidosis. In: *The metabolic basis of inherited diseases* (3rd edn) (ed. J. B. Stanbury, J. B. Wyngaarden, and D. S. Frederickson), p. 1548. McGraw Hill, New York.

Shioji, R., Furuyama, T., Onodera, S., Saito, H., Ito, H., and Sasaki, Y. (1970). Sjogren's syndrome and renal tubular acidosis. *American Journal of Medicine*, **48**, 456–63.

Simpson, D. P. (1971). Control of hydrogen ion homeostasis and renal acidosis. *Medicine*, **50**, 503–42.

Simpson, D. and Hecker, J. (1982). Glutamine distribution in mitochondria from normal and acidotic kidneys. *Kidney International*, **21**, 774–9.

Sly, W. S., White, M. P., Sundaram, V., Tashian, R. E., Hewett-Emmett, D., Guibaud, P., *et al.* (1985). Carbonic anhydrase II deficiency in 12 families with the autosomal recessive syndrome of osteoporosis with renal tubular acidosis and cerebral calcification. *New England Journal of Medicine*, **313**, 139–45.

Soriano, J. R., Boichis, H., and Edelmann, C. M. (1967). Bicarbonate reabsorption and hydrogen ion excretion in children with renal tubular cidosis. *Journal of Paediatrics*, **71**, 802–13.

Soriano, J. R. and Edelmann, C. M. (1969). Renal tubular acidosis. *Annal Review of Medicine*, **20**, 363–82.

Stapleton, T. (1949). Idiopathic renal acidosis. *Lancet*, **1**, 683–5.

Steele, T. W. and Edwards, K. D. G. (1971). Analgesic nephropathy. *Medical Journal of Australia*, **1**, 181–7.

Stein, J. C., Rector, F. C., and Seldin, D. W. (1968). The effect of acute metabolic acidosis on proximal tubular sodium reabsorption in the rat. *Journal of Clinical Investigation*, **47**, 93a.

Stone, D. K. and Xie, X. S. (1988). Proton translocating ATPases: Issues in structure and function. *Kidney International*, **33**, 767–74.

Szylman, P., Better, O. S., Chaimowitz, C., and Rosler, A. (1976). Role of hyperkalaemia in the metabolic acidosis of isolated hypoalderonism. *New England Journal of Medicine*, **294**, 361–5.

Taher, S. M., Anderson, R. J., McCartney, R., Popovitzer, M. M., and Schrier, R. W. (1974). Renal tubular acidosis associated with toluene 'sniffing'. *New England Journal of Medicine*, **290**, 765–8.

Tamarappoo, B. K., Sudhir, J., and Welbourne, T. C. (1990). Interorgan glutamine flow regulation in metabolic acidosis. *Minor Electolyte Metab.*, **16**, 322–30.

Verlander, J. W., Madsen, K. M., and Tisher, C. C. (1991). Structural and functional features of proton and bicarbonate transport in the rat collecting duct. *Seminars in Nephrology*, **11**, 465–77.

Wagner, S., Vogel, R., Lietzke, R., Koob, R., and Drenckhann, D. (1987). Immunochemical characterization of a band 3-like anion exchanger in collecting duct of human kidney. *American Journal of Physiology*, **253**, (2 Pt2), F213–31.

Welbourne, T. C. (1986). Effect of metabolic acidosis on hindquarter glutamine and alanine release. *Metabolism*, **35**, 614–18.

Wingo, C. S. (1989). Active proton secretion and potassium absorption in the rabbit outer medullary collecting duct. *Journal of Clinical Investigation*, **84**, 361–5.

Winsnes, A., Monn, E., Stokke, O., and Feyling, T. (1979). Congenital persistent proximal type of renal tubular acidosis in two brothers. *Acta Paediatrica Scandinavica*, **60**, 86108.

Wolf, A. V. (1947). Renal regular of water and some electrolytes in man, with special reference to their relative retention and excretion. *American Journal of Physiology*, **148**, 54–69.

Wrong, O. M. (1988). Urinary anion gap in hyperchloremic metabolic acidosis. *New England Journal of Medicine*, **319**, 585–6.

Wrong, O. M. (1991). Distal renal tubular acidosis: the value of urinary pH, PCO2 and NH4$^+$ measurements. *Paediatric Nephrology*, **5**, 249–55.

Wrong, O. M. and Davies, H. E. F. (1959). The excretion of acid in renal disease. *Quarterley Journal of Medicine*, **28**, 259–313.

Wrong, O. M. and Feest, T. G. (1976). Nephrocalcinosis. In: *Advances in medicine* (ed. D. K. Peters), vol. 12, p. 394–405. Pitman Medical, London.

Wrong, O. M. and Feest, T. G. (1980). The natural history of distal renal tubular acidosis. *Contributions in Nephrology*, **21**, 137–44.

Wrong, O. M., Feest, T. G., and MacIver, A. G. (1993). Immune-related, potassium-losing interstitial nephritis: a comparison with distal renal tubular acidosis. *Quarterley Journal of Medicine*, **86**, 513–34.

Wrong, O. M., Norden, A. G. W., and Feest, T. G. (1994). Dent's disease: a familial proximal renal tubular syndrome with low-molecular weight proteinuria, hypercalcuria, nephrocalcinosis, metabolic bone disease, progressive renal failure and a marked male predominance. *Quarterley Journal of Medicine*, **87**, 473–93.

York, S. E. and Yendt, E. R. (1966). Osteomalacia with renal bicarbonate loss. *Canadian Medical Association Journal*, **94**, 1329–42.

Zackai, E. H., Sly, W. S., McAlister, W. G. (1972). Microcephaly, mild mental retardation, short stature, and skeletal anomalies in siblings. *American Journal of Diseases of Children*, **124**, 111–5.

14.1

Bardet–Biedl syndrome

Patrick S. Parfrey, Jane Green, and John D. Harnett

Introduction

Traditionally, Laurence–Moon–Biedl syndrome has been described as characterized by retinal dystrophy, polydactyly, obesity, mental retardation, and hypogenitalism (Ammann 1970; McKusick 1988). However, it is likely that this syndrome comprises two genetic disorders: the Laurence–Moon and Bardet–Biedl syndromes (Bardet 1920; Biedl 1922; Schachat and Maumenee 1982; Lancet 1988). In the former, polydactyly is rare and spastic paraparesis dominates, whereas in the latter syndrome neurologic manifestations are very unusual and renal abnormalities are frequent (Harnett *et al.* 1988). We have suggested that the cardinal manifestations of Bardet–Biedl syndrome are dystrophic extremities, retinal dystrophy, obesity, hypogenitalism in males, and renal abnormalities (Green *et al.* 1989). This chapter will focus on the manifestations (Table 14.1.1) and management of Bardet–Biedl syndrome.

Heredity

Bardet-Biedl syndrome is an autosomal recessive condition (Ammann 1970). The probable consanguinity rate ranges from 35% to 45% among parents of affected patients (Bell 1958; Ammann 1970; Green *et al.* 1989). In studies comprising a defined population, the estimated prevalence of Bardet–Biedl syndrome was 1:17500 in Newfoundland (Green *et al.* 1989), 1:65000 in the Arab population of Kuwait (Faragand Teebi 1988), and 1:160000 in Switzerland (Ammann 1970). Although rare recessive conditions have been shown to cluster in a single isolated area, the geographic distribution of Bardet–Biedl syndrome patients does not show similar clustering. Newfoundland is a very large island with a population of 570000 scattered in small communities around the coastline. In the past, social contact between these outport communities was dependent on the sea and was impossible for several months of the year. Cases have been identified from several such communities. This lack of clustering was also seen in Switzerland (Ammann 1970) and the Netherlands (Stigglebout 1972).

The phenotypic expression of the syndrome displays not only interfamilial but also intrafamilial variation. This occurs especially for mental retardation, polydactyly, degree of obesity, reproductive dysfunction in females, and abnormalities of renal function (Green *et al.* 1989). Intrafamilial variation is less evident with respect to the type of retinal dystrophy, the presence of obesity, and the presence of abnormal renal calyces (Green *et al.* 1989).

The frequent observation of obesity, hypertension, diabetes mellitus, and renal disease in first-degree relatives (obligate gene carriers) and other blood relatives raises the possibility that

Table 14.1.1   The clinical spectrum of Bardet–Biedl syndrome

---

Cardinal manifestations:
1. Dystrophic extremities: brachydactyly, syndactyly
2. Retinal dystrophy
3. Trunkal obesity
4. Hypogenitalism in males
5. Renal structural anomalies: fetal lobulation, calyceal clubbing/cysts

Other important manifestations:
1. Polydactyly
2. Other ophthalmic manifestations
3. Mental retardation
4. Reproductive endocrine abnormalities in females
5. Diabetes mellitus
6. Hypertension and chronic renal failure

Bardet–Biedl heterozygotes may also develop these abnormalities (Croft and Swift 1990). However, in our studies we did not find strong evidence to support an increased risk of clinically important disease in heterozygote siblings (O'Dea *et al.* 1996). Two other syndromes, related in part phenotypically to Bardet–Biedl syndrome, are Biemond syndrome (characterized by iris coloboma) and Alstrom syndrome (characterized by deafness and diabetes mellitus).

Bardet–Biedl syndrome is genetically heterogeneous. In different families, linkage has been reported to chromosome 3 (Sheffield *et al.* 1994), chromosome 11q (Leppert *et al.* 1994), chromosome 15 (Carmi *et al.* 1995*a*), and chromosome 16q (Kwitek-Black *et al.* 1993). No linkage with these markers has been documented in other families. In 15 Newfoundland families one locus was linked to chromosome 3, eight were unlinked to the four known loci, and four more were uninformative. It has been suggested that there are phenotypic differences among patients with Bardet–Biedl syndrome linked to three different chromosome loci (Carmi *et al.* 1995*b*), but this requires confirmation in other families.

Causation

After five weeks of fetal development, the hands and feet begin to differentiate, the optic vesicle begins to invaginate, the cerebral hemispheres are well-marked, and the ureteral bud and gonads are present (Beck *et al.* 1985). Subsequently, the mesenchymal core of the peripheral part of the plate-like enlargement at the extremity of the limb bud becomes condensed to outline the digits, and the thinner intervening areas break down from the circumference toward the centre (Moore 1982). This process is carried out incompletely or may be arrested prematurely in Bardet–Biedl syndrome (Fig. 14.1.1).

During the second month of fetal development, the blind ends of the secreting renal tubules must establish communication with the blind ends of the collecting tubules derived from the metanephrogenic cap of the ureteral diverticulum (Gray 1985). Failure to do so leads to the formation of calyceal cysts.

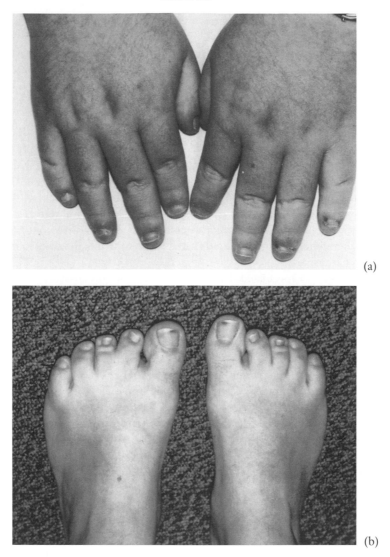

(a)

(b)

Fig. 14.1.1 (a) Dysmorphic hands and (b) feet in Bardet–Biedl syndrome, showing brachydactyly (broad stubby extremities) and syndactyly.

By the end of the eighth week, the hands and feet, the layers of the retina, the genitalia, and the kidneys have developed, and the cerebral cortex is differentiating (Moore 1982). Thus, it appears that fundamental directive genes, which should be operational at the end of the second month after conception, during the final stages of maturation of several organs, may be defective. The genetic heterogeneity of the syndrome suggests this process involves a cascade of enzymes genetically controlled from at least five different loci.

Toledo *et al.* (1977) have shown that the hypogonadism is due to the primary gonadal failure, implying that the expression of the sex chromosome is impaired in Bardet–Biedl syndrome. The prevalence of sex chromosome aneuploid is higher than expected by chance (Grossniklaus *et al.*

1988). Thus the chromosome that carries the defective gene may affect sex chromosome distribution and expression.

Bell (1958) has suggested that the genesis of Bardet–Biedl syndrome is interference with the smooth development of the hypothalamus, and Ammann (1970) has hypothesized that temporary fetal hydrocephalus is the basis of central nervous system involvement. There is little evidence of hypothalamic–pituitary hypofunction, however, and it is difficult to associate such a defect with maturational defects of the hands and kidneys (Green *et al.* 1989).

Some insight into the pathophysiology of retinitis pigmentosa in Bardet–Biedl syndrome is provided by the study of Corrocher *et al.* (1989) in five members of a family, two of whom were affected by Laurence–Moon–Biedl syndrome. A remarkable increase of polyunsaturated fatty acids (particularly arachidonic acid) and of cholesterol/phospholipid molar ratio was noted in the family. This pattern of membrane lipids was associated with an increment of malondialdehyde production and an increased activity of glutathione-peroxidase. Serum retinal and α-tocopherol were in the normal range whereas serum selenium was low in three out of five members. Moreover, the alteration of membrane lipids was associated with a decrease in maximal velocity of Li–Na counter transport.

Corrocher *et al.* (1989) speculated that the enrichment of polyunsaturated fatty acids on the cell membranes may represent a condition favouring lipoperoxidation. The photoreceptors of patients with Laurence–Moon–Biedl syndrome, who are affected by retinitis pigmentosa, have numerous inclusions of lipofuscin material which is considered a product of lipoperoxidation. If the increase of polyunsaturated fatty acids observed in erythrocytes is present on the membrane of photoreceptors, it might represent a condition favouring lipoperoxidation induced by light. This may explain the accumulation of lipofuscin material and the other retinal abnormalities observed in this disease. The time necessary for the light to oxidize the membrane lipids and the difference in the efficiency of the photoreceptor antioxidant system (which keeps the free radicals at physiological level) may explain why the blindness is not present at birth, but occurs within the first three decades of life.

Clinical manifestations (Table 14.1.1)

Dysmorphic extremities

Polydactyly is not a universal feature of Bardet–Biedl syndrome. It was found in 58% of Newfoundland patients (Green *et al.* 1989) and 69% of Swiss patients (Ammann 1970). Syndactyly, polydactyly, or both occurred in 90% of patients, and brachydactyly of the feet in all patients in our recent report (Fig. 14.1.1) (Green *et al.* 1989). Among 18 patients with polydactyly, the feet were affected in 89% and the hands in 50%. These data are similar to those of Klein and Ammann (1969), who found isolated hexadactyly to be twice as likely to affect the feet as the hands. This has been attributed to the later formation of toe anlagen in embryological development.

Obesity

Obesity is a characteristic feature of the Bardet–Biedl syndrome, as confirmed in large series (McKusick 1988; Green *et al.* 1989). It is most prominent in the trunk and proximal sections of the limbs. In our studies, 88% of the patients were above the 90th percentile of weight for height, and some were very obese. A further 8% had previously been obese (Green *et al.* 1989).

Renal disease (Table 14.1.2)

Renal failure is probably the major cause of death in Bardet–Biedl syndrome (Hurley *et al.* 1975; Churchill *et al.* 1981; O'Dea *et al.* 1996). Renal disease has been recognized frequently in this syndrome (Nadjmi *et al.* 1969; Alton and McDonald 1973; Bauman and Hogan 1973; Hurley *et al.* 1975; Churchill *et al.* 1981; Linne *et al.* 1986), but previous studies have been fraught with the problems of ascertainment bias. This was not a problem in our recent study (Harnett *et al.* 1988).

We evaluated renal structure and function in 20 of 30 patients with the disorder identified from ophthalmologic records in Newfoundland (Harnett *et al.* 1988). The mean age was 31 years, and seven were male. All 20 patients had structural or functional abnormalities of the kidneys or both. Three had end-stage renal disease. The remaining 17 patients had normal serum creatinine values and estimated creatinine clearances. Half of the subjects had hypertension. Fourteen of 17 patients could not concentrate urine above 750 mOsm per kilogram of body weight even after vasopressin, whereas all 10 normal controls could (Fig. 14.1.2). Urinary pH decreased below 5.3 after ammonium chloride administration in all 15 normal controls, but in only 13 of 18 patients.

Renal imaging

Calyceal clubbing or blunting was evident in 18 of our 19 patients studied by intravenous pyelography; 13 patients had calyceal cysts or diverticula (Fig. 14.1.3). Seventeen of 19 patients had lobulated renal outlines of the fetal type (Fig. 14.1.4). Four patients had diffuse renal cortical loss, but only two of these had renal insufficiency (Harnett *et al.* 1988).

Ultrasound was not as successful in identifying the communicating cysts/diverticula as intravenous pyelography (Cramer *et al.* 1988). The explanation may be the technical difficulty in examining these obese patients and in differentiating full calyces from adjacent cysts/diverticula. Also, as seen on IVP, the cysts/diverticula may enlarge following IVP-induced diuresis. Sonography was comparable to IVP in documenting cortical changes (Cramer *et al.* 1988).

Calyceal clubbing and cystic changes have been described previously in Laurence–Moon–Biedl syndrome (Alton and McDonald 1973) and have been attributed to vesicoureterial reflux (Hurley *et al.* 1975). Therefore, micturating cystography was performed in 17 of our patients.

Table 14.1.2 Renal abnormalities in patients with Bardet–Biedl syndrome (Green *et al.* 1989)

Abnormality	No. with abnormality	No. tested	%
Structural	20	21	95
Communicating cysts or diverticulae	13	21	62
Fetal-type lobulation	20	21	95
Diffuse cortical loss	6	21	29
Focal scarring	5	21	24
Functional			
Hypertension	18	29	62
Partial defect in urine concentration	14	17	82
Renal tubular acidosis			
Incomplete	5	19	26
Complete	1	19	5
End-stage renal disease	3	32	9

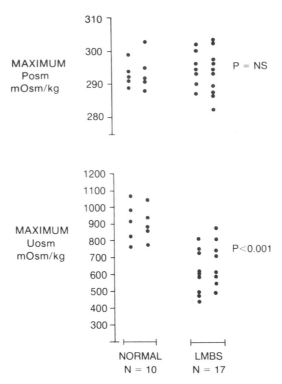

MAXIMUM
Posm
mOsm/kg

P = NS

MAXIMUM
Uosm
mOsm/kg

P<0.001

NORMAL
N = 10

LMBS
N = 17

Fig. 14.1.2   Plasma osmolality and urine osmolality after overnight fast in patients with Bardet–Biedl syndrome and controls. (Reprinted with permission from Harnett, *et al.* (1988). *N. Engl. J. Med.*, **319**, 615–18.)

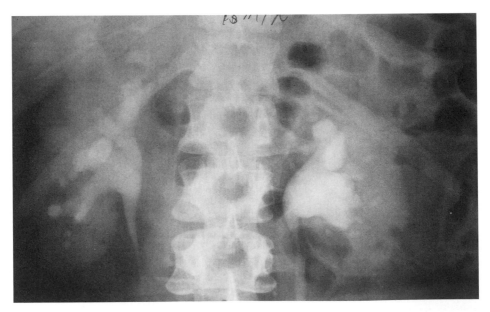

Fig. 14.1.3   Intravenous urogram in a patient with Bardet–Biedl syndrome showing the abnormal and blunted calyces, and several communicating cysts and diverticulae.

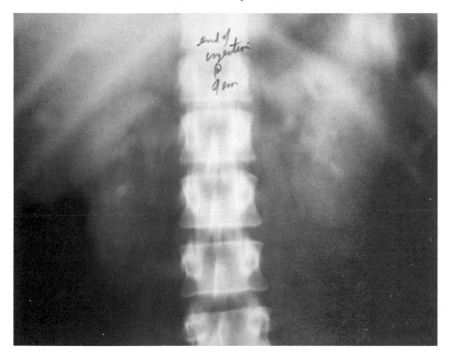

Fig. 14.1.4 Prominent lobulation in kidneys of patient with Bardet–Biedl syndrome.

The calyceal abnormalities were not related to vesicoureteral reflux and probably are dysplastic in nature (Cramer *et al.* 1988).

Persistent fetal lobulation in children with Bardet–Biedl syndrome has also been previously described (Alton and McDonald 1973; Patriquin 1987) but has not been as notable a feature in other reported cases as in our group. This lobulation is normally seen in the fetus and neonate but gradually disappears as the child matures and the lobes fuse (Patriquin 1987).

It appears that this combination of calyceal clubbing and pronounced diverticula, with lobulation, is characteristic and probably diagnostic of Bardet–Biedl syndrome. This may be particularly useful in the younger patient in whom eye changes are not yet advanced and the diagnosis is still in doubt (Cramer *et al.* 1988).

Prenatal and postnatal renal ultrasound may detect cortical and medullary cysts and other renal structural abnormalities (Ritchie *et al.* 1988; Garber and deBruyn 1991). Thus renal imaging is particularly important in investigating a child born with polydactyly, or a subsequent child of parents who have already had a child with Bardet–Biedl syndrome.

Pathology

A wide variety of histologic changes, including periglomerular and interstitial fibrosis, cystic dilatation of tubules, glomerular changes, and cortical medullary cysts, have been described in Laurence–Moon–Biedl syndrome (Hurley *et al.* 1975; Price *et al.* 1981). These changes may correlate with functional abnormalities, but no data to substantiate this correlation are avail-able. It is likely that many of these histological abnormalities are secondary to the primary renal defect.

Price *et al.* (1981) described marked ultrastructural alterations of glomerular basement membrane (GBM) comprising effacement of the trilaminar architecture, segmental irregular thickening, and accumulation of granular or fibrillar material within the inner third of the GBM. They suggested that the ultrastructural changes might be the primary glomerular abnormality in Bardet–Biedl syndrome. On the contrary, Tieder *et al.* (1982) reported four cases of Bardet–Biedl syndrome in which tubulointerstitial lesions were noted without specific ultrastructural changes in the GBM. A similar patient was subsequently reported in whom tubulointerstitial and vascular lesions were the most prominent abnormalities (Sato *et al.* 1988).

The natural history of renal impairment

We have prospectively followed 36 patients with Bardet–Biedl syndrome, 25% of whom have developed chronic renal insufficiency and 11% end-stage renal failure (O'Dea *et al.* 1996). The earliest age of onset of renal impairment was two years. By age 48, 25% of cases has chronic renal insufficiency (Fig. 14.1.5).

This data on ESRD contrasts with results of previous studies. Uraemia developed in five of nine patients (55%) from Montreal before the age of 15 years (Hurley *et al.* 1975). Linne and colleagues (1986) described six patients, five of whom had small kidneys and reduced glomerular filtration rates, and two of who had end-stage renal disease. Alton and McDonald (1973) have reported that 30% of patients with Laurence–Moon–Biedl syndrome died of uraemia. The reason for this discrepancy may be that the patients we evaluated have been identified through the ophthalmology service and were asymptomatic from a renal standpoint. Many of the previous reports may be biased in that the patients studied were referred because of a specific renal problem, and may represent the small group of patients with Bardet–Biedl syndrome who have more severe renal disease.

There are few reports on renal replacement therapy in this group of patients (Linne *et al.* 1986; Williams *et al.* 1988; Norden *et al.* 1991). In one report, a patient who had mild to moderate mental retardation, a severe visual defect, and moderate obesity was transplanted but was young and cooperative (Norden *et al.* 1991). We have a similar patient who has done extremely well after renal transplantation. In another of our patients renal replacement was considered, but following discussion with the parents it was not instituted because of severe physical and mental handicap.

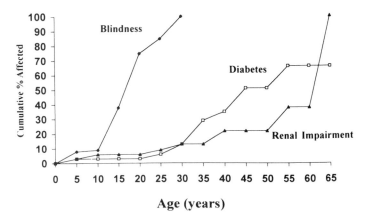

Fig. 14.1.5   The age of diagnosis of blindness, diabetes mellitus, and renal impairment in Bardet–Biedl syndrome. (Reprinted with permission from O'Dea, *et al.* (1996). *Am. J. Kid. Dis.*, **27**, 778.)

Retinal dystrophy

The retinal pigmentary changes are heterogeneous (Ammann 1970; Bergsma and Brown 1975) and are not usually those of classic retinitis pigmentosa (Ammann 1970).

In two of 28 patients studied in Newfoundland, the retina was not visible because of dense cataracts. Of the other 26 patients, only 8% had the fundoscopic appearance of typical retinitis pigmentosa, with dense bone-spicule pigmentation, pale optic discs, and attenuated vessels (Green *et al.* 1989). Eighteen patients (69%) had an atypical retinal dystrophy, with sparse pigmentation, central and peripheral atrophy, attenuated vessels, and mild to severe optic-disk pallor. Six patients (23%) had the appearance of severe macular dystrophy, with only sparse pigment clumping in the midperiphery. However, four of these six patients had decreased night vision at the time of presentation (Green *et al.* 1989). Because our patients were identified primarily through the Canadian National Institute for the Blind and the Ocular Genetics Clinic, there is a possibility of ascertainment bias. However, Ammann (1970) observed retinal dystrophy in 92% of the Swiss series, and Bell (1958) reported this finding in 94% of her series.

All patients who could be tested had markedly constricted visual fields, severe abnormalities of colour vision, raised dark-adaptation thresholds, and extinguished or minimal rod-and-cone responses on electroretinography (Green *et al.* 1989). Other ophthalmological disorders which are often associated with retinal dystrophies also occur (Table 14.1.3) (Green *et al.* 1989).

Visual acuity

In our recent report of 36 patients with Bardet–Biedl syndrome, 86% were legally blind (O'Dea *et al.* 1996). The blindness was usually incapacitating. At last examination, one patient had no light perception, 28% could only perceive light, 16% could see only hand movements, 28% could do no better than count fingers. The remaining 24% had visual acuity ≤20/200. The age of recorded legal blindness was five to 29 years of age. Fig. 14.1.5 shows that 25% of Bardet–Biedl patients were legally blind by age 13, 50% by age 18, and 100% by age 30 years. All five patients not yet legally blind were younger than 12 years. Other studies have found that visual acuity was moderately reduced at the beginning of their teens, after which it rapidly deteriorated by the age of 30 years (Klein and Ammann 1969; Runge *et al.* 1986; Leys *et al.* 1988). In those over 30 years

Table 14.1.3 Ophthalmologic abnormalities in patients with Bardet–Biedl syndrome (Green *et al.* 1989)

Characteristic	No. with disorder	No. tested	%
Blindness*	27	28	96
Retinal dystrophy	28	28	100
Myopia	12	16	75
Astigmatism	10	16	63
Nystagmus	14	27	52
Glaucoma	5	23	22
Posterior subcapsular cataracts	12	27	44
Mature cataracts or aphakia	8	27	30

*Registered as blind with Canadian National Institute for the Blind.

of age, 73% of our patients and 75% of Ammann's (1970) had visual acuity less than adequate for counting fingers.

Leys *et al.* (1988) studied the visual acuities and dark-adapted sensitivities of 12 children with Bardet–Biedl syndrome. All except one child were tested serially. In the first decade of life, visual acuity of all children was within two octaves of normal. In their second and third decades, in all but two patients the final visual acuity obtained was more than two octaves below normal. Dark-adapted sensitivities of all patients were, or became, significantly less than normal even in those patients whose period of follow-up was limited to the first decade of life. Of the 11 patients measured serially, seven showed a decrease in dark-adapted sensitivities of at least 0.5 log units during the follow-up period, and the last measured sensitivities of all patients were at least 2 log units less than the normal mean.

Photoreceptor defect

Ocular histopathology in a four-year-old boy with Bardet–Biedl syndrome, who had not yet developed end-stage disease, revealed photoreceptor cell degeneration without significant changes in retinal pigment epithelium (Runge *et al.* 1986). However, the type of photoreceptor-mediated dysfunction that is the earliest manifestation of Bardet–Biedl retinopathy (rod dysfunction, cone dysfunction, or both) is unknown.

Jacobson *et al.* (1990) studied visual function in 16 patients with the Bardet–Biedl syndrome. Visual acuity, kinetic perimetry, and electroretinography testing indicated a severe loss of central and peripheral vision and rod and cone function by the second or third decade of life. Light- and dark-adapted static perimetry in patients 10–15 years of age showed a parallel, and marked, loss of rod and cone sensitivity across the visual field. Patients with more advanced disease and no measurable peripheral visual field showed different patterns of central visual dysfunction. In the least affected patient, a 13-year-old boy, there was more rod than cone abnormality, as determined by electroretinography and static perimetry.

Mental retardation

This feature is difficult to study because it is profoundly influenced by visual acuity. The visual deficit may limit educational opportunities, and the inability to read history books or newspapers will diminish the amount of information that can be obtained. Therefore, an important observation from our recent studies is that only a minority of patients were mentally retarded when appropriate verbal and performance IQ tests for the visually impaired were used (Green *et al.* 1989). Because most patients with this syndrome have the potential for independent work, special education (which takes their visual handicap into account) is appropriate.

Bell (1958) and Amman (1970) found a much higher proportion of subjects with mental retardation than we did (Green *et al.* 1989). In Bell's study, the patients were not assessed quantitatively. In the Swiss study (1970), mild 'feeble-mindedness' was a characteristic of the majority, accompanied by labile and superficial emotion and mood. We also noted inappropriate mannerism and shallow affect in many of our patients. Their IQ scores for performance were generally better than their verbal scores, especially in the patient who had a good formal education. Six of our patients achieved the standard of grade 9, but often only after entering special education classes. One has a university degree and another is taking computer courses. Several did not receive specialized education, from which they could have benefited. Our data suggest that whereas emotional and intellectual development may be impaired in Bardet–Biedl syndrome, mental retardation is not a cardinal manifestation.

Hypogonadism

Men

Hypogenitalism is usually present in male Bardet–Biedl patients (Bell 1958; Ammann 1970; Green *et al.* 1989). Seven of eight men (88%) had small testes and very small penises in our study (Green *et al.* 1989). Two had low serum testosterone levels. Three of the eight patients had high basal follicle stimulating hormone (FSH) levels, and in all eight FSH responded to pituitary stimulation. One patient had high basal luteinizing hormone (LH) levels, three had supranormal responses to gonadotropin-releasing hormone, and in the remaining five the response was normal. Thus hypogenitalism was not due to hypopituitarism since to male patient was hypogonadotropic and all responded to gonadotropin-releasing hormone. Hypogonadium was probably primary in origin. Although the majority of our male patients had normal serum testosterone levels, the association of subnormal or normal virilization with primary gonadal failure is not uncommon is similar syndromes (Mozaffarian *et al.* 1979).

Toledo *et al.* (1977) have evaluated the hypothalamic–pituitary–gonadal function and performed testicular biopsies in three male siblings with Bardet–Biedl syndrome. They have suggested a trend to an evolving gonadal disorder that progresses throughout adult life. Another patient has been reported with germinal aplasia in one testis, incomplete spermatogenesis in the other testis, and a failure of the genitalia to respond to 11 months of testosterone treatment (Mozaffarian *et al.* 1979).

Women

The clinical picture is more heterogeneous is women, in whom poor development of the sexual organs is more difficult to measure than in men. No men with Bardet–Biedl syndrome have been reported to have fathered children whereas women with Bardet–Biedl syndrome have given birth to children (Bell 1958)—an event that occurred in two of our 12 female patients. Campo and Aaberg (1982) studied four women with Bardet–Biedl syndrome, none of whom had identifiable primary or secondary endocrine dysfunction. Three other woman with a normal hypothalamic–pituitary–gonadal axis have also been described (Leroith *et al.* 1980), as has a 27-year-old woman with normal baseline gonadotropin levels, a pubertal LH response, a somewhat blunted FSH response to gonadotropin-releasing hormone, and a normal prolactin response to thyrotropin-releasing hormone (Lee *et al.* 1986).

We have measured the serum gonadotropin responses to gonadotropin-releasing hormone in women with Bardet–Biedl syndrome. Only one of the 11 patients who were of reproductive age had hypogonadotropic hypogonadism whereas two were hypoestrogenemic but with high or normal gonadotropin levels. In several women the results were suggestive of polycystic ovary syndrome, with abnormally high LH levels and high normal prolactin levels. The latter syndrome is quite common in the general population (Polson *et al.* 1988). However, none of our patients were found to have large or cystic ovaries on ultrasonography. This may be partly because ovaries are difficult to visualize in obese women. The cause of the high LH levels in our patients was not evident. It may have been due to inadequate hypothalamic signals, an increased intra-ovarian ratio of androgen to oestrogen, or primary maturational arrest of the ovarian follicle.

Diabetes mellitus

Diabetes may be the direct cause of death in Bardet–Biedl syndrome (Escallon *et al.* 1989). In our recent follow-up of 38 patients with Bardet–Beidl syndrome, 12 (32%) had diabetes mellitus

(O'Dea *et al.* 1996). Two patients were insulin-dependent, four were prescribed oral hypoglycae-mic agents, and six were maintained on dietary management. Figure 14.1.5 shows that 25% of patients were diabetic by age 35 years and 50% by age 55. The ages of diagnosis ranged from 24–55 years. The rate of diabetes is higher in our cohort than in that of Klein and Ammann (14%) (1969), who found abnormal glucose tolerance in 14% of their 48 patients.

The cause of diabetes is unclear. Pancreatic abnormalities have not been reported from autopsies to account for the presence of abnormal glucose levels (Franke 1950; Fraccaro and Gastaldi 1953; Churchill *et al.* 1981). Obesity could lead to the development of diabetes by a reduction of cellular insulin receptors, which in turn leads to a decrease in insulin sensitivity and an increase in insulin levels (Olefsky and Kolterman 1981; Rizza *et al.* 1981). Diabetes in Bardet–Biedl syndrome is probably type II because all our patients had large increases in serum insulin levels after a glucose load (Green *et al.* 1989), suggestive of insulin resistance, and only a minority were insulin-dependent.

Hypertension

Twenty-five of 38 (66%) Bardet–Biedl patients were hypertensive, compared with only 11% (five of 45) of the unaffected siblings. Sixty per cent of the hypertensive Bardet–Biedl patients were treated with antihypertensive agents. Twenty-five per cent of Bardet–Biedl patients had elevated blood pressure by the age of 26 years, 50% by the age of 34, and 75% by the age of 53 (Fig. 14.1.6). In contrast, 25% of unaffected siblings were hypertensive by the age of 49 (p = 0.001).

Survival

In our study, eight of 38 (21%) Bardet–Biedl patients died by last follow-up (O'Dea *et al.* 1996). The ages of death ranged from one to 63. Three (38%) of these deaths were the result of end-

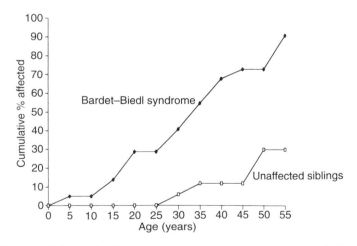

Fig. 14.1.6   The age of diagnosis of hypertension in patients with Bardet–Biedl syndrome and in their unaffected siblings. (Reprinted with permission from O'Dea, *et al.* (1996). *Am. J. Kid. Dis.*, **27**, 779.)

stage renal disease, two of congestive heart failure (both of whom had chronic renal failure), one of metastatic renal cancer who had chronic renal failure, one of pulmonary embolism and morbid obesity, and the eighth from respiratory failure and sepsis after surgery for Hirschsprung's disease at age one year. Thus, renal failure was present in 75% of patients at the time of death.

Of the 58 unaffected siblings, only one (1.7%) had died (as a result of a myocardial infarct at age 36). Fig. 14.1.7 shows the cumulative survival in 38 Bardet–Biedl patients and their 58 unaffected siblings. Life expectancy was significantly worse in patients with Bardet–Biedl syndrome than in their unaffected siblings, with 25% of Bardet-Biedl patients dead by the age of 44 years of age (p < 0.0001).

Diagnosis

Schachat and Maumenee (1982) have suggested that specific diagnostic criteria for Bardet–Biedl syndrome should include at least four of the following cardinal signs: mental retardation, obesity, hypogenitalism, polydactyly, and pigmentary retinopathy. We consider that mental retardation, if assessed quantitatively, is not usually present (although intelligence and affective responses are not optimal); hypogenitalism is infrequent in women; polydactyly occurs less frequently than brachydactyly and syndactyly; and a characteristic renal abnormality occurs often. Therefore, we suggest that the cardinal manifestations of Bardet–Biedl syndrome should be considered to include: retinal dystrophy, dystrophic extremities, obesity, hypogenitalism in men only, and renal disease (Green *et al.* 1989) (Table 14.1.1).

The early onset and severity of the various manifestations of this syndrome make early diagnosis of the syndrome essential if the patient's function is to be maximized. Only the feature of dysmorphic extremities may be recognized at birth. However, the presence of retinal

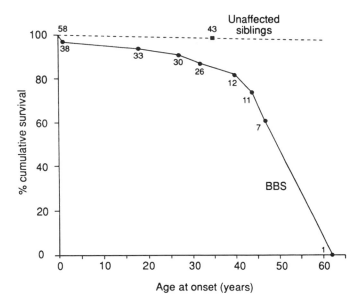

Fig. 14.1.7 The cumulative survival of patients with Bardet–Biedl syndrome and of their unaffected siblings. (Reprinted with permission from O'Dea, *et al.* (1996). *Am. J. Kid. Dis.*, **27**, 779.)

dystrophy, severe obesity, and renal structural changes should lead to an early diagnosis. The fact that many patients are not mentally retarded and do not become blind until their teen years suggests that special education could maximize patients' ability to function independently in adulthood. Screening for hypertension, abnormal glucose levels, and renal function is indicated because early treatment of these manifestations could be beneficial.

Investigation (Table 14.1.4)

The extent of investigations will depend upon the age of the patient. If an infant is suspected as having inherited the disease, or an infant has dystrophic extremities, then a renal ultrasound and intravenous pyelogram should be performed, and a complete ophthalmologic assessment undertaken. Milestones should be monitored and intelligence quotient measured as soon as possible. Follow-up should include ophthalmology assessment, weight and height, blood pressure measurement, blood urea and serum creatinine to assess glomerular filtration rate, serum sodium to monitor for nephrogenic diabetes insipidus, serum bicarbonate to monitor for renal tubular acidosis, and blood sugar. The development of polyuria, in the absence of diabetes mellitus, is an indication to test urine concentrating ability. The failure of urine osmolality to rise to normal following an overnight fast, and the failure of ADH administration to raise the urine osmolality above 750 mOsm/hg would confirm the diagnosis of nephrogenic diabetes insipidus. After puberty, the extent of primary gonadal failure can be assessed in males by measuring serum testosterone, follicle stimulating hormones, and luteinizing hormones, and in females by measuring serum estragon, follicle stimulating hormones, luteinizing hormones, and prolactin. An investigation protocol to assess the various manifestations of Bardet–Biedl syndrome is suggested in Table 14.1.4.

Management (Table 14.1.5)

Education

The most important intervention is the provision of special education. Rapid development of blindness in a very obese child, with mild to moderate mental retardation, may lead to education neglect. Consequently, education must take into account the degree of visual impairment as well as the intelligence of the child. Diligent education may produce an independent adult. Lack of education will produce an extremely dependent adult.

Diet

The propensity to obesity can be managed by early dietetic advice with calorie restriction. Achievement of normal body weight may prevent the development of diabetes mellitus. Should overt diabetes occur, oral hypoglycaemic agents may be effective and delay the prescription of insulin.

Renal disease

As the severity of renal disease is variable, the frequency of follow-up should be individualized. Follow-up should include monitoring of blood pressure, proteinuria, serum creatinine, and electrolytes.

Table 14.1.4 Investigation of Bardet–Biedl syndrome

Manifestation	Investigation
Obesity	Height and weight
Mental retardation	Intelligence quotient testing appropriate for those with visual impairment
Diabetes mellitus	Glucose tolerance test
Renal structure	Intravenous pyelogram Renal ultrasound
Renal-function	Blood urea Serum creatinine Creatinine clearance Serum bicarbonate Urine osmolality after overnight fast
Retinal dystrophy	Visual acuity Refraction Slit-lamp examination Intra-ocular pressure with tonometry Direct ophthalmoscopy Colour vision Visual fields Dark adaptation ? Electroretinography
Hypogenitalism Adult males:	Serum testosterone Serum luteinizing hormone Serum follicle stimulating hormone
Adult females:	Serum oestrogen Serum luteinizing hormone Serum follicle stimulating hormone Serum prolactin

Table 14.1.5 Management of Bardet–Biedl syndrome

1. Specialized education with low-vision aids
2. Regular ophthalmology follow-up
3. Dietary intervention to prevent or treat obesity and diabetes mellitus
4. Treatment of hypertension and chronic renal failure
5. Early discussion of end-stage renal disease therapy options with patient and/or guardian
6. Consideration of contraception in adult females
7. Genetic counselling of parents

The early onset of hypertension and renal impairment suggest that nephrological follow-up is necessary, with screening for these disorders, because early treatment of these manifestations could be beneficial.

The question of whether renal replacement should be instituted will arise. The extent of other disabilities should determine whether renal replacement therapy will be offered or accepted. None of the cardinal manifestations alone is a contraindication to transplantation (Norden *et al.* 1991), but taken together they do influence the decision.

The patient who is mentally competent and mobile is likely to do well on dialysis or after successful renal transplantation, even though vascular access or peritoneal dialysis may be difficult because of obesity, and steroid therapy may unmask diabetes. The blind, immobile, mentally retarded, housebound/institutionalized patient is unlikely to have a satisfactory quality of life on renal replacement treatment. In countries with limited dialysis facilities such patients will usually not be offered therapy. In those with unlimited access, informed parents/guardians may refuse dialysis for their child. Discussion of the issues involved should ensue soon after the diagnosis of chronic renal disease, and well before the necessity for dialysis. This will allow a rational and humane decision to be reached.

Ophthalmology

As several treatable ophthalmologic conditions such as myopia, glaucoma, and cataracts may develop (Table 14.1.3), regular ophthalmology follow-up should be provided.

Contraception

Although the sex hormone profile in adult females suggests an ovarian defect, some patients with Bardet–Biedl syndrome have become mothers. Consequently, neglect of contraceptive considerations is inadvisable.

Genetic counselling

Genetic counselling of families will be necessary. Because of the autosomal recessive inheritance pattern, parents of an affected child will be carriers. At present, carriers can only be recognized after they have had an affected child. At each subsequent pregnancy, for these carrier parents there is a 25% risk that the child will also be affected with Bardet–Biedl syndrome. There are as yet no genetic markers available for prenatal diagnosis, although renal ultrasound may reveal characteristic structural abnormalities. The variability of expression of the disease is such that it may be fatal in the first two decades of life or patients may survive for five decades or more.

References

Alton, D. J. and McDonald P. (1973). Urographic findings in the Bardet–Biedl syndrome, formerly the Laurence–Moon–Biedl syndrome. *Radiology*, **109**, 659–63.

Ammann, F. (1970). Investigations cliniques et genetiques sur le syndrome de Bardet–Biedl en Suisse. *J. Genet. Hum.*, **18** (Suppl.), 1–310.

Bardet, G. (1920). *Sur un syndrome d'obesite congenitale avec polydactylie et retinite pigmentaire (contribution a l'etude des formes cliniques de l'obesite hypophysaire)*. Thesis, University of Pairs, Paris.

Bauman, M. L. and Hogan, G. R. (1973). Laurence–Moon–Biedl syndrome: a report of two unrelated children less than 3 years of age. *Am. J. Dis. Child.*, **126**, 119–26.

Beck, F., Mofatt, D. B., and Davies, D. P. (1985). *Human embryology* (2nd edn), pp. 137, 168, 276. Blackwell, Oxford.

Bell, J. (1958). The Laurence–Moon syndrome. In: *The treasury of human inheritance* (ed. L. S. Penrose), part III, vol. 5, pp. 51–96. Cambridge University Press, London.

Bergsma, D. R. and Brown, K. S. (1975). Assessment of ophthalmologic, endocrinologic and genetic findings in the Bardet–Biedl syndrome. *Birth Defects*, **11**, 132–6.

Biedl, A. (1922). Ein Geschwisterpaar mit adiposogenitaler Dystrophie. *Dtsch. Med. Wochenschr.*, **48**, 1630. (Discussion).

Campo, R. V. and Aaberg, T. M. (1982). Ocular and systemic manifestations of the Bardet–Biedl syndrome. *Am. J. Opthalmol.*, **94**, 750–6.

Carmi, R., Rokhlina, T., Kwitek-Black, A. E., *et al.* (1995*a*). Use of a DNA pooling strategy to identify a human obesity syndrome locus on chromosome 15. *Hum. Mol. Genet.*, **4**, 9–13.

Carmi, R., Elbedour, K., Stone, E. M., and Sheffield, V. C. (1995*b*) Phenotypic differences among patients with Bardet–Biedl syndrome linked to three different chromosome loci. *Am. J. Med. Genet.*, **59**, 199–203.

Churchill, D. N., McManamon, P., and Hurley, R. M. (1981). Renal disease—a sixth cardinal feature of the Laurence–Moon–Biedl syndrome. *Clin. Nephrol.*, **16**, 151–4.

Corrocher, R., Guadagnin, L., de Gironcoli, M., Girelli, D., Guarini, P., Oliveri, O., *et al.* (1989). Membrane fatty acids, glutathione-peroxidase activity, and cation transport systems of erythrocytes and malondialdehyde production by platelets in Laurence–Moon–Biedl syndrome. *J. Endocrinol. Invest.*, **12**, 475–81.

Cramer, B., Green, J., Harnett, J., Johnson, G. J., McManaman, P., Farid, N., *et al.* (1988). Sonographic and urographic correlation in Bardet–Biedl syndrome (formerly Laurence–Moon–Biedl syndrome). *Urol. Radiol.*, **10**, 176–80.

Croft, J. B. and Swift, M. (1990). Obesity, hypertension and renal disease in relatives of Bardet–Biedl syndrome sibs. *Am. J. Med. Genet.*, **36**, 37–42.

Escallon, F., Traboulsi, E. I., and Infante, R. (1989). A family with the Bardet–Biedl syndrome and diabetes mellitus. *Arch. Ophthalmol.*, **107**, 855–7.

Farag, T. I. and Teebi, A. S. (1988). Bardet–Biedl and Larurence–Moon syndromes in a mixed Arab population. *Clin. Genet.*, **33**, 78–82.

Fraccaro, M. and Gastaldi, F. (1953). Le patologia della sindrome di Laurence–Moon–Biedl. *Folia Hereditary Pathology*, **2**, 177.

Franke, C. (1950). The gonads of the Laurence–Moon–Biedl syndrome: Three case reports with one partial autopsy. *J. Clin. Endocrinol.*, **10**, 108–12.

Garber, S. J. and deBruyn, R. (1991). Laurence–Moon–Biedl syndrome: renal ultrasound appearances in the neonate. *Brit. J. Radiol.*, **64**, 631–3.

Gray, H. (1985). *Anatomy of the human body* (30th edn) (ed. C. D. Clemente), pp. 1287, 1517. Lea & Febiger, Philadelphia.

Green, J. S., Parfrey, P. S., Harnett, J. D., Farid, N. R., Cramer, B. C., Johnson, G., *et al.* (1989). The cardinal manifestations of Bardet–Biedl syndrome, a form of Laurence–Moon–Biedl syndrome. *N. Engl. J. Med.*, **321**, 1002–9.

Grossniklaus, H. E., Muir, A., Bruner, W. E., Anneble, W., Dickerman, L. L., and Johnson, W. E. (1988). Sex chromosome aneuploidy and Bardet–Biedl syndrome. *Ophthalmol. Paed. Genet.*, **9**, 37–42.

Harnett, J. D., Green, J. S., Cramer, B. C., *et al.* (1988). The spectrum of renal disease in Laurence–Moon–Biedl syndrome. *N. Engl. J. Med.*, **319**, 615–18.

Hurley, R. M., Dery, P., Nogrady, M. B., and Drummond, K. N. (1975). The renal lesion of the Laurence-Moon-Biedl syndrome. *J. Pediatr.*, **87**, 206–9.

Jacobson, S. G., Borruat, F-X., and Apathy, P. P. (1990). Patterns of rod and cone dysfunction in Bardet-Biedl syndrome. *Am. J. Ophthalmol.*, **109**, 676–88.

Klein, D. and Ammann, F. (1969). The syndrome of Laurence–Moon–Bardet–Biedl and allied diseases in Switzerland: clinical, genetic and epidemiological studies. *J. Neurol. Sci.*, **9**, 479–513.

Kwitek-Black, A. E., Carmi, R., Duyk, G. M., *et al.* (1993). Linkage of Bardet–Biedl syndrome to chromosome 16q and evidence for non-allelic genetic heterogeneity. *Nature Genet.*, **5**, 392–6.

Lancet (1988). Laurence–Moon and Bardet-Biedl syndromes. *Lancet*, **2**, 1178.

Lee, C. S., Galle, P. C., and McDonough, P. G. (1986). The Laurence–Moon–Bardet–Biedl syndrome: case report and endocrinologic evaluation. *J. Reprod. Med.*, **31**, 353–6.

Leppert, M., Baird, L., Anderson, K. L., *et al.* (1994). Bardet–Biedl syndrome is linked to DNA markers on chromosome 11q and is genetically heterogeneous. *Nature Genet.*, **7**, 108–12.

Leroith, D., Farkash, Y., Bar-Ziev, J., and Spitz, I. M. (1980). Hypothalamic–pituitary function in the Bardet–Biedl syndrome. *Isr. J. Med. Sci.*, **16**, 514–18.

Leys, M. J., Schreiner, L. A., Hansen, R. M, Mayer, D. L., and Fulton, A. B. (1988). Visual acuities and dark-adapted thresholds of children with Bardet–Biedl syndrome. *Am. J. Opthal.*, **106**, 561–9.

Linne, T., Wikstad, I., and Zetterstrom, R. (1986). Renal involvement in the Laurence–Moon–Biedl syndrome. Functional and radiological studies. *Acta Paediatr. Scand.*, **75**, 240–4.

McKusick, V. A. (1988). *Mendelian inheritance in man: catalogs of autosomal dominant, autosomal recessive, and X-linked phenotypes* (8th edn), p. 834. Johns Hopkins University Press, Baltimore.

Moore, K. L. (1982). *The developing human: clinically oriented embryology* (3rd edn), pp. 78, 279, 366. W. B. Saunders, Philadelphia.

Mozaffarian, G., Nakhjavani, M. K., and Farahi, A. (1979). The Laurence–Moon–Bardet–Biedl syndrome: unresponsiveness to the action of testosterone, a possible mechanism. *Fertil. Steril.*, **31**, 417–22.

Nadjmi, B., Flanagan, M. J., and Christian, J. R. (1969). Laurence–Moon–Biedl syndrome associated with multiple genito-urinary tract abnormalities. *Am. J. Dis. Child.*, **117**, 352–7.

Norden, G., Friman, S., Frisenette, F. C., Persson, H., and Karlberg, I. (1991). Renal transplantation in the Bardet–Biedl syndrome, a form of Laurence–Moon–Biedl syndrome. *Nephrol. Dial. Transpl.*, **6**, 982–3.

O'Dea, D., Parfrey, P. S., Harnett, J. D., Hefferton, D., Cramer, B. C., and Green, J. (1996). The importance of renal impairment in the natural history of Bardet–Biedl syndrome. *Am. J. Kid. Dis.*, **27**, 776–83.

Olefsky, J. M. and Kolterman, O. G. (1981). Mechanism of insulin resistance in obesity and non-insulin dependent (type II) diabetes. *Am. J. Med.*, **70**, 151–68.

Patriquin, H. B. (1987). *Fetal lobation of the kidney: an ultrasonoanatomic correlation*. Poster exhibit, Internal Pediatric Radiology meeting, Toronto, 1987.

Polson, D. W., Adams, J., Wadsworth, J., and Franks, S. (1988). Polycystic ovaries—a common finding in normal women. *Lancet*, **1**, 870–2.

Price, D., Gartner, J. G., and Kaplan, B. S. (1981). Ultrastructual changes in the glomerular basement membrane of patients with Laurence–Moon–Bardet–Biedl syndrome. *Clin. Nephrol.*, **16**, 283–8.

Ritchie, G., Jequier, S., Luissier-Lazaroff. (1988). Prenatal renal ultrasound of Laurence–Moon–Biedl syndrome. *Pediatr. Radiol.*, **19**, 65–6.

Rizza, R. A., Mandarinol, G., and Gerich, J. E. (1981). Mechanisms of insulin resistance in man: Assessment using the insulin dose-response curve in conjunction with insulin receptor binding. *Am. J. Med.*, **70**, 169–76.

Runge, P., Calver, D., Marshall, J., and Taylor, D. (1986). Histopathology of mitochondrial cytopathy and the Laurence–Moon–Biedl syndrome. *Brit. J. Opthal.*, **70**, 782–96.

Sato, H., Saito, T., Kamakage, K., Kyogoku, Y., Furuyama, T., and Yoshinaga, K. (1988). Renal histopathology of Laurence–Moon–Biedl syndrome: Tubulointestitital nephritis without specific glomerular changes. *Nephron*, **49**, 227–8.

Schachat, A. P. and Maumenee, H., (1982). Bardet–Biedl syndrome and related disorders. *Arch. Ohthalmol.*, **100**, 285–8.

Sheffield, V. C., Carmi, R., Kwitek-Black, A., *et al.* (1994). Identification of a Bardet–Biedl syndrome locus on chromosome 3 and evaluation of an efficient approach to homozygosity mapping. *Hum. Mol. Genet.*, **3**, 1331–5.

Stigglebout, W. (1972). The Bardet–Biedl syndrome; including Hutchinson–Laurence–Moon syndrome. In: *Neuroretinal degenerations.* Vol. 13 of *Handbook of clinical neurology* (ed. P. J. Vinkin and G. W. Bruyn), pp. 1277–91. North Holland Amsterdam.

Tieder, M., Levy, M., Gubler, M. C., Gagnadoux, M. F., Broyer, M., Lavoste, M., *et al.* (1982). Renal abnormalities in the Bardet–Biedl syndrome. *Int. J. Pediat. Nephrol.*, **3**, 199–203.

Toledo, S. P. A., Medeiros-Neto, G. A., Knobel, M., and Mattar, E. (1977). Evaluation of hypothalamic pituitary–gonadal function in the Bardet–Biedl syndrome. *Metabolism*, **26**, 1277–91.

Williams, B., Jenkins, D., and Walls, J. (1988). Chronic renal failure: an important feature of the Laurence–Moon–Biedl syndrome. *Postgrad. Med. J.*, **64**, 462 4.

14.2

Structural tubulointerstitial disease: nephronophthisis

Michel Broyer and Claire Kleinknecht

Introduction

Nephronophthisis was first described by Fanconi *et al.* in 1951 in young siblings having prominent polyuria, anaemia, and progressive renal failure in the absence of haematuria, heavy proteinuria, and hypertension. At autopsy the kidneys were shrunken and had diffuse prominent tubulointerstitial lesions. Several reports confirmed the distinctive features of this disease, first in Europe (Royer *et al.* 1963) and then in the USA (Mangos *et al.* 1964). At the same time a disease with similar symptoms, including polyuria and progressive uraemia in the absence of other major urinary abnormalities, was reported in a child who had cysts in the renal medulla at autopsy. For this reason the disease was referred to as medullary cystic disease (MCD) (Smith and Graham 1945). These particular features were noted in several other cases (Hogness and Burnell 1954), and in 1961, Strauss reported a series of patients with renal failure often associated with anaemia and sodium loss and characterized by the presence of cysts in the renal medulla. Habib *et al.* in 1965 and Strauss and Sommers in 1967 stressed the similarity between the renal lesion of nephronophthisis and some cases of MCD.

Thus, after a period of nosologic confusion, it clearly appeared that Fanconi's nephronophthisis and Strauss's MCD were two terms designating the same entity. In fact, several questions remained since the cases reported by Strauss in 1961 affected mainly adults without familial occurrence and also because a dominant mode of inheritance was reported in patients described as having MCD (Goldman *et al.* 1966; Kliger and Sheer 1976). This is why some authors proposed to keep the term MCD for the cases occurring in the adult with a dominant inheritance, and the term nephronophthisis for the juvenile recessive form. However, this proposal was not applicable since an age limit is difficult to establish, and juvenile and adult forms coexist in the same family with either recessive (Swon and Eisinger 1972; Fillastre *et al.* 1976; Kleinknecht 1983) or dominant (Mongeau and Worthen 1967; Giangiacomo *et al.* 1975) inheritance.

This high degree of heterogeneity made a single entity unlikely, and this is why some authors prefer to speak of the MCD–nephronophthisis complex (Avashti *et al.* 1976; Waldherr *et al.* 1982). It remains nevertheless important, particularly in view of identification of the primary genetic deficit, to separate different forms of this complex into units which are as homogenous as possible. In this perspective it appears that a major group of patients share the same clinical morphological and genetic features as those described by Fanconi *et al.* in 1951, and can be considered as the most important of these units. This group will be described in this chapter as autosomal recessive nephronophthisis. This view recently received clear confirmation by the localization of the gene on the short arm of chromosome 2.

Autosomal recessive nephronophthisis

Autosomal recessive nephronophthisis is considered rare. It was, however, the original disease in 10–32% of children treated for uraemia (Betts and Forest-Hay 1971; Gomez-Campdera 1981; Waldherr *et al.* 1982) and in 7% of children with end-stage renal disease (ESRD) reported in the EDTA registry (Broyer *et al.* 1989). The disease is distributed evenly among males and females and has been mainly reported in Europe and North America, but cases have also been reported in Japan, South America, and Israel, as well as in children of Arab, Turkish, and Indian origin.

Clinical symptoms

The first symptom is a reduced urinary concentrating ability developing during childhood, around the age of four years, resulting in *polyuria polydypsia* and sometimes secondary enuresis. These symptoms persist until ESRD. Patients are normal at birth and develop normally during the first years or months of life (10 months to 20 years in the Enfants Malades series (Kleinknecht and Habib 1992). Clinical symptoms appear when the concentrating ability is markedly reduced and it may be the only renal dysfunction found during early usual investigations.

Polyuria is often paid little attention by the family and is often found from a clinical history. The development of hyposthenuria is usually associated with *growth retardation* characterized by a marked decrease in previously normal growth velocity. The other main clinical symptom is progressive renal failure which is constant, insidious, and sometimes remains undetected until the end stage (about 15% of cases). Note that glomerular filtration rate (GFR) is subnormal at presentation except for a few patients detected early or for children who are systematically examined after detection of an affected sibling. Typically oedema, haematuria, urinary tract infection, and proteinuria are absent in nephronophthisis. Hypertension is possible but rare before the end stage. *Anaemia* has been considered to be particularly severe and to occur early and was sometimes the presenting symptom. It has been shown, however, that anaemia does not precede severe renal insufficiency and that it parallels the decline of renal function as in most other renal disorders. *Metabolic acidosis* may be the presenting symptom and is often present at first evaluation if GFR is below 40 ml/mn. Excessive *sodium loss* is present in most patients with renal failure, but whether it can precede severe renal insufficiency has not been investigated. This is associated with tubular resistance to aldosterone mimicking pseudohypoaldosteronism type I (Eisenstein *et al.* 1992). Dramatic hyponatremic dehydratation episodes may occur due to inappropriate sodium intake, gastrointestinal disorder or anorexia; when associated with hyperkalaemia these episodes pose a risk of sudden death if the diagnosis has not been made previously. There is no evidence of proximal tubular dysfunction: glycosuria, hypophosphataemia, and hyperaminoacidaemia are absent. An unexplained association of the disease with red and blond hair has been described (Rayfield and Mc Donald 1972).

Despite poor visualization due to dilution, IVP shows a normal urinary tract and frequently a large bladder. Kidney size is normal or slightly reduced for height. Ultrasonography may be helpful in the diagnosis, showing medullary cysts and loss of corticomedullary differentiation or increased echogenicity in a kidney of normal or slightly reduced size (Garel *et al.* 1984). In fact, these signs are observed almost exclusively in patients with end-stage disease, and even then, inconstantly. The most important contribution of radiology is that it allows the exclusion of some other causes of renal failure such as renal hypoplasia or urinary tract malformation.

Natural history

The disease is always progressive, leading to ESRD which is often associated with sodium loss. Although hypertension may occur at this stage, it remains rare. The average onset of terminal chronic renal failure has been shown to occur at about 10–13 years of age; the range was from three to 23 years in the Enfants Malades series and from four to 20 years in another recently reported series (Hildebrandt *et al.* 1992). After kidney transplantation the disease does not recur on the graft.

Pathology

At the terminal stage, the prominent macroscopic feature is diffuse contraction of both kidneys with a finely granular surface. Cut sections show grossly visible cysts of variable size, irregularly distributed at the corticomedullary junction and in the outer medulla. Calyces and the pelvis appear completely normal.

Light microscopy examination reveals dramatic atrophy of the cortex and the medulla and diffuse tubulointerstitial damage. The most striking feature is extreme thickening of the tubular basement membrane which is often multilayered and wrinkled, staining strongly with periodic

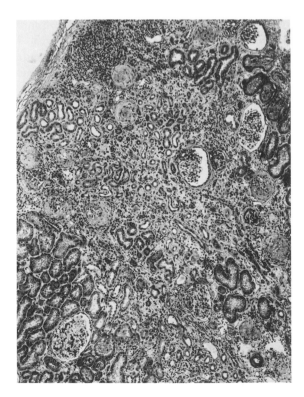

Fig. 14.2.1 Early stage of the disease. Segmental zone of interstitial fibrosis containing atrophic tubules with thickened basement membranes. Light microscopy (×80).

acid Schiff. Groups of tubules showing dilatation or marked compensatory hypertrophy alternate with groups of collapsed tubules. Diverticulum-like protrusions can be seen in the atrophic tubules. All segments of nephron are affected but the changes are prominent in the distal tubules, especially the ascending limb. Other tubules may show considerable attenuation or even disintegration of the basement membrane and there may be an abrupt transition from one abnormality to another, a feature which is said to be almost unique to this disease (Zollinger *et al.* 1980; Cohen and Hoyer 1986). Between the atrophic tubules there is moderate intertitial fibrosis, usually without inflammatory infiltrate. Glomeruli are often normal although some are completely sclerosed and others show periglomerular fibrosis; in some instances glomerular cysts are present. Arteries are usually normal. Immunofluorescence studies using anti-basement membrane antibodies show reduced tubular staining; Gubler *et al.* (1987) also found a complete loss of labelling with antibodies to laminin and type IV collagen within the central position of the thick tubular membrane, giving a railroad appearance which contrasted, however, with the findings of Cohen and Hoyer (1986). These observations suggest that the fundamental defect in this disease might be the production of abnormal tubular basement membrane. Electron microscopy examination was reported to show characteristic changes including thickening, splitting, attenuation, and granular disintegration of the tubular basement membrane with abrupt transitions between the alterations as mentioned with light microscopy (Zollinger *et al.* 1980). At the base of tubular epithelial cells a marked increase of microfilaments is observed.

Kidney biopsy at an early stage of the disease may show the presence of groups of atrophic tubules with irregularly thickened tubular basement membrane; lymphocytic and histiocytic infiltration has also been observed. Medullary cysts are rarely found at this stage.

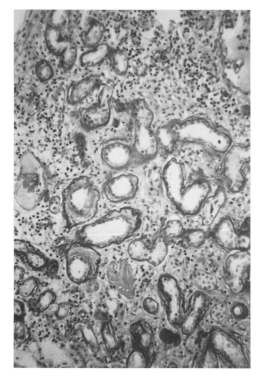

Fig. 14.2.2 Cortex. At high magnification various tubular changes are present. Some tubules are collapsed, others are surrounded by thickened tubular basement membranes. Note the laminated and wrinkled appearance of some segments of tubular basement membranes as well as the abrupt attenuation of others in the same tubular profile. Light microscopy; PAS stain (×120).

Pathogenesis

The data from immunofluorescence studies reported above suggest that the fundamental defect in this disease might be the production of abnormal tubular basement membrane. Analysis by two-dimensional electrophoresis of cellular extracts obtained after culture of tubular cells from small biopsy fragments of patients with nephronophthisis revealed several changes in protein composition, the main being the decrease of a polypeptide with a molecular weight of 120 kD (Bertelli *et al.* 1990). This alteration could be of pathogenetic relevance.

Genetics

The occurrence in siblings of both sexes and the frequency of consanguinity in the family history strongly favour an autosomal recessive mode of inheritance. In addition, heterozygous carrier parents have no detectable urinary abnormality. The finding of Antignac *et al.* (1993) gave evidence that the purely renal from of nephronophthisis is linked to chromosome 2p; the gene was localized to a region between D 2548 and D 2551 and this was confirmed using adjacent microsatellite markers (AFM 220 Ze 3 at the D2 S 160 locus), whereas the same markers excluded linkage with Senior–Loken syndrome. This suggests a genetic heterogeneity between pure nephronophthisis and nephronophthisis associated with extrarenal symptoms such as the Senior–Loken syndrome. The question of how many distinct disease entities are included in the nephronophthisis/medullary cystic disease complex is just beginning to be answered on the basis of molecular genetics.

Konrad *et al.* (1996) reported that large homozygous deletions of the 2q13 region found in 2/3 of cases are a major cause of juvenile nephronophthisis. Recently the gene was identified simultaneously by two different groups (Hildebrandt *et al.* 1997; Saunier *et al.* 1997). This gene encodes a novel protein with a putative src homology 3 domain and point mutations generating null mutants were reported in patients with hemizygous deletion. The absence of the protein product might interrupt a signalling pathway that normally regulates expression of specific tubular basement membrane component. Further characterization of this protein should provide some insight into the pathogenesis of the disease.

Associated disorders

Several disorders have been described in association with nephronophthisis-like nephropathies, with a frequency excluding coincidence.

1. Tapetoretinal degeneration

The most frequently associated anomalies involve the eyes. The classical Senior–Loken syndrome includes nephronophthisis and Leber's amaurosis with tapetoretinal degeneration. The criteria for diagnosis of eye involvement are early blindness, extinct electroretinogram, and progressive development of retinal pigmentation. According to Antignac *et al.* (1993), Senior-Loken syndrome and nephronophthisis are not dependent on the same gene. No dissociation was reported in affected families between eye and kidney disorders, suggesting a pleiotropic effect of one gene or a strong linkage between the genes for the two disorders.

Other eye anomalies have been reported in association with a nephronophthisis-like nephropathy such as coloboma (Dieterich and Straub 1980), catarct (Godel *et al.* 1979), retinitis pigmentosum of various origins, and even simple anomalies without extinction of ERG tracing (Bois and Royer 1970; Fillastre *et al.* 1976).

2. Central nervous system dysfunction

Cerebral involvement, particularly mental retardation and cerebellar dysfunction, has been reported. Mental retardation, reported in the initial series of Fanconi *et al.* (1951), coexisted with eye involvement in 50% of cases (Proesmans *et al.* 1975). Cerebellar ataxia, first described by Mainzer *et al.* (1970), was almost always reported in association with retinal degeneration and in some instances with bone anomalies or with mental retardation.

3. Skeletal involvement

Cone-shaped epiphysis has been observed, always in association with anomalies of the eye, liver, or brain (Mainzer *et al.* 1970).

4. Liver involvement

Hepatosplenomegaly with liver portal fibrosis but without bile duct proliferation was reported by Boichis *et al.* (1973) in three siblings in association with renal lesions consistent with nephronophthisis. Subsequently, several authors reported nephronophthisis with 'congenital hepatic fibrosis' (Proesmans *et al.* 1975; Witzleben and Sharp 1982). In all the reported cases the bile duct proliferation was mild and different from the classical hepatofibrosis found in recessive polycystic kidney disease. This point was more precisely shown by morphometric studies of ratios of bile ductules to connective tissue in hepatic portal tracts, which showed lower values for nephronophthisis than for recessive polycystic disease (Landing *et al.* 1990).

All the disorders associated with nephronophthisis represent either unique extrarenal involvement or occur with varying possibility of association. Although it has been reported that siblings could be affected with the same classical syndrome, there is obvious heterogeneity and it is doubtful whether these disorders belong to the same genetic entity. The existence of associated disorders must not be considered as evidence for nephronophthisis but should rather stimulate investigation for the feature(s) of another disease.

Diagnosis

Unlike nephronophthisis, the diagnosis of polyuria of other origin is usually straightforward. Central diabetes insipidus is responsive to vasopressin and nephrogenic diabetes insipidus starts after birth. Ultrasonography excludes other kidney diseases or urinary tract malformations which may be the cause of polyuria. Finally, the diagnosis is confirmed by histology and in 50% of cases by family history. The absence of medullary cysts does not preclude the diagnosis since they usually develop late in the course of the disease. On the other hand, the presence of medullary cysts is not diagnostic since they may develop in many other conditions. If there is no pathognomonic sign on histological examination, it seems reasonable to exclude patients with chronic tubulointerstitial nephritis without typical alteration of the tubular membrane, but it is difficult to determine whether some patients who do not show this alteration represent a variant or the same genetic entity.

Several syndromes with possible renal involvement may be misleading for diagnosis, such as the Bardet–Biedl syndrome and thoracic asphyxating dystrophy of Jeune (Donaldson *et al.* 1985). A few children developing symptoms in infancy and progressing rapidly to end-stage renal disease have been reported (Proesmans *et al.* 1976; Harris *et al.* 1980; Witzleben and Sharp 1982; Gagnadoux *et al.* 1989).

These patients had no cysts detectable by ultrasonography and renal histology differed from typical nephronophthisis by the absence of prominent thickening of the tubular basement membrane. Many of these patients had extrarenal symptoms. The nosological problem raised by these disorders should hopefully be solved by molecular genetics.

Autosomal dominant nephronophthisis–medullary cystic disease

Whether all cases reported as nephronophthisis or medullary cystic disease with dominant inheritance represent a homogeneous disease and to what extent they share the clinical and morphological features of recessive nephronophthisis is questionable.

The age at onset is often stressed as a major difference. The end stage is reached later than in the recessive form, from the third to the fourth decade of life or even later. The clinical symptoms reported in the dominant disease often clearly differ from those of recessive nephronophthisis. Haematuria, proteinuria, and severe hypertension were reported (Victorin *et al.* 1970; Makker *et al.* 1973), as were large cysts before the terminal stage. Extrarenal abnormalities have been reported more often in the dominant than in the recessive form. The main association is with gout and/or hyperuricaemia which probably represents a distinct entity (Warren *et al.* 1981). Finally, thickening of the tubular basement membrane, the prominent morphological feature of nephronophthisis, is absent, mild, or not mentioned in the dominant cases. Autosomal dominant inheritance was suggested by several instances of father-to-son transmission as well as transmission to children born from different marriage (Wrigley *et al.* 1973; Grateau *et al.* 1986). Variable penetrance is also suggested by some cases with normal parents and an affected relative (Victorin *et al.* 1970; Giangiacomo *et al.* 1975). A urinary concentrating defect in one of the parents was considered a mild form of the disease. Unfortunately, in only a minority of cases was the diagnosis ascertained in at least two generations by radiologic detection of cysts or examination of renal parenchyma.

In conclusion, the so-called dominant nephronophthisis–medullary cystic disease, an extremely rare condition, probably includes several different entities and may be considered to be completely different from recessive nephronophthisis.

References

Antignac, C., Ardery, C., Beckman, J., Benessy, F., Gros, F., Medhioub, M., *et al.* (1993). A gene for familial juvenile nephronophthisis (recessive medullary cystic kidney disease) maps to chromosome 2p. *Nature Genetics*, **3**, 342–5.

Antignac, C., Kleinknecht, C., and Habib, R. (1998). Nephronophthisis. In: *Oxford textbook of Clinical Nephrology*, 2d ed. (ed. M. Davison, S. Cameron, J. P. Grunfeld, D. Kerr, E. Ritz, and C. Winearls), Oxford University Press, Oxford, 1998, pp. 2417–26.

Arasthai, P. S., Erickson, D. G., and Gardner, K. D. (1976). Hereditary renal-retinal dysplasia and the medullary cystic disease-nephronophthisis complex. *Annals of Internal Medicine*, **84**, 157–61.

Bertelli, R., Ginevri, F., Candiano, G., Giardi, M. R., Tarelli, L. T., Meroni, M., *et al.* (1990). Tubular epithelium culture from nephronophthisis-affected kidneys: a new approach to molecular disorders of tubular cells. *American Journal of Nephrolology*, **10**, 463–9.

Betts, P. R. and Forest-Hay, I. (1973). Juvenile nephronophthisis. *Lancet*, **II**, 475–8.

Boichis, H., Passwell, J., Davod, R., and Miller, H. (1973). Congenital hepatic fibrosis and nephronophthisis. *Quarterly Journal of Medicine*, **42**, 221–33.

Bois, E. and Royer, P. (1970). Association de néphropathie tubulo-interstitielle chronique et de dégénérescence tapéto-rétinienne. *Archives Françaises de Pédiatrie*, **27**, 471–81.

Cohen, A. H. and Hoyer, J. R. (1986). Nephronophthisis—A primary tubular basement membrane defect. *Laboratory Investigation*, **55**, 564–72.

Dieterich, E. and Straub, E. (1980). Familial juvenile nephronophthisis with hepatic fibrosis and neurocutaneous dysplasia. *Helvetica Paediatrica Acta*, **35**, 261–7.

Donaldson, M. D. C., Warner, A. A., Trompeter, R. S., Haycock, G. B., and Chantler, C. (1985). Familial juvenile—Jeune's syndrome and associated disorders. *Archives of Disease in Childhood*, **60**, 426–34.

Donckerwolcke, R., Broyer, M., Chantler, C., and Rizzoni, G. (1996). Renal replacement therapy in children. In: *Replacement of renal function by dialysis*, 4th ed. (ed. C. Jacobs, C. M. Kjellstrand, K. N. Koch, and J. F. Winchester), Kluwer academic publishers Dordrecht, 1996, pp. 863–95.

Eisenstein, B., Davidovitz, M., Garty, B. Z., Shmueli, D., Ussim, A., and Stark, H. (1992). Severe tubular resistance to aldosterone in a child with familial juvenile nephronophthisis. *Pediatric Nephrology*, **6**, 57–9.

Fanconi, G., Hanhart, F., Albertini, A., Uhlinger, E., Dolivo, G., and Prader, A. (1951). Die familiäre juvenile nephronophthise. *Helvetica Paediatrica Acta*, **6**, 1–49.

Fillastre, J. P., Guenel, J., Riveri, P., Marx, P., Whitworth, J. A., and Kunh, J. M. (1976). Senior–Loken syndrome (nephronophthisis and tapeto-retinal degeneration); a study of 8 cases from 5 families. *Clinical Nephrology*, **5**, 14–19.

Gagnadoux, M. F., Bacri, J. L., Broyer, M., and Habib, R. (1989). Infantile chronic tubulo-interstitial nephritis with cortical cysts: variant of nephronophthisis or new disease entity? *Pediatric Nephrology*, **3**, 50–5.

Garel, K. D., Habib, R., Pariente, D., Broyer, M., and Sauvegrain, J. (1984). Juvenile nephronophthisis: sonographic appearance in children with severe uremia. *Radiology*, **151**, 93–5.

Giangiacomo, J., Monteleone, P. L., and Witzleben, C. L. (1975). Medullary cystic disease vs nephronophthisis: a valid distinction. *Journal of the American Medical Association*, **232**, 629–31.

Godel, V., Aiana, A., Nemet, P., and Lazar, M. (1979). Retinal manifestation in familial juvenile nephronophthisis. *Clinical Genetics*, **16**, 277–81.

Goldman, S. H., Walker, S. R., Merigan, T. C., and Gardner, K. D. (1966). Hereditary occurence of cystic disease of the renal medulla. *New England Journal of Medicine*, **274**, 984–92.

Gomez-Campdera, F. J. (1981). Nefronophtisis-analisis de 10 casos. *Medecina Clinica* (Barcelona), **77**, 230–5.

Grateau, G., Grunfeld, J. P., Droz, D., and Noel, L. H. (1986). La néphronophtise de l'adulte: une seule ou deux maladies. *Nephrologie*, **7**, 104–8.

Gubler, M. C. (1987). Ultrastructural and immunohistochemical study of renal basement membranes in familial juvenile nephronophthisis. In: *Renal basement membranes in health and disease* (ed. R. G. Price and B. G. Hudson), pp. 389–98.

Habib, R., Mouzet-Mazza, M. T., Courtecuisse, V., and Royer, P. (1965). L'ectasie tubulaire précalicielle chez l'enfant. *Annales de Pédiatrie*, **41**, 980–90.

Harris, H. W., Carpenter, T. O., Shanley, P., Rosen, S., Levey, R. H., and Harmon, W. E. (1986). Progressive tubulo-interstitial renal disease in infancy with associated hepatic abnormalities. *American Journal of Medicine*, **81**, 169–76.

Hildebrandt, F., Waldherr, R., Kutt, R., and Brandis, M. (1992). The nephronophthisis complex: clinical and genetic aspects. *Clinical Investigation*, **70**, 802–8.

Hildebrandt, F., Otto, E., Rensing, C., Nothwang, H. G., Vollmer, M., Adolphs, H., Hanusch, H., and Brandis, M. (1997). A novel gene encoding an SH3 domain protein is mutated in nephronophthisis type 1. *Nat. Genet.*, **17**, 149–53.

Hogness, J. R. and Burnell, J. M. (1954). Medullary cysts of the kidney. *Archives of Internal Medicine*, **93**, 355–66.

Kleinknecht, C. (1983). Néphronophtise. In: *Néphrologie pédiatrique* (ed. P. Royer, R. Habib, H. Mathieu, and M. Broyer), pp. 48–61, Flammarion.

Kliger, A. S. and Sheer, R. L. (1976). Familial disease of the renal medulla. A study of progeny in a family with medullary cystic disease. *Annals of Internal Medicine*, **85**, 190–4.

Konrad, M., Saunier, S., Heidet, L., Silbermann, F., Benessy, F., Calado, J., Le Paslier, D., Broyer, M., Gubler, M. C., and Antignac, C. (1996). Large homozygous deletions of the 2q13 region are a major cause of juvenile nephronophthisis. *Human Molecular Genetics*, **5**, 367–71.

Landing, B. H., Wells, T. R., Lipsey, A. I., and Oyemade, O. A. (1990). Morphometric studies of cystic and tubulo-interstitial kidney diseases with hepatic firbrosis in children. *Pediatric Pathology*, **10**, 959–72.

Mainzer, F., Saldino, R. M., Ozonoff, M. B., and Minagi, H. (1970). Familial nephropathy associated with retinitis pigmentosa, cerebellar ataxia and skeletal abnormalities. *American Journal of Medicine*, **49**, 556–62.

Makker, S. P., Grupe, W. E., Perrin, E., and Heymann, W. (1973). Identical progression of juvenile hereditary nephronophthisis in monozygotic twins. *Journal of Pediatrics*, **82**, 773–9.

Mangos, J. A., Opitz, J. M., Lobeck, C. C., and Cookson, D. U. (1964). Familial juvenile nephronophthisis—an unrecognized renal disease in the United States. *Pediatrics*, **34**, 337–45.

Mongeau, J. G. and Worthen, H. G. (1967). Nephronophthisis and medullary cystic disease. *American Journal of Medicine*, **43**, 345–55.

Proesmans, W., Van Damme, B., and Macken, J. (1975). Neophronophthisis and tapeto-retainal degeneration associated with liver fibrosis. *Clinical Nephrology*, **3**, 160–4.

Proesmans, W., Van Damme, B., Desmet, V., and Eeckels, R. (1976). Fatal tubulo-interstitial nephropathy with chronic cholestatic liver disease. *Acta Paediatrica Belgica*, **29**, 231–8.

Rayfield, E. J. and Mcdonald, F. D. (1972). Red and blonde hair in renal medullary cystic disease. *Archives Internes de Medecine*, **130**, 72–5.

Royer, P., Habib, R., Mathieu, H., and Courtecuisse, V. (1963). Les néphropathies tubulo-interstitielles chroniques idiopathiques de l'enfant. *Annales de Pédiatrie*, **39**, 620–33.

Saunier, S., Calado, J., Heilig, R., Silbermann, F., Benessy, F., Morin, G., Konrad, M., Broyer, M., Gubler, M. C., Weissenbach, J., and Antignac, C. (1997). A novel gene that encodes a protein with a putative src homology 3 domain is a candidate gene for familial juvenile nephronophthisis. *Hum. Mol. Genet*, **6**, 2317–23.

Smith, C. H. and Graham, J. B. (1945). Congenital medullary cysts of the kidneys with severe refractory anemia. *American Journal of Disease in Childhood*, **69**, 370–8.

Strauss, M. B. (1961). Clincial and pathological aspects of cystic disease of the renal medulla. An analysis of eighteen cases. *Annals of Internal Medicine*, **57**, 373–81.

Strauss, M. B. and Sommers, S. C. (1967). Medullary cystic disease and familial juvenile nephronophthisis. *New England Journal of Medicine*, **277**, 863–4.

Sworn, M. J. and Eisinger, A. J. (1972). Medullary cystic disease and juvenile nephronophthisis in separate members of the same family. *Archives of Disease in Childhood*, **47**, 278–81.

Victorin, L., Ljungqvist, A., Winberg, J., and Akesson H. O. (1970). Nephronophthisis—a uremic disease with hypotonic urine. *Acta Medica Scandinavia*, **188**, 235–56.

Waldherr, R., Lennert, T., Weber, H. P., Fodish, H. J., and Sharer, K. (1982). The nephronophthisis complex. *Virchows Archives: A Pathological Anatomy and Histopathology*, **394**, 235–54.

Warren D, J., Simmonds, H. A., Gibson, T., and Naik, R. B. (1981). Familial gout and renal failure. *Archives of Disease in Childhood*, **56**, 699–704.

Witzleben, C. L. and Sharp, A. R. (1982). Nephronophthisis—congenital hepatic fibrosis. An additional hepatorenal disorder. *Human Pathology*, **13**, 728–33.

Wrigley, K. A., Sherman, R. L., Ennis, F. A., and Becker, E. L. (1973). Progressive hereditary nephropathy—a variant of medullary cystic disease. *Archives of Internal Medicine*, **131**, 240–4.

Zollinger, H. U., Mihatsch, M. J., Edefonti, A., and Gaboardi, F. (1980). Nephronophthisis (medullary cystic disease of the kidney). *Helvetica Paediatrica Acta*, **35**, 509–30.

14.3

Multicentric osteolysis with nephropathy

Jean-Pierre Grünfeld

Introduction

Idiopathic osteolysis is a group of rare diseases of unknown cause characterized by progressive resorption of bones, primarily in the hands and feet. Monocentric osteolysis is differentiated from multifocal (or multicentric or essential) osteolysis. The latter form is known to be associated with nephropathy, and approximately 15 such observations have been reported (see recent reviews in Turner *et al.* 1987; Pai and Macpherson 1988; Shinohara *et al.* 1991).

Osteoarticular manifestations: 'Disappearing-bone disease'

The first symptoms usually appear in early childhood and consist of swelling and pain of the wrists, fingers, and ankles, simulating arthritic episodes. The major differential diagnosis is the polyarticular variety of juvenile rheumatoid arthritis. Subsequently, x-ray films show generalized osteopenia, soft-tissue wasting, and osteolysis; that is, symmetric dissolution of the carpal bones involving first the proximal row, then the distal row and distal ulna, and finally the proximal metacarpals (Fig. 14.3.1). After the onset of the carpal changes, the tarsal and other foot bones are involved. Elbows and knees are involved later in the sequence of events. These bone changes lead to limb deformities and severe musculoskeletal disability by adolescence.

Nephropathy

Typically, nephropathy appears several years after osteolysis has occurred. Proteinuria is the first abnormality, sometimes in the nephrotic range; it may develop as late as 12 years after the onset of skeletal disease. Microhaematuria, leukocyturia, or casts are rarely found. The onset of renal failure is often accompanied by severe hypertension. Hypercalcaemia and nephrocalcinosis are not found.

End-stage renal failure occurs from one to 17 years after the onset of proteinuria. Successful kidney transplantation has been performed in at least three cases (Gagnadoux *et al.* 1981; Turner *et al.* 1987; Pai and Macpherson 1988); none has suffered recurrence of the nephropathy on the transplanted kidney.

The early renal lesion has been described as focal and segmental glomerulosclerosis (Bennett *et al.* 1980; Hirooka and Hirota 1985; Shinohara *et al.* 1991). Discrete ultrastructural abnormalities of the glomerular basement membrane have been reported on a renal biopsy from a 2-year old affected girl (Bakker *et al.* 1996). Advanced glomerulosclerosis or global glomerular obsolescence is described in other cases. IgM deposits are found by immunofluorescence. In rare cases, tuft necrosis and crescents have been ascribed to malignant hypertension (Sybert and Motulsky

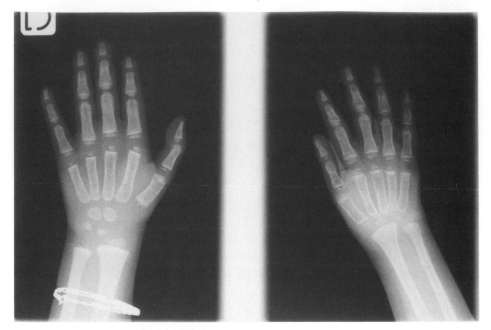

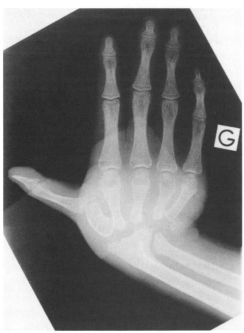

Fig. 14.3.1 Acro-osteolysis, carpal form. Three-year-old boy. Note marked loss of volume of the carpals which have almost disappeared. The base of the metacarpals is thin and sharp. The other hand is normal; (b) Radiograph of the father's hand. Complete disappearance of the carpals except for one bone. Shortening and deformation of the metacarpals. Deformation of the articular surface of the radius. Relative shortening of the third phalanges compared to the second. (Figures by courtesy of Professor Michel Broyer.)

1979; Turner *et al.* 1987). Arteriosclerosis and/or vascular proliferative changes are prominent in most cases.

Other manifestations

Various abnormalities outside of the triad arthritis—osteolysis—nephropathy have been described. In some families, affected individuals have a 'Marfan-like' habitus or chubby cheeks, protruding eyes, small chin, and 'doll-like' facial appearance (Carnevale *et al.* 1987). Other clinical associations include mental retardation in several patients, epilepsy, corneal opacity, pulmonary stenosis (Shinohara *et al.* 1991), myopathic changes, platybasia of the skull, odontoid hypoplasia, and cervical cord compression (Pai and Macpherson 1988).

The pathogenesis of the renal lesion is unknown. It has been suggested that some component of bone, liberated by its destruction, might trigger an immune response or exert a toxic effect on the kidney. These suggestions so far remain completely speculative.

Classification and genetics

The rarity of multicentric osteolysis has not prevented its categorization. Nephropathy is seen mainly in sporadic forms (Bennett *et al.* 1980; Hirooka and Hirota 1985; Pai and Macpherson 1988; Shinohara *et al.* 1991); however, despite some assertions, it may be found in inherited forms (Carnevale *et al.* 1987; Shurtleff *et al.* 1964). Type 1 multicentric osteolysis is inherited as an autosomal dominant trait. The case reported as sporadic by Gagnadoux *et al.* (1981) belongs in fact to this category since after kidney transplantation the affected man had an affected son (M. Broyer and M.F. Gagnadoux, personal communication), Type 2 multicentric osteolysis is an autosomal recessive disease. The Winchester syndrome overlaps with multicentric osteolysis; osteolysis involves primarily the phalanges. This syndrome (also called type 5 multicentric osteolysis) is an autosomal recessive disorder characterized also by short stature, contractures, coarse face, thick skin with hyperpigmentation, and peripheral corneal opacities (Hardegger *et al.* 1985).

References

Bakker, S. J. L., Vos, G. D., Verschure, P. D., Mulder, A. H., and Tiebosch, A. T. (1996). Abnormal glomerular basement membrane in idiopathic multicentric osteolysis. *Pediatric Nephrology*, **10**, 200–2.

Bennett, W. M., Houghton, D. C., and Beals, R. C. (1980). Nephropathy of multicentric osteolysis. *Nephron*, **25**, 134–8.

Carnevale, A., Canun, S., Mendoza, L., and del Castillo, V. (1987). Idiopathic multicentric osteolysis with facial anomalies and nephropathy. *American Journal of Medical Genetics*. **26**, 877–86.

Gagnadoux, M. F., Bacri, L., Gubler, M. C., and Broyer, M. (1981). Acroosteolysis nephropathy. Report of a case: natural history and treatment by hemodialysis and transplantation. *The International Journal Of Pediatric Nephrology*, **2**, 143–4.

Hardegger, F., Simpson, L. A., and Segmueller, G. (1985). The syndrome of idiopathic osteolysis. *Journal of Bone and Joint Surgery (Br.)*, **67**, 89–93.

Hirooka, M. and Hirota, M. (1985). Chronic nephropathy in idiopathic multicentric osteolysis. *The International Journal Of Pediatric Nephrology*, **6**, 145–50.

Pai, G. S. and Macpherson, R. I. (1988). Idiopathic multicentric osteolysis: Report of two new cases and a review of the literature. *American Journal of Medical Genetics*, **29**, 929–36.

Shinohara, O., Kubota, C., Kimura, M., Nishimura, G., and Takahashi, S. (1991). Essential osteolysis associated with nephropathy, corneal opacity, and pulmonary stenosis. *American Journal of Medical Genetics*, **41**, 482–6.

Shurtleff, B. D., Sparkes, R. S., Clawson, D. K., Guntheroth, W. G., and Mottel, N. K. (1964). Hereditary osteolysis with hypertension and nephropathy. *Journal of the American Medical Association*, **188**, 363–8.

Sybert, V. P. and Motulsky, A. G. (1979). Renal involvement in hereditary multiple osteolysis. *Lancet*, **i**, 52.

Turner, M. C., Gonzalez, O. R., Landing, B. H., and Lieberman, E. (1987). Multicentric osteolysis: report of the second successful renal transplant. *Pediatric Nephrology*, **1**, 42–5.

Section D
Metabolic disorders

15

Fabry's disease and the lipidoses

Robert J. Desnick and Christine M. Eng

Introduction

Originally described as a dermatologic curiosity by Fabry (1898), and independently by Anderson in the same year (1898), Fabry's disease is now recognized as an inborn error of metabolism resulting from the defective activity of the lysosomal enzyme, α-galactosidase A. The enzymatic defect, transmitted by an X-linked recessive gene, leads to the progressive deposition of neutral glycosphingolipids with terminal α-galactosyl moieties in the plasma and lysosomes of endotheli-al, perithelial, and smooth-muscle cells of the cardiovascular–renal system and, to a lesser extent, in reticuloendothelial, myocardial, and connective-tissue cells. Epithelial cells in the kidney, cornea, and other tissues contain the lysosomal glycolipid deposits, as do ganglion and perineural cells of the autonomic nervous system. The predominantly accumulated glycosphingolipids are globotriaosylceramide (Fig. 15.1) and galabiosylceramide, the latter being deposited primarily in renal lysosomes (Schibanoff *et al.* 1969). Progressive endothelial glycosphingolipid accumulation results in ischaemia and infarction and leads to the major clinical manifestations of the disease.

Onset of the disease in classically affected males usually occurs during childhood or adoles-cence, with periodic crises of severe pain in the extremities (acroparesthesias), the appearance of a characteristic skin lesion (which led to the descriptive name of *angiokeratoma corporis diffusum universale*), hypohidrosis, and the corneal and lenticular changes seen by slit-lamp microscopy. With increasing age, the major morbid symptoms of the disease result from the progressive infiltration of glycosphinglipid in the cardiovascular–renal system. Death usually occurs in adult life from renal, cardiac, and/or cerebral complications of their vascular disease. Prior to the availability of treatment by renal transplantation or dialysis, the average age of death for classical-ly affected males was about 41 years (Colombi *et al.* 1967). In contrast, a milder phenotype of Fabry's disease, known as the 'cardiac variant', was recently recognized (Desnick *et al.* 1995). Typically, these individuals present with cardiac manifestations and mild proteinuria in the fifth decade of life, and do not have angiokeratoma, hypohidrosis, corneal/lenticular lesions, or a history of acroparesthesias.

The frequency of Fabry's disease has not been determined; the disease is rare, and it is estimated that the incidence is about one in 40 000. Of more than 400 described cases of affected males, most are Caucasian; however, Black, Hispanic, American Indian, Egyptian, and Asian cases have been observed (Desnick *et al.* 1995).

Clinical manifestations

The classically affected hemizygote

Clinical manifestations in classically affected males result predominantly from the progressive deposition of globotriaosylceramide in the vascular endothelial and smooth-muscle cells (Table

Globotriaosylceramide (GL-3)

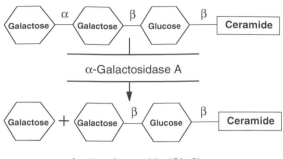

α-Galactosidase A

Lactosylceramide (GL-2)

Fig. 15.1 The metabolic defect in Fabry disease.

Table 15.1 Fabry's disease: major manifestations

Manifestation	Classical type	Cardiac variant
Age at onset	4–8 yr	>40 yr
Average age of death	41 yr	>60 yr
Angiokeratoma	+	–
Acroparathesias	+	–
Hypohidrosis	+	–
Corneal/lenticular opacity:	+	–
Heart	Ischaemia/MI	LVH/MI
Brain	TIA/strokes	–
Kidney	Renal failure	Mild proteinuria
Residual α-gal A activity	<1%	1–10%

15.1). Clinical onset usually occurs during childhood or adolescence but may be delayed until the second or third decade of life. Early manifestations include periodic crises of severe pain in the extremities (acroparesthesias), the appearance of vascular cutaneous lesions (angiokeratoma), hypohidrosis, and the characteristic corneal and lenticular opacities.

Kidney

Progressive glycosphingolipid deposition in the kidney results in proteinuria and other signs of renal impairment, with gradual deterioration of renal function and development of azotaemia in middle age. During childhood and adolescence, protein, casts, red cells, and desquamated kidney and urinary-tract cells may appear in the urine. Birefringent lipid globules with characteristic 'Maltese crosses' can be observed free in the urine and within desquamated urinary-sediment cells by polarization microscopy. With age, progressive renal impairment is evidenced by significant proteinuria, isosthenuria (specific gravities of 1.008 to 1.012), and alterations of other renal tubular functions, including tubular reabsorption, secretion, and excretion (Pabico *et al.* 1973). Polyuria and a syndrome similar to vasopressin-resistant diabetes insipidus occasionally develop. Gradual deterioration of renal function and the development of azotaemia usually occur in the third to fifth decades of life, although renal failure has been reported in the second decade (Sheth *et al.* 1983). Death most often results from uraemia unless chronic haemodialysis or renal transplantation is undertaken. The mean age at death of 106 hemizygous males who were not treated for uraemia was 41 years (Colombi *et al.* 1967), but occasionally an affected male has survived into his sixties.

Pain

The single most debilitating symptom of Fabry's disease is the pain. Two types have been described: episodic crises and constant discomfort (Wise *et al.* 1962; Lockman *et al.* 1973). The painful crises most often begin in childhood or early adolescence and signal clinical onset of the disease. Lasting from minutes to several days, these 'Fabry crises' consist of agonizing, burning pain initially in the palms and soles. Often the pain will radiate to the proximal extremities and other parts of the body. Attacks of abdominal or flank pain may simulate appendicitis or renal colic (Rahman *et al.* 1961). The painful crises are usually triggered by exercise, fatigue, emotional stress, or rapid changes in temperature and humidity. With increasing age, the periodic crises usually decrease in frequency and severity; however, in some patients, they may occur more frequently, and the pain can be so excruciating that the patient may contemplate suicide (Bagdale *et al.* 1968). Because the pain is usually associated with a low-grade fever and an elevated erythrocyte sedimentation rate, these symptoms frequently have led to the misdiagnosis of rheumatic fever, neurosis, or erythromelalgia (Bagdale *et al.* 1968; Johnston *et al.* 1968; Lockman *et al.* 1973; Sheth and Bernhard 1979).

Skin lesion

Angiectases may be one of the earliest manifestations and may lead to diagnosis in childhood. There is a progressive increase in the number and size of these cutaneous vascular lesions with age. Classically, the angiokeratomas develop slowly as clusters of individual punctate, dark red to blue–black angiectases in the superficial layers of the skin. The lesions may be flat or slightly raised and do not blanch with pressure. There is a slight hyperkeratosis notable in larger lesions. The clusters of lesions are most dense between the umbilicus and the knees and have a tendency toward bilateral symmetry. The hips, back, thighs, buttocks, penis, and scrotum are most commonly involved, but there is a wide variation in the pattern of distribution and density of the lesions. Involvement of the oral mucosa and conjunctiva is common, and other mucosal areas may also be involved. Variants without the characteristic skin lesions have been reported (Urbain *et al.* 1967) (see below). Although the angiectases may not be readily apparent in some patients, careful examination of the skin, especially the scrotum and umbilicus, may reveal the presence of isolated lesions. In addition to these vascular lesions, anhidrosis, or more commonly hypohidrosis, is an early and almost constant finding.

Cardiac and cerebral

With increasing age, the major morbid symptoms of the disease result from the progressive deposition of glycosphingolipid in the cardiovascular system. Cardiac disease occurs in most affected males. Early findings include left ventricular enlargement, valvular involvement, and conduction abnormalities (Ferrans *et al.* 1969; Becker *et al.* 1975). Mitral insufficiency is the most frequent valvular lesion and is typically present in childhood or adolescence. Involvement of the myocardium and possibly the conduction system results in electrocardiographic abnormalities which may show left ventricular hypertrophy, ST segment changes, and T-wave inversion. Other abnormalities, including arrhythmias, intermittent supraventricular tachycardias, and a short PR interval, have been described (Mehta *et al.* 1977; Efthimiou *et al.* 1986). Echocardiographic studies demonstrate an increased incidence of mitral valve prolapse and an increased thickness of the interventricular septum and the left ventricular posterior wall (Bass *et al.* 1980; Goldman *et al.* 1986). In addition, hypertrophic obstructive cardiomyopathy secondary to glycosphingolipid infiltration in the interventricular septum has been reported (Colucci *et al.* 1982). Late manifestations may include angina pectoris, myocardial ischaemia and infarction, congestive heart failure, and severe mitral regurgitation (Becker *et al.* 1975; Ferrans *et al.* 1969). These findings may be accentuated by systemic hypertension related to vascular involvement of renal parenchymal vessels.

Cerebrovascular manifestations result primarily from multifocal small-vessel involvement and may include thromboses, transient ischaemic attacks, basilar artery ischaemia, and aneurysm, seizures, hemiplegia, hemianaesthesia, aphasia, labyrinthine disorders, or frank cerebral haemorrhage (Bethune *et al.* 1961; Wise *et al.* 1962). Magnetic resonance imaging has proven useful in the evaluation of cerebrovascular involvement (Morgan *et al.* 1990), in fact, magnetic resonance imaging proved more effective in detecting lacunar infarcts than computerized tomography (Moumdjian *et al.* 1989).

Ocular features

Ocular involvement is most prominent in the cornea, lens, conjunctiva, and retina (Spaeth and Frost 1965; Sher *et al.* 1979). A characteristic corneal opacity, observed only by slit-lamp microscopy, is found in classically affected males and in most of their heterozygous female relatives. The earliest lesion is a diffuse haziness in the subepithelial layer. In more advanced cases, the opacities appear as whorled streaks extending from a central vortex to the periphery of the cornea. Typically, the whorl-like opacities are inferior and cream-coloured; however, they range from white to golden-brown and may be very faint. An identical, familial corneal dystrophy, termed *cornea verticillata*, was described by Gruber (1946); subsequent investigation of these patients revealed that they were hemizygous and heterozygous for Fabry's disease (Terlinde *et al.* 1982). An indistinguishable, drug-induced phenocopy of the Fabry corneal dystrophy occurs in patients on long-term chloroquine or amiodarone therapy (see 'Diagnosis').

Two specific types of lenticular changes have been described. A granular anterior capsular or subcapsular deposit has been observed in about one-third of classically affected males, but rarely in their heterozygous female relatives. Typically, these lenticular opacities are bilateral and inferior in position. They frequently appear in a 'propeller-like' distribution, i.e. wedge-shaped with their bases near the lenticular equator and aligned radially with the apexes toward the centre of the anterior capsule. A second, and possibly pathognomonic, lenticular opacity has been observed in both hemizygous and heterozygous individuals (Sher *et al.* 1979). It may be the first ocular manifestation to appear. The opacity is posterior, linear, and appears as a whitish, almost translucent, spoke-like deposit of fine granular material on or near the posterior lens capsule. These lines usually radiate from the central part of the posterior cortex. This unusual opacity has been termed the *Fabry cataract* and is best seen by retroillumination.

Other clinical features

Auditory and vestibular abnormalities have been described (Morgan *et al.* 1990). Several patients have had chronic bronchitis, wheezing respiration (Wise *et al.* 1962), or dyspnea with alveolar capillary block. In many hemizygotes, pulmonary function studies indicate a mild obstructive component, and primary pulmonary involvement has been reported in the absence of cardiac or renal disease (Kariman *et al.* 1978).

Lymphoedema of the legs may be present in adulthood without hypoproteinaemia, varices, or any clinically manifest vascular disease (Gemignani *et al.* 1979). This sign presumably reflects the progressive glycosphingolipid deposition in the lymphatic vessels and lymph nodes. Patients have presented with prominent lymphadenopathy as their only finding (Mayou *et al.* 1989). Many patients have varicosities and haemorrhoids. Priapism also has been reported (Wilson *et al.* 1973).

Episodic diarrhoea and, to a lesser extent, nausea, vomiting, and flank pain are the most common gastrointestinal complaints (Rowe *et al.* 1974; Nelis and Jacobs 1989). These symptoms may be related to the deposition of glycosphingolipid in intestinal small vessels and in the autonomic ganglia of the bowel (Sheth *et al.* 1981). Achalasia and jejunal diverticulosis, which may lead to perforation of the small bowel, have been described (Friedman *et al.* 1984). Although intestinal malabsorption has been reported, it is not a recognized feature of the disease. Radiologic studies may reveal thickened, edematous folds and mild dilatation of the small bowel, a granular-appearing ileum, and the loss of haustral markings throughout the colon, particularly in the distal segments (Rowe *et al.* 1974). The symptomatology and pathophysiology of the gastrointestinal involvement have been reviewed (Sheth *et al.* 1981; Rowe *et al.* 1974).

The cardiac variant

Affected males with a variant phenotype have been described who were essentially asymptomatic at ages when classical hemizygotes would be severely affected or would have expired from the disease (Desnick *et al.* 1995) (Table 15.1). Many of these variants were identified serendipitously during evaluation of other unrelated medical problems or of their family members. In contrast to patients with the classic phenotype who have no detectable α-galactosidase A activity, these variants have residual activity compatible with their milder phenotypes. Recent reports have described several patients with late-onset cardiac or cardiopulmonary disease (Clarke *et al.* 1971*a*; Bishop *et al.* 1981; Elleder *et al.* 1990; Ogawa *et al.* 1990; Sakuraba *et al.* 1990; Nagao *et al.* 1991; von Scheidt *et al.* 1991; Ishii *et al.* 1992). These 'cardiac variants' had cardiomegaly, typically involving the left ventricular wall and interventricular septum, and electrocardiographic abnormalities consistent with a cardiomyopathy. Others had hypertrophic cardiomyopathy and/or myocardial infarctions. They were essentially asymptomatic during most of their lives and did not experience the early classical manifestations, including acroparesthesias, angiokeratoma, corneal and lenticular opacities, and hypohidrosis. Most were diagnosed after the onset of cardiac manifestations and most were found to have mild proteinuria.

The heterozygote

The clinical course and prognosis of affected hemizygous males and classically affected heterozygous females differ significantly (Desnick *et al.* 1995). Heterozygotes experience little difficulty in adult life at ages when affected males already have severe renal and/or cardiac involvement. Although most biochemically documented or obligate heterozygotes are asymptomatic throughout a normal lifespan, with increasing age some manifest minor symptoms of the disease (Table 15.2). Approximately 30% of heterozygotes have a few, isolated skin lesions, less than 10% have acroparesthesias, and about 70% have the whorl-like corneal dystrophy (Franceschetti 1976). Renal findings in heterozygotes include hyposthenuria; the occurrence of erythrocytes, leukocytes, and granular and hyaline casts in the urinary sediment; proteinuria; and other signs of renal

Table 15.2 Clinical manifestations in heterozygotes for Fabry's disease

Manifestation	Estimated incidence* (%)	Remarks
Corneal dystrophy	~70	Useful for heterozygote identification
Angiokeratoma	~30	Single or isolated lesions
Acroparesthesias	<10	Infrequent; hands, feet, and lower abdomen
Hypohidrosis	<1	Rare variants†
Cardiac involvement	<1	Rare variants†
CNS involvement	<1	Rare variants†
Renal failure	<1	Rare variants†

*Based on review of over 122 heterozygous females, 1–85 years of age, evaluated by the authors.
†Rare female variants with 0–5% α-galactosidase A activity.

impairment. Some heterozygotes will develop cardiac involvement with advanced age (Broadbent *et al.* 1981). However, a few heterozygotes have been described with disease as severe as that observed in classically affected hemizygous males (Ferrans *et al.* 1969). In contrast, obligate heterozygotes (daughters of affected hemizygous males) without any clinical manifestations and with normal levels of leukocyte α-galactosidase A and urinary sediment glycosphingolipids have been reported (Rietra *et al.* 1975). Indeed, asymptomatic and symptomatic monozygotic female twins have been described (Levade *et al.* 1991). Such markedly variable expression is expected in females heterozygous for X-linked diseases due to random X inactivation. At the cellular level, heterozygotes for most X-linked enzymatic defects have two populations of cells, one with mutant and the other with normal enzymatic activity due to the random inactivation of one X chromosome in each cell early in embryogenesis. Ultrastructural examination of renal tissue from heterozygotes from classically affected families also demonstrated two populations of glomerular, interstitial, and vascular cells: one normal, the other with observed glycosphingolipid deposition (Gubler *et al.* 1978). To date, limited information is available on the heterozygous relatives of males with the cardiac variant phenotype.

Renal pathology and pathophysiology

Morphologically, Fabry's disease is characterized by widespread tissue deposits of crystalline glycosphingolipids which show birefringence with characteristic 'Maltese crosses' under polarization microscopy. In classically affected males, the glycosphingolipid is deposited in all areas of the body, occurring predominantly in the lysosomes of endothelial, perithelial, and smooth-muscle cells of blood vessels and, to a lesser degree, in histiocytic and reticular cells of connective tissue. Lipid deposits are also prominent in epithelial cells of the cornea and glomeruli and tubules of the kidney, in muscle fibres of the heart, and in ganglion cells of the autonomic system. Glycosphingolipid deposition does not occur in hepatocytes or in the liver sinus endothelium (Elleder 1985). In males with the cardiac variant phenotype, glycosphingolipid deposition has been documented in the lysosomes of myocytes and in the kidney tubular cells and, to a lesser extent, in glomerular cells (Desnick *et al.* 1995). Vascular endothelial involvement has been notably absent in cardiac variants (von Scheidt *et al.* 1991).

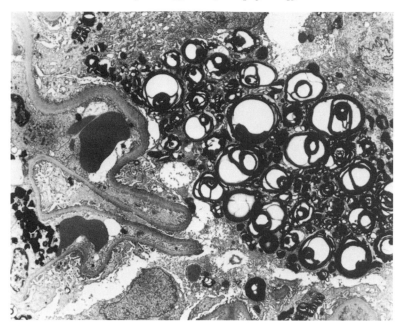

Fig. 15.2 Electron photomicrograph of a portion of a glomerulus from a classically affected male patient. Note the numerous concentric lamellar inclusions.

Renal pathology

The earliest lesions are due to the accumulation of glycosphingolipids in endothelial and epithelial cells of the glomerulus (Fig. 15.2) and of Bowman's space and in the epithelium of the loops of Henle and of distal tubules. The lesions of the renal vasculature are less prominent than those of the nephron, and renal architecture is maintained. In later stages, and to a lesser degree, proximal tubules, interstitial histiocytes, and fibrocytes may show lipid accumulation. Lipid-laden distal tubular epithelial cells desquamate and may be detected in the urinary sediment (Desnick *et al.* 1971). These cells have been shown to account for about 75% of the urinary cells shed by a classically affected hemizygote (Chatterjee *et al.* 1984). The early abnormalities in renal function have their basis in these lesions, the later and more severe renal changes are the result of glomerular sclerosis, progressive vascular lesions, and hypertension.

Concurrently, renal blood vessels are involved progressively and often extensively. An early finding is arterial fibrinoid deposits which may result from the necrosis of severely involved muscular cells (Pompen *et al.* 1947; Gubler *et al.* 1978). Other histologic changes in the kidney are the sequelae of non-specific, end-stage renal disease with evidence of severe arteriolar sclerosis, glomerular atrophy and fibrosis, pseudotubular proliferation of residual glomerular epithelium, tubular atrophy, and diffuse interstitial fibrosis. Renal size increases during the third decade of life, followed by a decrease in the fourth and fifth decades. The renal involvement has been the subject of comprehensive reviews (McNary and Loewenstein 1965; Burkholder *et al.* 1980).

The pattern of glycosphingolipid deposition in classically affected males with Fabry's disease, particularly its predilection for vascular endothelial and smooth-muscle cells, is uniquely different from that seen in other glycosphingolipidoses (Johnson and Desnick 1990). However, the origin of the accumulated glycosphingolipid substrates has not been fully clarified. A significant contribution comes from endogenous synthesis and subsequent lysosomal accumulation of terminal α-galactosyl-containing glycosphingolipids following autophagy of cellular membranous material containing these lipid substrates. Endogenous metabolism is a major source of substrate accumulation in avascular sites such as cornea and in neural cells, which presumably are protected from the increased circulating levels of globotriaosylceramide by the blood–brain barrier. In addition, the turnover of globotriaosylceramide, and particularly its precursor globotetriaosylceramide (globoside), which are present in higher concentrations in normal renal tissue than in any other tissue, are presumably responsible for the endogenous renal deposition of the Fabry substrate.

Renal pathophysiology

The observed abnormalities in renal function have their basis in lesions of the nephron and of the renal vasculature, and possibly in disorders of the posterior pituitary and hypothalamus. Glycosphingolipid deposits antedate clinical signs and symptoms. During this early period, the lesions of the renal vasculature are less prominent than those of the nephron, and renal architecture is maintained. The observed mild proteinuria may be explained by alteration of the glomerular epithelial cells and their foot processes (McNary and Lowenstein 1965) and/or by increased desquamation of lipid-laden tubular epithelial cells (Chatterjee *et al.* 1984).

Loss of renal concentrating ability with polyuria and polydipsia may occur well in advance of a significant decrease in glomerular filtration or evidence of renal failure (Pabico *et al.* 1973). The defect in concentrating ability may be due to decreased water permeability of the distal tubules and collecting ducts secondary to lipid deposition. The diabetes insipidus-like syndrome, which is not related to faulty electrolyte transfer in distal tubules, may result from tubular insensitivity to antidiuretic hormone or to combined dysfunction of the renal tubular cells and lesions of the glycosphingolipid-laden supraoptic nucleus and antidiuretic centre of the hypothalamus. The later and more severe renal changes are the result of vascular lesions and of systemic hypertension.

α-galactosidase A: the enzymatic defect in Fabry's disease

The enzymatic defect in Fabry's disease is the deficient activity of the lysosomal enzyme, α-galactosidase A. Following the identification of globotriaosylceramide and galabiosylceramide as the accumulated substrates in Fabry's disease (Sweeley and Klinasky 1963), Brady *et al.* (1967) synthesized globotriaosylceramide with a radiolabeled terminal galactosyl moiety and used the radiolabelled glycosphingolipid to demonstrate the presence of a galactosidase in normal intestinal tissue and its deficient activity in intestinal biopsy specimens from males with Fabry's disease. The anomeric specificity of the deficient galactosidase activity was determined in 1970 by Kint, who demonstrated that leukocytes from hemizygotes with Fabry's disease were deficient in an α-galactosidase activity when assayed with either synthetic substrate, *p*-nitrophenyl-α-D-galactoside or 4-methylumbelliferyl-α-D-galactoside (Kint 1970). The identification of the anomeric linkage was confirmed in subsequent spectroscopic and enzymatic studies, which demonstrated that globotriaosylceramide from Fabry kidney has an $\alpha 1 \rightarrow 4$ linkage in the terminal galactosyl moiety (Clarke *et al.* 1971*b*; Hakomori *et al.* 1971).

α-galactosidases A and B

Early studies with synthetic substrates revealed that classically affected hemizygotes had a level of α-galactosidase activity that was approximately 10–25% of that observed in the respective source from normal individuals (Desnick *et al.* 1973a). The residual α-galactosidase activity in Fabry hemizygotes was thermostable and was not inhibited by myoinositol, whereas 80–90% of the total α-galactosidase activity in normal individuals was thermolabile and myoinositol-inhibitable (Desnick *et al.* 1973a; Johnson *et al.* 1975). Based on these studies with synthetic substrates, the two activities initially were thought to represent α-galactosidase isozymes and were designated α-galactosidases A and B (Beutler and Kuhl 1972a). The two 'isozymes' were separable by electrophoresis, isoelectric focusing, and ion-exchange chromatography. Subsequently, the demonstration that polyclonal antibodies against α-galactosidase A or B did not cross-react with the other enzyme (Beutler and Kuhl 1972b), that only α-galactosidase A activity was deficient in hemizygotes with Fabry's disease, and that the genes for α-galactosidases A and B mapped to different chromosomes (Desnick *et al.* 1995) clearly established that these enzymes were genetically distinct. Thus, it was not surprising when α-galactosidase B was shown in 1977 to be an α-*N*-acetylgalactosaminidase, a homodimeric glycoprotein which hydrolyzed artificial and natural substrates with terminal α-*N*-acetylgalactosaminyl moieties (Schram *et al.* 1977), including various *O*- and *N*-linked glycopeptides and glycoproteins, glycosphingolipids, and the proteoglycan, cartilage keratan sulphate II (Desnick *et al.* 1995).

Physical and kinetic properties

The native α-galactosidase A from human sources is a protein of approximately 101 kDa (Bishop and Sweeley 1978). Polyacrylamide gel electrophoresis in the presence of sodium dodecylsulphate (SDS) has consistently shown a single diffuse subunit band of about 49 kDa, indicating that the enzyme has a homodimeric structure. The enzyme is a glycoprotein containing 5–15% asparagine-linked complex and high mannose oligosaccharide chains (Desnick *et al.* 1979; Bishop *et al.* 1986). The relatively heat-labile enzyme that catalyses the hydrolysis of substrates possessing terminal α-galactosidic residues, including various synthetic water-soluble substrates and naturally occurring glycosphingolipids and glycoproteins. Maximal activity of α-galactosidase A with the artificial substrate 4-methylumbelliferyl-α-D-galactopyranoside is obtained at pH 4.6. The Michaelis constant (K_m) of the reaction with this substrate is approximately 2 mM. (Bishop and Sweeley 1978; Desnick *et al.* 1973a).

Enzyme biosynthesis and processing

Biosynthetic studies in cultured human cells have shown that the α-galactosidase A glycoprotein subunit is synthesized as a precursor peptide which is processed to the mature lysosomal subunit (Lemansky *et al.* 1987). Metabolic labelling studies in cultured human fibroblasts (Lemansky *et al.* 1987) have identified an ~50 kDa precursor which was processed via 47–50 kDa intermediates over several days to a mature lysosomal form of 46 kDa. The transport to lysosomes is dependent on mannose-6-phosphate receptors, since the enzyme was secreted as a 52 kDa glycosylated precursor in mucolipidosis II cells or in the presence of NH$_4$Cl.

Residual activity in atypical hemizygotes

Among lysosomal storage disorders, the rate of clinical progression in Fabry's disease is among the slowest, reflecting the normally low rate of substrate metabolism. Therefore, variants with residual activity who are asymptomatic or express subtle renal and/or cardiac manifestations of the disease would be expected to present at an advanced age. Such rare variants have been described with milder manifestations of disease, including the 'cardiac variant' (see above; Table 15.2). In contrast to the classically affected hemizygotes, who essentially have no detectable α-galactosidase A activity, biochemical investigation of the atypical variants has revealed the presence of residual α-galactosidase A activity, consistent with the attenuation or absence of the characteristic clinical manifestations (Bach *et al.* 1982; Kobayashi *et al.* 1985; Rietra *et al.* 1975; Romeo *et al.* 1975).

Serveral of the reported cardiac variants have been the subject of biochemical studies. The 38-year-old Italian cardiac variant described by Clarke and colleagues (1971*a*) had urinary sediment globotriaosylceramide levels in the hetrozygote range and low levels of galabioasylceramide. His total α-galactosidase activity (A and B) in cultured skin fibroblasts and leukocytes was about 30% of normal. Subsequently, his residual α-galactosidase A activity in cultured fibroblasts was partially purified and shown to have kinetic and thermostability properties similar to α-galactosidase A from normal fibroblasts. About 20% of normal α-galactosidase A activity was detected in his fibroblasts, but the amount of enzyme protein was not measured (Romeo *et al.* 1975). The 42-year-old Italian cardiac variant with severe rheumatoid arthritis described by Bishop *et al.* (1981) had levels of α-galactosidase A activity that were about 1% of normal in plasma and urine. Immunoprecipitation with monospecific anti-α-galactosidase A antibodies demonstrated residual activity in granulocytes, lymphocytes, platelets, liver, and cultured fibroblasts ranging from 9–37% of the respective normal levels. The immunoprecipitated residual α-galactosidase A activity from fibroblasts had the same kinetic and physical properties as the immunoprecipitated enzyme from normal fibroblasts. Rocket immunoelectrophoresis studies demonstrated that the level of α-galactosidase A activity corresponded to the amount of enzyme protein. However, compared to the normal enzyme, the residual fibroblast α-galactosidase A was more thermolabile at pH 4.6 and 50°C, and significantly less stable at pH 7.4 and 37°C. This finding was consistent with the extremely low enzyme levels in plasma and urine. Interestingly, the levels of globotriaosylceramide in plasma and urinary sediment were both in the low heterozygote range. No lysosomal inclusions were observed in hepatocytes or Kupffer cells in percutaneously biopsied liver, although ultrastructural evidence of glycosphingolipid was observed in a kidney biopsy. These findings were consistent with a stability mutation, resulting in an enzyme with normal kinetics. In this variant, it appeared that 10–40% of normal intracellular activity was sufficient to prevent the major clinical manifestations of the disease. In addition, the finding of only 1% of enzymatic activity in the plasma and low levels of plasma globotriaosylceramide suggested that circulating enzyme was not required to catabolize the plasma substrate.

The molecular genetics of α-galactosidase A

Our understanding of human α-galactosidase A and Fabry's disease has been advanced dramatically by the isolation of the full-length cDNA and entire genomic sequences encoding this lysosomal enzyme (Bishop *et al.* 1986; 1988; Kornreich *et al.* 1989). The full-length cDNA sequence provided the primary structure of the enzyme precursor, including the signal peptide. The subsequent isolation and sequencing of the entire chromosomal gene for α-galactosidase A allowed characterization of the structural organization and regulatory elements of this housekeeping gene (Bishop *et al.* 1988; Kornreich *et al.* 1989). *In situ* hybridization, restriction fragment length polymorphism (RFLP) studies, and the recent isolation and analyses of yeast artificial chromosomes (YACs) containing the α-galactosidase A gene and flanking markers (Vetrie *et al.* 1993) provided both genetic and physical mapping of the α-galactosidase A gene to the q22 region of the X chromosome. Studies of the α-galactosidase A mutations in unrelated Fabry families have identified a variety of lesions underlying the molecular genetic heterogeneity of this disease. Most mutations have been private and occurred only in single pedigrees (see below). Characterization of these lesions will provide information on the nature and frequency of the mutations causing this disease as well as insights into the structure-function relationships of this lysosomal hydrolase. More accurate carrier diagnosis has become possible by identification of the specific lesions in families or by analysis of closely-linked polymorphisms (see 'Diagnosis'). The identification of the mutation in a given Fabry family will permit the precise diagnosis of other family members by the use of a mutation-specific restriction endonuclease digestion or the use of oligonucleotide probes corresponding to the normal and mutant gene sequences. Eukaryotic expression of the full-length cDNA has resulted in the production of large amounts of active enzyme for characterization, crystallization, and future trials of enzyme replacement (see 'Treatment').

Gene rearrangements

The frequency of gene rearrangements in the α-galactosidase A gene causing Fabry's disease was assessed in 165 unrelated patients by Southern hybridization analysis using the full length α-galactosidase A cDNA as a probe (Bernstein *et al.* 1989) or by multiplex PCR amplification of the entire α-galactosidase A coding region (Kornreich and Desnick 1993). The latter method determines the size of each of the seven exons in four PCR products that are simultaneously amplified, and provides rapid screening for large (>50–100 bp) insertions or deletions. By these two methods, one partial gene duplication and five partial gene deletions were identified (Bernstein *et al.* 1989; Kornreich *et al.* 1990), a frequency of about 3%, which is similar to that reported for other X-linked diseases. Of note, no total gene deletions were identified.

Coding region mutations

Approximately 75% of the mutations causing Fabry's disease are missense or nonsense mutations. Of the 57 coding region single-base alterations reported, 44 were missense mutations and 13 were nonsense mutations (Fig. 15.3). (Bernstein *et al.* 1989; Koide *et al.* 1990; Sakuraba *et al.* 1990; von Scheidt *et al.* 1991; Ishii *et al.* 1992; Davies *et al.* 1993; 1994; Eng *et al.* 1993; 1994*a*, *b*; Meaney *et al.* 1994; Ploos van Amstel *et al.* 1994; Madsen *et al.* 1995). Approximately half (30/57) of these coding region mutations were in exons 5 through 7. Although most of the missense and nonsense mutations were detected in classically affected hemizygotes, several missense mutations (P146S, N215S, M296V, Q279E, and R301Q) were identified in asymptomatic or mild variants of Fabry's disease, the 'cardiac variant' (see Table 15.2). Of the 14 CpG dinucleotides in the α-galactosidase A coding sequence, point mutations occurred in six (in codons 112, 143, 227, 301, 342, and 356). Codons 227 and 342 had mutations at both the C and G of their respective CpG dinucleotides. The high frequency of mutations at CpG dinucleotides is consistent with their recognition as mutational hot spots due to the deamination of methylcytosine to thymidine.

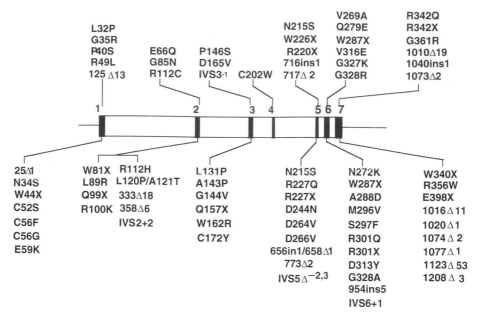

Fig. 15.3 Schematic of the α-galactosidase A gene indicating the relative position of the seven exons and listing the number of mutations identified in each. Numbers for deletions or insertions refer to nucleotide position in α-galactosidase A cDNA sequence. P40S = proline to serine substitution at codon 44; ins = insertion; Δ = deletion; IVS = intervening sequence.

RNA processing defects

Four mutations altering processing of the α-galactosidase A transcript have been described in classically affected hemizygotes (Fig. 15.3). These include a gt → gg single-base substitution in the 5′ donor consensus splice site of intron 2 (designated IVS2^{+2}) (Eng *et al.* 1993), a gt → tt substitution in the 5′ donor consensus splice site of intron 6 (IVS6^{+1}) (Sakuraba *et al.* 1992), a 2 bp deletion, tcagΔca, that disrupted the 3′ acceptor consensus splice site of intron 5 (IVS5$^{Δ-2,3}$) (Eng *et al.* 1993), and an AG → AT substitution in the 3′ acceptor site of intron 3 (Davies *et al.* 1994). The IVS6^{+1} mutation, which resulted in exon skipping, has been the most fully characterized (Sakuraba *et al.* 1992). Northern hybridization analysis of affected males initially detected a shortened 1.25 kb α-galactosidase A mRNA which was present at 50–60% of normal abundance. Heterozygotes had both the normal 1.45 kb and the shorter 1.25 kb transcript. RNase A protection analysis identified a deletion of about 200 bp that included all of exon 6. The exon 6 deletion resulted from a gt → tt substitution of the invariant 5′ donor splice consensus site of intron 6, causing abnormal splicing of the α-galactosidase A pre-mRNA.

Small insertions and deletions

Fourteen small deletions of 1 to 53 bp and three small insertions of 1 to 5 bp have been identified in the α-galactosidase A coding sequence in unrelated Fabry patients (Fig. 15.3) (Ishii *et al.* 1991; Davies *et al.* 1993; Eng *et al.* 1993; Ploos van Amstel *et al.* 1994; Madsen *et al.* 1995). Each of these rearrangements resulted in frameshift mutations that led to premature chain termination, with the exception of the 358de16 mutation which predicted the deletion of two amino acids, L120 and A121, and the in-frame substitution of histidine for asparagine and the 333de118 mutation which involved the in-frame deletion of the six amino acids from R112 to I117. These rearrangements were detected in classically affected hemizygotes with the exception of a three-base deletion (1208Δ3) in exon 7, which was identified in a patient with a later-onset, moderate disease phenotype (Eng *et al.* 1993).

Complex mutations

Two complex mutations, each involving two mutational events, were identified in exons 2 and 5 of the α-galactosidase A gene (Eng *et al.* 1994*b*).The exon 2 rearrangement resulted from a mutation(s) that altered the *underlined* two bases in the sequence AGC*TA*GCT to AGC*CA*ACT. The mutant sequence predicted the in-frame substitution of L120 and A121 to P120 and T121 (L120P and A121T). Interestingly, the eight-base region, including the two substituted bases, formed an inverted repeat. This rearrangement could be explained by two independent base substitutions involving a T to C transition and a G to A transition. Alternatively, this mutation may have resulted from the deletion of a T and a G followed by the duplication of each preceding base, leading to the mutated sequence AGCCAACT. The other complex rearrangement in exon 5 involved the insertion of an adenosine residue after nucleotide 654 (duplication of the A at position 654) and the deletion of the cytosine at position 656 (AT*C* CGA to A*A*T CGA). These base changes predicted an isoleucine to asparagine substitution at position 219 (I219N). Interestingly, the adenosine duplication was preceded by three other adenosine residues (nucleotides 651–653).

Common α-galactosidase A lesions causing Fabry's disease

Most of the reported mutations have been private (i.e. confined to a single Fabry pedigree). In fact, the discovery that two presumably unrelated families had identical mutations occasionally led to linking of two distant arms of the same pedigree. However, several mutations have been found in unrelated families of different ethnic or geographic backgrounds. These include N215S, R227Q, R227X, and R342Q mutations. The N215S was found in several unrelated cardiac variants who were asymptomatic or had mild disease manifestations (Elleder *et al.* 1990; Davies *et al.* 1993; Eng *et al.* 1993). R227Q and R227X, which occurred at a CpG nucleotide, were the most common mutations causing the classical phenotype. Taken together, they were found in 5% (eight of 148) of unrelated Fabry families studied (Eng *et al.* 1993), including families whose mutant alleles could be traced to Danish, English, German, Indian, Irish, Italian, and Polish ancestries. Two families with the R227Q mutation were of German descent, but a common ancestor or demographic region could not be identified. Codon 342 also contains a CpG dinucleotide and several apparently unrelated families have had either the R342Q or R342X mutations (Davies *et al.* 1993; Ploos van Amstel *et al.* 1994).

Genotype/phenotype correlations

Of the reported molecular lesions, classically affected males with no detectable α-galactosidase A activity had a variety of α-galactosidase A molecular lesions, including large and small gene rearrangements, splicing defects, and missense or nonsense mutations. In contrast, all of the asymptomatic or mildly affected cardiac variants (Table 15.2) had missense mutations which expressed residual α-galactosidase A activity. However, efforts to establish genotype/phenotype correlations have been limited since most Fabry patients had private mutations and attempts to predict the phenotype requires more extensive clinical information from unrelated patients with the same genotype. In addition, attempts to predict the clinical phenotype based on the type or location of a molecular lesion are premature. For example, the atypical mild mutations, N215S, Q279E, M296V, and R301Q, are all located in exons 5 and 6. However, other nearby missense mutations result in severe disease, such as S297F which is adjacent to M296V. The type of amino acid change (i.e. isofunctional vs. altered charge) also fails to predict a classical or mild phenotype. Thus, the clinical severity of private missense mutations detected in Fabry families with few or only young patients are difficult to predict; however, future crystallographic studies may provide useful structure-function information for genotype/phenotype correlations.

Diagnosis

Previously, the diagnosis of affected hemizygous males and heterozygous females was based on clinical findings and the levels of α-galactosidase A activity in easily obtained sources such as plasma and isolated lymphocytes or granulocytes. Since the gene encoding α-galactosidase A undergoes random X-inactivation, the expressed level of enzymatic activity in females heterozygous for the disease gene may vary significantly, thereby making accurate carrier detection difficult. The recent availability of the full-length cDNA and genomic sequences encoding human α-galactosidase A now permits the accurate molecular diagnosis of hemizygotes and heterozygotes through the identification of the precise lesion in the α-galactosidase A gene. In addition, the recent identification of simple sequence repeat polymorphism closely linked to the α-galactosidase A gene permits molecular diagnosis by linkage analysis in informative families whose specific mutations have not been determined (Caggana *et al.* 1997).

Clinical evaluation

The clinical diagnosis of classically affected hemizygous males is most readily made from the history and by observation of the characteristic skin lesions and corneal dystrophy. The most common childhood symptom before appearance of the cutaneous lesions is recurrent fever in association with pain of the hands and feet. The disorder has been often misdiagnosed as rheumatic fever, neurosis, erythromelalgia, or collagen vascular disease. Differential diagnosis of the cutaneous lesions must exclude the angiokeratoma of Fordyce (1896), angiokeratoma of Mibelli (Traub and Tolmach 1931), and angiokeratoma circumscriptum (Dammert 1965), none of which have the typical histologic or ultrastructural pathology of the Fabry lesion.

Presumptive diagnosis of hemizygotes can be made by observation of the characteristic corneal dystrophy upon slit-lamp examination and by demonstration of the birefringent inclusions in the urinary sediment. In contrast, males with isolated cardiac involvement (especially left ventricular hypertrophy), with or without mild proteinuria, should have their plasma and/or leukocyte α-galactosidase A activities determined. Also, all males with renal failure whose biopsy was not examined ultrastructurally should have their α-galactosidase A activity determined as described below.

Women suspected of being heterozygous carriers of the Fabry gene should be carefully examined for evidence of the corneal opacity and for isolated skin lesions, particularly on the breasts, back, trunk, and posterolateral thighs. Heterozygote detection also may be accomplished by the histologic finding of lipid-laden cells in biopsied skin and tissues or in the urinary sediment.

Biochemical diagnosis of affected hemizygotes

All suspect hemizygotes should be confirmed biochemically by the demonstration of deficient α-galactosidase A activities in plasma or serum, leukocytes, tears, biopsied tissues, or cultured skin fibroblasts. Classically affected hemizygotes usually have no detectable α-galactosidase A activity when the assay is performed with synthetic substrates for α-galactosidase A with the addition of α-N-acetylgalactosamine in the reaction mixture to inhibit the α-galactosidase B activity (Mayes *et al.* 1981). This assay modification permits the reliable diagnosis of classically affected hemizygotes.

Cardiac variants and other atypical hemizygotes may be detected by the presence of residual α-galactosidase A activity ranging from less than 5 to 35% of normal. Such variants have been detected with high levels of activity in plasma (~30%) and low levels (2–10%) in cellular sources; with absent or low levels in plasma and higher levels (5–25%) in cultured cells and tissues; as well as with low, but detectable residual activity in both plasma and cellular sources. In most variants studied, the levels of residual activity have been highest (20–30% of normal) in cultured skin fibroblasts. The kinetic and stability properties of the residual α-galactosidase A activity should be determined as well as the levels of globotriaosylceramide in various fluid and cellular sources.

Molecular diagnosis of Fabry heterozygotes

The biochemical identification of female carriers of the Fabry gene is less reliable. Many heterozygous females can be detected by intermediate levels of α-galactosidase A activity in various sources. However, due to random X-chromosomal inactivation, heterozygotes can express levels of enzymatic activity ranging from essentially zero to normal. Thus, reports of obligate heterozygotes with normal α-galactosidase A activity and no keratopathy (Spaeth and Frost 1965) are not unexpected and emphasize the need for precise carrier detection.

More recent molecular analyses of the specific gene defect in each family or the use of α-galactosidase A-specific RFLPs (Desnick *et al.* 1987) or closely linked X-chromosomal anonymous DNA sequences (MacDermott *et al.* 1987; Kornreich *et al.* 1992; Caggana *et al.* 1997) have provided more accurate heterozygote detection. The identification of a gene rearrangement, a restriction endonuclease cleavage site alteration, or a specific point mutation detectable by use of a specific restriction enzyme or synthetic oligonucleotide probe permits the precise diagnosis of heterozygotes in families with specific alterations. Recent advances in rapid DNA sequencing make more feasible the identification of mutations in all Fabry patients. Certainly, for all families in which the molecular lesion has been identified, precise molecular carrier detection should be offered. Alternatively, molecular diagnoses may be accomplished using indirect methods. These include the analysis of α-galactosidase A-specific RFLPs (Desnick *et al.* 1987) as well as for anonymous X-chromosomal polymorphic sequences which are closely linked to the α-galactosidase A locus (Desnick *et al.* 1987; MacDermott *et al.* 1987; Kornreich *et al.* 1992; Caggana *et al.* 1997).

Prenatal diagnosis

Prenatal diagnosis of Fabry's disease can be accomplished by the assay of α-galactosidase A activity in chorionic villi obtained at 10 weeks of pregnancy or in cultured amniotic cells obtained by amniocentesis at approximately 15 weeks of pregnancy. The prenatal diagnosis of an affected male fetus minimally requires the demonstration of deficient α-galactosidase A activity and an XY karyotype.

Genetics and family counseling

Fabry's disease is inherited as an X-linked recessive trait. All sons of hemizygous males will be unaffected but all daughters will be obligate carriers of the gene. On average, half the sons of heterozygous females will have the disease and half the daughters will be carriers. Genetic counselling should be offered to all families in which the diagnosis of Fabry's disease is made. Inheritance of the Fabry gene from hemizygotes and heterozygotes should be considered since both genotypes transmit the gene. In each extended family, all at-risk males should be diagnostically evaluated. All at-risk females in a pedigree should be examined clinically and biochemically for heterozygote identification. In addition, it may be necessary to carry out molecular studies in order to accurately determine the genotype of women at risk for inheriting the disease gene (see above, 'Molecular diagnosis of Fabry heterozygotes'). Fabry's disease has been detected antenatally from cultured fetal cells and amniotic fluid obtained by amniocentesis as well as from chorionic villi (see above, 'Prenatal diagnosis').

Family and vocational counselling should be provided, especially to families with affected children. Often, parents, teachers, and/or physicians misinterpret the excruciating pain experienced during childhood as malingering, especially in the absence of any objective physical or laboratory findings. Since physical exertion, emotional stresses, and fatigue as well as rapid changes in the environmental temperature and humidity can trigger these painful episodes, appropriate arrangements must be made with physical education teachers, employers, and other individuals to minimize or eliminate activities that may precipitate the painful crises. In addition, young affected males should be allowed to participate in selected sports or physical activities and be permitted to stop at their own discretion. Within this perspective, reasonable occupational and vocational objectives can be pursued. Vocational counselling should discourage occupations which require significant manual dexterity, physical exertion, emotional stress, or exposure to rapid changes in temperature or humidity.

Treatment

Medical management

In Fabry's disease, the chronicity of the clinical events causes severe debilitation and incapacity that extends over years. The single most debilitating and morbid aspect of Fabry's disease is the excruciating pain. The pathophysiological events that cause the incapacitating episodes of pain or the chronic burning acroparesthesias have not been clarified. Numerous drugs have been tried for the relief of these agonizing pains (Wise *et al.* 1962). With the exception of centrally acting narcotic analgesics, which have been only partially effective, conventional analgesic agents have not been helpful. However, prophylactic administration of low-maintenance dosages of diphenylhydantoin have been found to provide relief from the periodic crises of excruciating pain and constant discomfort in hemizygotes and heterozygotes (Lockman *et al.* 1973). Similarly, carbamazepine also provided pain relief (Lenoir *et al.* 1977). The combination of diphenylhydantoin and carbamazepine may significantly reduce the occurrence and severity of the pain (Atzpodien *et al.* 1975). Subsequent reports have further documented the effectiveness of diphenylhydantoin and/or carbamazepine in the prevention and amelioration of these debilitating episodes (Dupperrat *et al.* 1975). The potential side-effects of gingival hypertrophy with diphenylhydantoin and dose-related autonomic complications with carbamazepine, including urinary retention, nausea, vomiting, and ileus, have been recorded (Filling-Katz *et al.* 1989).

Care of patients with regard to cardiac, pulmonary, and central nervous system manifestations remains non-specific and symptomatic. Obstructive lung disease has been documented in older hemizygotes and heterozygotes, with more severe impairment in smokers; therefore, patients should be discouraged from smoking. Patients with reversible obstructive airway disease may benefit from bronchodilation therapy. Prophylactic oral anticoagulants are recommended for stroke-prone patients. Angiokeratoma can be removed for cosmetic appearance or other indications by argon laser treatment with little, if any, scarring (Hobbs and Ratz 1987).

Dialysis and renal transplantation

Since renal insufficiency is the most frequent late complication in classically affected patients with this disease, chronic haemodialysis and/or renal transplantation have become life-saving procedures (Donati *et al.* 1987). Contrary to an unfavourable early report (Maizel *et al.* 1981), more recent experience has indicated the clear benefit of transplantation for this disease (Donati *et al.* 1987). Successful transplantation will correct renal function, and the engrafted kidney will remain histologically free of endogenous glycolipid deposition (e.g. Mosnier *et al.* 1991) since the normal α-galactosidase A in the allograft will catabolize endogenous renal glycosphingolipid substrates. Reports of substrate accumulation in transplanted cadaveric kidneys have identified rare, isolated deposits, observable only by electron microscopy in infiltrating mononuclear cells (Mosnier *et al.* 1991) or non-glomerular capillary endothelial cells (Faraggiana *et al.* 1981; Friedlender *et al.* 1987). Presumably these endothelial cells were derived from the recipient and were α-galactosidase A deficient (Sinclair 1972). However, it is important to note that transplantation of kidneys from Fabry heterozygotes, which already may contain significant substrate deposition, should be avoided. In one reported case, transplantation of a heterozygous allograft resulted in renal dysfunction five years later (Popli *et al.* 1987). Therefore, all potential related donors must be carefully evaluated so that only unaffected or non-carrier individuals are chosen. Also, the immune function in Fabry hemizygotes has been shown to be similar to that in other uraemic patients, indicating that there is no immunologic contraindication to transplantation in this disease (Donati *et al.* 1984). However, the formation of anti-α-galactosidase A antibodies has been demonstrated following acute rejection (Voglino *et al.* 1988) in a recipient who was later shown to be CRIM-negative for the enzyme.

In addition to treatment of the renal failure, kidney transplantation has been undertaken to determine if the allograft could provide normal α-galactosidase A for substrate metabolism (Desnick *et al.* 1972*a*). Hypothetically, the normal kidney might metabolize the accumulated substrate by uptake and catabolism within the allograft and/or by the release of the active enzyme into the circulation for uptake and metabolism in other tissues such as the vascular endothelium. Although biochemical and/or clinical improvement has been reported in most recipients (e.g. Desnick *et al.* 1972*a*, 1973*b*; Maizel *et al.* 1981; Voglino *et al.* 1988), no biochemical effect could be demonstrated in other recipients (Clarke *et al.* 1972; Grünfeld *et al.* 1975). Several patients with successful engraftment, who survived for 10–15 years, have died from complications of cardiac disease (Kramer *et al.* 1984) or unrelated disorders (Mosnier *et al.* 1991). Thus, the use of renal allografts to alter the rate of progressive substrate accumulation remains unclear and further studies are required to document the long-term biochemical effects of this strategy. In view of these results, renal transplantation should be undertaken only in patients with clinically significant renal failure.

Enzyme replacement strategies

Attempts to replace the defective α-galactosidase A activity with normal enzyme have been undertaken *in vitro* and *in vivo*. Studies using partially purified α-galactosidase A from fig (Dawson *et al.* 1973), coffee bean (Osada *et al.* 1987), and human sources (Mayes *et al.* 1982) added to the media of cultured skin fibroblasts from Fabry hemizygotes demonstrated the ability of the exogenous enzyme to gain access to and catabolize the accumulated substrate, globotriaosylceramide. These *in vitro* studies indicated the feasibility of enzyme replacement and, in particular, demonstrated that low levels (<5%) of exogenous enzyme, particularly the high-uptake form (Mayes *et al.* 1982), were capable of normalizing substrate metabolism. The recent cloning of the full-length cDNA encoding α-galactosidase A (Kornreich *et al.* 1989) has stimulated efforts to use eukaryotic systems for the expression of large amounts of enzyme for future trials of replacement therapy. The stable overexpression of human α-galactosidase A in CHO cells permitted the large-scale production of both lysosomal and secreted forms of this enzyme for characterization and for future clinical trials of enzyme replacement (Ioannou *et al.* 1992). Only when large amounts of active enzyme are available will it be possible to properly evaluate the short- and long-term biochemical and clinical effects of enzyme replacement endeavours.

The lipidoses

This review of selected lipidoses is not comprehensive and was designed to highlight the renal aspects of these disorders (see Lipoprotein glomerulopathy in Chapter 12). References for more comprehensive reviews are given for each entry.

Gaucher's disease (deficient acid β-glucosidase activity)

Gaucher's disease results from the deficient activity of acid β-glucosidase and the resultant accumulation of the glycosphingolipid, glucosyl ceramide, primarily in the cells of the reticuloendothelial system (i.e. unique macrophages or 'Gaucher cells' in the bone marrow, liver, and spleen). The three subtypes of Gaucher's disease are distinguished by their clinical severity and course, and by the presence or absence of neurologic complications. Type 1 is the most common and does not have mental or neurologic involvement. This disease occurs predominantly in Jewish individuals of Central and Eastern European ancestry (Ashkenazi Jews) with a carrier frequency of about one in 20. Type 2 has its onset in infancy and is a fatal neurodegenerative disorder with death occurring in the first or second year of life. It is an extremely rare type and does not occur at increased frequency in any particular ethnic or demographic group. Type 3 begins in early childhood, has mild to severe neurologic involvement, and is very rare except in Sweden where most patients have been found. These three types of Gaucher's disease are allelic variants and are inherited as autosomal recessive traits.

Although the specific enzymatic defect was identified in 1965, the recent isolation of the acid β-glucosidase gene and the development of enzyme therapy have had a dramatic effect on the diagnosis, management, and treatment of this disease. The full-length cDNA and entire genomic sequence encoding acid β-glucosidase have been isolated and characterized (for review, see

Beutler and Grabowski 1995). To date, over 50 mutations have been detected in the gene. The identification of several common mutations in type 1 patients of Ashkenazi Jewish descent have permitted accurate carrier screening and improved prenatal diagnosis. In addition, certain genotype–phenotype correlations have been made for types 1, 2, and 3 disease (Sibille *et al.* 1993). More recently, enzyme replacement therapy with placental-derived or recombinant acid β-glucosidase has proven clinically efficacious for the treatment of patients with type 1 disease (Grabowski *et al.* 1995). Efforts are currently underway to develop gene therapy for Gaucher type 1 disease by the retroviral-mediated insertion of the acid β-glucosidase gene into pluripotential haematopoietic stem cells.

The pathologic descriptions of the kidney have focused on type 1 and type 2 disease. Occasionally, the kidney is involved with either typical Gaucher cells in the glomerulus or cells scattered either singularly or as groups throughout the interstitium (Chang-Lo *et al.* 1967). In addition, tubular epithelial cell involvement and Gaucher cells in the tubular lumen have been described (Chang Lo *et al.* 1967). There are no reports of clinically significant renal dysfunction in children (Frederickson and Sloan 1972; Brito *et al.* 1973). Significant proteinuria (20 g/day) has been reported, associated with acute glomerulonephritis (Chander *et al.* 1979). Occasional adults with type 1 disease may have clinically-manifest renal involvement, particularly proteinuria in severely involved patients who have been splenectomized, but usually it is secondary to other causes such as drug toxicity, hypertension, or other concurrent conditions. Several cases with renal involvement have been reviewed (Chander *et al.* 1979).

G_{M1} gangliosidosis type 1 (defective β-galactosidase activity)

G_{M1} gangliosidosis type 1 and its counterpart, galactosialidosis (defective β-galactosidase and α-neuroaminidase activities), present a unique phenotype among the lysosomal storage disorders. Many of the clinical manifestations are reminiscent of both the cerebral lipidoses and the mucopolysaccharidoses. G_{M1} gangliosidosis presents with neonatal seizures or poor feeding, a Hurler-like facial dysmorphia, and cherry-red maculae. These infants suffer from severe psychomotor retardation and usually die by two years of age (Suzuki *et al.* 1995). Hepatosplenomegaly, dysostosis multiplex, and foamy bone-marrow macrophages are present at birth, indicating the systemic accumulation of G_{M1} ganglioside and a keratan sulphate-like mucopolysaccharide (Okada and O'Brien 1968; O'Brien 1969). The infantile form of galactosialodosis has a similar phenotype characterized by coarse facies, cherry-red maculae, ascites, skeletal dysplasia, organomegaly, and foam cells in the bone marrow (d'Azzo *et al.* 1995).

Diagnosis is based on the typical phenotype of the infantile forms of G_{M1} gangliosidosis and galactosialidosis and the demonstration of deficient β-galactosidase activity in peripheral blood leukocytes in both disorders with the commercially available fluorogenic substrate 4-methylumbelliferyl-β-galactoside. The differential diagnosis should include galactosialidosis and Morquio B (mucopolysaccharidosis IVB), two disorders that also have this enzyme deficiency. Therefore, leukocytes should be assayed for α-neuraminidase activity and the urine of suspect patients should be tested for the presence of sialyloligosaccharides and keratin sulphate. In at-risk families, the prenatal diagnosis can be accomplished by assays of cultured amniocytes or chorionic villus samples.

The renal pathologic findings in the infantile form of G_{M1} gangliosidosis are attributable to the lysosomal accumulation in the glomerular epthelial cells of the amorphous keratan sulphate-like mucopolysaccharide and/or asialoglycoproteins (Okada and O'Brien 1968; O'Brien 1969). On histologic examination, cytoplasmic ballooning of epithelial cells is variably present in the proximal convoluted tubule and the loop of Henle (Landing *et al.* 1964), and the severity is age-related (Scott *et al.* 1967). The glomerular lesions of G_{M1} gangliosidosis are remarkably reminiscent of those in Fabry's disease. Ultrastructural studies (Scott *et al.* 1967) reveal extensive substrateengorged lysosomes in the glomerular epithelium and proximal convoluted tubule, with less involvement of arteriolar smooth muscle. In addition, small amounts of lamellar, lipid-like material have been found in the epthelial cells of the glomerulus and proximal convoluted tubule (Okada and O'Brien 1968).

G_{M1} ganglioside is increased 20-fold to 50-fold in the liver and spleen (Suzuki 1968). Presumably, the primary accumulated substrates in the kidney are the keratan sulphate-like material and asialoglycoproteins; these substrates account for the histochemical and morphologic observations of large amounts of amorphous, periodic acid–Schiff (PAS)-positive material in renal lysosomes.

Although the renal histologic lesions are extensive, impairment of renal function is not typically discribed in the infantile form of G_{M1} gangliosidosis, galactosialidosis, and Morquio B disease. Only one case report (Mihatsch *et al.* 1973) has documented preterminal decreases in creatinine clearance, with glycosuria and aminoaciduria, presumably due to proximal tubular dysfunction. More severe renal abnormalities may possibly be found if these children survive longer, as suggested by the renomegaly in the older children who have died from this disease (Landing *et al.* 1964).

G_{M2} gangliosidosis type 2 (defective β-hexosaminidase A and B activities)

G_{M2} gangliosidosis type 2, Sandhoff's disease, presents at three to nine months of age with failure to thrive. While many clinical features are shared by Sandhoff and Tay–Sachs disease, the organomegaly secondary to the storage of globoside clearly distinguishes Sandhoff's disease. Death usually occurs by five years of age due to intercurrent pulmonary infections (Desnick *et al.* 1972*b*).

On histopathologic examination, small granules that stain positive with Luxol fast blue, hematoxylin and eosin, Sudan IV, and PAS are seen in the glomerulus, tubules, and vascular endothelial cells. The epithelial cells of the glomerulus and tubules have patchy granular involvement, except for sparing of the lower collecting tubules (Dolman *et al.* 1973). Near the papilla, large, round eosinophilic bodies are described as being larger than the nuclei and staining faintly with Sudan IV. Ultrastructurally, these inclusions are lysosomes containing membranous, lamellar, osmophilic concretions similar to the cytoplasmic inclusion bodies observed in neurons from Tay–Sachs disease (Dolman *et al.* 1973).

The deficient activities of β-hexosamindase A and B in the kidney correlate well with the reported accumulation of globoside and the abnormal excretion of N-acetylneuramic acid and galactosamine-rich oligosaccharides (Sandhoff *et al.* 1968). Due to the major neurologic involvement, lack of renal functional impairment has not been well-documented.

Metachromatic leukodystrophy (defective arylsulphatase A activity)

The late infantile form of metachromatic leukodystrophy is an insidious disease of the nervous system that presents with difficulties with gait or coordination in the first to fourth year of life (Kolodny and Fluharty 1995). While early development is normal, progressive involvement of the nervous system leads to a vegetative state by seven to 10 years of age; death occurs some years later.

The major clinical pathologic changes are confined to the nervous system; however, on histopathologic examination, lesions have been found in the liver, gallbladder, adrenal glands, pituitary, and kidney. Renal lesions characteristically are confined to the tubular system; the proximal convoluted tubules, loops of Henle, and collecting tubules have a patchy distension of the cytoplasm by metachromatic granules (Kolodny and Fluharty 1995). Resibois' (1971) elegant ultrastructural study documented lamellar and prismatic inclusions of a lipid nature in the distal tubules. The collecting ducts, however, contain fewer, but much larger, cytoplasmic inclusions of membranous, lamellar material. These lamellated structures represent accumulated renal sulphatide, which results from a deficiency of lysosomal arylsulphatase A. Although the mono-hexosyl sulphatide that is found primarily in the brain is also present in the kidney, much larger quantities of dihexosyl sulphatide accumulate in the kidney; the latter sulphatide occurs only in certain other visceral tissues. These data suggest that the source of the accumulated renal sulphatide is endogenous. Despite the striking morphologic changes, there are characteristically no functional abnormalities, although one patient was described with proximal renal tubular acidosis.

Mucolipidosis II (UDP-N-acetylglucosamine-1-phosphotransferase deficiency)

Since its original description in 1965 (Leroy and Demars 1967), mucolipidosis II or I cell disease has presented a challenge and vexation to investigators of disorders of the lysosomal apparatus. Unlike most of the lysosomal storage diseases which result from a single defective enzyme activity, mucolipidosis II is characterized by multiple deficiencies of lysosomal hydrolase activities in certain tissues (particularly of mesenchymal origin) and marked elevations of these activities in the plasma and urine of affected patients (Tondeur *et al.* 1971). This disease is due to the defective activity of the enzyme UDP-N-acetylglucosamine-1-phosphotransferase (Reitman *et al.* 1981). The deficiency of this enzymatic activity results in a generalized abnormality of lysosomal hydrolase post-translational modification, which is required for trafficking of these enzymes to the lysosome through the mannose-6-phosphate-mediated pathway (Kaplan *et al.* 1977).

Clinically, patients with mucolipidosis II have progressive psychomotor retardation, severe growth failure, gingival hypertrophy, dysostosis multiplex, and a Hurler-like facial dysmorphia. Renal function is not impaired. Death usually occurs before the fourth year of life.

Striking foamy transformation of the visceral cells of Bowman's capsule is evident in the renal glomerulus (Martin *et al.* 1975; Kornfeld and Sly 1995), while only a few vacuoles are noted in the proximal convoluted tubule. Ultrastructurally, extensive lesions of the glomerular epithelium are seen; however, it is noteworthy that the foot processes are spared or slightly vacuolated. The interstitial cells, presumably fibroblasts, may have extensive vacuolation (Martin *et al.* 1975).

Martin and colleagues (1975) found that the vacuolated cells did not stain with PAS, Fiel–Nielson, toluidine blue O, Sudan black B, Sudan III, or oil red O after use of several fixatives. In addition, they found that no lysosomal hydrolase activity could be demonstrated in the visceral cells of Bowman's capsule while the loops of Henle and collecting ducts were histochemically stained for acid phosphatase, β-glucuronidase, and non-specific esterase.

Acknowledgements

This work was supported in part by a grant (1-578) from the March of Dimes Birth Defects Foundation and grants from the National Institutes of Health, including a research grant (R29 DK 34045 Merit Award), a grant (MO1 RR00071) for the Mount Sinai General Clinical

Research Center Program from the National Center of Research Resources, and a grant (P30 HD28822) for the Mount Sinai Child Health Research Center.

References

Anderson, W. (1898). A case of angiokeratoma. *British Journal of Dermatology*, **10**, 113.

Atzpodien, W., Kremer, G. J., Schnellbacher, E., Denk, R., Haferkamp, G., and Bierbach, H. (1975). Angiokeratoma corporis diffusum (Morbus Fabry). Biochemische Diagnostik im Blutplasma. *Deutsche Medizinische Wochenschrift*, **100**, 423.

Bach, G., Rosemann, E., Karni, A., and Cohen, T. (1982). Pseudodeficiency of α-galactosidase A. *Clinical Genetics*, **21**, 59.

Bagdale, J. D., Parker, F., Ways, P. O., Morgan, T. E., Lagunoff, D., and Eidelman, S. (1968). Fabry's disease: A correlative clinical, morphologic, and biochemical study. *Laboratory Investigation*, **18**, 681.

Bass, J. L., Shrivastava, S., Grabowski, G. A., Desnick, R. J., and Moller, J. H. (1980). The M-mode echocardiogram in Fabry's disease. *American Heart Journal*, **100**, 807.

Becker, A. E., Schoorl, R., Balk, A. G., and van Der Heide, R. M. (1975). Cardiac manifestations of Fabry's disease. Report of a case with mitral insufficiency and electrocardiographic evidence of myocardial infarction. *American Journal of Cardiology*, **36**, 829.

Bernstein, H. S., Bishop, D. F., Astrin, K. H., Kornreich, R., Eng, C. M., Sakuraba, H., *et al.* (1989). Fabry disease: Six gene rearrangements and an exonic point mutation in the α-galactosidase gene. *Journal of Clinical Investigation*, **83**, 1390.

Bethune, J. E., Landrigan, P. L., and Chipman, C. D. (1961). Angiokeratoma corporis diffusum (Fabry's disease in two brothers). *New England Journal of Medicine*, **264**, 1280.

Beutler, E. and Kuhl, W. (1972*a*). Purification and properties of human α-galactosidases. *Journal of Biological Chemistry*, **247**, 7195.

Beutler, E. and Kuhl, W. (1972*b*). Relationship between human α-galactosidase isozymes. *Nature New Biology*, **239**, 207.

Beutler, E. R. and Grabowski, G. A. (1995). Gaucher's disease. In: *The metabolic basis of inherited disease* (7th edn) (ed. C. R. Scriver, A. L. Beaudet, W. S. Sly, and D. Valle), p. 2641. McGraw Hill, New York.

Bishop, D. F. and Sweeley, C. C. (1978). Plasma α-galactosidase A. Properties and comparisons with tissue α-galactosidases. *Biochimica Biophysica Acta*, **525**, 399.

Bishop, D. F., Grabowski, G. A., and Desnick, R. J. (1981). Fabry disease: An asymptomatic hemizygote with significant residual α-galactosidase A activity. *American Journal of Human Genetics*, **33**, 71A.

Bishop, D. F., Calhoun, D. H., Bernstein, H. S., Hantzopoulos, P., Quinn, M., and Desnick, R. J. (1986). Human α-galactosidase A: Nucleotide sequence of a cDNA clone encoding the mature enzyme. *Proceedings of the National Academy of Sciences, USA*, **83**, 4859.

Bishop, D. F., Kornreich, R., and Desnick, R. J. (1988). Structural organization of the α-galactosidase A gene: Further evidence for the absence of a 3′ untranslated region. *Proceedings of the National Academy of Sciences, USA*, **85**, 3903.

Brady, R. O., Gal, A. E., Bradley, R. M., Martensson, E., Warshaw, A. L., and Laster, L. (1967). Enzymatic defect in Fabry's disease: Ceramide trihexosidase deficiency. *New England Journal of Medicine*, **276**, 1163.

Brito, T., Gomes dos Reis, V., Penna, D. O., and Camargo, M. E. (1973). Glomerular involvement in Gaucher's disease. A light, immunofluorescent and ultrastructural study based on kidney biopsy specimens. *Archives of Pathology*, **95**, 1.

Broadbent, J. C., Edwards, W. D., Gordon, H., Hartzler, G. O., and Krawisz, J. E. (1981). Fabry cardiomyopathy in the female confirmed by endomyocardial biopsy. *Mayo Clinic Proceedings*, **56**, 623.

Burkholder, P. M., Updike, S. J., Ware, R. A., and Reese, O. G. (1980). Clinicopathologic, enzymatic and genetic features in a case of Fabry's disease. *Archives of Pathology Laboratory Medicine*, **104**, 17.

Caggana, M., Ashley, G. A., Desnick, R. J., and Eng, C. M. (1997). Fabry disease: Molecular carrier detection and prenatal diagnosis by analysis of closely linked polymorphisms at Xq22.1. *American Journal of Medical Genetics*, **71**, 329.

Chander, P. N., Nurse, H. M., and Pirani, C. L. (1979). Renal involvement in adult Gaucher's disease after splenectomy. *Archives of Pathology and Laboratory Medicine*, **103**, 440.

Chang-Lo, M., Yam, L. T., and Rubenstone, A. I. (1967). Gaucher's disease. *American Journal of Medical Science*, **254**, 30.

Chatterjee, S., Gupta, P., Pyeritz, R. E., and Kwiterovich, P. O. (1984). Immunohistochemical localization of glycosphingolipid in urinary renal tubular cells in Fabry's disease. *American Journal of Clinical Pathology*, **82**, 24.

Clarke, J. T. R., Knaack, J., Crawhall, J. C., and Wolfe, L. S. (1971*a*). Ceramide trihexosidosis (Fabry's disease) without skin lesions. *New England Journal of Medicine*, **284**, 233.

Clarke, J. T. R., Wolfe, L. S., and Perlin, A. S. (1917*b*). Evidence for a terminal α-D-galactopyranosyl residue in galactosyl-galactosyl-glucosyl-ceramide from human kidney. *Journal of Biological Chemistry*, **246**, 5563.

Clarke, J. T. R., Guttmann, R. D., Wolfe, L. S., Beaudoin, J. G., and Morehouse, D. D. (1972). Enzyme replacement therapy by renal allotransplantation in Fabry's disease. *New England Journal of Medicine*, **287**, 1215.

Colombi, A., Kostyal, A., Bracher, R., Gloor, F., Mazzi, R., and Tholen, H. (1967). Angiokeratoma corporis diffusum–Fabry's disease. *Helvetica Medica Acta*, **34**, 67.

Colucci, W. S., Lorell, B. H., Schoen, F. J., Warhol, M. J., and Grossman, W. (1982). Hypertrophic obstructive cardiomyopathy due to Fabry's disease. *New England Journal of Medicine*, **2**, 926.

Dammert, K. (1965). Angiokeratosis naeviformis—a form of naevus telangiectatieus lateralis (naevus flammeus). *Dermatologica*, **130**, 17.

Davies, J. P., Winchester, B. G., and Malcolm, S. (1993). Mutation analysis in patients with the typical form of Anderson—Fabry disease. *Human Molecular Genetics*, **2**, 1051.

Davies, J. P., Christomanou, H., Winchester, B., and Malcolm, S. (1994). Detection of 8 new mutations in the α-galactosidase A gene in families with Fabry disease. *Human Molecular Genetics*, **3**, 667.

Dawson, G., Matalon, R., and Li, Y. T. (1973). Correction of the enzymatic defect in cultured fibroblasts from patients with Fabry's disease: Treatment with purified α-galactosidase from Ficin. *Pediatric Research*, **7**, 684.

d'Azzo, A., Andria, G., Strisciuglio, P., and Galijaard, H. (1995). Galactosialidosis. In: *The metabolic and molecular bases of inherited disease* (7th edn) (ed. C. R. Scriver, A. L. Beaudet, W. S. Sly, and D. Valle), p. 2741. McGraw-Hill, New York.

Desnick, R. J., Dawson, G., Desnick, S. J., Sweeley, C. C., and Krivit, W. (1971). Diagnosis of glycosphingolipidoses by urinary sediment analysis. *New England Journal of Medicine*, **284**, 739.

Desnick, R. J., Allen, K. Y., Simmons, R. L., Woods, J. E., Anderson, C. F., Najarian, J. S., *et al.* (1972*a*). Correction of enzymatic deficiencies by renal transplantation: Fabry's disease: *Surgery*, **72**, 203.

Desnick, R. J., Dean, K. J., Grabowski, G. A., Bishop, D. F., and Sweeley, C. C. (1979). Enzyme therapy XII. Enzyme therapy in Fabry's disease: Differential enzyme and substrate clearance kinetics of plasma and splenic α-galactosidase isozymes. *Proceedings of the National Academy of Sciences, USA*, **76**, 5326.

Desnick, R. J., Allen, K. Y., Desnick, S. J., Raman, M. K., Bernlohr, R. W., and Krivit, W. (1973*a*). Enzymatic diagnosis of hemizygotes and heterozygotes: Fabry's disease. *Journal of Laboratory Clinical Medicine*, **81**, 157.

Desnick, R. J., Allen, K. Y., Simmons, R. L., Woods, J. E., Anderson, C. F., Najarian, J. S., *et al.*

(1973*b*). Fabry disease: Correction of the enzymatic deficiency by renal transplantation. In: *Enzyme therapy in genetic diseases* (ed. R. J. Desnick, R. W. Bernlohr, and W. Krivit), p. 88. Williams and Wilkins, Baltimore, MD.

Desnick, R. J., Synder, P. D., Desnick, S. J., *et al.* (1972*b*). Sandhoff's disease: Ultrastructural and biochemical studies. *Advances in Experimental Biology*, **19**, 351.

Desnick, R. J., Bernstein, H. S., Astrin, K. H., and Bishop, D. F. (1987). Fabry disease: Molecular diagnosis of hemizygotes and heterozygotes. *Enzyme*, **38**, 54.

Desnick, R. J., Ioannou, Y. A., and Eng, C. M. (1995). α-Galactosidase A deficiency: Fabry disease. In: *The metabolic and molecular bases of inherited disease* (7th edn) (ed. C. R. Scriver, A. L. Beaudet, W. S. Sly, and D. Valle), p. 2741. McGraw-Hill, New York.

Dolman, C. L., Chang, E., and Duke, R. J. (1973). Pathologic findings in Sandhoff disease. *Archives of Pathology*, **96**, 272.

Donati, D., Sabbadini, M. G., Capsoni, F., Baratelli, L., Cassani, D., de Maio, A., *et al.* (1984). Immune function and renal transplantation in Fabry's disease. *Proceedings of the European Dialysis Transplant Association*, **21**, 686.

Donati, D., Novario, R., and Gastaldi, L. (1987). Natural history and treatment of uremia secondary to Fabry's disease: A European experience. *Nephron*, **46**, 353.

Dupperrat, B., Puissant, A., Saurat, J. H. Delanoe, J., Doyard, P. A., and Grünfeld, J. P. (1975). Maladie de Fabry. Angiokératomes présents à la naissance. Action de la diphénylhydantoïne sur les crises douloureuses. *Annales de Dermatologie et de Syphiligraphie*, **102**, 392.

Efthimiou, J., McLelland, J., and Bettridge, D. J. (1986). Short P-R intervals and tachyarrhythmias in Fabry's disease. *Postgraduate Medical Journal*, **62**, 285.

Elleder, M. (1985). Fabry's disease: Absence of storage as a feature of liver sinus endothelium. *Acta Histochemica*, **77**, 33.

Elleder, M., Bradová Smid, F., Budesinski Harzer, K., Kustermann-Kuhn, B., Ledvinová, J., Belohlávek Král, V., *et al.* (1990). Cardiocyte storage and hypertrophy as a sole manifestation of Fabry's disease. *Virchows Archiv fur Pathologische Anatomie*, **417**, 449.

Eng, C. M., Resnick-Silverman, L. A., Niehaus, D. J., Astrin, K. H., and Desnick, R. J. (1993). Nature and frequency of mutations in the α-galactosidase A gene causing Fabry disease. *American Journal of Human Genetics*, **53**, 1186.

Eng, C. M. and Desnick, R. J. (1994*a*). Molecular basis of Fabry disease: Mutations and polymorphisms in the human α-galactosidase A gene. *Human Mutation*, **3**, 103.

Eng, C. M., Niehaus, D. J., Enriquez, A. L., Burgert, T. S., Ludman, M. D., and Desnick, R. J. (1994*b*). Fabry disease: twenty-three mutations including sense and antisense CpG alterations and identification of a deletional hot spot in the α-galactosidase A gene. *Human Molecular Genetics*, **3**, 1795.

Fabry, J. (1898). Ein Beitrag Zur Kenntnis der Purpura haemorrhagica nodularis (Purpura papulosa hemorrhagica Hebrae). *Archives de Dermatologie et de Syphiligraphie*, **43**, 187.

Farraggiana, T., Churg, J., Grisham, E., Strauss, L., Prado, A., Bishop, D. F., *et al.* (1981). Light and electron microscopic histochemistry of Fabry disease. *American Journal of Pathology*, **103**, 247.

Ferrans, V. J., Hibbs, R. B., and Burda, C. D. (1969). The heart in Fabry's disease: A historical chemical and electron microscopic study. *American Journal of Cardiology*, **24**, 95.

Filling-Katz, M. R., Merrick, H. F., Fink, J. K., Miles, R. B., Sokol, J., and Barton, N. W. (1989). Carbamazepine in Fabry's disease: Effective analgesia with dose-dependent exacerbation of autonomic dysfunction. *Neurology*, **39**, 598.

Fordyce, J. A. (1896). Angiokeratoma of the scrotum. *Journal of Cutaneous Genitourinary Disease*, **14**, 81.

Franceschetti, A. T. H. (1976). Fabry disease. Ocular manifestations. In: *The eye and inborn errors of metabolism, birth defects: Orig Art Ser XII (3)* (ed. D. Bergsmu, A. J. Bron, and E. Cotlier), p. 195, Alan R. Liss, New York.

Frederickson, D. S. and Sloan, H. R. (1972). Glucosylceramide lipidoses: Gaucher's disease. In: *The metabolic basis of inherited disease* (3rd edn) (ed. J. B. Stanbury, J. B. Wyngaarden, and D. S. Frederickson), p. 730. McGraw Hill, New York.

Friedlender, M. M., Kopolovicm J., Rubingerm D., Silver, J., Drukker, A., Ben-Gershon, Z., *et al.* (1987). Renal biopsy in Fabry's disease eight years after successful renal transplantation. *Clinical Nephrology*, **27**, 206.

Friedman, L. S., Kirkham, S. E., Thistlethwaite, J. R., Platika, D., Kolodny, E. H. and Schuffler, M. D. (1984). Jejunal diverticulosis with perforation as a complication of Fabry's disease. *Gasteroenterology*, **86**, 558.

Gemignani, F., Pietrini, Y., Tagliavini, F., Lechi, A., Neri, T. M., Asinari, A., *et al.* (1979). Fabry's disease with familial lymphoedema of the lower limbs. *European Neurology*, **18**, 84.

Goldman, M., Cantor, R., Schwartz, M. F., Baker, M., and Desnick, R. J. (1986). Echocardiographic abnormalities and disease severity in Fabry's disease. *Journal of the American College of Cardiology*, **7**, 1157.

Grabowski, G. A., Barton, N., Pastores, G. M., Dambrosia, J. M., Banerjee, T. K., McKee, M. A., *et al.* (1995). Enzyme therapy in Gaucher disease type 1: Comparative efficacy of mannose-terminated glucocerebrosidase from natural and recombinant sources. *Annals of Medicine*, **122**, 33.

Gruber, H. (1946). Cornea verticillata. *Ophthalmologica*, **111**, 120.

Grünfeld, J. P., Leporrier, M., Droz, D., Bensaude, I., Hinglais, N., and Crosnier, J. (1975). La transplantation rénale chez les sujets atteints de maladie de Fabry. *Nouvelle Presse Medicale*, **4**, 2081.

Gubler, M. C., Lenoir, G., Grünfeld, J-P., Ulmann, A., Droz, D., and Habib, R. (1978). Early renal changes in hemizygous and heterozygous patients with Fabry's disease. *Kidney International*, **13**, 223.

Hakomori, S. I., Siddiqui, B., Li, Y. T., Li. S. C., and Hellerqvist, C. B. (1971). Anomeric structures of globoside and ceramide trihexoside of human erythrocytes and hamster fibroblasts. *Journal of Biological Chemistry*, **246**, 2271.

Hobbs, E. R. and Ratz, J. L. (1987). Argon laser treatment of angiokeratomas. *Journal of Dermatologic Surgery and Oncology*, **13**, 1319.

Ioannou, Y. A., Bishop, D. F., and Desnick, R. J. (1992). Overexpression of human α-galactosidase A results in its intracellular aggregation, crystallization in lysosomes, and selective secretion. *Journal of Cell Biology*, **119**, 1137.

Ishii, S., Sakuraba, H., Shimmoto, M., Minamikawa-Tachino, R., Suzuki, T., and Suzuki, Y. (1991). Fabry disease: Detection of a 13-bp deletion in α-galactosidase A gene and its application to gene diagnosis of heterozygotes. *Annals of Neurology*, **29**, 560.

Ishii, S., Sakuraba, H., and Suzuki, Y. (1992). Point mutations in the upstream region of the α-galactosidase A gene exon 6 in an atypical variant of Fabry disease. *Human Genetics*, **89**, 29.

Johnson, D. L., Del Monte, M. A., Cotlier, E., and Desnick, R. J. (1975). Fabry disease: Diagnosis of hemizygotes and heterozygotes by α-galactosidase A activity in tears. *Clinica Chimica Acta*, **63**, 81.

Johnson, D. L. and Desnick, R. J. (1990). Molecular pathology of Fabry's disease: Physical and kinetic properties of α-galactosidase A in cultured human endothelial cells. *Biochimica Biophysica Acta*, **538**, 195.

Johnston, A. W., Weller, S. D., and Warland, B. J. (1968). Angiokeratoma corporis diffusum. Some clinical aspects. *Archives of Diseases of Children*, **43**, 73.

Kaplan, A., Achord, D. T., and Sly, W. S. (1977). Phosphohexosyl components of a lysosomal enzyme are recognized by pinocytosis receptors on human fibroblasts. *Proceedings of the National Academy of Sciences, USA*, **75**, 5185.

Kariman, K., Singletary, W. V. Jr, and Sieker, H. O. (1978). Pulmonary involvement in Fabry's disease. *American Journal of Medicine*, **64**, 911.

Kint, J. A. (1970). Fabry's disease, α-galactosidase deficiency. *Science*, **167**, 1268.

Kobayashi, T., Kira, J., Shinnoh, N., Goto, I., and Kuroiwa, Y. (1985). Fabry's disease with partially deficient hydrolysis of ceramide trihexoside. *Journal of Neurological Science*, **67**, 179.

Koide, T., Ishiura, M., Iwai, K., Inoue, M., Kaneda, Y., Okada, Y., *et al.* (1990). A case of Fabry's disease in a patient with no α-galactosidase A activity caused by a single amino acid substitution of Pro-40 by Ser. *FEBS Letter*, **259**, 353.

Kolodny, E. H. and Fluharty, A. L. (1995). Metachromatic leukodystrophy. In: *The metabolic and molecular bases of inherited disease* (7th edn) (ed. C. R. Scriver, A. L. Beaudet, W. S. Sly, and D. Valle), P. 2693. McGraw-Hill, New York.

Kornfeld, S. and Sly W. S. (1995). I-cell disease and pseudo-Hurler polydystrophy: disorders of lysosomal enzyme phosphorylation. In: *The metabolic and molecular bases of inherited disease* (7th edn) (ed. C. R. Scriver, A. L. Beaudet, W. S. Sly, and D. Valle), p. 2495. McGraw-Hill, New York.

Kornreich, R., Desnick, R. J., and Bishop, D. F. (1989). Nucleotide sequence of the human α-galactosidase A gene. *Nucleic Acids Research*, **17**, 3301.

Kornreich, R., Bishop, D. F., and Desnick, R. J. (1990). α-Galactosidase A gene rearrangements in Fabry disease: Identification of short direct repeats at breakpoints in an *Alu*-rich gene. *Journal of Biological Chemistry*, **265**, 9319.

Kornreich, R., Astrin, K. H., and Desnick, R. J. (1992). Amplification of human polymorphic sites in the X-chromosome region q21.33 to q24: DXS17, DXS87, DXS287, and α-galactosidase A. *Genomics*, **13**, 70.

Kornreich, R. and Desnick, R. J. (1993). Fabry disease: Detection of gene rearrangements in the human α-galactosidase A gene by multiplex PCR amplification. *Human Mutation*, **2**, 108.

Kramer, W., Thormann, J., Mueller, K., and Frenzel, H. (1984). Progressive cardiac involvement by Fabry's disease despite successful renal allotransplantation. *International Journal of Cardiology*, **7**, 72.

Landing, B., Silverman, F., Craig, J., *et al.* (1964). Familial neurovisceral lipidosis. *American Journal of Diseases of Children*, **108**, 503.

Lemansky, P., Bishop, D. F., Desnick, R. J., Hasilik, A., and von Figura, K. (1987). Synthesis and processing of α-galactosidase A in human fibroblasts. Evidence for different mutations in Fabry disease. *Journal of Biological Chemistry*, **262**, 2062.

Lenoir, G., Rivron, M., Gubler, M. C., Dufier, J. L., Tome, F. S. M., and Guivararch, M. (1977). La maladie de Fabry. Traitement du syndrome acrodyniforme par la carbamazépine. *Archives Françaises de Pédiatrie*, **34**, 704.

Leroy, J. and Demars, R. I. (1967). Mutant enzymatic and cytological phenotypes in cultured fibroblasts. *Science*, **157**, 804.

Levade, T., Giordano, F., Maret, A., Marguery, M-C., Bazex, J., and Salvayre, R. (1991). Different phenotypic expression of Fabry disease in female monozygotic twins. *Journal of Inherited Metabolic Disease*, **14**, 105.

Lockman, L. A., Hunninghake, D. B., Krivit, W., and Desnick, R. J. (1973). Relief of pain of Fabry's disease by diphenylhydantoin. *Neurology*, **23**, 871.

MacDermot, K. D., Morgan, S. H., Cheshire, J. K., and Wilson, T. M. (1987). Anderson–Fabry disease. Close linkage with highly polymorphic DNA markers DXS17, DXS87, and DXS88. *Human Genetics*, **77**, 263.

McNary, W. and Lowenstein, L. M. (1965). A morphological study of the renal lesion in angiokeratoma corporis diffusum universale (Fabry's disease). *Journal of Urology*, **93**, 641.

Madsen, K. M., Hasholt, L., Sørensen, S. A., Fermer, M. L., and Dahl, N. (1995). Two novel mutations (L32P) and (G85N) among five different missense mutations in six Danish families with Fabry's disease. *Human Mutation*, **5**, 277.

Maizel, S. E., Simmons, R. L. Kjellstrand, C., and Fryd, D. S. (1981). Ten-year experience in renal transplantation in Fabry's disease. *Transplantation Proceedings*, **13**, 57.

Martin, J. J., Leroy, J. G., Farrioux, J. P., *et al.* (1975). I-cell disease (mucolipidosis II): a report on its pathology. *Acta Neuropathology (Berlin)*, **33**, 285.

Mayes, J. S., Scheerer, J. B., Sifers, R. N., and Donaldson, M. L. (1981). Differential assay for lysosomal α-galactosidases in human tissues and its application to Fabry's disease. *Clinica Chimica Acta*, **112**, 247.

Mayes, J. S., Cray, E. L., Dell, V. A., Scheerer, J. B., and Sifers, R. N. (1982). Endocytosis of lysosomal α-galactosidase A by cultured fibroblasts from patients with Fabry disease. *American Journal of Human Genetics*, **34**, 602.

Mayou, S. C., Kirby, J. D., and Morgan, S. H. (1989). Anderson–Fabry disease: an unusual presentation with lymphadenopathy. *Journal of the Royal Society of Medicine*, **82**, 555.

Meaney, C., Blanch, L. C., and Morris, C. P. (1994). A nonsense mutation (R220X) in the α-galactosidase A gene detected in a female carrier of Fabry disease. *Human Molecular Genetics*, **3**, 1019.

Mehta, J., Tuna, N., Moller, J. H., and Desnick, R. J. (1977). Electrocardiographic and vectorcardiographic abnormalities in Fabry's disease. *American Heart Journal*, **93**, 699.

Mihatsch, M., Ohnacker, H., Riede, U. N., *et al.* (1973). G_{m1}-gangliosidosis. Part II. Morphological aspects and review of the literature. *Helvetica Paediatrica Acta*, **28**, 521.

Morgan, S. H., Rudge, P., Smith, S. J. M., Bronstein, A. M., Kendall, B. E., Holly, E., *et al.* (1990). The neurological complications of Anderson–Fabry disease (α-Galactosidase A deficiency)—investigation of symptomatic and presymptomatic patients. *Quarterly Journal of Medicine*, **277**, 491.

Mosnier, J. F., Degott, C., Bedrossian, J., Molas,G., Degos, F., Pruna, A., *et al.* (1991). Recurrence of Fabry's disease in a renal allograft eleven years after successful renal transplantation. *Transplantation*, **51**, 759.

Moumdjian, R., Tampieri, D., Melanson, D., and Ethier, R. (1989). Anderson–Fabry disease: A case report with MR, CT, and cerebral angiography. *American Journal of Neurologic Radiology*, **10**, S69.

Nagao, Y., Nakashima, H., Fukuhara, Y., Shimmoto, M., Oshima, A., Ikari, Y., *et al.* (1991). Hypertrophic cardiomyopathy in late-onset variant of Fabry disease with high residual activity of α-galactosidase A. *Clinical Genetics*, **39**, 233.

Nelis, G. F. and Jacobs, G. J. A. (1989). Anorexia, weight loss, and diarrhea as presenting symptoms of angiokeratoma corporis diffusum (Fabry–Anderson's disease). *Digestive Disease Sciences*, **34**, 1798.

O'Brien, J. S. (1969). Generalized gangliosidosis. *Journal of Pediatrics*, **75**.

Ogawa, K., Sugamata, K., Funamoto, N., Abe, T., Sato, T., Nagashima, K., *et al.* (1990). Restricted accumulation of globotriaosylceramide in the hearts of atypical cases of Fabry's disease. *Human Pathology*, **21**, 1067.

Okada, S. and O'Brien, J. S. (1968). Generalized gangliosidosis: β–galactosidase deficiency. *Science*, **160**, 1002.

Osada, T., Kuroda, Y., and Ikai, A. (1987). Endocytic internalization of α-2-macroglobulin: α-galactosidase conjugate by cultured fibroblasts derived from Fabry hemizygote. *Biochemica Biophysica Research Communication*, **142**, 100.

Pabico, R. C., Atanacio, B. C., McKenna, B. A., Pamurcoglu, T., and Yodaiken, R. (1973). Renal pathologic lesions and functional alterations in a man with Fabry's disease. *American Journal of Medicine*, **55**, 415.

Ploos van Amstel, J. K., Jansen, P. P. M., de Jong, J. G. N., Hamel, B. C. J., and Wevers, R. A. (1994). Six novel mutations in the α-galactosidase A gene. *Human Mutation*, **3**, 503.

Pompen, A. W. M., Ruiter, M., and Wyers, J. J. G. (1947). Angiokeratoma corporis diffusum (universale) Fabry, as a sign of an unknown internal disease: Two autopsy reports. *Acta Medica Scandinavica*, **128**, 234.

Popli, S., Molnar, Z. V., Leehey, D. J., Daugirdas, J. T., Roth, D. A., Adams, M. B., *et al.* (1987). Involvement of renal allograft by Fabry's disease. *American Journal of Nephrology*, **7**, 316.

Rahman, A. N., Simcone, F. A., Hackel, D. B., Hall, P. W. III, Hirsch, E. Z., and Harris, J. W. (1961). Angiokeratoma corporis diffusum universale (hereditary dystopic lipidosis). *Transactions of the Association of American Physicians*, **74**, 366.

Reitman, A. L., Varki, A., and Kornfeld, S. (1981). Fibroblasts from patients with I-cell disease and pseudo-Hurler polydystrophy are deficient in uridine 5′ diphosphate-N-acetylglucosamine: Glycoprotein N-acetylglucosaminyl-phosphotransferase activity. *Journal of Clinical Investigation*, **67**, 1574.

Resibois, A. L. (1971). Electron microscopic studies of metachromatic leucodystrophy. IV. Liver and kidney alterations. *European Pathology*, **6**, 278.

Rietra, P. J. G. M., van den Bergh, F., and Tager, J. M. (1975). Properties of the residual α-galactosidase activity in the tissues of a Fabry hemizygote. *Clinica Chimica Acta*, **62**, 401.

Rietra, P. J. G. M., Brouwer-Kelder, E. M., de Groot, W. P., and Tager, J. M. (1976). The use of biochemical parameters for the detection of carriers of Fabry's disease. *Journal of Molecular Medicine*, **1**, 237.

Romeo, G., Urso, M., Piszcane, A., Blum, E., de Falco, A., and Ruffilli, A. (1975). Residual activity of α-galactosidase A in Fabry's disease. *Biochemical Genetics*, **13**, 615.

Rowe, J. W., Gilliam, J. I., and Warthin, T. A. (1974). Intestinal manifestations of Fabry's disease. *Annals of Internal Medicine*, **81**, 628.

Sakuraba, H., Oshima, A., Fukuhara, Y., Shimmoto, M., Nagao, Y., Bishop, D. F., *et al.* (1990). Identification of point mutations in the α-galactosidase A gene in classical and atypical hemizygotes with Fabry disease. *American Journal of Human Genetics*, **47**, 784.

Sakuraba, H., Eng, C. M., Desnick, R. J., and Bishop, D. F. (1992). Invariant exon skipping in the human α-Galactosidase A pre-mRNA: A g^{+1} to t substitution in a 5′-splice site causing Fabry disease. *Genomics*, **12**, 643.

Sandhoff, K., Andreae, U., and Jatzkewitz, H. (1968). Deficient hexosaminidase activity in an exceptional case of Tay–Sachs disease with additional storage of kidney globoside in visceral organs. *Pathologe Europe*, **3**, 278.

Schibanoff, J. M., Kamoshita, S., and O'Brien, J. S. (1969). Tissue distribution of glycosphingolipids in a case of Fabry's disease. *Journal of Lipid Research*, **10**, 515.

Schram, A. W., Hamers, M. N., and Tager, J. M. (1977). The identity of α-galactosidase B from human liver. *Biochimica Biophysica Acta*, **482**, 138.

Scott, R., Lagunoff, D., and Trump, B. (1967). Familial neurovisceral lipidosis. *Journal of Pediatrics*, **71**, 357.

Sher, N. A. Letson, R. D., and Desnick, R. J. (1979). The ocular manifestations in Fabry's disease. *Archives of Ophthalmology*, **97**, 671.

Sheth, K. J. and Bernhard, G. C. (1979). The arthropathy of Fabry disease. *Arthritis and Rheumatism*, **22**, 781.

Sheth, K. J., Werlin, S. L., Freeman, M. E., and Hodach, A. E. (1981). Gastrointestinal structure and function in Fabry's disease. *American Journal of Gastroenterology*, **76**, 246.

Sheth, K. J., Roth, D. A., and Adams, M. B. (1983). Early renal failure in Fabry's disease. *American Journal of Kidney Disease*, **2**, 651.

Sibille, A. R., Eng, C. M., Kim, S. J., Pastores, G. M., and Grabowski, G. A. (1993). Genotype–phenotype correlations in Gaucher disease type 1. *American Journal of Human Genetics*, **52**, 1094.

Sinclair, R. (1972). Origin of endothelium in human renal allograft. *British Medical Journal*, **11**, 15.

Spaeth, G. L. and Frost, P. (1965). Fabry's disease: its ocular manifestations. *Archives of Ophthalmology (Chicago)*, **74**, 760.

Suzuki, K. (1968). Cerebral G$_{m1}$ gangliosidois: Chemical pathology of visceral organs. *Science*, **159**, 1471.

Suzuki, Y., Sakuraba, H., and Oshima, A. (1995). β-galactosidase deficiency (β-galactosidosis): G$_{M1}$ gangliosidosis and Morquio B disease. In: *The metabolic and molecular bases of interited disease* (7th edn) (ed. C. R. Scriver, A. L. Beaudet, W. S. Sly, and D. Valle). McGraw-Hill, New York.

Sweeley, C. C. and Klinosky, B. (1963). Fabry's disease: Classification as a sphingolipidosis and partial characterization of a novel glycolipid. *Journal of Biological Chemistry*, **238**, 3148.

Terlinde, R., Richard, G., Lisch, W., and Ullrich, K. (1982). Ruckbildung der Cornea verticillata bei Morbus–Fabry durch Kontaktlinsen. Erste Beobachtungen. *Contactologia*, **4**, 20.

Tondeur, M., Vamos-Hurwitz, E., Mockel-Pohl, S., *et al.* (1971). Clinical, biochemical, and ultrastructural studies in a case of chondrodystrophy presenting the I-cell phenotype in tissue culture. *Journal of Pediatrics*, **79**, 366.

Traub, E. F. and Tolmach, J. A. (1931). Angiokeratoma. Comprehensive study of the literature and report of a case. *Archives de Dermatologie et de Syphiligraphie*, **24**, 39.

Urbain, G., Peremans, J., and Philippart, M. (1967). Fabry's disease without skin lesions. *Lancet*, **1**, 1111.

Vetrie, D., Bobrow, M., and Harris, A. (1993). Construction of a 5.2-megabase physical map of the human X chromosome at Xq22 using pulsed-field gel electrophoresis and yeast artificial chromosomes. *Genomics*, **15**, 631.

Voglino, A., Paradisi, M., Dompé, G., Onetti Muda, A., and Faraggiana, T. (1988). Angiokeratoma corporis diffusum (Fabry's disease) with unusual features in a female patient. *American Journal of Dermatopathology*, **10**, 343.

von Scheidt, W., Eng, C. M., Fitzmaurice, T. F., Erdmann, E., Hübner, G., Olsen, E. G. J., *et al.* (1991). An atypical variant of Fabry's disease confined to the heart. *New England Journal of Medicine*, **324**, 395.

Wilson, S. K., Klionsky, B. L., and Rhamy, R. K. (1973). A new etiology of priapism: Fabry's disease. *Journal of Urology*, **109**, 646.

Wise, D., Wallace, H. J., and Jellinck, E. H. (1962). Angiokeratoma corporis diffusum: A clinical study of eight affected families. *Quarterly Journal of Medicine*, **31**, 177.

16

Lecithin–cholesterol acyltransferase deficiency and the kidney

D.S. Harry and A.F. Winder

Introduction

In 1935, Sperry recognized that when human serum or blood was incubated, the free cholesterol concentration fell without any change in the total cholesterol. He correctly attributed this observation to the enzymatic esterification of free cholesterol with a fatty acid coming from the hydrolysis of a fatty acid-containing compound. In the early 1960s, Glomset published several papers on the nature of the enzyme involved which he designated as lecithin–cholesterol acyltransferase (LCAT) (Glomset 1962; 1963).

The role of LCAT in normal cholesterol metabolism

LCAT (phosphatidylcholine: sterol O-acyltransferase, EC 2.3.1.43) is a key enzyme in the extracellular, intraplasmatic, metabolism of cholesterol. Synthesized and secreted by the liver, LCAT is a glycoprotein with a mass of about 67 000 Daltons. The mature protein contains 416 amino-acid residues and has several sequences of hydrophobic amino acids, one of which is similar to sequences found in pancreatic and lingual lipases (Mclean *et al.* 1986*a*). About 25% of the total LCAT mass is carbohydrate that is covalently linked to four potential N-glycosylation sites (Yang *et al.* 1987).

LCAT circulates in the blood as a complex with high-density lipoproteins (HDL) and a cholesteryl ester transfer protein (CETP) (Fielding and Fielding 1980; Norum *et al.* 1989). It is activated by apolipoprotein A-1 and catalyses the transfer of the sn-2 fatty acid of phosphatidylcholine (lecithin) to the 3-hydroxyl group of free cholesterol on the surface of HDL particles. Cholesteryl ester and lysophosphatidylcholine (lysolecithin) are the products. The newly synthesized cholesteryl ester is transferred by the CETP to the core of very low-density lipoproteins (VLDL) and to the VLDL metabolic product, intermediate low-density lipoproteins (IDL). IDL are either removed rapidly from plasma by the liver or are further enriched with cholesteryl esters to become low-density lipoproteins (LDL) which carry the bulk of plasma cholesteryl esters (Albers and Segrest 1986). LDL are cleared by specific cell-surface receptors found on most tissues but primarily on hepatocytes. In this manner, LCAT maintains a concentration gradient of free cholesterol from peripheral tissues into HDL particles and eventually via LDL to the liver. This reverse cholesterol transport enables the liver to dispose of excess body cholesterol as bile acids (Fielding 1990), the only quantitatively important route for cholesterol excretion.

Familial LCAT deficiency

The importance of LCAT was emphasized in 1966 when the first case of familial LCAT deficiency was diagnosed (Norum and Gjone 1967). A 33-year-old woman was admitted to a Norwegian hospital with diffuse corneal opacities, anaemia, proteinuria, and hyperlipidaemia. She was thought to have chronic nephritis but renal function subsequently proved to be normal. Both plasma triglyceride and cholesterol levels were elevated with most of the cholesterol present not as cholesteryl ester but as free cholesterol. Plasma lecithin was increased but lysolecithin was low. No pre-β lipoproteins (VLDL) or α-lipoproteins (HDL) could be detected by lipoprotein electrophoresis (Table 16.1). Subsequently, the same clinical and biochemical features were observed in two of the patient's sisters. Studies on all three sibs demonstrated the absence of plasma LCAT activity. As there was no history of liver disease, in which LCAT can be secondarily reduced, or of kidney disease, the new inborn error of familial LCAT deficiency was ascribed to this group of patients. Two phenotypically distinct syndromes of LCAT deficiency have been described: 'classic' LCAT deficiency and fish-eye disease (FED) (McIntyre 1988). FED subjects also present with pronounced corneal opacification, levels of HDL protein and lipid at about 10% of normal, and a partial LCAT deficiency. This partial defect is associated with mutant forms of LCAT which have either lost the potential for esterifying cholesterol on HDL but not VLDL or LDL cholesterol (Karmin *et al.* 1993), or which can esterify HDL cholesterol but are only released into the plasma in very small amounts (Klein *et al.* 1993). The range of molecular defects associated with these defects continues to enlarge (Qu *et al.* 1995; Kuivenhoven *et al.* 1996). Compound double heterozygotes of LCAT deficiency, FED, and FED-like syndromes in which the LCAT reaction is impaired through structural mutations affecting apolipoprotein A–I have also been described (Frohlich *et al.* 1987; Funke *et al.* 1991a,b; Winder *et al.* 1993). In contrast to patients with classical LCAT deficiency, renal disease is not a feature of FED, presumably because cholesterol esterification in plasma does proceed through alternative lipoprotein substrates.

Genetics

Familial LCAT deficiency is inherited as an autosomal recessive trait. The gene for LCAT is found on the long arm of chromosome 16 in the region 16q22 and appears linked to the serum

Table 16.1 Lipid values in classic LCAT deficiency

Lipid	LCAT deficiency	Reference range
	(mmol/L)	
Cholesterol	4.8 ± 2.95	4.44 ± 6.8
Triglyceride	3.9 ± 4.06	0.77 ± 2.65
VLDL cholesterol	1.1 ± 0.70	0.26 ± 1.0
LDL cholesterol	2.3 ± 1.42	2.64 ± 4.9
HDL cholesterol	0.2 ± 0.14	0.80 ± 1.66
Cholesteryl ester as % total cholesterol	11 ± 9	65–75

Results are given as means ± SD from LCAT patients reported in the literature.

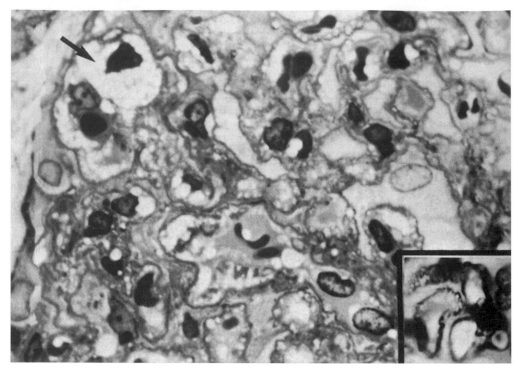

Fig. 16.1 The basement membrane contains many lacunae as seen by silver stains (inset) or on toluidine blue staining of plastic sections. A foam cell (arrow) lies in the mesangium separated by an endothelial cell from the capillary loop. (Toluidine blue × 1600). (Inset: periodic acid silver methenamine × 1600.)

α-haptoglobin locus (McIntyre 1988). It contains 6 exons and 5 introns and is expressed primarily if not solely in the liver (Mclean 1986a,b). Several mutations in the LCAT gene have been demonstrated in the familial disease, including mutations at codons 10, 83, 141, 147, 156, 228, and 239, (Karmin *et al.* 1993; Klein *et al.* 1993). So far, no common defect of the gene has been identified; each case family is caused by independent and different defects of the LCAT structural gene. Most FED cases for which a defect has been defined have a C–T substitution at codon 123 (threonine for isoleucine), away from the proposed active centre and consistent with changes in the structural organization of the enzyme affecting substrate access to the active centre and thus changing preferred lipoprotein substrates for the LCAT reaction from HDL to other lipoproteins in plasma (Assman *et al.* 1991).

The kidney in LCAT deficiency

In classical LCAT deficiency there is widespread accumulation of lipid in tissues, notably cornea, bone marrow, and spleen, arterial walls and renal parenchyma, and anaemia with target cells. The lipid is principally phospholipids and unesterified cholesterol. As more cases have been reported it is apparent that homozygotes can have accelerated atherosclerosis with mildly enhanced clinical expression; LCAT heterozygotes and FED cases are not affected.

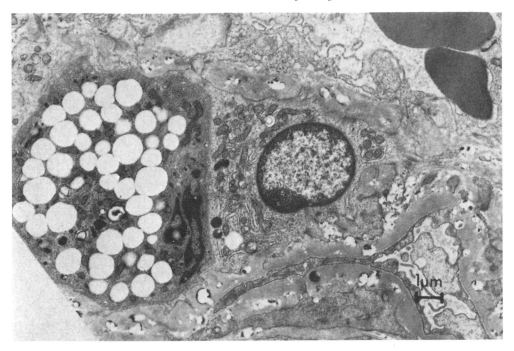

Fig. 16.2   Multiple vacuoles in cytoplasm of a mesangial cell giving appearance of an early foam cell. (×9600.)

Renal impairment with proteinuria evident before age 50 years is a common but not invariable feature, noted in seven out of eight cases in 1978 (Norum *et al.* 1989) and in 19 out of 21 cases in 1982 (Borysiewicz *et al.* 1982); about 66 cases of LCAT and FED are now reported from some 33 families (Assman *et al.* 1991; Kuivenhoven *et al.* 1996). One UK patient specifically reported as presenting without proteinuria (Winder and Bron 1978) has, 20 years later, developed macro-proteinuria and end-stage renal failure requiring dialysis, plus pancreatitis and hypertriglyceri-daemia, responsive in the short term to infusion of normal plasma (Watts *et al.* 1995). An Irish family presenting in the UK through one sister with unselective proteinuria and renal hyperten-sion (Borysiewicz *et al.* 1982) then had two further affected sisters without renal impairment, who remain so 15 years later. A brother with hypertension, blurred vision, and proteinuria had died age 55 years without diagnosis or post-mortem and before LCAT deficiency was recognized in the family (Borysiewicz *et al.* 1982). Renal biopsies and kidneys removed at transplantation in LCAT deficiency show arteriolar thickening with subendothelial lipid deposits, and mesangial foam cells (Borysiewicz *et al.* 1982; Norum *et al.* 1989) (Figs 16.1, 16.2, 16.3). Renal transplan-tation can restore adequate renal function without effect on lipoprotein abnormalities in plasma, but lipid changes similar to those in LCAT kidneys are seen in transplant biopsies and while renal function remains good (Flatmark *et al.* 1977; Myhre *et al.* 1977; Horina *et al.* 1993)

Lipoprotein changes in plasma include additional fractions in the LDL density range, with a large molecular weight component, LMLDL, incorporating albumin, showing some association with renal impairment (Gjone *et al.* 1974; Norum *et al.* 1989). However, in the Irish family described above, the association between LMLDL and renal impairment was not close, and a

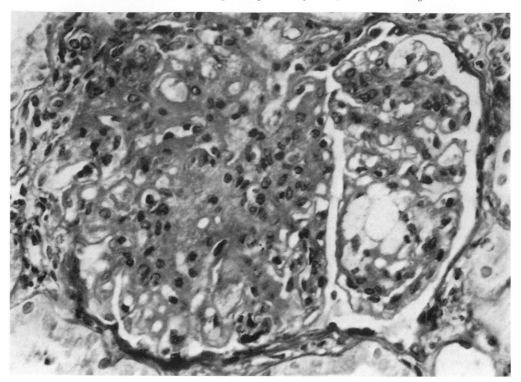

Fig. 16.3 Typical glomerulus showing foam cells and expanded mesangium with increased basement membrane-like material. (PAS × 400.)

specific contribution of LMLDL to the pathogenesis of renal lipid accumulation and decline is not definitely established. This has a bearing on treatment as levels of LMLDL, and of other lipid components in LCAT plasma probably derived from chylomicrons, decline on low total-fat diets (Norum *et al.* 1989). Thus, although these components are not specifically identified as contributing to renal and other lipid accumulation and organ damage, dietary control is recommended; there are no current reports of any change in clinical progression. Single or repeat infusions of fresh plasma do improve cholesterol esterification and transport in plasma, with associated changes in lipoprotein composition, but long-term studies or specific clinical benefits have not been reported (Norum and Gjone 1978; Murayama *et al.* 1984; Norum *et al.* 1989; Assman *et al.* 1991; Watts *et al.* 1995).

Diagnosis

LCAT deficiency, FED, or related syndromes can be suspected from the clinical presentation, including corneal opacification and the lipoprotein profile with marked deficiency of HDL and apo A–I in plasma. In LCAT but not FED the proportion of cholesterol in plasma in ester form is markedly reduced. Consanguinity should also be reviewed. LCAT activity and variant FED enzyme activity can now be directly determined (Chen and Albers 1982; Gillett and Ower 1992). Unravelling double heterozygosity and any contribution of apo A–I variants (Mclean *et al.*

1986*b*; Funke *et al.* 1991*a,b*) is more complex and specialist advice with family studies is recommended.

Treatment

Ideally, gene therapy or liver transplantation would be the treatments of choice for this syndrome, but no attempt to use either approach has been reported. Kidney transplantation, however, has been performed in several patients with LCAT deficiency. Although there is evidence of lipid deposition in the kidney within six months of transplantation, good renal function is maintained. Horina and colleagues (1993) reported good long-term results and stable kidney graft function in an LCAT-deficient subject 56 months after transplantation. Given that the five-year renal graft survival rate in patients without this disease is about 70–80%, then LCAT deficient patients with end-stage renal disease appear suitable for kidney transplantation.

References

Albers, J. J., and Segrest, J. P. (1986). Plasma lipoproteins. In: *Methods in ezymology*, Vol. 129. Academic Press, Florida.

Assmann, G., von Eckardstein, A., and Funke, H. (1991). Lecithin: cholesterol acyltransferase deficiency and fish-eye disease. *Current Opinion in Lipidology*, **2**, 110–17.

Borysiewicz, L. K., Soutar, A. K., Evans, D. J., Thompson G. R., and Rees, A. J. (1982). Renal failure in familial lecithin: cholesterol acyltransferase deficiency. *Quart. J. Med.*, **204**, 411–26.

Chen, C. H. and Albers, J. J. (1982). Characterisation of proteoliposomes containing apolipoprotein A–I: a new substrate for the management of LCAT activity. *J. Lipid Res.*, **23**, 680–91.

Fielding, P. E. and Fielding, C. T. (1980). A cholesteryl ester transfer complex in human plasma. *Proc. Nat. Acad. Sci. USA*, **77**, 3327–31.

Fielding, C. J. (1990). Lecithin–cholesterol acyltransferase. In: *Advances in cholesterol research* (ed. M. Esfahani and J. B. Swaney), pp. 271–314. The Telford Press, Caldwell.

Flatmark, A. L., Hovig, T., Myhre, E., and Gjone, E. (1977). Renal transplantation in patients with familial lecithin: cholesterol acyltransferase deficiency. *Transplantation Proc.*, **9**, 1665–71.

Frohlich, J., Hoag, G., McLeod, R., Hayden, M., Godin, D. V., Wadsworth, L. D., *et al.* (1987). Hypoalphalipoproteinaemia resembling fish-eye disease. *Acta Med. Scand.*, **221**, 291–8.

Funke, H., von Eckardstein, A., Pritchard, P. H., Karas, M., Albers, J. J., and Assmann, G. (1991*a*). A frameshift mutation in the human apolipoprotein A–I gene causes high-density lipoprotein deficiency, partial lecithin: cholesterol acyltransferase deficiency, and corneal opacities. *J Clin. Invest.*, **87**, 371–6.

Funke, H., von Eckardstein, A., Pritchard, P. H., Karas, M., Albers, J. J., Kastelein, J. J. P. (1991*b*). A molecular defect causing fish-eye disease: an amino-acid exchange in lecithin–cholesterol acyltransferase (LCAT) leads to the selective loss of alpha-LCAT activity. *Proc. Natl. Acad. Sci. USA*, **88**, 4855–9.

Gillett, M. P. T. and Owen, J. S. (1992). Cholesterol esterifying enzymes—lecithin: cholesterol acyltransferase and acylcoenzyme A:cholesterol acyltransferase (ACAT). In: *Lipoprotein analysis. A practical approach.* (ed. C. A. Converse and E. R. Skinner), pp. 187–201. IRL Press, Oxford.

Gjone, E., Blomhoff, J. P., and Skarbovic, A. J. (1974). Possible association between abnormal low-density lipoprotein and nephropathy in lecithin:cholesterol acyltransferase deficiency. *Clin. Chim. Acta*, **54**, 11–18.

Glomset, J. A. (1962). The mechanism of the plasma cholesterol esterification reaction: plasma fatty acid transferase. *Biochim. Biophys. Acta*, **65**, 128–35.

Glomset, J. A. (1963). Further studies on the mechanism of the plasma cholesterol esterification reaction. Biochim. *Biophys. Acta*, **70**, 389–95.

Horina, J. H., Wirnsberger, G., Horn, S., Roob, J. M., Ratschek, M., Holzer, H., *et al.* (1993). Long-term follow-up of a patient with lecithin–cholesterol acyltransferase deficiency syndrome after kidney transplantation. *Transplantation*, **56**, 233–6.

Karmin, O., Hill, J. S., Wang, X., and Pritchard, P. H. (1993). Recombinant lecithin–cholesterol acyltransferase containing a Thr123 to Ile mutation esterifies cholesterol in low-density lipoprotein but not in high-density lipoprotein. *J. Lipid Res.*, **34**, 81–8.

Klein, H-G., Santamarina-Fojo, S., Duverger, N., Clerc, M., Dumon, M-F., Albers, J. J., *et al.* (1993). Fish-eye syndrome: A molecular defect in the lecithin–cholesterol acyltransferase (LCAT) gene associated with normal α-LCAT-specific activity. *J. Clin. Invest.*, **92**, 479–85.

Kuivenhoven, J. A., Stalenhoef, A. F., Hill, J. S., Demacker, P. N., Errami, A., Kastelein, J. J., *et al.* (1996). Two novel molecular defects in the LCAT gene are associated with fish-eye disease. *Art. Thromb. Vasc. Biol.*, **16**, 294–303.

McIntyre, N. (1988). Familial LCAT deficiency and fish-eye Disease. *J. Inher. metab. Dis.*, **11** (Suppl. 1), 45–56.

McLean, J., Wion, K., Drayna, D., Fielding, C., and Lawn, R. (1986a). Human lecithin–cholesterol acyltransferase gene: complete gene sequence and sites of expression. *Nucl. Acid Res.*, **14**, 9387–406.

McLean, J., Fielding, C., Drayna, D., Dieplinger, H., Baer, B., Kohr, W., *et al.* (1986b). Cloning and expression of the human lecithin–cholesterol acyltransferase cDNA. *Proc. Natl. Acad. Sci. USA*, **83**, 2335–9.

Murayama, N., Asano, Y., Kato, K., *et al.* (1984). Effects of plasma infusion on plasma lipids, apoproteins and plasma enzyme activites in familial lecithin:cholesterol acyltransferase deficiency. *Eur. J. Clin. Invest.*, **14**, 122–9.

Myhre, E., Gjone, E., Flatmark, A., and Hovig, T. (1977). Renal failure in familial lecithin:cholesterol acyltransferase deficiency. *Nephron*, **18**, 239–48.

Norum, K. R. and Gjone, E. (1967). Familial plasma lecithin–cholesterol acyltransferase defiency. Biochemical study of a new inborn error of metabolism. *Scand. J. Clin. Invest.*, **20**, 231–43.

Norum, K. R. and Gjone, E. (1978). The effect of plasma transfusion on the plasma cholesteryl esters in patients with familial plasma lecithin: cholesterol acyltransferase deficiency. *Scand. J. Clin. Lab. Invest.*, **22**, 339–42.

Norum, K. R., Gjone, E., and Glomset, J. A. (1989). Familial lecithin–cholesterol acyltransferase deficiency including fish-eye disease. *The metabolic basis of inherited disease* (6th edn), (ed. C. R. Scriver, A. L. Bcaudet, W. S. Sly, and D. Valle), pp. 1181–94. McGraw Hill, New York.

Qu, S. J., Fan, H. Z., Blanco-Vaca, F., and Pownall, H. J. (1995). *In vitro* expression of natural mutants of human lecithin: cholesterol acyltransferase. *J. Lipid Res.*, **36**, 967–74.

Sperry, W. M. (1935). Cholesterol esterase in blood. *J. Biol. Chem.*, **111**, 467–78.

Watts, G. F., Mitropoulos, K. A., Al-Bahrani, A., Reeves, B. E. A., and Owen, J. S. (1995). Lecithin–cholesterol acyltransferase deficiency presenting with acute pancreatitis: effect of infusion of normal plasma on triglyceride-rich lipoproteins. *J. Intern. Med.*, **238**, 137–41.

Winder, A. F. and Bron, A. J. (1978). Lecithin–cholesterol acyltransferase presenting as visual impairment, with hypocholesterolaemia and normal renal function. *Scand. J. Clin. Lab. Invest.*, **38** (Suppl. 150), 151–5.

Winder, A. F., Owen, J. S., Vallance, D., Wray, R., Lloyd-Jones, D., and White, P. (1993). Fish-eye disease at 76 years. *Atherosclerosis*, **103**, 296.

Yang, C. Y., Manoogian, D., Pao, Q., Lee, F. S., Knapp, R. D., Gotto, A. M., *et al.* (1987). Lecithin–cholesterol acyltransferase. *J. Biol. Chem.*, **262**, 3086–91.

17

Nephropathic cystinosis: growing into adulthood

Linda K. Gallo and William A. Gahl

Introduction

Although nephropathic cystinosis has long been considered a renal disease of childhood, two major therapeutic interventions have transformed it into an adult disorder as well. First, renal transplantation has prolonged the lives of many cystinosis patients into the third and fourth decades. In particular, the 70–80 North American patients who had received a renal allograft prior to 1985 (Gahl *et al*. 1986) have now reached adulthood. Second, the cystine-depleting agent, cysteamine, has so favourably altered the natural course of cystinosis that many patients are now approaching adulthood without requiring a renal allograft (Gahl *et al*. 1987; Clark *et al*. 1992; Markello *et al*. 1993). Consequently, adult nephrologists and other physicians are increasingly called upon to manage the many renal and non-renal complications of long-standing cystinosis. These will be discussed below, but first it is helpful to become familiar with the disease in children.

The basic defect

Cystinosis is an autosomal recessive disorder in which the disulphide amino acid, cystine (Fig. 17.1), accumulates within cellular lysosomes. Different cell types store different amounts of cystine, ranging from five to 1000 times normal (Gahl *et al*. 1989). For example, the cystine levels of polymorphonuclear leukocytes and cultured fibroblasts are 50 to 100-fold elevated. In some cells, the cystine concentration exceeds its solubility, only 1–2 mM at neutral pH, and typical birefringent crystals form (Fig. 17.2). This occurs in the kidney, liver, rectal mucosa, cornea, conjunctiva, iris, retina, lymph node, bone marrow, spleen, macrophage, and muscle (Gahl *et al*. 1989).

In the late 1960s, cystinosis researchers identified the lysosome as the organelle storing cystine (Patrick and Lake 1968; Schulman *et al*. 1969; 1970). The source of the cystine is protein, which is degraded within the lysosome to its component amino acids, including cystine and the free thiol, cysteine (Gahl *et al*. 1989). In normal individuals, cystine and cysteine freely exit the lysosome (Gahl *et al*. 1982*b*) and enter the cytoplasm, where all cyst(e)ine assumes the reduced form because of the cytoplasm's high glutathione concentration. Cytoplasmic cysteine can be incorporated into protein or degraded to inorganic sulphate for excretion.

In patients with cystinosis, transport of cystine out of the lysosome is impaired. Elucidation of this basic defect occurred in 1982 by investigators making use of cystine dimethylester to load lysosomes with cystine to cystinotic levels. Amino-acid methylesters readily traverse the lysosomal membrane and undergo hydrolysis to the corresponding free amino acid within the acidic lysosome. After cystine dimethylester loading, the rates of cystine clearance from normal and

HOOC$\quad\quad\quad\quad\quad$COOH
$$\underset{\underset{\text{NH}_2}{|}}{\text{HC}} - \text{CH}_2 - \text{S} - \text{S} - \text{CH}_2 - \underset{\underset{\text{NH}_2}{|}}{\text{CH}} \quad\quad \text{HS} - \text{CH}_2 - \text{CH}_2 - \text{NH}_2$$

Cystine$\quad\quad\quad\quad\quad\quad\quad$Cysteamine

Fig. 17.1   Chemical structures of cystine and β-mercaptoethylamine (cysteamine).

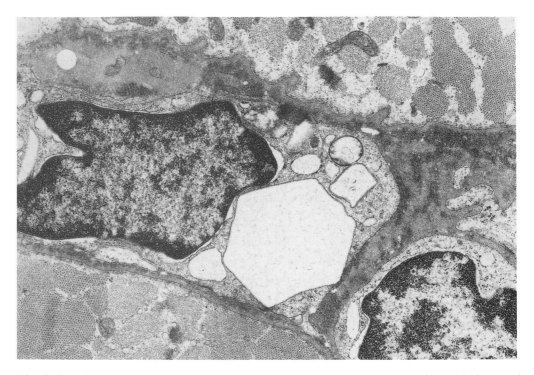

Fig. 17.2   Electron micrograph of cystine crystals inside the lysosome of a pericyte within muscle tissue. The hexagonal and rectangular shapes are typical. ×40 000. (Courtesy of the late Dr. T. Kuwabara, National Eye Institute.)

cystinotic lysosomes were compared (Gahl *et al.* 1982*b*). Cystinotic lysosome-rich fractions showed almost no loss of cystine after 45 minutes while normal lysosomal fractions lost cystine at a substantial rate. Experiments demonstrating saturation kinetics offered strong evidence for a carrier-mediated, or facilitated, lysosomal transport system (Gahl *et al.* 1982*a*) and counter-transport experiments provided definitive proof (Gahl *et al.* 1983). Investigators now recognize cystinosis as the prototypic lysosomal membrane transport defect.

Clinical manifestations in childhood

At birth and for the first few months of life, children with nephropathic cystinosis appear clinically normal. Symptoms usually appear between six and 12 months of age and include dehydration, failure to thrive, and electrolyte imbalance as a result of renal tubular Fanconi's syndrome (Gahl 1986; Krasnewich and Gahl 1991), which is characterized histologically by a 'swan neck' deformity of the proximal tubule (Teree *et al.* 1970). Cystinosis is the most common cause of Fanconi's syndrome in children. The renal tubules fail to reabsorb essential nutrients, resulting in the loss of amino acids, glucose, phosphorus, calcium, magnesium, sodium, potassium, bicarbonate, carnitine, water, and other small molecules. Juvenile-onset diabetes mellitus is often a preliminary diagnosis because of the glucosuria and polyuria, generally 2–4 litres per day. However, blood glucose levels are normal. The aminoaciduria is generalized and approximately 10-fold normal in amount. Phosphaturia causes hypophosphataemic rickets, curable with phosphate replacement. A tubular proteinuria also occurs, with 50-fold normal excretion of proteins of molecular weight 10000 to 50000 daltons (Waldman *et al.* 1973).

Progressive renal failure is the most serious threat to the survival of a child with cystinosis. Glomerular scarring and fibrosis proceed inexorably to uraemia. Though the rate of deterioration varies widely from one patient to another, renal demise occurs, on average, between nine and 10 years of age (Gretz *et al.* 1983; Gahl *et al.* 1990; Markello *et al.* 1993).

The extensive ophthalmic involvement of cystinosis begins with a patchy retinal depigmentation apparent as early as five weeks of age (Wong *et al.* 1967). No clinical abnormality accompanies this early finding. In the cornea, the presence of crystals on slit-lamp examination is pathognomonic for cystinosis. Although absent at birth, the crystals are usually present by one year of age. Initially, the crystals are found only in the anterior third of the cornea, but eventually the full thickness of the cornea becomes involved (Cogan *et al.* 1960). The conjunctivae of children and the irides of older patients also accumulate crystals. Photophobia, which produces considerable discomfort, occurs in almost all patients sometime between infancy and adolescence.

In the absence of specific cystine-depleting therapy, growth is severely retarded (Gahl *et al.* 1987). Nutritional deficiencies, chronic acidosis, renal damage, toxin retention, and cystine accumulation in bone and endocrine organs all contribute to a persistent failure to grow (Gahl 1986). Although single growth-hormone measurements and somatomedin-C levels are normal in patients with cystinosis (Lucky *et al.* 1977), therapy with recombinant human growth hormone has improved growth rates two to fourfold in several children (Wilson *et al.* 1989). However, in two pre-transplant patients treated with growth hormone, an accelerated rate of rise of serum creatinine values hastened the time to renal transplantation (Andersson *et al.* 1992).

Patients with nephropathic cystinosis occasionally have gastrointestinal problems such as vomiting, diarrhoea, and poor appetite. One seven-year-old boy developed ulcerative colitis; a colon biopsy showed crystal deposition in the lamina propria (Treem *et al.* 1988). Although hepatomegaly and splenomegaly can also occur (Gahl *et al.* 1986), they generally do not constitute a significant medical threat (Gahl 1986; Gahl *et al.* 1989).

Caucasian children with cystinosis are usually more lightly pigmented than their siblings. Typically, they have blond hair and blue eyes. Many cystinosis patients flush easily, avoid heat, and have a tendency to develop hyperthermia. Pilocarpine iontophoresis has shown a marked decrease in sweat volume, although sweat electrolytes and sweat-gland histology are normal (Gahl *et al.* 1984). Hypothyroidism often presents between five and 10 years of age (Lucky *et al.* 1977). This common complication of cystinosis may be due to destruction of the thyroid gland because of cystine storage; direct involvement of the anterior pituitary has not been demonstrated. Cystinosis does not affect intelligence adversely, nor do patients have an increased tendency toward infection.

For as yet unknown reasons, laboratory values are often abnormal. The sedimentation rate is usually high. Platelets may be elevated to twice normal values, and anaemia, not due to iron deficiency, is quite common (Gahl *et al.* 1989).

Diagnosis

Postnatal diagnosis can be made with the recognition of corneal crystals on slit-lamp examination by an experienced ophthalmologist. This finding is almost always present after one year of age. Cultured fibroblasts and polymorphonuclear leukocytes are easily accessible tissues in which to measure cystine levels, which are normally less than 0.2 nmol 1/2 cystine/mg cell protein. Individuals homozygous for cystinosis have leukocyte and fibroblast levels of 5–10 nmol 1/2 cystine/mg cell protein, while heterozygotes store less than 1.0 nmol 1/2 cystine/mg cell protein (Schneider *et al.* 1967). Levels of cystine in placental tissue can also be diagnostic (Smith *et al.* 1989). The use of kidney or bone-marrow biopsies solely for diagnosis is no longer necessary. Prenatal diagnosis can be performed on cultured fetal amniocytes (Schneider *et al.* 1974; States *et al.* 1975; Boman and Schneider 1981), chorionic villi (Gahl *et al.* 1985*a*; Smith *et al.* 1986), or cord blood (Boman and Schneider 1981).

Incidence, genetics, and cystinosis variants

Classical nephropathic cystinosis has an incidence of approximately one in 160 000 live births in North America where there are an estimated 300–400 cystinosis patients (Gahl *et al.* 1989). We estimate that approximately 100 of these patients have received a renal transplant. In the French province of Brittany, the incidence of cystinosis has been estimated as high as one in 26 000, while for the rest of France the estimate is one in 326 000 (Bois *et al.* 1976). Although it is considered a disorder of fair-skinned individuals of European descent, cystinosis does occur in blacks, Hispanics, Indians, Pakistanis, and people of Middle Eastern descent. The chromosomal location of the cystinosis gene is chromosome 17p. The inheritance pattern is autosomal recessive, with a 25% recurrence risk. Heterozygotes are never clinically affected.

Two variants of nephropathic cystinosis occur. Intermediate or adolescent cystinosis is an extremely rare disease manifest by more slowly progressive Fanconi's syndrome and glomerular damage with onset late in childhood (Pabico *et al.* 1980; Dale *et al.* 1981; Manz *et al.* 1982; Langman *et al.* 1985). Photophobia, growth impairment, and decreased skin and retinal pigmentation are often present. Cystine storage occurs in the cornea, conjunctiva, bone marrow, and kidney. Typically, patients become uraemic in their second or third decade of life and have leukocyte cystine levels of 2.5–5.0 nmol 1/2 cystine/mg protein. Consequently, cysteamine therapy is recommended for these patients (see below).

A third class of patients have an asymptomatic variant of cystinosis known as the benign or adult form (Lietman *et al.* 1966; Kraus and Lutz 1971). The kidneys do not appear to be affected, but crystals are present in the cornea, conjunctiva, and bone marrow. Except for photophobia, the lives of these rare individuals are entirely normal in length and quality.

Therapy

Prior to renal failure, children with nephropathic cystinosis receive medications aimed primarily at restoring renal losses due to Fanconi's syndrome. Replacement therapy may include citrate or bicarbonate, phosphate, potassium, vitamin D, calcium, sodium, magnesium, levothyroxine, and carnitine. Free access to water and bathroom privileges is essential.

In the past decade, significant benefit has also accrued from the use of cysteamine, a cystine-depleting agent. This compound was originally used to prevent damage from radiation (Bacq 1965) and acetaminophen poisoning (Chiu and Bhakthan 1978) because its thiol group traps reactive free radicals. A major breakthrough in the treatment of cystinosis occurred when Thoene *et al.* (1976) reported that cysteamine depletes cystinotic fibroblasts in culture of over 90% of their free cystine. The same degree of cystine-depleting efficacy was demonstrated in peripheral leukocytes when cysteamine was administered orally or intravenously to children with cystinosis.

In the mid-1980s, the mechanism of cystine depletion by cysteamine was elucidated. Cysteamine's amine group permits it to pass through plasma and lysosomal membranes. Once inside the acidic lysosome, the amine groups becomes positively charged. This helps the lysosome to retain cysteamine, which then participates in a disulphide interchange reaction with cystine (Gahl *et al.* 1985*b*). This produces cysteine, which freely leaves cystinotic lysosomes, and cysteine–cysteamine-mixed disulphide, which is carried out of the lysosome by a lysosomal membrane transport system for lysine, a structural analogue of the mixed disulphide (Pisoni *et al.* 1985). As a consequence, the cellular cystine content is dramatically decreased.

In 1978, a nationwide protocol was initiated to administer cysteamine to children with cystinosis who retained substantial residual renal function (Gahl *et al.* 1987). Up to 90 mg/kg/day of cysteamine free base was administered; the goal was to maintain leukocyte cystine levels below 1.0 nmole 1/2 cystine/mg of protein. The protocol was altered slightly in 1987 (Clark *et al.* 1992). Children were randomized to standard dose (1.3 gm free base/m^2/day) or high dose (1.95 gm free base/m^2/day) oral cysteamine/phosphocysteamine solution. Phosphocysteamine, the phospho-thioester of cysteamine, has cystine-depleting effects similar to those of cysteamine but does not have cysteamine's unpleasant taste and smell (Thoene and Lemons 1980; Smolin *et al.* 1988). In both the 1978 and 1987 protocols, cysteamine was given in divided doses every six hours, beginning with an initial dose of 10 mg/kg/day and increasing by 10/mg/kg/day every one to two weeks. The dosage frequency was dictated by pharmacokinetics. The greatest plasma cysteamine concentration and the best cystine depletion are achieved one hour after a dose (Jonas and Schneider 1982); depletion is minimal five to six hours after a dose.

Both national studies showed that cysteamine preserves glomerular function and improves growth in children treated early and long (Gahl *et al.* 1987; Clark *et al.* 1992). In fact, the second study has demonstrated that the mean creatinine clearance at the start of the protocol, 62 ml/min/1.73 m^2, was maintained for at least two years without any decrement whatsoever. The children also grew at a normal rate, although there was no catch-up growth. These remarkable findings are totally incompatible with the natural history of the disease.

Recent evidence also indicates that cysteamine therapy, when begun in the first year or two of life, allows the cystinotic kidney to *acquire* glomerular function (Markello *et al.* 1993), just as a normal kidney does. This finding emphasizes the importance of early cystine depletion; it is estimated that for every month of cysteamine therapy initiated between six months and two years of life, a year's worth of ultimate renal function is preserved. These triumphs in the maintainance of function are accompanied by strong evidence of parenchymal organ cystine depletion as well (Gahl *et al.* 1992). Children treated for up to 11 years with oral cysteamine have much lower muscle cystine levels than untreated patients the same age. Moreover, cystine concentrations in the liver, pancreas, lung, and kidney were dramatically reduced in a nine-year-old, cysteamine-treated boy compared with cystine values in the same tissues of an age-matched control (Gahl *et al.* 1992).

In several families with a family history of cystinosis, oral cysteamine therapy was initiated as early as three weeks of life. One child has had normal growth and renal function for eight years, without Fanconi's syndrome (da Silva *et al.* 1985). In three others, however, an attenuated renal Fanconi syndrome developed, but the younger children clearly experienced less serious complications of their disease than their older affected siblings (Reznik *et al.* 1991).

Although most patients tolerate cysteamine well, up to 15% have significant nausea and vomiting (Gahl *et al.* 1987). Lethargy and somnolence are occasionally observed in patients receiving too much cysteamine (over 90 mg/kg/day). All symptoms have been reversible on reduction of dosage or cessation of therapy. Virtually all children are annoyed by the foul taste and smell of cysteamine, so most patients prefer phosphocysteamine. However, in 1994, the United States Food and Drug Administration approved an encapsulated formulation of cysteamine bitartrate called Cystagon[R].

Since oral cysteamine does not affect corneal cystine crystals, topical cysteamine eyedrops (0.5%) have been used (Kaiser-Kupfer *et al.* 1987*b*; 1990). This therapy actually dissolves the corneal cystine crystals in young patients, and removes corneal haziness from older individuals (Fig. 17.3). Virtually all patients report marked relief of their corneal discomfort, and long-term

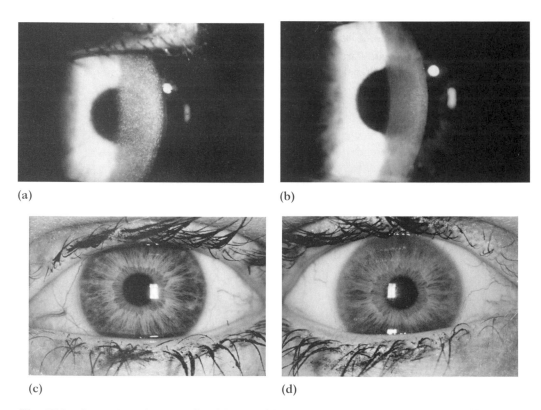

(a) (b)

(c) (d)

Fig. 17.3 Corneal cystine crystals with and without topical cysteamine therapy in a 20-year-old cystinosis patient. (a) Slit-lamp photograph of crystals in left cornea prior to cysteamine therapy; (b) slit-lamp photograph of left cornea after six months of diligent cysteamine eyedrop treatment; (c) clear left cornea after therapy; (d) right cornea, treated with placebo (normal saline), remains hazy after six months of treatment. (Courtesy of Dr. Muriel I. Kaiser-Kupfer, National Eye Institute.)

Table 17.1 Complications of nephropathic cystinosis in adults not treated with cysteamine

Disorder	Typical age of onset (years)	Frequency in adults (%)
Corneal crystals	1	100
Short stature	1	90
Hypothyroidism	10	80
Delayed puberty	16	80
Neurological deficits	20	5–10
Distal myopathy	20	20
Swallowing abnormalities (severe)	20	10
Pancreatic insufficiency	20	10
Decreased visual acuity	25	10–20

treatment reduces the frequency of corneal erosions. As always, early therapy is best since corneal crystal formation can be entirely prevented.

If oral cysteamine therapy in begun after three or four years of age, the patient will eventually require dialysis, a temporizing measure, or kidney transplantation, the definitive procedure. In general, cystinosis patients are excellent candidates for a renal allograft and do extremely well. Since kidneys from heterozygotes are normal, living related donors may be used without risk of disease recurrence. Biopsies of renal allografts from cystinosis patients have commonly shown crystals in interstitial cells (Malekzadeh *et al.* 1977; Langlois *et al.* 1981; Spear *et al.* 1989) and infrequently in the mesangium of the glomerulus, but these most likely represent migratory cells of host origin, such as macrophages (Spear *et al.* 1989). The longevity of kidneys transplanted into cystinosis patients is considered as good as or better than that for other recipients.

Cystinosis in adults

To date, the only way that children with cystinosis have become adults with cystinosis is via renal transplantation. As a result, affected adults carry with them all the medical difficulties of other transplant patients, i.e. risks of renal osteodystrophy, hypertension, and the depression of chronic disease, in addition to the specific complications of cystinosis (Table 17.1). These include visual impairment, neurologic deficits, hypothyroidism, pancreatic insufficiency, myopathy, and male infertility. In addition, most adults with cystinosis have a typical, aged facies resulting from a combination of their disease and their steroid use (Fig. 17.4). The more serious complications affect approximately half of all patients over age 20 and are generally progressive. Interestingly, any individual patient can have one or two complications and be spared the others. The oldest individual with nephropathic cystinosis is now in his late-thirties.

Ophthalmic involvement

One of the most serious complications of cystinosis with respect to quality of life is ophthalmic involvement. In a study of eight post-transplant patients aged 12–24 years, none of whom received long-term cysteamine treatment or topical eyedrops, all had massive accumulation of crystals in the stroma of the cornea and iris (Kaiser-Kupfer *et al.* 1986). Visual acuity was seriously impaired in four patients, with retinal dysfunction, colour blindness, and impaired

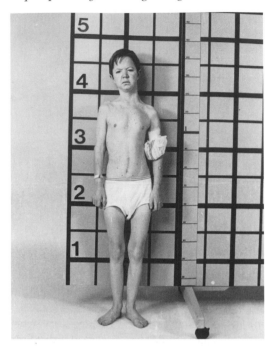

Fig. 17.4   Typical aged, cushingoid appearance of a 22-year-old post-transplant patient with nephropathic cystinosis. Note generalized muscle wasting.

night vision. Currently, five of our six patients over 30 years of age are legally blind. Other findings include debilitating blepharospasm, posterior synechiae, and crystals on the anterior lens surface and the retina. Complications such as photophobia, blepharospasm, corneal erosions, and reduced visual acuity significantly limit patients' activities, including school attendance, driving, and steady employment (Gahl and Kaiser-Kupfer 1987). All these ophthalmic abnormalities increase in frequency and severity with age. A few patients have had band keratopathy (Yamamoto *et al.* 1979), and pupillary block glaucoma has been described in a 19-year-old female (Wan *et al.* 1986). One 12-year-old boy required a corneal transplant to relieve the pain of his recurrent corneal erosions (Kaiser-Kupfer *et al.* 1987*a*).

Neurological complications

Neurologic findings are sporadic and rare but become more apparent as patients age. Mild cerebral atrophy was found in 12 of 14 patients aged 13–24 years who were examined by CT scan (Fink *et al.* 1989). In general, their neurological examinations were normal, although one 18-year-old woman with severe atrophy had an abnormal EEG and dementia. Another 23-year-old man had bradykinesia, dementia, and spasticity with mineralization of the internal capsules and periventricular white matter and marked cerebral atrophy. This individual died at age 28, and post-mortem examination showed severe cerebral involvement with multifocal cystic necrosis, dystropic calcification, spongy change, and vacuolization (Vogel *et al.* 1990). The majority of patients with neurologic involvement are transplant recipients, which raises the question of whether any of their central nervous system disturbances are secondary to chronic renal failure, dialysis, or immunosuppression.

Other nervous system complications include short-term memory loss (Jonas *et al.* 1987), difficulties with gait (Gahl *et al.* 1986; Vogel *et al.* 1990), transient ischaemia attacks (Gahl *et al.* 1986), and polyneuropathy (Almond *et al.* 1991). Autopsy results have shown cystine storage in virtually all tissues of the central nervous system, with the highest levels in the choroid plexus, dura, anterior pituitary, and basal ganglia (Jonas *et al.* 1987). Electron microscopy revealed needle-shaped and hexagonal crystals in the cytoplasm of white matter neurons and in basal ganglia pericytes. Necrosis and demyelination of the internal capsule and brachium pontis have been reported in one 19-year-old with cystinosis (Levine and Paparo 1982).

Myopathy

Skeletal muscle involvement is expressed as generalized atrophy, weakness (Jonas *et al.* 1987; Gahl *et al.* 1988*a*), swallowing dysfunction (Sonies *et al.* 1990), and dysarthria (Gahl *et al.* 1986; Vogel *et al.* 1990). One 22-year-old male with cystinosis and a renal allograft developed generalized muscle weakness and wasting over a two-year period (Gahl *et al.* 1988*a*). Proximal and distal muscles of all limbs showed atrophy and weakness. Respiratory muscles were also affected, and he died of food aspiration. Further studies have revealed a distal myopathy in 12 of 50 post-transplant patients studied at the National Institutes of Health (NIH) (Fig. 17.5). Hand-muscle biopsies in two individuals exhibited histologic characteristics of a vacuolar myopathy. One

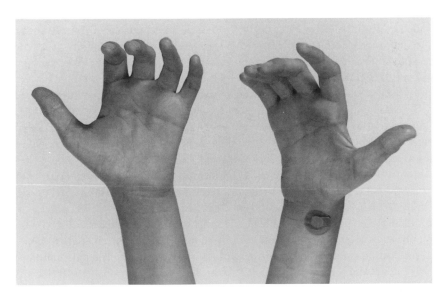

Fig. 17.5 Hand-muscle atrophy in 23-year-old man with cystinosis and a renal allograft. Note wasting of interosseous muscles. (Courtesy of Dr. Lawrence Charnas, NICHD.)

patient has now undergone a tendon reinsertion procedure to obtain increased hand strength; the results of this operation are currently pending.

Swallowing dysfunction, another late complication of nephropathic cystinosis, can be severe in older patients who may have profound oesophageal and pharyngeal dysphagia. Seven of nine individuals with cystinosis, aged 21–31, had abnormalities in all three phases of swallowing, i.e. oral, pharyngeal, and oesophageal (Sonies *et al.* 1990). This oropharyngeal muscle dysfunction can be life-threatening and is most likely due to damage caused by cystine accumulation in muscle cells, which have been shown to store cystine both *in situ* and *in vitro* (Harper *et al.* 1987). Certain eating and swallowing manoeuvres can assist in preventing food aspiration.

Other systemic involvement

Complications also occur in glandular systems. Pancreatic insufficiency involving both exocrine and endocrine dysfunction has been reported (Fivush *et al.* 1987; 1988). One 17-year-old, post-transplant patient developed chronic pancreatitis with steatorrhoea, weight loss, and decreased trypsinogen levels. The patient was responsive to pancreatic enzyme replacement, suggesting that the malabsorption was caused by pancreatic exocrine insufficiency. Five other post-transplant cystinosis patients were found to have severe hyperglycaemia and low insulin levels. Steroid therapy was probably not the sole cause of their hyperglycaemia because three of the patients became insulin-dependent two to seven years after their transplant while receiving minimal prednisone doses. Pancreatic tissue does store cystine so crystal deposits within the parenchyma most likely lead to organ destruction.

Sexual maturation may also be impaired in cystinosis. Both male and female patients usually undergo pubertal changes but they may be delayed until the middle to late teens (Gahl and Kaiser-Kupfer 1987; Ehrich *et al.* 1991; Chik *et al.* 1993). One 20-year-old woman with cystinosis and a renal allograft successfully delivered a healthy male infant, although she developed pre-eclampsia at 35.5 weeks of pregnancy (Reiss *et al.* 1988). Examination of the placenta showed cystine crystals only in the maternal portion. Because most females with cystinosis did not survive into their reproductive years prior to the availability of renal allografts, the true fertility rate is not known. Cystine accumulation and primary ovarian failure have been reported in a 22-year-old patient (Jonas *et al.* 1987).

The three male adults with cystinosis who have provided a semen sample have all been aspermic. Several other patients have hypergonadotropic hypogonadism (Chik *et al.* 1993), probably due to cystine crystal formation in the testes (Lucky *et al.* 1977; Gahl *et al.* 1988*b*). Testosterone replacement has benefited several patients by enhancing secondary sexual characteristics. Men with cystinosis can have erections and ejaculate.

Hypothyroidism is a common problem. The majority of North American patients over 10 years old who did not receive cysteamine but did receive a renal transplant have required thyroid supplementation (Gahl *et al.* 1986; Almond *et al.* 1991; Gahl *et al.* 1988*b*). In contrast, a German study found that the thyroid status of most children improved after successful renal transplantation, with only a few requiring treatment with thyroid hormone (Ehrich *et al.* 1991).

Growth retardation is universal and often persists in patients after transplantation (Malekzadeh *et al.* 1977; Gahl and Kaiser-Kupfer 1987; Gahl *et al.* 1988*b*; Ehrich *et al.* 1991). Adult males seen at the NIH average 146 cm in height (30 cm below the normal mean); females average 137 cm (26 cm below the normal mean). Bone age is usually several years delayed, suggesting that growth hormone therapy may be beneficial. However, once a patient reaches age 20, he or she will not grow regardless of the bone age. Immunosuppression therapy probably contributes to persistent growth inhibition. A few patients on cyclosporin A have demonstrated catch-up growth when compared to children treated with azathioprine (Ehrich *et al.* 1991).

Adenoidal hypertrophy, an unusual finding in early adulthood, has resulted in hearing loss in one 16-year-old male. Microscopic examination of the adenoidal lymphoid tissue revealed focal deposits of crystals, presumably cystine, which were predominantly extracellular (Rozenbaum *et al.* 1989).

Hepatomegaly occurs in fewer than half of all transplant patients (Gahl *et al.* 1986; Gahl and Kaiser-Kupfer 1987). Splenomegaly is even less common. A mild elevation of liver enzymes (SGOT, SGPT) occurs infrequently. Elevations of the sedimentation rate and serum cholesterol concentrations are seen in fewer than one-third of patients, with a frequency equivalent to that in pre-transplant patients. In one study, the mean $\pm$ SD platelet count for post-transplant patients was $255 \pm 109 \times 10^3/\text{mm}^3$, significantly less than the mean platelet count of $433 \pm 81 \times 10^3/\text{mm}^3$ in pre-transplant patients (Gahl *et al.* 1986).

Impact of cysteamine therapy

In the past, only renal tranplantation could bring cystinosis patients to adulthood. Now, the first children treated from infancy are in mid-adolescence. What can we expect for them as adults?

These individuals should be productive members of society. Although they require lifelong cysteamine therapy and replacement of renal losses, most should not require a renal allograft for decades and some should never need one (Markello *et al.* 1993). Based upon findings of parenchymal cystine depletion, we have every reason to expect that visual acuity and other ophthalmic functions will remain normal. Neurological, muscular, and swallowing difficulties should not occur. Patients should be spared the endocrine complications of cystinosis, including hypothyroidism, and proceed through puberty normally, with only slightly impaired growth parameters.

The same degree of optimism is not warranted for the current group of post-transplant patients beginning cysteamine therapy as adults. Although cysteamine apparently does not adversely affect the functioning of renal allografts, its beneficial effects may be limited to stabilizing the function remaining in affected organs rather than reversing deficiencies. Damaged neural, muscular, pancreatic, and retinal tissues are unlikely to repair themselves or regenerate even if years of cysteamine therapy effect chronic cystine depletion. Nevertheless, oral cysteamine provides the only real hope of preventing further deterioration of vital organs. In addition, cysteamine eyedrops can remove crystals from the corneas of adults and prevent corneal erosion; this has certainly improved the lives of many patients.

In spite of this area of success, much remains to be accomplished in the study of cysteamine's efficacy. We need to know if cysteamine crosses the blood–brain barrier, how to dose patients on dialysis, and whether there are any long-term side-effects of cysteamine therapy. Finally, the jury is still out on how beneficial cysteamine will be for patients who already have serious non-renal complications of cystinosis.

Conclusion

Cystinosis has come a long way from its fatal past, and now sits on the doorstep of adult physicians. These care-givers must adopt a multidisciplinary approach to the disease, remaining constantly attentive to new complications of persistent cystine storage. Only then will cystinosis complete its journey and be an orphan no longer.

References

Almond, P. S., Morel, P., Troppmann, C., Matas, A., Najarian, J. S., and Chavers, B. (1991). Progression of infantile cystinosis after renal transplantation. *Transplant Proc.*, **23**, 1386.

Andersson, H. C., Markello, T., Schneider, J. A., and Gahl, W. A. (1992). Effect of growth hormone treatment on serum creatinine concentration in patients with cystinosis and chronic renal disease. *J. Pediatr.*, **120**, 716–20.

Bacq, Z. M. (1965). *Chemical protection against ionizing radiation* (ed. Charles C. Thomas), pp. 16–26, 180–239. Springfield, Ill.

Bois, E., Feingold, J., Frenay, P., and Briard, M. L. (1976). Infantile cystinosis in France: genetics, incidence, geographic distribution. *J. Med. Genet.*, **13**, 434–8.

Boman, H. and Schneider, J. A. (1981). Prenatal diagnosis of nephropathic cystinosis. Pregnancy at risk ascertained through heterozygote diagnosis of parents. *Acta. Paediatr. Scand.*, **70**, 389–93.

Chik, C. L., Friedman, A., Merriam, G. R., and Gahl, W. A. (1993). Pituitary-testicular function in nephropathic cystinosis. *Ann. Intern. Med.*, **119**, 568–75.

Chiu, S. and Bhakthan, N. M. G. (1978). Experimental acetaminophen-induced hepatic necrosis: Biochemical and electron microscopic study of cysteamine protection. *Lab. Invest.*, **39**, 193–202.

Clark, K. F., Fanklin, P. S., Reisch, J. S., Hoffman, H. J., Gahl, W. A., Thoene, J. G., *et al.* (1992). Effect of cysteamine-HCl and phosphocysteamine dosage on renal function and growth in children with nephropathic cystinosis. *Clin. Res.*, **40**, 113A.

Cogan, D. G. and Kuwabara, T. (1960). Ocular pathology of cystinosis, with particular reference to the elusiveness of the corneal crystals. *Arch. Ophthalmol.*, **63**, 51–7.

Dale, R. T., Rao, G. N., Aquavella, J. V., and Metz, H. S. (1981). Adolescent cystinosis: a clinical and specular microscopic study of an unusual sibship. *Br. J. Ophthalmol.*, **65**, 828–32.

da Silva, V. A., Zurbrugg, R. P., Lavanchy, P., Blumberg, A., Suter, H., Wyss, S. R., *et al.* (1985). Long-term treatment of infantile nephropathic cystinosis with cysteamine. *N. Engl. J. Med.*, **313**, 1460–3.

Ehrich, J. H. H., Brodehl, J., Byrd, D. I., Hossfeld, S., Hoyer, P. F., Leipert, K-P., *et al.* (1991). Renal transplantation in 22 children with nephropathic cystinosis. *Pediatr. Nephrol.*, **5**, 707–14.

Fink, J. K., Brouwers, P., Barton, N., Malekzadeh, M. H., Sato, S., Hill, S., *et al.* (1989). Neurologic complications in long-standing nephropathic cystinosis. *Arch. Neurol.*, **46**, 543–8.

Fivush, B., Green, O. C., Porter, C. C., Balfe, J. W., O'Regan, S., and Gahl, W. A. (1987). Pancreatic endocrine insufficiency in post-transplant cystinosis. *Am. J. Dis. Child.*, **141**, 1087–9.

Fivush, B., Flick, J. A., and Gahl, W. A. (1988). Pancreatic exocrine insufficiency in a patient with nephropathic cystinosis. *J. Pediatr.*, **112**, 49–51.

Gahl, W. A., Bashan, N., Tietze, F., Bernardini, I., and Schulman, J. D. (1982*a*). Cystine transport is defective in isolated leukocyte lysosomes from patients with cystinosis. *Science*, **217**, 1263–5.

Gahl, W. A., Tietze, F., Bashan, N., Steinherz, R., and Schulman, J. D. (1982*b*). Defective cystine exodus from isolated lysosome-rich fractions of cystinotic leucocytes. *J. Biol. Chem.*, **257**, 9570–5.

Gahl, W. A., Tietze, F., Bashan, N., Bernardini, I., Raiford, D., and Schulman, J. D. (1983). Characteristics of cystine counter-transport in normal and cystinotic lysosome-rich leucocyte granular fractions. *Biochem. J.*, **216**, 393–400.

Gahl, W. A., Hubbard, V. S., and Orloff, S. (1984). Decreased sweat production in cystinosis. *J. Pediatr.*, **104**, 904–5.

Gahl, W. A., Dorfmann, A., Evans, M. I., Karson, E. M., Landsberger, F. J., Fabro, S. E., *et al.* (1985*a*). *First trimester fetal diagnosis. Chorionic biopsy in the prenatal diagnosis of nephropathic cystinosis* (ed. M. Fraccaro, G. Simmoni, and B. Brambti), pp. 260. Springer-Verlag, Berlin.

Gahl, W. A., Tietze, F., Butler, J. D., and Schulman, J. D. (1985*b*). Cysteamine depletes cystinotic leucocyte granular fractions of cystine by the mechanism of disulphide interchange. *Biochem. J.*, **228**, 545–50.

Gahl, W. A. (1986). Cystinosis coming of age. *Adv. Pediatr.*, **33**, 95–126.

Gahl, W. A., Schneider, J. A., Thoene, J. G., and Chesney, R. (1986). Course of nephropathic cystinosis after age 10 years. *J. Pediatr.*, **109**, 605–8.

Gahl, W. A. and Kaiser-Kupfer, M. I. (1987). Complications of nephropathic cystinosis after renal failure. *Pediatr. Nephrol.*, **1**, 260–8.

Gahl, W. A., Reed, G. F., Thoene, J. G., Schulman, J. D., Rizzo, W. B., Jonas, A. J., *et al.* (1987). Cysteamine therapy for children with nephropathic cystinosis. *N. Engl. J. Med.*, **316**, 971–7.

Gahl, W. A., Dalakas, M. C., Charnas, L., Chen, K. T., Pezeshkpour, G. H., Kuwabara, T., *et al.* (1988*a*). Myopathy and cystine storage in muscles in a patient with nephropathic cystinosis. *N. Engl. J. Med.*, **319**, 1461–4.

Gahl, W. A., Thoene, J. G., Schneider, J. A., O'Regan, S., Kaiser-Kupfer, M. I., and Kuwabara, T. (1988*b*). Cystinosis: Progress in a prototypic disease. *Ann. Intern. Med.*, **109**, 557–69.

Gahl, W. A., Renlund, M., and Thoene, J. G. (1989). *The metabolic basis of inherited disease. Lysosomal transport disorders: Cystinosis and sialic acid storage disorders* (6th edn) (ed. C. R., Scriver, A. L. Beaudet, W. S. Sly, and D. Valle), pp. 2619–47. McGraw-Hill, New York.

Gahl, W. A., Schneider, J. A., Schulman, J. D., Thoene, J. G., and Reed, G. F. (1990). Predicted reciprocal serum creatinine at age 10 years as a measure of renal function in children with nephropathic cystinosis treated with oral cysteamine. *Pediatr. Nephrol.*, **4**, 129–35.

Gahl, W. A., Charnas, L., Markello, T. C., Bernardini, I., Ishak, K. G., and Dalakas, M. C. (1992). Parenchymal organ cystine depletion with long-term cysteamine therapy. *Biochem. Med. Metab. Biol.*, **48**, 275–85.

Gretz, N., Manz, F., Augustin, R., Barrat, T. M., Bender-Götze, C., Brandis, M., *et al.* (1983). Survival time in cystinosis. A collaborative study. *Proc. Eur. Dial. Transplant Assoc.*, **19**, 582–9.

Harper, G. S., Bernardini, I., Hurko, O., Zuurveld, J., and Gahl, W. A. (1987). Cystine storage in cultured myotubes from patients with nephropathic cystinosis. *Biochem. J.*, **243**, 841–5.

Jonas, A. J. and Schneider, J. A. (1982). Plasma cysteamine concentrations in children treated for cystinosis. *J. Pediatr.*, **100**, 321–3.

Jonas, A. J., Conley, S. B., Marshall, R., Johnson, R. A., Marks, M., and Rosenberg, H. (1987). Nephropathic cystinosis with central nervous system involvement. *Am. J. Med.*, **83**, 966–70.

Kaiser-Kupfer, M. I., Caruso, R. C., Minkler, D. S., and Gahl, W. A. (1986). Long-term ocular manifestations in nephropathic cystinosis. *Arch. Ophthalmol.*, **104**, 706–11.

Kaiser-Kupfer, M. I., Datiles, M. B., and Gahl, W. A. (1987*a*). Corneal transplant in a boy with nephropathic cystinosis. *Lancet*, **1**, 331.

Kaiser-Kupfer, M. I., Fujikawa, L., Kuwabara, T., Jain, S., and Gahl, W. A. (1987*b*). Removal of corneal crystals by topical cysteamine in nephropathic cystinosis. *N. Engl. J. Med.*, **316**, 775–9.

Kaiser-Kupfer, M. I., Gazzo, M. A., Datiles, M. B., Caruso, R. C., Kuehl, E. M., and Gahl, W. A. (1990). A randomized placebo-controlled trial of cysteamine eye drops in nephropathic cystinosis. *Arch. Ophthalmol.*, **108**, 689–93.

Krasnewich, D. M. and Gahl, W. A. (1991). Cystinosis: A treatable lysosomal storage disease. *The Endocrinologist*, **1**, 111–18.

Kraus, E. and Lutz, P. (1971). Ocular cystine deposits in an adult. *Arch. Ophthalmol.*, **85**, 690–4.

Langlois, R. P., O'Regan, S., Pelletier, M., and Robitatille, P. (1981). Kidney transplantation in uremic children with cystinosis. *Nephron*, **28**, 273–5.

Langman, C. B., Moore, E. S., Thoene, J. G., and Schneider, J. A. (1985). Renal failure in a sibship with late-onset cystinosis. *J. Pediatr.*, **107**, 755–6.

Levine, S. and Paparo, G. (1982). Brain lesions in a case of cystinosis. *Acta Neuropathol. (Berlin)*, **57**, 217–20.

Lietman, P. S., Frazier, P. D., Wong, V. G., Shotton, D., and Seegmiller, J. E. (1966). Adult cystinosis—a benign disorder. *Am. J. Med.*, **40**, 511–17.

Lucky, A. W., Howley, P. M., Megyesi, K., Spielberg, S. P., and Schulman, J. D. (1977). Endocrine studies in cystinosis: compensated primary hypothyroidism. *J. Pediatr.*, **91**, 204–10.

Malekzadeh, M. H., Neustein, H. B., Schneider, J. A., Pennisi, A. J., Ettenger, R. B., Uittenbogaart, C. H., *et al.* (1977). Cadaver renal transplantation in children with cystinosis. *Am. J. Med.*, 63, 525–33.

Manz, F., Harms, E., Lutz, P., Waldherr, R., and Scharer, K. (1982). Adolescent cystinosis: renal function and morphology. *Eur. J. Pediatr.*, 138, 354–7.

Markello, T. C., Bernardini, I. M., and Gahl, W. A. (1993). Improved renal function in children with cystinosis treated with cysteamine. *N. Engl. J. Med.*, 328, 1157–62.

Pabico, R. C., Panner, B. J., McKenna, B. A., and Bryson, M. F. (1980). Glomerular lesions in patients with late-onset cystinosis with massive proteinuria. *Renal Physiol.*, 3, 347–54.

Patrick, A. D. and Lake, B. D. (1968). Cystinosis: electron microscopic evidence of lysosomal storage of cystine in lymph node. *J. Clin. Pathol.*, 21, 571–5.

Pisoni, R. L., Thoene, J. G., and Christensen, H. N. (1985). Detection and characterization of carrier-mediated cationic amino acid transport in lysosomes of normal and cystinotic human fibroblasts. *J. Biol. Chem.*, 260, 4791–8.

Reiss, R. E., Kuwabara, T., Smith, M. L., and Gahl, W. A. (1988). Successful pregnancy despite placental cystine crystals in a woman with nephropathic cystinosis. *N. Engl. J. Med.*, 319, 223–6.

Reznik V. M., Adamson, M., Adelman, R. D., Murphy, J. L., Gahl, W. A., Clark, K. F., *et al.* (1991). Treatment of cystinosis with cysteamine from early infancy. *J. Pediatr.*, 119, 491–3.

Rozenbaum, J. A., Trachtman, H., Gloster, E., and Goldstein, M. (1989). Hearing loss and adenoidal hypertrophy in an adolescent with nephropathic cystinosis. *Otolaryngol. Head Neck Surg.*, 101, 701–3.

Schneider, J. A., Bradley, K., and Seegmiller, J. E. (1967). Increased cystine in leukocytes from individuals homozygous and heterozygous for cystinosis. *Science*, 157, 1321–2.

Schneider, J. A., Verroust, F. M., Kroll, W. A., Garvin, A. J., Horger 3rd., E. O., Wong, V. G., *et al.* (1974). Prenatal diagnosis of cystinosis. *N. Engl. J. Med.*, 290, 878–82.

Schulman, J. D., Bradley, K. H., and Seegmiller, J. E. (1969). Cystine: compartmentalization within lysosomes in cystinotic leukocytes. *Science*, 166, 1152–4.

Schulman, J. D., Wong, V., Olson, W. H., and Seegmiller, J. E. (1970). Lysosomal site of crystalline deposits in cystinosis as shown by ferritin uptake. *Arch. Pathol.*, 90, 259–64.

Smith, M. L., Pellett, O. L., Cass, M. M. J., Kennaway, N. G., Buist, N. R. M., Buckmaster, J., *et al.* (1986). Prenatal diagnosis of cystinosis utilizing chorionic villus sampling. *Prenat. Diagn.*, 6, 195.

Smith, M. L., Clark, K. F., Davis, S. E., Greene, A. A., Marcusson, E. G., Chen, Y-J., *et al.* (1989). Diagnosis of cystinosis with use of placenta. *N. Engl. J. Med.*, 321, 397–8.

Smolin, L. A., Clark, K. F., Thoene, J. G., Gahl, W. A., and Schneider, J. A. (1988). A comparison of the effectiveness of cysteamine and phosphocysteamine in elevating plasma cysteamine concentration and decreasing leukocyte-free cystine in nephropathic cystinosis. *Pediatr. Res.*, 23, 616–20.

Sonies, B. C., Ekman, E. F., Andersson, H. C., Adamson, M. D., Kaler, S. G., Markello, T. C., *et al.* (1990). Swallowing dysfunction in nephropathic cystinosis. *N. Engl. J. Med.*, 323, 565–70.

Spear, G. S., Gubler, M. C., Habib, R., and Broyer, M. (1989). Renal allografts in cystinosis and mesangial demography. *Clin. Nephrol.*, 32, 256–61.

States, B., Blazer, B., Harris, D., and Segal, S. (1975). Prenatal diagnosis of cystinosis. *J. Pediatr.*, 87, 558–62.

Teree, T. M., Friedman, A. B., Kest, L. M., and Fetterman, G. H. (1970). Cystinosis and proximal tubular nephropathy in siblings. Progressive development of the physiological and anatomical lesion. *Am. J. Dis. Child.*, 119, 481–7.

Thoene, J. G., Oshima, R. G., Crawhall, J. C., Olson, D. L., and Schneider, J. A. (1976). Cystinosis: intracellular cystine depletion by aminothiols in vitro and in vivo. *J. Clin. Invest.*, 58, 180–9.

Thoene, J. G. and Lemons, R. (1980). Cystine depletion of cystinotic tissues by phosphocysteamine (WR638). *J. Pediatr.*, 96, 1043–4.

Treem, W. R., Rusnack, E. J., Ragsdale, B. D., Seikaly, M. G., and DiPalma, J. S. (1988). Inflammatory bowel disease in a patient with nephropathic cystinosis. *Pediatrics*, **81**, 584–7.

Vogel, D. G., Malekzadeh, M. H., Cornford, M. E., Schneider, J. A., Shields, W. D., and Vinters, H. V. (1990). Central nervous system involvement in nephropathic cystinosis. *J. Neuropathol. Exp. Neurol.*, **49**, 591–9.

Waldman, T. A., Mogielnicki, R. P., and Strober, W. (1973). *Cystinosis. The proteinuria of cystinosis: its pattern and pathogenesis* (ed. J. D. Schulman), pp. 55–66. DHEW Publication no. (NIH) 72–249, Government Printing Office, Washington, D.C.

Wan, W. L., Minckler, D. S., and Rao, N. A. (1986). Pupillary-block glaucoma associated with childhood cystinosis. *Am. J. Ophthalmol.*, **101**, 700–5.

Wilson, D. P., Jelley, D., Stratton, R., and Coldwell, J. G. (1989). Nephropathic cystinosis: improved linear growth after treatment with recombinant human growth hormone. *J. Pediatr.*, **115**, 758–61.

Wong, V. G., Lietman, P. S., and Seegmiller, J. E. (1967). Alterations of pigment epithelium in cystinosis. *Arch. Ophthalmol.*, **77**, 361–9.

Yamamoto, G. K., Schulman, J. D., Schneider, J. A., and Wong, V. G. (1979). Long-term ocular changes in cystinosis: Observations in renal transplant recipients. *J. Pediatr. Ophthalmol. Strabismus*, **16**, 21–5.

18

Glycogen storage diseases (von Gierke's disease)

Jean-Pierre Grünfeld

Introduction

The glycogen storage diseases (GSDs) include over 12 separate genetic defects that affect glycogen metabolism, primarily break down in liver or muscle, or both. Indeed, liver and muscle contain abundant quantities of glycogen. Since carbohydrate metabolism in the liver is responsible for plasma glucose homeostasis, GSDs with liver involvement are manifested by hepatomegaly and hypoglycaemia. In contrast, muscle glycogen provides substrates which enable the ATP generation necessary for muscle contraction. The presenting features of GSDs that affect the muscle are cramp, exercise intolerance, and progressive muscle weakness. In occasional cases, acute rhabdomyolysis may occur in these patients, leading to myoglobinuria and acute renal failure.

Type I glycogen storage disease (GSD-I) is a prototype of liver glycogenesis and is the only GSD in which primary renal involvement occurs. It was first described by von Gierke in 1929 and is also called 'von Gierke's disease'. It is an autosomal recessive inherited disorder. The most frequently encountered subtype, GSD-Ia (see below), is a very uncommon disease, with an incidence of one in 100 000 to 300 000 births (Lei *et al.* 1993; Talente *et al.* 1994).

Biochemical defect

GSD-Ia results from deficient glucose-6-phosphatase activity in liver, kidney, and intestine (Hers *et al.* 1989), with excessive accumulation of glycogen in these organs. Fat excess is also found in the liver. When glucose-6-phosphatase activity is deficient, the liver is unable to hydrolyze glucose from glucose-6-phosphate through normal glycogenolysis and gluconeogenesis.

Glucose-6-phosphatase is a single 35 kd protein which is the catalytic unit of a multicomponent complex, situated on the lumenal surface of the endoplasmic reticulum that gains access to substrates in the cytosol by means of associated translocases. Cloning of the glucose-6-phosphatase gene (Lei *et al.* 1993; 1995) opened identification of mutations in affected families from various populations (Chevalier-Porst *et al.* 1996; Parvari *et al.* 1997), the possibility of prenatal diagnosis (Qu *et al.* 1996; Lee *et al.* 1996; Parvari *et al.* 1997), and the hope of gene therapy, first in animal models of GSD-I (Lei *et al.* 1996; Kishnani *et al.* 1997). Glycogen storage disease type Ib (GSD-Ib) results from a deficiency of the glucose-6-phosphate translocase (which so far has not been purified) that transports glucose-6-phosphate into the lumen of the endoplasmic reticulum where it is hydrolyzed. Therefore, GSD-Ib patients are also unable to maintain euglycaemia, and they develop similar metabolic consequences as GSD-Ia patients. In addition, GSD-Ib patients have neutropenia and are prone to recurrent bacterial infections which suggests that the translocase has a role in regulating neutrophil function (Talente *et al.* 1994). The course of the infectious complications may be ameliorated by long-term administration of G-CSF (Wang *et al.* 1991).

Other GSD biochemical subgroups (Ic and Id) have been isolated, involving other putative translocases. Lei *et al.* have established that GSD type Ib and Ic patients have normal coding regions and intron/exon junctions of the glucose-6-phosphatase gene. The genetic defect(s) in these patients, phenotypically deficient in enzyme activity, remains to be elucidated. Other components of the glucose-6-phosphatase complex are important to the hydrolysis of glucose-6-phosphate (Lei *et al.* 1995).

Extrarenal features and therapy

Patients with GSD-I present with hypoglycaemia in the neonatal period or more commonly at three to four months of age. Seizures are common in children as night-time feedings are discontinued, or when a febrile illness causes decreased oral intake. Mental retardation is uncommon because the brain is protected by its ability to metabolize lactate which is present at high concentrations in the serum. Chronic hypoglycaemia triggers a sustained increase of counter-regulatory hormones such as cortisol. In childhood, this results in poor growth and delayed puberty; in adulthood, it leads to osteonecrosis, osteopenia, and frequent fractures, and probably contributes to muscle weakness (Talente *et al.* 1994). Symptomatic hypoglycaemia is uncommon in adults, even untreated. The affected children have doll-like faces with fat cheeks, relatively thin extremeties, proportional short stature, and protuberant abdomen due to hepatomegaly (but the spleen is normal). Liver test abnormalities are frequently found in adult patients. Hepatic adenomas, detected by ultrasonography, developed in 75% of cases in the adult series reported by Talente *et al.* (1994). Xanthoma and diarrhoea may be present and epistaxis is a frequent problem. Anaemia, refractory to iron supplementation, is a common finding in adults. Hyperlipidaemia (cholesterol and triglycerides) and fatty liver result from the large influx of adipose-derived fatty acids into the liver in response to low insulin and high glucagon and cortisol levels. Hyperlipidaemia is characterized by increased very low and low-density lipoprotein concentrations, and by increased levels of Apo B, C, and E, whereas Apo A and D levels are relatively normal or reduced. Patients with severe hypertriglyceridaemia are at risk of pancreatitis (Chen and van Hove 1995).

In the past 15 years, great progress has been made in the treatment of GSD-I. The current treatment is orally administered, uncooked cornstarch or nocturnal nasogastric infusion of glucose (see ref. in Chen and van Hove 1995). When diagnosis and initiation of therapy are early and when euglycaemia is maintained in this manner, the overall prognosis of the disease is much better, growth and pubertal development are normal, and it is hoped that some late complications will be prevented. Of interest, the treatment lowers cholesterol but does not normalize it (Chen and van Hove 1995). Liver transplantation has been performed in two patients with GSD-I (see review in Selby *et al.* 1993). It resulted in conversion to normal intermediary carbohydrate metabolism and elimination of the other metabolic derangements. Cloning of the glucose-6-phosphatase gene opens the possibility of prenatal diagnosis and the hope of gene therapy (Lei *et al.* 1993; 1995).

Renal findings

Renal disease in GSD-I was only recognized as a major complication in 1988 (Chen *et al.* 1988). This is not surprising since severe renal impairment is seen mainly in adults, i.e. in patients who have been adequately managed during childhood. Recent general reviews on renal involvement are available (Reitzma-Biereus *et al.* 1992; Chen *et al.* 1995). The paper by Talente *et al.* (1994) is also very helpful with regard to this. The authors have collected data on 37 adult patients with GSD-Ia and on five adult patients with GSD-Ib. Renal complications seem to be less prominent in the latter group, but no definitive statement can yet be made.

Fanconi–like syndrome

A Fanconi–like syndrome can occur, albeit rarely, in GSD-I (see review in Chen *et al.* 1990). The proximal renal tubular defects include increased urinary excretion of β_2-microglobulin, generalized amino-aciduria, hyperphosphaturia, and proximal renal tubular acidosis due to loss of bicarbonate in the urine. Glycosuria is not expected in view of the generally low blood glucose level. The Fanconi–like syndrome develops typically in young patients who have not received any specific therapy for GSD-I. Dietary therapy (see above) rapidly improves proximal renal tubular function. Proximal renal tubular dysfunction is therefore due to poor metabolic control, and is seen less frequently in appropriately detected and well-managed patients.

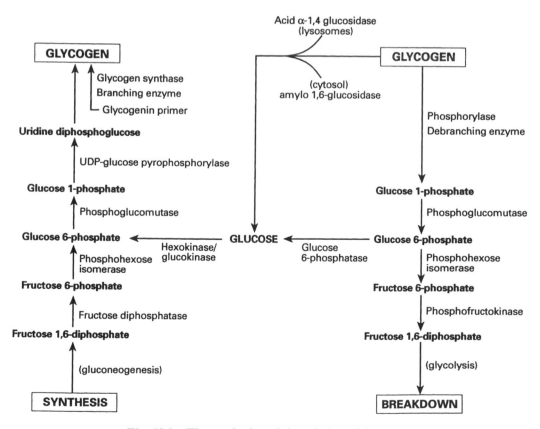

Fig. 18.1   The synthesis and degradation of glycogen.

Distal tubular acidosis

An incomplete form of distal renal tubular acidosis is probably the most frequent tubular disorder in GSD-I patients. In contrast to Fanconi's syndrome, it is observed in patients who have good metabolic control, without evidence of metabolic acidosis.

In the study by Restaino *et al.* (1993), all patients who were tested had evidence of impaired acid excretion. In response to an acid load, most patients had subnormal titrable acid and ammonia excretion; in five out of nine patients, urine pH did not decrease below 5.5. The metabolic block that occurs in GSD-I might impair renal production of ammonia. Indeed, renal gluconeogenesis (requiring the glucose-6-phosphatase enzyme) participates in acid excretion by providing a route for disposal of glutamine, thus generating ammonia available for urinary excretion. Two additional factors are associated with distal tubular acidosis and promote stone formation and nephrocalcinosis: hypocitraturia occurs as a result of enhanced proximal tubular reabsorption of citrate; hypercalciuria may also be a result of chronic acidosis. Furthermore, increased levels of 1,25 (OH) vitamin D (possibly due to reduced intake of phosphate) may result in enhanced intestinal calcium absorption and hypercalciuria (Restaino *et al.* 1993).

Hyperuricaemia; renal stones and nephrocalcinosis

Hyperuricaemia is a feature of GSD-I and is explained by the combination of increased synthesis of purine and a competitive inhibition of renal tubular excretion of urate by lactate. Uric acid stone has been very rarely reported. The improved metabolic control and, if necessary, the use of xanthine oxidase inhibitors have resulted in normalization of serum uric acid concentration (Chen *et al.* 1990).

Renal stones and/or nephrocalcinosis are common findings in GSD-I patients, mostly in adults. However, renal stones have been found in patients as young as three years of age (Restaino *et al.* 1993). Stone analysis showed predominant calcium oxalate monohydrate, and a small amount of calcium phosphate with little uric acid composition. Several factors may contribute to stone formation, such as distal renal tubular acidosis, hypocitraturia, hyperuricosuria, and hypercalciuria.

Focal and segmental glomerulosclerosis

This is by far the most common and serious renal abnormality seen in GSD-I (Chen *et al.* 1988; Obara *et al.* 1993; Chen and van Hove 1995). It mainly affects patients older than 20 years but can also be seen in younger patients. The disease is characterized by insidious onset of proteinuria and slowly progressive renal failure. Glomerular lesions (i.e. focal and segmental or global glomerulosclerosis) precede the tubulointerstitial lesions. Verani and Bernstein (1988) stated that thickening, lamellation, and glycogen deposition in the glomerular basement membrane were characteristic alterations associated with GSD-I.

Various factors may contribute to glomerulosclerosis in GSD-I. Enlargement of the kidneys is a common finding in GSD-I and is ascribed to glycogen accumulation. This finding was emphasized by von Gierke (19••). More recently, Obara *et al.* (1993) demonstrated enlargement of glomeruli on renal biopsies of two GSD-I patients. It has been shown in animal models that glomerular enlargement predisposes to the development of glomerulosclerosis (Ichikawa *et al.* 1991). Most GSD-I patients, regardless of age, have elevated glomerular filtration rate (GFR) associated with elevated renal plasma flow (Baker *et al.* 1989). Similar haemodynamic changes have been found associated with experimental models of glomerulosclerosis. In addition, similar alterations have also been documented in the stages preceding the appearance of nephropathy in patients with diabetes mellitus or sickle-cell disease. The mechanism of hyperfiltration in GSD-I is not clear. Obviously, hyperglycaemia does not occur. Protein intake is not high in these patients. Chen and van Hove indicate that plasma levels of atrial natriuretic peptide, growth hormone, and glycine are normal, and that infusion of lactic acid causes hyperfiltration, warranting further investigation of lactate (1995). Finally, glomerular hyperfiltration might be related to renal and glomerular enlargement, but some young GSD-I patients exhibit hyperfiltration despite normal-sized kidneys (Chen and van Hove 1995). There is some evidence that optimal and early metabolic control may delay, prevent or slow the progression of renal disease (Chen *et al.* 1990; Yokoyama *et al.* 1995; Wolfsdorf, Laffel and Crigler, 1997).

Hyperlipidaemia has aggravating or possibly triggering roles in the development of glomerulosclerosis, on the basis of observations in humans and animal models. The mechanisms of lipid-mediated renal injury have been reviewed (Keane 1994). Increase in fat intake in GSD-I patients has been followed by increase in proteinuria. Interactions between lipid abnormalities and enhanced renal production of thromboxane have been postulated by Chen and van Hove (1995).

Amyloidosis

AA amyloidosis has been reported in three GSD-I patients. One underwent liver and kidney transplantation (Poe and Snover 1988). The second has GSD-Ib disease and developed amyloid involvement of kidneys and thyroid (Kikuchi *et al.* 1990). The third patient developed renal amyloidosis five years after kidney transplantation (Chen and van Hove 1995). The latter two patients have a long-standing history of chronic inflammation of the bowel, a condition already noted in GSD-I and predisposing to secondary amyloidosis.

References

Baker, L., Dahlem, S., Goldfarb, S., Kern, E. F. O., Stanley, C. A., Egler, J., *et al.* (1989). Hyperfiltration and renal disease in glycogen storage disease, type I. *Kidney International*, **35**, 1345–50.

Chen, Y. T., Coleman, R. A., Scheinman, J. I., Kolbeck, P. C., and Sidbury, J. B. (1988). Renal disease in type I glycogen storage disease. *New England Journal of Medicine*, **318**, 7–11.

Chen, Y., Scheinman, J., Park, H., Coleman, R., and Roe, C. (1990). Amelioration of proximal renal tubular dysfunction in type I glycogen storage disease with dietary therapy. *New England Journal of Medicine*, **323**, 590–3.

Chen, Y. T. and van Hove, J. L. K. (1995). Renal involvement in type I glycogen storage disease. *Advances in Nephrology*, **24**, 357–65.

Chevalier-Porst, F., Bozon, D., Bonardot, A. M., Bruni, N., Mithieux, G., Mathieu, M., *et al.* (1996). Mutation analysis in 24 French patients with glycogen storage disease type 1a. *Journal of Medical Genetics*, **33**, 358–60.

Hers, H. G., van Hoof, F., and de Barsy, T. (1989). Glycogen storage diseases. In: *The metabolic basis of inherited disease* (ed. C. R. Scriver, A. L. Beaudet, W. E. Sly, and D. Valle) pp. 425–52. McGraw-Hill, Inc., New York.

Ichikawa, I., Ikoma, M., and Fogo, A. (1991). Glomerular growth promotors, the common key mediator for progressive glomerular sclerosis in chronic renal disease. *Advances in Nephrology*, **20**, 127–48.

Keane, W. F. (1994). Lipids and the kidney. *Kidney International*, **46**, 910–20.

Kikuchi, M., Haginoya, K., Miyabayashi, S., Igarashi, Y., Narisawa, K., and Tada, K. (1990). Secondary amyloidosis in glycogen storage disease type Ib. *European Journal of Pediatrics*, **149**, 344–5.

Kishnani, P. S., Bao, Y., Wu, J. Y., Brix, A. E., Lin, J. L., and Chen, Y. T. (1997). Isolation and nucleotide sequence of canine glucose-6-phosphatase mRNA: identification of mutation in puppies with glycogen storage disease type Ia. *Biochemical & Molecular Medicine*, **61**, 168–77.

Lee, W. J., Yang, C. H., Ho, E. S., Shih, A., Lin, L. Y., and Lin, W. H. (1996). Prenatal diagnosis in a Chinese family with type Ia glycogen storage disease by PCR-based genetic analysis. *Prenatal Diagnosis*, **16**, 1027–31.

Lei, K. J., Shelly, L., Pan, C. J., Sidbury, J. B., and Chou, J. Y. (1993). Mutations in the glucose-6-phosphatase gene that cause glycogen storage disease type Ia. *Science*, **262**, 580–3.

Lei, K. J., Shelly, L. L., Lin, B., Sidbury, J. B., Chen, Y. T., Nordie, R. C., *et al.* (1995). Mutations in the glucose-6-phosphatase gene are associated with glycogen storage disease types Ia and IaSP but not Ib and Ic. *Journal of Clinical Investigation*, **95**, 234–40.

Lei, K. J., Chen, H., Pan, C. J., Ward, J. M., Mosinger, B. J., Lee, E. J., *et al.* (1996). Glucose-6-phosphatase dependent substrate transport in the glycogen storage disease type-1a mouse. *Nature Genetics*, **13**, 203–9.

Obara, K., Saito, T., Sato, H., Ogawa, M., Igarashi, Y., and Yoshinaga, K. (1993). Renal histology in two adult patients with type I glycogen storage disease. *Clinical Nephrology*, **39**, 59–64.

Parvari, R., Lei, K. J., Bashan, N., Hershkovitz, E., Korman, S. H., Barash, V., *et al.* (1997). Glycogen storage disease type 1a in Israel: Biochemical, clinical, and mutational studies. *American Journal of Medical Genetics*, **72**, 286–90.

Poe, R. and Snover, D. C. (1988). Adenomas in glycogen storage disease type I: two cases with unusual histologic features. *Archives of Pathology and Laboratory Medicine*, **12**, 477–83.

Qu, Y., Abdenur, J. E., Eng, C. M., and Desnick, R. J. (1996). Molecular prenatal diagnosis of glycogen storage disease type Ia. *Prenatal Diagnosis*, **16**, 333–6.

Reitsma-Bierens, W. C. C., Smit, G. P. A., and Troelstra, J. A. (1992). Renal function and kidney size in glycogen storage disease type I, *Pediatric Nephrology*, **6**, 236–8.

Restaino, I., Kaplan, B. S., Stanley, C., and Baker, L. (1993). Nephrolithiasis, hypocitraturia, and a distal renal tubular acidification defect in type 1 glycogen storage disease. *Journal of Pediatrics*, **122**, 392–6.

Selby, R., Starzl, T. E., Yunis, E., Todo, S., Tzakis, A. G., Brown, B. I., *et al.* (1993). Liver transplantation for type I and type IV glycogen storage disease. *European Journal of Pediatrics*, **152**, (Suppl. 1), S71–S76.

Talente, G. M., Coleman, R. A., Alter, C., Baker, L., Brown, B. I., Cannon, R. A., *et al.* (1994). Glycogen storage disease in adults. *Annals of Internal Medicine*, **120**, 218–26.

Verani, R. and Bernstein, J. (1988). Renal glomerular and tubular abnormalities in glycogen storage disease type I. *Archives of Pathology and Laboratory Medicine*, **112**, 271–4.

von Gierke, E. (1929). Glykogenspeicher Krankheit der Leber und Nieren. *Beiträge zur Pathologischen Anatomie*, **82**, 497–513.

Wang, W. C., Crist, W. M., Inle, J. N., Arnold, B. A., and Keating, J. P. (1991). Granulocyte colony-stimulating factor corrects the neurtropenia associated with glycogen storage disease type Ib. *Leukemia*, **5**, 347–9.

Wolfsdorf, J. I., Laffel, L. M. B., and Crigler, J. F. (1997). Metabolic control and renal dysfunction in type I glycogen storage disease. *Journal of Inherited Metabolic Diseases*, **20**, 559–68.

Yokoyama, K., Hayashi, H., Hinoshita, F., Yamada, A., Suzuki, Y., Ogura, Y., *et al.* (1995). Renal lesion of type Ia glycogen storage disease: the glomerular size and renal localization of apolipoprotein. *Nephron*, **70**, 348–52.

19

The amyloidoses and familial Mediterranean fever

S.R. Nelson and M. Pras

Introduction

The understanding of 'amyloid' is advancing on several fronts, particularly the molecular genetics of the inherited forms of this condition. These inherited forms of amyloid may have their prodrome in childhood but most have their clinical manifestations in adolescent and adult life.

Rokitansky (1842) and others described physical deposits of a waxy, lard-like substance before Virchow (1854) termed them 'amyloid'. But it is Virchow who is recognized as the discoverer of the disease entity 'amyloidosis' because of his clinical description and observation that the deposits take up iodine in a manner similar to starch or cellulose. On the basis of this staining, Virchow concluded that they were made up of carbohydrate. A few years later, the chemists Kekule and Schmidt (1858) noted that they contained so much nitrogen that they were albuminous in nature. For many years the protein component has been the focus of amyloid research but recently the presence of the carbohydrate and glycosaminoglycan components has been re-examined. Manipulation of the latter may offer therapeutic options for the future in addition to present therapies.

Definition

Amyloid is a term which describes pathological deposits of extracellular proteinaceous fibrillar material, with particular features under the light and electron microscope. Characteristically, the deposits take up Congo red and show apple green birefringence when viewed under crossed polarized light (Puchtler 1962). Under high magnification, amyloid deposits show non-branching fibrils 7–9 nm in diameter and of variable length. Immunotactoid glomerulopathy shows a similar fibrillary pattern under the electron microscope but the fibrils are much larger than in amyloid, occasionally showing a tubular arrangement; they do not have typical Congo red staining and are excluded from the definition. In the majority of cases of this disease complex, different clinical amyloidotic syndromes are characterized by different proteins comprising the fibrils.

Pathophysiology

Amyloid deposits in tissues are notable for a lack of tissue reaction and it is the progressive accumulation of this inert material that causes problems by its physical presence. The deposits themselves are composed of protein fibrils which arise from the polymerization of low molecular weight proteins into a β-pleated sheet structure (80–85%) (Eanes and Glenner 1968), together with the glycoprotein serum amyloid P component (SAP) (10–15%) and glycosaminoglycan (5%). On the basis of this structural motif it was suggested that these deposits should be called the β-fibrilloses but the term 'amyloidosis' has remained. However, it is the type of protein in the fibril that is used to classify and determine the origin of the amyloid.

The various proteins contributing to the fibrils share some common features, including molecular weight (5–20 kd) and preponderance of β sheet structures, but these are diverse in origin. It appears that some proteins and peptides which possess β-pleated sheet configuration have a predisposition to forming amyloid fibrils. Fibrils have been created *in vitro* with synthe-sized fragments of β protein and with intact $β_2$ microglobulin molecules (Conners *et al.* 1985). In the amyloid deposits of familial amyloid polyneuropathy (FAP) most of the fibril is made up of variant point mutations of the transthyretin (TTR) protein but some normal transthyretin protein can also be found. The peptides forming amyloid fibrils may come from a precursor protein in excess (e.g. in AA amyloid derived from SAA), from genetic variants of normal peptides (e.g. FAP from abnormal transthyretin), or from cleavage products of a genetic variant precursor protein (e.g. apolipoprotein AI). The possible exception to this may be $β_2$ micro-globulin amyloidosis which is thought to be derived from whole normal molecules, although some workers believe variant molecules are also important. This type of amyloid is only seen as a complication of long-term dialysis.

Whilst forming only a small percentage of the fibrils the glycoprotein and glycosaminoglycan components of the amyloid are probably highly significant in its formation and relatively inert behaviour. The amyloid P component is structurally identical to its plasma precursor, SAP, and is bound in a calcium-dependent manner to the fibrils. In man there appears to be only one circulating and tissue form of this bianntenary glycoprotein (Hawkins *et al.* 1991). The plasma levels of SAP are similar in normal individuals and those with amyloidosis (Pepys *et al.* 1978) but the levels rise in renal failure (Nelson *et al.* 1991*a*). The cause of this is uncertain as the molecule is metabolized in the liver (Pepys *et al.* 1982).

The glycosaminoglycans present in the deposits are intimately associated with the fibrils and are more difficult to remove from the fibrils than the SAP (Nelson *et al.* 1991*b*). These very large molecules change dimensions depending on the pH and conductivity of their environment and it is speculated that they allow the protein monomers to come together to form fibrils of polymer-ized subunits. The classes of glycosaminoglycans present in amyloid deposits is disputed. They are likely to be of two restricted classes, heparan and dermatan sulphate both in a highly sulphated form (Nelson 1991*b*).

Historically, when amyloid was recognized in association with chronic infections/inflamma-tion it was classified as secondary amyloidosis; in the absence of an apparent predisposing factor it was termed 'primary amyloidosis'. Subsequently, the recognition of amyloid associated with ageing (senile amyloid) and its development in certain kindreds complicated this classification. With developments in protein chemistry it has been possible to analyse the protein subunit in a large number of cases and classify amyloid according to its precursor protein. For example, the designation AL amyloid is used to denote amyloid protein subunits derived from immuno-globulin light chains associated with plasma cell dyscrasias. Although there are no known hereditary forms of immunocyte-related amyloidosis, AL amyloid has been described separately in two sibship pairs and in cousins (Gertz *et al.* 1986).

In the hereditary amyloidoses, the deposition of amyloid occurs in several clinically distinct patterns. These patterns are described by their predominant clinical manifestations as nephro-pathic, neuropathic, cardiomyopathic, cerebral haemorrhagic, and cutaneous varieties and are shown in Table 19.1 along with their proven or presumptive precursor protein and ethnic groups in Table 19.2. The clinical patterns result from the site of deposition of the amyloid substance, but why these patterns occur is unknown. It appears not to be solely a function of

Table 19.1   Major clinical features in those hereditary amyloidoses with significant renal involvement

Disease	Major features	Renal involvement	Mode of inheritance	Age of onset of renal manifestation
FMF	Recurrent febrile serositis; synovitis	Common	A recessive	<20 years
Muckle–Wells	'Augue bouts'; Deafness	~25%	A dominant	30+
Ostertag	Nephrotic syndrome	Obligatory	A dominant	
FAP-1	Lower limb neuropathy; autonomic failure	Rare	A dominant	
FAP-3 lowa	Lower limb neuropathy; peptic ulceration	Common	A dominant	
Finish FAP	Corneal lattices; cranial nerve	Rare	A dominant	<30 years in the rare homogzyous

the precursor protein as two individuals both with an identical rare arginine 26 substitution in apolipoprotein Al were found to have clinically distinct patterns, one neuropathic and the other non-neuropathic.

Diagnosis

The presence of amyloid in organ systems may be suspected from history and clinical examination. In general, every case of unexplained nephropathy, cardiomyopathy, peripheral polyneuropathy (especially carpal tunnel syndrome as well as an unexplained hepatosplenomegaly), macroglossia, malabsorption, and adenopathy should draw attention to the possibility of systemic or localized amyloidosis. Laboratory tests such as echocardiography which demonstrate restrictive cardiomyopathy or ultrasound of the abdomen, demonstrating organomegaly, should increase the degree of suspicion, but a definite diagnosis can only be made by biopsy. Patients who are part of a known or suspected familial amyloidotic kindred at presentation can undergo biopsy with staining of material specifically directed at amyloid. Most unsuspected renal amyloid deposits are initially seen as homogenous eosinophilic material in the mesangium or loops of the glomerulus or in a perivascular distribution. Once suspected, specific Congo red staining can be performed to establish the diagnosis. Congo red must be prepared in standard conditions, used within one month of preparation, and appropriate control slides stained simultaneously to ensure accurate repeatable staining. Pre-treatment of a deposit with potassium permanganate has been used as a means of identifying amyloid A deposits as potassium permanganate is known to prevent Congo red staining in this type of amyloid. However, the test is not reliable, particularly as unusual amyloids may show a similar feature. Specific antibodies to the precursor proteins are the best routine technique for elucidating the amyloid type correctly but sequence analysis of the fibril protein is the gold standard and the means of identifying new amyloid types.

The recently developed technique of l-123-labelled SAP imaging can show the extent of

Table 19.2 Hereditary amyloid syndromes

	Kindred origin	Precursor protein	Substitution
Nephropathic			
FMF	Sephardic Jews; Turks; Armenians	SAA (104 amino acids)	AA 75–76 amino acids
Muckle–Wells	English; French German	SAA	
Ostertag phenotype	English	Apolipoprotein AI	60 Arg/Leu
Ostertag phenotype	Scandivanian	Apolipoprotein A1	26 Arg/Gly
Ostertag phenotype	English	Lysozyme	56 lle/Thr
Ostertag phenotype	English	Lysozyme	67 Asp/His
Ostertag phenotype	Peruvian	Fibrinogen	554 Arg/Leu
Ostertag phenotype	Irish; American	Fibrinogen	526 Val/Glu
Ostertag phenotype	American	Fibrinogen	Deletion frame shift
Neuropathic			
Type 1–Lower limb	Portuguese; Swedish; Japanese; Jewish	TTR	30 Met/Val
Type 2–Upper limb	German; Swiss	TTR	84 Ser/Isoleu
Type 3	Scottish; lowa	Apolipoprotein Al	26 Arg/Gly
Type 4–Cranial + Corneal	Finnish	Gelsolin	187 Aspg/Asp
Cardiomyopathic			
	Danish; Appalachian	TTR	?Met 110
		TTR	60 Ala/Threo
Cerebral haemorrhagic			
	Icelandic; Dutch	Cystatin C	68 Glu/Leu
		β-protein	β PP 695
Cutaneous			
	Many	Unknown	

amyloid involvement in many organs and give a quantitative assessment of the total amyloid deposition (Hawkins *et al.* 1990). This may reveal clinically unsuspected amyloid deposits, e.g. in the adrenal glands or more particularly in organs such as the spleen which are not amenable to biopsy. The technique utilizes the biochemical finding that all known amyloid deposits bind SAP in a calcium-dependent manner, and is therefore not influenced by the precursor protein type. Serum and genetic markers for each variant protein are also valuable as diagnostic tools and are dealt with separately in each section below.

Familial Mediterranean fever

'Benign paroxysmal peritonitis' was the title of the first paper describing this condition (Siegal 1945). A variety of other manifestations have subsequently been described and the development of amyloid indicates a far from benign outlook. It is an important disease entity to recognize as therapy is effective and life-saving. The serous inflammatory episodes characterizing this condition, which include peritoneal, pleural, and synovial inflammatory attacks accompanied by a fever, are usually brief, lasting 12–72 hours, but severe enough to incapacitate the patient. Peritonitis is the presenting feature in 90% of cases, synovitis and pleurisy are less common, while orchitis has been reported in few patients (Sohar *et al.* 1967). Occasionally, (mainly in children) bouts of fever occur without localizing signs. Skin involvement with pyrexia tends to affect the lower limbs with an erysipelas-like rash. Not all the attacks are brief and synovial attacks in particular may be prolonged, lasting weeks or months in 10% of patients (Sneh *et al.* 1977). Recovery of the affected joint is usually good although hip involvement may sometimes result in considerable loss of function (Sneh *et al.* 1977). FMF has been divided into two phenotypes: type 1 where renal amyloid follows repeated attacks of febrile serositis and type 2 where the renal symptoms (e.g. nephrotic syndrome) are the presenting feature. Diagnosis of type 2 is made if the patient or a member of their family subsequently develop typical serositis attacks. Unlike most other forms of familial amyloidosis, FMF appears to be an autosomal recessive condition with the putative gene located on the short arm of chromosome 16 (Pras *et al.* 1992). There have been a few families reported where the inheritance appears to be autosomal dominant (Reiman *et al.* 1954; Yuval *et al.* 1995).

Further studies of chromosome 16 have located the FMF gene to a 1Mb interval between the tuberous sclerosis (TSC2) gene and the CREB-binding protein. This region has in turn been subjected to rigorous analysis by two groups using the full panoply of genetic techniques (International FMF consortium 1997, French FMF consortium 1997). The FMF gene appears to encode a product which has a ret-finger protein domain making it part of the RoRet gene family. The predicted protein has been termed pyrin (by the international group) to link it with fever and marenostrin (by the French FMF group) to link it with its Mediterranean origins. Northern blot analysis has shown it to be expressed in granulocytes where by analogy to its homology with rpt-1 it may be expected to be a nuclear factor that down regulates the inflammatory response. FMF patients appear to have one of four single nucleotide changes which are clustered together at the C terminal of the predicted protein probably in a globular domain affecting its secondary structure.

FMF has been reported most frequently in Sephardic Jews, Anatolian Turks, Armenians, and less commonly in Ashkenazi Jews and Arabs. There are FMF cases in Ireland and isolated cases of FMF or 'FMF-like' cases in scandinavia and in other groups of European descent. Some of them have an autosomal dominant inheritance (see ref. in Karenko *et al.* 1992). The frequency of amyloidosis also varies between the susceptible populations and seems to affect a greater percentage of Sephardic Jews and Anatolian Turks than any other group (Pras *et al.* 1984). Diagnosis of FMF primarily rests on the patient's personal and family history, examination during febrile attacks, and the response to colchicine therapy. The localization of the relevant gene to the short arm of chromosome 16 (Pras *et al.* 1992) has allowed the use of micro-satellite markers to be regarded as a useful test in most affected families (Levy *et al.* 1996), in particular it can allow the pre-clinical diagnosis of this condition. Recently, the differential production of tumour necrosis factor from the blood of asymptomatic FMF patients when stimulated by lipopolysaccharide was shown to have a sensitivity of 86% and specificity of 70% when applied to a test population (Schattner *et al.* 1996). However, the complexity of the test may mean it does not enjoy a vogue outside FMF centres. For nephrotic patients in whom FMF-induced amyloidosis is a possible diagnosis, bone-marrow biopsy has an 80% pick-up rate for amyloid deposition and may avoid a potentially more hazardous renal biopsy (Sungar *et al.* 1993).

Careful documentation has shown that the appearance of amyloid bears no relationship to the type, frequency, or severity of attacks and in those with the so-called type 2 phenotype it develops prior to the attacks (Heller 1961*a,b*). It seems likely therefore that the predisposition to the febrile episodes and the development of amyloidosis is co-inherited rather than the amyloidosis occurring as a direct consequence of the febrile episodes. The series of 470 patients studied by Sohar *et al.* (1967) and Pras *et al.* (1982) before the introduction of effective therapy demonstrated the high mortality in children and young adults with 90% of deaths occurring in patients under 40 years old, including six deaths under the age of 10 years.

The amyloid deposits in FMF are found in the glomeruli, spleen, adrenals, lungs, and blood vessels of many organs but with sparing of the hepatic sinusoids. The renal manifestations start with intermittent asymptomatic proteinuria and progress through nephrotic syndrome to uraemia. The time course of this progression can be from five to 20 years. The precursor protein is serum amyloid A protein (SAA) which is one of the classic acute-phase reactant proteins. During attacks the SAA levels rise sharply above the already elevated baseline level. The gene which encodes the SAA proteins is located on the short arm of chromosome 11. The FMF gene on chromosome 16 does not encode the AA protein but influences the SAA gene by an aberrant expression of the gene or is expressed by another mechanism to form AA protein.

The natural history of this disease has been dramatically influenced by the introduction of colchicine as a prophylactic treatment (Goldfinger 1972). The dose required for relief of symptoms varies between 1 and 2 mg/day, which induces full remission in 75% of patients and reduces frequency, duration, and severity of attacks in the other 20%. This dose does not appear to be related to the previous severity of the disease. Increasing the dose above 2 mg/day does not appear to improve the results in the 5% of 'non-responders', whilst most workers regard less than 1 mg/day as being inadequate. Dose reduction is not required for children; in fact, as they suffer more frequent severe attacks, a greater percentage of them require 2 mg/day for control of their disease (Pras *et al.* 1984).

Colchicine given during an attack is not effective in reducing the severity of that particular episode. However, it reduces the frequency of attacks which ensures good compliance at least in type 1 (Zemer *et al.* 1974), and reduces if not abolishes the predisposition to amyloidosis. Indeed, there are some patients in whom the frequency of attacks has not been reduced but amyloidosis appears to have been prevented (Zemer *et al.* 1986). The side-effects of colchicine, i.e. diarrhoea, nausea, and rash are generally transient and do not preclude the continued use of the drug. Myoneuropathy with intermittent or progressive proximal muscular weakness and depressed tendon reflexes together with a 10 to 20-fold increase in creatinine kinase has been reported in patients treated for gout, and responds to colchicine withdrawal (Kuncl *et al.* 1987). Allergic reactions to the drug have been successfully treated by desensitization (Cabili *et al.* 1982).

Long-term follow-up of 350 children treated with colchicine for six to 13 years has shown that none of them developed amyloidosis whilst on treatment (Zemer *et al.* 1991). Omission of colchicine in three patients for 18–24 months led to proteinuria and two of these children progressed to end-stage renal failure (ESRF). Of those patients with proteinuria, at the initiation of therapy, 9 of 17 had resolution of the proteinuria, four remained stable, and four progressed to ESRF. Livneh *et al.* (1994) have recently reexamined their experience with colchicine therapy in FMF patients with renal amyloidosis. Colchicine compared with no treatment had a favourable effect on renal disease. However, in approximately 45% of the patients, the renal condition deteriorated during follow-up, despite colchicine therapy. These authors conclude that the therapeutic dosage of colchicine for amyloidosis of FMF is >1.5 mg/day, and that this dosage is effective only in patients with initial serum creatinine levels <1.5 mg/dl (or 133 µmol/L) (Livneh *et al.* 1994). Colchicine seemed to have no effect on the outcome of 48 pregnancies in the 31 women who conceived whilst on the drug, although aminocentesis is still recommended.

However, renal function may be compromised during pregnancy in patients whose serum creatinine is equal to or above 1.5 mg/dl (or 133 μmol/L) and 24-hour urine protein excretion equals or exceeds 2 g (Livneh *et al.* 1993). For those patients in ESRF, transplantation is an effective mode of therapy and colchicine should be continued not only to prevent recurrence in the graft but to prevent or delay progression of amyloid elsewhere such as in the myocardium, small bowel, liver, and thyroid.

Muckle–Wells syndrome

This syndrome, otherwise known as familial nephropathic amyloidosis with febrile urticara and deafness, was first described by Muckle and Wells in 1962. They had had the opportunity of studying four affected siblings, two of whom had post-mortem-proven amyloid, a third who died of renal failure, and the fourth who had febrile urticaria and deafness but with normal renal function. The family study included 101 persons over five generations; nine affected cases were discovered amongst 18 at-risk individuals which was entirely consistent with an autosomal dominant inheritance pattern with incomplete penetrance.

The febrile urticarial rash occurred frequently in episodes lasting 12–36 hours which were known in the family as 'ague bouts'. Typically, these bouts started in adolescence and continued thereafter. The rash was described as large geographic papules, 1–7 cm in diameter, involving the skin of the trunk and limbs which was aching or irritating. It was accompanied by severe malaise, rigors, lassitude, headache, and pains in the limbs and joints. Perceptive deafness started in the affected individuals in childhood and was gradually progressive. The inner ear, organ of Corti, and vestibular sensory epithelium were absent, the cochlear nerve was atrophic and the basilar membrane calcified in two cases at post-mortem. However, no amyloid was found in the ears.

During the attacks there was slight pyrexia and an elevated white count on some occasions. The erythrocyte sedimentation rate was raised between episodes and a polyclonal hypergamma-globulinaemia also noted. Another clinical feature of note was loss of libido for some 10–15 years prior to presentation. No obvious cause was found for this at post-mortem.

Three of the index cases died of uraemia between the ages of 39 and 57 (although their mother had died at 76 from a cerebrovascular incident, having suffered typical attacks of the 'ague' and renal disease). At post-mortem the kidneys were shrunken and between a quarter and half the normal size and infiltrated with amyloid. This is in distinct contrast to the usual picture of amyloid infiltration where renal size is preserved. In one of the cases amyloid was also found in the liver and spleen whilst in one other without hepatosplenic involvement, the adrenals had heavy amyloid infiltration.

In a meta-analysis of 78 patients with ague bouts and rash (Muckle 1979), one-third of the patients had nephropathy which was proven to be due to amyloid in half these cases. Nephropathy was not seen in the absence of 'ague bouts'.

Muckle–Wells syndrome can occur sporadically without a family history and in one such case the amyloid was proven to be of AA type (Linke *et al.* 1983). It is not proven whether the amyloid is a consequence of the repeated inflammatory episodes or is co-inherited in a manner similar to FMF. Therapy of this group would logically be directed in a manner similar to FMF with colchicine therapy, and a beneficial effect has been reported in one case (Schwarz *et al.* 1990).

Hereditary nephropathic amyloid of Ostertag type

Ostertag (1932) was the first to describe a familial form of amyloidosis of any type. The patients he recorded presented with nephrotic syndrome accompanied by hypertension and hepatosplenomegaly. He studied five cases affecting three generations of the same family. Further kindreds with similar features from Poland, Ireland, England, and America have been described. Ostertag type of nephropathic amyloidosis comprises a heterogenous group of diseases in which a progressive renal disease transmitted by a dominant gene is common to all families, but the amyloid fibrils are composed of different proteins which characteristically are deposited mainly in the kidneys (Tables 19.1 and 19.2). Not all of them have had hepatosplenomegaly and some individuals have had a sicca syndrome from amyloidotic infiltration of secretory glands. In most of these cases there has not been the opportunity to type the amyloid in detail. In three English kindreds the protein fibrils have been typed; two had variants of lysozyme (Pepys *et al.* 1993) whilst the third family had an apolipoprotein Al variant (Soutar *et al.* 1992). The lysozyme variants were both caused by point mutations in exon 2; in the first family altering codon 56 from isoleucine to threonine and in the second altering codon 67 from asparginine to histidine. As yet these are the only two families with a proven lysozyme related-disease. In addition to the features described by Ostertag, the first of these two families (Zalin *et al.* 1991) had petechiae or purpura occurring with minimal skin trauma since childhood. In the third kindred, a family member had a splenectomy for thrombocytopenia and bruising. Amino acid sequencing of amyloid fibrils extracted from this tissue and subsequent plasma sample analyses showed that the family had a variant of apolipoprotein A1 (Apo A1) amyloid. Apolipoprotein A1, the major apolipoprotein of plasma HDL, is a 243 amino acid protein synthesized in the liver with a molecular weight of 28 kD. The variant carries an additional charge due to a single-base substitution CTG (leucine) to CGG (arginine) in the codon for residue 60. The propositus and other affected members of the family were heterozygous for this variant Apo A1. The amyloid deposits contained only variant protein.

Other apolipoprotein Al variants

There have been 10 variants of Apo A1 described (Schonfeld 1990), all of which are extremely rare. In a population study of 32 000 subjects, no variants were found (von Eckardstein *et al.* 1990). One such variant with a substitution of arginine for glycine at position 26 has been associated with amyloidosis. This was reported by two different groups (Nichols *et al.* 1988; Jones *et al.* 1991) in clinically different phenotypes. Although the substitution occurred at the same place in the precursor protein, it degraded on analysis into fragments of different sizes, 9 and 11 Kd respectively. Again, the amyloid deposits contained only variant protein.

In the case reported by Nichols *et al.* (1988), the patient had Iowa-type hereditary amyloidosis which is classified as a familial amyloidotic polyneuropathy (FAP) type 3. It was first described by van Allen *et al.* (1969) in settlers in Iowa with ancestors from England, Ireland, and Scotland. The salient features are lower-limb neuropathy, peptic ulceration, and renal failure. These features are generally noted in the third and fourth decades and average lifespan from onset of clinical symptoms is 12 years (range 0.5 to 26 years) with death occurring from renal failure unless dialysis is instituted. Autonomic symptoms occur in many patients.

The family with amyloidosis reported by Jones *et al.* (1991) and earlier by Libbey (1987) was of Scandinavian descent living in Massachusetts. The index case had hypertension and impaired renal function at the age of 25 and died aged 43 years of hepatic encephalopathy with a functioning renal transplant. The amyloid affected most organs but the renal involvement was notable for sparing the glomeruli whilst extensively involving the interstitium between the tubules. The mother of the index case died aged 58 years from renal failure and post-mortem examination revealed liver, splenic, and bone-marrow involvement as well as extensive renal amyloid. In this family there was no evidence of peripheral neuropathy or peptic ulceration.

Recently, three fibrinogen variants have been described, each producing a phenotype of Ostertag type although without hepatomegaly (Benson *et al.* 1993; Uemichi *et al.* 1994; 1996). All three of the variants had an altered Aα chain, two by a substitution and one by a deletion, giving a frame shift and premature termination of the protein. The latter kindred is the first description of genomic deletion leading to an amyloidogenic product.

Familial amyloid polyneuropathies (FAP)

Renal involvement in the familial amyloid polyneuropathies (Table 19.1) other than type III Iowa variety is usually incidental rather than a major feature of the disease. All FAP diseases are transmitted in an autosomal manner with high penetrance. Type I Portuguese FAP was first reported by Andrade in 1952. The paraesthesia/hyperaesthesia presents commonly between the ages of 25 and 35 years and progresses proximally from the lower limbs; autonomic involvement is common. Death occurs from cachexia, infection, and/or cardiac failure some 10 to 12 years after onset of symptoms. The protein in the amyloid deposits is transthyretin (TTR) with a methionine substituted for valine in position 30. Transthyretin, formerly termed 'prealbumin' because it migrates in front of albumin electrophorectically, is synthesized by the liver and to a lesser extent by the choroid plexus. Four identical monomers, each of 127 amino acids, form the circulating tetramer. It transports thyroxine and serves as a retinol-binding protein. The detection of variant transthyretin genes, including that for type 1 Portuguese FAP, is now possible by restriction enzyme analysis of PCR-amplified genomic DNA (Nichols and Benson 1990). Prenatal diagnosis by chorionic villous sampling, the use of PCR, and restriction enzyme analysis is also possible (Morris *et al.* 1991). A recent development in the treatment of this distressing condition is liver transplantation (Holmgren *et al.* 1993; Parrilla *et al.* 1995). In all cases the progress of the disease was halted with evidence of improvement in clinical state in patients surviving more than six months. There was also electromyographic evidence of improvement in those patients followed up for more than 12 months.

In familial polyneuropathies with TTR-derived amyloidosis, renal involvement is not exceptional. In the Mayo Clinic series, 16% of the patients had renal involvement (Gertz *et al.* 1992*a*). In the Portuguese-type amyloid polyneuropathy with the Met 30 mutation in the TTR gene, 40 of 83 patients developed renal abnormalities and eight progressed to ESRD.

Type II FAP

This entity has been described in two kindreds (Rukavina *et al.* 1956; Mahloudji *et al.* 1969) and is characterized by diffuse upper-limb neuropathy and carpal tunnel syndrome. Renal involvement has been noted at post-mortem but renal failure has not been observed. The mean age of onset is 43 years (range 15 to 66 years). Vitreous opacities were the presenting feature in the Indiana family of Swiss descent (Rukavina *et al.* 1956). In these diseases the amyloid proteins that compose the fibrils are also TTR variants (Benson and Wallace 1989).

Type IV FAP (Finnish type)

The precursor protein in this amyloid is gelsolin (Maury 1991) which is an actin-modulating protein that occurs in a cytoplasmic and secretory form. In the common heterozygous form of this disease the patients present in their twenties with corneal dystrophy and lattice formation and progress over the next 10–20 years with worsening cranial neuropathy and distal sensorimotor neuropathy. They live to old age with only intermittent proteinuria as a sign of renal involvement. The rare homozygous variety has a more severe course in which renal failure develops usually before the age of 30 (Meretoja 1973; Maury 1993). A point mutation of the gene on chromosome 9 is believed to be responsible for the abnormal gelsolin (Kwiatkowski *et al.* 1988). The diagnosis of this condition can be established by oligonucleotide hybridization of PCR-amplified DNA from peripheral blood (Maury *et al.* 1990).

Other familial amyloidoses

Cardiomyopathic hereditary amyloidosis is notable for its lack of renal involvement. Both of the described forms are transthyretin variants and can be diagnosed from restriction fragment length polymorphism analysis of genomic DNA.

The Icelandic (cystatin C) variant and Dutch (Beta protein) variant, in which amyloidosis affects cerebral and meningeal blood vessels, present with sudden severe cerebral haemorrhages at a young age; there is no extracranial amyloid. Skin-limited amyloidoses, some of which are familial, are common in certain parts of the world, particularly amongst Orientals and South Americans. Generally, these have not been extensively investigated as there is a limited amount of biopsy material for analysis.

Management

None of the amyloidotic conditions described exclusively affect the kidneys and therefore management must be directed at the multisystem nature of the disease. The identification of the amyloid type and hence the understanding of its genetic transmission allow informed genetic counselling as discussed in Chapter X.

Once renal impairment has become clinically manifest, there are very few instances in which progressive renal failure can be halted. However, colchicine therapy has sometimes been associated with resolution of proteinuria in FMF. Both Dimethyl sulphoxide (DMSO) and colchicine have enjoyed a vogue in the treatment of non-FMF systemic amyloidosis. However, their clinical benefits are not proven and DMSO is very unpleasant for the patient to take. Topical DMSO can be a successful treatment for cutaneous amyloid.

There were several reports in the late 1970s and early 1980s which pointed to the poor outcome of renal replacement therapy in patients with amyloidosis and ESRF. The overall survival of these patients is still not as good as in the majority of renal failure patients (Fassbinder *et al.* 1991; Gertz *et al.* 1992*b*; Moroni *et al.* 1992; Ylinen *et al.* 1992). In the reported series, most of the patients had AA or AL amyloid and the commonest cause of death was cardiac related, followed by infection and malnutrition. Gertz *et al.* (1992*b*) reported a mean survival on dialysis for patients with AL amyloidosis of 8.2 months with death occurring largely from extrarenal, particularly myocardial, involvement (50%). The outcome of replacement therapy in the 37 patients with AA amyloidosis reported by Ylinen *et al.* (1992) showed a survival on dialysis of 82%, 46%, and 37% at 1,2, and 3 years respectively. Twelve per cent received renal transplants with survival rates of 70%, 62%, and 62% at 1,2, and 3 years respectively. The commonest cause of death was infection (39%) whilst cardiac causes were less common (17%), reflecting the differing patterns of organ involvement between these types of amyloid. Experience of dialysis in AA amyloid in Northern Italy (Moroni *et al.* 1992) showed a high drop-out rate (~30%) in the first month of starting replacement therapy but subsequently survival similar to the above series; they found no difference in outcome between those treated with CAPD or haemodialysis. For patients with cardiac involvement, CAPD is the preferred modality of dialysis. However, for those with low albumin from proteinuria or malabsorption through gut involvement, the loss of protein in the peritoneal dialysate may be sufficient to render the patient extremely hypoproteinemic and thus susceptible to peripheral oedema and infective complications. The overall peritonitis rates for these patients are higher than for the general CAPD population.

It is important to assess the adrenal reserve regularly in these patients as progressive adrenal involvement may occur. If adrenal failure is unrecognized in the face of infection, the clinical outcome may be adversely affected, particularly if the hypotension is attributed to cardiac involvement.

Large series of familial amyloidosis patients with renal transplants have not been reported, but the experience with FMF-transplanted patients shows that they do not tolerate high-dose cyclosporin (10–14 mg/kg) because they tend to suffer with gastrointestinal side-effects and muscle weakness (Siegal *et al.* 1986; Cohen *et al.* 1989; Sobh *et al.* 1994). However, Jacob *et al.* (1982) has reported good results on 2–3 mg/kg/day with a low rate of renal allograft rejection. Also, cyclosporine in low dose as part of a triple immunosuppressive regime with colchicine appears to be well-tolerated (Vergoulas *et al.* 1992). Livneh *et al.* (1992) found that the recurrence of amyloidosis in the transplanted kidney of FMF patients was slower in patients who had received a regular dose of colchicine greater than 1 mg/day compared with those patients who had received a lower dose of colchicine.

The use of the synthetic octapeptide octreotide has been reported as controlling diarrhoea in patients with familial amyloidotic polyneuropathy (Carvalho *et al.* 1992). Another development in this condition is the specific removal of the amyloidogenic transthyretin from plasma by immunoadsorption (Regnault *et al.* 1992). It is difficult to imagine, however, that lifelong immunoadsorption could be performed to prevent the onset of this disease. We must therefore look to developments in gene therapy to treat these conditions in the future.

References

Andrade, C. (1952). A peculiar form of peripheral neuropathy. Familial atypical generalised amyloidosis with special involvement of peripheral nerves. *Brain*, 75, 408–28.

Benson, M. D. and Wallace, M. R. (1989). Genetic amyloidosis: recent advances. *Advances in Nephrology*, 18, 129–38.

Benson, M. D., Liepnieks, J., Uemichi, T., Wheeler, G., and Correa, R. (1993). Hereditary renal amyloidosis associated with a mutant fibrinogen alpha chain. *Nature Genetics*, 3(3), 252–3.

Cabili, S., Shemer, Y., Revach, M., and Pras, M. (1982). Allergic reactions and desensitization to colchicine in familial Mediterranean fever. *Rheumatologie*, 12, 207–8.

Carvalho, M., Alves, M., and Luis, M. L. S. (1992). Octreotide—a new treatment for diarrhoea in familial amyloidotic poyneuropathy. *Journal of Neurology, Neurosurgery, and Psychiatry*, 55(9), 860–1.

Cohen, L., Boner, G., Shmeli, D., Yusim, A., Rosenfeld, J., and Shapira, Z. (1989). Cyclosporin poorly tolerated in familial Mediterranean fever. *Nephrology, Dialysis, and Transplantation*, 4, 201–4.

Conners, L. H., Shirahama, T., Skinner, M., Fenves, A., and Cohen, A. S. (1985). *In vitro* formation of amyloid fibrils from intact β_2-microglobulin. *Biochemical and Biophysical Research Communications*, 131, 1063–8.

Eanes, E. D. and Glenner, G. G. (1968). X-ray diffraction studies of amyloid filaments. *Journal of Histochemistry and Cytochemistry*, 16, 673–7.

Fassbinder, W., Brunner, F. P., Brynger, H., *et al.* (1991). Combined report on regular dialysis and transplantation in Europe, XX, 1989. *Nephrology Dialysis and Transplantation*, 6 (Suppl. 1), 31–3.

French FMF Consortium (1997). A candidate gene for familial Mediterranean fever. *Nature Genetics*, **17**, 25–31.

Gertz, M. A., Garton, J. P., and Kyle, R. A. (1986). Primary amyloidosis (AL) in families. *American Journal of Hematology*, **22**, 193–8.

Gertz, M. A., Kyle, R. A., and Thibodeau, S. N. (1992*a*). Familial amyloidosis: a study of 52 North American-born patients examined during a 30-year period. *Mayo Clinic Proceedings*, **67**, 428–40.

Gertz, M. A., Kyle, R. A., and O'Fallon, W. M. (1992*b*). Dialysis support of patients with primary systemic amyloidosis. A study of 211 patients. *Archives of Internal Medicine*, **152**(11), 2245–50.

Goldfinger, S. E. (1972). Colchicine for familial Mediterranean fever. *New England Journal of Medicine*, **287**, 1032.

Grateau, G., Baudis, M., and Delpech, M. (1991). Study of restriction fragment length polymorphism for serum amyloid P component gene in rheumatoid arthritis with amyloidosis. *Journal of Rheumatology*, **18**(7), 994–6.

Harats, N., Kluve-Beckerman, B., Skinner, M., Passo, M., Quinn, L., and Benson. (1989). Lack of association of a restriction fragment length polymorphism for serum amyloid P gene with reactive amyloidosis. *Arthritis and Rheumatism*, **32**(10), 1325–7.

Hawkins, P. N., Wootton, R., and Pepys, M. B. (1990). Metabolic studies of radio-iodinated serum amyloid P component in normal subjects and patients with systemic amyloidosis. *Clinical Investigation*, **86**, 1862–9.

Hawkins, P. N., Tennent, G. A., Woo, P., and Pepys, M. B. (1991). Studies *in vivo* and *in vitro* serum amyloid P component in normals and in a patient with AA amyloidosis. *Clinical Experimental Immunology*, **84**, 308–16.

Heller, H., Sohar, E., Gafni, J., and Heller, J. (1961*a*). Amyloidosis in familial Mediterranean fever. *Archives of Internal Medicine*, **119**, 539–50.

Heller, H., Sohar, E., and Pras, M. (1961*b*). Ethnic distribution and amyloidosis in familial Mediterranean fever. *Archives of Internal Medicine*, **107**, 539.

Holmgren, G., Ericzon, E. G., Groth, C. G., Steen, L., Suhr, O., Andersen, O., *et al.* (1993). Clinical improvement and amyloid regression after liver transplantation in hereditary transthyretin amyloidosis. *Lancet*, **341**, 1113–16.

International FMF Consortium (1997). Ancient missense mutations in a new member of the *RoRet* gene family are likely to cause familial Mediterranean fever. *Cell*, **90**, 797–807.

Jacob, E. T., Siegal, B., Bar-Nathan, N., and Gafni, J. (1982). Improving outlook for renal transplantation in amyloid nephropathy. *Transplant Proceedings*, **14**(1), 41.

Jones, L. A., Harding, J. A., Cohen, A. S., and Skinner, M. (1991). New USA family has apolipoprotein A1 (Arg26) variant. In *Amyloid and anyloidosis 1990* (ed. J. B. Natvig, O. Forre, G. Husby, A. Husebekk, B. Skogen, K. Slettern, *et al.*), pp. 385–8. Kluwer, Dordrecht, The Netherlands.

Karenko, L., Pettersson, T., and Roberts, P. (1992). Autosomal dominant 'Mediterranean fever' in a Finnish family. *Journal of Internal Medicine*, **232**, 365–9.

Kékulé, A. and Schmidt, M. B. (1858). In: *Cellular pathology* (ed. R. Virchow and Robert M. DaWitt), New York.

Kuncl, R. W., Duncan, G., Watson, D., Alderson, K., Rogawski, M. A., and Peper, M. (1987). Colchicine myopathy and neuropathy. *New England Journal of Medicine*, **316**(25), 1562–8.

Kwiatkowski, D. J., Mehl, R., and Yin, H. L. (1988). Genomic organization and biosynthesis of secreted and cytoplasmic forms of gelsolin. *Journal of Cell Biology*, **106**, 375.

Lanham, J. G., Meltzer, M. L., de Beer, F. C., Hughes, G. R. V., and Pepys, M. B. (1982). Familial amyloidosis of Ostertag. *Quarterly Journal of Medicine*, **201**, 25–32.

Levy, E. N., Shen, Y., Kupelian, A., Kruglyak, L., Aksentijevich, I., Pras, E., *et al.* (1996). Linkage disequilibrium mapping places the gene causing familial Mediterranean fever close to D16S246. *American Journal of Human Genetics*, **58**, 523–34.

Libbey, C. A. (1987). Case 50–1987 weekly clinicopathological exercises. *New England Journal of Medicine*, **317**(24), 1520–31.

Linke, R. P., Heilmann, K. L., Nathrath, W. B. J., and Eulitz, M. (1983). Identification of amyloid A protein in a sporadic Muckle—Wells syndrome. *Laboratory Investigation*, **48**(6), 698–704.

Livneh, A., Zemer, D., Siegal, B., Laor, A., Sohar, E., and Pras, M. (1992). Colchicine prevents kidney transplant amyloidosis in familial Mediterranean fever. *Nephron*, **60**, 418–22.

Livneh, A., Cabili, S., Zemer, D., Rabinovitch, O., and Pras, M. (1993). Effect of pregnanay on renal function in amyloidosis of familial Mediterranean fever. *Journal of Rheumatology*, **20**, 1519–23.

Livneh, A., Zemer, D., Langevitz, P., Laor, A., Sohar, E., and Pras, M. (1994). Colchicine treatment of AA amyloidosis of familial mediterranean fever. *Arthritis and Rheumatism*, **17**, 1804–11.

Mahloudji, M., Teasdall, R. D., Adamkiewicz, J. J., Hartmann, W. H., Lambird, P. A., and McKusick, V. A. (1969). The genetic amyloidosis. *Medicine*, **48**(1), 1–37.

Maury, C. P. J. (1991). Gelsolin-related amyloidosis. *Journal of Clinical Investigation*, **87**, 1195–9.

Maury, C. P. J. (1993). Homozygous familial amyloidosis, Finish type: demonstration of glomerular gelsolin-derived amyloid and non-amyloid tubular gelsolin. *Clinical Nephrology*, **40**(1), 53–6.

Maury, C. P. J., Kere, J., Tolvanen, R., and de la Chapelle, A. (1990). Finnish hereditary amyloidosis is caused by a single nucleotide substitution in the gelsolin gene. *FEBS*, **276**(1), 75–7.

Meretoja, J. (1973). Genetic aspects of familial amyloidosis with corneal lattice dystrophy and cranial neuropathy. *Clinical Genetics*, **4**, 173–85.

Moroni, G., Banfi, G., Montoli, A., Bucci, A., Bertani, T., Ravelli, M., *et al.* (1992). Chronic dialysis in patients with systemic amyloidosis: the experience in Northern Italy. *Clinical Nephrology*, **38**(2), 81–5.

Morris, M., Nichols, W., and Benson, M. (1991). Prenatal diagnosis of hereditary amyloidosis in a Portuguese family. *American Journal of Medical Genetics*, **39**(1), 123–4.

Muckle, T. J. (1979). The 'Muckle—Wells' syndrome. *British Journal of Dermatology*, **100**, 87–92.

Muckle, T. J. and Wells, M. (1962). Urticaria, deafness, and amyloidoses: a new heredo-familial syndrome. *Quarterly Journal of Medicine*, **31**(122), 235–48.

Nelson, S. R., Tennent, G. A., Sethi, D., Gower, P. E., Ballardie, F. W., Amatayakul-Chantler, S., *et al.* (1991*a*). Serum amyloid P component in chronic renal failure and dialysis. *Clinica Chimica. Acta*, **200**, 191–200.

Nelson, S. R., Lyon, M., Gallagher, J. T., Johnson, E. A., and Pepys, M. B. (1991*b*). Isolation and characterization of the integral glycosaminoglycan constituents of human amyloid A and monoclonal light-chain amyloid fibrils. *Biochemical Journal*, **275**, 67–73.

Nichols, W. C., Dwulet, F. E., Liepnieks, J., and Benson, M. D. (1988). Variant apolipoprotein A1 as a major constituent of a human hereditary amyloid. *Biochemical and Biophysical Research Communications*, **156**(2), 762–8.

Nichols, W. C. and Benson, M. D. (1990). Hereditary amyloidosis: detection of variant prealbumin genes by restriction enzyme analysis of amplified genomic DNA sequences. *Clinical Genetics*, **37**, 44–53.

Ostertag, B. (1932). Demonstration einer eigenartigen familiaren 'Paramyloidose'. *Zentralb. Allg. Pathol.*, **32**, 253–4.

Parrilla, P., Ramirez, P., Bueno, F. S., Robles, R., Acosta, F., Miras, M., *et al.* (1995). Clinical improvement after liver transplantation for type 1 familial amyloid polyneuropathy. *British Journal of Surgery*, **82**, 825–8.

Pepys, M. B., Dash, A. C., Markham, R. E., Thomas, H. C., Williams, B. D., and Petrie, A. (1978). Comparative clinical study of protein SAP (amyloid P component) and C-reactive protein in serum. *Clinical Experimental Immunology*, **32**, 119–24.

Pepys, M. B., Baltz, M. L., de Beer, F. C., Dyck, R. F., Holford, S., Breathnach, S. M., *et al.* (1982). Biology of serum amyloid P component. *Annals of New York Academy of Science*, **389**, 286–98.

Pepys, M. B., Hawkins, P. N., Booth, D. R., Vigushin, D. M., Tennent, G. A., Soutar, A. K., *et al.* (1993). Human lysozyme gene mutations cause hereditary systemic amyloidosis. *Nature*, **362**, 553–7.

Pepys, M. B., Rademacher, T. W., Amatayakul-Chanteler, S., Williams, P., Noble, G. E., Hutchinson, W. L., *et al.* (1994). Human serum amyloid P component is an invariant constituent of amyloid deposits and has a uniquely homogeneous glycostructure. *Proceedings of the National Academy of Science*, 91, 5602–6.

Pras, M., Bronshpigel, N., Zemer, D., and Gafni, J. (1982). Variable incidence of amyloidosis in familial Mediterranean fever amongst different ethnic groups. *Johns Hopkins Medical Journal*, 150, 22–6.

Pras, M., Gafni, J., Jacob, E. T., Cabili, S., Zemer, D., and Sohar, E. (1984). Recent advances in familial Mediterranean fever. *Advances in Nephrology*, 13, 261–70.

Pras, E., Aksentijevich, I., Gruberg, L., Balow, J. E., Prosen, L., Dean, M., *et al.* (1992). Mapping of a gene causing familial Mediterranean fever to the short arm of chromosome 16. *New England Journal of Medicine*, 326(23), 1509–13.

Puchtler, H., Sweat, F., and Levine, M. (1962). On the binding of Congo red by amyloid. *Journal of Histochemistry and Cytochemistry*, 10, 355–64.

Regnault, V., Costa, P. M., Teixeira, A., Rivat, C., Stolz, J. F., Saraiva, M. J., *et al.* (1992). Specific removal of transthyretin from plasma of patients with familial amyloidotic polyneuropathy: optimization of an immunoadsorption procedure. *International Journal of Artificial Organs*, 15, 249–55.

Reimann, H. A., Moadie, J., Semerdjian, S., and Sahyoun, P. F. (1954). Periodic peritonitis—heredity and pathology. *Journal of the American Medical Association*, 154, 1254–9.

Rokitansky, C. (1842). In: *Handbuch der pathologischen anatomie*, vol. 3. Braumuller & Seidel, Vienna.

Rukavina, J. G., Block, W. D., Jackson, C. E., Falls, H. F., Carey, J. H., and Curtis, A. C. (1956). Primary systemic amyloidosis: Review and an experimental, genetic and clinical study of 29 cases with particular emphasis on the familial form. *Medicine*, 35, 239–334.

Schattner, A., Gurevitz, A., Zemer, D., and Hahn, T. (1996). Induced TNF production *in vitro* as a test for familial Mediterranean fever. *Quarterly Journal of Medicine*, 89, 205–10.

Schonfeld, G. (1990). The genetic dyslipoproteinemias—nosology update 1990. *Athero*, 81, 81–93.

Schwarz, R. E., Dralle, H., Linke, R. P., Nathrath, W. B. J., and Neuman, K. H. (1990). Amyloid goiter and arthritides after kidney transplantation in a patient with systemic amyloidosis and Muckle–Wells syndrome. *American Journal of Clinical Pathology*, 92(6), 821–5.

Siegal, B., Zemer, D., and Pras, M. (1986). Cyclosporine and familial Mediterranean fever amyloidosis. *Transplantation*, 41, 793–4.

Siegal, S. (1945). Benign paroxysmal peritonitis. *Annal of Internal Medicine*, 23, 1.

Sneh, E., Pras, M., Michaeli, D., Shahin, N., and Gafni. (1977). Protracted arthritis in familial Mediterranean fever. *Rheumatology Rehabilition*, 16, 102–6.

Sobh, M., Refaie, A., Moustafa, F., Shokeir, N., Sally, S., and Ghoneim, M. (1994). Study of live donor kidney transplantation outcome in recipients with renal amyloidosis. *Nephrology Dialysis and Transplantation*, 6, 704–8.

Sohar, E., Gafni, J., Pras, M., and Heller, H. (1967). Familial Mediterranean fever: a survey of 470 cases and review of the literature. *American Journal of Medicine*, 43, 227–53.

Soutar, A. K., Hawkins, P. N., Vigushin, D. M., Tennent, G. A., Booth, S. E., Hutton, T., *et al.* (1992). Apolipoprotein A1 mutation Arg-60 causes autosomal dominant amyloidosis. *Procedings of the National Academy of Science*, 89, 7389–93.

Sungar, C., Sungur, A., Ruacan, S., Arik, N., Yasavul, U., Turgan, C., *et al.* (1993). Diagnostic value of bone-marrow biopsy in patients with renal disease secondary to familial Mediterranean fever. *Kidney International*, 44, 834–6.

Uemichi, T., Liepnieks, J. J., and Benson, M. D. (1994). Hereditary renal amyloidosis with a novel variant fibrinogen. *Journal of Clinical Investigation*, 93, 731–6.

Uemichi, T., Liepnieks, J. J., Yamada, T., Gertz, M. A., Bang, N., and Benson, M. D. (1996). A frame shift mutation in the fibrinogen Aα chain gene in a kindred with renal amyloidosis. *Blood*, 87, 4197–203.

van Allen, M. W., Frohlich, J. A., and Davis, J. R. (1969). Inherited predisposition to generalized amyloidosis. Clinical and pathological study of family with neuropathy, nephropathy and peptic ulcer. *Neurology*, **19**, 10–25.

Vergoulas, G., Papagiannis, A., Takoudas, D., Papanikolaou, V., Gakis, D., and Antoniadis, A. (1992). Renal transplantation and pregnancy in a patient with familial Mediterrranean fever amyloidosis taking triple drug immunosuppression and colchicine. *Nephrology, Dialysis and Transplantation*, **7**(3), 273–4.

Virchow, R. (1854). *Archives of Pathology, Anatomy, and Physiology*, **6**, 135.

von Eckardstein, A., Funke, H., Walter, M., Altland, K., Benninghoven, A., and Assmann, G. (1990). Structural analysis of human apolipoprotein A-1 variants. *Journal of Biological Chemistry*, **265**, 8610–17.

Woo, P., O'Brien, J., Robson, M., and Ansell, B. M. (1987). A genetic marker for systemic amyloidosis in juvenile arthritis. *Lancet*, **2**, 767–9.

Ylinen, K., Gronhagen-Riska, C., Honkanen, E., Ekstrand, A., Metsarinne, K., and Kuhlback, B. (1992). Outcome of patients with secondary amyloidosis in dialysis treatment. *Nephrology Dialysis and Transplantation*, **7**, 980.

Yuval, Y., Hemo-Zisser, M., Zemer, D., Sohar, D., and Pras, M. (1995). Dominant inheritance in two families with familial Mediterranean fever (FMF). *American Journal of Medical Genetics*, **57**, 455–7.

Zalin, A. M., Jones, S., Fitch, N. J. S., and Ramsden, D. B. (1991). Familial nephropathic and non-neuropathic amyloidosis: clinical features, immunohistochemistry, and chemistry. *Quarterly Journal of Medicine*, **81**(295), 945–56.

Zemer, D., Revach, M., Pras, M., Modan, B., Schor, S., Sohar, E., *et al.* (1974). A controlled trial of colchicine in preventing attacks of familial Mediterranean fever. *New England Journal of Medicine*, **291**, 932–4.

Zemer, D., Pras, M., Sohar, E., Modan, M., Cabili, S., and Gafni, J. (1986). Colchicine in the prevention and treatment of the amyloidosis of familial Mediterranean fever. *New England Journal of Medicine*, **314**, 1001–5.

Zemer, D., Livneh, A., Danon, Y. I., Pras, M., and Sohar, E. (1991). Long-term colchicine treatment in children with familial Mediterranean fever. *Arthritis and Rheumatism*, **43**(8), 973–7.

20

Genetic aspects of diabetic nephropathy

R.W. Bilous, S.M. Mauer, and G.C. Viberti

Introduction

Both insulin and non-insulin dependent diabetes mellitus (IDDM and NIDDM) are recognized as having a large genetic component in their pathogenesis. Identical twin studies (Barnett *et al.* 1981) and later HLA analysis in IDDM patients provided early evidence (Cudworth and Festenstein 1984). More detailed genetic analysis has demonstrated specific abnormalities in some NIDDM patients (Leahy and Boyd 1993).

Because diabetic nephropathy is known to affect a minority (albeit sizeable) of IDDM and NIDDM patients (approximately 25% cumulative incidence after 25 years duration in both types of diabetes) (Ballard *et al.* 1988; Hasslacher *et al.* 1989), there has been a considerable interest in trying to identify genetic factors in the individual predisposition to renal complications. Several studies have demonstrated a still unexplained excess prevalence of nephropathy in male diabetic patients (Andersen *et al.* 1983; Krolewski *et al.* 1985) but failed to find any significant or consistent association between HLA antigens and microvascular complications (Barbosa and Saner 1984). The demonstration that the vast majority of the >80-fold excess early mortality in IDDM patients was linked to the presence of proteinuria (Borch-Johnsen *et al.* 1985) has stimulated research into ways of identifying those patients most at risk of developing nephropathy.

This review will concentrate on those lines of research with a proven or likely genetic basis. Other potential pathophysiological mechanisms are outside the scope of this article.

Definitions and natural history of nephropathy

Diabetic nephropathy was first defined in 1951 as the presence of persistent proteinuria, detected by qualitative methods, in diabetic patients with no identifiable other renal disease (Wilson *et al.* 1951). The vast majority of these patients will have retinopathy, many will be hypertensive, and advanced cases will have a reduced glomerular filtration rate (GFR), but all of these clinical features are optional extras for the diagnosis. The peak incidence in IDDM patients is after 15–20 years duration (Kofoed-Enevoldsen *et al.* 1987) and progression to end-stage renal failure (ESRF) has been reported as more rapid in patients with diabetes diagnosed after puberty (Krolewski *et al.* 1985). In both IDDM and NIDDM patients there is an association with prolonged poor glycaemic control (Pirart 1978).

Diabetic patients who are progressing to overt renal disease excrete small quantities of albumin in their urine that are not detectable by routine dipstick tests, but are still above the levels found in normal non-diabetic subjects. This phenomenon has been termed 'microalbuminuria', has been defined as a urinary albumin excretion rate (UAER) of 30–300 mg/day (Walker and Viberti 1991), and represents early or incipient nephropathy. Patients with UAER <20 mg/day are termed 'normoalbuminuric' and those with UAER >300 mg/day as 'clinically proteinuric' or 'overtly nephropathic' or 'macroalbuminuric'. GFR may be high (so-called hyperfiltration) in all phases of nephropathy but declines at an average rate of 10 ml/min/year in the untreated, clinically proteinuric patient (Viberti *et al.* 1983). Blood pressure tends to rise steadily as nephropathy progresses (Microalbuminuria Collaborative Study Group 1993). Glomerular pathology (glomerulopathy) is more severe with advanced nephropathy and is correlated with the observed changes in GFR and levels of albuminuria (Mauer *et al.* 1984; Ellis *et al.* 1986*a*; Walker *et al.* 1992).

The excess mortality observed in proteinuric diabetic patients is due to renal failure and cardiovascular disease, particularly in NIDDM patients (Borch-Johnsen *et al.* 1985; Nelson *et al.* 1988).

Familial clustering of diabetic nephropathy

In the last few years, evidence favouring a strong familial predisposition to the development of kidney disease associated with diabetes has been mounting. Seaquist *et al.* (1989) examined nephropathy risk in IDDM multiplex families with a proband (the first of the siblings to develop diabetes) having a duration of diabetes of at least 10 years, and the sibling a duration of at least seven years. The probands with diabetic nephropathy consisted of 26 renal transplant recipients that had siblings with diabetes. Eleven probands free from diabetic nephropathy that had diabetic siblings were recruited from 400 multiplex families. The mean duration of diabetes among the probands exceeded 20 years in both groups. Two of the 12 diabetic siblings of probands free from diabetic nephropathy (17%) had urinary albumin excretion rates above 45 mg/24 hours. In contrast, 12 of the 29 siblings of probands with end-stage renal disease (ESRD) also had ESRD (41%) while 12 had UAER above 45 mg/24 hours and only 17% were normoalbuminuric. Thus the overall incidence of renal disease was 82% amongst this group of siblings (Fig. 20.1).

The work by Borch-Johnsen *et al.* (1992) largely confirmed these findings. They studied 24 probands with clinical nephropathy defined as UAER >300 mg/day and 34 normoalbuminuric probands with UAER <20 mg/day. There was a higher prevalence of overt nephropathy in siblings of probands with nephropathy (33%) than siblings of normoalbuminuric probands (10%; $p < 0.04$). In all, 43% of the siblings of probands with nephropathy had UAER >100 mg/ 24 hours as compared to 13% of siblings with normoalbuminuric probands (odds ratio 4.9, 95% confidence intervals (CI) 1.2–5.1) (Fig. 20.1). Although the odds ratio in this study was somewhat lower than that of Seaquist *et al.* (1989) (24.0; 95% CI 4.0–145), the two groups of probands were more clearly differentiated in the Seaquist study where the group with nephropathy was defined as having ESRD whereas in the study of Borch-Johnsen *et al.* (1992) overt proteinuria (UAER >300 mg/day) was the definition for the nephropathy group. Both of these studies were unable to separate genetic susceptibility from similarities due to shared environment. In the latter study, glycated haemoglobin (HbAlc) was loosely but significantly correlated in the probands and siblings ($r = 0.47$, $p = 0.001$). However, environmental and genetic factors potentially governing glycaemic control cannot be excluded.

In order to overcome this problem, a larger study of the cumulative incidence of nephropathy (defined as persistent dipstick positive proteinuria >300 mg/L) in 125 siblings of 110 probands has recently been reported (Quinn *et al.* 1996). By following patients from diagnosis of diabetes, the authors were able to calculate an incidence rate ratio which goes some way towards separating genetic and environmental influences. Both probands and siblings had a mean duration of diabetes >21 years and cumulative incidence of nephropathy for the group as a whole was 35%

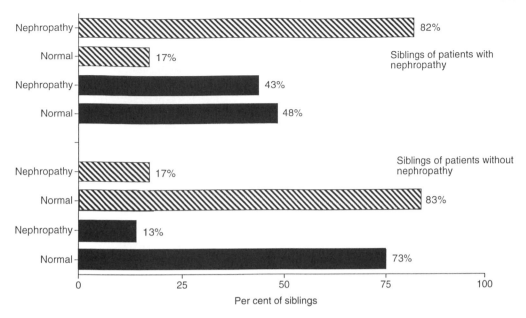

Fig. 20.1 Categorization of siblings of diabetic patients with (upper panel) and without (lower panel) diabetic nephropathy. (Adapted from Seaquist *et al.* (1989) hatched bars; and Borch-Johnsen *et al.* (1992) solid bars; with permission.) Nephropathy is defined as UAER >45 mg/day plus end-stage by Seaquist *et al.*; and as UAER >100 mg/day by Borch-Johnsen *et al.* Normal is defined as UAER <45 mg/day and <35 mg/day respectively.

after 30 years duration, similar to other reported series (Andersen *et al.* 1983; Krolewski *et al.* 1985; Hasslacher *et al.* 1989). The cumulative risk was much greater, however, for siblings of probands with nephropathy (71.5%) compared to those of probands with normal UAER or microalbuminuria (25.4%; p < 0.001). These data convert to an odds ratio of 2.6 (95% CI 1.2–5.5) if the definitions of nephropathy used by Borch-Johnsen *et al.* (1992) are used, which is not statistically different (p = 0.42) (Quinn *et al.* 1996). The authors also speculate that the large difference in cumulative risk (46.1%) is close to the 50% that would be expected if an autosomal dominant inheritance was operating.

These studies of familial predisposition to renal disease in IDDM patients are supported by observations in two generations of Pima Indians with NIDDM (Pettit *et al.* 1990). In these studies, after adjustment for age, systolic blood pressure, diabetes duration, and glucose concentration (all risk factors for nephropathy in this patient population), proteinuria occurred amongst 14% of their offspring if neither parent had proteinuria, 23% if at least one parent had proteinuria, and 46% if both parents had diabetes and proteinuria. However, failure to use a hard endpoint such as ESRD may have introduced a bias that would tend to underestimate the extent of familial aggregation of renal disease.

Ethnic studies

Diabetic patients of Asian ethnic origin in the United Kingdom have a greater prevalence of microalbuminuria and clinical nephropathy than age-, sex-, and diabetes-duration-matched

Europid subjects, and age- and sex-matched non-diabetic Asian controls (Allawi *et al.* 1988). This increase is reflected in the greater incidence of ESRF in Asian patients observed in Leicester (Burden *et al.* 1992). These authors performed a retrospective review of all patients enrolling onto renal replacement therapy programmes in the county from 1979–1988. They found that the incidence of diabetic nephropathy in the general population was 2.3 and 23.3 cases per million person-years per year for Europid and Asian subjects respectively. Interestingly, the relative risk for all causes of ESRF excluding diabetes is significantly higher in Asian subjects at 3.66.

African Americans with IDDM and NIDDM have a substantially increased risk for the development of diabetic nephropathy compared to whites (Cowie *et al.* 1989), although this risk appears greater in NIDDM patients. The findings amongst black NIDDM patients may be explained by their increased risk of hypertension and by the summation of two renal diseases, hypertensive and diabetic nephropathy. The increased risk of diabetic nephropathy amongst Israeli Jews of non-Ashkenazi origin more likely represents true predisposition to the development of diabetic renal disease based on ethnicity (Kalter-Leibovici *et al.* 1991). In this study, both prospectively followed glycaemic control and lower socio-economic status were significantly and independently correlated to albuminuria. The odds ratio for nephropathy risk increased as the quartile of glycaemic control worsened. However, even after adjusting for these variables, non-Ashkenazi origin still had an odds ratio of 2.0 for increased risk of all proteinuria, and 3.8 for overt nephropathy. Other ethnic groups illustrating an increased incidence of nephropathy and renal failure due to diabetes are the Pima Indians in Arizona (Nelson *et al.* 1988), the Nauruan Pacific Islanders (Collins *et al.* 1989), Mexican Americans (Pugh *et al.* 1988), and Maoris and Pacific Islanders living in New Zealand (Simmons 1996). Many of the ethnic groups described in the above studies have an increased prevalence of NIDDM *per se* which has been related to dietary and other lifestyle changes associated with immigration. Many have a lower socio-economic status (although this cannot be said for the Nauruans), and consequent problems of access to health care. Thus any inherited ethnic predisposition to nephropathy is difficult to dissociate from socio-economic and environmental conditions which may exacerbate other known risk factors for diabetes complications such as blood glucose control.

Hypertension and diabetic nephropathy

Diabetic patients who develop nephropathy will also develop arterial hypertension in most cases. Antihypertensive therapy has been shown to retard the rate of progression to ESRF in insulin-dependent diabetic patients with proteinuria (Parving *et al.* 1987). The effect of intensively treated hypertension in advanced nephropathy has been further underscored by the results of patient survival studies (Mathiesen 1989; Parving and Hommel 1989). Effective treatment of hypertension in cohorts of proteinuric IDDM patients was found to reduce cumulative mortality from rates ranging between 42% and 70% in cohorts not receiving antihypertensive therapy to rates between 13% and 18% during observation periods of eight and 10 years respectively.

An increase in systemic blood pressure in IDDM patients with microalbuminuria and incipient nephropathy has been reported by several groups (Mathiesen *et al.* 1984; Wiseman *et al.* 1984), and prospective studies in microalbuminuric IDDM patients have shown that the changes in UAER are related to changes in arterial pressure (Feldt-Rasmussen *et al.* 1986). These associations between blood pressure and albumin excretion rate have been shown to be independent of blood glucose control, and as renal function is generally well-preserved in microalbuminuric patients, it is less likely that the increase in blood pressure is a consequence of advanced renal functional impairment, even though microalbuminuric IDDM patients show more severe glomerulopathy than age- and diabetes-duration-matched normoallbuminuric patients (Walker *et al.* 1992). How these morphological changes are linked to the development of albuminuria and the increase in blood pressure remains to be elucidated, but may well be the result of adaptive responses to a decreasing filtration surface area secondary to an expanding mesangium. Studies in microalbuminuric patients alone are unlikely to resolve whether it is an increase in blood pressure consequent to glomerulopathy or an inherited predisposition to hypertension that makes the greater contribution to the development of diabetic nephropathy.

The reports of two longitudinal studies may shed light on the factors that influence the transition from normo to microalbuminuria in IDDM patients. In a study by Mathiesen *et al.* (1990), 209 normoalbuminuric, normotensive, IDDM patients were monitored for 60 months. Of the 205 patients who completed this study, seven progressed to persistent microalbuminuria. Initial blood pressure was similar but the albumin excretion rate was significantly greater and glycated haemoglobin was higher in the group of progressors. Significant increases in blood pressure were recorded in this group only after microalbuminuria had been present for approximately two years. These findings suggest that blood glucose control and the initial level of albumin excretion rate are the main determinants of microalbuminuria, and that microalbuminuria precedes the increase in blood pressure. However, this study has to be interpreted with caution as blood pressure was only measured yearly, to the nearest 5 mmHg, by different observers. The variation in these measurements was significantly greater than that of the UAER, which was measured four times a year by sensitive immunoassay, and this lack of precision could have misssed important changes of between 4 and 5 mmHg blood pressure.

In a prospective study by the Microalbuminuria Collaborative Study Group (1993), the development of persistent microalbuminuria was studied in 137 normoalbuminuric, normotensive IDDM patients over a four-year period. Twice-yearly measurements of blood pressure to the nearest 2 mmHg using a random zero sphygmomanometer, UAER, and HbAlc were recorded. Eleven patients progressed to persistent microalbuminuria and these subjects showed at baseline a significantly higher mean blood pressure (101 ± 2.4 versus 90 ± 0.9 mmHg; $p < 0.05$), UAER (14.8 [95% CI, 12.4–17.2] versus 4.3 [2.1–6.4] µg/min; $p < 0.05$), and glycated haemoglobin (10.4 ± 0.6 versus $8.9 \pm 0.2\%$; $p < 0.05$) than those patients whose UAER remained within the normal range (Fig. 20.2). A multiple logistic regression analysis of these data indicated that baseline UAER and blood pressure were significant determinants of microalbuminuria. Thus increases in blood pressure are taking place while albumin excretion is increasing within the normal range in the group of progressors. This finding has been confirmed by more recent data reported by Mathiesen *et al.* in their original cohort of patients, but with follow-up extended to 10 years (Mathiesen *et al.* 1995).

Although further studies in IDDM patients with a shorter duration of disease will be required to understand the chronological relationship between the early increases in UAER and blood pressure, some insight into this process comes from a study in Pima Indians developing NIDDM and proteinuria (Nelson *et al.* 1993). Systematic measurements of blood pressure were obtained in 356 Pima Indians before they developed diabetes and these were related to the onset of proteinuria, estimated by albumin : creatinine ratio, after the onset of diabetes. It was found that the incidence of proteinuria was three times greater in patients in the uppermost tertile of pre-diabetic blood pressure than in those patients in the lowermost tertile. Further, similar evidence has recently been reported in a five-year prospective study of NIDDM patients of Japanese origin

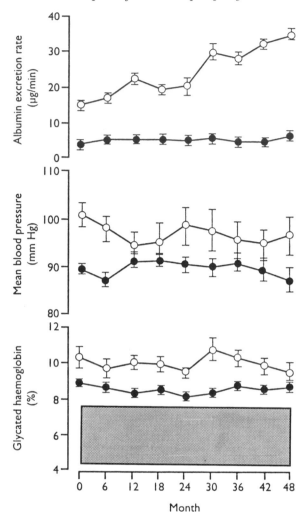

Fig. 20.2 Albumin excretion rate, mean blood pressure, and glycated haemoglobin levels in IDDM patients who progressed to persistent microalbuminuria (open circles; n = 11), and who remained normoalbuminuric (closed circles; n = 103) over a four-year follow-up. The shaded area represents the normal range for glycated haemoglobin. Data as geometric mean (×/÷ tolerance factor) for UAER and mean (± SD) for mean blood pressure and glycated haemoglobin. Reproduced from Microalbuminuria Collaborative Study Group (1993) with permission.

with normoalbuminuria (Haneda *et al.* 1992). The 32% of patients who developed microalbuminuria during the observation period were found to have higher arterial pressures at the start of normoalbuminuria and to increase their blood presure in parallel with the increase in UAER. These studies suggest that the pre-microalbuminuric evolutionary stages of diabetic nephropathy are associated with an elevation of the systemic arterial pressure in diabetic patients. This hypothesis is supported by evidence of a link between an inherited predisposition to hypertension and the risk of development of diabetic nephropathy in IDDM patients.

Family studies of blood pressure

Higher values of arterial pressure were measured in parents of IDDM patients with proteinuria and reported by Viberti *et al.* (1987). In a subsequent study in which information was collected by means of a questionnaire, Krolewski *et al.* (1988) found a significantly higher prevalence of arterial hypertension among the parents of IDDM patients with microalbuminuria and clinical nephropathy. More recently in a case–control study, Barzilay *et al.* (1992) showed that diabetic patients with advanced nephropathy not only had a greater prevalence of parental hypertension but also higher mean arterial blood pressures during adolescence (Table 20.1). Follow-up data in that study show that the relative risk of developing overt nephropathy was 3.3 if one or more parents were hypertensive. Together therefore, these studies strongly suggest that a family history of hypertension confers an increased susceptibility to the development of proteinuria in some groups of IDDM patients.

These findings could not be confirmed in a Danish study of IDDM patients with nephropathy (Jensen *et al.* 1990). In their study, the prevalence of hypertension was 25% in the parents of diabetic patients with nephropathy and 19% in the parents without nephropathy. However, the authors analysed only parents of diabetic patients who had developed nephropathy before the age of 31 years and did not assess any history of hypertension in deceased parents. Moreover, although proteinuric patients came from the total clinic population, the selection of the control uncomplicated group excluded infrequent attenders who may represent a group with poor control and possibly fewer complications. These individuals could theoretically represent a non-susceptible-to-complications, low blood pressure group, perhaps originating from families with lower blood pressures. This sampling strategy may thus have led to two results: on the one hand a reduction of the difference in blood pressure between parents of proteinuric patients and parents of control patients (by exclusion of families with lower blood pressures in this group) and

Table 20.1 Odds ratio for the contribution of various risk factors for hypertension to the later development of nephropathy in insulin-dependent diabetic patients. Data have been corrected for levels of glycaemic control. Adapted from Barzilay *et al.* (1992) with permission

Individual Characteristic	Odds ratio	P
Adolescent mean arterial pressure		
Below 25th centile	1.0	
Above 75th centile	1.9	0.042
Parental hypertension		
Neither parent	1.0	
One or both parents	3.3	0.009
Tertile of Na/Ll countertransport (mmol/L cells/hr)		
0.06–0.23	1.0	
0.24–0.40	2.5	
≥0.41	7.0	0.027

on the other, a comparison of relatively young parental groups in whom differences in arterial pressure may still not have emerged. In addition, there was a lack of correlation between parental and offspring blood pressures, the correlation coefficient reported (r = 0.03) is similar to levels usually found between spouses. Studies in the general UK population have reported a significant association between parental and offspring blood pressures (Gregory *et al.* 1990) and this relationship has been confirmed in diabetic patients (Keen *et al.* 1975). Thus methodological differences in population selection may account for these apparent discrepancies.

Other familial factors that might be involved in the development of diabetic nephropathy relate to the significant excess of cardiovascular disease in nephropathic diabetic patients (Borch-Johnsen *et al.* 1985). The familial aggregation of cardiovascular disease in diabetic patients with nephropathy was explored in a study of parental cardiovascular morbidity and mortality in two cohorts of IDDM patients with or without proteinuria (Earle *et al.* 1992). The prevalence of cardiovascular disease was found to be significantly greater in the parents of insulin-dependent diabetic patients with nephropathy (31 versus 14%; p <0.01), and the frequency of cardiovascular disease as a direct cause of death was also significantly higher (40 versus 22%; p <0.03). In this group of parents, the age- and sex-adjusted relative risk for cardiovascular disease was 2.9 (95% CI, 1.5–5.5; p <0.001), and a history of cardiovasular disease in the father was associated with a significantly increased risk of nephropathy in the diabetic offspring after controlling for age, gender, and duration of diabetes (odds ratio 3.2; 95% CI, 1.3–7.9; p <0.01). Among the diabetic patients with nephropathy a positive family history of cardiovascular disease was significantly more frequent in those who had suffered a cardiovascular event (odds ratio 6.2; 95% CI, 2–19; p <0.005). This study therefore indicates that a predisposition to cardiovascular disease increases the risk of nephropathy in diabetes and the risk of cardiovascular disease in IDDM patients with nephropathy, and suggests that both disorders may share similar pathogenic processes that may have a genetic or environmental basis.

Sodium–lithium (Na/Li) countertransport

A positive family history of arterial hypertension and/or cardiovascular disease will therefore help in the early identification of IDDM patients at risk of developing nephropathy, but its predictive accuracy remains relatively low. Studies of intermediate phenotypes related to the risk of hypertension and cardiovascular disease might improve our ability for early detection. One such factor that has been extensively studied is the red blood cell sodium–lithium countertransport activity (Na/Li CT). An increased activity of this membrane transport mechanism has been found to be associated with essential hypertension and some of its renal and cardiovascular complications (Canessa *et al.* 1980; Morgan *et al.* 1986; Carr *et al.* 1989; Nosadini *et al.* 1991). In IDDM patients, increased Na/Li CT rates have been found in patients with both microalbuminuria and clinical nephropathy (Krolewski *et al.* 1988; Mangili *et al.* 1988; Jones *et al.* 1990) and in NIDDM patients with hypertension and proteinuria, though not by all authors (Gall *et al.* 1991). Parents of proteinuric IDDM patients with high Na/Li CT have also been reported to have elevated values in one study (Walker *et al.* 1990) although not in another (Jensen *et al.* 1990), confirming the high heritability of the rates of Na/Li CT described in the general population (Boerwinkle *et al.* 1986) and in subjects with arterial hypertension (Hasstedt *et al.* 1988).

In support of this view is a report of a correlation between Na/Li CT rates in identical twins discordant for diabetes (Hardman *et al.* 1992). Forty-four identical twin pairs discordant for insulin-dependent diabetes were studied, and 44 age-matched, non-diabetic subjects acted as controls. Erythrocyte Na/Li CT levels were similar in the diabetic and non-diabetic twins (0.29 [95% CI 0.24–0.34] versus 0.25 [0.20–0.29] mmol/L cells/hour respectively; p = NS), but both values were higher than controls (0.19 [0.16–0.22]; p = <0.05). There was also a significant correlation between red blood cell Na/Li CT levels in twin pairs (r = 0.30; p = <0.05). Interestingly, systolic blood pressure was higher in the diabetic twins, but non-diabetic twins and the controls had similar values. There was a strong correlation between twins for both systolic and diastolic blood pressures (r = 0.75; p = <0.001, and r = 0.58; p = <0.01 respectively).

In a study of 185 unselected IDDM patients who attended their clinic consecutively, the prevalence of elevated Na/Li CT activity (i.e. >0.41 mmol/L red blood cells per hour) was found to be 21.5%, 42.8%, and 51.7% in normoalbuminuric, microalbuminuric, and clinically proteinuric patients respectively, a highly significant difference (p <0.005 by ANOVA) (Lopes de Faria *et al.* 1992*a*). The percentage of patients with proteinuria (microalbuminuria and overt proteinuria) significantly increased with increasing quartiles of the Na/Li CT distribution. In a multiple logistic regression analysis, Na/Li CT emerged as the most important factor related to proteinuria, followed by duration of diabetes, mean blood pressure, and glycated haemoglobin. Interestingly, the prevalence of Na/Li CT >0.41 mmol/L red blood cells per hour decreased consistently with the duration of diabetes in normoalbuminuric patients, reaching a low of 15% in those patients who had had diabetes for more than 20 years. These patients are at a much lower risk of developing nephropathy. An interaction was observed between Na/Li CT and blood glucose control as predictors of proteinuria, in that the highest frequency occurred in those patients with HbAlc values above the median and Na/Li CT rates above the normal range. These findings are in accord with those reported by Krolewski *et al.* (1988) and Barzilay *et al.* (1992) who showed that the risk of renal disease in their patients was greatly increased in those IDDM subjects with elevated Na/Li CT rates and who had an increased index of hyperglycaemia (Table 20.1).

Not all published studies have confirmed an association between increased Na/Li CT and nephropathy, however (Jensen *et al.* 1990; Elving *et al.* 1992; Rutherford *et al.* 1992*a*). Much discussion has revolved around the methodology of estimating Na/Li CT and several potential methodological confounding factors have been reviewed (Canessa *et al.* 1992; Rutherford *et al.* 1992*b*). It has also been found that Na/Li CT activity is affected *in vitro* by changing insulin concentration. It is possible that observed differences in Na/Li CT activity represent changes in both the affinity of the transporter for Na/Li exchange and maximum velocity, both of which are reduced in diabetes; whereas non-diabetic, hypertensive patients show a reduction in affinity only (Rutherford *et al.* 1992*b*). These authors suggest that the observations are more in keeping with a generalized abnormality in cell membrane fluidity rather than a genetically inherited defect of ion transport.

Attempts have been made to examine ways in which Na/Li CT may be linked to known or proposed pathophysiological mechanisms leading to diabetic complications. Na/Li CT activity is associated with lipid abnormalities in diabetic patients who have UAER spanning the normal to the microalbuminuric range (Jones *et al.* 1990). Circulating lipid abnormalities are known to occur in microalbuminuric patients before any loss of renal function (Jensen *et al.* 1988; Jones *et al.* 1989). The link between Na/Li CT on the one hand and arterial hypertension, lipid abnormalities, poor blood glucose control, and proteinuria (all risk factors for microvascular complications and macrovascular disease) on the other may find an explanation in an altered insulin sensitivity in these patients.

Insulin sensitivity

Using a hyperinsulinaemic euglycaemic clamp technique, Lopes de Faria *et al.* (1992*b*) studied two groups of normotensive, non-proteinuric, insulin-dependent diabetic patients with normal or elevated Na/Li CT, and demonstrated a greater resistance to peripheral insulin action in the group with high Na/Li CT activity. They also found a significant association between reduced insulin sensitivity and increased serum triglycerides, apolipoprotein B, and left ventricular hypertrophy. These data have provided a possible metabolic basis for the association of an altered cell membrane ion transport system known to be predictive of cardiovascular disease risk and other risk factors for vascular complications.

Reports in both IDDM and NIDDM patients indicate that reduced insulin sensitivity is associated with microalbuminuria (Groop *et al.* 1993; Yip *et al.* 1993*b*) which is a strong predictor of cardiovascular disease mortality in these individuals (Schmitz and Vaeth 1988; Mattock *et al.* 1992; Messent *et al.* 1992). That insulin insensitivity may be a critical primary factor is suggested by recent observations in first-degree relatives in IDDM patients with microalbuminuria (Yip *et al.* 1993*a*). These subjects displayed abnormalities of carbohydrate and lipid metabolism when compared to first-degree relatives of IDDM patients with normoalbuminuria, even though albumin excretion rates were almost identical in the two groups of relatives. Similar decreases in insulin sensitivity have recently been reported in first-degree relatives of NIDDM patients (Forsblom *et al.* 1995). Evidence supports the role of insulin insensitivity (and its accompanying metabolic syndrome) as a significant risk factor for cardiovascular disease in the general population (Foster 1989), and the potential importance of insulin insensitivity to the susceptibility to developing diabetic nephropathy was suggested by a preliminary report describing an association between polymorphism of the insulin receptor gene and the development of overt proteinuria in IDDM patients (Krolewski *et al.* 1992). These authors examined the insulin receptor locus and showed, using the restriction fragment enzyme, Rsa 1, that the genotype distribution in patients with microalbuminuria or clinical proteinuria departed significantly from Hardy–Weinberg equilibrium. This finding may provide a molecular basis for the observations of insulin insensitivity in patients developing nephropathy and would represent a further genetic explanation for nephropathy risk.

Sodium–hydrogen (Na/H) antiport activity

Na/Li CT has no known physiological function in man and it is of interest largely as a proxy marker of other membrane-based sodium exchangers. One such is the Na/H antiport which regulates intracellular pH, cell volume and growth, and is involved in sodium reabsorption in the proximal renal tubule (Mahnensmith and Aronson 1985). It might therefore be of importance to establish whether diabetic patients with or without nephropathy display any abnormality in this physiological transport system in their cells. An increased Na/H antiport activity has been reported in leukocytes of IDDM patients with microalbuminuria and clinical proteinuria (Ng *et al.* 1990*b*), but in order to overcome the potential problem of the effects of the disturbed diabetic environment on circulating cells, Trevisan *et al.* (1992*a*) measured Na/H antiport activity in serially passaged, cultured skin fibroblasts from IDDM patients with nephropathy. There was a significantly greater Na/H antiport activity in the fibroblasts from patients with, compared to those without, nephropathy, whose activity was comparable to a non-diabetic control group. Moreover, the incorporation of (^{3}H-) thymidine into the DNA in response to 10% fetal calf serum was significantly greater in the fibroblasts derived from the patients with nephropathy.

Thus cell growth is associated with an increased activity of the Na/H antiport in diabetic patients with renal disease. If these *in vitro* abnormalities in cell membrane Na/H transport and in cell growth operate under physiological conditions, it should be possible to identify *in vivo* morphological and functional changes consistent with the *in vitro* findings.

Studies in a group of hypertensive, short-term, IDDM patients without clinical proteinuria who had either an increased or normal Na/Li CT activity revealed that those with higher rates had larger kidneys and more marked left ventricular hypertrophy (Trevisan *et al.* 1992*b*). Proximal tubular reabsorption of sodium was significantly greater in those subjects with increased Na/Li CT activity. The *in vivo* morphological and functional abnormalities are therefore consistent with the *in vitro* findings in fibroblasts of enhanced cell growth and activity of the Na/H antiport, and all of these data taken together support the notion that IDDM patients who develop nephropathy have some intrinsic abnormality in their cell functional response to the metabolic disturbance of diabetes, which leads to the vascular changes responsible for renal and cardiovascular complications.

The abnormalties in function of the Na/H antiport seem unlikely to reflect modifications in the Na/H antiport gene. Studies in essential hypertension have shown no linkage of the Na/H antiporter gene with the development of raised blood pressure (Lifton *et al.* 1991) and so far no study has reported abnormalities of Na/H antiport gene expression in either patients with essential hypertension or diabetic nephropathy. On the other hand, preliminary studies suggest that some of the regulatory pathways of the Na/H exchange rate may be important for its hyperactivity in diabetic nephropathy. Inhibition of protein kinase C in leukocytes of IDDM patients with nephropathy has been shown to normalize the elevated activity of the Na/H antiporter (Ng *et al.* 1990*a*) while there is no effect on cells with normal baseline antiport activity. These preliminary observations and kinetic studies indicate that the degree of phosphorylation of the internal regulatory site for hydrogen transport may be a critical step for its overactivity. If this were to be proved, attention would turn to the genes coding for the different kinases involved in the phosphorylation processes which regulate the activity of the Na/H exchanger. It is becoming increasingly clear that in diabetic nephropathy the abnormality is likely to reside in the host cell response to the environmental dysregulation brought about by diabetes. This abnormal response is likely to affect different functions, including the production of extracellular matrices. Preliminary data suggests that collagen production is significantly increased in skin fibroblasts from IDDM patients with nephropathy (Lurbe *et al.* 1996), and fibronectin has been found to activate the Na/H antiporter in mouse fibroblasts (Schwartz *et al.* 1991). A number of cell types, including vascular smooth muscle cells and perhaps mesangial cells, are also likely to be similarly affected as indicated by studies in animal models of genetic arterial hypertension (Berk *et al.* 1989; Guicheney *et al.* 1991). Direct study of renal tissue from diabetic patients and their families may provide a way forward in our understanding of the genetic basis for the susceptibility to nephropathy.

Renal structural studies

Non-diabetic members of identical twin pairs discordant for IDDM have glomerular basement membrane (GBM) width and mesangial fractional volume measurements within the normal range (Steffes *et al.* 1985). In each instant, the diabetic member of the identical twin pair had greater values for GBM width and mesangial fractional volume than their non-diabetic twin. This was true of tubular basement membrane width as well. Many of the diabetic identical twins had values for GBM width and mesangial fractional volumes that were still within the range of normal, and could only be described as having lesions by virtue of the study of their non-diabetic, identical twin. However some of the diabetic twins were developing lesions quite quickly and had overt glomerulopathy. Thus the difference between individuals with IDDM appears to be the rate at which the lesions of diabetes develop rather than the direction of the structural abnormalities.

Interestingly, some of the non-diabetic members of the identical twin pairs had increased muscle capillary basement membrane (MCBM) width (Steffes *et al.* 1985), although there was no relationship with MCBM width in the sibling pairs. In the diabetic twins, MCBM width correlated with GBM width but not with tubular basement membrane width or mesangial volume. In the non-diabetic twins, MCBM width did not correlate with any measurement of renal structure. MCBM width does not appear to be a useful predictor of the risk of kidney disease in patients with diabetes (Ellis *et al.* 1986*b*), but there may be subtle abnormalities of basement membranes in non-diabetic members of families with IDDM patients. The observations that the width of MCBM is unrelated to suceptibility to renal injury may only confirm that this is not an appropriate marker of glomerulopathy risk. However, these data are compatible with the idea that in diabetic families, underlying cell or tissue characteristics are important in conferring susceptibility to, or protection from, important complications of diabetes, an idea first proposed in 1968 (Siperstein *et al.* 1968).

Studies of Fioretto *et al.* (1991) indicate that amongst IDDM sibling pairs the concordance in nephropathy incidence is based upon a concordance in glomerulopathy lesions. In these ongoing studies, 12 sibling pairs had renal biopsies and kidney-function studies performed. The duration of IDDM in the probands was 25 and in siblings 18 years (range 10–57 years). GFR averaged more than $100 \text{ml}/\text{min}/1.73 \text{m}^2$ in both groups. Correlation for GBM width in the probands of siblings was r = 0.71. Correlation for the degree of mesangial expansion in the siblings of probands was r = 0.87. There was less variance between siblings than among all patients for these variables. After correcting for duration of IDDM, the effect of sibship on lesions was still present. These data support a strong familial concordance for nephropathy risk and suggest that this might operate through a concordance in glomerular lesions.

Supporting the concept of risk factors intrinsic to the cellular function within the end organs themselves are studies of the rate of development of kidney lesions of diabetic nephropathy in transplanted kidneys residing for 6–14 years in IDDM diabetic kidney allograft recipients (Mauer *et al.* 1989). Although each recipient had end-stage diabetic glomerulopathy in his or her own kidneys, there was marked variability in the rate of development of mesangial expansion in the transplanted kidney. GBM width and fractional mesangial volume did not correlate significantly with several possible risk factors, including donor source (cadaver vs. living related), histocompatibility match, age of the recipient or donor, age at onset of diabetes, duration of diabetes before renal failure, immunosuppressive drug dose, or blood pressure post-transplantation. There was a direct albeit imprecise relationship between the light microscopic index of mesangial expansion and measures of glycaemic control (r = 0.61; p <0.01). These studies suggested that in a population that had uniformly demonstrated a high risk of development of nephropathy in their native kidneys, the risk was highly variable in normal kidneys placed into the same diabetic environment.

Mean glomerular volume and glomerular number are two structural factors that have been proposed as possible structural determinants of nephropathy progression and risk. Filtration surface area within the glomerulus is negatively correlated to mesangial expansion and positively correlated to mean glomerular volume (Ellis *et al.* 1986*a*). Mean glomerular volumes were significantly greater in a cohort of diabetic patients developing nephropathy after 25 years duration compared to a group with nephropathy after 15 years (2.13 ± 0.64 v $1.43 \pm 0.47 \times$

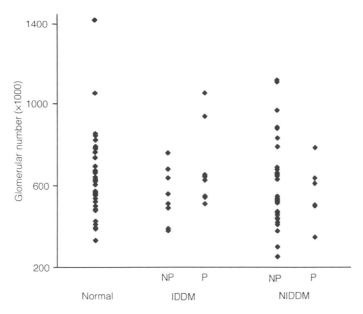

Fig. 20.3 Glomerular number in IDDM and NIDDM diabetic patients with (P) and without (NP) proteinuria, and in a group of age-matched, non-diabetic, control subjects. Note similar numbers in all groups. Adapted from Bendtsen and Nyengaard (1992) and Nyengaard and Bendtsen (1992) with permission.

$10^6 \mu m^3$; p <0.01) (Bilous *et al.* 1989). Studies in normal man have shown that mean glomerular volume relates to body size (Nyengaard and Bendtsen 1992), which is of course highly genetically determined. Barker and others have described associations between low birth weight and development of diabetes, hypertension, and cardiovascular disease in later life (Barker *et al.* 1990; 1993). They suggest that fetal growth retardation results in arrested organ development, particularly of the pancreatic islets and renal glomeruli. The discovery of a reduced glomerular number in babies dying of sudden infant death syndrome (Hinchliffe *et al.* 1993) and similar results in rats that have undergone intrauterine growth retardation (Merlet-Benichou *et al.* 1994) has led to a hypothesis of oligonephropathy as an explanation of hypertension risk in non-diabetic patients and nephropathy risk in diabetic subjects (Brenner *et al.* 1988; MacKenzie *et al.* 1996). The number of glomeruli per kidney is known to vary almost threefold between normal individuals (Bendtsen and Nyengaard 1992) and this variation is similar in diabetic patients which might support the oligonephropathy hypothesis. However, although there were fewer numbers of glomeruli in patients with advanced renal failure in the series of Bendtsen and Nyengaard (1992), there was a small subgroup of subjects with proteinuria who had a glomerular number that was not different from those patients without proteinuria (Fig. 20.3). If glomerular number were a determinant of nephropathy risk, one would have predicted fewer glomeruli in this subset. Furthermore, no correlation between glomerular number and birth weight was found in a cohort of Danish subjects, although it has to be said that none of them had a birth weight less than 2.5 kg (Nyengaard *et al.* 1996). In addition, not all studies have confirmed Barker's original observations (Paneth and Susser 1995). Longer-term prospective studies in large numbers of patients are urgently needed to explore these ideas.

All of these studies are compatible with the hypothesis that in addition to glycaemic control there are risk factors intrinsic to the kidney itself, some of which may be genetically determined. Although the nature of these risk factors remains to be elucidated, a further potential mechanism may be deduced from observations of immunofluorescent staining of renal extracellular basement membranes for plasma proteins in diabetic patients (Michael and Brown 1981). Studies comparing normal and diabetic kidneys suggest that albumin binds to renal extracellular membranes in diabetes relatively firmly, requiring incubation at very low pH for significant albumin release, and that IgG deposition in basement membranes in diabetes is restricted to IgG4 (Melvin *et al.* 1984). There is also increased staining of muscle capillary and sarcolemmal basement membranes for IgG and albumin in diabetic patients (Gohn *et al.* 1978). In non-diabetic HLA identical siblings of IDDM patients (including four discordant identical twin sets) there was no difference in MCBM width comparing the HLA identical siblings to the non-HLA identical sibling and normal controls. However, HLA identical siblings had increased muscle capillary and muscle extracellular membrane immunofluorescence for albumin compared to the other two groups (Barbosa *et al.* 1980). In addition, Chavers *et al.* (1984) found abnormal albumin deposition in dermal capillary basement membranes of some unaffected parents of IDDM patients. These studies suggest that there are underlying tissue abnormalties in family members of IDDM patients and further studies are indicated to determine the possibility of association of such tissue abnormalties with genetic factors which might predispose to serious diabetic complications.

Possible candidate genes

Three types of model have been proposed to explain the genetic component of nephropathy risk (Krolewski *et al.* 1992). In the additive model, hyperglycaemia is responsible for early renal damage giving rise to microalbuminuria, whereas subsequent progression to nephropathy and ESRD is determined by one or more genes. In an interactive model, the combination of hyperglycaemia and a genetic abnormaltiy in an individual would result in renal damage. This model would explain why some patients with long-term poor glycaemic control do not develop microvascular complications. Finally, a mixed model would combine these possiblities with hyperglycaemia plus a gene defect giving rise to early structural changes but subsequent progression is determined by a second set of genes.

Using these models, exploration of possible candidate genes in IDDM patients has been undertaken and reviewed recently by Chowdhury *et al.* (1995). Overall, the results have been disappointing with preliminary positive associations failing to be comfirmed by later (usually larger) studies. The best studied of these genes relates to the renin-angiotensin system (RAS).

There are several reasons why genetic abnormalities in the RAS may be important in the pathogenesis of nephropathy. Firstly, polymorphisms in the angiotensin-converting enzymes (ACE) gene are closely related to circulating ACE levels (Rigat *et al.* 1990) which converts angiotensin I to angiotensin II. Secondly, treatment of diabetic patients who have early nephropathy with ACE inhibitor agents prevents progression of albuminuria (Microalbuminuria Captopril Study Group 1996). Thirdly, the presence of an extra 287 base pair sequence in intron 16 of the ACE gene on chromosome 17 (termed the insertion or I genotype) has been associated with a lower incidence of myocardial infarction in subjects who are homozygous (II); those individuals without the extra sequence have been defined as the deletion or D genotype and homozygosity (DD) is linked to a greater risk of coronary heart disease (Cambien *et al.* 1992). As patients with diabetic nephropathy have an excess cardiovascular disease risk, insertion–deletion polymorphisms could be implicated in pathophysiology. Fourthly, polymorphisms of the angiotensinogen gene that link with essential hypertension have been described in non-diabetic subjects (Chowdhury *et al.* 1995). Finally, the development of microvascular complications has been linked to increased circulating levels of prorenin (Wilson and Luetscher 1990). Marre *et al.* (1994) studied 62 insulin-dependent patients with diabetic nephropathy defined as a UAER >30 mg/day, with 62 diabetic control subjects who were age-, sex- and duration-matched. The ACE genotype distribution for the insertion–deletion polymorphism was determined for all patients together with cirulating ACE levels. They found a significantly lower proportion of the insertion II genotype in patients with nephropathy (odds ratio 0.216, 95% CI 0.067–0.695; $p = 0.006$). Conversely, there was a slightly increased frequency of the D allele in insulin-dependent patients with nephropathy when compared to those without ($p = 0.0525$).

A second study (Doria *et al.* 1994) used a nested case–control design of 77 normoalbuminuric and 74 nephropathic patients (UAER >30 μm/min) with long-standing, insulin-dependent diabetes. DNA from these subjects was genotyped at the ACE locus by a restriction fragment-melting polymorphism (DdeI) and the two allele insertion–deletion previously studied by Cambien *et al.* (1992). This study found that the least common allele of the DdeI RFMP was significantly more frequent among cases with nephropathy than among controls (12.8 v 4.5%; $p < 0.05$). However, they could not confirm a statistically significant increase in the ACE gene deletion described by Cambien and Marre in the nephropathic subjects.

Two more recent studies in larger numbers of patients have also failed to confirm a link between the insertion–deletion polymorphism of the ACE gene and nephropathy in both insulin- (total n = 655) and non-insulin-dependent (n = 455) patients (Schmidt *et al.* 1995; Chowdhury *et al.* 1996). Some of this discrepancy may be related to methodological problems of mistyping the ACE genotype such that ID subjects may be misclassified as DD. Furthermore, the smaller numbers in the early reports may have been subject to survivor bias. Finally, all of the studies have used different definitions of nephropathy, which may bias any estimate of association.

Interestingly, a recent study in Denmark in 388 IDDM patients (198 with nephropathy) found a lower prevalence of cardiovascular disease in those with the II genotype, but no association with I/D polymorphism and nephropathy alone (Tarnow *et al.* 1995). The same workers have reported a study of 35 IDDM patients with nephropathy on captopril treatment and in whom the rate of fall of GFR in the 11 subjects with the DD genotype, compared to 24 who were ID or II, was significantly increased (5.7 versus 2.6 ml/min/year; $p = 0.01$) (Parving *et al.* 1996). This difference was not related to captopril dose or achieved levels of blood pressure control.

Although not all studies have confirmed the original association of insertion–deletion polymorphism and myocardial infarction, there is a consensus that the D allele is linked in some way to coronary heart disease (Singer *et al.* 1996). It is probable, however, that there is not a strong link to diabetic nephropathy itself, and it is therefore of little use in identifying those diabetic subjects at high risk of developing renal complications. These polymorphisms may, however, determine clinical outcome.

Two angiotensinogen gene polymorphisms (M235T + T174M) which have links to essential hypertension have been described in non-diabetic subjects, but two reports in large numbers of subjects have failed to demonstrate any association with nephropathy (Chowdhury *et al.* 1996; Schmidt *et al.* 1995).

Other proposed candidate genes have been studied, including those encoding for basement membrane proteins such as heparan sulphate proteoglycan and the ∝ 1 chain of type IV collagen; the insulin gene; and the aldose reductase gene. The results are largely preliminary, await confirmation from larger studies, and are summarized by Chowdhury *et al.* (1995).

Conclusion

The clustering of diabetic nephropathy in families and the increased prevalence in different ethnic groups is strongly suggestive of a genetic basis for diabetic nephropathy. Over the last few years, information exploring this proposal has been accumulating. These data seem to be pointing towards an interaction between basic renal structural parameters, cell membrane transport systems closely linked to proliferation and growth, and metabolic dysregulation including insulin insensitivity and hyperglycaemia as the major components. There are preliminary data supporting a genetic basis for each of these factors. In addition, a candidate gene approach has suggested a role for ACE gene polymorphism in determining cardiovascular morbidity in patients with nephropathy. We are sure that the continued study of this subject over the next few years will reveal a great deal more about this complex interrelationship and its basis of inheritance.

References

Allawi, J., Rao, P. V., Gilbert, R., Scott, G., Jarrett, R. J., Keen, H., *et al.* (1988). Microalbuminuria in non-insulin-dependent diabetes: its prevalence in Indian compared with Europid patients. *British Medical Journal*, **296**, 462–4.

Andersen, A. R., Christiansen, J. S., Andersen, J. K., Kreiner, S., and Deckert, T. (1983). Diabetic nephropathy in type I (insulin-dependent) diabetes: an epidemiological study. *Diabetologia*, **25**, 496–501.

Ballard, D. J., Humphrey, L. L., Melton, L. J. III, Frohnert, P. P., Chu, C-P., O'Fallon, W. M., *et al.* (1988). Epidemiology of persistent proteinuria in type II diabetes mellitus: population based study in Rochester, Minnesota. *Diabetes*, **37**, 405–12.

Barbosa, J., Cohen, R. A., Chavers, B., Michael, A. F., Steffes, M., Hoogwerf, B., *et al.* (1980). Muscle extracellular membrane immunofluorescence and HLA as possible markers of prediabetes. *Lancet*, **ii**, 230–3.

Barbosa, J. and Saner, B. (1984). Do genetic factors play a role in the pathogenesis of diabetic microangiopathy? *Diabetologia*, **27**, 487–92.

Barker, D. J., Bull, A. R., Osmond, C., and Simmonds, S. J. (1990). Foetal and placental size and risk of hypertension in adult life. *British Medical Journal*, **301**, 259–62.

Barker, D. J., Hales, C. N., Fall, C. H., Osmond, C., Phipps, K., and Clark, P. M. (1993). Type II (non-insulin-dependent) diabetes mellitus, hypertension and hyperlipidaemia (syndrome X): relation to reduced fetal growth. *Diabetologia*, **36**, 62–7.

Barnett, A. H., Eff, C., Leslie, R. D. G., and Pyke, D. A. (1981). Diabetes in identical twins: a study of 200 pairs. *Diabetologia*, **20**, 87–93.

Barzilay, J., Warram, J. H., Bak, M., Laffel, L. M. B., Canessa, M., and Krolewski, A. S. (1992). Predisposition to hypertension: risk factor for nephropathy and hypertension in IDDM. *Kidney International*, **41**, 723–30.

Bendtsen, T. F. and Nyengaard, J. R. (1992). The number of glomeruli in type I (insulin-dependent) and type II (non-insulin-dependent) diabetic patients. *Diabetologia*, **35**, 844–50.

Berk, B. C., Vallega, G., Muslin, A. J., Gordon, H. M., Canessa, M., and Alexander, R. W. (1989). Spontaneously hypertensive rat vascular smooth-muscle cells in culture exhibit increased growth and Na/H exchange. *Journal of Clinical Investigation*, **83**, 822–9.

Bilous, R. W., Mauer, S. M., Sutherland, D. E. R., and Steffes, M. W. (1989). Mean glomerular volume and rate of development of diabetic nephropathy. *Diabetes*, **38**, 1142–7.

Boerwinkle, E., Turner, S. T., Weinshilboum, R., Johnson, M., Richelson, E., and Sing, C. F. (1986). Analysis of the distribution of erythrocyte sodium lithium countertransport in a sample representative of the general population. *Genetic Epidemiology*, **3**, 365–78.

Borch-Johnsen, K., Andersen, P. K., and Deckert, T. (1985). The effect of proteinuria on relative mortality in type I (insulin-dependent) diabetes mellitus. *Diabetologia*, **28**, 590–6.

Borch-Johnsen, K., Norgaard, K., Hommel, E., Mathiesen, E. R., Jensen, J. S., Deckert, T., *et al.* (1992). Is diabetic nephropathy an inherited complication? *Kidney International*, **41**, 719–22.

Brenner, B. M., Garcia, D. L., and Anderson, S. (1988). Glomeruli and blood pressure. Less of one, more of the other? *American Journal of Hypertension*, **1**, 335–47.

Burden, A. C., McNally, P. G., Feehally, J., and Walls, J. (1992). Increased incidence of end-stage renal failure secondary to diabetes mellitus in Asian ethnic groups in the United Kingdom. *Diabetic Medicine*, **9**, 641–5.

Canessa, M., Adragna, N., Solomon, H. S., Connolly, T. M., and Tosteson, D. C. (1980). Increased sodium–lithium countertransport in red cells of patients with essential hypertension. *New England Journal of Medicine*, **302**, 772–6.

Canessa, M., Zerbini, G., and Laffel, L. M. B. (1992). Sodium activation kinetics of red blood cell Na/Li countertransport in diabetes: methodology and controversy. *Journal of the Americal Society of Nephrology*, **3**, 541–9.

Carr, S. J., Thomas, T. H., and Wilkinson, R. (1989). Erythrocyte sodium–lithium countertransport in primary and renal hypertension: relation to family history. *European Journal of Clinical Investigation*, **19**, 101–6.

Chavers, B., Etzwiller, D., Barbosa, J., Bach, F. H., and Michael, A. F. (1984). Albumin deposition in dermal capillary basement membrane in parents of type I (insulin-dependent) diabetic patients. *Diabetologia*, **26**, 415–19.

Chowdhury, T. A., Kumar, S., Barnett, A. H., and Bain, S. C. (1995). Nephropathy in type I diabetes: the role of genetic factors. *Diabetic Medicine*, **12**, 1059–67.

Chowdhury, T. A., Dronsfield, M. J., Kumar, S., Gough, S. L. C., Gibson, S. P., Khatoon, S., *et al.* (1996). Examination of two genetic polymorphisms within the renin-angiotensin system: no evidence for an association with nephropathy in IDDM. *Diabetologia*, **39**, 1108–14.

Cohn, R. A., Mauer, S. M., Barbosa, J., and Michael, A. F. (1978). Immunofluorescent studies of skeletal-muscle extracellular membrane in diabetes mellitus. *Laboratory Investigation*, **39**, 13–16.

Collins, V. R., Dowse, G. K., Finch, C. F., Zimmet, P. Z., and Linnane, A. W. (1989). Prevalence and risk factors for micro and macroalbuminuria in diabetic subjects and the entire population of Nauru. *Diabetes*, **38**, 1602–10.

Cowie, C. C., Port, F. K., Wolfe, R. A., Savage, P. J., Moll, P. P., and Hawthorne, V. M. (1989). Disparities in incidence of diabetic end-stage renal disease according to race and type of diabetes. *New England Journal of Medicine*, **321**, 1074–9.

Cudworth, A. G. and Festenstein, H. (1978). HLA genetic heterogeneity in diabetes mellitus. *British Medical Bulletin*, **34**, 285–9.

Doria, A., Warram, J. H., and Krolewski, A. S. (1994). Genetic predisposition to diabetic nephropathy. Evidence for a role of the angiotensin 1 converting enzyme gene. *Diabetes*, **43**, 690–5.

Earle, K., Walker, J. D., Hill, C., and Viberti, G. C. (1992). Familial clustering of cardiovascular disease in patients with insulin-dependent diabetes and nephropathy. *New England Journal of Medicine*, **326**, 673–7.

Ellis, E. N., Steffes, M. W., Goetz, F. C., Sutherland, D. E. R., and Mauer, S. M. (1986*a*). Glomerular filtration surface in type I diabetes mellitus. *Kidney International*, **29**, 889–94.

Ellis, E. N., Mauer, S. M., Goetz, F. C., Sutherland, D. E. R., and Steffes, M. W. (1986*b*). Relationship of muscle capillary basement membrane to renal structure and function in diabetes mellitus. *Diabetes*, **35**, 421–5.

Elving, L. D., Wetzels, J. F. M., De Pont, J. J. H. H. M., and Berden, J. H. M. (1992). Is increased erthrocyte sodium–lithium countertransport a useful marker for diabetic nephropathy? *Kidney International*, **41**, 862–71.

Feldt-Rasmussen, B., Mathiesen, E. R., and Deckert, T. (1986). Effect of 2 years of strict metabolic control on progression of incipient nephropathy in insulin-dependent diabetes. *Lancet*, ii, 1300–4.

Fioretto, P., Steffes, M. W., Barbosa, J., Sprafka, M., and Mauer, S. M. (1991). Glomerular structure in siblings with insulin-dependent diabetes mellitus (IDDM). *Journal of the American Society of Nephropathy*, **2**, 289. (Abstract).

Forsblom, C. M., Eriksson, J. G., Ekstrand, A. V., Teppo, A-M., Taskinen, M-R., and Groop, L. C. (1995). Insulin resistance and abnormal albumin excretion in non-diabetic, first-degree relatives of patients with NIDDM. *Diabetic Medicine*, **12**, 363–9.

Foster, D. W. (1989). Insulin resistance—a secret killer? *New England Journal of Medicine*, **320**, 733–4.

Gall, M-A., Rossing, P., Jensen, J. S., Funder, J., and Parving, H-H. (1991). Red cell Na/Li countertransport in non-insulin-dependent diabetics with diabetic nephropathy. *Kidney International*, **39**, 135–40.

Gregory, J., Foster, K., Tyler, H., and Wiseman, M. (1990). The dietary and nutritional survey of British adults. *Office of Population Censuses and Surveys, Social Survey Division*, pp. 250–61. HMSO, London.

Groop, L., Ekstrand, A., Forsblom, C., Widen, E., Groop, P-H., Teppo, A-M., et al. (1993). Insulin resistance, hypertension and microalbuminuria in patients with type 2 (non-insulin-dependent) diabetes mellitus. *Diabetologia*, **36**, 642–7.

Guicheney, P., Wauquier, I., Paquet, J. L., and Meyer, P. (1991). Enhanced response to growth factors and to angiotensin II of spontaneously hypertensive rat-skin fibroblasts in culture. *Journal of Hypertension*, **9**, 23–7.

Haneda, M., Kikkawa, R., Togawa, M., Koya, D., Kajiwara, N., Uzu, T., et al. (1992). High blood pressure is a risk factor for the development of microalbuminuria in Japanese subjects with non-insulin-dependent diabetes mellitus. *Journal of Diabetes and its Complications*, **6**, 181–5.

Hardman, T. C., Dubrey, S. W., Leslie, R. D. G., Hafiz, M., Noble, M. I., and Lant, A. F. (1992). Erythrocyte sodium–lithium countertransport and blood pressure in identical twin pairs discordant for insulin-dependent diabetes. *British Medical Journal*, **305**, 215–19.

Hasslacher, Ch., Ritz, E., Wahl, P., and Michael, C. (1989). Similar risks of nephropathy in patients with type I or type II diabetes mellitus. *Nephrology Dialysis and Transplantation*, **4**, 859–63.

Hasstedt, S. J., Wu, L. L., Ash, K. O., Kuida, H., and Williams, R. R. (1988). Hypertension and sodium–lithium countertransport in Utah pedigrees: evidence for a major locus inheritance. *Americal Journal of Human Genetics*, **43**, 14–22.

Hinchliffe, S. A., Howard, C. V., Lynch, M. R. J., Sargent, P. H., Judd, B. A., and van Velzen, D. (1993). Renal developmental arrest in sudden infant death syndrome. *Paediatric Pathology*, **13**, 333–43.

Jensen, J. S., Mathiesen, E. R., Norgaard, K., Hommel, E., Borch-Johnsen, K., Funder, J., et al. (1990). Increased blood pressure and sodium/lithium countertransport are not inherited in diabetic nephropathy. *Diabetologia*, **33**, 619–24.

Jensen, T., Stender, S., and Deckert, T. (1988). Abnormalities in plasma concentrations of lipoproteins and fibrinogen in type 1 (insulin-dependent) diabetic patients with increased urinary albumin excretion. *Diabetologia*, **31**, 142–5.

Jones, S. L., Close, C. F., Mattock, M. B., Jarrett, R. J., Keen, H., and Viberti, G. C. (1989). Plasma lipid and coagulation factor concentrations in insulin-dependent diabetics with microalbuminuria. *British Medical Journal*, **298**, 487–90.

Jones, S. L., Trevisan, R., Tariq, T., Semplicini, A., Mattock, M., Walker, J. D., et al. (1990). Sodium–lithium countertransport in microalbuminuric insulin-dependent diabetic patients. *Hypertension*, **15**, 570–5.

Kalter-Leibovici, O., Van Dyk, D. J., Leibovici, L., Loya, N., Erman, A., Kremer, I., *et al.* (1991). Risk factors for development of diabetic nephropathy and retinopathy in Jewish IDDM patients. *Diabetes*, **40**, 204–10.

Keen, H., Track, N. S., and Sowry, G. C. (1975). Arterial pressure in clinically apparent diabetics. *Diabete et Metabolisme*, **1**, 159–78.

Kofoed-Enevoldsen, A., Borch-Johnsen, K., Kreiner, S., Nerup, J., and Deckert, T. (1987). Declining incidence of persistent proteinuria in type 1 (insulin-dependent) diabetic patients in Denmark. *Diabetes*, **36**, 205–9.

Krolewski, A. S., Warram, J. H., Christlieb, A. R., Busick, E. J., and Kahn, C. R. (1985). The changing natural history of nephropathy in type 1 diabetes. *American Journal of Medicine*, **78**, 785–94.

Krolewski, A. S., Canessa, M., Warram, J. H., Laffel, L. M. B., Christlieb, A. R., Knowler, W. C., *et al.* (1988). Predisposition to hypertension and susceptibility to renal disease in insulin-dependent diabetes mellitus. *New England Journal of Medicine*, **318**, 140–5.

Krolewski, A. S., Doria, A., Magre, G., Warram, J. H., and Housman, D. (1992). Molecular genetic approaches to the identification of genes involved in the development of nephropathy in insulin-dependent diabetes mellitus. *Journal of the American Society of Nephrology*, **3**, S9–S17.

Leahy, J. C. and Bcyd, A. E. III. (1993). Diabetes genes in non-insulin-dependent diabetes mellitus. *New England Journal of Medicine*, **328**, 56–7.

Lifton, R. P., Hunt, S. C., Williams, R. R., Pouyssegur, J., and Lalouel, J. M. (1991). Exclusion of the Na–H antiporter as a candidate gene in human essential hypertension. *Hypertension*, **17**, 8–14.

Lopes de Faria, J. B., Friedman, R., Tariq, T., and Viberti, G. C. (1992*a*). Prevalence of raised sodium–lithium countertransport activity in type 1 diabetic patients. *Kidney International*, **41**, 877–82.

Lopes de Faria, J. B., Jones, S. L., MacDonald, F., Chambers, J., Mattock, M. B., and Viberti, G. C. (1992*b*). Sodium–lithium countertransport activity in normoalbuminuric insulin-dependent diabetic patients. *Diabetes*, **41**, 610–15.

Lurbe, A., Fioretto, P., Mauer, M., La Pointe, M. S., and Batlle, D. (1996). Growth phenotype of 'cultural skin' fibroblasts from IDDM patients with and without nephropathy and overactivity of the Na$^+$/H$^+$ antiporter. *Kidney International*, **50**, 1684–93.

MacKenzie, H. S., Lawler, E. V., and Brenner, B. M. (1996). Congenital oligonephropathy: the fetal flaw in essential hypertension? *Kidney International*, **49** (Suppl. 55), S30–S34.

Mahnensmith, R. L. and Aronson. P. S. (1985). The plasma membrane sodium–hydrogen exchanger and its role in physiological and pathophysiological processes. *Circulation Research*, **56**, 773–88.

Mangili, R., Bending, J. J., Scott, G., Li, L. K., Gupta, A., and Viberti, G. C. (1988). Increased sodium–lithium countertransport activity in red cells of patients with insulin-dependent diabetes and nephropathy. *New England Journal of Medicine*, **318**, 146–50.

Marre, M., Bernadet, P., Gallois, Y., Sauagner, F., Guyene, T., Hallab, M., *et al.* (1994). Relationships between angiotensin 1 converting enzyme gene polymorphism, plasma levels and diabetic retinal and renal camplications. *Diabetes*, **43**, 384–8.

Mathiesen, E. R., Oxenboll, B., Johansen, K., Svendsen, P. Aa., and Deckert, T. (1984). Incipient nephropathy in type 1 (insulin-dependent) diabetes. *Diabetologia*, **26**, 406–10.

Mathiesen, E. R., Borch-Johnsen, K., Jensen, D. V., and Deckert, T. (1989). Improved survival in patients with diabetic nephropathy. *Diabetologia*, **32**, 884–6.

Mathiesen, E. R., Ronn, B., Jensen, T., Storm, B., and Deckert, T. (1990). Relationship between blood pressure and urinary albumin excretion and development of microalbuminuria. *Diabetes*, **39**, 245–9.

Mathiesen, E. R., Ronn, B., Storm, B., Foght, H., and Deckert, T. (1995). The natural course of microalbuminuria in insulin-dependent diabetes: a 10-year prospective study. *Diabetic Medicine*, **12**, 482–7.

Mattock, M. B., Morrish, N. J., Viberti, G. C., Keen, H., Fitzgerald, A. P., and Jackson, G. (1992). Prospective study of microalbuminuria as a predictor of mortality in NIDDM. *Diabetes*, 41, 736–41.

Mauer, S. M., Steffes, M. W., Ellis, E. N., Sutherland, D. E. R., Brown, D. M., and Goetz, F. C. (1984). Structural-functional relationships in diabetic nephropathy. *Journal of Clinical Investigation*, 74, 1143–55.

Mauer, S. M., Goetz, F. C., McHugh, L. E., Sutherland, D. E. R., Barbosa, J., Najarian, J. S., *et al.* (1989). Long-term study of normal kidneys transplanted into patients with type 1 diabetes. *Diabetes*, 38, 516–23.

Melvin, T., Kim, Y., and Michael, A. F. (1984). Selective binding of IgG4 and other negatively charged plasma proteins in normal and diabetic human kidneys. *American Journal of Pathology*, 115, 443–6.

Merlct-Benichou, C., Gilbert, T., Muffat-Joly, M., Lelievre-Pegorier, M., and Leroy, B. (1994). Intrauterine growth retardation leads to a permanent nephron deficit in the rat. *Paediatric Nephrology*, 8, 175–80.

Messent, J. W. C., Elliott, T. G., Hill, R. D., Jarrett, R. J., Keen, H., and Viberti, G. C. (1992). Prognostic significance of microalbuminuria in insulin-dependent diabetes mellitus: a twenty-three year follow-up study. *Kidney International*, 41, 836–9.

Michael, A. F. and Brown, D. M. (1981). Increased concentration of albumin in kidney basement membranes in diabetes mellitus. *Diabetes*, 30, 843–6.

Microalbuminuria Collaborative Study Group (1993). Risk factors for the development of microalbuminuria in insulin-dependent diabetic patients: a cohort study. *British Medical Journal*, 306, 1235–9.

Microalbuminuria Captopril Study Group (1996). Captopril reduces the risk of nephropathy in IDDM patients with microalbuminuria. *Diabetologia*, 39, 587–93.

Morgan, D. B., Stewart, A. D., and Davidson, C. (1986). Relations between erythrocyte lithium efflux, blood pressure and family histories of hypertension and cardiovascular disease. Studies in a factory workforce and in a hypertension clinic. *Journal of Hypertension*, 4, 609–15.

Nelson, R. G., Pettitt, D. J., Carraher, M. J., Baird, H. R., and Knowler, W. C. (1988). Effect of proteinuria on mortality in NIDDM. *Diabetes*, 37, 1499–504.

Nelson, R. G., Pettitt, D. J., Baird, H. R., Charles, M. A., Liu, Q. Z., Bennett, P. H., *et al.* (1993). Pre-diabetic blood pressure predicts urinary albumin excretion after the onset of type 2 (non-insulin-dependent) diabetes mellitus in Pima Indians. *Diabetologia*, 36, 998–1001.

Ng, L. L., Simmons, D., Frighi, V., Garrido, M. C., and Bomford, J. (1990*a*). Effect of protein kinase C modulators on the leucocyte Na/H antiport in type 1 (insulin-dependent) diabetic subjects with albuminuria. *Diabetologia*, 33, 278–84.

Ng, L. L., Simmons, D., Frighi, V., Garrido, M. C., Bomford, J., and Hockaday, J. D. R. (1990*b*). Leucocyte Na/H antiport activity in type 1 (insulin-dependent) diabetic patients with nephropathy. *Diabetologia*, 33, 371–7.

Nosadini, R., Semplicini, A., Fioretto, P., Lusiani, L., Trevisan, R., Donadon, V., *et al.* (1991). Sodium/lithium countertransport and cardio-renal abnormalities in essential hypertension. *Hypertension*, 18, 191–8.

Nyengaard, J. R. and Bendtsen, T. F. (1992). Glomerular number and size in relation to age, kidney weight and body surface in normal man. *Anatomical Record*, 232, 194–201.

Nyengaard, J. R., Bendtsen, T. F., and Mogensen, C. E. (1996). Low birth weight—is it associated with few and small glomeruli in normal subjects and NIDDM patients? *Diabetologia*, 39, 1634–7.

Paneth, N. and Susser, M. (1995). Early origin of coronary heart disease (the 'Barker hypothesis'). *British Medical Journal*, 310, 411–12.

Parving, H-H., Andersen, A. R., Smidt, U. M., Hommel, E., Mathiesen, E. R., and Svendsen, P. Aa. (1987). Effect of anti-hypertensive treatment on kidney function in diabetic nephropathy. *British Medical Journal*, 294, 1443–7.

Parving, H-H. and Hommel, E. (1989). Prognosis in diabetic nephropathy. *British Medical Journal*, **299**, 230–3.

Parving, H-H., Jacobsen, P., Tarnow, L., Rossing, P., Lecerf, L., Poirier, O., *et al.* (1996). Effect of deletion polymorphism of angiotensin-converting enzyme gene on progression of diabetic nephropathy during inhibition of angiotensin-converting enzyme: observational follow-up study. *British Medical Journal*, **313**, 591–4.

Pettitt, D. J., Saad, M. F., Bennett, P. H., Nelson, R. G., and Knowler, W. C. (1990). Familial predisposition to renal disease in two generations of Pima Indians with type 2 (non-insulin-dependent) diabetes mellitus. *Diabetologia*, **33**, 438–43.

Pirart, J. (1978). Diabetes mellitus and its degenerative complications: a prospective study of 4400 patients observed between 1947 and 1973. *Diabetes Care*, **1**, 168–88 and 252–63.

Pugh, J. A., Stern, M. P., Haffner, S. M., Eifler, C. W., and Zapata, M. (1988). Excess incidence of treatment of end-stage renal disease in Mexican Americans. *American Journal of Epidemiology*, **127**, 135–44.

Quinn, M., Angelico, M. C., Warram, J. H., and Krolewski, A. S. (1996). Familial factors determine the development of diabetic nephropathy in patients with IDDM. *Diabetologia*, **39**, 940–5.

Rigat, B., Hubert, C., Alhenc-Gelas, F., Cambien, F., Corvol, P., and Soubrier, F. (1990). An insertion–deletion polymorphism in the angiotensin I converting enzyme gene accounting for half the variance of serum enzyme levels. *Journal of Clinical Investigation*, **86**, 1343–6.

Rutherford, P. A., Thomas, T. H., Carr, S. J., Taylor, R., and Wilkinson, R. (1992*a*). Changes in erythrocyte sodium–lithium countertransport kinetics in diabetic nephropathy. *Clinical Science*, **82**, 301–7.

Rutherford, P. A., Thomas, T. H., and Wilkinson, R. (1992*b*). Erythrocyte sodium–lithium countertransport: clinically useful, pathophysiologically instructive, or just phenomenology? *Clinical Science*, **82**, 341–52.

Schmidt, S., Schone, N., Ritz, E., and the Diabetic Nephropathy Study Group (1995). Association of ACE gene polymorphism and diabetic nephropathy? *Kidney International*, **47**, 1176–81.

Schmitz, A. and Vaeth, N. (1988). Microalbuminuria: a major risk factor in non-insulin-dependent diabetes. A 10-year follow-up study of 503 patients. *Diabetic Medicine*, **5**, 126–34.

Schwartz, M. A., Lechene, C., and Ingber, D. E. (1991). Insoluble fibronectin activates the Na/H antiporter by clustering and immobilizing integrin alpha$_5$ beta$_1$, independent of cell shape. *Proceedings of the National Academy of Science USA*, **88**, 7848–53.

Seaquist, E. R., Goetz, F. C., Rich, S., and Barbosa, J. (1989). Familial clustering of diabetic kidney disease: evidence for genetic susceptibility to diabetic nephropathy. *New England Journal of Medicine*, **320**, 1161–5.

Simmons, D. (1996). The epidemiology of diabetes and its complications in New Zealand. *Diabetic Medicine*, **13**, 371–5.

Singer, D. R. J., Missouris, C. G., and Jeffery, S. (1996). Angiotensin-converting enzyme gene polymorphisms. What to do about all the confusion. *Circulation*, **94**, 236–9.

Siperstein, M. D., Unger, R. H., and Madison, L. L. (1968). Studies of muscle capillary besement membranes in normal subjects, diabetic and prediabetic patients. *Journal of Clinical Investigation*, **47**, 1973–99.

Steffes, M. W., Sutherland, D. E. R., Goetz, F. C., Rich, S. S., and Mauer, S. M. (1985). Studies of kidney and muscle biopsy specimens from identical twins discordant for type 1 diabetes mellitus. *New England Journal of Medicine*, **312**, 1282–7.

Tarnow, L., Cambien, F., Rossing, P., Nielsen, F. S., Hansen, B. V., Lecerf, L., *et al.* (1995). Insertion–deletion polymorphism in the angiotensin I converting enzyme gene is associated with coronary heart disease in IDDM patients with diabetic nephropathy. *Diabetologia*, **38**, 798–803.

Tarnow, L., Cambien, F., Rossing, P., Nielsen, F. S. A., Hanssen, B. V., Ricard, S., *et al.* (1996). Angiotensinogen gene polymorphism in IDDM patients with diabetic nephropathy. *Diabetes*, **45**, 367–9.

Trevisan, R., Li, L. K., Messent, J., Tariq, T., Walker, J. D., Earle, K., *et al.* (1992*a*). Na/H antiport activity and cell growth in cultured skin fibroblasts of IDDM patients with nephropathy. *Diabetes*, **41**, 1239–46.

Trevisan, R., Nosadini, R., Fioretto, P., Semplicini, A., Donadon, V., Doria, A., *et al.* (1992*b*). Clustering of risk factors in hypertensive insulin-dependent diabetics with high sodium–lithium countertransport. *Kidney International*, **41**, 855–61.

Viberti, G. C., Bilous, R. W., Mackintosh, D., and Keen, H. (1983). Monitoring glomerular function in diabetic nephropathy. A prospective study. *American Journal of Medicine*, **74**, 256–64.

Viberti, G. C., Keen, H., and Wiseman, M. J. (1987). Raised arterial pressure in parents of proteinuric insulin dependent diabetics. *British Medical Journal*, **295**, 515–17.

Walker, J. D., Tariq, T., and Viberti, G. C. (1990). Sodium–lithium countertransport activity in red cells of patients with insulin-dependent diabetes and nephropathy and their parents. *British Medical Journal*, **301**, 635–8.

Walker, J. D. and Viberti, G. C. (1991). Aetiology and pathogenesis of diabetic nephropathy: clues from early functional abnormalities. In: *Textbook of diabetes* (ed. J. C. Pickup and G. Williams), pp. 657–70. Blackwell Scientific Publications, Oxford.

Walker, J. D., Close, C. F., Jones, S. L., Rafftery, M., Keen, H., Viberti, G. C., *et al.* (1992). Glomerular structure in type 1 (insulin-dependent) diabetic patients with normo and microalbuminuria. *Kidney International*, **41**, 741–8.

Wilson, D. M. and Luetscher, J. A. (1990). Plasma prorenin activity and complications in children with insulin-dependent diabetes mellitus. *New England Journal of Medicine*, **323**, 1101–6.

Wilson, J. L., Root, H. R., and Marble, A. (1951). Diabetic nephropathy. A clinical syndrome. *New England Journal of Medicine*, **245**, 513–17.

Wiseman, M., Viberti, G., Macintosh, D., Jarrett, R. J., and Keen, J. (1984). Glycaemia, arterial pressure and microalbuminuria in type 1 (insulin-dependent) diabetes mellitus. *Diabetologia*, **26**, 401–5.

Yip, J., Mattock, M., Sethi, M., Morocutti, A., and Viberti, G. C. (1993*a*). Insulin resistance in family members of insulin-dependent diabetic patients with microalbuminuria. *Lancet*, **341**, 369–70.

Yip, J., Mattock, M. B., Morocutti, A., Sethi, M., Trevisan, R., and Viberti, G. C. (1993*b*). Insulin resistance in insulin-dependent diabetes with microalbuminuria. *Lancet*, **342**, 883–7.

21

Sickle cell anaemia and renal disease

Stephen H. Morgan

Introduction

Human single-gene disorders have been the subject of intense genetic research for almost a century and have resulted in many hostorical advances leading to the evolution of 'molecular genetics' as a science. In 1949, Pauling suspected that an abnormal haemoglobin was the cause of sickle-cell anaemia (Pauling *et al.* 1949) and this was subsequently confirmed by Ingram (1956) who found a single amino acid substitution (valine for glutamic acid at position 6 of the beta-globin chain) altering the haemoglobin polypeptide sequence. This was the first demonstration, in any organism, that a mutation in a structural gene could produce such an alteration in an amino acid sequence.

In the commonest form of sickling disease, the abnormal haemoglobin (HbS) results from a point mutation in the beta-globin gene. This alters the corresponding mRNA codon from GA which codes for glutamic acid to GU which codes for valine at the sixth position from the N terminus. This difference alters the electrophoretic mobility of the beta-globin chain which at reduced oxygen tension leads to aggregation of HbS into rod-like masses which distort red cells into sickle shapes. HbC results from a similar substitution of glutamine for lysine. HbSC disease usually produces a clinically milder clinical course. An individual with one normal beta-globin gene and one sickle-cell disease gene (sickle trait) is usually clinically normal, although occasionally, if exposed to reduced inspired oxygen tension, such as under anaesthesia or at high altitudes, he or she may develop splenic or renal infarcts.

The life expectancy of patients with sickle-cell anaemia has improved considerably since 1960 when Sir John Dacie described it as 'essentially a disease of childhood'. In 1973, Diggs estimated a median survivial of 14.3 years for patients with HbSS disease with 20% of deaths occurring in the first two years of life and half between the ages of five to 30 years (Diggs 1973). More recent and large published series suggest a median survival of 42 years for men and 48 years for women with HbSS disease, with this improvement increasing to 60 years and 68 years respectively for HbSC disease (Leikin *et al.* 1989; Platt *et al.* 1994).

Prolonged survival in homozygous sickle-cell anaemia has highlighted the pathological effects of the disease at many sites, including the kidney. In some patients the changes produce only asymptomatic biochemical abnormalities. In others, papillary infarction and recurrent urinary tract infections present more difficult clinical problems. In 1974, the first report of prolonged survival of patients with sickle-cell anaemia on haemodialysis was seen (Friedman *et al.* 1974). Sickle-cell anaemia is, however, a relatively rare cause of progressive renal failure but this, as a complication, does significantly affect prognosis (Nissenson and Port 1989; Powars *et al.* 1991). It appears that patients with the Central African Republic beta-s gene cluster haplotype are genetically predisposed to, and more likely to, develop progressive shronic renal failure as well as other major organ damage (Powars *et al.* 1990).

Table 21.1   Renal abnormalities in sickle-cell anaemia

1. *Haemodynamic changes*
    Increased glomerular filtration
    Increased renal plasma flow
    Decreased filtration fraction
2. *Supranormal proximal tubular function*
    Increased reabsorption of phosphate and beta 2
        microglobulin
    Increased secretion of uric acid and creatinine
3. *Abnormalities of distal tubular function*
    Impaired potassium elimination
    Impaired concentration ability
    Impaired urinary acidification
4. *Glomerular abnormalities*
    Proteinuria
    Nephrotic syndrome
    Chronic renal failure
5. *Miscellaneous*
    Haematuria
    Papillary necrosis
    Recurrent urinary tract infections
    Acute renal failure

Renal manifestations of sickle-cell anaemia

The wide spectrum of functional and pathological disorders of the kidney in sickle-cell anaemia has been the subject of many recent reviews (Allon 1989; Statius van Eps 1992; Tomson 1992; Falk and Jennette 1994). The major abnormalities are summarized in Table 21.1. These complications develop more commonly in homozygous HbSS disease than in HbSC disease.

Tubular disorders

In childhood, many of the biochemical disorders of renal function observed—particularly impaired concentrating ability and a partial distal renal tubular acidosis—are reversible, and improve following repeated blood transfusion. By adolescence, however, they tend to become fixed (Statius van Eps 1992). Initially, these abnormalities are probably caused by increased viscosity within, and intermittent occlusion of, the vasa recta by microthrombi. This may be reduced by multiple transfusion. Eventually, however, these vessels become irreversibly obliterated with consequent ischaemia and multiple infarctions of the inner renal medulla with blunting and cavitation of the papillary tip, papillary necrosis, and calyectasis. An overlying parenchymal scar develops, characteristically depressing the capsular surface of the affected kidney. The contribution of chronic analgesic usage to the development of papillary necrosis is a debatable but potential factor.

One important practical aspect of these abnormalities is that the increased tubular secretion of creatinine observed in patients with sickle-cell anaemia produces an unreliable overestimate of glomerular filtration rate (GFR), if this is based on creatinine clearance alone (Allon *et al.* 1988).

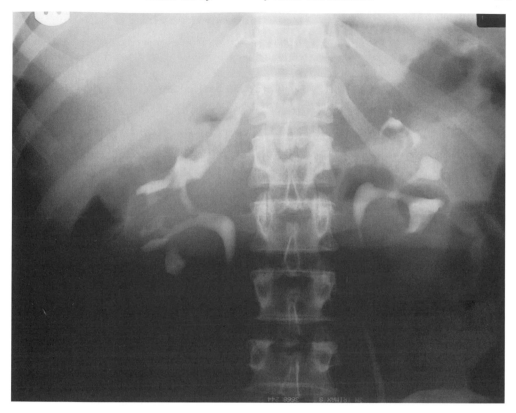

Fig. 21.1 IVU showing typical lesion of papillary necrosis.

Haematuria and papillary necrosis

Macroscopic haematuria and coincidentally observed microscopic haematuria, with or without gross papillary necrosis, are not infrequent events in sickle-cell anaemia. These complications may also develop in heterozygotes with sickle-cell trait and are often undiagnosed. Intravenous pyelography (IVU) remains the investigation of choice (Fig. 21.1) but should only be performed in well-hydrated patients. Gross, protracted, and life-threatening haematuria may occur as a result of relatively inconspicuous lesions of the papillae (Mostofi *et al.* 1957). Such bleeding is four to five times commoner in the left kidney than from the right. It is postulated that this is due to increased venous pressure on the left due to the longer renal vein. A protracted episode of haematuria may become a difficult clinical problem to the extent that nephrectomy and autotransplantation have sometimes been considered (Quinibi 1988). Obviously, other haemorrhagic disorders and pathologies should be excluded before considering such extreme intervention and, on the whole, conservative maneouvres including bed rest, maintaining a high flow of alkaline urine, exchange transfusion, and antifibrinolytic drugs should be considered initially.

Recurrent urinary tract infections—which may themselves precipitate a sickling crisis—are particularly common, even in the absence of established papillary scarring. The usual bacterial isolates are *E.coli*, *Enterobacter*, and *Klebsiella* and infections may often be asymptomatic.

Acute renal failure

Reversible acute tubular necrosis is well-recognized in sickle-cell anaemia, usually in the context of 'crises' with super added sepsis and volume depletion (Sklar *et al.* 1990). The possibility of an acute glomerulonephritis running a rapidly progressive course—precipitating a sickle crisis—should not be overlooked, and has on one occasion been missed (Gleadle *et al.* 1995). Acute rhabdomyolysis during a crisis, resulting in acute renal failure, is also described (Hassell *et al.* 1994).

Sickle-cell glomerulopathy

Low-grade proteinuria (<3.0 g/day) is relatively common in sickle-cell anaemia, and may occur in up to 26% of patients (Sklar *et al.* 1990; Falk and Jennette 1994). Nephrotic range proteinuria is the hallmark of 'sickle-cell glomerulopathy' and usually heralds an inevitable progression to end-stage renal failure (ESRF). Nonetheless, chronic renal insufficiency is relatively rare in sickle-cell anaemia, occurring in 4.2–18% of patients in large population surveys and usually developing between the second and fourth decade (Thomas *et al.* 1982; Powars *et al.* 1991; Falk *et al.* 1992). This particular complication reduces the median survival in sickle-cell anaemia from 51 years in non-uraemic patients to 27 years—even with early renal replacement therapy (Powars *et al.* 1991). In these patients there is an increased incidence of painful crises, transfusion requirement, pericardial and pleural effusions, and death from intracranial haemorrhage.

The pathology of sickle-cell glomerulopathy

Heavy proteinuria, reflecting glomerular injury, is more common and occurs earlier in HbSS than in other haemoglobinopathies (Falk *et al.* 1992). The commonest histological lesion is glomerular hypertrophy associated with focal and segmental glomerulosclerosis (FSGS), first described 40 years ago (Bernstein and Whitten 1960) and subsequently confirmed by other investigators (Pitcock *et al.* 1970; Bhathena and Sondheimer 1991; Verani and Conley 1991). Recent detailed studies have emphasized glomerular hypertrophy ('glomerulomegaly') as a significant feature of sickle glomerulopathy with an increase in average glomerular diameter and glomerular area by 35% and 80% respectively (Falk *et al.* 1992) (Fig. 21.2). Sclerotic segments often show non-specific immunofluorescence for IgM and C3.

The precise mechanism for the development of the histological changes observed in sickle-cell glomerulopathy remains unclear. Children with sickle-cell anaemia have a very high renal plasma flow and GFR, and some of the histological changes observed in adult patients may reflect 'hyperfiltration injury' (Falk and Jennette 1994). This may be exacerbated by ischaemic medullary damage which stimulates the release of vasodilator prostaglandins (Hatch *et al.* 1970). Angiotensin-converting enzyme inhibitors have a demonstrable role in reducing proteinuria and glomerular hyperfiltration injury in many unrelated glomerular disorders. This phenomenon has again been observed in heavy proteinuria complicating sickle-cell anaemia, but any clinical benefit has yet to be demonstrated (Falk *et al.* 1992; Falk and Jennette 1994).

Other glomerular lesions have been observed in sickle-cell anaemia, including classical post-streptococcal glomerulonephritis (Sushano and Lewy 1969; Roy *et al.* 1976), membranous glomerulonephritis (Elfenbein *et al.* 1974), and mesangiocapillary (membrano-proliferative) glomerulonephritis with or without crescent formation (Iskanadar *et al.* 1991; Gleadle *et al.* 1995). Heavy proteinuria and membranous changes as a result of renal vein thrombosis is, of course, theoretically potentially more likely in sickle-cell anaemia than in other nephrotic states.

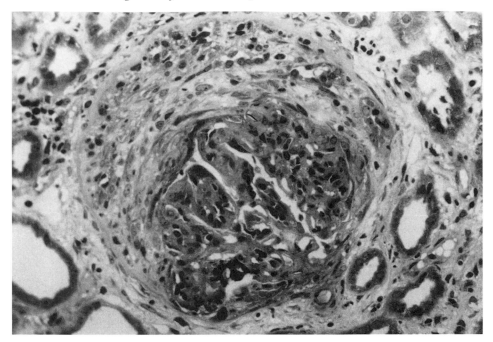

Fig. 21.2   Glomerulus with mesangiocapillary glomerulonephritis and glomerulomegaly.

It has been suggested that the variety of glomerular lesions observed in sickle-cell anaemia are the result of autologous immune complex disease due to the release of renal tubular epithelial antigen from ischaemic tubular cells (Straus *et al.* 1975; Ozwa *et al.* 1976), but no immune complex deposition has been observed in glomeruli, even early on in the natural history of sickle-cell glomerulopathy (Tejani *et al.* 1985). Chronic endothelial injury or mesangial phaghocytosis of fragmented red cells may produce misleading histological appearances resembling mesangiocapillary (membranoproliferative) glomerulonephritis, but without classical changes on immunofluorescence.

Hypertension in sickle-cell disease

Hypertension is unusual in populations with sickle-cell anaemia—less than in the black population as a whole (Johnson and Giorgio 1981) unless chronic renal insufficiency supervenes. It is postulated that this is due to a physiological environment analogous to that seen in Bartter's syndrome. Patients with sickle-cell anaemia have been found to have endogenous hyperreninism and increased production of renal prostoglandins along with histological changes within the renal medulla similar to that seen in Bartter's syndrome (Statius van Eps 1992).

Management of chronic renal failure in sickle-cell anaemia

The impact of chronic renal failure on mortality in sickle-cell disease has already been highlighted. General measures to avoid sickle crises and the risk of acute on chronic renal failure are obvious and include prompt treatment of urinary tract and other infections and pre-operative blood transfusion if HbS levels are greater than 20%. The loss of the ability to concentrate urine is a consistent abnormality in early sickle-cell nephropathy and puts these patients at particular risk of dehydration—another factor in the precipitation of crises.

The problem of end-stage renal failure

As chronic renal failure progresses to end-stage, there may be worsening anaemia, an increase in transfusion requirements, and an accompanying risk of iron overload (Morgan *et al.* 1982; Sherwood *et al.* 1985). As in other diseases which cause chronic renal failure, initiation of dialysis should be based on clinical assessment rather than absolute biochemical indices. Once a patient with sickle-cell anaemia is established on dialysis, regular transfusion—reducing the HbS percentage to less than 20–30%—appears to protect against sickle crises. Hostorical experience, however, suggests that in general patients fare badly on dialysis with difficult vascular access and the consequences of continuing and often extensive damage to other organs, particularly the heart (Tomson 1991).

Use of erythropoietin in sickle-cell anaemia

Reduced erythropoietin production occurs at an early stage in renal dysfunction associated with sickle-cell anaemia. The worsening anaemia, increased transfusion requirements, and risk of HLA sensitization in patients with advancing chronic renal failure, who may potentially be transplantable, have stimulated much interest in the use of recombinant human erythropoietin therapy (rHuEpo) (Roger *et al.* 1991; Steinberg 1991). Although the use of rHuEpo appears to stimulate a reticulocytosis and a significant increase in HbS levels, there is no beneficial or even significant rise in protective HbF and total haemoglobin, or reduction in transfusion requirements, even in weekly doses exceeding 300 units/kg (Tomson *et al.* 1992; Tomson 1993). Treatment of non-uraemic patients with sickle-cell anaemia with hydroxyurea appears to prolong red-cell survival and increase HbF levels (Rodgers *et al.* 1990) and this response may be augmented by rHuEpo (Rodgers *et al.* 1993). Whether the use of hydroxyurea in combination with rHuEpo will confer any benefit for patients with sickle-cell anaemia and ESRF remains unanswered.

Renal transplantation

Early reports of transplantation in sickle-cell anaemia suggested poor patient and allograft outcome (Chatterjee 1980) with an increased incidence of thrombotic cerebrovascular disease (Barber *et al.* 1987), transplant renal artery thrombosis (Donnelly *et al.* 1988), and an increase in sickling crises following correction of anaemia (Spector *et al.* 1978). Recurrence of classical sickle glomerulopathy has also been described three years after renal transplantation (Miner *et al.* 1987).

The overall clinical experience of renal transplantation in sickle-cell anaemia has, however, been small, as highlighted by a recent review from Baltimore, USA where of 1555 renal transplants performed between 1968 and 1993, only five were for sickle-cell anaemia (Montgomery *et al.* 1994). Adequate perioperative hydration and oxygenation along with pre-operative exchange transfusion if the HbS level is greater than 20–30% are recommended manoeuvres. Reported experience of renal transplantation from UK centres is minimal, but Chatterjee's updated report from North America (1987) suggests a one-year graft survival of 82% for live related allografts and 62% for cadaveric allografts.

The outlook for patients with sickle-cell anaemia and progressive renal failure still appears bleak. The recognition of a subset of patients with glomerulopathy by regular urinalysis and the early initiation of treatment with angiotensin-converting enzyme inhibitors may delay the progression of renal failure, as has been observed in diabetes mellitus, but this needs further analysis. The management of worsening anaemia as renal failure progresses is a continuing challenge.

References

Allon, M. (1989). Renal abnormalities in sickle-cell disease. *Archives of Internal Medicine*, **150**, 501–4.

Allon, M., Lawson, L., Eckman, J., Delaney, V., and Bourke, E. (1988). Effects of non-steroidal anti-inflammatory drugs on renal function in sickle-cell anaemia. *Kidney International*, **34**, 500–6.

Barber, W. H., Deirhoi, M. H., and Julian, B. A. (1987). Renal tranplantation in sickle-cell anaemia and sickle-cell disease. *Clinical Transplantation*, **1**, 169–75.

Bernstein, J. and Whiiten, C. F. (1960). A histological appraisal of the kidney in sickle-cell anaemia. *Archives of Pathology*, **70**, 407–18.

Bhathena, D. B. and Sondheimer, J. H. (1991). The glomerulopathy of homozygous sickle haemoglobin (SS) disease: morphology and athogenesis. *Journal of the American Society of Nephrology*, **1**, 1241–52.

Chatterjee, S. (1980). National study on natural history of renal allograft in sickle-cell disease or trait. *Nephron*, **25**, 199–201.

Chatterjee, S. N. (1987). National study of natural history of renal allograft in sickle-cell disease or trait: A second report. *Transplantation Proceedings*, **19**, 33–5.

Diggs, L. M. (1973). Anatomic lesions in sickle-cell disease. In: *Sickle-cell disease: diagnosis, management, education and research* (ed. H. Abramson, J. F. Bertles, and D. L. Wethers), pp 189–229. St Louis CV, Mosby.

Donnelly, P. K., Edmunds, H. E., and O'Reilly, K. (1988). Renal transplantation in sickle-cell disease. *Lancet*, **ii**, 229.

Elfenbein, I. B., Patchefsky, A., Schwartz, W., and Weinstein, A. G. (1974). Pathology of the glomerulus in sickle-cell anaemia with and without nephrotic syndrome. *American Journal of Pathology*, **77**, 357–76.

Falk, R. J., et al. (1992). Prevalence and pathological features of sickle-cell nephropathy and response to inhibition of antiotensin-converting enzyme. *New England Journal of Medicine*, **326**, 910–15.

Falk, R. J. and Jennette, J. C. (1994). Sickle-cell nephropathy. *Advances in Nephrology*, **23**, 133–47.

Friedman, E. A., Sreepada Roao, T. K., Sprung, C. L., et al. (1974). Uraemia in sickle-cell anaemia treated by maintenance haemodialysis. *New England Journal of Medicine*, **291**, 431–5.

Gleadle, J. M., Morgan, S. H., Landells, W. N., and Lumley, H. S. (1995). Crescentic glomerulonephritis in sickle-cell disease. *Nephrology, Dialysis and Transplantation*. In press.

Hassell, K. L., Eckman, J. R., and Lane, P. R. (1994). Acute multiorgan failure syndrome: a potentially catastrophic complication of severe sickle-cell pain episodes. *American Journal of Medicine*, **96**, 155–62.

Hatch, F. E., et al. (1970). Renal circulatory abnormalties in young adults with sickle-cell anaemia. *Journal of Laboratory and Clinical Medicine*, **76**, 632–40.

Ingram, V. M. (1956). A specific chemical difference between the globins of normal human and sickle-cell anaemia haemoglobin. *Nature*, **178**, 792–4.

Iskander, S. S., et al. (1991). Membrano-proliferative glomerulonephritis associated with sickle-cell disease in two siblings. *Clinical Nephrology*, **35**, 47–51.

Johnson, C. S. and Giorgio, A. J. (1981). Arterial blood pressure in adults with sickle-cell disease. *Archives of Internal Medicine*, **141**, 891–3.

Leikin, S. L., Gallagher, D., Kinney, T. R., Sloane, D., Klug, P., and Rida, W. (1989). Mortality in children and adolescents with sickle-cell disease. *Paediatrics*, **84**, 500–8.

Miner, D. J., Jorkasky, D. K., Perloff, L. J., Grossman, R. A., and Tomaszenski, J. E. (1987). Recurrent sickle-cell nephropathy in a transplant kidney. *American Journal of Kidney Diseases*, **4**, 306–13.

Montgomery, R., Zibari, G., Hill, G. S., and Ratner, L. E. (1994). Renal transplantation in patients with sickle-cell nephropathy. *Transplantation*, **58**, 618–19.

Morgan, A. G., Gruberca, and Serjeant, G. R. (1982). Erythropoietin and renal function in sickle-cell disease. *British Medical Journal*, **285**, 1686–8.

Mostofi, F. K., Vorder-Brugge, C. F., and Diggs, L. W. (1957). Lesions in kidneys removed for unilateral haematuria in sickle-cell disease. *Archives of Pathology*, **63**, 336–51.

Nissenson, A. R. and Port, F. K. (1989). Outcome of end-stage renal disease in patients with rare causes of renal failure. 1. Inherited metabolic disorders. *Quarterly Journal of Medicine*, **73**, 1055–62.

Ozawa, T., *et al.* (1976). Autologous immune complex nephritis associated with sickle-cell trait: diagnosis of the haemogloblinopathy after renal structural and immunological studies. *British Medical Journal*, **1**, 369–71.

Pauling, L., Itano, H. A., Singser, S. J., and Wells, J. C. (1949). Sickle-cell anaemia, a molecular disease. *Science*, **110**, 543–8.

Pitcock, J. A., *et al.* (1970). Early renal changes in sickle-cell anaemia. *Archives of Pathology*, **90**, 403–10.

Platt, O. S., Brambilla, D. J., and Wendell, F., *et al.* (1994). Mortalty in sickle-cell disease: life expectancy and risk factors for early death. *New England Journal of Medicine*, **330**, 1139–44.

Powars, D., Chan L. S., and Schroeder, W. A. S. (1990). The variable expression of sickle-cell disease is genetically determined. *Seminars in Haematology*, **27**, 360–76.

Powars, D., Elliott-Mills, D., and Chan, L., *et al.* (1991). Chronic renal failure in sickle-cell disease: risk factors, clinical course, and mortality. *Annals of Internal Medicine*, **115**, 614–20.

Qunibi, W. Y. (1988). Renal autotransplantation for severe sickle-cell haematuria. *Lancet*, i, 236–7.

Rodgers, G. P., Dover, G. J., Noguchi, C. T., Schechter, A. N., and Nienhuis, A. W. (1990). Haematological response of patients with sickle-cell disease to treatment with hydroxyurea. *New England Journal of Medicine*, **322**, 1037–45.

Rodgers, G. P., Dover, G. J., Uyesaka, N., *et al.* (1993). Augmentation by erythropoietin of the fetal-haemoglobin response to hydroxyurea in sickle-cell disease. *New England Journal of Medicine*, **328**, 73–80.

Roger, S. D., MacDougall, I. C., Thuraisingham, R. C., and Rain, A. G. G. (1991). Erythropoietin in anaemia of renal failure in sickle-cell disease. *New England Journal of Medicine*, **325**, 1175–6.

Roy, S., *et al.* (1976). Sickle-cell disease and post-streptococcal acute glomerulonephritis. *American Journal of Clinical Pathology*, **66**, 986–90.

Sherwood, J. B., Goldwasser, E., Chilcote, R., Carmichael, L. D., and Nagel, R. L. (1985). Sickle-cell anaemia patients have low erythropoietin levels for their degree of anaemia. *Blood*, **67**, 46–9.

Sklar, A. H., *et al.* (1990). A population study of renal function in sickle-cell anaemia. *International Journal of Artificial Organs*, **13**, 231–6.

Spector, D., Zachary, J. B., Sterioff, S., and Millan, J. (1978). Painful crises following renal transplanation in sickle-cell anaemia. *American Journal of Medicine*, **64**, 835–9.

Statius van Eps, L. W. (1992). Sickle-cell disease and the kidney In: *Oxford textbook of clinical nephrology* (ed. S. Cameron, A. M. Davison, J-P. Grunfeld, D. Kerr, and E. Ritz), pp. 700–20. Oxford University Press, Oxford.

Steinberg, M. H. (1991). Erythropoietin for anaemia of renal failure in sickle-cell disease. *New England Journal of Medicine*, **324**, 1369–70.

Strauss, J., *et al.* (1975). Nephropathy associated with sickle-cell anaemia: an autologous immune complex nephritis. *American Journal of Medicine*, **58**, 382–7.

Susmand, S. and Lewy, J. E. (1969). Sickle-cell disease and acute glomerulonephritis. *American Journal of Diseases of Childhood*, 118, 615–18.

Tejani, A., *et al.* (1985). Renal lesions in sickle-cell nephropathy in children. *Nephron*, 39, 352–5.

Thomas, A. N., Pattison, C., and Serjeant, G. R. (1982). Causes of death in sickle-cell disease in Jamaica. *British Medical Journal*, 285, 633–5.

Tomson, C. R. V. (1992). End-stage renal disease in sickle-cell disease: future directions. *Postgraduate Medical Journal*, 68, 775–8.

Tomson, C. R. V. (1993). Effect of recombinant human erythropoietin on erythropoiesis in homozygous sickle-cell anaemia and renal failure. *Blood*, 81, 9–14.

Tomson, C. R. V., Edmunds, M. E., Chambers, K., Bricknell, S., Feehally, J., and Walls, J. (1992). Effect of recombinant human erythropoietin on erythropoiesis in homozygous sickle-cell anaemia and renal failure. *Nephrology, Dialysis and Transplantation*, 7, 817–21.

Verani, R. R. and Conley, S. B. (1991). Sickle-cell glomerulopathy with focal segmental glomerulosclerosis. *Child Nephrology and Urology*, 11, 206–8.

Section E
Disorders associated with renal calculi

22

The primary hyperoxalurias

Stephen H. Morgan

Introduction

Although oxalate has a biological role in plants and fungi—providing a protective calcium oxalate exoskeleton—no useful function has been defined in man. Nonetheless, a normal adult will excrete up to 0.5 mmol/24 h of oxalate in the urine derived from diet and the endogenous metabolism of glyoxylate and ascorbic acid (vitamin C) (Fig. 22.1). An excess biological load of oxalate is potentially harmful as the calcium salt is very insoluble at physiological pHs (Hodgkinson 1977).

Oxalate is excreted by the kidney by a combination of glomerular filtration and net tubular secretion (Osswald and Hautmann 1979). The kidney's role in oxalate excretion makes it a prime target for calcium oxalate crystallization and the formation of renal calculi of parenchymal nephrocalcinosis if subjected to an increased plasma load and consequent hyperoxaluria. A decline in glomerular filtration rate (GFR) will, therefore, cause oxalate accumulation. If the plasma oxalate concentration reaches a critically high level resulting in plasma supersaturation with respect to calcium, tissue deposition of calcium oxalate will occur (systemic oxalosis). Blood vessels, myocardium, bone, and kidneys are the primary targets (Fayemi *et al.* 1979).

Hyperoxaluria may accompany a number of clinical disorders (Table 22.1), usually as a secondary consequence of hyperabsorption of ingested oxalate or because of an exogenous derangement of normal metabolic pathways. The primary hyperoxalurias (PH) comprise three inborn errors of metabolism, all of which may present similarly. This review will concentrate on primary hyperoxaluria type I (PH1), an autosomal recessive disorder of metabolism which has been particularly well-characterized over the past decade, but will make some comparisons with other primary disorders of oxalate metabolism.

Clinical aspects of the hyperoxalurias

Although the primary hyperoxalurias are metabolically and genetically distinct, clinically they may be indistinguishable, all commonly presenting with recurrent calcium oxalate urinary calculi in childhood or adult life.

In PH, a decline in GFR resulting from renal damage of any kind (obstructive stone disease, urinary infection, surgical intervention) will cause oxalate retention with a consequent rise in plasma oxalate concentration (Zarembski *et al.* 1966). If the GFR falls below 25 ml/min/1.73 m^2, plasma oxalate concentrations may attain critically high levels (Morgan *et al.* 1987) causing supersaturation of plasma and tissue deposition of calcium oxalate (systemic oxalosis). It is this propensity to develop systemic oxalosis that determines the clinical severity of this disease in any one particular patient.

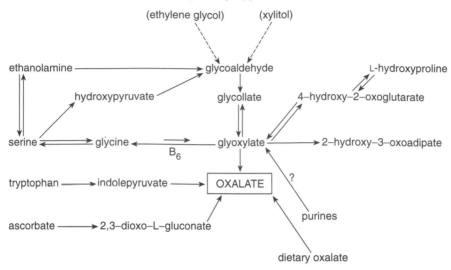

Fig. 22.1   Metabolic pathways to oxalate production in man.

Table 22.1   The hyperoxalurias

Primary hyperoxaluria
   Type 1 hyperoxaluria with glycolic aciduria
              (alanine: glyoxylate aminotransferase
              [AGT] deficiency)
   Type 2 hyperoxaluria with L-glyceric aciduria
              (D-glycerate dehydrogenase [DGDH]
              deficiency)
   Type 3 mild metabolic (intestinal
              hyperabsorptive) hyperoxaluria

Secondary hyperoxaluria
   Increased oxalate absorption
              Increased oxalate ingestion
              Small bowel disease, resection, or bypass
              Chronic pancreatic or biliary tract disease
   Metabolic derangement
              Excessive ascorbic acid ingestion
              Ethylene glycol poisoning
              Pyridoxine (vitamin B) deficiency
              Methoxyflurane anaesthesia
              Postprostatectomy glycine irrigation
              Aspergillus infection
   Chronic renal failure*

---

*Causes hyperoxalaemia rather than hyperoxaluria.

Clinical biochemistry

Typically, both plasma and urinary oxalate levels will be raised in all three disorders. PH2 is differentiated from PH1 and PH3 on the basis of urinary organic acid excretion. In addition to hyperoxaluria, patients with PH2 excrete an excess of L-glyceric acid, whilst those with PH1 and PH3 excrete glycolic acid in their urine.

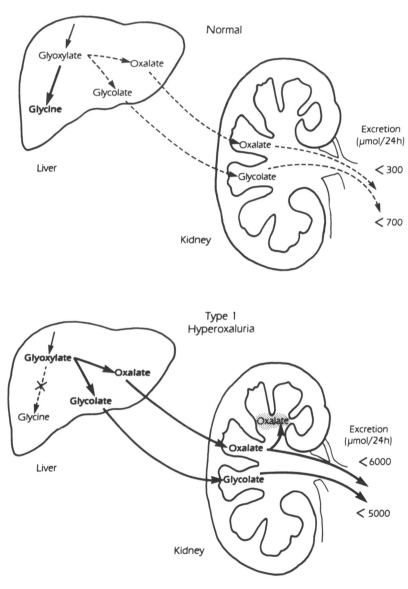

Fig. 22.2 Glyoxylate metabolism in normal man and patients with primary hyperoxaluria type 1 (alanine:glyoxylate aminotransferase deficiency). (From Morgan *et al.* (1989) with permission.)

Primary hyperoxaluria type 1 (PH1)

Essentially, the basis of the metabolic defect in PH1 reflects disordered glyoxylate metabolism resulting in the endogenous overproduction of oxalate and glycolate which are then excreted by the kidney. The solubility of oxalate is poor, and calcium oxalate calculi form when the urine becomes supersaturated.

In vivo metabolic studies have long implicated abnormal glyoxylate transamination as a possible cause of PH1 (Smith *et al.* 1964) (Fig. 22.2). This was originally ascribed to a deficiency of cytosolic 2-oxoglutarate:glyoxylate carboligase (Koch *et al.* 1967). The first direct evidence that the enzymatic defect was actually due to deficiency of alanine:glyoxalate aminotransferase (AGT) came when this enzyme was found to be markedly deplete in liver biopsies from two patients with PH1 (Danpure and Jennings 1986). To date, more than 150 patients with PH1 have been shown to have hepatic AGT deficiency (Danpure, personal communication). In addition to a reduction in AGT catalytic activity, many patients may be deficient in AGT immunoreactive protein (Danpure 1991). In about one-third of patients with PH1 immunoreactive AGT protein (normally exclusively localized within hepatocellular peroxisomes) (Kamoda *et al.* 1980; Cooper *et al.* 1988) has been mistargeted to mitochondria and unable to perform its metabolic function properly (i.e. glyoxylate detoxification) (Danpure *et al.* 1989*a*; Danpure 1991).

Pyridoxal phosphate is an essential cofactor for all aminotransferases. Pharmacological doses of pyridoxine hydrochloride (vitamin B_6 400–1000 mg daily) cause varying degrees of reduction in oxalate excretion in some but not all PH1 patients (Gibbs and Watts 1970; Watts *et al.* 1985*a*). Mutations deleting or affecting the affinity of the enzyme-binding site for pyridoxine as a cofactor may produce this range of therapeutic response. Urinary oxalate excretion can also be reduced by pyridoxine in patients with recurrent idiopathic calcium oxalate stones and in patients with PH3 (Gershoff and Prien 1967; Gill and Rose 1986). Pyridoxine appears safe in patients with primary hyperoxaluria despite the use of large pharmacological doses, and deleterious side-effects such as peripheral neuropathy have not been observed (Schaumberg *et al.* 1983).

A full-length cDNA encoding human AGT has been cloned and sequenced (Takada *et al.* 1990). The gene encodes a protein sequence of 392 amino acids and has been localized to chromosome 2q36–37 (Purdue *et al.* 1992). Causal mutations have only been defined in approximately 50% of patients with PH1 and do not form a basis for molecular diagnosis (Danpure 1991; Purdue *et al.* 1992).

Table 22.2 Clinical features of primary hyperoxaluria

Recurrent urinary tract stones
  Obstruction
  Urinary tract infection
  Surgical scarring
Progressive development of renal failure
Systemic oxalosis
  Further decline in GFR
  Cardiac conduction defects
  Synovitis
  Osteosclerosis
  Peripheral neuropathy
  Obliterative vasculitis

Table 22.3 Diseases in which peroxisomal dysfunction plays a major role

Zellweger syndrome*
Adrenoleukodystrophy
Acatalasia
Refsum's disease*
Hyperpipecolic aciduria
Chondroplasia punctatum rhizomelia
Leber amaurosis
Primary hyperoxaluria type 1*

*Associated with renal disease.

Subcellular histological analysis of liver biopsies from PH1 patients demonstrate normal numbers of relatively normal looking but slightly small peroxisomes. In comparison with other peroxisomal diseases (Table 22.3) PH1 is unrelated to any defect in lipid metabolism. Consequently, the clinical manifestations of PH1 differ significantly from those other peroxisomal disorders which are usually multisystemic, often with neurological involvement.

Primary hyperoxaluria type 2 (PH2)

This variant of PH was first described in 1968 (Williams and Smith 1968). Patients with this disorder have deficient activity of D-glycerate dehydrogenase, an enzyme which also has glycolate reductase activity (DGDH/GR).

A deficiency of DGDH allows hydroxypyruvate to be reduced by L-lactate dehydrogenase in the presence of reduced NADH. The resulting product is L-glycerate, an organic acid not usually found in urine (Tolbert 1981). The glycolate reductase (GR) activity of DGDH reduces the conversion of glyoxylate to glycolate. The subsequent conversion of glyoxylate to oxalate by L-lactate dehydrogenase then accounts for the hyperoxaluria characteristic of PH2.

Primary hyperoxaluria type 3 (PH3 mild metabolic hyperoxaluria)

This subgroup of 'idiopathic', recurrent, calcium oxalate stone-formers with modest hyperoxaluria and proportionately modest glycolic aciduria remains controversial in both its diagnosis and recognition (Gill and Rose 1986). Careful documentation of such patients has excluded any secondary factors predisposing to hyperoxaluria, and in particular no morphological or functionally definable intestinal lesions. The defect which produces PH3 has been postulated to be a primary abnormality resulting in isolated oxalate hyperabsorption from the bowel, which may be reversed by thiazide diuretics (Yendt and Cohanim 1986). More recently, an abnormality in conversion of pyridoxine to pyridoxal phospate has been suggested (Edwards and Rose 1991).

Clinical pathology

Although clinically indistinguishable, PH2 usually follows a more benign course than PH1, with only one patient reported to have progressed to end-stage renal failure (ESRF) (Williams and Smith 1968). Patients with PH2 do, however, appear much rarer, a total of only 21 patients to date documented in the world literature (Chlebeck *et al.* 1994). Although urinary calculi have

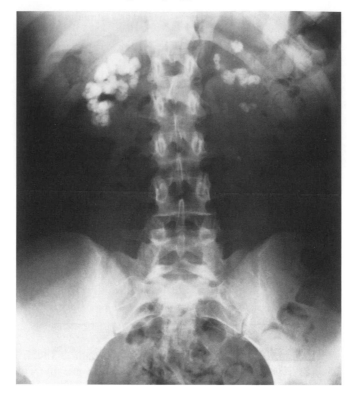

Fig. 22.3   Extensive bilateral staghorn calculi in a patient with hyperoxaluria.

been described as early as two months of age in PH2 (Seargeant *et al.* 1991), premature death is unusual. This is contrary to the overall clinical experience in PH1 where 50–80% of patients are dead or in ESRF by the end of their third decade (Hockaday *et al.* 1964; Latta and Brodehl 1990). Some patients with PH1 do, nonetheless, follow a relatively uneventful course, presenting with late-onset renal failure despite complete absence of hepatic AGT (Irish and Doust 1992).

Clinical presentation of PH1

An infantile form of PH1 is well described with ESRF and diffuse renal parenchymal oxalosis at presentation as early as two months (Leumann 1987). Renal calculi are not found but the renal parenchyma is characteristically echodense on ultrasonography or computerized tomography. This is useful in differentiating other causes of ESRF and crystalluria early in childhood, including disorders of purine metabolism (HGPRTase and APRTase deficiency).

More classically, patients with PH1 present between 2–18 years with recurrent urolithiasis and already significant renal functional impairment (Fig. 22.3).

There is considerable heterogeneity in the severity and rate of progression to end-stage failure in PH1, which may reflect the residual degree of hepatic AGT activity (Danpure *et al.* 1987). There is also considerable variability with respect to the partial or complete correction of oxalate overproduction in patients treated with pharmacological doses of pyridoxine hydrochloride

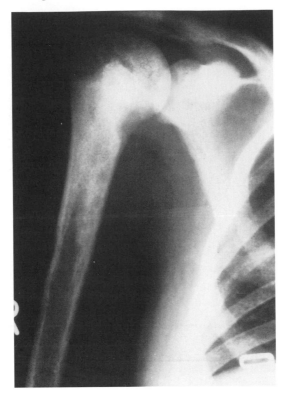

Fig. 22.4 Osteosclerosis in a patient with primary hyperoxaluria type 1 and ESRF.

(Vitamin B$_6$ 400–1000 mg daily) (Gibbs and Watts 1970; Watts *et al.* 1985*a*). Approximately 25% of patients with PH1 demonstrate a favourable response to pyridoxine. Pyridoxine-resistant patients follow a more indolent clinical course.

In PH1, recurrent urinary calculi may lead to loss of renal functional reserve as a result of vomiting and dehydration, infection, obstruction, and surgical scarring. As the GFR falls, systemic oxalosis develops with deposition of calcium oxalate at many sites, particularly in the tunica media of muscular arteries, myocardium, bone marrow, bone, synovium, vasa nevora, and kidneys (Figs 22.4 and 22.5). Clinically, this will lead to digital gangrene and difficult vascular access for dialysis, cardiomyopathy and cardiac conduction defects, destructive synovitis, and painful mononeuritis and osteosclerosis (Fig. 22.4). These systemic features (which will progress despite conventional dialysis) and accelerated renal failure account for the previously high mortality in PH1.

Diagnosis and assessment of patients with PH

The initial presentation of PH, as previously outlined, may range from recurrent urolithiasis to advanced systemic oxalosis with painful osteosclerosis and end-stage renal disease (ESRD).

In patients where there is a suspicion of PH, provided the GFR is greater than 10 ml/min, a diagnosis can be confirmed by assay of 24-hour urinary oxalate excretion. Biochemical

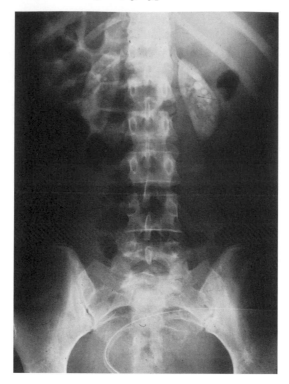

Fig. 22.5 Plain abdominal X-ray of a girl with primary hyperoxaluria type 1. Note the small, densely-calcified, end-stage kidneys and peritoneal dialysis catheter. (From Morgan and Moffat (1991) with permission.)

measurement of plasma and urinary oxalate excretion (POx and EUOx) was, in the past, unreliable as different assay techniques gave wide variations in normal ranges. *In vivo* techniques for measuring POx and oxalate metabolic pool size by radioisotope dilution yield consistent and reproducible results but remain a research tool (Watts *et al.* 1983). More reliable techniques for the measurement of POx and UEOx are now available, giving values that compare well with those derived from isotope-dilution techniques, and with a functional availability that makes them useful in clinical practice (Kasidas and Rose 1985; 1986).

Once a diagnosis of PH is biochemically confirmed, it may be further refined by measurement of urinary glycolate or L-glycerate. Should PH1 be confirmed it is vital to establish if the patient falls into a 'good prognosis' (pyridoxine-sensitive) group or a 'poor prognosis' (pyridoxine-resistant) group by measuring POx and UEOx before and after at least two months' treatment (vitamin B_6 400–1000 mg/day). In both groups it is essential to coordinate regular biochemical follow-up (GFR and POx) since oxalate retention increases dramatically as the GFR falls below 40 ml/min/1.73 m² with a consequent increased propensity for the development of systemic oxalosis (Morgan *et al.* 1987). Close biochemical surveillance also allows the appropriate initiation of renal replacement therapy.

When a diagnosis of PH1 is made it is important to establish a clinical 'baseline' for individual patients to monitor the development of significant systemic oxalosis. To this end, follow-up ECG, echocardiograms, skeletal survey, and bone densitometry are recommended. Computer-

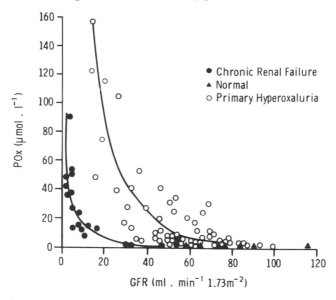

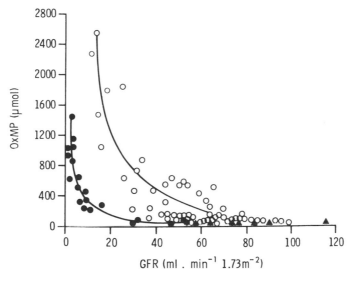

Fig. 22.6 Relationship between GFR and plasma oxalate concentration (POx) and oxalate metabolic pool size in eight patients with primary hyperoxaluria type 1 (○), studied by an *in vivo* isotopic method (Watts *et al.* 1983) sequentially over a six-year period. As the GFR falls, the effect of oxalate retention superimposed on overproduction results in expansion of the oxalate metabolic pools and a rise in POx. The effect of retention alone on these parameters is shown in a group of patients with non-hyperoxaluric renal failure (●). The normal range is shown for comparison (▲). (From Morgan *et al.* (1987) with permission.)

ized tomographic densitometry of the kidney is a particularly sensitive tool for documenting parenchymal oxalosis.

In patients presenting with advanced or end-stage renal failure and in whom there is a high suspicion of PH, urinary oxalate excretion is diagnostically unhelpful. The demonstration of a raised POx is also unhelpful since some patients with ESRD not due to PH will have a POx which lies in a similar range to patients with PH and ESRD (Morgan *et al.* 1987) (Fig. 22.6). In this instance a liver biopsy for AGT or DGDH assay is the only reliable route to diagnosis, and is essential if a kidney or kidney and liver transplant is to be considered (Morgan *et al.* 1990).

Prenatal diagnosis

With the discovery of the basic metabolic defect in PH1 came the viability of prenatal diagnosis by fetal liver biopsy. Unfortunately, the specific activity of AGT in fetal liver in the second trimester is much lower than that found postnatally and AGT activity is barely detectable before 14 weeks gestation. Plateau levels of AGT are reached at 21–24 weeks gestation allowing exclusion or confirmation (Danpure *et al.* 1988; 1989*b*) of diagnosis by a combination of immunoelectron microscopy of ultrasound-guided fetal liver biopsies.

Treatment of the primary hyperoxalurias

Strategies to limit stone formation

These empirical measures apply to patients with either PH1 or PH2. All patients with urinary stone disease should drink sufficient fluids to maintain a daily measured urine volume of three litres. As a 'rule of thumb', a glass of water for every waking hour is often suggested in addition to other fluids. Dietary restriction of both calcium and oxalate are recommended to reduce the contribution of both these ions to their concentration in the urine. Aggressive restriction of dietary calcium may, however, increase oxalate absorption from the bowel.

There has recently been encouraging reinterest in the long-term use of orthophosphate in patients with PH (Milliner *et al.* 1994). These agents reduce urinary supersaturation with calcium oxalate and urinary crystallization (Fredrick *et al.* 1963; Smith 1976; Brigman and Finlayson 1978). Oral alkali citrates may also confer benefit, particularly if started when a diagnosis of PH is made early on in the natural history of the disease (Luemann *et al.* 1993).

Management of established urolithiasis

This is largely dictated by standard urological practice and is not specific for calcium oxalate stones as a result of PH. It is, however, particularly important to avoid dehydration by prolonged pre-operative fasting.

Caution should probably be exercised with extracorporeal shock-wave lithotripsy as in one of the author's own patients and in patients anecdotally reported from other centres there has been accelerated acute or chronic renal dysfunction following the procedure (Barrett *et al.* 1988).

Management of established renal failure in PH1

Renal function usually deteriorates in the second decade in patients with pyridoxine-resistant PH1. Oxalate retention, superimposed on oxalate overproduction, leads to sudden expansion of the metabolic pool size and a sharp rise in POx (Fig. 22.6). Characteristically, the terminal illness is short, and unless renal excretory function is adequately replaced, death occurs from accelerated renal failure and the effect of systemic oxalosis.

Conventional dialysis techniques (standard or high-flux haemodialysis and continuous ambulatory peritoneal dialysis), although sufficient to control uraemia, do not provide sufficient oxalate clearance to counter overproduction of oxalate (Watts *et al.* 1984; Morgan *et al.* 1988; Sethi *et al.* 1988). Hence patients with PH1 managed in the long-term by standard dialysis techniques fall prey to the consequences of worsening systemic oxalosis. The poor subsequent physical health of such patients may jeopardize the success of a renal or a combined renal hepatic transplant (Morgan and Watts 1989; Watts *et al.* 1991*a,b*).

Lone renal transplantation has in general yielded poor results, often with delay in allograft function and a massive pre-operative oxalate load predisposing to intratubular and interstitial calcium oxalate deposition and allograft destruction. Successful strategies to optimize graft survival have included very early transplantation—before the GFR falls below 25 ml/min/1.73 m^2 (Watts *et al.* 1988), parathyroidectomy, vigorous (daily) pre-operative and postoperative haemodialysis, and post-transplantation hyperdiuresis (Scheinman *et al.* 1984; Scheinman 1991). There is some compelling evidence that transplant immunosuppression with cyclosporin A may accelerate renal parenchymal oxalosis although the precise mechanism is not clear (Noel *et al.* 1992).

Enzyme replacement therapy by liver transplantation in PH1

Because alanine:glyoxylate aminotransferase is only expressed to any significant extent in liver (Kamoda *et al.* 1980), it makes this organ uniquely suitable for use in enzyme replacement therapy in pyridoxine-resistant PH1. Orthotopic hepatic transplantation would introduce a supply of catalytically competent enzyme in the correct organ and subcellular location for substrate metabolism. A combined hepatorenal transplant would thus potentially correct the metabolic defect as well as replace the damaged primary target organ.

The first application of such controversial treatment was marred by the death of the patient in the immediate postoperative period from overwhelming cytomegalovirus infection (Watts *et al.* 1985*b*). Since then, over 100 such combined transplants and primary liver transplants have been performed in adult and paediatric patients with PH1. To date (Cochat and Watts 1995), the longest survival has been eight years with continued stable and near normal renal function. Biochemical resolution of the metabolic defect was illustrated in this patient with urinary glycolate excretion falling to within normal limits by one month post-transplant (Watts *et al.* 1987), in keeping with experience reported by other centres (Watts *et al.* 1991*a,b*). Long-term observation of patients receiving combined hepatorenal transplantation have also demonstrated radiological and histological improvement in osteosclerosis (Toussaint *et al.* 1993).

The rate of normalization of plasma and urinary oxalate levels may often be slow post-transplantation, particularly in those patients with a long history and especially those who have spent any length of time on renal replacement therapy prior to combined tranplantation. The plasma and urinary oxalate levels in such patients might take more than a year to normalize (Ruder *et al.* 1990). Even after successful combined transplantation, the newly grafted kidney may still be threatened by hyperoxaluria over this period of normalization (Lloveras *et al.* 1992).

In general, the metabolic outcome of liver tranplantation in PH1 is better if patients are transplanted before ESRF, so that combined renal transplantation is unnecessary (Cochat *et al.*

1989). This clinical option still remains somewhat controversial in view of the morbidity and irrevocability of liver transplantation as compared to lone renal transplantation.

Bibliography

Barratt, T. M., Von Sperling, V., Dillon, M. J., Rose, G. A., and Trompeter, R. S. (1988). Primary hyperoxaluria in children. In: *Oxalate metabolism in relation to urinary stone* (ed. G. A. Rose), pp. 83–101. Springer-Verlag, Berlin.

Brigman, J. and Finlayson, B. (1978). A survey of the effect of some drugs, chemicals and enzymes on calcium oxalate precipitation in the rat kidney. *Investigative Urology*, **15**, 496–7.

Broyer, M., Brunner, F. P., Brynger, H., *et al.* (1990). Kidney transplantation in primary oxalosis: data from the EDTA registry. *Nephrology Dialysis and Transplantation*, **5**, 332–6.

Chalmers, R. A., Tracey, B. M., Mistry, J., Griffiths, K. D., Green, A., and Winterhorn, M. H. (1984). L-glyceric aciduria (primary hyperoxaluria type 2) in siblings in two unrelated families. *Journal of Inherited Metabolic Diseases*, **7** (Suppl. 2), 133–4.

Chlebeck, P. T., Milliner, D. S., and Smith, L. H. (1994). Primary hyperoxaluria type II (L-glyceric aciduria). *American Journal of Kidney Diseases*, **23**, 255–9.

Cochat, P., Faure, J. L., Divry, P., *et al.* (1989). Liver transplantation in primary hyperoxaluria type 1. *Lancet*, **i**, 1142–3.

Cochat, P. and Scharer, K. (1993). Should liver transplantation be performed before advanced renal insufficiency in primary hyperoxaluria type 1. *Paediatric Nephrology*, **7**, 212–18.

Cochat, P. and Watts, R. W. E. (1995). *Nephrology, Dialysis and Transplantation*, **10** (Suppl. 8).

Cooper, P. J., Danpure, C. J., Wise, P. J., and Guttridge, K. M. (1968). Immunoelectron microscopic localization of alanine:glyoxylate aminotransferase in normal human liver and type 1 hyperoxaluric livers. *Biochemical Society Trans.*, **16**, 627–8.

Danpure, C. J. and Jennings, P. R. (1986). Primary alanine: glyoxylate aminotransferase deficiency in primary hyperoxaluria type 1. *FEBS Letters*, **201**, 20–4.

Danpure, C. J., Jennings, P. R., and Watts, R. W. E. (1987). The enzymological diagnosis of primary hyperoxaluria type 1 by measurement of alanine:glyoxylate aminotransferase activity in hepatic percutaneous needle biopsies. *Lancet*, **i**, 289–91.

Danpure, C. J., Jennings, P. R., Penketh, R. J., Wise, P. H., and Rodeck, C. H. (1988). Prenatal exclusion of primary hyperoxaluria type 1, *Lancet*, **i**, 367.

Danpure, C. J., Cooper, P. J., Wise, P. J., and Jennings, P. R. (1989*a*). An enzyme trafficking defect in two patients with primary hyperoxaluria type 1: peroxisomal alanine: glyoxylate aminotransferase rerouted to mitochondria. *Journal of Cell Biology*, **108**, 1345–52.

Danpure, C. J., Jennings, P. R., Penketh, R. J., Wise, P. J., Cooper, P. J., and Rodeck, C. H. (1989*b*). Foetal liver alanine: glyoxylate amino-transferase and the prenatal diagnosis of primary hyperoxaluria type 1. *Prenatal Diagnosis*, **9**, 271–81.

Danpure, C. J., Jennings, P. R., Mistry, J., Chalmers, R. A., McKerrell, R. E., Blakemore, W. F., *et al.* (1989). Enzymological characterization of a feline analogue of primary hyperoxaluria type 2: A model for human disease. *Journal of Inherited Metabolic Diseases*, **12**, 403–14.

Danpure, C. J. (1991). Molecular and clinical heterogeneity in primary hyperoxaluria type 1. *American Journal of Kidney Diseases*, **17**, 366–9.

Edwards, P. and Rose, G. A. (1991). Metabolism of pyridoxine in mild metabolic hyperoxaluria and primary hyperoxaluria type 1. *Urologia Internationalis*, **47**, 113–17.

Fayemi, A. O., Ali, M., and Braun, E. V. (1979). Oxalosis in haemodialysis patients. *Archives of Pathology and Laboratory Medicine*, **103**, 58–62.

Frederick, E. W., Rabkin, M. T., Richie. R. H., and Smith, L. H. (1963). Studies in primary hyperoxaluria 1: *in vivo* demonstration of a defect in glyoxalate metabolism. *New England Journal of Medicine*, **269**, 821–9.

Gershof, S. N. and Prine, E. L. (1967). Effect of daily MgO and vitamin B_6 administration to patients with recurring calcium oxalate kidney stones. *American Journal of Clinical Nutrition*, **20**, 393–9.

Gibbs, D. A. and Watts, R. W. E. (1970). The action of pyridoxine in primary hyperoxaluria. *Clinical Science*, **38**, 277–86.

Gibbs, D. A. and Watts, R. W. E. (1973). The identification of the enzymes that catalyse the oxidation of glyoxylate to oxalate in the 100 000 g supernatant fraction of human hyperoxaluric and control liver and heart tissue. *Clinical Science*, **44**, 227–41.

Gill, H. S. and Rose, G. A. (1986). Mild metabolic hyperoxaluria and its response to pyridoxine. *Urology International*, **41**, 393–6.

Hicks, N. R., Cranston, D. W., and Charlton, C. A. C. (1983). Fifteen-year follow-up of hyperoxaluria type II. *New England Journal of Medicine*, **309**, 796. (Letter).

Hockaday, T. D. R., Clayton, J. E., Frederick, E. W., and Smith, L. H. (1964). Primary hyperoxaluria. *Medicine*, **43**, 315–45.

Hodgkinson, A. (1977). *Oxalic acid in biology and medcine*. Academic Press, New York.

Irish, A. B. and Doust, B. (1992). Late presentation and development of nephrocalcinosis in primary hyperoxaluria. *Australian and New Zealand Journal of Medicine*, **22**, 48–50.

Kamoda, N., *et al.* (1980). The organ distribution of human alanine-2-oxoglutarate aminotransferase. *Biochemical Medicine*, **23**, 25–34.

Kasidas, G. P. and Rose, G. A. (1985). Continuous flow assay for urinary oxalate using immobilized oxalate oxidase. *Annals of Clinical Biochemistry*, **22**, 412–19.

Kasidas, G. P. and Rose, G. A. (1986). Measurement of plasma oxalate in healthy subjects, and in patients with chronic renal failure using immobilized oxalate oxidase. *Clinica Chima Acta*, **154**, 49–58.

Koch, J., Stokstad, E. L. R., Williams, H. E., and Smith, L. H. (1967). Deficiency of 2-oxoglutarate: glyoxylate carboligase activity in primary hyperoxaluria. *Proceedings of the National Academy of Science USA*, **57**, 1123–9.

Latta, K. and Brodehl, J. (1990). Primary hyperoxaluria type 1. *European Journal of Paediatrics*, **149**, 518–22.

Leumann, E. P. (1987). New aspects of infantile oxalosis. *Paediatric Nephrology*, **1**, 531–5.

Leumann, E., Hoppe, B., and Neuhaust, T. (1993). Management of primary oxaluria: efficacy of oral citrate administration. *Paediatric Nephrology*, **7**, 207–11.

Lloveras, J. J., Durand, D., Danpure, C., *et al.* (1992). Combined liver kidney transplantation in primary hyperoxaluria type 1: prevention of the recidive of calcium oxalate deposits in the renal graft. *Clinical Nephrology*, **38**, 128–31.

Milliner, D. S., Eickholt, J. T., Bergstrahl, E. J., Wilson, D. M., and Smith, L. H. (1994). Results of long-term treatment with orthophosphate and pyridoxine in patients with primary hyperoxaluria. *New England Journal of Medicine*, **331**, 1553–8.

Mistry, J., Danpure, C. J., and Chalmers, R. A. (1988). Hepatic D-glycerate dehydrogenase and glyoxalate reductase deficiency in primary hyperoxaluria type 2. *Biochemical Society Trans.*, **16**, 626–7.

Morgan, S. H., Purkiss, P., Watts, R. W. E., and Mansell, M. A. (1987). Oxalate dynamics in end-stage renal failure. Comparison with normal subjects and patients with primary hyperoxaluria. *Nephron*, **47**, 253–7.

Morgan, S. H., Maher, E. R., Purkiss, P., and Watts, R. W. E. (1988). Oxalate metabolism in end-stage renal disease: The effect of ascorbic acid and pyridoxine. *Nephrology, Dialysis and Transplantation*, **3**, 28–32.

Morgan, S. H. and Watts, R. W. E. (1989). Perspectives in the assessment and management of patients with primary hyperoxaluria type 1. *Advances in Nephrology*, **18**, 95–106.

Morgan, S. H., Bending, M. R. B., and Danpure, C. J. (1990). Exclusion of primary hyperoxaluria type 1 by percutaneous hepatic biopsy in end-stage renal failure. *Nephron*, **55**, 336–7.

Morgan, S. H. and Moffat, D. B. (1991). Inherited disease and congenital malformation. In: *Clinical atlas of the kidney* (ed. J. D. Williams, A. W. Asscher, D. B. Moffat, and E. Sanders), pp. 2.1–2.24. Gower Medical Publishing, London.

Noel, C., Pruvot, F. R., Talaska, A., *et al.* (1992). Transplantation for primary hyperoxaluria: role of oxalate crystal deposits in the occurrence of kidney failure. *Press Medicale—Paris*, **21**, 1997–8.

Osswald, H. and Hautmann, R. (1979). Renal elimination kinetics and plasma half-life of oxalate in man. *Urology International*, **34**, 440–50.

Purdue, P. E., Lumb, M. J., Fox, M., *et al.* (1991). Characterization and chromosomal mapping of a genomic clone encoding human alanine:glyoxylate aminotransferase. *Genomics*, **10**, 34–42.

Purdue, P. E., Lumb, M. J., Allsop. J., Minatogawa, Y., and Danpure, C. J. (1992). A glycine to glycine substitution abolishes alanine:glyoxylate aminotransferase activity in a subset of patients with primary hyperoxaluria type 1. *Genomics*, **13**, 215–18.

Rodby, R. A., Tyszka, T. S., and Williams, J. W. (1991). Reversal of cardiac dysfunction secondary to type 1 primary hyperoxaluria after combined liver–kidney transplantation. *American Journal of Medicine*, **94**, 498–504.

Ruder, H., Otto, G., Schutgent, R. B., *et al.* (1990). Excessive urinary oxalate excretion after combined renal and hepatic transplantation for correction of hyperoxaluria type 1. *European Journal of Paediatrics*, **150**, 56–8.

Schaumberg, H., *et al.* (1983). Sensory neuropathy from pyridoxine abuse—a new megavitamin syndrome. *New England Journal of Medicine*, **309**, 445–8.

Scheinman, J. I. (1984). The management of primary hyperoxaluria. *Kidney International*, **17**, 13–17.

Scheinman, J. I. (1991). Primary hyperoxaluria: therapeutic strategies for the nineties. *Kidney International*, **40**, 389–99.

Scheinman, J. I., Najarian, J. S., and Mauer, S. M. (1984). Successful strategies for renal transplantation in primary oxalosis. *Kidney International*, **25**, 804–11.

Seargeant, L. E., DeGroot, G. W., Dilling, L. A., Mallory, C. J., and Haworth, J. C. (1991). Primary oxaluria type 2 (L-glyceric aciduria): a rare cause of nephrolithiasis in children. *Journal of Paediatrics*, **118**, 912–14.

Sethi, D., Morgan, S. H., Purkiss, P., Curtis, J. R., and Watts, R. W. E. (1988). Oxalate clearance and metabolism in end-stage renal disease treated by high-flux haemodialysis. *Current Therapy in Nephrology (Karger)*, 379–81.

Smith, L. H., Hockaday, T. D., Efron, M. L., and Clayton, J. E. (1964). The metabolic defect of primary hyperoxaluria. *Transcripts of the Association of American Physicians*, **77**, 317–25.

Smith, L. H. and Williams, H. E. (1967). Treatment of primary hyperoxaluria. *Modern Treatment*, **4**, 522–30.

Smith, L. H. (1976). Application of physical, chemical, and metabolic factors to the management of urolithiasis. In: *Urolithiasis research* (ed. H. Fleisch, W. G. Robertson, L. H. Smith, and W. Valensieck), pp. 199–211. Plenum Press, New York.

Takada, Y., Kaneko, N., Esumi, H., Purdue, P. E., and Danpure, C. J. (1990). Human peroxisomal L-alanine:glyoxylate aminotransferase. Evolutionary loss of mitochondrial targetting signal by point mutation of the initiations codon. *Biochemical Jouranl*, **268**, 517–20.

Tolbert, N. E. (1981). Metabolic pathways in peroxisomes and glyoxysomes. *Ann. Rev. Biochem.*, **50**, 133–57.

Toussaint, C., De Pauw, L., Vienne, A., Gevenois, P. A., Quintin, J., Gelin, M., *et al.* (1993). Radiological and histological improvement of oxalate osteopathy after combined liver–kidney transplantation in primary hyperoxaluria type 1. *American Journal of Kidney Diseases*, **21**, 54–63.

Watts, R. W. E., Veall, N., and Purkiss, P. (1983). Sequential studies of oxalate dynamics in primary hyperoxaluria. *Clinical Science*, **65**, 627–33.

Watts, R. W. E., Veall, N., and Purkiss, P. (1984). Oxalate dynamics and removal rates during haemodialysis and peritoneal dialysis in patients with primary hyperoxaluria and severe renal failure. *Clinical Science*, **66**, 591–7.

Watts, R. W. E., Veall, N., Purkiss, P., Mansell, M. A., and Haywood, E. F. (1985a). The effect of pyridoxine on oxalate dynamics in three cases of primary hyperoxaluria (with glycolic aciduria). *Clinical Science*, **69**, 87–90.

Watts, R. W. E., *et al.* (1985b). Primary oxaluria (type 1). Attempted treatment by combined hepatic and renal transplantation. *Quarterly Journal of Medicine*, **57**, 697–703.

Watts, R. W. E., *et al.* (1987). Successful treatment of primary hyperoxaluria type 1 by combined hepatic and renal transplantation. *Lancet*, **ii**, 474–5.

Watts, R. W. E., Morgan, S. H., Purkiss, P., Mansell, M. A., Baker, L. R. I., and Brown, C. B. (1988). Timing of renal tranplantation in the management of pyridoxine-resistant type 1 primary hyperoxaluria. *Transplantation*, **45**, 1143–5.

Watts, R. W. E., Morgan, S. H., Danpure, C. J., *et al.* (1991a). Combined hepatic and renal transplantation in primary hyperoxaluria type 1: Clinical report of nine cases. *American Journal of Medicine*, **90**, 179–88.

Watts, R. W. E., Danpure, C. J., De Pauw, I.., and Toussant, C. (1991b). Combined liver and kidney and isolated liver transplantation for primary hyperoxaluria type 1: The European experience. *Nephrology Dialysis and Transplantation*, **6**, 502–11.

Will, E. J. and Bijvoet, O. L. (1979). Primary oxalosis. Clinical and biochemical response to high-dose pyridoxine therapy. *Metabolism*, **28**, 542–8.

Williams, H. E. and Smith, L. H. (1968). L-glyceric aciduria: a new genetic variant of primary hyperoxaluria. *New England Journal of Medicine*, **278**, 233–9.

Willis, J. E. and Sallach, H. J. (1962). Evidence for a mammalian D-glycerate dehydrogenase. *J. Biol. Chem.*, **237**, 910–15.

Yendt, E. R. and Cohanim, M. (1986). Absorptive hyperoxaluria: a new clinical entity—successful treatment with hydrochlorthiazide. *Clinical and Investigative Medicine*, **9**, 44–50.

Zarembski, P. M. A., Hodgkinson, A., and Parsons, F. M. (1966). Elevation of the concentration of plasma oxalic acid in renal failure. *Nature*, **212**, 511–12.

Further reading

Hillman, R. E. (1989). Primary hyperoxaluria. In: *The metabolic basis of inherited disease* (6th edn) (ed. C. R. Scriver, A. L. Beaudet, W. S. Sly, and D. Valle), vol. 1, pp. 933–44. McGraw-Hill, New York.

23

Cystinuria

Philippe Jaeger

Introduction

Cystinuria is an inherited disorder characterized by defective renal and intestinal transport of cystine as well as of arginine, lysine, and ornithine, the dibasic amino acids. Save the fact that cystine is the least soluble amino acid, cystinuria would have remained an experimental model to study transepithelial amino acid transports in man. Because of poor solubility of cystine, however, it is one of the disorders to look for in patients with renal stone disease (Halperin and Thier 1980; DeFronzo and Thier 1986 *a, b*).

Cystinuria has nothing to do with cystinosis. The latter is also an inherited disturbance of carrier-mediated transport of cystine, but across the lysosomal membrane. Because of abnormal efflux of this amino acid from the lysosomes, cystine accumulates within the cells, cystine crystals being thus deposited throughout the body, e.g. the kidney (Cole 1991).

Practical approach to the disease

Presentation of a 'typical' case

A 56-year-old man without relevant family history is sent by his general practitioner to a renal stone clinic because of recurrent nephrolithiasis refractory to standard 'common sense' dietary advice. The first episode of renal colic was at age 47, and the patient claims to have passed 'numerous stones' over the past nine years. He has been on a low-calcium diet for six years, and the penultimate stone allegedly contained calcium oxalate.

Physical examination: normal. Examination of urine sediment: normal. Sodium cyanide nitro-prusside screening test for cystine: negative. After one month back on free-choice diet, a 24-hour urine collection was ordered which revealed hypercalciuria (375 mg/24h), hyperuricosuria (925 mg/24h), normal oxalate (324 µmol/24H), and citrate (927 mg/24h). The recently passed stone (the only one the patient still had at home) was submitted for infrared spectrophotometry, the results of which showed mixed calcium oxalate and cystine. A second 24-hour urine collection was ordered which gave the following results:

cystine: 1138 mg/g creat (n:10–30), ornithine: 616 mg/g creat (n: 0–4)
lysine: 2262 mg/g creat (n: 7–48), arginine: 1237 mg/g creat (n < 150)

Diagnosis of cystinuria was thus made, nine years after the first stone was passed.

This case history raises numerous questions: why was the family history negative for renal stone disease, the urine sediment negative for cystine crystals, the nitroprusside screening test negative for purple hue, and the penultimate stone made of calcium oxalate? The answers are given below and should help to cover, in a practical way, pathophysiology, genetics, and diagnostics of cystinuria.

Pathophysiology

Why dibasic amino aciduria along with cystinuria?

As stated above, cystinuria does not originate from overproduction of cystine but from a transport defect of this amino acid at the renal tubular level. This explains why low–normal (as opposed to high–normal) serum levels of cystine are encountered in the disease. The defect also affects the intestinal epithelium, as evidenced by increased urinary excretion rates of putrescine and cadaverine (diamines derived from the metabolism of arginine and lysine in the intestine, which are then both absorbed and eliminated in the urine) (Halperin and Thier 1980).

In the kidney, there are at least seven transport systems for amino acids, all located along the pars recta of the proximal tubule (Scriver 1986) (Fig. 23.1). A transport system (*A*) that cystine shares with the three dibasic amino acids, lysine, arginine, and ornithine, is located in the luminal brush border membrane; separate transport systems which are specific for dibasic amino acids are located at level (*B*), and also in the basolateral membrane (*C*). A transport system specific for cysteine (*D*) (with SH-R configuration), one specific for cysteine, cystine, and the neutral amino acids (*E*), and one specific for lysine (*F*) are also located in the luminal brush border membrane, whereas one additional transport which appears to be specific for cystine is located in the basolateral membrane (*G*).

It is the first transport system which appears to be defective in classic cystinuria, thus explaining concomitant dibasic amino aciduria (DeFronzo and Thier 1986*a*). Occasionally,

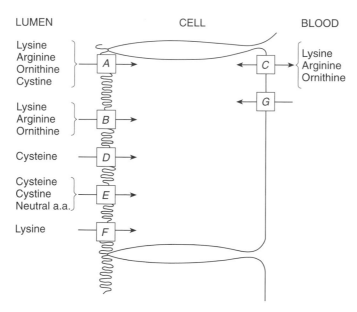

Fig. 23.1 The various transport systems for amino acids and their location in the membranes of a representative proximal tubular cell.

Table 23.1   Urinary excretion of cystine in normal subjects and patients with cystinuria

Reference	Normal range	Homozygous cystinuria	Heterozygous cystinuria		
			type I	type II	type III
Rosenberg *et al.* (1966)	10–50	>250	10–60	70–250	30–170
Kelly (1978)				65–141	19–31
Halperin and Thier (1980)	<60*	>400*			
Linari *et al.* (1981)		x̄ = 630*		x̄ = 228*	x̄ = 55*

Expressed as mg/g creat or as mg/24h (*).

however, one of the other systems may be defective, thus leading to hyperdibasic amino aciduria type 1 (*B*) or 2 (*C*), to isolated cystinuria (*D*), or to isolated lysinuria (*F*).

Why a negative family history?

Cystinuria is an autosomal recessive inherited disorder, which may be caused by mutations in rBAT, a gene coding for the cystine transporter (Calonge *et al.* 1994). Homozygous individuals excrete very high amounts of cystine (>400 mg/24 h or >250 mg/g creatinine) as well as of lysine, arginine, and ornithine. This is not the case for heterozygotes, however, as was demonstrated by Rosenberg *et al.* (1966) who ended up with three types of cystinuria. Heterozygotes of type I excrete normal amounts of cystine and dibasic amino acids (and thus do not form stones), whereas those of type II and III which excrete intermediate amounts may occasionally form renal stones (type II). There is a wide overlap in excretion of cystine between individuals heterozygous for type II and those heterozygous for type III (Table 23.1), although mean urinary cystine is higher in type II than in type III. Thus distinction between types II and III is based on the pattern of plasma response to oral cystine loading, which reflects the pattern of disturbance of intestinal transport of cystine and dibasic amino acids (Fig. 23.2). For instance, in type I, active intestinal transport of cystine is absent and in type II it is absent or severely reduced; thus, after oral loading with cystine, the plasma level of this amino acid does not rise, whereas in type III (with diminished although demonstrable active intestinal transport of cystine) it does.

The three varieties represent abnormalities in a single allele; indeed, compound (double) heterozygotes (I/II, II/III, I/III) have been observed whose levels of cystinuria and dibasic amino aciduria are similar to those of homozygous individuals.

Why a first stone at age 47?

Patients with idiopathic nephrolithiasis often present with hypercalciuria, hyperuricosuria, hyperoxaliuria, and/or hypocitraturia. Over the last few years it has become increasingly apparent that, as a rule, these metabolic abnormalities (usually generated by abnormal dietary habits) lead to renal stone disease only when added to an 'unsuspected' underlying disease such as medullary sponge kidney, abnormal metabolism of vitamin B_6, abnormal intestinal transport of citrate, or production of abnormally structured macromolecular inhibitors (Tamm–Horsfall protein, nephrocalcin). This is the 'powder keg and tinderbox' theory which we

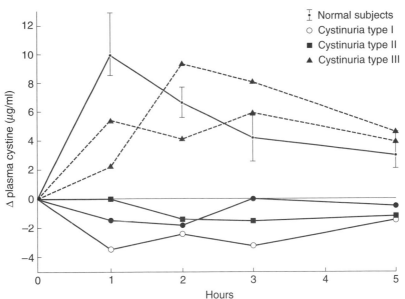

Fig. 23.2 Response of plasma cystine concentration to oral cystine load of 0.5 mmol/kg. Control values represent mean and range of results in three subjects. From Rosenberg *et al.* (1966). Reproduced by permission of the American Society for Clinical Investigation.

have recently proposed (Jaeger 1992). Heterozygosity for cystinuria may well correspond to such an unsuspected, underlying disease which the patient has inherited but which will only lead him to form stones at a time when nutritional abnormalities are also present. Several lines of arguments support this hypothesis. The first is the observation by Sakhaee *et al.* (1989) that hypercalciuria may be present in 19% of a population of cystinurics, hyperuricosuria in 22%, and hypocitraturia in 44%. The second is that mixed stones are not infrequently encountered in patients with cystinuria, thus illustrating that cystine may well form the nidus for calcium stones: mixtures of cystine, struvite, calcium oxalate, and calcium phosphate have all been found (Evans *et al.* 1982), and sometimes stones do not even contain cystine (Boström and Hanbraeus 1964). Thirdly the prevalence of heterozygosity for cystinuria underlying calcium oxalate stone-formers has been found in some series to reach values as high as 13.4% (Resnick *et al.* 1979), a figure which is reminiscent of that published for medullary sponge kidneys (Jaeger 1992).

Clearly, this explains why cystine urolithiasis may become clinically manifest at any time from infancy through to the ninth decade of life, although the mean age at which clinical manifestations occur is in the second to third decade (Halperin and Thier 1980).

Diagnostics

Why a normal urine sediment and a negative nitroprusside screening test?

The simplest screening test for cystinuria is microscopic examination of the urine sediment, looking for typical, hexagonal, 'benzene-ring' crystals (Halperin and Thier 1980). Though diagnostic, the presence of these crystals is only encountered in 17–26% of homozygous cystinurics (Dahlberg *et al.* 1977; Evans *et al.* 1982).

A sodium cyanide nitroprusside test should thus implement this examination when screening for cystinuria. 5 ml of urine are alkalinized with 5 drops of NH_4OH; 2 ml of 5% NaCN are added and the solution allowed to stand for 10 minutes. If, on addition of drops of 5% Na nitroprusside, a stable purple-red colour appears, the test is read as positive (Halperin and Thier 1980). There is a caveat: positive tests may also be seen in acetonuria, homocystinuria, and in patients receiving ampicillin, n-acetylcysteine, or another sulphur-containing drug (Pahira 1987). Since the detection limit is 75–125 mg cystine/g creatinine, it is apparent that the test will allow detection of homozygous or compound heterozygous stone formers who excrete more than 250 mg/g creatinine, but only some of the heterozygotes (Milliner 1990) whose urinary excretion of cystine is much lower (Table 23.1) (Kelly 1978).

How to make the diagnosis

A 24-hour urine collection for ion exchange chromatography quantification of urinary amino-acid excretion is the way to make a firm diagnosis and to differentiate homozygotes/compound heterozygotes from heterozygotes of type II or III (Table 23.1). This first step will help both clinical management and genetic counselling. Further characterization of cystinuria, i.e. discrimination of type II from type III, is at present largely of academic interest (Milliner 1990).

Why is it such a chronically troublesome disease?

It has been known for almost 20 years that renal stone-formers do not do well on a low-calcium diet compared with controls on placebo (Ettinger 1976). The reason for this appears to be substitution of hyperoxaluria (an aggressive risk factor) for hypercalciuria (a soft risk factor for nephrolithiasis) (Jaeger *et al*. 1985). The dietary advice given to the aforementioned patient may therefore have been counter-productive. Nonetheless, recurrent stone disease is the rule in cystinuria and urological/surgical procedures are frequently required. Abnormal creatinine levels may thus be encountered in as many as 50% of patients, chronic pyelonephritis in 19.4%, and unilateral nephrectomy in 9.7%, 3.2% of the patients ultimately requiring dialysis (Milliner 1990).

Is it a rare disorder?

The prevalence of cystinuria varies widely from one report/country to another: 1/12 500 in Canada, 1/17 000 in Australia, 1/18 000 in Japan, 1/20 000 in England, the extremes being 1/100 000 in Sweden and 1/2500 in Israeli Jews of Libyian origin (Milliner 1990). The mutant gene seems to be common with a frequency approaching 0.01. Among the functional homozygotes, the type I phenotype is the most common, i.e. 40–73% of families with cystinuria; among the incompletely recessive forms, type III heterozygoty is more common than type II.

Treatment

From a theoretical standpoint, four steps can be envisioned in the prevention of recurrence of cystinuric renal stone disease: dilution, solubilization, curtailment of production, and correction of the renal leak of cystine (Jaeger 1989). The same holds true to prevent growth and even dissolve existing stones, the other two goals of therapy of the disease.

Dilution

Within a pH range of 4.5 to 7.0, the solubility of cystine in urine is about 300 mg/L (Dent and Senior 1955). Assuming a urinary excretion rate of cystine 1000 mg/24 h in a patient with homozygous cystinuria, a fluid intake to provide 24-hour urine volumes of 3.4 litres will be needed to avoid precipitation of the amino acid in urine. Fluid should be evenly distributed throughout the day and in sufficient amounts so as to require voiding at least once a night (at which point more fluid should be taken).

The difficulty in actually maintaining stone-formers on such high fluid intakes for a long period of time is well-known. Motivation for such programmes, however, is probably stronger in cases of very active metabolic stone disease such as cystinuria than in cases of indolent idiopathic nephrolithiasis. Thus, for cystinuria, it is not surprising that reports of disease stabilization and stone dissolution from high fluid intake already appeared in the mid-1960s (Dent *et al.* 1965; Frimpter 1968). Clearly, fluid is the first line of therapy for the disease, and this is particularly true for heterozygotes who would only need to consume some 'additional' fluid to ensure reasonable urine dilution and prevent cystine precipitation.

Solubilization

Alkalinization

The solubility of cystine is influenced by the pH of the solvent. Above pH 7.5, cystine solubility in urine rises dramatically, reaching about 1000 mg/L at pH 8.0 (Dent and Senior 1955). Thus, urinary alkalinization may serve as a useful therapeutic adjunct to fluid intake. It can be achieved by ingestion of alkaline spring water, but also with bicarbonate-or citrate-containing preparations. 1–2 mEq/kg/day of alkali are needed to raise urine pH into the therapeutic range, i.e. 7.5–8.0. Here too, the alkali load has to be spaced throughout the 24–hour period. Acetazolamide given at bedtime may assist in achieving urine alkalinization during the night (Jaeger 1989).

The strategy, however, has its own hazards. Calcium phosphate may precipate, thus predisposing to nephrocalcinosis; as stated above, mixed cystine/calcium phosphate stones are known to occur in this context. Metabolic alkalaemia may be produced. In addition, the obligate sodium load linked to bicarbonate may be a limiting factor, for instance in patients with congestive heart failure. Nonetheless, alkalinization should always be undertaken as 'part two' of the therapeutic approach, and this is particularly true now that potassium citrate (for instance 3×30 mEq/day) has become widely available for this purpose.

Reduction of cystine to cysteine

Because cysteine is much more soluble in urine than cystine, the use of reducing agents to break the disulphide bond of cystine and convert the latter into cysteine sounded like a rational therapeutic approach to cystinuria as early as 1949. Ascorbic acid was first tried for this purpose (Rolnick 1949). As often happens, preliminary results were promising. After a daily dose of 5 g ascorbic acid, Asper and Schmucki (1982) even obtained a 48% reduction of urinary cystine in their patients with cystinuria. Clinical follow-up over two to three years was also encouraging: three relapses out of 31 patients treated by these authors (Asper and Schmucki 1982), and no relapse in four patients treated by Lux and May (1983). In both studies, however, an effervescent vitamin C preparation had been used, providing an alkali load leading urine pH to rise, which accounted at least in part for the protective effect of the manoeuvre. Therefore, to clarify the issue, Birwé *et al.* recently challenged the idea, administering pure ascorbic acid at 5 g/day over six days to normal volunteers and to patients with cystinuria (Birwé *et al.* 1991): urinary excretion of cystine decreased by 23% in controls and 11% in patients, i.e. a mild reduction, whereas cysteine excretion rose. Considering the fact that given in this form ascorbic acid will lead urine pH and citrate to fall, the manoeuvre is potentially lithogenic and should probably be abandoned.

Disulphide exchange reaction

As an alternative to breaking up the disulphide bond and generating cysteine (which is unstable in urine), there was the possibility of allowing cysteine to react with another thiol to form a new disulphide which might be more soluble in urine than cystine. The idea was first tested with D-penicillamine as early as 1963 (Crawhall *et al.* 1963). It soon became apparent that the penicillamine–cysteine disulphide is 50-fold more soluble than cystine. In addition, for reasons which remain obscure, D-penicillamine induces a reduction in total cystine excretion (i.e. cystine + cysteine + cysteine–penicillamine). Clinical experience has demonstrated that D-penicillamine given at 1–2 g/day in four divided doses does indeed lead urinary cystine to fall below 200 mg/g creatinine, i.e. values below the threshold of stone formation (Crawhall 1987). As expected, stabilization of stone disease and even dissolution of stones have been observed.

Unfortunately, the usefulness of the drug has been limited by the high prevalence of side-effects, e.g. gastrointestinal symptoms, impairment in taste and smell, dermatological complications, hypersensitivity reactions, haematological abnormalities (leukopenia), abnormal liver function tests, and renal complications (proteinuria), multiple symptoms being present in up to 67% of patients who often request interruption of treatment (Pak *et al.* 1986). It has been claimed, however, that the prevalence of these symptoms can be substantially reduced by starting treatment at a low dose and increasing it over a period of two months up to a maximum of 1.5–2 g/day (Halperin and Thier 1980).

Despite this, some patients cannot tolerate D-penicillamine. New disulphides were therefore tested. The first one, mercaptopropionylglycine (MPG), shares all the chemical properties of D-penicillamine and therefore also the serious side effects. Nonetheless, in a recently reported open study, only 30.6% of the patients had to stop taking MPG vs. 69% for D-penicillamine (Pak *et al.* 1986). MPG was equally effective as D-penicillamine in reducing cystine excretion, remission of stone formation being reached in 63–71% of the patients and individual stone formation reduced in 81–94%.

The second agent to be tested was captopril, an inhibitor of angiotensin-converting enzyme, which contains a sulphhydryl group. Added to urine, it binds to cysteine in exactly the same way as D-penicillamine does and forms a captopril–cysteine disulphide, the solubility of which is 200-fold higher than cystine. In 1987, Sloand and Izzo administered the drug (75 and 150 mg/day) to two patients with cystinuria for nine and 26 weeks, respectively. The urinary excretion rate of cystine decreased by 93% and 70%, respectively, and no side-effects were noted. Since then, at least 10 other patients with cystinuria have been treated with captopril: in two of them cystine excretion clearly was unaffected by the drug administered at 150 mg/day and 112.5 mg/day for five and two months, respectively (Aunsholt and Ahlbom 1990). In seven of them, however, captopril administered for one to five months at 150 mg/day led to an 11–82% decline in cystine excretion (Streem and Hall 1989). Two moles of captopril are needed to bind one mole of cystine. Thus, mechanisms other than the disulphide exchange reaction have to be postulated to account for the effect and further studies are needed to clarify this issue. It is our opinion that a simple haemodynamic effect of the drug on the renal handling of cystine has not been formally excluded in these studies.

Recently, other molecules have been found to efficiently engage into disulphide exchange reaction; for instance, meso -2-3-dimercaptosuccinic acid (DMSA), a heavy metal chelating agent, has been shown to form a mixed disulphide, two L-cysteine residues binding to one molecule of DMSA (Maiorino *et al.* 1989). The discovery of the formation of these cysteine–DMSA disulphides should encourage the evaluation of DMSA in the treatment of cystinuria. Another thiol compound, thiophosphate (WR2721), has been investigated *in vitro* but has not yet undergone clinical trials (Blackburn and Peterson 1984).

Curtailment of production

Cystine is generated from the essential amino acid, methionine, via transulphuration (Halperin and Thier 1980). Therefore, it was hoped that a low-methionine or a low-protein diet would lead to reduction of cystine excretion in patients with cystinuria. This has been shown to be the case, but the diet is difficult to tolerate (Jaeger 1989). In addition, for children, the diet is most questionable. Therefore, common sense suggests that cystinurics should avoid excessive protein intake, but at the era of development of so many new thiol compounds, a formal low-protein diet is probably not indicated any longer, even if fluid and alkali have failed to control the disease and penicillamine cannot be tolerated.

Correction of the renal leak

For some time, the ultimate goal in therapy of cystinuria has been correction of the renal leak, although it is probably wishful thinking. From a theoretical standpoint, the renal leak of cystine could be corrected by renal transplantation. Among the cystinurics who reached end-stage renal disease, at least three are known to have been successfully transplanted, i.e. with disappearance of cystine and dibasic amino aciduria (Kelly and Nolan 1968; Hotsma *et al.* 1983; Krizek *et al.* 1983). Nonetheless, renal transplantation cannot be envisioned as the approach to the problem.

In 1979, Miyagi *et al.* reported that glutamine given to one patient with cystinuria, either p.o. or IV, led to dramatic reduction of urinary excretion of cystine. Despite several attempts by various groups of investigators, the finding has still remained unconfirmed. Recently, however, we have shown that when given to patients on a high sodium intake (300 mmol/24 h), glutamine led to a sharp reduction of urinary cystine excretion, whereas when given on a normal sodium intake it did not (Jaeger *et al.* 1986). However, glutamine allowed reduction of cystine excretion only by the amount which had been excreted as a consequence of the high sodium intake, making it of limited interest as a therapeutic agent. On the other hand, during this manoeuvre, the role of sodium as a drive for urinary excretion of cystine suddenly became apparent: there was a positive correlation between urinary excretion rates of cystine and of sodium, an increment in sodium intake of 150 mmol/day 'leading' to one in cystine excretion of 650 μmol/24 h (Fig. 23.3). Therefore, a reduction of sodium intake in patients whose urinary excretion rate of cystine appears to correlate with it might merge as a valuable adjunct to other forms of therapy. At least two groups of investigators have confirmed this finding so far (Norman and Manette 1990; Peces *et al.* 1991), but the mechanisms governing the association remain unknow.

In conclusion, in a population of patients with renal stone disease, 1–2% have overt cystinuria and many more may have the incompletely recessive form of the disease. Improved understanding of the various facets of the disorder will undoubtedly lead to earlier diagnosis. High fluid intake, alkalinization of the urine, and dietary advice, e.g. avoidance of excessive protein and

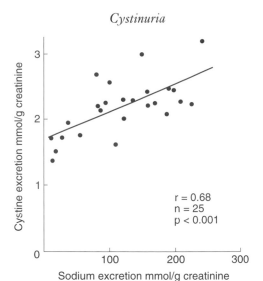

Fig. 23.3 Individual rates of excretion of cystine obtained in four patients with cystinuria and plotted as a function of urinary sodium excretion rate (n = 25, r = 0.68, p < 0.001). From Jaeger *et al.* (1986). Reproduced by permission of the *New England Journal of Medicine*.

sodium intake, are the core of the therapeutic strategy. For the rare patients whose disease remains refractory to this approach, further steps may be proposed such as prescription of thiol compounds, an area in which much research is being performed. In a near future therefore, dilution and solubilization of cystine will certainly be elegantly and efficaciously effected. Curtailment of production and correction of the renal leak of cystine remain attractive but distant goals. The search should nevertheless be pursued, in view of the particular problems which confront urologists, e.g. cystine stones which cannot be fragmented by modern techniques (Ginalski *et al.* 1992).

References

Asper, R. and Schmucki, O. (1982). Cystinurietherapie mit ascorbinsäure. *Urologia Internationalis*, **37**, 91–109.

Aunsholt, N. A. and Ahlbom, G. (1990). Lack of effect of captopril in cystinuria. *Clinical Nephrology*, **34**(2), 92–3. (Letter).

Birwé, H., Schneeberger, W., and Hesse, A. (1991). Investigations of the efficacy of ascorbic acid therapy in cystinuria. *Urological Research*, **19**, 199–201.

Blackburn, P. and Peterson, L. M. (1984). Thiol-disulfide interchange between cystine and N-2-mercaptoethyl-1, 3-diamino propane as a potential treatment for cystinuria. *Annals of Biochemistry*, **1**, 31–8.

Boström, H. and Hanbraeus, L. (1964). Cystinuria in Sweden: VII. Clinical, histopathological, and medico-social aspects of the disease. *Acta Medica Scandinavica*, **175** (Suppl. 411), 1.

Calonge, M. J., Gaspanini, P., Chillaron, J., *et al.* (1994). Cystinunia caused by mutations in rBAT, a gene involved in the transport of cystine. *Natwce, Genetics*, **6**, 420–5.

Cole, B. R. (1991). Cystinosis and cystinuria. In: *The principles and practice of nephrology* (ed. Jacobson, Striker, and Klahr), pp. 396–403. B.C. Decker Inc., Publishers, Philedelphia, Hamilton.

Crawhall, J. C. (1987). Cystinuria: an experience in management over 18 years. *Mineral and Electrolyte Metabolism*, **13**, 286–93.

Crawhall, J. C., Scowen, E. F., and Watts, R. W. E. (1963). Effect of penicillamine on cystinuria. *British Medical Journal*, **i**, 588–90.

Dahlberg, P. J., Van Den Berg, C. J., Kurtz, S. B., *et al.* (1977). Clinical features and management of cystinuria. *Mayo Clinic Proceedings*, **52**, 533–42.

DeFronzo, R. A. and Thier, S. O. (1986*a*). Renal tubular defects in phosphate and amino acid transport. In: *Physiology of membrane disorders* (ed. T. E. Andreoli, J. F. Hoffmann, D. D. Fanestil, and S. G. Schultz), pp. 1009–11. Plenum Press, New York.

DeFronzo, R. A. and Thier, S. O. (1986*b*). Inherited disorders of renal tubule function. In: *The kidney* (ed. B. M. Brenner and F. C. Rector), vol. 2, pp. 1310–13. W.B. Saunders Co., Philadelphia.

Dent, C. E. and Senior, B. (1955). Studies on the treatment of cystinuria. *British Journal of Urology*, **27**, 317–32.

Dent, C., Friedman, M., Green, H., and Watson, L. (1965). Treatment of cystinuria. *British Medical Journal*, **1**, 403–8.

Ettinger, B. (1976). Recurrent nephrolithiasis: natural history and effect of phosphate therapy. A double-blind controlled study. *American Journal of Medicine*, **61**, 200–6.

Evans, W. P., Resnick, M. I., and Boyce, W. H. (1982). Homozygous cystinuria: Evaluation of 35 patients. *Journal of Urology*, **127**, 707–9.

Frimpter, G. W. (1968). Medical management of cystinuria. *American Journal of the Medical Sciences*, **255**, 348–57.

Ginalski, J. M., Deslarzes, C., Asper, R., Jichlinski, P., and Jaeger, Ph. (1992). Rôle respectif de la taille, de la localisation et de la composition du calcul en tant que déterminant du succès thérapeutique après lithotritie par ondes de choc extracorporelles dans la lithiase rénale. *Néphrologie*, **13**, 83–6.

Halperin, E. C. and Thier, S. O. (1980). Cystinuria, *Contemporary Issues of Nephrology*, **5**, 208–30.

Hotsma, J. J., Koene, R. A. P., Trijbels, F. J. M., and Monnens, L. A. H. (1983). Disappearance of cystinuria after renal transplantation. *Journal of the American Medical Association*, **250**, 615.

Jaeger, P. (1989). Cystinuria: pathophysiology and treatment. *Advances in Nephrology*, **18**, 107–12.

Jaeger, P. (1992). Renal stone disease in the 1990s: the powder keg and tinderbox theory. *Current Opinion in Nephrology and Hypertension*, **1**, 141–8.

Jaeger, P., Portmann, L., Jacquet, A. F., and Burckhardt, P. (1985). Influence of the calcium content of the diet on the incidence of mild hyperoxaluria in idiopathic renal stone-formers. *American Journal of Nephrology*, **5**, 40–4.

Jaeger, P., Portmann, L., Saunders, A., Rosenberg, L. E., and Thier, S. O. (1986). Anticystinuric effects of glutamine and of dietary sodium restriction. *New England Journal of Medicine*, **315**, 1120–3.

Kelly, S. (1978). Cystinuria genotypes predicted from excretion patterns. *American Journal of Medical Genetics*, **2**, 175–90.

Kelly, S. and Nolan, E. P. (1978). Excretory rates in posttransplant cystinuric patients. *Journal of the American Medical Association*, **239**, 1132.

Krizek, V., Erben, J., Lazne, M., Navratil, P., and Svab, J. (1983). Disappearance of cystinuria after kidney transplantation. *British Journal of Urology*, **55**, 575.

Linari, F., Marangella, M., Fruttero, B., *et al.* (1981). The natural history of cystinuria: a 15-year follow-up in 106 patients. In: *Urolithiasis: clinical and basic research* (ed. L. H. Smith, W. G. Robertson, and B. Finlayson), p. 145. Plenum Press, New York.

Lux, B. and May P. (1983). Long-term observation of young cystinuric patients under ascorbic acid therapy. *Urologia Internationalis*, **38**, 91–4.

Maiorino, R. M., Bruce, D. C., and Aposhian, H. V. (1989). Determination and metabolism of dithiol-chelating agents. *Toxicology and Applied Pharmacology*, **97**, 338–49.

Milliner, D. S. (1990). Cystinuria. *Endocrinology and Metabolism Clinics of North America*, **19**(4), 889–907.

Miyagi, K., Nakada F., and Ohshiro, S. (1979). Effect of glutamine on cystine excretion in a patient with cystinuria. *New England Journal of Medicine*, **301**, 196–8.

Norman, R. W. and Manette, W. A. (1990). Dietary restriction of sodium as a means of reducing urinary cystine. *Journal of Urology*, **143**, 1193–5.

Pahira, J. H. (1987). Management of the patient with cystinuria. *Urologic Clinics of North America*, **14**, 339–46.

Pak, C. Y. C., Fuller, C., Sakhaee, K., Zerwekh, J. E., and Adams, B. V. (1986). Management of cystine nephrolithiasis with alpha-mercaptopropionylglycine. *Journal of Urology*, **136**, 1003–8.

Peces, R., Sanchez, L., Gorostidi, M., and Alvarez, J. (1991). Effects of variation in sodium intake on cystinuria. *Nephron*, **57**, 421–3.

Resnick, M. I., Goodman, H. O., and Boyce, W. H. (1979). Heterozygous cystinuria and calcium oxalate urolithiasis. *Journal of Urology*, **122**, 52–4.

Rolnick, H. C. (1949). Nephrolithiasis. In: *The practice of urology*, p. 798. J.B. Lippincott, Philadelphia.

Rosenberg, L. E., Downing, S. J., Durant, J. L., and Segal, S. (1966). Cystinuria: biochemical evidence for three genetically distinct diseases. *Journal of Clinical Investigation*, **45**, 365–71.

Sakhaee K., Poindexter, J. R., and Pak, C. Y. C. (1989). The spectrum of metabolic abnormalities in patients with cystine nephrolithiasis. *Journal of Urology*, **141**, 819–21.

Scriver C. R. (1986). Cystinuria. *New England Journal of Medicine*, **315**, 1155–57.

Sloand, J. A. and Izzo, J. L. (1987). Captopril reduces urinary cystine excretion in cystinuria. *Archives of Internal Medicine*, **147**, 1409–12.

Streem, S. B., and Hall, P. (1989). Effect of captopril on urinary cystine excretion in homozygous cystinuria. *Journal of Urology*, **142**, 1522–4.

24

Purine metabolism

R.W.E. Watts

Introduction

The inherited disorders of purine metabolism associated with renal disease are listed in Table 24.1. They are the sole cause of only a small proportion of all renal disease and are therefore best considered as part of the overall problem of purine, especially uric acid metabolism-related renal disease. Genetic factors may precipitate the occurrence or determine the severity of acquired disorders in this area. Conversely, environmental factors and acquired diseases modify the phenotypic expression of the primary genetic conditions.

The purines that cause renal disease are uric acid, sodium urate, xanthine, and 2, 8-dihydroxyadenine. The renal diseases due to uric acid and sodium urate are urolithiasis, chronic hyperuricaemic nephropathy, acute uric acid nephropathy, chronic sodium urate nephropathy associated with autosomal dominant gout, and hereditary renal hypouricaemia.

Diseases due to uric acid and/or sodium urate

Uric acid production

The plasma and urine uric acid are derived from dietary nucleoproteins and from the product of *de novo* purine synthesis whereby the purine ring is built up in a stepwise manner from glycine, bicarbonate, formate (the active one-carbon residue which is strictly designated as 'formyl'), and amino groups derived from aspartate and glutamine. Figure 24.1 shows the contribution which each of these molecules makes to the purine ring. Inosinic acid (IMP) is the product of the purine *de novo* synthesis sequence. IMP is converted to adenylic (AMP) and guanylic (GMP) acids by the purine interconversion and salvage reactions (Fig. 24.2). The degradation of AMP and GMP to uric acid via hypoxanthine and xanthine is also shown. AMP and GMP are further phosphorylated to the corresponding triphosphates (ATP and GTP) which are then converted to the 3′, 5′-cyclic nucleotides under the catalytic influences of adenylate cyclase and guanylate cyclase respectively.

The dietary intake of nucleoproteins is a major factor in diseases due to uric acid. The ingested adenine and guanine nucleotides are degraded to the free purine bases and hence to uric acid by enzymes in the intestinal juices and small intestinal mucosa without passing through the endogenous purine nucleotide, nucleoside, and purine-base metabolic pools. In summary, the uric acid levels in biological fluids depend on the nucleoprotein intake and on the relative activities of the enzymes catalysing the individual steps on the purine *de novo* synthesis, salvage, and degradation pathways.

Table 24.1 The inherited disorders of purine metabolism that cause renal disease

General area of the metabolic lesion	Specific enzyme abnormality	Main clinical effects	Inheritance
PRPP synthesis (prior to purine *de novo* synthesis)	Ribose phosphate pyrophosphokinase (phosphoribosylepyrophosphate synthetase) superactivity (EC 2.7.6.1)	Gout, urolithiasis (uric acid)	Sex-linked recessive
Purine salvage	Hypoxanthine phosphoribosyltransferase (EC 2.4.2.8) deficiency (Fig. 24.2, reaction 7)	Neurological. Gout, urolithiasis (uric acid)	Sex-linked recessive
	Adenine phosphoribosyltransferase (EC 2.4.2.7) deficiency (Fig. 24.2, reaction 8)	Urolithiasis (2,8-dihydroxyadenine	Autosomal recessive
Purine base degradation	Xanthine oxidase (xanthine dehydrogenase EC 1.2.3.2) deficiency (Fig. 24.2, reaction 9)	Urolithiasis (xanthine)	Autosomal recessive
	Xanthine oxidase and aldehyde oxidase (dehydrogenase EC 1.2.3.1) deficiency	Urolithiasis (xanthine)	Autosomal recessive
	Xanthine oxidase, aldehyde oxidase and sulphite oxidase (EC 1.8.2.1) deficiency	Neurological. Ocular lens dislocation, Urolithiasis (Xanthine)	Autosomal recessive
Renal tubule transport defects	Renal tubule reabsorption	Urolithiasis	Autosomal recessive
	Renal tubule excretion	Gout, renal failure	Autosomal dominant

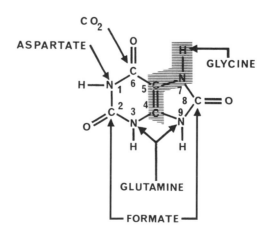

Fig. 24.1 The precursors of the individual carbon and nitrogen atoms of the purine ring.

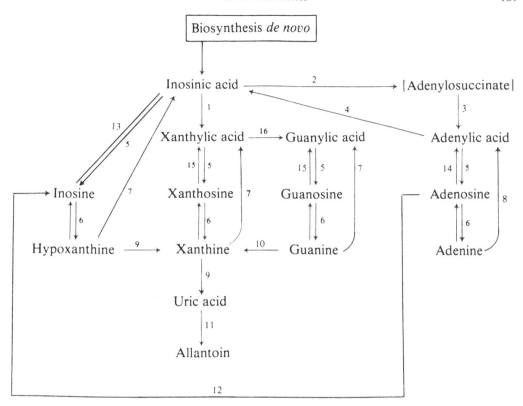

Fig. 24.2 Interconversion, conservation, and degradation pathways of the purine nucleotides, nucleosides, and bases. Key to enzymes: **1**, IMP dehydrogenase (EC 1.2.1.14); **2**, adenylosuccinate synthesis (EC 6.3.4.4); **3** adenylosuccinate lyase (EC 4.3.2.2); **4**, AMP deaminase (EC 3.5.4.6); **5**, 5′-nucleotidase (EC 3.1.3.5); **6**, purine nucleoside phosphorylase (EC 2.4.2.1); **7**, hypoxanthine phosphoribosyltransferase (EC 2.4.2.8); **8**, adenine phosphoribosyltransferase (EC 2.4.2.7); **9**, xanthine oxidase (EC 1.2.3.2); **10**, guanine deaminase (EC 3.5.4.3); **11**, urate oxidase (EC 1.7.3.3) (absent from human tissue); **12**, adenosine deaminase (EC 3.5.4.4); **13**, inosine kinase (EC 2.7.1.73); **14**, adenosine kinase (EC 2.7.1.20) [adenine deaminase (EC 3.5.4.2) which catalyses the deamination of adenine to hypoxanthine, occurs in some animal tissues but not in man]; **15**, unclassified nucleoside kinase; **16**, GMP synthetase (EC 6.3.4.1).

Uric acid stones

Uric acid is the major constituent of about 5% of urinary stones in Europe and North America. The incidence of uric acid stones is much higher in the Mediterranean and arid Middle Eastern countries where it may reach 50% of the total stone incidence. Most cases of uric acid urolithiasis are of multifactorial origin, environmental factors (nucleoprotein intake, climate, water intake, and the amounts of physiological crystallization inhibitors present in the urine) acting to modify the expression of the overall genetic background.

Hypoxanthine phosphoribosyltransferase (HPRT) deficiency

HPRT deficiency presents in two ways: the Lesch–Nyhan syndrome (Table 24.2) and the sex-linked recessive gout–urolithiasis syndrome.

Table 24.2   Clinical manifestations of virtually complete
hypoxanthine phosphoribosyltransferase (HPRT) deficiency
(Lesch–Nyham syndrome)

Muscle hypotonia
Delayed motor development
Torsion dystonia
Compulsive self-injurious behaviour
Aggressive behaviour
Dysarthria
Variable degree of intellectual deterioration in later childhood
Megaloblastic anaemia in some cases only
Hyperuricaemia and hyperuricaciduria (urolithiasis and gout)
Sex-linked recessive inheritance

Lesch–Nyhan syndrome

Muscle hypotonia is present from birth, although it is frequently not remarked on until poor head control is observed at about three months. Torsion dystonia, with its two components of abnormal posturing and episodic rigidity, is superimposed on the basic hypotonia which can be detected between the dystonic episodes. Dysarthria associated with dyskinesia of the mouth, pharynx, and larynx greatly limits the patient's ability to communicate and, coupled with the inability to even point accurately, leads to great frustration. It also complicates chewing and swallowing. Mental handicap is inconstant, at least in earlier childhood, usually of mild degree, and becomes more apparent in later childhood. The degree of apparent mental handicap is exaggerated by the extreme disorder of expressive motor function which exceeds the comprehension defect and by extrinsic factors such as lack of basic social and educational opportunities. The self-injurious behaviour usually begins at about two years of age. It is inconstant and some patients never show it. The patients feel pain normally, are aware of their compulsion, afraid of it, but are unable to control it. They may ask to have their limbs retrained or their teeth extracted. No structural or ultrastructural changes have been detected in the brain. Page *et al.* (1981) regard the self-injurious behaviour as the clinical hallmark of complete as opposed to partial HPRT deficiency. The results of computed tomography and electroencephalography are characteristically normal. The neurological manifestations usually antedate clinical evidence of uric acid urolithiasis and/or sodium urate nephropathy in these patients. However, a few present with either uric-acid stones or renal failure due to a combination of obstructive uropathy and sodium urate nephropathy in infancy or early childhood before the neurological disorder has been detected.

The sex-linked gout–urolithiasis syndrome due to HPRT deficiency

Sex-linked recessive urolithiasis with or without gout is the least severe end of the clinical spectrum of disease due to partial HPRT deficiency. The history of urolithiasis usually extends back at least to adolescence or early adulthood. There is marked hyperuric aciduria and a variable degree of hyperuricaemia which need not be particularly gross. Some patients present with severe urolithiasis and/or gout and minor neurological abnormalities such as mild spinocerebellar and/ or other long tract signs.

Biochemical diagnosis of HPRT deficiency

In an appropriate clinical context, the diagnosis is usually first suggested by high urine and serum uric acid concentrations. Hyperuricaemia may be only slight and an increase in the urinary uric acid excretion is a more reliable pointer. The urine uric acid to creatinine ratio should be examined in relation to the age of children and Kaufman *et al.* (1968) have published reference data. Satisfactory results are obtained if the urine is dried onto filter paper for transmission to the laboratory (McInnes *et al.* 1972). HPRT deficiency is diagnosed definitively by measuring the erythrocyte HPRT activity. The adenine phosphoribosyltransferase (APRT) activity and the phosphoribosylpyrophosphate (PRPP) concentration in the cells are raised. HPRT and APRT are measured on fresh lysate of washed blood cells or on washed cells which have been stored in the solid frozen state. PRPP measurements require a fresh blood sample. HPRT and APRT can also be measured on drops of dried blood on filter paper.

The asymptomatic female carriers of a mutant HPRT gene are identified by demonstrating their mosaicism with respect to $HPRT^+$ and $HPRT^-$ cells. This involves either autoradiographic studies of cultured skin fibroblasts (Halley and Heukels-Dully 1977) or phosphoribosyltransferase assays on multiple single-hair follicles (Gartler *et al.* 1971; McKeran *et al.* 1975). An alternative approach involves the use of the full-length cDNA probe for the HPRT gene (Jolly *et al.* 1983). Gibbs *et al.* (1986) reported a study of the practical usefulness of this approach.

The HPRT gene is located on the long arm of the X chromosome (regional assignment Xq26–q27.2). It is about 44 kilobases long and the 654 nucleotide coding region is divided into nine exons. This corresponds to 217 amino acids plus the initiating methionine residue which is removed by post-translational processing. The promotor region of the gene resembles that of other housekeeping genes* in that the CAAT- and TATA-base sequences found in most of the genes transcribed by RNA polymerase II are replaced by five copies of the sequence CGCGGG. There are numerous potential methylation sites in the 5′ flanking region of the gene (Patel *et al.* 1986). Nucleotide insertions, deletions, and point mutations have all been reported in the Lesch–Nyhan syndrome (Gibbs and Caskey 1987; Gibbs *et al.* 1990; Davidson *et al.* 1991). The nature of these genomic lesions cannot be correlated with the clinical phenotype.

The point mutations are widely scattered in the genome. There is some suggestion of clustering in the evolutionarily conserved regions predicted to be involved in hypoxanthine–guanine binding and in PRPP binding (Davidson *et al.* 1991). Studies of the three-dimensional structure of the normal human HPRT molecule and of mutant human HPRT molecules should demonstrate the impact that the nucleotide alterations and hence the amino acid substitutions have on the structure and function of HPRT. This may, in turn, provide a correlation between the changes at the genomic level and the clinical phenotype.

HPRT deficiency can be diagnosed prenatally by chorionic villus sampling (Gibbs *et al.* 1984, 1985, 1986; Stout *et al.* 1985) and in cultured amniocytes.

---

*Housekeeping genes direct the synthesis of enzymes catalysing the reactions of intermediary metabolism as opposed to structural proteins, hormones, etc. The 'promotor' region is the part of the gene to which RNA polymerase binds to initiate transcription. The TATA sequence designates the initiation of transcription in many eukaryotic genes. The CAAT region is the part of the nucleotide sequence about 75 base pairs upstream, that is, towards the 5′ end of the gene, from the starting point of eukaryotic gene transcription. It may be involved in binding RNA polymerase II.

Ribose phosphate pyrophosphokinase (PRPP synthetase) superactivity

The PRPP synthetase gene has been assigned to the long arm of the X chromosome (regional assignment Xq23 → 25). Recent work cited by Stone and Simmonds (1991) suggests that the two subunits of PRPP synthetase are encoded at separate sites on the X chromosome. Genes related to one of subunits (PRPS1) have also been reported on chromosomes 7 and 9. PRPP synthetase superactivity classically causes sex-linked recessive urolithiasis and/or gout. The patients usually present in adolescence or as young adults and there is marked hyperuricaemia with hyperuric aciduria. PRPP synthetase superactivity is a very rare cause of urinary stones. Sensorineural deafness is now recognized as a characteristic feature in some cases and a range of other neurological abnormalities, including autism (Nyhan *et al.* 1969; Becker *et al.* 1980), have also been reported in association with it (Simmonds *et al.* 1982; Becker *et al.* 1988; Stone and Simmonds 1991).

The definitive diagnosis is made by measuring the PRPP synthetase activity of blood-cell lysates. Cells from affected patients contain abnormally high concentrations of PRPP and this is presumed to increase the activity of amidophosphoribosyltransferase by altering the state of aggregation of subunits.

2,8-dihydroxyadenine stones (2,8-dihydroxyadeninuria APRT deficiency)

Clinical aspects

Patients with this autosomal recessive disorder (Simmonds *et al.* 1989) usually present in childhood, including early infancy, with radiotranslucent 2,8-dihydroxyadenine urinary stones. These are white or pale grey in colour, rough and friable. Some cases present with anuric renal failure due to multiple 2,8-dihydroxyadenine stones or with chronic renal failure due to renal intratubular precipitation (Gagné *et al.* 1994).

Biochemistry

There are two types of enzyme defect, designated types I and II. The type I defect is mainly found in Caucasians and the patients are homozygous or doubly heterozygous for mutations (null alleles) which leave virtually no catalytic activity. Type II patients have so far only been encountered in the Japanese. In these cases, the mutant enzyme has reduced affinity for the co-substrate 5-phosphoribosyl-1-pyrophosphate and shows abnormal kinetic properties with altered heat stability *in vitro*.

Lack of APRT leaves adenine available as a substrate for xanthine oxidase, which catalyses its oxidation to 2, 8-dihydroxyadenine. Treatment with allopurinol is therefore highly effective, immediately and in the long term. These stones are easily mistaken for uric acid stones because 2, 8-dihydroxyadenine reacts as uric acid in the widely used colorimetric assays. This problem does not arise with enzymological assays using uricase. Symptomatic and asymptomatic homozygotes for the enzyme defect can be identified by their increased excretion of adenine and 2,8-dihydroxyadenine. APRT deficiency is demonstrable in lysed blood cells and the heterozygotes have levels which are intermediate between the normal and homozygous individuals' values. The gene directing the synthesis of APRT has the assignment 16q22. It is 2.8 kB long, with 0.9 kB coding region, spread over 5 exons. The promotor regions contains five GC-rich regions and lacks the TATA and CCAAT sequences, features typical of an housekeeping gene. The enzyme is a dimer of subunit molecular weight 19481.

Xanthine stones (xanthinuria)

Clinical aspects

About one-third of patients with xanthinuria present at any age with radiotranslucent stones. The stones are usually smooth, soft, and yellow–brown in colour. Most cases of xanthinuria are discovered incidentally. Xanthinuric myopathy, a rare complication, presents in adult life with muscle 'tightness' and stiffness which is often, but not invariably, aggravated by exertion. The discomfort increases over a period of about 20 minutes after the exertion. There are no objective clinical abnormalities related to xanthinuric myopathy but electromyography and histology are compatible with a diffuse myopathic process.

Diagnostic biochemistry

The plasma and urine uric acid levels are characteristically less than about $0.06 \, \text{mmol} \, l^{-1}$ ($1.0 \, \text{mg} \, dl^{-1}$) and $0.30 \, \text{mmol}$ ($50 \, \text{mg}$) $24 \, h^{-1}$, respectively, when the patient is taking an unrestricted diet and the measurements are made colorimetrically. Such low values are very rare except in xanthinuria. For example, Harkness *et al.* (1983) searched the clinical biochemical data on 47420 unselected patients in a general hospital without finding a case of hypouricaemia due to xanthinuria, although they found two patients with isolated renal hypouricaemia.

The amounts of oxypurine (hypoxanthine plus xanthine) normally present in the plasma and urine are: 0.00–$0.15 \, \text{mmol} \, l^{-1}$ (0.00–$0.25 \, \text{mg} \, dl^{-1}$) and 0.07–$0.13 \, \text{mmol}$ (11–$22 \, \text{mg}$) $24 \, h^{-1}$, respectively. The corresponding values in xanthinuric patients are 0.03–$0.05 \, \text{mmol} \, l^{-1}$ (0.05–$0.09 \, \text{mg} \, dl^{-1}$) plasma and 0.60–$3.6 \, \text{mmol}$ (100–$600 \, \text{mg}$) $24 \, h^{-1}$ in the case of urine. Xanthine accounts for 60–90% of the total oxypurine excreted. This presumably reflects the more active metabolic turnover of hypoxanthine and its more efficient salvage by HPRT. The studies of Harkness *et al.* (1985) suggest that the plasma and urinary hypoxanthine and xanthine are mainly derived from adenine and guanine nucleotides, respectively (Fig. 24.2).

The genetic data are compatible with autosomal recessive transmission. Most of the obligatory heterozygotes show no clinical or biochemical abnormalities although some have raised hypoxanthine and xanthine levels in blood and urine with uric acid values in the lower part of the normal range. One patient has been shown to be CRM⁻ (Gibbs *et al.* 1976).

Muscle biopsies from xanthinuric patients contain crystals of hypoxanthine and xanthine (Chalmers *et al.* 1969).

Enzymology

There are three enzymological types of xanthinuria:

(1) xanthine oxidase (EC 1.2.3.2) deficiency only;
(2) combined deficiencies of xanthine oxidase and aldehyde oxidase (EC 1.2.3.1);
(3) combined deficiencies of xanthine oxidase, aldehyde oxidase, and sulphite oxidase (EC 1.8.2.1).

The patients who present clinically with xanthine urolithiasis have either the solitary xanthine oxidase deficiency or the combined xanthine oxidase and aldehyde oxidase deficiency.

The patients with the very rare deficiency of all three enzymes present in infancy with feeding difficulties, delayed psychomotor development, hypotonia, seizures, myoclonus, torsion dystonia, ataxia, and dislocation of the ocular lenses as in isolated sulphite oxidase deficiency. The plasma and urine uric-acid levels are low with elevated hypoxanthine and xanthine, and the patients are at risk of developing xanthine-containing stones. There is defective synthesis of a molybdopterin cofactor (Roesel *et al.* 1986) and this impairs the activity of the three tissue molybdoflavoprotein enzymes. Prenatal diagnosis is possible by measuring the sulphite oxidase activity of cultured amniocytes (Desjacquest *et al.* 1985).

An acquired combined enzyme deficiency due to molybdenum deficiency has been reported in a patient receiving total parential nutrition (Stone and Simmonds 1991). Sheep grazed on molybdenum-deficient pastures develop xanthine urinary stones.

Renal handling of urate

The pKa_1 of uric acid is 5.75 so that the uric acid/urate couple exists predominantly as the urate anion in plasma, but the ratio [uric acid]/[urate] changes materially within the physiological range of urine and renal tubular fluid pH values.

Uric acid/urate excretion involves glomerular filtration, tubular reabsorption, tubular secretion, and postsecretory reabsorption. The urate is freely filterable at the glomerulus. Ninety-nine per cent of the filtered urate is actively reabsorbed in the proximal convoluted tubule. An amount of urate equal to about 50% of the original filtered load is actively secreted in an unidentified, more distal region of the nephron. Tubular secretion is mainly responsible for maintaining a normal rate of uric acid excretion. It is strongly inhibited by pyrazinamide as well as by other anions (e.g. lactate). The decrement in uric acid excretion produced by pyrazinamide administration has been regarded as a measure of the tubular secretion of urate in man. Most of the secreted urate is reabsorbed in either the same or a more distal segment of the renal tubule. This postsecretory reabsorption is equal to about 40% of the original filtered load or four-fifths of the tubular secretory component and leaves the urinary urate excretion at about 10% of the original filtered load and the clearance in the range 6–11 ml min^{-1} $1.73 m^{-2}$.

In vitro studies by Werner *et al.* (1991) have demonstrated a urate/chloride exchanger in the brush border membrane of human renal proximal tubular epithelium. Urate ions enter the cell in exchange for chloride ions. The coexistence of this transport mechanism in the basolateral membrane of the cell would enable urate ions to pass from the epithelial cell lumen into the vascular compartment. The carrier has been also shown to have affinity for bicarbonate, hydroxyl, lactate, succinate, pyrazinoate, probenecid, and para-aminohippurate (PAH) ions. It is saturable and its transport of urate can be inhibited by pyrazinamide, probenecid, and lactate. It seems likely that the activity of this carrier operating differentially in different parts of the nephron may underlie the different aspects of the renal handling of the urate ion which were unravelled by the physiological studies of the actions of pyrazinamide *in vivo*.

Isolation of the urate/chloride exchanger protein and the gene directing its synthesis should enhance our understanding of both hereditary isolated renal hypouricaemia and of the genetic contribution to the aetiology of gout.

Isolated renal hypouricaemia

Renal hypouricaemia, which is due to a failure of the renal tubular reabsorption mechanism for urate, occurs in isolation (hereditary renal hypouricaemia) or as part of Fanconi's syndrome of

Table 24.3 Causes of hypouricaemia

1. Reduced xanthine oxidase activity
   (a) Xanthinuria (congenital xanthine oxidase deficiency)
   (b) Allopurinol administration

2. Renal hypouricaemia (renal tubule reabsorption defects)
   (a) Congenital
       (i) isolated
       (ii) associated with other reabsorption defects in Fanconi's syndrome
   (b) Acquired
       (i) uricosuria therapeutic and diagnostic agents
       (ii) toxic damage to the renal tubules
       (iii) extrarenal malignancies
       (iv) inappropriate secretion of antidiuretic hormone (SIADH)
3. Purine nucleoside phosphorylase (EC 2.4.2.1) deficiency

Table 24.4 Uricosuric substances

Acetohexamide	Indomethacin
ACTH	Meclofenamic acid
Adrenocorticosteroids	Naproxen
Aspirin (>4 g per day)	p-nitrophenylbutazone
6-azauridine	Orotic acid
Azopropazone	Phenylendandione
Benziodarone	Phenylbutazone
Benzbromarone	Probenecid
Carinamide	Phloridizin
Chlorproxithene	Radiocontrast agents:
Cinchophen	iopanoic acid
Dicoumarol	meglumine iodipamide
Ethylbiscoumacetate	calcium ipidate
Ethyl-p-chlorophenoxylbutyric acid	sodium diatrizoate
Glycine	Sulphinpyrazone
Halofenate	Zoxazolamine

multiple tubular reabsorption defects and it is a risk factor for urate urolithiasis. The lower limit of the reference range for plasma urate is about $60 \mu mol \, l^{-1}$ and the causes of plasma urate concentrations below this value are presented in Table 24.3. Most cases of renal hypouricaemia are due to medication, particularly to large doses of aspirin (>4 grams daily).

Isolated renal hypouricaemia is inherited in an autosomal recessive manner. It is a very rare anomaly, about 33 cases having been reported. Uric acid nephrolithiasis or mixed uric acid and calcium oxalate calculi are the only clinical complications. Isolated renal hypouricaemia and idiopathic hypercalciuria have been reported in association with one another (Sperling and de Vries 1980).

Table 24.5   Drugs which cause clinically significant urate retention

---

1. Diuretics*:
   (a) Thiazides and thiazide-related components
   (b) Loop diuretics (frusemide, bumetamide, ethacrynic acid)
2. Analgesics and anti-inflammatory agents:
   (a) Aspirin in low doses (<4 g per day)
   (b) Phenylbutazone in low doses
3. Drugs used in the treatment of tuberculosis:
   (a) Ethambutol
   (b) Pyrazinamide
4. Nicotinic acid (pharmacological doses)
5. Vasopressin

---

*Note: The potassium sparing agents (triamterene and amiloride) and spirinolactone do not have this effect.

Kaneko and his colleagues (1989) concluded, on the basis of studies performed on four patients with isolated renal hypouricaemia, that the renal handling of xanthine and hypoxanthine, especially xanthine, is similar to that of uric acid. These investigations were performed *in vivo* and involved observations of the effect of pyrazinamide on the renal clearance of the three purines. One patient with isolated renal hypouricaemia and decreased renal clearances of hypoxanthine and xanthine has been reported (Kawachi *et al.* 1991).

Perturbation of the renal handling of urate by drugs

An uricosuric action, sometimes unsuspected by the prescriber, is the commonest cause of hypouricaemia and hyperuricosuria. Whether a given substance produces uricosuria or urate retention often depends on the dose. Table 24.4 lists the drugs and some other substances which decrease the tubular reabsorption component of the urate excretory process and therefore cause uricosuria when given in the customary therapeutic doses. Some drugs cause clinically significant urate retention (Table 24.5) and this can complicate the diagnosis of gout.

Autosomal dominant hyperuricaemia and gout (familial hyperuricaemic nephropathy)

Most cases of primary gout are of multifactorial origin with contributions from both environmental and genetic factors. There is commonly a positive family history but without a pedigree indicating unifactorial (Mendelian) inheritance. Impaired overall renal function was common in gouty patients before allopurinol became available, the kidneys being damaged by microtophi containing sodium urate monohydrate crystals. This is now uncommon. However, there exist families in which the syndrome of hyperuricaemia, gout, and impaired renal function appears at an early age and follows an autosomal dominant pattern of inheritance. This involves direct transmission by the parents of either sex, both sexes being affected equally severely. The metabolic lesion in these patients causes reduced net renal clearance of urate (Calabrese *et al.* 1990; Reiter *et al.* 1995), and the primary pathophysiological abnormality appears to be diminished net tubular excretion of urate by the renal tubules. Such patients characteristically present with heavy proteinuria early in the evolution of their disease and they rapidly develop severe and potentially fatal renal failure. These patients are grossly hyperuricaemic, the degree of the hyperuricaemia being much greater than that which is commensurate with their degree of renal failure. Duncan and Dixon (1960) were the first to recognize the syndrome which was subsequently reported by Leumann and Wegmann (1983). The physiological investigation of these patients individually has been hampered by the fact that their overall renal function is reduced before they develop symptoms and further work is needed to identify more individuals with hyperuricaemia and normal renal function in families with hyperuricaemic nephropathy so that they can be studied from the point of view of their renal handling of urate and their urate dynamics *in vivo*. McDermott *et al.* (1984) published several extensive pedigrees fulfilling the criteria for autosomal dominant inheritance. Fig. 24.3 shows two examples. These workers demonstrated experimentally that the rate of purine *de novo* synthesis is not accelerated in this disease. This negative finding supports the concept of the fundamental pathological lesion being a defect in the renal tubular handling of the urate ion. Less severe expression of this defect causes the genetic component of the common type of gout patient in whom there may be a positive family history without unifactorial inheritance and in whom the disease usually presents in middle-aged men and about 20 years after the menopause in women (Puig *et al.* 1994). In these patients, who are commonly obese, the clinical expression is triggered by environmental factors, often a high nucleoprotein diet and/or alcohol.

The identification of the urate carrier protein (or proteins) and the gene (or genes) directing its (their) synthesis will permit a search for the specific mutations which predispose to the common clinical syndrome of gout. The recognition of the urate–chloride exchanger in the renal tubule epithelium by Roch-Ramel and her colleagues (Werner *et al.* 1991) may prove to have been the first step in that direction.

Alcoholic beverages affect overall purine metabolism in three ways by:

(1) in the case of beer, providing a source of additional exogenous, yeast-derived, purines for conversion to uric acid;
(2) increased degradation of hepatic adenine nucleotides during ethanol oxidation;
(3) increased generation of lactate due to alteration in the [NAD]/[NADH] ratio, induced by the oxidation of ethanol to acetaldehyde, the lactate competing with urate for the renal tubular transport system responsible for the active tubular excretion of urate and hence causing hyperuricaemia and gout.

The treatment of familial (autosomal dominant) hyperuricaemic nephropathy comprises measures to maintain normouricaemia, that is, the avoidance of major sources of dietary nucleoprotein and purine, moderation of alcohol intake, and the administration of allopurinol. The dose of allopurinol should be sufficient to maintain normouricaemia and should be relatively low in the presence of impaired renal function. Hyperuricaemic relatives of the propositi should be identified and treated before their renal function is impaired.

Sex-linked recessive hyperuricaemia and gout

Sex-linked recessive hyperuricaemia, gout, urinary calculi, and nephropathy occur in patients with HPRT deficiency and in those with PRPP synthetase superactivity. These metabolic lesions cause excessive purine *de novo* synthesis and hence hyperuricaemia and hyperuricosuria, the renal handling of urate not being primarily at fault.

Patients with this type of hyperuricaemic nephropathy should be treated by:

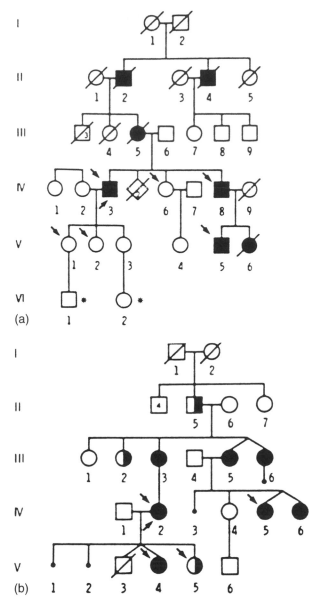

Fig. 24.3 (a) and (b) Pedigree charts for two families in which the abnormal gene causing autosomal dominant gout (familial hyperuricaemic nephropathy) is segregating. ■ ●, male and female subjects, respectively, with hyperuricaemia and renal failure; ◧ ◐, male and female subjects, respectively, with hyperuricaemia and normal renal function; □ ○, male and female subjects not known to be affected; ◈ subjects on whom no data are available; /, deceased; ↗, propositus; ↘, subjects whose rates of mononuclear cell purine synthesis *de novo in vitro* were measured: ⊙, n female subjects; ☐, n male subjects; *, babies who were examined clinically but not investigated further; ●, miscarriage. Reproduced with permission from (1984) *Clinical Science*, **67**, 249–58.

(1) a sufficiently large fluid intake to maintain a measured 24-hour urine volume of 3 litres;
(2) alkalinization of the urine;
(3) avoidance of major sources of dietary nucleoprotein and purines, and an excessive alcohol intake;
(4) allopurinol.

References

Becker, M. A., Raivio, K. O., Bakay, B., Adams, W. B., and Nyhan, W. L. (1980). Variant human phosphoribosylpyrophosphate synthetase altered in regulatory and catalytic function. *Journal of Clinical Investigation*, **65**, 109–20.

Becker, M. A., Puig, J. G., Mateos, F. A., Jiminez, M. L., Kim, M., and Simmonds, H. A. (1988). Inherited superactivity of phosphoribosylpyrophosphate synthetase: association of uric acid over-production and sensory neural deafness. *American Journal of Medicine*, **85**, 383–90.

Calabrese, G., Simmonds, H. A., Cameron, J. S., and Davies, P. M. (1990). Precocious familial gout with reduced fractional urate clearance and normal purine enzymes. *Quarterly Journal of Medicine*, **75**, 441–450.

Chalmers, R. A., Watts, R. W. E., Bitensky, L., and Chayen, J. (1969). Microscopic studies on crystals in skeletal muscle from two cases of xanthinuria. *Journal of Pathology*, **99**, 45–56.

Davidson, B. L., Tarlé, S. A., Van Antwerp, M., Gibbs, D. A., Watts, R. W. E., Kelley, W. N., et al. (1991). Identification of 17 independent mutations responsible for human hypoxanthine-guanine phosphoribosyltransferase (HPRT) deficiency. *American Journal of Human Genetics*, **48**, 951–8.

Desjacques, P., Mousson, B., Vianey-Liaud, C., Boulieu, R., Bory, C., Baltassat, P., et al. (1985). Combined deficiency of xanthine oxidase and sulphite oxidase: diagnosis of a new case followed by an antenatal diagnosis. *Journal of Inherited Metabolic Disease*, **8** (Suppl. 2), 117–18.

Duncan, H. and Dixon, A. St. J. (1960). Gout, familial hyperuricaemia, and renal disease. *Quarterly Journal of Medicine*, (NS), **29**, 127–35.

Gagné, E. R., Delard, E., Daudon, M., Noël, L. H., and Nawar, T. (1994). Chronic renal failure secondary to 2,8-dihgdroxyadenine deposition: the first report of recurrence in a kidney transplant. *American Journal of Kidney Diseases*, **24**, 104–7.

Gartler, S. M., Scott, R. C., Goldstein, J. L., Campbell, B., and Sparkes, R. (1971). Lesch–Nyhan syndrome: rapid detection of heterozygotes by use of hair follicles. *Science*, **172**, 572–4.

Gibbs, D. A., Allsop, J., and Watts, R. W. E. (1976). The absence of xanthine oxidase (EC 1.2.3.2) from a xanthinuric patient's milk. *Journal of Molecular Medicine*, **1**, 167–70.

Gibbs, D. A., McFadyen, I. R., Crawfurd, Md'A., de Muinck Keizer, E. E., Headhouse-Benson, C. M., Wilson, T. M., et al. (1984). First-trimester diagnosis of Lesch–Nyhan syndrome. *Lancet*, ii, 1180–3.

Gibbs, D. A., Headhouse-Benson, C. M., McFadyen, I. R., Crawfurd, Md'A., and Watts, R. W. E. (1985). Prenatal diagnosis of Lesch–Nyhan syndrome using a full-length cDNA probe for the HPRT gene. *Clinical Science*, **69** (Suppl. 12), 26.

Gibbs, D. A., Headhouse-Benson, C. M., and Watts, R. W. E. (1986). The use of a restriction fragment length polymorphism (RFLP) closely linked to the disease gene for carrier state and prenatal diagnosis. *Journal of Inherited Metabolic Disease*, **9**, 45–58.

Gibbs, R. A. and Caskey, C. T. (1987). Identification and localization of mutations at the Lesch–Nyhan locus by ribonuclease A cleavage. *Science*, **236**, 303–5.

Gibbs, R. A., Nguyen, P-N., McBride, L. J., Koepf, S. M., and Caskey, C. T. (1990). Multiplex DNA deletion detection and exon sequencing of the hypoxanthine phosphoribosyltransferase gene in Lesch–Nyhan families. *Genomics*, **7**, 234–5.

Halley, D. and Heukels-Dully, M. J. (1977). Rapid prenatal diagnosis of the Lesch–Nyhan syndrome. *Journal of Medical Genetics*, **14**, 100–2.

Harkness, R. A., Coade, S. B., Walton, K. R., and Wright, D. (1983). Xanthine oxidase deficiency and Dalmatian hypouricaemia: incidence and effect of exercise. *Journal of Inherited Metabolic Disease*, 6, 114–20.

Harkness, R. A., Coade, S. B., Simmonds, R. J., and Duffy, S. (1985). Effect of a failure of energy supply on adenine nucleotide breakdown in placentae and other fetal tissues from rat and guinea pig. *Placenta*, 6, 199–216.

Jolly, D. J., Okayama, H., Berg, P., Esty, A. C., Filpula, D., Bohlen, P., *et al.* (1983). Isolation and characterization of a full-length expressible cDNA for human hypoxanthine phosphoribosyltransferase. *Proceedings of the National Academy of Sciences USA*, 80, 477–81.

Kaneko, K., Fujimori, S., Kanbayashi, T., and Akaoka, I. (1989). Renal handling of hypoxanthine and xanthine in normal subjects and in cases of idiopathic renal hypouricaemia. In: *Purine and pyrimidine metabolism in Man VI. Part A: Clinical and molecular biology* (ed. K. Mikanagi, K. Nishioka, and W. N. Kelly), p. 309–15. Plenum Press, New York and London.

Kaufman, J. M., Green, M. L., and Seegmiller, J. E. (1968). Urine uric acid to creatinine ratio—a screening test for inherited disorders of purine metabolism. Phosphoribosyltransferase (PRT) deficiency in X-linked cerebral palsy and in a variant of gout. *Journal of Paediatrics*, 73, 583–92.

Kawachi, M., Kono, N., Mineo, I., Kiyokawa, H., Nakajima, H., Shimitzu, T., *et al.* (1991). Renal hypouricaemia associated with hyperoxpurinaemia due to decreased renal excretion of oxypurines: a new defect in renal purine transport. In: *Purine and pyrimidine metabolism in man VII. Part A: Chemotherapy, ATP depletion, and gout* (ed. R. A. Harkness, G. B. Elion, and N. Zöllner), p. 239–42. Plenum Press, New York and London.

Leumann, E. P. and Wegmann, W. (1983). Familial nephropathy with hyperuricaemia and gout. *Nephron*, 34, 51–7.

MacDermot, K., Allsop, J., and Watts, R. W. E. (1984). The rate of purine synthesis *de novo* in blood mononuclear cells *in vitro* from patients with familial hyperuricaemic nephropathy. *Clinical Science*, 67, 249–58.

McInnes, R., Lamm, P., Clow, C. L., and Scriver, C. R. (1972). A filter paper sampling method for the uric acid: creatinine ratio in urine. *Paediatrics*, 49, 80–4.

McKeran, R. O., Andrews, T. M., Howell, A., Gibbs, D. A., and Watts, R. W. E. (1975). The diagnosis of the carrier state for the Lesch–Nyhan syndrome. *Quarterly Journal of Medicine*, (NS), 44, 189–205.

Nyhan, W. L., James, J. A., Teber, A. J., Sweetman, L., and Nelson, L. G. (1969). A new disorder of purine metabolism with behavioural manifestations. *Journal of Paediatrics*, 74, 20–7.

Page, T., Bakay, B., Nissinen, E., and Nyhan, W. L. (1981). Hypoxanthine-guanine phosphoribosyltransferase variants: correlation of clinical phenotype with enzyme activity. *Journal of Inherited Metabolic Disease*, 4, 203–6.

Patel, P. I., Framson, P. E., Caskey, C. T., and Chinault, A. C. (1986). Fine structure of the human hypoxanthine phosphoribosyltransferase gene. *Molecular and Cellular Biology*, 6, 393–403.

Puig, J. G., Mateos, F. A., Miranda, M. E., Forres, R. J., De Miguel, E., De Ayela, C. P., Gill, A. A. (1994). Purine metabolism in women with primary gout. *American Journal of Medicine*, 97, 332–338.

Reiter, L., Brown, M., and Edmonds, J. (1995). Familial hyperuricaemic nephropathy. *American Journal of Kidney Diseases*, 21, 235–41.

Roesel, R. A., Bowyer, F., Blankenship, P. R., and Hommes, F. A. (1986). Combined xanthine and sulphite oxidase defect due to a deficiency of molybdenum cofactor. *Journal of Inherited Metabolic Disease*, 9, 343–7.

Simmonds, H. A., Webster, D. R., Wilson, J., and Lingham, S. (1982). An X-linked syndrome characterised by hyperuricaemia, deafness and neurodevelopmental abnormality. *Lancet*, 2, 68–70.

Simmonds, H. A., Sahota, A. S., and Van Acker, K. J. (1989). Adenine phosphoribosyltransferase deficiency and 2,8-dihydroxyadenine lithiasis. In: *The metabolic basis of inherited disease* (6th edn) (ed. C. R. Scriver, A. L. Beaudet, W. S. Sly, and D. Valle), p. 1029–44. McGraw-Hill, New York.

Sperling, O. (1989). Hereditary renal hypouricaemia. In: *The metabolic basis of inherited disease* (6th edn) (ed. C. S. Scriver, A. L. Beaudet, W. S. Sly, and D. Valle), pp. 2605–17. McGraw-Hill, New York.

Sperling, O. and de Vries, A. (1980). Hereditary renal hypouricaemia with hyperuricosuria and variably absorptive hypercalciuria and urolithiasis—a new syndrome. In: *Purine metabolism in man III, Part A Clinical and therapeutic aspects* (ed. A. Rapada, R. W. E. Watts, and C. H. M. M. De Bruyn), p. 149–53. Plenum Press, New York and London.

Stone, T. W. and Simmonds, H. A. (1991). *Purines: basic and clinical aspects*. Kluwer Academic Publications, Dordrecht.

Stout, J. T., Jackson, L. G., and Caskey, C. T. (1985). First-trimester diagnosis of Lesch–Nyhan syndrome: applications to other disorders of purine metabolism. *Prenatal Diagnosis*, **5**, 183–9.

Werner, D., Guisan, B., and Roch-Ramel, F. (1991). Urate transport in the proximal tubule of the human kidney. In: *Purine and pyrimidine metabolism in man VII. Part A: Chemotherapy, ATP depletion and gout* (ed. R. A. Harkness, G. B. Elion, and N. Zöllner), p. 177–80. Plenum Press, New York and London.

Section F
The phakomatoses

25

Renal manifestations of neurofibromatosis and tuberous sclerosis

D.S. Milliner and V.E. Torres

NEUROFIBROMATOSIS

Introduction

Neurofibromatosis is one of the most common inherited disorders and occurs in approximately one out of every 3000 births (Riccardi 1987). It is fundamentally a hamartomatous disorder of neural crest tissue. Neuroectodermal and mesodermal changes in neural structures and their accompanying blood vessels lead to diverse manifestations in multiple organ systems. Historically, as many as eight different subtypes of neurofibromatosis have been described, many with overlapping features (McKusick *et al.* 1992). In order to provide consistency in diagnosis and widely accepted recommendations for evaluation and management, a National Institutes of Health (NIH) consensus conference in 1987 considered all available information and recognized two main subtypes, termed NF1 and NF2 (National Institutes of Health 1988).

Neurofibromatosis type 1 is also known as von Recklinghausen's disease or 'peripheral' neurofibromatosis. It occurs in one in every 4000 births and accounts for approximately 85% of all cases of neurofibromatosis (National Institutes of Health 1988). Inheritance is autosomal dominant. The gene for NF1 has been localized to chromosome 17q11.2 (Barker *et al.* 1987). It contains 53 exons and the gene product, neurofibromin, is a ras GTPase activating protein (Cawthan *et al.* 1990; Viskochil *et al.* 1990). Due to unique structural qualities of the gene, including its very large size, the mutation rate is as high as one in 10 000 gametes (Riccardi 1987). Review of recent studies suggests a carrier incidence at birth of 0.0004, a gene frequency of 0.0002, and a proportion of cases due to new mutation of 0.56 (Littler and Morton 1990). Thus, half of affected patients will have no family history of neurofibromatosis. The majority of NF1 mutations described to date have involved nucleotide alterations that would be predicted to result in a loss of neurofibromin function (Upadhyaya *et al.* 1994; 1995). Prenatal testing is now available by the restriction fragment length polymorphism technique for informative families. Recent studies have suggested a high degree of penetrance (Ritter and Riccardi 1985).

Neurofibromatosis type 1 has heterogeneous manifestations. Approximately 30% of NF1 patients will develop significant medical problems related to the disease and many more will experience deformities, cosmetic problems, or other adverse effects (Holt 1978; Riccardi 1987). Central nervous system manifestations include mild to moderate learning disabilities in 25–40% of patients with NF1 and mental retardation in 5%. Seizures occur in 3%. Optic nerve gliomas are particularly common and are found in 15% of patients with NF1, but cause impairment in only 5% (Riccardi 1987). Central nervous system tumours, such as astrocytomas, may cause significant disability. Skin lesions are prominent and include cutaneous neurofibromas, subcutaneous neurofibromas, and plexiform neuromas which infiltrate adjacent normal tissue and may grow to large size. Plexiform neuromas often have features of both the cutaneous and subcutaneous lesions and frequently have overlying pigmentation and/or hair growth. The cutaneous tumours usually develop during childhood or adolescence. They tend to increase in size and number with age and often become more numerous or larger during puberty and pregnancy. Cafe-au-lait spots are characteristic and may be present at birth. They are typically found during early childhood, and the number tends to increase with age. Axillary and inguinal freckling may develop during adolescence. Angiomas and xanthrogranulomas of the skin are seen less often. Skeletal manifestations of NF1 include short stature, macrocephaly, vertebral dysplasia, scoliosis, limb-length discrepancy, pseudoarthroses, genu valgum, genu varum, and pectus excavatum. Craniofacial dysplasia occurs in 5% of patients with NF1 and frequently includes sphenoid wing dysplasia and facial asymmetry. The most common ocular finding is Lisch nodules, which are pigmented hamartomas of the iris. Ten per cent of patients will have Lisch nodules by age six, 50% by age 29, and nearly 100% by age 60 (Riccardi 1987). Orbital or periorbital plexiform tumours may cause proptosis and, with or without visual compromise, occur in 5% of children with NF1. Visceral neurofibromas may occur. The renal hilum is one of the most frequent sites of involvement (Riccardi 1987). Neurofibromas may rarely occur anywhere in the gastrointestinal tract and may cause bowel obstruction or bleeding. Paraspinal neurofibromas may result in neurologic compromise.

Malignant degeneration of neurofibromas is said to occur in 3–15% of patients with NF1, and other tumours are found with increased frequency as well (McKusick *et al.* 1992). The overall risk of malignancy has been reported as 4.2% for patients over the age of 21 years (Voutsinas and Wynne-Davies 1983). Sorensen and colleagues, in a nationwide cohort study in Denmark, noted malignancy in one-third of the 212 probands during 39 years of follow-up for a total relative risk of 2.5 (Sorensen *et al.* 1986). Female relatives with NF1 had a relative risk of malignancy of 1.9 and male relatives with NF1 of 0.9. Thirty-seven per cent of tumours originated in the central nervous system (Sorensen *et al.* 1986). Patients with NF1 have an increased incidence of embryonal malignancies, such as Wilms' tumour and rhabdomyosarcoma. Leukaemia (especially chronic myelogenous leukaemia) occurs in children with NF1 with greater frequency than in the general population. There is some evidence to suggest that there may be an increased incidence of neuroblastoma as well (Hope and Mulvihill 1981). Pheochromocytoma occurs in approximately 1/200 patients with neurofibromatosis type 1, if all ages are considered (Riccardi 1987). Neural crest-derived tumours, such as ganglioneuromas and glomus tumours, are also sometimes seen.

The expression of NF1 varies widely from patient to patient. Some have skin lesions only and others multisystem involvement or devastating central nervous system tumours or malignancy. In most patients, the manifestations increase with advancing age. It is important for the clinician to be aware of the types of problems that are likely to present during each stage of life, a topic nicely summarized by Riccardi (1987). Congenital or neonatal problems may include glaucoma, pseudoarthroses, sphenoid wing dysplasia, or large plexiform neuromas, the latter two of which may cause appreciable disfigurement. During early childhood, cafe-au-lait spots are typical. Developmental delay or symptoms referable to optic gliomas or large plexiform neuromas may become evident. Embryonal tumours are occasionally encountered. Seventy-five per cent of children manifest some clinical signs of the disease by two years of age (Riccardi 1987). During latency age, learning disabilities, signs and symptoms of optic gliomas, seizures, scoliosis, increasing size of plexiform neuromas, and the development of cutaneous tumours predominate. Some

Table 25.1   Diagnostic criteria for NF1 (National Institutes of Health 1987)

Must have two or more of the following:
1. Café-au-lait spots
   five of >0.5 cm in children
   six of >1.5 cm in adults
2. Two or more neurofibromas (any type) *or* one plexiform neuroma
3. Multiple axillary or inguinal freckles
4. Sphenoid wing dysplasia or congenital thinning or bowing of long bone cortex
5. Bilateral optic nerve gliomas
6. Two or more iris Lisch nodules
7. First-degree relative with NF1 by above criteria.

Table 25.2   Diagnostic criteria for NF2 (National Institutes of Health 1987)

1. Bilateral VIII nerve mass by CT or MRI
                    or
2. First-degree relative with NF2 and either
   (a) Unilateral VIII nerve mass
              or two of the following
   (b) Neurofibroma
       Meningioma
       Glioma
       Schwannoma
       Juvenile posterior subcapsular cataract

patients will begin showing Lisch nodules. Precocious puberty is occasionally seen. Adolescence may be marked by growth in cutaneous and subcutaneous tumours, increasing cafe-au-lait spots, sometimes by hypertension due to vascular lesions, delayed puberty, or neurofibrosarcomas. Early to mid adult life is notable for continued increase in number and size of cutaneous lesions, neurofibrosarcomas, and hypertension which may be due to a variety of aetiologies, including pheochromocytoma. During late adulthood, the disease tends to be quiescent and marked only by a slow increase in the size of cutaneous tumours and visceral or other neurofibromas.

Diagnostic criteria for NF1 are shown in Table 25.1. Plexiform neuromas are felt to be specific for NF1 (McKusick *et al.* 1992). Iris Lisch nodules, optic gliomas, and pseudoarthroses suggest NF1. Although cafe-au-lait spots may occur in other types of neurofibromatosis, they are typically more widespread and prominent in NF1.

Neurofibromatosis type 2, also known as 'central' neurofibromatosis, occurs in one of every 50 000 births and accounts for approximately 8% of individuals with neurofibromatosis. Inheritance is autosomal dominant. The gene for NF2 resides on chromosome 22q11.2 (Martuzar and Eldridge 1988). This gene encodes a novel protein which has been named Merlin (for moesin-ezrin-radixin-like-protein) or Schwannomin, with homology to a highly conserved family of proteins that have been postulated to connect the cytoskeleton to components of the plasma membrane (Kley *et al.* 1995). Vestibular schwannomas (acoustic neuromas) and other central nervous system tumours are characteristic. Patients may present with hearing loss, tinnitus, dizziness, unsteadiness of gait, headaches, or seizures. Bilateral eighth nerve tumours are diagnostic of NF2 (Table 25.2). Patients will occasionally be encountered who have features of both NF1 and NF2 and are difficult to classify.

A third type of neurofibromatosis (NF3) is recognized by some authors (McKusick *et al.* 1992) and includes intestinal neurofibromas, cafe-au-lait spots that are fewer in number and more pale than those of NF1, freckling, cutaneous neurofibromas (especially in the palm of the hand), bilateral acoustic neuromas, posterior fossa and upper cervical meningiomas, or paraspinal nerve fibromas. Notably, Lisch nodules and optic gliomas are not seen in NF3.

Renal and urinary tract involvement in neurofibromatosis

Renal or urinary tract involvement occurs most often in patients with NF1. It may be manifest as vascular lesions, renal parenchymal lesions, or tumours and their associated effects.

Vascular lesions

Vascular lesions are characteristic of neurofibromatosis and are found in both small and large vessels. The arterial changes are characterized by marked destruction of components of the arterial wall as well as the presence of tightly packed nodular masses of fused or formed cells. In a review of autopsy material in 18 patients with neurofibromatosis, Salyer and Salyer (1974) found vascular abnormalities in eight. The kidney was the most common site of involvement with renovascular changes in six of the eight. Some authors have suggested that the vascular lesions are of neural origin (Habib and Habib 1962; Salyer and Salyer 1974). Salyer and Salyer implicated Schwann cell proliferation and secondary degenerative fibrosis. Greene and colleagues (1974) and Finley and Dabbs (1988) demonstrated by electron microscopy and immunoperoxidase studies, respectively, intimal lesions which had the characteristics of smooth muscle, thus implicating mesodermal dysplasia. Although the histogenesis of vascular changes in neurofibromatosis remains controversial, the patterns of involvement and clinical manifestations are well-established.

Reubi (1945) was the first to describe the vascular lesions with later amplification by other authors (Feytrer 1949; Habib and Habib 1962; Greene *et al.* 1974; Salyer and Salyer 1974; Finley and Dabbs 1988). Small intralobular artery lesions consist of subintimal proliferation of fibroelastic-type cells with elongated nuclei arranged around a reduced vessel lumen. Medium-size arterial lesions (arcuate and intralobar arteries) show intimal proliferation and rupture of elastic laminae, allowing intimal aneurysms to form. Large vessels (including the main renal artery) often show nodular changes as well as hyperplasia and hyalinization of the intima, destruction of the media and elastic laminae, and aneurysmal dilatation. Mixed forms are seen. Vascular thromboses may be associated, further reducing the vessel lumen.

The consequences of the dysplastic lesions of arteries are diminished blood flow and eventual vascular obliteration which may or may not be accompanied by fibrosis. Small vessel changes, when occurring in the kidney, may result in localized areas of ischaemia or infarction and secondary hypertension (Smith *et al.* 1970; Diprete *et al.* 1990). When occurring in larger vessels, stenoses may result. Renal artery stenosis is particularly noteworthy and is a cause of hypertension in patients with NF1 (Mena *et al.* 1973; Tilford and Kelsch 1973). (Fig. 25.1). Stenoses may also occur in the abdominal aorta, celiac axis, iliac arteries, and other large arteries. Renal artery aneurysms are typically seen in association with other renal artery lesions and are commonly poststenotic. However, isolated aneurysms are also seen (Flynn and Buchanan 1979). Rarely such

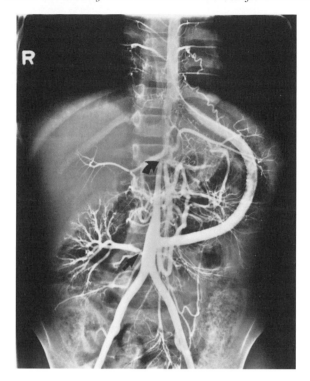

Fig. 25.1 Five-year-old girl with NF1 and hypertension. Angiography confirmed coarctation of the aorta and bilateral renal artery stenosis. Hypertension improved following bypass grafting of the aorta and right renal autotransplantation, but blood pressure increased again one year later. Repeat arteriogram shows restenosis at origin of autotransplanted renal artery (straight arrow). Left renal artery stenosis is also shown (curved arrow).

aneurysms may rupture, particularly during pregnancy (Tapp and Hickling 1969). In addition to the vascular lesions described above, true neurofibromas may develop in the adventitial layer and have the potential to compromise the vascular lumen of small or large vessels in the kidney or other organ systems. However, reports of clinical consequences of vascular compression from such lesions have been rare.

Renal parenchymal lesions

Renal parenchymal changes due to neurofibromatosis are uncommon. Polycystic changes of kidneys and liver have been reported in patients with NF1 (Siegelman *et al.* 1971; Varma *et al.* 1982). One of these patients (Siegelman *et al.* 1971) had an associated renal cell carcinoma. Given the reports of renal cysts and renal neoplasms in two other neurocutaneous syndromes (von Hippel–Lindau disease and tuberous sclerosis), these associations may be important despite the small number of reported cases to date. There have also been several reports of Wilms' tumour in patients with neurofibromatosis (Stay and Vawter 1977; Walden *et al.* 1977; Hope and Mulvihill 1981) and neurofibrosarcoma at an irradiation site in a patient with neurofibromatosis and Wilms' tumour (Chu *et al.* 1981).

A unique renal parenchymal abnormality, sclerosing peritubular nodules, has been reported in three members of a family with NF2 (Mandybur and Weiss 1981). The nodules appear to originate as concentric, peritubular proliferations of collagen-producing spindle cells. The cells of origin are believed to reside in the renal interstitium and have characteristics of fibroblasts as well as smooth-muscle cells (Mandybur and Weiss 1981). On ultrastructural examination, four stages of nodule development have been noted leading to progressive sclerosis and tubular destruction. Despite widespread involvement of the cortex, none of the patients reported had clinical manifestations of renal dysfunction.

Renal phosphate wasting and hypophosphataemic osteomalacia have been reported in association with neurofibromatosis (Melick *et al.* 1979; Hogan *et al.* 1986; Weinstein and Harris 1990) Konishi and colleagues (1991) reviewed 35 cases. All but three occurred in adults. The serum phosphate concentration was reported in 24 of the cases and ranged from 1.0–3.0 mg/dL with a mean of 1.94. Tubular reabsorption of phosphorus measured in eight patients was 71.9% ± 9.58% (mean ± SD). TMP/GFR reported in four patients ranged from 1.3–1.9 mg/dL. Serum calcium was reported in 19 of the patients and was 9.2 ± 0.7 mg/dL Only three patients had a serum calcium of less than 8.5 mg/dL. Serum concentrations of 25 hydroxy vitamin D were normal in six of seven patients tested. The patient with the low value had had a previous gastrectomy. Serum 1,25 dihydroxy vitamin D values were normal in all six patients in whom this metabolite was measured. In patients reported to date, evidence of generalized proximal tubular dysfunction is lacking. The pathogenesis of the renal phosphate wasting is unknown. Konishi *et al.* (1991) speculate that neurofibromata might produce a humoral factor which induces phosphaturia. Such a factor has been identified in extracts from dermal fibroangiomas in a patient with multiple epidermal nevus syndrome and hypophosphataemic rickets (Ashinberg *et al.* 1977). The possibility of an occult secondary tumour producing a similar humoral factor must also be considered in such patients. Pharmacologic doses of vitamin D, with or without phosphorus supplementation, were effective in ameliorating the osteomalacia in all but two of the patients. In one patient who did not respond favourably to treatment, overt hyperparathyroidism coexisted with osteomalacia, and the patient required parathyroidectomy (Weinstein and Harris 1990).

Tumours of the urinary tract

The collecting system of the kidneys, the ureters, and the bladder are occasionally affected by neurofibromatosis. The most common site of involvement is the bladder. Manifestations include renal pelvic neurofibromas (Mandybur and Weiss 1981), and retroperitoneal or pelvic neurofibromas (Cheong *et al.* 1990) causing extrinsic compression of the ureters and bladder (Melick *et al.* 1979) (Fig. 25.2) Sacral neurofibromas may result in a neurogenic bladder. Bladder neurofibromas are often initially manifest as haematuria, frequency, urgency, enuresis, or pain. Fifty per cent of reported cases have occurred in children (Blum *et al.* 1985). Large, plexiform neuromas of the bladder may cause upper urinary tract obstruction. (Clark *et al.* 1977; Rink and Mitchell 1983; Blum *et al.* 1985) Fibromatous tumours may involve prostate, urethra, seminal vesicles, or testes (Blum *et al.* 1985) and the genitalia may be involved in up to 35% of patients with bladder neurofibromatosis (Rink and Mitchell 1983). Malignant tumours have been rare (Blum *et al.* 1995). A single cases of a renal alimentary fistula has been reported in a 12-year-old patient with neurofibromatosis (Shokri 1968). Due to the progressive nature of neurofibromatosis, conservative management is recommended when possible. Surgical debulking of tumours is sometimes indicated. If significant obstruction occurs, urinary diversion may be required.

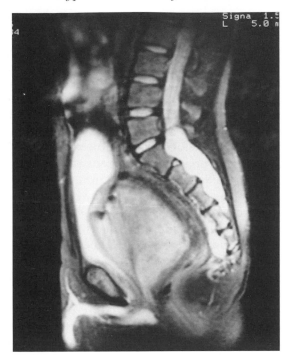

Fig. 25.2   Magnetic resonance imaging of a large neurofibroma causing bladder compression in a 10-year-old boy with neurofibromatosis.

Hypertension in neurofibromatosis

Hypertension in patients with neurofibromatosis requires careful evaluation. Although the majority of adults will have essential hypertension unassociated with the neurofibromatosis, a number of causes of hypertension particular to neurofibromatosis must be considered (Table 25.3). In children with neurofibromatosis, essential hypertension is unlikely. Diagnostic evaluation will usually disclose a specific cause, most often a vascular lesion such as renal artery stenosis, abdominal coarctation, or intrarenal vascular disease.

Renal artery stenosis due to renal artery dysplasia is the most common cause of hypertension during childhood and adolescence in patients with neurofibromatosis. Renal artery lesions occur with equal frequency in patients with mild or severe neurofibromatosis. The many case reports to date document a mean age at diagnosis of 14 years (Schurch *et al.* 1975). Seventy per cent of patients with renal artery stenosis are less than 16 years of age. The male to female ratio is 2:1 (Mallman and Roth 1986). Bilateral renal artery stenosis occurs in 33–40% of patients (Syme 1980; Mallman and Roth 1986). There is a predilection for the left renal artery in those with unilateral disease (3:1) (Blum *et al.* 1985). Renal artery stenoses in neurofibromatosis typically involve proximal portions of the artery, including the origin, more than 50% of the time (Schurch *et al.* 1975). This is in contrast to fibromuscular dysplasia in which 95% of lesions are in the distal two-thirds of the renal arteries (Hamson *et al.* 1967). Renal artery stenosis in neurofibromatosis is frequently accompanied by poststenotic dilatation which has a characteristic 'funnel' appearance on arteriography (Itzchak *et al.* 1974). Approximately 20–25% of patients with renal artery stenosis have associated coarctation of the aorta (Schurch *et al.* 1975). Coarctation of the abdominal aorta without renal artery stenosis is occasionally seen. A smaller number of patients show stenoses of other visceral arteries, such as coeliac, hepatic, iliac, or mesenteric arteries. Lesions of the thoracic aorta and pulmonary arteries have also been reported (Itzchak *et al.* 1974; Rowen *et al.* 1975). Aneurysms, most often of the renal arteries but occasionally of other visceral arteries, are a recognized consequence of the vascular disease of neurofibromatosis (Allan and Davies 1970; Fye *et al.* 1975; Pfau *et al.* 1976; Flynn and Buchanan 1979; Kuo *et al.* 1989). Aneurysms generally occur distal to renal artery stenosis but are occasionally seen independently and may be the cause of hypertension (Flynn and Buchanan 1979).

To date, treatment efforts have primarily been directed to dilatation, repair, or bypass of vascular stenosis. Angioplasty has been performed to dilate proximal renal artery lesions in a small number of patients, and results have been mixed (Baxi *et al.* 1981; Elias *et al.* 1985; Mallman and Roth 1986; Gardiner *et al.* 1988; Robinson *et al.* 1991). Surgical repair with bypass of the stenotic segment or transplantation of the kidney to iliac fossa have both been used successfully (Gill *et al.* 1976). However, progression of abdominal aortic coarctation and recurrent stenosis of the renal arteries have been reported following surgical repair (Schurch *et al.* 1975; Pollard *et al.* 1989). Results of angioplasty and surgical repair may also be limited by coexisting intrarenal vascular lesions or microvascular changes in the kidney (Schurch *et al.* 1975; Pfau *et al.* 1976; Lonstein and McKinley 1979; Kuo *et al.* 1989). Partial (Greene *et al.* 1974; O'Regan and Mongeau 1983; Elias *et al.* 1985) and total nephrectomy (Tilford and Kelsch 1973; Elias *et al.* 1985) have also been performed but should be avoided, if possible, in view of the progressive nature of the vascular changes and in the interest of preserving functioning kidney tissue. Medical management has been successful in some patients (O'Regan and Mongeau 1983; Tenschert *et al.* 1985) but entails the potential for reduced perfusion pressure to one or both kidneys, and in the case of abdominal coarctation, to the lower extremities as well. Angiotensin-converting enzyme inhibitors should be used with particular caution in such circumstances. Elias and colleagues (1985) reviewed treatment outcomes of 49 patients with neurofibromatosis and renovascular hypertension due to renal artery stenosis. Twenty-five had unilateral lesions. Of 23 treated surgically, 16 (76%) had cure of hypertension, 4 (19%) were improved, and 1 (5%) failed. No outcome information was available in the remaining two patients. Of 24 patients with bilateral renal artery lesions, 18 had surgical treatment. This included five patients who failed to improve following balloon angioplasty and subsequently had surgery. Eight (44%) were cured, nine (50%) improved, and one (6%) failed. Eight patients were treated medically (two with unilateral and six with bilateral renal artery stenosis). Six did not improve and one died. The remaining patient had improved blood pressure following removal of an intracranial mass despite bilateral renal artery stenosis.

Extrinsic compression of the renal artery is rare, occurring in only 4% of cases of neurofibromatosis with documented renal vascular hypertension (Schurch *et al.* 1975). There are rare reports of extrinsic compression of the renal artery by neurofibromas (Lynch *et al.* 1972; Schurch *et al.* 1975) and by a non-neurofibromatous vascular band (Watson and Osofsky 1981). Intrarenal small-vessel disease may be a cause of hypertension in patients with neurofibromatosis (Smith *et al.* 1970; Bourke and Gatenby 1971; Schurch *et al.* 1975; Pfau *et al.* 1976; Finley and Dabbs 1988) and is important in that repair of concomitant abdominal coarctation or renal artery stenosis will not result in resolution of hypertension. Coarctation of the abdominal or thoracic aorta may result in hypertension. When the lesions of abdominal coarctation and bilateral renal artery stenosis coexist (Fig. 25.1), management can be complex. Pheochromocytomas occur in 0.5–8% of patients with NF1. (Samvelson and Axelsson 1981; Sorensen *et al.* 1986; Riccaroli 1987; Huson *et al.* 1988; Kaufman 1993) (Fig. 25.3) They may be bilateral. Although usually benign, malig-

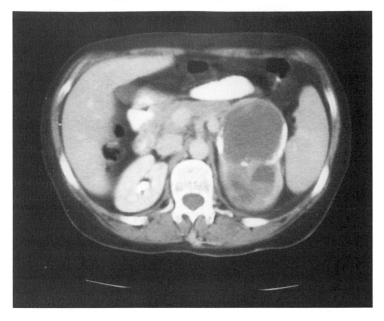

Fig. 25.3 Computerized tomography scan showing a large pheochromocytoma with haemorrhage, infarction, and calcification in a 49-year-old woman with NF1.

nant cases have been reported (Okada and Shozawa 1984). Occasionally, pheochromocytomas have been found during diagnostic assesments for problems other than hypertension in patients who have normal blood pressures.

Rare causes of hypertension in neurofibromatosis include central nervous system lesions and catecholamine secretion by benign neurofibromas. A 14-year-old girl with neurofibromatosis had severe hypertension due to a cerebellar glioblastoma. Although she had concomitant renal artery stenoses and coarctation of the abdominal aorta, her hypertension improved following removal of the cerebellar tumour (Guthrie *et al.* 1982). A hyperadrenergic state has been documented in patients with massive cervical neurofibromas (Rubenstein *et al.* 1981; Riccardi and Eichner 1986). These tumours secrete excessive amounts of catecholamines, particularly norepinephrine, and may mimic pheochromocytoma.

Among 106 paediatric patients with neurofibromatosis evaluated by O'Regan and Mongeau (1983), eight had hypertension and five of the eight had vascular lesions. These included three patients with bilateral renal artery stenosis and intrarenal vascular stenosis, one with a hypoplastic renal artery and hypoplastic kidney, and another patient with abnormal vessels to a hypoplastic left upper pole. Thus, 5% of children in the series were found to have renal vascular hypertension. Two of the patients had transient hypertension of undetermined aetiology and one had hypertension due to reflux renal scarring unrelated to neurofibromatosis. Among children with renal artery lesions, three of 27 (11%) (Daniels *et al.* 1987) and eight of 54 (14.8%) (Deal *et al.* 1992) were found to have neurofibromatosis. During childhood and adolescence, the most common cause of hypertension in patients with neurofibromatosis is renal artery stenosis. Intrarenal vascular disease and coarctation of the aorta are less common. Pheochromocytoma is rare.

In adults with neurofibromatosis, essential hypertension is more common than secondary forms. The incidence of renal artery stenosis as a cause of hypertension in adult patients with neurofibromatosis has been estimated at less than 1%. (60) Pheochromocytomas are found primarily in adult patients (Tilford and Kelsch 1973). Multiple causes of hypertension, such as renal artery stenosis, renal small vessel disease, abdominal coarctation, intrarenal aneurysms, and pheochromocytoma, not infrequently coexist (Ahlmen *et al.* 1972; Kremen *et al.* 1985; Tenschert *et al.* 1985; Riccardi and Eichner (1986).

Prevalence of renal and urinary tract abnormalities in patients with neurofibromatosis

The prevalence of renal and urinary tract abnormalities in neurofibromatosis is difficult to assess. Reports in the literature are limited by selection bias, emphasis on certain populations (for example, paediatric vs. adult), and variable approaches to case detection.

Histories of 300 patients with neurofibromatosis seen at the Mayo Clinic from 1982 to 1992 were reviewed. Two hundred and sixty-six patients (88.6%) met NIH consensus conference criteria for NF1, 27 (9%) met criteria for NF2, three patients (1%) had features of both NF1 and NF2, and four (1.3%) were felt by staff geneticists to have neurofibromatosis of another type. The number of patients with hypertension, the per cent of the study population at risk, and causes of hypertension are designated by age in Table 25.4. As reported in other series, renal artery stenosis was seen primarily in patients less than 20 years of age. Renal artery stenosis was bilateral in three of seven patients and unilateral in four (two left, two right). A seven-year-old with bilateral disease and stenosis of multiple small renal arteries developed recurrence of left renal artery stenosis following surgical repair. A 12-year-old boy with bilateral renal artery stenosis also had a left upper pole renal infarct, coarctation of the abdominal aorta, and stenosis of the mesenteric artery. A 12-year-old boy with unilateral renal artery stenosis had a generalized arteriopathy, including coarctation of the abdominal aorta, occlusion of the origin of the left main renal artery (contralateral to the stenosis), and multiple aneurysms of renal, splenic, and lumbar arteries. One patient with hypertension at 21 years of age was found to have an infarct distal to a renal artery aneurysm. Pheochromocytoma was seen predominantly in patients ages 20–49 and was bilateral in two. In addition, one 46-year-old hypertensive patient had a right adrenal mass but normal urine metanephrines. A 37-year-old woman with hypertension had bilateral adrenal masses but no evidence of secretory activity. A 50-year-old patient was normotensive and urine metanephrines and catecholamines were normal despite CT scan findings strongly suggestive of pheochromocytoma. Thus, a total of 10 patients had pheochromocytoma (3.3%) which was a cause of hypertension in at least seven (2.3%) (Table 25.4).

Table 25.3   Causes of hypertension in neurofibromatosis

Renal artery stenosis
Coarctation of aorta
Pheochromocytoma
Renal artery aneurysms
Renal artery compression by neurofibroma
Intrarenal vascular disease
Posterior fossa tumours
Catecholamine production by cervical neurofibroma

Table 25.4 Causes of hypertension in patients with neurofibromatosis: Mayo Clinic findings

Age, yrs	At risk n	↑BP n	Per cent	Renal artery stenosis	Pheochromocytoma	Aneurysm	Essential	Other	Incomplete evaluation
0–9	300	2	0.7%	2	0	0	0	0	0
10–19	273	8	2.9%	4	0	0	0	1	3
20–29	222	6	2.7%	0	2	1	1	0	2
30–39	157	9	5.7%	1	2	0	0	3	3
40–49	89	7	7.9%	0	2	0	0	1	4
50–59	48	6	12.5%	0	0	0	3	1	2
60–69	30	7	23.3%	0	1	0	1	0	5
70–79	17	0	0	0	0	0	0	0	0
80–89	2	0	0	0	0	0	0	0	0
TOTAL	300	45	15.0%	7	7	1	5	6	19

Of the five patients with 'essential' hypertension, one had thorough evaluation to rule out secondary causes. The remaining four had mild blood pressure elevations, readily controlled with small doses of antihypertensive agents. Many patients, particularly those greater than 40 years of age, had incomplete diagnostic evaluation for their hypertension. Although most of them likely had essential hypertension, it was not possible to exclude vascular disease as the cause. Among those patients in the 'other' category, one 18-year-old had transient hypertension during two pregnancies, a 30-year-old had hypertension secondary to increased intracranial pressure, a 34-year-old had significant hypertension that resolved following treatment of his alcoholism, and two had adrenal masses demonstrated by CT scanning but normal urinary metanephrines and catecholamines. A 56-year-old had a small right kidney with delayed uptake. No arteriogram was performed.

Five patients had intrarenal lesions related to neurofibromatosis. These included a 12-year-old with multiple renal artery aneurysms, a 21-year-old with an infarct distal to an aneurysm, and a 12-year-old with intrarenal vascular lesions also leading to infarction. A 33-year-old woman had neurofibrosarcoma infiltrating the left kidney and a 42-year-old woman had renal phosphate wasting with severe osteomalacia. Four other patients had renal parenchymal disorders that may or may not have been related to neurofibromatosis, including a 17-year-old with haematuria, proteinuria, and an active urine sediment; a 21-year-old with an active urine sediment and good renal function; a 48-year-old with biopsy documented crescentic glomerulonephritis; and a 62-year-old with proteinuria not further evaluated.

Fourteen patients had urologic complications of neurofibromatosis. Included are eight patients with neurogenic bladder, a 2-year-old with embryonal rhabdomyosarcoma, a 7-year-old with a plexiform neurofibroma involving the bladder wall with bilateral partial ureteral obstruction, an 18-year-old with a retroperitoneal mass displacing the kidney and ureter, an 18-year-old with a diffuse neurofibroma of the bladder causing clots and gross haematuria, and two patients in their 40s, each with a mass displacing the ureter.

Recommendations for long-term management

Neurofibromatosis is a progressive disorder. In addition to ongoing management of specific, identified problems in the kidneys or urinary tract and management of hypertension, patients also require ongoing surveillance for other problems resulting from the disease. The consensus conference of the NIH (1988) recommends annual evaluations by a physician familiar with neurofibromatosis, even in asymptomatic patients. For patients with NF1, the history should focus on cognitive or psychomotor deficits, pain, disturbances of vision, evidence of neurologic deficits, and constipation. The physical examination must include attention to blood pressure, scoliosis or other skeletal anomalies, macrocephaly, focal neurologic deficits (impaired vision, ptosis, optic atrophy), proptosis, and assessment of existing or new neurofibromas. In young patients, attention to growth velocity and learning disabilities or developmental delay is important, as is evidence of precocious or delayed puberty. Laboratory tests such as CT scans and MRI imaging are unlikely to be of value in asymptomatic patients. For patients with NF2, an annual evaluation should focus on changes in hearing, signs or symptoms indicating loss of vestibular function, and signs or symptoms suggestive of increased intracranial pressure or intraspinal neoplasms. Patients with NF2 or at risk of NF2 should have at least one MRI of the head by puberty, even if asymptomatic. During adult life, annual audiograms and brain stem auditory-evoked responses provide a non-invasive way to detect eighth nerve tumours. MRI with gadolinium using 'acoustic' cuts should be performed every two to three years in patients with NF2 and those at risk of NF2. Other tests should be performed as indicated by clinical findings. For all patients with neurofibromatosis, patient and family education, family screening, and genetic counselling are of importance.

TUBEROUS SCLEROSIS COMPLEX

Introduction

Tuberous sclerosis complex (TSC) is an autosomal dominant disease that appears to affect cell migration and differentiation in a variety of organs with the possible exceptions of peripheral nervous system, meninges, skeletal muscles, and pineal gland (Gomez 1988; 1991). As in the case of neurofibromatosis, it has been suggested that derivatives of neural crest cells constitute the chief elements involved in the lesions of TSC (Johnson *et al.* 1991; Lallier 1991). Linkage studies to a variety of genetic markers indicate that TSC is genetically heterogeneous, with at least two gene loci, TSC-1 in chromosome 9q32–q34 (Fryer *et al.* 1987; Connor and Sampson 1991; Haines *et al.* 1991; Janssen *et al.* 1991) and TSC-2 near the PKD 1 locus in chromosome 16q13 (Kandt *et al.* 1992). The TSC-2 gene has been identified. It contains 41 exons and encodes a protein of approximately 198 kd which has been named tuberin. The function of tuberin is not well understood but it contains domains with Rap1GAP and transcriptional activities (Wienecke *et al.* 1995; Tsuchiya *et al.* 1996). The TSC-1 gene has also been recently identified. The corresponding 130 kd protein has been named hamartin (van Slegtenhorst *et al.* 1997). The prevalence of TSC at birth may be as high as 1 : 5800 (Osborne *et al.* 1991). TSC is due to the new mutations in 60–70% of the patients (Hunt and Lindenbaum 1984; Wiederholt *et al.* 1985; Fryer *et al.* 1987; Sampson *et al.* 1989; Connor and Sampson 1991; Haines *et al.* 1991; Janssen *et al.* 1991; Shepherd *et al.* 1991).

Diagnostic criteria and general manifestations

The name 'tuberous sclerosis of the cerebral convolutions' was coined by Désiré-Magloire Bourneville in 1880 when he described the potato-like hardening of the hypertrophic cerebral gyri in a 15-year-old epileptic, hemiplegic, and mentally defective girl (Bourneville 1880; 1900). The diagnostic significance of the facial angiofibromas (adenoma sebaceum) was first pointed by Vogt as a component of the classical triad (seizures, mental retardation, and facial angiofibromas) in 1908. (Vogt 1908) None of the elements of this triad is essential for the diagnosis of TSC. Other organs may be involved with characteristic lesions. The severity of the involvement, size, number, and location of the lesions is very variable, even in members of the same family. Clinical criteria were developed by Gomez (1988; 1991) to assist in the diagnosis of TSC (Table 25.5).

The neurologic manifestations of TSC relate to the presence of cortical tubers and subependymal glial nodules or giant cell astrocytomas and include seizures, infantile spasms, hemiplegia, hemianopsia, and disorders of mentation. Mental subnormality and abnormal behaviour are usually associated to the onset of generalized seizures in the first years of life. Patients with TSC and cortical tubers who never had seizures have normal intellect. With the increasing recognition of mild forms of TSC, the frequency of seizures and mental retardation in this disease has

Table 25.5   Clinical findings leading to a diagnosis of TSC

1. Neurologic (definite diagnosis: single with histologic confirmation; multiple by imaging or ophthalmoscopy)
    (a) Cortical tuber
    (b) Subependymal glial nodule/giant cell astrocytoma
    (c) Retinal hamartoma
2. Dermatologic (definite diagnosis)
    (a) Facial angiofibromas
    (b) Fibrous forehead plaque
    (c) Ungual fibroma
    (d) Shagreen patch (histologic confirmation)
3. Visceral (presumptive diagnosis)*
    (a) Multiple renal angiomyolipomas
    (b) Multiple cardiac rhabdomyomas
    (c) Multiple renal cysts and an angiomyolipoma
    (d) Pulmonary lymphangiomyomatosis and a renal angiomyolipoma
4. Suggestive: Hypomelanotic skin macules, enamel pits, hamartomatous rectal polyps; radiographic sclerotic bone patches and cysts; angiolipoma of kidney, liver, adrenal, or gonads; thyroid adenoma (papillary or fetal type); infantile spasms

*Individuals with only these findings have borne children with TSC.

decreased (Webb *et al.* 1991; Webb and Osborne 1991). The subependymal glial nodules or giant cell astrocytomas become symptomatic as they grow and obstruct the cerebrospinal fluid circulation and cause signs of increased intracranial pressure or seizures. Retinal hamartomas are usually asymptomatic.

The skin signs of TSC include facial angiofibromas (adenoma sebaceum), fibrous plaques, ungual fibromas, shagreen patches, and hypomelanotic skin macules. Hypomelanotic macules are the earliest and most common skin manifestation of TSC, occurring in 90% of the patients (Fitzpatrick 1991). They are best detected under Wood's light. Three types of hypomelanotic macules have been described: polygonal, 'ash-leaf', and 'confetti'. Although not the most common, the confetti-like macules have been claimed to be the most characteristic (Fitzpatrick 1991). Facial angiofibromas occur only in 50% of the patients and are rarely found before three years of age. Fibrous plaques can be found at a younger age and involve the forehead, eyelid, cheek, or scalp. Ungual fibromas and shagreen patches do not develop until the second decade.

Extrarenal visceral manifestations of TSC include cardiac rhabdomyomas, vascular dysplasia, pulmonary lymphangiomyomatosis, hamartomas, rectal polyps, angiomyolipomas of the liver, adrenal glands or gonads, and papillary or fetal-type thyroid adenomas. Cardiac rhabdomyomas occur very early, in the fetus after the 26th gestational week or in young infants, and tend to decrease in size or disappear on serial echocardiograms (Lie 1991). Aortic and intracranial aneurysms and aortic coarctation are rare manifestations of TSC. Pulmonary lymphangiomyomatosis is also uncommon, affects women in the third or fourth decade of life, and can cause a spontaneous pneumothorax, chylothorax, hemoptysis, and respiratory failure.

Renal and urinary tract manifestations

The main renal manifestations of TSC are angiomyolipomas, cysts, and renal cell carcinomas. Other associations rarely recognized include renal interstitial disease, focal segmental glomerulosclerosis, glomerular microhamartomas, renal artery stenosis, ureteropelvic junction stenosis, and horseshoe kidney.

Angiomyolipomas

Angiomyolipomas are benign tumours composed of abnormal thickened wall vessels that lack a well-developed internal elastic lamina and of varying amounts of spindle, smooth, muscle-like cells and adipose tissue (Farrow *et al.* 1968). They are found in about 0.3–2.1% of kidneys at routine autopsy (Reese and Winstanley 1958; Hajdu and Foote 1969). Because these figures largely exceed both the frequency of symptomatic angiomyolipomas in the general population and the estimated prevalence of TSC, it is obvious that most patients with angiomyolipomas never have symptoms and do not have TSC. Symptomatic angiomyolipomas in patients without TSC are usually single and mainly found in middle-aged women (Oesterling *et al.* 1986; Blute *et al.* 1988). On the other hand, angiomyolipomas in patients with TSC are usually multiple and bilateral (Bernstein *et al.* 1986; Stiwell *et al.* 1987; Benstein and Robbins 1991).

Prior to the introduction of sonography and computed tomography, the pre-operative diagnosis of an angiomyolipoma could rarely be made with certainty, because the angiographic characteristics of these lesions (serpentine vessels, saccular aneurysms, and puddling of contrast medium) are not specific and can occasionally be observed in malignant renal tumours (Heckl *et al.* 1987). The non-invasive diagnosis of angiomyolipoma requires the identification of fat in the tumour (increased echogenecity on ultrasound and low attenuation on CT) (Fig. 25.4) (Totty *et al.* 1981; Bosniak *et al.* 1988; Uhlenbrock *et al.* 1988). Therefore, the diagnostic accuracy depends

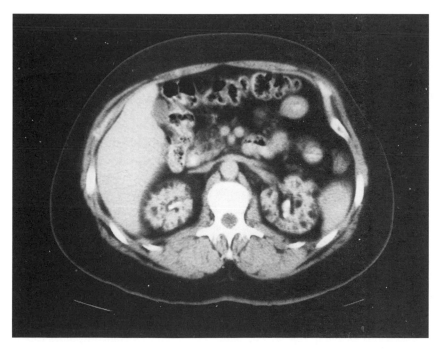

Fig. 25.4 Multiple small angiomyolipomas detected by computerized tomography in a 50-year-old man.

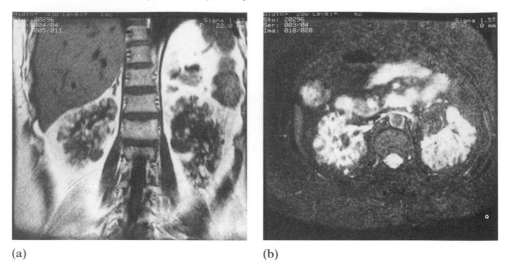

(a)   (b)

Fig. 25.5   Multiple small angiomyolipomas detected by magnetic resonance imaging in a 45-year-old woman. The angiomyolipomas give a high signal intensity on the T1-weighted images (a) and reduced signal intensity on the T2-weighted images with fat saturation (b).

on the amount of fat tissue in the tumour. Ultrasonography may be more sensitive than computed tomography for detection of small angiomyolipomas since the fatty tissue is highly echogenic, and lesions smaller than 1 cm may be difficult to diagnose on CT because of the partial volume effect. The use of 5 mm thin sections and unenhanced scans improve the accuracy of CT in detecting fat in small lesions in which partial volume effect may be significant. On the other hand, the specificity of CT may be superior to that of ultrasound in differentiating small angiomyolipomas from perinephric or renal sinus fat. CT scan may also be superior to ultrasound for detection of small angiomyolipomas in a diffusely hyperechoic kidney. More recently, magnetic resonance imaging has been added to the evaluation of these tumours, and in some cases, it may be more sensitive in demonstrating the fat in the tumour (Uhlenbrock *et al.* 1988). On MRI, the fat gives a high-signal intensity on T1-weighted images and an intermediate signal on T2 weighted images (Fig. 25.5). Occasionally, the distinction between an angiomyolipoma and a renal cell carcinoma cannot be reliably established by any imaging techniques. In this situation, ultrasound or CT-guided fine needle aspiration biopsy has been proposed to help differentiate between a renal angiomyolipoma and a renal cell carcinoma and avoid surgical exploration (Taavitsainen *et al.* 1989; Sant *et al.* 1990). At present, the safety and efficacy of this approach is not clearly defined and our preference in this setting is to proceed with surgical exploration.

Renal angiomyolipomas are benign tumours but can be locally invasive, extending into perire-nal fat or, more rarely, the collecting system, renal vein, and even in the inferior vena cava and right atrium (Kutcher *et al.* 1982; Rothenberg *et al.* 1986; Camónez *et al.* 1987). Lymph nodal and splenic involvement are usually thought to represent multicentricity rather than metastatic spread (Bloom *et al.* 1982; Hulbert and Graf 1983). The main manifestations of the renal angiomyolipomas relate to their potential for haemorrhage (hematuria, intratumoral, or retro-peritoneal haemorrhage) and mass effect (abdominal or flank mass and tenderness, hypertension, renal insufficiency) (Oesterling *et al.* 1986; Blute *et al.* 1988). Angiomyolipomas can also cause fever of unknown origin (Vekemans *et al.* 1987). The tumour size correlates with the presence or absence of symptoms. Small angiomyolipomas are usually, but not always, asymptomatic. Micro-haematuria is commonly reported in surgical studies but is rarely observed in patients with asymptomatic angiomyolipomas. The risk for serious haemorrhage from an angiomyolipoma appears to be increased during pregnancy, possibly due to hormonal changes and an increased blood volume, which may cause these tumours to rupture and bleed (Lewis and Palmer 1985; Petrikovsky *et al.* 1990). It has been suggested that hypertension in patients with angiomyolipo-mas is caused by compression of the adjacent kidney by the tumour and release of renin, as cure of the hypertension following the surgical removal of the tumour has been observed in some cases (Futter and Collins 1974). Nevertheless, the majority of patients with renal angiomyolipomas have normal blood pressure and most of those with pre-existing hypertension remain hyperten-sive following the surgical removal of the angiomyolipoma (Hajdu and Foote 1969; Mukai *et al.* 1992). In addition, peripheral renin activity in these patients has been normal or low, suggesting a volume expanded state (Futter and Collins 1974; Green *et al.* 1990). Bilateral renal angiomyol-ipomas can destroy enough renal tissue to cause significant impairment of renal function.

Renal cysts

Cystic disease is the second most common renal manifestation of TSC (Bernstein *et al.* 1986; Stillwell *et al.* 1987; Robbins and Bernstein 1988; Bernstein and Robbins 1991). The number of cysts may range from one or few to innumerable and macroscopically indistinguishable in the absence of angiomyolipomas from polycystic kidney disease. These cysts can develop from any segment of the nephron. When their number is limited and the size is small, they are predomi-nantly cortical. In some cases, glomerular cysts may prefominate. It has been suggested that the epithelial lining of these cysts is distinctive and unique to TSC. The cells are large and acido-philic and contain large, hyperchromatic nuclei with occasional mitotic figures.

The appearance of the cysts on ultrasound, CT, or MRI is identical to that of benign simple cysts or polycystic kidney disease. In the absence of angiomyolipomas it may be impossible to differentiate radiologically TSC from autosomal dominant polycystic kidney disease (Fig. 25.6).

The major clinical problem associated with severe cystic changes in TSC is the development of hypertension and renal failure. Because cystic kidneys may be the presenting manifestation of TSC, this diagnosis should be considered in children with renal cysts and no family history of polycystic kidney disease (Wenzl *et al.* 1970; Stapleton *et al.* 1980; Dommergues *et al.* 1982; Avni *et al.* 1984; Berant and Alon 1987; Miller *et al.* 1989). The renal cystic involvement in TSC is particularly prominent in certain families, suggesting a genetic predisposition (O'Callaghan *et al.* 1975; Mitnick *et al.* 1983; Durham 1987). A recent study suggests that the majority, if not all, patients with TSC presenting with polycystic-like kidneys at an early age have a contiguous gene syndrome with deletions affecting both the TSC-2 and the PKD1 genes (Brook-Carter *et al.* 1994). This early presentation of TSC with polycystic kidneys is often associated with hyperten-sion, even at a stage when the renal function is normal (Okada *et al.* 1982). The pathogenesis of this hypertension is not known but several patients have been found to have elevated peripheral renin activities (Meyrier *et al.* 1980; Yu and Sheth 1985). These patients are likely to develop renal failure in the second or third decades of life.

Renal cell carcinoma

Whether patients with TSC are at an increased risk for renal cell carcinoma has been controver-sial. The large, hyperchromatic, pleomorphic nuclei with occasional mitotic figures of the

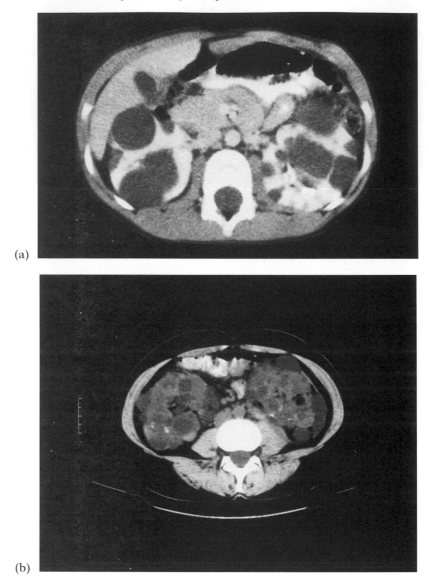

Fig. 25.6 Tuberous sclerosis complex mimicking polycystic kidney disease. (a) Multiple, bilateral renal cysts without angiomyolipomas in a seven-year-old boy with tuberous sclerosis complex; (b) multiple, bilateral renal cysts and angiomyolipomas in a 31-year-old woman with tuberous sclerosis complex.

spindle, smooth, muscle-like cells in the angiomyolipomas have been a source of confusion with malignant tumours. In the last two decades, however, an increasing number of renal cell carcinomas have been diagnosed in these patients using strict criteria (Gutierrez *et al.* 1979; Lynne *et al.* 1979; Chan *et al.* 1983; Graves and Barnes 1986; Taylor *et al.* 1989; Ohigashi *et al.* 1991; Washecka and Hanna 1991). The increased risk for renal cell carcinoma in TSC has also been supported by observations in the Eker rat. This strain of rats, which develops spontaneous renal

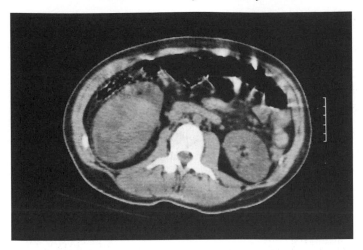

Fig. 25.7 Large mass in the lower pole of the right kidney without evidence of fat by CT in a 23-year-old man with tuberous sclerosis. At surgery this mass was later found to be a renal cell carcinoma.

cell carcinomas, has a 6.3 kb insertional mutation at the intron 30 of the TSC-2 gene (Yeung *et al.* 1994; Kobayashi *et al.* 1995). In addition to renal cell carcinomas, other tumours such as oncocytomas or leiomyosarcomas have been observed less often (Srinivas *et al.* 1985; Green 1987; Fernández de Sevilla *et al.* 1988).

The association of a renal cell carcinoma with TSC should be suspected in cases of enlarging lesions with no fatty tissue demonstrable by sonogram, CT, or MRI (Fig. 25.7) and when intratumoural calcifications which occur very rarely in uncomplicated angiomyolipomas are present (Honey and Honey 1977; Suslavich *et al.* 1979; Shapiro *et al.* 1984; Ahuja *et al.* 1986; Weinblatt *et al.* 1987).

The natural history of renal cell carcinomas associated with TSC is different from that of sporadic renal cell carcinomas. In a review of 19 patients, 81% were female, the median age at diagnosis was 28 years, and 43% were bilateral (Srinivas *et al.* 1985). The prognosis of these tumours is not as favourable as initially thought, as three of these 16 patients died of metastatic disease.

Other renal lesions

An infrequent presentation of TSC is that of a chronic tubulointerstitial disease (Mirouze *et al.* 1963; Kleinknecht *et al.* 1976; Hervé *et al.* 1982; De Paepe *et al.* 1987; Schillinger *et al.* 1988). A hyperplastic appearance of the interstitial stroma with areas of spindle cell, smooth muscle, and fibroblastic cells, as well as inflammatory cellular infiltrates and interstitial fibrosis have been reported. Renal mass reduction caused by angiomyolipomas, cysts, or interstitial fibrosis may result in glomerular hyperfiltration, moderate degrees of proteinuria, and focal segmental glomerulosclerosis (Schillinger *et al.* 1985; 1988). Intraglomerular microhamartomatous lesions of probable mesangial origin have been described (Nagashima *et al.* 1988). TSC rarely involve medium size and large vessels, including the renal arteries. Some cases of renal artery stenosis have been reported (Rolfes *et al.* 1985). Finally, the association with stenosis of the ureteropelvic junction and horseshoe kidneys have also been noted (Golji 1961; Ortiz Cabria *et al.* 1990).

Mayo clinic findings

Between 1940 and 1992, 403 patients were seen at the Mayo Clinic with the diagnosis of TSC (Torres *et al.* 1993). One hundred and sixty-four of these patients had sonographic or CT studies of the kidneys on at least one occasion. Angiomyolipomas were not observed in the first year of age but were present in 37% of the children between one and five years of age. After age five, angiomyolipomas were observed in 41% of males and 63% of females. Six patients had diffusely hyperechoic kidneys. Cysts were detected in 20% of male and 9% of female patients. Cysts were detected more often with increasing age, but one patient presented with large polycystic kidneys at seven months of age. Five additional patients had large polycystic kidneys. Four patients had a renal cell carcinoma. Hypertension was diagnosed in 1% of the patients without angiomyolipomas or cysts, 15% of the patients with angiomyolipomas without cysts, and 30% of the patients with cysts. Impairment of renal function was observed in none of the patients without angiomyolipomas or cysts, 15% of the patients with angiomyolipomas only, and 17% of the patients with cysts. Five of the six patients with polycystic kidneys had hypertension and moderate-to-severe renal insufficiency. Nine patients underwent partial or total nephrectomies for pain, life-threatening gross haematuria, or retroperitoneal haemorrhage. Two additional patients were treated by selective arterial embolization. In two patients, the retroperitoneal haemorrhage occurred during pregnancy.

Forty-nine of these 403 patients are known to have died (Shepherd *et al.* 1991; Torres *et al.* 1993). The cause of death was a brain tumour or status epilepticus in 19, renal disease in 11, and pulmonary lymphangiomyomatosis in four. Of the 11 patients with a renal cause of death, six died of renal failure, three died of retroperitoneal haemorrhage (one on dialysis and two with preserved renal function), and two died of metastatic renal cell carcinoma. One patient with a non-renal cause of death was treated by maintenance haemodialysis. Of the eight patients who had reached end-stage renal failure at the time of their deaths, three had large polycystic kidneys, two had small contracted cystic kidneys, and two had experienced progressive renal insufficiency following unilateral nephrectomies for angiomyolipomas. The details of the renal pathology in one patient are not available.

Recommendations for long-term management

For appropriate genetic counselling, first-degree relatives of a patient with TSC, if still of reproductive age, should undergo a thorough examination. This should include a meticulous examination of the skin with the Wood lamp, ophthalmologic examination with dilatation of the pupils, cranial computerized tomography with contrast, and a renal ultrasound (Cassidy *et al.* 1983). Some authors also suggest examination of the teeth for pitted enamel hypoplasia and X-rays of the skull, hands, and feet to search for bony sclerosis and bone cysts (Hauser and Anton-Lamprecht 1987; Lygidakis and Lindenbaum 1987). Others suggest that the value of an extensive radiologic investigation is doubtful with the exception of a cranial computerized tomography (Fryer *et al.* 1990). If all of these examinations are negative, non-penetrance or germ-line mosaicism cannot be ruled out, but the likelihood is low.

Prenatal diagnosis of tuberous sclerosis has been made in some cases by sonographic identification of cardiac rhabdomyomas or cerebral tumours during the late-mid and third trimester (Muller *et al.* 1986; Platt *et al.* 1987). DNA analysis can be used in the first trimester to exclude the diagnosis of tuberous sclerosis in families in which linkage to chromosomes 9q32q34 or 16p13 has been demonstrated (Connor *et al.* 1987).

Renal angiomyolipomas are benign lesions and often require no treatment. The increased frequency and size of the angiomyolipomas in women and the reports of haemorrhagic complications during pregnancy suggest that female sex hormones may contribute to the growth of these lesions. It seems, therefore, appropriate to caution patients with multiple angiomyolipomas on the potential risk of pregnancy and oestrogen administration. In pulmonary lymphangiomyomatosis, which is a more life-threatening condition than multiple renal angiomyolipomas, oophorectomy, radium ablation of the ovaries, progesterone administration, antiestrogens, and androgens have been used (Bush *et al.* 1969; Banner *et al.* 1981; Michel *et al.* 1983; El Allaf *et al.* 1984; Adamson *et al.* 1985; Clemm *et al.* 1987). Whether any of these treatment modalities have had any beneficial effect on the development and growth of the renal angiomyolipomas is not known. Because of the potential that angiomyolipomas have for growth and development of complications, annual re-evaluation with ultrasonography or CT is necessary (Oesterling *et al.* 1986; Blute *et al.* 1988). Indications for intervention include symptoms such as pain or haemorrhage, growth with compromise of functioning renal parenchyma, and an inability to exclude an associated renal cell carcinoma. When an associated malignancy can be excluded, the treatment should be to spare as much renal tissue as possible. Renal sparing surgery such as enucleation or partial nephrectomy should be used. Some lesions, because of their size or central location, may be more amenable to selective arterial embolization (Eason *et al.* 1979; Earthman *et al.* 1986; Van Baal *et al.* 1990; Jonsson *et al.* 1991). This procedure is often facilitated by the presence of one or more large hypertrophic feeding vessels. This technique has been found to be effective and safe with a low rate of complications, including haemorrhage and infection.

The mainstay of the treatment of the cystic disease associated with TSC is strict control of the hypertension. Surgical decompression of these kidneys has been considered, but the experience available in patients with autosomal dominant polycystic kidney disease does not suggest that surgical decompression has, at least in the short term, a beneficial effect (Elzinga *et al.* 1992).

Early detection of a renal cell carcinoma is essential for the successful management of this complication. The association of a renal cell carcinoma with TSC should be suspected in cases of enlarging lesions with no fatty tissue demonstrable by sonogram, CT, or MRI and when intratumoral calcifications, which occur very rarely in uncomplicated angiomyolipomas, are present. In these cases, fine needle aspiration biopsy, or, preferably in our opinion, surgical exploration should be performed. Because of the frequent bilaterality of the lesions in TSC, renal sparing surgery should be performed whenever possible (Oesterling *et al.* 1986; Blute *et al.* 1988).

Acknowledgements

The authors thank Dr. Pamela Karnes for her review of the neurofibromatosis portion of the manuscript and helpful suggestions.

References

Adamson, D., Heinrichs, W. L., Raybin, D. M., and Raffin, T. A. (1995). Successful treatment of pulmonary lymphangiomyomatosis with oophorectomy and progesterone. *American Review of Respiratory Diseases*, **132**, 916.

Ahlmen, J., Bergentz, S. E., Ohlsson, L., and Hood, B. (1972). Two causes of hypertension in a subject with generalized neurofibromatosis. *Scandinavian Journal of Urology and Nephrology*, **6**(1), 94–8.

Ahuja, S., Loffler, W., Wegener, O-H., and Ernst, H. (1986). Tuberous sclerosis with angiomy-olipoma and metastasized hypernephroma. *Urology*, **28**, 413–19.

Allan, T. N. K. and Davies, E. R. (1970). Neurofibromatosis of the renal artery. *British Journal of Radiology*, **43**, 906.

Ashinberg, L. C., Solomon, L. M., Zeiss, P. M., Justice, P., and Rosenthal, I. M. (1977). Vitamin D-resistant richets associated with epidermal nevus syndrome: demonstration of a phosphaturic substance in the dermal lesions. *Journal of Pediatrics*, **91**, 56–60.

Avni, E. F., Szliwowski, H., Spehl, M., Lelong, B., Baudain, P., and Struyven, J. (1984). L'atteinte rénale dans la sclérose tubéreuse de Bourneville. *Annales de Radiologie*, **27**, 207–14.

Banner, A. S., Carrington, C. B., Emory, W. B., Kittle, F., Leonard, G., Ringus, J., *et al.* (1981). Efficacy of oophorectomy in lymphangioleiomyomatosis and benign metastasizing leiomyoma. *New England Journal of Medicine*, **305**, 204.

Barker, D., Wright, E., Nguyen, K., Cannon, L., Fain, P., Goldgar, D., *et al.* (1987). Gene for von Recklinghausen neurofibromatosis is in the pericentromeric region of chromosome 17. *Science*, **236**(4805), 1100–2.

Baxi, R., Epstein, H. Y., and Abitbol, C. (1981). Percutaneous transluminal renal artery angioplasty in hypertension associated with neurofibromatosis. *Radiology*, **139**(3), 583–4.

Berant, K. M. and Alon, U. (1987). Polycystic kidneys as the presenting feature of tuberous sclerosis. *Helv. Paediat. Acta.*, **42**, 29–33.

Bernstein, J., Robbins, T. O., and Kissane, J. M. (1986). The renal lesions of tuberous sclerosis. *Semin. Diagn. Pathol.*, **3**, 97–105.

Bernstein, J. and Robbins, T. O. (1991). Renal involvement in tuberous sclerosis. *Ann. NY Acad. Sci.*, **615**, 36–49.

Bloom, D. A., Scardino, P. T., Ehrlich, R. M., and Waisman, J. (1982). The significance of lymph nodal involvement in renal angiomyolipoma. *Journal of Urology*, **128**, 1292–5.

Blum, M. D., Bahnson, R. R., and Carter, M. F. (1985). Urologic manifestations of von Recklinghausen neurofibromatosis. *Urology*, **26**(3), 209–17.

Blute, M. L., Malek, R. S., and Segura, J. W. (1988). Angiomyolipoma: Clinical metamorphosis and concepts for management. *Journal of Urology*, **139**, 20–4.

Bosniak, M. A., Megibow, A. J., Hulnick, D. H., Horii, S., and Raghavendra, B. N. (1988). CT diagnosis of renal angiomyolipoma: the importance of detecting small amounts of fat. *American Journal of Radiology*, **151**, 497.

Bourke, E. and Gatenby, P. B. B. (1971). Renal artery dysplasia with hypertension in neurofibromatosis. *British Medical Journal*, **3**(776), 681–2.

Bourneville, D-M. (1880). Sclérose tubéreuse des circonvolutions cérébrales: Idiotie et épilepsie hémiplégique. *Archives de Neurologie*, **1**, 81–91.

Bourneville, D-M. and Brissaud, E. (1900). Idiotie et epilepsie symptomatiques de sclérose tubéreuse ou hypertrophique. *Archives de Neurologie*, **10**, 29–39.

Brook-Carter, P. T., Peral, B., Ward, C. J., Thompson, P., *et al.* (1994). Deletion of the TSC-2 and PKD1 genes associated with severe infantile polycystic kidney disease: a contiguous gene syndrome. *Nature Genetics*, **8**, 328–32.

Bush, J. K., McLean, R. L., and Sieker, H. O. (1969). Diffuse lung disease due to lymphangiomyoma. *American Journal of Medicine*, **46**, 645.

Camúñez, F., Lafuente, J., Robledo, R., Echenagusia, A., Pérez, M., Simo, G., *et al.* (1987). Demonstration of extension of renal angiomyolipoma into the inferior vena cava in a patient with tuberous sclerosis. *Urology and Radiology*, **9**, 152–4.

Cassidy, S. B., Pagon, R. A., Pepin, M., and Blumhagen, J. D. (1983). Family studies in tuberous sclerosis; evaluation of apparently unaffected parents. *Journal of the American Medical Association*, **248**, 1302–4.

Cawthon, R., Weiss, R., Wu, G., *et al.* (1990). A major segment of the neurofibromatosis type 1 gene: cDNA sequence, genomic structure, and point mutations. *Cell*, **62**, 193–201.

Chan, H. S. L., Daneman, A., Gribbin, M., and Martin, D. J. (1983). Renal cell carcinoma in the first two decades of life. *Pediatric Radiology*, **13**, 324–8.

Cheong, L. L., Khan, A. N., and Bisset, R. A. L. (1990). Sonographic features of a renal pelvic neurofibroma. *Journal of Clinical Ultrasound*, **18**(2), 129–31.

Chu, J., O'Connor, D. M., and Danis, R. K. (1981). Neurofibrosarcoma at irradiation site in a patient with neurofibromatosis and Wilms' tumor. *Cancer Journal for Clinicians*, **31**(6), 333–5.

Clark, S. S., Marlett, M. M., Prudencio, R. F., and Dasgupta, T. K. (1977). Neurofibromatosis of the bladder in children: case report and literature review. *Journal of Urology*, **118**, 654–6.

Clemm, C., Jehn, U., Wolf-Hornung, B., Siemon, G., and Walter, G. (1987). Lymphangioleiomyomatosis: a report of three cases treated with tamoxifen. *Klin. Worchenschr.*, **65**, 391.

Connor, J. M., Lughlin, S. A. R., and Whittle, M. J. (1987). Frist trimester prenatal exclusion of tuberous sclerosis. *Lancet*, **i**, 1269.

Connor, J. M. and Sampson, J. (1991). Recent linkage studies in tuberous sclerosis Chromosome 9 markers. *Ann. NY Acad. Sci.*, **615**, 265–73.

Daniels, S. R., Loggie, J. M. H., McEnery, P. T., and Towbin, R. B. (1987). Clinical spectrum of intrinsic renovascular hypertension in children. *Pediatrics*, **80**(5), 698–704.

Deal, J. E., Snell, M. F., Barratt, T. M., and Dillon, M. J. (1992). Renovascular disease in childhood. *Journal of Pediatrics*, **121**(3), 378–84.

De Paepe, J. P., Michel, L., Pirson, Y., Squifflet, J. P., and Alexandre, G. (1987). Transplantation rénale et sclérose tubéreuse de Bourneville. *Acta. Chir. Beig.*, **87**, 376–81.

DiPrete, D., Abuelo, J. G., Abuelo, D. N., and Cronan, J. J. (1990). Acute renal insufficiency due to renal infarctions in a patient with neurofibromatosis. *American Journal of Kidney Disease*, **15**(4), 357–60.

Dommergues, J. P., Pollet, F., Valayer, J., Roset, F., and Aicardi, J. (1982). Maladie polykstique rénale àrévélation précoce Première manifestation d'une sclérose tubéreuse de Bourneville. *Arch. Fr. Pediatr.*, **39**, 31–2.

Durham, D. S. (1987). Tuberous sclerosis mimicking adult polycystic kidney disease. *Australian and New Zealand Journal of Medicine*, **17**, 71–3.

Earthman, W. J., Mazer, M. J., and Winfield, A. C. (1986). Angiomyolipomas in tuberous sclerosis: subselective embolotherapy with alcohol, with long-term follow-up study. *Radiology*, **160**, 437–41.

Eason, A. A., Cattolica, E. V., and McGrath, T. W. (1979). Massive renal angiomyolipoma: preoperative infarction by balloon catheter. *Journal of Urology*, **121**, 360–1.

El Allaf, D., Borlee, G., Hadjoudj, H., Henrard, L., Marcelle, R., and Van Cauwenberge, H. (1984). Pulmonary lymphangioleiomyomatosis. *European Journal of Respiratory Diseases*, **65**, 147.

Elias, D. L., Ricketts, R. R., and Smith, R. B. (1985). Renovascular hypertension complicating neurofibromatosis. *American Surgeon*, **51**(2), 97–106.

Elzinga, L. W., Barry, J. M., Torres, V. F., Zincke, H., Wahner, H. W., Swan, S., *et al.* (1992). Cyst decompression surgery for autosomal dominant polycystic kidney disease. *Journal of the American Society of Nephrology*, **2**, 1219–26.

Farrow, G. M., Harrison, E. G. Jr., Utz, D. C., and Jones, D. R. (1968). Renal angiomyolipoma: a clinic opathologic study of 32 cases. *Cancer*, **22**, 564.

Fernández de Sevilla, T., Muñiz, R., Palou, J., Banús, J. M., Alegre, J., Garcia, A., *et al.* Renal leiomyosarcoma in a patient with tuberous sclerosis. *Urologic Internationalis*, **43**, 62–4.

Feytrer, F. (1949). Uber die vasculare neurofibromatose. *Virchows Archiv A Pathological Anatomy and Histopathology*, **317**, 221.

Finley, J. L. and Dabbs, D. J. (1988). Renal vascular smooth muscle proliferation in neurofibromatosis. *Human Pathology*, **19**(1), 107–10.

Fitzpatrick, T. B. (1991). History and significance of white macules, earliest visible sign of tuberous sclerosis. *Ann. NY Acad. Sci.*, **615**, 26–35.

Flynn, M. P. and Buchanan, J. B. (1979). Neurofibromatosis, hypertension, and renal artery aneurysms. *Southern Medical Journal*, **73**(5), 618–20.

Fryer, A. E., Connor, J. M., Povey, S., *et al.* (1987). Evidence that the gene for tuberous sclerosis is on chromosome 9. *Lancet*, **i**, 659–61.

Fryer, A. E., Chalmers, A. H., and Osborne, J. P. (1990). The value of investigation for genetic counselling in tuberous sclerosis. *Journal of Medical Genetics*, **27**, 217–23.

Futter, N. G. and Collins, W. E. (1974). Renal angiomyolipoma causing hypertension: A case report. *British Journal of Urology*, **46**, 485–7.

Fye, K. H., Jacobs, R. P., and Roe, R. L. (1975). Vascular manifestations of von Recklinghausen's disease. *Western Journal of Medicine*, **122**(2), 110–15.

Gardiner, G. A., Freedman, A. M., and Shlansky-Goldberg, R. (1988). Percutaneous transluminal angioplasty: delayed response in neurofibromatosis. *Radiology*, **169**(1), 79–80.

Gill, P. G., Marshall, V. R., and Ludbrook. (1976). Autotransplantation of the kidneys: A case study with special reference to vascular neurofibromatosis. *Vasa*, **5**(3), 245–8.

Golji, H. (1961). Tuberous sclerosis and renal neoplasms. *Journal of Urology*, **85**, 919–23.

Gomez, M. R. (1988). Criteria for diagnosis. In: *Tuberous sclerosis* (2nd edn) (ed. M. R. Gomez), pp. 9–19. Raven Press, New York.

Gomez, M. R. (1991). Phenotypes of the tuberous sclerosis complex with a revision of diagnostic criteria. *Ann. NY Acad. Sci.*, **615**, 1–7.

Graves, N. and Barnes, W. F. Renal cell carcinoma and angiomyolipoma in tuberous sclerosis: Case report. *Journal of Urology*, **135**, 122–3.

Green, J. A. S. (1987). Renal oncocytoma and tuberous sclerosis. *South African Medical Journal*, **71**, 47–8.

Green, J. E., Adams, G. W., Shawker, T. H., Sax, F. L., Koeller, D. M., and Zasloff, M. A. (1990). Hypertension and renal failure in a patient with tuberous sclerosis *Scuthen Medical Journal*, **83**, 451–4.

Greene, J. F., Fitzwater, J. E., and Burgess, J. (1974). Arterial lesions associated with neurofibromatosis. *American Journal of Clinical Pathology*, **62**(4), 481–7.

Guthrie, G. P., Tibbs, P. A., McAllister, R. G., Stevens, R. K., and Clark, D. B. (1982). Hypertension and neurofibromatosis case report. *Hypertension*, **4**(6), 894–7.

Gutierrez, O. H., Burgener, F. A., and Schwart, S. (1979). Coincident renal cell carcinoma and renal angiomyolipoma in tuberous sclerosis. *American Journal of Radiology*, **132**, 848–50.

Habib, R. and Habib, E. C. (1962). Les lesion vasculaires de laboratory neurofibromatose de von Recklinghausen. *Societe Anatomique De Paris*, **10**(1), 47–53.

Haines, J. L., Amos, J., Attwood, J., Bech-Hansen, N. T., Burley, M., Conneally, P. M., *et al.* (1991). Genetic heterogeneity in tuberous sclerosis Study of a large collaborative dataset. *Ann. NY Acad. Sci.*, **615**, 256–64.

Hajdu, S. I. and Foote, F. W. (1969). Angiomyolipoma of the kidney: report of 27 cases and review of the literature. *Journal of Urology* **102**, 396–401.

Harrison, E. G. Jr., Hant, J. C., and Bernatz, P. E. (1967). Morphology of fibromuscular dysplasia of the renal artery in renovascular hypertension. *American Journal of Medicine*, **43**, 97.

Hauser, I. and Anton-Lamprecht, I. (1987). Electronmicrosurgery as a means for carrier detection and genetic counseling in families at risk of tuberous sclerosis. *Human Genetics*, **76**, 73–80.

Heckl, W., Osterhage, H. R., and Frohmüller, H. G. W. (1987). Diagnosis and treatment of renal angiomyolipoma. *Urologia Internationalis*, **42**, 201–6.

Hervé, J. P., Chevet, D., Cledes, J., Lepogamp, P., Leroy, J. P., and Meyrier, A. (1982). L'insuffisance rénale chronique de la sclérose tubéreuse de Bourneville. *Journal of Nephrology*, **3**, 49–50.

Hogan, D. B., Anderson, C., Mackenzie, R. A., and Crilly, R. G. (1986). Case report: hypophosphatemic osteomalacia complicating von Recklinghausen's neurofibromatosis: increase in spinal density on treatment, *Bone* **7**(1), 9–12.

Holt, J. F. (1978). Neurofibromatosis in children. *American Journal of Roentgenology*, **130**, 615–39.

Honey, R. J. and Honey, R. M. (1977). Tuberose sclerosis and bilateral renal carcinoma. *British Journal of Urology*, **49**, 441–6.

Hope, D. G. and Mulvihill, J. J. (1981). Malignancy in neurofibromatosis. *Advances in Neurology*, **29**, 33–56.

Hulbert, J. C. and Graf, R. (1983). Involvement of the spleen by renal angiomyolipoma: metastasis or multicentricity? *Journal of Urology*, **130**, 328.

Hunt, A. and Lindenbaum, R. H. (1984). Tuberous sclerosis: a new estimate of prevalence within the Oxford region. *Journal of Medical Genetics*, **21**, 272–7.

Huson, S. M., Harper, P. S., and Compston, D. A. S. (1988). von Recklinghausen neurofibromatosis: A clinical and population study in south-east Wales. *Brain*, **6**, 1355–81.

Itzchak, Y., Katznelson, D., Boichis, H., Jonas, A., and Deutsch, V. (1974). Angiographic features of arterial lesions in neurofibromatosis. *American Journal of Roentgenology*, **122**(3), 643–7.

Janssen, L. A. J., Povey, S., Attwood, J., Sandkuyl, L. A., Lindhout, D., Flodman, P., *et al.* (1991). A comparative study on genetic heterogeneity in tuberous sclerosis: Evidence for one gene on 9q34 and a second gene on 11q22–23. *Ann. NY Acad. Sci.*, **615**, 306–15.

Johnson, W. G., Yoshidome, H., Stenroos, E. S., and Davidson, M. M. (1991). Origin of the neuron-like cells in tuberous sclerosis tissues. *Ann. NY Acad. Sci.*, **615**, 211–19.

Jonsson, E., Sueoka, B. L., Spiegel, P. K., Richardson, J. R. Jr., and Heaney, J. A. (1991). Angiographic management of retroperitoneal hemorrhage from renal angiomyolipoma in polycystic kidney disease. *Journal of Urology*, **145**, 1248–50.

Kandt, R. S., Haines, J. L., Smith, M., Northrup, H., Gardner, R. J. M., Short, M. P., *et al.* (1992). Linkage of an important gene locus for tuberous sclerosis to a chromosome 16 marker for polycystic kidney disease. *Nature Genetics*, **2**, 37–41.

Kaufman, J. J. (1993). Pheochromocytoma and stenosis of the renal artery. *Surgery, Gynecology and Obstetrics*, **156**(1), 11–15.

Kleinknecht, D., Haiat, R., Frija, J., and Mignon, F. (1976). Sclérose tubéreuse de Bourneville avec bicuspidie aortique et insuffisance rénale. *La Nouvelle Presse Médicale*, **5**, 1196–8.

Kley, N., Whaley, J., and Seizinger, B. R. (1995). Neurofibromatosis type 2 and von Hippel–Lindau disease: from gene cloning to function. *Glia*, **15**, 297–307.

Kobayashi, T., Hirayama, Y., Kobayashi, E., *et al.* (1995). A germline insertion in the tuberous sclerosis (TSC2) gene gives rise to the Eker rat model of dominantly inherited cancer. *Nature Genetics*, **9**, 70–4.

Konishi, K., Yamakawa, H., Hanaoka, H., Nakamura, M., Suzuki, H., Davatchi, F., *et al.* (1991). Case report: hypophosphatemic osteomalacia in von Recklinghausen neurofibromatosis. *American Journal of the Medical Sciences*, **301**(5), 322–8.

Kremen, A. F., Hill, E., and Kremen, A. J. (1985). Pheochromocytoma, renal artery stenosis, and lymphocytic lymphoma associated with von Recklinghausen's neurofibromatosis: A case report and literature review. *Minnesota Medicine*, **68**(2), 99–101.

Kuo, J. Y., Okada, Y., Takeuchi, H., Yoshida, O., Suzuki, H., and Kim, Y. C., (1989). Neurofibromatosis associated with renovascular hypertension due to stenosis and aneurysm of the left renal segmental artery: report of a case. *Urologia Internationalis*, **44**(3), 177–80.

Kutcher, R., Rosenblatt, R., Mitsudo, S. M., Goldman, M., *et al.* (1982). Renal angiomyolipoma with sonographic demonstrations of extension into the inferior vena cava. *Radiology*, **14**, 755–6.

Lallier, T. E. (1991). Cell lineage and cell migration in the neural crest. *Ann. NY Acad. Sci.*, **615**, 158–71.

Lewis, E. L. and Palmer, J. M. (1985). Renal angiomyolipoma and massive retroperitoneal hemorrhage during pregnancy. *West Journal of Medicine*, **143**, 675–6.

Lie, J. T. (1991). Cardiac, pulmonary, and vascular involvements in tuberous sclerosis. *Ann. NY Acad. Sci.*, **615**, 58–70.

Littler, M. and Morton, N. E. (1990). Segregation analysis of peripheral neurofibromatosis (NF1). *Journal of Medical Genetics*, **27**, 307–10.

Lonstein, J. E. and McKinley, C. R. (1979). Neurofibromatosis and hypertension: A case report. *Spine*, **4**(3), 220–7.

Lygidakis, N. A. and Lindenbaum, R. H. (1987). Pitted enamel hypoplasia in tuberous sclerosis patients and first-degree relatives. *Clinical Genetics*, **32**, 216–22.

Lynch, J. D., Sheps, S. G., Bernatz, P. E., Remine, W. H., and Harrison, E. G. (1972). Neurofibromatosis and hypertension due to pheochromocytoma or renal artery stenosis. *Minnesota Medicine*, **55**(1), 25–31.

Lynne, C. M., Nadji, M., Carrion, H. M., Russel, E., Bakshandeh, K., and Politano, V. A. (1979). Renal angiomyolipoma, polycystic kidney, and renal cell carcinoma in patient with tuberous sclerosis. *Urology*, **14**, 174–6.

McKusick, V. A., Francomano, C. A., and Antonarakis, S. E. (1992). Neurofibromatosis (von Recklinghausen's disease; neurofibromatosis, type I; NF1). In: *Mendelian inheritance in man. Catalogs of autosomal dominant, autosomal recessive, and X-linked phenotypes* (10ty edn), vol. 1, pp. 759–67. John Hopkins University Press, Baltimore.

Mallmann, R. and Roth, F. J. (1986). Treatment of neurofibromatosis associated renal artery stenosis with hypertension by percutaneous transluminal angioplasty. *Clinical and Experimental Hypertension*, **8**(4–5), 893–9.

Mandybur, T. I. and Weiss, M. A. (1981). Sclerosing peritubular nodules: A hereditary renal abnormality in von Recklinghausen's disease. *Human Pathology*, **12**(8), 704–12.

Martuza, R. L. and Eldridge, R. (1988). Neurofibromatosis 2. *New England Journal of Medicine*, **318**, 684–8.

Melick, R. A., Larkins, R. G., Greenberg, P. B., and Wark, J. D. (1979). Osteomalacia due to unusual causes presenting in adults. *Australian and New Zealand Journal of Medicine*, **9**(3), 253–7.

Mena, E., Bookstein, J. J., Holt, J. F., and Fry, W. J. (1973). Neurofibromatosis and renovascular hypertension in children. *American Journal of Roentgenology*, **118**(1), 39–45.

Meyrier, A., Rainfray, M., Roland, J., and Merlier, J. (1980). Sclérose tubéreuse de Bourneville avec insuffisance rénale chronique traitée par hémodialyse et transplantation. *Néphrologie*, **1**, 85–8.

Michel, J. M., Diggle, J. H., Brice, J., Mellor, D. H., and Small, P. (1983). Two half-siblings with tuberous sclerosis, polycystic kidneys and hypertension. *Dev. Med. Child Neurol.*, **25**, 239–44.

Miller, I. D., Gray, E. S., and Lloyd, D. L. (1989). Unilateral cystic disease of the neonatal kidney: a rare presentation of tuberous sclerosis. *Histopathology*, **14**, 529–32.

Mirouze, J., Barjon, P., Jaffiol, C., Baumelou, H., and Marty, M. (1963). L'urémie de la maladie de Bourneville (A propos de deux observations). *Journal D'Urologie et de Néphrologie*, **69**, 639–47.

Mitnick, J. S., Bosniak, M. A., Hilton, S., Raghavendra, B. N., Subramanyam, B. R., and Genieser, N. B. (1983). Cystic renal disease in tuberous sclerosis. *Radiology*, **147**, 85–7.

Mukai, M., Torikata, C., Iri, H., Tamai, S., Sugiura, H., Tanaka, Y., *et al.* (1992). Crystalloids in angiomyolipoma 1. A previously unnoticed phenomenon of renal angiomyolipoma occurring at a high frequency. *American Journal of Surgical Pathology*, **16**, 1–10.

Muller, L., DeJong, G., Falck, V., Hewlett, R., Huner, J., and Shires, J. (1986). Antenatal ultrasonographic findings in tuberous sclerosis. *South African Medical Journal*, **69**, 633–8.

Nagashima, Y., Ohaki, Y., Tanaka, Y., Misugi, K., and Horiuchi, M. (1988). A case of renal angiomyolipomas associated with multiple and various hamartomatous microlesions. *Virchows Archiv A Pathological Anatomy and Histopathology*, **413**, 177–82.

National Institutes of Health Consensus Development Conference Statement (1987). Neurofibromatosis, meeting report, Bethesda, MD, July 13–15, 1987. *Neurofibromatosis*, **1**, 172–8.

O'Callaghan, T. J., Edwards, J. A., Tobin, M., and Mookerjee, B. K. (1975). Tuberous sclerosis with striking renal involvement in a family. *Archives of Internal Medicine*, **135**, 1082–7.

Oesterling, J. E., Fishman, E. K., Goldman, S. M., and Marshall, F. F. (1986). The management of renal angiomyolipoma. *Journal of Urology*, **135**, 1121–4.

Ohigashi, T., Iigaya, T., and Hata, M. (1991). Coincidental renal cell carcinoma and renal angiomyolipomas in tuberous sclerosis. *Urologia Internationalis*, **47**, 160–3.

Okada, R. D., Platt, M. A., and Fleishman, J. (1982). Chronic renal failure in patients with tuberous sclerosis association with renal cysts. *Nephron*, **30**, 85–8.

Okada, E. and Shozawa, T. (1984). von Recklinghausen's disease (neurofibromatosis) associated with malignant pheochromocytoma. *ACTA Pathologica Japonica*, **34**(2), 425–34.

O'Regan, S. and Mongeau, J. G. (1983). Renovascular hypertension in pediatric patients with neurofibromatosis. *International Journal of Pediatric Nephrology*, **4**(2), 109–12.

Ortiz Cabria, R., Blanco Parra, M., and Rodriguez de la Rua Roman, J. (1990). Esclerosis tuberosa patologia renal multiple presentacion de un caso. *Actas Urologicas Espanolas*, **14**, 310–13.

Osborne, J. P., Fryer, A., and Webb, D. (1991). Epidemiology of tuberous sclerosis. *Ann. NY Acad. Sci.*, **615**, 125–7.

Petrikovsky, B. M., Vintzileos, A. M., Cassidy, S. B., and Egan, J. F. X. (1990). Tuberous sclerosis in pregnancy. *American Journal of Perinatology*, **7**, 133–5.

Pfau, A., Luttwak, E., Rosenmann, E., and Schwartz, A. (1976). Neurofibromatosis and hypertension. *Urology*, **8**(6), 586–9.

Platt, L. D., Devore, G. R., Horenstein, J., Pavlova, Z., Kovacs, B., and Falk, R. E. (1987). Prenatal diagnosis of tuberous sclerosis: the use of fetal echocardiography. *Prenatal Diagnosis*, **7**, 407–11.

Pollard, S. G., Hornick, P., Macfarlane, R., and Caine, R. Y. (1989). Renovascular hypertension in neurofibromatosis. *Postgraduate Medical Journal*, **65**, 31–3.

Reese, A. J. M. and Winstanley, D. P. (1958). The small tumour-like lesions of the kidney. *British Journal of Cancer*, **12**, 507–16.

Reubi, F. (1945). Neurofibromatosis et lesions vasculares. *Schweizerische Medizinische Wochenschrift*, **75** (Suppl.), 463.

Riccardi, V. M. and Eichner, J. E. (1986). *Neurofibromatosis: phenotype, natural history, and pathogenesis*. Johns Hopkins University Press Baltimore.

Riccardi, V. M. (1987). Neurofibromatosis. Diseases with autosomal dominant inheritance. In: *Neurocutaneous diseases: A practical approach* (ed. M. R. Gomez), pp. 11–29. Butterworth, Massachusetts.

Rink, R. C. and Mitchell, M. E. (1983). Genitourinary neurofibromatosis in childhood. *Journal of Urology*, **130**, 1176–9.

Ritter, J. L. and Riccardi, V. M. (1985). von Recklinghausen neurofibromatosis (NF1): An argument for very high penetrance and a comparison of sporadic and inherited cases. *American Journal of Human Genetics*, **37**, A135.

Robbins, T. O. and Bernstein, J. (1988). Renal involvement. In: *Tuberous sclerosis* (2nd edn) Raven Press, New York. (ed. M. R. Gomez), pp. 133–46.

Robinson, L., Gedroyc, W., Reigy, J., and Saxton, H. M. (1991). Renal artery stenosis in children. *Clinical Radiology*, **44**(6), 376–82.

Rolfes, D. B., Towbin, R., and Bove, K. E. (1985). Vascular dysplasia in a child with tuberous sclerosis. *Pediabic Pathology*, **3**, 359–73.

Rothenberg, D. M., Brandt, T. D., and D'Cruz, I. (1986). Computed tomography of renal angiomyolipoma presenting as right atrial mass. *Journal of Computenzed Assisted Tomography*, **10**, 1054–6.

Rowen, M., Dorsey, T. J., Kegel, S. M., and Ostermiller, W. E. (1975). Thoracic coarctation associated with neurofibromatosis. *American Journal of Diseases of Children*, **129**(1), 113–15.

Rubenstein, A. E., Mytilin E.O.U.C., Yahr, M. D., *et al.* (1981). Neurotransmitter analysis of dermal neurofibromas: Implications for the pathogenesis on treatment of neurofibromatosis. *Neurology*, **31**, 1184–8.

Salyer, W. R. and Salyer, D. C. (1974). The vascular lesions of neurofibromatosis. *Angiology*, **25**(8), 510–19.

Sampson, J. R., Scahill, S. J., Stephenson, J. B. P., Mann, L., and Connor, J. M. (1989). Genetic aspects of tuberous sclerosis in the west of Scotland. *Journal of Medical Genetics*, **26**, 28–31.

Samuelsson, B. and Axelsson, R. (1981). Neurofibromatosis: A clinical and genetic study of 96 cases in Bottenberg, Sweden. *Acta Dermato-Venereologica*, **95**, 67.

Sant, G. R., Ayers, D. K., Bankoff, M. S., Mitcheson, H. D., and Ucci, A. A. Jr. (1990). Fine-needle aspiration biopsy in the diagnosis of renal angiomyolipoma. *Journal of Urology*, **143**, 999–1001.

Schillinger, F., Montagnac, R., Grapin, JL., Birembaut, P., and Hopfner, C. (1985). L'insuffisance rénale de al sclérose tubéreuse de Bourneville: une nouvelle forme d'atteinte glomérulaire par hyperfiltration? *Journal of Nephrology*, 6, 219–23.

Schillinger, F., Montagnac, R., Grapin, J. L., Schillinger, D., and Bressieux, J. M. (1988). Le rein au cours de la sclérose tubéreuse de Bourneville. *Rev. Méd. Interne.*, 9, 61–6.

Schurch, W., Messerli, F. H., Genest, J., Lefebvre, R., Roy, P., Cartier, P., *et al.* (1975). Arterial hypertension and neurofibromatosis: renal artery stenosis and coarctation of abdominal aorta. *Canadian Medical Association Journal*, 113(9), 879–85.

Shapiro, R. A., Skinner, D. G., Stanley, P., and Edelbrock, H. H. (1984). Renal tumors associated with tuberous sclerosis: The case for aggressive surgical management. *Journal of Urology*, 132, 1170–4.

Shepherd, C. W., Beard, C. M., Gomez, M. R., Kurland, L. T., and Whisnant, J. P. (1991). Tuberous sclerosis complex in Olmsted County, Minnesota, 1950–1989. *Archives of Neurology*, 48, 400–1.

Siegelman, S. S., Zavod, R., and Hecht, H. (1971). Neurofibromatosis, polycystic kidneys, and hypernephroma. *New York State Journal of Medicine*, 71(2), 2431–3.

Shepherd, C. W., Gomez, M. R., Lie, J. T., and Crowson, C. S. (1991). Causes of death in patients with tuberous sclerosis. *Mayo Clinic Proceedings*, 66, 792–6.

Shukri, A. M. (1968). Reno-alimentary fistulae. *British Journal of Surgery*, 55(7), 551–4.

Smith, C. J., Hatch, F. E., Johnson, J. G., and Kelly, B. J. (1970). Renal artery dysplasia as a cause of hypertension in neurofibromatosis. *Archives of Internal Medicine*, 125, 1022–6.

Sorensen, S. A., Mulvihill, J. J., and Nielsen, A. (1986). Long-term follow-up of von Recklinghausen neurofibromatosis: survival and malignant neoplasms. *New England Journal of Medicine*, 314(16), 1010–15.

Srinivas, V., Herr, H. W., and Hajdu, E. O. (1985). Partial nephrectomy for a renal oncocytoma associated with tuberous sclerosis. *Journal of Urology*, 133, 263–5.

Stapleton, F. B., Johnson, D., Kaplan, G. W., and Griswold, W. (1980). The cystic renal lesion in tuberous sclerosis. *Journal of Pediatrics*, 97, 574–9.

Stay, E. J. and Vawter, G. (1977). The relationship between nephroblastoma and neurofibromatosis. *Cancer*, 39, 2550–5.

Stillwell, T. J., Gomez, M. R., and Kelalis, P. P. (1987). Renal lesions in tuberous sclerosis. *Journal of Urology*, 138, 477–81.

Suslavich, F., Older, R. A., and Hinman, C. G. (1979). Calcified renal carcinoma in a patient with tuberous sclerosis. *American Journal of Radiology*, 133, 524–6.

Syme, J. (1980). Neurofibromatosis as a cause of renovascular hypertension. *Australasian Radiology*, 24(1), 62–6.

Taavitsainen, M., Krogerus, L., and Rannikko, S. (1989). Aspiration biopsy in renal angiomyolipoma. *Acta Radiol.*, 30, 381–2.

Tapp, E. and Hickling, R. S. (1969). Renal artery rupture in a pregnant woman with neurofibromatosis. *Journal of Pathology*, 97(2), 398–402.

Taylor, R. S., Joseph, D. B., Kohaut, E. C., Wilson, E. R., and Bueschen, A. J. (1989). Renal angiomyolipoma associated with lymph-node involvement and renal cell carcinoma in patients with tuberous sclerosis. *Journal of Urology*, 141, 930–2.

Tenschert, W., Holdener, E. E., Haerter, M. M., Senn, H., and Vetter, W. (1995). Secondary hypertension and neurofibromatosis: bilateral renal artery stenosis and coarctation of the abdominal aorta. *Klinische Wochen-Schrift*, 63(13), 593–6.

Tilford, D. L. and Kelsch, R. C. (1973). Renal artery stenosis in childhood neurofibromatosis. *American Journal of Diseases of Children*, 126(5), 665–8.

Torres, V. E., King, B. F., Holley, K. E., Blute, M. L., and Gomez, M. R. (1994). The kidney in the tuberous sclerosis complex. In: *Advances in Nephrology*, pp. 43–90. Mosby-YearBook, St. Louis.

Totty, W. G., McClennan, B. L., Melson, G. L., and Patel, R. (1981). Relative value of computed – tomography and ultrasonography in the assessment of renal angiomyolipoma. *Journal of Computerized Assistal Tomography*, 5, 173–8.

Tsuchiya, H., Orimoto, K., Kobayashi, T., and Hino, O. (1996). Presence of potent transcriptional activation domains in the predisposing tuberous sclerosis (Tsc2) gene product of the Eker rat model. *Cancer Research*, 56, 429–33.

Uhlenbrock, D., Fischer, C., and Beyer, H. K. (1988). Angiomyolipoma of the kidney Comparison between magnetic resonance imaging, computed tomography, and ultrasonography for diagnosis. *Acta Radiol.*, 29, 523–6.

Upadhyaya, M., Shaw, D. J., and Harper, P. S. (1994). Molecular basis of neurofibromatosis type 1 (NF1): mutation analysis and polymorphisms in the NF1 gene. *Human Mutations*, 4, 83–101.

Upadhyaya, M., Maynard, J., Osborn, M., *et al.* (1995). Characterisation of germline mutations in the neurofibromatosis type 1 (NF1) gene. *Journal of Medical Genetics*, 32, 706–10.

Van Baal, J. G., Lips, P., Luth, W., Bakker, P., Davis, G., Karthaus, P., *et al.* (1990). Percutaneous transcatheter embolization of symptomatic renal angiomyolipomas: a report of four cases. *Netherlands Journal of Surgery*, 42, 72–7.

van Slegtenhorst, M., de Hoogt, R., Hermans, C., Nellist, M., Janssen, B., Verhoef, S., *et al.* (1997). Identification of the tuberous sclerosis gene TSC1 on chromosome 9q34. *Science*, 277, 805–8.

Varma, S. C., Talwar, K. K., Kaushik, S. P., and Sharma, B. K. (1982). Association of von Recklinghausen's neurofibromatosis with adult polycystic disease of kidneys and liver. *Postgraduate Medical Journal*, 58(676), 117–18.

Vekemans, K., Van Oyen, P., and Denys, H. (1987). Renal angiomyolipoma as a cause of fever of unknown origin. *British Journal f Urology*, 60, 271–8.

Viskochil, D., Buchberg, A. M., Xu, F., *et al.* (1990). Deletions and a translocation interrupt a cloned gene at the neurofibromatosis type 1 locus. *Cell*, 62, 187–92.

Vogt, H. (1908). Zur diagnostik der tuberösen sklerose. *Z Erforsch Behandl Jugendl Schwachsinns*, 2, 1–12.

Voutsinas, S. and Wynne-Davies, R. (1983). The infrequency of malignant disease diaphyseal aclasis and neurofibromatosis. *Journal of Medical Genetics*, 20, 345–9.

Walden, P. A. M., Johnson, A. G., and Bagshawe, K. D. (1977). Wilms' tumour and neurofibromatosis. *British Medical Journal*, 1, 813.

Washecka, R. and Hanna, M. (1991). Malignant renal tumors in tuberous sclerosis. *Urology*, 37, 340–3.

Watson, D. J. and Osofsky, S. G. (1981). Renovascular hypertension with a neural band across the renal artery in neurofibromatosis. *Southern Medical Journal*, 74(9), 1145–6.

Webb, D. W., Fryer, A. E., and Osborne, J. P. (1991). On the incidence of fits and mental retardation in tuberous sclerosis. *Journal of Medical Genetics*, 28, 395–7.

Webb, D. W. and Osborne, J. P. (1991). Non-penetrance in tuberous sclerosis. *Journal of Medical Genetics*, 28, 417–19.

Weinblatt, M. E., Kahn, E., and Kochen, J. (1987). Renal cell carcinoma in patients with tuberous sclerosis. *Pediatrics*, 80, 898–903.

Weinstein, R. S. and Harris, R. L. (1990). Hypercalcemic hyperparathyroidism and hypophosphatemic osteomalacia complicating neurofibromatosis. *Calcified Tissue International*, 46(6), 361–6.

Wenzl, J. E., Lagos, J. C., and Albers, D. D. (1970). Tuberous sclerosis presenting as polycystic kidneys and seizures in an infant. *Journal of Pediatrics*, 77, 673–6.

Weiderholt, W. C., Gomez, M. R., and Kurland, L. T. (1982). Incidence and prevalence of tuberous sclerosis in Rochester, Minnesota, 1950 through 1982. *Neurology*, 35, 600–3.

Wienecke, R., König, A., and DeClue, J. E. (1995). Identification of tuberin, the tuberous sclerosis-2 product: tuberin possesses specific RaplGAP activity. *Journal of Biological Chemistry*, 270, 16409–14.

Yeung, R. S., Xiao, G-H., Jin, F., *et al.* (1994). Predisposition to renal carcinoma in the Eker rat is determined by germ-line mutation of the tuberous sclerosis 2 (TSC2) gene. *Proceedings of the National Academy of Science USA*, **91**, 11413–16.

Yu, D. T. and Sheth, K. J. Cystic renal involvement in tuberous sclerosis. *Clinical Pediatrics*, **24**, 36–9.

26

von Hippel–Lindau syndrome

Hartmut P.H. Neumann, Jörg Laubenberger,
Ulrich Wetterauer, and Berton Zbar

This chapter is dedicated to the memory of Michele Filling-Katz, M.D., National Institute of Health, Bethesda, Maryland, USA, who performed modern radiological studies in VHL with outstanding accuracy and lost her young life in a private tragedy.

Introduction

von Hippel–Lindau syndrome (VHL) is a cancer-prone inherited disorder of adulthood involving many organs and organ systems (Figs 26.1 and 26.2, Table 26.1). The reported prevalence in different populations was 1 : 38 000–1 : 53 000 (Maher *et al.* 1991; Neumann and Wiestler 1991). The disease predominantly affects the eyes (retinal angiomatosis), central nervous system (haemangioblastoma of the cerebellum, brainstem, and spinal cord), adrenal glands and paraganglia (phaeochromocytoma), kidneys (renal cysts, renal cell carcinoma), and pancreas (pancreatic cysts). Rare manifestations involve among other organs the epididymis (epidydimal cystadenoma) and inner ear (endolymphatic sac tumour). Renal involvement by von Hippel–Lindau sysdrome is not well-known and the disease is often simply regarded as involving tumours only of the eye and the cerebellum within the same patient. However, von Hippel–Lindau syndrome has a wide spectrum of morbidity, and the renal manifestations remain a central problem with regard to treatment. Nephrology textbooks often do not discuss von Hippel–Lindau syndrome. Here we intend to fill this gap, but also draw attention to an important gene which has been identified and characterized in 1993 and is important for oncogenesis of renal cell carcinomas (Latif *et al.* 1993).

Historical remarks

Eugen von Hippel (1867–1938) (Fig. 26.3) was a German ophthalmologist who became director of the University Eye Clinic in Göttingen. In Heidelberg, he studied and published the clinical findings of *A very uncommon disease of the retina* in two patients in 1904 (von Hippel 1904) and added, after enucleation of one affected eye, *The anatomical basis of the very uncommon disease of the retina described by me* in 1911 (von Hippel 1911). He interpreted the lesion as of vascular origin and created the term 'angiomatosis retinae', often also called von Hippel's disease. The clinical description, however, was first given by Deval (1862), and the histology presented by Collins (1894), who called it 'capillary naevus'.

Arvid Lindau (1892–1952) (Fig. 26.4) was a Swedish pathologist, director of the Institute of Pathology and Bacteriology at the University of Lund. His outstanding pioneering work, comprising his thesis *Studies of cerebellar cysts—pathogenesis and relations to angiomatosis retinae*, was

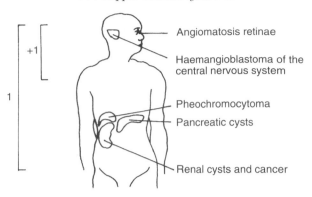

Fig. 26.1 Principal lesions and minimal criteria of VHL. The clinical diagnosis for VHL requires either in one individual two lesions, one in the eyes or CNS and one of any principal lesion, *or* eye or CNS lesions in one individual and one of the principal lesions in a relative.

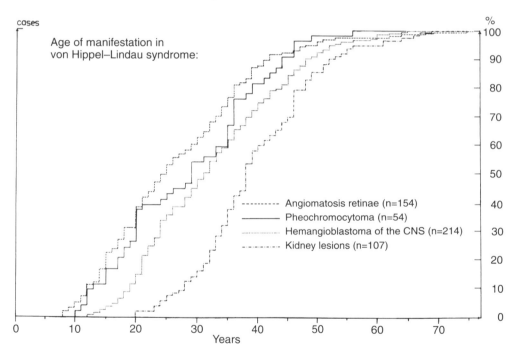

Fig. 26.2 Cumulative age distribution of angiomatosis retinae, phaeochromocytoma, haemangioblastoma of the CNS, and kidney lesions in VHL. (From Neumann 1987*a*.)

published in 1926 (Lindau 1926) and contained personally studied cases from Sweden and from Denmark, Germany, and Czechoslovakia, and included an extensive review of the literature. His autopsy series contained coincidental tumorus lesions of the kidneys, the adrenal glands, and the liver, as well as cysts in the pancreas and epididymis which he summarized under the term 'angiomatosis of the central nervous system complex'. The first description of a cerebellar haemangioblastoma was made by Jackson (1872).

Fig. 26.3 Eugen von Hippel. Courtesy of his daughter, Mrs. Chemin-Petit, Berlin.

Fig. 26.4 Arvid Lindau with his wife during his voluntary stay at Prof. Aschoff's Institute of Pathology at the University of Freiburg in 1927. Courtesy of his son, Jan Lindau, Lund, Sweden.

VHL was identified as a genetic disease and its autosomal dominant mode of inheritance was recognized by the Danish physician, Møller (1929). An extensive review of the history of the disease was made by Melmon and Rosen (1964).

Kidney lesions

Age, sex, symptoms

Renal lesions of von Hippel–Lindau syndrome are detected either from symptoms or from asymptomatic leions found by screening investigations (Figs 26.5–26.8) in affected patients or apparently healthy relatives at genetic risk. The mean age at detection of renal lesions is approximately 35 years (Neumann 1987a, Lamiell *et al.* 1989, Poston *et al.* 1995, Chauveau *et al.* 1996) (Fig. 26.2). The youngest patient with renal cancer was 16 years-old (Keeler and Klauber 1992). Sporadic renal carcinoma occurs approximately 20 years later than renal cell carcinoma in VHL (Wagle and Scal 1970). In general, renal lesions in VHL are detected later than those in the eye, central nervous system (CNS), or adrenal medulla and paraganglia. The sex ratio (males/females) of renal lesions in those affected was 1.4–1.7 (Levine *et al.* 1982, Neumann 1987a) and no difference in the age of manifestation of renal lesions was observed.

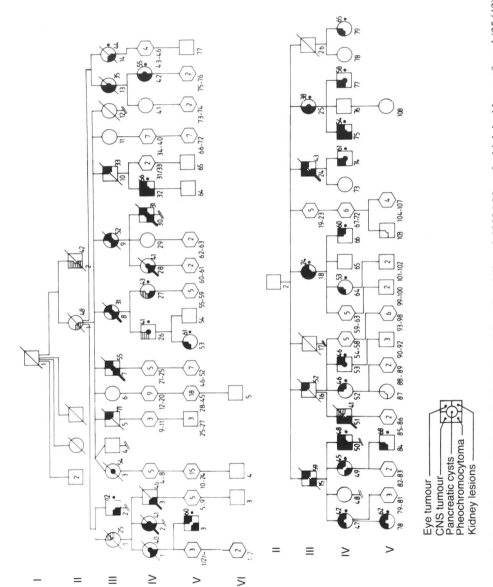

Fig. 26.5 Pedigree of the large Hawaiian VHL kindred. (Adapted from Lamiell *et al.* 1989.) Note the high incidence of renal (25/42) and pancreatic (19/42) lesions. This family has a mutation of nucleotide 686 thymin to cytosin that changes a leucine to proline.

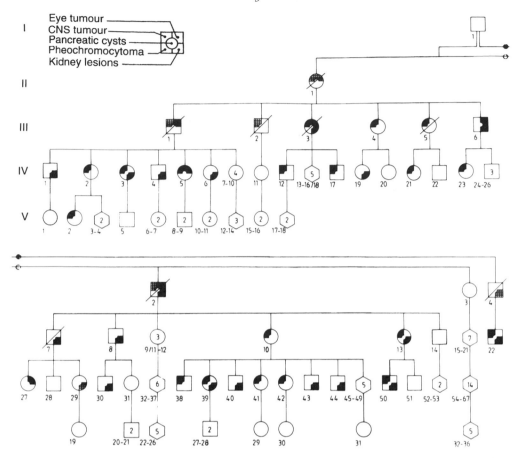

Fig. 26.6 Pedigree of the large Newfoundland VHL kindred. (Adapted from Green *et al.* 1986.) Originally, one renal cell carcinoma was reported, later a 14% incidence of renal lesions (Lamiell *et al.* 1989). Note the high incidence of phaeochromocytoma (20/37) and absence of pancreatic lesions. This family has a mutation of nucleotide 712 cytosin to thymin that changes an arginine to tryptophane.

Symptoms may be caused either by lesions confined to the organ or by metastatic cancer. Loin pain or complaints of an abdominal mass and, infrequently, gross haematuria are reported mainly in patients with large tumours. Hypertension, deterioration of renal function, and proteinuria have rarely been observed in VHL patients with renal lesions, and cysts as numerous as in polycystic kidney disease are very seldom too (Frimodt-Møller *et al.* 1981, Chauveau *et al.*, 1996).

Incidence of kidney involvement and clinical types of VHL

Kidney lesions have been found in up to 60% of VHL subjects at autopsy (Horton *et al.* 1976). On average, 33% of those affected show renal cysts and/or cancer (Lamiell *et al.* 1989). Remarkable interfamilial variations have been observed that reflect different mutations in the VHL gene. The two largest, extensively studied families are living on two islands, Hawaii and Newfoundland, and include 43 and 38 affected patients, respectively (Green *et al.* 1986; Lamiell *et al.* 1989).

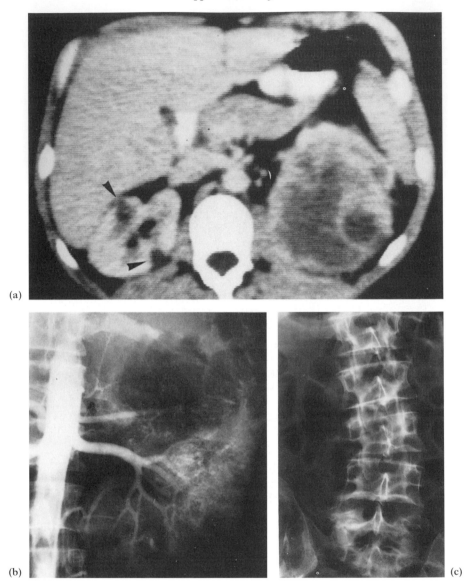

(a)

(b)   (c)

Fig. 26.7   Metastatic renal cancer in a 36-year-old male. (a) CT. Note a left, huge, partially necrotic, renal tumour and two cysts (arrows) in the right kidney; (b) angiography; (c) tumourous destruction of a lumbar vertebral body (arrow).

The pedigrees are shown in Figs 26.5 and 26.6. In the Hawaiian family, 63% of those affected have renal cysts and carcinoma and 37% pancreatic lesions, whereas phaeochromocytoma was only recently observed in a single case. In contrast, the Newfoundland kindred showed an incidence of 53% for phaeochromocytoma, but renal lesions in only 18% of those affected (Green *et al.* 1986; Lamiell *et al.* 1989). In the Freiburg–von-Hippel–Lindau syndrome study, there are 14 families with pheochromocytomas but without renal carcinomas (Neumann *et al.* 1993).

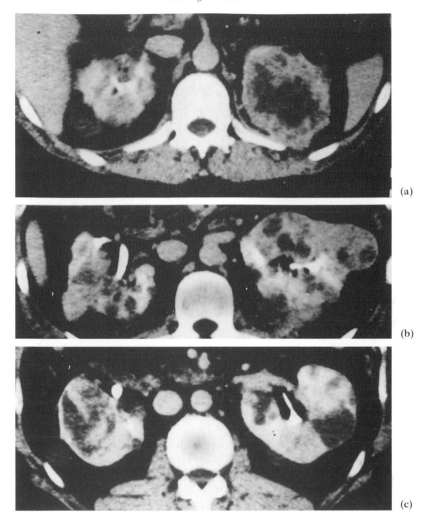

(a)

(b)

(c)

Fig. 26.8 Kidney lesion detected by screening in a 45-year-old male. Note the cystic lesion of borderline density (60 HE) which was shown to be a tumour by angiography. Contrast enhanced CT scan.

Because of these clinical variations, VHL is classified into type 1 (with renal cancer and without pheochromocytoma), type 2A (without renal cancer and with pheochromocytoma), and type 2B (with both manifestations—rare).

Radiological imaging

Modern imaging techniques are important in the detection and management of renal lesions in von Hippel–Lindau syndrome. Because there is a lifelong risk of developing cancer, regular investigations are recommended. High-resolution imaging techniques and precise documentation of individuals and kindreds are indispensable for the early diagnosis and monitoring of growing cysts and tumours. Ionizing radiation exposure should be minimized. Ultrasound is a

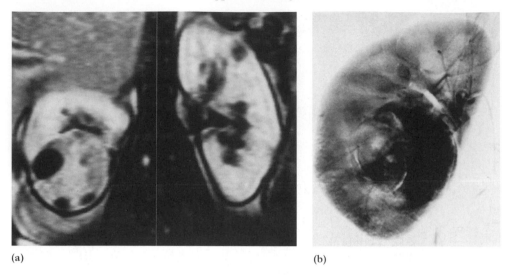

(a)   (b)

Fig. 26.9   Cysts and cancer of the kidney in VHL shown by Gadolinium-enhanced MR imaging. Incidental finding in a 36-year-old female patient. (a) MR imaging; (b) angiography of the right kidney.

well-established method for the detection of renal cysts and tumours. However, its accuracy depends on the operator. IV-enhanced computerized tomography (CT) is more sensitive (Jennings *et al.* 1988; Choyke *et al.* 1990) and clearly superior in exact documentation (Figs 26.7 and 26.8), and should be performed at least once, beginning in late youth or early adulthood (Green *et al.* 1986, Lamiell *et al.* 1989, Maher *et al.* 1990*a*).

The position of angiography in renal VHL lesions has not yet been formally evaluated. Despite good vascularization, angiography findings of such tumours may be disappointingly faint (Fig. 26.7*b*), and were found to be inadaequate for identification of renal cell carcinoma in VHL (Miller *et al.* 1991).

Magnetic resonance imaging (MRI) (Fig. 26.9) is evolving as a versatile technique for regularly repeated investigation. So far, only limited experience with this method in VHL has been published; accuracy similar to CT has been indicated (Sato *et al.* 1988; Choyke *et al.* 1990).

Pathology

Gross morphology

The characteristic renal findings in VHL are cysts and tumours. In most patients, both kidneys are affected but sizes of cysts and tumours vary considerably. Multifocal lesions are typical and the surface of the organs is frequently altered. The sectioned solid mass has the same yellowish colour as sporadic renal cell carcinoma. The tumours are often well-encapsulated, the cysts filled with clear fluid or blood.

Histology (Fig. 26.10)

The histology of renal cysts demonstrates a continuum from simple cysts with a single layer of epithelium, through atypical proliferative cysts with stratification of epithelial lining cells and

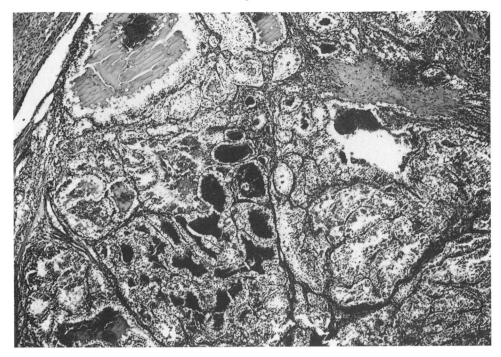

Fig. 26.10 Histological findings of a renal tumour in VHL. Clear cell carcinoma—in part, cystic (non-papillary type).

focal atypical epithelium, to carcinoma, present as complex projections into cyst lumina (Malek and Green 1971; Bernstein *et al.* 1987; Solomon and Schwartz 1988; Spencer *et al.* 1988; Ibrahim *et al.* 1989). The size of a cyst does not correlate with the presence or absence of malignancy (Lee *et al.* 1977; Solomon and Schwartz 1988). Solid renal tumours in von Hippel–Lindau syndrome are clear-cell carcinomas. Metastases occur in regional lymph nodes, lung, liver, and bone, but rarely within the CNS (Horton *et al.* 1976, Neumann *et al.* 1992). Renal tumours in von Hippel–Lindau syndrome have seldom been haemangioblastomic (Christoferson *et al.* 1961).

Treatment and prognosis

The treatment of renal lesions in VHL is surgical. Bilateral and multifocal development of renal lesions is typical in VHL, but radical treatment, such as bilateral nephrectomy, requires permanent kidney-replacement therapy, e.g. dialysis. Because of this dilemma, treatment of renal tumours in VHL is difficult and has been discussed controversially. Renal malignancies in VHL have been treated by tumour enucleation, partial nephrectomy, bench surgery (on an excised kidney with reimplantation to spare apparently healthy tissue), bilateral nephrectomy, or staged bilateral nephrectomy (Lamiell *et al.* 1989). An aggressive approach has been recommended by a number of authors (Mullin *et al.* 1976; Fetner *et al.* 1977; Gersell and King 1988). In 1980, a plea was made for conservation of sufficient functional kidney tissue for as long as possible (Pearson *et al.* 1980). This conservative approach has been subsequently recommended by others (Das *et al.* 1981; Levine *et al.* 1982; Malek *et al.* 1987; Spencer *et al.* 1988; Novick and Streem 1992) and is currently the method of choice (Poston *et al.* 1995; Steinbach *et al.* 1995; Chauveau *et al.* 1996). The postoperative result can be best controlled by duplex sonography which shows perfusion in all areas of the kidneys.

Patients with VHL rarely need renal dialysis unless they have had bilateral nephrectomies. Renal transplantation has been done for some VHL patients, usually using cadaveric donors (Peterson *et al.* 1977; Lamiell *et al.* 1989). After long-term follow-up, no donor kidney has been reported to develop cysts or tumours. Moreover, post-transplant immunosuppressive therapy has not seemed to influence the natural history of extrarenal lesions in patients with VHL. In retrospective studies, cerebellar haemangioblastoma is the leading cause of death in von Hippel–Lindau syndrome and renal cell carcinoma comes second (Neumann 1987*b*; Lamiell *et al.* 1989). In a study in East Anglia in the UK, renal cell carcinoma was the first cause of death (Maher *et al.* 1990*b*). The prognosis of CNS tumours has been ameliorated considerably since the introduc tion of microneurosurgery (Neumann *et al.* 1992). It can therefore be expected that the prognosis of von Hippel–Lindau syndrome will, in the future, depend substantially on effective manage-ment of the renal lesions.

Other manifestations

The frequent and rare lesions of von Hippel–Lindau syndrome are listed in Table 26.1, and the recommended screening programme in Table 26.2.

Eye

Angiomatosis retinae (Fig. 26.11) may cause severe impairment of vision uni- or bilaterally as a result of retinal detachment. Blindness or near-blindness typically happens without preceding symptoms and without pain. It can occur in childhood or youth and may remain unnoticed until routine examination, such as vision tests in school or on application for a driving licence. The classic ophthalmological finding (Collins 1894; von Hippel 1904) is a round, red tumour of the

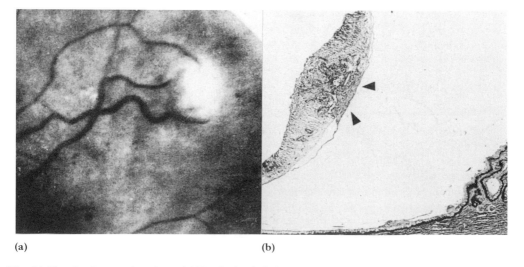

(a)   (b)

Fig. 26.11 Angiomatosis retinae. (a) Typical ophthalmoscopic findings with a round tumour (T) and a pair of tortuous feeding vessels; (b) histology showing retinal detachment by a peripheral angioma (arrows); cc = corpus ciliare.

retina with a pair of feeding vessels showing an increase in diameter and tortuosity. Multifocal and bilateral lesions are frequently observed (Ridley *et al.* 1986). Histologically, the tumour is identical to haemangioblastoma of the CNS (Lindau 1926). Detection of peripheral angiomatosis can be done by direct ophthalmoscopy, using Goldmann's three-mirror contact glass which has proven to be reliable. However, small lesions are difficult to detect with this technique. They can be identified earlier by fluorescein angiography, because the poor quality of the vessels causes leakage of the fluorescein (Moore *et al.* 1991).

Laser-beam treatment is the method of choice for retinal angiomas. This very effective therapy has only rare and transient side-effects (Welch 1977; Ridley *et al.* 1986). Delicate localization are angiomas near the macula, angiomas adjacent to large retinal vessels, and angiomas near the optic disc. Decisions for treatment in such cases are difficult and follow-up observations may be justified. Angiomas should be treated only by an experienced opthalmologist. The major complication of untreated retinal angiomatosis is impairment of vision by retinal detachment.

Central nervous system

Haemangioblastoma of the CNS (Fig. 26.12) is frequently (in up to 80% of cases) localized to the cerebellum and produces a large cyst, whereas the solid tumour itself is only a small mural nodule (Lindau 1926; Lamiell *et al.* 1989; Neumann *et al.* 1992). This is the classical morphology of Lindau's tumour. However, 25% of cerebellar haemangioblastomas are not cystic. Brainstem, medulla oblongata, and spinal cord are other important sites (Browne *et al.* 1976; Neumann *et al.* 1992), and lesions may cause syringomyelia (Fig. 26.12b). Histological investigation reveals

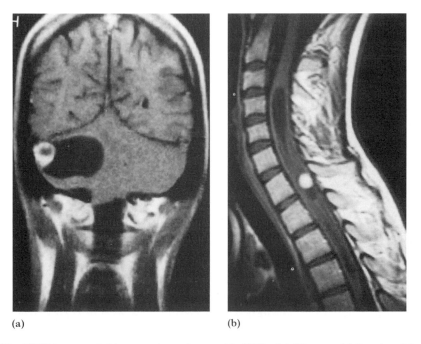

(a)   (b)

Fig. 26.12 CNS haemangioblastoma in patients with VHL. (a) 26-year-old female with symptomatic cystic cerebellar haemangioblastoma. Gadolinium-enhanced MRI; (b) 22-year-old female with asymptomatic cervical haemangioblastoma. Note two areas of syrinx, one adjacent to the tumour. Gadolinium-enhanced MRI.

Table 26.1   Frequent and rare lesions in von Hippel–Lindau syndrome

Eye:	Retinal angiomas[1]	49%
	Haemangioblastoma of the optic nerve (Henkind and Benjamin 1976)	
CNS:	Haemangioblastoma[1]	54%
	Astrocytoma	0.5%
	Choroid plexus papilloma (Blamires and Maher 1992)	
	Ependymoma (Horton *et al.* 1976; Neumann 1987*a*)	
	Neuroblastoma (Burns *et al.* 1987; Neumann 1987*a*)	
Kidney:	Renal cell carcinoma[1]	26%
	Renal cysts[1]	30%
Pancreas:	Multiple cysts[1]	26%
	Serous cystadenoma	1%
	Islet cell tumour	1%
	Haemangioblastoma (Lamiell *et al.* 1989)	
	Adenocarcinoma (Lamiell *et al.* 1989)	
Adrenal gland, paraganglia:	Phaeochromocytoma[1] (adrenal and extra-adrenal)	29%
	Haemangioblastoma (Burns *et al.* 1987)	
Pituitary gland:	Adenoma	0.5%
Apud cells:	Carcinoid	1%
Epididymis:	Cystadenoma[1] and cysts	13%
Testis:	Germ-cell tumour (Cendron *et al.* 1991)	
Mesosalpinx:	Cystadenoma (Gersell and King 1988; Korn *et al.* 1990)	
Liver:	Cysts	1%
	Angioma, adenoma, carcinoma (Goodman *et al.* 1964; Horton *et al.* 1976; Lamiell *et al.* 1989)	
Spleen:	Cysts	0.5%
	Angioma (Horton *et al.* 1976)	
Lung:	Cysts	
	Angioma (Horton *et al.* 1976)	
Bone:	Cysts (Brandt 1921)	
Skin:	Angioma	0.5%
	Angioblastoma (Horton *et al.* 1976)	
Ear:	Endolymphatic sac tumour	0.5%

Presented are the incidences in the Freiburg VHL register at December 1995, including 228 patients. Rare lesions not observed in the register are cited from literature.

[1]Denotes principal lesions in VHL (from Neumann and Zbar 1997).

numerous vessels and foam cells, in between which may be found altered astrocytes or glial cells. Metastases have been reported only occasionally (Neumann *et al.* 1992). Histological differentiation of haemangioblastoma of the CNS and metastases of renal cell carcinoma in von Hippel–Lindau syndrome can be difficult (Goodbody and Gamlen 1974; Isaac *et al.* 1956) and requires special staining techniques (Andrew and Gradwell 1986; Clelland and Treip 1989; Frank *et al.* 1989).

Symptoms are caused by cerebellar dysfunction or increased intracranial pressure, often initially provoking investigations of the upper intestinal tract because of nausea and vomiting. Spinal haemangioblastomas (Fig. 26.12b) cause segmental neurological deficits and may produce paraplegia or even tetraplegia in advanced stages. Approximately 20% of haemangioblastomas of the CNS are due to von Hippel–Lindau syndrome, whereas 80% are sporadic (Neumann and Wiestler 1991). Multifocal tumours are a striking feature of familial tumours (Neumann *et al.* 1992). The imaging method of choice is Gadolinium-DPTA contrast-enhanced MR which detects very small tumour nodules in the cerebellum in the T1-weighted images. T2-weighted images provide no additional information (Filling-Katz *et al.* 1989). In addition to MRI of the brain, a Gadolinium-DTPA-enhanced MRI scan of the spinal cord should always be performed (Fig. 26.12). Cerebellar lesions require neurosurgical treatment if symptomatic. In most cases, increased intracranial pressure as a result of occlusive hydrocephalus is the cause of sudden deterioration. Using microsurgical techniques, postoperative mortality decreased enormously (Constans *et al.* 1986; Neumann *et al.* 1989; Boughey *et al.* 1990; Resche *et al.* 1993). Although microsurgery of haemangioblastoma of the CNS has considerably improved the surgical results, multifocal tumour development and recurrence remain a serious problem in the clinical management of VHL carriers (Neumann *et al.* 1992). Spinal lesions may need treatment only if symptomatic. Among alternative therapeutic approaches, radiosurgery is a candidate to replace classic neurosurgery. Preliminary reports are promising but larger series are still missing (Warnick 1993).

Adrenal medulla and paraganglia

The fourth, most frequent lesion resulting in severe morbidity in von Hippel–Lindau syndrome is phaeochromocytoma (Fig. 26.13) (Horton *et al.* 1976; Atuk *et al.* 1979; Green *et al.* 1986; Neumann 1987*a*). This tumour accounts for 3–5% of deaths (Neumann 1987*b*; Lamiell *et al.* 1989); a fatal outcome may occur especially in late pregnancy or during childbirth (Green *et al.* 1986) since the tumour is mainly found at a younger age (Fig. 26.2). Nearly all patients have a history of palpitations, sweating attacks, and headaches, and intermittent or permanent hypertension. The diagnosis of phaeochromocytoma is based on elevated circulating or excreted catecholamines, and radiological documentation of the tumour(s). Twenty-four-hour urine assays should include noradrenaline, adrenaline, their methoxylated derivatives, and vanillylmandelic acid; valuable plasma assays are noradrenaline and adrenaline. 123- or 131-iodine-metaiodobenzyl-guanidine scintigraphy (MIBG) (Fig. 26.13a) has a sensitivity of about 95% for tumour localization and is an excellent method for simultaneous documentation of multiple phaeochromocytomas (Shapiro *et al.* 1985; Neumann *et al.* 1993). A similar high sensitivity (95%) was found for MRI using T1- and T2-weighted techniques (Fig. 26.13b), and is currently recommended as the method of choice for radiological imaging, whereas CT scanning (Fig. 26.13c) is inferior (Neumann *et al.* 1993). In von Hippel–Lindau syndrome, extra-adrenal and multifocal phaeochromocytoma is common (Neumann 1987*a*) and should be considered, whereas malignant phaeochromocytoma seems to be very rare (Atuk *et al.* 1979; Levine *et al.* 1982; Sato *et al.* 1988). The therapy is surgery sparing normal adrenal tissue, if the pheochromocytoma is symptomatic. Pre-operative MIBG scintigraphy and MRI are important to localize extra-adrenal pheochromocytoma (Hoffman *et al.* 1982). Precautionary adequate alpha and beta receptor blockade should be applied and constant perioperative supervision of blood pressure and heart rate is required. Manipulation can cause a sudden elevation of catecholamines in the blood circulation and severe hypertension and arrhythmia during the operation (Hull 1986).

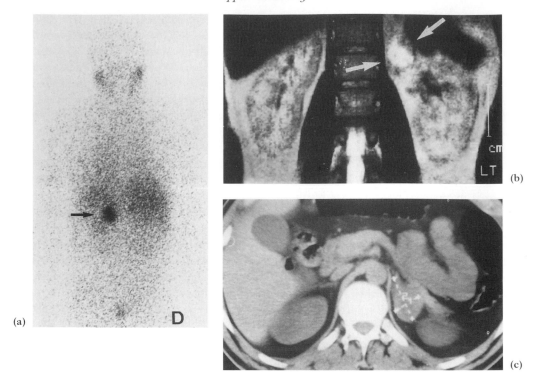

(a) (b) (c)

Fig. 26.13 Phaeochromocytoma of the left adrenal gland found by screening in a 29-year-old male with intermittent hypertension, member of a VHL kindred, overlooked by abdominal ultrasound. (a) 123 iodine-metaiodobenzyl-guanidine scintigram (arrow: tumour, D: right); (b) coronal T2-weighted MR imaging (arrow: tumour); (c) CT (tumour marked).

Pancreas

Pancreatic cysts (Fig. 26.14) are a classical feature of von Hippel–Lindau syndrome. In older reports (Horton *et al.* 1976), these lesions were found at autopsy, indicating that symptoms are, in general, absent, a finding which is confirmed by the Freiburg–von Hippel–Lindau syndrome study. The great majority of the affected report no or minor abdominal discomfort (Neumann *et al.* 1991). Exocrine or endocrine failure was restricted to very few patients (Fishman and Bartholomew 1979) and, as a rule, therapeutic interventions should be avoided. For diagnostic imaging, abdominal ultrasound, CT, and MRI can be used (Neumann *et al.* 1991). For initial radiological documentation, CT is recommended (Choyke *et al.* 1990). Involvement of the pancreas can be restricted to a few cysts, but frequently cysts are scattered over the entire organ and can lead to enormous enlargement of the pancreas. Obstruction of the pancreatic and biliary ducts has been reported in only a few instances (Beerman *et al.* 1982). Serous cystademona of the pancreas may represent a variation of pancreatic involvement in von Hippel–Lindau syndrome and has been found in some cases (Beerman *et al.* 1982; Neumann *et al.* 1991). Its biological behaviour was always benign and no treatment was needed.

Pancreatic islet cell tumours have been found in some kindreds (Hull *et al.* 1979; Cornish *et al.* 1984; Lamiell *et al.* 1989; Binkowitz *et al.* 1990). Other malignancies, such as pancreatic adeno-carcinoma, are very rarely observed (Lamiell *et al.* 1989).

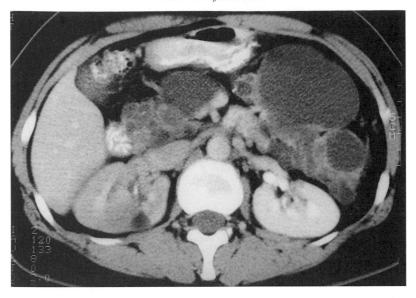

Fig. 26.14 Pancreatic cysts, asymptomatic lesions in a 29-year-old female member of a VHL kindred. CT screening.

Table 26.2 Recommended screening programme for von Hippel-Lindau syndrome

Extensive pedigree evaluation*
Physical examination, including blood pressure measurement and neurological status*
Ophthalmoscopy*
MR imaging of brain and spinal cord using Gadolinium DTPA**
CT of the abdomen with IV contrast medium***
(Sonography of the abdomen*)
Sonography of the testes***
24-hour urine catecholamine assay*
EDTA blood sampling for molecular genetic analysis

* Starting at age six.
** Starting at age 12.
*** In adulthood.

Epididymis

Cysts or cystic tumours of the epididymis are found in a number of VHL families with an incidence of up to 39% in males (Melmon and Rosen 1964; Macrae and Newigin 1968; Tsuda *et al.* 1976; Lamiell *et al.* 1989; Choyke *et al.* 1990). Histologically, these lesions are cystadenomas. The tumours are often bilateral and can cause obstruction of seminal ducts and thus infertility (de Souza *et al.* 1985; Witten *et al.* 1985). The diagnostic method of choice is sonography.

Endolymphatic sac tumour

This lesion is a very rare tumour of the inner ear (Lo *et al.* 1993; Delisle *et al.* 1994). Seemingly, most patients with endolymphatic sac tumour have VHL. The tumours can lead to uni- or even bilateral hearing loss. Treatment is surgical, and patients with complete hearing loss can be provided with a cochlear implant (Kempermann *et al.* 1996).

Rare lesions

Rarely, lesions in other organs and atypical lesions in principally affected organs have been observed in von Hippel–Lindau syndrome. Mostly, cysts, angiomas, or haemangioblastomas are observed. It remains to be shown whether atypical lesions are actually caused by the underlying genetic defect. For choroid plexus papilloma, this has already been shown by molecular genetic studies (Blamires and Maher 1992).

Genetics

The VHL gene was cloned in 1993 after six years of intensive effort (Latif *et al.* 1993). This section of the chapter will summarize information obtained on the molecular anatomy of the VHL gene, on the mutations that produce VHL disease, and on VHL gene expression during murine embryogenesis.

VHL is inherited as an autosomal dominant trait. A single genetic locus near the tip of the short arm of chromosome 3 (3p25-26) is responsible for the disorder. Clinical heterogeneity is a well-known feature of VHL (Glenn *et al.* 1991; Neumann and Wiestler 1991). Some VHL families contain members affected with pheochromocytomas while others do not. This clinical observation, together with the results of mutation analysis, forms the basis of a new proposed classification of VHL. There is a remarkable correlation between the disease classification and the type of VHL mutation (below).

VHL may occur in individuals without a family history of the illness. The proportion of cases of new VHL mutations is not known. In the National Cancer Institute of the USA (NCI) series, there were 6/114 families that met strict criteria for a new VHL mutation (both parents of the affected individual were living; no evidence of VHL was detected in either parent during screening at the NCI).

Positional cloning of the VHL gene

The VHL gene was isolated by positional cloning, a strategy that has proved useful in the isolation of a number of human disease genes. Positional cloning relies on genetic and physical mapping methods to define precisely the interval that harbours the disease gene. The first step in the positional cloning of the VHL gene was taken by Seizinger *et al.* who demonstrated by linkage analysis that the VHL gene was linked to *RAF1*, a proto-oncogene located near the tip of the short arm of chromosome 3 (3p25-26) (Seizinger *et al.* 1988). This result was confirmed by Vance *et al.* (1990), Maher *et al.* (1990*a*), Hosoe *et al.* (1991), and Pericak-Vance *et al.* (1993). Hosoe *et al.* demonstrated that VHL was linked to D3S18, a polymorphic DNA marker isolated by Donis-Keller *et al.* (1987). Multipoint linkage analysis indicated that the most likely location for VHL was in the interval bounded by RAF1 and D3S18 (Hosoe *et al.* 1991). Seizinger *et al.* (1991) also demonstrated that VHL was located distal to RAF1 in the interval between RAF1 and D3S719. Polymorphic DNA markers D3S601 and D3S720 were identified in the interval between RAF1 and the distal flanking markers; D3S601 and D3S719 did not recombine with VHL. To further narrow the region that harboured the VHL gene, D3S601 and LIB12-48 were used to construct a pulsed field gel electrophoresis (PFGE) map of the VHL region (Yao *et al.* 1993). Affected members of more than 100 VHL families were studied by PFGE in an attempt to identify germline deletions in the VHL gene; three families were identified (Yao *et al.* 1993). These germline deletions were overlaping and provided a precise physical localization for the VHL disease gene.

Kuzmin *et al.* (1994) isolated and characterized yeast artificial chromosomes (YACs) surrounding D3S601. A YAC contig was assembled and used to isolate cosmids. One cosmid, located entirely within the three nested deletions, detected conserved sequences and was used to isolate two cDNAs. The gp 7 cDNA detected intragenic mutations in the germline of affected individuals and was shown to be the VHL gene.

Evidence that the VHL gene is a tumour suppressor gene

The available evidence suggests that the VHL gene is a tumour suppressor gene for specific cell types in the retina, CNS, adrenal gland, kidney, pancreas, and epididymis. Loss of heterozygosity for polymorphic markers located on 3p has been demonstrated in clear cell carcinomas of the kidneys, pheochromocytomas, and CNS hemangioblastomas. In VHL families where it was possible to trace the parental origin of the chromosome 3p sequences, the chromosome 3p bearing the wild-type allele was lost (Tory *et al.* 1989). The consistent loss of the wild-type allele of a disease gene in an inherited cancer syndrome is a hallmark of a tumour suppressor gene. These observations suggest that normal function of the VHL gene is required for control of cell growth in certain specific cell types.

Characterization of the VHL gene

The partial gp 7 cDNA contained 1.65 kb of DNA. Extension of the cDNA in the 5′ direction provided an additional 0.3 kb of DNA. The gp 7 cDNA detects a 5 kb message expressed in all adult tissues that have been tested (brain, heart, kidney). The message was originally estimated at 6–6.5 kb. Comparison of the gp 7 sequence with the database indicates that the VHL gene encodes a novel protein. The only homology that was detected was with a cell surface membrane of *Trypanasoma brucei*. The cDNA sequence lacks domains that would suggest a DNA binding protein, enzymatic activity, nuclear localization, or membrane localization.

The structure of the VHL gene is shown in Fig. 26.5; the cDNA contains 3 exons. There is a long 3′ untranslated region. The open reading frame encodes a putative protein of 852 nucleotides (but see below). The region 5′ of this cloned DNA has been examined for additional exons by sequence analysis and by hybridization to Northern blots in an attempt to detect the VHL message. No evidence was obtained for additional 5′ exons.

The transcription start sites and promoter of the VHL gene are located within exon 1. Transcription is initiated around a putative SPI binding site about 60 bp upstream from the first AUG codon in the VHL mRNA. Several putative transcription factor binding sites, notably for nuclear respiratory factor 1 and PAX, were found upstream of the transcription start sites. A minimal region of 106 bp was delineated. The promoter sequence does not contain TATA and CCAAT boxes (Kuzmin *et al.* 1995).

Translation of the VHL gene

Recent work has focused on determining the location of the translation start sites of the VHL gene. Exon 1 contains two possible translation start sites. The two AUG codons were evaluated for ability to support translation. An *in vitro*-coupled transcription/translation assay and an *in vivo* transient transfection assay were used to test the ability of the VHL cDNA to support expression of the protein. Three proteins, 18, 30, and 36kd were expressed from the VHL cDNA, both *in vitro* and *in vivo*. Based on the pattern of antisera reactivity, the 30 and 18kd proteins were considered to be the products of translation from the first and second AUG codons, respectively. The 36kd protein is most likely a post-translationally modified derivative of the 30kd protein. The predicted size of the protein initiated at the first AUG codon is 213 amino acids and at the second AUG is 160 amino acids. These proteins would be predicted to be 23kd and 18kd. The VHL gene shows alternative splicing; a VHL message is expressed with or without exon 2. That makes the number of proteins that can be produced from the genome equal to 4: consisting of 119, 160, 172, and 213 amino acids. The major conclusion of these studies is that the VHL gp 7 cDNA could support translation of more than one human VHL protein from overlapping, in frame, open reading frames. So far, the NCI laboratory has not identified the VHL protein in human tissues, suggesting that the VHL protein may be expressed at lower levels or have a rapid turnover. It is not known which protein(s) acts as tumour suppressor(s) and which proteins are produced in different tissues. Differences in distribution of VHL isoforms might contribute to the tissue-specific pattern of neoplasia in VHL.

Characterization of the VHL protein

The VHL gene has been expressed in *E. coli* and Cos cells. Polyclonal antibodies have been prepared and studies performed in a rabbit reticulocyte *in vitro* translation system and in monkey kidney (Cos) cells. The size of the protein detected in these systems was 18, 30, and 36kd. The predicted sizes of the proteins are 18 and 23kd.

Function of the VHL gene product

Considerable effort has been directed toward identification of the function of the VHL protein. The VHL protein has been found to bind to elongins B and C and to negatively regulate the rate of transcription elongation (Duan *et al.* 1995). The VHL protein has also been shown to regulate the expression of vascular endothelial growth factor (VEGF).

VEGF is a protein involved in capillary permeability and new blood vessel formation (angiogenesis). In clear-cell renal carcinoma cells lacking a functional VHL protein, VEGF is overproduced and not regulated properly (Wizigmann-Voos *et al.* 1995; Siemeister *et al.* 1996). For example, during oxygen deprivation cells increase production of VEGF, while during normoxic conditions cells decrease production of VEGF. Clear-cell renal carcinoma cells lacking functional VHL protein are unable to regulate VEGF production in response to environmental oxygen concentration.

Expression of the VHL gene during murine embryogenesis

VHL expression in human kidney and during embryogenesis was analysed by *in situ* mRNA hybridization with 35 S-labelled antisense VHL probes derived from human and mouse VHL cDNAs. During embryogenesis, VHL expression occured in all three germ-cell layers and their derivatives. Enhanced expression was most apparent in the epithelial components of the lung, kidney, and eye (Kessler *et al.* 1995).

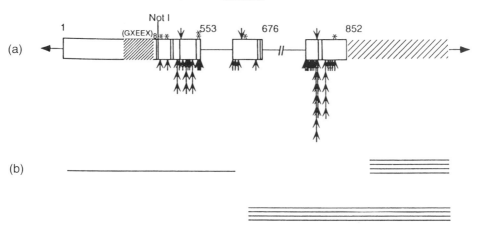

Fig. 26.15   (a) and (b). Molecular anatomy of the VHL gene and of germline mutations in the VHL gene. The 3 exons of the VHL gene are illustrated (rectangles). Exon 1 contains nucleotides 1–553; exon 2, 554–676; and exon 3, 677 to 852. Arrows pointing downward indicate insertions. Arrows pointing upward indicate nucleotide substitutions. Asterisk indicates a stop codon. A vertical line within an exon indicates a deletion. Note the hot spot for mutations located at nucleotides 712 and 713. Note that all germline mutations occur 3′ to the Not I site in exon 1; (b) extent of germline deletions are shown for nine families (Chen *et al.* 1995).

VHL gene mutations

As with any human disease gene, the critical questions are: what types of mutations produce the disease? Where are the disease-producing mutations located? Are there hot spots for mutations? Are there correlations between genotype and phenotype? Some human inherited disorders are caused by a single type of mutation in a single location within the gene. VHL is remarkable in that disease is produced by many types of mutation. The mutations are scattered throughout the gene. About 40% of the germline mutations are predicted to produce a truncated VHL protein (Fig. 26.15).

At the NCI, germline mutations were detected in 75% of 114 VHL families (Chen *et al.* 1995). Large deletions accounted for about 21% of the mutations, 58% of mutations were missense, 14% of mutations were microdeletions/insertions, and 7% were nonsense (Fig. 26.16). There was a striking correlation between the clinical type of VHL and the type of mutation (Fig. 26.16). Ninety-six per cent of VHL type 2 (with pheo) families had missense mutations in the VHL gene. VHL type 1 (without pheo) was produced by large deletions, missense mutations, nonsense mutations, and microdeletions/insertions. A mutation hot spot was detected at nucleotides 712 and 713 (codon 238). The mutation hot spot was associated with VHL type 2B and has been observed by the Cambridge group (Crossey *et al.* 1994). The major conclusion from our observations is that a full-length VHL protein is not required to produce retinal angiomas, renal cell carcinomas, or haemangioblastomas.

Large families with inherited multisystem cancer provide excellent models for defining relationships between particular phenotypes and mutations. These large families may segregate some but not all of the neoplasms associated with the disease. VHL provides an excellent example of families of this type. Specific phenotypes were associated with mutations at nucleotides 505, 712,

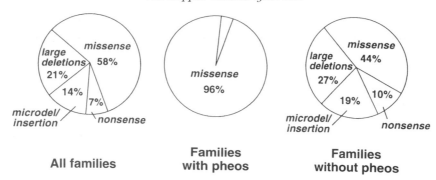

All families **Families with pheos** **Families without pheos**

Fig. 26.16   Pie diagram shows the proportions of families with Von Hippel-Lindau disease found to have different types of mutations. Note that 96% of VHL families with pheochromocytoma had missense mutations (Chen *et al.* 1995).

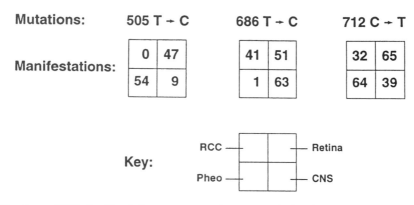

Fig. 26.17   Large VHL families define genotype–phenotype relationships. The proportion of affected family members with renal cell carcinoma (RCC), retinal angiomas, CNS hemangioblastomas, and pheochromocytomas are shown for a representative large family with 505, 686, and 712 mutations (Chen *et al.* 1995). Note that affected members of the family with the 505 mutations had frequent pheochromocytomas but no renal cell carcinoma; members of the family with the 712 mutations had frequent pheochromocytomas and renal cell carcinoma.

and 713 (Burns *et al.* 1987) (Fig. 26.17). Members of a large family with a 505 T to C mutation had pheochromocytomas, angiomas, haemangioblastomas without RCC, or pancreatic cysts. This mutation has been found to be quite frequent in families with VHL in the Black Forest, Germany and was also present in two families from Pennsylvania, USA (Brauch *et al.* 1995). Members of another large family with a 712 C to T mutation define another VHL phenotype. These individuals had pheochromocytomas, angiomas, haemangioblastomas with renal cell carcinomas, and pancreatic cysts.

Genetic testing

It is now possible to identify asymptomatic carriers of the VHL gene by testing for the mutation characteristic of a particular family. Because of the heterogeneity of disease-producing mutation, identification of the disease-producing mutation in an individual VHL family is labour-intensive. So far, more than 140 distinct germline mutations in the VHL gene have been identified (Glavac *et al.* 1996; Zbar *et al.* 1996); in approximately 70% of families with clinically confirmed VHL, the germline mutations can be detected. Once identified, the mutation information becomes of considerable value to any family member seeking knowledge of disease-carrier status. Distinguishing VHL gene carriers from their normal relatives spares those individuals found not to carry the gene the expense and inconvenience of repeated medical testing.

Treatments are available that may reduce the morbidity and mortality of the disease. The correlation between genotype and phenotype will guide the physician in choice of screening tests and in prognosis. For example, patients with the 505 mutation appear to have a better prognosis than patients with the 712–713 mutation. Mutation detection may be useful in the diagnosis of VHL in patients with an equivocal clinical history; for example, in patients with single or bilateral retinal angiomas without a family history of angiomas or other tumours associated with VHL; or in patients with a family history of clear-cell renal carcinoma without any other manifestation of VHL.

If genetic testing is part of genetic counselling in candidates for VHL or in so far unidentified carriers in families of clinically confirmed VHL, a number of aspects must be considered carefully before such analyses are initiated. These include information on the test, implications of a positive and negative result, possibility that the test may not be informative, options for risk estimation without genetic testing, risk of passing a mutation to children, technical accuracy of the test, fees involved in testing and counselling, risks of psychological distress, risks of insurance or employer discrimination, confidentiality issues, and options and limitation of medical surveillance and screening following testing.

Identification of VHL germline mutation carriers can cause psychological burden and possibly insurance disadvantages; it is, however, the basis of timely detection of VHL-associated lesions and opens new avenue for effective treatment. Therefore, VHL is summarized among the (few) diseases in which genetic testing is recommended (Statement of the American Society of Clinical Oncology 1996).

References

Andrew, S. M. and Gradwell, E. (1986). Immunoperoxydase-labelled antibody staining in differential diagnosis of central nervous system haemangioblastomas and central nervous system metastases of renal carcinomas. *Journal of Clinical Pathology*, **39**, 917–19.

Atuk, N. O., McDonald, T., Wood, T., Carpenter, J. T., Walzak, R., Donaldson, M., *et al.* (1979). Familial pheochromcytoma, hypercalcemia and von Hippel–Lindau disease. A ten-year study of a large family. *Medicine* (Baltimore), **58**, 209–18.

Beerman, M. H., Fromkes, J., Carey, L. C., and Thomas, F. B. (1982), Pancreatic cystadenoma in von Hippel–Lindau disease; an unusual cause of pancreatic and common bile duct obstruction. *Journal of Clinical Gastroenteroly*, **4**, 537–40.

Bernstein, J., Evan, A. P., and Gardner, K. G. (1987). Epithelial hyperplasia in human polycystic kidney diseases. Its role in pathogenesis and risk of neoplasia. *American Journal of Pathology*, **129**, 92–101.

Binkowitz, L. A., Johnson, C. D., and Stephens, D. H. (1990). Islet cell tumour in von Hippel–Lindau disease: increased prevalence and relationship to the multiple endocrine neoplasias. *American Journal of Radiology*, **155**, 501–5.

Blamires, T. L. and Maher, E. R. (1992). Choroid plexus papilloma. A new presentation of von Hippel–Lindau (VHL) disease. *Eye*, **6**, 90–2.

Boughey, A. M., Fletcher, N. A., and Harding, A. E. (1990). Central nervous system haemangioblastoma: a clinical and genetic study of 52 cases. *Journal of Neurology, Neurosurgery, and Psychiatry*, **53**, 644–8.

Brandt, R. (1921). Zur Frage der Angiomatosis retinae. *Albrecht von Graefes Archiv der Ophthalmologie*, **106**, 127–65.

Brauch, H., Kishida, T., Glavac, D., Chen, F., Pausch, F., Höfler, *et al.* (1995). Nucleotide 505 germline mutation in the VHL tumor suppressor gene correlates with pheochromocytoma in von Hippel–Lindau disease. *Human Genetics*, **95**, 551–6.

Browne, T. R., Adams, R. D., and Robertson, G. H. (1976). Haemangioblastoma of the spinal cord. Review and report of five cases. *Archives of Neurology*, **33**, 435–41.

Burns, C., Levine, P. H., Reichman, H., and Stock, J. L. (1987). Case report: Adrenal haemangioblastoma in von Hippel–Lindau disease as a cause of secondary crythrocytosis. *American Journal of the Medical Sciences*, **30**, 119–21.

Cendron, M., Wein, A. J., Schwartz, S. S., Murtagh, F., Livolski, V. A., and Tomaszewski, J. E. (1991). Germ cell tumour of testis in a patient with Von Hippel–Lindau disease. *Urology*, **37**, 69–71.

Chauveau, D., Duvic, C., Chrétien, Y., Paraf, F., Droz, D., Melki, P., *et al.* (1996). Renal involvement in von Hippel–Lindau disease. *Kidney International*, **50**, 944–51.

Chen, F., Kishida, T., Yao, M., Hustand, T., Glavac, D., Dean, J. R., *et al.* (1995). Germline mutations in the von Hippel–Lindau disease tumor suppressor gene: correlations with phenotype. *Human Mutation*, **5**, 66–75.

Choyke, P. L., Filling-Katz, M. R., Shawker, T. H., Gorin, M. B., Travis, W. D., Chang, R., *et al.* (1990). von Hippel–Lindau disease: radiologic screening for visceral manifestations. *Radiology*, **174**, 815–20.

Christoferson, L. A., Gustafson, M. B., and Petersen, A. G. (1961). von Hippel–Lindau Disease. *Journal of the American Medical Association*, **178**, 280–2.

Clelland, C. A. and Treip, C. S. (1989). Histological differentiation of metastatic renal carcinoma in the cerebellum from cerebellar haemangioblastoma in von Hippel–Lindau's disease. *Journal of Neurology, Neurosurgery, and Psychiatry*, **52**, 162–6.

Collins, E. T. (1894). Two cases, brother and sister, with peculiar vascular new growth, probably primarily retinal, affecting both eyes. *Transactions of the Ophthalmologic Society of the United Kingdom*, **14**, 141–9.

Constans, J. P., Meder, F., Maiuri, Donzelli, R., Spaziante, R., and de Divitiis, E. (1986). Posterior fossa hemangioblastomas. *Surgical Neurology*, **25**, 269–75.

Cornish, D., Pont, A., Minor, D., Coomles, J., and Bennington, J. (1984). Metastasic islet cell tumour in von Hippel–Lindau disease. *American Journal of Medicine*, **77**, 147–50.

Crossey, P. A., Richards, F. M., Foster, K., Green, J. S., Prowse, A., Latif, F., *et al.* (1994). Identification of intragenic mutations in the von Hippel–Lindau disease tumour suppressor gene and correlation with disease phenotype. *Human Molecular Genetics*, **8**, 1303–8.

Das, S., Egan, R. M., and Amar, A. D. (1981). von Hippel–Lindau syndrome with bilateral synchronous renal cell carcinoma. *Urology*, **18**, 599–600.

Delisle, M. B., Uro, E., Rouquette, I., Yardeni, E., and Rumeau, J. L. (1994). Papillary neoplasm of the endolymphatic sac in a patient with von Hippel–Lindau disease. *Journal of Clinical Pathology*, **47**, 959–61.

de Souza Andrade, J., Bambirra, E. A., Otacilio, J. B., and de Souza, A. F. (1985). Bilateral papillary cystadenoma of the epififymis as a component of von Hippel–Lindau syndrome: Report of a case presenting as infertility. *Journal of Urology*, **133**, 288–9.

Deval, C. (1862). *Traité théorique et practique des maladies des yeux*. C. Albessard et Bérard, Paris.

Donis-Keller, H., Green, P., Helms, C., Cartinhour, S., Weiffenbach, B., Stephens, *et al.* (1987). A genetic linkage map of the human genome. *Cell*, **51**, 319–37.

Duan, D. R., Pause, A., Burgess, W. H., Aso, T., Chen, D. Y. T., Garrett, K. P., *et al.* (1995).

Inhibition of transcription elongation by the VHL tumor suppressor protein. *Science* (Washington), **269**, 1402–6.

Fetner, C. D., Barilla, D. E., Scott, T., Ballard, J., and Peters, P. (1977). Bilateral renal cell carcinoma in von Hippel–Lindau syndrome: treatment with staged bilateral nephrectomy and hemodialysis. *Journal of Urology*, **117**, 534–6.

Filling-Katz, M. R., Choyke, P. L., Patronas, N. J., Gorin, M. B., Barba, D., Chang, R., *et al.* (1989). Radiologic screening for von Hippel–Lindau disease. The role of enhanced MRI in the central nervous system. *Journal of Computer Assisted Tomography*, **13**, 743–55.

Fishman, R. S. and Bartholomew, L. G. (1979). Severe pancreatic involvement in three generations in von Hippel–Lindau disease. *Mayo Clinic Proceedings*, **54**, 329–31.

Frank, T. S., Trojanowski, J. Q., Roberts, S. A., and Brooks, J. J. (1989). A detailed immunohistochemical analysis of cerebellar haemangioblastoma: an undifferentiated mesenchymal tumour. *Modern Pathology*, **2**, 638–51.

Frimodt-Møller, P. C., Nissen, H. M., and Dyreborg, U. (1981). Polycystic kidneys as renal lesion in Lindau disease. *Journal of Urology*, **125**, 868–70.

Gersell, D. J. and King, T. C. (1988). Papillary cystadenoma of the mesosalpinx in von Hippel–Lindau disease. *American Journal of Surgical Pathology*, **12**, 145–9.

Glavac, D., Neumann, H. P. H., Wittke, C., Jaenig, H., Masek, O., Streicher, T., *et al.* (1996). Mutations in the VHL tumor suppressor gene and associated lesions in families with von Hippel–Lindau disease from Central Europe. *Human Genetics*, **98**, 271–80.

Glenn, G. M., Daniel, L. N., Choyke, P., Linehan, W. M., Oldfield, E. A., Gorin, M. B., *et al.* (1991). von Hippel–Lindau disease distinct phenotypes suggest more than one mutant allele at the VHL locus. *Human Genetics*, **87**, 207–10.

Glenn, G. M., Linehan, W. M., Hosoe, S., Latif, F., Yao, M., Choyke, P., *et al.* (1992). Screening for von Hippel–Lindau disease by DNA polymorphism analysis. *Journal of the American Medical Association*, **267**, 1226–31.

Goodbody, R. A. and Gamlen, T. R. (1974). Cerebellar haemangioblastoma and genitourinary tumours. *Journal of Neurology, Neurosurgery, and Psychiatry*, **37**, 606–9.

Goodman, M. D., Kleinholz, J. G., and Peck, F. C. (1964). Lindau disease in the Hudson valley. *Journal of Neurosurgery*, **21**, 97–103.

Green, J. S., Bowmer, M. I., and Johnson, G. J. (1986). von Hippel–Lindau disease in a Newfoundland kindred. *Canadian Medical Association Journal*, **134**, 133–46.

Henkind, P. and Benjamin, J. V. (1976) Vascular anomalies and neoplasms of the optic nerve head. *Transactions of the Ophthalmologic Society of the United Kingdom*, **96**, 418–23.

Hoffman, R. W., Gardner, D. W., and Mitchell, F. L. (1982). Intrathoracic and multiple abdominal pheochromocytomas in von Hippel–Lindau disease. *Archieves of Internal Medicine*, **142**, 1962–4.

Horton, W. A., Wong, V., and Eldridge, R. (1976). von Hippel–Lindau disease. *Archives of Internal Medicine*, **136**, 769–77.

Hosoe, S., Brauch, H., Latif, F., Glenn, G., Daniel, L., Bale, S., *et al.* (1991). Localization of the von Hippel–Lindau disease gene to a small region of chromosome 3. *Genomics*, **8**, 634–40.

Hull, C. J. (1986). Phaeochromocytoma diagnosis, preoperative preparation and anaesthetic management. *British Journal of Anaesthesiology*, **58**, 1453–68.

Hull, M. T., Warfel, K. A., Muller, J., and Higgins, J. T. (1979). Familial islet cell tumours in von Hippel–Lindau disease. *Cancer*, **44**, 1523–6.

Ibrahim, R. E., Weinberg, D. S., and Weidner, N. (1989). Atypical cysts and carcinomas of the kidneys in the phacomatoses. *Cancer*, **63**, 148–57.

Isaac, F., Schoen, J., and Walker, P. (1956). Unusual case of Lindau disease, cystic disease of kidneys and pancreas with renal and cerebellar tumours. *American Journal of Radiology*, **75**, 912–20.

Jackson, H. (1872). A series of cases illustrative of cerebral pathology: Cases of intracranial tumours. *Medical Times* (London), **2**, 541–68.

Jennings, A. M., Smith, C., Cole, D. R., Jennings, C., Shortland, J. R., Williams, J. L., *et al.* (1988). von Hippel–Lindau disease in a large British family: clinicopathological features and recommendations for screening and follow-up. *Quarterly Journal of Medicine*, **251**, 233–49.

Kadir, S., Kerr, W. S., and Athanasoulis, C. A. (1981). The role of arteriography in the management of renal cell carcinoma aassociated with von Hippel–Lindau disease. *Journal of Urology*, **126**, 316–19.

Keeler, L. L. and Klauber, G. T. (1992). von Hippel–Lindau disease and renal cell carcinoma in a 16-year-old boy. *Journal of Urology*, **147**, 1588–91.

Kees, A. (1980). Malignes karzinoid und phäochromozytom bei von Hippel–Lindau'scher ekrankung. *Klinische Wochenschrift*, **92**, 218–21.

Kempermann, G., Neumann, H. P. H., Scheremet, R., Volk, B., Mann, W., Gilsbach, J., *et al.* (1996). Deafness due to bilateral endolymphatic sac tumours in a case of von Hippel–Lindau syndrome. *Journal of Neurology, Neurosurgery, and Psychiatry*, **61**, 318–20.

Kessler, P. M., Vasavada, S. P., Rackley, R. R., Stackhouse, T., Duh, F-M., Latif, F., *et al.* (1995). Expression of the von Hippel–Lindau tumor suppressor gene VHL in human fetal kidney and during mouse embryogenesis. *Molecular Medicine*, **1**, 457–66.

Korn, W. T., Schatzki, S. C., Disciullo, A. J., and Scully, R. E. (1990). Papillary cystadenoma of the broad ligament in von Hippel–Lindau disease. *American Journal of Obstetrics and Gynecology*, **163**, 596–8.

Kuzmin, I., Stackhouse, T., Latif, F., Duh, F-M., Geil, L., Gnarra, J., *et al.* (1994). One-megabase yeast artificial chromosome and 400-kilobase cosmid-phage contigs containing the von Hippel–Lindau tumor suppressor and CA (2+)-transporting adenosine triphosphatase isoform 2 genes. *Cancer Research*, **54**, 2486–91.

Kuzmin, I., Duh, F-M., Latif, F., Geil, L., Zbar, B., and Herman, M. I. (1995). Identification of the promoter of the human von Hippel–Lindau gene. *Oncogene*, **10**, 2185–94.

Lamiell, J. M., Salazar, F. G., and Hsia, Y. E. (1989). von Hippel–Lindau disease affecting 43 members of a single kindred. *Medicine* (Baltimore), **68**, 1–29.

Latif, F., Tory, K., Gnarra, J., Yao, M., Duh, F-M., Orcutt, M. L., *et al.* (1993). Identification of the von Hippel–Lindau disease tumor suppressor gene. *Science*, **260**, 1317–20.

Lee, K. R., Wulfsberg, E., and Fepes, J. J. (1977). Some important radiological aspects of the kidney in von Hippel–Lindau syndrome, the value of prospective study in an affected family. *Radiology*, **122**, 649–53.

Levine, E., Collins, D. L., Horton, W. A., and Schimke, R. N. (1982). Computed tomographic screening of the abdomen in von Hippel–Lindau disease. *American Journal of Radiology*, **139**, 505–10.

Lindau, A. (1926). Studien über Kleinhirnzysten. Bau, Pathogenese und Beziehungen zur Angiomatosis retinae. *Acta Pathologica et Microbiologica Scandinavica*, **Suppl. I**, 1–129.

Lo, W. W. M., Applegate, L. J., Carberry J. N., *et al.* (1993). Endolymphatic sac tumors: radiologic appearance. *Radiology*, **189**, 199–204.

Macrae, H. M. and Newigin, B. (1968). von Hippel–Lindau disease: a family history. *Canadian Journal of Ophthalmology*, **3**, 28–34.

Maher, E. R., Bentley, E., Yates, J. R. W., Barton, D., Jennings, A., Fellows, I. W., *et al.* (1990*a*). Mapping of von Hippel–Lindau disease to chromosome 3p confirmed by genetic linkage analysis. *Journal of Neurology Science*, **100**, 27–30.

Maher, E. R., Yates, J. R. W., Harries, R., Benjamin, C., Harris, R., Moore, A. T., *et al.* (1990*b*). Clinical features and natural history of von Hippel–Lindau disease. *Quarterly Journal of Medicine*, **283**, 1151–63.

Maher, E. R., Iselius, L., and Yates, J. R. W. (1991). von Hippel–Lindau disease: a genetic study. *Journal of Medical Genetics*, **28**, 443–7.

Malek, R. S. and Green, L. F. (1971). Urologic aspects of von Hippel–Lindau syndrome. *Journal of Urology*, **106**, 800–1.

Malek, R. S., Omess, P. J., Benson, R. C., and Zincke, H. (1987). Renal cell carcinoma in von Hippel–Lindau syndrome. *American Journal of Medicine*, **82**, 236–8.

Melmon, K. L. and Rosen, S. W. (1964). Lindau's disease: review of the literature and study of a large kindred. *American Journal of Medicine*, **36**, 595–617.

Miller, D. L., Choyke, P. L., Walther, M. M., Doppman, J. L., Kragel, P. J., Weiss, G. H., *et al.* (1991). von Hippel–Lindau disease: inadequacy of angiography for identification of renal cancers. *Radiology*, **179**, 833–6.

Møller, H. U. (1929). Familial angiomatosis retinae et cerebelli. Lindau's disease. *Acta Ophthalmologica*, **7**, 244.

Moore, A. T., Maher, E. R., Rosen, P., Gregor, Z., and Bird, A. C. (1991). Ophthalmological screening for von Hippel–Lindau disease. *Eye*, **5**, 1–5.

Mullin, E. M., DeVere White, R., Peterson, L. J., and Paulson, D. F. (1976). Bilateral renal carcinoma in von Hippel–Lindau disease. *Urology*, **8**, 475–8.

Neumann, H. P. H. (1987*a*). Basic criteria for clinical diagnosis and genetic counselling in von Hippel–Lindau syndrome. *Journal of Vascular Diseases*, **16**, 220–6.

Neumann, H. P. H. (1987*b*). Prognosis of von Hippel–Lindau syndrome. *Journal of Vascular Diseases*, **16**, 309–11.

Neumann, H. P. H., Eggert, H., Weigel, K., Friedburg, H., Wiestler, O. D., and Schollmeyer, P. (1989). Hemangioblastoma of the central nervous system: a ten-year study with special reference to von Hippel–Lindau syndrome. *Journal of Neurosurgery*, **70**, 23–30.

Neumann, H. P. H., Dinkel, E., Brambs, H. J., Wimmer, B., Friedburg, H., Volk, B., *et al.* (1991). Pancreatic lesions in the von Hippel–Lindau syndrome. *Gastroenterology*, **101**, 465–71.

Neumann, H. P. H. and Wiestler, O. D. (1991). Clustering of features of von Hippel–Lindau syndrome: evidence for a complex genetic locus. *Lancet*, **337**, 1052–4.

Neumann, H. P. H., Eggert, H. R., Scheremet, R., Schumacher, M., Mohadjer, M., Wakhloo, A. K., *et al.* (1992). Central nervous system lesions in von Hippel–Lindau syndrome. *Journal of Neurology, Neurosurgery, and Psychiatry*, **55**, 898–901.

Neumann, H. P. H., Berger, D. P., Sigmund, G., Blum, U., Schmidt, D., Parmer, R. J., *et al.* (1993). Pheochromocytomas, multiple endocrine neoplasia type 2 and von Hippel–Lindau disease. *New England Journal of Medicine*, **329**, 1531–8.

Neumann, H. P. H., Lips, C. J. M., Hsia, Y. E., and Zbar, B. (1995). von Hippel–Lindau syndrome. *Brain Pathology*, **5**, 181–93.

Neumann, H. P. H. and Zbar, B. (1997). Renal cysts, renal cancer, and von Hippel–Lindau disease. *Kidney International*. In press.

Novick, A. C. and Streem, S. B. (1992). Long-term follow-up after nephron-sparing surgery for renal cell carcinoma in von Hippel–Lindau disease. *Journal of Urology*, **147**, 1488–90.

Pearson, J. C., Weiss, J., and Tanagho, E. A. (1980). A plea for conservation of kidney in renal adenocarcinoma associated with von Hippel–Lindau disease. *Journal of Urology*, **124**, 910–12.

Pericak-Vance, M. A., Nunes, K. J., Whisenant, E., Loeb, D. B., and Small, K. W. (1993). Genetic mapping of dinucleotide repeat polymorphisms and von Hippel–Lindau disease on chromosome 3p25–26. *Journal of Medical Genetics*, **30**, 487–91.

Peterson, G. J., Codd, J. E., Cuddihee, R. E., and Newton, W. T. (1977). Renal transplantation in von Hippel–Lindau disease. *Archives of Surgery*, **112**, 841–2.

Poston, C. D., Jaffe, G. S., Lubensky, I. A., Solomon, D., Zbar, B., Linehan, W. M., *et al.* (1995). Characterization of the renal pathology of a familial form of renal cell carcinoma associated with von Hippel–Lindau disease: Clinical and molecular genetic implications. *Journal of Urology*, **153**, 22–6.

Resche, F., Moisan, J. P., Mantoura, J., De Kersaint-Hilly, A., André, M. J., Perrin-Resche, I., *et al.* (1993). Haemangioblastoma, haemangioblastomatosis and von Hippel–Lindau disease. *Advances of Technical Standards of Neurosurgery*, **20**, 197–304.

Ridley, M., Green, J., and Johnson, G. (1986). Retinal angiomatosis: the ocular manifestations of von Hippel–Lindau disease. *Canadian Journal of Ophthalmology*, 21, 276–83.

Sato, Y., Waziri, M., Smith, W., Frey, E., Yuh, W. T. C., Hanson, J., *et al.* (1988). von Hippel–Lindau disease: MR imaging. *Radiology*, 166, 241–6.

Seizinger, B. R., Rouleau, G. A., Ozelius, L. J., Lane, A. H., Farmer, G. E., Lamiell, J. M., *et al.* (1988). von Hippel–Lindau disease maps to the region of chromosome 3 associated with renal cell carcinoma. *Nature*, 332, 268–9.

Seizinger, B. R., Smith, D. I., Filling-Katz, M. R., Neumann, H. P. H., Green, J. S., Choyke, P. L., *et al.* (1991). Genetic flanking markers refine diagnostic criteria and provide insights into the genetics of von Hippel–Lindau disease. *Proceedings of the North Atlantic Academy of Science*, 88, 2864–8.

Shapiro, B., Copp, J. E., Sisson, J. C., Eyre, P. L., Wallis, J., and Beierwaltcs, W. H. (1985). Iodine-131 metaiodobenzylguanidine for the locating of suspected phaeochromocytoma: experience in 400 cases. *Journal of Nuclear Medicine*, 26, 576–85.

Siemeister, G., Weindel, K., Mohrs, K., Barleon, B., Martiny-Baron, G., and Marme, D. (1996). Reversion of deregulated expression of vascular endothelial growth factor in human renal carcinoma cells by von Hippel–Lindau tumor suppressor protein. *Cancer Research*, 56, 2299–301.

Solomon, D. and Schwartz, A. (1988). Renal pathology in von Hippel–Lindau disease. *Human Pathology*, 19, 1072–9.

Spencer, W. F., Novick, A. C., Montie, J. E., Streem, S. B., and Levin, H. S. (1988). Surgical treatment of localized renal cell carcinoma in von Hippel–Lindau disease. *Journal of Urology*, 139, 507–9.

Statement of the American Society of Clinical Oncology: Genetic testing for cancer susceptibility. (1996) *Journal Clinical Oncology*, 14, 1730–6.

Steinbach, F., Novik, A. C., Zincke, H., Miller, D. P., Williams, R. D., Lund, G., *et al.* (1995). Treatment of renal cell carcinoma in von Hippel–Lindau disease: a multicenter study. *Journal of Urology*, 153, 1812–16.

Tory, K., Brauch, H., Linehan, M., Barba, D., Oldfield, E., Filling-Katz, M., *et al.* (1989). Specific genetic change in tumours associated with von Hippel–Lindau disease. *Journal of North Atlantic Cancer Institute*, 81, 1097–101.

Tsuda, H., Fukushima, S., Tokakashi, M., Hikosaka, Y., and Hayashi, K. (1976). Familial bilateral papillary cystadenoma of the epididymis: report of 3 cases in siblings. *Cancer*, 37, 1831–9.

Vance, J. M., Small, K. W., Jones, M. A., Stajich, J. M., Yamaoka, L. H., Roses, A. D., *et al.* (1990). Confirmation of linkage in von Hippel–Lindau disease. *Genomics*, 6, 565–7.

von Hippel, E. (1904). Über eine sehr seltene Erkrankung der Netzhaut. *Albrecht von Graefes Archiv der Ophthalmologie*, 59, 83–6.

von Hippel, E. (1911). Die anatomische Grundlage der von mir beschriebenen 'sehr seltenen Erkrankung der Netzhaut'. *Albrecht von Graefes Archiv der Ophthalmologie*, 79, 350–77.

Wagle, D. G. and Scal, D. R. (1970). Renal cell carcinoma—review of 256 cases. *Journal of Surgery and Oncology*, 2, 23–32.

Warnick, S. (1993). Dealing with brain tumors. *VHL Family Forum*, 1, 10–11.

Welch, R. B. (1977). Fluorescein angiography in sickle-cell retinopathy and von Hippel–Lindau disease. *Ophthalmology Clin.*, 17, 137–54.

Witten, F. R., O'Brien III, D. P., Sewell, C. W., and Wheatley, J. K. (1985). Bilateral clear-cell papillary cystadenoma of the epididymides presenting as infertility: an early manifestation of von Hippel–Lindau syndrome. *Journal of Urology*, 133, 1062–4.

Wizigmann-Voos, S., Brier, G., Risau, W., and Plate, K. H. (1995). Up-regulation of vascular endothelial growth factor and its receptors in von Hippel–Lindau disease-associated and sporadic hemangioblastomas. *Cancer Research*, 55, 1358–64.

Yao, M., Latif, F., Orcutt, M. L., Kuzmin, I., Stackhouse, T., Zhou, F. W., *et al.* (1993). von Hippel–Lindau disease: identification of deletion mutations by pulsed-field gel electrophoresis. *Human Genetics*, **92**, 605–14.

Zbar, B., Kishida, T., Chen, F., Schmidt, L., Maher, A. R., Richards, F. M., *et al.* (1996). Germline mutations in the von Hippel–Lindau disease (VHL) gene in families from North America, Europe, and Japan. *Human Mutation*, **8**, 348–57.

27

Wilms' tumour

Christopher D. Mitchell

Introduction and definition

Wilms' tumour, the most common genito–urinary malignancy of childhood, is a triphasic embryonal neoplasm consisting of varying proportions of blastema, stroma, and epithelium. It develops from proliferation of the metanephric blastema, possibly in the absence of normal stimulation from the metanephric ducts, to produce differentiated tubules and glomeruli. Although the specific histological appearance was described by Max Wilms in 1899, the eponym is now loosely applied to virtually any malignant tumour arising in the kidney in childhood, some of which are pathologically, clinically, and probably genetically distinct.

Embryology

Some knowledge of renal embryology will aid in understanding some of the complexities of histological classification of childhood renal tumours; it will also provide a framework for understanding the genetic processes at work during renal development.

Three successive renal systems, the first two of which are vestigial, develop in man (Fitzgerald 1994). The first is the pronephros which, save for the caudal end of the pronephric duct, disappears at about 30 days gestation. The second vestigial system, the mesonephros, appears as the pronephros regresses. Renal tubules are formed in intermediate mesoderm in the thoraco-lumbar region and are invaginated by capillary tufts developing *in situ*. The distal ends of the tubules open into the persisting, caudal end of the pronephric duct, now referred to as the mesonephric duct. The third and final renal system arises as the ureteric bud develops from the dorsal aspect of the mesonephric duct, close to its point of entry into the cloaca. The bud extends into the intermediate mesoderm behind the lower end of the mesonephros and this stalk then acquires a lumen, forming a ureter. The lumen invades the advancing bud and, at its cephalic end, dilates to form a renal pelvis. Adjacent cells in the intermediate mesoderm then multiply to form a metanephric 'cap' of blastema which invests the invaginated ureteric bud around the pelvis. The cells of the ureteric bud divide, forming in turn first the major and minor calyces, then the collecting tubules, and finally the nephrons. This wave of differentiation spreads outward into the metanephric cap. Contact between blastema and ducts seems critical to this orderly succession of events.

Epidemiology

The annual incidence of Wilms' tumour is around eight per million children under the age of 15 years. There are both racial and regional variations in incidence, so that the previously held view

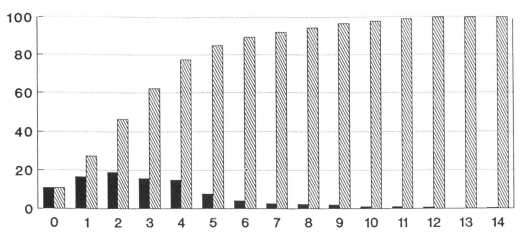

Fig. 27.1 Proportion of Wilms' tumour cases diagnosed per year of life (United Kingdom Child Cancer Study Group data, 361 cases, absolute numbers of cases for each year are given at the top of each bar).

that the incidence was constant throughout the world (the 'index' tumour) is not correct (Parkin *et al.* 1988). The risk of developing Wilms' tumour is approximately one in 10 000 live births. The tumour accounts for about 8% of childhood malignancies so, in incidence, ranks fifth among the solid tumours of childhood, after central nervous system tumours, lymphoma, neuroblastoma, and soft-tissue sarcoma. The tumour occurs with equal frequency in boys and girls, with a peak incidence in the third year. Although very rare in the neonatal period (Hrabovsky *et al.* 1986), over 75% of children affected are under four years of age and at least 90% under seven years at diagnosis Barnes, personal communication; Breslow and Beckwith 1982 (Fig. 27.1), with only a very few being diagnosed after the age of 11 years.

Genetics

The initial clues to the location within the human genome of the Wilms' tumour gene came from the study of patients with other phenotypic abnormalities which were frequently associated with the subsequent development of the tumour. Various congenital abnormalities—most frequently genito-urinary anomalies, aniridia, and mental retardation—are associated with Wilms' tumour. Aniridia may be familial (two-thirds of cases) or sporadic (one-third of cases) (McKusick 1986). Wilms' tumour, however, is associated almost exclusively with the sporadic form. The incidence of aniridia in the general population is about one in 50 000; in contrast, the incidence among children with Wilms' tumour has been reported to be as much as one in 73 (Miller *et al.* 1964), a 700-fold excess risk. When genito-urinary anomalies and mental retardation occur together, the syndrome is known as the AGR (aniridia–genitourinary–retardation) triad (Riccardi *et al.* 1978; Francke *et al.* 1979). This triad is an example of a contiguous gene syndrome and was of great importance in the isolation of the WT1 gene as affected patients have approximately a 50% risk of developing Wilms' tumour (Narahara *et al.* 1984).

It is important to differentiate between those cytogenetic changes detectable in somatic cells, the most accessible of which are lymphocytes, and those seen in tumour cells. While changes in somatic cells indicate the approximate location of genes whose mutation results in predisposition to a malignancy, changes in tumour cells may reflect mutations subsequent to the initiating mutation that contribute to tumour progression. Virtually all of the AGR group of patients have a deletion affecting the short arm of chromosome 11, which is visible in cytological preparations. Although the precise extent of each deletion varies, the 11p13 region is always involved. These observations suggest the presence of a gene whose deletion or other mutation results in Wilms' tumour, and place both this gene and that for sporadic aniridia in the same subregion of 11p13 (see Cowell *et al.* 1989 for review).

Additional evidence of a locus important in the genesis of Wilms' tumour comes from observations on loss of heterozygosity. The two-mutation hypothesis of cancer (Knudson 1971) predicts that a number of malignancies—chiefly the childhood embryonal ones—arise as the result of two rate-limiting mutations. The presence of a visible chromosome deletion in a small number of children with Wilms' tumour has prompted the suggestion that the deletion constitutes the first mutation. Any mutation affecting the homologous allele would lead to the complete inactivation of the hypothetical Wilms' gene, and might result in the development of malignancy. These hypothese were strengthened by the outcome of experimental observations in retinoblastoma (see Cowell 1989 for review). The principle of these experiments is that DNA probes, which detect unique sites within the human genome, may be used to find variations in the length of DNA fragments produced when genomic DNA is subjected to digestion by restriction enzymes. Such polymorphic variations arise as the normal and continuing process of mutation generates or removes sites of recognition of restriction enzymes. These so-called restriction fragment-length polymorphisms are inherited in a straightforward Mendelian fashion. If an individual is heterozygous for a particular probe—that is, has a different fragment length from each allele—one can distinguish the maternally and paternally derived chromosomes. With these techniques, it has been shown that the majority of Wilms' tumours in patients who are heterozygous for DNA markers on the short arm of chromosome 11 appear to have lost one allele, resulting in homo- or hemizygosity (Fearon *et al.* 1984; Koufos *et al.* 1984; Orkin *et al.* 1984). The mechanisms by which such a loss of heterozygosity could occur are shown in Fig. 27.2. In view of the 'two-mutation' hypothesis advanced by Knudson (1971), it is of interest that the mean age of onset of bilateral Wilms' tumour is significantly lower than that of the unilateral (Breslow and Beckwith 1982). One implication of this finding is that bilateral cases may have inherited a predisposing germline mutation from an unaffected parent, as is found in retinoblastoma, where up to 40% of cases are familial, and where transmission of predisposing germline mutations has been confirmed (Dunn *et al.* 1988; Zhu *et al.* 1989).

The precise order of the genes within the chromosome 11p13 region was indicated in a patient with a 'visible' deletion associated with Wilms' tumour, mental retardation, and genito-urinary abnormalities, but not aniridia (Turleau *et al.* 1984*a*). The chromosomal abnormality was del (11)(p11p13) with the distal breakpoint in the distal part of the p13 band. Thus, the aniridia locus lies distal to that for Wilms' tumour, probably between 11p13.3 and 11p13.6. Other genes in the 11p13 region are for catalase (Junien *et al.* 1980) and the β subunit of follicle-stimulating hormone (FSH) (Glaser *et al.* 1986). The probable gene order is centromere–catalase–Wilms'–aniridia–FSHb–telomere (Turleau *et al.* 1984*b*; Levis *et al.* 1985; Porteous *et al.* 1987; Cowell *et al.* 1989). The presence in the 11p13 region of other genes important in genito-urinary development may be inferred from the various genito-urinary abnormalities seen in association with Wilms' tumour, and the finding of a t(11; 2) (p13; p11) in a stillborn fetus with Potter's syndrome (Porteous *et al.* 1987). Chromosome translocation breakpoints that lie near the Wilms' tumour locus (Simola *et al.* 1983; Lewis *et al.* 1985; Boehm *et al.* 1988) were important in strategies

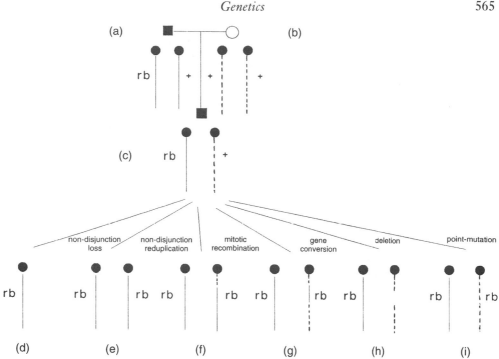

Fig. 27.2 Inactivation of homologous alleles. In (a), both chromosomes 11 are depicted by dotted lines and carry the wild-type gene at the presumed Wilms' tumour locus. In (b), one of these genes has undergone an inactivating mutation, in this instance by point-mutation of a single base. The chromosome bearing the mutation is depicted by a solid line. In (c) to (h) are depicted the mechanisms by which a second mutation can result in inactivation of the homologous locus on the normal chromosome. In (c), mitotic non-disjunction results in hemizygosity for all loci, whereas in (d) there has been reduplication of the abnormal chromosome resulting in homozygosity for all loci. Mitotic recombination (e) and gene conversion (f) result in homozygosity over short distances of the chromosome. An interstitial deletion, (g), results in hemizygosity for a few loci. A second pointmutation inactivates only the remaining normal Wilms' tumour locus (h).

designed for cloning the gene responsible for Wilms' tumourigenesis (Bickmore *et al.* 1988). Figure 27.3 indicates the extent of some of the deletions reported in Wilms'–AGR patients.

These strategies led to the cloning of aniridia-associated chromosome breakpoints and the location of a candidate gene for sporadic aniridia (Gessler *et al.* 1989), which has subsequently been identified as a human homologue of the mouse gene PAX-6 (Ton *et al.* 1991), and in 1990, the isolation of a candidate WT1 gene (Call *et al.* 1990; Gessler *et al.* 1990). Evidence that the WT1 gene was involved in Wilms' tumourigenesis came from the finding that mutations within WT1 were associated with genito-urinary abnormalities and hereditary Wilms' tumours (Pelletier *et al.* 1991*a*), that there were mutations of the retained WT1 homologue in the tumours of patients with the WAGR syndrome (Baird *et al.* 1992), and homozygous WT1 point mutations in sporadic unilateral Wilms' tumours (Coppes *et al.* 1993*b*). It should be noted though, that not all Wilms' tumours contain mutated copies of WT1 (Little *et al.* 1993; Varanesi *et al.* 1994), even when heterozygosity for chromosome region 11p13 has been lost (Cowell *et al.* 1993), suggesting that other genetic loci may be important.

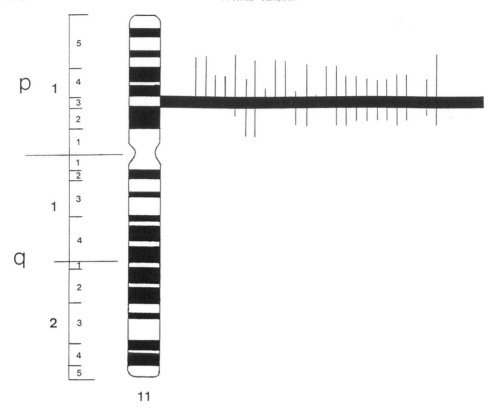

Fig. 27.3 Extent of chromosome 11 deletions in AGR patients. Chromosome 11 is shown on the left of the figure; deletions are indicated by the vertical bars on the right. The common region of overlap is shown by the solid horizontal line. Many of the deletions end within this region.

The WT1 gene is encoded by 10 exons; the messenger RNA is the result of a complex pattern of alternative splicing (Haber *et al.* 1991). The WT1 protein is 45–49 kd in size. It contains functional domains that indicate transcriptional regulatory activity but the identity of the genes controlled by WT1 during development remain unknown. Nevertheless, it is known that in reconstitution experiments, transient high expression of WT1 results in the suppression of activity of growth-inducing genes such as early growth response-1 (EGR-1), insulin-like growth factor-II (IGF2), and the A-chain of platelet-derived growth factor (PDGFA) (Rauscher 1993). In addition, WT1 has recently been found to form a complex with p53 protein, an association which enhances the transcriptional repression possessed by WT1 (Mahaswaran *et al.* 1993).

Other tumour suppresser genes, such as p53 or RB1, are expressed ubiquitously; in contrast, WT1 has a very restricted pattern of expression. During normal differentiation, WT1 expression is limited to condensing mesenchyme, renal vesicles, and glomerular epithelium. Expression of WT1 within the kidney peaks at about the time of birth and then declines rapidly as the organ achieves its finally differentiated form (Pritchard-Jones *et al.* 1990; Buckler *et al.* 1991). The regions of expression are all thought to the sites of origin of Wilms' tumour. This differentiation-related expression in the kidney contrasts with the continuous expression seen in mesothelial cells, Sertoli cells of the testis, and granulosa cells of the ovary (Pelletier *et al.* 1991*b*).

Table 27.1 Incidence of associated anomalies in Wilms' tumour patients

All genito-urinary abnormalities	2.6%
Hemihypertrophy	2.5%
Aniridia	0.68%
Beckwith–Wiedemann syndrome	0.21%

There are, in addition, a number of other disorders which are also associated, such as Beckwith–Wiedemann syndrome (see below) (Beckwith 1963; Wiedemann 1964), Denys–Drash syndrome (Denys *et al.* 1967; Drash *et al.* 1970), and Perlman syndrome (Perlman *et al.* 1973; 1974). The isolation of the WT1 gene and discovery of other molecular features has improved our understanding of the predisposition posed by these latter three syndromes (Table 27.1)

The classical transforming oncogenes such as *ras* or *myc* acquire their oncogenic ability as the result of activating mutations which, phenotypically, are dominant. The antioncogenes in their wild-type state suppress malignancy; inactivating mutations result in loss of suppressing activity so that malignancy can then develop. As a single normal allele is sufficient to provide continued normal cellular function, it follows that both alleles must be inactivated and that, phenotypically, these mutations are recessive. In the case of retinoblastoma, mutations within the RB1 gene, while causing malignancy, do not result in an extended phenotype. Children with small, cytogenetically visible deletions may well be phenotypically normal apart from their tumours. Some mutations in WT1, however, appear to be dominant and to cause an extended phenotype very different to that seen in patients with the AGR triad. The Denys–Drash syndrome (Denys *et al.* 1967; Drash *et al.* 1970) consists of male pseudohermaphroditism, mesangial sclerosis of specific appearance (Habib *et al.* 1985), and Wilms' tumour. The diagnosis may be made in the presence of the second feature alone (Jadresic *et al.* 1988; 1990). As a group, these patients develop Wilms' tumours earlier in life than is the case in patients without the syndrome, and at a rate compatible with the presence of one predisposing mutation of the two required for tumour development (Mitchell, unpublished observations), a situation reminiscent of that arising in bilateral retinoblastoma.

Following the isolation of the WT1 gene, intragenic mutations affecting one allele were found in a group of 10 patients with the Denys–Drash syndrome. In nine of the cases, the mutations lay within exon 9 (zinc finger III) and in the remaining case in exon 8 (zinc finger II). Wilms' tumours from three of the patients and a granulosa cell tumour from a further patient all showed reduction to homozygosity for the mutation-bearing WT1 allele. Analysis of two families confirmed that the mutations had arisen *de novo* in the affected individuals (Pelletier *et al.* 1991*c*). Further examples of mutations within WT1, usually point mutations in exon 9, have since been described in Denys–Drash syndrome patients (Baird *et al.* 1992; Coppes *et al.* 1993*a*).

It has already been noted that not all sporadic Wilms' tumours contain mutations within WT1 are homozygous within sporadic Wilms' tumours. This observation suggests that there may be other genetic loci of importance in Wilms' tumourigenesis, and that, at a genetic level, Wilms' tumour is a heterogeneous disorder, quite unlike retinoblastoma. The existence of genetic loci other than that on chromosome region 11p13 is supported by several other lines of evidence, including chromosome studies of tumours, extended observations on loss of heterozygosity, and family studies.

If a mutant gene lying in the chromosome region 11p13 predisposes to Wilms' tumour, then karyotypic abnormalities of the same region should be evident in sporadic cases of the tumour unassociated with the AGR triad. Several reports have confirmed this conjecture. Kaneko *et al.* (1983) describe a patient with a normal constitutional karyotype in whose tumour a deletion of 11p13 was the only chromosomal abnormality. In two other patients. however, both copies of chromosome 11 were normal but there were translocations involving chromosome 1 and 16. One of nine patients reported by Kondo *et al.* (1984) and six of 14 patients reported by Douglass *et al.* (1985) had 11p abnormalities. In Douglass' study, there were simple deletions as well as others resulting from complex chromosomal translocations. Slater and De Kraker (1982) reported 1p abnormalities in three of 11 tumours and, in a later review (Slater *et al.* 1985), reported that 11p deletions were the most common abnormalities, being found in 13 of 38 tumours. The next most commonly involved region was 1q; chromosome 16 was also frequently involved. In the largest single series (Solis *et al.* 1988), rearrangements involving chromosome 1 were the most common, occurring in five of 20 tumours, followed by abnormalities of chromosomes 7 and 16; only two tumours had rearrangements involving region 11p. Thus, although chromosome region 11p13 is involved at a cytogenetic level, abnormalities are also noted in a number of other locations, principally 16q and 1p. The case for a locus within chromosome region 16q has been further strengthened by the finding of loss of heterozygosity for markers that lie in this region (Coppes *et al.* 1992, Maw *et al.* 1992). Abnormalities of chromosome 1 are frequently seen in a variety of tumours and so this finding may be non-specific.

The phenomenon of loss of heterozygosity and its occurrence within the chromosome region 11p13 has already been mentioned. In some patients, the distance over which heterozygosity has been lost is restricted to 11p13 although in others it covers most of the short arm of the chromosome. There is also a group of patients in whom the phenomenon is restricted to the 11p15 region (Wadey *et al.* 1990; Coppes *et al.* 1992). This locus has now been designated WT2. At this point an explanation of genomic imprinting and its relevance to Wilms' tumour is necessary.

During the process that leads to loss of heterozygosity there is, theoretically, an equal chance of the allele of chromosome 11 retained in the tumour being of either maternal or paternal origin. However, it appears that the maternal allele is consistently lost from Wilms' tumours, with persistence of the paternal allele (Schroeder *et al.* 1987; Williams *et al.* 1989; Pal *et al.*, personal communication). By inference, therefore, it is the paternal allele that bears the initiating mutation. These findings suggest the presence of genomic imprinting, an epigenetic phenomenon whereby expression of genes is dependent on their parental origin. It has, for example, been proposed that the maternal genome largely determines embryonic development, whereas the paternal genome largely determines development of the extraembryonic tissues (Hall 1990).

A model, based on the phenomenon of genomic imprinting that accounts for this observation and the suggestion that Wilms' tumour arises as a result of only two rate-limiting steps has been proposed by Wilkins (1988). This hypothesis suggests that Wilm's tumour arises from the faulty interaction of two pairs of genes—a Wilms' regulatory gene pair and a 'transforming' gene pair. Imprinting would normally inactivate the transforming gene on the maternally derived copy of chromosome 11, leaving active the paternally derived homologue. In normal cells the transforming gene is then suppressed by the Wilms' regulatory genes. If the maternal copy of the Wilms' regulatory gene is inactivated by mutation, followed by loss of the paternal homologue of chromosome 11, then the activity of the remaining maternal copy of the transforming gene will remain low because it is imprinted. Conversely, if the paternal copy of the Wilms' regulatory gene is inactivated, followed by loss of the maternal homologue, then the remaining paternally-derived transforming gene will be expressed at high level.

The link between 11p15 region and Wilms' tumour noted above is further strengthened by its association with Beckwith–Wiedemann syndrome (BWS), which is characterized by viscerome-galy, macroglossia, hyperinsulinaemic hypoglycaemia, and a predisposition to a number of different malignancies, including Wilms' tumour (Beckwith 1963; Wiedemann 1964). In some patients the overgrowth is asymmetrical, which is recognizable clinically as hemihypertrophy. A few patients with BWS have been found to have a duplication of part of the short arm of chromosome 11, resulting in triplication of the 11p15 region (Waziri *et al.* 1983; Pueschel and Padre-Mendoza 1984; Turleau *et al.* 1984*c*). The majority of patients have two grossly normal copies of chromosome 11, but both of these copies are paternally derived, a phenomenon termed 'uniparental isodisomy'. In patients with triplication of 11p15, two of the copies are paternal in origin (Grundy *et al.* 1991; Henry *et al.* 1991). These observations suggest that the gene respon-sible for BWS is one which normally is expressed only by the paternal allele. Where both copies of the gene are paternally derived there is double the normal level of expression and the result is the overgrowth that characterizes the syndrome. Thus, BWS is an example of a condition caused by inappropriate inheritance of genes which are subject to genomic imprinting. Genetic linkage studies in the rare families with Beckwith–Wiedemann syndrome also indicate that the locus for the condition lies in the chromosome region 11p15 (Koufos *et al.* 1989; Ping *et al.* 1989).

Insulin-like growth factor II (IGF2) is an obvious candidate gene because of its location at chromosome region 11p15, because it is subject to imprinting with expression restricted to the paternal allele, and because it is overexpressed in Wilms' tumours as a consequence of expression from both alleles (Reeve *et al.* 1985; Scott *et al.* 1985; Ogawa *et al.* 1993; Ranier *et al.* 1993).

Perlman syndrome is another, although very rare, condition that constitutes a predisposition to Wilms' tumour. Only 11 children with the condition have been reported in the world literature. A further three cases have been seen at the Hospital for Sick Children in London (Grundy *et al.*, personal communication). Superficially, there is a resemblance to Beckwith–Wiedemann syndrome, but the two conditions are distinct (Grundy *et al.* 1992). Perlman syndrome is characterized by fetal gigantism, high mortality rate in early life, a distinctive facial appearance, mental retardation, and genito-urinary abnormalities, including a high risk of devel-oping Wilms' tumour. The syndrome was first recognized as an association between bilateral metanephric hamartomas and nephroblastomatosis in two siblings ((Liban and Kozenitsky 1970). Subsequently, similarly affected siblings, one of whom had Wilms' tumour, were reported (Perlman *et al.* 1973; 1974; Neri *et al.* 1984; Greenberg *et al.* 1986; Perlman 1986; Hamel *et al.* 1989). The facial appearance is very characteristic and quite distinct from that seen in Wiede-man–Beckwith syndrome. The features include deep-set eyes, a small, short nose with depressed nasal bridge, an inverted V-shaped upper lip, and low-set ears. There is macrocephaly, macro-somia, nephromegaly, hepatomegaly, and islet-cell hyperplasia. The neonatal death rate is high (10/14 cases). All four children who survived the neonatal period developed Wilms' tumour, which was bilateral in three of the cases, and a Wilms' tumour was found at autopsy in a fifth patient who died at the age of four days. Nephroblastomatosis has been noted in the majority of Perlman syndrome patients and Wilms' tumour is the only associated malignancy reported so far.

Although Perlman syndrome clearly constitutes a strong predisposition to Wilms' tumour, no cytogenetic or molecular data have yet been reported which indicate the basis of the predisposition.

Despite speculation to the contrary, the incidence of familial Wilms' tumour is extremely low. The United Kingdom Children's Cancer Study Group has found only one family with clear-cut Mendelian-dominant inheritance—three patients out of 670 on record (Barnes, personal

Table 27.2 Frequency of presenting symptoms (data from the first United Kingdom Wilms' tumour study)

Abdominal mass	74%
Fever	1%
Pain	44%

communication). The first National Wilms' tumour study, in North America, reported 20 patients (1%) with one or more relatives affected by the tumour. However, in only one case had a parent been affected and in only seven had a sibling been affected (Breslow and Beckwith 1982). Only one patient developed bilateral tumours. The vast majority of Wilms' tumours are, therefore, sporadic.

Although the occurrence of familial Wilms' tumour is extremely rare, it has been possible to perform linkage studies in a few large affected families and demonstrate that the predisposition is not linked to markers within either chromosome region 11p13 or 11p15 (Grundy *et al.* 1988; Huff *et al.* 1988) not to the locus on chromosome region 16q (Huff *et al.* 1992). The location of the familial locus remains unknown.

Clinical features

Most children with Wilms' tumour are well and present only because they have an abdominal mass detected by a parent or other person. Symptoms such as abdominal pain, haematuria, and fever do occur (Ledlie *et al.* 1970; Barnes, personal communication) (Table 27.2) but generally the contrast with the clinical picture of abdominal neuroblastoma, the major differential diagnosis, is marked. Physical examination should include a search for the stigmata of the various associated conditions, such as hemihypertrophy, Beckwith–Wiedemann syndrome, genital abnormalities, and aniridia. Hypertension, which may arise from excessive renin production, vascular compression by the tumour, or as part of pre-existing renal disease, occurs in a few patients and may be sufficiently severe to require treatment. The blood pressure must, therefore, be measured. Abdominal examination reveals a smooth, rounded, or lobulated mass arising in the loin; it may be possible to feel the attached normal kidney. The mass is usually ballotable and does not move with respiration, thus allowing distinction from liver or spleen. The previously held view that abdominal examination should not be repeated for fear of tumour rupture or tumour emboli is unfounded. Any metastases present at diagnosis—usually pulmonary—will only rarely be detected by clinical examination.

Investigations

The objectives of investigation are to confirm the diagnosis, delineate the extent of the tumour, determine that the contralateral kidney is functional, discover any metastases, and ensure that the child is fit enough to undergo anaesthesia and surgery.

A blood count may detect anaemia resulting from haemorrhage into the tumour; there may also be thrombocytosis in response to haemorrhage. Urinalysis, particularly for protein, and measurement of serum electrolytes, urea, and creatinine should detect any gross abnormalities of renal function. A 'spot' estimation of vanilmandelic acid (VMA) is essential to exclude neuroblastoma, especially in hypertensive children, if immediate surgery is contemplated. No imaging technique can exclude neuroblastoma with complete accuracy, and some are intrarenal. There are two reasons for taking care to exclude the diagnosis of neuroblastoma: first, immediate surgery may not then be appropriate; and second, catecholamine-secreting tumours pose particular anaesthetic problems, which should be recognized pre-operatively.

An abdominal ultrasound scan is the imaging investigation of choice for determining the organ of origin, the extent of any spread within the abdomen, the patency of the inferior vena cava, and for detecting any involved lymph nodes. It is important to know that the contralateral kidney is functioning adequately before surgery. Patients with a solitary functioning kidney will require 'individual' management akin to that for patients with bilateral tumours, usually with primary chemotherapy and delayed surgery in an attempt to preserve the maximum of functioning nephrons. Conventionally, function has been assessed by intravenous urography, which can delineate the inferior vena cava (although not distinguish compression from invasion) and also provides good images for planning any subsequent radiotherapy. A dimercaptosuccinic acid (DMSA) scan is an alternative. Some radiologists and urologists hold the view that normal renal size and indices of renal function are sufficient to exclude a non-functioning contralateral kidney. Those centres able to scan the chest by computed axial tomography may use the excretion of contrast at the end of that examination as an indication of function of the contralateral kidney.

Posteroanterior and lateral chest radiographs are mandatory in the exclusion of pulmonary metastases. The place of computed tomography for the detection of pulmonary metastases in Wilms' tumour is not yet established. It seems reasonable to use the most sensitive technique in the search for metastatic disease, but it is not yet clear that the increase in sensitivity will significantly improve the outcome. A report by the United Kingdom Children's Cancer Study Group showed that a number of patients have metastases detected by computed tomography that are not found by conventional radiography (31 out of 142), and that just over 25% of these patients will relapse (7 out of 31). However, relapses were commoner in patients who were otherwise stage I than those who were stages II–V. Overall, four of the seven patients were salvaged using second-line treatment (including two of three stage I patients) (Owens *et al.* 1995). These data suggest that the majority of higher stage patients will have their pulmonary disease adequately treated by their stage-appropriate chemotherapy and should not have their initial treatment intensified. A North American study found pulmonary disease by scanning but not by conventional radiography in 11 of 124 children (Wilimas *et al.* 1988), but there was no significant difference in the relapse rate between that small group and the larger number of patients whose lung lesions could be seen on ordinary radiography.

Postoperatively, other imaging investigations may be indicated by specific histological findings. A ^{99}Tc bone scan is indicated after the diagnosis of the so-called 'bone-metastasizing renal tumour' (also called clear–cell sarcoma; see below). An additional radiological survey of the skeleton is unnecessary. In rhabdoid Wilms' tumour a CT scan of the head should be done to exclude the presence of an intracranial second tumour (Bonnin *et al.* 1984).

Prognostic features

It is important to acknowledge that prognostic factors arise as an artefact of treatment regimens. If treatment was uniformly successful, or a disease uniformly fatal, there would be no prognostic factors. In Wilms' tumour the recognition of prognostic factors has allowed the stratification of treatment, thus enabling the direction of intensive treatment to patients with 'bad risk' disease and the refinement of treatment for patients with 'good risk' disease. The most important prognostic factors in Wilms' tumour are histological appearance and stage (Breslow *et al.* 1978; 1985; 1986), features first delineated by the series of national Wilms' tumour studies conducted in North America.

Pathology

Two broad groups of tumours may be recognized by their histological appearances; by far the larger group has 'favourable' appearances (see Beckwith 1986 for review).

Favourable histology

The major proportion of the favourable group consists of classical triphasic tumours, in which epithelial, blastemal, and stromal elements are all present. There is debate about the origin of the stromal elements which may be a true component of the tumour but could be a proliferation of normal vascular and connective tissue caused by the proximity of malignant cells. The occasional finding of an undifferentiated sarcomatous stroma weighs against the latter suggestion. The presence of such a stroma is not itself a sign of poor prognosis. Some triphasic tumours may have rhabdomyoblastic differentiation, such that the cells resemble fetal rhabdomyoblasts, often with cross-striations. This appearance is not unfavourable but it must not be confused with the 'malignant rhabdoid tumour of the kidney' which is a variant with poor prognosis (see below). Another form of triphasic Wilms' tumour that may not have such a favourable outlook has infiltrating tongues of tumour growing in vessels (Malone and Risdon, personal communication). At present, this observation appears restricted to stage I (see below) tumours. The monomorphic epithelial variant, usually found in children less than one year of age, is easily recognized as it appears to consist entirely of primitive tubules. This appearance has a very favourable prognosis.

Unfavourable histology

Anaplasia is an unfavourable feature occasionally observed in triphasic tumours where it is characterized by large (>4 times normal) hyperchromatic nuclei, an increased nuclear: cytoplasmic ratio, and abnormal (e.g. tripolar) mitoses. Anaplasia in Wilms' tumour is often a patchy, focal change which may escape notice unless a deliberate search is made, including widespread sampling, with blocks cut every centimetre across the widest diameter of the tumour. The appearances are often best recognized by scanning the slide at low power. Anaplasia is the only unfavourably type of appearance seen in tumours developing in the setting of one of the predisposing syndromes such as aniridia.

The major unfavourable histological types are probably distinct tumours rather than true variants of Wilms' tumour. The bone-metastasizing renal tumour of childhood was first reported by Kidd (1970), and it was later separately identified by Marsden and Lawler (1978) from the United Kingdom, and by Beckwith and Palmer (1978) from America: they all describe a distinctive neoplasm with a particular propensity for skeletal metastasis and aggressive clinical behaviour. The incidence of reported bone metastases was 76% of 38 cases in the British series, and 17% of 75 cases in the American series.

In the third National Wilms' tumour study, the bone-metastasizing tumour comprised nearly 6% of cases, making it the most frequent form of 'unfavourable' histology. Its age distribution is similar to that of Wilms' tumour. There appears to be a distinct male preponderance for this type in both the American and British series, although not as great as originally suggested. There have been no reports of bone-metastasizing renal tumour in patients with a Wilms' tumour-associated condition such as sporadic aniridia.

The other unfavourable type is the malignant rhabdoid tumour, first recognized by Beckwith and Palmer (1978) in their report from the first national Wilms' tumour study. It is the least common of the unfavourable entities and was found in only 2% of patients entered in the national (American) studies. The age distribution is markedly different to that of Wilms' tumour, with nearly half the patients being diagnosed in the first year of life (Weekes *et al.* 1989 for review). It is also associated with second primary tumours of various types (usually primitive neuroectodermal tumours) arising in the midline of the posterior intracranial fossa (Bonnin *et al.* 1984). The intracranial tumour may precede or follow the renal tumour. Hypercalcaemia has been reported in a number of cases of malignant rhabdoid tumours (Rousseau-Merck *et al.* 1982; Mitchell *et al.* 1985), but may also occur in congenital mesoblastic nephroma.

Other variants and renal tumours

Congenital mesoblastic nephroma is a rare, distinctive tumour of the infantile kidney, with a characteristically benign outcome. It was first recognized as a distinct entity by Bolande *et al.* (1967; see Bolande 1973 for review). There have been reports of local recurrences and metastases but in only one of these was the patient less than three months of age. Review of the specimen showed that tumour extended to the margin of resection. There have been other recurrences in patients over three months of age; the microscopic appearances were of dense cellularity and numerous mitotic figures. Vascular invasion and tumour rupture have also been associated with an unfavourable outcome. Fortunately, most congenital mesoblastic nephromas are recognized in the early weeks of life when the chances of recurrence are minimal if resection margins are adequate.

A review of 290 patients with Wilms' tumour treated at St Jude Children's Hospital (Fernandes *et al.* 1988) showed that three had neoplasms compatible with the histological diagnosis of 'teratoid Wilms' tumour', a term used to describe a tumour that has the classical triphasic appearance but with more diverse cell types and tissues (Variend *et al.* 1984). These tumours must be distinguished from true intrarenal teratomas which must be of intrarenal origin but must show also evidence of non-renal differentiation. Beckwith (1986) considers that intrarenal teratomas, teratoid Wilms' tumour, and classical Wilms' tumour form a continuum. Two of the patients described by Fernandes *et al.* (1988) had bilateral tumours extending into the renal pelvis, causing ureteral obstruction and renal failure. Beckwith (1986) has also suggested that botryoid growth into the renal pelvis is evidence of the tumour's origin from intralobar (deep) nephroblastomatosis (see below), that intralobar nephroblastomatosis is an early defect in nephrogenesis, and that tumours derived from it are more likely to include diverse cell types and tissues.

Renal cell carcinoma is rare in childhood. Raney *et al.* (1983) reviewed 20 cases and found that most presented with pain and haematuria. Half of the patients died of metastatic disease at a median of one year from diagnosis. There was a strong correlation between survival and tumour stage (using the staging system of the National Wilms' tumour study), but age was also an important factor–all six of six patients aged less than 11 years survived compared with only four of 11 over that age). Radiotherapy and chemotherapy appeared to have little influence on the outcome; adequate surgical resection was the only effective treatment. Occasionally, in contrast to the condition in adults, renal cell carcinoma in childhood can be chemo-responsive, and non-resectable tumours can become resectable. The usual regimen in these few cases has been cyclophosphamide, vincristine, and Adriamycin.

　　The incidence of Wilms' tumour in the adult is difficult to determine because many cases have been included with renal cell carcinoma. About 200 cases of adult Wilms' tumour have been reported, with the majority faring badly. Byrd *et al.* (1982) reviewed those patients over 16 years of age who had been enrolled in the national Wilms' tumour studies. The median age at presentation was 25 years and the most common presenting symptom was pain. The most common signs were an abdominal mass and haematuria. No patient had bilateral disease, but there were more patients with stage III and IV disease than in childhood. Despite treatment according to the recommendations of the study, the actuarial survival was only 24% at three years, suggesting that, despite the improvements in treatment of childhood Wilms' tumour, in the adult it is still a life-threatening disease.

Nephroblastomatosis

Nephroblastomatosis, first described by Hou and Holman (1961), is defined as the persistence of metanephric blastema or its incompletely differentiated derivatives beyond the 36th week of gestation. It is a rare, incidental discovery in childhood autopsies, but is found more commonly in association with Wilms' tumour, with a frequency of 15–30%. It is also found in a number of other genetic conditions associated with Wilms' tumour, but in the absence of malignancy (see Beckwith 1986 and Bove and McAdams 1985 for reviews). These associations have led to the suggestion that nephroblastomatosis is a precursor of Wilms' tumour, a view supported by the finding of a chromosome 11p deletion in nephroblastomatosis tissue from a patient with a normal somatic karyotype (Heidemann *et al.* 1986). Another school of thought is that the lesions are a developmental anomaly that may be related to the genesis of Wilms' tumour, but which is neither a precursor of, nor a predisposition to, tumour development.

　　Beckwith (1986) has proposed a classification of nephroblastomatosis into intralobar (deep), perilobar (superficial), mixed, and a rare panlobar form. The most common form of nephroblastomatosis is of multiple, small nodules lying superficially in the subcapsular cortex. Occasionally, a continuous subcapsular layer may be formed which can result in clinically detectable renal enlargement. The lesions of superficial perilobar nephroblastomatosis tend to enlarge with age and to become well-differentiated and well-defined. Proliferative nodules of monophasic embryonal epithelium may also be seen, with rosetting or a more differentiated tubular or papillary pattern, and prominent mitotic activity. Such lesions can be indistinguishable from Wilms' tumour, hence the name Wilms' tumourlets. The intralobar or deep form of nephroblastomatosis (Machin and McCaughey 1984) is usually a solitary nodule consisting of tubules and blastema. The association with Wilms' tumour is clear as the lesion is seldom recognized in the absence of a tumour. In these circumstances the tumours are often multifocal or bilateral, and are usually predominantly stromal or blastemal with minimal epithelial differentiation. The rarest (panlobar) form is bilateral and involves the whole renal parenchyma apart from the medullo-pelvic area. This variant has not been associated with Wilms' tumour, probably because of limited survival.

　　In those patients whose tumours are judged to be 'unresectable', initial pathological diagnosis may depend on percutaneous 'trucut' biopsy specimens. There is concern that these may not provide a representative sample of the tumour and may fail to reveal unfavourable features such as anaplasia. Pre-operative treatment may then mask the unfavourable features in the eventually resected specimen, and result in undertreatment. In a review of 26 pre-treatment trucut samples

(Pritchard, personal communication), no unfavourable features were found in 23 samples or in the eventual resection specimens. In one case, there was anaplasia both in the biopsy and the resection specimens. However, in two cases, there was anaplasia in the resection but not in the biopsy. This small study shows that it is possible to diagnose Wilms' tumour successfully in biopsies, and suggests that unfavourable features will not be eradicated by pre-operative chemotherapy. It does, however, demonstrate that unfavourable features may not be detected by percutaneous biopsy, and illustrates that the findings from biopsies must be interpreted with care.

Staging systems

Several staging systems have been used for Wilms' tumour, evolving as successive studies have redefined the criteria for each stage. The major contribution to these systems has been from the North American national studies. The system for the first and second of these studies defined group I as those tumours limited to the kidney, the capsule intact, no rupture during removal, and no residual tumour beyond the line of resection. Group II tumours were defined as those extending beyond the kidney, but completely resected. Thus the tumour could penetrate beyond the pseudocapsule into perirenal soft tissue, periaortic lymph nodes, or renal vessels, provided that there was no residual tumour beyond the line of resection. Group III tumours included all those with residual non-haematogenous spread, confined within the abdomen. This group included those tumours biopsied or ruptured before or during surgery, implants on peritoneal surfaces, lymph nodes beyond the periaortic chains, and those not resectable because of local invasion into vital structures. Group IV tumours comprised all cases of haematogenous spread, and group V were those cases with simultaneous or metachronous bilateral tumours.

Changes in the groupings after the first trial followed the realization that there was a group of tumours with variant histological appearances ('unfavourable histology') that conferred a worse outcome, as did the presence of involved lymph nodes. Those patients with unfavourable tumours had such poor survival regardless of stage that they were subsequently treated by the most intensive means. The presence of involved lymph nodes downgraded patients from group II to group III so that they received radiotherapy and more intensive chemotherapy. In the third

Table 27.3 The staging system of the third North American national Wilms' tumour study

Stage I	Tumour limited to the kidney and completely excised. Surface of renal capsule intact; no tumour rupture; no residual tumour apparent beyond margin of excision.
Stage II	Tumour extends beyond kidney but is completely excised; regional extension of tumour; vessel infiltration; tumour biopsy or local spillage of tumour confined to flank. No residual tumour apparent at or beyond margins of excision.
Stage III	Residual non-haematogenous tumour confined to the abdomen. Lymph-node involvement of hilum, periaortic chains or beyond; diffuse peritoneal contamination by tumour spillage; peritoneal implants; tumour extends beyond resection margins, either microscopically or macroscopically; tumour not completely removable because of local infiltration into vital structures.
Stage IV	Deposits, beyond stage III, in lung, liver, bone, brain.
Stage V	Bilateral renal involvement at diagnosis.

national study the groups were renamed 'stages', and the stages were redefined on the basis of information acquired during the first two studies. This staging system is summarized in Table 27.3. Stage I was unchanged; stage II was redefined to include patients previously in group II, but in addition those who had been biopsied or in whom the tumour had ruptured provided that the spill was confined to the flank. From the second national study it was noted that local spillage at operation or renal vein invasion did not adversely affect outcome. Patients so affected were upgraded from stage III to stage II, with a concomitant reduction in therapy. Because of its adverse prognosis, lymph-node involvement at the hilus or periaortic chain was downgraded from group II to stage III. Stages IV and V were unchanged. Studies by the United Kingdom Children's Cancer Study Group have confirmed the validity of these staging systems.

Treatment

Surgical considerations

Despite advances in chemotherapy, surgical resection remains the fundamental treatment for Wilms' tumour. According to the strategies of the American national and United Kingdom Children's Cancer Group studies, the information gained by histopathological study of the resected specimen directs the rational use of subsequent therapy.

Before the development of adjuvant chemotherapy, the outcome of purely operative treatment reflected the risks of major abdominal surgery in small children and the systemic nature of cancer, in that those who survived surgery had a high chance of developing metastases. Much of the early improvement in outcome was due to improved surgical and anaesthetic techniques, the development of intravenous fluid therapy, and blood transfusion. The improvement in survival of patients treated at a single British centre is shown in Fig. 27.4 (Williams 1972; Bond 1975; Pritchard, personal communication).

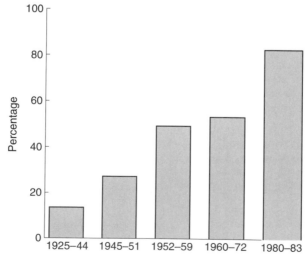

Fig. 27.4 Absolute three-year survival for patients seen at the Hospital for Sick Children, London, during the time periods specified.

It is essential that surgery for Wilms' tumour should start with a generous transverse abdominal incision so that examination of the abdominal cavity can be thorough and to ease the manipulation of the tumour during its removal. It is important that both kidneys are properly inspected before any excision is begun. The contralateral kidney must be mobilized and inspected carefully on all surfaces for previously undetected tumour. The remainder of the abdominal cavity must then be examined. If the contralateral kidney and remainder of the abdominal cavity are normal and the tumour is resectable, the operation then proceeds with the mobilization of surrounding structures, at this stage disturbing the tumour as little as possible. The ureter is dissected free, transected, and a plane of cleavage developed towards the renal pelvis and its associated vessels. The vein, which lies anterior to the artery, is mobilized so that the artery can be tied first. The vein is then tied and the tumour mobilized. Finally, the tumour with associated tissue is removed *en bloc* with care to avoid rupture and contamination of the abdominal cavity. Para-aortic lymph nodes are then biopsied, especially if they are enlarged.

The three major contraindications to surgery are (1) bilateral disease, (2) a large 'fixed' tumour, and (3) hepatic invasion. In general, 'heroic' surgery is no longer appropriate as chemotherapy will shrink tumours very effectively, sparing the child a radical operation with its attendant risks. Particular problems may arise with very large tumours overlying the major blood vessels. Care is needed to avoid the inadvertent ligation of contralateral renal vessels, the superior mesenteric artery, or even the aorta and inferior vena cava. Tumour thrombus in the renal vein or inferior vena cava is usually revealed by the pre-operative ultrasound. Occasionally, it is only discovered at operation. In these circumstances the inferior vena cava should be mobilized so that control can be established above and below the thrombus, before removal is attempted.

'Second-look' surgery, when a definitive operation is performed some time after an initial open biopsy, poses no particular problems save for that of obtaining enough mobilization of a previously mobilized kidney to allow full inspection.

Specific postoperative measures include close monitoring of urine output for 48 hours and adequate pain relief with either a morphine infusion or an epidural anaesthetic. Paralytic ileus, a consequence of mobilization of the bowel, may be accentuated by treatment with vincristine, but this is a rare complication.

Although North American practice remains steadfastly in favour of immediate surgery followed by adjuvant therapy dictated by the surgical stage, there is increasing recognition that pre-operative treatment may be of benefit in some circumstances. It seems inappropriate to subject a child with disseminated disease to immediate surgery for removal of the primary tumour until control of the metastases has been established. In those patients with very large tumours it may be beneficial to use pre-operative chemotherapy to shrink the tumour so as to facilitate the resection. It is also possible that good, early response may define groups of patients with more favourable disease in whom treatment can be minimized. Set against these hopes though, must be the fact that the national Wilms' tumour study (NWTS) staging system has only been validated in patients subjected to immediate surgery.

In the third national Wilms' tumour study (NWTS 3), 131 children were judged to have primarily unresectable disease. The patients were assigned a pre-treatment stage and then treated accordingly. The four-year survival for this group of patients was only 74% compared to 88% for those patients having immediate surgery (Ritchey *et al.* 1994). In the first United Kingdom Children's Cancer Study Group Wilms' tumour study (UKW1), 23 patients (6% of the total number studied) had initially unresectable disease, but instead of being assigned a pre-treatment stage were all treated as stage III patients with four-drug chemotherapy and, in those patients with local residual disease after delayed surgery, 30 Gy flank or whole abdominal irradiation

(Pritchard *et al.* 1995). Unfortunately, the outcome for this small group of patients is not analysed separately from other stage III patients and so it is impossible to judge the relative merits of these two approaches. The International Society of Pediatric Oncology (SIOP) group has pursued pre-operative treatment for many years and produced persuasive evidence that such a policy improves the stage at the time of surgery (see below). In an attempt to resolve the issues posed by the findings from these three cooperative groups, the UKCCSG is currently conducting a prospective randomised trial comparing immediate surgery with six weeks of chemotherapy and delayed surgery.

Chemotherapeutic considerations

Stratification of therapy, based on the extent of the primary tumour, presence of involved lymph nodes or metastases, and the extent of any tumour spillage at operation, is the key to rational use of chemotherapy. Reduction in therapy for 'good risk' patients and more intensive therapy for 'bad risk' patients results in fewer adverse effects of treatment in the former group, while achieving good survival in the latter.

The first national Wilms' tumour study in North America was the first concerted attempt to analyse postoperative chemotherapy and radiotherapy systematically (D'Angio *et al.* 1976). That study and its successors (D'Angio *et al.* 1981, 1989) have been instrumental in devising prognostic stages and in their revision, as has already been noted. Equally important has been the steady progress in delineating optimal treatment within the various disease stages. The major findings in the national series are summarized in Table 27.4. At the end of the third national study, therapy had been significantly reduced for stage I patients, who appeared to need only 10 weeks of adjuvant chemotherapy and no radiotherapy. In stage II patients, by using a more intensive

Table 27.4 Summary of the findings of the North American National Wilms' Tumour Studies (NWTS)

First study	
Group I	Patients <2 years of age do not require radiotherapy
Group II/III	Actinomycin D plus vincristine is better than either alone
Group IV	Pre-operative vincristine is of no benefit
Other findings	Unfavourable histology, lymph-node involvement are adverse factors
Second study	
Stage I	No patients benefit from radiotherapy, regardless of age—6 months of vincristine and actinomycin D is as good as 15 months
Stages II, III, IV	Addition of Adriamycin to vincristine and actinomycin D improves survival
Other findings	Stages II and III had the same survival—local spillage and invasion of renal vein did not affect outcome
Third study	
Stage I	Ten weeks therapy with actinomycin D/vincristine is as effective as 6 months
Stage II	Intensive vincristine/actinomycin D is as effective as three drugs—addition of radiotherapy does not enhance survival
Stage III	Intensive vincristine/actinomycin D is as effective as three drugs—10 Gy as effective as 20 Gy
Other findings	Addition of cyclophosphamide to vincristine/actinomycin D/Adriamycin does not improve survival

regimen of vincristine and actinomycin D, neither Adriamycin with its associated cardiotoxicity nor radiotherapy were required. For stage III disease, the intensive two-drug regimen was as effective as the three-drug one, and it had been possible to reduce radiotherapy from 20 Gy to 10 Gy. The addition of cyclophosphamide to Adriamycin, actinomycin D, and vincristine did not enhance survival of stage IV or 'unfavourable histology' patients. The use of Adriamycin appeared specifically to improve the outlook for patients with bone-metastasizing renal tumour. Strategies for malignant rhabdoid tumour of the kidney probably ought to be quite different from those used for the other renal tumours of childhood. Results from the third national study are shown in Table 27.5 (D'Angio *et al.* 1989).

The United Kingdom Children's Cancer Study Group has built its study in part on the results of these American national studies and also on those of United Kingdom Medical Research Council trials (Lennox *et al.* 1979; Morris-Jones *et al.* 1987). In the first United Kingdom Wilms' trial, stage I patients treated with 10 weeks of vincristine at weekly intervals, followed by five three-weekly doses, had 98% survival at two years, suggesting that actinomycin D can be avoided in these patients. In the second Wilms' trial this treatment was reduced still further to 10 weeks of vincristine at weekly intervals only, without diminution of relapse-free survival. As with the American national studies, the recognition of unfavourable histology and the adverse impact of lymph-node metastases has led to the use of more aggressive therapy for these patients, with an improvement in their overall survival, so that the current two-year disease-free survival of patients with unfavourable histology, stages I to III, is around 50%. Results for the first United Kingdom study are given in Table 27.6 (Pritchard *et al.* 1995).

Table 27.5 Results of the third National Wilms' Tumour Study (NWTS3)

Stage	Two-year relapse-free survival (%)	Two-year	overall survival (%)
I	92	97	Ten weeks of vincristine and actinomycin D
II/III	87	91	15 months of vincristine, actinomycin D, and doxorubicin
III	78	86	Vincristine, actinomycin D, and 10 Gy
IV and unfavourable histology	72	81	

Table 27.6 Results for the first United Kingdom Wilms' Tumour Study (UKW1)

Stage	Three-year EFS (%)	Three-year OS (%)	Six-year EFS (%)	Six-year OS (%)
I	90	96	89	96
II	85	94	85	93
III	82	83	82	83
IV	58	65	50	65

EFS = event free survival; OS = overall survival.

Unlike the American or British studies, the cooperative European studies run by the SIOP have concentrated on the use of pre-operative therapies in an effort to reduce surgical morbidity, particularly tumour rupture. In the first ISPO study, patients were randomized either to immediate surgery or to pre-operative radiotherapy (20 Gy) (Lemerle *et al.* 1976). The frequency of tumour spillage at operation was significantly reduced by radiotherapy. Although there was no difference in the overall survival, recurrence-free survival was better in the rupture-free group. The second SIOP study was non-randomized and observational: some patients had immediate surgery at the discretion of the investigator, usually because the tumour was thought to be suitable for primary resection; others received pre-operative radiation (20 Gy) and five doses of actinomycin D. Again, a reduced incidence of tumour rupture was found with pre-operative treatment. The fifth SIOP study (Lemerle *et al.* 1983) compared pre-operative chemoradiotherapy, as used in the second, with pre-operative chemotherapy, consisting in this instance of two five-day courses of actinomycin D and four weekly doses of vincristine. There were no significant differences in freedom from recurrence or overall survival, or in the frequency of tumour spillage, indicating the equal efficacy of the chemotherapy and the chemoradiotherapy. When the chemotherapy of the fifth SIOP study was compared with the immediate surgery of the first, an additional benefit of chemotherapy in the later study was the lower stage of disease found at operation. Thus, the proportion of stage I patients increased from 22% to 48% with a concomitant reduction in the proportion with stage II, node-negative tumours (45% to 32%) and stage II, node-positive or stage III tumours (33% to 19%). In the sixth SIOP study, in which all patients received pre-operative chemotherapy, stage II, node-negative tumours did not benefit from postoperative radiotherapy (Voute *et al.* 1987). By extrapolation from these findings it would appear that with the SIOP approach around 80% of patients would not need radiotherapy and still achieve a survival rate of 88–92%; in the third American national study, 70% of patients with favourable histology, non-metastatic tumours did not require radiotherapy (D'Angio 1983) and similar survival rates were achieved.

Radiotherapeutic considerations

Radiotherapy is now used less and in lower doses in the treatment of Wilms' tumour because of its local deleterious effects on growing tissues. The general trend has been to reduce the dose delivered as successive trials have indicated that dose reduction does not compromise cure rates.

The radiation dose originally recommended varied from 18 Gy to 24 Gy in children aged over 40 months, delivered through parallel opposed, megavoltage photon portals, with daily treatment fractions of up to 2 Gy. For patients in groups I and II, the irradiation portal covered the kidney and the associated tumour, as defined on the pre-operative intravenous urogram. The other border came across the midline to encompass the whole of the vertebral bodies but not the contralateral normal kidney. Group III patients and those in groups I and II with intraoperative tumour spillage were treated with whole abdominal radiation from the domes of the disphragm to the pelvic floor and to the lateral reflections of the peritoneum. The recommended doses were 25 Gy in three weeks for children under four years of age, and 35 Gy in four weeks to those over four years, delivered in 1.5 Gy daily fractions with shielding of the contralateral kidney and liver so that their dosage did not exceed 15 Gy and 30 Gy, respectively. The results of this trial suggested that whole abdominal radiation was not necessary if tumour spillage was restricted to the flank. The local recurrence rate was only 12%. At first it was thought that radiotherapy had been instrumental in producing this low rate (Tefft *et al.* 1976), but later it became clear that there was no difference in the local or distant rate of relapse dependent on radiation dosage (D'Angio *et al.* 1978). The second national study showed that omission of radiotherapy in all stage-I patients was safe. Data from the third study suggested that reduction of dosage from 20 Gy to 10 Gy in stage III patients was unsatisfactory, as this was associated with a number of local relapses. Currently, the fourth national study is exploring a reduction of the dose to the renal bed to 10 Gy in conjunction with three-drug chemotherapy in stage III patients with favourable histology.

Special problems

Bilateral tumours

Bilateral tumours provide a particular challenge, and here the key is 'conservation of nephrons'. Initial surgery in these circumstances is limited to establishing the histological diagnosis, either by open or closed (trucut) biopsy from both kidneys, because the histology can differ between them. Chemotherapy is then instituted. Once a maximal response has been obtained, the operation is usually bilateral partial nephrectomy. If these procedures will not clear the residual tumour and preserve adequate renal function, then 'bench surgery' has been advocated. Here, the kidney is removed and residual tumour resected; the kidney is then reimplanted. In the presence of extensive nephroblastomatosis, where there could be a subsequent metachronous tumour, it has been suggested that surgery should be conservative (Heidemann *et al.* 1985). Approaches similar to those outlined for bilateral tumours may be useful in these patients.

Data from SIOP studies (Coppes *et al.* 1987) show that the highest local stage is important in determining prognosis, and that children with synchronous tumours do better than those with metachronous tumours. In addition, children with metachronous tumours tend to be younger at diagnosis than those with synchronous tumours (13.2 vs. 32.1 months).

Resection of bilateral tumours with preservation of renal function may be impossible in a few children. It may be necessary to remove both kidneys, with renal transplantation after a period of dialysis. This strategy, though, is one of last resort, and should not be contemplated until conventional therapies have clearly failed.

Wilms' tumour in patients with single kidneys

Very occasionally, Wilms' tumour will be found in a patient with a single functioning kidney. Management should follow the guidelines for patients with bilateral tumours as preservation of normal, functioning renal tissue is critical. Thus, initial chemotherapy with careful monitoring of response and timing of definitive surgery will provide the most favourable result. Immediate nephrectomy followed by dialysis, chemotherapy, and then transplantation would be an option, but one fraught with many additional problems so that it is best avoided if at all possible.

Wilms' tumour in patients with pre-existing renal disease

In these patients, variations in management will be dictated by the type and prognosis of the pre-existing disease. Where there is likely to be inexorable progression to end-stage renal failure there seems little virtue in delaying surgical removal of the tumour and associated kidney. If necessary, dialysis can be instituted to supplement residual renal function. The timing of transplantation is more difficult, but to avoid the complexity of simultaneous cancer chemotherapy and transplantation immunosuppression it seems better to delay transplant until chemotherapy has been completed and enough time has elapsed for recurrence of malignancy to be unlikely. In practice, this period would be about two years from completion of chemotherapy.

Recurrence of Wilms' tumour in the transplanted kidney is extremely unlikely because Wilms' tumorigenesis is due to local rather than systemic factors. Similarly, there are no grounds for modifying immunosuppression after transplantation.

Follow-up and screening investigations

The place of repeated 'screening' investigations in patients with conditions associated with, or predisposing to, Wilms' tumour has not been established. Often the physicians taking care of such patients are not primarily oncologists and may not recognize all of the issues involved when making a decision to start screening. Some physicians propose that repeated screening permits earlier detection of clinically occult tumours and leads to an improvement in outcome. Others note that tumours may be clinically detectable only a few weeks after apparently normal (usually ultrasound) screening.

There are two separate issues to consider. First, what is the evidence that screening of presymptomatic, predisposed children will lead to earlier detection of tumours? Second, will detection of presymptomatic tumours result in fewer deaths or less treatment-related morbidity (as less therapy would be necessary for lower-stage disease)? Palmer and Evans (1983) reviewed nine patients with Wilms' tumour, known to have aniridia, who had been screened routinely by intravenous urography in an attempt to diagnose their tumours presymptomatically; an unsuspected tumour was detected in only one patient. It was concluded that urography was inefficient for such screening and suggested that ultrasonography might be better. There is less morbidity with ultrasound but there is no published evidence that it is more useful than intravenous urography. It is also most unlikely that presymptomatic detection will reduce the chances of death. The most important prognostic factor is the histological type, and the two groups of unfavourable histology do not occur in any of the predisposing conditions. As stage is, in part, linked to histology (i.e. unfavourable histological types tend to be a higher stage at diagnosis), it seems unlikely that morbidity would be much influenced either. Thus, the weight of evidence is that presymptomatic screening by any currently available method is insensitive and unlikely to influence the subsequent course of therapy or outcome. It is even possible that in such circumstances the 'normal' scan may provide false reassurance and so delay diagnosis. It seems more sensible to explain to parents that the child has a condition which may predispose to Wilms' tumour, to teach them to examine the child's abdomen, and to encourage them to seek medical advice if they are at all concerned. It remains unclear whether routine screening investigations are warranted.

During and after treatment, investigation is aimed at detecting early local or distant relapses. Generally, local relapses are less frequent than pulmonary relapse. Chest radiographs (posteroanterior and lateral) should be obtained regularly during treatment and continued afterwards over the time when relapse is most likely to occur. Pulmonary relapse may be clinically undetectable until quite advanced, whereas local (abdominal) relapses are usually more overt. Typically, therefore, chest radiographs should be obtained every nine weeks during treatment, every two months for the first year, and every three months for the second year after completion of treatment. Stage IV patients should continue to have chest radiographs three-monthly for a further year. Screening for local relapse need not be so frequent and abdominal ultrasonography at completion of treatment and then six-monthly for two years is enough. Other sites of relapse

Table 27.7   Follow-up investigations

During treatment	
Chest radiograph (PA and lateral)	Every nine weeks
Abdominal ultrasound	Every six months, unless initially inoperable, when more frequent imaging will be required
(Bone scan in bone-metastasizing months from start of therapy)	renal tumour at three, six, and 12
Off treatment	
Chest radiograph (PA and lateral)	Eight-weekly for first year, 12-weekly for second year (and for additional year in stage IV patients)
Abdominal ultrasound	Six-monthly for two years
(Bone scan in bone-metastasizing renal tumour: six-monthly for two years)	

are rare, even (despite its name) in bone-metastasizing renal tumour in which pulmonary metastases are most common. Thus, patients with this tumour need radionuclide bone scans, if at all, only at six-monthly intervals for two years. A suggested system for follow-up investigations is outlined in Table 27.7.

Patterns and treatment of relapse

The most frequent site of relapse overall is the lungs. In the second and third American national Wilms' tumour studies, this site accounted for 58% of all relapses; abdominal relapse accounted for a further 29% (Grundy *et al.* 1989). These findings differ from those of the first study where 74% of relapses were pulmonary and only 18% abdominal (Sutow *et al.* 1982). This difference is not accounted for by the cessation of radiotherapy for stage I and II because the relapse rates at each site were identical in irradiated and non-irradiated patients. It may reflect a greater efficacy of chemotherapy on pulmonary micrometastases compared to those in other sites. In the fifth SIOP study, 54% of all relapses were isolated pulmonary events, the remainder being in other or multiple sites (Lemerle *et al.* 1983). Sixteen per cent of all relapses involved the abdomen, but only in association with other sites. Isolated pulmonary relapse accounted for 41% of all relapses in the first United Kingdom study, with abdominal relapses accounting for 24%, and the remaining 35% being patients with multiple simultaneous sites of relapse (Pinkerton, personal communication).

Both British and American studies (Groote-Loonen *et al.*, personal communication; Grundy *et al.* 1989) have found factors that identify increased likelihood of salvaging relapsed patients. Tumours with favourable histology that recurred only in the lungs, or in the abdomen, and where radiotherapy had not been included in the primary treatment, or that occurred more than 12 months from diagnosis, were all associated with a more favourable outcome. Patients with relapsed, unfavourable histology tumours had poor survival regardless of the site or timing of relapse.

Retrieval therapy is, in part, dictated by the therapies previously used. Initial surgery may not be necessary for non-irradiated abdominal recurrences of tumours with favourable histology when radiotherapy and further chemotherapy can be given—an important consideration if the tumour appears not to be resectable. If not previously used, radiotherapy is indicated for multiple pulmonary relapses and is used in conjunction with salvage chemotherapy. Apart from the three standard agents—vincristine, actinomycin D, and Adriamycin—other agents useful in relapse include isophosphamide or VP16 (Groote-Loonen *et al.*, personal communication).

Prognosis

With the use of modern anaesthetic and surgical techiques and the rational application of combination chemotherapy, the majority of patients with Wilms' tumour will be cured. In part, this is because most patients will present with histologically favourable, low-stage disease, but there have also been genuine advances in chemotherapy. The overall survival from the fifth SIOP trial was 86% at three years, with a relapse-free survival of 71%. Results for the better arm of treatment for each stage of the third American national study and those from the first United Kingdom study are shown in Table 27.5. Thus, the vast majority of Wilms' tumour patients are cured, many with minimal short- or long-term morbidity.

Stage V patients are often treated in a very 'individualized' fashion, and so the available findings are usually those of single centres. Data collected from 22 ISPO centres indicate an overall survival of 64% with a follow-up of six years.

Future prospects

The two continuing clinical challenges in Wilms' tumour are to refine therapy in patients with good prognosis so as to minimize treatment-related morbidity and to improve therapy for poor prognosis and relapsing patients so that their survival improves. Advances in the understanding of the genetic basis of Wilms' tumour may help define more precisely patients with good and poor prognosis than the clinical staging currently in use. Stage I tumours with favourable histology already receive minimal treatment, but the recognition of highly favourable histological or genetic patterns may define a group who need no adjuvant chemotherapy. Pre-operative chemotherapy may provide a route to overall reduction of chemotherapy and obviation of radiotherapy. Improvement in treatment of cases of unfavourable histology awaits the development of novel strategies.

References

Baird, P. N., *et al.* (1992). Identification of mutations in the WT1 gene in tumours from patients with the WAGR syndrome. *Oncogene*, **7**, 91–7.

Beckwith, J. B. (1963). Extreme cytomegaly of the fetal adrenal cortex, omphalocele, hyperplasia of the kidneys and pancreas, and Leydig cell hyperplasia: another syndrome? Communication to the Western Society for Pediatric Research, November 11.

Beckwith, J. B. (1986). Wilms' tumor and other renal tumors of childhood. In: *Pathology of neoplasia in children and adolescents* (ed. M. W. B. Finegold), pp. 313–32. Saunders, Philadelphia.

Beckwith, J. B. and Palmer, N. F. (1978). Histopathology and prognosis of Wilms' tumour: results from the first National Wilms' tumour study. *Cancer*, **41**, 1937–48.

Bickmore, W., Christie, S., van Heyningen, V., Hastie, N. D., and Porteous, D. J. (1988). Hitchhiking from HRAS1 to the WAGR locus with CMGT markers. *Nucleic Acid Research*, **16**, 51–60.

Boehm, T., *et al.* (1988). The T-ALL specific t(11; 14) (p13; q110) translocation breakpoint cluster region is located near to the Wilms' tumour predisposition region. *Oncogene*, **3**, 691–5.

Bolande, R. P. (1973). Congenital mesoblastic nephroma of infancy. *Perspectives in Pediatric Pathology*, 1, 227–50.

Bolande, R. P., Brough, A. J., and Izant, R. J. (1967). Congenital mesoblastic nephroma of infancy. *Pediatrics*, 40, 272–8.

Bond, J. V. (1975). Prognosis and treatment of Wilms' tumour at Great Ormond Street Hospital for Sick Children, 1960–72. *Cancer*, 36, 1202–7.

Bonnin, J. M., Rubinstein, L. J., Palmer, N. F., and Beckwith, J. B. (1984). The association of embyronal tumours originating in the kidney and in the brain. A report of seven cases. *Cancer*, 54, 2137.

Bove, K. E. and McAdams, A. J. (1985). The nephroblastomatosis complex and its relationship to Wilms' tumour: a clinicopathologic treatise. *Perspectives in Pediatric Pathology*, 3, 185–222.

Breslow, N. E., *et al.* (1978). Prognostic factors for patients without metastases at diagnoses. Results of the national Wilms' tumour study. *Cancer*, 41, 1577–89.

Breslow, N. E., *et al.* (1985). Prognostic factors for Wilms' tumour patients with non-metastatic disease at diagnosis. Results of the second national Wilms' tumour study. *Journal of Clinical Oncology*, 3, 521–31.

Breslow, N. E., *et al.* (1986). Clinicopathologic features and prognosis for Wilms' tumour patients with metastases at diagnosis. *Cancer*, 58, 2501–11.

Breslow, N. E. and Beckwith, J. B. (1982). Epidemiological features of Wilms' tumour: results of the national Wilms' tumour study. *Journal of the National Cancer Institute*, 68, 429–36.

Buckler, A. J., Pelletier, J., Haber, D. A., Glaser, T., and Housman, D. E. (1991). Isolation, characterization, and expression of the murine Wilms' tumor gene (WT1) during kidney development. *Molecular and Cellular Biology*, 11, 1707–12.

Byrd, R. L., Evans, A. E., and D'Angio, G. J. (1982). Adult Wilms' tumour: effect of combined therapy on survival. *Journal of Urology*, 127, 648–51.

Call, K. M., *et al.* (1990). Isolation and characterisation of a zinc finger polypeptide gene at the human chromosome 11 Wilms' tumour locus. *Cell*, 60, 509–20.

Coppes, M. J., *et al.* (1987). Prognosis of bilateral Wilms' tumour (BWT) is SIOP 1, 2, and 5. Abstract 122, ISPO Proceedings, Jerusalem.

Coppes, M. J., *et al.* (1992). Loss of heterozygosity mapping in Wilms' tumor indicates the involvement of three distinct regions and a limited role for non-disjunction or mitotic recombination. *Genes Chromosom. Cancer*, 5, 326–34.

Coppes, M. J., Campbell, C. E., and Williams, B. R. G. (1993a). The role of WT1 in Wilms' tumorigenesis. *FASEB Journal*, 7, 886–95.

Coppes, M. J., Liefers, G. J., Paul, P., Yeger, H., and Williams, B. R. G. (1993b). Homozygous somatic WT1 point mutations in sporadic unilateral Wilms' tumour. *Procedures of the National Academy of Science USA*, 90, 1416–19.

Cowell, J. K. (1989). Recessive oncogenes and antioncogenes. In: *Handbook of experimental pharmacology*. vol. 94(2): *Chemical carcinogenesis and mutagenesis* (ed. C. Cooper and P. L. Grover). Springer, Heidelberg.

Cowell, J. K., Wadey, R. B., Buckle, B. B., and Pritchard, J. (1989). The aniridia—Wilms' tumour association: molecular and genetic analysis of chromosome deletions on the short arm of chromosome 11. *Human Genetics*, 82, 123–6.

Cowell, J. K., Groves, N., and Baird, P. N. (1993). Loss of heterozygosity all 11p13 in Wilms' tumour does not necessarily involve mutations in the WT1 gene. *British Journal of Cancer*, 67, 1259–61.

D'Angio, G. J. (1983). ISPO and the management of Wilms' tumour. *Journal of Clinical Oncology*, 1, 595–6.

D'Angio, G. J., *et al.* (1976). The treatment of Wilms' tumour. Results of the first national Wilms' tumour study. *Cancer*, 38, 633–46.

D'Angio, G. J., *et al.* (1978). Radiation therapy of Wilms' tumour. Results according to dose, field, postoperative timing, and histology. *International Journal of Radiation Oncology, Biology, and Physics*, 4, 769–80.

D'Angio, G. J., *et al.* (1981). The treatment of Wilms' tumour: results of the second national Wilms' tumour study. *Cancer*, **47**, 2302–11.

D'Angio, G. J., *et al.* (1989). The treatment of Wilms' tumour. Results of the third national Wilms' tumour study. *Cancer*, **64**, 239–60.

Denys, P., Malvaux, P., van den Berghe, H., Tanghe, H., and Proestmans, W. (1967). Assocaition d'un syndrome anatomo-pathologique de pseudohermaphroditisme masculin, d'une tumeur de Wilms, d'une nephropathie parenchymateuse et d'un mosaicisme XX/XY. *Archives Francais Pediatrie*, **24**, 729–39.

Douglass, E. C., Wilimas, J. A., Green, A. A., and Look, A. T. (1985). Abnormalities of chromosome 1 and 11 in Wilms' tumour. *Cancer Genetics and Cytogenetics*, **14**, 331–8.

Drash, A., Sherman, F., Hartman, W. H., and Blizzard, R. M. (1970). A syndrome of pseudohermaphroditism, Wilms' tumour, hypertension, and degenerative renal disease. *Journal of Pediatrics*, **76**, 585–93.

Dunn, J. M., Phillips, R. A., Becker, A., and Gallie, B. L. (1988). Identification of germline and somatic mutations affecting the retinoblastoma gene. *Science*, **241**, 1797–800.

Fearon, E. R., Vogelstein, B., and Feinberg, A. P. (1984). Somatic deletion and duplication of genes on chromosome 11 in Wilms' tumours. *Nature*, **309**, 176–8.

Fernandes, E. T., Parham, D. M., Ribeiro, R. C., Douglass, E. C., Kumar, A. P. M., and Wilimas, J. (1988). Teratoid Wilms' tumour: the St Jude experience. *Journal of Pediatric Surgery*, **23**, 1131–4.

Fitzgerald, J. H. T. (1978). *Human embryology: a regional approach*, pp. 1–205. Harper & Rowe, London.

Francke, U., Holmes, T. B., Atkins, L., and Riccardi, V. M. (1979). Aniridia–Wilms' tumour association; evidence for specific deletion of 11p13. *Cytogenetics and Cell Genetics*, **24**, 185–92.

Gessler, M., Simeola, K. O. J., and Bruns, G. A. P. (1989). Cloning breakpoints of a chromosome translocation identifies the AN2 locus. *Science*, **244**, 1575–8.

Gessler, M., *et al.* (1990). Homozygous deletion of in Wilms' tumours of a zinc-finger gene identified by chromosome jumping. *Nature*, **343**, 774–78.

Glaser, T., *et al.* (1986). The beta subunit of follicle-stimulating hormone is deleted in patients with aniridia and Wilms' tumour, allowing a further definition of the WAGR locus. *Nature*, **321**, 882–7.

Greenberg, F., Stein, F., Gresik, M. V., Finegold, M. J., Carpenter, R. J., Riccardi, V. M., *et al.* (1986). The Perlman familial nephroblastomatosis syndrome. *American Journal of Medical Genetics*, **24**, 101–10.

Greenberg, F., Copeland, K., and Gresik, M. V. (1988). Expanding the spectrum of the Perlman syndrome. *American Journal of Medical Genetics*, **29**, 733–76.

Grundy, P., Koufos, A., Morgan, K., Li, F. P., Meadows, A. T., and Cavenee, W. K. (1988). Familial predisposition to Wilms' tumour does not map to the short arm of chromosome 11. *Nature*, **336**, 375–6.

Grundy, P., Breslow, N., Green, D. M., Sharples, K., Evans, A. E., and D'Angio, G. J. (1989). Prognostic factors for children with recurrent Wilms' tumour: results from the second and third national Wilms' tumour study. *Journal of Clinical Oncology*, **7**, 638–47.

Grundy, P., Telzerow, P., Paterson, M. C., *et al.* (1991). Chromosome 11 uniparental isodisomy predisposing to embryonal neoplasms. *Lancet*, **338**, 1079–80.

Grundy, P. E., Telzerow, P. E., Breslow, N., Moksness, J., Huff, V., and Paterson, M. C. (1994). Loss of heterozygosity for chromosomes 16q and 1p in Wilms' tumors predicts an adverse outcome. *Cancer Research*, **54**, 2331–3.

Grundy, R. G., Pritchard, J., Baraitser, M., Risdon, M., and Robards, M. (1992). Perlman and Wiedemann–Beckwith syndromes: two distinct conditions associated with Wilms' tumour. *European Journal of Paediatrics*, **151**, 895–8.

Haber, D. A., Sohn, R. L., Buckler, A. J., Pelletier, J., Call, K. M., and Housman, D. E. (1991).

Alternative splicing and genomic structure of the Wilms' tumor gene, WT1. *Procedures of the National Academy of Science USA*, **88**, 9618–22.

Habib, R., *et al.* (1985). The nephropathy associated with male pseudohermaphroditism and Wilms' tumour (Drash syndrome): a distinctive glomerular lesion—report of 10 cases. *Clinical Nephrology*, **24**, 269–78.

Hall, J. G. (1990). Genomic imprinting: review and relevance to human diseases. *American Journal of Human Genetics*, **46**, 857–73.

Hamel, B. C. J., Mannens, M., and Bokkerink, J. P. M. (1989). Perlman syndrome: Report of a case and results of molecular studies. *American Journal of Human Genetics*, **45**(4), A48.

Heidemann, R. L., Haase, G. M., Foley, C. L., Wilson, H. L., and Bailey, W. C. (1985). Nephroblastomatosis and Wilms' tumour: clinical experience and management of seven patients. *Cancer*, **555**, 1446–51.

Heidemann, R. L., McGavran, L., and Waldstein, G. (1986). Nephroblastomatosis and deletion of 11p. The potential etiologic relationship to subsequent Wilms' tumor. *American Journal of Pediatric Hematology and Oncology*, **8**, 231–4.

Henry, I., Bonaiti-Pellie, C., Chehensse, V., *et al.* (1991). Uniparental paternal disomy in a genetic cancer-predisposing syndrome. *Nature*, **351**, 665–7.

Hou, L. T. and Holman, R. L. (1961). Bilateral nephroblastomatosis in a premature infant. *Journal of Pathology and Bacteriology*, **82**, 249–55.

Hrabovsky, E. E., Othrsen, H. B., deLorimier, A., Kelalis, P., Beckwith, J. B., and Takashima, J. (1986). Wilms' tumor in the neonate: a report from the national Wilms' tumor study. *Journal of Pediatric Surgery*, **21**, 385–7.

Huff, V., Compton, D. A., Chao, L.-Y., Strong, L.C., Geiser, C. F., and Saunders, G. F. (1988). Lack of linkage of familial Wilms' tumour to chromosomal band 11p13. *Nature*, **336**, 377–8.

Huff, V., *et al.* (1992). Non-linkage of 16q markers to familial predisposition to Wilms' tumour. *Cancer Res*, **52**, 6117–120.

Jadresic, L., Dillon, M. J., Grant, D. B., Pritchard, J., and Barratt, T. M. (1988). The nephropathy associated with male pseudohermaphroditism and nephroblastoma. *Pediatric Nephrology*, **2**, C149. (Abstract).

Jadresic, L., *et al.* (1988). The nephropathy associated with male pseudohermaphroditism and nephroblastoma. *Pediatric Nephrology*, **2**:C149(abstract).

Junien, C., *et al.* (1980). Regional assignment of catalase (CAT) gene to band 11p13. Association with the aniridia–Wilms' tumourgonadoblastoma (WAGR) complex. *Annals of Genetics*, **28**, 165–8.

Kaneko, Y., Kondo, K., Rowley, J. D., Moohr, J. W., and Maurer, H. S. (1983). Further chromosome studies on Wilms' tumour cells of patients without aniridia. *Cancer Genetics and Cytogenetics*, **10**, 191–7.

Kidd, J. M. (1970). Exclusion of certain renal neoplasms from the category of Wilms' tumor. *American Journal of Pathology*, **59**, 16a.

Knudson, A. G. (1971). Mutation and cancer: statistical study of retinoblastoma. *Proceedings of the National Academy of Science USA*, **68**, 820–3.

Kondo, K., Chilcote, R. R., Maurer, H. S., and Rowley, J. D. (1984). Chromosome abnormalities in tumour cells from patients with sporadic Wilms' tumour. *Cancer Research*, **44**, 5367–81.

Koufos, A., *et al.* (1984). Loss of alleles at loci on human chromosome 11 during genesis of Wilms' tumour. *Nature*, **309**, 170–2.

Koufos, A., *et al.* (1989). Familial Wiedemann–Beckwith syndrome and a second Wilms' tumor locus both map to 11p15.5. *American Journal of Human Genetics*, **44**, 711–19.

Ledlie, E. M., Mynors, L. S., Draper, G. J., and Gorbach, P. D. (1970). Natural history and treatment of Wilms' tumour: an analysis of 335 cases occurring in England and Wales, 1962–1966. *British Medical Journal*, **4**, 195–200.

Lemerle, J., *et al.* (1976). Pre-operative versus postoperative radiotherapy, single versus multiple courses of actinomycin D in the treatment of Wilms' tumors. Preliminary results of a controlled clinical trial conducted by the International Society of Pediatric Oncology (ISPO). *Cancer*, **38**, 647–54.

Lemerle, J., *et al.* (1983). Effectiveness of preoperative chemotherapy in Wilms' tumor: results of an International Society of Pediatric Oncology (ISPO) clinical trial. *Journal of Clinical Oncology*, **1**, 604–10.

Lennox, E. L., Stiller, C. A., Morris-Jones, P. H., and Kinnier-Wilson, L. M. (1979). Nephroblastoma: treatment during 1970–73 and the effect on survival of inclusion in the first MRC trial. *British Medical Journal*, **2**, 567–9.

Lewis, W. H., Goguen, J. M., Powers, V. E., Willard, H. F., and Michalopoulos, J. (1985). Gene order on the short arm of human chromosome 11: regional assignment of the LDH-A gene distal to catalase in two translocations. *Human Genetics*, **71**, 249–53.

Liban, E. and Kozenitzky, I. L. (1970). Metanephric hamartomas and nephroblastomatosis in sibs. *Cancer*, **25**, 885.

Little, M. H., *et al.* (1993). Evidence that WT1 mutations in Denys-Drash syndrome patients may act in a dominant-negative fashion. *Hum Mol Genet*, **2**, 259–64.

Machin, G. A. and McCaughey, W. T. E. (1984). A new precursor lesion of Wilms' tumour (nephroblastoma): intralobar multifocal nephroblastomatosis. *Histopathology*, **8**, 35–53.

McKusick, V. A. (1986). *Mendelian inheritance in man* (7th edn). Johns Hopkins University Press, Baltimore.

Mahaswaran, S., *et al.* (1993). Physical and functional interaction between WT1 and p53 proteins. *Procedures of the National Academy of Science USA*, **90**, 5100–4.

Marsden, H. B. and Lawler, W. (1978). Bone-metastasising renal tumour of childhood. *British Journal of Cancer*, **38**, 437–41.

Maw, M. A., *et al.* (1992). A third Wilms' tumor locus on chromosome 16q. *Cancer Research*, **52**, 3094–8.

Miller, R. W., Fraumeni, J. R., and Manning, M. D. (1964). Association of Wilms' tumor with aniridia, hemihypertrophy, and other congenital malformations. *New England Journal of Medicine*, **27**, 922–7.

Mitchell, C. D., Harvey, W., Gordon, D., Womer, R. B., Dillon, M. J., and Pritchard, J. (1985). Rhabdoid Wilms' tumour and prostaglandin-mediated hypercalcaemia. *European Paediatric Haematology and Oncology*, **2**, 153–7.

Morris-Jones, P., Marsden, H. B., Pearson, D., and Barnes, J. (1987). MRC second nephroblastoma trial, 1974–78: long-term results. Abstract 121, ISPO Proceedings, Jerusalem.

Narahara, K., *et al.* (1984). Regional mapping of catalase and Wilms' tumour–aniridia, genito-urinary abnormalities, and mental retardation triad loci to the chromosome segment 11p13.05–p13.06. *Human Genetics*, **66**, 181–5.

Neri, G., Martini-Neri, M. E. M., Katz, B. E., and Opitz, J. M. (1984). The Perlman syndrome: familial renal dysplasia with Wilms' tumor, fetal gigantism and multiple congenital anomalies. *American Journal of Medical Genetics*, **19**, 195–207.

Ogawa, O., Eccles., M. R., Szeto, J., *et al.* (1993). Relaxation of insulin-like growth factor II gene imprinting implicated in Wilms' tumour. *Mature*, **362**, 749–51.

Orkin, S. H., Goldman, D. S., and Sallan, S. E. (1984). Development of homozygosity for chromosome 11p markers in Wilms' *Nature*, **309**, 172–4.

Owens, C. M., Dicks-Mireaux, C., Burnett, S. J. D., Veys, P. A. and Pritchard, J. Results of the 2nd Wilms' tumor study of the United Kingdom Children's Cancer Study Group. *American Journal of Radiology*. In press.

Palmer, N. and Evans, A. E. (1983). The association of aniridia and Wilms' tumor: methods of surveillance and diagnosis. *Medical and Pediatric Oncology*, **11**, 73–5.

Parkin, D. M., Stiller, C. A., and Draper, G. J. (1988). The international incidence of childhood cancer. *International Journal of Cancer*, **42**, 511–20.

Pelletier, J., Bruening, W., Li, F. P., Haber, D. A., Glaser, T., Housman, D. E. (1991*a*). WT1 mutations contribute to abnormal genital system development and hereditary Wilms' tumour. *Nature*, **353**, 431–4.

Pelletier, J., Schalling, M., Buckler., A. J., Rogers, A., Haber, D. A., and Housman, D. (1991*b*). Expression of the Wilms' tumor gene WT1 in the murine urogenital system. *Genes. Dev.*, 5:1345–56.

Pelletier, J., *et al.* (1991*c*). Germline mutations in the Wilms' tumor supresor gene are associated with abnormal urogenital development in Denys–Drash syndrome. *Cell*, **67**, 437–47.

Perlman, M. (1986). Perlman syndrome: familial renal dysplasia with Wilms' tumor, fetal gigantism, and multiple congenital anomalies. *American Journal of Medical Genetics*, **25**, 793–5.

Perlman, M., Goldberg, G. M., Bar-Ziv, J., and Danovitch, G. (1973). Renal hamartomas and nephroblastomatosis with fetal gigantism: a familial syndrome. *Journal of Paediatrics*, **83**, 414–18.

Perlman, M., Levin., M., and Wittels, B. (1974). Syndrome of fetal gigantism, renal hamartomas, and nephroblastomatosis with Wilms' tumor. *Cancer*, **35**, 1212–17.

Ping, A. J., *et al.* (1989). Genetic linkage of Beckwith-Weidemann syndrome to 11p15. *Am. J. Hum. Genet* **44**, 720–23.

Porteous, D. J., *et al.* (1987). HRAS–1 selected chromosome transfer generates markers that co-localize aniridia- and genitourinary dysplasia-associated translocation breakpoints and the Wilms' tumor gene within band 11p13. *Proceedings of the National Academy of Sciences USA*, **84**, 5355–9.

Pritchard, J., *et al.* (1995). Results of the United Kingdom Children's Cancer Study Group (UKCC-SG) first Wilms' tumor study (UKW-1). *Journal of Clinical Oncology*, **13**, 124–33.

Pritchard-Jones, K., Fleming, S., Davidson, D., *et al.* (1990). The candidate Wilms' tumour gene is involved in genitourinary development. *Nature*, **346**, 194–7.

Pueschel, S. M. and Padre-Mendoza, T. (1984). Chromosome 11 and Beckwith–Weidemann syndrome. *Journal of Pediatrics*, **104**, 484–5.

Rainier, S., Johnson, L. A., Dobry, C. J., Ping, A. J., Grundy, P. E., and Feinberg, A. P. (1993). Relaxation of imprinted genes in human cancer. *Nature*, **362**, 747–9.

Raney, R. B., Palmer, N., Sutow, W. W., Baum, E., and Ayala, A. (1983). Renal-cell carcinoma in children. *Medical and Pediatric Oncology*, **11**, 91–8.

Rauscher III, F. J. (1993). The WT1 Wilms' tumor gene product: a developmentally regulated transcription factor in the kidney that functions as a tumor suppressor. *FASEB Journal*, **7**, 896–903.

Reeve, A. E., Eccles, M. R., Wilkins, R. J., Bell, G. I., and Millow, L. J. (1985). Expression of insulin-like growth factor-II transcripts in Wilms' tumour. *Nature*, **317**, 258–60.

Reeve, A. E., Sih, S. A., Raizis, A. M. and Feinberg, A. P. (1989). Loss of alleleic heterozygosity at a second locus on chromosome 11 in sporadic Wilms' tumour cells. *Molecular and Cellular Biology*, **9**, 1799–803.

Riccardi, V. M., Sujansky, E., Smith, A. C., and Francke, U. (1978). Chromosome imbalance in the aniridia—Wilms' tumor association: 11p interstitial deletion. *Pediatrics*, **61**, 604–10.

Ritchey, M. L., *et al.* (1994). Management and outcome of inoperable Wilms' tumour—a report of national Wilms' tumour study 3. *Annals of Surgery*, **220**, 683–90.

Rousseau-Merck, M. F., *et al.* (1982). An original hypercalcemic infantile renal tumour without bone metastasis: heterotransplantation to nude mice. *Cancer*, **50**, 85–93.

Schroeder, W. T., *et al.* (1987). Non-random loss of maternal chromosome 11 alleles in Wilms' tumours. *American Journal of Human Genetics*, **40**, 413–20.

Schwartz, C. E., Haber, D. A., Stanton, V. P., Strong, L. C., Skolnick, M. H., and Housman, D. E. (1991). Familial predisposition to Wilms' tumor does not segregate with the TW1 gene. *Genomics*, **10**, 927–30.

Scott. J., *et al.* (1985). Insulin-like growth factor-II gene expression in Wilms' tumour and embryonic tissues. *Nature*, **317**, 260–2.

Simola, K. O. J., Knuutila, S., Kaitila, I., Pirkola, A., and Pohja, F. (1983). Familial aniridia and translocation t(4; 11) (q22; p13) without Wilms' tumour. *Human Genetics*, **63**, 158–61.

Slater, R. M. and De Kraker, J. (1982). Chromosome number 11 and Wilms' tumour. *Cancer Genetics and Cytogenetics*, **5**, 237–45.

Slater, R. M., De Kraker, J., Voute, P. A., and Delamare, J. F. M. (1985). A cytogenetic study of Wilms' tumour. *Cancer Genetics and Cytogenetics*, **14**, 95–109.

Solis, V., Pritchard, J., and Cowell, J. K. (1988). Cytogenetics of Wilms' tumours. *Cancer Genetics and Cytogenetics*, **34**, 223–34.

Sutow, W. W., *et al.* (1982). Prognosis in children with Wilms' tumor metastases prior to or following primary treatment. Results from the first national Wilms' tumour study. *American Journal of Clinical Oncology*, **5**, 339–47.

Tefft, M., D'Angio, G. J., and Grant, W. (1976). Post-operative radiation therapy for residual Wilms' tumour. Review of group III patients in the national Wilms' tumour study. *Cancer*, **37**, 2768–72.

Ton, C. C. T., *et al.* (1991). Positional cloning and characterization of a paired box- and homeobox-containing gene from the aniridia region. *Cell*, **67**, 1059–74.

Turleau, C., DeGrouchy, J., Nihoul-Fekete, T., Dufier, J. L., Chavin-Colin, F., and Junien C. (1984*a*). Del 11p13/nephroblastoma without aniridia. *Human Genetics*, **67**, 455–6.

Turleau, C., De Grouchy, J., Tournade, M. F., Gagnadoux, M. F., and Junien, C. (1984*b*). Del 11p/aniridia complex. Report of three patients and review of 37 observations from the literature. *Clinical Genetics*, **26**, 356–62.

Turleau, C., De Grouchy, J., Chavin-Colin, F., Martelli, H., Voyer, M., and Charlas, R. (1984*c*). Trisomy 11p15 and Beckwith–Wiedemann syndrome. A report of two cases. *Human Genetics*, **67**, 219–21.

Varanesi, R., *et al.* (1994). Fine structure analysis of the WT1 gene in sporadic Wilms' tumour. *Proc. Nat. Acad. Sci. USA*, **91**, 3554–58.

Variend, S., Spicer, R. D., and MacKinnon, A. C. (1984). Teratoid Wilms' tumour. *Cancer*, **53**, 1936–42.

Voute, P. A., *et al.* (1987). Preoperative chemotherapy (CT) as first treatment in children with Wilms' tumor. Results of the ISPO nephroblastoma trials and studies. Abstract 123, ISPO Proceedings, Jerusalem.

Wadey, R. B., *et al.* (1990). Loss of heterozygosity in Wilms' tumour involves two distinct regions of chromosome 11. *Oncogene*, **5**, 901–7.

Waziri, M., Patil, S. R., Hanson, J. W., and Bartley, J. A. (1983). Abnormality of chromosome 11 in patients with features of Beckwith–Weidemann syndrome. *Journal of Pediatrics*, **102**, 873.

Weekes, D. A., Beckwith, J. B., Mierau, G. W., and Luckey, D. W. (1989). Rhabdoid tumor of the kidney. A report of 111 cases from the national Wilms' tumor study center. *American Journal of Surgical Pathology*, **13**, 439–58.

Wiedemann, N. R. (1964). Complexe malformatif familial avec hernie ombilicale et macroglossie: un syndrome nouveau? *Journeau de Genetique Humaine*, **13**, 223–32.

Wilimas, J. A., Douglass, E. C., Magill, H. L., Fitch, S., and Hustu, H. O. (1988). Significance of pulmonary computed tomography at diagnosis in Wilms' tumour. *Journal of Clinical Oncology*, **6**, 1144–6.

Wilkins, R. J. (1988). Genetic imprinting and carcinogenesis. *Lancet*, **i**, 329–31.

Williams, I. G. (1972). *Tumours of childhood—a clinical treatise*, pp. 103–4. Heinemann, London.

Williams, J. C., Brown, K. W., Mott, M. G., and Maitland, N. J. (1989). Maternal allele loss in Wilms' tumour. *Lancet*, **i**, 283–4.

Wilms, M. (1899). *Die mischgeschwulste der nieren*, pp. 1–90. Arthur Georgi, Leipzig.

Zhu, X., *et al.* (1989). Preferential germline mutation of the paternal allele in retinoblastoma. *Nature*, **340**, 312–13.

28

Mitochondrial cytopathies and other rare inherited diseases affecting the kidney

J. Stewart Cameron

Introduction

There are a large number of rare inherited disorders, in many of which survival is limited and the conditions are rarely if ever seen in renal units dealing with adult patients. These conditions are more the subject of specialist paediatric nephrology, and accounts of them have been given by Crawfurd (1988), Gilbert–Barness *et al.* (1989), McKusick (1990), Barness and Opitz (1993), and Clarren (1994). This brief account is confined to inherited disorders which are likely to be encountered, albeit rarely in most cases, in adult clinics and which are not dealt with elsewhere in this book. Some rare inherited disorders affecting the glomeruli are dealt with elsewhere in this book, including familial dysautonomia, acro-osteolysis, collagen type III nephropathy, and familial fibronectin glomerulopathy.

Mitochondrial cytopathies with renal involvement

Until recently it was believed that these syndromes were rare, confined to childhood, and involved the nervous and muscular systems predominantly. Now it is clear that they may present at any age with manifestations in almost any organ, including the kidney, and often include apparently unrelated manifestations in multiple organs, although a single organ system may be affected for a long period (Johns 1995). It is certain that they are underdiagnosed in many areas of medicine (Munnich *et al.* 1992). An area of particular interest in nephrology is tubulointerstitial failure of obscure origin, particularly when followed or accompanied by other apparently bizarre and unrelated manifestations (Szabolcs *et al.* 1994).

Mitochondrial DNA

Human mitochondrial (mtDNA) (Luft 1994; Wallace 1994; Johns 1995) is a closed circular molecule of length 16.5 kb which encodes small (12S) and large (16S) ribsosomal RNA (rRNA), 22 transfer RNAs (tRNA), and 13 key subunits of the polypeptide enzymes of the respiratory chain.

The mitochondrial respiratory chain (Fig. 28.1) is a very complex metabolic pathway comprising about 100 polypeptides. Most of these are encoded by nuclear DNA (nDNA) and only 13 by the mtDNA. mtDNA is transcribed polycystronically and further processed into mature messenger RNAs (mRNAs). At least one of these transcription factors is encoded in nDNA. In addition,

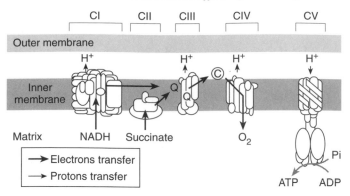

Fig. 28.1 The respiratory chain. Complexes I to V are coded for partly by mitochondria and partly by nuclear DNA. Complex I (NADH CoQ reductase) oxidizes NADH produced by either the Krebs cycle or fatty acid oxidation. Electrons are transferred to complex IV (cytochrome c oxidase) which oxidizes reduced cytochrome c. Complex V mediates synthesis of ATP. Protons extruded by complexes I, III, and IV accumulate in the intermembrane space and can be used for further ATP synthesis.

nDNA codes for proteins involved in mtDNA replication and repair. Thus interactions between the nucleus and the mitchondria are expected, and genes encoded within the nucleus and its product may interfere with mtDNA and its gene product. Mutations of nDNA, mtDNA, or both may constitute the genetic basis of mitochondrial diseases.

Mitochondria are the only sources of extranuclear DNA in humans. During egg fertilization, the sperm contributes only its nDNA to the zygote. In contrast, the mother transmits her mtDNA to her offspring and only her daughters can transmit mtDNA to the next generation. Thus inheritance does not follow conventional Mendelian laws. During cell division, mitochondria are randomly distributed among daughter cells. When an mtDNA mutation arises, it creates an intracellular mixture of normal or wild-type and mutant molecules called heteroplasmy. Subsequently, as the mutant and normal mtDNAs are randomly distributed into daughter cells during mitotic or meiotic replication, a percentage of mutant and normal molecules drifts within the cell towards either pure mutant or pure normal (homoplasmy), whereas others remain heteroplasmic (Rötig *et al.* 1995). This accounts for the clinical heterogeneity of mitochondrial diseases. A threshold number of mutant mtDNA molecules must be present for the disease to be expressed in a given tissue. This threshold may vary in different tissues according to the dependence of the tissue on oxidative metabolism. Thus in the first case of mtDNA deletion diagnosed by renal biopsy (Szabolcs *et al.* 1994), approximately 90 per cent of mtDNA was deleted in renal tubular cells whereas only 50 per cent of mutant mtDNA was found in blood leucocytes.

Mitochondrial cytopathies

Muscles and the central nervous system are the most commonly affected, and various syndrome complexes have been described (Chinnery and Turnbull 1997). These include the MERRF syndrome, with myoclonic epilepsy and the histological appearance of 'ragged red fibre' disease in muscles stained with Gomori trichrome, which represent subsarcolemmal collections of abnormal mitochondria. On electron microscopy the mitochondria appear abnormal, with the appearance of a parking lot seen from the air, with crystalline inclusions. Others have the MELAS syndrome of mitochondrial encephalopathy, lactic acidosis, and stroke-like episodes. Other disorders include the Kearns–Sayre syndrome (external ophthalmoplegia, pigmentary retinopathy, myopathy, and cardiac conduction defects) and Leigh's syndrome (subacute necrotizing encephalomyelopathy). Apart from the progressive and ultimately fatal muscular weakness, which is particularly prominent after exercise, deafness and other neurological manifestations are common.

Although mitochondrial cytopathies are traditionally regarded as neuromuscular disorders, a much broader spectrum of clinical features is now known to be present (Chinnery and Turnbull 1997). Cardiac muscle and its conduction system, the haemopoietic system, and the endocrine pancreas are commonly affected, with the appearance of diabetes mellitus (for a review of the most common syndromes likely to be encountered see Egger *et al.* (1981), Munnich *et al.* (1992), and Luft (1994)). These different features may occur at different times or synchronously in single patients. The basic defect is in electron transport in mitochondria, principally cytochrome c oxidase. Thus the energy supply to cell is insufficient. Hyperlactataemia is a valuable clue to the presence of mitochondrial cytopathies, although absence of this feature does not exclude the diagnosis.

Renal syndromes in mitochondrial cytopathy

The renal syndromes of mitochondrial cytopathy have often been overlooked (Grünfeld *et al.* 1996; Niaudet and Rötig 1996, 1997; Buemi 1997) because of the prominent associated features such as deafness, blindness, diabetes mellitus, and muscular weakness. Not surprisingly in view of the high energy requirement of the renal tubules, renal syndromes centre round tubulopathies, including Fanconi syndromes (Ogier *et al.* 1988; Niaudet and Rötig 1996, 1997). Some patients do not show a full Fanconi syndrome but only aminoaciduria: most patients presented during childhood, and myopathy and neurological problems were the most frequent associated problem. Disease was severe, and half died within the first year of life.

Isolated renal tubular acidosis (Eviatar *et al.* 1990), or Bartter-like disease (Goto *et al.* 1990), together with hypercalciuria and nephrocalcinosis (Matsutani *et al.* 1992; Rötig *et al.* 1992; Niaudet *et al.* 1994; Rötig *et al.* 1995) have been described as well. Tubulointerstitial nephritis is seen with chronic renal insufficiency (Mori *et al.* 1991; Szabolcs *et al.* 1994) which may present in later life. The latter authors were able to demonstrate abnormal mitochondria within the tubules on renal biopsy (Fig. 28.2), and it is possible that a larger proportion of obscure tubulointerstitial disease relates to unrecognized mitochondrial dysfunction; for example one case was diagnosed as nephronophthisis (Donaldson *et al.* 1984). Glomerular disease may also be present. Brun *et al.* (1992) described two siblings with a *nephrotic syndrome* and focal segmental glomerulsclerosis, and three other nephrotic patients with the MELAS syndrome have been described from Japan (Yoneda *et al.* 1989; Ban *et al.* 1992; Matsushita *et al.* 1993), two of whom had focal segmental glomerulosclerosis, as well as another case from in France (Rötig *et al.* 1994*b*). Two patients presented in *acute renal failure*, one with the Kearns-Sayre syndrome (Zupanc *et al.* 1991), the other with the MELAS syndrome (Hsieh *et al.* 1995), apparently the result of secondary electrolyte problems compounded by functionally hypoxic tubules.

Finally, as many as 1 to 2 per cent of patients with isolated diabetes mellitus, mostly non-insulin-dependent, may arise from disease of mtDNA (Ballinger *et al.* 1992; Froguel and Vionnet 1995). In addition, some families suffer diabetes in a setting of multisystem involvement, such as the Wolfram or DIDMOAD syndrome in which diabetes insipidus, optic atrophy, and deafness are also present (Rötig *et al.* 1994), as a result of mutations in mtDNA.

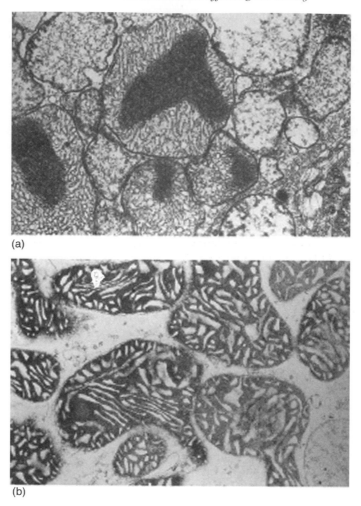

(a)

(b)

Fig. 28.2　Abnormal cristae in mitochondria within renal tubular cells in a 7-year-old girl with tubulo-interstitial renal disease. Abnormal mitochondria in the tubules on light or electron microscopy may give a clue to the diagnosis of mitochondrial cytopathy in tubulointerstitial disease of apparently obscure origin. (Magnification 9000 ×.) (Reproduced with permission from Szabolcs *et al.* (1994).).

Investigation for suspected mitochondrial disease

The main route to a diagnosis of mitochondrial cytopathy is a awareness of its existence. The presence of bizarre, apparently unrelated symptoms in patients with renal disease, especially in children and adolescents, should rouse suspicion at a clinical level. Patients may be misdiagnosed as Alport's syndrome because of associated deafness (Jansen *et al.* 1997), as nephronopthisis or non-specific tubulointerstitial disease, unless prominent extra-renal manifestations are present. In particular, minor degrees of muscle involvement may be overlooked. Determination of the resting plasma lactate concentration, which is usually elevated, is a key investigation; the lactate:

pyruvate ratio is increased also. However, a normal plasma lactate does not exclude the diagnosis, and studies on cerebrospinal fluid may be more informative. Mention has already been made of the unusual appearances of mitochondria in affected tissues seen by electron microscopy, and this may alert to the diagnosis. Muscle biopsy in cases without apparent muscle involvement may show the 'ragged red fibre' pattern on Gomori staining. Studies by polarography of oxygen consumption of isolated mitochondria or whole cells from biopised material of affected tissues establish the diagnosis further. Finally, studies using Southern blot analysis have shown deletions of mtDNA ranging from 2–9 kb in patients with a Fanconi syndrome, although less commonly point mutations have also been seen, for example the tRNA$^{Leu(URR)}$ mutation present in over 80% of sufferers from the MELAS syndrome (Jansen *et al.* 1997).

Treatment

There is no effective treatment for most of the conditions described above, except for associated acidosis, but renal physicians should be aware of the dangers of hypoxia and of some drugs (valproate, barbiturates, tetracyclines, chloramphenicol) which interfere with the action of the respiratory chain. Other possible therapies, including vitamins K and C, and riboflavin, are reviewed by Niaudet and Rötig (1997).

Gräsbeck–Imerslund syndrome (proteinuria with vitamin B$_{12}$ malabsorption)

This rare autosomal recessive syndrome (Gräsbeck *et al.* 1960; Imerslund 1960) presents in infants as a megaloblastic macrocyctic anaemia with associated subnephrotic proteinuria, which is usually highly selective (Becker *et al.* 1977) but has also been reported as non-selective (Rumpelt and Michl 1979), or even of tubular pattern (Geisert *et al.* 1975). Aminoaciduria may also be present. The syndrome seems to be seen most often in Scandinavia (Nevanlinna 1980), but cases have been reported from Germany (Becker *et al.* 1977), Israel (Ben Bassat *et al.* 1969), and elsewhere (Lin *et al.* 1994) including the United Kingdom (Uttley *et al.* 1975) and a case from South America (cited by Becker *et al.* (1977)).

Ileal biopsies show a normal morphology and the absorptive defect is confined to vitamin B$_{12}$. Hypertension is absent and the outlook for renal function is benign, but a need for vitamin B$_{12}$ supplementation persists throughout life. Although severe neurological manifestations may be present and respond to parenteral vitamin B$_{12}$ (Salameh *et al.* 1991), the proteinuria does not change during successful treatment.

The renal histology is variable (Gräsbeck *et al.* 1960; Becker *et al.* 1977; Collan *et al.* 1979; Rumpelt and Michl 1979). Normal glomeruli, mesangial expansion, and 'membranous' nephropathy have been reported on optical microscopy. Podocyte foot process fusion (Becker *et al.* 1977) and abnormalities of both the capillary basement membrane (Collan *et al.* 1979) and the podocytes (Rumpelt and Michl 1979) have been described on electron microscopy. The underlying defect which determines the specific defect in vitamin B$_{12}$ absorption and the proteinuria remains unknown.

Wiskott–Aldrich syndrome (Hitzig and Truniger 1996)

The principal manifestations of the Wiskott–Aldrich syndrome are immune deficiency and thrombocytopenia, sometimes with purpura, eczema, bloody diarrhoea, and ear infections in boys. Infection and/or bleeding are often fatal in infancy, and survivors may develop leukaemia or lymphoma. In addition, a variety of immune or autoimmune disorders have been described in these patients, including impaired skin graft rejection, but normal T-blast transformation, and raised IgA with low IgM concentrations in serum. The fundamental defect seems to be a disordered expression of a 66-kDa intracellular protein, a small GTPase of the Rho family which interacts with Cdc42, which in turn controls the surface expression of many molecules in immune cells (Featherstone 1996).

Inheritance of this complex syndrome is consistent with an X-linked recessive pattern (Crawfurd 1988, pp. 441–3), and female heterozygotes may show low platelet counts and abnormal platelet function. The gene has been localized to Xp11.22–23 in a region of high gene density (Deray *et al.* 1994).

Renal disease has been described in a number of survivors who may have had an incomplete form of the disease (Spitler *et al.* 1980; De Santo *et al.* 1988–9; Hitzig and Truniger 1996) as well as Henoch-Schönlein purpura in a female heterozygote (Lasseur *et al.* 1997). Haematuria, casts and proteinuria up to the nephrotic range with concomitant oedema have been noted, but the renal histology has been determined in only a few cases. Gutenberger *et al.* (1970) and Standen *et al.* (1986) described familial thrombocytopenia, increased IgA, and renal disease in several family members. Renal biopsy showed proliferative glomerulonephritis or interstitial nephritis. A patient studied in our unit had a vasculitic picture clinically, which has also been reported in a number of patients without renal involvement. A crescentic glomerulonephritis showing prominent mesangial IgA deposition was present in the renal biopsy, as in the case described by De Santo *et al.* (1988–9); an evolution into endstage renal failure occurred within 2 years of onset. This patient was later transplanted successfully under minimal immunosuppression (Webb *et al.* 1993). The patient described by Hitzig and Truniger (1996) and a brother of that of Fischer *et al.* (1996) also showed IgA nephropathy, but in the former case only mild mesangial proliferative disease was present. In Fischer *et al.*'s family both brothers evolved into renal failure and one was transplanted, but under immunosuppression the patients developed severe cytomegalovirus infection and died. Another successful transplant has been reported however (Meisels *et al.* 1995) although this patient, unlike ours, was capable of developing clinical rejection.

X-linked granulomatous disease

In two-thirds of patients chronic granulomatous disease is an X-linked condition affecting males in whom the defective gene at Xq 21.1 leads to the absence of a 90-kDa component of cytochrome b. The remaining patients usually have a less severe disease, inherited in an autosomal recessive manner, due to a defect in a cytosolic factor necessary for the respiratory burst. Female heterozygotes carrying the X-linked form of the disease frequently develop systemic lupus erythematosus. The functional defect in both types is defective phagocytosis, associated with impaired chemiluminescence of neutrophils and impaired reduction of the dye nitroblue tetrazolium. Clinical presentation is usually in infancy, with skin sepsis which becomes deeper, resulting in abscess formation, and chronically discharging sinuses from regional lymph nodes.

Alibadi *et al.* (1989) described 50 per cent of the children in their series as having recurrent pyelonephritis associated with retroperitoneal lymphadenitis, granuloma formation, and obstruction. Antibiotics were required to treat the infections, but ureterolysis was necessary in one patient and two had nephrectomies. It is not yet clear whether these findings are typical of other series of this rare inherited disorder, but urinary tract imaging should be performed in any child or young adult presenting with a urinary tract infection. Interstitial cystitis has also been reported (Kontras *et al.* 1971). Sclerosing glomerulonephritis was noted in one family (Dilworth and Mandell 1977).

Branchio-oto-renal dysplasia

There are various associations between malformed ears, hearing loss, and renal anomalies (Crawfurd 1988). One of the more common and better delineated of these syndromes is usually called the branchio-oto-renal dysplasia syndrome. The gene for this condition has been mapped to chromosome 8q. One family with both the trichorhinopharyngeal and branchio-oto syndromes has been reported in which an inherited rearrangement of chromosme 8q involving band 8q13.3 has been documented (Haan *et al.* 1989). Further refined mapping of the gene is consistent with this genetic localization (Kumar *et al.* 1994; Li Ni *et al.* 1994). The gene involved has been identified and is a human homologue of the *Drosophilsa eyes absent* gene (Abdelhak *et al.* 1997).

The branchio-oto-renal syndrome is inherited as an autosomal dominant condition; the prevalence about one in 40 000. Patients present with hearing loss; sensorineural, middle-ear and mixed types have all been described. Branchial fistulas and abnormalities of the pinna (usually described as 'cup-shaped') together with pre-auricular pits or clefts (Fig. 28.3) may also be present. Structural renal abnormalities of various types are associated, including renal dysplasia, aplasia, duplication defects, and bladder anomalies (Widdershoven *et al.* 1983). One family with cystic kidneys in the branchio-oto-renal syndrome has been described (Melnick *et al.* 1976). The phenotypic expression varies from family to family, with some having the branchial anomalies and hearing loss without renal dysplasia.

This condition may be more common than is realized. A study of 400 children with hearing problems in Montreal showed 19 with pre-auricular pits, and four families out of nine who consented to further investigation had branchio-oto-renal dysplasia (Fraser *et al.* 1980). Certainly, the pre-auricular area should be examined in all patients with renal anomalies or with renal failure of obscure origin and deafness. A number of patients enter endstage renal disease if the renal anomalies are severe.

Orofaciodigital syndrome type 1

This a rare (1:250000 live births) multiple congenital syndrome of multiple anomalies (Donnai *et al.* 1987), consisting of oral frenulae and clefts, hypoplasia of the nasal alae, hamartomata of the tongue, symmetrical digital shortening, together with mental retardation in about fifty per cent of cases. Inheritance patterns are suggestive of an X-linked disease lethal to males, resulting in apparent expression only in female heterozygotes, and has recently been mapped to Xp22.2–Xp22.3 (Feather *et al.* 1997*b*). However, up to three quarters of recorded cases seem to be sporadic without a family history. Renal findings suggest polycystic kidney disease, and this has been diagnosed as a coincidental anomaly in the past, with a slow evolution into renal failure. However, Feather *et al.* (1997*a*) have shown in one kindred that the cysts were mainly glomerular in origin. Clues to the diagnosis (apart from the associated anomalies, which may be minor e.g. bilaterally shortened fingers) are what appears to be polycystic kidney disease affecting only female members of a family, with a pseudo-dominant inheritance.

Smith–Lemli–Opitz syndrome

Children with this relatively common autosomal recessive syndrome (carrier rate) present with poor growth, microcephaly, various degrees of mental retardation, hypotonia, and incomplete development of the external genitalia in males. Glomerulosclerosis has also been described. The facies is dysmorphic and characteristic (Fig. 28.4). Other structural anomalies of the gonads, limbs, and digits may be seen in some cases (Pober 1990). It is inherited in an autosomal recessive

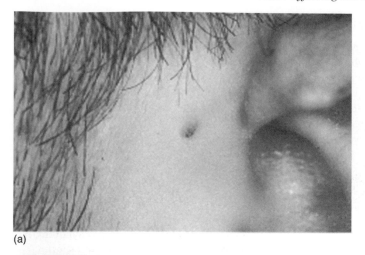

(a)

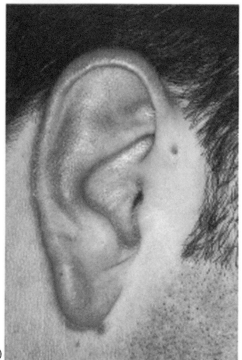

(b)

Fig. 28.3 Pre-auricular pits in the branchio-oto-renal syndrome. A variety of pits and clefts can be seen, together with abnormalities of the pinna which may be simplified and cup-shaped.

fashion, but the location of the gene is uncertain. A defect in cholesterol biosynthesis at the 7-dehydrocholesterol to cholest-5-en-3β-ol step has been described (Tint *et al.* 1994), with accumulation of the former and depletion of the latter in plasma and body fluids. How this relates to the clinical manifestations remains obscure, but they could be the result of cholesterol deficiency during fetal development, with lack of 7-dehydrocholesterol for insertion into membranes.

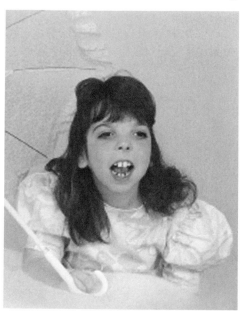

Fig. 28.4 The Smith–Lemli–Opitz syndrome in a 10-year-old girl. The characteristic facies of up-turned nose, micrognathia, and ptosis can be seen. (Case described by Tint *et al.* (1994) with the permission of Dr Ellen Roy Elias, The Floating Hospital for Children, Boston, MA.)

It is interesting that some inhibitors of cholesterol synthesis lead to renal abnormalities in animals (Barbu *et al.* 1988), and about two-thirds of cases show a variety of renal anomalies including dysplasia, hypoplasia, and anomalies of urinary drainage (Cherstvoy *et al.* 1975).

Cystic fibrosis

Cystic fibrosis is a relatively common recessive inherited condition (one in 19 healthy Caucasian individuals are carriers) arising from mutations in the cystic fibrosis transmembrane conductance regulator gene located at 7q.21.3–22.1 which codes for a cAMP-regulated Cl$^-$ channel in the apical membrane of secretory epithelia (Coutelle *et al.* 1993). The decrease in volume of secretions is insufficient to explain the very viscid secretions produced from the bronchial glands, and there is also blockage of pancreatic ducts and pancreatic exocrine failure. These viscid bronchial secretions lead to recurrent and persistent pulmonary infections which, until the advent of antibiotics, were usually fatal in childhood. However, an increasing number of patients now survive into their twenties, thirties, and even forties.

In the past various renal changes were described at post mortem (Abramowsky and Swinehart 1982), including amyloidosis and glomerulosclerosis, but more recently it has become evident that proteinuria and glomerulonephritis are rather frequent in these long-standing cases of cystic fibrosis. Whether the glomerulonephritis relates to the underlying disease or to the chronic infections suffered by patients with cystic fibrosis is not clear; the predominant species of nephritis is IgA nephropathy (Melzi *et al.* 1991), as in two personal cases, and crescentic nephritis has been seen also. Secondary amyloidosis would be expected and has been recorded (Glenner 1986; McGlennan *et al.* 1986; Melzi *et al.* 1991), with a full nephrotic syndrome in some cases (Gaffney *et al.* 1993) and evolution to renal failure in others (Melzi *et al.* 1991). In addition, vasculitis has been found in older patients (Finnegan *et al.* 1989), usually ANCA-positive and with clinically evident nephritis in three cases. One of Finnegan's patients had Henoch–Schönlein purpura. Antineutrophil cytoplasmic antibodies (ANCA) have been found in children with cystic fibrosis and infections but without clinical vasculitis (Efthamiou *et al.* 1991), an interesting observation in view of the controversy as to the pathogenetic significance of these antibodies. One-third of patients have hypercalciuria, and microscopic nephrocalcinosis is visible in the other 90 per cent, including infants (Katz *et al.* 1988).

Cockayne syndrome

Cockayne syndrome is an autosomal recessive disorder characterized by a variety of clinical features of which photosenstitivity, precocious senile appearance, poor growth, neurological abnormalities, sensorineural deafness, and pigmentary retinopathy are common (Nance and Berry 1992). The basic lesion appears to be a defect in the repair of DNA after damage, particularly by ultraviolet irradiation (Van Hoffen *et al.* 1993). Death usually occurs in early life, but some patients survive into adulthood. Renal symptoms consisting of hypertension, mild proteinuria or a nephrotic syndrome (Reiss *et al.* 1996), and declining renal function in some cases leading to renal failure affect about one in 10 patients. A generalized thickening of the glomerular basement membrane is seen on renal biopsy (Hirooka *et al.* 1988; Sato *et al.* 1988) or focal segmental glomerulo-sclerosis (Reiss *et al.* 1996).

Orotic aciduria

This rare condition (Webster *et al.* 1995) arises from defects in one of two multienzymes of pyrimidine synthesis, now usually called multienzyme pyr 5,6 or uridine monophosphate synthase; the two enzymic activities expressed by the single protein are orotidine 5′- monophosphate decarboxylase and orotate phosphoribosyl transferase. Deficiency of either leads to the excretion of large amounts of orotic acid. The condition is inherited as an autosomal recessive pattern, with the gene being located near 3q13.

Clinical manifestations include megaloblastic anaemia, diarrhoea, growth retardation, and cardiac malformations in some patients. The large excretion of very insoluble orotic acid leads to a 'sludge' of crystals within the urinary tract, with colic, haematuria, and obstruction at all levels from the renal pelvis to the urethra, one or more of which have affected about half the reported cases. The urine is clear initially but then throws down a profuse sediment. Treatment with uridine is successful but must be maintained lifelong. A high urine output is also desirable to help solubilize the orotic acid.

Familial hypo/hyperparathyroidism, deafness, and renal disease

Bilous *et al.* (1992) described a family showing this conjunction with an apparently dominant inheritance in which the renal component appeared to be dysplasia. The combination of disorders raises the question of whether this family were in fact suffering from a transmissible mitochondrial cytopathy (see above) or an unusual type of Alport's syndrome. This may be a different condition from the family described by Barakat *et al.* (1977), in which the renal component was a nephrotic syndrome in four siblings; the pattern of inheritance was not clear, but appeared to be recessive.

In contrast, Edwards *et al.* (1989) described a family in which the propositus presented with hypercalcaemia and parathyroid hyperplasia was found. Inheritance was consistent with an autosomal recessive pattern and appeared to be distinct from Alport's syndrome; ocular examination was normal.

Optic nerve disorders and renal disease

Ocular abnormalities have been associated with renal disease in a number of families (Bron *et al.* 1989; Weaver *et al.* 1988; Leyes *et al.* 1997). The ocular component has varied from microphthalmos to coloboma, or the optic nerve appearance described as the 'morning glory' optic disc (Weaver *et al.* 1998) after the flower of that name (*Convolvulus*) (Fig. 28.5). Renal failure has ensued in some family members. These conditions have now been associated with mutations in one of the nine *PAX* transcription genes, *PAX2* (Sanyanusin *et al.* 1995; Schimmenti *et al.* 1997) located at 10q24–5, which is expressed in the ureteric bud and is involved in kidney and eye development. The spectrum of renal abnormalities includes renal agenesis, vesicoureteric reflux and hypoplasia, these conditions are described in more detail in Leys *et al.* (1997).

Charcot-Marie-Tooth disease

This is a group of inherited peripheral neuropathies principally affecting the legs and arising from myelin degeneration, commonly presenting as a mixed neuropathy with weakness and pes cavus during childhood and adolescence. The syndrome has a diverse inheritance: type 1A, the commonest is a dominant condition of variable penetrance which results from a mutation in the myelin protein Po (myelin protein zero, MPZ) gene on chromosome 1. Type 1B also dominant from mutations at chromosome 17p11.2 for peripheral myelin protein PMP22. X-linked disease is associated with varied mutations in the gene for a gap protein, connexin 32 (Chance and Fischbeck 1994).

A dozen patients have been described with renal disease since the first description of three cases from Canada (Lemieux and Neemeh 1967; Hanson *et al.* 1970; Lennert *et al.* 1976; Castillo *et al.* 1982; Guillot *et al.* 1984; Hara *et al.* 1984; Gherardi *et al.* 1986; Lloveras *et al.* 1986), as well as two unpublished personal cases. The presenting feature in all was proteinuria of up to

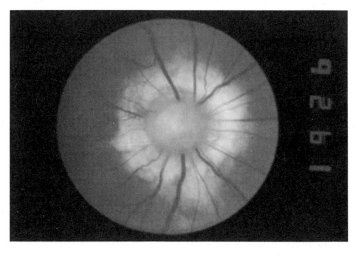

Fig. 28.5 The 'morning glory' appearance of the optic nerve which may be associated with renal disease, sometimes accompanied by renal failure. (By courtesy of Dr David Calver.)

nephrotic dimensions, associated with focal segmental glomerulosclerosis in all patients. Most of the patients were young, but one was 60 years of age (Moulin *et al.* 1984). Rapid progression to end-stage renal failure and resistance to treatment has been seen in most, but some have shown a more benign evolution (Martini *et al.* 1985). Half of the patients with renal disease also had sensineural deafness, rare in other affected patients. This has led to a misdiagnosis of Alport's syndrome in some, but the characteristic appearances of the glomerular basement membrane seen in Alport's syndrome were absent, except in one case which appears to represent two diseases in one family (Gregory *et al.* 1991). Because of the variable penetrance only one half of the patients with renal disease had a family history, so the condition must be considered in any patient with FSGS who presents peripheral neuropathy.

Why such patients should develop progressive FSGS remains unclear, unless autonomic neuropathic regulatory failure is present within the intrarenal circulation, since familial dysautonomia is also associated with FSGS.

Alagille's syndrome

This syndrome of chronic cholestasis arising from a paucity of bile ducts is associated with a characteristic facies together with skeletal, ocular, and cardiovascular abnormalities. The gene, whose function remains unknown, is located at 20p12 (Spinner *et al.* 1994). A mesangiopathic glomerulopathy has been described, with fibrillary deposits and foam cells (Habib *et al.* 1987; Russo *et al.* 1987), which correlates with the severity of the hyperlipidemia and resembles that seen in patients with LCAT deficiency (see Chapter 16). Medullary cysts have also been described (Russo *et al.* 1987), as well as cystic dysplastic kidneys (Martin *et al.* 1996). One of Russo *et al.*'s patients had appearances similar to membranous nephropathy, with positivity for IgG and complement. Otherwise, the basement membranes show, on electron microscopy, a lamellated appearance. Usually the clinical manifestations of the glomerulopathy are mild, but renal failure may appear during adult life and its management may be influenced strongly by the associated problems, especially as concomitant liver transplantation may be required.

α_1-antitrypsin deficiency

α_1-antitrypsin is a circulating acute phase 52 kD glycoprotein, a member of the serpin (serine proteinase inhibitor) family synthesized in the liver and in macrophages, which antagonizes a wide range of proteolytic enzymes important in inducing inflammation especially neutrophil elastase (Carrell *et al.* 1994). The locus is located at 14q.31.2 and the synthesis of the molecule is controlled by two codominant genes which affect disease susceptibility. About 1:2500 of the Caucasian population are homozygous for type Z (PiZZ), and have a plasma concentration of enzyme below the effective level. The main effect of this deficiency is on the lung with early onset of severe emphysema, and on the liver, with accumulation of the mutant molecule within hepatocytes, leading to cirrhosis (Lomas *et al.* 1992). Liver disease is often evident in infancy or childhood, whilst the emphysema tends to have a later onset.

Renal disease is frequently seen (Davis *et al.* 1992) especially in children with severe liver disease, much less so in emphysematous adults. The most common pattern observed has been mesangiocapillary glomerulonephritis type I (Davis *et al.* 1992; Strife *et al.* 1983) in affected children, but crescentic nephritis has been described also principally in adults, usually with concomitant anti-neutrophil antibody associated (ANCA)-positive vasculitis (Lévy *et al.* 1985; Lewis *et al.* 1985; Lévy 1986; Fortin *et al.* 1991; Mazodier *et al.* 1996). The ANCA may be directed against proteinase 3 (Savidge *et al.* 1995), and a full Wegener's syndrome may be seen (Mazodier *et al.* 1996). Griffith *et al.* (1996) make the interesting observation that the c-ANCA anti-PR3 antibody is associated with the ZZ phenotype, p-ANCA with the S allele. Further Segelmark *et al.* (1995) suggested an influence of the Z allele on outcome on vasculitis as a whole. Henoch-Schönlein purpura was noted in two adult patients (Elzouki *et al.* 1995). In another patient hepatic transplantation led to regression of the mesangiocapillary glomerulonephritis (Elzouki *et al.* 1997) thus proving the causality of the association.

The pathogenesis of the nephritis or vasculitis is not clear: the absence of the α_1-antitrypsin from the plasma could facilitate intraglomerular or vascular inflammation (Esnault 1997), but the PiZZ itself has been demonstrated within glomerular immune aggregates (Davis *et al.* 1992) suggesting that perhaps it might act as an antigen to provoke nephritis. IgA has usually been reported alone or as well as IgG in glomerular immune aggregates but the origin of the IgA (gut, bone marrow) is not yet known.

Inherited disorders of renal tubular transporters

Along the length of the renal tubule some 40 different transporters are inserted into the apical or basolateral membranes and creating the polarity of the tubular eipthelium (López-Nieto and Brenner 1997). Mutations in the majority of these transporters have now been described leading to such well-known syndromes described elsewhere in this book as cystinuria and other aminoacidurias, glycosurias, hypophosphataemia, renal tubular acidosis of various types, Dent's disease and idiopathic hypercalciuria, and nephrogenic diabetes insipidus.

Recently it has been realized that three inherited diseases depend upon mutations in ion transporters in the tubule: Bartter's syndrome, the clinically-related Gitelman's syndrome, and Liddle's syndrome (Pearce 1998).

Bartter's and Gitelman's syndrome

Batter's syndrome and Gitelman's syndrome were first described in 1962 and 1966, respectively (Bartter, *et al.* 1962, Gitelman, *et al.* 1966). For more than three decades, these two syndromes have not be accurately differentiated by many clinicians. Recent progress in cell physiology and molecular genetics has established the molecular mechanisms involved, and has clearly individualized the two syndromes. Both syndromes, often familial, include metabolic alkalosis and hypokalemia due to renal wasting, but other features are distinctive.

Bartter's syndrome is a severe, often congenital syndrome, recognized before the age of 6 years. The neonatal form is revealed by polyhydramnios during pregnancy, premature delivery, failure to thrive and polyuropolydipsia. High plasma renin and aldosterone and juxtaglomenular cell hyperplasia have also been recognized, but anti-aldosterone agents do not correct the biochemical abnormalities. Hyperprostaglandism has been documented, mostly in the pre/neonatal form (Seyberth, *et al.* 1985). Bartter's syndrome is characterized by a defect in NaCl reabsorption in the thick ascending limb of the loop of Henle. This also accounts for hypercalciuria (or high molar urinary calcium/creatinine concentration ratio) and nephrocalcinosis in some patients. The patients act as if they were ingesting chronically a loop diuretic. Indeed an almost identical syndrome in adult is produced by divictic abuse and may be confused with the inherited form.

Three molecular defects have been identified in the autosomal recessive form of Bartter's syndrome, all affecting NaCl reabsorption in Henle's loop, at three different sites: the Na^+-K^+-$2Cl^-$ contransporter (NKCC2) inhibited by bumetamide-furosemide, located at the apical membrane; the potassium apical channel (ROMK); and the basolateral Cl⁻ channel (CLCNKB) (Simon *et al.* 1997; Simon *et al.* 1996*a*; Simon *et al.* 1996*b*). The last defect is the most prevalent. However, the molecular abnormality, as well as the mode of inheritance, are so far unknown in some families. The clinical presentation is similar in these three forms, except nephrocalcinosis which is not observed in families with CLCNKB mutations. Most families investigated are consanguineous and affected patients are homozygous for the inactivating mutations.

Gitelman's syndrome is revealed in children after 8 years of age of often in adults. Symptoms due to potassium deficit (tetany, muscle weakness) are often mild or absent. Urinary calcium excretion (or molar urinary calcium/creatinine concentration ratio ≤0.2) is low (Bettinelli, *et al.* 1992). Nephrocalcinosis is not found. Serum magnesium concentration is low in all patients, whereas it is decreased in only 20 to 30% of th patients with Bartter's syndrome. Chondrocalcinosis develops in some cases and is probably related to magnesium deficit. Prostaglandin excretion is normal and renin and aldosterone levels are often within normal range.

A single molecular defect has been found in autosomal recessive Gitelman's syndromes, involving the thiazide-sensitive Na-Cl contransporter localized at the apical membrane of the cells of the distal convoluted tubule and connecting segment (in humans) (Simon, *et al.* 1996*c*). This explains why the patients act as if they were chronically ingesting thiazide diuretics. Most patients are composite heterozygotes, the gene mutation inherited from the mother being different from that inherited from the father.

Liddle's syndrome and pseudohyperaldosteronism type I

In 1963 Liddle *et al.* described a familial autosomal dominant hypokalaemic hypertension with features which mimicked primary aldosteronism, but in which plasma aldosterone and renin concentrations were very low and there was resistance to spironolactone. Liddle and colleagues postulated that this abnormality must be the result of a defect in a renal tubular transporter, an hypothesis later proved correct by disappearance of the hypertension and hypokalaemia following renal transplantation in several patients.

Clinical presentation is usually in childhood or early adult life, but it may be seen in infancy. Severe hypertension mimicking Conn's syndrome is the usual mode of onset, and diagnosis may be missed for long period whilst a diagnosis of Conn's syndrome or renal artery stenosis is sought unsuccessfully. However, the low aldosterone and renin are diagnostic in this situation. Volume expansion from sodium retention suppresses renin secretion. The syndrome was shown by studies 30 years later in the original family to arise from a mutation in the amiloride/triamterene-sensitive sodium channel located in the luminal surface of the principal cells of the cortical collecting duct (Shimkets *et al.* 1994). This has three sub-units, designated α, β and γ. The first is responsible for conductance and the latter two regulate the transport. The transporter is widely distributed in cells and it and its mutations are not confined to renal epithelium or epithelial cells (Oh and Warnock 1997).

The gene for the β chain is located on chromosome 16p 12.2–13.1 (Shimkets *et al.* 1994*a*), and mutations in either the β- or the γ-subunit (coded on chromosome 12p13.1pter) lead to increased conductance with sodium entry and potassium exit down their electrochemical gradients, which give rise to the clinical syndrome (Shimkets *et al.* 1994; Hansson *et al.* 1995). In contrast, mutations of the α chain lead to the channel being closed and a syndrome mimicking hypoalderosteronism (pseudohypoaldosteronism type I) (Chang *et al.* 1996).

Treatment of Liddle's syndrome is with amiloride or triamterene, which blocks the open channel, raises plasma potassium and controls the hypertension. The importance of this rare type of inherited hypertension is that it forms a model of how single gene mutations can lead to a hypertensive state, and thus to the idea of candidate genes being able to explain how essential hypertension might arise as a multigenic disease involving tubular cation transporters (Williams and Fisher 1997; Warnock 1998).

References

Abdelhak, S., Kalatzis, V., Heilig, R., Compain, S., Samson, D., and Vincent, C. (1997). A human homologue of the Drosophila eyes absent gene underlies branchio–oto–renal (BOR) syndrome and identifies a novel gene family. *Nature Genetics*, 15, 157–64.

Abramovsky, C.R. and Swineheart, G.L. (1982). The nephropathy of cystic fibrosis. *Human Pathology*, 13, 934–9.

Alibadi, H., Gonzalez, R., and Quie, P.G. (1989). Urinary tract disorders in patients with chronic granulomatous disease. *New England Journal of Medicine*, 321, 706–8.

Ballinger, S.W. *et al.* (1992). Maternally transmitted diabetes and deafness associated with 10.4 kb mitochondrial DNA deletion. *Nature Genetics*, 1, 11–15.

Ban, S.I., Mori, N., Saito, K., Mizukami, K., Suzuki, T., and Shiraishi, H. (1992). An autopsy case of mitochondrial enecephalomyopathy (MELAS) with special reference to extraneuromuscular abnormalities. *Acta Pathologica Japonica*, 42, 818–24.

Barakat, A.Y., D'Alabora, J.B., Martin, M.M., and Jose, P.A. (1977). Familial nephrosis, nerve deafness, and hypoparathyroidism. *Journal of Pediatrics*, 91, 61–4.

Barbu, V. *et al.* (1988). Cholesterol prevents the teratogenic effects of AY 9944: importance of timing of cholesterol supplementation to rats. *Journal of Nutrition*, 110, 2310–12.

Barness, E.G. and Opitz, J.M. (1993). Renal abnormalities in malformation syndromes. In: *Pediatric Kidney Disease* (2nd edn) (ed. C.M. Edelmann Jr), pp. 1067–1119. Little Brown, Boston, MA.

Bartter, F.C., Pronove, P., Gill, J.R.J., and MacCardle, R.C. (1962). Hyperplasia of the juxtaglomerular complex with hyperaldosteronism and hypokalemic alkalosis. *American Journal of Medicine*, 33, 811–28.

Becker, M., Rotthauwe, H.W., Weber, H.-P., and Fischbach, H. (1977). Selective vitamin B_{12} malabsorption (Imerslund–Gräsbeck syndrome). Studies on gastroenterological and nephrological problems. *European Journal of Pediatrics,* 124, 139–53.

Ben Bassat, J., Feinstein, A., and Ramot, B. (1969). Selective vitamin B_{12} malabsorption with proteinuria in Israel. *Israel Journal of Medical Sciences*, 5, 62–8.

Bettinelli, A., Bianchetti, M.G., Girardin, E., Caringella, A., Cecconi, M., Appiani, A.C., *et al.* (1992). Use of calcium excretion values to distinguish two forms of primary renal tubular hypokalemic alkalosis: Bartter and Gitelman syndromes. *The Journal of Pediatrics*, 120, 38–43.

Bilous, R.W. *et al.* (1992). Brief report: autosomal dominant familial hypoparathyroidism, sensorineural deafness and renal dysplasia. *New England Journal of Medicine*, 327, 1069–74.

Bron, A.J., Burgess, S.E., Awdry, P.N., Oliver, D., and Arden, G. (1989). Papillo-renal syndrome. An inherited association of optic disc dysplasia and renal disease. Report and review of the literature. *Ophthalmological Paediatrics and Genetics*, 10, 185–98.

Brun, P., Ogier, H., Romero, N., Bocquet, L., Gubler, M.-C., and Loirat, C. (1992). Syndrome néphrotique avec hyalinose segmentaire et focale au cours d'une cytopathie mitchondriale. *Pédiatrie*, 47, 23.

Buemi, M. *et al.* (1997). Renal failure from mitochondrial cytopathies. *Nephron*, 76, 249–53.

Carrell, R.W., Whisstock, J., and Lomas, D.A. (1994). Conformational changes in serpins and the mechanism of α_1-antitrypsin deficiency. *American Journal of Respiratory and Critical Care Medicine*, 150, s171–6.

Castillo, G., Bilbao, F., Prats-Viñas, J.M. *et al.* (1982). Glomerulosclerosis focal, hipertensión arterial y sordera neurosensorial en la enfermedad de Charcot-Marie-Tooth. *Nefrología*, **2**, 61–5.

Chance, P.F., and Fischheck, C.H. (1994). Molecular genetics of Charcot Marie Tooth disease. *Human Molecular Genetics*, **3** Sept. No 1, 1503–7.

Chang, S.S., Grunder, S., Hanukoglu, A., *et al.* (1996). Mutations in sub-units of the epithelial sodium channel cause salt wasting with hyperchloraemic acidosis, pseudohyperaldosteronism type 1. *Nature Genetics*, **12**, 248–53.

Cherstvoy, E.D. *et al.* (1975). The pathological anatomy of the Smith–Lemli–Opitz syndrome. *Clinical Genetics*, **7**, 383–7.

Chinnery, P.F., and Turnbull, D.M. (1997) Mitochondrial medicine. *Quarterly Journal of Medicine*, **90**, 657–67.

Clarren, S.K. (1994). Inherited renal disorders. In: *Pediatric Nephrology* (2nd edn) (ed. M.A. Holliday, T.M. Barrett, and E. Avner), pp. 491–514. Little Brown, Boston, MA.

Collan, Y., Lahdevirta, J., and Jokinen, E.J. (1979). Selective vitamin B_{12} malabsorption with proteinuria. Renal biopsy study. *Nephron*, **23**, 297–303.

Coutelle, C., Caplen, N., Hart, S., Huxley, C., Williamson, R. (1993). Gene therapy for cystic fibrosis. *Archives of Disease in Childhood*, **68**, 437–43.

Crawfurd, M. D'A. (1988). *The Genetics of Renal Tract Disorders*. Oxford University Press.

Davis, I.D., Burke, B., Freese, D., Sharp, H.L., and Kim, Y. (1992). The pathologic spectrum of nephropathy associated with α_1-antitrypsin deficiency. *Human Pathology*, **23**, 57–62.

Deray, J.M., Ochs, H.D., and Francke, V. (1994). Isolation of a novel gene mutated in Wiskott–Aldrich syndrome. *Cell*, **78**, 635–44.

De Santo, N.G. *et al.* (1988–9). IgA glomerulopathy in Wiskott–Aldrich syndrome. *Child Nephrology and Urology*, **9**, 118–20.

Dilworth, J.A. and Mandell, G.L. (1977). Adults with chronic granulomatous disease. *American Journal of Medicine*, **63**, 233–43.

Donaldson, M.D.C., Warner, A.A., Trompeter, R.S., Haycock, G.B., and Chantler, C. (1984). Familial juvenile nephronophthisis, Jeune's syndrome, and associated disorders. *Archives of Disease in Childhood*, **60**, 426–34.

Donnai, D., Kerzin-Storrar, L., and Harris, R. (1987). Familial orofaciodigital syndrome type I presenting as adult polycystic kidney disease. *Journal of Medical Genetics*, **24**, 84–7.

Edwards, B.D., Patton, M.A., Dilly, S.A., and Eastwood, J.B. (1989). A new syndrome of autosomal recessive nephropathy, deafness and hyperparathyroidism. *Journal of Medical Genetics*, **26**, 289–93.

Efthamiou, J., Spickett, G., and Lane, D. (1991). Antineutrophil cytoplasmic antibodies, cystic fibrosis and infection. *Lancet*, **337**, 1037–8.

Egger, J., Lake, B.D., and Wilson, J. (1981). Mitochondrial cytopathy. A multisystem disorder with ragged red fibres on muscle biopsy. *Archives of Disease in Childhood*, **46**, 741–52.

Elzouki, A.-N., Sterner, G., and Eriksson, S. (1995). Henoch-Schönlein purpura and alpha 1-antitrypsin deficiency. *Nephrology Dialysis Transplantation*, **10**, 1454–7.

Elzouki, A.N., Lingren, S., Nilsson, S., Veress, B., and Eriksson, S. (1997) Severe alpha-1 antitrypsin deficiency (PiZ homozygosity) with membranoproliferative glomerulonephritis and nephrotic syndrome, reversible after orthotopic liver transplantation. *Journal of Hepatology*, **26**, 1403–7.

Esnault, V.L. (1997). ANCA-positive vasculitis and alpha-1 antitrypsin deficiency: could free ANCA antigens released by neutrophils mediate vasculitic lesions? *Nephrology Dialysis Transplantation*, **12**, 249–51.

Eviatar, L. *et al.* (1990). Kearns–Sayre syndrome presenting as renal tubular acidosis. *Neurology*, **40**, 1761–3.

Feather, S.A., Woolf, A.S., Donnai, D., Malcolm, S., and Winter, R.M. (1997*b*) The oro-facial-digital syndrome type 1 (OFD1), a cause of polycyctic disease and associated amlformations, maps to Xp22.2-Xp22.3. *Human Molecular Genetics*, **6**, 1163–7.

Feather, S.A., Winyard, P.J.D., Dodd, S., and Woolf, A.S. (1997*a*). Oro-facial-digital syndrome type 1 is another dominant polycystic kidney disease: clinical, radiological and histopathological features of a new kindred. *Nephrology Dialysis Transplantation*, **12**, 1354–61.

Featherstone, C. (1996). How does one gene cause the Wiskott-Aldrich syndrome? *Lancet*, **348**, 950.

Finnegan, M.J. *et al.* (1989). Vasculitis complicating cystic fibrosis. *Quarterly Journal of Medicine*, **72**, 609–21.

Fischer, A., Binet, I., Oertli, D., Bock, A., and Thiel, G. (1996). Fatal outcome of renal transplantation in a patient with the Wiskott-Aldrich syndrome. *Nephrology Dialysis Transplantation*, **11**, 2077–9.

Fortin, P.R., Frazer, R.S., Watts, C.S., and Esdaile, J.M. (1991). α_1-antitrypsin deficiency and necrotizing vasculitis. *Journal of Rheumatology*, **18**, 1613–6.

Fraser, R.C., Sproule, J.R., and Halal, F. (1980). Frequency of the branchio-oto-renal (BOR) syndrome in children with profound hearing loss. *American Journal of Human Genetics*, **7**, 341–9.

Froguel, P. and Vionnet, N. (1995). Genetics of non-insulin dependent diabetes mellitus: from genes to disease. *Advances in Nephrology*, **24**, 157–63.

Gaffney, K., Gibbons, D., Keogh, B., and Fitzgerald, M.X. (1993). Amyloidosis complicating cystic fibrosis. *Thorax*, **48**, 949–50.

Geisert, J., Luckel, J.-C., Lutz, D., and Beyer, P. (1975). Les protéinuries de type tubulaire chez l'enfant. *Annales de Pédiatrie*, **22**, 297–300.

Gherardi, R., Belghiti-Deprez., D., Hirbec, G., Bouche, P., and Lagrue, G. (1985). Focal glomerulosclerosis associated with Charcot-Marie-Tooth disease. *Nephron*, **40**, 357–61.

Gilbert Barness, E.F., Opitz, J.M., and Barness, L.A. (1989). Hereditable malformations of the kidney and urinary tract. In: *Inheritance of Kidney and Urinary Tract Diseases* (ed. A. Spitzer and E.Avner). Kluwer, Boston, MA.

Gitelman, H.J., Graham, J.B., and Welg, L.G. (1966). A new familial disorder characterized by hypokalemia and hypomagnesemia. *Transactions of the Association of American Physicians*, **79**, 221–35.

Glenner, G.G. (1986). Reactive systemic amyloidosis in cystic fibrosis and other disorders associated with chronic inflammation. *Archives of Pathology and Laboratory Medicine*, **110**, 873–4.

Goto, Y., Itami, N., Kajii, N., Tichimaru, H., Endo, M., and Horai, S. (1990). Renal tubular involvement mimicking Bartter syndrome in a patient with Kearns–Sayre syndrome. *Journal of Pediatrics*, **116**, 904–10.

Gräsbeck, R., Gordin, R., Kantero, I., and Kühlback, B. (1960). Selective B_{12} malabsorption and proteinuria in young people. *Acta Medica Scandinavica*, **167**, 289–96.

Gregory, M.C., Terreros, D., Kashtan, C.E. *et al.* (1991). Ultrastructural and clinical evidence of Alport syndrome in a kindred with Charcot Marie Tooth disease. *Journal of the American Society of Nephrology*, **2**, 254.

Griffith, M.E., Lovegrove, J.U., Gaskin, G., Whitehouse, D.B., and Pusey, C.D. (1996). C-antineutrophil cytoplasmic antibody in vasculitis patients is associated with the Z allele of alpha-1-antitrypsin, and p-antineutrophil cytoplasmic antibody positivity with the S allele. *Nephrology Dialysis Transplantation*, **11**, 438–43.

Grünfeld, J.-P., Niaudet, P., and Rötig, A. (1996). Renal involvement in mitochondrial cytopathies. *Nephrology Dialysis Transplantation*, **11**, 760–1.

Guillot, M., Gubler, M.C., Aicardi, J., Broyer, M., Landthaler, G. and Parain D. (1984). Nephropathy associated with Charcot-Marie-Tooth (CMT) disease. *International Journal of Pediatric Nephrology*, **6**, 232 (abstract).

Gutenberger, J. *et al.* (1970). Familial thrombocytopenia, elevated serum IgA levels and renal disease: report of a kindred. *American Journal of Medicine*, **49**, 729–41.

Haan, E.A. *et al.* (1989). Tricho-rhino-phalangeal and branchio-oto syndromes in a family with an inherited rearrangement of chromosome 8a. *American Journal of Medical Genetics*, **32**, 490–4.

Habib, R., Dommergues, J.P., Gubler, M.C. *et al.* (1987) Glomerular mesangiolipidosis in Alagille syndrome (arteriohepatic dysplasia). *Pediatric Nephrology*, 1, 455–64.

Hanson, P.A., Farber, R.E., and Armstrong R.A. (1970). Distal muscle wasting, nephritis and deafness. *Neurology*, 20, 426–34.

Hansson, J.H., Nelson-Williams, C., Suzuki, H. *et al.* (1995). Hypertension caused by a truncated epithelial sodium channel gamma subunit: genetic heterogeneity of Liddle's syndrome. *Nature Genetics*, 11, 76–82.

Hara, M., Ichida, F., Higuchi, A., Tanizawa, T., and Okada, T. (1984). Nephropathy associated with Charcot-Marie-Tooth disease. *International Journal of Pediatric Nephrology*, 5, 99–102.

Hirooka, M., Hirota, M., and Kamada, M. (1988). Renal lesions on Cockayne syndrome. *Pediatric Nephrology*, 2, 239–43.

Hitzig, W.H., and Truniger, B. (1996). Wiskott–Aldrich syndrome—a truly interdisciplinary problem. *Nephrology Dialysis Transplantation*, 11, 2093–2095.

Hsieh, F., Gokh, R., and Dworkin, L. (1996). Acute renal failure and the MELAS syndrome, a mitochondrial encephalomyelopathy. *Journal of the American Society of Nephrology*, 7, 647–52.

Imerslund, O. (1960). Idiopathic chronic megaloblastic anaemia in children. *Acta Paediatrica Scandinavica*, 49 (Supplement 119).

Jansen, J.J. *et al.* (1997). Mutation of mitochondrial tRNA$^{Leu(URR)}$ gene associated with progressive kidney disease. *Journal of the American Society of Nephrology*, 8, 1118–24.

Johns, D.R. (1995). Mitochondrial DNA and disease. *New England Journal of Medicine*, 333, 638–44.

Katz, S.M., Krueger, L.J., and Falkner, B. (1988). Microscopic nephrocalcinosis in cystic fibrosis. *New England Journal of Medicine*, 319, 263-6.

Kontras, S.B., Bodenbender, J.G., McClare, C.R., and Smoth, J.P. (1971). Interstitial cystitis in chronic granulomatous disease. *Journal of Urology*, 105, 575–8.

Kumar, S. *et al.* (1994). Refining the region of branchio-oto-renal syndrome and defining the flanking markers on chromosome 8q by genetic mapping. *American Journal of Medical Genetics*, 55, 1188–94.

Lasseur, C., Allen, A.C., Deminière, C., Aparicio, M., Feehally, J., and Combe, C. (1997). Henoch Schönlein purpura with immunoglobulin A nephropathy and abnormalities of immunoglobulin A in a Wiskott-Aldrich syndrome carrier. *American Journal of Kidney Diseases*, 29, 285–7.

Lemieux, G., and Neemeh, J.A. (1967). Charcot Marie Tooth disease and nephritis. *Canadian Medical Association Journal*, 97, 1193–8.

Lennert, T.H., Hanefeld, F. and Bernstein, J. (1976). Charcot-Marie-Tooth disease and chronic nephropathy. Abstracts, 10th meeting of the European Society for Paediatric Nephrology, Barcelona, June 3–7 1976, p. 34.

Lévy, M., Gubler, M.C., Hadchouel, M., Niaudet, P., Habib, R., and Odièvre, M. (1985). Déficit en en alpha-1-antitrypsine et atteinte rénale. *Néphrologie*, 6, 65-70.

Lévy, M. (1986). Severe deficiency of alpha-1-antitrypsin associated with cutaneous vasculitis, rapidly progressive glomerulonephritis, and colitis. *American Journal of Medicine*, 81, 363 (letter).

Lewis, M. *et al.* (1985). Severe deficiency of alpha-1-antitrypsin associated with cutaneous vasculitis, rapidly progressive glomerulonephritis, and colitis. *American Journal of Medicine*, 79, 489–94.

Leys, A., Proesmans, W., and Devriendt, K. (1997). The eye and the kidney. In: *Oxford textbook of clinical nephrology, 2nd edition*. Eds Davison, A.M., Cameron, J.S., Grünfeld, J.-P., Kerr, D.N.S., Ritz, E., Winearls, C. pp. 2787–808. Oxford University Press, Oxford.

Li Ni *et al.* (1994). Refined localisation of the branchiootorenal syndrome gene by linkage and haplotype analysis. *American Journal of Medical Genetics*, 51, 176–84.

Liddle, G.W., Bledsoe, J., and Coppage, W.S. (1963). A familial disorder simulating primary hyperaldosteronism but with negligible aldosterone secretion. *Transactions of the American Association of Physicians*, 76, 199–213.

Lin, S.H., Sourial, N.A., Lu, K.C., and Huseh, E.J. (1994). Imerslund–Gräsbeck syndrome in a Chinese family with distinct skin lesions. *Journal of Clinical Pathology*, 47, 956–8.

Lloveras, J.J., Salles, J.P., Durand, D., Suc, J.M., and Rascol, A. (1986). Focal glomerulosclerosis and Charcot-Marie-Tooth disease: not a chance association? *Nephron*, **43**, 231 (letter).

Lomas, D.A., Evans, D.Ll., Finch, J.T., and Carrell, R.W. (1992). The mechanism piZ α_1-antitrypsin accumulation within the liver. *Nature*, **357**, 605–7.

Lópes-Nieto, C.E. and Brenner, B.M. (1997). Molecular basis of inherited disorders of renal solute transport. *Current Opinion in Nephrology and Hypertension*, **6**, 411–21.

Luft, R. (1994). The development of mitochondrial medicine. *Proceedings of the National Academy of Sciences of the United States of America*, **91**, 8731–8.

McGlennan, R.C., Burke, B.A., and Dehner, L.P. (1986). Systemic amyloidosis complicating cystic fibrosis. A retrospective pathologic study. *Archives of Pathology and Laboratory Medicine*, **110**, 879–84.

McKusick, V.A. (1990). *Mendelian Inheritance in Man. Catalog of Autosomal Dominant, Autosomal Recessive and X-linked Phenotypes*. Johns Hopkins University Press, Philadelphia, PA.

Martin, S.R., Garel, L., and Alvarez, F. (1996). Alagille's syndrome with cystic kidney disease. *Archives of Disease in Childhood*, **74**, 232–5.

Martini, A., Ravelli, A., and Burgio, G.R. (1985). Focal segmental glomerulosclerosis and Charcot-Marie-Tooth disease. *International Journal of Pediatric Nephrology*, **6**, 151 (letter).

Matshushita, T., Sano, T., Nakano, S., Matsuda, H., and Okada, S. (1993). Successful mitral valve replacement for MELAS. *Pediatric Neurology*, **9**, 391–3.

Matsutani, H. *et al.* (1992). Partial deficiency of cytochrome oxidase with isolated proximal tubular acidosis and hypercalciuria. *Child Nephrology and Urology*, **12**, 221–4.

Mazodier, P., Elzouki, A.-N.Y., Segelmark, M., and Eriksson, S. (1996). Systemic necrotizing vasculitides in severe alpha$_1$-antitrypsin deficiency. *Quarterly Journal of Medicine*, **89**, 599–611.

Meisels, I.S. *et al.* (1995). Renal allograft rejection in a patient with the Wiskott-Aldrich syndrome. *Transplantation*, **59**, 1214–15.

Melnick, M. *et al.* (1976). Familial branchio-oto-renal dysplasia: a new addition to the branchial arch syndromes. *Clinical Genetics*, **9**, 25–34.

Melzi, M.L., Constantini, D., Giani, M., Claris Appiani, A., and Giunta, A.M. (1991). Severe nephropathy in three adolescents with cystic fibrosis. *Archives of Disease in Childhood*, **66**, 1444–7.

Mori, K., Narahara, K., Ninomiya, S., Goto, Y., and Nonaka, I. (1991). Renal and skin involvement in a patient with complete Kearns–Sayre syndrome. *American Journal of Medical Genetics*, **28**, 583–7.

Moulin, B., Godin, M., Ducastelle, T., Landthaler, G., and Fillastre, J.P. (1984). Charcot-Marie-Tooth disease (CMTD), nerve deafness and glomerulonephritis (GN). Abstracts, IXth Congress of the International Society of Nephrology, Los Angles 1984, p. 114A.

Munnich, A. *et al.* (1992). Clinical aspects of mitochondrial disease. *Journal of Inherited Metabolic Disorders*, **15**, 448–55.

Nance, M.A. and Berry, S.M. (1992). Cockayne syndrome: review of 140 cases. *American Journal of Medical Genetics*, **42**, 68–84.

Nevanlinna, H.R. (1980). Selective malabsorption of vitamin B$_{12}$. In *Population Structure and Genetic Disorders* (ed. A.W. Eriksson, H.R. Nevanlinna, P.L. Workman, and R.K. Norio), pp. 680–2. Academic Press, London.

Niaudet, P. and Rötig, A. (1996). Renal involvement in mitochondrial cytopathies. *Pediatric Nephrology*, **10**, 368–73.

Niaudet, P. *et al.* (1994). Deletion of mitochondrial DNA in a case of de Toni–Debré–Fanconi syndrome. *Pediatric Nephrology*, **8**, 164–8.

Niaudet, P., and Rötig, A. (1997). The kidney in mitochondrial cytopathies. *Kidney International*, **51**, 1000–7.

Norden, G., Frimans, S., Frisenette-Finch, C., Persson, H., and Karlberg I. (1991). Renal transplantation in the Bardet–Biedl syndrome, a form of Laurence–Moon–Biedl syndrome. *Nephrology, Dialysis and Transplantation*, **6**, 982–3.

Ogier, H. *et al.* (1988). De Toni–Fanconi–Debré syndrome with Leigh syndrome revealing severe muscle cytochrome c oxidase deficiency. *Journal of Pediatrics*, **112**, 734–9.

Oh, Y. and Warnock, D.G. (1997). Expression of amloride-sensitive sodium channel β subunit gene in human B lymphocytes, *Journal of the American Society of Nephrology*, **8**, 126–9.

Pearce, S.H.S. (1998). Straightening out the renal tubule: advances in the molecular basis of the inherited tubulopathies. *Quarterly Journal of Medicine*, **91**, 5–12.

Pober, B. (1990). Smith–Lemli–Opitz syndrome. In: *Birth defects encyclopedia* (ed. M.L.Buyse), pp. 1570–2. Blackwell Scientific, Dover, MA.

Reiss, U. *et al.* (1996). Nephrotic syndrome, hypertension and adrenal failure in atypical Cockayne syndrome. *Pediatric Nephrology*, **10**, 602–5.

Rötig, A. *et al.* (1992). Maternally inherited duplication of the mitochondrial genome in a syndrome of proximal tubulopathy, diabetes mellitus, and cerebellar ataxia. *American Journal of Medical Genetics*, **50**, 364–70.

Rötig, A. *et al.* (1994). Deletion of mitochondrial DNA in a case of early-onset diabetes mellitus, optic atrophy and deafness (Wolfram syndrome, MIM 222300). *Journal of Clinical Investigation*, **91**, 1095–8.

Rötig, A. *et al.* (1995). Renal involvement in the mitochondrial disorders. *Advances in Nephrology*, **24**, 367–78.

Rumpelt, H.J. and Michl, W. (1979). Selective vitamin B_{12} malabsorption with proteinuria (Imerslund–Majman–Gräsbeck syndrome): ultrastructural examinations on renal glomeruli. *Clinical Nephrology*, **11**, 213–17.

Russo, P.A., Ellis, D., and Hashida, Y. (1987). Renal histopathology in Alagille's syndrome. *Pediatric Pathology*, **7**, 557–68.

Salameh, M.M., Banda, R.W., and Mohdi, A.A. (1991). Reversal of severe neurological abnormalities after vitamin B_{12} replacement in the Imerslund–Gräsbeck syndrome. *Journal of Neurology*, **238**, 349–50.

Sanyanusin, P., Schimmenti, L.A., Ward, T.A., Pierpont, M.E.M., Sullivan, M.J., Dobyns, W.B., and Eccles, M.R. (1995). Mutation of the *PAX2* gene in a family with optic nerve colobomas, renal anomalies and vesicoureteral reflux. *Nature Genetics*, **9**, 358–64.

Sato, H., Saito, T., Kurosawa, K., Ootaka, T., Furuyama, T., and Yoshinaga, K. (1988). Renal lesions in Cockayne syndrome. *Clinical Nephrology*, **29**, 206–9.

Savidge, J.A., Chang, L., Cook, L., Burdon, J., Daskalakis, M., and Doery, J. (1995). α_1-antitrypsin deficiency and anti-proteinase-3 antibodies in anti-neutrophil cytoplasmic antibody (ANCA)-associated systemic vasculitis. *Clinical and Experimental Immunology*, **100**, 194–7.

Schimmenti, L.A., Cunliffe, H.E., McNoe, L.A. *et al.* (1997). Further delineation of renal–coloboma syndrome in patients with extreme variability of mutations. *American Journal of Human Genetics*, **60**, 869–78.

Segelmark, M., Elzouki, A.-N., Wieslander, J., and Eriksson, S. (1995). PiZ gene of α_1-antitrypsin as a determinant of outcome in PR3-ANCA-positive vasculitis. *Kidney International*, **48**, 844–50.

Seyberth, H.W., Rascher, W., Schweer, H., Kuhl, P., Mehls, O., and Schärer, K. (1985). Congenital hypokalemia with hypercalciuria in preterm infants: A hyperprostaglandinuric tubular syndrome different from Bartter syndrome. *Journal of Pediatrics*, **107**, 694–701.

Simon, D.B., Bindra, R.S., Mansfield, T.A., Nelson-Williams, C., Mendoca, E., Stone, R., *et al.* (1997). Mutations in the chloride channel gene, CLCNKB, cause Bartter's syndrome type III. *Nature Genetics*, **17**, 171–8.

Simon, D.B., Karet, F.E., Hamdan, J.M., Dipietro, A., Sanjad, S.A., and Lifton, R.P. (1996*a*). Bartter's syndrome, hypokalaemic alkalosis with hypercalciuria, is caused by mutations in the Na-K-2Cl cotransporter NKCC2. *Nature Genetics*, **13**, 183–88.

Simon, D.B., Karet, F.E., Rodriguez-Soriano, J., Hamdan, J.H., Dipietro, A., Trachtman, H., *at al.* (1996*b*). Genetic heterogeneity of Bartter's syndrome revealed by mutations in the K+ channel, ROMK. *Nature Genetics*, **14**, 152–6.

Simon, D.B., Nelson-Williams, C., Bia, M.J., Ellison, D., Karet, F.E., Molina, A.M., *et al.* (1996*c*). Gitelman's variant of Bartter's syndrome, inherited hypokalaemic alkalosis, is caused by mutations in the thiazide-sensitive Na-Cl cotransporter. *Nature Genetics*, **12**, 24–30.

Shimkets, R.A., Warnock, D.G., Bositis, C.M. *et al.* (1994). Liddle's syndrome: heritable human hypertension caused by mutations in the beta subunit of the epithelial sodium channel. *Cell*, **79**, 407–14.

Spinner, N.B. *et al.* (1994). Cytologically balanced t(2;20) in a two-generation family with Alagille syndrome: cytogenetic and molecular studies. *American Journal of Human Genetics*, **55**, 238–43.

Spitler, L.E., Wray, B.B., Mogerman, S., Miller, J.J., O'Reilly, R.J., and Lagios, M. (1980). Nephropathy of the Wiskott–Aldrich syndrome. *Pediatrics*, **66**, 391–8.

Standen, G.R., Lillicrap, D.P., Matthews, N., and Bloom, A.L. (1986). Inherited thrombocytopenia, elevated serum IgA and renal disease: identification as a variant of the Wiskott–Aldrich syndrome. *Quarterly Journal of Medicine*, **59**, 401–8.

Strife, C.F., Hug, G., Chuck, G., McAdams, A.J., Davis, C.A., Kline, J.J. (1983). Membranoproliferative glomerulonephritis and α_1-antitrypsin deficiency in children. *Pediatrics*, **71**, 88–92.

Szabolcs, M.J. *et al.* (1994). Mitochondrial DNA deletion: a cause of chronic tubulointerstitial nephropathy. *Kidney International*, **45**, 1388–96.

Tint, G.S. *et al.* (1994). Defective cholesterol biosynthesis associated with the Smith-Lemli-Opitz syndrome. *New England Journal of Medicine*, **330**, 107–13.

Torralbo, A. *et al.* (1995). Morning glory optic disc anomaly associated with chronic renal disease. *Nephrology Dialysis Transplantation*, **10**, 1762–4.

Uttley, J., MacDonald, M.K., and Uttley, U. (1975). Renal ultrastructure in the Imerslund syndrome. *Abstracts, 9th Meeting of the European Society of Paediatric Nephrology, Cambridge, 1975*, p. 58.

Van Hoffen, A., Natarajan, A.T., Mayne, L.V., Van Zeeland, A.A., Mullenders, L.H., and Venema, J. (1993). Deficient repair of the transcribed strand of active genes in Cockayne syndrome. *Nucleic Acids Research*, **21**, 5890–5.

Wallace, D.C. (1994). Mitchondrial DNA sequence variation in human evolution and disease. *Proceedings of the National Academy of Sciences of the United States of America*, **91**, 8739–46.

Warnock, D.G. (1998). Liddle syndrome: an autosomal dominant form of human hypertension. *Kidney International*, **53**, 18–24.

Weaver, R.G., Cashwell, L.F., Lorentz, W., Whiteman, D., Geisinger, K.R., and Ball, M. (1988). Optic nerve coloboma associated with renal disease. *American Journal of Medical Genetics*, **29**, 597–605.

Webb, M.C., Andrews, P.A., Koffman, C.G., and Cameron, J.S. (1993). Renal transplantation in Wiskott–Aldrich syndrome. *Transplantation*, **56**, 747–8, 1585.

Webster, D.R., Becroft, D.M.O., and Suttle, D.P. (1995). Hereditary orotic aciduria and other disorders of pyrimidine metabolism. In: *The Metabolic and Molecular Bases of Inherited Disease* (7th edn) (ed. C.L.Scriver, A.L.Beaudet, W.S.Sly and D.Valle), pp. 1799–1837. McGraw-Hill, New York.

Widdershoven, J., Monnens, L., Assmann, K., and Cremers, C. (1983). Renal disorders in the branchio-oto-renal syndrome. *Helvetica Paediatrica Acta*, **38**, 654–7.

Williams, G.H. and Fisher, N.D. (1997). Genetic apporach to diagnostic and therapeutic decisions in human hypertension. *Current Opinion in Nephrology and Hypertension*, **6**, 1345–52.

Yoneda, M., Tanaka, M., and Nishikimi, M. (1989). Pleotropic molecular defects in energy-transducing complexes in mitochondrial encephalomyopathy (MELAS). *Journal of Neurological Science*, **92**, 143–58.

Zupanc, M.L., Moraes, C.T., Shanske, S., Langman, C.B., Ciafaloni, E. and DiMauro, S. (1991). Deletion of mitochondrial DNA in patient with combined features of Kearns-Sayre and MELAS syndromes. *Annals of Neurology*, **43**, 680–3.

INDEX

Note: page numbers in *italics* refer to figures and tables